William Manchester's
THE LAST LION:
WINSTON SPENCER CHURCHILL;
ALONE:
1932–1940

"The best Churchill biography for the plain readers of this generation . . . Exhaustive . . . interesting. Even readers who know the basic story will find much that is new, much to make them angry again."—*Newsweek*

"Stirring. . . . As Manchester points out several times, it's as if the age, having produced a Hitler, then summoned Churchill as the only figure equal to the task of vanquishing him. The years 'Alone' are the pivotal years of Churchill's career." —*The Boston Sunday Globe*

"History in the grand manner. . . . Vivid and interesting. . . . Here Manchester tells again the familiar but always instructive story of Churchill's unheeded fight to arouse the European democracies (and their even sleepier transatlantic ally) to the menace of Hitler."—*The Washington Post*

"Superb. . . . Pulls together the multitudinous facets of one of the richest lives ever to be chronicled. . . . Churchill and Manchester were clearly made for each other."—*Chicago Tribune Book World*

"The best, destined to be the most memorable and the most lasting [Churchill biography]. . . . Manchester brings new insights, new information, and a new approach."—William L. Shirer

"Compelling reading."—*The Times* of London

"He sounded the alarm about the terrible plot being hatched inside Hitler's deranged mind . . . told with skill and vivid anecdotes . . . the story continues to shock and horrify."—*Time*

Books by William Manchester

Biography

History

Essays

Fiction

Diversion

Memoirs

THE LAST LION

Winston Spencer Churchill:
Alone,
1932–1940

William Manchester

History with its flickering lamp stumbles along the trail of the past,
trying to reconstruct its scenes, to revive its echoes, and kindle with
pale gleams the passion of former days.

> —Winston Churchill
> Speech in the House of Commons
> November 12, 1940

BANTAM BOOKS TRADE PAPERBACKS
NEW YORK

To

BILL SHIRER

who saw it from the other side

and saw it first

❦ ❦

"Ich hatt' einen Kameraden . . ."

Then out spake brave Horatius,
  The Captain of the Gate:
"To every man upon this earth
Death cometh soon or late.
And how can man die better
  Than facing fearful odds,
For the ashes of his fathers,
And the temples of his gods?"

Thomas Babington Macaulay, *Lays of Ancient Rome*
Memorized by Churchill at age thirteen

ARRAY

ILLUSTRATIONS

Churchill and Anthony Eden walk down Whitehall in late August 1939.
  (*The Illustrated London News Picture Library*)
Churchill is appointed First Lord of the Admiralty, September 1939.
  (*United Press International*)
In the first month of the war Randolph marries Pamela Digby.
  (*Mary Soames Collection*)
New York Times, May 11, 1940.
  (*Copyright © 1940 by The New York Times Company. Reprinted by permission*)
Winston Spencer Churchill becomes Prime Minister of Great Britain.
  (*Cecil Beaton Photograph, courtesy of Sotheby's, London*)

CHRONOLOGY

1932 MacDonald is puppet P.M.; Tories, led by Baldwin, have power
Depression; hunger riots; Royal Navy mutiny
Roosevelt elected president of U.S.
Nazis lack majority in Reichstag
WSC researches *Marlborough* in Germany
His meeting with Hitler canceled after WSC criticizes Nazi anti-Semitism
WSC publishes *Amid These Storms*
His daughter Diana marries
Son Randolph quits Oxford for journalism

1933 Named chancellor, Hitler seizes power
Reichstag destroyed by fire
British leaders begin visits to Hitler; see Germany as shield against U.S.S.R.
Toynbee, Lippmann also among his admirers
British policy: unilateral disarmament
Eden enthusiastically supports it
WSC publishes first *Marlborough* volume
He builds intelligence network in London and Berlin
Cites German rearmament in Parliament, is labeled "scaremonger"

1934 Hindenburg dies; Hitler becomes Führer, spends ten billion pounds yearly on arms
The Times kills stories that might offend him
WSC's first major speech on air defense
Baldwin pledges RAF will never be No. 2
WSC creates a lake at Chartwell
Publishes second *Marlborough* volume
Clementine's South Seas voyage

1935 Hitler repudiates Versailles, signs naval treaty with Britain, invokes anti-Semitic laws
Labour denies Hitler aggressive, opposes rearmament

Baldwin's first confession: admits Luftwaffe stronger than RAF, but
    his popularity unaffected
Baldwin becomes P.M.
Mussolini invades Ethiopia
General election — Tory victory
Randolph runs as Tory at West Toxteth, is defeated
Hoare-Laval deal exposed
Diana divorces, marries Duncan Sandys, MP
Her sister Sarah becomes chorus girl

1936   King George V dies; Edward VIII is King
        Randolph loses by-election at Ross and Cromarty; his candidacy an
            embarrassment to WCS
        SMALL NAZI FORCE INVADES RHINELAND
        FRENCH, WITH 350,000 TROOPS, BACK OFF
        Cliveden/Blickling set rejoices
        WSC: "Stop it! Stop it! NOW is the appointed time!"
        Civil war in Spain
        WSC publishes third *Marlborough* volume
        Baldwin's second confession: he concealed RAF inferiority to win
            election
        Hitler and Mussolini form Axis, opposing democracies
        WSC leads huge Albert Hall rally to support rearmament and League
            of Nations
        He errs, backing King in marriage crisis
        Shouted down in Parliament; his movement falters
        King abdicates; WSC is discredited
        Sarah marries vaudeville performer

1937   Axis backs Spanish Fascists
        Baldwin retires, Chamberlain is P.M.
        Makes appeasement his foreign policy
        Halifax visits Hitler — appeasement starts
        WSC publishes *Great Contemporaries*

1938   Year of "The Lambeth Walk"
        Il Duce's Ethiopian conquest recognized by Britain
        Eden quits cabinet
        ANSCHLUSS; HITLER SEIZES AUSTRIA
        WSC proposes Grand Alliance to confront Hitler

Chamberlain rejects it; says Reich would be angered

WSC publishes 2 books and 59 articles, yet faces bankruptcy; proposes to sell Chartwell, quit Parliament, go into business. Saved by last-minute loan

In House Sandys documents lack of antiaircraft defense; government wants to prosecute for revealing official secrets

MUNICH: CHAMBERLAIN SELLS OUT CZECHS

Duff Cooper resigns as first lord of the Admiralty

WSC denounces Munich Agreement

Both WSC and Hitler now travel armed

Attempt by disaffected constituents to oust WSC from House — applauded by Hitler — fails

Parliamentary inquiry exonerates Sandys

WSC compares P.M.'s judgment with his own in devastating speech at Chingford

1939   At Château de l'Horizon, WSC puts ex-king in his place

Fascists triumphant in Spain

WSC survives second attempt by appeasers to unseat him

HITLER SEIZES ALL CZECHOSLOVAKIA, ENTERS PRAGUE

Chamberlain announces Polish guarantee

Mussolini conquers Albania

WSC toils to meet debt payments

After Prague, British public begins to turn toward him

Billboards: "WHAT PRICE CHURCHILL?"

WSC suggests Britain, France, Russia form defensive alliance against Hitler

Soviet foreign commissar Litvinov formally proposes it

French enthusiastic, but Chamberlain, anti-Bolshevik, vetoes it

Stalin dismisses Litvinov, appoints Molotov

Molotov turns from Allies, signs pact with Hitler

Allies pledge support for Poland

WSC tours Maginot Line

HITLER INVADES POLAND

ALLIES DECLARE WAR ON GERMANY

Italy proclaims neutrality

WSC named first lord of the Admiralty

Nazis and Soviets partition Poland

Ark Royal torpedoed in Scapa Flow

Russia invades Finland
RN defeaats *Graf Spee*

1940   British prisoners rescued from *Altmark*
Finns surrender to Soviets
Chamberlain: Hitler "missed the bus"
GERMANY INVADES DENMARK, NORWAY
WSC masterminds ill-starred Norway campaign

May 10, 1940
NAZIS INVADE LOW COUNTRIES, FRANCE
WSC BECOMES PRIME MINISTER

MAPS

AUTHOR'S NOTE

THIS WORK is a biography, not a history. The two are often confused, and understandably so, for both recount the past. But there is a distinction. History is a chronological account of prior events. Biography focuses on one figure, exploring the significance of his life by examining "the earthly pilgrimage of a man," in Thomas Carlyle's words, or, in Sir Edmund Gosse's, by presenting "the faithful portrait of a soul in adventure by life."

In the view of this writer, there can be no enlightening life which does not include an account of the man's times. This need for context is even greater when the central figure is a towering statesman. It is impossible to understand Churchill and his adversaries in the 1930s, for example, without grasping the British revulsion against the horrors of World War I. If a man casts a long shadow, as Churchill did, extensive research leads to lengthy books. I propose to cover the life of Churchill in three volumes. Three volumes is a lot. But he deserves at least a triptych if one is to meet the exacting standard set down by Paul M. Kendall of the University of Kansas. The biographer, he writes in *Encyclopaedia Britannica*,

seeks to elicit from facts, by selection and design, the illusion of a life actually lived. Within the bounds of given data, the biographer seeks to transform plain information into illumination. . . . His achievement as a biographer will be measured, in great part, by his ability to suggest the sweep of chronology and yet to highlight the major patterns of behavior that give a life its shape and meaning.

My personal encounters with Sir Winston Churchill were confined to a five-day Atlantic crossing aboard the *Queen Mary* in January 1953, when he was in his last premiership. Subsequently, I visited No. 10 Downing Street. But when I undertook my present task I was remembered by members of his family and entourage. Their hospitality, when I set about the ten-year job of researching and writing *The Last Lion*, honored me and moved me. Thus began the most ambitious literary venture of my life, which included taped interviews of such diversity and length that their transcription required a full year. Those are essential to *The Last Lion*'s scholarly foundation.

I am particularly grateful to Martin Gilbert, MA, Fellow of Merton

College, Oxford, and official biographer of Sir Winston Churchill, for his time, his generosity, his kindness in guiding me toward sources, and for his invaluable narrative and document volumes.

My debt to Lady Soames, DBE, née Mary Churchill, is immense, for her recollections of her father, her patience in answering my inquiries, and her role as my tour guide through the rooms, the grounds, and the outer buildings of Chartwell, in one of which, her father's studio, I saw — perhaps gaped at would be more accurate — nearly five hundred of her father's paintings. They are stunning, and serve to confirm Sir Isaiah Berlin's conclusion that Churchill was "the largest human being of our times."

The late Sir John Colville, CB, CVO, Honorary Fellow, Churchill College, Cambridge, retired RAF fighter pilot, author, and private secretary to three prime ministers — chiefly Churchill — was cooperative, forthcoming, and encouraging throughout. To assist me he devoted hours he could have spent in more urgent causes, and did so with that understated charm which is the mark of an English gentleman, almost convincing me that there was nothing he would rather do.

Among others who were most helpful to me were surviving "Churchillians," as Sir John called them: Sir William Deakin, DSO, MA; Sir Fitzroy Maclean, CBE, MP (C); the late Lord Boothby, KBE; Sir David Pitblado, KCB, CVO; Sir John Martin, KCMG, CB, CVO; the late Lord Soames, PC, GCMG, GCVO, CH, CBE; Lieutenant General Sir Ian Jacob, GBE, KBE, CB, DL; Anita Leslie; Sir David Hunt, CBE, OBE, DFC; Lord Bonham-Carter; young Winston Churchill, MP, grandson of his namesake; the late Oscar Nemon; the late, gallant Viscount Head, PC, GCMG, KCMG, CBE; the late Lord Duncan-Sandys, who was Churchill's son-in-law; and five of Churchill's secretaries — Grace Hamblin, OBE, Jane Williams, Kathleen Hill, Vanda Salmon, and Cecily ("Chips") Gemmell. I should also express my appreciation to Wing Commander R. M. Sparkes, RAF, who took me through the Annexe — Churchill's wartime bunker and the site of the Cabinet War Room as it had been in 1945 — long before it was opened to the public.

With the exception of one member of the Royal Family, no one refused to be interviewed and taped. The late Harold Macmillan (Lord Stockton) set an entire day aside for me; so did the late Lord Butler of Saffron Walden ("Rab"); so did the ineffable Malcolm Muggeridge. All questions I posed (including some which were clearly impertinent) were answered by Lady Avon, the widow of Anthony Eden; the late Lady Diana Cooper, widow of Alfred Duff Cooper, Viscount Norwich; the historian A. J. P. Taylor; Lord Strauss; Lord Hailsham; the Rt. Hon. Malcolm MacDonald, OM, PC, MP, son of Ramsay and a cabinet minister in Churchill's wartime national government; Lord Geoffrey Lloyd; R. L. James, the retired headmaster of Harrow; Lord Selkirk; Noel Mander; George Malcolm Thompson; Denis Kelly; Alan MacLean; Elizabeth Gilliatt; John Grigg; Sir Charles Martin; Richard Hill; Lord Southbridge; Graham Norton; and certain Americans who enjoyed a special relationship with Churchill: the late Virginia Cowles, Kay Halle, and the late Averell Harriman. Mrs. Harriman provided immense help and encouragement, though classifying Pamela Harriman as American or British presents difficulties. As Averell was, she is very active in the U.S. Democratic party. However, she was born Pamela Digby, the daughter of the eleventh Lord Digby, KG, DSO, MC, TD, and her first husband was Randolph Churchill. As Winston's daughter-in-law and the widow of one of the greatest statesmen in American history, she is, so to speak, an English-speaking Union unto herself.

In addition to taped interviews, the primary biographical sources for this book are specified in the back of the work. Material is cited from, among others, the 300 collections of private papers in the Churchill College Archives Centre at Cambridge University; Hansard's record of parliamentary debates; the private papers of prime ministers and the minutes of cabinet meetings now stored in the Public Record Office, Kew, Surrey; and over a hundred collections of personal papers which remain in private hands. Historical sources include British, French, German, and U.S. foreign policy documents and — in translation — those of the Polish, Italian, and Russian governments.

William L. Shirer was an indispensable source for the background of events in Germany and France during these troubled years.

On my own behalf, and that of my archival research assistants in England, I should like to express my gratitude for the assistance and advice of Correlli Barnett and Dr. Michael Hoskin (Keepers of the Archives at Churchill College, Cambridge), Sir William Hawthorne (Master of Churchill College at the time of our research), Captain Stephen Roskill, RN (Fellow of the College), and archivists Pat Bradford and particularly Marion Stewart, who seemed to have even the most elusive document at her fingertips; G. H. Martin (Keeper of the Public Record Office in Kew) and his colleagues Mrs. P. Piper, N. A. M. Rodger, and Dr. M. J. Subb; H. S. Cobb and F. Johnson (Record Office, House of Lords); Christine Kennedy (Nuffield College Library, Oxford); D. G. Vaisey (Department of Western Manuscripts in Oxford's Bodleian Library — "Bodley"); Dr. B. S. Benedikz (Special Collections, University of Birmingham); D. A. Clarke and G. E. A. Raspin (British Public Library — formerly the British Museum Library — and British Library of Political and Economic Science, University of York); Gordon Phillips (*Times* Archive); Colin Watson (Obituary Department of *The Times*); A. E. Cormack and R. F. Barker (Royal Air Force Museum, Hendon); D. M. Smith and C. C. Webb (Borthwick Institute of Historical Research); F. Bailey (Naval Historical Society, Ministry of Defence); E. C. Blayney (Foreign and Commonwealth Office); Philip A. H. Brown, A. N. E. D. Schofield, and D. H. Bourke (British Library); Mrs. K. F. Campbell (Library and Records Department, Foreign and Commonwealth Office); Eric Ceadel (Librarian, Cambridge University Library); Jacqueline Kavanagh (Written Archives Officer, BBC Written Archives Centre); L. H. Miller (Librarian, Ministry of Defence); Margaret Townsend (Editor's Secretary, *News of the World*); Judith A. Woods (Archivist, the Labour Party Library); V. E. Knight (Librarian, University of Liverpool); L. R. Day (Science Museum Library, University of Liverpool); Kay Chapman and R. J. B. Knight (National Maritime Museum); Peter McNiven (University of Manchester); Diana Grimwood Jones and Gillian Grant (St. Anthony's College, Oxford); Patricia Methven (Liddell Hart Centre for Military Archives, King's College, University of London); R. A. W. Suddaby (Imperial War Museum); and John Spencer-Churchill, eleventh Duke of Marlborough, who gave me the freedom of Blenheim Palace.

I am indebted to T. Chadbourne Dunham, professor emeritus of German at Wesleyan University, who checked my translations from the German, and to the graceful and bilingual Kathryn I. Briggs, who performed the same service with translations from the French.

I am grateful to Peter Day, Nigel Viney, and Richard Langworth, the International Churchill Society's keeper of the flame, for their meticulous review of the final manuscript in the interests of historical accuracy, and to Perry Knowlton, Adam Deixel, and I. Gonzalez at the Curtis Brown literary agency, who provided access to Churchill's American royalty statements.

My assistant, Margaret Kennedy Rider, has been loyal and tireless, as always. As my chief researcher in England, Deborah Baker once more proved imaginative and perceptive. Betsy Pitha assisted nobly in the annotation, as did Virginia Creeden, who was also invaluable in securing permission to quote from letters, diaries, documents, and published works. The staff of the Firestone Library at Princeton University was especially helpful. I am again grateful for the support and assistance provided by the staff of Wesleyan University's Olin Memorial Library, led by J. Robert Adams, Caleb T. Winchester Librarian. Particularly helpful were Joan Jurale, head reference librarian; Edmund A. Rubacha and Suzanne Javorski, reference librarians; Margaret Halstead, reference secretary; Erhard F. Konerding, documents librarian; and Steven Lebergott, chief of interlibrary loans. Other members of the staff who were especially helpful were Alan Nathanson, bibliographer, and Ann Frances Wakefield and Dale Lee.

Finally, I once more acknowledge my gratitude to Don Congdon, my literary agent of forty years; Roger Donald, vice president and publisher of Trade Adult Books, Little, Brown and Company; and, last but foremost in the final stages of text revision, Peggy Leith Anderson, whose manuscript editing skills are unmatched in my long experience.

W.M.

Wesleyan University
December 1987

THE STORY THUS FAR

A Synopsis of
THE LAST LION: WINSTON SPENCER CHURCHILL;
Visions of Glory: 1874–1932

T HE GRANDSON of a duke, Winston Churchill was born in splendrous Blenheim Palace during the autumn of 1874, when the British Empire was the world's mightiest power. Almost immediately the infant was entrusted to his plump nanny, "Woom," who became his only source of childhood happiness. His father, Lord Randolph Churchill, a brilliant if erratic member of Parliament — he was, briefly, chancellor of the Exchequer — actually loathed Winston. The boy's breathtakingly beautiful American mother, Jennie, devoted most of her time to sexual intrigue, slipping between the sheets with handsome, powerful men in Britain, in the United States, and on the Continent. Her husband was in no position to object. He was an incurable syphilitic.

Winston rebelled against school authority, first becoming a disciplinary problem and then, at Harrow, the lowest-ranked scholar in the lower form. His dismal academic record ruled out Oxford or Cambridge, so he went to Sandhurst, England's West Point. On February 20, 1895, less than a month after his father's death from paresis, young Churchill was commissioned a second lieutenant and gazetted to the Fourth Hussars, preparing to embark for India. In Bangalore Churchill succeeded where his schoolmasters failed. During the long, sweltering siestas, he educated himself, reading Plato, Aristotle, Gibbon, Macaulay, Schopenhauer, and poring over thousands of pages of parliamentary debates. Developing a flair for the language, he found he could earn money writing newspaper and magazine articles and books. At the same time he felt strong stirrings of ambition. He would, he decided, seek a seat in Parliament. But first he must become famous. Ruthlessly manipulating his mother's lovers (who included the Prince of Wales), he managed to appear wherever the fighting was fiercest. By 1899 he was in South Africa. Taken prisoner in the Boer War by the Boers, he managed a sensational escape from a POW stockade, making his way across three hundred miles of enemy territory to freedom. His breakout made him a national figure. Returning home, he was elected to Parliament while Victoria still reigned.

In the House of Commons his rise was meteoric. At thirty-three he was a cabinet minister. Appointed president of the Board of Trade, he joined with David Lloyd George, the new chancellor of the Exchequer, in the move to abolish sweated labor despite die-hard peers in the House of Lords. In 1908, working in tandem, they conceived and then guided through the Commons an unprecedented program of liberal legislation: unemployment compensation, health insurance, and pensions for the aged, all of them to be financed by taxes on the rich and the landed gentry. Winston denounced the aristocracy in savage speeches, and titled relatives stopped speaking to him. But he had a new, exciting supporter: Clementine Hozier, who became Mrs. Winston Churchill in 1908. Long afterward the groom said that they had "lived happily ever afterwards." In fact, they remained deeply in love until his death nearly sixty years later.

When the Central Powers, led by Germany and Austria-Hungary, plunged all Europe into the Great War of 1914–1918, Churchill had anticipated it. Since 1911 he had been first lord of the Admiralty. The fleet was ready. But on the western front the great armies were locked in a bloody, hopeless stalemate. It would be years before either side could hope for victory in the west. Churchill saw a way to break the deadlock. He proposed that the Allied navies open a new front in the eastern Mediterranean, exploiting the weakness of the Central Powers' unstable ally, Turkey. If the Dardanelles strait were forced by battleships, Constantinople would fall within hours. The French and British could then join hands with their Russian ally and sweep up the Danube into Hungary, Austria, Bavaria, and Württemberg, ripping open the Second Reich's undefended southern flank.

Today military historians agree that the Dardanelles strategy could have ended the war in 1916 with a German defeat. But a timid British admiral, who had been sweeping all before him, turned tail at the first sign of resistance — even as the Turks, believing themselves beaten, abandoned their forts on the strait and began the evacuation of their capital. Then equally incompetent British generals botched the landings on Gallipoli Peninsula, which flanked the Dardanelles. The British public demanded a scapegoat, and Churchill, as the stratagem's most flamboyant advocate, was dismissed from the Admiralty. He joined the army, crossed to Flanders, and, as a lieutenant colonel, commanded a battalion in the trenches.

After the Versailles peace conference, in which he played no part, he became secretary for war and air, and established the Royal Air Force. Then, as colonial secretary, he was responsible for Britain's postwar diplomacy in the Middle East. He planned the Jewish state, created the nations of Iraq and Jordan, and picked their rulers. It was typical of Churchill, whatever the question, that he would open with a ferocious stance. Negotiations would lead to compromise and solution. Thus he responded to postwar IRA terrorism by creating a force of Black and Tans — former British soldiers who became terrorists themselves. Yet in the end it was he who befriended Michael Collins, the IRA guerrilla leader, and who piloted the Irish Free State treaty through Parliament.

In 1922 Lloyd George's coalition government fell and was succeeded by Stanley Baldwin's Conservatives. As a Liberal, and then as a Liberal Free Trader, Churchill ran for Parliament in three elections and was defeated each time. Changing parties, he won as a Tory in 1924 and was appointed chancellor of the Exchequer — traditionally, a step away from the prime ministry — by Baldwin. His appointment was in fact unwise. Rejecting the counsel of John Maynard Keynes and accepting instead the advice of the Bank of England, he returned Britain to the gold standard. Markets abroad couldn't afford British exports. A coal miners' strike led to a crippling general strike. Winston founded a strike-breaking newspaper; then, after the strike had failed, he took up the coal miners' cause and fought the mine owners, including a close Churchill relative, for higher pay and safer pits.

After Ramsay MacDonald's Labour party won the election of 1929, Winston held the Exchequer post in the Tory shadow cabinet, which would return to power when Labour's slim majority disappeared. But before that could happen, he fell again. The issue was a grant of dominion status for India, putting her on a level with Canada, South Africa, Australia, and New Zealand. He, like Disraeli, regarded the British Raj as the brightest jewel in England's imperial crown. He told Parliament that India was "a geographical term. It is no more a united nation than the Equator." Facing a stone wall of hostile Tories, Churchill resigned from the shadow government on January 27, 1931. Less than seven months later a new government was formed, and in November what might have been Churchill's place at the Exchequer was filled by Neville Chamberlain. Thrice fallen from grace — the Dardanelles, the lost elections, and now India — Churchill had become a political pariah, out of joint with the times.

In the early 1920s, a small legacy and £20,000 in royalties from sales of his six-volume history of the Great War had permitted him to buy Chartwell Manor, a country home near the small Kent town of Westerham, where he did most of his writing. John Kenneth Galbraith has pointed out that administrations suspicious of intellectuals unwittingly make substantial contributions to scholarship and writing. "It comes about," he wrote, "from not employing the scholars or scribes." During Churchill's long spell as a backbencher he wrote and published a million words.

His chief concern was that Britain might be vanquished by a tacit conspiracy between Prussian aggression and English pacifism. Typically in the House of Commons, he would contemplate his colleagues, then lower his head like a bull confronting a matador and slowly shake it. After a pitifully weak MP revolt against government policy, Aneurin Bevan encountered him in the smoking room and asked: "What have you been up to? We haven't seen much of you in the fight lately." "Fight?" growled Winston, sweeping the room with a challenging glance. "I can't see any fight. All I can see in this Parliament is a lot of people leaning against each other."

THE LION CAGED

CHARTWELL. 1932. EARLY MORNING.

THE FIRST olive moments of daylight, anticipating the imminent appearance of the sun over the English Channel, disclose a wide, misty, green plain descending to the South Downs and the sea. This is the great Weald of Kent. It is a peculiarity of the Weald's terrain — demonstrated in the shrouded past by Romans, Saxons, and Normans — that it would be quite defenseless should an enterprising foe cross the Channel. Were any force to prepare for an invasion, its campfires on the far shore would be visible from nearby Dover. But now, fourteen years after the Armistice of 1918, the Weald is an idyll of peace, and the explorer on foot finds that it possesses camouflaged delights. Its smooth breast, for example, is not entirely unbroken. The pastureland, sloping upward toward London, is cleaved by a shallow valley. This combe rises to a timbered crest. There, among eighty sheltering acres of beech, oak, lime, and chestnut, stands the singular country home of England's most singular statesman, a brilliant, domineering, intuitive, inconsiderate, self-centered, emotional, generous, ruthless, visionary, megalomaniacal, and heroic genius who inspires fear, devotion, rage, and admiration among his peers.[1]

At the very least he is the greatest Englishman since Disraeli, a quaint survivor of Britain's past who grapples with the future because he alone can see it. His past is illustrious; in the House of Commons he has, at one time or another, held every important ministry save those of prime minister and foreign secretary. Now, however, he is a backbencher — an elected member of Parliament excluded from the cabinet. In his fifty-eighth year, he is already regarded as an anachronism. He first became a household word as a gallant young British officer, a loyal subject of Queen Victoria, handsome and recklessly brave, serving alongside the Buffs in battles on India's northwest frontier, with Kitchener at Khartoum, and in the Boer War — all symbols of the nation's imperial pride, which he fiercely defends despite flagging allegiance elsewhere in the realm. He is mocked for failures which were not his, notably his strategy to force the Dardanelles in 1915. He seems less a figure of the twentieth century (which he loathes) than of the nineteenth — or, reaching even farther back, of Renaissance versatility. The wide sweep of his interests and activities embraces literature, painting, philosophy, hunting, polo, military science, the history of the United States — even architecture, bricklaying, and landscaping. Indeed, many of the shining ponds and pools and the happy waterfalls between the Weald and the manor were created by him, wearing hip-high Wellingtons and excavating the rich earth with his hands.[2]

Tree-locked and silent at dawn, Chartwell's immediate grounds further testify to his stamina. On the south side of the mansion, a garden surrounded by pleasant red brick — walled by him — invites his guest to peer inside the "Mary Cot," a brick playhouse which he built for his nine-year-old daughter. Between the playhouse and the great house lie his orchard of fruit trees and a tennis court of barbered grass he shaped for his wife, Clementine. Eastward, the flushed sky reveals a lawn terrace; northward, his heated swimming pool and ponds inhabited by black swans and "Churchill's goldfish" (actually golden orfe). He is planning to cement into Chartwell's north wall, overlooking the pool, the family's coat of arms and its Spanish motto, so appropriate in these years of his political exile: *Fiel Pero Desdichado* — Faithful but Unfortunate.

On the grounds are various lesser buildings. A painting studio. A white cottage with two bedrooms houses Maryott White, Mary's governess — "Nana" to the little girl but "Cousin Moppet" to the others. She and Nellie Romilly, Clementine's sister, are two of Mrs. Churchill's relatives in residence, sharing the household tasks. Another cottage is planned; Winston expects to finish it in 1939; then he and Clemmie will move into it, leaving the mansion to their son, Randolph. It is startling to realize that all this is less than twenty-five miles from Hyde Park corner. There men on soapboxes tell crowds, who nod in agreement, that society is rushing toward catastrophe. In eight years it will be upon them, but here all is serene. The sound of heavy guns, the roar of hostile bomb-laden aircraft overhead, arrowing toward London, are unimaginable. Quietude lies like a comforting veil over the house and grounds; Winston's 1932 Daimler 35/120 six-cylinder Landaulette seems an intrusion. He would do without the motorcar if he could; he despises automobiles, and if he encounters a traffic jam on one of those infrequent occasions when he himself is at the wheel, he simply drives on the sidewalk.

The house is a metaphor of its squire. It is above all staunch. On the outside the red bricks meet neatly; within, the walls are upright. Studs join beams with precision, doors fit sensibly. Like the householder it is complex, and, like him, steeped in the past. Most of the existing structure dates from the fifteenth century, but annals record an owner in 1350, and the oldest part of the building, now occupied by Churchill's study, was built twenty years after the Battle of Hastings, making it ten years older than Westminster Hall. After acquiring it for £5,000 in the early 1920s, he spent £18,000 on renovations. The front is stately, almost classic in its simplicity. The door frame, which Winston acquired from a London dealer, originally belonged to some other great country home when Victoria was a very young queen; the wood is silvered by age, and its pilasters and scrolls strike a baroque note. The back of the mansion is craggy, a consequence of the master's many accretions.

At daybreak the air is fresh and cool, but by midmorning it will be uncomfortably warm, and the mullioned, transomed windows are open. There is an exception. Those in Churchill's bedroom are puttied shut. He likes the country, but not country air; drafts, he believes, invite common colds, to which he has been susceptible since childhood. There is also the matter of noise. Any noise, especially if high-pitched, is an abomination. The jangling of cowbells will destroy his train of thought. But whistling, notes W. H. Thompson, the Scotland Yard detective who serves as his bodyguard from time to time, is the worst: "It sets up an almost psychiatric disturbance in him — intense, immediate, and irrational. I have seen him expostulate with boys on the street who were whistling as he passed."[3]

Daybreak brings movement to Chartwell's grounds. Sleep still envelops master, mistress, and their four children — Diana, twenty-three and about to be married; Randolph, twenty-one and already a problem (he has been drinking double brandies since he was eighteen); titian-haired Sarah, dreaming of fame on the stage at eighteen; and, in the bedroom above her, little Mary, who mercilessly taunts Sarah about her beaux. The pets are up and about, however. Trouble, Sarah's chocolate-colored spaniel, Harvey, Randolph's fox terrier, and Mary's Blenheim spaniel Jasper, a gift of the Duchess of Marlborough, are investigating the rosebushes and anointing them. Winston's pet cat, a marmalade named Tango, stretches himself; so does Mickey, a tabby cat. A fox trots up from the studio; horses begin to snort; a small black goat strides across the orchard; a goose wanders about aimlessly.

Presently people appear. Because today is a special occasion — all the children are home — the cook is Mrs. Georgina Landemare. These days Mrs. Landemare is here on and off, but like many other Westerham folk she will eventually be absorbed by Chartwell and the needs of its master. Already there are eighteen servants, including a butler, a footman, and an assistant gardener, who now arrives from his home in nearby Westerham to prowl the grounds in his daily search for the cigar butts Winston discarded yesterday, to use in his pipe. Most of the staff are natives of nearby Westerham. Both his secretaries, Grace Hamblin and Violet Pearman ("Mrs. P."), live within walking distance. Since childhood they have known Frank Jenner, the Westerham taxi driver who sometimes carries Churchill to Parliament and back and also serves as Chartwell's handyman; and Harry Whitbread, the laborer who taught Churchill to lay bricks and returns from time to time to work beside him. All of them, regardless of political persuasion, are proud of their eminent neighbor, though far from awed. Whitbread lectures him on how workingmen see social issues; Winston is attentive and thanks him afterward. The town delights in Churchillian lore. Once a month Westerham's barber trims his fringe of hair in his bedroom. Recently a temporary replacement asked him how he would like his hair cut. Churchill replied: "A man of my limited resources cannot presume to have a hairstyle. Get on and cut it."[4]

Chartwell is Churchill's sanctuary, his great keep. All his forays into tumultuous London politics are made from this sure base. However harsh the storms in the House of Commons, or the attacks on him in the press, here he is among friends and on grounds which, to him, epitomize his island nation. To him the essence of Chartwell is that it is completely, utterly, entirely *English*.

As one of the great advocates of the British Empire, he remembers the dictum of Queen Victoria: "I think it very unwise to give up what we hold." His struggle against England's pledge to free India has cost him much. But on matters of principle he has never learned how to compromise. *He does not know how to give in.*

Had he yielded on India, he could have looked to broader, brighter horizons. But he believes in his star. And if he can be spectacularly wrong he can also be terrifically right. If we are to follow his victories and his defeats — they will be many — we must try to define him, to identify him. One way is to follow him through a typical day at Chartwell. It is worthwhile if only because he will be forever remembered, not only as a great statesman, but also as one of history's great originals.

🦁   🦁

The spacious cream drawing room overlooks the Weald. Beneath the prismatic gleams of its eighteenth-century chandeliers, an exquisite little clock stands upon a mahogany Louis XVI *bureau à cylindre*. Now, at 8:00 A.M., it chimes. Above, in the householder's study, the sound is echoed as another clock also tells the hour. Simultaneously a sibilant rustle of Irish linen sheets breaks the hush in Churchill's bedroom a few feet away, as he sits bolt upright and yanks off his black satin sleep mask. *He*, not the sun, determines when he will greet the new day. Fumbling on the bedside table, he rings the bell for his valet-cum-butler, or, as Churchill calls him, "my man."[5]

Churchill's man is called David Inches by the rest of the household, and like his master he is considered eccentric, "a tremendous character," in the words of Grace Hamblin, Winston's chief secretary, "always overworked, always perspiring, sometimes drunk!" Awaiting him, Churchill peers around, rumpled but remarkably alert in view of the fact that he retired, as is his custom, only six hours ago. Poised thus, he is surrounded by Churchilliana. Elsewhere, Chartwell's decor reflects Clementine Churchill's understated upper-class elegance; but her husband is a flamboyant swashbuckler, a throwback to the Cavaliers or the Elizabethan patriciate with its aristocratic disdain for the opinions of others. Thus this most personal part of the mansion is decorated, not with implicit grace, but with explicit flourish — an ornate Fabergé cigar box, engraved plates of gold and silver, and, standing in solitary splendor, a gold-headed walking stick engraved "to my youngest minister." This last was his wedding present from King Edward VII and a reminder of the 1880s, when Edward was Prince of Wales and he and Winston's mother, Jennie, were intimate — an evocation of the first decade of the new century, when young Winston was a rising power in the Edwardian Parliament.[6]

A minute passes; two minutes. No valet. Winston fumes; the Churchillian lower lip juts out. His bizarre daily schedule deceives visitors who think it disorderly. Those who live at Chartwell know better. Though very odd, it *is* a schedule — is, in fact, a rigid one. Young F. W. D. ("Bill") Deakin will soon leave his don's rooms at Christ Church, Oxford, and become chief researcher (at a mere £300 a year) for Winston's multivolume biography of his great ancestor John Churchill, the first Duke of Marlborough. Long afterward Deakin will recall: "He was totally organized, almost like a clock. His routine was absolutely dictatorial. He set himself a ruthless timetable every day and would get very agitated, even cross, if it was broken." He is very cross now. His valet is often dilatory, though today the blame is not his. Lately the bell has not been working properly. And though Churchill is now bellowing, his shouts are unheard. That is partly his fault. The walls in this part of the mansion are thick. By puttying all the crevices he has effectively soundproofed the room.[7]

Raging, he flings aside the counterpane, leaps out, stamps his bare foot like a spoiled child, and then stalks dramatically across the room, crossing the threshold and reaching the landing in pursuit of his man. This happens from time to time, and the effect is sometimes spectacular, for Churchill sleeps naked and remains so on such sorties. He will don a robe when visiting other homes, "in deference," as he puts it, to his hosts' "views of propriety," but at Chartwell he feels free to roam around nude; as one of his servants will later explain, it seems "completely natural to him." It did not seem natural to a young housemaid who has just left his employ. Looking up the stairwell one morning she beheld, on the top step, Winston Leonard Spencer Churchill in the buff — all 210 pounds of him, a massive pink man with a bald, smooth dome and broad if slightly stooped shoulders, glaring down at her, as one of Winston's secretaries remembers, "like a laser beam." The girl fled the house shrieking. She has sent for her belongings and her pay.[8]

At long last Inches arrives, sweating and offering profuse apologies. The Churchill children delight in mimicking him, but their father values his man; despite his tippling and other flaws, the valet knows the daily Churchillian drill. He opens the day properly, carrying in a tray bearing his master's first meal of the day: orange juice from a bottle (Winston detests freshly squeezed juice), and a cooked English breakfast, with, as the pièce de résistance, a small steak, a chicken leg, or a cutlet Churchill ordered set aside at last evening's dinner for this very purpose. There is also a small dish of jam, usually black cherry. If the jam has been forgotten Winston will lie there propped up on pillows, pouting and refusing to touch anything on the tray until it appears.[9]

Rising, he moves toward the bathroom with an alacrity surprising for his age and weight and quickly shaves himself with a safety razor while his valet draws the first of his two daily baths. Like preparing the breakfast, this requires precision. Churchill will not enter the tub until it is two-thirds full and the bath thermometer registers 98 degrees. Once in, he demands that the temperature be raised to 104 degrees. Inches, obedient, again opens the hot spigot. The water has now reached the brim. Winston likes it that way; on his instructions the bath's overflow drain has been sealed off. This is splendid hydrotherapy, but like his immodest excursions beyond his bedroom door, it invites disaster. He likes to play in his bath, and when on impulse he turned a somersault, "exactly like a porpoise," a spectator recalls, the tub overflowed, damaging the ceiling below and, worse, drenching the frock coat of an eminent Frenchman there who called to pay his respects. Now a special drain has been installed. Churchill lolls in his bath, reciting Kipling, rehearsing speeches or lectures he will soon deliver, or singing, not in the virile baritone familiar in Parliament, but in a soft, high tone.[10] Elsewhere in the great building Sarah ("Mule," he fondly calls her) has risen and is playing the most popular hit of the season on her phonograph:

Night and day
You are the one . . .

Sarah's father prefers to recall melodies which evoke the England of his youth, long before 1914 and Armageddon, when, as he wrote afterward in his history of the Great War, "the world on the verge of catastrophe was very brilliant," when "nations and empires crowned with princes and potentates rose majestically on every side, lapped in the accumulated treasures of the long peace"[11] — when young patricians like Lieutenant Winston S. Churchill, subaltern of horse in Her Britannic Majesty's Fourth Hussars, lived like gods here and throughout the vast British Empire. Talleyrand once observed that those who did not live under *l'ancien régime* did not know what true *douceur de vivre* meant. Being an aristocrat in the Victorian and Edwardian eras had been *fun,* and Winston never tires of singing the great hit of the Boer War, when his escape from an enemy prisoner-of-war camp made him a national hero:

> *Good-bye, Dolly, I must leave you,*
> *Though it breaks my heart to go;*
> *Something tells me I am needed*
> *At the front to meet the foe!*

Nor of booming out Victorian England's anthem of imperial conquest:

> *It's the soldiers of the Queen, my lads,*
> *Who've been the lads, who've seen the lads,*
> *In the fight for England's glory, lads,*
> *Of her world-wide glory let us sing!*

In the England of 1932, glory has become a discredited word. After "the glorious dead" of 1914–1918, the word "glory" now soils the air. Therefore, when he warns of a Germany obsessed with a yearning for vengeance, crowds heckle him or drift away. He is no tribune of the people now. Although he believes in radical social solutions, he remains a traditionalist in all else. And tradition, he holds, begins at home. The ritualistic unfolding of a Chartwell day, from dawn to Kent's long blue twilight, is for him a kind of private pageant. He enjoys it; he considers it as efficient as it is delightful, and he never doubts — nor does anyone else sleeping beneath this roof — that he alone is qualified to be the playwright, producer, director, stage manager, and, of course, hero of the performance.

It is time for the star to don his first costume. Emerging from his bath pink and clean, he waits impatiently until Inches has toweled him dry and then slips into one of two worn-out cherished dressing gowns. The more subdued is dark blue velvet; the other, a riot of green and gold displaying a scarlet dragon coiled sinuously around his plump torso. His valet has been busy during his bath. Churchill will remain in bed all morning, and for a man with his tender skin this invites bedsores. Therefore Inches has brought a basket of large sponges, which he now deftly thrusts between the sheet and the most vulnerable parts of the Churchillian anatomy as his master yaws this way and that.[12]

The tray has gone. Remaining within reach are the jam and a weak (three-ounce) scotch and soda — always Johnnie Walker Red — which the prostrate Winston will sip occasionally over the next four hours in the tradition of Palmerston, Pitt, and Baldwin. However, the legend that he is a heavy drinker is quite untrue. Churchill is a sensible, if unorthodox, drinker. There is always some alcohol in his bloodstream, and it reaches its peak late in the evening after he has had two or three scotches, several glasses of champagne, at least two brandies, and a highball, but his family never sees him the worse for drink. He remarks: "We all despise a man who gets drunk." And, after an exchange of views on drinking: "All I can say is that I have taken more out of alcohol than alcohol has taken out of me." He encourages absurd myths about his alcoholic capacity, however, partly to furbish his macho image, which needs it because he cries so often in public ("I'm a blubberer," he cheerfully tells friends), and partly because Europeans still like to think that their leaders are men who can hold their liquor. Winston tipples off and on all day but never gets drunk.[13]

Having tasted this first scotch, he is ready for one of the children's pug dogs, who leaps upon the bed, trembling with joy, tail wagging furiously. Churchill then lights his first cigar of the day. His valet is custodian of Chartwell's cigar hoard, which will eventually grow to over three thousand, all from Havana, mostly Romeo y Julietas and La Aroma de Cubas, kept in a tiny room between this chamber and his study on shelves labeled "wrapped," "naked," and "large." Friends and admirers have sent Winston countless cigar cutters, and he carries one on his watch chain. He never uses them, however. Instead, he moistens one end of a fresh cigar, pierces it with a long match, blows through it from the other end to clear a passage, and lights it from the candle that always stands by his bed. During the course of a day he may consume ten or more cigars, but he seldom smokes one through. Indeed, most of the time they will be unlit. He simply chews them and never inhales. If one becomes hopelessly frayed, he may wrap it in gummed brown paper, calling this improvisation a "bellyband."[14]

The morning papers are neatly stacked by the bed, with *The Times* and the *Daily Telegraph* on top and the *Daily Worker* on the bottom. Editorials are read first, frequently with such intense concentration that the newsprint may become hopelessly smeared with jam. That is a servant's problem, not his; when Winston has finished a page, he simply lets it slide to the floor. All in all, he devotes two hours to the press, occasionally stepping into his slippers and striding toward his wife's bedroom to call her attention to this or that item. It may be a mere statistic representing an increase in Germany's mineral ore imports, but he sees significance in it. Or she may arrive at *his* bedside on a similar errand. Although they never breakfast together, each starts the day with the same rite.[15]

As he glares at the last pages of the *Worker,* Mrs. P. or Grace Hamblin — later to be joined by Kathleen Hill — enters the room. It is important that she do so boldly, even noisily; her employer is not deaf, but he dislikes surprises. If someone glides in, he will rise wrathfully and roar: "Goddammit!" As she prepares to take dictation, he riffles through the morning mail, which she has sorted into three piles: affairs of state, private correspondence, and letters from the general public. As a young author he had written his mother, "My hand gets so cramped. I am writing every word twice & some parts three times." Now he seldom puts a word on paper himself — except when affixing his signature, correcting galley proofs, or writing close friends and his immediate family — and he normally uses fountain pens, blue ink for correspondence, red for proofs. The humblest correspondent receives a reply, but the secretary writes it. Winston merely outlines in the most general way what he wants said and she, familiar with his style and his love of anachronistic phrases ("sorely tried," "most grieved," "keenly elated," "pray give me the facts," "highly diverted"), fills it out. Important letters require more thought and longer searches for the right word. Once the mail has been cleared away, memoranda dictated, and visitors greeted — he will receive anyone except the King in his bedchamber — he may summon a researcher after glancing through proofs, and say: "Look this up," or "Find out about this." The researcher may be asked to read certain documents aloud. Or Churchill may turn to speeches. By noon the cadences of his prose have begun to trot; by 1:00 P.M. they are galloping. In the words of Mrs. Hill, he would often be "dashing around in shorts and undershirt and a bright red cummerbund while I trotted behind him from room to room with a pad and pencil struggling to keep pace with the torrential flow of words." One has the impression of a man in a desperate hurry, not even dressed yet, already behind the day's schedule — which is, in fact, the case.[16]

He is approaching his daily lunch crisis. The meal is to be served at 1:15 P.M.; often, eminent guests are arriving. And he is never there to greet them. He deplores this tardiness in himself yet cannot break it, though everyone at Chartwell knows the explanation: he systematically underestimates, usually by about five minutes, the length of time he needs to do everything, from shaving to wriggling about while his valet dresses him. Its most hair-raising consequences come while he is traveling. Once at Coventry station a close friend was pacing the platform beside an infuriated Clementine. The conductor was signaling all aboard when Winston finally came in sight. Clemmie told the friend: "Winston's a sporting man; he always gives the train a chance to get away." Even at Chartwell his dilatoriness is a source of distress for both his family and the manor's staff. Once a manservant conspired against him by setting his bedroom clock ahead. It worked for a while, because he scorned that offspring of trench warfare the wristwatch, remaining loyal to his large gold pocket watch, known to the family as "the turnip," which lay beyond his grasp. After his suspicions had been aroused, however, the game was up; he exposed it by simply asking morning visitors the time of day.[17]

Eventually a communal effort by all available servants propels their master, roughly dressed, down into the drawing room, which he enters with a beaming Here-I-am-at-last expression. If the assembled guests include newcomers under the impression that it is a normal upper-class British home, they are swiftly disillusioned by the greetings exchanged between the Churchills. Instead of "Hullo," they utter elementary animal sounds: "Wow-wow!" or "Miaow!" In the family, Christian names are replaced by exotic *petits noms*. Clementine addresses her husband as "Pug," he calls her "Cat." The children are "Puppy Kitten" (Diana), "the Chumbolly" (Randolph), "Mule" (Sarah), and "Mouse" (Mary).

At the round oaken dining room table on the floor below, Churchill chooses to sit facing eastward (making that the head of the round table), looking out across his terrace toward the largest of his artificial lakes. The servants place a candle in a silver Georgian holder by his setting. He will need it when, after one of his long monologues, he finds that his cigar has gone out. As he approaches his chair it is evident that he anticipates the meal with relish. Although he scorns exercise, his appetite is always keen. He cannot, however, be considered a gourmet. Intricate dishes are unappreciated by him; for lunch he prefers Irish stew, Yorkshire pudding with "good red beef," as he calls it, or an unsauced whiting with its tail in its mouth. Furthermore, he is a confirmed anthropomorphist; he has adopted many of Chartwell's chickens as pets, has even given them names and speaks of them as his "friends." So there is no fowl. He would be troubled by the thought that he was devouring one of them.[18]

To Churchill a meal without wine would not be a meal at all. In his ten years as squire of Chartwell he has yet to pass a day without confronting a shining bottle of champagne, always at dinner and often at lunch also. As a youth he declared: "A single glass of champagne imparts a feeling of exhilaration. The nerves are braced; the imagination is stirred; the wits become more nimble." A bottle produces the contrary effect: "A comatose insensibility." He confines himself to a single glass now. Apart from his contempt for the fiction that red meat and white wine do not mix, his drinking habits are characteristic of upper-class Englishmen. He regards the American martini as barbaric, and when Jan Christiaan Smuts arrives and presents him with a bottle of South African brandy he takes a sip, rolls it around on his tongue, then rolls his eyes, and, beaming at his old friend, says: "My dear Smuts, it is excellent." He pauses. "But it is not brandy." At the end of lunch, after a glass of port with a plain ice and a ripe Stilton, he greets the appearance of Hine, *real* brandy, with a blissful smile and the reaming of a fresh cigar. Brandy, he believes, is essential to a stable diet, and the older the bottle the better. Although uninebriated, he becomes more genial, more affable, more expansive, radiating reassurance.[19]

Sir John Colville, who will later serve as private secretary to three prime ministers, including Churchill, may well have been right in arguing that Churchill's friends are — except for the absence of boors and the garrulous — notable for their variety. They include the witty, the ambitious, the lazy, the dull, the exhibitionists, the talented, the intellectual, and above all the honorable. But the most gifted will appear at dinner. And his guests are all *friends*. In London, even in his pied-à-terre at No. 11 Morpeth Mansions, where he stays while attending Parliament, he is embattled. He needs no snipers here.

But neither are guests confined to lickspittles and sycophants. Himself a celebrity before the turn of the century, before the word had entered common usage, Churchill relishes the company of others in the public eye. His favorite American, the financier Bernard Baruch, visits here whenever in England. T. E. Lawrence, now serving in RAF ranks under an assumed name, roars up on his motorcycle and, knowing that the spectacle will enchant Mary, appears at dinner in his robes as a prince of Arabia. Charlie Chaplin entertains them all with his pantomime and mimicry. Winston asks whether he has chosen his next role. "Yes," Chaplin replies: "Jesus Christ." Churchill pauses, then asks, "Have you cleared the rights?"

Among the regulars at the table are two MPs who remain loyal to Winston in these years of his political eclipse: the handsome young Robert J. G. ("Bob") Boothby and Brendan Bracken, a brash adventurer and self-made millionaire notable for his pug nose, granny glasses, disheveled mop of flaming red hair, and the extraordinary rumors, which he encourages, that he is his host's illegitimate son. Winston finds this gossip highly amusing. Clementine does not. (She once confronted her husband and demanded to know whether the stories were true. He replied: "I've looked the matter up, but the dates don't coincide.") Clemmie is the only participant who is never intimidated by her husband's deep frowns and hissing wrath, and her dislike of Bracken, revealed by gesture, glance, and edged voice, is stark. Churchill admires her spirit — "God," he later confides in a friend, "she dropped down on poor Brendan like a jaguar out of a tree" — but remains silent. Others at the table wonder why. Undeniably Bracken is gifted and able. But his behavior, even in this most tolerant of homes, is atrocious. Recently he went through Clementine's scrapbook with shears, scissoring out articles of Winston's career.[20]

And Winston, for reasons which reveal more about him than Bracken, enjoys the younger man's company. Men who have done something with their lives interest him — indeed, they are the only men who do. He is particularly impressed by military men; any winner of the Victoria Cross is embraced, and when he meets Sir Bernard Freyberg, the New Zealand war hero, Churchill insists that the embarrassed Freyberg strip so that his host can count his thirty-three battle scars. Similarly, men who have amassed fortunes while he has struggled year after year with creditors, hold enormous appeal for him. That is part of Bracken's charm.

It also explains, in part, Winston's fondness for Baruch, though Baruch's appeal is broader. He is an American, he is Jewish, he recognizes the menace of an aggressive Germany, and Churchill is indebted to him for an extraordinary act of shrewdness and generosity. Winston was badly hurt in the Wall Street Crash three years ago. Had it not been for Baruch, however, it would have been much worse; he could have spent the rest of his life in debt. He is not a born gambler; he is a born *losing* gambler. In New York at the time, he dropped into Baruch's office and decided to play the market, and as prices tumbled he plunged deeper and deeper, trying to outguess the stock exchange just as he had tried to outguess roulette wheels on the Riviera. In Wall Street, as in Monte Carlo, he failed. At the end of the day he confronted Baruch in tears. He was, he said, a ruined man. Chartwell and everything else he possessed must be sold; he would have to leave the House of Commons and enter business. The financier gently corrected him. Churchill, he said, had lost nothing. Baruch had left instructions to buy every time Churchill sold and sell whenever Churchill bought. Winston had come out exactly even because, he later learned, Baruch even paid the commissions.[21]

Bracken can't match that. Being British and in Parliament, however, he can serve his idol in other ways. In the House he is scorned as Winston's "sheepdog," his "lapdog," or — this from Conservative leader Stanley Baldwin — his faithful *chela*, the Hindi word for minion. But uncritical admiration is precisely what Churchill needs. He is in the third of what will be ten years of political exile to the back benches. No other statesman in the country's political history will have served so long a Siberian sentence, and he would have to have a heart of stone not to be grateful for Bracken's steadfast, unquestioning allegiance.[22]

Churchill may even be flattered by the stories that he fathered a son on the wrong side of the blanket. Those closest to him agree that he is undersexed; some suggest that the explanation lies in the promiscuity of his beautiful, wanton mother. The historian A. J. P. Taylor will reflect: "She moved from one man to another. And it's possible, I don't say this is the only explanation, that Churchill's really almost extreme chastity was a reaction to his mother's lack of it. There are other possibilities. He may have been weakly sexed biologically, or the explanation may have been psychological. He once remarked: 'The reason I can write so much is that I don't waste my essence in bed.' " Winston didn't marry until his thirty-fourth year, and there is every reason to believe that he was a virgin bridegroom. Despite frequent separations from Clemmie, who disapproves of the lush Riviera and spends her holidays with the children at spartan resorts on the North Sea, or a hotel near Rugby, he has committed but one act of infidelity, at Golfe-Juan, on the Mediterranean, with a divorced, titled Englishwoman whose seductive skills and sexual experience far exceeded his. To one who cherishes his reputation for mischievousness, whispers that a fellow MP is his bastard may not be altogether unwelcome.[23]

Bracken is one of his two most striking disciples. The other, in many ways Brendan's opposite, complements him. Born in Germany of an American mother, Frederick A. Lindemann took his doctorate at the University of Berlin in 1910, continued his scientific studies in Paris and Brussels, confirmed Einstein's refinement of Planck's quantum theory, and, as a member of the Royal Aircraft Establishment in the Great War, organized London's kite balloon barrage. After the Armistice he was appointed professor of experimental philosophy at Oxford and recognized as one of Europe's leading physicists. Now in 1932 "the Prof," as everyone in the Churchill family calls him, has just published his *Physical Significance of the Quantum Theory*. His Oxford colleagues now believe that his best work is behind him; Professor Derek Jackson notes that the younger generation regards him "as more of a theoretical physicist devoid of experimental ability." Churchill disagrees, and so will history.[24]

Lindemann's achievements cannot be impeached, but in his own way he can be trying. Even by Chartwell's standards he is odd. Indeed, he seems to be everything Winston is not. Tobacco in any form is anathema to him. He lives largely on the whites of eggs and is a vegetarian and teetotaler, except when as a guest here, he bows to his host's insistence that he consume exactly 32 cubic centimeters of brandy a day. He always wears a bowler, even on a warship or in the cockpit of an RAF fighter. His valet and secretary, Harvey, who drives his huge, unwieldy limousine, is his double, matching his attire of the day shirt by shirt, sock by sock, and bowler by bowler.[25]

The Prof will follow Churchill anywhere. Winston's motives for cultivating him are very different. Lindemann's many talents include a matchless gift as an interpreter of science for laymen. In the words of Sir John Colville, Lindemann can "simplify the most opaque problem, scientific, mechanical or economic," translating technical jargon into language which provides "a lucid explanation" and sacrifices "nothing of importance." Churchill loathes scientific terminology. He never even mastered public school arithmetic. The Prof provides him with the essential facts when he needs them without disrupting his concentration on other matters. Like radar, Lindemann's "beautiful brain," as Churchill calls it, will prove worth several divisions in the struggle to save England from Adolf Hitler. Less than ten years from now he will arrive at No. 10 Downing Street with clear, accurate charts which, by replacing statistics, present displays showing England's stockpiles of vital raw materials, the rate at which ships are being launched on the Clyde, the Tyne, and Barrow, and Britain's production of tanks, artillery, small arms, and warplanes in terms the prime minister can understand with what Colville calls "infallible skill and punctuality."[26]

It is a measure of Churchill's own accomplishments that he can inspire a man with whom he shares little except a common affection for Americans. The Prof has little use for others. Like many of his laboratory colleagues, he never applies the scientific method in judging society. He is in fact a snarl of prejudices. So profound is his misogyny that he has not spoken to his only sister for fifteen years. His sole recreation is tennis. He is a champion of Sweden, an achievement all the more remarkable because, to discourage women from regarding him as a sex object, he plays in the hottest weather wearing thick black ribbed socks and a heavy shirt tightly buttoned at the wrists.[27]

This is not at all Churchillian, though modern feminists would regard Winston as a stereotype of male chauvinism. He opposed woman suffrage until Clementine converted him, wouldn't dream of soliciting a woman's advice on matters of national policy, and dropped the idea of writing an article for *Collier's* on the prospects of a woman becoming prime minister of England because he thought the idea laughable. Nevertheless, he admires Englishwomen of his class and enjoys their company — provided, of course, that they are attractive and don't attempt to discuss topics reserved for members of his own sex. As a man who reached his majority in 1895, when Victorian gentlemen never used the words "breast" or "leg" if ladies were present, he assumes that they are innocents who must be shielded from the brutal facts of life and that feminine beauty is unaccompanied by carnal desire.

If Chartwell's guest book is a reliable index, the only ladies who will be invited to lunch in Churchill's heaven — with the one great exception of his longtime friend Lady Violet Bonham Carter, née Asquith — will be escorted, and even they will be required to confine themselves to smiling when their host makes a clever remark, nodding vigorously when he has expressed an opinion, and expressing no opinion of their own. This is not sexist, however, because it also applies to gentleman guests. Winston means to dominate them and cheerfully acknowledges it; his own idea of a fine meal is to dine well and then discuss a serious topic — "with myself as chief conversationalist." It isn't even conversation; unlike Lloyd George he is a poor listener, has little interest in what others have to say, and, if he is not the speaker, withdraws into silent communion with himself while his interior monologue, the flow of private rhetoric, soars on. His daughter Mary will recall that "small talk or social chitchat bored Winston profoundly — but he rarely suffered from it, since he completely ignored it, pursuing his own themes."[28]

In London he will give those who disagree with him a fair hearing; two of his favorite aphorisms are "I would rather be right than consistent" and "In the course of my life I have often had to eat my words, and I must confess that I have always found it a wholesome diet." But at Chartwell, with a pony of brandy in one hand and a cigar in the other, he is inclined to bully those who challenge him. And the fact is that few dare try. Lords Birkenhead and Beaverbrook could. Birkenhead — F. E. Smith before his ennoblement — would cross foils with Churchill and win as often as he lost. It is perhaps significant that F.E. became Winston's best friend. And the man has not drawn breath who can intimidate Beaverbrook, the great press lord, known to the Churchills as "the Beaver," who, when he first met Churchill in 1911, was plain Max Aitken, a Canadian upstart. During one visit here he declined wine with his Stilton. "Port is the brother of cheese," his host said in lordly reproach. "Yes," Max flashed back, "and the sister of gout." But Birkenhead has lain in his grave two years, and Beaverbrook, though Churchill's once and future ally, will seldom be seen at Chartwell in this decade. The feisty Beaver, for all his shrewdness, shares the almost unanimous conviction of England's ruling classes that

Winston — whom he calls a "busted flush" — exaggerates the emerging Nazi menace; like his fellow press lords he believes Hitler's friendship worth cultivating and assures his readers — he will reassure them every year, even when the sands are running out in 1939 — that "there will be no war."[29]

Lacking peers in colloquy, Churchill rules his table as an absolute monarch. His expression radiates benevolence, his arms are spread to embrace everyone there; then, having opened all hearts, he speaks of today's guest of honor, usually an old friend. Then his visage darkens, he points a threatening finger, and all await the inevitable consignment of a transgressor — never present — to his doom. Today's wretch turns out to be Thomas Babington Macaulay, who dared slander John Churchill, the first Duke of Marlborough. The great duke's great-great-great-great-great-great grandson thunders his verdict: "It is beyond our hopes to overtake Lord Macaulay. We can only hope that truth will follow swiftly enough to fasten the label 'liar' to his genteel coattails."[30]

Guests say afterward that the host is so fascinating they cannot remember what they ate. Political scientist and historian Harold Laski observes that many of them, in trying to remember all Winston's mots, overlook the flaws in his reasoning. Other critics note that Churchill has no small talk, though as the American writer Virginia Cowles asks, "Why should anyone want small talk when Churchill is at the peak of his form?" Certainly no one here tries to stop him. Later, biographer Lady Longford will write that "his set-pieces were . . . so brilliant that few listeners wished to interrupt. Similarly, they recognized that he was self-centered precisely because he had an interior vision which must be brought to the light of day. They felt privileged to assist."[31]

Absolutely secure here, he can laugh at himself and encourage others to join him. "Megalomania," he says, referring to his domineering manner, "is the only form of sanity." He has just published a collection of his magazine articles under the title *Thoughts and Adventures* (*Amid These Storms* in the United States) and, as usual, he has sent copies to friends and acquaintances in high places. Opening an envelope bearing the royal crest, he reads aloud an acknowledgment from the Duke of Gloucester: "Dear Winston. Thank you for your new book. I have put it on the shelf with the others." And he relishes and retells the story of how F.E., his adversary when Winston was the Liberal member for Dundee, set a Tory rally roaring with laughter by interrupting his speech to say: "I see from the *Dundee Advertiser* — I mean the newspaper, not the politician. . . ." Like a man trying on neckties, he tests his phrases at lunch, watching faces to measure their effect. "An immense responsibility," he ruminates, "rests upon the German people for this subservience to the barbaric idea of autocracy. This is the gravamen against them in history — that, in spite of all their brains and courage, they worship power, and let themselves be led by the nose."[32]

The last drop of brandy is gone. He gives the empty bottles a glance, not of regret, but of affection; he will paint them, he announces, and call the completed canvas *Bottlescape*. Through the meal his visage has been kaleidoscopic: somber, mischievous, bored, proud, arrogant, magnanimous, despairing, indifferent, exalted, contemptuous, adoring. Now it screws up, creasing his laugh lines, and he makes a crowing, expiratory sound in his throat — signs, as his friends know, that he is about to amuse them, perhaps with that odd brand of self-mockery to which British soldiers and parliamentarians alike turn in times of adversity.[33]

They are right. He tells of taking his annual Riviera holiday without his valet. This, for a patrician of his generation, was a momentous decision. He had never even been on a bus or even seen the tube. In traveling alone he felt he was "striking a blow for equality and fraternity," but misadventures plagued him all the way, and he describes each, relishing the details. His guests laugh; it is a good story. But it is more. Winston cannot get through the day without servants, and he assumes this is true of all gentlemen. It *was* true in his youth, but is no longer. Later Colville, his assistant private secretary, will ask leave to become an RAF fighter pilot. Winston hates to see a valuable member of his staff go, but it is a request he, of all men, cannot refuse. Alone together, "Jock" and Winston *are* equals; the first Lord Colville became a peer in 1604. The younger man, like Winston, is a Harrovian; his Cambridge college is Trinity; his club, White's. Churchill, the quondam hussar, grandly declaims: "The RAF is the cavalry of modern war." But he is shocked when Colville tells him he will first serve in the ranks as an aircraftsman, second class. Winston protests: "You mustn't — you won't be able to take your man!" It hasn't crossed his mind that a civil servant earning £400 a year, about $32.30 a week, could hardly afford a valet.[34]

Should his visitors include a guest of great eminence, Churchill will offer to show him round Chartwell's grounds. Otherwise, he proceeds with his first afternoon activity: feeding his golden orfe, ducks, and swans. Donning a Stetson — if there is a chill in the air, he will also wear an overcoat — he heads for a broad wicker chair beside the goldfish pond, calling ahead, "Arf! Arf!" or "Yoick! Yoick!"

They rush to greet him, though a servant, a step behind him, has what they want. Twice a month Frank Jenner collects a blue baby-food tin at the local railway station. Within, packed in sawdust, are maggots, the caviar of goldfish gourmets. Winston offers a lidful of maggots to the fish; when it is empty he holds out the lid to be refilled. Nearby a wooden box contains bread crumbs. These Churchill feeds to the ducks and swans.

The feeding is an integral part of the Churchillian day. After it, he sinks into the wicker chair, dismisses his servant, and remains, companionless and immobile, for at least a half hour. A table beside the chair bears another weak Johnnie Walker and soda, a box of cigars, a pagoda-shaped ashtray, and a container of long Canadian matches, useful in a rising wind. The squire of Chartwell prefers solitude here. Long afterward, servants will recall his reciting Housman and Kipling to himself, or reading, or simply staring out across the Weald, alone with his reflections, a great hunched figure whose cigar smoke mingles with the many scents of an English country home, including, in season, the fragrance of freshly cut grass.

His interest in all creatures on his estate is unflagging. As a young Colonial Office under secretary he had been an enthusiastic hunter of wild game, but those days are past. Now he holds a kitten to his face and murmurs, "Darling." It is true that he kicked a large tabby cat who played with the telephone cord when he was speaking to the lord chancellor of England, shouting, "Get off the line, you fool!" — and hastily telling the chancellor, "Not you!" But afterward he offered the cat his apologies, which he never extends to human beings, cajoling the pet, cooing, "Don't you love me anymore?" and proudly telling his valet at breakfast next day, "My Mickey came to see me this morning. All is forgiven."[35]

In his reverence for all living creatures Churchill approaches ascetic Jainism. Butterflies are sacred. So are predators. He loses two Siberian geese to foxes, but when a fox trap is proposed, he shakes his head, saying, "I couldn't bear to think of them being hurt." Similarly, when a heron raids his ponds he merely covers them with wire netting, forbidding his staff even to scare the bird away. A sheet of frosted glass occupies one wall of the guests' bathroom in a friend's Mediterranean villa. During one of Winston's visits there, he observed that the bathroom light attracted night moths, who, fluttering against the glass, were easy prey for lurking lizards. He winced and gritted his teeth when the lizards chewed up their victims, but vetoed his valet's suggestion that the lizards be frightened away by tapping on the window. They were obeying a law of nature, he said, and ought not be punished.[36]

When a black swan falls ill, he does not hesitate to summon the keeper of the London Zoo. A goat sickens, and Whitehall's Ministry of Agriculture is consulted. Arriving home at 3:00 A.M. after a late session of

Parliament and learning that there has been no afternoon feeding at the pond, he rouses a maid to hold a flashlight while he makes amends to his piscatorial friends. All this is vexing to the sleepy maid. She is relieved when a new secretary becomes an overnight heroine in Winston's eyes. Something extraordinary has been happening to the fish. They are turning white and dying. Winston is stumped; so is his gardener. Then the girl pipes up: "I know what's wrong. They have fungus." Churchill gives her a lowering look. How, he rumbles, does she know? She replies that her parents have an aquarium. He asks: "And how do you treat it?" She answers: "You put in a salt solution and gradually the fungus drops off. If you act quickly enough they can be saved." He does, they are, and during the healing period he drives up to London and consults experts at the zoological gardens in Regents Park. On his return he summons the young secretary. "Do you know what they told me?" he asks. "They said exactly what *you* said." He beams at her. "Oh, I think you are a *very clever* secretary! You know what goes wrong with fish. Henceforth, you will attend them." He is delighted, the staff is delighted. The feelings of the girl, who has been at Chartwell long enough to know that her other duties will continue, are mixed.

Winston is, among other things, a dog's best friend. Observing one manservant's poodle limping, he tells him to send it to a veterinarian, and when the pet returns well two weeks later, he pays the bill. One of Chartwell's animals vexes him; Mary's dog, it seems, has never been properly housebroken. Winston mutters darkly: "He commits at least three indiscretions a day." Mary is worried about her dog. But her father cannot bring himself to intervene, and the pug continues to enjoy his unsanitary ways.

Still recuperating from a traffic accident he suffered months before in New York, Churchill lays no bricks these days. But he cannot remain idle. He is, Bill Deakin notes, "incapable of inactivity," and Cousin Moppet writes: "Winston has so many irons in the fire that the day is not nearly long enough." During one of his Johnsonian lunches he remarks: "Broadly speaking, human beings may be divided into three classes: those who are billed to death, those who are worried to death, and those who are bored to death." Though heavily billed (he has just settled £1,600 of his son's debts), and deeply worried about the events stirring central Europe, he is never bored. To Virginia Cowles, a weekend guest, he says: "With all the fascinating things there are to do in the world, some people while away their time playing Patience. Just fancy!"[37]

Since his physician has banned bricklaying, he heads for his studio, telling a member of his staff to fetch his brushes, easel, and palette. He intends to paint "one of my beloved cats" or to re-create on canvas a still life from photographs taken from their latest visit to Cannes or Marrakech. "If it weren't for painting," he tells a friend, "I couldn't live. I couldn't bear the strain of things."

Winston designed the studio. Inside, it is small but very lofty, providing maximum light. In constructing it, he put wooden slats along the interior walls; incompleted canvases went there. Eventually the slats will become shelves, supporting some five hundred finished paintings. He paints few people and no violence, but the full body of his work provides an overview of his travels: the Acropolis, Stromboli, the canals of Amsterdam, Scandinavian fjords, Pompeii, Rome, Rotterdam, Passchendaele, Ypres, Vimy Ridge, Messines, Menin, Waterloo, Scapa Flow, Ulster, Balmoral, Devonshire, and Kent. Cathedrals fascinate him. So do ruins; he had to be dragged away from Pompeii. And he finds waterfalls irresistible. He spent days at his easel by the roaring Jordan. On his finished canvas there is an illusion of moving water; one can almost catch the sound of it.

His painting methods are purely Churchillian. Confronted by a virgin canvas, he moves rapidly and decisively, giving the scene a swift appraisal and then slapping on the oils, reacting instinctively to a single theme: a villa, a temple, sailboats at low tide. Inspector Thompson, after hours of watching him at his easel, writes: "I would think that the man's inner spirit is superbly calm and that he paints from it — never from the mind or intellect." Thomas Bodkin, director of the National Gallery of Ireland, thinks successful professional painters might learn a lot from Winston: "He does not try to say two things at the same time. . . . The dominant motive is never obscured by irrelevancies." After a careful examination of Winston's canvases, Sir John Rothenstein, director of the Tate Gallery and one of England's most eminent art critics, judges them to be works "of real merit which bear a direct and intimate relationship to his outlook on life. In these pictures there comes bubbling irrepressibly up his sheer enjoyment of the simple beauties of nature."[38]

If he has chosen not to paint this afternoon, he may summon a "Miss" and enter the study to make a start on the day's work, an article for an American magazine, perhaps, or a piece for Fleet Street. Or he may read in his bedchamber, listening to BBC music, provided it is *his* kind of music — *H.M.S. Pinafore, The Pirates of Penzance,* and *The Mikado,* or French military marches. Once more Chartwell hears the poignant counterpoint of father and daughter. Sarah is playing the nostalgic:

> *April in Paris —*
> *Chestnuts in blossom . . .*

while Churchill is exuberantly tapping his feet in rhythm to:

Randolph is growing a beard, which, his father writes, "makes him look perfectly revolting. He declares he looks like Christ. To me he looks like my poor father in the last phase of his illness."[40]

Mary has just returned from the local school, where she is a day student; Cousin Moppet will now read to her. Like the others she hails her father as "Pa-*pah.*" After replying ("Puppy Kitten," "Mule," etc.) he may examine his firearms. He likes them; he has never forgotten the Mauser that saved his life in the last great charge of British cavalrymen at Omdurman. He is also an extraordinary marksman, perhaps because a weapon, like a paintbrush, does exactly what it is told to do and never argues back. Automobiles quarrel with him; he is the worst driver in England. When he tried to fly he nearly killed himself; if he takes to the dance floor all other couples leave it. But with his Mannlicher, .32 Webley Scott, or Colt .45, which require only a keen eye and a steady hand, he is a dead shot. Later, at the age of seventy, he will challenge the accuracy of guards officers and General of the Army Dwight D. Eisenhower. Of Winston's ten shots, one will hit the fringe of the bull's-eye; the other nine will be dead center. The elite guardsmen will scatter theirs. Poor Ike will miss the target completely.

Now Churchill may withdraw and don a silk sleeping vest for a siesta, a custom he had observed in 1895 as a young war correspondent in Cuba, where the climate imposed it and custom sanctioned it. The temperature in his bedchamber is always exactly 74 degrees Fahrenheit. Yet he insists on the vest. Slipping into it, and drawing the sleep mask over his eyes, he slides between fresh linen sheets. He never requires more than a few seconds to drift off. Moments after his cheek touches the pillow, before his valet has even left the room, Winston is slumbering. He can do this almost anywhere. In automobiles or aboard planes he carries a special pillow; he dons the mask, curls his head down into his chest like a mother hen, and enjoys absolute rest until the journey's end. At Chartwell his siesta may last two hours. Refreshed, he joins his family at 5:00 P.M., usually playing cards with Clemmie or Randolph in the drawing room. Bridge is rarely played because he never wins. Furthermore, it is a relatively new game and therefore suspect. He prefers mah-jongg, backgammon, gin rummy, and bezique, a forerunner of pinochle. Usually played with two thirty-two-card packs, bezique can be traced to the 1600s; its antiquity qualifies it for Churchillian amusement.

As the drawing room clock strikes 7:00 P.M., he mounts the stairs for his second daily bath. During these ablutions he likes an audience, old companions who at appropriate moments will laugh, murmur approval, express indignation, and understand his arcane references to political upheavals on the Continent and parliamentary intrigue in London. If no close friends are among his guests, he may send for a research assistant and review their progress with *Marlborough*. As a last resort, Winston will summon a Miss to sit outside and take dictation during pauses in his soaping, rinsing, and splashing. Before his valet guides him into his dinner jacket, he signs the day's mail and then dawdles, putting on another record, or fashioning a bellyband, or singing "Abdullah Bulbul Amir" to the thirty-eighth verse. Dinner, the day's main event, is scheduled to be served at 8:30. He may reach the drawing room by 8:45.

It is lunch on a far grander scale, with more guests, of greater distinction, silvery buckets of iced champagne, Churchill presiding in his grandest manner, and several courses. Among the foods likeliest to be served are clear soup, oysters, caviar, Gruyère cheese, pâté de foie gras, trout, shoulder of lamb, lobster, dressed crab, *petite marmite*, scampi, Dover sole, chocolate éclairs, and, of course, roast beef and Yorkshire pudding. Winston never eats tripe, crumpets, sausages, cabbage, salami, sauerkraut, corned beef, or rice pudding. Clemmie, who knows his preferences, has briefed the cook on what is to be on the menu. He decides when meals are to be served, he determines who is to be invited.

If he has been in London recently, different versions of his latest witticisms have been repeated in the clubs of Pall Mall and St. James's, in drawing rooms of the West End and the City's counting rooms. Asked now to confirm them, he nods as he gropes for a match or the stem of his wineglass, pausing occasionally to correct a verb or alter syntax. He tells of how, crossing Parliament Square, he ran into Lord Londonderry, his cousin and frequent adversary. Londonderry, hoping to drive home a point, had asked him: "Have you read my latest book?" Winston chortles his reply: "No, I only read for pleasure or profit." In the House of Commons he had remarked upon Sir Stafford Cripps's "look of injured guilt." So many cabinet ministers wanted ennoblement that he had protested: "They can't all have peerages; there ought to be some disappearages." One member of the government had protested that this was a slur; Churchill shot back: "I know of no case where a man added to his dignity by standing on it."[41]

It is difficult to keep up with a host who can set such a pace. Nevertheless the dinner is not a one-man show. Guests have been invited for luster, not servility. David Lloyd George has been in Parliament ten years longer than Churchill and an awesome prime minister for six. Sir Archibald Sinclair — who, when Churchill led a battalion in the trenches, served as his second in command — is about to assume leadership of the

Liberal party, which, with fifty-nine seats in the House, holds the balance between Labour and the Conservatives. Alfred Duff Cooper and Anthony Eden, both of whom were decorated for bravery in France, hold subcabinet posts in the government and will soon become full-fledged ministers, Duff Cooper at the War Office and Eden as foreign secretary.

Late in life Mary will recall: "The 'basic' house party, enlarged by other guests, usually formed a gathering it would be hard to beat for value. There was little warming up; the conversation plunged straight into some burning or vital question. But the talk was by no means confined to politics; it ranged over history, art, and literature; it toyed with philosophical themes; it visited the past and explored the future. The Prof and his slide rule were much in demand on all scientific problems. Sometimes the conversation was a ding-dong battle of wits and words between, say, Winston and Duff Cooper, with the rest of the company skirmishing on the sidelines and keeping score. The verbal pyrotechnics waxed hot and fierce, usually dissolving into gales of laughter." Then, she remembers, conversation "usually dwindled" as everyone wanted to "share the main 'entertainment,' " which was almost always "a dramatic and compelling monologue from Winston." Frequently he would recite "Horatius," and "this was very popular with the children, as we could join in 'the brave days of old' bits."[42]

All his guests meet his conversational standards: "The man who cannot say what he has to say in good English cannot have very much to say that is worth listening to." None hesitates to speak up when he pauses for breath. Winston is unresentful of this. As Sir David Hunt, one of Churchill's private secretaries, will recall long afterward: "He has been accused of excessive addition to the monologue; there was certainly a tendency that way but he was always tolerant of interjections from his listeners if they were relevant or amusing." Collin Brooks, the newspaper editor, in comparing Churchill in the House with Churchill at Chartwell, notes that the style of his public speeches, "slow in pace and heavy in emphasis," yields, in the privacy of his home, to "a quicker flow." Winston's casual quips "sparkle and sting, but the talk is unhurried, with occasional pauses, for effect or to hold his listeners while he gropes for the right word." Intense or gay, he infuses his discussions of grave issues with gusto and what one guest will recall as "verbal gymnastics and mental pyrotechnics . . . often rounded off by a sudden colloquial that from most other people would be an anticlimax."[43]

Brooks sets down one of Winston's observations about politics: "Our weakness today is not in the decline of Parliament itself, but in the diminished interest which the press gives to it. It is, indeed, heartbreaking for any man to go down day after day in these turbulent times to deliver

speeches which, by the content, if not by their form, are of great impor-
tance, and to realize that they are heard by but a few hundreds of his fellow
Members, and read by but a scattering of people who habitually read
Hansard."[44]

But he did not invite them here to complain about his political isolation. He introduces other themes, and, being completely uninhibited, will
from time to time burst into song. One guest recalls attending the theatre
in 1926 on the evening the general strike ended. He sat directly behind
Winston and Clemmie. Now he wonders whether Churchill remembers
the show. Churchill not only remembers *Lady Be Good,* starring the
Astaires; he can, and does, croon the lyrics of all its tunes. His memory is
extraordinary. Lady Violet will remember how "he could quote back to me
words of which I had no recollection, and when I asked: 'Where does that
come from?' he replied: 'You said it' or 'You quoted it to me' — sometimes
remembering the time and the place. He could not forget what he liked,
except occasionally on purpose, when his own past utterances conflicted
with his present attitudes." To illustrate a point he quotes a poem he read
in *Punch* fifty years ago and has not seen since.[45]

After the ladies have left and the men are gathered around him for
port, brandy, and cigars, he will sit until 10:00 P.M., or later, talking of
his school days, the great political issues of the past, the MPs who fought
over them, battlefields of his youth, strategic innovations in the American
Civil War. Using salt shakers, cutlery, and brandy goblets, he can reenact
any battle in that war, from Bull Run to Five Forks, citing the troops
engaged on either side, identifying the commanders, describing the passage at arms, the aftermath. Reflections on any conceivable subject succeed
one another in his racing brain. The plight of mankind, he muses, is "all
the fault of the human mind being made in two lobes, only one of which
does any thinking, so we are all right-handed or left-handed; whereas, if
we were properly constructed, we should use our right and left hands with
equal force and skill according to circumstances. As it is, those who can
win a war well can rarely make a good peace, and those who could make
a good peace never win."

At least one guest finds it difficult to picture Churchill as a peacemaker,
noting Winston's account "of how he first came under fire when he was
twenty-one, of his boyish delight in the proximity of danger, or his glee
that he was actually 'seeing the real thing.' " The hazards and discomforts
of war, Winston argues, strengthen a young man's character. Certainly
they had strengthened his. But war was very different then. The indus-
trial/technological revolution had not yet cranked out the appliances of
death — machine guns, shrapnel shells, land mines — which were taking
so frightful a toll in the twentieth century. In South Africa, at the crucial

battle of Majuba in 1881, the British lost just 92 men. By contrast, over 400,000 young British soldiers had fallen in 1916 and 1917 in the Somme and Passchendaele campaigns — in vain, with no strategic gains. In 1932 few Englishmen know that as a young war correspondent he had written: "War, disguise it as you may, is but a dirty, shoddy business, which only a fool would play at," or that he declared after the Armistice in 1918: "War, which was cruel and magnificent, has become cruel and squalid."[46]

But in his youth he *had* thought it magnificent. In his first book he wrote: "Nothing in life is so exhilarating as to be shot at without result," and "There are men who derive as stern an exaltation from the proximity of danger and ruin, as others from success." It is this very trait — and his longing to be on a battlefield, watching what he calls "the fun of the good things" — which worries all but the most devoted of his followers. His critics call him "a genius without judgment," a man with "a zigzag streak of lightning in the brain," the only cabinet minister who gloated when Britain declared war on Germany in 1914.

Because of the general revulsion against another European war, and because Churchill's judgment has been discredited since the failure of the Dardanelles campaign, men will shrug and turn away when he predicts, accurately, that Hitler will come to power in Germany, and that once Hitler has moved into the Kanzlei — the German chancellery in Berlin — their only hope of avoiding another general war will lie in following his advice: shoring up England's defenses, or, that failing, in turning to a leader who possesses not only vision and intellect, but also a capacity for brutality, faith in the superiority of his race, and a positive relish at the prospect of grappling with a nation of warriors led by a demagogue who represents everything he loathes — in short, to Winston Churchill.

The great difference between the two is that Hitler wants war and will actually be annoyed by Britons and Frenchmen who propose to give him what he wants without a fight, while Churchill, though a born warlord, is prepared to sacrifice all save honor and the safety of England to keep the peace. Hitler's *Mein Kampf* is a difficult book, but no one who has struggled through it can doubt that the author is a killer obsessed with *Blutdurst*, bloodthirstiness. Churchill, on the other hand, after telling his guests that he has already begun research on a major project which will follow *Marlborough*, a four-volume *History of the English-speaking Peoples*, gloomily adds: "I doubt if I shall finish it before the war comes." If he does and an English victory is "decisive," he says, "I shall have to add several more volumes. And if it is not decisive no more histories will be written for years."

It is eleven o'clock. Churchill sees his overnight guests to their rooms and, as they retire, begins his working day. Only after entering his employ will Bill Deakin discover, to his astonishment, that Churchill lacks a large private income, that he lives like a pasha yet must support his extravagant life with his pen. The Churchill children are also unaware that, as Mary will later put it, the family "literally lived from book to book, and from one article to the next." Her mother, who knows, prays that each manuscript will sell. Luckily, they all do, with the exception of one screenplay for Alexander Korda, and editors and publishers, both in Britain and America, pay him the highest rates. His output is prodigious. During backbencher years, from early 1931 to late 1939, he will publish eleven volumes and over four hundred articles, many of them hack work ("Sport Is a Stimulant in Our Workaday World," "The Childless Marriage Threatens Our Race," "What Other Secrets Does the Inventor Hold?") in *Strand Magazine, Sunday Pictorial, Daily Mail, The Times, Saturday Review, Answers, Sunday Telegraph, Sunday Chronicle, Collier's, Sunday Dispatch, Pictorial Magazine, Sunday Times, Pictorial Weekly, The Listener, Pearson's Magazine, Daily Sketch, Evening Standard, Sunday Express, News of the World, Jewish Chronicle,* and *Daily Telegraph.* His annual earnings will average £20,000, or $96,000. During the same period he will deliver 368 speeches for which he is, of course, paid nothing. He will reject some commissions: a history of Parliament because the sum is inadequate, nearly $30,000 for a speaking tour in the United States because the mounting crises on the Continent keep him in England, and $50 from William S. Paley, president of the Columbia Broadcasting System, for an appraisal of Nazi activity in Austria. Paley asks CBS correspondent William L. Shirer to make the approach. Shirer, appalled by the paltry sum, phones Winston at the House of Commons. Called out of the chamber, Churchill says he will do it for $500. Paley decides he isn't worth it, and a fragment of history is lost.[47]

Winston's Chartwell study is a writer's dream. Entering through the Tudor doorway with its molded architrave, one looks up and up — the ceiling has been removed, revealing vaulting rafters and beams which were in place long before the Renaissance. One's second impression — and it is strong — is a reminder of the greatest enigma in Churchill's life. Despite his parents' disgraceful neglect of him in his early years, a bronze cast of Jennie's hand lies on one windowsill. The desk and the bureau-bookcase with Gothic glazing were Lord Randolph's. The most prominent painting on the walls depicts his father writing. On the level of awareness, Winston reveres the memory of both his parents, but the resentment has to be there. His suppression of it is doubtless a heavy contributor to his periodic spells of depression, and his combativeness arises from the need to

Billy McCoy was a musical boy . . .
And then the hammock starts a-swingin'
And the bells begin a-ringin'
While he's sittin' at that 'pianna'
There on the Alabama,
Playin' the Oceana Roll!

MGM pioneers the renting of films to those who can afford them, other studios follow, and Alexander Korda sees to it that Churchill has priority. His taste in films, as in music, is middlebrow — Lew Ayres in *All Quiet on the Western Front,* Fredric March in *Dr. Jekyll and Mr. Hyde,* Douglas Fairbanks, Jr., and Richard Barthelmess in *The Dawn Patrol,* and Charles Laughton, Winston's favorite actor, in *The Sign of the Cross.* His taste in literature is more eclectic. Here his interests are professional. His leisure reading, serious and frivolous, strengthens his grasp of his mother tongue. In Chartwell's library one can glimpse the landscape of his mind. Among the books he has read, and often reread, are Gibbon's five-volume *Decline and Fall of the Roman Empire,* William James's *The Varieties of Religious Experience,* J. A. Froude's *History of England,* Sir Richard Burton's sixteen-volume *Arabian Nights,* the King James Bible, and C. S. Forester's biography of Nelson. Later he will devour Forester's Hornblower novels, John Paget's *The New "Examen,"* Winwood Reade's *The Martyrdom of Mankind.* He likes to dip into books of verse and later quote them at meals. His favorite poets are Kipling, Housman, and Rupert Brooke. If in the mood for mere amusement, he plucks out novels by the Brontës, Fielding's *Tom Jones,* Scott's *Rob Roy,* Trollope's political novels (particularly *The Duke's Children*), P. G. Wodehouse's fatuities, or the tales of Kipling, R. L. Stevenson, and Somerset Maugham, the only modern novelist whose skills he admires.[39]

He enjoys being cosseted — F. E. Smith said "Winston is a man of simple tastes; he is always prepared to put up with the best of everything." But although the grandson of a duke could move in the highest social circles, his leisure is largely confined to Chartwell and its grounds. Only rarely can he be coaxed away for a weekend elsewhere. His greatest pleasures lie here. On a bright afternoon he will stroll around the grounds, greeting those who are home. He is an indulgent father. Like many another man who suffered in his childhood, he has spoiled his children, especially Randolph, despite their mother's pleading, sowing winds from which he will later reap whirlwinds. Diana is sorting out the first of her trousseau. Sarah is mooning about, playing her records, savoring memories of her success in the Kitkat Players, an amateur troupe; sulking because her parents refuse to support her yearning to become a chorus girl.

find another outlet for his anger. Significantly, he works not at his father's magnificent mahogany desk with gleaming claw feet, but at a high Disraeli desk of unvarnished deal with a slanting top, designed by Winston and fashioned by a local carpenter — a reminder that Victorians liked to write standing up.

His appearance heralded by the *harff, harff* of his slippers, he enters the room in his scarlet, green, and gold dressing gown, the cords trailing behind him. Before greeting his researcher and the two secretaries on duty tonight, he must read the manuscript he dictated the previous evening and then revise the latest galleys, which arrived a few hours earlier from London. Since Churchill's squiggled red changes exceed the copy set — the proofs look as though several spiders stained in crimson ink wandered across the pages — his printers' bills are shocking. But the expense is offset by his extraordinary fluency. Before the night is out, he will have dictated between four thousand and five thousand words. On weekends he may exceed ten thousand words. Once his family presented him with a Dictaphone. He was delighted. It seemed miraculous. He could dictate alone; one of the secretaries could transcribe the Dictabelt later. After a productive session, he went to bed triumphant, only to be told upon wakening that it was all wasted. He had forgotten to turn the device on. Everything was lost. "No more gadgets!" he roared, and stuck to the old system till his death.

Churchill has developed what biographer Philip Guedalla calls a faculty for "organizing large works." If he is researching a speech, a magazine essay, or a newspaper article, he needs little help. But for a major effort — his four-volume *Marlborough* or his *History of the English-speaking Peoples* — he requires a staff, most of them young Oxford graduates to whom he assigns readings and investigations; they then submit précis or memoranda which he studies between bursts of dictation. Among those thus engaged (at very small wages — £300 to £500 a year) are Deakin, John Wheldon, Keith Feiling, Maurice Ashley, Charles Hordern, and Ridley Pakenham-Walsh, both the last two former military officers. For a man approaching sixty, Winston does a great deal of his own field work, touring Marlborough's European battlefields — he is amazed at their enormity — but he hasn't time to rummage through the archives at Blenheim, translate old Flemish documents, or pore over the dispatches of William of Orange. So his staff does it for him.

This in no way diminishes his achievements. Deakin will remember that he, Winston, and the "shorthand-typists," as Churchill calls his secretaries, would sometimes "work on Marlborough until three or four in the morning. One felt exhilarated. Part of the secret was his phenomenal, fantastic power to concentrate on what he was doing. And he communicated

it. You were absolutely a part of it — swept into it. I might have given him
some memorandum before dinner, four or five hours before. Now he
would walk up and down dictating. My facts were there, but he had seen
it in deeper perspective. My memorandum was only a frame; it ignited his
imagination." Winston asks him to write a summary of the election of
1710, and, Deakin will recall, "He read this without any comment at all
and then dictated what he wanted to write in his book. . . . He translated
it into integral power and things he understood in contemporary terms, but
it was a transformation that was very special. His penetrating insight
revealed insights I had completely missed."[48]

Because tonight's major project is a parliamentary speech, the researcher's tasks are complete before midnight. Those of the shorthand-typists are
about to begin. Two will be on hand, to work shifts, and they will have
assembled the necessary tools: scrap paper, shorthand notebooks, pens,
pencils, rulers, erasers, scissors, paste, rubber bands, copy paper, carbon
paper, an assortment of green tags, a copy of Vacher's *Parliamentary
Companion Guide*, and Winston's "klop" or "klopper" — a powerful paper
punch. Winston despises staplers. Instead the klop perforates a batch of
paper; he then threads a piece of string through the hole and attaches it to
a tag. In a public address the pages must be in order, and he has an
irrational fear that someone will sabotage him, reversing pages. Right up
to the moment of delivery he will be nervously checking to reassure
himself that they are in sequence.

Sometimes, as Cecily ("Chips") Gemmell will recall, the opening hour
is "ghastly." There is no diverting him. A stenographer peers through a
window and observes blithely: "It's dark outside." Churchill, giving her
a bleak look, replies pitilessly: "It generally is at night." His creative flow
is blocked; he will prowl around, fling himself into a chair, bury his head
in his hands and mutter, "Christ, I've got to do this speech, and I can't do
it, I *can't*." On such occasions, Inspector Thompson notes, Winston is "a
kicker of wastebaskets, with an unbelievably ungovernable bundle of bad
temper. It is better to stay away from him at such times, and this his family
seeks to do."[49]

But the help has no choice. In time a word will come; then another
word; then a prolonged search for the right phrase, ending, after a prolonged mumbling to himself, with a chortle of delight as he finds it. But
his pace is still halting; Sir John Martin, one of his principal private
secretaries, will later recall it as a long process, "while he carefully savored
and chose his words, often testing alternative words or phrases in a low
mutter before coming out loudly with the final choice." He is trying to
establish rhythm, and once he has it, his pace quickens. Beginning where
he will begin in the House, he opens with what MP and diarist Harold

Nicolson calls "a dull, stuffy manner, reciting dates and chronology," but as he progresses he takes a livelier tone, introducing his familiar quips and gestures. Most writers regard the act of creativity as the most private of moments, but for Churchill it is semipublic; not only is the staff on hand, but any guest willing to sacrifice an hour's sleep is also welcome.

In Parliament he stands when speaking. Here he paces. In the House of Commons pacing is impossible, so he has adopted a different mode of delivery there. Nicolson notes: "His most characteristic gesture is strange indeed. You know the movement that a man makes when he taps his trouser pockets to see whether he has got his latch-key? Well, Winston pats both trouser pockets and then passes his hands up and down from groin to tummy. It is very strange."[50]

In Parliament his wit will flash and sting, but members who know him well are aware that he has honed these barbs in advance, and only visitors in the Strangers' Gallery are under the impression that his great perorations are extemporaneous. F.E. once referred to "Churchill's carefully prepared impromptus." Peter E. Wright, who had been among Churchill's colleagues during the Gallipoli crisis of 1915, notes: "Mr. Churchill cannot, as is well known, improvise very easily; telling as his speeches are, they are wrought, rehearsed, and often half read. To produce it all, Mr. Churchill, in his books and in his speeches, heaves like a mountain." But so, Wright adds, do other MPs, with disappointing results, whereas, "if Mr. Churchill's throes are volcanic, so is the result — a burning flood of lava, often uneven and tumultuous, but sweeping and splendid in its general effect."[51]

It is the product of toil, sweat, and frequent tears. On the average he spends between six and eight hours preparing a forty-minute speech. Frequently, as he dictates passages which will stir his listeners, he weeps; his voice becomes thick with emotion, tears run down his cheeks (and his secretary's). Like any other professional writer, he takes his text through several drafts before it meets his standards; but even in its roughest stages it is free of cant and bureaucratic jargon. Where Stanley Baldwin has said "a bilateral agreement has been reached," Churchill makes it "joined hands together." The "Local Defence Volunteers" become the "Home Guard." One sure way of rousing his temper is to call a lorry a "commercial vehicle" or alter "the poor" to "the lower-income group." He wages a long, and, in the end, successful campaign to ban the civil service's standard comment "The answer is in the affirmative" to a simple "Yes." A Churchillian text includes such inimitable phrases as "the jaws of winter," "hard and heavy tidings," and — neither Pitman nor Gregg is equal to this — "a cacophonous chorus." In both conversation and dictation he uses words with great precision and insists that others do the same. On a trip his physician comments: "I hope you did not catch cold sitting on the balcony in the chill night air." His patient, smiling mischievously, corrects him: "Portico, not balcony, Charles."[52]

Most of the action takes place in his study, but it can be unsettling even there. Once at 3:00 A.M. Winston uncharacteristically opened a window. Immediately a bat entered. The young woman on duty, more frightened of her employer than of this new uninvited immigrant of the Chartwell pet colony, closed her eyes and kept taking down words while Churchill pursued the bat with a poker, drove it back out, and slammed the window shut — meantime not missing a phrase. Another time a fire broke out in the study. Churchill's voice continued until, enveloped in smoke, his croaks and gasps became incomprehensible. By then a half-dozen servants had arrived. The flames had been smothered and all windows opened. The secretary, who had also been on duty the Night of the Bat, as the staff now called it, vanished. ("I headed for the loo," she recalls.) Churchill convened a court of inquiry on the spot, demanding the name of the arsonist. Kathleen Hill looked at him and said evenly, "You." She pointed at the remains of the cigar butt in the charred seat of an overstuffed chair. He scowled darkly, turned, and shouted, *"Where's Miss?"*[53]

His secretaries are required to take down every audible word from him; he often changes his mind in midpassage, but he may change it back. If he says "I was going" and adds after a pause "I decided to go," they type: "I was going. I decided to go." They spell one another from time to time, not because they are exhausted; he wants to see what he had said in cold type. He will revise it in his red ink, redictate it, and scrutinize it again. Occasionally he will add a paragraph. When at last he has a final version, it will be typed, on a machine with outsized type, on small pieces of paper, eight by four inches, the whole lot klopped and strung to a tag. The speech will be set in broken lines to aid his delivery, "speech form," or "psalm form," as Lord Halifax calls it. After Hitler becomes absolute master of the Third Reich, Churchill tells the House of Commons:

> I have on more than one occasion
> Made my appeal that the Führer of Germany
>   Should become the Hitler of peace.
>
> When a man is fighting in a desperate conflict
> He may have to grind his teeth and flash his eyes;
>   Anger and hatred nerve the arm of strife.
>
> But success should bring a mellow, genial air
> And, by altering the mood to suit the new circumstances,

Preserve and consolidate in tolerance and goodwill
What has been gained by conflict.

Thus, when Churchill rises to speak in the House, he holds in his hand not notes on the issues he means to address, but the entire text of what he intends to say. To be sure, he may say a few words suitable to the occasion, commenting on the remarks of previous speakers, but the rest is a set piece, though few know it. Because his delivery gives an illusion of spontaneity and the notes include stage directions ("pause; grope for word" and "stammer; correct self"), each of his speeches is a dramatic, vibrant occasion.

It would be pleasant to report that his relationship with his staff is genial, that he treats them as he would his daughters, and that he is particularly patient with new secretaries. In fact, he is nothing of the sort. He treats them like servants. A. J. P. Taylor calls him an "atrocious" taskmaster, and his attitude toward his employees is difficult to understand or, at times, even to excuse. He can summon each of his pets by name, recite poetry by the hour, and remember the exact circumstances under which he learned of a certain event fifty years earlier, but he knows the names of only three or four of his eighteen servants and stenographers. They are "the tall Miss with blue eyes" or "the man with ginger hair." Newcomers find his lisp an obstacle — they simply do not understand what he is saying — but he makes no allowance for that. Chips Gemmell will remember that during her first session she "sat there terrified; I couldn't understand a word he was saying, and I couldn't keep up with him. I thought, this is a nightmare. This isn't happening. So I went plop, plop, quite convinced it wasn't real." Winston didn't read her typescript until the team assembled in the study the following evening. He glanced through the first two pages, his face passing through deeper and deeper shades of red and his frown growing more savage, until he rose, flung the sheets on the floor, stamped his feet, and screamed: "You haven't got one word in fifty right! *Not one word in fifty! NOT ONE WORD IN FIFTY!*"[54]

She froze. So did Elizabeth Nel, when, on the evening of her secretarial baptism, she found her machine had been set at single, not double, spacing. With Churchill rattling along, uncharacteristically fluent at this early hour, she had no time to switch. After she had passed him the first page, she will recall, "he went off like a rocket. I was a fool, a mug, and idiot: I was to leave his presence and one of the others was to appear." Later she was given a second chance, and, still later, a third. She was understandably nervous, and "my apprehensions were seldom ill-founded. More often than not it would come skimming back to me with a few red alterations on it, sometimes to the accompaniment of remarks disparaging to my education and sense of hearing."[55] Yet their misunderstandings are completely understandable. Who can blame a stenographer who types "lemons" when he means the Greek island of Lemnos, mistakes "fretful" for "dreadful," or "perfervid" for "perverted"? Winston can and does; he rages and stamps his feet. (Foot-stamping is his outlet with women, a substitute for obscenities; if only men were present he would cut loose with a string of short Anglo-Saxon oaths "mostly beginning," as he once put it, "with the earlier letters of the alphabet.") One young woman wrote home:

Not in a very good temper this morning. He suddenly said "Gimme t—gr—spts—pk." Interpreting this as "Give me a toothpick," I leapt up, looked round and then started rummaging in the bag where such necessities should be kept. After less than 20 seconds he said, very bored and superior "now Miss Layton just stop playing the bloody ass and" . . . . Presently, after dictating something, he found I'd put "Somehow I think it right" (which was what I thought he'd said). So fairly patient, he said "no, no, I said *now the time is right*" (with accents like that). So I did it again. Gave it back. There was a roar of rage. "God's teeth, girl, can't you do it right the second time? I said *ripe ripe ripe — P P P*." I should, perhaps, have realized, but he hadn't mentioned that "right" was "wrong." However he forgave me for the rest of the day.

Occasionally the secretaries guess at a word, trusting to chance rather than provoke certain wrath by asking: "What did you say, sir?" Any break in his creative flow is intolerable to him. When a girl reaches the bottom of a page she must remove paper, carbon, and second sheet, then insert a new set and roll it into place. Winston makes no allowance for this. He barks: "Come on! Come on! What are you waiting for?" The crackling of carbon and the flimsy second sheets is almost as intolerable to him as whistling. He splutters: "Don't fidget so with that paper! Stop it!" His tantrums would be more bearable if he apologized afterward or complimented them on work well done. He never does either. When one of the secretaries carries on the night after one of his outbursts, he may mutter, "There. I knew you could do it." Or, if one bursts into tears: "Good heavens, you mustn't mind me. We're all toads beneath the harrow, you know." Once a manservant stood up to him. The result was a blazing row. At the end of it Churchill, his lower lip jutting, said: "You were very rude to me, you know." The servant, still seething, replied: "Yes, but you were rude, too." Churchill grumbled: "Yes, but I am a great man."[56] At Chartwell this is the last word. Later the servant will say: "There was no answer to that. He knew, as I and the rest of the world knew, that he was right." Elizabeth Nel, after reciting her very legitimate grievances, adds: "Neither I nor anyone else considered this treatment unfair. . . . I used to wonder how long his patience would last, if he would not one day say, 'Go, and never let me see you again.' " Phyllis Moir, another member of the secretarial pool, will recall Winston on the phone, telling her to fetch him certain papers: "Mr. Churchill was standing by the telephone, his face very red and very angry, stamping his feet and sputtering with rage. He literally tore the papers out of my hand and savagely stammered an incoherent answer into the mouthpiece." She adds loyally: "Mr. Churchill is not the sort of man to apologize to anyone, but he would go out of his way to say something appreciative and his whole manner made you feel he was ashamed of his bad behavior." In this instance, she explains, he expressed his shame by failing to turn on her wrathfully after he had hung up. Instead he asked her if she was enjoying the countryside.[57]

It seems hardly adequate. Neither does his forgiveness "for the rest of the day" seem appropriate redress for browbeating a girl who mistook his lisped "ripe" for "right." The blunt truth is that Winston has never considered himself a toad beneath the harrow, and for the best of reasons: he isn't one. No humble man would outflank a traffic jam by driving on pavement. He believes he is a superior being, entitled to exceptional forbearance as well as special privilege and not subject to judgment by the rules of polite society. This is, of course, arguable. What is striking is that those who work for him, toiling long hours, underpaid, and subject to savage, undeserved reprimands, agree with him. They feel the sting of his whip. Yet he continues to command their respect, even their love. Those who are shocked by Churchill's treatment of his employees all have this in common: they never worked for him.

Sometime between 2:00 and 4:00 A.M. he quits, leaving the others to sort out ribbon copies and carbons, clean up the study, and, if the night's dictation has included manuscript, prepare a packet for the London courier. In his bedroom he divests himself of his trousers and velvet slippers; then, in one great overhead swoop, yanks the rest of his clothing up, away, and across the chamber. In a gesture that is more narcissistic than remedial, he faces the mirror in his bedroom and brushes his strands of hair straight down over his ears, saying to his valet, with dubious authority, "That's the way to keep your hair, Inches." He asks him for "my eye blinkers," slips the sleep mask in place, and is soon breathing the deep, slow breaths of the slumberer. His dreams, he tells his family, are often of his father, who died prophesying Winston would be a failure. In 1932 it would be hard to find more than a dozen men of Parliament or Fleet Street who would think that prediction laughable.

A Fever over Europe

VICTORIA Regina — "the Old Queen," still a vivid memory among Englishmen in their forties — would have been shocked speechless. Here was London, the most civilized city in the world, and there in its streets were the rabble, identifiable by their ragged clothes, their faces clenched in rage, and, when they raised their voices, the unmistakable accents of their class. To affluent spectators, the rioting seemed illusory. Many were looking at the poor, really *looking* at them, for the first time in their lives. Usually the patriciate encountered them only in servile roles, and the privileged had been raised to ignore them, even to speak of them in their presence as though they were not there. But in 1932, with the Depression at rock bottom, the poor could not escape notice. There were too many of them, and they were too angry.

A London constable needed only a brief glance to distinguish between the classes. Shaw's *Pygmalion* to the contrary, it wasn't just a matter of clothes, expressions, and accents. No speech therapist or couturier could alter their posture, mannerisms, and physique. Lower-class diets were so poor that emergency programs were needed to provide them with fruit, vegetables, and, for each schoolchild, 2.67 ounces of milk a day. Generations of malnutrition, of stooping in tunnels or bending over textile looms, had given workmen slight stature, poor posture, coarse complexions, weak eyesight, and hollow chests; and even among nubile women, breasts were small and limp. Individually they were unattractive and easily overpowered. But when they coalesced into a mob they could constitute a threat to the tall, fair, erect gentry. Of course, the gentry did not dream of meeting force with their own force. It was, as most of them said, a matter for the police.

Those of less insensitive conscience were shocked. Yet they shouldn't have been. There had been plenty of warnings. People were edgy. The city's celebrated civility was beginning to fray. Every household in Mayfair or Belgravia had its tales, hushly told, of rude beggars who had accosted ladies outside Harrods or St. Paul's and grew ugly if denied sixpence. And Whitechapel had actually insulted a member of the Royal Family. The Prince of Wales's brother Prince "Bertie" — the future King George VI — had paid a compassionate visit to the city's starving East End. According to sworn testimony, published in *The Times,* His Royal Highness had been driven back by ragged cockneys shaking grimy fists and shouting: "Food! Give us food! We don't want royal parasites!"[1]

This lèse-majesté was the prelude to the riots of October 1932. The first seems to have been spontaneous. The cockneys who had defied royalty had been released by the magistrate with a warning. Emboldened, they decided to sortie into the city proper. The sheer size of the multitude was frightening. They poured into the streets by the thousands, and soon they were bearing down on Lambeth Bridge. Twenty times the bobbies launched truncheon charges; finally, as a last resort, they blocked their bridgehead with lorries parked hubcap to hubcap. The barricade held until the bruised, scarred, and exhausted throng fell back.[2]

The second onslaught, a march on London from the outer reaches of the country, was more menacing. Its moves had been carefully planned by a dour, disheveled youth named W. A. L. Hannington, "Wal" to his men and "Red Wal" in the London newspapers. The men behind him called their trek a hunger march. It was a long one. They had come from towns as far as western Wales and northern Scotland, bearing a petition for relief signed by a million unemployed workers, with the expectation that the prime minister would receive their delegation. In the countryside local charities fed the marchers, but after a cabinet minister told the House of Commons that Bolsheviks were behind their protest and it was "up to the Communists to feed them," they were given few handouts in the capital.[3]

Their enormous petition was too cumbersome for the street brawlers to carry, so they checked it at Charing Cross Station and then swarmed up the Strand to Trafalgar Square, stoning limousines and using tree branches — hacked off in Hyde Park — to club well-dressed men. Bobbies waded into them, swinging billy clubs, and broke their momentum at Marble Arch. England's most sacred political institutions, it seemed, were safe. Then it was learned that a second column, five thousand strong, had emerged from concealment in Green Park and was crossing St. James's Park, in their rear. Debouching by the Guards Memorial, this mob advanced on No. 10 Downing Street. The only policeman in sight was the single bobby who, by tradition, stands by the prime minister's front door.

At this point, less than four hundred yards from their objective, the marchers' luck turned against them. The open ground between the rioters and the entrance to Downing Street was occupied by the parade ground of the Royal Horse Guards. As long as anyone could remember, the only duty of these cavalrymen had been to perform ceremoniously for admiring tourists. Now, preparing to fight for King and Country, they buckled on their glittering helmets, mounted their handsome steeds, drew their gleaming sabers from their polished scabbards, and formed a very thin red line. The sheer weight of the mob could have overwhelmed them, but the marchers, most of them in London for the first time, seemed awestruck. They wavered and milled around. By the time they had regrouped, reserves from Bow Street were there in force, sending them reeling back toward Trafalgar Square. Anticlimax followed. At Charing Cross Station, where they produced their claim check, a courteous clerk explained that the petition, with its million signatures, had been classified as an incentive to riot and confiscated by Scotland Yard. Beaten and bitter, they rode home on British railroads, which, relieved to see them dispersed, charged only token fares.[4]

※   ※

Television did not exist, and radio news was closely monitored by Sir John Reith, czar of the BBC, so the failed demonstrations had little impact on the British public. Few, if any, could have predicted that the suppressed riots, with their threat of social upheaval, would later play a role in the formation of the most disastrous foreign policy in the history of Britain and its empire. The significance of the incidents was largely overlooked by Fleet Street. It was a dreary time; people were less interested in momentous events than in escapism.

In the early thirties, the average Englishman's exposure to American culture — and he enjoyed it immensely — was chiefly confined to motion pictures, now in the transition period between silent films and talkies. In Westerham, the local cinema was The Swan. Winston Churchill, trudging up its steps with little Mary in tow to see MGM's lavish *Ben-Hur,* was, at least in this, typical of his countrymen. Like them he loved Westerns. His favorite was *Destry Rides Again,* with Tom Mix. He favored movies featuring drama, excitement, action, slapstick — Cecil B. DeMille's *The Sign of the Cross,* Douglas Fairbanks in *The Iron Mask,* Walt Disney's anthropomorphic Mickey Mouse cartoons, and the Marx Brothers at the peak of their lunacy. With the arrival of sound had come popular music from abroad: "Singin' in the Rain," "Beyond the Blue Horizon," "Tiptoe through the Tulips," and Marlene Dietrich, at twenty-nine huskily serenading Emil Jannings with "Falling in Love Again" in Josef von Sternberg's first German talkie, *Der blaue Engel.* For Britons who preferred to buy British, homemade pickings were slim, with one shining exception: Noel Coward. These were the years when Gertrude Lawrence, young Laurence Olivier, Beatrice Lillie, and Coward himself played roles he had created, when his name was writ large on the hoardings of four London theatres: *Private Lives* at the Phoenix; *Cavalcade* at the Drury Lane; *Words and Music* at the Adelphi; and, at His Majesty's Theatre, *Bitter Sweet*.

In the back gardens of their semidetached bungalows in Streatham or Battersea, British housewives' gossip and snobbery had always served as shields against unpleasantness. The most exciting rumors in 1932 centered on the Royal Family, especially the world's most eligible bachelor, HRH the Prince of Wales, now thirty-eight. It was no secret that King George and Queen Mary were putting heavy pressure on their middle-aged heir to marry *someone* suitable; they had just spent over £10,000 renovating and redecorating Marlborough House, at the west end of Pall Mall, making it both comfortable and elegant for their new daughter-in-law, whoever she might be. Of course the Prince would find a bride soon, the housewives told one another, hanging clothes out to dry. He knew his duty. And, they added, nodding vigorously, he would marry well, giving Great Britain a future queen who would become the pride of the Empire.

The Empire! The mere mention of it aroused patriotic Britons like Churchill, made them brace their backs and lift their eyes. If there was any fixed star in their firmament it was an abiding faith in the everlasting glory of their realm — Dominions, Crown Colonies, protectorates, Chinese treaty towns — which, in sum, was over three times the size of the Roman Empire at its height: 475 million people, 11 million square miles, ninety-one times the area of Great Britain, encompassing a quarter of both the earth's surface and its population. The fourth edition of *The Pocket Oxford Dictionary* defined "imperial" as "magnificent"; "imperialism" as the "extension of the British Empire for protection of trade, union of its parts for defence, internal commerce, etc."; and "imperialist" as an "advocate of British imperialism."

Britons still scrupulously observed Empire Day, giving schoolchildren a half-holiday. They joined or encouraged the British Empire League, the British Empire Union, the Victoria League, and the Patriotic League of Britons Overseas. They cried "Hear, hear" when the new viceroy of India, Lord Willingdon, foresaw "a Great Imperial Federation, when we can snap our fingers at the rest of the world." Baldwin declared: "The British Empire stands firm, as a great force for good. It stands in the sweep of every wind, by the wash of every sea." Colin Cross, the historian, has observed that "with authority reaching to every continent, the British

Empire was literally a world power; indeed in terms of its influence it was the only world power."[5]

Historian James Morris has written of the Empire: "Most Britons still considered it, all in all, a force for good in the world. . . . The Monarchy was still immensely popular in most parts of the Empire, even in India, even in Ireland." Schoolboys in the United Kingdom and the United States alike were taught that in battle the British "always won," as indeed they had in every major war since the eighteenth century.

All the imperial trappings were kept intact. The prime ministers of the Dominions continued to meet in London, ostensibly to coordinate economic policies, though none were forthcoming. Dominion children studied books with such chapter titles as "The Thread That Binds Our Race," and Boy Scouts — not only in the Empire but also in America — wore broad-brimmed Boer War hats and shared with the South African police the motto "Be Prepared." Lord Beaverbrook's newspapers, particularly the London *Daily Express,* made expansion of the imperial domain a crusade. Graduates of "Oxbridge" — Oxford and Cambridge — still sailed abroad to spend lifetimes as imperial proconsuls, looking forward, late in life, to the rewards of CMG, KCMG, or GCMG. In New Delhi, at state banquets, the viceroy's entrance into the dining hall was preceded by two elegantly uniformed aides-de-camp; and when the orchestra played "God Save the King," the Indian servants in their gold and scarlet liveries stood poised behind each guest.[6]

And yet . . .

There were signs, for those who could read them, that the Empire was, in Churchill's gloomy words, on a "downward slurge." *La belle époque* was over. Most of the Crown's subjects, abroad as well as at home, felt comfortable with imperialism. With the exception of the *Daily Worker,* every British newspaper supported it. Few, even in Ireland, were offended when the thick voice of their sovereign was identified on radio for his annual, unbearably boring Christmas broadcast ("Another year has passed . . .") by an announcer with a plummy accent as "His Britannic Majesty, by Grace of God and of the United Kingdom of Great Britain and Ireland and of the British Dominions beyond the Seas, King, Defender of the Faith, Emperor of India." But the mystique was fading; indeed, for some it had already gone.[7]

Earlier generations of Englishmen had found colonial uprisings endlessly fascinating. They had pored over newspaper accounts (many written by young Churchill) and tacked pages of the *Illustrated London News* — depicting the Mutiny, Chinese Gordon's Last Stand, Kitchener at Omdurman, and the expeditions relieving Boer sieges of Ladysmith, of them crippled and maimed, destined to be public wards for the remainder of their lives. Add to these the nearly half-million young widows and fatherless children, and one finds that two years after the war 3.5 million Britons, nearly 10 percent of the population, were receiving a pension or an allowance.[10]

     ❊   ❊

In the year of the Wall Street Crash, when Robert Graves's American publisher issued *Goodbye to All That,* his powerful evocation of service in the trenches, the *Nation* thought it striking "not that he tells the truth about the war but that it took him so long to discover it." But the lag applied not only to Graves; it was characteristic of an entire British literary generation. The most extraordinary thing about England's disenchantment with the war is that it didn't surface for over ten years. The reading public had been fed the self-serving memoirs of those responsible for the disaster and the thin fictional gruel of Bulldog Drummond and Richard Hannay. Those who had remained home were simply incapable of absorbing the truth. Aging Tommies told them that sixty thousand young Englishmen had fallen on the first day of the battle of the Somme without gaining a single yard. *Sixty thousand!* It *couldn't* be true. Those who said so must be shell-shocked.[11]

The coalescence came in 1929. On January 21 the curtain rose on the first of what would be 594 London performances of *Journey's End,* the ultimate in antiwar plays, by Robert C. Sherriff, a thirty-three-year-old former insurance man who had served in the East Surrey Regiment's Ninth Battalion through the bloody spring of 1917. Its audiences left the Savoy Theatre stunned but primed, now, for Graves's memoir; for Edmund Blunden's *Undertones of War;* for the German novelist Erich Maria Remarque's *Im Westen nichts Neues,* which appeared that spring in Berlin and was immediately translated by a London publisher as *All Quiet on the Western Front;* and, the following year, for Siegfried Sassoon's *Memoirs of an Infantry Officer.*[12]

The Great War may have been the first historic event in which reality outstripped the imagination. In the 1980s it is difficult to grasp the public innocence of that earlier generation, and how it recoiled when confronted at last by the monstrous crimes which had been committed in the name of patriotism. As time passed, the yeast of bitterness worked in the public mind and its emotions. By 1932 readers had accepted Sassoon and Graves as sources of the revealed word, and traveling troupes were presenting *Journey's End* in every post of the Empire. Newspapers and magazines picked up the now-it-can-be-told theme; pacifism became as fashionable as war fever had been less than twenty years earlier. On February 9, 1933, the Oxford Union voted 275 to 153 to approve the resolution "that this House will in no circumstances fight for King and Country." Eight months later, in what may have been the most significant by-election of the decade, a Tory in London's East Fulham, whose Conservative majority after the last campaign had been fourteen thousand votes, was swamped by an obscure Labour challenger. Labour's man had told the constituency that he would "close every recruiting station, disband the Army and disarm the Air Force," and demanded that England "give the lead to the whole world by initiating immediately a policy of general disarmament." His victory margin was five thousand votes, representing an extraordinary swing of 26 percent. It was no accident. Over the next four months constituencies ranging widely in character but representative of the country's mood elected antiwar candidates by margins ranging from 20 to 25 percent.[13]

Churchill was alarmed. In the House of Commons he was the League of Nations' chief supporter, but the league now faced a trembling future. He became preoccupied with national security. Unilateral disarmament would be madness, he told Parliament. The by-elections also distressed Stanley Baldwin, leader of the Conservative party, but his response was very different. To him the loss of safe seats was a grave matter. If the voters wanted disarmament, he decided, that was what he would give them.[14]

The real threat to British security, His Majesty's Government held, lay within. Indeed, Conservative MPs believed that the menace faced them just across the well of the House of Commons, on the Labour benches. Actually, His Majesty's Loyal Opposition was itself a mildly conservative party, and had proved it in 1924 while occupying the front bench for nine months. Many of its members were former Liberal MPs who had switched parties once they saw that Labour was the only realistic alternative to Tory rule. Nevertheless, Conservatives believed that if England was to remain the England they knew and loved, they must remain in power.

Until now British Communists had all been members of the working class, or shabby young men wearing steel-rimmed glasses who mouthed the weary party line in Hyde Park, responding to questions with incomprehensible jargon and quotations from Marx, Engels, and Lenin. In the early 1930s communism became respectable, then fashionable, then a distinction among intellectuals and university undergraduates. Among the Communist Party of Great Britain (CPGB) members were W. H. Auden, Christopher Isherwood, and Stephen Spender. Oxford's October Club, a CPGB cell, had three hundred dues-paying students. Cambridge started later, but soon one of every five Cambridge men had signed on, among them one H. A. R. ("Kim") Philby.

Those who dismissed this as an example of British eccentricity, or of typical undergraduate irresponsibility, were silenced by news from the United States, the world's most affluent nation. Ragged mobs of the homeless and penniless were occupying U.S. public buildings — including one statehouse — and twenty-five thousand war veterans, arriving in Washington with their families to plead for relief, were routed with tear gas and bayonets. American recruits to the party included John Dos Passos, Sherwood Anderson, Erskine Caldwell, and Edmund Wilson, who called Russia "the moral top of the world, where the light never really goes out."

Every generation cherishes illusions which baffle its successors (who passionately defend their own), but intellectuals are expected to view the world with healthy skepticism. Those who visited the Soviet Union in the starkest years of the Depression were so easily deceived, so eager to accept the flimsiest evidence, so determined to believe the most transparent misrepresentations, that one feels that some of the scorn directed nowadays at the appeasers of Nazi Germany should be reserved for men who ought to have known better. Bernard Baruch asked Lincoln Steffens, "So you've been over into Russia?" and Steffens replied: "I have been over into the future, and it works."[15]

He had seen what Stalin wanted him to see, on a rigged tour, the kind generals stage for visiting politicians. Everything paraded by him had worked, but he had not seen into the future or even the present. As one of the most celebrated journalists of his time, Steffens should have investigated his host's policy of collectivization and its ghastly results. Only a willing dupe could say of such a holocaust that it worked. If it did, so did Auschwitz.

Actually, the moral top of Edmund Wilson's world, where the light never really went out, had entered a period of murk which masked monstrous crimes — crimes which were suspected but not acknowledged until Nikita Khrushchev revealed them in 1957 — all committed in the name of the people they were destroying. The catastrophe had begun with Lenin's death in 1924. Churchill, his archenemy, nevertheless recognized Lenin's greatness: "The strong illuminant that guided him was cut off at the moment when he had turned resolutely for home. The Russian people were left floundering in the bog. Their worst misfortune was his birth; their next worst — his death."[16]

Lenin had left a vague "political testament" which recommended that Joseph Stalin, then secretary-general of the Communist party's Central Committee, be dismissed. Stalin suppressed this document and, in his role as secretary-general, joined two accomplices in a ruling triumvirate which expelled Stalin's chief rival, Leon Trotsky. (Eventually, Stalin would order the murders of his accomplices and Trotsky.) Stalin consolidated his position as master of the Kremlin, and by 1932 the Soviet Union was in the grip of a reign of terror which would reach its peak in the great purges of 1934–1938. To the world, however, Stalin insisted that his rule was benign. In the early summer of 1932, interviewed by the German biographer Emil Ludwig, he denied that he was a dictator, denied that he reigned by fear, and declared that the "overwhelming majority" of the laboring population in the U.S.S.R. was behind him. Their support, he said, accounted for the "stability of Soviet power," not "any so-called policy of terrorism."

At that time no Russian translation of *Mein Kampf* existed, but in this exchange Stalin had instinctively followed a principle set down in Adolf Hitler's tenth chapter: "The great masses of the people . . . will more easily fall victims to a big lie [*eine grosse Lüge*] than to a small one." Everything the Russian dictator had told Ludwig was the exact opposite of the truth. Soviet peasants were already in the toils of a misery far more wretched than anything known under the czars. Abandoning Lenin's managed economy, with its quasi-capitalistic incentives, Stalin had launched a series of five-year plans moving twenty-five million farmers from their lands into collectives. Troops and secret police rounded up protesters and murdered, exiled, or imprisoned them in an expanding net of concentration camps which systematically worked them to death. Nevertheless, collectivism failed. The Ukrainians were devastated by famine. Stalin rejected their appeal for help and actually exported grain while ten million of them starved to death.

By the autumn of 1932 England's ruling classes were afraid of their own countrymen, and their fear alarmed Labour, whose MPs heard wild tales of plots by His Majesty's Government to turn Britain into a police state. Hugh Dalton, MP, son of a clergyman but a committed socialist, visited Stafford Cripps, a member of the Labour hierarchy. Dalton wrote in his diary that Cripps "thinks there is a grave danger of Fascism in this country," that Metropolitan-Vickers, the munitions manufacturers, "are 'probably supplying arms to British Fascists.' " Cripps, Dalton wrote, believed that "Churchill will probably defeat the Government on India next spring and form a Government of his own, with a Majority in this Parliament and then 'introduce Fascist measures' and 'there will be no more general elections.' " Dalton, appalled, thought that "this seems to me to be fantastic and most profoundly improbable." But Harold Laski echoed Cripps, telling Dalton that he had "heard 'from an inside source' that members of the [all-party national] Government are discussing the advisability of not having a General Election in 1936, nor till such later date as the Government advises the King that it would be safe to return to party politics."[17]

Cripps and Laski were looking into the wrong closets. British politics were unthreatened by communism. But the domestic disorders, the dole, and the increase in CPGB memberships profoundly affected His Majesty's Government's foreign policy. HMG's subsequent dealings with a resurgent Germany make no sense unless seen in counterpoint with Tory anxiety. The London hunger riots had, or so it seemed to them, been a sign that England's class system was disintegrating. The remarkable stability of British society was rooted in a social contract whose origins lay in the medieval relationship between lord and serf. Within the memory of living men, employees could be arrested for the most trivial of offenses, and an employer was entitled to police help in finding a runaway employee. Under the Prevention of Poaching Act, suspicious constables had possessed the power to stop and search anyone in "streets, highways, and public places."[18]

Although unwritten and largely unspoken, the terms of the social contract were handed down from generation to generation and seldom challenged. Now the hunger riots had changed all that. The precise distinctions between the classes would never be the same. If mobs could roam London, those in power reasoned, their troubles with the lower middle, working, and underclasses had just begun. They were right, but wrong to blame Moscow and its British minions. Englishmen kept their places when they and their families were fed, clothed, and housed. The unemployed, however, knew no such restraint. The man without a situation took little risk, and might attract attention to his cause, by stoning limousines, joining a demonstration — or joining the Communist party. To those in power such men, by their very numbers, were alarming. Nearly a quarter of the country's work force was jobless, and in some dark pockets the figure reached 50, 60, or even 70 percent. England had to export or die. That was the fate of an island nation. Now goods lay in mountainous stacks in warehouses or on wharves. Desperate, His Majesty's Government adopted draconian measures — £24,149,060 in new taxes and £2,344 in spending cuts.

Among those affected by the cuts were British tars. An able seaman's pay was reduced from four shillings a day (ninety-seven cents) to three shillings (seventy-three cents). Shattering three centuries of tradition, men of the Royal Navy mutinied. Over thirteen thousand of His Majesty's sailors anchored in Cromarty Firth, Scotland — men whose ships bore such proud names as *Nelson, Repulse,* and *Valiant* — defied their officers, sang "The Red Flag," and elected leaders for what can only be called their own soviet. Only a handful were punished. Their pay was restored. The Admiralty angrily denounced HMG's capitulation, calling it a ghastly precedent. The government agreed but said it had had no choice.

And, of course, the grim facts did bear political implications. In December 1929 there had been just 3,200 Communists in Britain, 550 of them organized in cells. Now the hammer and sickle was carried through the heart of London. Membership in the CPGB was growing rapidly as the Depression deepened, increasing by 140 percent, then 259 percent, then 282 percent. And these were only the hard-core, card-carrying members. The number of sympathizers was far larger; in two by-elections the Communist candidates received, respectively, 31.9 and 33.8 percent of the vote.

At the same time, Communists everywhere had become more militant and more submissive to Moscow. This was one result of the Comintern's Tenth Plenum in 1929. Stalin had decreed that local deviations from the party line be suppressed and that all loyal members move to set "class against class." They were told to fight, not only capitalism, but also the labor movement. Since the Comintern had been founded to "accelerate the development of events toward world revolution," the threat to established order everywhere was open. In London it was taken seriously; to conservative Englishmen the possibility of a Communist Britain seemed very real.

Several Tories with strong influence on their party's leadership contemplated executing a momentous pivot in the history of British diplomacy. No one spoke of it publicly, nor was it whispered in the House of Commons smoking room. Even as theory, it was still in the fetal stage, and it might never come to term. Only a few Conservatives were committed to it. But others, including members of the party hierarchy, thought it had merit.

They pondered Benito Mussolini's popularity in Italy, where, by 1932, he had been ruling for ten years. It had been a good decade for Italians. *Il Duce*'s dreams of building another Roman Empire evoked a tepid response, but his managed economy had prospered; his countrymen's standard of living had risen. His goals, a biographer notes, had "a great appeal to many people in Italy in the years immediately following World War I; the Russian Revolution had terrified the leaders of the Italian financial and industrial community, and Mussolini's program seemed to many of them to be an effective means of countering any similar development in their own country."

British intelligence reported that in Germany, also suffering from the Depression, Adolf Hitler was following the Duce's lead, presenting himself to the Ruhr's *Schlotbarone* (smokestack barons) as a shield against the Reds. Hitler's National Socialist German Workers' Party — National-

Kimberley, and Mafeking — to the walls of their homes. Challenges to the supremacy of the Union Jack had stirred their blood, and they had responded eagerly to calls to the Flag, Duty, Race, and the White Man's Burden. In the early 1930s millions of Britons, especially the elderly, members of the upper class, and those who had reached their majority before 1914, still felt that way. But imperial enthusiasm was dwindling among the working classes and the young. They were weary of the White Man's Burden. The new mood was caught by Aldous Huxley; to him the Raj resembled the Old Man of Thermopylae, who never did anything properly. "For some reason," young Jock Colville wrote in his diary, "no subject is more boring to the average Englishman than the British Empire."[8]

British imperialism was, in fact, an idea whose time was going. The issue had already been decided. In the House of Commons the master blueprint governing the imperial future, the Statute of Westminster of 1931, decreed that the Mother Country and her dominions were "autonomous communities within the British Empire, equal in status, in no way subordinate to each other in any aspect of their domestic or foreign affairs, though united by a common allegiance to the Crown, and freely associated as members of the British Commonwealth of Nations."

George V, who treasured his legacy, watched in dismay as his imperial role beyond England's shores shrank to that of a posturing mascot. Confused, he minuted in November 1929, on the eve of the Depression: "I cannot look into the future without feelings of no little anxiety about the continued unity of the Empire." His apprehensions were well founded, though perhaps for reasons too cosmic for him to grasp. Empires are the sequelae of historical accidents. England, an island and therefore a trading nation, had gained control of the high seas just as colonies became ripe for plucking. As long as sea power remained dominant, imperial institutions were invincible; under Victoria it was British policy to keep the Royal Navy — 330 warships, manned by 92,000 tars — larger than the combined navies of any other two powers.[9]

Air power would prove to be the ultimate blow to the Empire's role as the world's one superpower, but the first great blow to the imperial future had been dealt by the Great War. In the red month of August 1914, when England's poet laureate promised Oxford and Cambridge students that if they enlisted they would find "Beauty through blood," all 450 million subjects of the Empire went to war, bound by a single declaration from their king-emperor. They sprang to arms in a trance of ardor, even elation. By Armistice Day 3,190,235 of the King's subjects had fallen in the slime and gore of trench warfare, 1,165,661 killed in action, 962,661 of them from Great Britain. Over 2 million soldiers had been wounded, thousands sozialistische Deutsche Arbeiterpartei, "Nazi" for short — had remained obscure as long as the German economy flourished. Now the country's industrialists, alarmed by the growing strength of communism in the working class, looked upon the Nazis with increasing approval.

At the time, the fear of Moscow was understandable. The Soviet Comintern, dedicated to the overthrow of other governments, was not just noisy; it was working, undermining the foundations of Western civilization from within. Communism was still new, virile, and virulent; cheerful tributes to it by leftists in the democracies drove democratic rightists, who were equally blind, toward Hitler. As T. R. Fehrenbach neatly states, "The Conservative Government of Great Britain, the one real order-keeping power in the world, was too intent upon the threatened social revolution to see the imminent nationalist revolt Hitler's Germany was mounting against the democratic world." They persuaded themselves, as Fehrenbach puts it, that a Germany ruled by Nazis could become "a counterpoise against the national and revolutionary ambitions of the Soviet Union."[19]

This was the rationale for the policy emerging in Whitehall and the Quai d'Orsay, of befriending the dictator states and appeasing their resentment of their postwar plight. The signs in Germany, to the men in high Tory councils, were encouraging. They pointed to the imminent establishment of a strong anti-Soviet regime in Berlin. Should that happen, they intended to befriend its leaders. Together, they believed, Englishmen and Germans had the stamina to forge a shield Comintern agents could never penetrate.

❧   ❧

If Britain succeeded in courting Germany, His Majesty's Government would have a lot of explaining to do, much of it to Englishmen who had been targets of Mausers and Krupp howitzers for four years and could never have prevailed without the gallant poilus who fought with them shoulder to shoulder, even when the Allied line nearly collapsed in the last spring of the war. An understanding with Berlin would mean the rejection of Britain's fellow democracy. Questions in the House would be endless. But as the new men saw it, the time had come to put wartime bitterness aside. France, they felt, lacked vigor, determination, and sound business sense.

The French *were* exhausted. In *France même* — France outside Paris — the country was quiescent. The fertile northern provinces had been transformed into a wasteland of crumbling trenches and rusting barbed wire; over half the Frenchmen between the ages of twenty and thirty-two — 1,385,000 — had been killed there between 1914 and 1918. The survivors were too maimed, or too feeble, to lift the tricolor in triumph. To be sure, the City of Light, the nation's capital, still glowed. Under the chestnut trees of the Champs Élysées, fashion reporters who had penetrated the closely guarded private openings of the city's grand couturiers forecast lower waists, straighter lines, fuller sleeves, and high, wide, and handsome shoulders. Hats were to be saucy: Arab fezzes, clown and cossack caps. Chanel would offer gloves of 18-karat spun gold, Regny an evening gown which could be converted into a bathing suit, and Rouff a naughty evening gown, with a zipper extending from the throat straight down to the bottom hem "for moonlight bathing," or, as cynics pointed out, "swift coupling."

In all world capitals it was assumed — it had, indeed, become a newspaper cliché — that France possessed "the finest army in the world." In London those pushing for a divorce from Paris and a remarriage in Berlin spread rumors of plans for a French preemptive war against the new German state. *The Times,* possibly floating a trial balloon, warned: "In the years that are coming there is more reason to fear for Germany than to fear Germany."[20]

Actually, confidence in the army of the Third Republic had been illusionary since 1917, when fifty-four French divisions — 750,000 men — had mutinied. Officers had been beaten and even murdered; an artillery regiment had attempted to blow up the Schneider-Creusot munitions plant; trains had been derailed; 21,174 men deserted outright. Trenches were abandoned, and had the Germans known there was no one on the other side of no-man's-land, they could have plunged through and won the war. The bitterness of the poilus survived the Armistice; their leaders told them their side had won, but they knew, in Churchill's words, that victory had been "bought so dear as to be almost indistinguishable from defeat."[21]

Gallic military thinking was now wholly defensive. On January 4, 1930, both houses of the National Assembly had voted to build, on the Franco-German border, a great wall to be named for the minister of war, André Maginot. It would cost seven billion francs when completed in 1935. To be sure, the line did not protect the wooded Ardennes, but Marshal Philippe Pétain dismissed fears for the forest: *"Elle est impénétrable."* This judgment by the hero of Verdun was unchallenged. To young journalist William L. Shirer, arriving at the Arc de Triomphe in 1925, it seemed that "no other country on the Continent could challenge France's supremacy. The nightmare of the German threat, which had haunted the

French for so long, had been erased." Their àncient foe, prostrate in defeat, its army reduced to a token force, its leadership "forbidden by the Versailles Treaty to build warplanes or tanks, or heavy guns or submarines or battleships, and saddled with the burden of reparations, was no longer a menace."[22]

That, too, was illusion. Germany was not the Germany the Allies thought they had created at Versailles, and France seemed to be drifting into a strengthless *oubli*. Alistair Horne, the popular British historian, saw "the urge for national *grandeur*" replaced by "a deep longing simply to be left in peace." In its capital, however, the mood quickened. It could be felt in the Café Flore and the Deux Magots, for example, the haunts of young Jean-Paul Sartre and his mistress, Simone de Beauvoir; in the *rêves fantastiques* of Jean Giraudoux and Jean Cocteau; in the Revue Nègre, the Ballet Suedois, the Ballet Russe, the extravagant theatre of Sergey Diaghilev, the fox trot *dansomanie*, Josephine Baker, Inkichinoff's film *La Tête d'un homme*, the Prevert brothers' film *L'Affaire est dans le sac*; and — the favorites of all the left-wing critics — the new stars Gilles and Julien, a pair of pacifist anarchists who performed in a Montmartre cabaret and then on the stage at Bobino's, wearing black sweaters and making songs like *"Le Jeu de massacre"* instant hits after singing them just once. The manic mood, Horne wrote, was "Anything for *spectacle.*" This was the France of legend: the land of tumbling francs, tumbling governments, and saucy, tumbling *filles*.[23]

La Force de l'âge (*The Prime of Life*), Simone de Beauvoir's memoir of the late 1920s and early 1930s, provides a more perceptive picture. Her depiction of French intellectuals contrasts starkly with the rising Nazi *Wildheit* in Berlin, where the excesses and decadence of the postwar decade were yielding to a flirtation, and then a lethal embrace, between philistinism and savagery. To be sure, there was ferocity in the French capital, too, as Communist gangs fought with members of the Croix de Feu, the Action Française, the Jeunesse Patriotes, and, later, Le Francisme, the most bizarre of the leagues. But they were a lunatic fringe; the intelligentsia considered them vulgar and so never mentioned them or even acknowledged their existence. "Peace seemed finally assured," de Beauvoir wrote in the fall of 1929. She felt she was living in "a new 'Golden Age,' " that the swelling of the Nazi ranks across the border was "a mere fringe phenomenon, without any serious significance." She, her lover Sartre, and their friends watched the Nazi seizure of power "quite calmly," she later wrote, and while she briefly noted the Nazi expulsion of Einstein, she was more dismayed by the closing of Berlin's Institute of Sexology.[24]

"We refused," she later wrote, "to face the threat which Hitler's behavior constituted to the world." Henri Barbusse wrote in *Le Monde* that the Nazis could not possibly put Germany's economy back on its feet; it was doomed, and after the collapse the German proletariat would reclaim its heritage. *Marianne*, a radical-socialist weekly, preached a steady pacifist line, coupled with announcements that if Hitler became chancellor he would soon be overthrown. In 1932 Romain Rolland drew up a manifesto, published in *Le Monde* and *Europe* and signed by André Gide, among others, which called upon all members of the French intelligentsia to vow "resistance against war." Writers, thinkers, academicians, continued to predict — despite mounting evidence to the contrary — that the two nations were moving toward a Franco-German rapprochement. Every leftist, every intellectual, was shouting simultaneously: "Down with fascism!" and "Disarmament NOW!" Even as Germany's army swelled with illegal recruits, France's intelligentsia, de Beauvoir wrote, saw "no threat to peace"; the only danger was "the panic that the Right was spreading in France, with the aim of dragging us into war." In 1914 "the whole of the intellectual elite, Socialists, writers, and all," had "toed a wholly chauvinistic line." Their lesson "forbade us to envisage the very possibility of a war."[25]

This perilous illusion was not limited to France's intellectual community. Barbusse's shocking novel of the trenches, *Le Feu*, reached millions who had never heard of Sartre, Romain Rolland, Louis Aragon, André Gide, or Paul Eluard. Barbusse died in 1935, just as Hitler was becoming a household name in French provinces; over 300,000 readers followed his coffin to Père Lachaise Cemetery in Paris. Insulated in their Gallic world, the people for whom the Führer and his Reich were sharpening their swords assumed that everyone who had suffered in the trenches, or knew and loved those who had, shared their disgust of fighting. They should have been more attentive. There is a revealing vignette in *La Force de l'âge*. Sartre and de Beauvoir are boating down the Elbe to the rock of Heligoland. Sartre strikes up a conversation with a fellow passenger, a forty-year-old German wearing a black peaked cap and a morose expression. The German tells Sartre that he had been a sergeant in the Great War, and, his voice rising, says: "If there is another war, this time we shall not be defeated. We shall retrieve our honor." Sartre thinks the poor fellow feels shamed because his side lost; being simple, the ex-sergeant needs reassurance that war's horrors lie in the past, never to return. He mildly remarks that there is no need of war; everyone wants peace. But he is facing a *sorte* he has never seen before: a real *Kämpfer* (warrior), incapable of forgetting or forgiving. Glaring, the man replies, "Honor comes first. First we must retrieve our honor." De Beauvoir wrote: "His fanatical tone alarmed me. . . . Never had I seen hatred shine so nakedly [*à nu*] from any human face." She tried to reassure herself "with the reflection that an ex-serviceman is bound to hold militaristic views," yet added, "How many such were there, who lived only for the moment when the great day of revenge would come?"[26]

🦁   🦁

Churchill was warning of Germany's yearning for revenge, but the casual visitor to Berlin that fall of 1932 would have seen few signs of it. The Zitadelle — the monumental government buildings over which the kaisers had reigned — seemed more effete than Paris and devoid of that indefinable tone which had once given the city its Lutheran ambience: an air of hard, clean, righteous high purpose, of noble masculinity, of spartan Prussian virtues at their most demanding and most admirable. Now all that was gone. Berlin was, in fact, conspicuous for its lack of any virtue whatever. It had become the new Babylon.

Before the Great War it had been Paris which had seethed with sinful romance, illicit intrigue; if you wanted to spend a weekend with your young secretary, you asked Cook's to book you a suite near the Place de l'Étoile. In those days Pigalle, the mean streets behind *Les Halles*, the notorious *maisons de joi* in the winding little rue de la Huchette, a block from Notre Dame, had been the most lurid attractions for those exploring what then passed for European decadence. No more: it now was Berlin. "Along the Kurfürstendamm," wrote Stefan Zweig, "powdered and rouged young men sauntered, and in the dimly lit bars one might see men of the world of finance courting drunken sailors"; while at transvestite balls, "hundreds of men costumed as women and hundreds of women as men danced under the benevolent eye of the police."[27]

Over two million young German women were destitute widows. The more desperate (and attractive) of them became prostitutes, seeking prey in the alleys near the Hauptbahnhof. Among them were muscular whores with whips and mothers in their early thirties, teamed with their teenaged daughters to offer *Mutter-und-Tochter* sex. Tourists were shocked by the more infamous night spots: the Kabarett Tingle-Tangle, the Apollo, the Monokel (*"die Bar der Frau"* — for lesbians), and the White Mouse, whose most sensational performer, and the role model for thousands of German girls in the Weimar years, was Anita Berber, who danced naked, mainlined cocaine and morphine, and made love to men and women sprawled atop bars, bathed in spotlights, while voyeurs stared and fondled one another. Anita was dead at twenty-nine. So, by then, was the Weimar Republic.

It was in these years that Europeans began importing not only movies but also the most trivial and seamiest exports of American mass culture. Everyone knew about Prohibition gangsters, and how they led to political corruption. That made them attractive, even fascinating. Viennese, Romans, Berliners, and Parisians formed cults around *les bandits américains*, as they were called in France, and, in one Lutzow-Platz graffito, *"die Häuptlinger der Chicagoer und New-Yorker Unterwelt — Al Capone, Jack Diamond, und Lucky Luciano."* So sedulously had they been aped in Italy that twenty-two-year-old Alberto Moravia devoted his first novel, *Gli indifferenti* (*The Time of Indifference*), to a devastating parable of depravity in Rome. New Orleans' Mardi Gras was the model for Germany's new *Faschingszeit;* the Tiller Girls at Berlin's Scala Theater were a frank imitation of the Ziegfeld chorus line; a clever wisecracker was a *Schnauze* (big mouth). Night clubs featured bands mimicking — and sometimes unintentionally parodying — American jazz combos. Week after week an advertisement ran in Munich's *Süddeutsche Monatshefte* crying: *"So dürfen Sie nicht Charleston tanzen!"*[28]

It had become fashionable to blame the global Depression on the collapse of the New York Stock Exchange three years earlier. Certainly the Crash was an important link in the chain; but the causes, the implications, and the sequence of events were international and too complex to be within the range of understanding then. The Great War had impoverished victors and vanquished alike. The Allies, however, believed they could recover their losses by making the losers pay. It was one of history's more tragic errors.

Once they began computing the cost of civilian property damage — not to mention what was called "the estimated capitalized value" of the five million Allied fighting men killed in the war — the Allied statesmen found themselves dealing with stupendous sums, billions of dollars. At Versailles they finally arrived at a rough figure: $31,530,500,000. This was their reparations bill, they declared, and Germany must pay it. The Allies, under the threat of renewed fighting, demanded an immediate down payment of five billion dollars — nearly thirty-three billion in 1980s currency. Also, the Germans must pay off Belgium's war loans. Also, interest on the unpaid balance. Also, a 26 percent tax on all German exports.

The terms were exorbitant, vindictive, and preposterous. John Maynard Keynes denounced Versailles as "a Carthaginian Peace." Churchill, who disapproved of the entire treaty, especially the punitive clauses, called the reparations "monstrous" and "malignant." Actually, there was no way that the leaders of the new German republic, struggling to find its feet in Weimar, could meet this absurd bill. They tried. But their government had no international credit. Germany's prewar commercial system had been destroyed by the Allied blockade. Rich Germans, anticipating heavy taxation, were fleeing abroad with their fortunes. After seven months, the mark sank to an all-time low: five million to the dollar. Then it dropped out of sight.

As the worldwide economic crisis deepened, Americans rescued the tottering German republic, first with loans and then with outright gifts of over ten million dollars. Once the New York stock market crashed, however, Wall Street had to look to its own. Helpless, Weimar staggered on the brink of ruin, maintaining the appearance of solvency by feats of legerdemain. Anti-Americans, forgetting the huge gifts, blamed Germany's plight on the United States. Some Tories even resented the fact that Churchill's mother had been American. Stanley Baldwin spoke contemptuously of "the low intellectual ability" of people in the United States; Neville Chamberlain agreed with him.

On one count Americans were guilty. European respect for U.S. diplomacy had been skidding since President Woodrow Wilson's departure from Versailles. In 1919 the U.S. Senate had rejected the Versailles covenants, including membership in the League of Nations, Wilson's creation, and his pledge to guarantee France's borders. After Wilson's death a succession of Republican presidents, reflecting the mood of U.S. voters, had been turned inward, devoting their attention to domestic issues. During the interwar years this doctrine was christened isolationism. At the same time, America's leaders kept nagging their former allies to pay their unpayable war debts. England could easily have paid her war debts to the United States had France paid *her* debts to England. But France was flat broke, which meant the British were stuck, which meant handsacross-the-sea met in a clammy grasp. Washington was unsympathetic. President Calvin Coolidge didn't want to hear about the Exchequer's problems; he wanted cash. He said: "They hired the money, didn't they?" Before the war Americans had been popular in Europe. But by the early 1930s Washington's repeated insistence that the hired money be repaid merely heightened the tension Over There.

Even more troubling was the U.S. absence from Geneva. It had dealt a devastating blow to the League of Nations. But in turning their backs on the problems of other great powers American isolationists were not alone. Immediately after the signing of the peace treaties in 1919 London drifted into a mild form of the American introversion, and one by one the chancelleries on the Continent followed their example, leaving the intricacies of external affairs to their foreign ministries.

The professional diplomats, delighted, turned to what they did best, assembling in huge conferences, immaculate in their striped trousers, wing collars, and pince-nez, solemnly initialing pacts and protocols which were later signed, on their recommendation, by their governments. By the end of the 1920s plenipotentiaries had bound the Continent in a fantastic web of signed documents bearing waxed seals and streaming ribbons, documents which, had they been honored, would have kept the peace. Czechoslovakia, Yugoslavia, and Rumania were linked in the Little Entente. France was pledged to the defense of Poland; Italy to Yugoslavia, Albania, Hungary, and Austria. The climax was the cluster of pacts solemnized at Locarno, Switzerland, in 1925. Locarno guaranteed the German-French and German-Belgian frontiers and provided for the arbitration of any disputes between Germany on the one hand, and France, Belgium, Poland, and Czechoslovakia on the other. Finally, to assure the territorial integrity of the Czechs, France signed a separate treaty promising to declare war on Germany if the Germans violated Czechoslovakia's borders. Italy and Britain joined in the mutual guarantee of peace in western Europe, and though British obligations were vague, Britain was already pledged to stand by France in any war.

The Wilhelmstrasse had sent a delegation to Locarno. Its legates moved gracefully through the great halls, elegant and charming, clicking heels, kissing hands, and in the "spirit of Locarno," as it was being hailed, added their signatures to the others on December 1, 1925. Foreign correspondents were baffled. Why were Germans there? These pacts were negotiated by nations with armies and navies. As a military power Germany had ceased to exist. The Treaty of Versailles had drawn the Junkers' teeth. Their army, or Reichswehr, as it had been renamed, could not exceed 100,000 men, including officers. Even tiny Belgium outnumbered them. They were allowed no military aircraft, no General Staff, no conscription, and no manufacture of arms and munitions without written permission from the triumphant Allies. Their navy was restricted to six battleships, six light cruisers, twelve torpedo boats — and no submarines. Weimar Germany was forbidden fortification of her own frontiers, and a demilitarized buffer zone, the Rhineland, separated her from the French and Belgians. Violation of any of these provisions were to be regarded as a declaration of war, punishable by an Allied military occupation of the German republic. Thus manacled, the defeated country constituted a threat to no one. Her delegation, the inquiring newspapermen were told, had been invited to Locarno as a gracious gesture, a sign that the wounds of 1918 were healing.[29]

Veteran correspondents were skeptical. The foreign policies of great powers, they knew, are not guided by generosity. Nor were they in this instance. The fact was that the Germans had acquired their invitations by diplomatic blackmail. Versailles had stigmatized not one, but two great nations; the victors had turned their backs on both the defeated Second Reich, excluded from the peace conference, and the new Soviet Union, which in 1917 had taken Russia — then an Allied power, fighting Germany — out of the war. Walter Rathenau, a brilliant Weimar statesman, had seized his chance. Taking advantage of a Genoa conference at which European diplomats were discussing the economic prospects of the Continent, he had slipped away to meet a Bolshevik delegation at nearby Rapallo. Since the Russians had not participated in the 1919 peace settlement, they could join Germany in renouncing all war claims. Extensive agreements, signed at the same time, drew them closer together. Two months later, on June 24, 1922, Rathenau was murdered by right-wing German nationalists. But the Rapallo Treaty stood.[30]

The Allies had been shocked. They realized, for the first time, that the independent German government could make important commitments without their consent. Thus the invitation to Locarno. There, Rathenau's successor, Gustav Stresemann, smoothly reassured them. Nervous Allied ministries were reminded that Germany was their shield against the Soviet Union.

🦁　🦁

Germany's former enemies listened carefully, wanting to believe. The Second Reich was dead. They cherished the hope that a stable German republic would serve as a bulwark against Russian adventurism. Another Allied incentive was anxiety; they knew that the kaiser's embittered officer corps refused to believe their army had been defeated on the battlefield and that the fighting qualities of German men were awesome.

A third motive was guilt. The Great War, by bankrupting both sides and destroying an entire generation of future leaders, eroded the confidence of the victors. Man, shocked by his inhumanity to man, was uncomfortable; he sought ways to ease his conscience. The transformation was not achieved overnight, but as the years passed a feeling deepened in London and Paris that the Central Powers had been shabbily treated at the Versailles peace conference. Allied casualties had been appalling, but at least they knew the jubilation of winning. When Germany and the two weaker members of her alliance had laid down their arms, they had lost 3,393,193 dead and 8,267,532 wounded. In defeat every conceivable humiliation had been visited upon them. Private property abroad belonging to German citizens had been summarily confiscated. The Kiel Canal and the country's five great rivers had been designated international waterways, like the English Channel or the Mediterranean. German representatives at the peace conference had been forced to sign the treaty's Article 231, accepting responsibility "for causing all the loss and damage to which the Allied and Associated Governments and their nationals have been subjected as a consequence of the war imposed upon them by the aggression of Germany and her allies."

Friedrich Ebert, provisional president of the new Weimar Republic, had called it "unbearable." The chancellor cried: "May the hand wither that signs this treaty!" The Allies, unmoved, issued an ultimatum. If the terms were not accepted, Allied troops would invade Germany. Ebert appealed to wartime chief of staff Paul von Hindenburg. Could such an attack be resisted? No, the field marshal replied, but he could not "help feeling that it were better to perish than sign such a humiliating peace [*Schmachfrieden*]." This was an outright evasion of responsibility. Because of it, Ebert, unsupported by the officer corps — the men who had actually lost the war — approved the treaty nineteen minutes before the Allied ultimatum ran out. It was an inauspicious start for the German republic.[31]

In November 1932 Churchill urged revision of Versailles "in cold blood and in a calm atmosphere and while the victor nations still have ample superiority, [rather] than to wait and drift on, inch by inch and stage by stage, until once again vast combinations, equally matched confront each other face to face." As the searing memoirs, best-selling novels, gripping plays, and popular films put the conflict in a new perspective, newspapers on both sides revealed the vast profits reaped by munitions tycoons. Holding the Germans solely responsible for the tragedy of 1914–1918, people now realized, had distorted the truth and violated the honor of the losers. It had amounted to an imposition of vindictive conditions on helpless men, forbidden, at the time, even to protest.[32]

By the early 1930s, however, the strongest emotion aroused in Germany's neighbors was primitive terror. The Germans knew it; they had deliberately provoked it in two wars, and had even given it a name, *Schrecklichkeit* (frightfulness). The nineteenth-century Prussian strategist Karl von Clausewitz had encouraged it as a means of shortening wars by putting the enemy "in a situation in which continuing the war is more oppressive to him than surrender." Teutonic troops, armed and dangerous, *were* frightful. They had practiced *Schrecklichkeit* in 1914, when bands of French and Belgian guerrillas defending their own soil had led to German executions of civilians, hostages, and prisoners of war. "Suddenly," Barbara Tuchman writes, "the world became aware of the beast beneath the German skin."[33]

In the 1920s and 1930s, accounts of these crimes were suppressed by pacifists in *das Ausland*, that revealing German term which welded all nations outside the Reich into a single collective noun. The new line was that all tales of German atrocities in the Great War had been Allied propaganda. But Belgians who had treated their invaders with disrespect had in fact been led before firing squads as early as the second day of the war. German records proved it. If Belgian refugees slowed the German advance, hostages were picked at random and killed.[34] One can find their gravestones today, inscribed: *"1914: Fusillé par les Allemands"* — "Shot by the Germans."

It was the dread of another such nightmare which provided the more powerful drive behind the grid of interlocking treaties culminating at Locarno. Even after Versailles, Germany remained the most powerful nation in Europe, with a population exceeding that of either Britain or France by thirty million. Geographical position alone seemed fated to guarantee Germany domination of Europe. Hitler's Nazis attracted the attention of chancelleries of Europe as Hitler set forth his goals, giving priority to the union of all Germans in a greater Germany. The very idea made foreign ministries tremble. Were it achieved, the smaller nations would confront a monolith of eighty-two million Teutons. A reconstituted Reich under strong leadership could reassemble the kaiser's dismantled juggernaut.[35]

Thus German signatures on the Locarno Pact had been welcomed. Despite Germany's violation of Belgian neutrality in 1914 — dismissing the Wilhelmstrasse's written pledge not to do so as *"ein Fetzen Papier"* ("a scrap of paper") — it was still inconceivable that a civilized nation would break its word. Great powers did not invade other states until war had been formally declared. If Locarno and Weimar's other postwar commitments were to be treated as scraps, diplomacy would be meaningless. Therefore, foreign ministries watched the tumultuous course of German politics in 1932 with increasing uneasiness. The Nazis were scum, men bereft of honor as Europe's ruling classes understood it. Late in the year a French agent, burrowed in the Wilhelmstrasse, sent the Quai d'Orsay a shocking report on the ten-year-old Russo-German treaty which Walter Rathenau had negotiated in Rapallo. A secret protocol, drafted by Foreign Minister Rathenau himself, had specified that the Russians would set aside tracts of land where the Germans would lay new foundations for the development of armament technique. There, too, German bombers and fighter planes were being assembled and German pilots, navigators, and bombardiers trained. The agent in Berlin was absolutely reliable. His French control in the Deuxième Bureau was badly shaken, but after he had regained his poise he felt baffled by one detail. Rathenau's assassins had been identified and interrogated. Their militant nationalism was clear. They wanted a new, rearmed Reich. Why had they slain a diplomat who had rendered their cause so priceless a service? The decoded reply was: "Rathenau was a Jew."[36] The Quai d'Orsay was dumbfounded. Would they, they wondered, *ever* understand the Germans?

In Berlin the world's longest breadline stretched down the Kurfürstendamm. Over fifteen million Germans were on the dole. In the streets husky, brown-shirted storm troopers (*Sturmtrupper*), wearing their high-crowned caps and black-on-white-on-red swastikas (*Hakenkreuz*, literally "hooked cross"), clubbed and battered men suspected of leftist sympathies, Jews of every age and sex, and anyone who failed to raise a stiff-armed *heil* when a Nazi band marched past under the banner *"Deutschland erwache!"* ("Germany awake!")

None of this was, in itself, extraordinary. In 1932 hunger and bloodshed haunted every great capital. But there was a significant difference in German turmoil. The drafters of Versailles had mutilated the kaiser's Second Reich in every way except the one which counted most. The internal structure of Wilhelmine Germany had been left intact. Because the judges in Weimar courtrooms had belonged to the prewar privileged class and regarded the republic as a puppet regime installed by enemies of the Reich, Nazi street fighters who murdered their political opponents in broad daylight, with dozens of witnesses testifying against them, received suspended sentences and five-mark fines. At the same time, supporters of the republic were sentenced to long prison terms for revealing, in speeches or newspapers, that the Reichswehr was rebuilding the army in defiance of Germany's pledge to the Allies. Franz L. Neumann writes: "It is impossible to escape the conclusion that political justice is the blackest page [*schwärzeste Seite*] in the life of the German Republic."[37]

Leniency was extended even to those rightists for whom the aristocracy had little sympathy. After the Armistice, Munich became the center of revolutionary conspiracies, including the successful plot to kill Rathenau and Hitler's unsuccessful putsch of 1923, an act of high treason in which nineteen men lost their lives while the Nazi leader fled the scene and hid from the police. Tracked down and arrested, Hitler spent only nine months in Landsberg prison, cosetted by every comfort the warden could provide, including writing materials. When he left his spacious "cell," he carried the manuscript of *Mein Kampf* under his arm, and as he emerged from the prison gate his supporters hailed him as a victorious hero.[38]

Until the Depression the Nazis had been a lunatic fringe. In 1928 they polled some 810,000 votes — 2.6 percent of those cast. The economic crises brought them swollen rolls and made Hitler a national figure. Oswald Spengler wrote: "In the heart of the people the Weimar Constitution is already doomed!" Two elections — in 1930 and 1932 —

demonstrated that the Nazis, although shy of a working majority, had emerged as the country's largest political party. It was also the most violent. "We want a dictatorship!" Hitler cried, and his deputies left no doubt of their scorn for democratic procedures. In the Reichstag and the Prussian Diet they wore their uniforms, swung their fists and clubs, and disrupted any session which seemed about to reach agreement on a substantive issue by hurling any object which came to hand, including, according to one account, "inkwells, water bottles, desk drawers, chairs, ledgers, broken table legs." Having driven all others from the chamber, the Nazis "spent the next half-hour triumphantly roaring old war songs."

With few exceptions, Churchill among them, foreign politicians were unalarmed by Hitler. To *Time,* amused by his pretentiousness, Hitler was a "bristle-lipped, slightly pot-bellied" forty-three-year-old who often "stroked his tuft of brown mustache." Those with no command of the German tongue regarded him as a comical figure bearing a close resemblance to Charlie Chaplin. Even foreign correspondents underrated him. They reasoned that the heart of the Nazi constituency lay in the lower middle class, and that the upper classes would be alienated by the party's leader, whose wartime rank had been that of corporal.[39]

Until 1932 they had been right. National Socialism had been a stigma. Among well-born Germans, the Nazi party was regarded as coarse. But that autumn they were beginning to understand that the door of history had been shut on their Augustan Age of princes and potentates and plumed marshals and glittering little regular armies — on all the fanfaronade that had marked their disciplined, secure world. In the waning autumn of 1932, when Americans were voting Franklin D. Roosevelt into the White House, the German patriciate was reassessing its view of Hitler. The eminent *Deutsche Allgemeine Zeitung,* always reflective of their opinion, abruptly abandoned its hostile treatment of National Socialism and urged Reich President Hindenburg to overcome his "strong personal dislike" of the Nazi leader and appoint him chancellor "in the interests of that tranquillity required for business revival."[40]

Once Hitler moved, he moved fast. Nazi deputies, though still short of an absolute majority, outnumbered the Social Democrats nearly two-to-one and dominated the Reichstag. Nevertheless, Field Marshal Hindenburg, Ebert's successor to the figurehead post of president, refused to appoint Hitler chancellor. The Chancellor Crisis followed. Running the government was impossible without the Nazi deputies, who, on Hitler's orders, vetoed each Hindenburg nominee for the office. Then Franz von Papen and General Kurt von Schleicher, the two strongest conservatives, agreed on a remarkable solution. Name Hitler chancellor, they told the Reich president, and they would manipulate him. Pandora's box was thereupon pried open, and on January 30, 1933, Hitler was sworn in as chancellor, or, as he preferred to be called, Reich chancellor — chancellor of the Empire. His expression, caught by a cameraman, was one of ecstasy. With his grasp of the Teutonic mind, he knew that now, having acquired *Autorität* by legal means, he would be accepted and obeyed by the German people, and that if he continued to pay lip service to Weimar's constitution, he could use it to destroy itself.[41]

He appointed Hermann Göring president of the Reichstag, and Göring moved into the Präsidentenpalast (Reichstag President's Palace). An underground passage, part of the central heating system, connected the Präsidentenpalast and the Reichstag building. Less than a month after Hitler became chancellor — five days before a new election — an arsonist or arsonists entered the Reichstag building through this tunnel and set it ablaze. Hitler swiftly exploited the tumult; he persuaded the anxious, confused Hindenburg to sign a decree for the protection of *Volk und Staat* which, in effect, put the entire country under martial law. The chancellor could and did gag his political opponents, terrorize them, and silence all but the boldest, who were arrested. Over four thousand figures in public life, including Reichstag deputies, were thrown into jail. Later the hard core of his opposition were moved to Dachau, the first Nazi concentration camp, and never knew freedom again.

As the election campaign approached its climax the Nazis, needing money, sought it from the titans of German industry. Göring invited them to the Präsidentenpalast — to respecters of *Autorität* the invitation had the force of a command — and on arrival they were seated in carefully arranged armchairs, with Gustav Krupp von Bohlen in the place of honor and four I. G. Farben directors immediately behind him. Hitler entered and faced them. "We are about to hold the last election," he began, and paused to let the full implications of that sink in. Naturally, he said, the transition to National Socialism would be smoother if the party was swept in by a landslide. Therefore, he solicited their support. In backing a dictatorship they would be backing themselves: "Private enterprise cannot be maintained in a democracy." Using his "authority and personality," he assured them, he would not only eliminate the Communist threat; he would abolish the trade unions and restore the Wehrmacht to its former glory. "Regardless of the outcome" at the polls, there would be "no retreat." If he lost he would stay in office "by other means . . . with other weapons." The chancellor sat down and Krupp sprang up to express "the unanimous feeling of the industrialists in support of the chancellor." Göring reminded them of the point of the meeting. Dr. Hjalmar Schacht, the Nazi financial wizard, cried more bluntly: "And now, gentlemen, pony up!" Once again

Krupp, as senior man, rose to pledge a million marks, and Schacht collected two million more from the others.[42]

Financed by German industrialists, Hitler led the bloodiest election campaign in European history. Every night trucks bearing squads of brown-shirted storm troopers thundered down streets and alleys all over the country, breaking down doors, dragging away their critics to be beaten and tortured. Bonfires blazed on hilltops and the storm troopers held torchlight parades, singing the party anthem. By day other party columns marched down thoroughfares, public address loudspeakers brayed martial music. Billboards were plastered with Nazi posters. Swastikas decorated telegraph poles.

It worked. The Nazis polled 17,277,180 votes; the Social Democrats 7,181,629. With the support of sympathetic nationalist deputies, Hitler could muster an absolute majority in the Reichstag. He needed more than that, however. His immediate goal was passage of an enabling act giving him dictatorial powers. Only a constitutional amendment could grant that, and amendments required two-thirds of the deputies. To the new chancellor, this presented no obvious problem; armed with his extraordinary decree, he could bar opposition deputies from entering Reichstag sessions, or, if they became unruly, arrest them.

But Hitler, though evil, was an evil genius; he recognized the necessity of mollifying the old Wilhelmine order, particularly the officer corps. If they backed him, the country would feel a sense of continuity, strengthening the impression of Nazi legitimacy. Thus he announced that the Third Reich's first Reichstag would convene in Potsdam's Garrison Church, the very temple of Prussianism, where the Hohenzollern sovereigns had prayed and Frederick the Great lay buried. He turned the session into an obsequious tribute to Hindenburg. André François-Poncet, the French ambassador, wrote that after this performance, "how could . . . the Junkers and monarchist barons . . . hesitate to grant him their entire confidence, to meet all his requests, to concede the full powers he claimed?"[43]

Two days later, in the Kroll Opera House in Berlin, the Reichstag voted 444 to 84 to give Hitler his dictatorial powers. The Enabling Act of March 23, 1933, transferred from the deputies to their chancellor the powers to make laws, control the budget, ratify treaties with foreign countries, and initial constitutional amendments. Thus ended the fourteen-year German republic. *Autorität* had been punctiliously observed every step along the way. "It was no victory," wrote Spengler, "for enemies were lacking."[44]

❧   ❧

In one of his more magnanimous moments, Churchill said of the Reich's future führer: "I admire men who stand up for their country in defeat, even though I am on the other side." Hitler, he added, had "a perfect right to be a patriotic German if he chose." Winston's son, Randolph, then a journalist, had accompanied the Nazi leader during his first, peaceful 1932 campaign, and later, when the returns showed a sharp increase in Nazi voters, Randolph had sent him a telegram of congratulation. His father, however, was less enthusiastic now. In Hitler's speeches, *The Times* had reported, he was demanding *Wehrfreiheit* (military freedom), a euphemism for German rearmament. Many MPs thought he might have a point, that *Wehrfreiheit* was worth discussing. In May 1932 Churchill asked them: "Do you wish for war?" Two months later he declined to join those acclaiming the Lausanne Conference, which had virtually ended reparations. How, he wondered, would Germany spend the money she owed the Allies? He felt apprehensive. Germany might rearm, he said, and cited a recent warlike statement by Hitler, "who is the moving impulse behind the German government and may be more than that soon."[45]

Churchill and Hitler almost met. Although still shaky from his New York automobile accident, Winston was moving ahead in mid-1932 with the research for his biography of his great ancestor, the first Duke of Marlborough. In the summer of 1932, he and a small entourage of friends and relatives toured Marlborough's old battlefields on the Continent. After a day on the field at Blenheim, he rested in Munich's Regina Hotel. The Nazis were, of course, aware that he was in the country. Inevitably, the Churchill party was approached, and their envoy was skillfully chosen. Ernst ("Putzi") Hanfstaengl was a Harvard graduate, a friend of Randolph's, and the millionaire son of a German father and a wealthy American mother. He was also the man who had given Hitler asylum after the aborted Nazi putsch of 1923. Putzi joined the Englishmen for cocktails. After he had played some of Churchill's favorite tunes on a lobby piano, they dined together.

The issue of German politics was raised almost immediately. Putzi offered to introduce Winston to his idol. Nothing would be easier, he said; Hitler came to the hotel every evening at five o'clock and would be delighted to meet so great a British statesman. It was all arranged, and then Churchill disarranged it. He asked Hanfstaengl: "Why is your chief so violent about the Jews? I can quite understand being angry with Jews who have done wrong or who are against the country, and I understand resisting them if they try to monopolise power in any walk of life; but what is the sense of being against a man simply because of his birth? How can any man help how he is born? Tell your boss for me that anti-Semitism may be a good starter, but it is a bad stayer."

Putzi's face fell. The next day he solemnly informed Winston that the meeting was off; Hitler had other plans. Since Churchill and his party remained at the Regina for a full week with no further overtures, he concluded that his disapproval of Nazi anti-Semitism had blacklisted him. So it had, but the story has an interesting envoi. Hitler had told Hanf-staengl: "In any case, what part does Churchill play? He is in the opposition and no one pays any attention to him." Putzi shot back: "People said the same thing about you." For this and other flippancies, Putzi, who had not only sheltered Hitler but had also given generously to his war chests, would later flee for his life, thus joining the extraordinary exodus from Germany of the blameless and the gifted. Hitler, in effect, exiled German intellectual life. During his first year in power he drove 1,600 scholars out of the country, including a quarter of the Heidelberg faculty and five Nobel laureates.[46]

In Parliament Churchill continued to urge revision of Versailles but vehemently opposed *Wehrfreiheit*, warning that accepting equality of armaments "would be almost to appoint the day for another European war — to fix it as if it were a prize-fight." Sounding the alarm even before Hitler moved into the chancellery, he wrote in the *Daily Mail* on October 17, 1932, that General Schleicher had "already declared that whatever the Powers may settle, Germany will do what she thinks fit in rearmament. Very grave dangers lie along these paths, and if Great Britain . . . encouraged Germany in such adventures, we might in an incredibly short space of time [be] plunged into a situation of violent peril." He told the House: "Now the demand is that Germany should be allowed to rearm. Do not delude yourselves. Do not let His Majesty's Government believe — I am sure they do not believe — that all that Germany is asking for is equal status. . . . That is not what Germany is seeking. All these bands of sturdy Teutonic youths, marching through the streets and roads of Germany, with the light of desire in their eyes . . . are not looking for status. They are looking for weapons."[47]

Perhaps nothing underscores the difference between German and British moods in the early 1930s so starkly as the political activities of their university undergraduates. In Oxford they were vowing never to fight, even in defense of England, while in Heidelberg, H. R. Knickerbocker of the *New York Evening Post* found, nearly three out of every four students were dues-paying Nazis. A German historian points out that Heidelberg, like Oxford, had preserved its "traditionalist, socially exclusive structure," but that the German youths from privileged families were suppressing student groups supporting the republic in Berlin by "a powerful union of nationalist, *völkisch*-oriented, and above all dueling fraternities." They campaigned strenuously against what they called the "Jewification" of the universities. Weimar's Ministry of Culture tried to end discrimination against "non-Aryan" undergraduates, but this merely brought "a further radicalization, increasing disorders and a further growth of National Socialist propaganda." Even "the majority of German writers," according to Günter Grass, "made no attempt to defend the republic, while not a few of them deliberately held it up to ridicule."[48]

The rightward drift in academe and the intellectual community was of profound significance. In Germany, as in England, most undergraduates came from upper-class families. Because their commitment to National Socialism was often decisive in determining parental commitment, the trend toward the hakenkreuz enlisted the lives, the fortunes, and the sacred honor of the country's traditional ruling oligarchies, including their children, who would inherit tomorrow's Germany.

Meantime, the Oxford Union's resolution that it would "in no circumstances fight for King and Country" had aroused Churchill's wrath. He called it an "abject, squalid, shameless avowal," a "very disquieting and disgusting symptom." Its impact abroad, he said, would be disastrous. He thought "of Germany, with its splendid clear-eyed youth marching forward. . . burning to suffer and die for their fatherland," and of "Italy, with her ardent Fascisti." He said: "One can almost feel the curl of contempt upon the lips of the manhood of all these peoples when they read this message sent out by Oxford University in the name of young England."[49]

In early 1934 Oxford's Tories invited him to speak, and he accepted — unwisely, for it was impossible for him to force entry into the locked minds of British undergraduates in the early 1930s; earlier, the Cambridge Union had voted 213 to 138 for "uncompromising" pacifism. But he couldn't resist a fight. He agreed to appear and answer twelve prepared questions. That part of the evening went well. It was afterward, during a general discussion, that he ran into trouble. Among the five hundred students present was a German Rhodes scholar, Adolf Schlepegrell. Schlepegrell pointed out that Versailles had specified a Saar plebiscite, scheduled for 1935, to determine whether it would join France or Germany. Since the population was German, the results were a foregone conclusion. Schlepegrell suggested a generous gesture — an immediate withdrawal of French troops stationed there. Churchill, in his most combative mood, rejected the idea. Germany must abide by the letter of Versailles, he said, because she "started the war," thereby "plunging the whole world into ruins." The young German quickly asked: "Does Mr. Churchill believe that the German people, the men and women who live in Germany today, are responsible for the war? Would he please answer 'yes' or 'no.' " Winston looked straight at him and replied: "Yes." The youth bowed to him and, amid tremendous applause from his fellow students, walked out of the hall.[50]

Ironically, when Schlepegrell returned to Germany — where he had become a newspaper hero — the authorities found that one of his grandmothers had been Jewish, and this disqualified him from taking a bar examination. Eventually he became a naturalized British citizen and served as a political intelligence officer during World War II. So Churchill won in the end. But that sequel lay in the future, unknown, on that evening when he walked out on Winston and humiliated him in the eyes of Oxford. Nor was that all. Later in the discussion, after the German's departure, Churchill declared British rearmament "essential for us to be safe in our island home," and the audience, to his surprise and consternation, burst into laughter. He repeated the phrase, and the laughter grew so raucous, and so prolonged, that he could not continue.[51]

A half-century later their mirth seems incomprehensible. Yet how could a generation informed by *Journey's End* and *All Quiet on the Western Front* have responded differently? They believed that Churchill was crying wolf. And they knew his alarm was groundless. As the new year arrived, a catchy tune from Walt Disney's *Three Little Pigs* was on everyone's lips:

> *Who's a-fraid of the big bad wolf, big bad wolf, big bad wolf?*
> *Who's a-fraid of the big bad wolf? Tra la la la la!*

PART ONE

SHOALS

NUMBER 10 Downing Street, at that time the most famous address in the world, is one of three gracious seventeenth-century houses built by George Downing, a Harvard man who returned to the country of his birth, became a Cromwellian civil servant, and designed No. 10, No. 11, and No. 12 as "large and well-built houses, fit for persons of honour and quality, each house to have a pleasant prospect into St. James's Park." Originally the properties of the Earl of Lichfield, they passed into royal hands when his lordship was undone by reckless gambling.[1]

Not all of No. 10's subsequent occupants were people of quality. King Charles II, the most promiscuous of the Stuarts, used it to house his kept women, who, when neglected by him, solicited passersby from windows and charged them fees. In 1732 King George II presented the building to Sir Robert Walpole, Britain's first prime minister, and ever since then it has been the London home of his successors (except Lord Salisbury, who preferred to live in his magnificent London mansion), just as No. 11 is the residence of the chancellor of the Exchequer and No. 12 the workplace of government whips. Because Walpole was also responsible for the kingdom's money, the front door of No. 10 bears a worn brass plate reading: "First Lord of the Treasury."[2]

If, during Churchill's last years as tenant, you were a young American foreign correspondent bearing an invitation to call here, that plate was the first thing you would have seen after the bobby at the door confirmed your appointment and checked your identity. Inside, on the ground floor, the house at first appeared to be, not the teeming hive of a world leader, but a lovely, somewhat quaint relic of the Restoration. Jock Colville has recalled that in the 1930s the atmosphere was that of any other comfortable upper-class London home, and that even after the outbreak of World War II Neville Chamberlain "disliked being disturbed, telephonically or otherwise, at weekends or after dinner at 10 Downing Street." But in some respects appearances were deceptive. There was more to No. 10 than at first

met the eye — tunnels linked the building with No. 11 and No. 12, and
the rear of No. 10 joined the much larger Lichfield House, another
possession which became crown property when the cards turned against the
unlucky Lichfield.[3]

State rooms occupied the floor above, and a creaking old elevator led
to the top floor, where the prime minister and his wife lived in guarded
privacy. Most intriguing, however, for one who cherished the past, was
the Cabinet Room on the ground floor. Outside, a row of coat pegs bore
the names of the cabinet ministers, and a dapper man in striped trousers
checked the P.M.'s appointments and studied documents from institutions
responsible to No. 10's householder — that morning the documents came
from, among others, the British Museum, the Church of England, and the
ancient universities. Baize double doors led to the elegant cabinet chamber,
centered on a dark, gleaming table. A secretary sat at a Victorian desk near
the door; tall, well-proportioned windows overlooked the Horse Guards.
The cabinet met at 11:00 A.M. on Tuesdays and Thursdays, but its
members waited outside until the prime minister, seated with the secretary
to the cabinet beside him, summoned them.[4]

Winston had first occupied a minister's chair at this table in 1908, at
the age of thirty-three, when the entire world awaited decisions made here,
and the future of millions, living in British possessions which most ministers hadn't even seen, depended on their judgments. In the last quarter of
the twentieth century the greatness of the British Empire is a memory
shared by a fraction of the population. The world was very different in
1932. Neither the United States nor the Soviet Union was a superpower.
Powerful armies were found elsewhere, but Britannia continued to rule the
world's waves, and her imperial resources were almost inexhaustible. The
roar of the British lion was still deafening — not only in Europe, but in
every time zone. In the aftermath of Waterloo an English journalist first
observed that "the sun never sets upon the Union Jack." That was still true
in the twenty-one-year interwar period which followed the Armistice of
1918, when decisions around this table, counterpoised with those made in
Berlin's Reich Chancellery, profoundly altered the course of history.

Over the centuries No. 10 has been the home of men whose luster was not
limited to Britain and whose names are household words, among them
Chatham, Pitt, Melbourne, Peel, Palmerston, Disraeli, Gladstone, and
Lloyd George. Although he had earlier been regarded as a future prime
minister, during the 1930s Fleet Street saw Churchill as a wine which had
passed its point. Still vigorous, still brilliant, he was nevertheless out of
tune with the times. He was distrusted, disliked — even hated — by those
who did not share his conviction that Germany threatened the peace and

England must arm to defend her shores. The leaders of England's three political parties were convinced that Hitler would never make war if his demands were met with diplomatic finesse. In those years, when Britain was losing her eminence as the world's mightiest power, Churchill was pitted against three tenants of No. 10 whom Englishmen would prefer to forget, three political mediocrities who presided over disastrous policies which reduced Britannia to an embattled island struggling to survive — a struggle that only Churchill and his small band of followers, who would finally succeed them on the first stroke of twelve, believed could be won.

Who were they?

Ramsay MacDonald was of humble origins — a bastard, actually. In his early years he joined the socialist Fabian Society, and in 1924 he became England's first Labour prime minister. All his life he had been a pacifist; in 1914 he had condemned Britain's entry into the Great War, and his foreign policy concentrated on the limitation, and then the elimination, of armaments. Bewildered by the worldwide Depression, he was, by the early 1930s, a ruin of the man he had been. "The wretched Ramsay," Churchill wrote his wife, "is almost a mental case — he'd be far better off in a Home." His most striking weakness was his vanity. Leonine, with a magnificent thatch of snowy hair, he wanted to remain prime minister despite his repudiation at the polls in 1931. Stanley Baldwin, the leader of the Conservative party, was more interested in power than titles. Baldwin suggested that MacDonald remain at No. 10 as the leader of a coalition, the "National Emergency Government," while Baldwin actually took the reins in the House as its lord president. MacDonald agreed. On June 7, 1935, however, he and Baldwin exchanged offices. Two years later he was dead.

Stanley Baldwin, "S.B.," the ultimate politician, was a plain, unsophisticated, and outwardly modest man, affectionately known to Tory ladies as the "Dear Vicar." Yet he was the most powerful prime minister since Walpole; in one form or another, either singly or jointly with MacDonald, he held supreme power, with two short intervals, for fourteen years, from 1923 to 1937. He had no interest in events on the Continent; indeed, anything beyond England's shores, including her empire, bored him. His instructions to the Foreign Office were to avoid agreements with Russia, "keep us out of war," and buy "peace at any price." Bob Boothby recalled: "If at any time after 1929 you had asked him where he was going, he would have had difficulty in answering the question." Short and thick-set, he was the personification of John Bull; in an ambiguous comment, Churchill said that Baldwin "represented in a broad way some of the strengths and many of the infirmities of our island race."[5]

"Good Old Neville," Baldwin's successor as prime minister in 1937, was the son of the great Joseph Chamberlain, who considered him "entirely unsuitable for a political career." Lloyd George declared that Neville's vision was no greater than that of "a provincial manufacturer of bed-steads," and once he had found his footing at No. 10 the French gave him the sobriquet *Monsieur J'aime Berlin*. His half brother Austen was an eminent statesman and one of Churchill's few allies in his struggle to prepare England for the coming Nazi onslaught, but Neville was the narrowest of prime ministers. He is still the least understood. His image is that of a weakling waving a frail umbrella while cowering before fearsome Hitler. In fact, he was decisive, self-confident, and — as re-vealed in his diaries and his letters to his two sisters — domineering. Most of his life had been devoted to business, chiefly in Birmingham. He did not stand for Parliament until his fiftieth year. Sir John Simon, an admirer, wrote that when colleagues came to Neville he would "listen in a business-like fashion to what one had to say, and then state his conclusions with the finality of a General Manager conducting his company's affairs." Cham-berlain once told Ivan Maisky, the Soviet ambassador, he felt that "if only we could sit down at a table with the Germans and run through all their complaints and claims with a pencil, this would greatly relieve all ten-sions." Later he said: "I don't believe myself that we could purchase peace at a lasting settlement by handing over Tanganyika to the Germans, but if I did I would not hesitate for a moment to do so." He was passionately antiwar, in large part because it meant government interference in private enterprise, and the manufacture of armaments which would be useless when peace returned. All in all he was preeminently a man of the thirties, "highly competent," in the words of Telford Taylor, the historian and lawyer, "but grim and graceless." J. C. Davidson, later Viscount David-son, described him as "a good Lord Mayor of Birmingham in a lean year." Chamberlain, Churchill said, looked at foreign affairs "through the wrong end of a municipal drainpipe."[6]

The arena where prime ministers and other Englishmen in public life perform — and whence, in Churchill's prime, the British Empire was ruled — is astonishingly small. Its length, between Trafalgar Square and Parliament, is six hundred yards; its breadth, from the Victoria Em-bankment along the Thames eastward to St. James's Park, three hundred yards. Within this small neighborhood are Downing Street, the Admi-ralty, Westminster Abbey, Parliament, Scotland Yard, and the Palace of Whitehall, now occupied by the Home Office, Commonwealth Office, and Foreign Office (called the FO or simply Whitehall). In World War II Churchill's bunker, an underground war room, lay beneath Storey's Gate, where Birdcage Walk, flanking the park, starts. The walk ends a thousand yards away at Buckingham Palace. On the opposite side of the

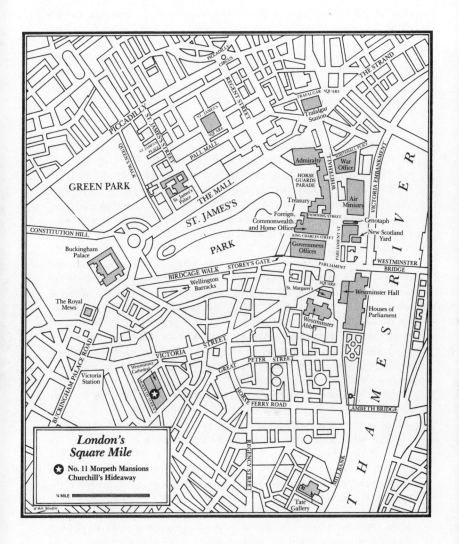

London's Square Mile

★ No. 11 Morpeth Mansions
Churchill's Hideaway

¼ MILE

GREEN PARK

PICCADILLY CIRCUS

REGENT STREET

THE STRAND

TRAFALGAR SQUARE

Trafalgar Station

ST. JAMES'S SQUARE

PALL MALL

ST. JAMES'S STREET

ST. JAMES'S PLACE

St. James's Palace

QUEEN'S WALK

THE MALL

ST. JAMES'S

PARK

Admiralty

HORSE GUARDS PARADE

War Office

WHITEHALL PLACE

WHITEHALL

Treasury

Air Ministry

Foreign, Commonwealth and Home Offices

DOWNING STREET

Cenotaph

New Scotland Yard

KING CHARLES STREET

PARLIAMENT ST

VICTORIA EMBANKMENT

CONSTITUTION HILL

Buckingham Palace

Government Offices

PARLIAMENT

WESTMINSTER BRIDGE

BIRDCAGE WALK

STOREY'S GATE

SQUARE

Wellington Barracks

St. Margaret's

Westminster Hall

The Royal Mews

Houses of Parliament

BUCKINGHAM PALACE ROAD

VICTORIA STREET

Westminster Abbey

Victoria Station

Westminster Cathedral

GREAT PETER STREET

MORPETH STREET

HORSE FERRY ROAD

MILLBANK

LAMBETH BRIDGE

T H A M E S   R I V E R

REGENCY STREET

TATE GALLERY

Tate Gallery

d'Art Studio

park is the Mall, St. James's Palace, Pall Mall, and all the famous clubs, including White's, the Oxford and Cambridge, the Athenaeum, Brooke's, the Reform, which was the haven of Liberal MPs, and the site of the Carlton, its Tory equivalent until the Luftwaffe leveled it during the Blitz. Churchill's flat at No. 11 Morpeth Mansions on Morpeth Terrace was within walking distance of the entire area. His daughter Mary remembers it as a " 'maisonette-flat-duplex' — just off the unfashionable end of Victoria Street and opposite the Roman Catholic cathedral."[7]

Except for Buckingham Palace, whose householder is excluded from great decisions, these are the haunts of the powerful. Their epicenter is the Palace of Westminster, parts of which were built in the eleventh century after the Battle of Hastings. Westminster was a triumph of Victorian exuberance, with over a thousand rooms, a hundred staircases, over two miles of corridors, and an eight-acre roof. Towering, vast, Gothic, built in asymmetric style, and topped by Big Ben, which was installed in 1858, Westminster has an interior which is the accomplishment of an entire generation of skilled craftsmen, who embellished the palace's robing rooms, private suites for parliamentary leaders, its ancient crypt and cloisters, division lobbies, smoking rooms, libraries, processional gallery, and, of course, the two Houses of Parliament — the House of Lords, with seats for 1,100 peers, and the House of Commons, which is too small to accommodate all 635 members of Parliament. That was deliberate. Regular attendance is rare, intimacy encourages lively debate, and "a crowded House," in historic moments, creates a dramatic sense of urgency.

The Commons, now rebuilt, was Churchill's principal forum for over forty years, and it should be envisaged as he knew it, unchanged in 225 years, with its timbered ceiling beneath which lay the well and carved chair of the Speaker, who determined which members of Parliament should have the floor and could intervene when the rules of the House were violated. On either side of the Speaker's dais, stretching away from him to the far end of the chamber, rose five tiers of benches upholstered in green. An aisle — "the gangway" — cuts across each tier at midpoint. On the Speaker's right sat MPs of the party in power; on his left, facing them across the well, were MPs of the Opposition. The lowest bench extending from the Speaker's right to the gangway was reserved for the government — the prime minister and his ministers. It was called the front bench or the Treasury Bench, sharing a common ancestor with the brass plate adorning the door of No. 10.

Backbenchers — "private members" — sat wherever they liked, or, in a crowded House, wherever they could find room. Because of his past glories, however, by tacit understanding the first seat beyond the gangway on the lowest tier was reserved for Winston Churchill, the member for Epping. He cherished it; his father, Lord Randolph Churchill, also a rebel, had sat there in the 1880s. Only the width of the narrow gangway separated Winston from the governments he attacked so unmercifully throughout the 1930s. But his maxim was: "Never give in, never give in, never, never, never, never . . . never give in, except to convictions of honour or good sense."

❦   ❦

Hitler had been vexed by Putzi Hanfstaengl's jeu d'esprit, and understandably so. It was true that both Putzi's Nazi idol and his British dinner companion were out of office, and certainly no one was paying much attention to the visitor from England, either here or in his own country. But Hitler, whose political antennae were exceptionally acute, knew how anxiously informed Europeans, and particularly *Auslandspolitiker,* were following his rising star. What he did not know was the keenness with which Churchill was watching him, or how doggedly Churchill would stalk him for twelve years, until the Führer of the Third Reich lay dead by his own hand in the ruined Reich Chancellery garden, a corpse enveloped by the writhing flames of a Viking funeral, while the blackened hulks of what had once been Berlin collapsed all round him.

Precisely when Winston became aware of freedom's archenemy is uncertain. In his World War II memoirs he wrote of his stay in Munich, shortly before the Nazis came to power, "I had no national prejudice against Hitler at this time. I knew little of his doctrine or record and nothing of his character."[8] But that is an astonishing lapse of memory. By then he had been well informed about Hitler for two years, had published several appraisals of him, and had repeatedly warned the House of the imminent threat in central Europe. His perception was exceptional; an extraordinary number of his peers were completely hoodwinked.

Once he had moved into the chancellery, Hitler had let it be known that his door would be open to English political figures, and pilgrimages to him became fashionable. His guests returned glowing with optimism, reporting that the Reich chancellor, despite his savage rhetoric, was eager to reach a political settlement with other nations, an agreement exorcizing the threat of war for a decade. In retrospect this is puzzling. Diplomats had already forged such a settlement in two great treaties meant to guarantee peace, not for ten years, but for the rest of the century. The first had been signed at Versailles in 1919. Versailles was now discredited in the eyes of

many, having sown seeds of resentment in Germany, but the Locarno Pact, enthusiastically signed by Germany in 1925, remained unslandered.

Yet within a decade of the Locarno agreement, Englishmen of power and influence were discussing new solutions as though this pact, despite its popularity in Germany, did not exist. Lord Lothian wrote *The Times:* "The central fact today is that Germany does not want war and is prepared to renounce it as a method of settling her disputes with her neighbors" — which is precisely what Germany *had* renounced, in writing, at Locarno. Thomas Jones, who had been in and out of Whitehall for a quarter century, wrote in his diary: "Rightly or wrongly, all sorts of people who have met Hitler are convinced that he is a factor for peace." Even after the German chancellor's aggressive intentions had become clear, Jones accompanied Lloyd George to Munich's Braunhaus — Nazi headquarters — and returned with the conviction that "Hitler does not seek war with us. He seeks our friendship. If we fail him, he will turn elsewhere and we shall be sorry to have refused him" — which, of course, was precisely the response their Braunhaus host had meant to invoke.[9]

Of greater interest, however, were the impressions of Jones's distinguished traveling companion. Meeting the press after he had been closeted with Hitler for an hour, Lloyd George said he regarded him as "the greatest living German," and had "told him so to his face." Back in England, Lloyd George wrote for the *Daily Express* — out of office like Churchill, he was struggling to make ends meet on his £300 salary as an MP, and journalism was a source of income for political celebrities — that the leader of the Nazis was "a born leader, a magnetic, dynamic personality with a single-minded purpose": to keep the peace. Lloyd George declared that with Hitler at the helm Germany would "never invade any other land." A year later he wrote to T. Philip Conwell-Evans, another admirer of the Nazis and one of Lothian's closest friends, of "the admiration which I personally feel for [Hitler]. . . . I only wish we had a man of his supreme quality at the head of affairs in our country today."[10]

No trap is so deadly as the one you set for yourself. Vernon Bartlett, a British journalist with a large following, spent forty minutes in Hitler's study. Afterward he wrote of his host's "large, brown eyes — so large and so brown that one might grow lyrical about them if one were a woman." Actually, Hitler's eyes were blue. Nazi goals were even applauded by Anglican clergymen, a group of whom expressed "boundless admiration for the moral and ethical side of the National Social programme, its clear-cut stand for religion and Christianity, and its ethical principles, such as its fight against cruelty to animals, vivisection, sexual offences, etc."[11]

Later there would be repentance, but the moving finger had writ, and neither sackcloth and ashes, nor magnums of tears could wash out a word of it. And none but Churchill, it seemed, was immune. The impressions of Sir John Simon, His Majesty's foreign secretary from 1931 to 1935, are among the most memorable. In Hitler he saw not arrogance but a man "rather retiring and bashful and of a certain mystical temperament . . . unconcerned with affairs in Western Europe." Later he described him to King George as "an Austrian Joan of Arc with a moustache." One expects more from Arnold Toynbee, but Toynbee, equally spellbound by the Reich chancellor, declared that he was "convinced of his sincerity in desiring peace in Europe and close friendship with England." The most painful toast to Hitler, for Americans, is a Walter Lippmann column which appeared in the *New York Herald Tribune* on May 19, 1933. Lippmann had heard a speech by the new chancellor, and described it as a "genuinely statesmanlike address," providing convincing "evidence of good faith." He told his readers: "We have heard once more, through the fog and the din, the authentic voice of a genuinely civilized people. I am not only willing to believe that, but it seems to me that all historical experience compels one to believe it." He went further. Persecuting the Jews served a purpose by "satisfying" Germans' yearning to "conquer somebody"; it was "a kind of lightning rod which protects Europe."[12] Walter Lippmann was a Jew.

Churchill didn't believe it. Ever since the Armistice he had been poring over reports from Berlin and Munich, winkling out evidence of a revanchist Germany. In 1924, when the future führer was still doing time after his failed putsch in Munich, Winston had warned that "the soul of Germany smoulders with dreams of a War of Liberation or Revenge." That August he told readers of the Hearst newspaper chain that "German youth, mounting in its broad swelling flood, will never accept the conditions and implications of the Treaty of Versailles." Over the years Hitler confirmed this view, and by 1930 he was declaring openly that once a National Socialist government had been formed, he and his *Strassenkämpfer* (street fighters) would "tear the covenants signed at Versailles into shreds." Then they would rearm. "I can assure you," he said in his thick, coarse voice, "that when the National Socialist movement is victorious in this struggle, the November 1918 revolution will be avenged and heads will roll."[13]

Using diplomatic channels, Churchill made his views of the Nazis clear to the Germans. Among the classified documents seized when Allied troops entered Foreign Minister Joachim von Ribbentrop's office on the Wilhelmstrasse in 1945 was a memorandum encoded K567878/A283, an appraisal written on October 18, 1930, by a German counselor posted to his government's London embassy. He reported that he had spent the past two days at a weekend house party where he had encountered "Mr.

Winston Churchill." Churchill had expressed his opinions of National Socialism "in cutting terms" (*"mit schneidenem Wort"*), remarking that it had "contributed towards a considerable deterioration in Germany's external position." His indictment of Hitler was specific. He believed him to be a congenital liar and was convinced, in the diplomat's words, that although Hitler had "declared that he has no intention of waging a war of aggression, he, Churchill, is convinced that Hitler or his followers will seize the first available opportunity to resort to armed force." Later, after the Nazis had seized power, Fritz Hesse, the press attaché in Germany's London embassy, called on Winston to sound him out again. He was told that with Hitler in power there was only one solution to the "German problem" — "If a dog makes a dash for my trousers, I shoot him down before he can bite." Hitler, after reading this, muttered that Churchill was a *"Deutschenfresser"* — a devourer of the Germans. Each man, therefore, was wary of the other from the outset.[14]

Political genius lies in seeing over the horizon, anticipating a future invisible to others. Churchill first warned of the approaching war in the Hearst papers on March 31, 1931, when Berlin and Vienna had announced the formation of a customs union. He wrote: "Beneath the Customs Union lurks the *'Anschluss'* or union between the German mass and the remains of Austria." Once that happened France's dwindling population would see "the solid German block of seventy millions producing far more than twice her number of military males each year, towering up grim and grisly." Nor would France be the only nation under the Teutonic shadow. Czechoslovakia had "3,500,000 Austrian-Germans in their midst. These unwilling subjects are a care." And an Anschluss would mean that Czechoslovakia would not only be weakened by "the indigestible morsel in its interior" but would also be "surrounded on three sides by other Germans." The Czechs would "become almost a Bohemian island in a boisterous fierce-lapping ocean of Teutonic manhood and efficiency."

This was to be one of Churchill's themes throughout the 1930s. The Germans, he told readers of the *Strand* in 1935, constituted "the most industrious, tractable, fierce and martial race in the world." And Hitler, having risen "by violence and passion," was "surrounded by men as ruthless as he." Churchill wanted England to pursue a policy leading to a "lasting reconciliation with Europe." But one could not deal with men who lied and murdered, men without honor or decency, led by a ruthless demagogue upon whose orders armed men tramped "from one end of the broad Reich to another." Single-handedly Hitler was reversing the decision reached on the battlefield in 1918. "That is where we are today," Churchill concluded, "and the achievement by which the tables have been completely turned upon the complacent, feckless, and purblind victors deserves to be reckoned a prodigy in the history of the world, and a prodigy which is inseparable from the personal exertions and the life-thrust of a single man."[15]

In the House he spoke to empty seats, dozing MPs, and disapproving frowns. Once the cry "Winston's up!" had brought members scurrying from the lobby and the smoking room. Now — like Edmund Burke six generations earlier, warning Parliament that unless the government changed its policy, Britain would lose her American colonies — he was largely ignored. There is a time to be eloquent, and there is a time when eloquence is wasted. Many of his greatest addresses, writes an Oxford historian, were delivered before "inattentive or skeptical audiences." To Sir John Wheeler-Bennett, who was in Germany, the 1930s were a period in which he, "like so many others, tried desperately to convince those in authority of the growing menace of National Socialism." They "failed miserably." It was "in those days," Wheeler-Bennett recalls, that "Winston was a tower of strength and comfort to us, the one British statesman who understood the warning which we sought to give, and who perceived, in all its starkness, the danger of a fresh outbreak of the *Furor Teutonicus*."[16]

England, to paraphrase Melville, seemed cloaked in a damp, drizzly, foggy November of the soul. So did France. In his Paris home at 110, boulevard Raspail, Major Charles de Gaulle was writing *Vers l'armée de métier*, advancing his concept of a small professional army, mobile and highly mechanized, which, he believed, should replace the reigning static theories of war symbolized by the Maginot Line. In the London murk Churchill, with his moral compass, knew exactly where he was, but few Englishmen even glimpsed him. Sir Robert Vansittart, "Van," the permanent under secretary of the Foreign Office, wrote: "Left or Right, everybody was for the quiet life." To those who saw what lay ahead, the quietude was excruciating. Franklin Roosevelt, sworn in as president five weeks after Hitler became Reich chancellor, was lifting American hearts with his fireside chats, and an MP suggested to Churchill that MacDonald or Baldwin try the same thing. "If they did," said Winston, "the fire would go out."[17]

Lady Astor — née Nancy Langhorne of Danville, Virginia — was rarely reflective of the British public's mood, but threading the maze of parliamentary intrigue with consummate skill, she always knew who was welcome at No. 10 Downing Street and who was not, even when those who were not included her. Joseph Stalin, receiving a British delegation headed by Nancy and George Bernard Shaw, had bluntly asked her about Winston's political prospects. Her eyes had widened. *"Churchill?"* she had said. She gave a scornful little laugh and replied, "Oh, he's *finished*."

Afterward, in Red Square, Shaw told the waiting press that he found the Soviet Union admirable, and would, indeed, advise young men from all over the world to pack up and settle in it. Nancy smiled and nodded, which, Virginia Cowles points out, was "reprehensible, because up until then she had been a tremendous anti-Bolshevik, denouncing the slaughter of the Russians in speech after speech." Winston's rhetorical weapons were of larger bore. He fired his broadside in the *Sunday Pictorial*, pointing out that the lady in question "denounces the vice of gambling in unmeasured terms, and is closely associated with an almost unrivaled racing stable. She accepts Communist hospitality and flattery, and remains the Conservative member for Plymouth." The Russians, he said, "have always been fond of circuses and traveling shows," and "here was the world's most famous intellectual Clown and Pantaloon in one, and the charming Columbine of the capitalist pantomime."[18]

In Parliament Churchill was supported by five MPs at most. The power of the party whips in those days was immense. Their effectiveness, Churchill wrote, combined with the "lethargy and blindness" of the three parties, made this "one of those awful periods which recur in our history, when the noble British nation seems to fall from its high estate, loses all sense of purpose, and appears to cower from the menace of foreign peril, frothing pious platitudes while foemen forge their arms." A. J. P. Taylor observes that Winston had "periods of great distinction when he seemed right at the front, and he had a gift for sliding down the ladder again. His life was one of snakes and ladders. Until the very end of the 1930s, there were more snakes than ladders. Before then, his reputation, in a sense, was at its lowest ebb." He had served twenty years in one cabinet or another, but because of his stand against independence for India, the "majority of the party," recalled Harold Macmillan, then a Conservative MP, not only "regarded his attitude as reactionary and unrealistic," but also questioned "the soundness of his judgment." The consequence, Macmillan believed, was that "all his warnings about the German threat and the rise of Nazism, as he himself has described, were in vain." Baldwin told his whips to keep a sharp eye on the outcast and to foster the view, Lord Winterton recalled, that Churchill was "an erratic genius; that he was utterly unreliable"; he had caused "unnecessary trouble to the Prime Minister and to all his colleagues in every Cabinet in which he has served by his volubility in disregarding every opinion except his own." In sum, according to Boothby, "The breach between Winston and the Conservative leaders was complete."[19]

In these years Churchill, in Lady Longford's words, was often "far away from the 'clatter and whirlpool,' beached, like one of the boats he painted." The British left, led by Clement Attlee and pledged to pacifism and disarmament, deeply distrusted him. Thus he outraged MPs on both sides of the Commons. But in Parliament, at least, traditional civility was observed. Outside Westminster was another matter. Afterward he said there had been "much mocking in the Press" about his fall from grace. The political cartoonists in *Punch*, the *Daily Herald*, the *Express*, and above all David Low in Beaverbrook's *Evening Standard* were brutal. Public appearances became an ordeal for him. Chosen rector of Edinburgh University, he was unable to deliver his rectorial address; students hostile to his calls for a strengthened national defense repeatedly shouted him down until he gave up and left the platform. A particularly ugly book published in 1931 was *The Tragedy of Winston Churchill*. Disregarding all evidence, including the findings of the Dardanelles Commission, the author wrote: "Overriding the considered opinions of every seaman who knew his job, he [Churchill] rushed blindly into that wretched fiasco of the Dardanelles. He had great gifts but 'nothing to offer' any member of any party." The author asked, "What has been Mr Churchill's career in reality but the tragedy of the brilliant failure, of whom it has been repeatedly said that he secretly despises those who pass him on the road to office and power?"[20]

Churchillian apocrypha has it that he was unwounded by all this, that throughout he was supremely confident that his hour would strike. On the contrary, his daughter Mary remembers, he was "far from resigned to his exclusion from the exercise of power"; the slanders, libels, and the distortions of his long career "hurt him deeply." In the House an MP launched a personal attack on him, saying: "All his political life has been notorious for changing opinions, just like the weathercock, which vacillates and gyrates with the changing winds. It is about time this House took notice of this menace." When Winston cited figures on the growing (and illegal) Nazi Luftwaffe and all but begged the government to strengthen the Royal Air Force, Sir Herbert Samuel, an eminent Liberal, compared him to "a Malay running amok."[21]

His old acquaintances and former colleagues were convinced that he was misjudging the Nazis as he had India. Beaverbrook wrote that Churchill had "been everything to every party. He has held every view on every question. . . . He is utterly unreliable in his mental attitude." After Hitler became chancellor, the Beaver predicted that "Winston Churchill will retire from Parliament. It is really the best thing for him to do." Hindenburg died, Hitler's power grew, and Max convinced himself that Winston's speeches were stanzas in a swan song. "Now that he seems to have reconciled himself to the part of a farewell tour of politics, he speaks better than for years past." Beaverbrook's biographer writes: "It became clear even to Churchill that Beaverbrook was no longer on his side, nor even sympathetic to him."[22]

Nevertheless, the two men occasionally saw one another. Beaverbrook's devotion to his newspapers approached that of a *religieux;* Churchill always produced good copy, so the Beaver paid him to write a column every other week for the *Evening Standard.* Malcolm Muggeridge was a young reporter for the *Standard;* at the next desk was Winston's son. Randolph, now in his early twenties, was already difficult, constantly quarreling with his father and nearly everyone else who crossed his path. Churchill would nod briefly at his son as he passed through the *Standard*'s office with his fortnightly piece. Muggeridge recalls that Winston "just looked awful. You'd say to yourself, 'There's a guy who's not well, or down on his luck, or dead broke.' If you knew he was a politician you'd think, 'He's washed out, he's had his chance and now he's through.' " Randolph rarely mentioned his father in the office, but one afternoon, as he watched him depart, he said to Muggeridge, "He's in a terrible state." Then, in an amused tone: "He misses his toys." Muggeridge asked, "What toys?" Randolph said: "His dispatch boxes."[23]

※   ※

Even before Hitler became chancellor, British intelligence had confirmed Churchill's unofficial estimates, based on his private sources of information, that the Nazis had over 400,000 storm troopers in uniform. During the Chancellor Crisis, Churchill had told the House: "I do not know where Germany's parliamentary system stands today, but certainly military men are in control of the essentials." Each concession which had been made to them, he said, each softening of the Versailles agreement, "has been followed immediately by a fresh demand." To him the peril was clear. If the Germans were permitted to reassemble their military juggernaut, every nation bordering the Reich would be in mortal danger. These, he said, were facts. The British people were being told lies. The prime minister and his cabinet had developed a "habit of saying smooth things and uttering pious platitudes and sentiments to gain applause." He could not recall "any time when the gap between the kind of words which statesmen used and what was actually happening in many countries was so great as it is now."[24]

MacDonald and Baldwin should have been aware of the threat. The British ambassador in Berlin, Sir Horace Rumbold, was an exceptional diplomat. In early March 1933, less than four days after Hindenburg had signed the emergency decree, Rumbold sent the Foreign Office a lengthy assessment of the new regime. The Nazis, he reported, had brought out "the worst traits in German character, i.e. a mean spirit of revenge, a tendency to brutality, and a noisy and irresponsible jingoism." In the heart of the capital, whippings and clubbings could be seen in every block and every park, even the Tiergarten. Rumbold regretted the failure of foreign opinion "to have fully grasped the fact that the National-Socialist programme is intensely anti-Jewish." It was no passing phase: "The imposition of further disabilities . . . must therefore be anticipated, for it is certainly Hitler's intention to degrade, and if possible expel the Jewish community from Germany."[25]

The ambassador knew this dispatch would be unwelcome to both the prime minister and the Foreign Office, but he continued to send them stark appraisals, including an account of the March 23 Enabling Act and its immediate consequences. The Nazis, he wrote, had ordered local burgomasters to "carry on anti-Jewish propaganda among the people." Jews were being "systematically removed from their posts" throughout the civil service because of "the accident of race." Youths were being enrolled in infantry training programs, boys under sixteen were subject to military training, pilots were being recruited for a Luftwaffe — all in open defiance of Versailles. The departure of "so many writers, artists, musicians, and political leaders has created for the moment a kind of vacuum [because] they numbered among their following the intellectual life of the capital and nearly all that was original and stimulating in the world of arts and letters." Most ominous of all, Jews, together with "Social Democrats, Communists, and non-political critics of Nazi policy" were being seized and sent to "large concentration camps" which were "being established in various parts of the country, one near Munich" — it was Dachau — "being sufficiently large to hold 5,000 prisoners."[26]

The ambassador was genuinely alarmed. He told Foreign Secretary Simon that he viewed the future with "great uneasiness and apprehension. . . . Unpleasant incidents are bound to occur during a revolution, but the deliberate ruthlessness and brutality which have been practiced [here] seem both excessive and unnecessary. I have the impression that the persons directing the policy of the Hitler Government are not normal. Many of us, indeed, have a feeling that we are living in a country where fanatic hooligans and eccentrics have got the upper hand."[27]

Rumbold was quietly replaced by Sir Eric Phipps, the British minister in Vienna. But Phipps also found the Nazis outrageous. He told the American ambassador that Hitler was "a fanatic who would be satisfied with nothing less than the dominance of Europe"; that although the Nazis would not invade neighboring countries until 1935, "war is the purpose here"; and that he had actually been approached by the Wilhelmstrasse with a suggestion that Germany and England divide Europe between them, to which he replied that such an agreement would "mean the end of international morality." The Nazis, never troubled by the principle of diplomatic immunity, opened the British pouches and read these reports before they reached London. Hitler told Lord Londonderry that he hated "the looks of Sir Eric" and felt relations between the two countries would be vastly improved if Britain were represented "by a 'more modern' diplomat who showed, at least, some understanding of the changes taking place in Germany."[28]

"What are we to do?" a disconcerted Baldwin asked Thomas Jones. His predecessors would have known precisely what to do. The German führer would have been told that Great Britain did not welcome foreign advice in determining ambassadorial appointments. But Jones reflected the new statesmanship when he wrote in his diary, "If it is our policy to get alongside Germany, the sooner Phipps is transferred elsewhere the better." He should be replaced, Jones thought, by someone "unhampered by professional diplomatic tradition" who could "enter with sympathetic interest into Hitler's aspirations." A candidate had already nominated himself. He was Sir Nevile Henderson, Britain's representative in Argentina. Henderson had let the Foreign Office know that he had regarded Phipps's assignment to Germany a "most unsuitable appointment" and that wags said "there is no British Embassy in Berlin at all, only a branch of the Quai d'Orsay." So Phipps was retired "at his own request" and Henderson took over. His colleagues quickly nicknamed him "our Nazi ambassador to Berlin." Hermann Göring and he became fast friends. Labour MP Josiah Wedgwood noted how he resembled those MPs who had "flocked to Germany at Hitler's invitation, in like manner," forgetting their "duty and their country's standards."[29]

But British diplomats and visiting Englishmen were not the government's sole sources of what was happening in Berlin. In the early years of the new regime, Paul Joseph Goebbels's Propaganda Ministry concentrated on preaching its glories to the German people. Cultivation of the foreign press was of lesser concern. As it happened, this was the high summer of foreign correspondents. The best of them — who covered Europe — were intelligent, well-read men, fluent in several languages, who had developed contacts and sources across the full spectrum of society, in the Reich and beyond. Long before Hitler came to power they knew of Nazi brutality and had sent accounts of it home.[30]

Even after Goebbels decided that something must be done about the foreign press in Berlin, little was. His problem was compounded by geography. Germany's capital, like England's, represented a concentration of great power in a small neighborhood. But in London a combination of ceremonial pomp, the discouraging mazes of Whitehall, and a tradition

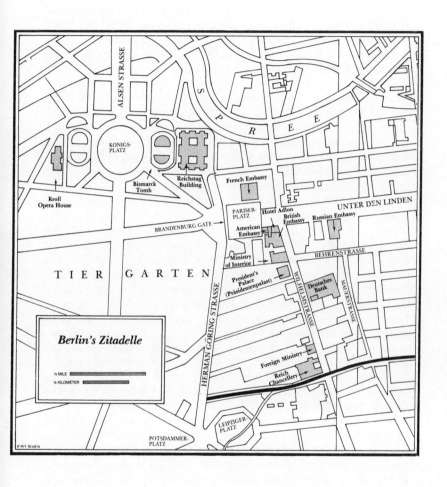

ALSEN STRASSE

S P R E E

KONIGS-
PLATZ

Bismarck
Tomb

Reichstag
Building

French Embassy

Kroll
Opera House

PARISER-
PLATZ

Hotel Adlon
British
Embassy

UNTER DEN LINDEN

Russian Embassy

BRANDENBURG GATE

American
Embassy

T I E R   G A R T E N

Ministry
of Interior

BEHRENSTRASSE

President's
Palace
(Präsidentenpalast)

Deutsches
Bank

WILHELMSTRASSE

MAUERSTRASSE

Berlin's Zitadelle

¼ MILE

¼ KILOMETER

HERMAN GÖRING STRASSE

Foreign Ministry

Reich
Chancellery

LEIPZIGER-
PLATZ

d'Art Studio

POTSDAMMER-
PLATZ

of studied rudeness toward outsiders created a web of safeguards which could be penetrated only by an insider of Churchill's stature. The heart of the Reich was more vulnerable. In the Zitadelle the great ministries stood shoulder to shoulder along the Wilhelmstrasse, with Hitler's huge new chancellery at the southern end. People wandered in and out on the flimsiest of excuses. The northern end of the Wilhelmstrasse ended at the Linden. There, the Pariser-Platz and the Brandenburg Gate marked the eastern edge of the Tiergarten, Berlin's largest and loveliest park, which spread westward behind the black, burned-out hulk of the Reichstag building. The Reichstag now met in the Kroll Opera House, four hundred yards inside the park. In the midst of all this, on the Pariser-Platz, the best possible strategic location, stood the Hotel Adlon, where the most gifted correspondents lived and worked. Because they continued to be dedicated and resourceful, the outside world was told what was happening even when diplomats in the Berlin embassies were silenced.[31]

Certainly England's envoys were under pressure to be mute. Civil servants who criticized Hitler were warned that it was "unpatriotic," as Lothian put it, "to refuse to believe in the sincerity of Germany." The British vice-consul in Hanover, a retired army officer turned businessman, sent Whitehall a partial account of German preparations for war. The Nazis, concerned that the full extent of their secret rearmament might be disclosed, demanded his recall, and Sir John Simon obliged without asking the Wilhelmstrasse for an explanation or the vice-consul for his version. In London's Foreign Office, however, Hitler was beset by critics beyond his reach. His most formidable foe in the diplomatic establishment was Permanent Under Secretary Vansittart — arrogant, sometimes wrong, but dead right about Nazi Germany — who ran the ministry regardless of which party was in office. Ralph Wigram, beneath Vansittart, shared his hostile view of the Nazis, and so, farther down the ladder, did young Duncan Sandys. Sandys had been Rumbold's third secretary in Berlin. After the ambassador was dismissed, he returned to the FO in London determined that the foreign secretary should know his views. When a dispatch from Britain's Berlin embassy reached his desk — a fresh appraisal of Hitler's intentions — Sandys attached a comment proposing that FO diplomacy anticipate the future. Specifically, he wrote, the demilitarized Rhineland buffer state, between Germany and France, would soon become an issue. The Nazis were preparing to march in. Talks between Britain and France now would assure joint action when they did. If no action was contemplated, the Wilhelmstrasse should be told so now; the democracies could demand, and get, a quid pro quo. If they meant to fight, Hitler ought to know that, too; he might back away from the risk. It was a shrewd, prophetic note, but the foreign secretary rejected it with the

scribble: "We cannot consider hypothetical issues." Sandys promptly resigned, entered politics, was elected to Parliament, and joined the small
band of Churchillians.

Van remained in the FO, arguing that the Nazis' savagery in their own
country could not be divorced from the growing possibility of aggression
beyond their borders; one had only to read *Mein Kampf* to know that. The
journalist Vernon Bartlett protested that it was "unfair" to judge Hitler by
his book; its expansionist passages had been written ten years earlier, when
the author was depressed and imprisoned. Van dismissed that as a non
sequitur and went on to say that "from the very outset of the regime" in
Berlin he had felt "no doubt whatever about the ultimate intentions of the
Nazis." It was, in his opinion, "an open secret that anything said by Hitler
is merely for foreign consumption and designed to gain time. . . . Nothing but a change of the German heart can avert another catastrophe," and
that was "unlikely to come from within, for the true German nature has
never changed."[32]

Any accomplished continental diplomat would have seen the significance in a Vansittart minute reporting that the Nazis were determined to
make their Reich "first in Europe." England could not tolerate domination
of the Continent by *any* nation. Churchill defined the principle for the
Conservative Members Committee on Foreign Affairs: "For four hundred
years the foreign policy of England has been to oppose the strongest, most
aggressive, most dominating power on the Continent, and particularly to
prevent the Low Countries" — Belgium, Luxembourg, and Holland —
"falling into the hands of such a power." This had been England's guiding
light in its struggles against Philip II of Spain, Louis XIV of France,
Napoleon, and the kaiser. Each time, he reminded them, Britain had
"joined with the less strong powers, made a combination among them, and
thus defeated and frustrated the continental military power, whoever he
was, whatever nation he led. Thus we preserved the liberties of Europe
. . . and emerged after four terrible struggles with an ever-growing fame
and widening Empire, and with the Low Countries safely protected in
their independence."[33]

The House stirred uneasily when Churchill, who, whatever his flaws,
had been more hostile to the Bolshevik regime than any other Englishman
in public life, told them — on the very day the Enabling Act became law
in the Reich — that Nazi Germany was a greater threat than the Soviet
Union. "We watch with surprise and distress," he said, "the tumultuous
insurgence and ferocity and war spirit, the pitiless ill-treatment of minorities, the denial of normal protections of civilized society to large numbers
of individuals solely on the grounds of race."[34] In any prewar Parliament,
so eloquent an appeal to the most cherished of British virtues —

decency — would have touched off a demonstration. Now the chamber was silent. The difficulty was that any political coalition becomes indistinguishable from a single-party state. There is no responsible opposition. With Labour's MacDonald as the King's first magistrate, guided by the Tory Baldwin as his éminence grise, the coalition government disciplined everyone but the party mavericks, most of whom accepted Lloyd George's assessment of Hitler anyway.

※   ※

T he appeasers distrusted France, blamed her for the punitive Versailles clauses, felt Germany had been wronged, and were determined to make restitution. Lord Lothian declared that it was Britain's moral obligation to support the Germans in their struggle to "escape from encirclement" (the encircling powers, presumably, being France, Switzerland, Austria, Czechoslovakia, Poland, Holland, Belgium, and Luxembourg) "to a position of balance." He neglected to add that any shift in the status quo would mean the liquidation of legitimate governments. At Versailles the 1914–1918 holocaust had been blamed on the Germans. Now the fashionable scapegoat was Germany's ancient enemy. "Lady Astor," *The Week* reported, "is obsessed with a vivid personal dislike of the French." As late as November 7, 1936, a member of the cabinet told his ministerial colleagues that Francophobia was increasing in England because the French were an obstacle to Britain "getting on terms with the dictator powers."[35]

The British yearning to accommodate their former enemies took peculiar forms. Upper-class Englishmen had been bred to handle foreign affairs with grace and subtlety. But many of the new breed of German diplomats were boorish. Therefore, envoys from Whitehall, eager to court them, tried to teach the Wilhelmstrasse manners. On August 22, 1932, for example, Sir Maurice Hankey, secretary of the cabinet and of the Committee of Imperial Defence (CID), sent a long memorandum to Prime Minister MacDonald, expressing apprehension over the likelihood that the Germans' claim to *Wehrfreiheit* — the right to rearm — would be "conducted with their usual clumsy and tactless way," which "might have a disastrous effect." He proposed making a demarche, after consulting the French, urging the Germans to postpone their demands. This failing, Britain should attempt to persuade the Wilhelmstrasse "to make their proposals in as harmless a form as possible."[36]

The foreign secretary, Sir John Simon, had his own euphemism for the rebuilding of the Reich's armed might. It was "parity." His resolve — and the cabinet's — was to sanction an expanding German army while disarming the French, until, after an infinite number of carefully monitored phases, both nations possessed the same number of soldiers, tanks, artillery pieces, warplanes, and warships.

The Times thought it "essential" that the Germans be permitted "to build the forbidden weapons at once." Restoring Germany's martial might would restore her pride and strengthen her feelings of security; then Germany and England, "in company," would launch a program of genuine, large-scale disarmament. The prime minister was first impressed, then inspired. Thus was the seed of the extraordinary MacDonald Plan implanted. Its first tenet was that England, as the conscience of Europe, would divest herself of her most formidable weapons. The press, the universities, labor unions, and every sounding board of public opinion would enthusiastically endorse the plan. When the League of Nations Union conducted a nationwide poll, the Peace Ballot, it found that 10.4 million Britons favored international disarmament, while 870,000 — about 8 percent — opposed it.[37]

As Churchill later wrote, "The virtues of disarmament were extolled in the House of Commons by all parties. On June 29, 1931, Ramsay MacDonald, looking forward to the first World Disarmament Conference, had proudly announced in the House that the dismantling of England's armed forces had been "swift, patient, and persistent," and that although it had gone "pretty near the limit," he intended to make "still further reductions" once he had persuaded other European governments to follow suit. His first target would be Paris. Germany, stripped of her defenses, constituted no threat to the peace, but the huge French army could attack across the Rhine at any time.[38]

Churchill instantly replied that the French army, far from being dangerous, was the strongest guarantee of peace on the Continent. Moreover, the chancelleries of eastern Europe, from the Baltic to the Black Sea, "look to France for guidance and leadership." If the French followed MacDonald's advice and sent half their poilus home, he continued, those states between Germany and Russia would be lost, leaderless, and ripe for the plucking. Britain must be armed — "England's hour of weakness is Europe's hour of danger." He urged the prime minister to abandon his mission: "The sudden disappearance or undue weakness of that factor of unquestionable French military superiority may open the floodgates of measureless consequence."[39]

Even as he had risen to speak, other members had begun drifting out of the chamber. Winston, they told one another, had always been against disarmament. Every MP knew it; they discounted it; he would make no converts here. But he had his readers, and as the diplomats convened in

Geneva, he toiled in his Chartwell study urging close scrutiny of all proposals by the conferees in Switzerland. In the *Daily Mail* he wrote that "millions of well-meaning English people" were praying for a successful conference. That, he said, was their vulnerability: "There is such a horror of war in the great nations who passed through Armageddon that any declaration or public speech against armaments, although it consisted only of platitudes and unrealities, has always been applauded; and any speech or assertion which set forth the blunt truths has been incontinently relegated to the category of 'warmongering.' "[40]

Despite MacDonald's optimism, the first round of talks at Geneva ended in July 1932 after five months of frustration. Nothing had been accomplished. Sixty nations, the United States and the U.S.S.R. among them, had sent delegations, but every session ended in a deadlock between the Germans, who insisted on permission to rearm before any other item on the agenda could be even considered, and the French, who argued that the disarmament of all European states be supervised, and then monitored, by an international police force. MacDonald, undiscouraged, laid plans for resuming the conference.

To Churchill the negotiations were highly suspect. He believed, quite simply, that military weakness invited attack, a view more controversial then than it has since become. As early as September 9, 1928, he had written a friend: "We always seem to be getting into trouble over these stupid disarmament manoeuvres, and I personally deprecate all these premature attempts to force agreements on disarmament." Was it likely, he asked in the *Daily Mail* of May 26, 1932, that France, with twenty million fewer people than Germany, and half the number of youths coming to military age every year, would deprive herself "of the mechanical aids and appliances on which she relies to prevent a fourth invasion in little more than a hundred years?" The goals of disarmament were admirable, but they would never be "attained by mush, slush, and gush." The hard and bitter truth was that lasting demilitarization of Europe could only be "advanced steadily by the harassing expense of fleets and armies, and by the growth of confidence in a long peace."[41]

Convalescing from paratyphoid, Churchill was confined to Chartwell during the opening of Parliament's disarmament debate of November 10, 1932, and missed Sir John Simon's affirmation that it was the objective of British policy to find a "fair meeting of Germany's claim to the principle of equality." Baldwin, supporting disarmament as the only way to peace, spoke of what he called "the terror of the air." Enemy bombers, he said, could hammer London into the earth like a hot white saucer. No defense against them was possible: "I confess that the more I have studied this question, the more depressed I have been at the perfectly futile attempts that have been made to deal with this problem." He thought that "the man on the street" should "realize that there is no power on earth that can protect him from being bombed." Whatever happened, he said, "the bomber will always get through."[42]

Baldwin had raised, or perhaps stumbled upon, one of the thorniest military issues of the time. The weight of professional military opinion was on his side. In England, Italy, the United States, France, and Germany, most air strategists subscribed to what was called the Douhet Theory. Shortly before his death in 1930, an Italian airman, General Giulio Douhet, had published *The War of 19 — ,* in which he argued that armies and navies should be relegated to defensive roles while bomber fleets won the war. Any nation investing heavily in air defense was risking defeat, he wrote, for "No one can command his own sky if he cannot command his adversary's sky." His most important convert was Nazi air force chief Hermann Göring, the 1918 ace, with his treasured memories of the Red Baron and the wind in the wires. Unfortunately for Göring, one aging RAF officer thought Douhet's thesis fatally flawed. He was Air Chief Marshal Sir Hugh Dowding, who would later command the RAF in the Battle of Britain. Dowding and eminent British scientists, colleagues of the Prof, convinced Churchill that every offensive weapon could be countered by imaginative, intrepid defenders. They cited fast fighters and trained antiaircraft crews; later they would brief Winston on RDF, an acronym so secret that until the war only a handful of men would know of it. It represented "radio direction finding" — or, as the Americans were to christen it, radar.[43]

In the *Daily Mail* of November 17, Churchill called on the government to look to Britain's defenses: "If Geneva fails, let the National Government propose to Parliament measures necessary to place our Air Force in such a condition of power and efficiency that it will not be worth anyone's while to come here and kill our women and children in the hope that they may blackmail us into surrender." Six days later he addressed the House on the issue. He had studied Baldwin's speech and thought it needlessly pessimistic. It had "created anxiety," he said, "and it created also perplexity." S.B. had left an unjustified impression of "fatalism, and even perhaps of helplessness." The time had come not to dismantle the RAF, but to expand it. "Why should we fear the air?" he asked. "We have as good technical knowledge as any country." He pressed the government to "consider profoundly and urgently the whole position of our air defense."

Of the French, he said, "They only wish to keep what they have got, and no initiative in making trouble would come from them." He was "not an alarmist" (this drew jeers) and did not "believe in the imminence of war" (more jeers). But, he continued, "the removal of just grievances of the vanquished ought to precede the disarmament of the victors."[44]

*   *   *

Diplomatic conversations and disarmament pacts seemed tiresome to Britons in those years. The Depression persisted, and they sought diversion in the yo-yo craze, three trunk murders, and the exceptional seductive prowess of the middle-aged rector of Stiffkey, who prowled London teashops, persuading an astonishing number of young waitresses to slip into toilets with him, assume awkward positions, and copulate. Defrocked, the vicar found employment as a tamer of lions and was eaten by one. The popular songs of the era were played in slow, almost lugubrious measures: "How Deep Is the Ocean," "Say It Isn't So," and "With My Eyes Wide Open, I'm Dreaming," which, Churchill later suggested, ought to have been Ramsay MacDonald's theme as the prime minister crossed the Channel in February 1933 and entrained for Geneva, where the plan bearing his name would highlight the agenda of the resuming disarmament talks.[45]

Churchill was not impressed. In Parliament he produced a copy of the Swiss newspaper *La Liberale Suisse* and quoted from the leading article. Prime Minister MacDonald's call for "German equality in armaments," he said, was depicted in the Swiss paper as raising suspicions "all over the Continent" that England wanted to "help Germany at the expense of her neighbours." The Swiss, he continued, saw it as "part of a deliberate plot by which the British Prime Minister is pursuing those pro-German sympathies which he has had for so many years. It is devised in order to bring about the defeat or paralysis of France at the hands of Germany and Italy, and so to expose the small nations to the ambition of the Teuton mass." Churchill tossed the paper aside. "Of course it is not true," he told the House, but "you see how small countries work out these proposals."[46]

MacDonald had called the Continent a house "inhabited by ghosts." It wasn't, said Churchill; "Europe is a house inhabited by fierce, strong, living entities. Poland, recreated at Versailles, is not a ghost: Poland is a reincarnation." But he was anxious about Teutonic influences. Poland's national character, like Germany's, was marred by a livid streak of anti-Semitism; the "odious conditions now ruling in Germany" might spread across the border "and another persecution and pogrom of Jews [begin] in this new area." Czechoslovakia — "the land of Good King Wenceslas" — had also emerged from Versailles "with its own dignity established." To be sure, there were Germans living within its borders, but they had always lived there, as inhabitants of the Austro-Hungarian Empire. Neither they nor their ancestors had ever been citizens of the Reich.

Indeed, he continued, at the Versailles peace conference, "No division was made of the great masses of the German people. . . . No attempt was made to divide Germany. . . . No State was carved out of Germany. She underwent no serious territorial loss, except the loss of Alsace and Lorraine, which she herself had seized only fifty years before. The great mass of Germans remained united after all that Europe had passed through, and they are more vehemently united today than ever before."[47]

The response in Germany was outrage. The *Birmingham Post*'s Berlin correspondent cabled: "Today's newspapers are full with 'sharp warnings' for England, introduced by headlines about . . . Mr Winston Churchill's 'impudence.' " Winston had no intention of lowering his voice. Eleven days later he told the Royal Society of St. George that the greater peril lay not in Berlin, but in British "defeatist doctrines" arising from "the mood of unwarrantable self-abasement into which we have been cast by a powerful section of our own intellectuals." He said: "Nothing can save England if she will not save herself. If we lose faith in ourselves, in our capacity to guide and govern, if we lose our will to live, then indeed our story is told."[48]

The House did not shout him down, but it came close, when his attacks on MacDonald took a more personal turn. Returning from Geneva, all smiles, the prime minister of the coalition briefed Parliament on the various proposals he had initialed, all of immense importance, he assured them, though he astonished and embarrassed his admirers by adding, "I cannot pretend that I went through the figures myself." Winston snapped up that line, noting that though MacDonald was unfamiliar with the numbers, he had taken "responsibility for them. It is a very grave responsibility. If ever there was a document upon which its author should have consumed his personal thought and energy it was this immense disarmament proposal." This was harshly critical perhaps, but still permissible. Other of Winston's observations, however, were incendiary: speaking on March 23, Churchill described the prime minister as "our modern Don Quixote," returning with the "somewhat dubious trophies" collected among the "nervous tittering of Europe." In Churchill's opinion, the proceedings in Geneva had been "a solemn and prolonged farce." He hoped that MacDonald would now take "a good rest, of which I have no doubt he stands in need," and then devote himself to "the urgent domestic tasks which await him here," leaving "the conduct of foreign affairs, at any rate for a little while, to be transacted by competent ambassadors through the normal and regular diplomatic channels."[49]

Harold Macmillan, who was elated, later recalled "hearing the speech from the back benches and the impression made by his formidable attack," but Winston himself saw the "look of pain and aversion" on the faces round him. Even while he was in the midst of it, the protests had begun. MacDonald's four years in Downing Street, he said, "have brought us nearer to war and made us weaker, poorer, and more defenceless." This touched off cries of "No, no, no!" Turning toward those who had interrupted him, Winston replied, "You say 'No.' You have only to hear what has been said here today to know that we have been brought much nearer to war." And when they cried, "By whom?" he said sensibly that he didn't "wish to place it on one man," but when a single individual had held "the whole power of foreign affairs for four years," nothing was to be gained "by pretending that there is no responsibility to be affixed anywhere." Once he sat down MPs from all three parties rose, variously deploring "a disgraceful personal attack on the Prime Minister," which was "thoroughly mischievous," and "mean and contemptible." Winston himself was described as "a disappointed office-seeker," the pursuer of a "personal vendetta" who was trying to "poison and vitiate the atmosphere" which MacDonald and his foreign secretary had tried to create in Switzerland.[50]

As usual Winston had a bad press. The *Northern Echo* called his performance "vitriolic," one of "the most audacious he has delivered," a "furious onslaught." The *Daily Dispatch* reported: "The House was enraged, in an ugly mood — towards Mr Churchill." So it was. It was perhaps a sign of the contempt MacDonald felt for his critic that he chose a thirty-six-year-old Foreign Office under secretary to reply for the government. Churchill's fear of Germany was groundless, the young diplomat told the House; the Germans merely wanted to replace their small long-service army by a larger, short-service militia. It was unfortunate that the member from Epping had thought so solemn a matter as foreign affairs an occasion for "quips and jests." To hold the prime minister accountable for deteriorating international relations was "a fantastic absurdity."

So said Anthony Eden in the House of Commons on March 23, and under his debonair manner he seemed honestly puzzled. Eden had fought in France as a young officer in the King's Royal Rifle Corps; he had fought in the trenches, been gassed and decorated. As a Tory he disagreed with MacDonald on most domestic issues, but in pursuing a lasting European peace he felt they should "all pull together," as in the Eton boating song, "steady from stroke to bow." How could anyone misinterpret the prime minister's reply to the rising Nazis? It was certain, Eden earnestly told the House, to "secure for Europe that period of appeasement which is needed." If appeased, Hitler's anger would vanish; his fear of encirclement would disappear; the Nazis, freed from anguish and insecurity, would become sensible, stable neighbors in a Europe free of rancor. The House gave him a standing ovation — Churchill and those around him remained seated. The MacDonald Plan was supported by Conservatives, Labour, and Liberals alike. Its essence was simple. The Nazis were entitled to bear arms. At the same time, Germany's former enemies should take the first long steps toward disarmament. And the first country to spike its guns should be that aggressive, martial, bellicose country — France.[51]

Appease *vt* Pacify, conciliate: *esp:* to buy off (an aggressor) by concessions usu. at the sacrifice of principles — **appeasable** *adj* — **appeasement** *n* — **appeaser** *n*

So defined, the word implies a slur, but Eden had used it in its original meaning — to bring to peace, pacify, quiet, or settle. In that sense it has been in the language for five centuries and appears in Chaucer, Spenser, and Samuel Johnson. Churchill had employed it after the general strike of 1926 in describing his approach to the negotiation of a settlement between miners and the owners of coalfields. As an aspersion, however, it had been introduced in the House of Lords on November 5, 1929. The speaker had been the dying Lord Birkenhead, F. E. Smith. Condemning Britain's conciliatory tactics toward advocates of Indian independence, F.E. called them "appeasers of Gandhi." Eventually, Telford Taylor notes, "the word became a symbol of weak and myopic yielding when resistance would be bolder and, in the long run, safer."[52]

Churchill used it as a stigma in 1933, when the coalition's determination to meet the German dictator's demands became clear to him. Appropriately, the first cabinet minister to rebuke Churchill outside the House for his attack on MacDonald was the man who would become known to history as the archpriest of appeasement. Speaking to his Birmingham constituency on March 24, Neville Chamberlain deplored Churchill's abuse of his talent "to throw suspicion and doubts in the minds of other Governments who have not expressed such feeling." He declared it England's duty to make "every effort," exert "every influence," and "act as mediators" to preserve the peace by reconciling estranged countries. The British government wanted to avoid all wars between nations because — and this was a typical Chamberlain touch — "they thereby destroy the possibility of markets for ourselves."[53]

Appeasement became evangelical; indeed, for some the line between foreign policy and religion became blurred. Thomas Jones denounced Vansittart's hostility toward the Nazis; Baldwin commented: "I've always said you were a Christian." Rage, wrote Margot Asquith, the widow of the prime minister, should be met with Christian love. "There is only one way of preserving Peace in the world, and getting rid of yr. enemy, and that is to come to some sort of agreement with him — and the *viler* he is, the more you must fight him with the opposite weapons than his." She concluded: "The greatest enemy of mankind today is *Hate*."[54]

As for mistreatment of the Jews — some said this and some said that. After all, no one could deny that Jews were, well, *different*. Churchill, an ardent Zionist since 1908, could speak for himself, but here as in so many ways he was unrepresentative of England's upper classes. This was over ten years before the Holocaust. The martyrdom of Jews in the 1940s would strip anti-Semitism of its respectability, but in the 1930s it was a quite ordinary thing to see restaurants, hotels, clubs, beaches, and residential neighborhoods barred to people with what were delicately called "dietary requirements." As late as the 1950s the *Pocket Oxford Dictionary* defined *Jew* as "1. *n.* Person of Hebrew race; (fig.) unscrupulous usurer or bargainer. 2. *v.t.* (colloq.). Cheat, overreach." Contempt for them was not considered bad form. They were widely regarded as unlovable, alien, loud-mouthed, "flashy" people who enriched themselves at the expense of Gentiles. Some even said the Germans who abused them were only getting back a little of their own. As Martin Gilbert and Richard Gott observed: "Even England was not free of anti-semitism. Not all Hitler's criticisms of Jews were discounted. Rumbold hated the anti-semitism of the new Germany; other Englishmen were less certain in their condemnation."[55]

One of Churchill's relatives, a peer and an anti-Semite, argued that Anglo-German friendship was mandatory if Western civilization was to be preserved. Churchill replied: "You cannot expect the English people to be attracted by the brutal intolerance of Naziism." But, he was asked, how brutal *are* the Nazis? Britons wondered whether Nazi excesses were sufficiently outrageous to permit a deterioration of relations between London and Berlin — thereby forfeiting what many believed could be a lasting peace. *The Times* thought not. The "shouting and exaggeration" in the new Reich, it assured its readers, was "sheer revolutionary exuberance"; Hitler's men, feeling "themselves to be the only true patriots, are enjoying the sound of their own unrestrained voices." The trouble was that the noise, the ugly language, and the accounts of bestial conduct didn't stop. Be patient, counseled *The Times;* hysteria was un-British: "Anxious Germans may rest assured that all this is not deliberately misconstrued by foreigners." Most *Times* leaders on foreign policy were written by editor Geoffrey Dawson or Robert Barrington-Ward, a fellow Oxonian, both of whom shared Lothian's conviction that France and Russia were conspiring to deny Germany her rank among the great powers, a place, Dawson said, "to which she is entitled by her history, her civilization, and her power."[56]

Barrington-Ward told a friend that Nazi outrages were "largely the reflex of the external persecution to which Germans have been subjected since the war." Englishmen's commitment to fair play, he added, obligated them to help the victimized country "escape from encirclement" and achieve "equality," the code phrase which meant rearmament. History has credited the Nazis for the restoration of the Reich's military might, but some Englishmen had anticipated them. In the summer of 1932, Franz von Papen, then chancellor, declared that the shackles of Versailles were *"unerträglich"* ("intolerable"). *The Times* — which the Germans believed was the voice of the government — weighed the chancellor's complaint, found it justifiable, and called for "the timely redress of grievances."[57]

Once Hitler had been sworn in and his *Strassenkämpfer* began unsheathing their long knives, the British government took the remarkable position that the detailed reports from two of its most eminent ambassadors, describing conditions in the Third Reich, were based on misunderstandings, distortions, and unconfirmed rumors. Speaking in Newcastle, Lord Lothian said that the Germans "have passed through a tribulation which we have never known. We should receive in no niggardly spirit the offers" — they were, of course, demands — "made to the world by Herr Hitler."[58]

The prime minister agreed. According to one Wilhelmstrasse document which came into British hands when Berlin fell in May 1945, MacDonald assured Germany's ambassador to Britain, Leopold von Hösch, that he knew there were no atrocities, no beatings, no desecration of synagogues — that everything England's own envoys had reported, was, in short, a lie. MacDonald explained that he understood "very well the character of, and the circumstances attending, a revolution." According to *The Times,* Baldwin told Hösch that England was "entirely willing to work closely . . . with a Germany under the new order" — *"die Neuordnung."* It is startling to read this Nazi phrase, so freighted with evil, quoted by a once and future prime minister in the columns of *The Times.* Doubtless Baldwin had not grasped its implications. But he should have. And he should have spoken out. His silence, his refusal to see, hear, and speak evil of the Nazi chancellor was characteristic of the response among England's ruling classes. If they offended him, they told one another, he would become hostile, and his hostility would blind him to reason.[59]

Vernon Bartlett thought his countrymen altogether too smug about democracy. Although it "suits us," he wrote, it "may not suit other people." Even Bartlett could not defend the imprisonment of Jews who had committed no crime and of former Reichstag critics of National Socialism. But, he wrote, "the Government now proposes to get rid of the concentration camp [*sic*] without much delay." Sir Thomas Moore, a respectable MP with a distinguished university career behind him, was another early admirer of Hitler. He joined the Anglo-Germany Fellowship and spent half his time in Germany, where, he reported, he had been unable to find any trace of the abuses Rumbold and Phipps described. After the Nazi chancellor had been in power eight months, Moore wrote in the *Sunday Dispatch,* "If I may judge from my personal knowledge of Herr Hitler, peace and justice are the key words of his policy." The next year he wrote "Give Hitler a Chance," calling the chancellor, now führer, "absolutely honest and sincere."[60]

War between the Germans and Communist Russia was a prospect with twin appeals to Britain's upper classes, reflecting their pacifism and their fear of bolshevism. But before the two totalitarian giants could meet at a common border, momentous events would be necessary in intervening states: Poland, Czechoslovakia, Austria, Hungary, Rumania, Latvia, Lithuania, and Estonia. The appeasers thought that it would be rather a good thing if Hitler began meddling there. J. L. Garvin, editor of *The Observer*, owned by Lord Astor, wrote that before a "constructive peace" could be established, "a large part of 'Eastern Europe' proper should be reconstructed under German leadership." The extraordinary Lord Lothian, who held no office, sailed to Germany and solemnly informed Hitler that "Britain has no primary interests in Eastern Europe." This folly was summed up by the Rumanian foreign minister. He said sadly: "Germany has her plans. Do other countries have their plans? If the other powers are without plans, we will be forced to go along with Germany."[61]

Lords Astor and Lothian were not only forfeiting future allies; they were also overlooking the fact that Britain *did* have interests in the buffer states between Russia and Germany. France was bound by treaty to go to war should any other country invade Czechoslovakia. And Britain was pledged to follow France's declaration with her own. In November 1933, in the Wilhelmstrasse, Konstantin von Neurath, the Nazi foreign minister, read a minute from Hösch. MacDonald had suggested that Hitler make a state visit to England. Neurath scrawled across the memorandum: "*Unsinn!*" — "Nonsense!" And so it was. Why run such a risk when British aristocrats were already giving what even Hitler hadn't dared ask for?

🦁   🦁

Churchill was right — the Geneva conference was doomed — but no one in Parliament would congratulate him on his foresight. In those days faith in disarmament was a creed, and to slight it was poor politics. But then, Churchill was a poor politician. Although the most gifted speaker of his age, he was clumsy, even inept, in manipulating the House, the intricate maneuvering of which Baldwin was master. Neither, in the opinion of prominent Labour leader Clement Attlee, was he a great parliamentarian, "mainly, of course, because he was too impatient to master the procedures." He was also capable of appalling political misjudgments. By resigning from Baldwin's shadow cabinet in 1931 over the India issue, thereby repeating his father's aristocratic disdain for consequences, he assured his exclusion from every prewar ministry and made the eventual designation of Neville Chamberlain as prime minister — with all that entailed — inevitable.

But no British politician in this century has matched Winston's skill in keeping himself in the public eye. In 1899, when Winston was still in his mid-twenties, G. W. Steevens, the great Victorian journalist, met him on the boat home from India and wrote in the *Daily Mail* that Churchill might become, among other things, "the founder of a great advertising business." Certainly he was a matchless self-advertiser. Even as a back-bencher, he made news by his dramatic presence in the House of Commons, by his soaring speeches, by parliamentary tricks which just skirted the borderline of propriety, and by his way of digging into a pocket, producing classified documents, and reading selected passages aloud, with all the gaudy panache he alone could display, to an astonished House, press gallery, and public.[62]

Now and then he would enter the chamber carrying a prop. If he had nothing else, at crucial moments he would produce his watch and play with it. Parliament was aware of his diversions, sometimes amused, often annoyed. Yet everything he did was just within the rules. Once, when an Opposition speaker had the floor, Winston lowered his great head and began to swing it back and forth in widening arcs. Backbenchers grinned and then chuckled. The victim said icily: "I see the Right Hon[orable] Gentleman shaking his head. I wish to remind him that I am only stating my own opinion." "And I," said Churchill, "am only shaking my own head." Another time, when an MP was approaching the end of a very long address and was drawing breath, pausing before his peroration, Churchill destroyed it by growling, "Rubbish." Anticipating an attack on an argument he himself had presented at the last session, he entered the chamber sucking a jujube — a lozenge — and pocketed it as he sat down. His opponent had just begun to pick up momentum when Winston began searching his jacket, vest, and trousers. At first he was surreptitious, as though anxious not to distract the listening MPs, but gradually one MP after another noticed that he was digging into his pockets, ever harder, ever more frantically. Laughter began, and the speaker, trembling with justifiable rage, asked: "Winston, what are you *doing?*" Churchill said meekly, "I am looking for my jujube."

The speaker's colleagues raised indignant shouts, but when they quieted down he reminded them that he always enjoyed a noisy House and told them why: "Honorable Members opposite will give me credit for not being afraid of interruptions and noise. It even would be much easier to be shouted down continually or booed down, because I have not the slightest doubt that I could obtain publicity for any remarks I wish to make, even if they are not audible in the House." He did not add, though they knew it, that he could also make money doing it, selling his text in Fleet Street at a handsome price. And if his tactics offended MPs on both sides of the well, he could always win back their hearts. The House of Commons is no less susceptible to flattery than each of its members, and when he digressed for a moment to recall a critical issue in the recent past, concluding, "All through these convulsions the House of Commons stood unshaken and unafraid," they felt, as Lord Chandos puts it, "that they had been in a battle and had just been decorated."

Splendid prose, wrote Hazlitt, should be accompanied by vehemence and gesture, a dramatic tone, flashing eyes, and "conscious attitude" — a precise description of Churchillian delivery. A consummate performer, he would rise, when recognized by the Speaker, with two pairs of glasses in his waistcoat. Perching the long-range pair on the end of his nose at such an angle that he could read his notes while giving the impression that he was looking directly at the House, he gave every appearance of speaking extemporaneously. If the occasion called for quoting a document, he produced his second pair and altered his voice and manner so effectively that even those who knew better believed that everything he said when *not* quoting was spontaneous.

As a youthful MP he had excelled at the set piece but faltered in the give-and-take of debate; Arthur Balfour, prime minister from 1902 to 1905, had chided him, calling his "artillery" impressive "but not very mobile." It was mobile now, and frequently sardonic. "It is wonderful how well men can keep secrets they have not been told," he said, and, "Too often the strong, silent man is silent because he has nothing to say," and, describing Lloyd George's criticism of his hostility toward Nazi Germany, "It revealed a certain vein of amiable malice." Sir Samuel Hoare, a coalition minister, was a favorite target. Winston said of him: "He never resents the resentment of those to whom he has been rude." But the coalition government must be allowed its day: "Where there is a great deal of free speech there is always a certain amount of foolish speech."[63]

Although this was said in a bantering tone, it reflected Churchill's absolute faith in democracy. If the electorate preferred to be governed by fools, they should be. Of course, that did not make folly wisdom. He did not share the view that sagacity lies in the masses, and in thwarted moments he would quote Hazlitt: "There is not a more mean, stupid, dastardly, pitiful, selfish, spiteful, envious, ungrateful animal than the Public. It is the greatest of cowards, for it is afraid of itself." The man of honor remained true to himself, even though drawn through the streets in a tumbril. He scorned opinion polls: "It is not a good thing always to be feeling your pulse and taking your temperature. Although one has to do it sometimes, you do not want to make a habit of it. I have heard it said that a Government should keep its ear to the ground, but they should also remember that this is not a very dignified attitude." He was often called irrational and cheerfully admitted it. So, he replied, was politics; so was human experience. It did not, he observed, "unfold like an arithmetical calculation on the principle that two and two make four. Sometimes in life they make five, or minus three, and sometimes the blackboard topples down in the middle of the sum and leaves the class in disorder and the pedagogue with a black eye. The element of the unexpected and the unforeseeable is what gives some of its relish to life, and saves us from falling into the mechanic thraldom of the logicians."[64]

Churchill was celebrated as a polemicist, but many of his flashing moments in the House were sheer fun. Rising to pay tribute to a fellow member on his golden wedding anniversary, Winston touched off a parliamentary cachinnation by beginning: "I rise to commit an irregularity. The intervention I make is without precedent, and the reason for that intervention is also without precedent, and the fact that the reason for my intervention is without precedent is the reason why I must ask for a precedent for my intervention." One of his baiters was Edith Summerskill, a feminist MP. Every time he said "man" during one of his addresses she interjected "or woman." After several such interruptions he paused, turned to her, and said: "It is always the grammarian's answer that man embraces woman, unless otherwise stated in the text." A rash new member called his thrusts slanders. Winston replied: "He spoke without a note and almost without a point." And after crossing foils several times with a Welsh Labour member and anticipating another demand from him to which his only response could be an unqualified negative, he had "Nothing doing" translated into Welsh and memorized it. The entire House was stunned when the Welshman, having made his claim, sat down and Churchill rose to growl: *"Dym a grbl."*

In a rare moment of humility he acknowledged to the House that it had put up with a lot from him. Since he first took his seat in the chamber, he said, "I have always said to myself one thing: 'Do not interrupt,' and I have never been able to keep to that resolution." Nor had he succeeded in curbing his savage tongue; he confessed that he could not recall "any expression of scorn or severity" used against him by his critics which "has come anywhere near the language I have been myself accustomed to use. . . . In fact, I wonder that a great many of my colleagues are on speaking terms with me."[65]

He could indeed be vicious. And he could bide his time. Ten years earlier Churchill and Michael Collins, founder of the Irish Republican Army, had established the Irish Free State, and won an Eire referendum despite opposition from Eamon de Valera. Now, with Collins and all other rivals murdered, De Valera had waded to power through their blood. In his first venture into foreign affairs he encouraged Mussolini's absurd claims in Ethiopia. Winston remarked: "Mr. De Valera, oblivious to the claims of conquered peoples, has given his croak. No sooner has he clambered into the imperial box than he hastens to turn his thumb down upon the first prostrate gladiator he sees." He prepared a trap for a Labour MP and spent four months waiting to spring it. Eventually the man stumbled, the House jeered, and the stumbler lost his temper. Winston pounced: "There is no one more free with interruptions, taunts, and jibes than he is. He need not get so angry because the House laughs at him: he ought to be pleased when they only laugh at him."[66]

Often he was at his most dangerous when he seemed bored. Hunched over in his seat below the gangway, within spitting distance of the Treasury Bench, he would appear to be inattentive to the business before the House. His eyes would close; he would breathe heavily. It was an ambush, of course, and twice MPs on the opposite side of the House lurched into it. The first asked loudly: "Must you fall asleep when I am speaking?" Winston replied: "No, it is purely voluntary." The second, more cautious, merely inquired whether he was asleep. Winston immediately answered: "I wish to God I were!" And he could stifle an effective jab with a sharper retort. As he finished a scathing attack on the cabinet, a backbencher called: "The Right Hon[orable] Gentleman, like a bad bridge player, blames his cards." Churchill snapped: "I blame the crooked deal."[67]

But these were minor prey. His great adversaries were the leaders of the national government — the coalition — who kept him out of the cabinet despite his long and brilliant ministerial career, which outshone any of theirs. Ramsay MacDonald, the prime minister, no longer spoke to him. Winston had called him "the boneless wonder," the "greatest living master of falling without hurting himself," and the man who possessed "the gift of compressing the largest number of words into the smallest amount of thought." He dismissed Neville Chamberlain as "a greater Birmingham." His chief target was Baldwin, the ringmaster of the coalition, who ruled the House as lord president, using MacDonald as a puppet and grooming Neville as his successor. Observing an elderly member listening to the lord president through an ear trumpet, Churchill rumbled: "Why does that idiot deny himself his natural advantage?"[68]

During one evening session, when it became obvious to every man in the House that the lord president had Luftwaffe and RAF production figures hopelessly muddled, Winston called him "no better than an epileptic corpse," and when asked what should be done if Baldwin died in office, he replied, "Embalm, bury, and cremate. Take no chances!"[69]

A young MP, an admirer of the lord president, delivered an emotional plea for unilateral disarmament and was so incautious as to approach Winston in the smoking room and ask his opinion of it. "Why, I thought it was very good," Winston replied. "It must have been good, for it contained, so far as I know, all the platitudes known to the human race, with the possible exceptions of 'Prepare to meet thy God' and 'Please adjust your dress before leaving.' "

His own taunts in the House were carefully prepared to observe parliamentary custom. There was a line between ridicule, which was permissible, and personal insults, which were not. Churchill had been in Parliament since 1901; he knew exactly where the line lay — knew, for example, of Parliament's list of banned words, which included "black-guard," "dog," "guttersnipe," and "swine." One young Labour MP, unaware of the list, had used all these in a ferocious assault on Churchill, thereby deeply offending not only Winston but the entire House. Attlee took the man aside; he told him he would have to go to Chartwell and apologize. The chastened MP drove to Kent and knocked on the front door. Churchill's valet answered. The man stated his name and mission and was asked to wait. Winston was in the toilet, moving his bowels. The valet stood in the hall outside, delivered his message, and waited. After a long moment Churchill said: "Tell him I'm on the privy and can take only one shit at a time."[70]

On the military balance between Germany and those who had conquered her armies less than twenty years earlier, Churchill was not only the most knowledgeable backbencher in the House; he was better informed than many senior diplomats on the Wilhelmstrasse. Some of his information was acquired routinely. As one of the monarch's senior privy councillors, he was on several distribution lists. He received copies of other, more sensitive documents because in 1931 he had asked Ramsay MacDonald for access to figures on the strength of England's armed forces. MacDonald found military matters dull, even trivial; he casually approved the request and then, apparently, forgot about it. It was one of those bureaucratic decisions which become self-perpetuating, remaining in effect unless withdrawn.

Among the documents to reach Chartwell was a Foreign Office assessment of Britain's defenses. The FO had found them pitiful. To double the blow, military intelligence reports, which also found their way to Churchill in the mid-1930s, disclosed that Germany had begun to rearm even before Hitler came to power. The Weimar Republic had started it in 1929, when only 2.6 percent of the German electorate supported Hitler. British agents found that the republic had spent two million pounds more than the British on "artillery, small arms ammunition and anti-gas material." Winston learned that the British embassy in Berlin, submitting its annual report in 1929, had stated that "the necessary jigs and patterns and gauges for the manufacture of modern weapons are being prepared and stocked in various factories all over Germany."[71]

By contrast, the Royal Navy in the 1930s was, in Telford Taylor's words, "sadly down-at-the-heels." During the two interwar decades only two capital ships were commissioned, and in 1929 the Labour government cut cruiser replacement and suspended work on the Empire's Singapore base. On May 31, 1933, when the delegates in Geneva were debating reciprocal inspections of one another's military establishments, the ministers responsible for Britain's armed forces told the cabinet that such inspections would "expose to the world our grave shortage of war supplies." One of Churchill's constituents asked him: "Don't you think it high time that the British lion showed its teeth?" He growled: "It must go to the dentist first."[72]

In the beginning many of Winston's informants were obscure and had small tales to tell: men returning from Germany — engineers, foreign correspondents, bankers, salesmen, tourists, professors, British officers who had traveled in mufti — and diplomats from neutral countries who passed data and appraisals through third parties or sometimes arrived unexpectedly on Chartwell's threshold. Refugees from the new Reich were interviewed, and those with scientific backgrounds were closely questioned by the Prof, who seemed to spend less and less time at Oxford and more and more advising Winston on radar, missiles, aircraft design, and high explosives. Everything found its place in Winston's jigsaw puzzle. He even established a relationship with Maisky, the Soviet ambassador to Britain, and met with him at regular intervals until the end of the 1930s.

British contacts close to the seats of power were, of course, much more useful. It is England's homogeneity and class insularity which make it seem small; in the public school network, referrals by mutual friends to mutual friends may lead anywhere, even to the sovereign. Here, as so often in his life, Churchill's membership in the privileged class was a great advantage. His informants included his second cousin Lord Londonderry, from 1931 to 1935 secretary of state for air in the coalition cabinet; Sir Henry Strakosch, an official adviser to the cabinet; and John Baker White, director of the Economic League, who collected details about German rearmament, found the government unreceptive to them, and turned the lot over to Churchill, who, he drily recalls, became very affable "when I made it clear that we did not want to be paid."[73]

Winston's chief secretary, Violet Pearman, befriended Wing Commander Torr Anderson, holder of the Distinguished Flying Cross. Anderson was troubled by Britain's air defenses, or lack of them, and spilled it out to Mrs. P. in a Westerham tearoom. She returned to Chartwell with him in tow, and after a long conversation with Anderson, Winston acquired a pipeline into the RAF, the service which worried him most.

Mrs. P.'s tasks included sorting the daily mail. It was enormous, it came from everywhere, and it fell into patterns. The high fever of militarism was throbbing throughout Germany. Duff Cooper, financial secretary at the War Office in the early 1930s and a parliamentarian marked for higher office, spent September of 1933 driving through Germany and Austria. He wrote Winston that throughout the Reich, "everywhere and at all times of the day and night there were troops marching, drilling, singing." Duff Cooper was convinced that the Reich was readying itself for war, preparing to fight any country at any time, "with more general enthusiasm than a whole nation has ever put into such preparation." A retired British lieutenant colonel, known for his hospitality to continental youths visiting the United Kingdom, wrote Winston: "I dined with four young Nazi students a week ago. They had been sent over to tell England what the Hitler movement was doing to the youth of Germany. It all sounded very unpleasant, though they seemed to like it. They made no secret of their belief that within three or four more years Germany would be at war."[74]

Among Churchill's chief sources was Major Desmond Morton, slim, elegant, with hooded eyes and a handsome mustache, whose country cottage conveniently lay just over the hill from Chartwell. In 1917 Morton had been shot through the heart at Arras; he had survived to join military intelligence, where, after the Armistice, he had worked under Churchill, who was then secretary for war and air. Seconded to the Foreign Office, Morton found himself idle much of the time. He knew Churchill was researching *The World Crisis,* his six-volume history of the Great War, and so, in a neighborly way, he volunteered to help. The offer was eagerly accepted; they became friends. Morton's name first appears in the Churchill papers in a letter from Clementine to Winston, then touring the United States. The brief mention is dated August 31, 1929: "Major Morton dined with us & helped keep in countenance Mr Lennox Boyd who was surrounded by a cloder of (6) cats."[75]

The reference was casual, and deliberately so. Winston shared everything with his wife — at the outbreak of hostilities in 1914, when he was first lord of the Admiralty, she had known more about Royal Navy activities than most cabinet ministers — and seven months earlier the relationship between Churchill and Morton had been transformed and was now delicate, even perilous. The major had been appointed to an extraordinarily sensitive post — chief of the Committee of Imperial Defence's Industrial Intelligence Centre, with official instructions to "discover and report the plans for manufacture of armaments and war stores in foreign countries." He shared Winston's anxiety over German militarism. Because their homes were within strolling distance of each other, the two men could meet casually. Long before Hitler unveiled the Luftwaffe, Churchill knew, through Morton, that thousands of young Nazi aviators and members of national glider clubs had been carefully organized and were prepared, on a signal from Berlin, to expand and deploy into fighter and bomber squadrons.[76]

Late in the fifth month of the Third Reich, June 1933, Morton telephoned Chartwell and suggested an immediate rendezvous. British intelligence had just received a most secret report from Group Captain J. H. Herring, the air attaché in Berlin. The Nazis had begun production of warplanes. Hitler had ordered all owners of civilian aircraft to register with his new Air Ministry, which meant, wrote Herring, that "a process of mobilisation is in progress"; in effect, Hitler was "already engaged in building an air force." The attaché added a prediction. Once the registration was over and the command structure in place, "all German aviation will remain a Government controlled branch of public life so long as the Nazi regime lasts."[77]

Morton continued to be a vital source of classified information, but he was not alone. Today Churchill's intelligence net seems amateurish; his informants would be quickly picked up by MI5, the internal security service. Luckily for them — and, later, for England — Scotland Yard had not yet formed a special branch to ferret out civil servants and military officers who became what were later described as security risks. Henry Stimson, an American patrician of the time, reasoned: "The only way to make a man trustworthy is to trust him; and the surest way to make him untrustworthy is to distrust him and show your distrust."[78] Later this article of upper-class faith would be exploited by Cambridge men who became Soviet agents, but the men who kept Churchill informed were faithful to King and Country.

It was during the disarmament talks in Switzerland that Winston hit his mother lode of intelligence. He found that although he was a pariah in the House of Commons, certain British civil servants in key positions regarded him as heroic. Equally useful was Winston's long career in the governments of Campbell-Bannerman, Asquith, Lloyd George, and Baldwin. He was known to hundreds of men in public life, the City, Fleet Street, and — most important — those who worked in shabby little offices opening off the long, bleak corridors of Whitehall. During his twenty years in office Winston had headed seven different ministries. He and Sir Robert Vansittart, for example, had been friends since 1902. The civil servants knew that soon England's survival might be at stake. As Michael Creswell, deputy head of the Foreign Office's Central Department, put it, they felt that their political leader, the foreign secretary, Sir John Simon, did not want to know "uncomfortable things."[79]

And so, even as Hitler consolidated his power, the first trickle of reports and memoranda not meant for Winston's eyes began to find their way there. It grew to a steady, broadening stream, until, as Professor Herbert G. Nicholas of Oxford puts it, Churchill, "supported by a small but devoted personal following," was able to "build up at Chartwell a private information centre, the information of which was often superior to that of the government."[80] The civil servants who were among his sources were the highly educated, well-connected, understated and underpaid men who really governed England and the Empire. The prime minister and cabinet made policy, but they relied on the briefings of their permanent under secretaries and the tiers of veteran specialists below them. Civil servants remained in place while governments came and went. They belonged to no party. But they knew when Britain's interests were in danger and Britons misinformed. Sir John Simon received daily reports from Vansittart, Ralph Wigram, and their staffs. If Simon distorted the truth in the House of Commons, the men in the FO swore and kicked their wastebaskets, but it had been happening for generations, and they had grown resigned to it. There was, however, a distinction between manipulation in the interests of political expediency and what amounted to treachery — compromising England's very existence.

The line had always existed. Every sensible man had known when it had been crossed. But in the past the incidents had been rare. Now, however, the line was being traversed so often that it had become blurred beyond recognition. The quiet men in bowlers, each with his rolled umbrella and his copy of *The Times*, became increasingly troubled. Several decided to approach Churchill. It was a momentous move. They were risking not only their careers, but also imprisonment, for, as one informant reminded Winston, the government "always has the Official Secrets Act to fall back upon." Under this remarkable piece of legislation, which would be unconstitutional in the United States, the disclosure of any government information, even if the purpose is to expose wrongdoing, is a crime. As Anthony Lewis pointed out in the *New York Times*, the act "intimidates the press and limits public discussion of policy." If the scholar of today concludes that Churchill saved England, the meticulous, often anonymous men who faced ruin and jail yet still put their country first also deserve to be remembered.[81]

Their first important contact with Chartwell came in the spring of 1933, when tension in Britain's Geneva delegation led to a split in the Foreign Office. A. C. Temperley, one of the frustrated British delegates, said aloud what had been on everyone's mind — that to talk of disarmament while Hitler secretly armed was absurd. Then he put it in writing: "Can we afford to ignore what is going on behind the scenes in Germany?" If the Nazis were unchecked, he wrote, Hitler would settle for nothing less than annexation of all of Europe. He proposed an ultimatum: tell Berlin to stop arming, and, if the Nazis balked, add a "hint of force." He was confident that it would work. At this point Nazi arrogance was all facade; Germany was "powerless before the French army and our fleet. Hitler, for all his bombast, must give way. Strong concerted action . . . should prove decisive. . . . There is a mad dog abroad once more and we must resolutely combine either to ensure its destruction or at least its confinement until the disease has run its course."

In the margin of Temperley's minute Vansittart scrawled his "entire agreement"; then he urged Eden to distribute copies to members of the cabinet and then have it read to them. It was done — "to no effect," Van wryly noted. Reginald ("Rex") Leeper, head of the FO's News Department, snatched up the fallen standard. Temperley had addressed his note to Leeper, knowing that Leeper wanted Britain to challenge Nazi rearmament. Following the cabinet's rejection of the suggested ultimatum, Leeper said he knew exactly how and when to trap the Nazis — now, at the conference in Geneva. After one of the Nazi delegates had spoken "in the best Hitlerian manner," he suggested, the Britons and Frenchmen should rise "one after another" and expose what was happening in the Ruhr. Leeper knew this was a "sensational step," he wrote, but if the Geneva talks continued on their present course, the conference would "drift to its certain death" and the munitions factories in the Ruhr would continue with increasing momentum.[82]

The prime minister and Simon had been pursuing a different approach. On June 16, 1932, MacDonald had met with Franz von Papen, then Germany's chancellor, and the result had been a reduction of the German reparations liability to a token sum — three thousand marks. Although Churchill was highly critical of the Treaty of Versailles, he believed in abiding by the rules of diplomacy; such bilateral agreements on the side, violating this or that clause, diminished the integrity of the whole. And Hitler — who was loutish even in small triumphs — roused Winston's wrath by announcing with a smirk that the three thousand marks "would be worth only a few marks in a few months." Churchill angrily told the House that the massive American loans of the 1920s, meant to support German reparations payments, had actually been used by the

Germans to modernize their industries — factories which could turn out arms faster than those in Britain and France. He wanted a firm reply to the German challenge.

But the coalition was marching to the beat of a different drummer. Offending the Germans, the foreign secretary argued, would be disastrous. He and the prime minister were determined to return from Switzerland with Germany's signature on a disarmament treaty, and if there was too high a price to pay, no one sitting around the table mentioned it. Leeper's proposal was therefore rejected. The consequences of jettisoning it were graver than anyone there knew; it led to Winston's deep penetration of the Foreign Office, directly across the street from No. 10. The FO became the most valuable beam in his intelligence structure: Churchillians there included Vansittart, Rex Leeper, and — in the FO's inner sanctum, the Central Department — Ralph Wigram, the department's head, together with his immediate subordinates, Michael Creswell and Valentine Lawford.

Everyone remembers Wigram as a man of immense charm. Lawford's first impression of him was one of "gentleness, young looks, shyness, modesty, economy of language." After Eton and Oxford he had risen almost effortlessly, drawing assignments at all the choice embassies. In 1933, aged forty-three, a Commander of St. Michael and St. George (CMG), he was brought back to the Foreign Office and, the following year, appointed counsellor. Beginning on the day Hitler became dictator of Germany, Wigram and Vansittart had watched developments in the Third Reich with growing concern. Now they agreed to share their information with Churchill. On October 26, 1934, Wigram sent his first significant report to Chartwell through Creswell and Morton. The Central Department had learned, he wrote, that the Nazis were "working for an army of offensive strength; in two years they expect to have 1,000 warplanes ready for combat." The threat was not immediate. They would "have to be mad . . . to try any games in the immediate future." However, he wrote, by 1938, "we shall be faced by a very, very much stronger Germany." The Central Department had acquired a transcription of a long conversation between Hitler and Admiral Erich Raeder, dated June, and ending: "The Führer demands complete secrecy on the construction of the U-boats." By November 19, 1934, the counsellor's anxiety had further increased. Hitler now led an army of 300,000 men, and its ranks were growing every day. The kaiser's Generalstab — the army's General Staff, outlawed at Versailles — was back in power. Since Hitler took over, Wigram pointed out, the Reichswehr had stopped publishing its annual list of officers. Otherwise, their swollen rolls would betray the Reichswehr's rapid expansion.[83]

Wigram recommended that the British government begin the immediate stockpiling of strategic materials and industrial retooling for armaments manufacture. Soon the Reich's military establishment would be strong enough to defy enforcement of Versailles by the Allies. This, he predicted, would be revealed by the Germans themselves. Before their might was great enough "to wage an aggressive war," Hitler would be demanding this and that, showing off his army to blackmail other European powers. The Nazis, the counsellor's report predicted, would become "increasingly arrogant and definitely aggressive. Instead of emitting protests and airing grievances Germany will make demands and assert rights." When the Führer possessed the greatest war machine in the world, he would turn his "attention to the absorption of Austria and the penetration of central Europe." Wigram's recommendations came at the end of this minute. If Britain accepted Nazi military might as a fait accompli, France would be alienated. Once the Western democracies' front was broken, no other combination of continental nations would dare resist the Führer. Therefore he proposed that Whitehall and the Quai d'Orsay "arraign" the Reich before the League of Nations, charging it with violations of Versailles. This strategy, he suggested, would "give us an opportunity for informing public opinion clearly of the nature of German rearmament." So warned, the Belgians and the Dutch would, in Wigram's judgment, join the anti-Nazi alliance.

Read today, this yellowing document reveals a sagacity and vision seldom matched in Britain's archives. Yet after its submission to the foreign secretary, the prime minister, and the rest of the cabinet, it was returned with comments which could only be interpreted as hostile, or, at best, indifferent. Before a debate in the House senior civil servants would walk up to Parliament and enter the "briefing box." There they would respond to ministerial questions. Creswell recalls: "One felt again and again that for them the important thing was to get through the debate. . . . What was happening in the world wasn't in the forefront of their mind." They hadn't studied the FO's assessments and appreciations; at most they had glanced through them. And that was what protected the secret of the civil servants' Churchill connection. Reading the transcriptions of those parliamentary debates today, one can only imagine the ministers' astonishment as Churchill rose to face them and reel off facts and figures that seemed to have come from nowhere — but were always confirmed afterward. Had Simon, say, or Hoare done his homework, they would have realized that Churchill had access to documents stamped "Most Secret."

At first the drill was Wigram-to-Creswell-to-Morton-to-Churchill. Then Ava Wigram came to Chartwell for the weekend, bearing analyses her husband had drawn up for a government that didn't want them. In time

Ralph joined his wife, staying overnight. If a matter was urgent, however, an exchange in London was quicker and safer. Wigram's home was at 4 North Street (now Great Peter Street), three blocks from Parliament and a brief stroll from Churchill's pied-à-terre in Morpeth Mansions.

Although Churchill never wrote of their meetings — their existence was unknown until Creswell revealed them nine years after Winston's death — one can surmise how they must have appealed to his romantic imagination: the furtive telephone conversation; hurrying down the foggy streets; the risk of discovery; the eager anticipation, afterward, of opening the plain unmarked buff envelope containing plans and details his foes in Parliament didn't know he had; visualizing their dismay if they knew — picturing, with ever greater gusto, the horror of Hitler if *he* knew.

Wigram's information was hard, precise, and tersely told. Churchill would read the latest FO accounts of the Luftwaffe's growing strength; reports (as early as May 1935) of Nazi propaganda campaigns among the Sudeten Germans in Czechoslovakia; columns of figures on artillery, tanks, and other Nazi armaments; and advance copies of Hitler's speeches. Winston had to disguise his sources, and sometimes lose a debate when he had the clinching facts in his hands, but in time he became as well informed as the prime minister and in some ways more so, because certain documents, inconsistent with the catechism of appeasement, were suppressed or altered before they reached the P.M.'s desk. Winston, however, had seen the originals, and seen them first. Long afterward, Sir John Colville, who became one of his principal aides, looked through Winston's papers of the 1930s and was astounded by what he found. Colville wrote: "Why the Government allowed . . . its servants to supply ammunition to its principal critic and gadfly, I have never understood." Neither the prime minister nor the foreign secretary would have approved, Colville reasoned, and after World War II, he recalled, he "asked Churchill this question direct and was given an uncharacteristically evasive answer. In fact all Winston said was: 'Have another drop of brandy.' "[84]

Although ill served by ministers who refused to recognize the truth, the British public, enjoying a free press, was aware of some of the more flagrant abuses in the Third Reich. On May 10, 1933, Nazis had celebrated their contempt for learning by building an enormous bonfire of books, incinerating all works on psychology and philosophy and all written by Jews, socialists, and liberals. On July 1 Nazi fliers began dropping leaflets and urging all Austrians to support the country's tiny Nazi party in plans to overthrow the government of Engelbert Dollfuss, which, though Fascist, had come to office through free elections. If that didn't work, Hitler confided to subordinates, he would have Dollfuss killed.

On July 14 the Reich chancellor dissolved the coalition of parties which had brought him to power. Any political speech or pamphlet not endorsed by the Nazis was *verboten*. Of Germany's three greatest newspapers, the 230-year-old *Vossische Zeitung,* comparable to *The Times* of London and the *New York Times,* was forced to close; the *Berliner Tageblatt*'s Jewish owner was driven out of business, and the *Frankfurter Zeitung*'s editorial hierarchy, largely Jewish, was replaced by Nazis. *Völkischer Beobachter* and *Der Angriff,* the two official Nazi organs, glorified Nazi street terrorists and ran flattering front-page pictures of those responsible for the desecration of synagogues. Germans who protested Nazi outrages were sent to Dachau or other, newer stockades. Teachers were told in the official publication of their profession, *Der Deutsche Erzieher,* that *Mein Kampf* was their *"unfehlbarer Leitstern"* ("infallible star"). Those who actually read the book could have had no doubts that the chancellor's infallible star would eventually lead their children to far-flung battlefields.

Central Europe lay under an "evil and dangerous" cloud, Churchill told an audience of his constituents in Theydon Bois after reading Group Captain Herring's report in 1933. "No one," he said, "can watch the events which are taking place in Germany without increasing anxiety about what their outcome will be. At present Germany is only partly armed and most of her fury is turned upon herself. But already her smaller neighbors, Austria, Switzerland, Belgium, and Denmark, feel a deep disquietude. There is grave reason to believe that Germany is arming herself, or seeking to arm herself, contrary to the solemn treaties exacted from her in her hour of defeat." He told the House: "At a moment like this, to ask France to halve her army while Germany doubles hers, to ask France to halve her air force while the German air force" — here he must have been sorely tempted to quote Herring — "remains whatever it is, is a proposal likely to be considered by the French Government, at present at any rate, as somewhat unreasonable."[85]

In Geneva, however, there was little support for the Quai d'Orsay's lonely stand. This may puzzle those who remember the great alliance of 1914–1918. But England and France had been enemies for nearly a thousand years before then, leaping back and forth across the Channel to fly at each other's throats. In Geneva the French believed they were conducting themselves *sans peur et sans reproche*. Actually they weren't. To their new allies in eastern Europe the delegates from Paris asked not "What can we do for you?" but "What can you do for us?" The instinctive French response to battlefield disasters, in 1870 and 1914 — it would be heard again in 1940 — was the wail: *"Nous sommes trahis!"* ("We are betrayed!"). As other nations in Geneva drew away from them, the French foreign minister declared: "Henceforth France will guarantee her security by her own means." Alistair Horne comments: "For sheer arrogant folly [this declaration] is hard to beat."[86]

Had the Geneva disarmament talks continued, British Foreign Office documents reveal, France herself would have been betrayed by her greatest ally; but the conference never reached that point. On March 27 Japan, offended by the League of Nations' censure of her Manchurian aggression, had announced that she would quit the league. It was a precedent and Hitler liked it. He had been provoked by the conferees' decision that his storm troopers — there were now 500,000 of them — counted as fighting men, and he declared that league overflights, checking upon the Reich's compliance with any agreement, were *"beschimpfend"* ("insulting"). In the light of French provocations, said the Wilhelmstrasse, the German Reich refused to apologize for its glorious past. Nor need it give reasons for its present position. The Reich was a sovereign state, though it was not being treated like one, which was intolerable and *"unverschämt"* ("shameless").[87]

President Roosevelt had tried to free the conferees from their gridlock by suggesting a ban on all offensive weapons. Privately, Hitler was furious. Nevertheless, he saw great political possibilities in the message from the White House, and on May 17, 1933, he exploited them in a deeply moving, breathtakingly meretricious speech before the Reichstag. FDR, he said, had earned the *"warmem Dank"* of the Reich. He accepted the president's proposals and stood ready to scrap the Reich's offensive weapons the moment other powers did the same. Germany was indeed prepared to disband her entire military establishment, together with uniforms, weapons, and ammunition, under the same circumstances, and would sign any nonaggression treaty, "because she does not think of attacking but only of acquiring security." The National Socialists cherished no ambition to *"germanisieren"* ("Germanize") other nations: "Frenchmen, Poles, and others are our neighbors, and we know of no event, compatible with history, which can conceivably change this reality."[88]

The speech constituted the basic draft of what diplomats came to call Hitler's *Friedensrede* (peace speech), to be delivered before the Reichstag after each German act of aggression, assuring the world that no one wanted peace more than he did, that he had just made his last territorial claim upon Europe. His reply to Roosevelt was a fraud, of course, but it was the work of a master swindler, and it took almost everyone in. London's *Daily Herald*, the official organ of the Labour party, declared that Hitler, as a trustworthy statesman, should be taken at his word. The conservative weekly *Spectator* called him the hope of a tormented world; to *The Times* his claim was "irrefutable."[89]

But there was a catch, and Churchill had spotted it. Implicit in Hitler's offer to disarm whenever other powers did likewise was Nazi Germany's assertion of its right to rearm unchallenged by *Ausländer*. Winston made this point in the House, and after the first few minutes the chamber emptied. The German chancellor had given the MPs a present, the illusion that he had no intention of becoming a warlord, and Churchill was trying to take it away. Beaverbrook wrote a friend that "if he continues on his present course, I would not be surprised if Baldwin put a veto on him in his constituency. And believe me, Baldwin can do it."[90]

Yet every time Churchill seemed on the verge of being driven out of politics, Hitler came to his rescue by building his brutal record, outrage succeeding outrage, each a flagrant betrayal of his most recent *Friedensrede*. His lightning prewar strokes startled a sane world unable to grasp the stark fact that he was not sane. On October 14, 1933, without warning, he made three announcements. The important one was that Germany was withdrawing from both the disarmament conference and the League of Nations. But there was more. One arose from the eternal language problem. Lord Hailsham, MacDonald's secretary for war, had told Hitler that German rearmament would violate Versailles, answerable, under the treaty's terms, by sanctions. In German, *Sanktionen* implies armed invasion; therefore Hitler added that if the league attempted to impose sanctions, his new minister of defense, General Werner von Blomberg, would order German troops to fight. Blomberg did in fact instruct his soldiers to man the Reich's frontiers and "hold out as long as possible." However, as he and his fellow officers were well aware, that wouldn't be long. Serious German resistance was impossible, and they were horrified.[91]

They were not, however, politicians. Hitler, the transcendent politician, knew that he couldn't lose, because in his third and final announcement he declared that he had dissolved the Reichstag and was submitting his decision to quit Geneva to a national plebiscite. No democracy, he knew, would intervene in a German election. He could also be certain of the results. The ballots would offer a single-party Nazi slate of Reichstag nominees, and the plebiscite — which, carefully worded, omitted the disarmament issue, turning the poll into a *ja–nein* on the Versailles treaty — would be held on November 12, the day after the anniversary of the hated Armistice. *Ausländskorrespondenten* — foreign correspondents — skeptical by profession and especially distrustful of the Nazis, monitored the election and reluctantly agreed that it was fair. The results were astounding. Some 96 percent of the electorate went to the polls and 95 percent of them approved of Germany's Geneva walkout. Nazi candidates for the Reichstag received 92 percent of the vote. *Ausländspolitiker* — political leaders in other countries — could no longer speculate over whether the Nazi chancellor had the support of his people.

In the entire history of the Reich, no German leader, including the kaiser, had matched his popularity.[92]

The diplomats droned on in Switzerland, and in June 1934 the last truncated session adjourned. The chairman had been Arthur Henderson, a Labour MP, who, as a tribute to his tireless efforts in Geneva, was declared winner of the Nobel Peace Prize. In his closing words, according to a contemporary account, he openly charged France with "responsibility for its failure to accomplish any practical results." The French furiously denied it, and history confirms them. Their peers, however, did not.[93]

❧   ❧

The breadline on Berlin's Kurfürstendamm had vanished. The Third Reich had become the only great power without massive unemployment, beggary, or hunger — a country freed from the shackles of the worldwide Depression. Since Hitler had moved into the Reich Chancellery on January 30, 1933, Germany's income had doubled; production had risen 102 percent; her *Volk* were riding a crest of affluence, euphoria, and throbbing patriotism not seen since their fathers had lustily marched off to war twenty years earlier. The Aladdin with the lamp was Reichsbank president Dr. Hjalmar Schacht. To foreign economists he seemed to be a magician. His genius was undeniable, but he possessed an extraordinary advantage, a gift of power from Hitler. Exercising this authority, Schacht created credit for a country without liquid capital or monetary reserves by manipulating the currency. So adroit was his jugglery that at one point bankers assigned the mark 237 different values.[94]

Europe had never seen anything like it, but Americans had. Under Roosevelt the new economists had been fueling a recovery a full year before August 1934, when Hitler appointed Schacht the Reich's economics minister. There was a difference, however. Germany was now bankrupt, and with a trade deficit approaching a half-billion marks Schacht was, under the laws of the German republic, a counterfeiter. In the City of London or in Wall Street his wizardry would have consigned him to prison. But in the Third Reich he was quite safe. Members of the government were untroubled by legalities, courts, and traditional stock trading principles. Indeed, the central fact about Nazi Germany, obvious now but visible to only a few at the time, is that it was a criminal conspiracy. When President Hindenburg died on August 2, 1934, at the age of eighty-six, Hitler announced that he was combining his office of chancellor with that of the dead president. He then appointed himself *Führer* — leader. This, unlike Hitler's appointment as chancellor, was illegal. In taking this step, Hitler committed a major felony under the German constitution, which stipulated that if a president should die while in office, his title and powers should pass, not to the chancellor, but to the president of the supreme court, to be safeguarded by him until the people could cast their votes in a new election.[95]

Laws are effective only when authorities enforce them and society submits. But in Germany the felons were the men invested with the greatest authority, and the handful of brave demonstrators who protested the transformation of a democracy into a dictatorship were beaten by the *Strassenkämpfer* and found themselves, not their assailants, facing criminal charges. The *Strassenkämpfer*, Hitler biographer Alan Bullock writes, "had seized control of the resources of a great modern State; the gutter had come to power." Hitler now announced his second nationwide plebiscite, this one on his assumption of dictatorial rule. Virtually no voices of dissent were heard from the universities, the eminent Jews having already left; from Germany's industrialists, who had in fact contributed heavily to Nazi election funds after he had promised to abolish trade unions; or from officeholders sworn to protect and defend the constitution now being raped. None even resigned in protest. On August 19, 1934, after a week of massive Nazi rallies, torchlight parades, and storm troopers marching through neighborhoods roaring, *"Wir wollen das Gesetz — sonst Mord und Totschlag!"* ("We want power — otherwise death and destruction!"), the plebiscite was held. Over 42.5 million Germans went to the polls — 95 percent of those registered — and 38 million, nine out of every ten, voted *ja*.[96]

The self-anointed Führer declared that he was now head of state and commander in chief of the country's military establishment. Every German officer was required to swear an oath of loyalty to him. The officer corps knew how momentous this step was. The kaiser had never dreamed of asking personal allegiance. The oath bound them not to the government or even the country, but to the commands of a single individual whose stability, even then, was widely questioned. Nevertheless, to their eternal shame, each of them pledged "by God" that he would "render unconditional obedience to Adolf Hitler, the Führer of the German Reich and people, Supreme Commander of the Armed Forces, and will be ready as a brave soldier to risk my life at any time for this oath." Hitler was now absolute ruler of Europe's most powerful state, a phenomenon unknown to the Continent since Napoleon.

Meanwhile, anti-Semitism, which had troubled Churchill from the outset, was becoming increasingly vicious. His informants reported that all over Germany *Bierkeller,* motion picture theatres, shops, and restaurants were displaying prominent signs reading *"Juden unerwünscht"* ("Jews not welcome"). Day-to-day existence was becoming increasingly difficult for non-Aryans. *"Für Juden kein Zutritt"* ("Jews not admitted") placards hung outside grocery and butchers' shops; they could not enter dairies to buy milk for their infants, or pharmacies to fill prescriptions, or hotels to find lodging. At every turn they were taunted: *"In dieser Stadt ist Juden der Zutritt streng verboten"* ("Jews absolutely forbidden in this city"); *"Juden bretreten diesen Ort auf eigene Gefahr"* ("Jews enter this place at their own risk"); and, at a dangerous highway curve on the west bank of the Rhine opposite Mannheim: *"Vorsicht! Scharfe Kurve! Juden 100 km!"* ("Caution! Sharp Curve! Jews 60 mph!").[97]

Visitors attending the Berlin Olympics in 1936 would ask how Germany had ended the breadlines and found jobs for the jobless. Their hosts suavely assured them that the Führer had solved the Depression in Germany by expanding public works programs and stimulating private enterprise. It sounded plausible, and the tourists left believing it. Yet any persistent searcher for the real source of the Reich's booming economy could have found it by visiting the Ruhr valley — the Ruhrgebiet — and the industrial areas of the Rhineland, where the great factories of Krupp, Thyssen, Flick, and I. G. Farben, looming like *kolossale* cathedrals through the smoke belching from their smokestacks, were working shifts around the clock. It was, for those who saw it, a vision of stark Teutonic power. In the peak years of Victorian energy, when England had been called "the workshop of the world," Londoners had a word for the sound of their toiling city. It was the Hum. Now the Ruhr was Germany's *Bienenstock* — its beehive. But the yield of a beehive is benign; the Ruhr's sweating workers were intent on building a more powerful military juggernaut than the army General Erich Ludendorff had guided in 1918.

No one who held high office in the 1920s, Churchill included, can be completely absolved of responsibility for the shocking deterioration of England's defenses between the wars. After the Armistice Lloyd George's government, at Winston's urging, had adopted a "ten-year rule" — an assumption, in drawing up service budgets, that "no great war is to be anticipated within the next ten years." Year after year the principle was reaffirmed. Ministers saw no reason to drop it. Germany was disarmed; Russia still in turmoil; France pacifistic; America isolationist. Nevertheless, as early as 1929 Basil Liddell Hart had written in the *Daily Telegraph* that "every important foreign power has made startling, indeed ominous, increases of expenditure on its army" and declared that the British government "would be false to its duty to this nation if it reduced our slender military strength more drastically." The Admiralty recommended building a submarine base at Hong Kong. "For what?" asked Winston. "A war with Japan! But why should there be a war with Japan? I do not believe there is the slightest chance of it in our lifetime."[98]

Churchill had an unusual, if unorthodox, grasp of military strategy, but was weak on tactics. In hindsight his observations of weapons seem odd. "The submarine," he wrote, "is not now regarded as the menace it used to be." Similarly, he told readers of the *News of the World* that he doubted "very much" whether the tank "will ever again see the palmy days of 1918. . . . Nowadays the anti-tank rifle and the anti-tank gun have made such great strides that the poor tank cannot carry thick enough skin to stand up to them." Anticipating "How Wars of the Future Will Be Waged," he envisioned "great prepared lines of fortifications which it will be very difficult indeed for the other army to break through. . . . The idea that enormous masses of mechanical vehicles and tanks will be able to overrun these fortifications will probably turn out to be a disappointment." He foresaw deadlock; any ground gained "will very often be only as moles." Doubtless there would be new developments, but nothing dramatic: "One thing is certain about the next war; namely, that the armies will use their spades more often than they use their bayonets."[99]

He also underestimated air power. In 1936 the first reports of civil war in Spain led him to conclude that events there demonstrated "the limitations rather than the strength of the air weapon" and proved that "so far as the fighting troops are concerned, aircraft are an additional complication rather than a decisive weapon." This, he felt, together with "the undoubted obsolescence of the submarine . . . should give a feeling of confidence and security so far as the seas and oceans are concerned, to the western democracies." On one point he had no doubt whatever. No warplane, he declared, could sink a warship. Over a decade had passed since Brigadier General William ("Billy") Mitchell, the American airman, had proved it could be done — proved it by actually doing it, sending six obsolete battleships to the floor of the Atlantic. But as late as January 14, 1939, Churchill told subscribers to *Collier's* that "even a single well-armed vessel will hold its own against aircraft."[100]

A friend of his later recalled a dinner party in the mid-1930s: "Winston was laughing at the idea that any bombers could put ships out of commission. He thought it ridiculous, so terribly funny. He said to get a ship you would have to be sure to put the bomb down the funnel. He had been told it had to go down the funnel or these armor-plated ships wouldn't blow up. . . . You know, he was making this great joke about the whole thing. I just remember how he amazed me at the time. Of course, the bomb didn't have to go down the funnel at all."

Winston's most striking tactical gaffe was a memorandum he sent to

Neville Chamberlain, then prime minister, only six months before the Munich Agreement, and it sharply criticized the two fighter planes which would prove to be England's salvation in 1940. On March 12, 1938, Churchill wrote: "We have concentrated upon the forward-firing fixed gun Fighter (Hurricane and Spitfire). The latest developments increasingly suggest that hostile aircraft can only be engaged with certainty on parallel or nearly parallel courses, hence that the turret type of equipment will be paramount." This revealed a total failure to grasp the evolution of aerial rearmament. Churchill was thinking in terms of the Tiger Moth and other old wood-and-fabric two-gun biplanes. To send such slow, fragile aircraft against the Nazis' Messerschmitt fighters would have meant the sacrifice of the RAF, followed by catastrophe; the Luftwaffe's bombers, arriving in fleets, would have leveled their targets, unchallenged by a single British fighter pilot.[101]

But if he misunderstood armored warfare, so did every officer on Britain's Imperial General Staff; and if he underrated air power and believed it would be ineffective against capital ships, the Admiralty agreed with him. The essence of England's armaments dilemma was not inaccurate views on weaponry. The real problem was that the most powerful and influential men in Britain were determined not to offend Hitler. And in this matter Churchill's vision was clear. He warned that whenever absolute rulers assemble great armies, they eventually make war: "Dictators ride to and fro upon tigers which they dare not dismount. And the tigers are getting hungry." Appeasing Germany was folly, he said; Hitler would spare no one; and there was no refuge in neutrality, no sense in urging the Nazis to turn their wrath against others or pursue a policy based on the hope that the Führer would be satisfied with half a loaf — even the whole loaf would leave him unglutted; he would never stop until he was stopped by force. British rearmament was therefore essential.

After the Japanese seized Shanghai in 1932 the cabinet had quietly dropped the ten-year rule, adding, however, that expenditures on arms would be determined by existing economic conditions. Existing economic conditions being what they were, arms budgets were depressed, and England, as Churchill put it, remained a "rich and easy prey." Winston said: "No country is so vulnerable and no country would better repay pillage than our own"; with London "the greatest target in the world," Britain was "a kind of tremendous, fat, valuable cow tied up to attract the beast of prey."[102]

Yet except for Austen Chamberlain, who as foreign secretary had been the architect of Locarno, no eminent parliamentarian backed Winston's calls for rearmament and for binding military alliances with European states under the shadow of the swastika. Even England's Chiefs of Staff were wary of commitment to other states; without such pacts, they argued,

Britain could choose when and where to apply pressure. Alliances — even a League of Nations alliance — would mean that each member nation would be obliged, at the very least, to apply sanctions to an aggressor, who in response could declare war on England. Anthony Eden agreed with the chiefs. Answering Churchill in the House of Commons on one occasion, he had said that "where I differ, with respect, from my Right hon Friend the Member for Epping, is that he seems to conceive that in order to have an effective world consultative system nations have to be heavily armed. I do not agree. . . . General disarmament must continue to be the ultimate aim."[103]

Labour regarded Churchill's demands for rearmament with a suspicion which can only be called paranoid. Clement Attlee, the party's deputy leader, denounced all arms appropriations and denied that Hitler's attentions were aggressive. He told Parliament: "We are back in a prewar atmosphere . . . in a system of alliances and rivalries and an armaments race," adding: "We deny the proposition that an increased British air force will make for the peace of the world." In the military estimates of HMG — His Majesty's Government, the prime minister and his cabinet — which were so inadequate in Churchill's view, Attlee discerned familiar, sinister themes. They were "nationalist and imperialist delusions . . . far more wild than any idealist dreams of the future we hold." He declared: "We on our side are for total disarmament because we are realists." When Winston recited a list of over twenty-four German factories producing airframe components and "considerably more" than eight plants turning out parts for warplane engines to be assembled by Heinkel, Junker, and Dornier, "on whose behalf the majority of other factories are working," Attlee replied that anyone could draw up lists. One Labourite suggested that Baldwin was building a force which could be sent "abroad to fight in foreign countries." Vansittart, who knew the MP had indicted the government of the wrong country, read that a Labour party conference had recommended a policy "subordinating our defense to the permission of Geneva, abolishing allegiance and loyalty to England, and pledging British citizens to a world-commonwealth which would 'override any national duty in time of war.' " They had decided to take this position, they explained to the press, because "we have abandoned the whole idea of the national order." In his memoirs Van acidly noted: "Hitler hadn't."[104]

Churchill's isolation in Parliament seems remarkable now. England was not ready for him. Whenever Hitler loomed large in headlines, Britons plunged their heads deeper into the sand. And their leaders joined them. Sir John Wheeler-Bennett, a British expatriate living in Germany, had first judged Hitler as "a man of sense . . . who does not want war," then, when his vision cleared, tried to persuade his countrymen at home that the Nazi regime was evil. He failed, he came to believe, because in Britain the "forces of apathy, of wilful myopia and of general delusion in high places were too strong for us."[105]

Neville Chamberlain told Nancy Astor that when he moved from No. 11 Downing Street to No. 10 he intended to be his "own Foreign Minister." His half brother Austen chided him: "Neville, you must remember you don't know anything about foreign affairs." Neville thought he knew a great deal, however, and his fellow ministers, especially Baldwin, found him impressive. He convinced them that Hitler would never attack France, the Low Countries, and Britain. The Führer, he said, wanted to move against Russia, not the West.

Actually, Hitler intended to turn south first. On the first page of *Mein Kampf* he had declared that a rejoining of Austria and Germany was a "goal to be pursued with every means [*mit allen Mitteln*], all our lives," and had melded both countries into a single proper noun: *Deutschösterreich*. His motive, as Churchill saw it, was to open "to Germany both the door of Czechoslovakia and the more spacious portals of southeastern Europe." His chief obstacle was Chancellor Engelbert Dollfuss, no tribune of the people but a leader who had risen through free elections. In the summer of 1934 Austrian Nazis, acting on Hitler's orders, plotted to murder Dollfuss and arrest everyone in his cabinet. At noon on July 25, ten of them, dressed in Austrian army uniforms, passed the chancellery sentries unchallenged. Bursting into the chancellor's office they shot him and left him on a sofa bleeding to death, ignoring his pleas for a priest. But their cabinet roundup was flawed; among the ministers they failed to capture was Kurt von Schuschnigg, a man of action. On Schuschnigg's orders Austrian troops overpowered the plotters. He hanged them while Mussolini, jealous of German designs on Austria, rushed fifty thousand troops to the Brenner Pass. This was the kind of language Hitler understood. He lay low, leaving Austria, in Churchill's phrase, "on the hob."

Even *The Times* commented that the assassination of Dollfuss "makes the name of Nazi stink in the nostrils of the world." But the appeasers were also shocked by the executions in Vienna and the Duce's threat of armed intervention. Somehow Schuschnigg's violence, and Mussolini's threat of it, blurred the brutal assassination of a national leader on orders from — and not even Germany's most ardent British supporters doubted the instigator's identity — another head of state. It was part of the tragedy of the 1930s that the democracies always gave Hitler a second chance, and he never failed to profit from it. Next time his plan to seize Austria would be foolproof and his armed might overwhelming.

It was Ludendorff's concept of *totaler Krieg*, total war, which gave the Reich's feverish boom its identity: *deutsche Wehrwirtschaft*, or German war economy. While the House of Commons haggled over petty appropriations for the services and debated whether men in the Royal Navy should be paid a living wage, all German shops were retooling to prepare for war so thoroughly that victory would be inevitable. Within a year of Schacht's appointment his staff had completed plans to convert 240,000 plants for total war. Lord Eustace Percy later wrote in awe of how Germany succeeded, "in little more than five years, not only in mobilizing a nation and abolishing its unemployment, but in equipping a great army and bringing the dreams of a new strategy within the bounds of reality." At the time, he added, English observers, official and unofficial, had "considered this feat wholly incredible."[106]

In 1945 Georg Thomas, the German general who served as Schacht's military liaison officer, published an account of Nazi rearmament in the 1930s. He wrote: "History will know only a few examples of cases where a country has directed, even in peacetime, all its economic forces deliberately and systematically toward the requirements of war, as Germany was compelled [*sic*] to do in the period between the two world wars." The army hierarchy was grateful, and particularly aware of its debt to the Reich's economic czar. In the mid-1930s, on Schacht's sixtieth birthday, *Militärwochenblatt*, the official army periodical, paid tribute to him as "the man whose skill and great ability" had made it possible for "an army of 100,000 men" to swell to "its present strength."[107]

But what *was* its present strength? The Foreign Office was monitoring the German press and radio, studying reports from its intelligence sources in the Reich, and struggling to establish figures, or at least approximations, of Hitler's growing might. The Nazis were gambling with time. Versailles notwithstanding, on assuming the chancellorship in 1933 Hitler had told Germany's generals that he wanted heavy army recruitment to start immediately. The generals were aghast at his military goals. Walter Görlitz's history of the German General Staff clearly documents their doubts. It would be 1942 or 1943, they believed, before they could present him with a reliable military instrument. But Hitler knew them better than they knew themselves. He said he wanted the Reichswehr tripled by October 1, 1934. And the generals nearly made it.[108]

Winston's intelligence apparatus was now almost complete, and the information he assembled was somber. Others shared his alarm; Vansittart remembers that "Wigram, made desperate by our danger, asked leave to leak some of my figures. . . . After all they *were* my figures, given to me personally for the good of the world and if necessary for its enlightenment. Indeed the donor had only risked his life on condition that I use them, and the moment had come." Some of the data arriving at Chartwell were almost unbelievable. Meeting in executive session, the cabinet in early 1934 had decided to sell 118 Rolls-Royce Merlin engines to the German government. Chamberlain had declared that approval of the sale was a matter of principle; trade, like religion, should recognize no frontiers. The engines, he said, had been designed for civilian use, and he refused to yield ground when an Air Ministry minute pointed out that they could also "be used in small fighter planes." When word of this transaction first reached Churchill, he dismissed it as preposterous; but then the actual bill of lading arrived in a plain envelope. Immediately he proposed a total ban on aircraft deliveries abroad. The Royal Air Force needed every plane it could get, he said, and none should be sold to *any* other country — certainly not to Nazi Germany. Chamberlain, speaking for the cabinet, rejected his proposal because the trade policy of His Majesty's Government required that "deficiencies in the Defence Forces should be made up with the least possible interference with the export trade."[109]

It is significant that HMG thought it necessary to make a formal reply to Winston, who, on the face of it, was merely another backbencher. But in England's ruling classes, little is as it seems. Historic policy decisions, including some which Walter Bagehot incorporated in *The English Constitution*, have been made by men who never held public office or were even elected to Parliament. It is what one *is* that counts; Churchill carried with him his lineage, his former eminence, and a presence so commanding that he dominated a room the moment he entered it. He might be mocked in the House of Commons, his calls to arms dismissed as "warmongering" or "scaremongering." But he was heard; he was seen. No one, however haughty, dismissed him with one of those rude, infuriating stares which Englishmen of position hand down from generation to generation, as though by gene.

Winston himself, when aroused, could be intimidating, a tremendous advantage in a leader. Unfortunately his hubris made it impossible for him to play the sneak. Because he was the least devious of men, his informants often lost sleep wondering whether he might unwittingly betray their confidences. Vansittart, a fellow patrician (and at times an infuriating snob), was the most visible of them; to those whose spiritual homes were Lothian's Blickling Hall and the Astors' Cliveden — citadels of appeasement — his hostility to Hitler had made him the most dangerous man in Whitehall, although he was, at this time, beyond the reach of his critics. Lesser men worried about the possibility that Churchill might compromise them. Mrs. P., anxious about the informant she had recruited in Westerham, sent Winston a note: "Cmdr Anderson told me very seriously that he had never been frightened in life before, but he is of this, ie that the fact of the vast number of German pilots" — the Nazis had trained over 8,000 — "may come out. IT MUST NOT BE DIVULGED OPENLY as it would implicate not only him, but Wing Commander Goddard, whom he must not harm. The number must be camouflaged." And Major G. P. Myers, in reporting that General Aircraft Ltd. had built only twenty-three Hawker Furies (fighters), reminded Winston: "I am an employee of General Aircraft Ltd. and as such would lose my position were the source of this information disclosed by mischance."[110]

To those threatened by it, Churchill's carelessness in shielding such informants constituted a major defect. Certainly it was a flaw. So was his lack of consideration for those who served him, and (this became more conspicuous after he moved into No. 10) the callousness with which he discarded men for whom he had no further use. Ingratitude is not attractive. But the man who stood against Nazi Germany when his peers ridiculed him — and who later refused to quit when those around him believed England's cause lost, thereby saving Western civilization — is surely entitled to a few warts.

Not so Stanley Baldwin. In the mid-1930s he possessed more prestige and political power than any prime minister since the death of Queen Victoria. Yet in history he is a cypher. Clearly he relished his popularity and knew how quickly it would vanish if he warned the country to prepare for another four years in the trenches and barbed wire of France and Flanders. Everyone would turn on him, including his sovereign. In 1935, when Sir Samuel Hoare succeeded Simon as foreign secretary, Baldwin gave him one instruction — "Keep us out of war, we are not ready for it." And when Hoare kissed hands within the hour, George V urged him to resolve diplomatic crises with compromises. "I have already been through one war," he moaned. "How can I go through another? If I am to go on, you must keep us out of one."[111]

Churchill, hammering away at the need for collective security, remained far from the mainstream. Writing in the *Daily Mail* on July 13, 1934, he reaffirmed his support of the League of Nations, urging agreements, under the sanction and authority of the league, between anxious nations with standing armies: "If you want to stop war, you gather such an aggregation of force on the side of peace that the aggressor, whoever he may be, will not dare challenge. . . . It is no use disguising the fact that there must be and there ought to be deep anxiety in this country about Germany. This is not the only Germany which we shall live to see, but we have to consider that at present two or three men, in what may well be a desperate situation, have their grip on the whole of that mighty country."

In 1934 the BBC decided to broadcast a series of talks by prominent Englishmen on "Causes of War." The first two speakers declared that wars were fostered by armaments manufacturers ("merchants of death"), by "nationalism" (a pejorative alias for patriotism), and by networks of treaties, specifically the encirclement of Germany, which was called "a gratuitous affront to German pride." On Friday, November 16, when Churchill's turn came, his message was very different. Diplomatic attempts to isolate the Third Reich were "the encirclement of an aggressor," and the only alarming thing about it was that the circle seemed too fragile to contain the rising tide of Teutonic fury. If containment failed, a series of crises would "lead to war. Great Wars usually come only when both sides think they have good hopes of victory." He knew, he said, that some of his listeners would think none of this threatened them. But they must remember that only a few hours away "there dwells a nation of nearly seventy millions of the most educated, industrious, scientific, disciplined people of the world, who are taught from childhood to think of war and conquest as a glorious exercise, and death in battle as the noblest fate for man. There is a nation which has abandoned all its liberties in order to augment its collective might. There is a nation which with all its strength and virtues is in the grip of intolerance and racial pride unrestrained by law." He went on:

At present we lie within a few minutes' striking distance
    of the French, Dutch, and Belgian coasts,
        and within a few hours of the great aerodromes of Central Europe.
        We are even within cannon-shot of the Continent.
            So close as that!

Is it prudent, is it possible, however much we might desire it,
    to turn our backs upon Europe and ignore what may happen there? . . .
        I hope, I pray, and on the whole, grasping the larger hope,
        I believe, that no war will fall upon us,

But . . . if you look intently at what is moving towards Great Britain,
    you will see that the only choice open
        is the grim old choice our forefathers had to face, namely,

Whether we shall submit to the will of the stronger nation
    or whether we shall be prepared
        to defend our rights, our liberties, and indeed our lives.[112]

By now a few elder statesmen were drifting toward his standard, and on November 28 Leopold Amery and Sir Robert Horne joined his small group of supporters when he moved to "humbly represent to Your Majesty that, in the present circumstances of the world, the strength of our national defences, and especially of our air defences, is no longer adequate to secure the peace, safety, and freedom of Your Majesty's faithful subjects." Speaking to the motion, Winston reasoned that only a strong British military presence would guarantee peace. He reasoned — and was jeered for reasoning — that "to urge preparation of defence is not to assert the imminence of war. On the contrary, if war was imminent preparations for defence would be too late." *Now* was the time for Britain to strengthen her ramparts. Parliament could not wish away the fact that German munitions factories were working around the clock — that rearmament dominated all other issues in the Third Reich, while Hitler Youth were taught "the most extreme patriotic, nationalistic and militaristic conceptions." The greatest peril to England was the Reich's building of a mighty air arm: "However calmly surveyed, the danger of attack from the air must appear most formidable." It was also unique. "Never in our history have we been in a position where we could be blackmailed, or forced to surrender our possessions, or take some action which the wisdom of the country would not allow it to do. . . . And yet, as I am going to show, this is the kind of danger which is coming upon us in a very short time unless we act upon a great scale and act immediately."

The time had arrived, he said, "when the mystery surrounding the German rearmament must be cleared up." The brutal fact was that "Germany already, at this moment, has a military air force — that is to say, military squadrons, with the necessary ground services, and the necessary reserves of trained personnel and material — which only awaits an order to assemble in full open combination; and that this illegal air force is rapidly approaching equality with our own." In less than three years the Luftwaffe would be "nearly double" the size of the RAF. And his estimate did not include some four hundred Nazi mail planes which could be converted into long-distance bombers "in a few hours" by removing passenger accommodations and fitting in bomb racks, racks which "are already made and kept in close proximity to the machines."

All Britain was vulnerable to Nazi bombers; modern aircraft traveling 200, 230, and even 240 miles an hour possessed an "enormous range. . . . The flying peril is not a peril from which one can fly. It is necessary to face it where we stand. We cannot possibly retreat. We cannot move London. We cannot move the vast population which is dependent upon the estuary of the Thames."[113]

Characteristically, Churchill had singled out one issue — air power — and would set all else aside when the RAF/Luftwaffe question arose. The year ahead would be crowded with crises, and he would play an active role in all of them, but he would always return to the question of

England's strength in the air, for there England's very life was at risk. It was the linchpin of his military policy, linked to his call for collective security as diplomatic policy. If European states threatened by Nazi aggression agreed to confront Hitler with a solid phalanx of nations, as Napoleon had been confronted at Leipzig, the RAF's Fighter Command need never fly into battle.

Facing the hostility of all three party leaders — Baldwin, Attlee, even Liberal leader Archie Sinclair — the old lion braced himself and demanded emergency appropriations to establish an air force "substantially stronger" than Germany's. If Britain lost her lead, "even for a month," it should be considered "a high crime against the state." The turnout in the last election, he reminded them, was the largest in Britain's history, and the people had voted, above all things, for the maintenance and security of their native land. "That was the emotion which brought us into power, and I venture to say: Do not, whatever be the torrent of abuse which may obstruct the necessary action, think too poorly of the greatness of our fellow countrymen. Let the House do its duty. Let the Government give the lead, and the nation will not fail in the hour of need."[114]

Frances Stevenson, Lloyd George's mistress, watched the speech from the Strangers' Gallery. In her diary she wrote that she did not think Winston "spoke as well as usual. But I suppose it was the *matter* of the speech that was more important than the delivery. . . . There was imagination in it too, coupled with a patriotism that was almost imperialistic."[115]

Baldwin rose to reply for the government. He was skeptical of Winston's information. It was "extraordinarily difficult" to acquire accurate figures on German air strength; in that respect the Third Reich was "a dark continent." But in his position he had access to highly classified reports, he said, and he could assure the House that it was "not the case" that the German air arm was "rapidly approaching equality with us"; alarmists to the contrary, Germany's strength was "not fifty percent" of England's. In his reply to Churchill he said: "I cannot look further forward than the next two years," but "such investigations as I have been able to make lead me to believe that his figures are considerably exaggerated." Indeed, no other conclusion was reasonable, because "the Royal Air Force is far superior to German air power" and would hold a margin of 50 percent superiority.

Baldwin then made a formal pledge, to Parliament, his king, and his country:

His Majesty's Government are determined in no condition to accept any position of inferiority with regard to what air force may be raised in Germany in the future.[116]

What possessed Stanley Baldwin, the shrewdest of politicians, to climb out so far on so brittle a limb — and for the second time within the year? On that earlier occasion, March 8, 1934, in the face of heated questioning from Churchill, Baldwin had assured Parliament: "Any Government of this country — a National Government more than any, and this Government — will see to it that in air strength and air power this country shall no longer be in a position inferior to any country within striking distance of our shores."[117] Now, as then, Baldwin wanted to silence Churchill, and he had, but the price was exorbitant. He had also been swayed by his craving for peace, of course, and his enjoyment of great personal popularity in the country. Still another explanation is that he ran what parliamentarians call an "easy" government, letting his ministers handle decisions in their departments while he acted as chairman of the board. So great was his indifference to diplomacy that the Foreign Office came to think of itself as a remote kingdom. Finally, the possibilities of error were multiplied by an irrational factor: Baldwin and those around him had repeatedly refused to believe that Hitler was what Hitler was. They had, in short, developed the political equivalent of a mental block.

If Baldwin had shut his mind to what was happening in Europe, however, he certainly knew the meaning of a solemn vow. No public school boy could survive the sixth form without a rigid sense of honor, and Baldwin, a Harrovian, knew how the Game was Played. But appeasement had begun to corrode the character of its evangelists. They were learning how to break promises and survive.

The immediate aftermath of Baldwin's November pledge is more interesting than the pledge itself, for it reveals the deeper motives of the men then governing England, ministers of the Crown who believed they were preserving the peace when in fact they were assuring the inevitability of war — and the end of Britain's role as a great power. When Baldwin committed his government to setting aside £130,000 for Britain's defenses, to abolish their "worst deficiencies," his own chancellor of the Exchequer cut him off at the pass. Bargaining relentlessly in cabinet meetings, Neville Chamberlain succeeded in paring down the £130,000 to £75,000 and finally to £25,000.

Although Chamberlain's position on rearmament would blur after he moved from No. 11 Downing Street to No. 10, as chancellor he fought every appeal for funds from the War Office, the Admiralty, and the Air Ministry. If Clausewitz saw war as a science, the chancellor viewed it as a business, or at any rate as an enterprise to be managed in the style of successful businessmen. When pondering decisions he liked to make a steeple of his hands and ruminate, looking out across the Horse Guards as to a mote in the middle distance. It was meaningless rite. His was a closed mind. Like Baldwin he was suspicious of innovations and of intellect. His Majesty's Government's position was that it would not prevent scientists or any other private citizens from preparing for war, provided they pay for it out of their own pockets and do nothing to obstruct the nation's business. Lord Weir, a Scottish manufacturer who also served as an adviser to the Air Ministry, said that an RAF expansion would do precisely that, so the project was shelved. Chamberlain explained to the House: "What we have to do is carry through in a limited period of time, measures which will make exceptionally heavy demands on industry and upon certain classes of skilled labour, without impeding the course of normal trade." He was willing to accept larger arms budgets, but believed that, for financial reasons, there must be a limit. That limit meant the gap between Britain's defense establishment and Germany's would continue to widen.[118]

In January 1935 two British peers visited the Reich Chancellery, on the Wilhelmstrasse, where they held vague discussions with Hitler on the subject of arms limitations. The talks were inconclusive, but since the Führer hadn't actually closed any doors, the FO was cautiously optimistic. Sir John Simon proposed that as foreign secretary he call at the chancellery and explore treaty possibilities. Arrangements were made and a meeting scheduled for March 6. Simon and Eden were packing on March 5 when the German ambassador telephoned to say that the talks would have to be postponed. The Führer had caught "a cold" ("*Erkältung*") and was in bed, miserable and short-tempered.

The Foreign Office was familiar with diplomatic colds. Other sources in Berlin confirmed what was suspected: Hitler was furious at Britain. From Chartwell Churchill wrote Clementine that Hitler had flown "into a violent rage and refused to receive Simon. . . . This gesture of spurning the British Foreign Secretary from the gates of Berlin is a significant measure of the conviction which Hitler has of the strength of the German Air Force and Army."[119]

There was an explanation for the Führer's *Zorn*. In London Baldwin's pledge to keep the RAF supreme in the sky had already begun to look wobbly. The fragments of information about German air strength pieced together by the Foreign Office were, as Michael Creswell put it, "most alarming." The Central Department had discussed the data, and Ralph Wigram had drawn up a memorandum for the cabinet. His latest information, assembled and analyzed, revealed that by 1936 the German air arm would surpass France's and exceed Britain's "very greatly." There was now no doubt, Wigram had concluded, that Nazi Germany was "out for superiority."[120]

Even Chamberlain had realized that something must be done. On March 4, therefore, His Majesty's Government had issued a White Paper on air defense. In it, HMG deplored the swiftness of Nazi rearmament, which, together with the belligerence of the government in Berlin, was identified as contributing to a general European "feeling of insecurity." The government therefore announced plans to expedite air force increases and proposed a major additional defense appropriation. Churchill was elated. He wrote Clementine that "all the frightened nations are at last beginning to huddle together."[121]

If Churchill was encouraged by the proposed increases, Hitler was enraged — hence his refusal to meet with Simon. Ralph Wigram wrote: "One wonders if in this 'rage' there is not also a design to make [it] difficult for the Govt here . . . to challenge the German rearmament." That, he pointed out, "would be entirely in the tradition of German diplomacy." Three days later Vansittart minuted: "All this is a far more overt German interference in British internal politics than anything the Soviets have done."[122] The Labour MPs remained pacifists to the man. Attlee moved to censure the government for recommending the increases. Though the Labour censure motion was defeated soundly, an air estimates debate was scheduled for Tuesday, March 19.

Meantime, Hitler was neither coughing nor sneezing. Instead he was unusually active, pacing his huge office in the Reich Chancellery, pondering a momentous move. Before April 1, he had promised General Ludwig Beck, an honorable officer who believed Germany's secret buildup was dishonorable, he would denounce the Versailles *Diktat* as *null und nichtig*. The time seemed ripe. The Versailles carbuncle had been festering long enough. Now he would lance it. To be sure, it would be awkward if France drew her sword. Her 352,000 poilus in metropolitan France could rout his half-formed army. But his instincts told him that they would shrink from force. He decided to test them. Air Minister Göring was told to announce the existence of the Luftwaffe. Everyone already knew it was there, but coming from a Reich minister the announcement would mean a formal, public rejection of the *Diktat*. London and Paris could either fight or submit. His instincts were right. They submitted. On March 9 Göring made his declaration, and the Quai d'Orsay was silent.

The following Saturday, March 16, with the British prime minister and his cabinet relaxing in their remote country homes, Hitler took the next step. After formally renouncing the Versailles treaty he decreed that all German youths were subject to conscription. The next day was Germany's annual Memorial Day, *Heldengedenktag*. The officer corps, wearing decorations and dress uniforms, gathered in the State Opera House to observe the occasion, the "spiked helmets of the old Imperial Army," writes William Shirer, who was there, "mingling with the . . . sky-blue uniforms of the Luftwaffe, which few had seen before."[123]

Churchill had tried again and again to tell Parliament that Germany was on a war footing. As he later wrote in the *Strand*, "the full terror of this revelation" now broke "upon the careless and imprudent world," as Hitler cast aside "concealment." He saw but one solution. France must use her superiority while she still had it.[124] But as Hitler had anticipated and Churchill had feared, France did nothing of the sort. In Geneva the French weakly lodged a protest at Germany's "violation of international law." The League of Nations condemned the Führer's decrees but rejected all proposals of punitive action, including sanctions.

In the House of Commons on March 19, Sir Philip Sassoon, parliamentary under secretary at the Air Ministry, announced that the RAF would be further strengthened by forty-one and a half squadrons over the next four years. During the past four months, he admitted, "the situation has deteriorated. There has been a great acceleration . . . in the manufacture of aircraft in Germany." However, he assured the House, "at the end of this year we shall still have a margin, though I do not say a margin of 50 percent."[125]

Churchill's sources unanimously, and vehemently, disagreed. The cabinet, he learned, was aware of the "potential superiority of German air power" but had concluded that Britain must learn to live with it. Baldwin must have known that the air debate would produce a stormy session, and any doubts he may have harbored had been dispelled by a letter from Churchill, who bluntly told him that he meant to raise the issue of the Reich's growing strength. "I believe," he wrote, "that the Germans are already as strong as we are and possibly stronger." The March 4 White Paper, because of its inadequacy, could actually widen the gap between the two air forces. Then: "This will of course run contrary to your statement that 'this country shall no longer be in a position inferior to any country within striking distance of our shores.' " He ended ominously: "I shall argue that according to such knowledge as I have been able to acquire, this is not being made good, as will be rapidly proved by events."[126]

On Tuesday, March 19, he made this threat good. Backbenchers, he told the House, were beginning to lose faith in the credibility of His Majesty's Government. He picked up the previous day's *Daily Telegraph* and quoted: " 'Between 250 and 300 military aircraft have been added to Germany's total since November.' " At that rate, the Nazis could have another 1,500 warplanes by 1936.

I must submit to the House that the Lord President was misled in the figures he gave last November, quite unwittingly, no doubt, because of the grave difficulty of the subject. At any rate, the true position at the end of this year will be almost the reverse of what he stated to Parliament. . . . I am certain that Germany's preparations are infinitely more far-reaching than our own. So that you have not only equality at the moment, but the great output which I have described, and you have behind that this enormous power to turn over, on the outbreak of war, the whole force of German industry.[127]

Laying before the House a string of precise figures, he went on: "At the end of the year, when we were to have had a 50 percent superiority over Germany, they will be at least three and four times as strong as we." He demanded that RAF expansion be redoubled.

Attlee's Labourites were outraged. The government's position was more nebulous. Baldwin chose Under Secretary Sassoon to answer the attack. To what extent Sassoon's reply was based on duplicity — Baldwin's duplicity or Sassoon's — and to what degree on ignorance by either or both, is matter for speculation. The record merely tells us that Sassoon rose, addressed himself to Winston, and said vaguely: "I do not think I can follow him into a morass of figures which must be, after all, very largely conjectural." Sassoon denied that the Luftwaffe would become "50 percent stronger than ours either on the basis of first-line strength or on the basis of total number of aircraft. So far as we can at present estimate, we shall still, at the end of this year, possess a margin of superiority."[128]

Baldwin again questioned Winston's evidence. It was incredible to him that the Luftwaffe could mount a serious challenge to the RAF. He could, it seemed, be convinced by only one man: Adolf Hitler. And that, amazingly, is what happened. Hitler had everything to gain by remaining silent, leaving His Majesty's Government comfortable in its false security. But in this, as in all else, he was unlike other men. Curing himself of his cold, he impulsively invited Simon and Eden to Berlin on March 25, less than a week after Parliament's air debate, and told them that the Reich had "reached parity with Great Britain as far as their respective air forces are concerned." Simultaneously, Goebbels released this electrifying news to the press. The Luftwaffe, the Führer told Simon, was a bulwark against bolshevism. He was alert to "the Russian danger," he said, though he seemed to be "a solitary prophet in the desert." He added confidently: "But later people will find out that I was right."[129]

Churchill wrote Clementine: "The political sensation of course is the statement by Hitler that his air force is already as strong as ours. This completely stultifies everything that Baldwin has said and incidentally vindicates all the assertions that I have made. I suspect in fact that he is really much stronger than we are."[130] Hitler had told Simon and Eden that according to his information the RAF had 1,045 first-line aircraft; since he was claiming parity, that, presumably, was the present strength of the Luftwaffe. But German intelligence had blundered. The British were nowhere near as formidable as he believed them to be. According to Air Ministry archives the RAF had only 453 first-line warplanes. Britain was in deep trouble unless she acted swiftly, but as summer approached and the days grew warmer it was often difficult to find any movement at all in Whitehall.

Parliament awaited a response from the front bench. And waited. And waited. In the *Daily Mail* of April 4 Churchill urged the government to make preparations for converting "the whole of our industry, should it become necessary, to various forms of munition production." Three days later Ralph Wigram arrived at Chartwell for an overnight stay. With him he brought a February 27 analysis by Creswell, comparing the relative air strengths of Britain and Germany. The Air Ministry report on RAF strength was only one of several sources; they varied greatly, but all confirmed Hitler. Actually the Führer had inflated the operational strength of his air arm, but Nazi "training, design, and production were proceeding apace and expanding rapidly," Telford Taylor writes. "The [operational] base was rapidly broadening, and by 1936 the threat of German air power would become reality."[131]

Given this momentum, and the inertia at No. 10, the threat was already real, and on May 2 Churchill spoke in the House of Commons:

When the situation was manageable it was neglected, and now that it is thoroughly out of hand, we apply too late the remedies which then might have effected a cure. There is nothing new in the story. It is as old as the Sibylline books. It falls into that long dismal catalogue of the fruitlessness of experience and the confirmed unteachability of mankind. Want of foresight, unwillingness to act when action would be simple and effective, lack of clear thinking, confusion of counsel until the emergency comes, until self-preservation strikes its jarring gong — these are the features which constitute the endless repetition of history.[132]

He bluntly told the House: "It cannot be disputed that both in numbers and in quality Germany has already obtained a marked superiority over our Home Defence Air Force." At Chartwell Wigram had told Churchill that the Foreign Office staff was profoundly disturbed by the facts the FO was reporting to His Majesty's Government and HMG's abuse of them, and a remarkable instance of this had occurred only a few days earlier, on April 30. By April 1937, MacDonald had told the Ministerial Committee on Defence Requirements, "Germany will have 1,512 aircraft, and we shall have 740." He asked: "Is this a situation that the Government can explain and defend in the House?" Chamberlain replied firmly that they couldn't and shouldn't; if they were to remain loyal to Baldwin they were "bound to maintain the position" that his pledge had not been broken. Should they acknowledge the mistake, he said, they would "give Germany the impression that we are frightened." His proposal, which his colleagues accepted, was that air power should be judged not from the number of fighters and bombers in an air force, but by an intangible "air strength." Secretary for Air Londonderry eagerly fell in line. Luftwaffe training, he said, "is inferior to ours." RAF flying skills were so finely honed, and British airplane designers and manufacturers were so imaginative and competent, that to say "Germany is stronger" would be incorrect. Therefore Britain had, in effect, retained parity.

The Foreign Office and Air Ministry experts protested that this was mendacity. The parliamentary under secretary for foreign affairs produced a sheaf of reports demonstrating that German pilots and planes, far from being "behind in training and equipment," were in the lead. Even if Luftwaffe air expansion ended in 1937, aerodynamic engineers said, Britain might not catch up until 1942, which meant that in the interval German diplomacy could exploit the gap.

Baldwin considered a cover-up and rejected it. A parliamentary inquiry could destroy him and give Churchill a national forum from which he could emerge as Britain's hero. So, to the consternation of a majority of his ministers, he announced that he had decided to make a clean breast of things. Addressing the House on May 22, nearly two months after Hitler's revelation, he quoted his pledge and followed it with what might be called his first confession:

With regard to the figure I gave in November of German air strength, nothing that has come to my knowledge since then makes me think that figure was wrong. I believed at the time it was right. Where I was wrong was in my estimate of the future. There I was completely wrong. . . . Whatever responsibility there may be — and we are perfectly ready to meet criticism — that responsibility is not that of any single Minister; it is the responsibility of the Government as a whole, and we are all responsible, and we are all to blame.[133]

"The horror of that moment," the King went on, "I shall never, never forget!"

"You will, though," the Queen said, "if you don't make a memorandum of it."

The fact that Stanley Baldwin had made a personal pledge to Parliament and England was ignored. Privately he blamed the Foreign Office. But FO figures which would have alerted him had gone to the Air Ministry. Vansittart recalled: "S.B. did not know the true position, either because the Air Ministry had not given my figures to him, or because it took them with salt, or because it had different ones of its own. Or perhaps they just got into a box and stayed there."

Intelligence, Van noted, "was becoming increasingly hard to operate in Germany, because informants, if detected, died slow and horrible deaths. Money was no longer enough for the risk of vastly improved tortures. Yet the facts were there. If S.B. had none, he was the rasher to say that we had a 50 percent margin."[134] The implications of the new situation were profoundly disturbing. Working at maximum capacity, British industry could turn out 1,250 planes in two years. Safety required twice as many.

Churchill expected a dramatic surge of public opinion, or at the very least a formal parliamentary inquiry. The conviction that he and England had been cheated burned in him. In April he had written Clementine: "How discreditable for the Government to have . . . misled Parliament upon a matter involving the safety of the country." Two days later he had written her again: "It is a shocking thing when a Government openly commits itself to statements on a matter affecting the public safety which are bound to be flagrantly disproved by events."[135]

But he had not thought it through. If the government fell, who would succeed? In other circumstances he might have expected a coalition, but both the Labour and Liberal parties had opposed *any* arms appropriations. Unmoved by Hitler's disclosures, they continued to plan waging the 1935 election campaign, now imminent, against "Tory armaments." Sinclair delivered a long speech in Parliament on "the question of private profits being made out of the means of death," and expressed astonishment at Winston's "dangerous argument" that vast sums should be spent on the RAF "in view of the financial conditions of the country and the intolerable burdens of our national debt and taxation." Lloyd George declared that Germany had been treated "as a pariah." She had, he said, been "driven into revolution" by the architects of Versailles (of whom he had been one) and demanded that her grievances be "put right."

Meanwhile, Baldwin was traveling around the country, puffing his pipe and assuring relieved audiences that England was safe. "His statements were wrong," Churchill wrote in an unpublished memorandum, "but they were everywhere accepted . . . by the British public." Winston blamed Fleet Street. His indictment was unjustified; as Lord Londonderry noted, press comment was "vehement." British reporters entering Germany confirmed the existence of the swelling army and the sense of urgency among the generals. In detailed dispatches the *Daily Telegraph* reported that the Luftwaffe was "already equipped with practically double the number of firstline military aircraft available in the country for the purposes of home defence." No sensible man could doubt now that Churchill had been right and Baldwin wrong. Londonderry wrote that the unmasking of the Baldwin pledge "came as a rude shock to the British public." In an open apology to Winston for having "ignored" his warnings, the *Daily Express* prophesied: "The reaction of the British public to the Nazi rearmament will be plain and positive."[136]

It wasn't, though. To a British colonel, a survivor of the Dardanelles expedition twenty years earlier, Churchill wrote that he was "astounded at the indifference" which had been the country's response to "the fact that the Government have been utterly wrong about the German air strength," and in a despairing note to Clemmie he said that the Nazis were "not only substantially stronger than we are," but were "manufacturing at such a rate that we cannot catch them up."[137]

By summer it was clear that the Dear Vicar had not only weathered the rearmament crisis; he was more popular than ever. Later Churchill recalled bitterly: "There was even a strange wave of enthusiasm for a Minister who did not hesitate to say he was wrong. . . . Conservative Members seemed angry with me for having brought their trusted leader to a plight from which only his native manliness and honesty had extricated him; but not, alas, his country." He wrote a friend: "When I first went into Parliament the most insulting charge which could be made against a Minister — short of actual malfeasance — was that he had endangered the safety of the country. . . . Yet such are the surprising qualities of Mr. Baldwin that what all had been taught to shun has now been elevated into a canon of political virtue."[138]

🦁   🦁

The revelations emanating from Germany — the announcement of the Luftwaffe, the overt rejection of Versailles and the resumption of conscription, the claim of air parity with Britain — had shaken all Europe, and reverberations continued through the spring. Mussolini at that time was committed to neither Germany nor the democracies. The Duce admired Hitler's style but worried about Austria. He liked it as it was, a buffer between Italy and the Reich, but he knew the Führer had designs upon it. Therefore he had agreed to meet Ramsay MacDonald and Premier

Pierre-Étienne Flandin for a three-power conference in Stresa, Italy. There, in April, the three leaders had declared that they would "oppose by all appropriate means any unilateral repudiation of treaties which may endanger the peace of Europe." This formation of the "Stresa Front" was followed by negotiations between Paris and Moscow for a Franco-Soviet military alliance. Stalin's foreign commissar then signed a similar pact with Czechoslovakia, though this was odd: the two countries lacked a common border; if Soviet troops were to rescue the Czechs, they would have to cross Poland or Rumania, both of whom historically regarded Russia as their bête noir. [139]

Hitler, deciding that Europe needed more reassurance, summoned the Reichstag on May 21 and delivered another *Friedensrede*, declaring that Germany would never dream of threatening other countries, that the Reich "has solemnly recognized and guaranteed France her frontiers," including the renunciation of "all claims to Alsace-Lorraine," and — at a time when Nazi *Strassenkämpfer* were storming through the streets of Vienna, clubbing Austrian pedestrians who had failed to greet them with the stiff-armed *Hitlergruss* — that "Germany neither intends nor wishes to interfere in the internal affairs of Austria, to annex Austria, or to conclude an Anschluss." [140]

In London *The Times* rejoiced. The Führer's speech was "reasonable, straightforward, and comprehensive. No one who reads it with an impartial mind can doubt that the points of policy laid down by Herr Hitler may fairly constitute the basis of a complete settlement with Germany — a free, equal and strong Germany instead of the prostrate Germany upon whom peace was imposed sixteen years ago." But the only settlement the Führer wanted was one achieved by conquest. On the evening of May 21, a few hours after his *Friedensrede*, he issued a secret decree reorganizing the Reich's military establishment. The name Reichswehr, a reminder of the hated Weimar regime, was replaced by the prouder, more aggressive Wehrmacht; the Ministry of Defense was rechristened the Ministry of War. General Blomberg, the war minister, was designated commander in chief of the armed forces. Under Blomberg, Göring headed the Luftwaffe, Raeder the navy, and Werner von Fritsch the army. Beck became chief of the Generalstab. In a few months, the War Academy would ceremoniously reopen, and the men Hitler had chosen to lead Germany in the coming war would speak eloquently of "the spirit of the Old Army." The tempo of the Reich's martial music was *accelerando*.

Had *The Times* known of this, Dawson's enthusiasm might have been tempered, but there can be little doubt that the paper's course would have remained unaltered. Very likely, excuses would have been found for

Hitler. How Dawson and Barrington-Ward remained so blind to developments in central Europe is unfathomable. It is not as though information was withheld from them. Norman Ebbutt, the paper's Berlin correspondent, filed accurate, perceptive dispatches on Nazi Germany for over three years, until the summer of 1937, when the Nazis, realizing that there seemed to be virtually no limit to the humiliation and intimidation London would accept rather than risk war, expelled him. Ebbutt's editors read his stories; they knew what was happening in the Third Reich, though their readers often did not; his dispatches were frequently rewritten or suppressed by Dawson, who, after five years of jumping through Hitler's hoops, merely wondered at the man's ingratitude. He wrote H. G. Daniels, his Geneva correspondent: "I do my utmost, night after night, to keep out of the paper anything that might hurt their [Nazi] susceptibilities. I can really think of nothing that has been printed now for many months past to which they could possibly take exception as unfair comment."[141]

The Führer, meantime, had made England an offer which any proud government would have rejected. In November 1934 he had told the British ambassador that Germany, in building up her navy, would agree to limit it to 35 percent of the size of the Royal Navy, with parity, or something close to it, in submarines. He had repeated his proposal to Lord Lothian in January, to Simon again in March, and on May 21 before the Reichstag, vowing that there would be no escalation of demands. He recognized "the overpowering importance, and hence the justification of the British Empire to dominate the seas," and he was determined to "maintain a relationship with the British people and state which will prevent for all time a repetition of the only struggle there has been between the two nations." He added: *"Für Deutschland ist sie endgültig"* ("For Germany this is final").[142]

The Times found Hitler's proposal "sincere" and "well considered," and the prime minister and his cabinet agreed. Baldwin, at that point still lord president, received Joachim von Ribbentrop, the Reich's ambassador-at-large, to review the details. In less than two weeks S.B. intended to cast MacDonald aside and move into No. 10 himself. It was time he dealt directly with the Germans. He had negotiations in mind, but it turned out that there was no room for them; Hitler, Ribbentrop explained, had committed himself to the Reichstag and could not retreat. However, he quickly added, the Führer would never dream of naval rivalry with Britain, though submarines were an exception to the 35 percent ratio; there the Germans meant to limit themselves to four vessels for every five British subs, except in cases of *"Notwendigkeit"* ("necessity"). Baldwin accepted on the spot, then called in a small group of ministers and laid it all before them.[143]

Even the most devout parishioner has moments of doubt, and now and then one finds a true believer in appeasement straying, if only a few steps, from the garden path. It happened at this point to Sir John Simon. Usually Simon was among the most devout. But for a moment in 1935 he was shaken; during the opening talks with German naval officers and Wilhelm-strasse diplomats he lost his temper, delivered a heated lecture on the unwisdom of ratios, and stalked from the room. He was the only member of the cabinet who refused to endorse the treaty. His successor as foreign secretary, Sir Samuel Hoare, spoke sharply in the House on July 11 about "those people" — he meant Churchill and the Churchillians — "who seem to take a morbid delight in alarms and excursions, in a psychology, shall I say, of fear, perhaps even of brutality." He called them "alarm-mongers and scaremongers." The pact with Germany, he noted, had been greeted by the people with glee. It was "an agreement profitable alike to peace and to the taxpayer."[144]

Hoare and the rest of His Majesty's Government overlooked a great deal. Hitler had driven a wedge between the allied nations on the Reich's western front, the two powers his generals feared most. At the same time he had ended Germany's diplomatic isolation, imposed by the rest of Europe after he had quit the League of Nations and abrogated Versailles. And with a stroke of the pen England — which had nothing to gain from the naval pact — was shattering what remained of Versailles' claims to legitimacy. Germany, as she continued to rearm, could no longer be accused of breaking her word. It was perhaps true, as Eden told the French diplomat Alexis Léger, that the limitations imposed at Versailles no longer meant much. But "it should have been apparent," Telford Taylor writes, "that for the British to countenance a reborn German Navy, including U-boats, would deeply wound French and Italian feelings."[145] Moreover, with an Anglo-Italian crisis over Ethiopia imminent, the timing of the pact was atrocious.

Two backbenchers in the House saw this: Lloyd George and Churchill. The Welsh firebrand was very old now, and his flame was flickering low, but Winston was fine, fit, and fierce. Speaking immediately after Hoare, he damned the agreement. Britain, he said, had struck a very poor bargain. The assumption that the Nazis would observe the still untested rules of submarine warfare was, he said, "the acme of gullibility." He pointed out that Britain had "condoned this unilateral violation of the Treaty [of Versailles]" without conferring with any of "the other countries concerned." At the very moment when European salvation depended on a "gathering together of Powers" fearing the "rearmed strength of Germany," England had chosen "to depart from the principle of collective security in a very notable fashion." The French would moan but cling desperately to Britain, their only sure ally. The Italians could go elsewhere. And, he predicted, they would.

But the most perilous feature of the pact, said Churchill, was that it took no account of Britain's worldwide responsibilities. Germany, he reminded Parliament, had no overseas possessions. Britain had an empire. He knew there were men in the chamber who disapproved of the Empire, but it still existed, and until Parliament decided otherwise, the government was obliged to shield the Dominions, Crown Colonies, and protectorates. The 100-to-35 ratio was comforting only if the Royal Navy were confined to the North Sea.

He paused, scowled, and then lashed out: "What a windfall this has been for Japan! Observe what the consequences are. . . . The British Fleet, when this [German] programme is completed, will be largely anchored in the North Sea." Now "the whole advantage of having a great naval base at Singapore upon which a battle fleet can be based" — to protect, he pointed out, imperial domains including Australia and New Zealand — "is greatly affected by the fact that when this German fleet is built we shall not be able to keep any appreciable portion of the British Fleet so far from home." The path to peace did not lie in bilateral agreements. War could be prevented only by collective security. And now His Majesty's Government had abandoned that. Admirers of the German regime might rejoice, but he was troubled. Before he rose, he reminded the House, the right honorable gentleman preceding him had talked of alarm-mongers and scaremongers. He accepted those epithets. One could do worse. "It is better to be alarmed and scared now than to be killed hereafter."[146]

The issue rankled. Later he noted that the *Daily Herald* had quoted Baldwin as saying, "We shall have to give up certain of our toys — one is 'Britannia rules the waves.' " Here Baldwin was attacking, not only Churchill's position, but also one of the three patriotic anthems Winston treasured most, the other two being "Land of Hope and Glory" and "The British Grenadiers." Churchill drew attention to the prime minister's misquotation. "It is, 'Britannia, rule the waves' — an invocation, not a declaration of fact. But if the idea 'Rule Britannia' is a toy, it is certainly one for which many good men from time to time have been ready to die." Yet at the time he said privately that very few Britons seemed ready to die for anything anymore; the entire country seemed crippled by a national *défaillance*. He had spoken to them in the tongue of Victoria's England, itself a dead language, and there were no interpreters.[147]

*   *   *

The Anglo-German Naval Agreement was signed on June 18, 1935 —
Hitler sent Ribbentrop to London as his personal emissary — eleven days
after Baldwin succeeded MacDonald at No. 10, thereby becoming prime
minister *de jure* as well as *de facto*. Less than three months had passed since
the Führer made public the fact that Germany had renounced Versailles
and was rearming. Europe, the United States, and Japan took note of
Britain's cynical disregard of her Versailles obligations, and Mussolini,
deciding he could now safely flout the League of Nations Covenant,
ordered his generals to plan an invasion of Ethiopia, to take place after the
rainy season ended.[148]

The most baffling aspect of this diplomatic debacle was Britain's treatment
of her great ally across the Channel. In a spectacular understatement, Eden
had pointed out to his ministerial colleagues that the French, when they
learned of the agreement, might have "reservations." Certainly they were
entitled to them. Hoare told the cabinet that it was "essential" to humor the
Germans in certain small requests, among them a pledge that the French
be told none of the treaty's provisions. France also had a first-class navy,
and the new agreement would put her ships within range of German naval
gunners. Yet His Majesty's Foreign Office could not even tell the Quai
d'Orsay how many ships Hitler could build, their size, and their
categories — battleships, heavy cruisers, light cruisers, destroyers,
U-boats. Actually, the pact permitted the Nazis to construct five battleships
whose armament and tonnage outclassed any vessels in the Royal
Navy — this had been accomplished by a mistranslation of one clause —
together with twenty-one cruisers, sixty-four destroyers, and, in practice,
an unlimited number of submarines.[149]

French loyalty to the triumphant entente of 1914–1918 was vital to
England's safety. If war were declared, it would be France's job to contain
the German army; at most the British could send but five divisions to the
Continent at the outset and six later. But beginning with Hitler's defiant
rejection of Versailles and continuing through the imminent crises in the
Rhineland, Austria, Czechoslovakia, and Poland, France was to be the
passive member of the 1918 entente, deferring to the British, accepting
decisions made in Whitehall. The patriciate ruling England enjoyed their
dominant role, accepting Gallic docility without question. They had never
understood why anyone should question their judgment and thought the
French were merely being sensible.

Churchill shared the illusion of France's defensive strength. Speaking
in the House three days after Hitler's defiant acknowledgment of German
rearmament, Winston said: "The frontiers of Germany are very much
nearer to London than the sea-coasts of this island are to Berlin, and

whereas practically the whole of the German bombing air force can reach London with an effective load, very few, if any, of our aeroplanes can reach Berlin with any appreciable load of bombs."[150] He considered this warning dire. He did not anticipate England's plight if Nazi bombers were based on *French* airfields — directly across the Channel. Carrying blockbuster bombs, they could then devastate London and Britain's great industrial cities, including their armaments factories, in the Midlands. Even Churchill's imagination could not encompass such a calamity. The possibility that the Germans could actually conquer France and overrun Paris, using over a million superb infantrymen behind a great panzer force, was never raised. He still believed that the French army was "the finest in the world."

🦁   🦁

Having predicted Hitler's outrages throughout 1935, Winston was treated with new respect in Parliament, but, he later wrote, although the House "now listened to me with close attention, I felt a sense of despair." The year had seen a series of triumphs for the Führer and humiliating defeats for the democracies. Baldwin, Churchill now knew, was hopeless. He recalled, from an 1883 issue of *Punch*, lines he had memorized as a young schoolboy in Brighton:

> *Who is in charge of the clattering train?*
> *The axles creak and the couplings strain;*
> *And the pace is hot, and the points are near,*
> *And Sleep has deadened the driver's ear;*
> *And the signals flash through the night in vain,*
> *For Death is in charge of the clattering train.*[151]

Baldwin was asleep at the throttle, so Winston decided that *he* must become the engineer, or at any rate the conductor or stoker — in short, a member of the government's crew and therefore a participant in the formulation of policy. On August 2, 1935, Parliament passed the Government of India Act, charting the course which would lead to Indian independence and, at the same time, ending Winston's six-year struggle to keep India in the Empire. He had quit the Tory leadership because of its decision to end the Raj, but now India was no longer an issue. He was free to concentrate on the Nazi menace, and, as he saw it, to rejoin his old cabinet colleagues. On August 25 he addressed an open letter to his Epping constituents, a eulogy to the glories of British India, which ended: "We have done our best and we have done our duty; we cannot do more."

As a propitiary gesture he invited G. D. Birla, one of Mahatma Gandhi's chief lieutenants, to lunch.* Afterward, Birla wrote Gandhi that the luncheon had been "one of my most pleasant experiences" in England. His host, he reported, had said, "Mr. Gandhi has gone very high in my esteem since he stood up for the untouchables," and had then gone on to express the hope that a Congress party regime would bring "improvement in the lot of the masses, morally as well as materially. I do not care whether you are more or less loyal to Great Britain. I do not mind about education, but give the masses more butter." Winston had told Birla: "I am genuinely sympathetic towards India. You need not expect anything but silence or help from us." Later Attlee introduced Churchill to Jawaharlal Nehru. According to him, the two old Harrovians "got on splendidly. Winston said how he had admired Nehru's courage in standing up to rioters and Nehru said he had enjoyed reading Winston's books. They chatted most amicably and something like real confidence was established, and to the best of my knowledge never diminished."[152]

In the weeks before November's general election, no Tory campaigned more tirelessly for Conservative candidates than Churchill. He offered his services to the party's central office, and they scheduled him to deliver major addresses in Wanstead, Hull, Biggleswade, Epping, Woodford, and South Chingford. He would decide his own strategy, of course, but Baldwin had chosen the ground on which the party as a whole would fight. The issues would be the Anglo-German Naval Agreement, trade and shipping, and public works. Actually, as Macmillan later recalled, Baldwin's own campaigning was "somewhat disingenuous. His speeches were admirably devised to suit all shades of opinion." He declared, *"No great armaments!"* That pleased the pacifists. Advocates of lower taxes wanted to stress the government's refusal to join Hitler in an arms race; Baldwin preferred an agreement with Hitler, which, he said, provided solid evidence that hardheaded, no-nonsense Britons could deal with dictators.[153]

Hitler, Baldwin's audiences were reassured, was not the menace he had been made out: "There may be Governments deliberately planning the future, leading reluctant or unsuspecting people into the shambles. . . . I confess that in my own political experience I have not encountered Governments possessed of all these malevolent qualities. Most Governments seem not much better or worse than the people they govern." To those like Leo Amery, who privately predicted that appeasement might encourage dictators, Chamberlain, speaking for the prime minister, heatedly replied

* For a full account of Churchill's struggle against Gandhi's campaign for Indian independence, see volume one of this work, pages 830 ff.

that this was a "mischievous distortion." The choice, he said, was "whether we shall make one last effort at Geneva for peace and security" or submit in a "cowardly surrender" to warmongerism, which would hold them up to "the shame of our children and our children's children." It was Chamberlain's strength that he never doubted that events would vindicate him; it was his fate that they would condemn him. Baldwin was the same, and the tragedy for both was that they lived long enough to know it.[154]

Churchill remained faithful to the cadence of his own drummer. Tory whips had approached him, advising him his prospects in the party would brighten if he refrained from fresh attacks on the Nazis until after the election. Winston replied that although that was the prime minister's line, it wasn't his. While Baldwin was dismissing the Nazi threat, Winston, in speeches and in articles for the *Daily Mail* and *Strand,* told his audiences the Ruhr's "great wheels revolve . . . disgorging weapons" for "the already largely war-mobilized arsenals and factories of Germany." As the campaign reached the home stretch he delivered a major address in Parliament, reminding members that Hitler was still spending £800 million a year — $3.9 billion at the then current rate of exchange — on arms. He said: "We cannot afford to see Naziism in its present phase of cruelty and intolerance, with all its hatreds and all its gleaming weapons, paramount in Europe," and he noted that he was being joined by fresh converts in the House. Only yesterday Lloyd George, finally aware of the Nazi peril, had performed an act of contrition in the House. Winston said that neither Lloyd George "nor His Majesty's Government will, I imagine, disagree today with the statement that Germany is already well on her way to becoming, and must become incomparably, the most heavily armed nation in the world and the nation most completely ready for war."[155]

There could be no doubt, he declared, that Nazi plans of European conquest existed. "Germany is an armed camp," he told Parliament. "The whole population is being trained from childhood up to war." And: "The German air force is developing at great speed and in spite of ruthless sacrifice of life." In "The Truth about Hitler," published in the November 1935 *Strand,* he wrote of how the Führer, after secretly rearming, had "sprung forward armed to the teeth, with his munitions factories roaring night and day, his aeroplane squadrons forming in ceaseless succession, his submarine crews exercising in the Baltic, and his armed hosts trampling from one end of the broad Reich to the other." Condemning Hitler's "ferocious doctrines," and predicting that they would be carried out with "brutal vigour," he wrote that German soil was "pock-marked" with concentration camps, where masses of Germans, from "world-famous scientists" to "wretched little Jewish children," were persecuted. Nothing could save a Jew from imprisonment and torture. "No past services, no proved patriotism, even wounds sustained in war," could prevent atrocities against people "whose only crime was that their parents had brought them into the world." Churchill referred skeptics to *Mein Kampf*, where Jews were described as "a foul and odious race." But the inmates of these camps were not all Jewish. Under Hitler "the slightest criticism" of the Führer and his criminal regime was "an offence against the State."[156]

The British ambassador in Berlin reported that Churchill's attacks on Hitler were widely covered in German newspapers, some of which "point out that the speech has special importance in view of Mr. Churchill's almost certain inclusion in the next Cabinet." There was no such certainty, of course, but throughout the thirties Winston seemed more formidable abroad than in England — a consequence, perhaps, of his perception and his eloquence. On October 30 Ralph Wigram minuted: "Mr. Churchill is making himself very unpopular in Germany," and the ambassador reported that the tone of Winston's piece "is much resented here." Desmond Morton, however, cabled Chartwell that "Germany did not like it — but resentfully admires it in private. It is right that Germany should realize that we are not all lulled into weak-livered complacency."[157]

Hitler read a translation of the *Strand* piece. According to Wigram's sources, he all but flung himself on the carpet and drummed his heels on the floor. Libels against the Reich's head of state, the Wilhelmstrasse officially warned the British embassy in Berlin, were "intolerable." Wigram sent the protest to Churchill, including the infuriated Führer's question to Britain's ambassador: "What is to be the fate of the Anglo-German Naval Agreement if the writer of this article is to be the Minister of the British Navy?" When this reached Wigram he wrote in the margin: "I don't know what exactly this means: but if Churchill knew that Hitler had said this" — as though Winston wouldn't know, and within hours — "he might well say that it was only another proof of the necessity of strong armaments — otherwise we shall have Germans telling us who shall & shall not be in office in this country."[158]

An unexpected consequence of this was a clumsy Nazi attempt to discredit Churchill in his own constituency. Broadcasts by the London correspondent for *Völkischer Beobachter* identified him as "an unscrupulous political intriguer," who, unless HMG repudiated him, might become a threat to world peace. His aunt Leonie Leslie wrote him: "Oh Winston! What a grand speech and *how* I am enjoying the abuse from Germany which I hear on the wireless." The British naval attaché in Berlin wrote him from Warsaw: "I had to wait until I left Germany to write & say how wonderful I thought your speech — as the Germans are so annoyed with you for telling the truth that no letters addressed to you would ever have got out of the country." He reminded Winston of a conversation between them in the spring of 1933 and commented: "I have never forgotten what you said then about the Nazis. Two & a half years in Berlin has shown everything you said then is true today. The Germans have only learnt one thing from the War —& that is *never* to go to war again until they are absolutely ready, & certain, of victory. No chances next time! The Germans fear, & I hope, you WILL be 1st Lord — or Minister of Defence! Please don't give me away."[159]

The Nazi reaction to Churchill's speeches and writings during the 1935 election campaign mirrored the future. Indeed, over the years one of the most persuasive witnesses to Churchill's effectiveness abroad was Adolf Hitler. In speeches to his people he said: "If there is any man in the world who is authorized to speak for Germany, then I am that man and no one else. . . . The German regime is entirely a matter for the German people and I will never allow any such foreign schoolmasters or governesses to interfere with it." When Winston spoke of the fate of Austria and Czechoslovakia, two democracies which lay helpless in Hitler's path, Hitler cried: "I can only ask — Good Lord [*du meine Güte*]! After all, what is a democracy? Who defines it? Has the Almighty perhaps handed the key to democracy to such people as Churchill? I am only the advocate of Germany. I am not like Churchill, and God knows what oppositionists, who style themselves advocates of the world. If Churchill says: 'How is it that a Head of State can cross swords with a British parliamentarian?' I must say: 'Churchill, feel yourself honored.' " And: "Churchill said the German regime should be destroyed by forces within Germany. . . . I can assure this gentleman, who appears to live on the moon, that forces opposed to the regime do not exist in Germany. There is only one force — the National Socialist movement and its leadership and armed forces. I cannot stop this man from rising to high office, but I can assure you that I will prevent him from destroying Germany." And: "If Churchill came to power in Great Britain instead of Mr. Chamberlain we know it would be his aim to unleash immediately a world war against Germany. He makes no secret of it." And: "I assume it is his desire to steal our weapons and to bring about again our fate of 1918. I can tell Churchill that it happened only once and that it will not happen again!"[160]

On Thursday, November 14, Britain voted. By evening it was clear that the Conservatives, winning 432 seats, had retained their overwhelming majority in the House of Commons. Labour had won 154 seats, a gain; the

Liberals 21, a loss. Churchill was among the few Conservatives actually to increase his plurality; he polled over 10,000 votes more than his two opponents combined. That evening he dropped by Albert Hall to watch the results posted. Once the outcome was certain, he took a cab to Stornoway House, where Lord Beaverbrook was throwing a victory party. Beaverbrook's first words to Churchill were: "Well, you're finished now. Baldwin has so good a majority that he will be able to do without you." Twelve years later, in an unpublished note, Winston wrote: "I was taken aback and offended by this." A "man like Mr. Baldwin," he had believed, "would not be influenced . . . about my joining the Government by the size of his majority."[161]

When he had resigned from Baldwin's shadow cabinet nearly five years earlier, Churchill had told Vansittart: "I have cheerfully and gladly put out of my mind all idea of public office." Van knew that was untrue. "Without office he was miserable," he wrote, "although I could never understand why. The big boy without a bauble had at his command every other gift in the world, and much attention if small assent. He should have been radiantly happy as the greatest of his time, probably of all time." Van had pointed out to him that should he become one of the cabinet's twenty-two ministers, the only consequence would be an increase in his frustration. Churchill believed the government thought well of him. Vansittart knew he was wrong: "Right and Left he was in bad odor for his gloomings. The Left called him 'the darling of the die-hards,' who proved too faint-hearted to back him." And the right regarded him a renegade. "The pity was great" for both Winston and himself, Van recalls, "for a lone voice can accomplish nothing, and in the last analysis a British public servant can do little to serve the State. We both pegged away, he with orations, I with comments and memoranda."[162]

In June, when Baldwin moved into No. 10, he had appointed Hoare as Simon's successor at the FO and replaced Londonderry with the abler Sir Philip Cunliffe-Lister, an admirer of Churchill. The new air minister's greatest achievements were to be his promotion of new fighter planes: the Hawker Hurricane, first tested five months after he took office, and the Spitfire, whose prototype flew four months later. In the House Winston had continued what he later described as his "severe though friendly" criticism of the government. He supported the government's position, in Geneva and elsewhere, with increasing frequency. "It is a terrific decree in life," George Meredith wrote, "that they must act who would prevail." A backbencher could not act. Vansittart notwithstanding, a minister could. In previous cabinets Churchill had found that he could often sway decisions. As his desire for a seat on the Treasury Bench grew, so did the frequency with which he praised Baldwin in public. In October he had written him:

"If yr power is great, so also are yr burdens — and yr opportunities. I think you ought to go to the country at the earliest possible moment, & I hope you will do so. . . . I will abide with you in this election, & do what little I can to help in the most serviceable way." It is impossible to miss the hunger in these last words.[163]

This, then, was how matters stood when Beaverbrook told Churchill that Baldwin didn't need him. Six months had passed since Winston had last spoken disparagingly of the P.M. His ministerial experience surpassed that of any other man in the House save Lloyd George. Despite slighting references to his age (in May a Tory MP had patronized him: "Although one hates to criticise anyone in the evening of his days . . .") he was at the height of his powers. And he yearned for office. This longing was inexplicable to Vansittart, but Winston found no pleasure in playing the independent critic. His imagination, his energy, and his capacities could be best expressed only when he occupied a seat of power. He hoped to be given the Admiralty but would take what he could get. Therefore he left London for Chartwell and awaited a call from Baldwin.[164]

It never came.

He remained near the telephone for six suspenseful days, and then, abandoning hope, sank into one of his deepest depressions, unable even to paint. Actually, Baldwin had toyed with the idea of bringing him into the government earlier, when he had reshuffled the cabinet after taking over as P.M. Dawson had talked him out of it, arguing that senior members of the party would be resentful and, moreover, that Churchill would be "a disruptive force, especially since foreign relations and defense will be uppermost."[165]

Ironically, Churchill's greatest handicap among his fellow Tories is now seen as a source of his splendor. Far more suspicion and disfavor in the party were aroused by the strength and coherence of his convictions than by his stinging phrases in the House or his undisguised lust for office. "No strongly centralized, political organization," Isaiah Berlin noted, "feels altogether happy with individuals who combine independence, a free imagination, and a formidable strength of character with stubborn faith and a single-minded, unchanging view of the public and private good."[166]

After the November 14 landslide, other Conservatives joined *The Times* editor in urging Baldwin to keep Churchill out. Nancy Astor wrote him: "Don't put Winston in the Government — it will mean war at home and abroad. I know the depths of Winston's disloyalty — and you can't think how he is distrusted by *all* the electors of the country." Three days after the election Thomas Jones wrote in his diary: "Winston will be kept out, I think." Later in the day, when the decision had been made, he noted with relief that the government had "kept clear of Winston's enthusiasm for ships and guns."[167]

To Jones, Baldwin said: "One of these days I'll make a few casual remarks about Winston. . . . I've got it all ready. I am going to say that when Winston was born lots of fairies swooped down on his cradle with gifts — imagination, eloquence, industry, ability, and then came a fairy who said 'No one person has a right to so many gifts,' picked him up and gave him such a shake and twist that with all these gifts he was denied judgment and wisdom. And that is why we delight to listen to him in the House but do not take his advice."[168]

But no fairy tale was responsible for Churchill's disappointment. Baldwin was swayed by other, less enchanting motives. One was recrimination. The Dear Vicar's geniality was legendary, but he would have been masochistic not to nurse the wounds Winston had inflicted on him in the past. In one of Baldwin's less affable moments he snapped: "Winston is part of the flotsam and jetsam of political life thrown up on the beach." Those around him agreed. Neville Chamberlain came close to the truth when, arguing against giving Churchill a ministry, he commented that his powers of persuasion might convince the cabinet to increase rearmament, which would have pressed the Treasury to produce funds. The Depression was still a grave problem. The City and the Bank of England were wedded to stable prices and a stable pound. Deficits were considered wicked, except in wartime, and deplorable even then. As A. J. P. Taylor puts it: "The secret of Pandora's box which Schacht had opened in Germany and which the American New Deal had also revealed, was still unknown to the [British] Government." Taylor believes that the MacDonald, Baldwin, and Chamberlain administrations "feared to offend economic principles even more than to offend Hitler."[169]

Apprehension over the reaction in Berlin was a factor, though Churchill's conclusion was that Baldwin had denied him office to pay "some of his debt to the pacifist deputation which he had received in the last days of the election." The truth was more ignoble. It hadn't occurred to Winston that a British prime minister, in selecting his cabinet, would bow to German sensitivities. He was wrong. According to Lady Longford, in considering a cabinet reshuffle, "Baldwin felt less inclined than ever to annoy Hitler by including the bellicose Churchill." Years later Boothby said: "Many people asked why Mr. Churchill, who had held the offices of first lord of the Admiralty, secretary of state for war, secretary of state for air, and minister of munitions, had not been appointed. The answer is quite simple. He would have roused, disturbed, and rearmed the country."[170]

Winston felt he had to leave England for at least six weeks. Afterward he wrote that he had "agreeable consolations. I set out with my paintbox for more genial climes without waiting for the meeting of Parliament."[171] Like all Churchillian holidays, this one would be a working vacation, largely devoted to writing the third volume of his Marlborough biography.

It seemed to be an excellent time for a Conservative member of Parliament to be absent from London. The situation in northeastern Africa had become critical; Italian troops massed in the horn of East Africa, on the frontiers of the Italian Somaliland, had invaded Ethiopia, or Abyssinia, as it was called then, undeterred by a commitment Sam Hoare had made to the League of Nations in Geneva. Slapping the lectern with the flat of his hand, the foreign secretary had declared: "The League stands, and my country stands with it for . . . steady and collective resistance to all acts of unprovoked aggression!" The press and the overwhelming majority of league delegates had agreed with Belgium's revered Paul Hymans: "The British have decided to stop Mussolini even if that means using force."[172] But they hadn't. In Geneva, Hoare, schooled at Harrow and Oxford, the very model of an English gentleman, had sown the seeds, not of resolve, but of hypocrisy.

PART TWO

REEF

S URVEYORS establishing landmarks work from several known reference points, and those who wish to view the past in perspective may adopt a similar technique. In the mid-1930s Europe's anticipation of the future began its swing from the unthinkability of war to the thinkability of it to the fatalistic acceptance of its inevitability. The omens were unmistakable. In March 1935 Hitler had announced that Germany was rearming; eleven days after Baldwin replaced MacDonald as prime minister in June the calamitous Anglo-German Naval Agreement was signed; and, after the Tory landslide in November, the redemption of Hoare's vow came due. Dead ahead lay the three pivotal crises: Ethiopia, the Rhineland, and Spain.

Using a boundary dispute as an excuse, Italy had begun its east African buildup in February 1935. Emperor Haile Selassie withdrew his troops twenty miles behind his frontier to avoid the kind of incident Mussolini was seeking, but the Duce would not be denied; he declared that he intended to use every weapon at hand, including poison gas, which had been outlawed by international convention. Hoare's warning speech in Geneva was delivered on September 11, a month before the fighting began. The historian of the league wrote that "it would be difficult to exaggerate the effect of his electrifying address, putting Mussolini on notice."[1]

It was Hoare's finest hour, though he hadn't meant it to be; to the end of his life he insisted that the world had simply misunderstood him, he hadn't intended to sound resolute. The fact is that he had been carried away by his own rhetoric. It had been his intention to suggest obliquely that if the league should censure any rupture of the Ethiopian frontier, invoking mild sanctions against Italy, the Duce might be bluffed into backing off. This, in Hoare's words, would infuse "new life" into the league's "crippled body." But bluffs work only if the other side thinks them real. And Italian intelligence agents, after burgling the British embassy in Rome, knew Britain had no intention of using force — had, in fact, no force available to use. Royal Navy ships routinely cruised the Mediterranean, but none carried ammunition. Therefore Mussolini felt quite safe when, as it was reported to Hoare, he appeared on his balcony, jutted his jaw to the cheers of the throng below, and cried that Britain was trying to "rob" Italians of "a place in the sun."[2]

Churchill's steady eye was still fixed on Nazi Germany. England and France needed allies, and the best possible solution to that problem was a strong, united League of Nations. Compared with Hitler's Reich, he told Parliament, Ethiopia was "a very small matter." Nevertheless, he had read with pride that the foreign secretary had taken a stand for the independence of the ancient mountain kingdom confronting Italian invasion. It was, he said, a matter of honor. The League of Nations was "fighting for its life. Probably it is fighting for all our lives. But it is fighting." He believed that the league "has passed from shadow into substance, from theory into practice, from rhetoric into reality. We see a structure always majestic, but hitherto shadowy, which is now being clothed with life and power, and endowed with coherent thought and concerted action. We begin to feel the beatings of a pulse which may, we hope, some day . . . restore a greater measure of health and strength to the whole world."[3]

Actually, he was troubled. His feelings about the issue were far more ambivalent than he publicly acknowledged. In the last war the Allies had barely beaten the Germans with Italy on their side. Backing the league made sense if all the member nations observed its covenant. If they didn't, Britain's stand would prove disastrous, for Italy would be alienated. And Ethiopia was not, in his view, a moral issue. Like most men of his generation, he regarded blacks as an inferior race. In Cuba, fresh out of Sandhurst, he had written that he distrusted "the negro element among the insurgents." He never outgrew this prejudice. Late in life he was asked whether he had seen the film *Carmen Jones*. He had walked out on it, he replied, because he didn't like "blackamoors."[4]

Berlin, not Rome, remained the enemy capital. To him Ethiopia was a "wild land of tyranny, slavery, and tribal war." He later wrote: "In the fearful struggle against rearming Nazi Germany which I could feel approaching . . . I was most reluctant to see Italy estranged, and even driven into the opposite camp." Moreover, Britain and France were in an awkward position. Arguably they were Italy's accomplices, because in April at Stresa they had not done what they ought to have done. At the end of the conference Mussolini had made a point of excluding Africa from the mutual agreement to abstain from aggression. The Allied diplomats decided not to argue the point. In Churchill's words, "Everyone was so anxious for Mussolini's support in dealing with Germany that it was felt undesirable at that moment to warn him off Abyssinia, which would obviously have very much annoyed him."[5]

Now they were facing the consequences. On August 21, when east Africa's rainy season was still holding Italian troops in check, Hoare and Eden, now minister for League of Nations affairs, had approached Winston for his advice. According to Hoare's record of their talk, Churchill had "showed himself deeply incensed at the Italian action," had "urged reinforcement of Britain's Mediterranean Fleet," and, above all, had stressed the need for "collective" action — not in the service of the league's ideals, but because of his "main interest in the League as a defence against Hitler." Churchill explained, noted Hoare, that "if the League now collapsed in ignominy," it would mean "the destruction of the bond that unites British and French policy and of the instrument that might in the future be chiefly effective as a deterrent to German aggression."[6]

He said as much in Parliament, supporting Hoare's pledge because the integrity of the league was at stake, but adding that he could not envisage Haile Selassie in the role of martyr. "No one," he said, "can keep up the pretense that Abyssinia is a fit, worthy, and equal member of a league of civilized nations." The sanctity of the League Covenant was still paramount, however; he proposed that the British government leave no doubt in Mussolini's mind that England was prepared to observe the covenant "even to the point of war."[7]

The issue was moot and still is. As Telford Taylor writes: "In retrospect, it seems that the wisest course, if bold, would have been to play the game of collective security to the hilt and bring Mussolini down, even if it meant a war, in which Italy would have had no allies. But benefit might also have been derived from a more cautious, if cynical, policy of keeping the Duce on the side of the angels in Europe by allowing him a bit of deviltry in Africa."[8]

As it happened, neither course had been given a chance. In "The Hollow Men" T. S. Eliot had written:

> *Between the idea*
> *And the reality . . .*
> *Falls the shadow.*

Rome's new legions struck southward from Eritrea on October 3, 1935, erupting across the frontier in a festive mood, trumpets blaring and huge battle flags rippling overhead. But even before they could reach Haile Selassie's troops the banners were discarded, the trumpets mute, and the Duce's gladiators bogged down in the wild, pathless terrain. Then the African defenders, attacking to drive them back, proved unexpectedly fierce. Evelyn Waugh described the Italian fighting, if that is the word for it, in his satirical *Scoop*. But events in the diplomatic arena were even more absurd. The British delegation in Geneva rallied the support of fifty nations in condemning Italy as the aggressor. Asked how far he would go in backing the covenant, Churchill replied, "The whole way with the whole lot."[9]

The league voted overwhelmingly to impose economic sanctions upon the Italians, but Baldwin's list of sanctions suggested that the prime minister had developed a bizarre taste for black humor. Among the items denied to the aggressor were camels, mules, donkeys, and aluminum — a metal so available in Italy that it constituted one of the country's chief exports. Unmentioned were the raw materials essential to the waging of war: steel, iron, coal, and, most remarkably, oil. Had they been deprived of petroleum, Mussolini's mechanized columns would have vanished in the ravines and chasms separating them from the Ethiopian capital, Addis Ababa. Indeed, had Baldwin been serious, he could have achieved an even quicker end to the Italian offensive by simply closing the Suez Canal to the Duce. It was suggested. Eden and his colleagues in Geneva answered that if Mussolini's patience were tried he might lose his temper and spread the war to the Continent, or launch a "mad dog" assault on His Majesty's Mediterranean Fleet.

This opéra bouffe gained in lunacy as it went along. Ice skating was Hoare's passion. En route to Switzerland, and accompanied by Vansittart, he broke his journey on Saturday, December 7, to confer with France's premier, Pierre Laval. Together they concocted a plan which would end the Ethiopian war by ceding two-thirds of the country to Italy — including vast tracts she could never win by force of arms — leaving Haile Selassie with the remainder of his territory and a corridor through Italian territory to the Red Sea. If Mussolini balked, the emperor would be given a different corridor running through the adjoining colonies of Britain or France. Elated, Hoare entrained for the Swiss village of Zuoz, laced on his skates, glided across the frozen lake, and fell, breaking his nose. Churchill, upon learning of the cynical intrigue in Paris, growled, "Too bad it wasn't his neck."[10]

The conspirators had agreed to keep their scheme secret until their governments had approved of it, but *Paris-Soir* acquired the complete text before Hoare even reached Zuoz, and on Monday the details were on every front page in the world. Churchill was in Majorca. Friends persuaded him that he was lucky to be abroad, so he decided to stay outside Barcelona, painting and writing in the serene countryside. There was no serenity in England; in the House a Labourite proposed that a new sign be erected over the league portals: "Abandon half, all ye who enter here — half your territory, half your prestige." In a letter to *The Times*, Harold Macmillan declared that were the Hoare-Laval plan approved, Britain would be party to a conspiracy "to undermine the very structure which a few weeks ago the nation authorized us to underpin. I have never attended the funeral of a murdered man, but I take it that at such a ceremony some distinction is made between the mourners and the assassins."[11]

The Hoare-Laval scheme, a loser from the beginning, now became an albatross. Mussolini, Haile Selassie, Baldwin, and Laval's cabinet all denounced it. On December 17 Randolph sent his father a full account. Relations between the two were strained — and would soon be strained further — but Churchill had found his son a resourceful reporter. Randolph wrote that "Baldwin, Hoare, and Vansittart" had "planned this shameful surrender," and "are extraordinarily confident of the outcome." Outraged public opinion on the other side of the Channel forced Laval from office, and the day after Randolph's report the British cabinet voted overwhelmingly — Neville Chamberlain was the sole exception — to demand Hoare's resignation. Desmond Morton wrote to Churchill: "Baldwin has completely lost every shred of confidence. He is believed to have sacrificed his friend, not because that friend made an error in method, but because he believed it was the only hope of saving his own skin."[12]

In hindsight it seems that Churchill's wisest course would have been to reject his friends' advice and return to London the moment the scandal broke. But he still believed his chances of reaching office were greater if he kept his sword sheathed and let others attack the prime minister. Indeed, from October 1935 to March 1936 he neither wrote nor spoke a single word criticizing the prime minister in public. Even his memoirs are bland on the Hoare-Laval deal; he merely comments that Vansittart, preoccupied with the Nazi menace, wanted to strengthen the Anglo-French entente "with Italy in their rear a friend and not a foe."[13]

Perhaps the most perceptive glimpse of Churchill during the Ethiopian crisis is provided by Vincent Sheean, the American foreign correspondent. Sheean, like Churchill, Lloyd George, the writer Michael Arlen — and, later, the Duke and Duchess of Windsor — was a friend of Maxine Elliott, a rich retired actress whose white, terraced villa in Cannes, the Château de l'Horizon, offered exotic asylum to celebrities.

"Churchill first became visible to me," Sheean wrote, "in a red bathrobe over bathing trunks; he wore a large, flopping straw hat, and slippers and a cherubic grin." He was defensive on the Ethiopia issue, but never evasive. When an elegant Frenchwoman pointed out that the British Empire had been built by the sort of small wars Italy was now waging, Winston smiled benevolently and said: "Ah, but you see, all that belongs to the unregenerate past, is locked away in the limbo of the old, the wicked days. The world progresses." That, he said, explained the purpose of the

League of Nations. Winston declared that the Duce was "making a most dangerous and foolhardy attack upon the whole established structure." The results were "quite incalculable. Who is to say what will come of it in a year, or two, or three? With Germany arming at breakneck speed, England lost in a pacifist dream, France corrupt and torn by dissension, America remote and indifferent — Madame, my dear lady, do you not tremble for your children?"[14]

In such company he never criticized His Majesty's Government, but his letters are full of it. After four days with Lloyd George at the Hotel Mamounia in Marrakech, he wrote Clementine that Britain was "getting into the most terrible position, involved definitely by honour & by contract in almost any quarrel that can break out in Europe" with her "defences neglected" and the cabinet "less capable a machine for conducting affairs that I have ever seen." He believed that the "Baldwin-MacDonald regime has hit this country very hard indeed, and may well be the end of its glories."[15]

Clemmie replied that "I really would not like you to serve under Baldwin, unless he really gave you a great deal of power and you were able to inspire and vilify the Government." The political situation at home, she wrote, was "depressing." She saw, as he did not, how powerful his position would be if, when his hour struck, he were free of any tainted association with the appeasers. Afterward he agreed, writing of his years in the wilderness: "Now one can see how lucky I was. Over me beat the invisible wings." Anthony Eden, less fortunate, emerged slightly stained. He had nearly resigned when he learned of the Hoare-Laval agreement, but Baldwin persuaded him to remain and then appointed him foreign secretary. Eden was only thirty-eight. He looked like a man of the future. But Churchill thought him a poor choice. He wrote home: "I expect the greatness of his office will find him out."[16]

It was Eden, in his new role, who had to tell the House that what Austen Chamberlain had described as the Ethiopian "madness" was over. It wasn't quite; but clearly the old kingdom was doomed to become an Italian colony. Lloyd George rose in a terrible fury. He said: "I have never before heard a British Minister . . . come down to the House of Commons and say that Britain was beaten . . . and that we must abandon an enterprise we had taken in hand." He pointed at the front bench. "Tonight we have had the cowardly surrender, and there are the cowards."[17]

In itself, the seven-month Ethiopian war was of little consequence. But the implications of the Hoare-Laval fiasco were far-reaching. By the time Haile Selassie's capital fell, the League of Nations had been destroyed as a force for peace and a referee of international disputes. At the same time, British hopes for an Anglo-Italian alliance, based on Mussolini's determination to keep Austria free of Nazi rule, had vanished in the quarreling between London and Rome. Neville Chamberlain, Baldwin's designated successor, had written off collective security as a bad debt. The Stresa Front, the Duce's handiwork, lay in ruins, and though he himself was to blame, he resigned from the league in a blind rage and sent his son-in-law and foreign minister, Count Galeazzo Ciano, to Hitler's Berghof retreat on the Obersalzberg, overlooking the resort town of Berchtesgaden. Informal discussions there led to serious talks in Berlin. The climax came in a fateful speech by Mussolini, delivered in Milan's Piazza del Duomo on November 1, 1936. In it he added a phrase to history, declaring, "The Berlin conversations have resulted in an understanding between our two countries. . . . This Rome-Berlin line is not a diaphragm but rather an axis around which can revolve all those European states with a will to collaboration and peace." "Rome-Berlin Axis" would be on front pages all over the world for the next seven years. Thus Germany, though uninvolved throughout, was the one beneficiary of the Ethiopian travesty. The naval treaty with Britain had been Hitler's first giant step in freeing his country from the diplomatic quarantine imposed on it after he had violated treaties bearing the signatures of Germany's leaders. Now two clumsy Allied politicians had freed him of that odium. In foreign chancelleries, at least, the Reich was once more respected as a great power.[18]

Today Hoare's conspiracy with Laval would mean the destruction of his political career. But fifty years ago members of the old boy network could survive almost any disgrace. Hoare's career was switched to a siding, but Baldwin had already marked him down as the next first lord of the Admiralty, and subsequently he served as home secretary, lord privy seal, secretary for air, and ambassador to Spain, after which he moved over to the House of Lords as Viscount Templewood. The great mass of the British people had a short memory and paid little attention to upper-class quid pro quo. In 1935 Baldwin merely advised Hoare to lie low for the present. The future viscount understood; he knew the rules; he must stiffen his lip and do his penance when old friends declined to be seen with him just now.

He was, therefore, startled to receive a graceful letter, bearing a Morocco postmark, from Winston Churchill. Winston wrote "to congratulate you on the dignity of yr speech of resignation, & to tell you how vy sorry I am at what has happened. . . . After so much work & worry I daresay the breathing space will be welcome." Like the hypochondriac who always arrives at the bedside of the sick, Winston rarely failed to provide consolation for political casualties. But Hoare was uncomforted. That same day he had been subjected to the unkindest cut of all — and from his sovereign at that. Following the timeless custom, he had resigned his office by riding to Buckingham Palace and surrendering his seals of office to

King George V. The King said: "Do you know what they're all saying? No more coals to Newcastle, no more Hoares to Paris!" When Eden arrived to kiss hands and claim the seals, the monarch repeated his royal jest and added that he had been puzzled by Hoare's response. "You know," he said, "the fellow didn't even laugh."[19]

🦁　🦁

Churchill had ended his letter to Hoare: "We are moving into a year of measureless perils." The first blow of 1936 was the death of the King, at Sandringham, in January. Winston was still in Morocco when he learned of it from a *News of the World* cable, which offered him £1,000 — three times an MP's annual salary — to write a tribute to George V. He dictated the piece to Mrs. Pearman on a train between Tangier and Marrakech and dispatched it only three days after the new monarch, Edward VIII, had begun his reign. Winston had known Edward for twenty-five years, and to his "joyous and gay" memories of their long association, as he now wrote him, there was also the "hope that Your Majesty's name will shine in history as the bravest and best beloved of all the sovereigns who had worn the island Crown."[20]

Within hours of his return to London he was engulfed in politics. Since Hitler's early days in power, Churchill had been urging Baldwin to create a new cabinet post, a minister of defense who would coordinate all three services. Support for the office had been growing in Parliament ever since, and now Baldwin agreed. But who would he name? Most MPs didn't even ask; the appointment of Churchill was assumed. Austen Chamberlain wrote his sister: "In my view there is only one man who by his studies, and special abilities, and aptitudes, is marked for it, and that man is Winston Churchill." At one time or another Churchill had borne ministerial responsibility for the War Office, the Admiralty, and the RAF. The previous November, when he had been excluded from the post-election cabinet shake-up, Harold Nicolson had written in his diary: "Clemmie tells me that Winston has not yet been approached. It looks as if he were going to be left out till February." It was February now. H. A. Gwynne of the *Morning Post,* a harsh critic of Churchill for over twenty years, nevertheless took the matter as "settled." Harold Macmillan and Lord Castlereagh were openly backing him, and *Cavalcade* magazine reported that even "left-wing Conservatives, who were hostile to Winston over the India question, now take the line that if there must be a defence minister, Winston Churchill is the man." Anthony Crossley, a young Conservative MP, parodied the arguments against Churchill's appointment:

> *But Winston were worst, with his logic accursed*
> *For he'll scorn our impartial endeavour.*
> *He'll make up his mind, right or wrong, with the first,*
> *And how shall we temporise ever?*
> *Let's have soldier or sailor or peer or civilian,*
> *Whatever his faults, so they not be Churchillian.*[21]

The inner circle around Baldwin — the members, so to speak, of the Dear Vicar's congregation — were not amused. They were thinking along other lines. Secretary to the Cabinet Hankey wanted a "sound man," someone who "will work and not upset the psychology of the whole machine." Warren Fisher, permanent under secretary of the Treasury, thought that the minister "should be a disinterested type of man, with no axe to grind or desire to make a place for himself" — a qualification which would have ruled out every gifted man in the House. Hoare, untouched by the letter which had wished him well in his dark hour, sang Churchill's dispraises with the prime minister and emerged to write Neville Chamberlain jubilantly: "On no account would he [Baldwin] contemplate the possibility of Winston in the Cabinet for several obvious reasons, but chiefly for the risk that would be involved by having him in the Cabinet when the question of his (S.B.'s) successor became imminent." News of this reached Chartwell. Sir Roger Keyes wrote Churchill that, encountering Baldwin in one of Westminster's halls, he had told him that Churchill "would be a very good appointment both in your interests and those of the Country." "I cannot only think of my interests," Baldwin remarked, turning away. "I have to think of the smooth working of the machine." The two minds — one preoccupied with the country, the other with the party machine — could not meet.[22]

Churchill, at Chartwell, remained on tenterhooks. He wrote Clemmie on February 21: "There is no change in the uncertainty about my affairs. Evidently B. desires above all things to avoid bringing me in. This I must now recognize. But his own position is much shaken, & the storm clouds gather." She replied: "My darling, Baldwin must be mad not to ask you to help him. Perhaps it is a case of 'Those whom the Gods wish to destroy. . . .' " Ten days later he wrote her: "The Defence business is at its height. Baldwin is still undecided. . . . Now this morning the DT [*Daily Telegraph*] comes out as the enclosed, wh is the most positive statement yet & the latest — & from a normally well-informed quarter. Anyhow I seem to be still *en jeu*."[23]

Baldwin didn't want Churchill, but since the Ethiopian debacle his prestige had dwindled, and support for Winston was growing in the House and in Fleet Street. It was at this moment, when events hung in a delicate balance, that Winston was sandbagged by his impetuous son. Churchill had a premonition of disaster from this quarter. On the day after Christmas he had written Randolph from Rabat: "It would in my belief be vy injurious to me at this junction if you publish articles attacking the motives & character of Ministers, especially Baldwin & Eden. I hope therefore you will make certain this does not happen. If not, I shall not be able to feel confidence in yr loyalty & affection for me."[24]

Randolph honored his father's request; he wrote no pieces critical of anyone else in the government. He did something worse. He announced that he would stand for Parliament, running against the national government's incumbent — Ramsay MacDonald's son Malcolm, a member of Baldwin's cabinet. Winston wrote Clemmie that Randolph had "put a spoke in my wheel." Later he wrote her: "You will see how unfortunate and inconvenient such a fight is to me. 'Churchill v MacDonald.' " It was worse: Lord Rothermere, the press lord, had assigned Baldwin's son Oliver "to write up Randolph, which he is apparently ready to do, and to write down Malcolm. . . . So we shall have Ramsay's son, Baldwin's son, and my son — all mauling each other in this remote constituency." Churchill was apprehensive that the prime minister might interpret Randolph's candidacy "as a definite declaration of war by me." Then he surmised that no other interpretation was possible: "I should think that any question of my joining the Government was closed by the hostility which Randolph's campaign must excite." Yet he still hoped for a post.[25]

Winston did not appear in Scotland to speak for his son. He wanted to; Brendan Bracken advised against it. They compromised by agreeing that Churchill should release a brief statement to the press, concluding with the mild observation that with "parliamentary government under grievous challenge in the present age . . . undue pressure should not be put by the Central Government upon a free choice of the constituency." That fell far short of a ringing endorsement, but the assumption that he was behind his son's challenge remained. *The Times* as much as said so. Winston wrote the proprietor of the paper that he was "surprised to read in the leading article of Saturday's 'Times' on the Ross and Cromarty by election, an insinuation that I had prompted my Son's candidature. As a matter of fact, I strongly advised him to have nothing to do with it. Naturally, as a Father, I cannot watch his fight . . . without sympathy; but I am taking no part in it. . . . In these circumstances the innuendo of your leading article is neither true nor fair."[26]

But the skeptics included the Scots voters, who, when they went to the polls, turned the contest into a rout. Malcolm MacDonald's victory was extraordinary. Of the 17,343 votes cast, 2,427 — less than 14 percent —

were for Randolph. Boothby wrote Winston that while he was "sorry," he believed that "a little chastening at this particular juncture will not necessarily be to his ultimate disadvantage." There was, Boothby continued, "more sympathy & friendly feeling" for Randolph "than he suspects. But, my God, you don't challenge that machine with impunity." The *Edinburgh Evening News* wrote bitingly: "By emphasizing the unpopularity of the Churchillians' attitude, the decisive defeat of Mr Randolph Churchill in Ross and Cromarty seems to be regarded as another nail in the political coffin of Mr Winston Churchill, either as a candidate for the Admiralty or Cabinet Minister charged with the coordination of Defence Services." Friends visiting Chartwell were careful to avoid any mention of the by-election, though they could see Winston's hurt, a wound sharper than any inflictable by a serpent's tooth.[27]

The prime minister thought Winston lacked judgment. Yet on his instructions, the cabinet was taking the first of the steps Churchill had demanded. On March 3, the government published a new Defence White Paper, revealing plans to build an aircraft carrier, two new battleships, and five battle cruisers; recruit six thousand Royal Navy ratings; raise four motorized infantry battalions; modernize antiaircraft defense and field artillery; and build 224 more Spitfires and Hurricanes. Fleet Street called it a bid for carte blanche, and indeed the White Paper itself declared: "Any attempt to estimate the total cost of the measures would be premature."[28]

Backbenchers were startled. It seemed hardly possible that such a program could get past the Exchequer without Neville's approval. Nor had it. He had suggested the vague wording, reasoning that "it would probably be advisable to avoid figures which could be added up to a larger amount than public opinion is expecting." The appropriation endorsed by the cabinet was £400 million, to be spread over the next five years. Since Nazi Germany was spending over twice that much on arms every year, the outlay which troubled Chamberlain seems rather less than exorbitant. It was in fact quite inadequate; RAF strength would rise from 1,512 front-line aircraft to only 1,736. To Churchill a strong England was one capable of defending itself. To Chamberlain it meant balanced budgets. "The British government," in the words of A. J. P. Taylor, "still lived in the psychological atmosphere of 1931: more terrified of a flight from the pound than of defeat in war. . . . The confidence of the City of London came first; armaments came second." Furthermore, the program outlined in the White Paper specified that it must be carried out "without impeding the course of normal trade." In other words, Britain would observe business as usual.[29]

Although the step was in the right direction, Churchill told Parliament on March 10, it was far too short. He could not feel that the new policy "has done full justice to the anxiety which the House feels about the condition of our national defences." Money was irrelevant and should not even be a consideration: "When things are left as late as this, no high economy is possible. That is the part of the price nations pay for being caught short." Churchill had been startled to read in the press, and even to hear remarks in the House smoking room, "giving a general impression that we are overhauling Germany now. . . . The contrary is true. All this year and probably for many months next year Germany will be outstripping us more and more." It would "not be possible for us to overtake Germany and achieve air parity, as was so solemnly promised," until the Germans reached a saturation point and decided to end expansion of the Luftwaffe. Then England could bridge the gap. "But this day will be fixed by Germany, and not by us, whatever we do." He believed that if London and Paris acted promptly, as he later wrote, there was "still time for an assertion of collective security." But "virtuous motives, trammelled by inertia and timidity, are no match for armed and resolute wickedness. A sincere love of peace is no excuse for muddling hundreds of millions of humble folk into total war. The cheers of weak, well-meaning assemblies soon cease to echo, and their votes soon cease to count. Doom marches on."[30]

※   ※

Doom appears in many forms, but none more naked than fixed bayonets. Even as Labour and Liberal pacifists were fuming that Baldwin, prodded by the warmonger Churchill, was returning England to its militant, imperialist past, genuine militarism was forming ranks on a riverbank 375 miles to the east. On the moonbright Rhine it was Friday, March 6, 1936. Night was thickening. In London's Savoy ballroom that evening, couples were dancing to the popular American tune "Red Sails in the Sunset." Across the Atlantic, where it was still afternoon, teenagers leaving school were arguing over the Lucky Strike Hit Parade's ranking of "In the Chapel by the Moonlight," "The Way You Look Tonight," and "Pennies from Heaven." In Atlanta Margaret Mitchell, an obscure newspaperwoman, was correcting proof for her first novel — she had named her heroine Pansy and titled the book *Tomorrow Is Another Day*, but her editor had changed them to Scarlett and *Gone with the Wind*. Meanwhile, for the first time since 1918, the hobnailed boots of German soldiers would march. Adolf Hitler's first invasion would begin at daybreak.

After the failure of his Austrian coup two years earlier, the Führer had been looking for a quick military victory elsewhere, and increasingly he had found himself looking westward, toward the Rhineland. Although it was the French who had christened this seventeen-year-old state *la région zone démilitaire,* it remained a part of the Reich, inhabited by Germans and including within its borders some of their greatest cities — Cologne, Aachen, Frankfurt, and Düsseldorf — industrial hubs separated by lovely vineyards producing some of the world's finest wines. Here the Versailles peacemakers had carved out, from land on both banks of the Rhine, a strip of territory thirty-one miles wide. French troops had occupied the zone after the war but left early at British urging. Under the treaty, Germany was forbidden to billet troops or build fortifications there. The buffer had been designed to provide France and Belgium with security, or at least a warning, should the Germans decide to give the Schlieffen Plan a second try and knife swiftly westward. Even more important, the zone was the keystone to France's arch of postwar alliances with Poland and Czechoslovakia. If the Germans attacked eastward, the French could race across the Rhineland and strike at the Ruhr, the Reich's industrial heartland and the center of its armaments works, including Krupp's flagship plant, the Gusstahlfabrik, in Essen.

At Versailles the losers had had no choice, but six years later Germany had freely joined the Locarno Pact, accepting the demilitarized zone as a permanent buffer. Should German troops enter the zone under any pretext, the Locarno agreement provided, they would be guilty of "an unprovoked act of aggression," and the other European powers bound by Locarno — France, Britain, Belgium, and Italy — would have not only the right, but the duty, to expel them from the Rhineland by force. Before 1914 generations of Rhinelander children had been taught to sing *"Die Wacht am Rhein,"* with its rousing challenge: "The Rhine, the Rhine, the German Rhine! Who guards tonight our Stream Divine?" In Wilhelmine Germany the reply had always been: the Sword of Germany. But for the past eighteen years guards had been unnecessary, for under Locarno soldiers of France or Belgium who entered the buffer would also have been guilty of *une violation de propriété.* The zone was one of the few postwar political achievements blessed by the Führer; as late as his *Friedensrede* of May 21, 1935, delivered to the Reichstag, he had hailed the unarmed Rhineland as the Third Reich's "contribution" to European peace. The Reich, he had solemnly declared, would "unconditionally respect" the "territorial" provisions of Versailles and the pledge, freely made by the republic of Germany at Locarno, to honor the inviolability of the Rhineland.[31]

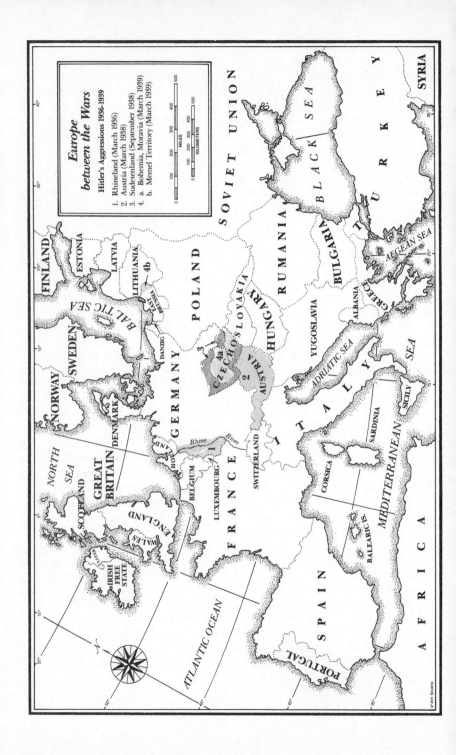

Europe between the Wars

Hitler's Aggressions 1936-1939

1. Rhineland (March 1936)
2. Austria (March 1938)
3. Sudetenland (September 1938)
4. a. Bohemia, Moravia (March 1939)
   b. Memel Territory (March 1939)

MILES

0   100   200   300   400   500

KILOMETERS

0   100   200   300   400   500

© Art Studio

Churchill was suspicious. The Führer, he believed, was likelier to remain faithful to his "great lie" credo, set forth in *Mein Kampf*. Winston had adopted, as a working thesis, the assumption that any given foreign policy statement by Hitler was the exact opposite of the truth. On January 17, eight months after the May *Friedensrede*, he wrote Clemmie that if his intelligence sources were right, the Führer was planning a major announcement which "may well be that Germany will . . . reoccupy the neutral zone with troops and forts." Should that happen, he wrote, the French with British help would be obliged to drive the invaders out. He added: "Baldwin and Ramsay, guilty of neglecting our defences in spite of every warning, may well feel anxious not only for the public but for their own personal skins."[32]

He was wrong about the British reaction but right about Hitler's intentions. Three weeks *before* promising to respect the territorial integrity of the Rhineland, the Führer had ordered the OKW (Oberkommando der Wehrmacht), the high command of Germany's armed forces, to draw up plans for seizing it. The operation was encoded *Schulung* (Schooling) and was, according to the Führer, to be "executed by a surprise blow at lightning speed," with "only the very smallest number of officers" to be informed. Meanwhile he was building an excuse for aggression. He began with the same Reichstag speech, observing, in an aside, that the mutual assistance treaty between France and Russia, initialed two months previously but not yet ratified by the Chamber of Deputies, would alter the status of Locarno by introducing "an element of insecurity."[33]

The French government knew what was coming. As early as October 21, 1935, the Deuxième Bureau informed the ministry that German troops were "actively preparing" to invade the zone; on October 21 the French high command sent an alert to the Quai: "The hypothesis of a German repudiation of the Rhineland statutes must be envisaged before the autumn of 1936, at the latest." The most plausible warnings came from the able French ambassador in Berlin. After a lengthy talk with the Führer in November, André François-Poncet wrote that Hitler had lost his temper *"dans une longue tirade contre le pacte franco-soviétique qu'il considérait comme criminel."* François-Poncet was convinced that Hitler now awaited only the appropriate moment to attack.[34]

Laval wired the French ambassador in London on January 11, 1936, advising him that four German divisions had been moved to the Rhineland's border. In Whitehall, the FO acknowledged receipt of the message but made no comment. A week later Laval and his cabinet learned from General Maurice Gamelin, the French commander in chief, that intelligence reports left little doubt that the Germans would invade the zone "as soon as possible." Again the British were informed; again the FO was unresponsive. This silence troubled Pierre-Étienne Flandin, who had succeeded Laval as *ministre des affaires étrangères,* and in the last week in January, Flandin crossed the Channel, officially to join the mourners at George V's state funeral but actually to discuss the approaching crisis with Eden.[35]

The timing was unpropitious. During the past eight months relations between the two allies had become strained; after the Anglo-German Naval Agreement and the Hoare-Laval affair, France seethed with Anglophobia. "With Hitler against bolshevism!" cried *L'Ami du peuple,* and in *Gringoire* the fiery journalist Henri Béraud raged: "I hate England. I hate her by instinct and by tradition. I say, and I repeat, that England must be reduced to slavery!" Knowledge of all this had preceded Flandin to London, and diplomatic jargon did not ease the tension. Men charged with managing a nation's foreign affairs are expected to rise above petty bickering, but Eden's reception of Flandin on Monday, January 27, 1936, was frosty. On Tuesday the Frenchman talked to Baldwin. Flandin had come to ask precisely what Britain planned to do if Hitler attempted to seize the Rhineland. To his consternation, neither Englishman would say. When he pressed them, they countered by asking him what *France* would do. It was hardly the sort of encouragement one is entitled to expect from an ally.[36]

Eden's own account of the French minister's mission is almost self-incriminating. To Flandin's question, he wrote, he had "replied that the French attitude to a violation of the Rhineland was clearly a matter for the judgment of the French government. . . . If they wished to negotiate with Hitler, they should do so; if they intended to repel a German invasion of the zone, they should lay their military plans. Any forcible action would depend on France." His "impression" was that "while not prepared to use force to defend the zone," his French guest had been "equally reluctant to negotiate about it." The young foreign secretary even entertained the uncharitable thought that Flandin "might be tempted" to "put the blame for inaction on either count elsewhere." In a cable to the British ambassador in Paris, Eden warned against "hypothetical" discussions and added: "Taking one thing with another, it seems undesirable to adopt an attitude where we would either have to fight for the zone or abandon it in the face of German reoccupation. It would be preferable for Great Britain and France to enter betimes into negotiations with the German Government for the surrender on conditions of our rights in the zone while such surrender still has bargaining power."[37]

None of this makes sense. You cannot bargain rights over territory which you are not prepared to defend. If the Allies meant to surrender the Rhineland — and an invitation to open negotiations would tell the Germans that they did — there was nothing left to discuss. The Germans would know they could march into a void, encountering no opposition. But the appeasers assumed that everyone preferred peace to war.

In the early hours of that Saturday, March 7, 1936, darkness and patchy fog lay over long stretches of the ancient Rhine, a river beloved by German poets and a source of exasperation to foreign conquerors from Caesar to Eisenhower, Bradley, and Montgomery. Despite the hour, few Rhinelanders were asleep. All week hearsay had been spreading among them, gathering in momentum, and it was accurate to the last particular. In Germany even the rumors were precise.

As the first streaks of dawn flushed the sky they heard a faint hum coming from the direction of Berlin. It grew to a growl which reached a thundering crescendo as Messerschmitt fighters, flying in tight V formations and bearing the broken cross of the German Reich on their wings, swarmed out of the eastern sky, circled the spires of Cologne Cathedral, and raced back eastward. Then the infantry began approaching from the right bank. Brawny young soldiers in the old, familiar coal-scuttle helmets crossed the bridges on bicycles and entered the squares of cities and towns in the demilitarized zone. Crowds already gathered there murmured their approval, a susurration which rose to an ovation as German battalions wearing red carnations in their belts goose-stepped over the Rhine and into the square under the eyes of their commanding officers, who stood, in full uniform, their medals twinkling, on small platforms which had miraculously appeared to give them eminence. The *Volk* in the squares rejoiced. Local Nazi leaders, many of them *Oberbürgermeisters*, appeared in their sausage-tight *Sturmtruppen* uniforms to lead the singing:

Deutschland, Deutschland über alles . . .

And then the Nazi anthem, the "Horst Wessel Song":

Die Fahne hoch! Die Reihen dicht geschlossen.
S.A. marschiert mit ruhig festem Schritt. . . .

Raise the banners! Stand rank on rank together.
S.A. march on, with steady, quiet tread. . . .[38]

The entire Rhineland was aflame with excitement, but the world was unaware of Hitler's move until, at the stroke of noon, he addressed the Reichstag in the Kroll Opera House, his deep, resonant voice thundering that the German Reich no longer felt "bound" by Locarno. Therefore, in the "interests of the basic rights of its people to the security of their frontier and the safeguarding of their defense," he had "reestablished, as from today, the absolute and unrestricted sovereignty of the Reich in the demilitarized zone of the Rhineland." The Reichstag exploded in delirium. Its six hundred deputies stiffened their right arms in *Hitlergrussen* and bellowed "Heil! Heil! Heil! Heil! Heil!" until the Führer raised his hand to silence them. "Men of the German Reichstag!" His deep voice was throbbing now. He vowed at "this historic moment," while German troops were on the march, that he would never yield to force in *"Wiederherstellung der Ehre"* ("restoring the honor of our people"). But neither would he threaten other nations. He pledged that "now, more than ever," he would work toward understanding between the people of all European countries, "particularly our Western neighbor nations."[39]

This was Hitler at his wiliest. Here he was speaking, not to the Reichstag, but to Frenchmen, Belgians, Italians, and Britons frightened of bolshevism. In an ingenious distortion of carefully worded state documents, he embroidered his argument that the Russo-French agreement was a breach of Locarno directed against the Reich — that it might even force France to join the Soviet Union in a war against Germany. France, said the Führer, "has destroyed the political system of the [Locarno] pact, not only in theory but in fact." Then, in a characteristic *Friedensrede* touch, he offered a string of meaningless carrots: immediate negotiations for a new demilitarized zone on both sides of the Franco-German and Belgo-German frontiers; the return of the Reich to the League of Nations; a twenty-five-year nonaggression pact between France and Germany; nonaggression treaties between the Reich and France, Czechoslovakia, Poland, and the smaller countries of eastern Europe. Deeply moved, he paused, his eyes moist and his voice choked. Then he made his last two vows. First, he once more pledged: *"Wir haben in Europa keine territorialen Fordernungen zu stellen"* ("We have no territorial demands to make in Europe"). And then: *"Deutschland wird niemals den Frieden brechen!"* ("Germany will never break the peace!").[40]

The cheering went on and on, but the diplomats, who had to inform their governments, and the foreign correspondents, who had to tell the world, slipped out. Shirer was among them. He observed a few generals making their way out toward the Tiergarten. Their smiles seemed forced. Then he encountered Blomberg and was shocked at his appearance: "His face was white, his cheeks twitching." In his diary Shirer wrote: "You could not help detecting a nervousness."[41]

War Minister Blomberg, General Fritsch, General Beck, and a handful of other senior members of the army hierarchy were now convinced that Nazi Germany would collapse within a week or less. Blomberg bore the immediate responsibility; hence his pallor and his nervous tic. In deciding to invade the buffer zone Hitler had acted in defiance of their advice. The generals knew that the occupation, stripped of the Führer's thespian eloquence and his hand-picked, carefully rehearsed battalions now camped on forbidden soil, was a gigantic scam. By canceling leaves and putting every trained poilu into battle dress, France could retake the Rhineland in a matter of hours. Outnumbering the half-trained, inadequately equipped Wehrmacht conscripts ten to one, the French infantrymen would be supported by tanks and the finest artillery in the world. Blomberg had agreed to assume command only after receiving written assurance from the Führer that he could take "any military countermeasures" he felt appropriate. If he so much as glimpsed a single French bayonet, he intended to beat "a hasty retreat" back across the Rhine. [42]

And that, in the opinion of the *Militärbehörden* — the senior military authorities on Behrenstrasse — would be the end of Adolf Hitler. How many generals had discussed the approaching debacle and shared in planning how to exploit the aftermath is unknown. Blomberg and Beck were excluded; the disgrace of the Führer would also reflect on the army, they were to be the commanding officers, and if they acknowledged defeat before the operation began, their honor would be compromised. But almost certainly a majority of the Generalstab believed France was committed, by a treaty Hitler had approved, to take military action against the presence of German troops in the demilitarized zone. The moment the French infantry moved, calling his bluff, the same treaty required Britain to support France with her own armed forces. The fledgling Wehrmacht would be routed. Hitler and his Nazis would be the laughingstock of Europe. Once the German people realized that they had been betrayed, a military government would move into the Reich Chancellery pending a constitutional convention and free elections. [43]

It is impossible to overestimate the strength of the belief within Germany's officer corps that France's advantage was overwhelming. Ten years later General Alfred Jodl, who became Hitler's chief of staff, would testify to it before the Nuremberg tribunal. At the time of the Rhineland coup, he said, "Considering the situation we were in" — they knew Gamelin had thirteen French divisions near the frontier — "the French covering army could have blown us to pieces." Afterward Hitler himself acknowledged it. His interpreter, Paul Schmidt, heard him say: "A retreat on our part would have spelled collapse." Still later he said: "The forty-eight hours after the march into the Rhineland were the most nerve-racking [*die aufregendste Zeitspanne*] in my life. If the French had then marched into the Rhineland, we would have had to withdraw with shame and disgrace [*mit Schimpfe und Schande zurückziehen müssen*], for the military resources at our disposal would have been wholly inadequate for even a moderate resistance."[44]

But in that blustery March week of 1936, Hitler, unlike his generals, saw the Rhineland as a risk worth taking. How much he knew of the democracies' impotence is unfathomable, but he had been surprised by the feeble Allied response to his earlier moves. In these years, before he became intoxicated with his own triumphs, his intuitive grasp of how far he could go with Allied leaders was uncanny.

Nearly an hour passed before François-Poncet could cable Flandin a terse summary of Hitler's new sensation. Premier Albert Sarraut immediately summoned his inner cabinet, including the minister of war, General Joseph-Léon-Marie Maurin, and the constable of France, Généralissime Gamelin. Their talks were already under way when the text of Hitler's Reichstag speech arrived.[45]

A large crowd of Parisians had begun to gather outside the Hotel de Ville. They seemed more curious than angry, though P. J. Phillips of the *New York Times* cabled his foreign editor: "Rather than submit to this last crushing piece of Teutonism France will fight." That was precisely what the premier and three of his civilian ministers wanted to do, but they had no Bonaparte, nor even a Foch, to lead the troops of their Third Republic. After setting forth the basic facts, Sarraut turned to Gamelin and asked him what the army proposed to do. According to the premier's testimony before a postwar investigating committee established by the French National Assembly at the insistence of wartime Resistance leaders, the premier expected France's commander in chief to unroll a map revealing swift, imaginative maneuvers which would drive the intruders back across the Rhine. Instead, Gamelin mildly asked permission to take *"les premières mesures de précaution."* Asked what those were, he replied that he wanted to recall soldiers on furlough, move reinforcements toward the frontier, and begin preparations to send up more troops should that seem advisable.[46]

Sarraut was aghast. Gamelin was planning the classic dispositions of a Saint-Cyr-l'École graduate whose native soil is threatened by an invasion. "Naturally," the *généralissime* said, "there is no question of forcing the Rhine, on which the Germans are virtually entrenched already." He then ran through what Sarraut later called "the whole gamut of perils." If France advanced into the Rhineland, the German riposte would be an "attack on us through Belgium, aerial bombing in Paris . . . attacks by submarines, artillery bombardment of our Rhine cities, Strasbourg, Mulhouse. . . ." He went on and on. Joseph Paul-Boncour, minister for League of Nations affairs, interrupted to tell the general that he would like to see him in Mainz — a German industrial city ninety miles from the

French border — "as soon as possible." That, Gamelin replied, was *une autre affaire.*" He would like nothing better, he added, "but first you must give me the means."

At first they didn't understand. As commander in chief he was entrusted with all the military means the country possessed. Maurin entered the discussion; presently the two generals were in animated conversation, and slowly the premier and his civilian ministers comprehended. The soldiers were discussing a *mobilisation générale*, costing thirty million francs and consisting first of putting a million men in positions which, with the Maginot Line, would permit the army to shield France. But that, the exasperated Sarraut pointed out, wasn't the problem. There were no signs that the Nazis had designs on French soil, at least not now. They *had* invaded a buffer zone where no soldier of either nation had the right to bear arms — a neutral land essential to France's survival and her diplomatic commitments in eastern Europe. The generals looked at one another, shrugged, and spread their hands in a gesture which could only be interpreted as *"Hélas, la politique!"*[47]

The baffled premier explained that he simply wanted an *opération de police*, with Gamelin using his vast superiority in infantry strength, firepower, and air power — the few Nazi aircraft, unarmed, were based on airstrips too far away to intervene in a swift expulsion. It was an *absurdité*. The invaders had three battalions; the poilus would overwhelm them. "After all," Sarraut told his commander in chief, "you have just a symbolic force in front of you."

Shirer was reporting that "for the first time since 1870 gray-clad German soldiers and blue-clad French troops face each other across the upper Rhine." The world awaited the response in Paris to this gross violation of Versailles and Locarno. Had it known the truth, it would have been incredulous. The elected leaders of France were begging their high command to put up their fists. And the generals were refusing. Gamelin and Maurin were immovable. The *généralissime*, backed by his war minister, insisted that his army was *"une force purement défensive."* Asked to propose an alternative, he suggested that the government lodge a vigorous protest with the League of Nations.

Sarraut asked Gamelin point-blank: "If we act alone against Germany, without allies, what will be the prospect?" The general said that at first, "given the present conditions," the French would have *"la prépondérance,"* but in a long war Germany's industrial power and numerical superiority might tip the balance.[48]

There was a long silence as they pondered the implications of this: another four years — perhaps more than four — of trenches, barbed wire, incessant shellfire, *attaques en masse* which gained a hundred yards at most, "leaving the dead," as Scott Fitzgerald had written, "like a million bloody rugs," and the legless or blind stumbling around the country while desperate young widows became streetwalkers. All this, and the possibility that France would be defeated in the end.

Then someone pointed out that the premier had assumed they would be acting without allies. France was allied with Britain in the west, and, in the east, with Czechoslovakia, Poland, and Russia. Locarno had specifically committed Italy, Belgium, and Britain to support the French in expelling troops or weapons Germany sent into the zone. And the Locarno powers weren't the only countries affected by Nazi aggression in the Rhineland. Aides were summoned, instructed to place telephone calls; they slipped back with promises of support from the Poles, the Czechs, and the Rumanians. Even Austria, bound to France by no pact, was ready to back her. The Belgians and the Italians had adopted attitudes of cautious reserve.[49]

France's most powerful ally, of course, lay across the Channel. "Above all," as Churchill later observed, the French "had a right to look to Great Britain, having regard to the guarantee . . . against German aggression, and the pressure we had put upon France for the earlier evacuation of the Rhineland." His Britannic Majesty's ambassador to France, Sir George Clark, didn't wait for a telephone call from a Sarraut aide. On instructions from Anthony Eden, he hastened to the Quai d'Orsay and insisted *"très vigoureusement,"* according to Flandin, that France take "no military measures which commit the future before prior consultation with the British Government." Sarraut and Flandin, trying to consult Whitehall by telephone, discovered what Hitler already knew — that on weekends most leaders of the English government were inaccessible. Eden was available but unhelpful. When Charles Corbin, France's ambassador to London, called on him he was told that no decision could be reached before Monday. Corbin reported to the Quai that Eden had "abstained, despite my insistence, from giving me any indication of his own views." Corbin had mentioned Britain's treaty commitment; Eden, he said, had "maintained silence."[50]

Sarraut was affronted, but France, lacking a moat to separate her from the Germans, needed Britain more than the British needed her, and after an interval the premier put his pride in his pocket and authorized Flandin to inform the British that rather than take an "isolated position," the French government preferred "to confer with the other powers party to Locarno."[51]

Eden handled the French with a duplicity they did not deserve. Among the information Eden withheld from Flandin was that after lunch on Saturday he had driven to Chequers, the country home of prime ministers. In Eden's words, "Baldwin said little, as was his wont on foreign affairs.

Though personally friendly to France, he was clear in his mind that there would be no support in Britain for any military action by the French. I could only agree."[52]

Back in the Foreign Office that afternoon, the foreign secretary drafted a long memorandum for submission to the cabinet Monday morning, and then a statement he would deliver in the House of Commons afterward. Any ultimatum to the Germans, he wrote, or even a strong note demanding that the Wehrmacht evacuate its troops in the buffer zone "should certainly not be made unless the powers concerned are prepared to enforce it by military action." Hitler's seizure of the zone, he felt, "has deprived us of a useful bargaining counter" — he was still trapped in that non sequitur — but above all, "We must resist any attempt to apply financial and economic sanctions" against Germany. At this point — and the situation in the zone would remain unchanged throughout the crisis — fewer than five thousand German soldiers had been posted within twenty miles of the French frontier. They were not deployed for battle, and they lacked tank support.[53]

Eden told Corbin on Sunday that there would be no British reinforcements. Reluctantly he agreed to fly over on Tuesday for talks with other Locarno diplomats, provided "it be understood" that those attending the conference would not be asked to agree "on concrete propositions." The French minister concluded that France's only hope of salvation lay in changing Eden's mind, or in persuading Englishmen who made or influenced the government's decisions to change it for him.[54]

That would be difficult. The *Daily Herald* (Labour) had already insisted that Hitler be taken at his word. Lord Lothian approved of the German invasion, remarking that, "after all, they are only going into their own back garden," a statement that has been widely, and mistakenly, attributed to *The Times*. It would not, however, have been out of place there; Dawson's editorial was headed "A Chance to Rebuild," and although it opened by describing the Nazi coup as "Herr Hitler's invasion," Dawson scorned the "sensationally minded," who had called it "an act of 'aggression.' " As he saw it, the Germans were understandably afflicted by a "deep, instinctive fear — the dread of encirclement," and the Rhineland had become, in their eyes, "more than a badge of inferior status, a source of military weakness to a Power which might one day become involved in a war on both sides again."[55]

Nancy Astor, Tom Jones, and Attorney General Sir Thomas Inskip were guests that weekend at one of Lord Lothian's house parties at Blickling Hall. The host and his party prepared a comment on Hitler's seizure of the Rhineland and telegraphed it to Baldwin. They "wholeheartedly" endorsed the Führer's act, urged that the Nazi "entrance to the zone" be ignored in the light of peace proposals before the Reichstag, and suggested that seizure of the buffer zone should be regarded as an "assertion . . . of equality and not an act of aggression." Tom Jones wrote in his diary that he intended to persuade Baldwin to accept Hitler's proposal at its face value even before discussing it with the cabinet. Harold Nicolson, a wise diarist, noted that the general mood "is one of fear. Anything to keep out of war. . . . On all sides one hears sympathy for Germany. It is all very tragic and sad."[56]

Ambassador Corbin, listening to Eden's speech in the diplomatic gallery of the House Monday afternoon, found it discouraging. Thankfully, the foreign secretary said, there was "no reason to suppose that the present German action implies a threat of hostilities." He scolded the Germans' disrespect for treaties. The invasion had "profoundly shaken confidence in any engagement into which the Government of Germany may enter" — it is a pity that Neville Chamberlain, sitting beside Eden, did not write that down and commit it to memory — but His Majesty's Government would study the Führer's new "peace proposals seriously and objectively" to see whether they would shore up "the structure of peace."[57]

Eden flew to Paris accompanied by Lord Halifax and Ralph Wigram, but the conference was sterile. The French foreign minister wanted immediate action — ejecting the Germans from the Rhineland while imposing economic, financial, and military sanctions against the aggressor. Eden noted: "The gravity of Flandin's statements exceeds anything which has been said before." He opposed meeting force with force, and to Flandin's surprise and dismay the Belgian premier agreed. The Italian ambassador, after bitterly reminding them that his country was still under league sanctions, folded his arms, lifted his chin, and spoke not another word.[58]

As they broke up, Eden said he was "glad that there was no intention of trying to reach decisions at this meeting." Flandin, who had convened the conference with precisely that intention, looked directly into Eden's eyes and said prophetically: "Negotiations will end in nothing, or rather, they will sanction a new retreat. And this time the retreat will be decisive, for it will generate a whole series of retreats."[59]

The following morning the British cabinet met to hear the foreign secretary's report. In the Quai, Eden had been bland and elusive, but in Downing Street he could be frank. He said he was convinced that if the Germans were permitted to keep the Rhineland, and to fortify it, war would be inevitable in two years — a war which "would be fought under very unfavourable conditions." The difficulty, he said, was that Sarraut and Flandin did not reflect the views of the typical Frenchman. France was "pacifist to the core"; in battle she would be an unreliable ally. Alfred Duff

Cooper, the new secretary for war, disagreed. He too believed that war was inevitable, but he thought that the time to stand up to Hitler was now. French morale would rise, he thought, once the French army had received its marching orders. According to cabinet minutes, he pointed out that "in three years' time" — 1939 — "Germany would have 100 divisions and a powerful fleet." Even with Parliament's adoption of the most recent White Paper, England could not match Nazi rearmament stride for stride, and "We should not, relatively, therefore, be in a better position."[60]

But the rest of the cabinet, including the prime minister, felt otherwise. Baldwin even opposed an appeal to the League of Nations. At some point, he said, "it would be necessary to point out to the French" that intervention in the Rhineland would not only let loose "another great war. . . . It would probably . . . result in Germany going Bolshevik." The first lord of the Admiralty and the secretary for air acknowledged that their position was "a disadvantageous one." One of Baldwin's ministers observed that "public opinion" strongly opposed Allied intervention in the neutral zone. Another concurred. And this was a government whose respect for public opinion was profound. In the end they decided to do nothing. Indeed, Baldwin observed, peace was "worth taking almost any risk."[61]

Quiet and efficient, British civil servants were taken for granted by most cabinet ministers, and when political issues arose they were treated brusquely or even ignored, despite the fact that most of them belonged to the same class and had gone to the same schools. Sir Robert Vansittart, forceful, knighted, and destined for a peerage, was an exception. Ralph Wigram was farther down the ladder. In Paris he had sat behind Eden and Halifax, speaking only when asked for a date, a statistic, a protocol, or technical advice. Nevertheless, Wigram had vehemently agreed with Flandin, believing a policy of drift now would be fatal, and afterward he had a private word with him. If the Locarno powers were to reconvene in London Thursday, he asked, why not move the league council's meeting there, rather than Geneva? The hope of action was small, but whatever the Locarno decision, it would gain prestige if promptly endorsed by the League of Nations. Flandin warmly agreed, and spoke to the others. It was done. But Wigram was still troubled, and once he returned to British soil he drove straight to Chartwell.

Although he was exiled from public life in England, Churchill's political statements continued to be closely studied in foreign chancelleries by those who sensed that eventually his hour would strike. Adolf Hitler continued to be among them. The Führer loathed Churchill and always spoke of him with undisguised malice, but he could not ignore him. In the beginning his insults were merely ugly. Winston, he said, was "a nervous old hen." You couldn't "talk sense" to such a man, the Führer said; he was merely *"ein romantischer Phantast"* — a romantic dreamer. However, once Churchill opened up with his heavy rhetorical artillery, Hitler's invective also escalated. "The gift Mr. Churchill possesses is the gift to lie with a pious expression on his face and to distort the truth. . . . His abnormal state of mind can only be explained as symptomatic of either a paralytic disease or a drunkard's ravings!" After his offer of nonaggression treaties, meant to blur the jagged edge of his thrust into the Rhineland, Hitler predicted that "only the Churchill clique" would "stand in the way of peace."[62]

Actually, the Rhineland crisis had broken at an awkward time for Winston. When the Foreign Office phoned Chartwell and read him a translation of Hitler's March 7 speech, he instantly saw it for what it was: "comfort for everyone on both sides of the Atlantic who wished to be humbugged." But because he still expected a summons to No. 10 and a cabinet appointment, he suppressed his most compelling instincts and spared Baldwin's government.[63]

In public, and especially in House debates, Churchill was civil, almost subdued. Parliament was amused; Winston, for once, was maneuvering for office. He had been sounding his trumpet of alarm for over three years now. His notes had been clear and true, yet they had neither altered the government's foreign policy nor slowed the rush toward catastrophe. Since he couldn't give up, he had redoubled his efforts to wedge his way into a seat at the cabinet table, where, he thought, he could control the clattering train. Winston believed, and virtually every parliamentary correspondent and MP not in office shared his conviction, that he would soon be appointed to the office, still vacant, of minister of defense.

Yet though he had spared the prime minister, Winston had not remained mute after Nazi troops burst into the Rhineland. He and Austen Chamberlain had formed a team, working in tandem to arouse the House by spelling out the consequences if the Nazi coup were to pass unchallenged. Austria would be the Führer's next objective, Churchill predicted, and Austen pointed out that "if Austria perishes Czechoslovakia becomes indefensible." Once Hitler had mastered eastern Europe, they both told the House, he would turn westward, stalking France and Britain. Some MPs, Churchill observed, thought the French were exaggerating the danger. He told them: "If *we* had been invaded four times in a hundred years, we should understand better how terrible that injury is." In France and Belgium, he said, "the avalanche of fire and steel which fell upon them twenty years ago" was still "an overpowering memory and obsession." He asked: "How should we feel if — to change the metaphor — we saw a tiger, the marks of whose teeth and claws had scarred every limb of our bodies, coming toward us and crouching within exactly the distance of a single spring?"[64]

In his diary Neville Chamberlain wrote that Winston had "made a constructive and helpful speech." On one point, however, Churchill had been adamant, and Neville's failure to assign it importance, or even mention it, reveals the moral gap between the two men. Both Austen and Winston emphasized Hitler's grave damage to the sanctity of treaties. Britain, they held, must remain faithful to her every vow. There was, Churchill said, much goodwill in England toward Germany, and an abiding hope that "the three great peoples of Western Europe may join hands in lasting friendship. But" — he paused — "it ought not even to be necessary to state that Great Britain, if called upon, will honor her obligations both under the Covenant of the League and under the Treaty of Locarno." In an article for the *Evening Standard* he amplified on this theme, appealing to Hitler "and the great disconsolate Germany he leads," urging them to place themselves "in the very forefront of civilisation" by "a proud and voluntary submission, not to any single country or group of countries, but to the sanctity of treaties and the authority of public law, by an immediate withdrawal from the Rhineland." It was like telling Rasputin to use his knife and fork. Still, Churchill had mentioned neither the past nor present sins of the men on the Treasury Bench.[65]

Wigram, reaching Chartwell late in the evening on Wednesday, March 11, found Churchill eager for news. After listening to an account of the Paris meeting, Winston decided he must talk to Flandin before anyone in the government saw him. Breaking the habit of a lifetime, he rose at dawn and drove to his London flat in Morpeth Mansions. Flandin arrived there by taxi at 8:30 A.M. He told Winston he intended to propose simultaneous mobilization by Britain and France of all land, air, and sea forces; producing a sheaf of papers, he read aloud what Churchill afterward called "an impressive list" of support from Poland, Czechoslovakia, Austria, Yugoslavia, Rumania, and the three Baltic states. "There was no doubt," Churchill wrote, "that superior strength still lay with the Allies of the former war. They had only to act to win." Winston told the French minister that in his "detached private position" there was little he could do, but he guided him to others, like Duff Cooper, who had a voice in the government, and that evening he gave a dinner for him. Influential Englishmen heard Flandin out and left promising to do what they could.[66]

Churchill himself had left the table earlier. The House of Commons Foreign Affairs Committee was holding a late session, and he had asked to be heard. There he repeated his insistence that Britain keep her Geneva and Locarno pledges. Alec Douglas-Home, a future prime minister, took notes at the meeting. He recorded that Winston produced Flandin's papers and then "drew a dramatic picture of all the countries of Europe hurrying to assist France and ourselves against Germany." The next speaker was Hoare, who ridiculed Churchill's argument. "As regards Winston's references to all the nations of Europe coming to our aid," he said, "I can only say that in my estimate these nations are totally unprepared from a military point of view." It was Douglas-Home's impression that after Churchill had spoken "a substantial proportion" of the committee was "prepared to see this country go to war." But Hoare, he thought, had "definitely sobered them down."[67]

It seems remarkable that no one there sought expert opinion on *Germany's* military preparedness. If they were unaware that the Wehrmacht was only a shadow of its future self, they surely knew Hitler had introduced conscription barely a year earlier. Doubtless the smaller countries were unprepared. All Europe was, even the nations that had made a fetish of rearmament; the Italians were proving that in Ethiopia. Nevertheless, all had standing armies of trained men. The MPs can hardly have doubted that Hitler would have backed down if encircled by an alliance of France, Great Britain, and the chain of states, swiftly forged by Flandin, on the Reich's eastern and southern fronts. It seems strange that Hoare, so recently disgraced, could discredit Churchill with so flimsy an argument.

But all the meetings held in London in that second week of March were peculiar. On Thursday, Neville Chamberlain entered in his diary: "March 12, talked to Flandin, emphasising that public opinion would not support us in sanctions of any kind." Flandin had replied that at the very least Britain could declare an economic boycott. Neville rejected that, though he offered to give up "a colony" in the interests of peace. The appeasers thought their empire a great bargaining counter, when in fact Hitler wanted none of it. The Third Reich, Ribbentrop had explained to Eden, wanted its *Lebensraum* (living space) in Europe, preferably to the east. In a deep leather chair at his club, Halifax reread Hitler's *Friedensrede* of March 7 and found a passage he had overlooked. In denouncing the Franco-Soviet treaty, the Führer charged that it not only violated Locarno but had also introduced "the threatening military power of a mighty empire into the center of Europe by the roundabout way of Czechoslovakia, which has signed an agreement with Russia." Halifax rang for a Carlton servant and told him he wanted an atlas with a more detailed map of Czechoslovakia. The man returned empty-handed. The map, he explained, had already been checked out by another member, Neville Chamberlain.[68]

Policy is often determined in camera, which is why contemporaneous public opinion, formed amidst the convulsion of historic events, is shaped by incomplete, often distorted, information. In London that week of conferences in St. James's Palace — one of the Locarno powers and the other of the Council of the League of Nations — the press was admitted only to the public meetings. It was at one of them that a friend saw Wigram, sitting at Eden's side, "looking increasingly disillusioned and depressed." The entire Foreign Office establishment had been shaken by the government's failure to respond to Hitler's challenge. The foreign secretary's conduct completely baffled them. And a few of them decided to tell him so. On the initiative of Rex Leeper, they converged on Eden's Whitehall office. He told them he shared their concern. But he doubted that the British people were ready for war. Most of the FO believed that Hitler's *Friedensrede* offer of nonaggression treaties was fraudulent, and that his invasion of the Rhineland was as great a threat to England as an invasion of Belgium; greater, say, than a conquest of Austria.[69]

Leeper therefore proposed a nationwide campaign to awaken all Britain to the Nazi menace, persuading the country to "abandon an attitude of defeatism vis-à-vis Germany." The need, he said, was for "bold and frank speeches, not hesitating to call a spade a spade and not shirking from unpleasant truths." Eden agreed, but on reflection decided that the idea was impractical. It would divide the country and politicize the Foreign Office. In the end Leeper and his colleagues decided to turn to Churchill. He would lead, and they would support him behind Baldwin's back.[70]

Wigram couldn't wait. Vansittart, who had given him permission to leak data to "selected publicists,"* was dismayed when Wigram gave this mandate the broadest possible interpretation. He called a press conference in his Lord North Street home and gave Flandin the floor. Abandoning diplomatic language the French minister spoke straight to the point. He said: "Today the whole world, and especially the small nations, turn their eyes toward England. If England will act now, she can lead Europe. You will have a policy, all the world will follow you, and you will thus prevent war. It is your last chance. If you do not stop Germany now, all is over. France cannot guarantee Czechoslovakia any more because that will become geographically impossible." If Britain did not act, he continued, France, with her small population and obsolete industry, lay at the mercy of a rearmed Germany. Franco-German friendship was impossible; "the two countries will always be in tension." He acknowledged that England

---

* *Publicist*, one of the most abused words in the English language, means "a writer versed in international law," or, loosely, "any writer, as a journalist, on matters of public policy." Walter Lippmann was a publicist. Publicity men are *not*.

could reach a fragile understanding with the Nazis now, but it would not last; if Hitler were not stopped "by force today, war is inevitable."[71]

The reporters returned to Fleet Street and wrote straightforward accounts of Flandin's appeal, which their editors buried. Everyone in Whitehall expected Baldwin to loose a lightning bolt, destroying Wigram, but his irregularity was ignored. Thoughtful Englishmen wavered, hawks one day and doves the next. Harold Nicolson summed up the quandary in a letter to his wife, Vita Sackville-West, that Thursday, March 12. "If we send an ultimatum to Germany, she ought in all reason to back down," he wrote. But what if she didn't? Then, he said, "We shall have war." He assumed that the Nazis would lose, but, he asked, what would be "the good of that? It would only mean communism in Germany and France." At that his line of reason broke. It wouldn't happen that way, he decided, because "the people of this country absolutely refuse to have a war. We should be faced by a general strike if we even suggested such a thing. We shall therefore have to climb down ignominiously and Hitler will have scored." Indecision was the equivalent of a Nazi triumph, and by the end of the week a swelling majority of MPs, diplomats, and journalists decided that Hitler would emerge the winner of the Rhineland crisis — that he had, indeed, already won.[72]

Flandin, offended and disheartened by the British press's lack of attention and the failure of his meeting with Chamberlain, again arrived at Morpeth Mansions. Churchill shared his anguish but could offer nothing but advice. As he later wrote: "I advised M. Flandin to demand an interview with Mr. Baldwin before he left." Darkness had fallen when the French minister's taxi turned off Whitehall and into Downing Street. The prime minister appeared at the threshold of No. 10 to receive his troubled guest. Baldwin was gracious. Once the amenities were over and they began to talk, however, he told his guest that his cause was lost. Explaining diffidently that he "knew little of foreign affairs" — quite true, but an astonishing admission from the leader of the world's one superpower, vulnerable, through its empire, to major disorders all over the world — he said he did know the feelings of his people, "and they want peace." Flandin protested. The peace would be unbroken. Not a shot would be fired. If faced by a police action the Germans would quickly evacuate the Rhineland. According to Flandin, the prime minister replied: "You may be right, but if there is *even one chance in a hundred* that war would follow from your police action, I have not the right to commit England."[73]

The behavior of both men is baffling. What commitment was Flandin seeking? According to his later version, he merely asked Baldwin to give the French a free hand. But France was a sovereign power. She needed no one's permission to act. Churchill had recognized this weakness in Flandin's first visit to England, before the invasion. He had thought it feckless of Flandin to come to Downing Street, cap in hand, urging the prime minister to honor England's treaty obligations and send British troops to join the French in a Rhineland counterattack. Statesmen shouldn't beg; "Clemenceau or Poincaré," he later noted, "would have left Mr. Baldwin no option." If France moved to meet her Locarno commitments — even though England refused to honor hers — Baldwin's approval would be unnecessary and irrelevant. It was the postwar verdict of the French parliamentary investigating committee that during the Rhineland crisis Premier Sarraut and his cabinet, unable to make up their own minds, were asking the British to do it for them. Churchill would have done it; Baldwin didn't. He said repeatedly: "England is not in a state to go to war." Back in the Faubourg Saint-Germain, Flandin described his call at No. 10 to Sarraut and his cabinet, concluding, "I understood that evening that I would not obtain, despite my efforts, British acceptance of our military intervention in the Rhineland." In other words, *"Nous sommes trahis."* In Berlin, Shirer scrawled in his diary: "Hitler has got away with it!" And so he had. The Führer immediately ordered a nationwide plebiscite to ask the *Volkes* whether they approved of the coup, and 98.8 percent voted *ja.*[74]

In Parliament that same month Winston reflected: "When we think of the great power and influence which this country exercises we cannot look back with much pleasure on our foreign policy in the last five years. They have certainly been very disastrous years." He spoke slowly, his voice heavy: "Five years ago all felt safe; five years ago we were all looking forward to peace, to a period in which mankind would rejoice in the treasures which science can spread to all classes if conditions of peace and justice prevail. . . . Look at the difference in our position now! We find ourselves compelled once again to face the hateful problems and ordeals which those of us who worked and toiled in the last struggle hoped were gone forever."

He summed up the outcome of the latest crisis: "What is, after all, the first great fact with which we are confronted? It is this. An enormous triumph has been gained by the Nazi regime. . . . The violation of the Rhineland is serious from the point of view of the menace to which it exposes Holland, Belgium, and France. It is also serious from the fact that when it is fortified . . . it will be a barrier across Germany's front door, which will leave her free to sally out eastward and southward by the back door."[75]

This speech was ignored. Macmillan recalls that at that time Winston's "speeches and demands . . . however effective in themselves, were injured because of the general doubt as to the soundness of his judgement," and Lady Longford described him as "the disregarded voice of Cassandra."[76]

Painter Paul Maze wrote Churchill, "Half England is hardly aware of the situation." That was understating it. The masses of the British people, few of whom knew where or what the Rhineland was, had returned with relief to their daily routines. Sir Oswald Mosley was planning an anti-Semitic demonstration, the Cunarder S.S. *Queen Mary* was ready for launching, George Orwell's *Keep the Aspidistra Flying,* having received mixed reviews, was selling poorly, and early vacationers in Brighton heard music hall "vocalists," as they were now called, croon:

> *These foolish things*
> *Remind me of you . . .*

Nazism had become fashionable in London's West End. Ladies wore bracelets with swastika charms; young men combed their hair to slant across their foreheads. Paul Maze continued: *"Do* write to the papers all you can. The German propaganda spread about is most harmful, especially in Mayfair society!"[77]

The Führer still had many admirers in Parliament and a lofty one (King Edward VIII) in Buckingham Palace. Germanophilia in the British upper classes had begun as an open, closely reasoned cause, but as the nature of Nazism became evident, with Churchill lifting rocks to show the creatures scurrying below, its character had changed. Martin Gilbert and Richard Gott observed that, "the more it was opposed and the more it was shown to be inadequate, if not erroneous, the more it transformed itself into a hidden obsession." The faithful plotted in the dark, behind closed doors. Sympathy for the Germans, "originally a mood to be proud of," Gilbert and Gott wrote, "became, with the brutalization of German politics, a mood of whispers and cabals." *The Times* echoed *Der Angriff* and *Völkischer Beobachter;* much was made of the joint Saxon heritage shared by pure-blooded Britons and German Aryans (and *not* by Jews). British criticism of the Third Reich was deeply resented in Berlin, and the British embassy there was always quick to apologize for it.[78]

The Quai d'Orsay and the Foreign Office, bruised and shaken, had done their best to paper over the debacle with new documents, exchanges of formal letters, and sealed covenants. Flandin wearily told the British he would accept Hitler's coup provided the reoccupation remained *symbolique* and unfortified — a provision which England could not possibly guarantee. Nevertheless, Eden and the FO went to work, persuading the other signatories to accept the Nazi fait accompli. Meanwhile, the League of Nations council went through the motions of condemning Germany for her treaty violations. On the day of the council's finding, twelve irreclaimable days had passed since the Führer's nervous battalions had crossed the Rhine bridges. Since no one even raised the question of imposing sanctions on the aggressor, the condemnation was a meaningless gesture, serving only to demonstrate the league's hollow authority and shrunken prestige.

The repercussions were not over. In 1918, when Ludendorff was plunging his bloody fists into the snakelike line of Allied trenches winding from the Swiss border to the Channel, the northern anchor of the defense had been held by King Albert's stubborn Belgians. Now Albert had lain in his grave for two years and the country was ruled by Leopold III, frivolous, shallow, and callow. After the fall of the Rhineland, Leopold decided that Britain and France were no longer reliable allies. He renounced the military alliance Albert had signed with the democracies twenty years earlier and acquired written releases from Paris and London. This meant that at the outbreak of war French troops could not enter Belgium until a Nazi invasion had been confirmed. "In one stroke," writes Alistair Horne, the British military historian, "the whole of her [France's] Maginot Line strategy lay in fragments."[79]

By March 26, less than three weeks after a few thousand poorly equipped Wehrmacht troops had cowed the armed might of France, photographs of the rising system of concrete fortresses Hitler was building opposite the Maginot Line — the Siegfried Line — came into Churchill's possession, and during the first week in April he received detailed reports. Shielding his sources, he shared the substance of the reports with the House. In a remarkably prescient speech he pointed out that these redoubts would permit Nazi troops to be "economised on that line," enabling "the main force to swing round through Belgium and Holland." If that happened, and the two Low Countries fell "under German domination," England would be in mortal peril, a terrifying prospect, he said, which was "brought very much nearer to this island by the erection of the German fortress line." Nor was that all. "Look east," he continued. "There the consequences of the Rhineland fortification may be more immediate. . . . Poland and Czechoslovakia, with which must be associated Yugoslavia, Rumania, Austria and some other countries, are all affected very decisively the moment this great work of construction has been completed."[80]

Parliament was unmoved. It was characteristic of the late 1930s that His Majesty's Government — and the vast majority of His Majesty's subjects — assumed that each crisis was the last, and that Hitler could be taken at his word when he assured them that he would press no further claims upon Europe. Churchill warned them now: "When you are drifting down the stream of Niagara, it may easily happen that from time to time you run into a reach of quite smooth water, or that a bend in the river or a change in the wind may make the roar of the falls seem far more distant. But" — his voice dropped a register, and only those who strained could hear — "*your hazard and your preoccupation are in no way affected thereby.*"[81]

On May 18 the Reich's foreign minister, Baron Konstantin von Neurath, received William Bullitt, Franklin Roosevelt's friend and the American ambassador to France. Neurath could scarcely have spoken more plainly. In his report to the State Department Bullitt quoted Neurath as declaring that it would be "the policy of the German Government" to take no new action beyond Germany's borders "until the Rhineland has been digested. . . . Until the German fortifications have been constructed on the French and Belgian frontiers, the German Government will do everything possible to prevent rather than encourage an outbreak by the Nazis in Austria and will pursue a quiet line with regard to Czechoslovakia." Neurath's parting words to Bullitt were: "As soon as our fortifications are constructed and the countries of Central Europe realize that France cannot enter German territory at will, those countries will begin to feel very differently about their foreign policies and a new constellation will develop."[82]

If public men of vision are tough, as Churchill was, they endure. If they are not, and most are not, they perish or live out their lives in lonely exile. The future may serve as an appellate court. It cannot, however, award retroactive damages, and so Ralph Wigram can never be redeemed. He was not a weak man. Nevertheless, Hitler's successful smash-and-grab coup had, in Churchill's words, dealt Wigram "a mortal blow." The crisis had subjected him to an unbearable strain. Valentine Lawford, one of Wigram's subordinates, notes that the "purely physical demands of those twelve days had been almost intolerable; and they had still further enfeebled the frail organs of a frail body." After Flandin had left London, Wigram forced himself to tour the occupied Rhineland. There he was shocked to see little children, coached by German soldiers, play "grenades" with snowballs. He returned to his Lord North Street home, as Ava Wigram later wrote Churchill, "and said to me, 'War is now *inevitable*, and it will be the most terrible war there has ever been. I don't think I shall see it, but you will. Wait now for bombs on this little house.' " He felt a sense of personal guilt. He told her, "I have failed to make the people here realize what is at stake. I am not strong enough to make the people here understand. Winston has always, always understood, and he is strong and will go on to the end." Several months later, writes Henry Pelling, Fellow of St. John's College, Cambridge, "depression overtook him and he committed suicide."[83]

Vansittart phoned the news to Winston. Churchill wrote Clementine,

"I was deeply shocked & grieved. . . . I thought him a grand fellow."
Meantime Clementine, skiing in Austria, had read Wigram's obituary in
The Times, and their letters crossed in the mail, hers reading: "He was a
true friend of yours & in his eyes you cd see the spark wh showed an inner
light was burning — His poor wife will be overwhelmed with grief."
Bearing a wreath, Winston attended the funeral, near Hayward's Heath,
with Vansittart, Bracken, and Maze. Afterward they brought the young
widow and the Wigrams' five-year-old mongoloid child back to Chartwell
for lunch. Churchill was amazed to learn — it is astonishing that a statesman who owed so much to civil servants should not have known — that,
as he wrote Clemmie, "there appears to be no pension or anything for
Foreign Office widows." In another note he added: "Poor little Ava is all
adrift now. She cherished him [Ralph] & . . . he was her contact with gt
affairs. Now she has only the idiot child."[84]

The last phrase jars. So does Churchill's mention of Wigram in his
memoirs. To be sure, Winston wrote that his death "was an irreparable loss
to the Foreign Office, and played its part in the miserable decline of our
fortunes," but then he adds that Wigram "took it too much to heart. After
all, one can always go on doing what one believes to be his duty, and
running ever greater risks till knocked out." Churchill, Boothby noted,
could be cruel. It seems less than generous thus to stigmatize Wigram,
suggesting that he had deserted his post in his country's hour of need. Yet
that seems to have been Winston's final opinion. One feels that in one of
his combative moods, Churchill would have sympathized with General
Patton for slapping a soldier broken by the shock of battle. Winston had
been hammered and tempered and shaped by ordeals beyond Wigram's
imagining. And, of course, Wigram would have been no match for
Hitler. Churchill knew he was, or would be, if he could only reach the
helm.[85]

Now, over two years since Winston had first urged the appointment of a
minister of defense to preside over the three services, Baldwin prepared to
make the appointment. He had been under great pressure from the press
and Parliament to name Churchill. Even Neville Chamberlain, for once in
agreement with his half brother, had said: "Of course, if it is a matter of
military efficiency, Winston is no doubt the man." In his memoirs
Churchill recalled that "I was naturally aware that this process was going
on. In the debate of March 9" — Monday, two days after the Rhineland
invasion, when the House first confronted the developing crisis — "I was
careful not to derogate in the slightest degree from my attitude of severe
though friendly criticism of Government policy."[86]

He wrote to Clemmie, insisting, "I do not mean to break my heart whatever happens," but of course he craved office. In the same letter he examined the prospects of the two candidates most prominently mentioned in the press and reported that neither really wanted the job — Neville Chamberlain "because he sees the premiership not far away" and Sir Kingsley Wood "because he hopes to be Chancellor of the Exchequer then and anyhow does not know a Lieutenant-General from a Whitehead torpedo." Thus, he reasoned, "it may all come back to your poor pig."[87]

Baldwin's reservations about Winston remained; and he had to consider his eventual successor. One of Neville Chamberlain's biographers writes: "The party would not have the immediate return of Hoare. If the new Ministry went to Churchill, it would alarm those Liberal and Central elements who had taken his exclusion as a pledge against militarism, it would be against the advice of those responsible for interpreting the party's general will, and would it not when Baldwin disappeared raise a disputed succession?"[88]

Churchill, Neville Chamberlain, and Kingsley Wood were not the only names which were submitted for the new ministry; the secretary of state for air, Lord Swinton (formerly Philip Cunliffe-Lister), and Walter Runciman, the president of the Board of Trade, were being considered. And so, by Hoare, was Hoare. Speaking from the back benches the injured ice skater skated on very thin ice indeed by making what a friend recalls as "a curiously distasteful bid for office." Neville Chamberlain noted it in his diary: "He began well but shocked the House by an elaborate tribute to S.B. which sounded like an obvious and clumsy bid for power and created a thoroughly bad impression."[89]

Actually, the prime minister preferred Hoare for the post, but nothing could be done until he had been rehabilitated. Baldwin and those around him also shied away from the thought of what they called "a strong personality" in the new ministry. These and other "niceties and gravities," as a Chamberlain biographer called them, had been "well weighed" for a full month, the month that ended during the Rhineland crisis.[90]

Nazi aggression, one might think, should have lent support to Winston's candidacy. At this, of all times, it seems inconceivable that Baldwin would pick a weak man to supervise the defense of England. Nevertheless, that was what he did. Baldwin said outright: "If I pick Winston, Hitler will be cross." In his biography of Chamberlain, Keith Feiling writes that the Rhineland was "decisive against Winston's appointment"; it was "obvious that Hitler would not like it." As the prime minister's heir apparent, Chamberlain encouraged Baldwin to think along these lines. He suggested that Baldwin choose a man "who would excite no enthusiasm" and "create no jealousies." The prime minister agreed. On Saturday, March 14 — exactly a week since German troops had crossed the Rhine — he

Chartwell: Churchill's sanctuary, home, and great keep.

Churchill's study, in the oldest part of Chartwell, which dates from 1086, twenty years after the Battle of Hastings.

Churchill in his study.

The Churchill coat-of-arms, with its motto—fitting for this period of his life—"Faithful but unfortunate."

Winston, Clementine, Diana, Randolph, and friends entertain Charlie Chaplin *(far right)* **at Chartwell.**

Clementine bathing in
Chartwell's swimming
pool, one of Winston's
creations.

A life mask of
Clementine, taken by
Paul Hamann, a German
artist, in the early 1930s.

Major (later Sir) Desmond Morton, a member of Churchill's intelligence net and a Chartwell neighbor.

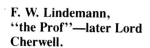

F. W. Lindemann, "the Prof"—later Lord Cherwell.

Brendan Bracken.

A Chartwell guest: French socialist Leon Blum, former Premier of France.

Albert Einstein *(right)* , another 1930s guest, in Chartwell's rose garden.

Jack Churchill and Clementine play bezique.

Accompanied by her parents, Sarah "comes out"—is formally presented at the Court in Buckingham Palace—in 1932.

Diana and her father leaving Morpeth Mansions in December 1932 for her marriage at St. Margaret's, Westminster, where Winston and Clementine had wed on September 12, 1908. Diana's marriage ended in divorce three years later.

Winston, Clementine, and Randolph hunt with the Duke of Westminster's boarhounds in Normandy, January 20, 1933.

Mary, aged thirteen, visibly excited, is flanked by her parents en route to Westminster Hall to hear loyal addresses from both Houses of Parliament, celebrating the Silver Jubilee of King George V and Queen Mary, May 9, 1935.

Diana's second marriage, to Duncan Sandys, MP, September 16, 1935.

After electing Churchill Lord Rector of Edinburgh University, students chair him through the city streets.

A shooting party, representing the power elite confronted by
the Führer of the Third Reich. *(Left to right)* Geoffrey Dawson,
editor of *The Times* and an implacable foe of Churchill's;
Lieutenant-Colonel R. Lane Fox, MP (later Lord Bingley);
Neville Chamberlain; Lord Halifax; and Sir Roger Lumley
(later Earl of Scarbrough, K.G.).

Sir Horace Wilson,
Chamberlain's *éminence grise*.

David Lloyd George, Britain's World War I Prime Minister, and Churchill in November 1934. A year earlier the BBC, pandering to Nazi Germany, banned both of them and Sir Austen Chamberlain, a distinguished former Foreign Secretary, from taking part in a series of political broadcasts.

announced that he was establishing, not a ministry of defense, but a ministry for coordination of defense. Its leader, the new cabinet member, would be Sir Thomas Inskip.[91]

Inskip? Fleet Street and Parliament were incredulous. The name was familiar but had been attached to no political achievements. As a youth Inskip had seriously considered becoming a missionary. Called to the bar instead, he had taken silk, and, for most of the past fourteen years, had been England's solicitor general or attorney general. Macmillan recalled that he lacked "the slightest glimmer of that ruthless determination, by which alone such an office could have been made effective at such a time." Until now he had never before been proposed or even considered for a high cabinet post. A search of *The Times* files reveals that his only notable public effort had been a successful campaign to suppress revisions of the Anglican prayer book. His appointment had been suggested to the prime minister by Chamberlain and David Margesson, the Tories' chief whip, on the ground that he was "the safest man." Now, rising from the front bench for his maiden speech as watchdog of Britain's security, Inskip confessed: "I may say, with all sincerity, that it never occurred to me — I say this in all seriousness — that I would ever be able to discharge this duty even if it were offered to me. . . . I do not claim to be a superman."[92]

In *The Gathering Storm,* the most personal of his six books on World War II, Churchill wrote that Baldwin had selected "an able lawyer, who had the advantages of being little known himself and knowing nothing about military subjects." He also set down his deeper, emotional reaction to the Inskip appointment: "To me this definite, and as it seemed final, exclusion from all share in our preparations for defence was a heavy blow." Bitterness was uncharacteristic of him, but in three acrid sentences he revealed his naked anger, his feeling that England had been placed in even greater peril, and he himself personally violated: "Mr. Baldwin certainly had good reason to use the last flickers of his power against one who had exposed his mistakes so severely and so often. Moreover, as a profoundly astute party manager, thinking in majorities and aiming at a quiet life between elections, he did not wish to have my disturbing aid. He thought, no doubt, that he had dealt me a politically fatal stroke, and I felt he might well be right."[93]

He added, accurately, that the "Prime Minister's choice was received with astonishment by press and public." Macmillan later commented that "Astonishment is almost an understatement. Even the most defeatist and most adulatory of the Prime Minister were aghast." Winston's friends were in shock. Lord Lloyd recalled Lindemann telling him that Baldwin's choice was "the most cynical thing that has been done since Caligula appointed his horse as consul." One of Lloyd George's young parliamentary protégés called it "another glaring instance of the stupidity of party politics, which always denies a nation the services of most of its best men," and Anthony Crossley added two more verses to his venomous parody:

> *Did you dare, Father Churchill, did you dare to expect*
> *   A summons to the Council again,*
> *In the face of the feeling that haunts the elect*
> *   That they scoffed at your warnings in vain?*

> *You're polite to the small and you're rude to the great,*
> *   Your opinions are bolder and surer*
> *Than is seemly today in an office of state —*
> *   You've even insulted the Führer.*[94]

Churchill had proposed a five-man cabinet team to supervise preparedness. To the three traditional posts of air, war, and Admiralty he would have added a minister of supply, with a defense minister presiding over the four. Given the complexities of total war, he argued, a ministry of supply was vital. Its responsibilities would include the manufacture of arms and equipment, the policing of profiteers, and agreements with the trade unions, who would become mutinous if, say, excessive profits for defense industries were not restrained. Baldwin, unimpressed, merely told Inskip to "coordinate" defense. He gave him no instructions on what that vague word meant, no power to enforce his decisions, and no professional advisers. It is difficult to grasp what he expected from a committed pacifist who had never worn a uniform nor heard the sound of gunfire, who — at a time when military strategy depended on an understanding of new weapons, including mastery of radar, upon which England's very survival would depend — had never even flown in an airplane, and whose only previous encounter with Britain's defense establishment had been a consequence of his opposition to rephrasing the Anglican service for burial of the dead at sea.

> *Alice laughed. "There's no use trying," she said; "one can't believe impossible things."*
> *"I daresay you haven't had much practice," said the Queen.*

Passed over for a cipher when he had been supremely qualified, Churchill was now free to unsheathe his broadsword again. But to sulk or fume would have diminished him. "I had to control my feelings," he later wrote, "and appear serene, indifferent, detached." Of course, he was not capable of detachment. Nor should he have been. Someone had to sound the alarm bell after Göring, contemptuous of the Allies' pusillanimity, announced that between four million and five million "active, intelligent, valiant Germans" were working "night and day" in the munitions factories of the Ruhr to arm the expanding Wehrmacht. In the *Evening Standard* Winston expressed astonishment that Parliament and the British people should ignore this boast and its implications. The Reich, he wrote, "is arming more strenuously, more scientifically and upon a larger scale, than any nation has ever armed before. . . . Surely these are facts which ought to bulk as large in ordinary peaceful people's minds as horse-racing, a prize fight or nineteen-twentieths of the current newspaper bill of fare." Over the next several days the *Standard* received a thick sheaf of letters from outraged subscribers protesting the publication of such "nationalistic" articles by England's "number one warmonger."[95]

He was in fact the country's number one peacemonger, the last champion of the League of Nations and therefore of collective security, the only policy which could have thwarted Hitler before the war which he alone wanted destroyed Europe's dominance of the globe. Once other countries had been knitted in a "strong confederacy for defence and peace," Winston told an inattentive House, "they should give Germany an absolute guarantee of the inviolability of German soil and a promise that if anyone offended her all will turn against that one, and if she strikes at anyone all will stand by and defend that victim." He ended: "Let us free the world from the approach of a catastrophe, carrying with it calamity and tribulation beyond the tongue of man to tell." Later he would be remembered as a great war leader, but no man ever fought harder for peace.[96]

Delivering the first report of progress in the new ministry, Inskip braced his stocky legs and, turning his curiously bunched face to the House, spoke confidently of "a swelling tide of production," reporting that "forty new aerodromes have been or are being acquired." In fact the new ministry had already acquired a reputation for slackness. Desmond Morton passed Winston a detailed analysis of Inskip's speech. "A swelling tide of production"? There was, said Morton, "nothing of the kind"; the only steps being taken were "to get industry into a condition *eventually* to produce what is required." Inskip's staff had contacted fifty-two firms, asking whether they would turn out armaments; fourteen agreed to manufacture munitions, "but none of them, not even the fourteen who have accepted firm contracts, have yet entered into production." The "forty new aerodromes" were simply forty fields which Inskip's staff had inspected accompanied by real estate agents. "The forty pieces of ground have not yet even been acquired."[97]

In the House in July, Inskip continued to sing hymns of exultation. To be sure, he acknowledged, Britain's heavy reliance on imported machine tools was unfortunate, and he further conceded that English factories would be unable to turn out shells for at least two years. But he felt certain that the government's "hope and trust" would assure the recruitment of enough skilled workers to man the machines. Churchill, troubled, replied that it would be unwise for him to set forth his case "in open debate in this Chamber. . . . The times have waxed too dangerous for that." Parliament's Foreign Affairs Committee, meeting behind closed doors, had heard Winston out. Harold Nicolson was there and thought his presentation unanswerable. Ranging beyond defense, Winston pointed out that were the Germans given a free hand in eastern Europe, as they had asked, within a year they would be dominant from Hamburg to the Black Sea. England, in that case, would be faced by the most formidable coalition since the fall of Napoleon. But a majority of the committee members belonged to Baldwin, and "what they would really like," Nicolson wrote, "would be a firm agreement with Germany and possibly Italy by which we could purchase peace at the expense of the smaller states. This purely selfish policy would to my mind make an Anglo-German war quite certain within twenty years."[98]

Churchill would have preferred to ignore Inskip himself, knowing that his criticism would invite charges of jealousy. But he could not remain seated when the new minister told the House that defense preparations for England would "of course" be circumscribed because interference with the country's commerce, and the everyday lives of its people, was unthinkable. Winston challenged him. Inskip, he said, had "made a very important pronouncement" in explaining that he was "working under peace conditions." There were, he pointed out, "many conditions" between peacetime and wartime: "preparatory conditions, precautionary conditions, emergency conditions." He had been under the impression that the new ministry had been created to recommend which of them should be adopted now. Churchill cited fresh data from Germany, obtained "from a source which I cannot divulge." Checking these figures against those published by the Nazi regime, he had found that they confirmed one another, revealing that Hitler had spent twenty billion marks preparing for war since coming to power, and, during 1935, another eleven billion — far in excess of Churchill's earlier estimate.

What, he asked, was England's new defense ministry doing? It was "drifting and dawdling as the precious months flow out." No member should be under the illusion, he said, that the balance could be redressed later by a massive appropriation of funds. The House had just approved the expenditure of fifty million pounds on munitions. But only twenty million could be spent because the gun and shell plants "and, above all, the aeroplane factories," had inadequate stockpiles of raw materials, lacked workers with the right skills, and hadn't retooled. One must also consider the workmen at the forges, lathes, and drills, he said, again raising the issue of profiteering. As minister of munitions in the last war he had learned that "you cannot do anything without a working arrangement with the trade unions"; they would not cooperate "so long as they think there are a lot of greedy fingers having a rakeoff." It is a measure of both the government's incompetence and its contempt for Churchill that another two years would pass before Inskip's ministry met with Labour's leaders.[99]

"A slow sort of country!" said the Queen. "Now, here, you see, it takes all the running you can do, to keep in the same place. If you want to get somewhere else, you must run at least as fast as that!"

❦   ❦

As usual Winston sat down to a faint ripple of applause. After the last division — MPs vote, literally, by dividing, leaving the chamber through one of two exits, "aye" or "no" — members scurried out into Parliament Square, pausing there to buy newspapers. The newsstand dealers were well stocked. As the season wore on, they had found, MPs were buying more papers every week. The news was extremely interesting, and became even more so when warm weather arrived. On May 5, the Duce's ragged legions finally straggled into the Ethiopian capital of Addis Ababa. Two months later, on Thursday, July 2, the League of Nations bowed to the inevitable, and discontinued all sanctions against Italy. Now, on July 18, Generalissimo Francisco Franco, *El Caudillo* and former chief of Spain's General Staff, broadcast a manifesto from his outpost in the Canary Islands, proclaiming a Fascist revolt against the country's republican government.

It is difficult to recapture the intense passions aroused throughout Europe and much of the United States by the bitter, bloody three-year Spanish Civil War. It was, among other things, a religious war. Loyalists, as the defenders of the republic were known, were not only hostile to the church; they tortured priests, raped nuns, and slaughtered innocents. Roman Catholics committed atrocities equally vile. The republic was Spain's legitimate government, but it had proved incapable of governing a nation in social and economic turmoil.

Labour had remained inflexibly pacifist, but in Edinburgh in October, at the party's first annual meeting after Franco's revolt, delegates were split over whether England should remain aloof in Spain. Cripps expressed the familiar Labour policy in an open letter to the Glasgow *Forward,* urging that "every possible effort should be made to stop recruiting for the armed forces. . . . Suppose you won another imperial victory, what then? British Fascism would be less brutal than German, but the world situation would be no better. Another Versailles peace, another period of acute suffering for the workers, and then the next war. That's all." On the first day of the conference Arthur Greenwood introduced a resolution calling for nonintervention in Spain, and it passed, 1,836,000 to 510,000 — 3.6 to 1.[100]

But within the party a great anguished turning had begun, a growing realization that pacifism had been discredited — that the only effective answer to Fascist and Nazi aggression was to cross swords with it. (The most astute of the pacifists, for whom George Orwell would speak two years later in his *Homage to Catalonia,* had also begun to question Moscow's motives in backing the Loyalist cause.) On October 7, 1936, two days after Greenwood's resolution, the Spanish issue was raised again, in a moment of high drama. The conference was addressed by Señora Dolores Ibarruri, celebrated by Spanish Loyalists as *La Pasionaria.* Her English was flawless — she was the daughter of a Scotswoman — and she spoke movingly of insurgent atrocities, Republican heroism, and hope for a new, socialist Spain. She ended: "We know that we are holding your hand over the distance. But if you wish this atrocious war to end soon, come and help us. Think of the precious gift that is being wasted — of the lives of our youth. Do not tarry. Now you know the truth. Now you know what the situation is. Come and help us. Come and help us. Scotsmen, ye ken noo."[101]

It was, Hugh Dalton recalled, "a magnificent performance, and it swept the whole Conference to its feet. We all rose and sang 'The Red Flag.' " Dalton then moved that Britain meet her responsibilities, as a member of the League of Nations, by preserving "the people's rights and liberties, the continuance of democratic institutions, and the observance of international law" by rearming, the quicker the better. Attlee warned the conference that if they passed the motion they would increase the risk of a general European war and Cripps tried to shelve it, but the delegates' blood was up. The measure passed, 1,738,000 to 657,000 — 2.6 to 1. Labour's parliamentary party — the MPs — did not all approve of this transformation, but Churchill's crusade for a stronger Britain no longer seemed quixotic.[102]

Awakening from their pacifist dream, Labourites and intellectuals invested the Republican cause with a romantic nimbus, reflected in their slogan, *"No pasarán!"* ("They shall not pass!"). One young Communist undergraduate came to symbolize the swing from the submissiveness of pacifism to the aggressive mood of youths prepared to sacrifice their lives in the struggle against fascism. John Cornford, returning to Cambridge from the Edinburgh meeting, called for volunteers — students who wanted to fight Franco's troops by joining the ranks of the Loyalist army. He organized them into Brigades XI and XIV (Loyalists used military terms loosely — a "brigade" could range in size from a force of thousands to a few hundred, or even less than a hundred). He himself then crossed to the Iberian Peninsula and joined 145 other Englishmen in No. 1 Company, Twelfth Battalion, XIV Brigade. On December 27, 1936, he turned twenty-one. On that day, or the following day, he was killed in action. His body was never recovered.[103]

The Loyalist leadership was infested with Communists, but as Harold Macmillan put it, "Many young men — by no means all with Socialist sympathies — joined the International Brigade to support the Spanish Government, and battled heroically for their faith." After Hitler had called them "Jews and Communists," a German staff officer advising Franco reported sardonically: "They may be Jews and Communists, but they fight like Germans and beat Italians." Spain, in the words of A. J. P. Taylor, "provided for the generation of the thirties the emotional experience of a lifetime."[104]

The young idealists did not, however, reflect the views of the older generation, particularly those guiding Britain's political destinies. Hoare, who did, hoped "Fascists and Bolsheviks would kill each other off." At the Admiralty the sea lords heartily favored Franco; Harold Nicolson, ever the moderate, considered Loyalist Madrid "a mere Kerensky Government at the mercy of an armed proletariat," though "Franco and his Moors are no better." Without waiting for action in Berlin or Rome, Eden in August announced an embargo on arms to Spain, hoping, as he wrote Baldwin, that "we might, by setting an example, do our best to induce . . . Germany and Italy to follow suit."[105]

Germany and Italy did the exact opposite. Mussolini sent Franco over sixty thousand troops. The Führer directed Göring to take the first steps in what became a half-billion-mark program, shipping tanks, warplanes, and artillery, all accompanied by German technicians. One of the Führer's motives was to use the Iberian Peninsula as a proving ground for the Reich's new weapons. Alfried Krupp first tested six batteries of his 88's as they later became known and feared by World War II Allied infantrymen, in the siege of Madrid, and was pleasantly surprised; designed as antiaircraft guns, they were also effective against tanks and infantrymen. Krupp sent prototypes of his new U-boats to Spain, including the mammoth *Deutschland*. The Italians did likewise.

That was a mistake. One or more commanders, eager for action, torpedoed British and French merchantmen. In London the sea lords, so ardently pro-Franco that they wanted Eden to join Berlin and Rome in recognizing his government, attributed the losses to submarines of "unknown' origin." But their origin was unknown to no one, and nothing was surer to arouse the fury of Englishmen than firing on the red ensign. Angry questions were raised in Parliament. Chamberlain, speaking for the government, said that nothing could be done. "I have been through every possible form of retaliation," he declared on June 20, "and it is absolutely clear that none of them can be effective unless we are prepared to go to war with Franco, which might possibly lead to war with Germany, and in any case would cut right across [the] policy of general appeasement." Nevertheless, in the fall of 1937, Eden persuaded the French to join the Royal Navy in depth-charge attacks on Axis submarines. Berlin and Rome raised trivial objections, but they could do little more without confessing their guilt. Significantly, decisive action resolved the issue. As they quibbled, the Admiralty in London and the Amirauté in Paris began sweeping Spanish waters with a fleet of eighty destroyers. Overnight the submarine threat vanished. "Open piracy," Eden told the House, had ended.[106]

Hitler's most memorable contribution to the Caudillo's arsenal was the Condor Legion, a *Luftwaffeneinheit* (squadron) of bombers which inspired one of Pablo Picasso's most celebrated paintings. The civilized world was deeply shocked when it read that on April 27, 1937, nine waves of Heinkels, armed with 550-pound bombs and piloted by Germans in Spanish uniforms, had conducted a massive raid on Guernica, killing 1,654 civilians, most of them women and children. Foreign correspondents in the vicinity confirmed the early Loyalist reports. The burning question was: "Who was responsible?" Eden asked Ribbentrop whether Germany would agree to an international investigation; Hitler personally rejected the proposal as "entirely outside the bounds of possibility." Instead he blamed the Russians; Guernica, he said, was a *"bolschewistische"* outrage, whereupon Mussolini, now being gradually obscured by the Führer's lengthening shadow, called it *"bolscevico"* violence.[107]

Churchill's immediate response to the outbreak of fighting in Spain had been to damn the Loyalists as the more wicked of two wicked causes. "Naturally," he later wrote, "I was not in favor of the Communists. How could I be, when if I had been a Spaniard they would have murdered me and my friends?" In the *Evening Standard* of August 10, 1936, he wrote that the "constitutional and would-be Republic" had found itself "sliding steadily toward the Left . . . falling into the grip of dark, violent forces coming ever more plainly into the open, and operating by murder, pillage and industrial disturbance." Atrocities were being committed by both sides, he acknowledged, but he dwelt more luridly on the "nightly butcheries" of the Loyalists. Encountering the Republican ambassador at a reception, he turned away from the diplomat's outstretched hand, dramatically muttering, "Blood, blood, blood."[108]

Yet he was among the few who understood Hitler's role in Spain, and he was particularly troubled by the prospect of driving Mussolini deeper into the Nazi camp. In his view, advocating the use of British strength on any Iberian battlefield was absurd. Apart from the courting or alienating of Italy, Britain and the Empire had no stake in Spain. Indeed, Winston saw, an outright Anglo-French commitment to either side — given their military deficiencies, particularly in the air — would be madness. The "Spanish convulsion," he declared, could evoke but one response: "Send charitable aid under the Red Cross to both sides, and for the rest — keep out of it and arm." In August he added: "It is of the utmost importance that France and Britain should act together in observing the strictest neutrality themselves and endeavoring to induce it in others. This Spanish welter is not the business of either of us." He remembered what the Duke of Wellington had said: "There is no country in Europe in . . . which foreigners can intervene with so little advantage as Spain." In victory, he believed, Franco would be an ingrate, and as Hitler would discover, Winston was right.[109]

Those who regarded Churchill as a man of principle were baffled. They shouldn't have been. He had always nailed his colors to the mast, but not always to the same mast. His sole concern now was the safety of his country. William James once wrote that men of genius differ from ordinary men not in any innate quality of the brain, but in the aims and purposes on which they concentrate and in the degree of concentration which they manage to achieve. Napoleon, himself great, called it the mental power *"de fixer les objets longtemps sans être fatigué"* — to concentrate on objectives for long periods without tiring. Churchill possessed it. His eyes were focused on Hitler to the exclusion of all else. Earlier, when the Japanese invaded Manchuria, he had expressed doubts that the League of Nations "would be well-advised to have a quarrel with Japan. . . . I hope we shall try in England to understand a little the position of Japan, an ancient state, with the highest sense of national honor and patriotism and with a teeming population and a remarkable energy." One doubts that he would have been so indulgent had Malaya, Australia, and the Raj been threatened by Nipponese bayonets then.[110]

He reviled Hitler, but spoke enigmatically of Mussolini and the Caudillo. In Cannes he told Vincent Sheean that to him Ethiopia, the Rhineland, and Spain were not unrelated incidents, that they "involve the whole structure of Europe, with possibilities of realignment carrying the promise of deadly danger to England." It struck Sheean that Churchill's "patriotism was rapidly engulfing all other sentiments," that his "awareness of the danger to England drove out whatever had originally prepared him for benevolence toward the Fascist principle, and he was willing, in the end, to work with the extreme left if necessary to defeat the paramount enemy. This evolution I saw." At their last parting, with Franco on the verge of triumph, Sheean observed that Churchill, "saddened and made solemn by the whole thing, perceived the importance of the victory for Hitler and Mussolini, and regarded the fall of the Republic as a blow to England."[111]

Harold Macmillan remembered "Churchill talking to me with great energy on this [aspect] of the Spanish question. He decided to declare himself neutral, for his eye was on the real enemy." Italy, as he saw it, was not England's real enemy. In his memoirs he would write that Britain was "justified in going so far with the League of Nations against Italy as we could carry France," but he knew the French could not be carried far. At the time he said: "We are not strong enough to be the lawgiver and the spokesman of the world." There was poignance here, for in his youth — before 1914 destroyed Britain's paramountcy — they had been both.[112]

As Franco's Nationalists gained the upper hand, he urged the House not to repeat the Ethiopian fiasco: "It is no use once again leading other nations up the garden path and then running away when the dog growls." As Sheean had seen, once the tide of battle favored the Nationalists, Churchill turned away from them. In the *Daily Telegraph* he wrote on December 30, 1938, that "the British Empire would run far less risk from the victory of the Spanish Government than from that of General Franco," and a few months later he told subscribers to the *Telegraph* that "the British Conservative Right Wing, who have given him [Franco] such passionate support, must now be the prey of many misgivings." Since the German threat had absolute priority, he told the House, Britain should refuse to take sides in Spain, though "I will not pretend that, if I had to choose between Communism and Naziism, I would choose Communism." He added: "I hope I will not be called upon to survive in a world under a Government of either of these dispensations. I feel unbounded sorrow and sympathy for their victims."[113]

However qualified, this was a remarkable turnabout for the man who, in the turmoil after the Armistice, had led the attempt to stifle bolshevism in its cradle. But he had executed remarkable pivots before: in the first decade of the century, when, as a young MP, he had fought to provide the poor with unemployment insurance, pensions for the aged, and insurance for the sick; again, by joining the IRA's Michael Collins in the early 1920s to create the Irish Free State; and yet again, after the general strike of 1926, by leading the struggle for the underpaid, ill-housed, ill-fed British coal miners. If a foolish consistency is the hobgoblin of little minds, Winston was disqualified.

At the urging of Vansittart and Leeper, Churchill in 1936 embarked on a strenuous campaign to awaken Britain through public lectures and newspaper articles, beginning on April 3 in the *Evening Standard*. His cry of alarm, published in the most prominent newspapers of fourteen countries, warned that without concerted action by the nations now lying under the shadow of the swastika, "such civilisation as we have been able to achieve" would be reduced by renewed warfare to "pulp and squalor." The peoples of Europe, "chattering, busy, sporting, toiling, amused from day to day by headlines and from night to night by cinemas," were nevertheless "slipping, sinking, rolling backward to the age when 'the earth was void and darkness moved upon the face of the waters.' " Surely, he argued, "it is worth a supreme effort — the laying aside of every impediment, the clear-eyed facing of fundamental facts, the noble acceptance of risks inseparable from heroic endeavour — to control the hideous drift of events and arrest calamity on the threshold. Stop it! Stop it! Stop it!!! NOW is the appointed time."

Time increased Hitler's momentum. His triumph in the Rhineland had heightened the Third Reich's prestige throughout Europe and dealt England and France a deep wound, all the more painful because it was self-inflicted. The damage to Britain had been particularly grievous; in 1914 the French had gone to war because, facing invasion, they had no choice, but the British, who could have remained on the sidelines — where the Germans had begged them to stay — had fought to defend Belgian neutrality. Other small countries had assumed that they too could rely on the righteous might of history's greatest empire. Now that England had shown the white feather, recruits swelled the ranks of Nazi parties in Austria, Czechoslovakia's Sudetenland, western Poland, and the Free City of Danzig. New parties raised the hakenkreuz in Bulgaria, Rumania, and Hungary; and in May a Fascist plot was exposed in Estonia. On July 11 Churchill gloomily wrote Sir Hugh Tudor, with whom he had stood shoulder to shoulder when Ludendorff launched his great triad of offensives on March 21, 1918: "Everything is getting steadily worse on the Continent. A good deal of work is of course going on here, but all about two years behind."[114]

By now Churchill had gathered a formidable mass of data about war preparedness from Morton, Anderson, and the FO. He could not reveal it in open session without further endangering the national security, however, and Baldwin refused his request for secret session. The prime minister did agree to receive a delegation representing both houses of Parliament, and they met on July 28 and 29. There Churchill presented an extraordinary array of facts detailing German air strength, identifying his sources as French to protect his informants. He went on to discuss, among other matters, "night-flying under war conditions"; the need to recruit more university graduates as pilots and to train more navigators; the gap between planning aircraft production and actual delivery; the want of spare parts; the vulnerability of England's "feeding ports" of London, Bristol, Liverpool, and Southampton; the need for an "alternative centre of Government" if London were bombed flat; proposals to build underground storage tanks to protect the country's fuel oil from attack; radar; industrial mobilization; and the shortages of machine guns, bombs, searchlights, trench mortars, and grenades. He stopped short of recommending that the nation's industry be put on a war footing, but he did suggest that "we ought not to hesitate to impinge on a certain percentage — 25 percent, 30 percent . . . and force them and ourselves to that sacrifice." He said: "The months slip by rapidly. If we delay too long in repairing our defences, we may be forbidden by superior power to complete the process. . . . I say there is a state of emergency. We are in danger as we have never been in danger before."[115]

After Churchill had finished, Tom Jones wrote in his diary, "all subsequent speeches were an anti-climax." He was wrong. The most memorable remarks were Stanley Baldwin's. The prime minister observed that he could not "deal in detail with the many points that have been raised." He and Neville had discussed the implications of an all-out effort to prepare the country for the worst, he said, and had concluded that the adverse "effect on trade" would be too high a price to pay. Any disturbance of peacetime production "might throw back the ordinary trade of the country for many years," inflicting grave damage on the nation's economic health "at a time when we might want all our credit."[116]

Winston could not imagine how British credit could be useful if Hitler's headquarters were in Buckingham Palace, the Reichstag met in the House of Commons, and all Englishmen in public life were herded into concentration camps. Baldwin assured him it would never come to that. As the City said, the prime minister was a practical man, a "sound" man. Churchill's figures, he said, were "exaggerated" — unaware that most of them had appeared in the weekly reports he initialed and passed on, apparently unread — and, raising doubts about "the peril itself," he recited the worn litany that Hitler's Reich was a shield against the Bolshevik bogey. Germany had no designs on Western Europe, he told them, because

"West would be a difficult programme for her." The Führer wanted "to move East, and if he should move East, I should not break my heart." In all events, he was not going to get England into a war "for the League of Nations or for anybody else." If war broke out, he said, "I should like to see the Bolshies and the Nazis doing it." To Churchill this begged the question. Germany, not Russia, threatened the peace. His fear was that the Tory rank and file, championing Franco's brand of Red-baiting, would join Hitler's camp followers. After the meeting broke up he wrote Corbin at the French embassy that one of his "greatest difficulties" was "the German talk that the anti-Communist countries should stand together." Should Léon Blum — the new French leader, a socialist — support the Spanish Loyalists, he said, "the dominant forces here would be pleased with Germany and Italy, and estranged from France. . . . I do not like to hear people talking of England, Germany and Italy forming up against European Communism. It is too easy to be good."[117]

The unforgivable sin of a commander, said Napoleon, is to "form a picture" — to assume that the enemy will act a certain way in a given situation, when in fact his response may be altogether different. The first Allied response to the Nazi regime had been prompted by the universal loathing among decent men of modern war's senseless slaughter. But revulsion is a frail foundation for a foreign policy. As Hitler's belligerence became clearer, Baldwin, Chamberlain, their fellow appeasers in England, and *les apaisers* in France assured one another that he would fight the Russians and leave them alone. But wishing didn't make it so, and they should have known that; Baldwin himself had described Hitler as a "lunatic" with whom "you can never be sure of anything," adding that "none of us know what goes on in that strange man's mind." Therefore, in the autumn of 1936, he called for his fiddlers three — Samuel Hoare (now first lord of the Admiralty), Lord Halifax (lord privy seal), and Neville Chamberlain (Exchequer) — and moved toward what they thought was firmer ground.[118]

It was quicksand. Their new mantra was *diplomacy* — negotiation as a sensible alternative to war. Britain's honor, they told the public, would be preserved; the negotiating table, not the battlefield, was where differences between England and Germany would be resolved. They were convinced that Hitler had his price. Some of them believed this even after all their assumptions, and much of London, lay in ruins. Devoted to peace, they could not understand that the ruler of Nazi Germany disdained negotia-

tions, enjoyed bloodshed — including the shedding of German blood —
and therefore preferred military conquest. Churchill understood because
of the aggressive drives lying deep in his own complex personality. He
worked tirelessly to avoid hostilities, but if the Führer was determined to
fight, the prospect of unsheathing the sword of England struck no terror
in Winston's heart. All other remedies having been exhausted, he would
wield it with relish.

Unfortunately it was a blunt, rusting weapon in 1936, and its hilt lay
beyond his reach anyhow. Those who held it despised it. And on November 7, after King Edward VIII had opened the new session of Parliament,
they all but discarded it. Although the exhausted prime minister was
confined to Chequers on doctor's orders — only a handful knew that the
King's yearning for an impossible marriage was responsible for his
exhaustion — his cabinet, meeting in Downing Street and knowing he
would approve, set the course which would lead to Munich less than two
years later.

Inskip was first to speak. The devout Anglican had no prayer for the
League of Nations. Collective security, he said, was dead; after Ethiopia
and the Rhineland, confidence in it had simply "disappeared." He proposed it be succeeded by broadening "the appeasement of Germany's
economic conditions." This was the new diplomacy, which had its critics
even within the government. Foreign Secretary Eden and Secretary for
War Duff Cooper disagreed. The government, they argued, should give
absolute priority to preparing a credible response to Nazi aggression within
a year. Hoare protested that this would trigger an "immense upheaval,"
weakening England in the long run, and William Ormsby-Gore, the
colonial secretary, remarked that Britain's close ties with France were
"widely resented in the country."

Everyone awaited Chamberlain's decision. He would move into No.
10 in a few months; his voice would be decisive. After a long pause he
adopted a firm, if reasonable, tone. He saw no alternative to a widening of
the search for appeasement. The issue of "national safety" was hard to
oppose, he said, but as chancellor of the Exchequer he was "concerned that
the cost of defence programs was mounting at a giddy rate." The latest
White Paper had led to the appropriation of £400 million. Should the flow
of funds continue at the present rate, rumors of an unbalanced budget
would spread. If that happened — and his tone left no doubt that he viewed
the possibility as calamitous — they might discover that Britain's credit
abroad was "not so good as it was a few years ago."[119]

In the discussion the chancellor's most enthusiastic supporter was the
minister of health, Kingsley Wood. Wood's forte, and no one could do it
better, was tidying files, updating appointment books, and — he was a

wizard at this — keeping interoffice memos moving. After four years as Chamberlain's parliamentary private secretary, he had risen in the postal, telegraph, and telephone services. Baldwin, impressed by the alacrity with which his mail arrived, made inquiries about Kingsley Wood and was told that he was "a sound man." Soon Chamberlain would appoint him secretary of state for air, assigning him responsibility for the RAF with the enthusiastic approval of *The Times*, which hoped he would "increase the number of aeroplanes with the same bright suavity with which he has increased the number of telephone subscribers." Duff Cooper wrote of him: "He clings to the idea of friendship with Germany and hates the thought of getting too closely tied up with the French."[120]

The cabinet approved Chamberlain's position, and thus his emerging policy was established. To preserve Britain's financial resources, they would reach some sort of agreement with Hitler. The vote was not, however, unanimous. Eden, Duff Cooper, and Minister of Transport Leslie Hore-Belisha, veterans of the trenches, disagreed with the chancellor, thereby numbering their days in office, for Chamberlain had little patience with men who, after he had given them clear instructions, argued about them. Already it was said of those rallying to his standard that each was "like a naught in arithmetic that makes a place but has no value of its own."

> "Reeling and Writhing, of course, to begin with," the Mock Turtle replied, "and the different branches of Arithmetic — Ambition, Distraction, Uglification, and Derision."

Kept abreast of developments at No. 10 by his FO informants, Churchill had seen Chamberlain's move coming. His intelligence net had provided new evidence that Parliament's appropriations, which Chamberlain thought improvident, would prove pitifully inadequate should Hitler let slip the dogs of war. Next to air power, a matter of life or death for Britain, Winston took a personal interest in the tank corps. The tank had been his conception, originally meant to mash German barbed wire for British soldiers swarming over their parapets and across no-man's-land; he had forced it on a reluctant War Office and seen its triumphant performance in the Great War's last battles. Although he had yet to grasp the role it would play in the next conflict, he knew Allied tanks had to be strong enough to match Germany's. On the evening of October 27, Brigadier P. C. S. Hobart, commander of England's only tank brigade, arrived at Morpeth Mansions in mufti and laid before him the full extent of Britain's mobile armor. Its medium tanks, the world's best in 1918, were now hopelessly obsolete, surpassed in quality and quantity by those of Germany, Russia, Italy, and even isolationist America.

In the air Britain continued to lag; Wing Commander Anderson, taking his greatest risk yet, sent Churchill a diagram dated October 6 and stamped "for official use only," pinpointing the exact location and strength of all RAF operational, training, and administrative units, together with its chain of command. The most dismaying report to reach Morpeth Mansions came from Squadron Leader H. V. Rowley, who had returned from the Reich only a few days earlier. He wrote: "The development of air power in Germany has left me in a somewhat dazed condition, but with one fact firmly in my mind, and that fact is that they are *now* stronger in the air than England and France *combined*."[121]

Armed with all this, Churchill struck. The cabinet had endorsed Chamberlain's proposal, thereby giving formal approval to Baldwin's meandering appeasement by adopting it as His Majesty's foreign policy. Winston laid his facts before Austen Chamberlain and other members of the delegation Baldwin had so recently received and reassured. All joined in a phalanx which petitioned the prime minister to schedule a two-day debate on the country's defenses. Since most of them were elder statesmen of his own party, he had no choice. At long last Churchill would have it out with him with the House of Commons as spectators, and, in a sense, as jurymen.

In 1897, as a twenty-three-year-old cavalry officer stationed in India, Winston had written a striking essay, "The Scaffolding of Rhetoric." Unpublished but found among his papers after his death, it dealt with diction, rhythm, accumulation of argument, analogy, and — approvingly — "a tendency to wild extravagance of language." Extravagance did not, however, mean verbosity; he preferred short words because "their meaning is more ingrained in the national character and they appeal with greater force to simple understanding than words recently introduced from the Latin and the Greek." The key to a speaker's impact on his audience, he believed, was sincerity: "Before he can inspire them with any emotion he must be swayed by it himself. . . . Before he can move their tears his own must flow. To convince them he must himself believe." If he has grasped all these, young Winston had written, his is the most precious of gifts: "He who enjoys it wields a power more durable than that of a great king. He is an independent force in the world. Abandoned by his party, betrayed by his friends, stripped of his offices, whoever can command this power is still formidable."

Now, nearly forty years later, abandoned by his party, betrayed by friends, and stripped of office, Churchill himself had grasped and mastered rhetorical skills, and in the RAF debate of 1936 his range, force, and depth held the House rapt and brought Stanley Baldwin to his knees. On November 11, the first day of the debate, Winston's hapless victim was Inskip. Under Winston's pitiless questioning, the defense minister admitted that England could put up only 960 warplanes to match the Luftwaffe's front-line strength of 1,500. Churchill then asked him when the government proposed to reach a decision on the proposal to establish a ministry of supply. Inskip was stammering, contradicting himself, evading the issue with vague promises to "review" the matter "in a few weeks," when Hoare intervened.

Mr. Hoare: All that my right hon. Friend quite obviously meant — and I repeat it — is that we are constantly reviewing it.

Mr. Churchill: You cannot make up your minds.

Mr. Hoare: It is very easy to make interjections of that kind. He [Churchill] knows as well as anyone in the House . . . that the situation is fluid.[122]

In a lengthy exchange Hoare repeatedly used the word "fluid." It was among the notes in Churchill's hands when he rose the following afternoon. His sense of history, of irony, and of retribution prompted him to adopt a tactic which struck a profound chord among those who had followed his long struggle, including, in the Strangers' Gallery, Lady Violet Bonham Carter, with her lifelong emotional commitment to him. Exactly two years earlier Churchill had moved an amendment declaring that Britain's security from attack, especially in the air, was "no longer adequate." It was then that Stanley Baldwin had made his formal pledge — a personal commitment — to maintain British military superiority in the air. Now Winston moved the identical amendment with the same cosponsors: Amery, Guest, Winterton, Horne, and, in place of Bob Boothby, who was abroad, Colonel John Gretton.

The prime minister's vow was at forfeit, and there was no way to redeem it. Only twenty-four hours earlier Inskip had acknowledged to the House that the RAF was outnumbered by Göring's fleets of Heinkels, Messerschmitts, Junkers, and Focke-Wulfs. This was Winston's day to speak for all who knew that sooner or later England must confront Hitler, and to observe it he had worked through the night, dictating and revising passages to polish one of his most brilliant philippics. The amendment of November 1934, he reminded the House, had been "the culmination of a long series of efforts to warn the Government of looming dangers." Producing a discolored old newspaper, he quoted a *Times* account of one of his own 1933 speeches. He had said: "During the last four or five years the world has grown gravely darker. . . . We have steadily disarmed, partly with a sincere desire to give a lead to other countries, and partly through the severe financial pressure of the time. But a change must now be made. We must not continue longer on a course in which we alone are growing weaker while every other nation is growing stronger."[123]

Unheeded, he had therefore moved his amendment the following year, and exacted Baldwin's promise. In so doing, he now reminded the House, he had been "much censured by leading Conservative newspapers, and I remember that Mr Lloyd George congratulated the Prime Minister, who was then Lord President, on having so satisfactorily demolished my extravagant fears."

That was the background: his concern in 1933 and, in 1934, his warning, which had been dismissed as "alarmist." What would have been said then, he now wondered aloud, had he predicted what had actually happened since? Imagine that he had prophesied that Nazi Germany would spend billions of marks on weapons, creating a stupendous arsenal by organizing her industries for war "as the industries of no country have ever been," building "a gigantic air force," introducing conscription, occupying the Rhineland and fortifying it "with great skill," launching a large submarine fleet "with our approval, signified by treaty," and forming a standing army of thirty-nine divisions "of highly equipped troops," with another eighty divisions "rapidly being prepared" — all momentous events which threatened the peace of Europe and defied covenants signed by the German government. Assume that he had foretold the disarray of the smaller powers in eastern and central Europe, the Belgian declaration of neutrality — "which, if the worst interpretation proves to be true, so greatly affects the security of this country" — and the transformation of Italy from an Anglo-French ally to an Axis partner — "Italy, whose industry is so much smaller, whose wealth and credit are a small fraction of this country's," yet who boasts an army of "eight million bayonets."

He continued relentlessly: "Suppose all that had been forecast. Why, no one would have believed in the truth of such a nightmare tale. Yet just two years have gone by and we see it all in broad daylight. Where shall we be this time in two years? I hesitate to predict."

But some things seemed certain. During 1937 the Wehrmacht would outnumber the French and increase in efficiency. The gap between the Luftwaffe and the Allied air forces — particularly the long-range bombers — would continue to grow. The French and British rearmament programs "will not by themselves be sufficient." Therefore, the Western democracies should "gather round them all the elements of effective collective security . . . assembled on the basis of the Covenant of the League of Nations." It was his great hope that "we may succeed again in achieving a position of superior force" and "not repeat the folly which we committed when we were all-powerful and supreme," but instead "invite Germany to make common cause with us in assuaging the griefs of Europe and opening a new door to peace and disarmament."

The House was waiting, quiet but alert. They knew he had not risen to propose joining hands with Hitler. He always opened with feints, often with studied praise of those he meant to execute. No one, he said, could withhold sympathy from Inskip, who "from time to time lets fall phrases or facts which show that he realizes, more than anyone on that bench it seems to me, the danger in which we stand." One such phrase "came from his lips the other night." In justifying his weak ministerial performance, he had called the period before he had taken office "years that the locust hath eaten." Churchill intended to weave locusts in and out of his speech, but here he merely observed that "from the year 1932, certainly from the beginning of 1933, when Herr Hitler came to power, it was general knowledge in this country that serious rearmament had begun in Germany." Then, with a genial smile, he turned toward the prime minister and expressed his pleasure at seeing him back in the chamber, "restored to vigour . . . recuperated by his rest and also, as we hear, rejuvenated." Knowing Baldwin, Churchill said, he felt sure that he would not wish any "shrinking" from "real issues of criticism" over "his conduct of public affairs." At any rate, Winston intended to "proceed in that sense."

Now, like Ulysses, he bent his bow. His expression hardened; joviality faded; there was bite in his voice as, without taking his eyes off Baldwin, he declared that in matters of national security "there rests upon him inevitably the main responsibility for everything that had been done, or not done." From his waistcoat he produced a piece of paper and let the arrow fly, slowly reciting Baldwin's promise of March 8, 1934:

Any Government of this country — a National Government more than any, and this Government — will see to it that in air strength and air power this country shall no longer be in a position inferior to any country within striking distance of our shores.

The House was still, but Churchill's voice rose, as though he meant to be heard above a din: "Well, sir, I accepted that solemn promise." He recalled that some of his friends, men less trusting than he, had demanded particulars, and Baldwin had then "showed less than his usual urbanity in chiding those Members for even venturing to doubt the intention of the Government to make good in every respect the pledge which he had so solemnly given in the afternoon." Now, cuttingly, Winston said: *"I do not think that responsibility was ever more directly assumed in a more personal manner."*

Baldwin was set up. Everyone expected an immediate attack on him. Baldwin himself did, and of course Winston knew that, so he left him hanging there and briefly dealt with what at first seemed to be the less incendiary issue of ministerial supervision of the armed forces. "The proper organization," he said, "is four Departments — the Navy, the Army, the Air, and the Ministry of Supply, with the Minister for the Co-ordination of Defence over the four." He observed that "practically everyone in the House is agreed upon this," and — the tone was sharpening again — if Inskip "had known as much about the subject when he was appointed" as he must have learned by now, he would have insisted upon the reorganization. Now, committed, he stubbornly refused to alter his stand; he argued that a supply ministry would do more harm than good, disturb or delay military programs, upset the country, destroy trade, demoralize finance, and turn the country into "one vast munitions camp." But then, surprisingly, Inskip had told the House, " 'The decision is not final.' It would be reviewed again in a few weeks." Churchill turned on him and asked: "What will you know in a few weeks about this matter that you do not know now, that you ought not to have known a year ago, and have not been told any time in the last six months? What is going to happen in the next few weeks which will invalidate all these magnificent arguments by which you have been overwhelmed, and suddenly make it worth your while to paralyze the export trade, to destroy the finances, and to turn the country into a great munitions camp?"

In the next minute Hoare wished he had never heard the word "fluid."

The First Lord of the Admiralty . . . said, "We are always reviewing the position." Everything, he assured us, is entirely fluid. I am sure that that is true. Anyone can see what the position is. The Government simply cannot make up their minds, or they cannot get the Prime Minister to make up his mind.

So they go on in strange paradox, decided only to be undecided, resolved to be irresolute, adamant for drift, solid for fluidity, all-powerful to be impotent. So we go on preparing more months and years — precious, perhaps vital to the greatness of Britain — for the locusts to eat. They will say to me, "A Ministry of Supply is not necessary, for all is going well." I deny it. "The position is satisfactory." It is not true. "All is proceeding according to plan." We know what that means.

He was on them now, his vowels soaring and his consonants crashing as he reeled off dates, figures, and information new to those not on the front bench, revealing that 140,000 young Englishmen had volunteered for the territorials (reserves) only to find there were neither arms nor equipment for them; painting the shocking picture of the tank corps ("Nothing has been done in the years that the locusts have eaten for them"); decrying the army's lack of antitank weapons, antiaircraft weapons, wireless sets. In comic relief, he related the story that a friend of his had come upon "a number of persons engaged in peculiar evolutions, genuflections and gestures." He thought they must be gymnasts, evangelists, or "lunatics out for an airing," but found instead, they were "a Searchlight Company of the London Territorials who were doing their exercises as well as they could without having the searchlights." He waited a full moment, then ripped: *"Yet we are told there is no need for a Ministry of Supply."*

Many MPs had been in the smoking room or the lobby when he rose, but word spread that this was worth watching, and the House had become crowded. Winston had assumed an almost biblical pose, his feet planted apart, his body immobile save for his head, which slowly toiled back and forth as his eyes swept the chamber and he told off his wrath in heavy cadence: "If we go on like this, and I do not see what power can prevent us from going on like this, some day there may be a terrible reckoning, and those who take the responsibility so entirely upon themselves are either of a hardy disposition or they are incapable of foreseeing the possibilities which may arise."

Everyone anticipated what was coming next, and now, after one of those staged Churchillian entr'actes in which he feigned confusion, breaking the tension by appearing to fumble for a memorandum and then grope for a word, he resumed his stand, and, moving into another octave, turned to "the greatest matter of all, the air." On Tuesday night, he recalled, Hoare had given them "the assurance that there is no foundation whatever for the statement that we are 'vastly behindhand' with our Air Force programme. It is clear from his words that we are behindhand. The only question is, what meaning does the First Lord attach to the word 'vastly'? He also used the expression, about the progress of air expansion, that it was 'not unsatisfactory.' One does not know what his standard is. . . ."

He broke off. This pause was heavy. Other MPs, whenever within earshot of Hoare, had left his sacrifice of Ethiopia unmentioned. Winston had cared little about the African kingdom; what rankled was Hoare's mortal blow to the League of Nations, which, he believed, represented Europe's greatest hope of salvation. To him sabotaging the principle of collective security forfeited any right to pity. He glowered at Hoare across the gangway and said slowly: "His standards change from time to time. In that speech of the eleventh of September [to the League of Nations] *there was one standard*, and in the Hoare-Laval Pact *there was clearly another*."

Lowering his key Churchill told the House, in general terms, of the July deputation to Baldwin. Baldwin had said Winston's facts and figures were "exaggerated," but after checking them over the ensuing three months, Churchill had found them to be absolutely accurate, "and were it not that foreign ears listen to all we say, or if we were in secret session, I would repeat my statement here." A lucid, rapid-fire summation of Europe's balance of air power followed, comparing British and German might and reminding the House that "We were promised most solemnly by the Government that air parity with Germany would be maintained by the home defence forces. At the present time, putting everything at the very best, we are . . . only about two-thirds as strong as the German air force." Once more his baleful eye fell on Hoare. The first lord had confirmed Churchill's estimates of both Luftwaffe and RAF strength, yet said: "I am authorised to say that the position is satisfactory." Winston declared: "I simply cannot understand it. Perhaps the Prime Minister will explain the position."

The House, he submitted, had no choice but to demand an inquiry by six to eight "independent Members, responsible, experienced, discreet," who would "make a brief report to the House, whether of reassurance or of suggestion for remedying the shortcomings. That, I think" — and this was the first sign that he would not confine his fire to the Treasury Bench—"is what any Parliament worthy of the name would do in these circumstances. . . .I hope that Members of the House of Commons will rise above considerations of party discipline, and will insist upon knowing where we stand in a matter which affects our liberties and our lives." Before approaching his peroration he delivered a straight shot at Baldwin. "I should have thought that the Government, and above all the Prime Minister, whose load is so heavy, would have welcomed such a suggestion."

Then:

Owing to past neglect, in the face of the plainest warnings, we have now entered upon a period of danger greater than has befallen Britain since the U-boat campaign was crushed. . . . The era of procrastination, of half-measures, of soothing and baffling expedients, of delays, is coming to its close. In its place we are entering a period of consequences. . . . Germany may well reach the culminating point of her gigantic military preparations. . . . If we can shorten this period in which the German Army will begin to be so much larger than the French Army, and before the British Air Force has come to play its complementary part, we may be the architects who build the peace of the world on sure foundations.[124]

Here another speaker would have ended. But Winston was not finished with them. The quintessential Churchill of the 1930s stood proudly alone. He had not been swayed by public opinion. But others had, and he meant to put them on notice. If he offended them they had it coming. One cannot imagine Franklin Roosevelt condemning Congress, or Hitler — though he could have done it with impunity — the Reichstag. Churchill could, and did, damn the House of Commons. And it was the finest passage in his speech. Harold Nicolson, watching, noted: "His style is more considered and slower than usual, but he drives his points home like a sledge-hammer."[125] Even *The Times* described his coda as "brilliant":

Two things, I confess, have staggered me, after a long parliamentary experience, in these debates. The first has been the dangers that have so swiftly come upon us in a few years, and have been transforming our position and the whole outlook of the world. Secondly, I have been staggered by the failure of the House of Commons to react effectively against those dangers. That, I am bound to say, I never expected. I would never have believed that we should have been allowed to go on getting into this plight, month by month and year by year, and that even the Government's own confessions of error would have produced no concentration of parliamentary opinion and force capable of lifting our efforts to the level of emergency. I say that unless the House resolves to find out the truth for itself it will have committed an act of abdication of duty without parallel in its long history.[126]

Baldwin's reply — halting in delivery and appalling in content — has, in the words of one historian, "haunted his reputation to and beyond the grave." "He speaks slowly," Nicolson wrote, "and with evident physical effort." One of the whips whispered: "This will take three months energy out of him." Toward the end of his speech, Nicolson thought his voice was as "limp as if he were a tired walker on a long road. The House realizes that the dear old man has come to the end of his vitality."[127]

The result was shocking. He was talking extemporarily — he usually did; that was part of his charm — but for once his celebrated candor betrayed him. He said: "I want to speak to the House with the utmost frankness. . . . The difference of opinion between Mr. Churchill and myself is in the years 1933 onwards." After reminding them of the financial crisis then, and remarking that in establishing and enforcing policy "a democracy is almost always two years behind the dictator," he declared: "I put before the whole House my own views with an appalling frankness." Speaking of 1933 and 1934, he reminded them that "at that time there was probably a stronger pacifist feeling running through the country than at any time since the war."

Suddenly he was talking, not about the threat to British lives and homes, but of votes, campaign slogans, and by-elections in which any candidate "who made the most guarded reference to the question of defence was mobbed for it." That, he said, "was the feeling of the country in 1933.

My position as the leader of a great party was not altogether a comfortable one." After the East Fulham results, in which a previously safe Tory seat was lost resoundingly "on no issue but the pacifist," he had asked himself "what chance there was within the next year or two of that feeling being so changed that the country would give a mandate for rearmament? Supposing I had gone to the country and said that Germany was rearming and that we must rearm, does anybody think that this pacific democracy would have rallied to that cry at that moment? I cannot think of anything that would have made the loss of the election from my point of view more certain."[128]

From my point of view. Surely this admits of but one interpretation. Tory victories were more important to Stanley Baldwin than the specter of Luftwaffe bombers overhead. Even *The Times*, after Baldwin's death a decade later, sadly concluded in its editorial columns that "what he sacrificed to political expediency obscured the real issue, delayed the education of public opinion, and impeded the process of rearmament, on the speed of which the success of any conceivable foreign policy then depended."

Baldwin has his defenders. Had the coalition lost, they point out, power would have passed to the parliamentary Labour party, which opposed any rearmament whatsoever. It is true that Labour didn't want it done. But then, Baldwin hadn't really done it. In 1935, urging support for Conservative candidates, he had told crowds that despite the ugly stories from Germany, "I confess that in my own political experience I have not encountered Governments possessed of all these malevolent qualities," and adopted as his rallying cry, "No great armaments!"[129]

To Churchill the argument that "the Government had no mandate for rearmament until after the General Election" was "wholly inadmissible":

The responsibility of Ministers for the public safety is absolute and requires no mandate. It is in fact the prime object for which Governments come into existence. The Prime Minister had the command of enormous majorities in both Houses of Parliament ready to vote any necessary measures of defence. The country has never yet failed to do its duty when the true facts have been put before it, and I cannot see where there is a defence for this delay.[130]

Afterward Londonderry wrote Winston: "SB's admission was a very remarkable one." The prime minister, he noted, had never acknowledged that "the country was running risks. In fact his lips were sealed. We told him and Neville of the risks, but they were too frightened of losing bye-elections." In a postscript Londonderry added: "Neville was really the villain of the piece because he as Chancellor blocked everything on the grounds of Finance." Nevertheless, Churchill's later indictment of Baldwin's confession stands: "It carried naked truth about his motives into indecency. That a Prime Minister should avow that he had not done his duty in regard to national security because he was afraid of losing the election was an incident without parallel in our political history."[131]

This second confession that he had broken his pledge, coming eighteen months after the first, shocked all England. Baldwin's prestige plummeted. William James had written: "Truth *happens* to an idea. It *becomes* true, is *made* true by events." Now it was happening to the Dear Vicar. "Today," Morton wrote Churchill, "his name is mud." Only a year earlier, Macmillan recalled, his prestige was "higher than it had ever been. He was universally trusted. He stood on a pinnacle." A few days before the general election in which Baldwin took so much pride he had delivered a memorable address to the Peace Society, speaking first of the generation shattered in France and Flanders, and then, on the issue of peace: "Everything that we have and hold and cherish is in jeopardy." He had spoken eloquently of the beauty which war could destroy. But he had not addressed the issue of how that destruction could be prevented. He was, writes Telford Taylor, "too easily swayed by the perils of the moment, too little governed by the dangers of the future."[132]

For the prime minister the past year had been a year of almost unrelieved disaster: Hoare-Laval; his unseemly reward of Hoare's groveling encomium by returning him to the cabinet; the even more unsuitable appointment of Inskip; the loss of the Rhineland; his humiliating, unsuccessful attempts to wring concessions from Mussolini and Hitler after their illegal conquests; and now Churchill's philippic, followed by his own shocking admission that he had put party before country.

Baldwin's friends were worried, concerned about both his health and his emotional stability. Distress signals had been visible for some time. Since February he had been afflicted with spells of disabling fatigue, and on April 30 Tom Jones found him swallowing pills which he told Jones relieved "nervous exhaustion." After a thorough examination, his physician found him free of functional disorders. His patient, he concluded, was simply worn out.[133]

The prime minister planned to retire, moving into the House of Lords as Earl Baldwin of Bewdley. He wanted to leave the memory of a final accomplishment before departing, but now, learning that their island's ramparts were insecure, Englishmen were outraged. He was unaccustomed to public hostility and, unlike Churchill, unprepared to face it down. To paraphrase one of sociologist David Riesman's similes, Winston was guided by a built-in gyroscope which would carry him toward his objective through tumult, while the prime minister relied on a kind of sociological radar — signals from the voters — to determine his course.

Despairing of Parliament, and hoping to form a nucleus of support beyond its walls, Winston had begun turning to tiny organizations which were struggling to waken the nation to its peril. In June 1935, at the request of Lady Bonham Carter, he had addressed one such group, Focus, at a Victoria Hotel luncheon. Clearly Focus was not the germ cell for a mass movement. Indeed, all present agreed that it should have neither rules nor members, and only sixteen people were present anyway. Nevertheless, the meeting was important, for they were all eminent and came from varied backgrounds and political convictions — Conservatives, Liberals, Labourites, aristocrats, and a representative of the working class. Winston became the group's natural leader. As his stock rose in the aftermath of Baldwin's mortification, he became increasingly active in the World Anti-Nazi Council, whose chairman was Sir Walter Citrine, general secretary of Britain's powerful Trade Union Congress. Here, for the first time, Churchill found common cause with socialists. He urged them to spread the word that Englishmen of all classes, from "the humblest workman" to "the most bellicose colonel" must form ranks against the growing danger. To this sympathetic audience Churchill declared that the government must adopt the policy of uniting all countries from the Baltic to the Aegean, including the Soviet Union, in an agreement to "stand by any victim of unprovoked aggression," with each nation pledging "a quota of armed force."[134]

He was speaking daily now and writing for newspapers each evening, knitting into his texts information from new sources, which included Viscount Cecil of Chelwood (the former Lord Robert Cecil), a member of the League of Nations Union. At Chartwell Churchill received Robert Watson-Watt, the inventor of radar, who told him of the Air Ministry's "unwillingness to take emergency measures" to test his devices — a measure even Inskip had supported, though Baldwin and a majority of the cabinet overruled him. Each of the service ministries shared Winston's sense of urgency, though in the government, as Martin Gilbert writes, "there was increasing Cabinet resentment at what was considered interference by him and . . . his constant appeals to Ministers and civil servants for greater vigilance."[135]

At its second meeting the Anti-Nazi Council established yet another movement, the Defence of Freedom and Peace. Churchill thought he had a better name for it: Arms and the Covenant, representing a policy of rearmament and collective security under the League of Nations Covenant. Citrine and other Labourites shied away from that. They were embarrassed; the parliamentary socialists, led by Attlee, still backed the league but not rearmament. Nevertheless, they agreed that Churchill should deliver the chief address at the movement's first great rally at the Albert Hall on December 3, 1936. He wanted broad support, and he was getting it. To Austen Chamberlain he wrote of the "robust spirit" among Labour's leaders, adding, "I have been surprised to find the resolution and clarity of thought which have prevailed among them, and the profound sense of approaching danger from the growing German power."[136]

The great rally exceeded all expectations. Winston later recalled: "We had the feeling that we were on the threshold of not only gaining respect for our views but of making them dominant." Lady Violet Bonham Carter, arriving, found "huge crowds surging around Albert Hall," with "groups of communists and fascists distributing leaflets and attempting demonstrations." In the Green Room, where the speakers assembled, she found Citrine, Sir Archibald Sinclair, and three peers, including Lord Allen of Hurtwood, a conscientious objector in the last war. It was meant to be, and bore every sign of becoming, a massive demonstration demanding action and a moment of personal triumph for Churchill. With similar rallies scheduled throughout the country during the following week, the movement could hardly be ignored by the government. Arms and the Covenant — the press had adopted Winston's more striking phrase — seemed on the verge of making history. It appeared that the only man who could derail it was the King of England. And that is exactly what happened.[137]

🦁   🦁

Lady Violet's "expectancy," she wrote, "was pierced by a sharp 'needle' of apprehension. I knew Winston could never think of two things at once. Would his eye be 'off the ball' tonight?" As he entered the Green Room, she later wrote, she "knew at a glance that my anxiety was justified. His face was sombre and overcast. He went straight up to Citrine and said that he felt that at this critical juncture in our affairs he must make some statement." According to Citrine, Winston said "People will expect some statement from me."[138]

Thus the curtain rose for the final act in one of the sorriest episodes in Churchill's career: the abdication crisis of 1936. Everyone within earshot knew what he meant; they had all read the lead editorial in that morning's *Times*. What they did not know was that just as he was leaving Morpeth Mansions to come here Churchill had received the text of a broadcast Edward VIII proposed to deliver to the nation. Citrine was appalled that Winston would even mention the issue in public. The audience, he replied, would certainly not expect any such statement; this meeting had nothing to do with the sovereign. "You will certainly be challenged," Citrine said, "and if no one else does I will." Winston, taken aback, said, "I must consider my position." In Violet's version Citrine went even further, declaring "quite firmly that if this was Mr. Churchill's intention, he [Citrine] could not take the chair. This cinched the matter. . . . But though Winston was obliged to bow to Citrine's ultimatum, I could see how much he minded being overridden."[139]

The press agreed that all the speakers received "a tumultuous reception." Churchill heard "prolonged cheering"; Violet felt "throughout my own speech that I had never spoken to a more responsive and inspiring audience." Churchill spoke last. Violet wrote: "He got a tremendous reception, and of course he made a good speech. (He could not make a bad one.) But many of us felt that he was not at the zenith of his form, and of course we knew why. His heart and mind were engaged elsewhere."[140]

Mystery enshrouds what happened next. Churchill later wrote that he heard a man cry, "God Save the King," and, "on the spur of the moment," told the hall: "There is another grave matter which overshadows our minds tonight. In a few minutes we are going to sing 'God Save the King.' I shall sing it with more heartfelt fervour than I have ever sung it in my life." Then, according to his version, he described Edward VIII as "a cherished and unique personality" and said he expected Parliament "to discharge its functions in these high constitutional questions." He trusted, he said, that "the British nation and the British Empire and . . . the British people" would not "be found wanting in generous consideration for the occupant of the Throne."[141]

This account has entered history virtually unchallenged. So reliable a source as Macmillan believed the fall of Winston's rising star, and Baldwin's remarkable comeback, began that night "in the Albert Hall, [when] Churchill said a few words of sympathy for the King." Lord Strauss, then an MP and later a member of Winston's wartime cabinet, recalled that "Churchill made a dramatic speech in support of the King at an Albert Hall meeting. It just killed the meeting."[142]

Yet no one who was on or near the platform that evening recalled him saying a word about the sovereign, and therefore, by implication, about what had become delicately known as "the royal marriage crisis." Citrine — who had vowed to challenge Winston if he spoke up for Edward — did not hear him do so. Nobody was standing closer to Winston, or watching him with a keener eye, than Violet. It was her recollection that "at the end of the meeting he commented to Mr. Eugen Spier on the enthusiasm with which the audience had sung the National Anthem, which he had interpreted as an endorsement of his attitude on the royal marriage issue." One can only assume that the sentiment was in Churchill's heart at the time, and that later he believed he had given voice to it. He was wrong. He was also wrong in his assumption that the lusty singing of the anthem signified support for the King. Any gathering of Britons would have done the same at the end of a patriotic rally.[143]

Actually, the sovereign's subjects were furious with him. When they learned over the next few days that Winston had decided to be his chief defender — and (inaccurately) that he had advised the King to "Raise the drawbridge, lower the portcullis, and tell them to come and get us!" — they transferred their rage to Churchill, with shattering results for the great cause he led. The elaborate schedule of rallies meant to follow the first one in Albert Hall was canceled. Chamberlain assured a relaxed cabinet that Arms and the Covenant was dead. The government would deal with Hitler, he said, not by matching him bomb for bomb, Short Lee-Enfield for Mauser, Spitfire for Messerschmitt, but by extending the hand of friendship and appeasement. Surely Hitler realized that his demands had to stop at some point. Churchill talked as though the Germans wanted all Europe. It was absurd. If they had it, whatever would they do with it? And, obviously, the wild stories of storm troopers leading anti-Semitic pogroms were rubbish. If the persecutions were as widespread as Winston claimed, Hitler would get wind of them and jail those responsible. But to hear Churchill you would think that the Führer wanted to kill every Jew in Europe![144]

Ich dien — I serve — is the motto of the princes of Wales, who mostly serve by standing and waiting for their reigning parent to die, at which instant they mount the throne, with the formal coronation following a year or so later. In the nine centuries since the Norman Conquest of 1066, thirty-five men and six women (if you include William and Mary's Mary) have reigned over England and her possessions. In Buckingham Palace, Windsor Castle, Sandringham, or any of the other royal estates, an English sovereign is an awesome personage, possessing so much wealth that no one can fix an exact sum. It fluctuates, like the stock market — or like the devotion of the Crown's subjects toward their sovereign.

In the dim, distant, blurry centuries of absolute monarchies, a king's power was exactly that: he had the absolute right to make war without consulting anyone, taxing as he pleased, raping, murdering, pillaging, and committing arson with license. This despotic rule was tempered only by his conscience, provided he had one, and the knowledge that if he alienated too many resourceful vassals, he might be overthrown. Beginning with the signing of the Magna Carta at Runnymede in 1215, the King's authority was limited by this agreement or that, with an occasional spurt of restric-

tions followed by generations with none. In 1837, when Victoria's delightful silvery voice was first heard at Kensington Palace, a member of
Parliament could not become prime minister without "the confidence of the
Crown." When Walter Bagehot's *The English Constitution* was published
thirty years later, the sovereign was left with three great rights: to be
consulted, to encourage, and to warn. These were deliberately vague; a
great monarch like Victoria could dominate — even alter policy — by
spotting opportunities with her celebrated "drill eye," by insisting on daily
consultations, and by skillfully encouraging and admonishing prime ministers and their cabinets. Strong-minded as she was, however, Victoria saw
the steady erosion of her power as suffrage broadened. There was little left
by 1894, the fifty-eighth year of her reign, when her son's eldest son's
eldest son was born and christened Edward Albert Christian George
Andrew Patrick David. The House of Commons congratulated Queen
Victoria on the infant's birth, but Keir Hardie, Labour's first member of
Parliament, delivered a remarkable prophecy: "From childhood onward
this [boy] will be surrounded by sycophants and flatterers and will be
taught to believe himself as of a superior creation. . . . He will be sent on
a tour round the world, and probably rumours of a morganatic marriage
will follow and the end of it all will be that the country will be called upon
to foot the bill."[145]

By 1911, when the youth was invested as Prince of Wales, the occupant
of the throne had become a puppet. His father, George V, could not utter
a public word without the prime minister's approval; when he addressed
Parliament, he was handed a manuscript written by others and was warned
not to stress this word or that.

Nevertheless, George V learned to enjoy his job, and like most men of
his generation he had been raised to follow the path of Duty. The Prince
was another matter. Edward reached maturity when the sheath of discipline, among royalty as well as commoners, was yielding to self-indulgence
and the pursuit of pleasure. During Stanley Baldwin's first premiership, in
the 1920s, he and the Prince exchanged sharp words on several occasions.
Everything about His Royal Highness — his dress, his contempt for
convention, the company he kept, his enthusiastic performances on dance
floors — strengthened the doubts of those who thought him an unsuitable
heir to the crown. He agreed with them. Anita Leslie, Winston's cousin,
witnessed an appalling scene between the Prince and his father. The Prince
screamed that he didn't want the throne, and, when his father grew angry,
staged a royal temper tantrum. Deeply distressed, the monarch strode out
the door. Shortly thereafter, the King died.[146]

His difficult son, now Edward VIII, became, among other things,
Defender of the Faith — the faith of the Church of England, which did

not recognize divorce. Britain's first bachelor king since the mad George III, 176 years earlier, Edward was now forty-two, and both his subjects and the Royal Family thought it time he acquired a queen. So did he; in his autobiography he wrote, with a careless air which would have dismayed Bagehot, that his "rolling stone was beginning to seek a resting place." He had enjoyed relationships with many women, but there was a curious pattern to them. He stared right through lovely girls and headed for their mothers. He not only sought out women whose childbearing years were over or ending; he was especially attracted to those already married.[147]

His search had ended late in his tenure as Prince of Wales, when he discovered, or was discovered by, Mrs. Wallis Warfield Spencer Simpson, a charming Baltimore adventuress of genteel if threadbare origins who had learned, like Becky Sharp, to live by her wits. Beginning her womanhood "in greatly reduced circumstances," Baltimoreans said, she supported herself "in greatly seduced circumstances." Wallis lacked beauty but possessed something rarer. She was *smart*. Violet eyes, dark hair, a magnolia complexion, and a stunning figure, combined with the great gift of being a good listener, made her popular everywhere. In 1916 she had married a naval officer. Divorcing him, she eloped with her best friend's husband, Ernest Simpson, a wealthy shipping man. Simpson's work often brought him to London; he was always accompanied by his wife, and upon being introduced to her at a garden party, the Prince of Wales found he could not take his eyes off her. How often they saw one another, or in what circumstances, is unknown, but after Edward became monarch she began divorce proceedings against her second husband. The divorce case was a seamy one of middle-aged adultery, and as it began toiling its way through His Majesty's courts of law that year, there were those who trembled at the possibility that His Majesty himself might be named in the proceedings.[148]

Early in February 1936, less than a month into the new reign, Stanley Baldwin was told that his new sovereign intended to marry Mrs. Simpson as soon as her decree was final. The bearer of the news was a third party, however, and the prime minister dismissed it as incredible. Sir Walter Monckton, Edward's chief confidant, later wrote: "I thought throughout, long before as well as after there was talk of marriage, that if and when the stark choice faced them between their love and his obligations as King-Emperor, they would in the end make the sacrifice, devastating though it may be."[149]

Nevertheless, Monckton was troubled, and on July 7 he called on Churchill to seek advice. Clementine once called Winston "the last believer in the divine right of kings." It was almost impossible for him to think unkind thoughts about any occupant of England's throne. But he was aware of Wallis. At the time of George V's death, he later wrote in an unpublished memorandum of events, "it was known through wide circles of politics and society" that Edward "had formed a deep attachment for Mrs. Simpson." However, he continued, "although branded with the stigma of a guilty love, no companionship could have appeared more natural, more free from impropriety or grossness." If the man existed with whom Wallis had enjoyed a platonic friendship, his name is lost to history. Yet Churchill wrote that first as prince, and now as king, Edward simply "delighted in her company, and found in her qualities as necessary to his happiness as the air he breathed." Winston drew the peculiar inference that her presence was "a safeguard."[150]

At No. 11 Morpeth Mansions that Tuesday evening Monckton told him all he knew, which was less than the whole truth. Mr. Simpson was now living with another woman, he said, and on the strength of that Wallis was seeking her freedom. Monckton added that while the King had no thought of marrying her, his strong "possessive sense" would be gratified were she a free woman. Indeed, even now he contemplated inviting her to Balmoral Castle, the royal residence in Scotland.[151]

Churchill frowned. His view of what happened when two worldly figures of opposite sex were alone together may have been distorted, but he knew what was and was not done in public. The divorce itself, he said, would be "most dangerous." Gossip was one thing; court proceedings were "in another sphere." If the woman gained her freedom under Wallis's circumstances, "it would be open to any Minister of Religion to say from the pulpit that an innocent man had allowed himself to be divorced on account of the King's intimacies with his wife." He urged "most strongly" that "every effort should be made to prevent such a suit." He also opposed, with all his vigor, any appearance by Mrs. Simpson at Balmoral. Edward must be reminded "that his friendship [with Mrs. Simpson] should not be flaunted in the eyes of the public." Later, he wrote, he learned that this advice "was not at all pleasing to Mrs Simpson," who had "expressed surprise that I should have been 'against her.' " Thursday evening Churchill dined with the King at York House. Edward had not yet received Monckton's report; he asked Churchill whether they had met. Winston nodded. What, asked Edward, had they discussed? Churchill answered in one word: "Gossip." Later he wrote: "His Majesty looked at me hard, but did not pursue the subject." And when Monckton did relay Winston's advice, the King ignored it.[152]

On October 4 Wallis took a house in Regents Park, and three weeks later at Ipswich she was awarded a decree nisi. It could not become absolute, and she could not remarry, until six months had passed. Nevertheless, the story was on the front page of every American newspaper. Not so in England.

The British press, responding to a personal appeal from their sovereign, suppressed the story. In fact, when Churchill wrote that the affair was common knowledge among "wide circles of politics and society," he was referring to the people *he* knew, the highest reaches of the upper class. The rest of Britain was ignorant of the marriage crisis. Even Anthony Eden was unaware of it until Baldwin, returning from vacation on October 12, astonished him by asking: "Have you had any letters about the King?" The young foreign minister replied: "No, not so far as I know; why should I have?" The answer awaited Eden, he later wrote, when he returned to the Foreign Office and "found there had been letters from overseas, where there was no press restraint. . . . They wrote of the King and Mrs. Simpson and her impending divorce suit and they were critical." Throughout the summer and early autumn, the Dominions and the Americans had been following with keen interest what H. L. Mencken called "the greatest story since the resurrection."[153]

Afterward Philip Guedalla said of Baldwin that he had handled the King "with a firmer touch than [he had] the King's enemies." Weary and fragile though he was, baffled by the glowering events on the Continent, the Dear Vicar nevertheless retained his sensitive domestic antennae. "Here, indeed," Macmillan recalled, "was a matter upon which his special talents and his lovable personality had their full play. The King's problem was, at it were, a supreme 'family' problem. Nobody could handle this kind of thing more skilfully or more sympathetically than Baldwin, or with a surer touch." He had been praying for the chance to score one last triumph. He could have hoped for none greater than this.[154]

But monarchs, even constitutional monarchs, are intimidating to those who have been brought up to revere the Crown, and this sovereign was displaying a cunning, evasive side no one in Parliament had noticed in him before. He had lied to Monckton, to his solicitor, and to his own family. Despite his solemn assurances, the terrible truth was that his intentions toward Wallis were honorable. He *did* intend to marry her. Finally, he laid the awful truth before his mother. Queen Mary, seething with rage and grief, told him that it was his constitutional duty to inform the prime minister at once.[155]

On Monday, November 16, he did so. Baldwin was convinced that Britons would not have Mrs. Simpson on any terms — as queen, as titled consort, or as morganatic wife. Had he been discreet, His Majesty might have kept her as his mistress, but since she was already a household word in the United States and the Dominions, sooner or later Fleet Street would make her a British celebrity. Moreover, any surreptitious arrangement was unacceptable to the King. She must become his wife, he insisted, and must share his throne. Baldwin told him that was unthinkable. The King remained adamant. Obviously, there was only one solution. Edward VIII must abdicate and be succeeded by his brother the Duke of York, "Bertie," as King George VI. Apparently both His Majesty and the prime minister recognized the inevitability of this from the outset, but neither could mention it to the other, let alone outsiders. In Cannes, whence she had gone, "the Baltimore woman," as the press now called her, was unaware that her next name was likely to be, not Wallis Regina, but Mrs. Windsor.

Baldwin's next move was obligatory; he had to report this conversation to the cabinet, leaders of the opposition parties, elder statesmen, and key figures in the House of Lords. Thus informed, Lord Salisbury led a small group of outraged senior parliamentarians to No. 10 the next day. It was their position, Salisbury said, that though they would not be shocked by a commoner who wanted "to marry his mistress," the situation was very different when "a man born to sublime responsibilities" was "ready to jeopardize them, as it seems, in order to gratify his passion for a woman of any sort." Salisbury had invited Churchill to join this delegation, but Winston had declined. He agreed with the delegates, he explained, but were he to commit himself now, he "would lose all influence over the King." Instead, he planned a personal appeal to His Majesty, arguing that just as millions of other Englishmen in his generation had "made every sacrifice in the War, so he must now be willing to make this sacrifice for his Country." Here Winston encountered a problem. He had a good case, but to state it he must see His Majesty, and Baldwin wouldn't permit that; he was keeping Edward secluded in the royal lodge at Fort Belvedere. Anyone wanting to call on him must be screened by the prime minister, who had approved only a handful of applicants, notably the Archbishop of Canterbury and Geoffrey Dawson of *The Times*.[156]

At this point a certain illogic began to creep into Winston's thinking. On Wednesday of the following week, Baldwin, seeking nonpartisan support in Parliament, told Churchill, Attlee, and Sinclair that should the King refuse to abandon his marriage plans, he and his cabinet would resign; he asked what their response would be. Attlee and Sinclair quickly replied that neither would accept the seals of prime minister. Churchill said his attitude was "a little difficult," but he would "certainly support the Government." He was convinced that the King would abandon his marriage plans. At the same time, he saw no reason why, after Wallis was again free, they should not "continue to see one another outside marriage." Even if one accepts his view of their relationship as a sexless friendship, this would constitute an invitation to scandal which, as he himself had told Monckton, could only tarnish the Crown. Furthermore — and here he raised an issue which would loom ever larger as the crisis grew — Churchill deplored talk of a swift decision. He saw no reason to be "hasty." This was merely a royal "infatuation." In time, he predicted, two or three months at most, it would pass and His Majesty would come to his senses. Baldwin, who had studied the expression on the King's face when he spoke of Wallis, knew better.[157]

Churchill did see that the essential "difficulty," as he wrote Salisbury, had risen since Wallis's decree nisi. It was a "point of honour that a man should marry the woman who divorces herself or is divorced on his account." This problem was "insuperable, unless the lady in question herself spontaneously gives the release." He therefore approved the dispatch of a mission to Cannes with that objective. One was formed. Lord Beaverbrook led it; he was perhaps the only man in Edward's kingdom audacious enough to ask his monarch's intended "to renounce all idea of marriage, morganatic or otherwise, with the King." All she had to do, he explained, was withdraw her petition for an absolute divorce. Winston believed that would end the crisis. His hopes were high. In a letter praising Beaverbrook he wrote: "He is a tiger in a fight . . . a *devoted* tiger! Very scarce breed." But if Beaverbrook was a tiger, Wallis was a man-eater. She coldly informed him and all the other King's men that should their sovereign decide to marry, she would place no obstacles in his path.[158]

Until now the public had been unaware of the impasse. Their ignorance ended on December 2, when the Right Reverend Alfred Blunt, bishop of Bradford, inadvertently touched off a furor by criticizing the King's poor churchgoing record. The press seized upon the occasion to comment on Wallis in Bradford, Leeds, Manchester, Nottingham, Darlington, and Birmingham newspapers. No power on earth could keep the crisis out of *The Times* the next day. The cabinet met in emergency session. Duff Cooper proposed that the coronation move forward as planned and the marriage issue be raised after the King had been crowned in May. But he was a minority of one. Were his course followed, the others told him, the monarchy, the very symbol of unity, would become the eye of a storm tearing Britain and the Empire apart, with the possibility that a King's party might be formed — a throwback to the days when the royal court vied with the House of Commons in governing the nation. Duff Cooper was also reminded that the prime minister had other duties, among them rearmament and foreign policy in Spain, Geneva, and Ethiopia. This was incontestable. Macmillan sympathized with the King, but he later emphasized that "apart from the personal problems involved, grave injury was done to the public interest from a wider point of view. During many weeks — the whole of the late summer and autumn — the Prime Minister and his leading colleagues . . . were occupied with the complications and distractions of this affair at a vital period."[159]

Baldwin declared the matter must be swiftly resolved. The cabinet agreed. That evening the King once more told the prime minister that his decision to marry Wallis was irreversible; Baldwin again replied that the government's position was unalterable. The need for a solution being urgent, there was no point in continuing the deadlock. But Churchill did not know that. As Baldwin and Edward conferred, Winston rose in the House to ask that "no irrevocable step" be taken until Parliament could be consulted. His appeal was greeted by angry murmurs. He and Beaverbrook then met with the King's solicitor and endorsed Edward's wish to address the nation. Within the hour Baldwin vetoed any royal broadcast as "thoroughly unconstitutional."

The Times leader the following morning — the day of the Albert Hall meeting — was the opening gun in Dawson's campaign against the marriage. He wrote of "a grave constitutional issue" arising from "a conflict between the KING'S intentions and the advice of his Ministers," and observed that "the high office which HIS MAJESTY holds is no man's personal possession. It is a sacred trust, handed down from generation to generation." The path of a sovereign was not easy, particularly one "who has reached middle age without the blessing of a happy marriage," but His Majesty must understand that the monarchy itself would be "weakened if ever private inclinations were to come into open conflict with public duty and be allowed to prevail." Edward was stung. In his memoirs he would write bitterly: "The press creates; the press destroys. All my life I had been the passive clay that it had enthusiastically worked into the hackneyed image of a Prince Charming. Now it had whirled around and was bent upon demolishing the natural man who had been there all the time."[160]

Emotionally, Churchill was becoming a loose cannon, making contradictory statements as he tried to reconcile the unsuitable marriage with his devotion to the Crown. Lunching with Sir Walter Citrine, he said very quietly, "I shall defend him. I think it is my duty." It was also a violation of his assurance to Salisbury, and Citrine, startled, said, "What? Irrespective of what he has done?" Winston, according to his companion, "looked grave, and, putting his hands on his breast, he said with emotion, 'He feels it here.' "[161]

Those closest to Churchill were appalled. His daughter Mary recalls that Clementine "disagreed profoundly. She saw something else very clearly, too," Mary remembers. "She realized that Winston's championship of the King's cause would do him great harm, and that he would be accused of making political capital out of this crisis." Harold Nicolson wrote that Churchill's "line" was "let the King choose his girl." But there was more to it than that. Later Winston's physician observed: "King and country, in that order, that's about all the religion Winston has." Yet he, too, missed the point. Part of it was Churchill's deep, unquestioning loyalty to those he had befriended. One of his secretaries recalls that even if a man had publicly disgraced himself, he would say, "I don't want to hear it. This man is my friend."[162]

Lady Violet Bonham Carter, after trying to reason with him about the issue and being "met by black hostility," concluded, as Clementine had, that he was "quite oblivious" to the public's distaste for "a hole-and-corner morganatic marriage." Violet wrote that "his championing of Edward VIII was inspired by a romantic loyalty. He would have been prepared to stand alone beside his King against a world of arms." Winston himself said much the same thing later: "I should have been ashamed if, in my independent and unofficial position, I had not cast about for any lawful means, even the most forlorn, to keep him on the Throne of his fathers." This was intuitive, not reasonable; it was as though the King had called: "Now who will stand on either hand / And keep the bridge with me?" Two had sprung forward: Beaverbrook and Churchill. But their incentives were very different. Later Beaverbrook said he had been trying to "get" Baldwin. Winston, aroused, hotly replied: "*I* wasn't trying to 'get' anyone. I wanted to save the King."[163]

It couldn't be done, and when, the day after *The Times* editorial and the Albert Hall rally, Edward asked the prime minister if he might see Churchill, as "an old friend" with whom he might "talk freely," Baldwin agreed. He knew he had won. He had just told His Majesty that the cabinet wanted a decision during the weekend — it was now Friday — or, if possible, this evening. Edward had replied: "You will not have to wait much longer." He hadn't wanted the crown; he wouldn't fight for it. Conservative MP Henry Channon wrote in his diary: "The King told [the Duke of Kent] that over two years ago while he knew he was an excellent Prince of Wales and liked the job, he nevertheless felt that he could never 'stick' being King as he put it, he was afraid of being a bad one. He could never tolerate the restrictions, the etiquette, the loneliness; so perhaps if the issue had not arisen something else would have."[164]

Yet His Majesty did not reveal this submissiveness to Churchill, who went to Fort Belvedere on the evening of December 4 under the impression that he could save him, nor did he mention Baldwin's time limit and his tacit acceptance of it. Churchill's impression was that Edward "wanted a fortnight to think the matter over." Winston had assumed that the prime minister would give him no less than a month. He said: "Your Majesty need not have the slightest fear about time. If you require time there is no force in this country which would or could deny it to you. Mr. Baldwin would certainly not resist you." He added a piece of advice. The King should not "on any account leave the country." That would "produce the worst possible impression"; everyone would say he had "gone to meet Mrs. Simpson." Edward demurred; he had no intention of seeing her, but thought "a complete change in the Alps" was what he needed. Nevertheless, he dropped the idea. Winston was his friend and champion; he couldn't quarrel with him. In his memoirs he would write: "When Mr Baldwin had talked to me about the Monarchy, it had seemed a dry and lifeless thing. But when Mr Churchill spoke it lived, it grew, it became suffused with light."[165]

Saturday morning Winston sent the prime minister a complete account of his audience with the King and prepared a statement for publication in the Sunday papers. It opened: "I plead for time and patience." There was no conflict between King and Parliament, he argued, because Parliament had not been consulted, nor allowed to express an opinion, and for a monarch to abdicate "upon the advice of the Ministry of the day" would be without precedent. Because Mrs. Simpson's decree would not be absolute until April 1937, the marriage could not be celebrated until spring, and "for various reasons" it might "never be accomplished at all." Surely "the utmost chivalry and compassion" should be shown "toward a gifted and beloved King torn between private and public obligations and duty."[166]

Churchill's assurance that the King "need not have the slightest fear about time" had been ill-advised. Actually, Baldwin told his senior ministers that same Sunday, "This matter must be finished before Christmas." According to Monckton, who was there, Chamberlain insisted even that was too much time; the uncertainty, he said, was "hurting the Christmas trade." And word of the King's fatalistic acceptance of dethronement was spreading. Beaverbrook had phoned Churchill with the bad news: "Our cock won't fight." Winston, refusing to give in, drafted a compromise statement for His Majesty. In it the King would give the cabinet veto power over his marital plans, should the question arise in April. Sinclair cosigned the proposal, but when it reached Fort Belvedere the King rejected it "on the grounds," as Winston later wrote Boothby, "that it would not be honourable to play for time when his fundamental resolve was unchanged, and he declared it unchangeable." After that, Churchill added, "No human effort could have altered the course of events."[167]

Unfortunately, before word of the King's response reached him, Winston had blundered into the worst political mauling of his life. Bob Boothby, one of a handful of MPs who had remained loyal to him, had been his weekend houseguest at Chartwell; there he had noted that Churchill was "silent and restless and glancing into corners," like "a dog . . . about to be sick on the carpet." Later Boothby told a friend his premonition, on Sunday, that "Winston was going to do something dreadful," but that he never dreamed he would come into the House of Commons and be "sick right across the floor."[168]

Monday, December 13, Churchill attended a meeting of the Anglo-French Luncheon Club, and, according to Boothby, arrived in Parliament "drunk, for the first and only time in his life." It was Question Time. The prime minister was at his best, patiently answering queries about the crisis. The House was friendly; MPs had spent the weekend taking the pulse of their constituencies and had found little support for Edward. "What is so tragic," Harold Nicolson wrote Vita,"is that now that people have got over the first sentimental shock, they *want* the King to abdicate. I mean opinion in the House is now almost wholly anti-King." MPs, he wrote, were saying that " 'If he can first betray his duty . . . there is no good in the man.' "[169]

As Winston took his seat Baldwin was explaining, rather disingenuously, that His Majesty was still weighing his decision and that until he reached it the government would make no move. Winston later acknowledged in his letter to Boothby that he "did not sufficiently realise how far the Prime Minister had gone to meet the views I had expressed. I ought of course to have welcomed what he said. . . ." Instead, oblivious to the proceedings he was interrupting, he rose to defend his press statement of the day before. He began: "May I ask my right hon. Friend whether he could give us an assurance that no irrevocable step will be taken before the House has received a full statement —" That was as far as he got. The House rose as one man in a spectacular display of collective fury. Macmillan recalled "the universal hostility shown to him from every quarter — Conservatives, Socialists, and Liberals." Winterton, who served in the House of Commons for forty-seven years, called the demonstration "one of the angriest manifestations I have ever heard directed against any man in the House of Commons." Individual cries were audible — "Drop it!" "Order!" "Twister!" — but most voices joined in a wordless, derisive, ear-splitting roar.[170]

In his diary Leo Amery wrote that Churchill was "completely staggered by the unanimous hostility of the House," and Nicolson noted: "Winston collapsed utterly in the House. . . . He has undone in five minutes the patient reconstruction work of two years." Winston himself felt "entirely alone in a wrathful House of Commons. I am not, when in action, unduly affected by hostile currents of feeling," but now it was "almost physically impossible to make myself heard." Nevertheless, he stood defiantly, in his familiar fighting stance, his jaw thrust forward and his expression grim, until, to his astonishment, the Speaker ruled him out of order for attempting to deliver a speech during Question Time. Flushed, he turned to Baldwin, and, according to Beaverbrook, shouted: "You won't be satisfied until you've broken him, will you?" Then he stalked out, followed only by Brendan Bracken. It was, *The Times* declared the next morning, "the most striking rebuff in modern parliamentary history."[171]

So extraordinary a spectacle suggests motivation which lay deeper than the immediate issue, in which Churchill, after all, had played a minor role, and an ineffectual one at that. Indeed, the entire response to the Simpson affair, public and private, seems to have been an overreaction. It had "completely absorbed the public interest," in Boothby's opinion, because "here, at last, was something that was moving and exciting without being dangerous." One could safely commit oneself; whichever way it went, the solution would not be a matter of life or death. Therefore, Britons could release the tension arising from frustration over rearmament and the growing likelihood of another European war. They had brooded over Churchill's recitation of alarming facts, resenting his insistence that they face the growing danger. As events vindicated him, that exasperation grew. Now, when he was clearly wrong, they made him the target of their chagrin. In raging at him they were raging at the prospect of another great conflict, one they did not deserve and for which, as they saw it, they bore no responsibility.[172]

After the Churchill shutdown, events moved swiftly toward a denouement. On Thursday, December 16, the King signed the Deed of Abdication, stipulating that his reign would end at noon the following day. Baldwin brought it to the House of Commons that same afternoon, had it read by the clerk, and then delivered an excellent speech tracing the course of the crisis from its origins. Holding up the signed document, he declared: "No more grave deed has ever been received by Parliament, and no more difficult, I may say repugnant, task has ever been imposed upon a Minister."[173]

That last part was not entirely true. Encountering Harold Nicolson afterward, Baldwin said, "I had a success, my dear Nicolson, at the moment I most needed it." Coming after a year crowded with disappointments, the acclaim over his masterstroke can hardly have been repugnant. But no one begrudged him it. In the *Evening Standard* Churchill wrote that the prime minister had "never spoken with more force or more parliamentary skill." His own brief account to the House of his action during the crisis — pointing out that he had been acting based on the limited information then available to him, was heard next — heard first in distrustful silence, then with sympathy, and finally with what Hansard's record described as "loud cheers." In his diary Amery wrote: "Winston rose in face of a hostile House and in an admirably phrased little speech executed a strategical retreat."[174]

On Friday Churchill lunched at Fort Belvedere, working with the King on the text of his abdication broadcast. As Edward wrote in his memoirs, it was an address which any "practiced student of Churchilliana could spot at a glance," with such phrases as "bred in the constitutional tradition by my father" and "one matchless blessing, enjoyed by so many of you and not bestowed on me — a happy home with his wife and children." Afterward Winston wrote of his host, "His mettle was marvellous." So it should have been. Edward was free of duties he detested; soon he would be reunited with his love, and he could devote the rest of his life to pleasure as His Royal Highness, the Duke of Windsor, the title his brother was about to bestow upon him — although, at the insistence of the Royal Family and to Edward's anger, Wallis would be denied the honorific Her Royal Highness. But she would be a duchess, which was a lot more than anyone in Baltimore would have predicted. At the end of his luncheon with Winston, Edward glanced at his watch and realized that "I ceased to be King." As he saw Churchill off, he wrote, "there were tears in his eyes. I can still see him standing at the door; hat in one hand, stick in the other. Something must have stirred in his mind; tapping out the solemn measure with his walking stick, he began to recite, as if to himself." The something was from Andrew Marvell's ode on the beheading of King Charles I:

> *He nothing common did or mean*
> *Upon that memorable scene.* [175]

But in the streets of London children were chanting a different couplet:

> *Hark! The herald angels sing,*
> *Mrs. Simpson pinched our King.*

That was not all she had pinched. Listening to the former king's broadcast at Chartwell with Bill Deakin, Churchill was moved to tears, not by his own prose but by its implications. For him, and for those working to strengthen the defense of England, the crisis had been disastrous. Afterward he wrote: "All the forces I had gathered together on 'Arms and the Covenant,' of which I conceived myself to be the mainspring, were estranged or dissolved, and I was myself so smitten in public opinion that it was the almost universal view that my political life was at last ended." [176]

Certainly his campaign for preparedness was a casualty. Violet Bonham Carter wrote that many of his loyal followers "expressed to me (and no doubt to others) the view that if he continued to lead us our cause would be hopelessly compromised." Had it not been for the Simpson crisis, Macmillan believed, Arms and the Covenant "might have succeeded in shaking the already weakened position of the Prime Minister. We might have been able to force a change of policy or of Government or both. Alas! . . . All the effect of the Albert Hall meeting was destroyed — first by the Abdication and secondly by the catastrophic fall in Churchill's prestige."[177]

In an angry letter written immediately after the shutdown in the House, Boothby had reminded Winston of their agreement that "you were going to use all your powers," which could have been "decisive" in a successful resolution of the royal marriage issue. "But this afternoon you have delivered a blow to the King, both in the House and in the country, far harder than any that Baldwin ever conceived of. You have reduced the number of potential supporters to the minimum possible — I shd think now about seven in all. *And you have done it without any consultation with your best friends and supporters.*" Boothby wanted "to follow you blindly" because, as he wrote in a second letter, "I believe, passionately, that you are the only man who can save this country, and the world, during the next two critical years." But now the Churchillians were under attack by men who had been on the verge of conversion to Winston's cause. One of them had been prepared "to send a series of cables to friends of his in the Australian Government . . . under the aegis of your authority," but now refused to do so. Boothby pointed out that it was "only when you rely on the power of clear disinterested argument, based on your unrivalled intellect and experience, with *the solid central mass of the House of Commons,* that you rise to the position of commanding authority which you should always occupy."[178]

At the new king's coronation in Westminster Abbey in May, Winston leaned toward Clementine and whispered: "You were right. I see now the other one wouldn't have done." But a public apology was impossible for him, and an acknowledgment of error nearly so. On Christmas Day he wrote Lloyd George, vacationing in the West Indies: "It has been a terrible time here. . . . You have done well to be out of it" — as though the Welsh radical, with his humble origin and scorn for aristocracy, would have risked his career to save a man who had abandoned a kingdom for a woman. To the Duke of Westminster, Churchill wrote: "It is extraordinary how Baldwin gets stronger every time he knocks out someone or something important to our country." But had Edward been important to England, and to the cause Churchill championed, he would not have appeared in Germany, on his honeymoon, striding down the middle of a street lined with Nazis extending their arms in a *Hitlergruss* — and returning the greeting with a stiff-armed *heil* of his own.*[179]

---

* A touched-up photograph of this scene, showing Edward with his right hand by his side, was published around the world. The original, described above, is in the possession of one of the American prosecutors at Nuremberg.

Churchill, the strategist and statesman, could not recognize the achievement of Baldwin, the political technician. Macmillan grudgingly admired the feat which left "Baldwin's authority . . . immensely strengthened and Churchill's fallen almost to nothing." Nicolson, singling out "the supremacy of Baldwin" as the chief consequence of the Simpson affair, quoted "a leading Labour man" as saying to him: "Thank God we have S.B. at the top. No other man could have coped with this." Nicolson was proud of "how unanimous the House really is in times of crisis. There has been no hysteria and no party politics." Actually, of course, there had been both: hysteria in the outburst against Churchill, and, in Baldwin's triumph, Tory gains equivalent to a victory at the polls.[180]

In the end Winston grasped the extent of his debacle and was plunged into gloom. In Paris after the abdication he told Beaverbrook, "My political career is over." The Beaver replied, "Nonsense," but later he wrote: "It was only by chance that he was a Member of Parliament when the war broke out." After the war Bernard Baruch reminded Churchill how, in 1936, "your political career seemed ended, and you wondered whether you should enter some business." The Albert Hall rally had turned to ashes. When Lord Davies urged Winston to rouse the nation by embarking on a public speaking campaign, Churchill replied that he thought there was a tendency to "overrate the value of public meetings," that at "the present time non-official personages count for very little," and that "one poor wretch may easily exhaust himself without his even making a ripple upon the current of opinion. If we could get access to the broadcast [sic] some progress could be made. All that is very carefully sewn up."[181]

Indeed it was; the appeasers, secure once more, and still convinced that Churchill was a dangerous provocateur, took every opportunity to muzzle him. The cabinet reviewed a BBC plan for a new series of broadcasts on European affairs. Duff Cooper, again a minority of one, thought all knowledgeable Englishmen should be invited to speak; the rest of the cabinet voted to exclude "independent expression of views." Secretary to the Cabinet Hankey suggested that Winston's privilege, as a privy councillor, to see copies of Air Ministry replies to his criticisms of the RAF be discontinued. "So far as I can see," he said, "there is no advantage in continuing this controversy with Mr Churchill." Baldwin approved, then quickly reversed himself when Winston phoned threatening to circulate his own memoranda "to any of my friends I might think fit." The government knew how accurate Winston's information was, though as yet none of them had made it a major issue.[182]

He knew — and told Inskip — that Britain's rearmament was falling "ever more into arrears," and that the country's weakness in the air was "marked and deplorable." Lord Rothermere, who had been staying at

Berchtesgaden as the Führer's first overnight foreign guest, wrote Churchill that the Führer "professes great friendship for England but it will be friendship on his terms and not ours." Rothermere predicted that "even without a great war Britain and France will be practically vassal states before the end of the present decade. The idea that we cannot fight is spreading all over England." In the *Evening Standard* on February 5, 1937, Winston wrote that fifteen million Czechs now lived "under the fear of violent invasion, with iron conquest in its wake." There the Goebbels "hate-culture continues, fostered by printing press and broadcast," and at any time Berlin's propaganda might be directed against Belgium, Holland, Sweden, Switzerland, even Britain.[183]

All this deepened his melancholy. Clementine and fourteen-year-old Mary were staying at the Flexen Hotel in Zürs am Arlberg, skiing in the Austrian Alps. Winston was alone at Chartwell with Deakin, working on *Marlborough,* and, as he wrote his wife, turning out "articles to boil the pot." Yet they weren't enough; unpaid bills lay in a heightening pile on his desk. Even the weather was cheerless — bleak and gray, with a heavy, pounding rain which confined him and his easel to one end of the drawing room, where he erected dust sheets to protect the furniture and peered out, painting what he could see. At last it cleared. Cecil Roberts, a journalist and an old acquaintance, called and found him seated by Chartwell's lake, hunched over, staring at his swans. Winston spoke mournfully of the imminent changing of the guard at No. 10, with Baldwin moving out and Chamberlain in. He said, "There's no plan of any kind for anything. It is no good. They walk in a fog. Everything is very black, very black."[184]

And as his debts mounted and his gloom deepened, England's indebtedness to Stanley Baldwin rose. He had kept that undesirable woman out of Buckingham Palace, and now, in his final deed for his homeland, he joined Chamberlain in telling Tory MPs that if they felt they must deplore totalitarianism and aggression, they must not name names. It was important, he said, to avoid "the danger of referring directly to Germany at a time when we are trying to get on terms with that country."[185]

Fleet Street cheered. So did Britain. These were men of *peace.*

> *"When I use a word,"* Humpty Dumpty said, *in rather a scornful tone,*
> *"it means just what I choose it to mean — neither more nor less."*
>
> *"The question is,"* said Alice, *"whether you* can *make words mean so many different things."*
>
> *"The question is,"* said Humpty Dumpty, *"which is to be master — that's all."*

PART THREE

UNDERTOW

CHURCHILL'S popularity touched bottom in the months following the royal marriage crisis. After the holidays Randolph brought the American writer Virginia Cowles to a Chartwell lunch. Late in life she recalled: "The year 1937 was one of the most painful in Churchill's life. His influence had fallen to zero, partly because of the Abdication Crisis, partly because Hitler and Mussolini remained quiet and people began to feel that perhaps there would not be a war after all." Exploring the grounds, she found him "down by the pond, in a torn coat and battered hat, prodding the water with a stick, looking for a pet goldfish which seemed to have disappeared." The goldfish was retrieved; his prestige in London was not.[1]

On May 27, 1937, six days after the coronation of George VI in Westminster Abbey, Stanley Baldwin resigned, departing, wrote Churchill, "in a glow of public gratitude and esteem." Harold Nicolson noted in his diary, "No man ever left in such a blaze of affection." At the abbey the applause for Baldwin had rivaled that for the King. Dawson's editorial declared that the Dear Vicar had "revealed himself as the authentic spokesman of the nation" — a startling accolade; until then Dawson had reserved that role for *The Times* — and, he continued, the crowds had "cheered him just because they had come to look upon him as the embodiment of their own best interests." At No. 10 that evening, as the maids packed, the departing P.M. became Earl Baldwin of Bewdley, Knight of the Garter, while his lordship's ladyship was invested as a Dame of the British Empire. "All hearts seem open at the moment," S.B. wrote Halifax. "It is wonderful. I feel tired, happy, and at peace." Churchill, of course, did not join the chorus. Instead he said: "Well, the light is at last out of that old turnip."[2]

History has coupled Baldwin's name with Neville Chamberlain's, though they were very different men, leaving No. 10 with different legacies. S.B. approved of appeasement, but passively; unsure of himself

in foreign affairs, he waited for other governments — particularly
Germany's — to take the initiative. Chamberlain, never troubled by self-
doubt, gave the policy drive. As Churchill later wrote, S.B.'s "vague but
nonetheless deep-seated intuition" had been succeeded by the "narrow,
sharp-edged efficiency" of an "alert, businesslike, opinionated, and self-
confident" man. Macmillan thought the new P.M. "only too sure that he
was right on every question. Baldwin's attitude to problems was largely one
of temperament and feeling; Chamberlain approached them with a clear,
logical mind. The only trouble was that when he was wrong he was terribly
wrong."[3]

Part of Baldwin's charm had been his air of boundless tolerance; he had
refused openly to take offense even when offense was deliberate. Chamberlain, on the other hand, "was resentful of criticism even from his
supporters," Leo Amery wrote in his memoirs. "It seemed to him akin to
insubordination, and no team could get on without discipline." Eden and
Duff Cooper, outspoken men with independent minds, were all but ignored in cabinet meetings. At first Eden had been delighted by Chamberlain's ascent of what Disraeli called "the greasy pole." He had told Halifax
that it would be a great relief "to have a Prime Minister who would take
some interest in the foreign side." Eden was less pleased when he learned
that Neville meant to be his own foreign minister, and that when the P.M.
did seek advice on foreign affairs, he sought it from two other ministers
who had presided over the Foreign Office: Simon and Hoare. Simon,
Hoare, Halifax, and Chamberlain himself formed what Fleet Street called
"the Big Four." The lesser three refrained from contradicting Chamberlain or challenging his judgment. "Both by instinct and training," wrote
Hoare, "I was bound to find myself in accord with Chamberlain's ideas."
In other words, if you wanted to get along, you went along.[4]

As they veered away from traditional British foreign policies and
turned down the garden path, the appeasers seemed wholly unaware of
Hitler's great design, blueprinted in *Mein Kampf* and now emerging as an
alarming reality. They preferred to concentrate on political intrigue. Halifax, lord president in Chamberlain's cabinet, had his eye on Eden's office
at the FO, and Chamberlain was seriously considering the switch, despite
the fact that in the first year of the new government Halifax demonstrated
how imperfect his grasp of diplomacy was. On November 17, 1937, he
became the first member of a British cabinet to call on the Führer at
Berchtesgaden, accepting an invitation which had pointedly excluded the
French. When the car arrived he remained seated. Viscounts do not open
doors for themselves. He saw a man's black trousers just outside. Assuming they were those of a footman, he muttered impatiently about the delay
until the shocked chauffeur whispered hoarsely, *"Der Führer! Der Führer!"*

Wrenching the door open, Halifax made matters worse by explaining why he had not done what he ought to have done. Adolf Hitler was the last man to enjoy being mistaken for a servant, and he glared as only he could. The noble lord laughed heartily. It was not a propitious overture. When Halifax reported back to No. 10 the P.M. agreed that the misunderstanding was a great joke, however, and that, for Halifax, was what counted. He told Chamberlain of Hitler's solution for the turmoil in India: "Shoot Gandhi." That, too, amused the P.M. It occurred to neither of them that the Führer had been serious.[5]

Chamberlain was appalled when the House of Commons voted to debate Halifax's trip. Determined to forge bonds of friendship and trust with the Third Reich, he was dismayed by the possibility that the Führer, who understood neither a free press nor parliamentary debates, might be offended by critics over whom the P.M. had no control. He sent Eden word that he hoped nothing would be said to "upset the dictators." It was a vain hope; on December 21, 1937, Winston delivered a powerful speech. Twice, he noted, the Nazi foreign minister had been invited to London; twice the invitation had been rejected. Halifax's mission, Churchill said, was an unseemly response to obduracy and bound to offend the French. He attached "the greatest significance to the relations we have with France." The security of the two democracies was "founded upon the power of the French Army and the power of the British Fleet." Noting that since Hitler had become Reich chancellor and Führer "the Germans in Czechoslovakia" had loudly denounced "the form of government under which they have to live," he expressed the hope that no more Europeans would come under Nazi rule; they would suffer for it — "particularly the Jews." It was unspeakable, he said, the timbre of his voice rising, that Hitler should plot to exterminate a race from the society "in which they have been born," or that, from their earliest years, "little children should be segregated, and that they should be exposed to scorn and odium. It is very painful."[6]

Chamberlain had been following a different line of thought. Over the holidays he read Stephen Roberts's *The House That Hitler Built*, a powerful indictment of National Socialism by an eminent Australian scholar, but he wrote his sister Ida: "If I accepted the author's conclusions I should despair, but I don't and won't. Fortunately I have recently had a 'scintillation' on the subject of German negotiations. It has been accepted promptly and even enthusiastically by all to whom I have broached it and we have sent for [Nevile] Henderson [the British ambassador in Berlin] to come and talk it over with us."[7]

Churchill watched the evil stirring in central Europe and felt strengthened in his conviction that it was time, and past time, that Britain looked to her defenses. An unimpeachable source had sent him a tentative draft of the Führer's *Fall Grün*, or Case Green, a plan to invade Czechoslovakia with three Wehrmacht corps in two or three months. Another informant had written Chartwell of the frantic attempts in eastern Europe's capitals "not to provoke Germany" and how the Nazi hierarchy was "convinced that we would be neutral if they attacked Czechoslovakia." Still another had provided him with figures on the RAF's loss of new aircraft due to inexperienced pilots and incompetent, untrained mechanics.[8]

But Chamberlain, certain there would be no war, saw no future for the armed forces. Churchill was standing against the tide, and on March 16, 1937, he had lost his most prestigious ally in the campaign to waken England when Sir Austen Chamberlain died. "Nothing can soften the loneliness or fill the void," he wrote Lady Chamberlain. "In this last year I have seen more of him and worked more closely with him than at any time in a political and personal association of vy nearly forty years."[9]

As the character of Neville's foreign policy emerged — alliances with Italian fascism and German Nazism, leaving France out and thus, by washing England's hands of old quarrels, assuring peace for Britain — ministers would hear less and less of it from the prime minister himself. The new householder at No. 10 rarely received anyone. Visitors appearing at the door were greeted by Sir Horace Wilson, a deferential man of hooded eyes and soft voice who had entered the civil service at the time of the Boer War. As chief industrial adviser to the government he had proved indispensable to Chamberlain during Neville's six years as chancellor of the Exchequer. On taking over the reins from Baldwin, the new P.M. appointed Sir Horace head of the civil service and head of the Treasury. Although never elected to office and unknown to the British public, Chamberlain's adviser held more power than most members of the cabinet, and he served his master as Rasputin had served the last czar. By the end of 1937 he would build for himself, writes W. J. Brown, "a more powerful position in Britain than almost anybody since Cardinal Wolsey. . . . His influence was almost wholly bad. . . . In all the critical years, when swift, bold, strong action alone could have served our need, Wilson's temporising, formula-evolving mind reinforced and emphasized the weakness of the Prime Minister." The Big Four made headlines, but it was Wilson, working through Chamberlain — whose faith in him was boundless — who became the high priest of appeasement.[10]

In a spirit of reconciliation Churchill had volunteered to appear at the Conservative convention to second the nomination of Chamberlain as leader of the party, but it was a wasted gesture. He was never a bearer of grudges; nevertheless, Sir John Colville recalled, he always retained "some bitterness toward 'the caucus' which, first under Baldwin and then under

Chamberlain," had kept him "out of office throughout the nineteen-thirties." His nominating speech, delivered at Caxton Hall on May 31, 1937, was not quite what the Tories had come to hear. After paying ritualistic tribute to Neville's accomplishments as chancellor in stimulating foreign trade and restoring England's foreign credit ("a memorable achievement"), he put the Conservatives on notice: he intended to continue on his lonely, unpopular path. The role of leader, he said, had never been interpreted as "dictatorial or despotic"; the House "still survives as the arena of free debate." He felt confident, he said — though he felt no such thing — that Chamberlain, "as a distinguished Parliamentarian and House of Commons man," would "not resent honest differences of opinion," and that party opinion would "not be denied its subordinate but still rightful place in his mind." In his diary one Tory MP described it as "an able, fiery speech not untouched by bitterness."[11]

Even Nicolson chose not to march under Churchill's banner. To his wife, Vita, he wrote: "Don't be worried, my darling. I'm not going to become one of the Winston brigade. My leaders are Anthony [Eden] and Malcolm [MacDonald]." Eden's following outmatched Churchill's, still limited to Boothby, Bracken, and Duncan Sandys, Winston's son-in-law since his 1935 marriage to Diana.[12]

There can be little doubt that Chamberlain was the choice not only of Conservative MPs but of the general public, and that Churchill was seen as a scaremonger. Sir John Reith saw to it that he was seldom heard over the BBC, and in that Reith had the full backing of the prime minister; twice in one week Horace Wilson summoned Reith to No. 10 to warn him that Chamberlain disapproved of broadcasting excerpts from parliamentary speeches critical of the government. Excerpts in which the P.M. chided his critics were another matter. Like all evangelists he observed two standards, arrogating all power to himself when his own cabinet disagreed with him, and, whenever possible, gagging eloquent critics.[13] But he could never have got away with it had his countrymen disagreed. The voices of 1930s appeasement fall strangely on the ear today; at the time a consensus of Englishmen not only thought them sensible, but those who argued otherwise were scorned, vilified, and even accused of treason. That same year British crowds packed cinemas to see Frank Capra's *Lost Horizon*, based on the novel by James Hilton. Early in the film the protagonist, Robert Conway — memorably played by Ronald Colman — bitterly reproaches himself for his flawed character. As a pacifist he had believed that Great Britain should dismantle her army, scuttle the Royal Navy, destroy all RAF bombers and fighter planes, and beat her swords into plowshares. Should hostile troops arrive on English soil, he had argued, they should be greeted politely and asked what they wanted, and be immediately given it. But when he was appointed foreign secretary with extraordinary powers, his nerve had failed him. When the movie was shown to Tommies and GIs in the early 1940s it required heavy editing. The uniformed audiences knew what Hitler would have done had he stumbled upon Shangri-La, whose inhabitants were clearly non-Aryan.

Early in 1938, as he had intimated to his sister, Neville struck out boldly. The prime minister's inspiration was christened "colonial appeasement." In *Mein Kampf,* and in his demagogic speeches to Nazi mass rallies, the Führer had bitterly denounced the "theft" of Germany's pre-1914 colonies at Versailles. Chamberlain believed that if the colonies were returned, Hitler would stop plotting to seize neighboring countries on the Continent. He presented his idea to the cabinet as a plan to court Nazi friendship by opening "an entirely new chapter in the history of African colonial development," under which the Reich would be "brought into the arrangement by becoming one of the African Colonial Powers . . . by being given certain territories to administer." Henderson and Halifax enthusiastically backed it. Eden's support was muted. The P.M. looked at him sharply. It was an omen.[14]

Horace Wilson assembled a task force of civil servants to draft documents for the transfer of colonial possessions. Halifax told Ribbentrop, Hitler's ambassador to the Court of St. James's, that England was "urgently trying to make concessions"; Eden, still loyal to Chamberlain, assured the Nazi ambassador that His Majesty's Government's "earnest desire" was a quid pro quo — colonies for the Reich and, for England, "a greater feeling of security," which would require some kind of arms agreement.[15]

At this point, the French, alarmed at reports from London, challenged the concept of colonial appeasement and Colonial Secretary Ormsby-Gore put a spoke in its wheel. Eden had pointed out that Britain's moral superiority would be less plausible if, like Hitler and Mussolini, she shredded agreements and flouted compacts — which, Chamberlain's colonial secretary now reminded him, would be entailed in such a deal. The territories which had once belonged to Germany flew the Union Jack now, but that didn't mean that they belonged to Britain; the League of Nations had mandated them to the English with the understanding that Englishmen would better the lot of the native populations. That pledge would clearly be shattered if they were turned over to the Third Reich, which had withdrawn from the league and taken the official view that blacks, like Jews, belonged to an inferior race and should be so treated.

But the appeasers, like all fundamentalists, held facts in contempt. One of England's most respected intellectuals, R. W. Seton-Watson, wrote heatedly that "the convenient thesis of Germany's unfitness to administer colonies is as untrue as it is insulting, and should be recanted." After Hitler's Rhineland coup and the Anglo-German Naval Agreement, it was argued, the Versailles treaty and the League of Nations had become feeble precedents. Dawson, back in his role as self-appointed spokesman for forty million Britons, wrote that "British public opinion is probably far ahead of the Government" in its conviction that a stable relationship with Germany should be the sole objective "of our foreign policy." Englishmen, he declared, had "little sympathy with the view" that the Third Reich should be bound by "limits imposed twenty years ago."[16]

Now a rift appeared among the appeasers. Hitler refused the quid pro quo on armaments. Eden argued that that should be the end of it. So did Churchill's cousin Lord Londonderry, who thought all Germany's former colonies should be returned but believed it essential that Britain get something in exchange. He was, he told a friend, "very anxious lest our conciliatory trend" be interpreted in Berlin as weakness, and he feared that when the Germans became strong enough they would seek to redress their grievances "by force of arms. . . . It appears to me that by the shilly-shallying policy of the Government we are slowly but surely drifting toward this position."[17]

Actually that was already Chamberlain's position. By February 1938, two years after the House of Commons had first debated the issue of German colonial claims — and despite the vehement protests of Eden — he cabled Nevile Henderson in Berlin that he would accept less quid than quo. To "justify" the exchange to the British public, he wanted the Nazis to offer something "towards safeguarding the peace of Europe." He withdrew his request for a broad limitation of armaments and said an agreement on aerial bombing would be enough. When Ribbentrop rejected that, too, Chamberlain caved in. They could settle the colonial issue now. It wouldn't even be used as a bargaining chip in future negotiations.[18]

Chamberlain sent Hitler a new offer. African colonies which had never belonged to Germany — and had therefore been unmentioned at Versailles — would be "redistributed." They were now the property of France, Belgium (the Congo), and Portugal (Angola), but they would be a present from England to the Reich. Hitler understood this kind of language. It was his own. Intrigued, he asked what would happen if the Belgians and Portuguese objected. Chamberlain replied that not only Portugal and Belgium but also "presumably" France would "in the end cooperate in the settlement." At present, however, it was essential that no word of his new plan reach Paris, "much less" Lisbon or Brussels. They would "merely be informed" that talks had been held to discuss issues "concerning Germany and England." Unfortunately for this scheme, Britain had a free press. Henderson explained to the Führer that Chamberlain lacked his absolute control over newspapermen. However, the ambassador continued, he had spoken to "about eighty" men from Fleet Street and had "earnestly emphasized" the need for discretion. At the same time Halifax happily sent the Wilhelmstrasse word that "measures taken" by the BBC guaranteed that broadcasts "eliminated discussion regarding colonies." In London Horace Wilson noted that Halifax had taken "special pains" to keep the country ignorant of the deal. Wilson expressed "hope that he has been successful."[19]

Chamberlain was running fantastic risks. In exchange for a phantom promise to calm British nerves, he was laying territories belonging to three imperial powers — none of which had been consulted, or would be told of the decision until it had been made — on the diplomatic table. Luckily for him, the Reich chancellor rejected his proposal. Once again Hitler fooled everyone, including his own diplomats. As late as November 10, 1937, Baron Ernst von Weizsäcker, the Wilhelmstrasse's equivalent of Vansittart, had written: "From England we want colonies. . . . The British need for tranquillity is great. It would be profitable to find out what England would be willing to pay for such tranquillity." And so it was. Hitler had begun to acquire a sense of Chamberlain, a feel for his weaknesses. As for the colonies, he brusquely told the amazed Henderson on March 3, he had no use for them. They "would only be a burden for me." The colonial question, he said, "can wait for four, six, eight, or even ten years." The British ambassador asked for something more definite, and Hitler promised a written reply, but Henderson, as he wrote in his memoirs, "left Berlin a year and a half later without having received it." Belatedly Henderson realized that the issue of Germany's prewar colonies had been a red herring, that it was not "understanding with Great Britain" that Hitler wanted; it was "dominion in Central and Eastern Europe."[20]

❦   ❦

The P.M. had been courting Mussolini, hoping to sign him up before Hitler could, but the Führer was a more skillful seducer. Eden knew it, and so did Kurt von Schuschnigg, the Austrian minister who had hanged the Nazi murderers of Chancellor Dollfuss in 1934 and had now himself become chancellor. Schuschnigg had been the object of both Hitler's and Mussolini's manipulations. In the summer of 1936 the Duce had persuaded him that a rapprochement with the Third Reich was desirable, and the result — a joint communiqué published on July 11, 1936 — declared that Austria would "maintain a policy based on the principle that Austria acknowledges herself to be a German State," while the Reich recognized "the full sovereignty of the Federal State of Austria." It was a bad bargain. Secret clauses stipulated the muzzling of the Viennese press and amnesty for Nazi "political prisoners" in Austrian jails — many of them storm troopers convicted of murdering Jews and critics of the Führer.[21]

A devout Catholic and a born leader, Schuschnigg nevertheless knew that his small army would be helpless against Hitler's Wehrmacht and Luftwaffe. And Mussolini, when asked whether he could continue to guarantee the Austrian frontiers, was now evasive. Schuschnigg was pondering a restoration of the Hapsburg dynasty as his last available safeguard when, on February 12, 1938, Hitler summoned him to the Berghof, his villa in the Bavarian mountains. Berlin had announced that the meeting had been called to foster better relations between the two countries; nonetheless, Schuschnigg was wary. He was not a man to be intimidated, but the Führer had yet to meet the man he couldn't break.

The Führer's methods were rarely subtle. Wearing the brown tunic of a Nazi storm trooper and flanked by German generals — a shocking breach of protocol, particularly to an Austrian of impeccable old-world Viennese manners — he led his uneasy guest to his second-floor study, with its enormous picture window overlooking the snow-capped Alps. In his later account of the meeting, *Ein Requiem in Rot-Weiss-Rot* (Red-White-Red, the national colors of Austria), Schuschnigg described what followed as "somewhat one-sided [*einseitig*]."[22]

Actually it was outrageous. The Austrian addressed Hitler as "Herr Reichskanzler," as diplomatic courtesy required; the Führer rudely referred to him as "Schuschnigg." Hitler spoke in harsh and contemptuous tones. Gazing out beyond the Alps, toward Austria, he declared: "I have a historic mission, and this mission I shall fulfill because Providence has destined me to do so. . . . Who is not with me will be crushed [*kommt unter die Räder*]." Austria was too weak to defend herself against his Wehrmacht and would be without allies. Italy? He and Mussolini saw things "eye to eye [*im reinen*]." France could have stopped him at the Rhineland; now "it is too late for France." And England? He had an understanding with the British; "England will not lift one finger for Austria [*keinen Finger für Österreich rühren*]." To Schuschnigg it seemed that Hitler might as well be speaking Hindustani; he was "a man from another world."

But in the end his tremendous, hypnotic force won. After eleven hours of insults and threats — at one point Hitler screamed: "I have only to give an order, and your ridiculous defenses will be blown to bits [*zerstoben*]!" — Schuschnigg crumbled. He accepted the Führer's ultimatum, signing a two-page "agreement" drafted by Ribbentrop. All jailed Austrian Nazis were to be freed, their party was recognized as legitimate, and three pro-Nazis were to become members of the cabinet, including the infamous Arthur Seyss-Inquart, who, as minister of the interior, would wield dictatorial powers over the police and security.[23]

Hitler reported all this to a cheering Reichstag, praising Schuschnigg's "understanding" and his "warmhearted willingness" to bring Austria and the Reich closer. This provoked a snort from Churchill: "When a snake wants to eat his victims he first covers them with saliva." The repercussions were felt in every world capital, though not by every world leader. On February 16, the day the Austrian cabinet was rebuilt to suit Hitler, Chamberlain's cabinet met to consider an RAF appeal for larger appropriations. Foreign Secretary Eden and First Lord of the Admiralty Duff Cooper thought it overdue. Chancellor of the Exchequer Simon argued against it on the ground that higher taxes would imperil Britain's "present standard of financial prosperity." Chamberlain agreed. So did Inskip; though responsible for defense coordination, he took the line that the Foreign Office should set about "reducing the scale of our commitments and the number of our potential enemies." This could only mean continued appeasement of Germany and Italy, and when Chamberlain said, "Hear, hear," Eden flushed.[24]

Relations between the prime minister and his young foreign secretary were approaching the breaking point. In January President Roosevelt had cabled Chamberlain, proposing that European leaders convene in Washington to discuss their differences. The prime minister was annoyed — according to Sir Alexander Cadogan, Vansittart's deputy at the Foreign Office, Chamberlain "had an almost instinctive contempt for the Americans" — and he rejected Roosevelt's offer without consulting Eden, stiffly replying that he believed he could reach agreements with the dictators, with Mussolini first. His Majesty's Government was prepared "to recognise *de jure* the Italian occupation of Abyssinia, if they found that the Italian Government on their side were ready to give evidence of their desire to contribute to the restoration of confidence and friendly relations."[25]

In Churchill's opinion Chamberlain's rebuff to the president's overture effectively ended, as he wrote in his memoirs, "the last frail chance to save the world from tyranny other than by war." If this seems extravagant, one must reflect on Churchill's reasoning, which Eden had adopted. Roosevelt, as Churchill wrote, was "running great risks in his own domestic politics by deliberately involving the United States in the darkening European scene." And he knew the democracies could not survive in Europe without

American support. Roosevelt was not a man you could insult twice. His message had been graceful, even deferential; now he knew he and Neville Chamberlain could never mesh. FDR realized that at some time Hitler must be turned back. If Great Britain fell, FDR could buy peace for a generation, but by then the position of the United States would be hopeless. Already local admirers of the Nazis were swinging clubs in the streets of Latin American capitals. Therefore the president, like Churchill, was determined to establish a special relationship between England and America.[26]

Chamberlain preferred agreements with Germany and Italy to America's goodwill. And he and those around him saw the foreign secretary as an obstacle to this policy. This is somewhat puzzling. To the British and American publics, Eden later came to be regarded as a shining figure overshadowed only by Churchill. Actually, he was more cautious than ambitious; until late in the decade there was little difference in principle between him and the prime minister whose friendship and confidence he had enjoyed. With Hitler threatening Austria, he told the cabinet, he did not want to put himself "in the position of suggesting a resistance which we could not in fact furnish." Nevertheless, Chamberlain persuaded Hankey that Eden had been "swayed by a lot of sloppy people in the F.O." In Rome, Lady Ivy Chamberlain, Austen's widow, proudly wearing a new Fascist party badge, reported that Eden was regarded there "with strong dislike and distrust." The prime minister was turning to people like her for private diplomacy, or sending messages abroad over his own name, thus bypassing and humiliating the foreign secretary. Why? The likeliest explanation is that Chamberlain, as Eden had told a friend, had a certain sympathy for dictators, "whose efficiency appealed to him."[27]

The climax came in late February. Hitler had browbeaten Schuschnigg on a Saturday. Eden's turn came the following week. He had invited the Italian ambassador to England, Dino Grandi, to confer with him at the Foreign Office. Acting on instructions from Rome, Grandi refused and asked for a meeting with Chamberlain to discuss the Führer's insistence on further concessions from Schuschnigg. The prime minister agreed and sent Eden instructions to join them when they met on Friday, February 18. Thus the British foreign secretary was in the extraordinary position of facing a de facto alliance between the envoy of a potential enemy and his own prime minister, which, as Telford Taylor suggests, "must be well-nigh unique in diplomatic annals."[28]

British intelligence had informed Eden that Hitler had decided to seize Austria by force and Mussolini had agreed not to intervene. Grandi, prompted by the P.M., denied that there was any such understanding and added that unless Britain were sympathetic toward Mussolini's policies,

Italian hostility toward His Majesty's Government would harden. After Grandi left, Eden wrote in his diary: "N.C. became very vehement . . . and strode up and down the room saying with great emphasis 'Anthony, you have missed chance after chance. You simply cannot go on like this.' " After following the star of appeasement for five years, Eden had found it to be tinsel. Only a week earlier he had promised an audience in Birmingham that he would agree to "no sacrifice of principles and no shirking of responsibilities merely to obtain quick results," that peace could be preserved only "on a basis of frank reciprocity with mutual respect." Now, unless he broke that vow, he had to quit. On Saturday the prime minister told his cabinet that he had decided to open direct negotiations with the Duce. Eden resigned in disgust the next day, and his under secretary quit with him.[29]

Halifax, appointed to succeed him, was delighted. Chamberlain was relieved, and no one in Parliament was surprised. Chamberlain filled the under secretary's void by appointing R. A. ("Rab") Butler. Butler called at the German embassy, described his close relationship with Sir Horace Wilson, told Hitler's diplomats that his primary objective was "close and lasting cooperation" with the Reich, and said he would "do all I can" to promote it. The embassy, which had reported to the Wilhelmstrasse that Wilson was "decidedly pro-German," now sent word that Butler also "has no prejudices against us."[30]

Readers of *The Times* were under the impression that anyone who spoke out in Eden's behalf would be a lone voice. Actually, the country was more divided than Dawson acknowledged. As England's most eminent journalist, he came under fire in Oxford. A young Fellow asked him why the FO, with *The Times*'s approval, devoted so much space to Mussolini and other Fascists when "It isn't they who are the danger. It is the Germans who are so powerful as to threaten all the rest of us together." Dawson revealed the depth of the void left when honor had been abandoned: "To take your argument at its own valuation — mind you, I'm not saying I agree with it — but if the Germans are so powerful as you say, *Oughtn't we to go in with them?*"[31]

Winston had reservations about Eden — he thought him weak at times and capable of unsound judgment — but he knew he had been a brave officer in France and would never compromise England's honor in the name of a sham peace. Later he described the impact of the news on him:

Late in the night of February 20, a telephone message reached me as I sat in my old room at Chartwell . . . that Eden had resigned. I must confess that my heart sank, and for a while the dark waters of despair overwhelmed me. In a long life I have had many ups and downs. During all the war soon to come and in its darkest times. . . . I slept sound and awoke refreshed, and had no feelings except appetite to grapple with whatever the morning's boxes might bring. But now, on this night of February 20, 1938, and on this occasion only, sleep deserted me. From midnight till dawn I lay in my bed consumed by emotions of sorrow and fear. There seemed one strong young figure standing up against long, dismal, drawling tides of drift and surrender, of wrong measurements and feeble impulses. My conduct of affairs would have been different from his in various ways; but he seemed to me at this moment to embody the life-hope of the British nation, the grand old British race that had done so much for men, and had yet some more to give. Now he was gone. I watched the daylight slowly creep in through the windows, and saw before me in mental gaze the vision of Death.

He sent Eden a note, advising him on what line to take in his resignation speech and urging him not to "allow your personal feelings of friendship to yr late colleagues to hamper you in doing full justice to yr case."[32]

Hurt and angry, Eden spoke to the House on February 21: "I should not be frank if I were to pretend that it is an isolated issue. It is not." Without actually mentioning the rebuff to Roosevelt or Hitler's designs on Austria, he said slowly: *"Within the last few weeks upon one most important decision of foreign policy which did not concern Italy at all the difference was fundamental."* His peroration was a paraphrase of the speeches Winston had been delivering for over five years: "I do not believe that we can make progress in European appeasement if we allow the impression to gain currency abroad that we yield to constant pressure. . . . I am certain in my own mind that progress depends above all on the temper of the nation, and that temper must find expression in a firm spirit. That spirit I am confident is there. Not to give voice to it is I believe fair neither to this country nor to the world."[33]

Churchill spoke the next day. Citing recent "acts of bad faith" by Fascists and Nazis, he said he thought "this was an inopportune time for negotiations with Italy." Furthermore, "the dictator Powers of Europe are striding from strength to strength and from stroke to stroke, and the Parliamentary democracies are retreating abashed and confused." All in all, he said, "This has been a good week for the Dictators. It has been one of the best they have ever had. The German Dictator has laid his hand upon a small but historic country, and the Italian Dictator has carried his vendetta to a victorious conclusion against my right Hon friend the late Foreign Secretary. . . . All the might, majesty, dominion and power of the British Empire was no protection to my right Hon friend. Signor Mussolini has got his scalp." The prime minister's contempt for Americans was widely known. Churchill foresaw the time when the United States might be desperately needed as a British ally. But after this disgraceful episode, "millions of people there who are our enemies have been armed with a means to mock the sincerity of British idealism, and to make out that we are all Continental people tarred with the same brush." That, he said, was a staggering blow. Britain's old policy, he noted, had been to build up the League of Nations. Chamberlain openly scorned the league. Churchill asked: "Is the new policy to come to terms with the totalitarian Powers in the hope that by great and far-reaching acts of submission, not merely by sentiments and pride, but in material Factors, peace may be preserved?" He reminded them of Britain's weak defenses, of the loss of the Rhineland, of the drama in Austria, now approaching a tragic climax, and added: "We do not know whether Czechoslovakia will not suffer a similar attack." To turn away from the Americans was folly, he said, facing Chamberlain and concluding: "I predict that the day will come when at some point or other, on some issue or other, you will have to make a stand, and I pray God that when that day comes we may not find that through an unwise policy we are left to make that stand alone."[34]

After thirty years of marriage the Churchills had reached the age at which familial bonds loosen. All the children except Mary, now in her midteens, were grown. Diana, nearly thirty, had married the son of Sir Abe Bailey, a wealthy South African and a friend of Winston's; three years later she divorced him and married Duncan Sandys. Now she was the mother of two. Randolph, in his late twenties, had been engaged to a girl from Cleveland, Ohio, until his mother talked him out of it. Her motive had been his happiness, but the real winner was the girl. Despite his distinguished name and his leonine features, the Churchills' only son was a grim prospect for any bride, or, indeed for anyone who crossed his path. Already he had as many enemies as his father. The constitution of one club had actually been amended to read: "Randolph Churchill shall not be eligible for membership." During one dinner-party argument he shouted at an executive of British Petroleum: "You have nothing to contribute to this. You are only a clerk in an oil store." He was a chain-smoker, and late in his life, when a tumor was discovered in his alimentary canal, many hoped for the worst. They were disappointed. It was benign. Lord Stanley of Alderly learned of the surgery while standing at the bar in White's. "What a pity," he said, "to remove the one part of Randolph that is not malignant." Both parents shared the responsibility for having raised a cad, though Winston's guilt was more conspicuous. Remembering his own wretched school years, he had approved of his son's contempt for Etonian discipline. After only four terms at Christ Church, Randolph came down from Oxford to launch his public career by a lecture tour of the United States. Everyone in the family except Winston, Mary recalls, thought the scheme "a hare-brained adventure."[35]

Eventually — and perhaps inevitably — the youth turned on his father. One mealtime after another erupted in terrible rows between the two, often in the presence of eminent guests. It became, in Colville's words, "a sad and sorry relationship." The climax followed a January 1938 visit to Chartwell by Leslie Hore-Belisha, the war minister. A few weeks later Churchill sent him a small gift. It was a typical Churchillian gesture — magnanimity toward a man whose company he enjoyed despite their disagreements on the government's defense policy. One evening during dinner *en famille* he was highly critical of Hore-Belisha's role in shaping that policy. Randolph interrupted to say that since he felt that way, the invitation to the war minister and the gift must have been meant to curry favor. The rest of the family gasped. Young Churchill meant to be ironic, but he must have known that his father's personal honor was no joking matter. Outraged, Winston stopped speaking to his son. Randolph wrote him the next day, not to apologize, but to reproach him for "relapsing into moody silence." Churchill replied: "I thought yr remark singularly unkind, offensive, & untrue; & I am sure no son shd have made it to his father. Your letter in no way removes the pain it has caused me, not only on my own account but also on yours, & also on account of our relationship. . . . I really cannot run the risk of such insults being offered to me, & do not feel I want to see you at the present time."[36]

As the years passed, Colville recalled, "the worm turned, and when Randolph arrived, resolved to be good and peaceful, it would be Winston who launched an attack." Thus their relationship deteriorated, never sinking to the depths of Winston's with his own father but nevertheless a source of pain for the entire family. The intriguing question arises: Where was Randolph's mother? The answer is that she was there but might just as well not have been. Aloof, silent, eyes averted, Clementine by her whole manner proclaimed that she had warned her husband, he hadn't listened, and this was the result. But the son felt uncomfortable with his mother, too. Later, after he had married Pamela Digby, he told her that Clementine "hated" him. That was absurd, but friends of the family thought her an unusual mother. Until the last quarter of the twentieth century, the wives of Britain's public men balanced their obligations to their husbands against those to their children. Most compromised. To Clementine, Winston always came first. Mary recalls that he and his career "consumed the cream of her thought and energy." That was not entirely true. She "never became a yes-woman," in Mary's words, "or lost her capacity for independent thought." Certainly she had a strong mind of her own. When Pamela was having difficulties with her young husband, Clemmie advised her: "Pack up, take the children, leave *and don't tell him where you're going*. You can't imagine how kind and sweet he'll be when you return."[37]

In all events, the Chumbolly — his *petit nom* in childhood — had become a problem. So had "Mule," Sarah, now in her early twenties, green-eyed and stunning, with titian hair and milk-white skin. Her mother wrote a friend: "Sometimes she looks absolutely lovely — but on the other hand she can look like a moping raven." She moped when she didn't have her way. In the end she always had it; she was her father's favorite; he could deny her nothing. She decided on a theatrical career and got it, beginning in the chorus line of C. B. Cochran's "Young Ladies," which, according to Pamela, was "a London revue of girls who danced fairly naked — as naked as you could get in those days. That was not really what her parents had in mind for their daughter." Then, while playing in *Follow the Sun*, she fell in love with a music hall comedian, Vic Oliver, a thirty-three-year-old Viennese, thought to be Jewish, who had already been married twice. The response of her parents was a vehement *No*. They wouldn't budge; neither would she. After a year of quarreling she bolted to New York, where Vic was working. Winston sent Randolph after her and engaged American lawyers to stop the marriage, but since she was legally of age, they were helpless. On Christmas Eve, 1936, two weeks after Edward's abdication, Sarah became Mrs. Victor Oliver. The newspapers made a carnival of the affair, and Randolph's public denunciation of them made everything worse. Hankey wrote Chartwell, "We both sympathise with you two," and even Baldwin wrote that he wanted Churchill "to know that I felt with you from my heart when I read in the papers of certain domestic anxieties that must have caused you pain. I know you well enough to realize how closely these things touch you." In the end, a family friend says, "Sarah broke Winston's heart, and he hers."[38]

That left Mary, the Chartwell child — unlike the others, she could remember no other home — with the companionship of an astonishing array of pets: lambs, bantams, a Blenheim spaniel, a beige-colored pug dog, and a marmalade cat, two fox cubs, and three goats, one of whom produced twins while the other gave birth to triplets, and all of whom ate the cherry trees, to Clementine's indignation. Sarah had learned French in a Paris finishing school from Georges Bidault, then obscure but later foreign minister of France; Mary was taught at Chartwell during school holidays by Madame Gabrielle l'Honoré, a discovery of Clemmie's. A nearby riding school provided Mary with mounts. Her relationship with her mother, she now recalls, was "respectful and admiring rather than close," though Clementine had taken her skiing in the Arlberg mountains.

After ten days, Winston received a report on their first Zürs expedition: "Mary fell down 19 times. . . . Today I am going in a sleigh as I am really bored with tumbling down!" The letter was signed: "Your bruised & struggling but undaunted Clemmie."[39]

Sometimes husband and wife spent holidays together. They were welcomed at Blenheim and Lou Sueil by the Marlboroughs; at Taplow by Lord and Lady Desborough; at Trent Park by Sir Philip Sassoon; and the Duke of Westminster (known as Bendor to his friends) was their host at his several homes in England, France, and Scotland. But these were relatives or very old friends. Other patricians felt awkward with them. Winston's criticism of the new Germany was considered bad form — even disloyal to His Majesty's Government. And his manners were odd. How could you entertain a man who wouldn't laugh at anti-Semitic jokes? His wife was almost as bad, and in some ways worse. She would even walk out on her own guests at Chartwell, something one didn't *do*. Mary recalls that "her victims were never the timid, however tedious, but the brash and powerful," and her "basic and undying radicalism also made high Tories and most very rich people potential targets for her scorn." Twice at Chartwell she humbled a British general. Leaving her guests to bathe before dinner, she told his aide-de-camp that she looked forward to seeing him in a half hour. The general said that his ADC didn't dine with him. Clementine turned on him and said: "In my house, General, I invite whom I wish and I don't require your advice." The ADC dined. The second time, the general muttered the threadbare old military myth that all politicians are dishonest. She rose starchily and said: "If that is your view, General, you should leave Chartwell at once. I shall arrange to have your bags packed." He stammered his apologies.[40]

Usually, however, the Churchills took separate vacations. Winston's painting was his release, his escape valve, and he found the "paintatious" Riviera, as he called it, irresistible. "I paint all day, and so far as my means go, gamble after dark," he happily wrote the former Edward VIII, now Duke of Windsor, in the early spring of 1937. He was seeing a lot of Edward and Wallis. To Clemmie he wrote from Maxine Elliott's Château de l'Horizon:

The Windsors dine here and we dine back with them. They have a lovely little palace next door to La D [La Dragonnière, Lord Rothermere's villa at Cap Martin]. Everything extremely well done and dignified. Red liveries, and the little man himself dressed up to the nines in the Balmoral tartan with dagger and jabot etc. . . . I am to dine with him tomorrow night with only Rothermere. No doubt to talk over his plans for returning home. They do not want him to come, but they have no power to stop him.[41]

British expatriates on the Mediterranean liked to think of their society as neo-Edwardian, and those who could afford it were as idle as only the idle rich can be. But Churchill was a working man. Typically, he wrote his wife: "I have stayed in bed every morning and made great progress with the book. We have averaged fifteen hundred words a day, though nominally on vacation. I shall have a lot for you to read when you come home." His occasional forays into Riviera diversion were, almost without exception, disappointing. He was taking lessons in what he called a "very pretty dance. We take three steps and give a hop." He added ruefully: "I always hop at the wrong time, which, I am afraid, provokes small minded people to laugh."[42]

Nevertheless, the creature comforts of the expatriate society appealed to the hedonistic streak in him; if he was well supplied with Pol Roger, fed by a great chef, and offered his choice of the best cigars, the identity of his suppliers was of little interest to him. As a statesman he was fiercely incorrupt, but on holiday he could be had — for a stiff price, to be sure — by women like Maxine Elliott and "Daisy," the daughter of the Duc de Decacazes, known in newspaper columns as "Mrs. Reginald Fellowes," though Mr. Fellowes was invisible. Daisy spent a great deal of her valueless time trying to seduce Winston, but between his paint box, printers' galleys, losing money on the green baize of the Riviera's gaming tables, monologues over brandy, and the pleasures of the table, he had no time for the pleasures she had in mind and may indeed have been unaware of her intentions. He would always find women mysterious. He had Clementine; that was enough for him.

It was not always enough for her, however. Late in life she told Mary, "It took all my time and strength just to keep up with him." This was hyperbole. Certainly, being Mrs. Winston Churchill required rare stamina. Fortunately, Clemmie had it. Indeed, she had enough to pursue her own pleasures, which were very unlike his. She didn't write, paint, gamble, or enjoy the company of *gens du monde;* she didn't like Maxine and wouldn't speak to Daisy. "Her favorite holiday," her youngest daughter recalls, "was to stay in a modest but comfortable hotel in some beautiful or interesting place," where, in the company of congenial people, she would "spend a week or two sightseeing and gallery visiting in an unhurried fashion." Winston disliked sightseeing, and he loathed being part of a tour group which would pause, in this gallery or that museum, while a guide explained what the tourists should appreciate and why. If so trapped, Churchill would stand on the outer fringe of the party, seething with frustration because he wasn't talking, couldn't even interrupt, and therefore wasn't the center of attention.[43]

Ambitious politicians try to project an image of radiant health, and to his admirers Churchill was the robust personification of John Bull. But he had been prey to ills since childhood. Some of his vacations were taken on doctor's orders; others were interrupted by bouts of influenza or infectious fevers. Once, when en route to Venice — where he expected to holiday with Clemmie, Randolph, Sarah, and the Prof — he had been stricken by paratyphoid in Bavaria. His condition was grave; a return to England was out of the question; he lay in a Salzburg sanitarium for two weeks, unable even to raise his head. His confinement continued through a third week, and he abandoned all hope of reaching Italy. He could write, however, and his bank balance, which was always in and out of the red, made work essential. Still in the sanitarium, he began a series of twelve articles on "The World's Great Stories," commissioned by Lord Riddell for *News of the World*. Back at Chartwell he wrote his cousin the Duke of Marlborough that he was "rather battered, but in another week I shall be alright. It was an English bug which I took abroad with me, and no blame rests on the otherwise misguided continent of Europe."[44]

Clementine, now moving gracefully into her fifties, shared with her husband the same peculiar mélange of exceptional energy and an unreliable constitution. As the Chamberlain government approached the end of its first year, with Halifax and the prime minister negotiating agreements with Italy — thus assuring Mussolini's support in any future European conflict, they confidently told the House — Clemmie took the cure in the Pyrenees at Cauterets, near Lourdes. Winston celebrated the following Christmas without her; she was resting on a South Pacific beach in the French colonial archipelago Îles sous le Vent. Perhaps enforced pleasure whetted her appetite for more. A splendid horsewoman, she rode often, and she played tennis with increasing skill, often with the Prof, who had made her an exception to his misogyny. She swam, hunted boar at Bendor's invitation, and beginning in 1936, the year of the Rhineland crisis, had improved her skiing while holidaying with her sister-in-law Lady Gwendeline ("Goonie") Churchill and Venetia Montagu, spending long hours après-ski by firesides in Zürs or Lenzerdeide, trying to forget the troubling present with tales of the serene past.[45]

Her most cherished memories of those interwar years were of a spectacular voyage halfway round the world in the second winter of the Third Reich, roughly the period between the Nazis' murder of Austrian chancellor Dollfuss and Hitler's announcement that Germany was rearming in defiance of Versailles. Clementine was an enchanted guest aboard Lord Moyne's yacht *Rosaura*. Moyne — who would be assassinated ten years later in Cairo by Jewish terrorists — was sailing off on one of those whimsical adventures, evocative of *King Kong*, which spiced the idle life of wealthy Englishmen between the wars. His destination was Komodo, an obscure island in what is now Indonesia, reportedly inhabited by "dragonlike monster lizards." Moyne intended to capture some for the London zoo. These creatures actually existed — one member of the party photographed a twelve-foot lizard with a pig in its jaws, and Moyne brought back two smaller specimens — but the real purpose of the trip was to visit exotica and to escape the gloom and vulgarity of Europe. Her husband and children saw her off at Victoria Station, and in her first letter she wrote that at the moment of departure, seeing "you all collected on the platform, I thought how much I love you all, and above and more than them all *you* my darling Winston. . . . You all looked so sweet and beautiful standing there, and I thought how fortunate I am to have such a family. Do not be vexed with your vagabond Cat — She has gone off toward the jungle with her tail in the air, but will return presently to her basket and curl down comfortably. . . ."

Clementine on the high seas was — at least at the outset — the quintessential Clementine. As she lay in her stateroom, she wrote home, she could "contemplate the photographs of my family erected on the chest of drawers." She had begun "an enormous piece of needlework which Venetia made me bring. I have got 144 reels of silk with which to quilt it & I calculate that even if I sew all day & never catch a butterfly or dragon I could not finish it before my return!" After thirty years of marriage her intimate letters to Churchill, and his replies, were as charming as an exchange between honeymooners. On New Year's Day she wrote from Madras: "Oh my Darling, I'm thinking so much of you & how you have enriched my life. I have loved you very much but I wish I had been a more amusing wife to you. How nice it would be if we were young again." He replied that she had written

some words vy dear to me about my having enriched yr life. I cannot tell you what pleasure this gave me, because I always feel so overwhelmingly in yr debt, if there can be accounts in love. It was sweet of you to write this to me, & I hope & pray I shall be able to make you happy & secure during my remaining years, and cherish you my darling one as you deserve, & leave you in comfort when my race is run. What it has been to me to live all these years in yr heart & companionship no phrases can convey. Time passes swiftly, but is it not joyous to see how great and growing is the treasure we have gathered together, amid the storms & stresses of so many eventful & to millions tragic & terrible years?[46]

Winston's domestic stresses, during his wife's absence, were trivial but irksome to a man trying to sway Parliament and write the opening passages of his next Marlborough volume. His eminent ancestor fascinated him, though he saw some of his warts; Marlborough had "far less pride than the average man," he wrote Clemmie, and was in fact capable of "grovelling." It was "only in the field and in his love for Sarah that he rises to the sublime. Still Mars and Venus are two of the most important deities in the classical heaven." It was maddening to descend from the eminence of character analysis to cope with the fox who was devouring his geese, an astonishing explosion among Chartwell's canine population, and feverish young Churchills who, he reasoned, ought to be too old to catch infectious childhood diseases. Discovering that every bitch on the grounds was giving birth to litters of puppies, Winston unmasked the culprit. He was Mary's pug, a slave of lust. But Mary couldn't be admonished; she had whooping cough. Randolph was home with a severe case of jaundice. Sarah was pale and tired, a consequence, her father wrote her mother, of "dancing practically four hours a day as well as going to balls. . . . I have therefore told her that she must not go to balls on any night when she practises dancing." As to the puppies, he had "banished all dogs from our part of the house. . . . I really think you will have to buy a new strip of carpet outside my landings."[47]

Another writer would have cut his schedule to the bone and concentrated on his manuscripts. But it was part of the Churchill syndrome that despite diversions he had absolute concentration during the hours set aside for work, and that other activities were actually necessary to fuel this power. One activity was social intercourse; he needed people as ships need water. The Prof's arrival for a two-day visit delighted him. So did the unexpected appearance of his eldest daughter at a moment when she was most needed. "I was sitting down last night to eat my New Year's dinner as I thought in solitude," he wrote his wife, "and in marched Diana looking absolutely lovely. She had come on her own to keep me company."[48]

Working with his hands was equally important. Every day he laid bricks, building a wall which, he promised Clemmie, would be completed when she arrived home. That ought to have been enough, but he also launched two major landscaping projects: turning a peninsula on one Chartwell lake into an island, where the geese could nest safe from the fox, and creating a ha-ha, or sunk fence, beyond the swimming pool to permit one's eye to plunge "across a valley of unbroken green." All this was to be accomplished in one week by hiring an enormous mechanical digger for twenty-five pounds. He assured his wife the digger would "do more than forty men do." Indeed, he added, it was capable of feats beyond the competence of people "as he is a caterpillar and can walk over the most sloppy fields without doing any harm."[49]

Note: the contraption was a "he." Winston, the ultimate anthropomorphist, invested every object, animate or inanimate, with a personality and
assigned it a personal pronoun. Mary simply described the contrivance as
"the monster." And she was right. The "digger drama," as it came to be
known at Chartwell, began when the machine clanked into view with all
the grace of a heavy tank. Winston regarded the creature with admiration,
which was transformed into uneasiness, alarm, pity, and, finally, fury. In
his next letter to Clemmie he wrote that the project was proving "a bigger
and longer business than I had expected. It will take a fortnight in all."
Nearly a month later he reported in exasperation that the digger had
broken down, had fallen into a pit and, despite his heroic efforts to
extricate it, had been idle for three weeks. Four hydraulic jacks were
rented; with their help "the animal emerged from his hole." Churchill
doubted "if I shall get out of it under £150." Altogether the mechanical
digger was on his property, with its expenses mounting, for ten weeks. As
the day for its departure approached, it became the object of a profound
Churchillian study, the results of which were reported to Chartwell's
absent mistress: "The animal is very strong with his hands but feeble with
his caterpillar legs, and as the fields are sopping, they had the greatest
difficulty in taking him away. They will have to lay down sleepers all the
way from the lake to the gate over which he will waddle on Monday. I shall
be glad to see the last of him."[50]

At last, on March 8, he wrote: "The digger has gone, thank God." His
wife knew how to restore his spirits. From Singapore she wrote: "What
tremendous works you are doing. . . . I'm *delighted* about the Ha-ha.
Please do *not* throw back *too* much earth on the garden side or the slope
might look too sudden. . . . How lovely it will be when your beautiful
wall reaches the end." Thus far in her trip she had been playing a familiar
role as Winston's eyes and ears; she had inspected the great Singapore
dockyard and noted how the government's cuts in defense spending had
reduced its effectiveness, and she had marched into the city's largest
bookshop and asked "if there were a brisk demand for your books." She
was told that a condensed version of *The World Crisis,* his history of World
War I, had "gone very well," and the second Marlborough volume was
"going better than the first. They had sold 12 sets of Marlborough & had
5 more on order. I think this is rather good when you realise how
expensive it is."[51]

At about this time Clementine left civilization, put away the needlework, turned away from her family photographs, and forgot her straitlaced
upbringing. The *Rosaura* was headed for the most exotic islands in the
world: Borneo, Celebes, the Moluccas, New Caledonia, the New
Hebrides, New Britain, and the Solomons. "This is the genuine article!"

she wrote in a euphoric burst, "unchartered [*sic*] seas, unexplored territory, stark naked savages." Churchill, vaguely troubled, perhaps goaded
by a flicker of intuition, replied that it made him gasp "to look at the map
& see what enormous distances you have covered . . . and it depresses me
to feel the *weight* of all that distance pressing down upon us both. How glad
I shall be when you turn homewards, & when the mails will be closing up
together, instead of lagging & widening apart!" He had reason for anxiety.
Clementine was in the presence of danger. That included physical danger;
at one point she became separated from the rest of the party, lost in an
almost impenetrable patch of dense tropical jungle; she was soaked in a
sudden rainstorm, terrified of the lizards and snakes around her, her
screams unheard until the yacht's second officer came crashing through the
undergrowth to rescue her. She wrote: "I almost kissed him."[52]

She was, in fact, in a kissing mood. And the greater peril lay there.
Among the unhappier facts of life is that desire peaks in the two sexes at
disparate ages. "The elementary notion of standardization," Mencken
noted, "seems never to have occurred to the celestial Edison." A male is
lustiest at fifteen; the average female reaches the heights of passion in her
mid-thirties. Churchill had always been a sublimator. All who were close
to him agree that he was weakly sexed, even in youth, and in his sixties his
volcano was virtually extinct. In Parliament a fellow MP whispered to him
that his trousers were unfastened. "It makes no difference," Winston
replied wryly. "The dead bird doesn't leave the nest."[53]

Clementine, however, was vulnerable. The setting conspired against
her. Cruising through tropical seas, past lush, nameless islands heavy with
the scent of exotic flowers, she felt transported. Like a Maugham
heroine — strong-minded, puritanical, even prim — she met a romantic
unattached man and fell in love. The man was Terence Philip, a handsome, wealthy art dealer seven years younger than she. In any affair, La
Rochefoucauld observed, one partner is the lover and the other the beloved. Philip was the beloved. Long afterward Clementine conceded that
the initiative had been hers, adding, "But he made me love him." Mary
compares the relationship between them to "a fragile tropical flower which
cannot survive in grayer, colder climes." Clementine came to her senses.
She was not meant for enchantment; her destiny was inseparable from
Churchill's. Late in life, in a nostalgic letter, she summed up the magic of
those three months beneath the Southern Cross, saying, in effect, that she
had briefly known the transient rapture of Cinderella at the ball; then the
clock struck and she fled. Of course, she missed Philip. They met several
times, and that summer she suggested to Churchill that she take another
trip. She wrote a friend: "It's very nice to be back but Oh Dear I want to
start out again very badly! Mr. Pug is very sweet but now he says

'NO.' . . ." Even before she returned he had written her: "I think a lot about you my darling Pussie . . . and rejoice that we have lived our lives together; and have still some years of expectation in this pleasant vale. . . . I feel this has been a gt experience and adventure to you & that it has introduced a new background to yr life, & a larger proportion; and so I have not grudged you your long excursion; but now I do want you back."[54]

She brought back one souvenir, an exquisite Bali dove which lived, at Chartwell, in a lovely wicker cage. It could not last there long; perhaps she had known that. After its death she buried it in the walled garden, beneath the sundial. Today one can read the epitaph she had carved round the sundial's base:

> HERE LIES THE BALI DOVE
>
> *It does not do to wander*
> *Too far from sober men*
> *But there's an island yonder,*
> *I think of it again.*

By 1937 Churchill's isolation in the House of Commons was almost complete; as his daughter Mary notes, "his gradual estrangement from the Conservative party's leadership, due to his . . . campaign for rearmament and confrontation with the growing power of Germany, made the probability of his being offered office increasingly remote." The quarantine of him was effective among and in the organs of entrenched power, notably *The Times* and the BBC. But Winston reached millions of readers with his powerful articles — over a hundred in 1937 alone, including fortnightly pieces in Beaverbrook's *Evening Standard,* which were syndicated in the *Glasgow Evening News,* the *Aberdeen Evening Express,* the *Belfast Telegraph,* the *Adelaide Advertiser,* the *East African Standard,* and the *Madras Mail;* translations in Brussels, Rotterdam, Copenhagen, Stockholm, Oslo, Tallinn, Kaunas, Zurich, Lausanne, Prague, Bucharest, Cracow, Buenos Aires, Trondheim, Lucerne, Budapest, and Belgrade; and a weekly essay in *News of the World. News of the World* was disdained by the mighty for its sensationalism and its pandering to the working class, but with an audience of four million members it could not be scorned by a man struggling to rouse the country, and Churchill was in no position to pick his forum anyhow. On November 3, 1937, he wrote the *News's* publishers, grandly describing it as "a wonderful platform from which to address the stable, sagacious, good-humoured, kind-hearted mass of the British nation, and I value the opportunity of doing so, quite apart from the handsome payments which you make."[55]

Handsome was the right word; on December 18, 1937, after he had agreed to write sixteen *News of the World* articles in 1938, he received a check for £4,500. William L. Shirer knew Randolph as a fellow journalist in the late 1930s and learned something of Winston's finances from his son. Randolph, he writes, explained that "his father lived mainly from a syndicated weekly [*sic*] newspaper column sold around the world. There were over two hundred subscribers, he said, who paid a total of around $2,000 a week, of which Churchill received some £300, or $1,500, a fairly comfortable income. But not one that was making him really rich." Yet Winston insisted upon continuing to live as though he were, and most Englishmen, including some who knew him well, would have been astounded to know that all his life he had been just a few steps — sometimes very few — from his creditors.[56]

Abroad he was taken more seriously than in Parliament. He was, as he described himself, "a private member of Parliament, but of some prominence." Newspaper publishers who held him in contempt would have preferred to ignore him, but their reporters gave him celebrity status, knowing he always made good copy. At one time or another, photographs of him laying bricks must have been seen by every Briton. When a British tailors' magazine deplored his wardrobe, it was news, even in the United States. Léon Blum, the French statesman, visited Chartwell to ask his advice. French generals invited him to tour the Maginot Line. He went and, after inspecting it, painted it. His following in France was large; when George VI and his queen made a state visit to Paris, the Churchills were invited to all the royal functions, always *bien placés* — better seated, indeed, than the British ambassador. Among Clementine's papers, when she died, was a Versailles menu dated July 21, 1938, and signed by her partners on both sides: M. Gabriel Hanotaux, a celebrated author, now forgotten, and Marshal Philippe Pétain, the hero of Verdun, whose performance in World War II would be less illustrious.[57]

Among those who recognized Churchill's potential should war come was the man who was going to make it all happen. Several months before Eden's resignation Ambassador Joachim von Ribbentrop, on Hitler's instructions, asked Winston to call on him at the German embassy in London. The excuse was one of Churchill's columns in Beaverbrook's *Evening Standard;* Winston had written that a recent speech by Ribbentrop had been misrepresented. But there was more to it than that. Envoys of great powers did not deign to discuss articles in newspapers of their host country; lesser men on their staffs did it for them. And when Churchill appeared at the German embassy on May 21, 1937, the column wasn't even mentioned. The matter discussed was so momentous that they were closeted for over two hours. The Führer, his ambassador said, proposed to guarantee the integrity of the British Empire. Churchill replied that the Royal Navy had been doing that for centuries and needed no help. Nevertheless, Ribbentrop declared that the Third Reich would "stand guard" over it; all he asked in return was a "free hand" in eastern Europe. The Reich, he explained, needed lebensraum for its increasing population. Winston, intrigued, asked how much living space Hitler wanted.[58]

Strolling up to a wall map, the Nazi blandly ticked off the Reich chancellor's shopping list: all of Poland, all of the Ukraine, and the Soviet republic of Byelorussia, including the Pripet Marshes. Churchill stared at the map. The Reich's land mass would be quintupled, from 182,000 square miles to 760,000. Great Britain had less than 89,000. After a long pause he replied that although Britons were "on bad terms with Soviet Russia" and "hated Communism as much as Hitler," they didn't hate it *that* much. He could only speak for himself, but he felt certain that no British government would tolerate German "domination of Central and Eastern Europe." According to Churchill, Ribbentrop "turned abruptly away" and said, "In that case, war is inevitable. The Führer is resolved. Nothing will stop him and nothing will stop us." Churchill urged him not to "underrate England," and particularly not to "judge by the attitude of the present administration." Britain, he said, "is a curious country, and few foreigners can understand her mind. . . . She is very clever. If you plunge us all into another great war, she will bring the whole world against you like last time." The Nazi said heatedly, "Ah, England may be very clever, but this time she will not bring the world against Germany." Because he thought the incident should be "put on record," Churchill later wrote, he "reported it at the time to the Foreign Office."[59]

It was not news there. The FO was, however, surprised by Hitler's decision to approach Churchill, his most implacable enemy, apparently in the belief that he could frighten him with Teutonic *Schrecklichkeit*. It was also noted wryly that this was one of those rare occasions in which Winston arrived in Whitehall as the bearer of news. Usually it was the other way round; the situation map he kept at Chartwell was almost as detailed, and as accurate, as those in Whitehall. He had begun on a small scale, but now his business as the receiver of stolen goods — state secrets not meant for the eyes of a private MP, however prominent — was booming. At Chartwell and in his Westminster flat he pored over classified British documents and reports on the latest developments in eight continental capitals. In London his informants included three members of Chamberlain's cabinet; in the world of science, technology, and the intelligentsia were Sir Eustace Tennyson d' Eyncourt and Sir William Beveridge; in the War Office, the chief of the Imperial General Staff (first Sir Cyril Deverell, and then, in 1939, Sir Edmund Ironside), a brigadier, and two colonels; in the RAF, an air chief marshal, a wing commander, a group captain, and a squadron leader; and in the Admiralty, a vice admiral (Sir Reginald Henderson), a rear admiral, a captain, and a brilliant young commander, Lord Louis Mountbatten. He had the support of almost every man in the top echelon of the Foreign Office. Ribbentrop had thought his message would stun Winston, and had been taken aback by his ready reply. In fact, he had only confirmed what Churchill had already known — from Vansittart's agent in Göring's office — for several months.

He relied on Van for material from the Wilhelmstrasse, but his data on the RAF's inadequacies, which created such consternation on the front bench, came directly from officers who were risking court-martial if found out. Group Captain Lachlan MacLean, who had commanded a company of Gurkha Rifles in France before transferring to the Royal Flying Corps in 1916, had drawn up a savage indictment describing the RAF's obsolete equipment and concluded that were war to come in the next three or even five years, "We shall be powerless to retaliate, at any rate in the air." Wing Commander Anderson acquired a copy and sent it to Churchill, who replied that he would like to meet the author. According to MacLean's account, "Accompanying Anderson I was introduced to Winston in his flat in Westminster and he congratulated me on the paper and we discussed the air rearmament." Subsequently Anderson would tell MacLean that Churchill needed data for a speech in the House. MacLean would prepare a memorandum "and I would let him have these papers and would perhaps go to Churchill's flat for a discussion." The arrangement evolved, he recalled, "into my sending to Winston's personal secretary, Mrs Pearman, papers on the more significant events in the air rearmament." In less than seven months the two RAF officers met Churchill, either in Morpeth Mansions or at Chartwell, seven times. Inevitably, they met Lindemann. Papers were exchanged on such arcane topics as RDF and "Times of Flight and Trajectory Tables" — dull to the layman, but essential to Britain's survival three years later.[60]

Eminent guests from abroad whose names are inscribed in Chartwell's guest book include the Rumanian foreign minister Nicolae Titulescu; former German chancellor Heinrich Brüning; Pierre Cot, the French air minister; and Britain's ambassador to Belgrade, who approved Churchill's plan to visit Yugoslavia and urge the formation of a European alliance to confront Nazi aggression. These visitors would stay for dinner. British civilian informants would arrive for tea at Chartwell or "elevenses" in his London flat, leaving behind them, when they departed, copies of blueprints, charts, diagrams, minutes of cabinet meetings, and confidential reports to the prime minister, all of which belonged in locked, guarded files at the War Office, the Admiralty, the Air Ministry, or Downing Street.

In bed the following morning, sipping his breakfast highball, Winston would compare them with information from the Wilhelmstrasse and the Linden; reports from the mistresses of the Duce's intimate advisers; foreign ministries from Helsinki to Athens; and straightforward *en clair et net* dispatches from the French. Churchill regularly exchanged data with three successive prime ministers, Blum, Flandin, and Édouard Daladier. Typically, he wrote Daladier in early 1938, asking for a cross-check of "information I have been able to gather from various sources about the present and prospective strength of the German Army." He put it at forty divisions "now at full war-strength," four of them armored, with another twenty divisions ready by October 1, and still another thirty-six in trained reserves. This represented a sevenfold jump in one year, an expansion of military strength without precedent in peacetime. Moreover, another twelve Austrian divisions would be added if Hitler's Anschluss succeeded and was followed by conscription there. Daladier consulted his War Office in the rue St. Dominique, checked the Deuxième Bureau, and replied that they were "entirely in accord with you." Even Desmond Morton was impressed. "I am astonished," he wrote to Winston, "by your knowledge of detail on Defence matters."[61]

All this did not pass the Treasury Bench unnoticed. Nor was it meant to. Espionage is usually covert. Information so acquired is exploited without the knowledge of the spies' victims; if made public it becomes valueless, and agents may be blown. But Churchill's motives were political; he meant to reverse the course of Britain's military policy. Throughout the fall of 1937 and into 1938 he continued to receive disturbing reports from Anderson, Morton, and, through MacLean, A.; Chief Marshal Sir Edgar Ludlow-Hewitt of the RAF. In the House of Commons his remarks on Britain's lack of preparedness grew sharper. So did the criticism of his criticism, but as Morton wrote him, he was "not the first to have told the truth and become heartily unpopular for it." Even if prophecies proved true, Morton continued, men had "the habit of crucifying the prophet or . . . they exterminate him with a gas cloud — of propaganda. However, they have not silenced you yet, so there is some hope for the Empire still."[62]

In the eyes of His Majesty's Government, press lords like Beaverbrook, and most members of Parliament, Churchill's concerns were largely irrelevant. To them, war between Britain and Nazi Germany wasn't even a remote possibility. Differences between the British Empire and the

German Reich would be resolved at negotiating tables. Since Britain was prepared to give Hitler whatever he wanted, why should a drop of blood be spilled, or England's rising productivity be threatened by a bloated arms budget?

Churchill was painfully aware that His Majesty's Government regarded him as a meddler and a Cassandra. Yet his figures — which were also HMG's figures — cried for action. In the fall of 1937 the Air Ministry, looking ahead to December 1939, had found that the RAF would have only 1,736 aircraft as against Germany's 3,240. More urgently, Chamberlain had invited a Luftwaffe mission headed by General Erhard Milch to spend a week inspecting the RAF's latest models on the ground and reviewing a fly-past. On October 12, Group Captain Mac-Lean sent word of this to Chartwell. MacLean had inferred, not unreasonably, that the Nazis, suspecting the inadequacies of England's air force, were coming "to find confirmation of their suspicions." Once they had grasped Britain's weakness in the air — and they could scarcely miss it; the aircraft they would be examining weren't even fully equipped — their discovery, MacLean wrote, "must inevitably influence German policy. . . . We are bluffing with the sky as the limit, without holding a single card, and we have then invited our opponents to come round and see what cards we hold, trusting to sleight of hand to put across a second bluff."[63]

Alarmed, Churchill was also in a quandary. There was no way to withdraw the invitation to Germany without making things worse. But it was time the government moved quickly to heal its sickly air force. His latest data, as he wrote Sir Maurice Hankey, could not be discussed in the House of Commons because "of the present dangerous world situation." He had decided to lay the facts before Hankey, who, as secretary to both the cabinet and the Committee of Imperial Defence, carried weight in the government. Hankey was aware of the problem; he had written Inskip that if the country realized how vulnerable Britain was to aggression HMG would be "forced to undertake late in the day panic measures." On October 16 Winston sent him MacLean's report, omitting the author's name and identifying him only as "a high staff officer of the RAF." He added, "I trust to our friendship and your honour that its origin is not probed. But look at the facts!"[64]

To his dismay, Hankey chose to ignore the facts. Instead he replied with an unexpected, lengthy rebuke. He was, he said, "a good deal troubled by the fact of your receiving so many confidences of this kind," particularly since Winston was "a critic of the Departments under whom these Officers serve" and they were ignorant "of the wider factors" in national policy. If they had grievances, they should speak to their senior officers or to the cabinet minister representing their service. "Backstairs" information, he wrote, should be discouraged "because it breeds distrust and has a disintegrating effect on the discipline of the Services." In a stiff reply, Churchill said he had not expected a "lengthy lecture," and "you may be sure I shall not trouble you again in such matters."[65]

By now His Majesty's Government was aware that Churchill had become a spymaster, and the hunt for his sources within the government — the "rotten apples," as Horace Wilson called them — was on. Not long after Churchill's exchange with Hankey, MacLean resigned from the RAF, reportedly under pressure. But those pursuing a military alliance were after bigger game. In the Foreign Office, Vansittart, with his swagger and arrogance, was the apple likeliest to be tainted. Since moving into No. 10 with Chamberlain, Wilson had been stalking the FO's permanent under secretary, judging him, Churchill wrote in his war memoirs, "as hostile to Germany." In HMG's view criticism of the Third Reich blackened a man's name. The prime minister had dismissed Van's warnings of German aggression as "hysterical," and Wilson had called the under secretary "an alarmist" who "hampers all attempts of the Government to make friendly contact with the dictator states," adding that "his influence over Anthony Eden is very great."[66]

At that time Eden, still foreign secretary, could have fought for Vansittart, and his decent instincts prodded him to do it. But as Gilbert and Gott put it, he "unwisely and rashly bowed to the wind" when Chamberlain declared that Van must be replaced by Sir Alexander Cadogan, a protégé of Horace Wilson. Vansittart had thirty-six years of diplomatic experience, but Cadogan, as a zealous believer in appeasement and the promise of an Anglo-German alliance, was likelier to sympathize with Chamberlain's conviction that the Third Reich should become Britain's most favored nation.[67]

On January 1, 1938, Vansittart was kicked upstairs and given the empty title of chief diplomatic adviser to the government. Cadogan would run the Foreign Office. The Germans were delighted; Ernst von Wörmann, chargé d'affaires at Hitler's London embassy, minuted that Van could no longer issue instructions to British envoys in foreign capitals, nor would classified material be channeled through him; he would see documents only "as required" by Cadogan. The fact that he was permitted to remain in his old office deceived no one. His "dismissal," as Churchill rightly called it, stunned Whitehall. There was no precedent for it; traditionally, permanent under secretaries held office until they died or chose to retire. Winston heard the news in Paris, where, after a month's holiday at the Château de l'Horizon, he was staying at the British embassy, conferring with Daladier, who would be premier in the next French government, and Alexis Léger, secretary general at the Quai d'Orsay. The fall of his great FO ally left Churchill distraught. The British ambassador,

Sir Eric Phipps, reported to London that Winston could "hardly talk of anything else," that he "thought Van's displacement was a very dangerous thing, that it would be represented as a victory for pro-Germans in England, that it would arouse the suspicions of the French, etc etc." Phipps, himself an appeaser, wrote Hankey that he was "honestly perturbed at the fuss over Van's appointment." But Churchill saw the significance of Vansittart's fall. "No one more clearly realised or foresaw the growth of the German danger," he later wrote, "or was more ready to subordinate other considerations to meeting it," and now "the whole responsibility for managing the Foreign Office passed out of his hands."[68]

Emboldened, a few months later the appeasers actually tried to imprison one of Churchill's few parliamentary followers. Duncan Sandys had his own clandestine sources; on June 17, 1938, armed with facts and figures, he sent the War Office a question — concerning London's air defenses — which clearly revealed access to classified information. Summoned by the attorney general, he was told that unless he disclosed the name of his informant, he would be prosecuted under the Official Secrets Act. Sandys told his tale in Parliament and requested the appointment of a select committee to study the applicability of the act to MPs carrying out their official duties. Winston delightedly wrote Lord Hugh Cecil, one of his oldest friends — he had been best man when Churchill married Clementine thirty years earlier — "The fur is going to fly."[69]

Tempers were up, and skyrocketed the next day when Sandys informed a crowded House that as a reserve officer he had been ordered to appear, in uniform, before a court-martial. This, he submitted, was a "gross breach" of Parliamentary privileges. He was backed by Attlee and Sinclair, the Labour and Liberal leaders, and, of course, by his father-in-law, who tartly remarked that an act designed to protect the national defense should not shield ministers who had neglected national defense. When the House cleared Sandys without dissent, Oliver Harvey of the Foreign Office noted in his diary, "I hear Winston is in the highest spirits over it." The appeasers, unchastened, reopened the inquiry on a technicality. It compounded the original blunders; Churchill took advantage of every opportunity to maul his critics. To a fellow MP he wrote that he was "quite content with my corner seat."[70]

Of course he wasn't, but a political outcast enjoys a freedom denied those charged with responsibility, and this was particularly true in Winston's case; even Hankey had conceded that he was "a leading Statesman . . . patriotic beyond criticism." As such he had been visited by the German air mission and briefed by Ambassador Joachim von Ribbentrop.[71]

🦁   🦁

Central to the appeasers' creed was the assumption that no one wanted war. They did not know, or refused to believe, that the German chancellor was an exception. Thus the victorious allies of 1918 "slept," as Churchill put it, while Germany, not answerable to voters, trained armies, built ships, and sent swarms of bombers and fighter planes into the sky. On November 5, 1937, Hitler had summoned his generals and senior diplomats to announce an irrevocable decision. Germany must make war. He was not getting any younger, and he wanted to fight, wanted to see his armies take action while he was still vigorous and capable of exercising direct command. The Wehrmacht and Luftwaffe were ordered to prepare for battle, which could come "as early as 1938."

In the Reich Chancellery that day he had rambled on for four hours and fifteen minutes, raising the possibility of war between Japan and France; denouncing France and England, the two "hate-filled" (*"hasserfüllte"*) countries; and sounding the ritualistic demand for lebensraum. He had chosen to prolong the war in Spain, he said, because among other things, the issue might bring Italy into armed conflict with Britain and France. This would open the way for Germany to resolve the Czech and Austrian questions. He added that "annexation of Czechoslovakia and Austria" would mean improved strategic frontiers, new sources of food, the assimilation of twelve million more "Germans," and, best of all, enough young men to form twelve new divisions. Of course, if Germany were to make use of this war between Italy and the democracies, "the attack on the Czechs" (*"Überfall auf die Tschechei"*) would have to be carried out with "lightning speed" (*"blitzartig schnell"*). Then — for the last time, as it turned out — he had agreed to answer questions from his subordinates.[72]

Three men stood up to him: Generals Blomberg and Fritsch and Foreign Minister Neurath. They pointed out what everyone there knew: to predict war between Britain and Italy was absurd. Moreover, Czechoslovakia had been supported by a military alliance with France since 1925 — and by the Franco-Soviet alliance since 1936. Less than two months earlier the French foreign minister had stressed that France would fulfill her obligations "whatever the form of the aggression if the aggression is certain"; unofficially, the Foreign Office had let it be known that a British declaration of war on Germany would follow.[73]

Hitler ignored all this. Within three months the dissenters had all been dismissed. Neurath was replaced as foreign minister by Ribbentrop, though (like Vansittart) he was given an impressive new title to save his prestige abroad. But Blomberg and Fritsch, the leaders of Germany's military elite, were destroyed, and Hitler, being Hitler, did it in the coarsest possible way. Blomberg was cashiered on the ground that his wife had once been a prostitute; Werner von Fritsch, the Wehrmacht's commander, was disgraced by a preposterous assertion that he was a homosexual who practiced sodomy in a dark alley near Berlin's Potsdam Hauptbahnhof on a demimonde figure known as Bayernsepp (Bavarian Joe). Stunned, too proud even to dignify such an accusation with an answer, the aristocratic officer told the Führer that he would respond only to a court-martial. Hitler had no evidence — there was none to be had — and he had no intention of letting the officer corps caste pass judgment on one of its own. He simply ordered Fritsch to retire, and the general, having taken the oath to obey his führer under all circumstances, vanished into obscurity. On February 4, 1938, Hitler proclaimed himself *Kriegsherr* (warlord), assuming personal command over Germany's armed forces. His dictatorial powers would remain unchecked until his death.[74]

It was time, the Führer decided, for Austrian independence to mount the scaffold. In the Berghof he had granted Schuschnigg's homeland a reprieve, but it was short; he was not a patient man. Eight days after the distraught Austrian chancellor returned to Vienna, the Führer staged one of his frenzied performances before the Reichstag. He raved that "political separation from the Reich must not lead to the deprivation of rights — that is, the general rights of self-determination [*Selbstbestimmung*]. . . . To the interests of the German Reich belongs the protection of those German peoples who are not in a position to secure, by their own efforts, their political and spiritual freedom." He ordered Jodl and Göring to mobilize their men and call up the reserves, confronting Schuschnigg with 4,126,200 superbly trained men — Versailles, had it been enforced, would have limited them to 100,000 — against Austria's 38,000 soldiers, many of German stock and therefore of doubtful loyalty.[75]

But how many Austrians wanted to join the Third Reich? In the *Evening Standard* on March 4 Churchill estimated that two-thirds of Schuschnigg's countrymen were prepared to defend their independence. The following day he was challenged by Unity Mitford, his wife's cousin. Unity had strong Nazi sympathies. She had been among Hitler's traveling companions since he became Reich chancellor five years earlier. Now she wrote "Dear Cousin Winston" that he, like most Englishmen, was "very misinformed about Austrian affairs, which are consistently misrepresented by the British press." She had been in Vienna when her führer had torn his strip off the Austrian chancellor, and she wrote:

The jubilation which broke out among all classes must have been one of the most tremendous demonstrations of belief the world has ever seen. . . . Everyone looked happy & full of hope for the future. . . . In Graz, Linz, and Vienna I witnessed demonstrations in which the people went mad with joy and one could not move in the streets for people shouting "Heil Hitler! Anschluss!" & waving Swastika flags. By night, the hills around Vienna were ablaze with bonfires in the shape of Swastikas.

She predicted that "a free plebiscite would result in *at least* 80% for the Nazis."[76]

Churchill passed this along to Georg Franckenstein, a veteran diplomat and Austria's envoy in London, asking for advice and assuring him that his reply would be confidential. Franckenstein pointed out that the Austrian Nazis were purposefully noisy and highly visible because they wanted to create the impression that they formed a majority, and he agreed that "there was much jubilation among the National Socialists after Hitler's speech." But while the Nazis were "displaying the greatest possible activity," the majority of people, at Schuschnigg's expressed wish, were remaining quiet and orderly "to avoid conflict and bloodshed which might lead to German intervention." Franckenstein had consulted several informed, objective observers about Nazi strength in Austria; "some suggested 25%, others 35%, but all were agreed that the majority in the country is in favor of an independent Austria."[77]

Chamberlain had applauded the "negotiations," at the Berghof. To what extent the P.M. was misled by his hopes and his advisers can never be determined, but the documents prove that in crises he was capable of lying to Parliament and the country. Once back in Vienna, Schuschnigg and Guido Schmidt, his under secretary of foreign affairs, had described their ordeal in detail, including the Führer's ultimatum. They had briefed envoys of all the powers, particularly England's, and William L. Shirer, who was there at the time, read the British legation's unsparing account before it was cabled to London. Even Ambassador Henderson, whose admiration for the Third Reich approached Unity Mitford's, wrote that Austria's chancellor had been "threatened and browbeaten, and under menaces accepted an arrangement of which he thoroughly disapproved." Furthermore, the Viennese correspondents of the *Daily Telegraph* and *The Times* had telephoned accurate reports of Hitler's *Schrecklichkeit* in the Berghof. Dawson didn't always print dispatches from his correspondents in Europe, but those he suppressed he sent to No. 10. Thus it is impossible to argue that the prime minister did not really know what had happened at the Führer's alpine retreat. On the contrary, he was keenly aware that Austria's independence was gravely imperiled. Nevertheless, he told the House on March 2 that

what happened was merely that two statesmen had agreed upon certain measures for the improvement of relations between their two countries. . . . It appears hardly likely to insist that just because two statesmen have agreed on certain domestic changes in one of two countries — changes desirable in the interest of relations between them — that one country renounced its independence in favor of the other. On the contrary, the Federal Chancellor's [Schuschnigg's] speech of February 24 contained nothing that might convey that the Federal Chancellor himself believed in the surrender of the independence of his country.[78]

Actually, Schuschnigg's address to the Austrian Bundestag, delivered after his return from the Berghof, had been an act of desperate courage. The federal chancellor declared that Austria would make no more concessions to the Nazis. "We must," he declared, "call a halt and say 'Thus far and no farther [*Bis hierher und nicht weiter*].' " He swore that the country would never surrender its independence, giving it a rallying cry: *"Rot-Weiss-Rot bis in den Tod!"* ("Red-White-Red till we're dead!").[79]

Obviously, defying Hitler was highly dangerous. He had already murdered one Austrian chancellor. His Austrian Nazis, who were if anything more brutal than the Reich's, roamed the streets in mobs — twenty thousand in Graz alone — hauling down their nation's flags and raising hakenkreuz banners. The police, acting on instructions from Seyss-Inquart, made no attempt to restrain them. In Vienna, the Karlsplatz was swarming with hysterical Nazis screaming *"Sieg Heil! Heil Hitler!"* and demanding that Schuschnigg be lynched. But the federal chancellor was made of sterner stuff than the men then ruling the British Empire, who were afraid to challenge Hitler. On March 9 Schuschnigg announced a national plebiscite to be held on Sunday, March 13. His countrymen would be asked whether or not they wanted a free, independent, Christian, united Austria: *Ja oder Nein?*[80]

In a note to Churchill, Ambassador Franckenstein jubilantly wrote that the Austrian voters would settle the "'duel' between Miss Mitford and myself." But the next day — Thursday, March 10 — the ambassador was less sanguine. Leo Amery gave a lunch for him at 112 Eaton Square. Harold Nicolson noted that the Austrian seemed "anxious and depressed." They congratulated him, Nicolson continued, upon "Schuschnigg having declared a plebiscite and having been so brave as to stand up to Hitler," but "he does not seem to think that his courage will avail very much."[81]

Until the plebiscite issue arose, Hitler had not planned an immediate

Anschluss, an outright annexation of Germany's southern neighbor; he merely wanted Austria as a vassal state. Hitler's goal had been to dominate Austria by undermining Schuschnigg, overthrowing him, and installing a government of Austrian Nazis. Schuschnigg's radio broadcast Wednesday evening, the ninth, announcing the plebiscite, was one of three developments which led Hitler to decide that Austria must and *could* be annexed, abolished as a nation, and integrated as part of the Reich.

The other two developments were the reactions to the broadcast in Rome and London. Before perpetrating the outrage, the Führer had to be certain Austria would be isolated. His brag to Schuschnigg about Austria's lack of allies had been equivocal; at that time he had no assurance that Italy, France, and Britain would remain aloof. In the case of France it hardly mattered. Churchill had warned his guests from Paris that their unstable governments gravely diminished their prestige in foreign chancelleries. Camille Chautemps's regime fell that Thursday; the country would lack a premier for a month; meantime, action was impossible.

Schuschnigg had hoped for more from Italy — four years earlier Mussolini had helped abort the Nazi coup when Dollfuss was murdered — but when he consulted him about the plebiscite, the Duce replied: *"C'è un errore!"* Hitler didn't know that, however, and on Thursday, as his troops deployed on the southern border of the Reich in attack formation, he sent Mussolini a preposterous letter, declaring that Austria was in "a state of anarchy," that the Austrians and Czechs were plotting to invade Germany with "at least twenty million men," and that Schuschnigg's failure to meet his "more than moderate" demands "made a mockery" of "a so-called plebiscite." Friday the Duce, still smarting from Anglo-French attempts to thwart his conquest of Ethiopia, sent word that Austria would be "immaterial" to him. The Führer danced with joy and told the messenger: "Tell Mussolini I will never forget him for this. . . . Never, never, never, no matter what happens!"[82]

The dictators, unanswerable to public opinion, could act like that. British statesmen couldn't; they had to satisfy their colleagues, their consciences, and, ultimately, their constituents. So the Chamberlain government resorted to hypocrisy. HMG took the position that Britain's armed forces were too weak to challenge the rearmed Reich (overlooking its responsibility for that weakness) and that Hitler's feelings of insecurity must be stroked with reassurances. In Berlin, Henderson wrote, "The big question which all Germans asked themselves was, 'What will England do?' " His own recommendation was: Nothing. "His Majesty's Government," he explained in his memoirs, was in no "position to have saved Austria by [its] actions." Besides, he added — and here his rationalization is remarkable — "the case against Hitler was not yet a cast-iron one.

Austria was German, and many Austrians were wholeheartedly in favor of union with the Reich." Determining *how* many had been the purpose of the plebiscite, but Henderson dismissed the plebiscite as Schuschnigg's "final mistake" and "the throw of a desperate gambler." It apparently occurred to none of the appeasers that the chancellor of an independent country, in resolving to poll his countrymen on whether they wished to surrender their independence, might be acting, not only within his rights — the legality of his move could scarcely be challenged — but wisely. Henderson triumphantly concluded, "The love of peace of the British public was too great for it to approve of a war in which the moral issue was in any possible doubt."[83]

Within an hour of Schuschnigg's broadcast on Wednesday, Goebbels had been whipping up German rage against him, and Churchill gloomily told a Manchester audience the next evening: "The horizon has not lightened in the last few months — or in the last few hours." By Thursday the question of what England would do had become urgent, and the ball was in the foreign secretary's court. Halifax and Ribbentrop were closeted for several hours, after which Ribbentrop sent a telegram which surfaced after the war among other German foreign policy documents in Nuremberg. "England will do nothing with regard to Austria," Ribbentrop reported, even if Germany resorted to naked force, provided there was "a very quick settlement."[84]

That was straightforward, if ignoble. More humbug began Friday morning. Ribbentrop breakfasted at his London embassy with Thomas Jones, Astor, Inskip, and a German diplomatic aide. The guests had been carefully picked; all were eager to hear Ribbentrop's justification of whatever Hitler was going to do, as were many others in England. As early as 1936, when Ribbentrop was the Reich's new ambassador to the Court of St. James's, he had been approached by Lord Lothian, who expressed the hope that German seizure of Austria, despite the attendant battles and bloodshed, would not lead to a "breach of faith" between His Majesty's Government and the Wilhelmstrasse.[85]

Thomas Jones, typically, had written Lady Grigg: "I keep on and on and on, preaching against the policy of ostracizing Germany, however incalculable Hitler and his crew may be. . . . We have abundant evidence of the desire of all sorts of Germans to be in friendly terms with us." Jones, it should be noted, had been elected to no office; in 1930 he had retired as deputy secretary to the cabinet, far below Vansittart in official protocol. Astor had been a delegate to the League of Nations seven years earlier and had retired to private life. Inskip, foundering in a job for which he was so singularly ill suited, was the only cabinet member at the breakfast. But

Ribbentrop knew these men made vital decisions and would be fertile ground for his rationalizations.[86]

After the Friday breakfast Jones noted in his diary that Ribbentrop "was clearly in a state of active apprehension. . . . He did tell us that Schuschnigg had acted without consultation with his Nazi colleagues and this rankled." No one had pointed out that Schuschnigg, remembering Dollfuss, may have assumed that any such consultation would have ended with himself a cadaver. But Ribbentrop's breakfast guests were not completely gulled. "Walking away," Jones wrote, "we said to each other that R. had not been frank about the Berchtesgaden [Berghof] interview"; they had heard "the account given by Schuschnigg to our Austrian ambassador — that the interview was the most terrible experience of his life." Yet Jones remained convinced that England had to go "to absurd lengths" in offering Hitler the other cheek. This reasoning had lost the Rhineland; now Austria was sliding down the Nazi maw.[87]

Ribbentrop was, in fact, only in town to wind up his London affairs, as Hitler had appointed him foreign minister of the Third Reich. Breakfast at the Reich embassy was followed by a farewell lunch at No. 10, with Ribbentrop as the P.M.'s guest of honor and Churchill as an impotent if bemused spectator. Because Winston was the most unpopular Englishman in the great stone piles lining the Wilhelmstrasse, Chamberlain would have enjoyed omitting his name from the guest list, but that was impossible. The prime minister could hardly give the Nazis veto power over visitors to his home. And Churchill was a world celebrity who had been a member of six British cabinets; if he were cut, there would be an uproar in the House.

There were sixteen at the table, including Winston and Clementine. About halfway through the meal an FO messenger brought Cadogan an envelope. Van's successor read it, walked round the table, and handed it to Chamberlain. By now Churchill was alert, sensing danger. Afterward he recalled: "I could not help noticing the Prime Minister's evident preoccupation." On a signal from her husband, Mrs. Chamberlain rose, saying, "Let us *all* have coffee in the drawing-room." Winston felt that "a kind of restlessness pervaded the company, and everyone stood about ready to say good-bye to the guests of honour." The Ribbentrops were merry and voluble, however; Churchill guessed that this was a "manoeuvre to keep the Prime Minister away from his work and the telephone." Finally the P.M. said: "I am sorry. I have to go now to attend to urgent business." In parting, Churchill bowed to Gertrud von Ribbentrop and "in a valedictory vein" murmured: "I hope England and Germany will preserve their friendship." She gave him a rude stare and snapped: "Be careful you don't spoil it."[88]

Placed as far as possible from the guest of honor, Churchill had been beyond earshot of the exchanges between Chamberlain and Ribbentrop and left No. 10 under the impression that the diplomatic transaction, whatever it had been, was over. Within an hour, however, even without Van, he knew the contents of the FO luncheon message. Two telegrams from the British delegation in Vienna had reported that at 5:50 A.M. the Germans had closed their Austrian border at Salzburg, that Wehrmacht divisions were massed all along the frontier between the two countries, and that at 10:00 A.M. Seyss-Inquart, on instructions from Hitler, had appeared in Schuschnigg's office to insist that plans for the plebiscite be canceled. Told that the alternative would be bloodshed, Schuschnigg, with his pitifully small army, capitulated. But yielding to one Nazi ultimatum quickly led to another. The Führer now followed with demands that Schuschnigg resign, that Seyss-Inquart succeed him as federal chancellor, and that his first official act be an appeal to the Reich Chancellery in Berlin, asking that the Wehrmacht enter Austria to "restore order." One way or another, 100,000 German troops would cross the border at 10:00 P.M. and move swiftly to envelop Vienna.

Churchill missed fireworks at No. 10 — a row which sharply defined the cultural abyss between the appeasers and the appeased — and the rainbow that followed. Englishmen cherished civility and good manners as social lubricants. German aristocrats — often cousins, several times removed, of their counterparts in England — shared their conviction. Until Hitler moved into the Reich Chancellery, the men in striped *Hosen* from the Wilhelmstrasse were celebrated for their breeding, their mastery of exquisite diplomatic language, and their meticulous observance of international treaties. Elaborate, almost choreographed manners had always graced relations between powers, however bloody the deeds. "When you have to kill a man," as Churchill later said, "it costs nothing to be polite."[89]

But the division between the Old Boys lunching at No. 10 that Friday, March 11, 1938, and the Nazi foreign minister representing his omnipotent führer cut deep. For the first time in history, the power of a European state was rooted in its lower middle class. Ribbentrop had appropriated his "von" from a distant aunt and affected noble origins. His sole distinction, before he caught the Führer's eye, had been his matinee profile, which had won him the hand of his boss's daughter, thereby ending his drab, ill-paid, exhausting career as a commercial traveler roaming Europe and hawking wines. Had he been an Englishman, he could never have been admitted to a London club, not to mention to a Tory cabinet. To Chamberlain and his cabinet, trying to persuade one another that he was acceptable in their circle, he remained an enigma, entertained by them only because he had been designated the formal representative of what was, by the third month of 1938, the greatest military power in the world. England's patricians had never dealt with such Europeans in affairs of state.

Before arriving for lunch, Ribbentrop knew of Hitler's first ultimatum to Schuschnigg — call off the plebiscite or face a German invasion. And shortly afterward word reached him of the second ultimatum, demanding that Seyss-Inquart replace Schuschnigg as chancellor. Yet he had given no indication that anything was amiss when, moments before Cadogan handed Chamberlain news of these developments from the British legation in Vienna, the prime minister told him of his "sincere wish and firm determination to clear up German-British relations." After studying the two telegrams the prime minister gave his honored guest a quizzical look and asked why German troops were massing on their Austrian border. With a straight face Ribbentrop replied that he believed they were there for "spring training." Clearly Chamberlain was unsatisfied, but it was not the sort of conversation a prime minister pursues over lunch, particularly when the most eloquent English critic of his foreign and defense policies is at the other end of the table, gazing at him intensely.[90]

Only after the others had departed did Chamberlain invite Ribbentrop and Halifax into the drawing room. By then additional reports of the Führer's ultimatum and its sequelae had arrived from Vienna. Chamberlain read them aloud. "The discussion," as Ribbentrop reported to the Führer afterward, "took place in a tense atmosphere." To his surprise, Halifax, who had been so unctuous at the Berghof, was "more excited than Chamberlain, who outwardly at least appeared calm and cool-headed." The Nazi statesman responded by doing what Nazis did best; rather than defend the indefensible, he simply denied "the truth of the reports." The Englishmen asked no questions, accepted the remarkable charge that British diplomats in Vienna had concocted everything, and cheerfully accompanied Ribbentrop to the door. His "leave-taking," he reported to the Führer, "was entirely amiable, and even Halifax was calm again."[91]

In an attempt to make Hitler's strong-arm diplomacy seem less brutal, Ribbentrop had not only lied to his hosts; he had also underestimated them. Accepting Austria as a state within the Reich's sphere of influence was one thing; naked bayonets were another. By the time the Nazi foreign minister had returned to his embassy, it had occurred to Chamberlain and Halifax that their guest had been less than candid with them. It was Ribbentrop, they recalled, who had denounced the Schuschnigg plebiscite as "a fraud and a swindle" and "a violation of the letter and spirit of the Berchtesgaden agreement." Within an hour they learned that Seyss-Inquart had proclaimed himself chancellor of Austria, that Hitler was preparing a broadcast promising his new subjects "a real plebiscite" to be supervised by the

SS (the Führer's private army) and the Gestapo (state secret police), and declaring that Schuschnigg was a fugitive. Halifax persuaded a reluctant Geoffrey Dawson to condemn what was now clearly a coup, and in an emergency cabinet meeting Chamberlain expressed shock at the "manner" of the annexation, calling it "distressing" and "a typical illustration of power politics." Henderson was instructed to deliver a formal note to the Wilhelmstrasse declaring that "His Majesty's Government feel obliged to register a protest in the strongest possible terms."[92]

But Henderson had already sandbagged British objections by telling Göring that Austria had fallen victim to "Schuschnigg's ill-conceived and ill-prepared folly." And words after an event have little force anyhow. Before the Anschluss, Halifax had encouraged it, and during Schuschnigg's last bitter hours in office he had telegraphed him that he could not "take the responsibility" of advising him to take measures "which might expose [your] country to dangers against which His Majesty's Government are unable to guarantee protection" — this despite Britain's Stresa pledge to guarantee Austrian independence.[93]

In Berlin, Neurath accepted the British note. Long afterward, Henderson acknowledged that "protests without the resolute intent to use force if they were disregarded were not going to stop the German troops, which were already on the march." Considering the Rhineland fiasco two years earlier, he realized "Germany had become too strong to be impressed by empty gestures, which merely confirmed those like Ribbentrop in their opinion that Britain would put up with anything rather than fight. Lung power was no match for armed power."[94]

In Nicolson's diary one senses the momentum, the rush of events that weekend. On Friday evening, March 11, he noted Schuschnigg's capitulation after "a pathetic farewell broadcast saying that he is yielding to 'brutal force.'" Saturday Hitler crossed the border and entered Linz, where he had spent his boyhood. Göring, reproached by the vacillating Henderson, replied with "a diatribe against Schuschnigg's lack of good faith." Nicolson, mingling with his working-class constituents, wrote: "They are all anti-Chamberlain, saying 'Eden has been proved right.'"[95]

At No. 10 on Saturday Chamberlain told the cabinet that Eden, in opposing friendly approaches to the Duce, had been proved wrong: "It might be said that we were too late in taking up the conversation with Italy. . . . Signor Mussolini would have moved troops to the Brenner Pass at the time of the Berchtesgaden talks, but he had not felt sure of his position in the Mediterranean." Cadogan blamed his predecessor, Vansittart ("an idiot with an idée fixe — all facade and nothing else"), for being obsessed with Austria "when we can't do anything about it." But to the prime minister, Eden remained the scapegoat. Writing his sister the next day Chamberlain reflected that "very possibly this might have been prevented if I had had Halifax at the Foreign Office instead of Anthony." He added: "What a fool Roosevelt would have looked like if he had launched his precious proposal. What would he have thought of us if we had encouraged him to publish it, as Anthony wanted us to do? And now we too would have made ourselves the laughing stock of the world." Chamberlain did not consider that a prime minister who had wined and dined with the Nazi foreign minister while Hitler was seizing Austria might look like a bigger fool and a greater laughingstock.[96]

Mapping out strategy for a forthcoming parliamentary debate on military policy, Horace Wilson had written to Chamberlain on Thursday predicting that Churchill would demand an air defense inquiry. Now he noted that at the cabinet meeting the P.M. decided that "an enquiry should be refused and refused flatly and firmly, the decision to be adhered to notwithstanding any criticism that may be raised during the debate." According to the meeting's official minutes, all present were informed "that the Right Hon Winston Churchill was intending to attack the Government on the inadequacy of their Air Force programme, and to support the motion of the Opposition for an enquiry into the Air Ministry. It was suggested that a speech belittling our efforts might have a very adverse effect on the international position just now," when dealings with Germany might be better served "by creating the impression of force." How the Nazis could be gulled when they already knew the frailty of Britain's defenses — particularly the RAF — was among the questions unraised by the cabinet.[97]

It is Sunday, March 13, the day Schuschnigg had set for his plebiscite, but 100,000 German troops, led by General Heinz Guderian's Second Panzer Division and the SS *Leibstandarte Adolf Hitler* are being pelted with flowers by their Austrian admirers — Goebbels calls it a *"Blumenkrieg"* ("flower war"). Seyss-Inquart presents his führer with a proclamation declaring that Austria no longer exists. It is now the Ostmark, "a province of the German Reich."

By Monday the Austrian scene is clearer. The enthusiasm of the crowds cheering Wehrmacht and Waffen SS troops is beyond doubt, but they are a minority. Churchill writes Unity Mitford: "It was because Herr Hitler feared the free expression of opinion that we are compelled to witness the present dastardly outrage." The Führer has added another seven million subjects to his expanding Reich, while seizing a military position of priceless strategic value without the firing of a single shot.[98]

In permitting the Führer to take Austria, the governments of Europe have betrayed tens of thousands of anti-Nazis, not only Austrians but also German citizens of Austria. Many have fled for their lives and choke the roads to Czechoslovakia, Poland, and Hungary. Some are turned back at the border; others, more affluent, possess passports and are passed through the frontier roadblocks, only to be rejected because they have no visas. Acquiring these documents is, for thousands, a matter of life or death. When they return to the Austrian capital their visa applications at the British and French consulates are rejected. In Vienna alone seventy thousand are arrested. Before the month is out virtually all who tried to flee have been shot by SS firing squads, have died by their own hands, or have been sent to the Reich's new Austrian concentration camps.

No photographs of the refugees appear in *The Times*. Instead, Dawson runs pictures of Austrian Nazis beaming on Wehrmacht battalions, creating an impression of a tumultuous, wildly enthusiastic welcome from all their countrymen. It is a shocking distortion; foreign tourists and foreign correspondents, particularly the Americans, give it the lie. Shirer is among them. Later he will recall that "the behavior of the Vienna Nazis was worse than anything I had seen in Germany. There was an orgy of sadism."[99]

In one of his syndicated newspaper columns Churchill writes, "The Austrian Nazis are a peculiarly virulent type who carried pillage, corruption and brutality beyond the wide limits of political discretion." Reports reaching Chartwell from his Austrian informants confirm him. An emaciated, haggard Schuschnigg will spend the next seven years in Dachau and then Neidendorf, a concentration camp in the South Tyrol, whence he will be rescued by American troops just as a Gestapo guard is about to execute him. The litany of misery which will end there may be glimpsed in Churchill's post-Anschluss mail from Austrian informants: "My many friends in this city are in the depths of despair"; ". . . many sickening incidents. A family of six Jews have just shot themselves, a few houses down the street"; "Yesterday morning I saw two well-dressed women forced to their knees to scrub out a 'Heil Schuschnigg!' on the pavement." Churchill writes Dawson, asking why this side of the story is unreported and is frostily told: "There is no doubt, I think, that the impression of jubilation was overwhelming."[100]

That would have been enough to satisfy his readers two years earlier. But the mood of the British public has shifted since the Rhineland. MPs hear from their constituents: even if most Austrians wanted to live under the swastika, those who don't have rights, too; are they being persecuted? Replies from the Foreign Office are vague. The temper of the upper classes has also changed. Their wealth has permitted them to visit the Continent often. The Rhineland was declassé; one couldn't have been seen there by one's equals, gaping at the Cologne Cathedral like shopkeepers' wives on tour. Hitler's seizure of it menaced few of their peers. Austria is another matter. They have friends there, even cousins, in Vienna, in lodges on the slopes of the Austrian Alps, and in shooting boxes in the deep, dark evergreen woods. And now they are worried about them. Among the worriers are Lady Londonderry, Lady Halifax, and the wife of the British prime minister. Ambassador Henderson cannot fob these people off with excuses. They send him names. He submits the lists to Ribbentrop, inquiring as to their whereabouts. The Reich's foreign minister replies that he finds their interest "incomprehensible. The British Government never lifted a finger for the victims of the Schuschnigg regime." It is an insolent note, and inauspicious. The Germans are beginning to feel like Germans again — like the Germans of the Second Reich, Bismarck's great creation in the wake of Prussia's victory over Louis Napoleon's France in 1871, memorable for its faith in Blood and Iron, its allegiance to *ein Volk, ein Kaiser, ein Reich,* the pigheadedness of its Junker leaders, and the rising hauteur of their officers, monocled and rude, who slapped "insolent" civilians in Alsace-Lorraine, and expected even German ladies to step in gutters and let them pass.[101]

Neurath strengthens this impression of arrogance by returning Henderson's initial note of protest with the comment: "Relations between the Reich and Austria can only be regarded as an internal affair of the German people which is no concern of third powers. . . . For this reason the German Government must from the outset reject as inadmissible the protest lodged by the British Government." If His Majesty's envoy wants proof of Seyss-Inquart's telegram inviting the Führer's troops into the Ostmark, he will find it "already published in the German press."[102]

🦁   🦁

On Monday, March 14, Nicolson heard the P.M. make "a dry statement" in the Commons, "giving little indication of real policy." The House had expected to hear more about Austria, but there seemed to be a conspiracy on the Treasury Bench (and in the FO, under its new permanent under secretary) to sidestep the Anschluss and turn to other matters. Of Hitler's conquest the prime minister declared: "The hard fact is that nothing could have arrested what actually happened — unless this country and other countries had been prepared to use force." A backbencher called: "What about rearmament?" Chamberlain's reply was evasive; the government "would make a fresh review" of the subject and "in due course we shall announce what further steps we may think it necessary to take."

Nicolson wrote: "There is a sense of real national crisis." But it was felt in neither Downing Street nor the corridors of Whitehall. [103]

Since the defrocking of Vansittart the Foreign Office had drifted under uncertain leadership. Cadogan, whose office gave him such wide discretionary powers that they rivaled Halifax's, seemed incapable of contemplating meeting force with force. As early as Saturday, March 12, he wrote in his diary: "We are helpless as regards Austria — that is finished. We *may* be helpless as regards Czechoslovakia. . . . Must we have a death-struggle with Germany again? . . . I'm inclined to think not. But I shall have to fight Van . . . and all the forces of evil. God give me courage. So far we've not done wrong."[104]

A month before the crisis, after Schuschnigg's mortification at Berchtesgaden, Cadogan had "almost" wished that "Germany would swallow Austria and get it over," and now that Hitler had devoured it he wrote Nevile Henderson: "Thank goodness, Austria's out of the way. I can't help thinking we were very badly informed about that country. . . . We should evidently have been very wrong to try to prevent *Anschluss* against the wishes of a very considerable proportion of the population. After all, it wasn't our business: We had no particular feelings for the Austrians: We only forbade *Anschluss* to spite Germany."[105]

Churchill was ready with an answer for both the prime minister and the Foreign Office during that same House session Monday. Nicolson wrote: "Winston makes the speech of his life." Churchill's instinctive response to the Anschluss had been that the issue should be laid before the League of Nations. He and Lord Cecil had approached Halifax with that suggestion, but the foreign secretary told them that "such procedure would be of no practical advantage in redressing the present situation." So Churchill offered the House of Commons a foreign policy which, we now know, would almost certainly have led to a military coup in Berlin, toppling the Nazi regime. [106]

Churchill saw the need for British unity, British action, and a firm policy to discourage new aggression. He surveyed the wreckage in Austria, submitting that the damage had been great. Nazi mastery of Vienna, "the center of all the communications of all the countries which formed the old Austro-Hungarian Empire, and of all the countries lying to the southeast of Europe," threatened the entire Danube basin, particularly Czechoslovakia, which had been "the greatest manufacturing area" in the Austro-Hungarian Empire. No doubt its name "sounds outlandish" to English ears, he said, but the Czech army was "two or three times as large" as Britain's, its munitions supplies were triple Italy's, and "they are a virile people; they have their treaty rights, they have a line of fortresses, and they have a strongly manifested will to live freely." At present, however, they were isolated. [107]

As Leo Amery had pointed out earlier in the day, England lacked a foreign policy. The country should acquire one, Churchill said, and swiftly. "Why," he asked the House, "should we assume that time is on our side?" Each day dawned on a Reich stronger than the day before. Parliament was "in no position to say tonight, 'The past is the past.' We cannot say 'The past is past' without surrendering the future." Churchill's proposed geopolitical concept, he declared, would assure peace for Britain and indeed for all European nations alarmed by Hitler's huge, teeming Wehrmacht.[108]

Winston told the House that England's neglected defenses were too shaky for her to stand alone against the pullulating Reich and the lands it dominated: "Over an area inhabited perhaps by 200,000,000 people Naziism and all it involves is moving on to absolute control." Even a rearmament crash program would be inadequate. Britain, he said, needed allies. The House was alert. They knew where Winston's line of thought was leading, and a few catcalls were heard from Tory backbenchers. He said quickly: "I know that some of my hon. Friends on this side of the House will laugh when I offer them this advice. I say, 'Laugh, but listen.' "[109]

Those who listened heard an imaginative, closely reasoned plan to confront Nazi aggression with an interlocking alliance of nations, each country inadequate in itself, but together mighty enough to give pause to Hitler's generals, if not to Hitler himself. Churchill directed their attention to the three states of the Little Entente: Czechoslovakia, Rumania, and Yugoslavia. Each was a power of the second rank, "but they are very vigorous states, and united they are a Great Power." The first had the Skoda munitions plants, the second oil, the third minerals and raw materials — and all had large armies. The Anschluss had driven "a wedge" into the Little Entente, but if that had roused them, perhaps the price was not exorbitant. Each faced a simple choice: "to submit, like Austria, or else to take effective measures while time remains to ward off the danger and, if it cannot be warded off, to cope with it." Coping, he said, could include widening the Little Entente by offering membership to other Danube countries lying in Hitler's path: Hungary and Bulgaria. That would thwart the Reich's drive for lebensraum in the east. Meantime Britain, with France, should vow to declare war on Germany if Hitler attacked any country in eastern Europe. Should Churchill's alliance become a reality, Germany's Generalstab would face the specter they had sworn to avoid since 1918: a two-front war. Winston turned on the jeering backbenchers; his voice rose: "Our affairs have come to such a pass that there is no escape without running risks. On every ground of prudence as well as of duty I urge His Majesty's Government to proclaim a renewed, revivified, unflinching adherence to the Covenant of the League of Nations. What is there ridiculous about collective security? The only thing that is ridiculous about it is that we haven't got it."

But Churchill knew that restoring the balance of power, however practical, reasonable, and even essential, would not in itself satisfy a British public still haunted by the memory of a million British corpses in the trenches. Winston believed in statecraft on a higher level, and he believed the British public could be swayed at this level. He insisted that there must be a "moral basis" for British rearmament and foreign policy, that only on those terms could the British people be united. Parliament could on this basis "procure their wholehearted action, and" — Churchill, typically, included America in his plan — "stir the English-speaking people throughout the world."

Meantime, he argued for the virtual encirclement of the Third Reich. Treaties binding Europe's Western democracies and the Danube states in a united front would turn back German aggression, and England would regain the security she had lost in 1914. He closed:

If a number of states were assembled around Great Britain and France in a solemn treaty for mutual defence against aggression; if they had their forces marshaled in what you may call a Grand Alliance; . . . if all this rested, as it can honourably rest, upon the Covenant of the League of Nations, in pursuance of all the purposes and ideals of the League of Nations; if that were sustained, as it would be, by the moral sense of the world; and if it were done in the year 1938 — and, believe me, it may be the last chance there will be for doing it — then I say that you might even now arrest this approaching war. Then perhaps the curse which overhangs Europe would pass away. Then perhaps the ferocious passions which now grip a great people would turn inwards and not outwards in an internal rather than an external explosion, and mankind would be spared the deadly ordeal towards which we have been sagging and sliding month by month. . . . Before we cast away this hope, this cause and this plan, which I do not at all disguise has an element of risk, let those who wish to reject it ponder well and earnestly upon what will happen to us if, when all else has been thrown to the wolves, we are left to face our fate alone.[110]

Such a speech, and such a proposal, coming from a senior statesman known throughout Europe, could not be ignored or set aside for future "study" and "discussion." In Moscow, Maksim Litvinov, the Soviet foreign commissar, praised the Grand Alliance strategy, condemned the Anschluss as an act of aggression and a threat to the chain of small countries between the Soviet Union and the Reich, and — though Churchill had not mentioned Russia as a grand ally — declared that his government was ready "to participate in collective actions . . . checking the further development of aggression and eliminating the increased danger of a new world massacre." The U.S.S.R., he said, was "prepared immediately to take up in the League of Nations or outside of it the discussion with other Powers of the practical measures which the circumstances demand."[111]

Ambassador Maisky delivered Litvinov's statement to the Foreign Office, which, by diplomatic custom, was bound to respond within a week. France was also heartened; Joseph Paul-Boncour, the minister now presiding over the Quai d'Orsay, submitted a similar demarche through Corbin, his ambassador in London. Halifax received these overtures with elegant courtesy, expressing a gratitude for Russian and French interest which he did not feel. The noble lord despised Bolsheviks and was a lifelong Francophobe. "The French are never ready to face up to realities," he remarked after Corbin had departed; "they delight in vain words and protestations." Cadogan agreed. Although Paul-Boncour had been in politics since 1899 — serving variously as minister of war, minister of labor, and premier except between 1914 and 1918, when he had commanded an infantry battalion and won the Croix de Guerre — Cadogan thought him "not a Foreign Minister who at so serious a moment could be a worthy partner in a discussion of the European crisis."[112]

Nicolson despaired. "A sense of danger and anxiety hangs over us like a pall. Hitler has completely collared Austria; no question of an *Anschluss*, just complete absorption." Later in the same entry he noted, without dissent, a colleague's argument that "the Government have betrayed the country and that the Tories think only of the Red danger and let the Empire slide. I am in grave doubts as to my own position. How can I continue to support a Government like this?" Looking back, Lord Boothby damned sheep and shepherds alike:

From 1935 to 1939 I watched the political leaders of Britain, in Government and in Opposition, at pretty close quarters; and I reached the conclusion, which I have not since changed, that with only two exceptions, Winston Churchill and Leopold Amery, they were all frightened men. On four occasions Hitler and his gang of bloody murderers could have been brought down, and a second world war averted, by an ultimatum. . . . Every time we failed to do it. And four times is a lot. The reasons for it, I am afraid, can only be ascribed to a squalid combination of cowardice and greed; and the British ministers responsible, instead of being promoted, should have been impeached.[113]

Nevertheless, Churchill's vision — challenging Hitler with a broad coalition of nations threatened by Nazi aggression — reached the hearts of millions. In London the *Star* expressed gratitude that "one man spoke out in Parliament last night, and made a speech which fitted the hour." Liddell Hart sent the War Office a memorandum pointing out that "we are blind if we cannot see that we are committed to the defence of Yugoslavia," adding that the French "military situation largely turns on the existence of a Czechoslovakian distraction to Germany's power of concentration in the West." According to minutes of a March 16 meeting, Halifax told the cabinet that "public opinion was moving fast in the direction of placing the defences of the country more nearly on a war footing." The prime minister, nodding slowly, replied that he was well aware of the nation's mood, and knew it was entitled to a statement or broadcast from him, but "at the moment he himself did not feel clear how far we are to go, or in what direction."[114]

Chamberlain was, in fact, tempted by Churchill's soaring proposal. Napoleon had been overwhelmed by a coalition of allied powers led by England; why not crush Hitler by the same strategy? But forming an alliance wasn't Chamberlain's style. Like Baldwin he felt uncomfortable with foreigners; he didn't really trust them, and their differences in national character seldom stirred his curiosity. On March 21, scarcely nine days after the Anschluss, Dawson quoted the P.M. as saying he had "come clear around from Winston's idea of a Grand Alliance to a policy of diplomatic action and no fresh commitments."[115]

The eight days in between had been filled with debate — Churchill and his supporters on one side, HMG on the other. Austria had gone down almost unnoticed, it seemed, and while Churchill's idea of a Grand Alliance had been aimed at securing the future of all Europe, in those eight days the spotlight was turned upon one country, Hitler's next target: Czechoslovakia.

By universal agreement the Reich's warlord was either a madman or a genius. In neither case could he be expected to behave like ordinary men, and he rarely did. General Alfred Jodl, the Wehrmacht's chief of operations, had worked with him for five years. He believed that at last he understood him. Yet when the Anschluss had been accomplished, Jodl wrote in his diary: "After the annexation, the Führer indicated that he is in no hurry to solve the Czech question." In fact, Hitler was rapidly revising *Fall Grün*, Case Green, the plans for a surprise attack on Czechoslovakia first drafted by Blomberg nine months earlier.[116]

How Case Green could have surprised anyone now seems inexplicable. In his Reichstag speech of February 20, when he declared that "over ten million Germans live in two of the states adjoining our frontiers," Hitler was including the three million Czechoslovakians of German descent — the *Sudetendeutsche* — living in the northern part of the country, in the shadow of the Sudeten (Sudetic) Mountains. Prague had trembled when he warned: "It is unbearable for a world power to know there are racial comrades at its side who are constantly being afflicted by the severest suffering for their sympathy with the whole nation. . . . The German Reich intends to protect those German peoples who live along its frontiers and cannot, by their own efforts, secure their political and spiritual freedom [*ihre politische und geistige Freiheit*]."[117]

London newspapers had carried brief accounts of disturbances in the Sudetenland, but British opinion was not, at this time, concerned with Czechoslovakia as a whole. Nor, until then, was Hitler. It was on his hit list, but rather far down. Now the Sudetendeutsche were forcing his hand. Their part of Czechoslovakia had never belonged to Germany. Nevertheless, the Führer's intoxicating performance had spawned five pseudo-Nazi parties in the Sudetenland, of which the noisiest, and probably the largest, was the Sudetendeutsche Heimatfront (Sudeten German Home Front) with its political arm, the Sudetendeutsche Partei (SDP), led by one Konrad Henlein, an otherwise unprepossessing gymnastics teacher with a fanatical loyalty to Germany's charismatic leader. One of the Heimatfront's most effective talents was to send gangs of SDP bullies into Czech communities and deliberately create *Grenzzwischenfälle* (border incidents). These scuffles revealed the Heimatfront's ardor (and violence); they also won broad sympathy for the group among the Germans. Hitler's countrymen remembered his campaign pledge to unshackle Germans enslaved in other countries. He was under pressure to deal with Czechoslovakia — but he was not irked; this was the kind of pressure he liked.

Actually, the Czechs had been extraordinarily tolerant of the boisterous Nazis who lived under their flag and were spoiling for a fight. In recent years President Eduard Beneš had been wary and tactful, but he was unreassured by Göring's "word of honor" (*"Ehrenwort"*) that the Czechs had nothing to fear from the Reich. In the Third Reich, Beneš knew, honor had acquired new meanings. The word was, for example, engraved on the daggers of SS men. He believed the Sudetenland riots were being orchestrated in Berlin as pretexts for intervention by Reich troops, and by the spring of 1938 he was absolutely right.

Churchill had long foreseen a jeopardized Czechoslovakia should a vindictive, rearmed Germany emerge in central Europe. As early as February 13, 1925, he had urged a redrawing of national borders in eastern Europe, contending that "real peace" would be elusive as long as regions with large German populations lay outside Germany's borders, only to be told that any change in frontiers would mean "tearing up" the Versailles treaty. On March 31, 1931 — two years before Hindenburg appointed Hitler chancellor — he told readers of the Hearst papers that Tomáš Masaryk, the country's first president, and Beneš had "refounded an ancient nation. . . . They have established a strong state on the broad basis of social democracy and anti-communism." But if Germany and Austria were reunited, "Czechoslovakia would lie in dire peril."[118]

The more Hitler pondered Czechoslovakia, the more he concluded that its very existence was an affront to him. Its birth at Versailles was enough to condemn it. Moreover, it lacked ethnic integrity; Hungarians, Ruthenians, Slovaks, Germans, and Czechs had all been spliced into the ancient Kingdom of Bohemia, and, if that weren't enough, the splicers had been Masaryk and Beneš, both intellectuals and believers in democracy. These men had then committed the ultimate sin in the Führer's eyes: they had transformed their country into the most prosperous, progressive, and enlightened nation in eastern Europe.

Until 1938 neither Hitler nor Henlein contemplated outright annexation. Most Sudeteners — about 18 percent of the country's fifteen million people — had intermarried with Czechs of other ethnic stock. Henlein could not speak for them; indeed, thousands of them were refugees from the Reich he admired, and thousands of others thanked God they didn't live under the hakenkreuz. Nevertheless, the Führer had concluded that the SDP had a future and he would invest in it. Beginning in 1935 the Sudeten party received fifteen thousand marks a month from the Wilhelmstrasse.

On May 19, 1935, the SDP had shown astonishing strength at the polls, winning 1,250,000 votes, three out of every five German votes cast, making it the second largest party in the national parliament. In the House of Commons Churchill called this demonstration of support "a very considerable fact, having regard to the energy which the German people, when inspired by the Nazi spirit, are able to exercise." It was, he said, one of several alarms set off by the success of the German dictatorship; "not only [was] the supreme question of self-preservation" involved, "but also the human and the world cause of the preservation of free Governments and of Western civilisation against the ever-advancing forces of authority and despotism."[119]

There was cause for alarm: by the summer of 1936 Nazi parties had appeared in Poland, the Baltic States, and the Free City of Danzig, where men wearing the swastika in their lapels held all key positions in the government. On July 21 Churchill wrote Lord Rothermere: "My information tallies with yours, that Czecho-Slovakia will soon be in the news." It was; the Czechs were rapidly rearming and building a powerful line of fortifications along the German frontier. Goebbels accused them of letting the Russians build military airfields on their soil, opening a campaign of denunciation and recrimination resembling his attacks on the Austrian government on the eve of Chancellor Dollfuss's murder. On February 5, 1937, Churchill wrote in the *Evening Standard* that "at any moment a quarrel may be picked with [the Czechs] by a mighty neighbor. Already they see the directions given in the regimented German press to write them down, to accuse them of being Communists, and, in particular, of preparing their airports for a Russian assault upon Germany. Vain to protest their innocence, vain to offer every facility for German or neutral inspection of their arrangements."[120]

In June 1937 Winston received a long report from one of his most reliable informants, Sheila Grant Duff, a cousin of Clemmie's and an Oxford graduate who was living in Prague. Western Czechoslovakia, she wrote, was kept in constant turmoil by gangs of Sudeten Germans who roamed the streets at night, clubbing Jews, looting their shops, and desecrating synagogues. She cited two of Henlein's Nazis, who claimed they had been ill-treated by Czech policemen: "This could be used to launch the '*Gegenmassnahmen*' [countermeasures] which the German press has threatened." Sheila was worried about the future of the Czech state. She implored Winston to "do everything in your power to make our attitude firm and unfaltering. The crisis has never been so great and I am convinced that only a stand on our part can overcome it. Czechoslovakia is, for the moment, almost entirely dependent on us." Writing in October to Lord Londonderry — who continued to believe that Anglo-Nazi friendship was possible — Winston pointed out that any arrangement with the Germans would entail giving them a "free hand so far as we are concerned in Central and Southern Europe. This means that they would devour Austria and Czecho-Slovakia as a preliminary to making a gigantic middle Europe-block. It would certainly not be in our interests to connive at such policies of aggression."[121]

The Chamberlain government, however, clearly agreed with Lord Londonderry, and continued to refuse to allocate adequate funds for defense. In February 1938, the secretary for air, Lord Swinton, having been blocked in his earlier proposals, again submitted an RAF budget, this one representing "the minimum for security." Attempts to match the Luftwaffe's overwhelming superiority in fighter planes were abandoned; the RAF would settle for enough aircraft to meet German "bombers that could be used against this country." Inskip said that would be too expensive. He proposed cutting back not only Britain's first-line air strength but also the reserve. Halifax, supporting him, stressed "every possible effort to get on good terms with Germany," which, as a code phrase of the time, meant refraining from war preparations which might arouse the Führer's wrath. Summing up the discussion, Chamberlain told his ministers what they already knew — that he attached "great importance to . . . the mainte- nance of our economic stability." Despite Swinton's appeal for a swift decision, the record shows that "no final decision was reached on policy for expansion of the Air Force." Action on the Admiralty budget was also deferred for a year.[122]

Meanwhile, the Czechoslovakian bomb continued to tick. One of Churchill's sources, traveling through eastern Europe, sent Chartwell an appraisal underscoring the determination of small countries not "to pro- voke Germany," while the Germans themselves "are convinced that we would be neutral if they attacked Czechoslovakia." The Czechoslovakian mood was described as "desperate." In Prague, Beneš reflected bitterly on a Versailles misjudgment, the drawing of his country's frontiers. The Sudeten Mountains, which he had fortified to repel a German attack, were an integral part of the very region inhabited by Henlein's Teutonic con- stituents. If they were annexed by Hitler, those strongholds would become part of the Reich, leaving the rest of Czechoslovakia defenseless.[123]

The tumultuous events in Vienna in March set off huge demonstrations in the Sudetenland, irresponsible talk of "going home to the Reich," and heightened harassment, including Sudetendeutsche clubbing of Czechs living along the German border. At Eger twenty-five thousand Sudeten- deutsche demonstrated as church bells pealed; at Saaz fifteen thousand paraded down streets chanting, *"Ein Volk, ein Reich, ein Führer!"* Until now the Germans had enjoyed prosperity and peace in Czechoslovakia, but the Führer would tell the world that they were martyrs, that they were "subjected to unspeakable suffering at the hands of Prague sadists because Aryan blood coursed through their veins." And decent Englishmen in public life, including a decent prime minister and his decent cabinet, would hesitate to challenge this absurd indictment because open disbelief would "provoke" Hitler. In reality, Hitler needed no provocation. He now meant to destroy the Czech state and incorporate it into the Reich.[124]

Immediately after Churchill's proposal for a Grand Alliance, Cadogan had discussed it with Chamberlain and Halifax, and had left with the impres- sion that they were giving it serious consideration. He disagreed, and his report to the FO reflected it. His position was not, however, acceptable to his colleagues, among them his assistant under secretary, Sir Orme Sar- gent, a protégé of Vansittart. In a memorandum to Cadogan, Sargent saw the Anschluss as the first step in a Nazi "policy of expansion" which would reduce "all the weak and disorganized countries of the Danubian basin . . . to a position, both politically and economically, of vassal states."[125]

It became the task of William Strang, Ralph Wigram's successor as head of the FO's Central Department, to sort it all out. Strang proposed three possible courses of action, ending with a wretched alternative, "a negative one," in his words, "not advanced on its own positive merits," but on the assumption that England was too weak to make any other response. In that event, Britain should "try to persuade France and Czechoslovakia that the best course would be for the latter to make the best terms she can with Germany while she can perhaps still do so in more favorable conditions than would obtain later."[126]

That was the option Cadogan found most appealing. He recommended that Britain make no commitment to support France in fulfilling her pledge to join the Czechs if they were attacked. In his diary that night, March 16, he wrote: "I shall be called 'cowardly' but after days and nights of thinking, I have come to the conclusion that it is the least bad. We *must* not precipitate a conflict now — we shall be smashed. . . . That is the policy of the line of least resistance, which the Cabinet will probably take." He was right. After Churchill's speech Chamberlain wrote his sister Ida that "the plan of the 'Grand Alliance,' as Winston calls it, had occurred to me long before he mentioned it. . . . I talked about it to Halifax." They had found it "a very attractive idea," he continued; "indeed, there is almost everything to be said for it until you come to examine its practicability. From that moment its attraction vanishes. You have only to look at the map to see that nothing that France or we could do could possibly save Czechoslovakia from being overrun by the Germans." He had reached the conclusion that "we could not help Czechoslovakia — she would simply be a pretext for going to war with Germany." But he intended to remain flexible. Should the Sudeten Germans agree to a sensible solution, he was "not sure that in such circumstances I might not be willing to join in some joint guarantee with Germany of Czech independence." Here, surely, was foreign policy with a clogged drain. Chamberlain refused to join France in defending the integrity of Czechoslovakia, but he might sign on with the Nazis. In Berlin, Henderson spoke as though a Nazi-British alliance were already a reality. He openly referred to "those blasted Czechs," and, when a diplomat on his staff began a dispatch to the Foreign Office, "There is no such thing as Czechoslovakia," made a marginal note agreeing that this was "largely true."[127]

The Times urged the Czechs to negotiate with Hitler; Czech stubbornness, it declared, could lead to war. *The Times* also reported a speech by Alan Lennox-Boyd, one of Winston's personal friends, who had told an audience in Biggleswade that Hitler could "absorb Czechoslovakia and Great Britain would remain secure." Boothby sent Churchill a cutting of this story and called it "an incitement to Germany to get on with the job."[128]

Even as Lennox-Boyd spoke, Churchill flung down his own gauntlet in the *Evening Standard*. Obviously, he wrote, Prague must make every effort to provide its Germanic minority with "every form of good treatment and equal citizenship, not incompatible with the safety of the State," but he had every reason to believe that this was being done already. The real danger, as he saw it, was that the Germans might create incidents and use them to justify an invasion of Czechoslovakia. He therefore welcomed the French reassurance that France would keep her word and fulfill treaty obligations to support the Czechs if they were victims of an unprovoked attack. He added: "A further declaration of the intentions of the British Government in such an event must be made."[129]

Thus, at the inner cabinet meeting of March 18, the government faced two Churchillian challenges: his call for a Grand Alliance and a demand that the government join France in a defensive alliance with Czechoslovakia. Chamberlain had asked the military Chiefs of Staff whether they were ready for war. He knew the answer; though his rearmament record was better than Baldwin's, it could hardly be compared to Hitler's. Production of the Hawker Hurricanes had begun five months earlier; the gull-winged Spitfire, now being redesigned to accommodate four additional machine guns (for a total of eight), had followed. Both were superior to the Luftwaffe's best fighters, but tightfisted budgets meant only a handful could be put in the sky now. Therefore, the Air Ministry's reply to the prime minister concluded that the RAF "cannot at the present time be said to be in any way fit to undertake operations on a major war scale." The Admiralty and the War Office agreed that Britain was "at a stage of rearmament when we are not ready for war." After these précis had been reviewed by the inner cabinet, according to the minutes summarizing the meeting, Halifax said they demonstrated "conclusively" that it "behooved us to take every step that we could and to use every argument that we could think of to dissuade France from going to the aid of Czechoslovakia."[130]

But this argument was specious in itself. The questions the P.M. had put to the chiefs had been highly selective, and minority reports had been suppressed. For example, Air Chief Marshal Sir Hugh Dowding, who headed the RAF's Fighter Command and would lead it during the Battle of Britain, believed that the speed and high rate of climb which marked Britain's new fighters, combined with the chain of radar towers now rising along England's southeast shores, demonstrated that hostile bombers could be intercepted in clear weather, when 60 percent of enemy raids could be expected. Radar also meant that continuous fighter patrols could be discontinued, and radar accuracy was improving every day.

Halifax had previously told his FO advisers that negotiations for Churchill's alliance would by their very nature be protracted, proving "both a provocation and an opportunity for Germany to dispose of Czecho-slovakia" before the ink had dried. Colonial Secretary Ormsby-Gore thought the commitment would be "bad and dangerous"; Lord President Hailsham believed it would "hasten an attack" on the Czechs; Minister for Defence Inskip called Czechoslovakia "an unstable unit in Central Europe"; and Chancellor of the Exchequer Simon, agreeing, added that it was a "very artificial creation with no roots in the past." (The border between Germany and the Sudetenland had endured for two hundred years.) The decisive voices, however, were those of the foreign secretary and the prime minister. Halifax advanced the remarkable argument that without a formal commitment both France and Germany would be kept "guessing," and would be less inclined to precipitate a general war. Chamberlain agreed. England, he told the cabinet, was "in no position from the armament point of view" to go to war — the responsibility for that plight was un-mentioned — and France was "in a hopeless position. . . . No effective help could be swiftly brought to Czechoslovakia," and if the Reich could get what it wanted through negotiation, there was "no reason to suppose that [it] would reject such a procedure in favor of one based on violence." The British should take the initiative in pursuing a solution "more accept-able to Germany." The cabinet agreed that it would be "a mistake to plunge into a certain catastrophe in order to avoid a future danger that might never materialize." Bringing pressure on Prague to yield to Sudetendeutsche demands was, Halifax acknowledged, "a disagreeable business" to be accomplished "as pleasantly as possible." He endorsed the prime minister's conclusion "that we must decline to undertake any fresh commitment in regard to Czechoslovakia and that we must try and persuade Dr. Beneš and also the French Government that the best course would be for Czechoslo-vakia to make the best terms she could with Germany," meanwhile "im-pressing on the French . . . the imperative necessity . . . of arriving at some amicable and permanent settlement."[131]

Afterward Halifax told Cadogan that the members had been "unani-mous" in agreeing that "Czechoslovakia is not worth the bones of a single British grenadier." That was not entirely candid. Duff Cooper, first lord of the Admiralty, had protested the note to the French as a "cold refusal to give any support to France" which "read like a declaration of isolation." If France and Germany went to war, he argued, "we should have to fight too, whether we like it or not, so we might as well say so."[132]

To the world outside No. 10 and even to backbenchers, Chamberlain and his cabinet gave the impression that they believed that the Germans and Czechs would reach a sensible settlement of their differences. In such a tangled web England could not be blindly committed by French decisions, but should war come, the Union Jack would fly beside the tricolor — or so the world outside supposed. In fact, the prime minister and his foreign secretary were determined that *under no circumstances* should England and France go to war to save Czechoslovakia. On March 21 Halifax told Foreign Office aides that the great thing was "to dissuade France from going to the aid of Czechoslovakia." Or, as Hilaire Belloc put it while lunching with Duff Cooper, Chamberlain's policy was:

> *Dear Czecho-Slovakia,*
> *I don't think they'll attack yer*
> *But I'm not going to back yer.*[133]

🦁   🦁

As part of their report to the prime minister, the combined chiefs, in an assessment which would have amazed their counterparts in Berlin, had declared it to be "certain that Germany could overrun the whole of Czechoslovakia in less than a week." That Friday, March 18, Chamberlain told the cabinet of his conviction that Hitler's concern was limited to the Sudetenland — that he had no designs on the rest of the country because it was his policy "to include all Germans in the Reich but not to include other nationalities." It was not one of Neville's more prescient statements, but he enlarged upon it the following Thursday afternoon in a House of Commons foreign policy debate. His Majesty's Government, he said, had decided to stand aloof from continental alliances. If France chose to go to war over the Sudetenland, Britain would not be committed to join her. In Czechoslovakia, the prime minister said, British "vital interests" were not concerned. Of course, the French had been told that legalities were irrelevant "in the case of two great countries like Britain and France, with long associations of friendship, with interests closely interwoven, devoted to the same ideals of democratic liberty, and determined to uphold them." An aide-mémoire to that effect had been sent to the British ambassador in Paris. The Russians had received no such assurance.[134]

As Churchill rose to respond, Virginia Cowles, in the Strangers' Gallery for the first time, "looked down," she wrote, "on the sea of black coats and white faces." To her Winston first "seemed only one man of many; but when he spoke his words rang through the House with terrible finality." As he often did, he attributed to Chamberlain opinions Chamberlain did not hold. He was glad to hear that Britain's arrangements for mutual defense with the French republic amounted to a defensive alliance. But "why not say so?" he asked. "Why not make it effective by a military convention of the most detailed character?" A similar commitment might be made to the Czechs, not "a permanent or automatic pledge," but one contingent upon "an act of violent aggression" by the Germans. Unless the Nazi pressure on Prague were counterbalanced by other great powers, the democratic state Beneš and Masaryk had founded "will be forced to make continuous surrenders, far beyond the bounds of what any impartial tribunal would consider just or right, until finally her sovereignty, her independence, her integrity, have been destroyed." It was absurd, said Churchill, to pretend that England could remain detached, and naive to believe that the Sudeten crisis would be Hitler's last: "The might behind the German Dictator increases daily. His appetite may grow with eating. The forces of law and freedom have for a long time known nothing but rebuffs, failures, and humiliations. Their influence would be immensely increased by any signs of concerted action and initiative and combination." England should be committed not only to Paris and Prague but to the integrity of every state which might come within range of Wehrmacht artillery.[135]

Great danger lay, he continued, in growing complacent during lulls in Hitler's demands: "After a boa constrictor has devoured its prey, it often has a considerable digestive spell." Each Nazi outrage — the defiant unveiling of the Luftwaffe and conscription, the seizure of the Rhineland and then its fortification — had been followed by a pause. "Now," he said,

after Austria has been struck down, we are all disturbed and alarmed, but in a little while there may be another pause. . . . Then people will be saying, "See how the alarmists have been confuted; Europe has calmed down, it has all blown over, and the war scare has passed away." The Prime Minister will perhaps repeat what he said a few weeks ago, that the tension in Europe is greatly relaxed. *The Times* will write a leading article to say how silly those people look who on the morrow of the Austrian incorporation raised a clamor for exceptional action in foreign policy and home defence, and how wise the Government were not to let themselves be carried away by this passing incident.

To take such an attitude, he said, was indefensible, a flagrant defiance of the facts. Every day, every week, the people of Austria were being subjected "to the rigors of Nazi domination." Every hour, every minute, the forces "of conquest and intimidation" were regrouping for another assault. Soon "another stroke" would fall. "What I dread," he told the House, "is that the impulse now given to active effort may pass away when the dangers are not diminishing, but accumulating and gathering, as country after country is involved in the Nazi system, and as their vast preparations reach their final perfection."

He was nearing the end. The Commons was still as still. He lowered his head and continued, the slight impediment in his speech adding to the drama of his delivery as he followed the psalm form of his notes:

> For five years I have talked to the House
>   on these matters — not with very great success.
>
> I have watched this famous island
>   descending incontinently, fecklessly,
>   the stairway which leads to a dark gulf.
>
> It is a fine broad stairway at the beginning,
>   but after a bit the carpet ends.
>
> A little farther on there are only flagstones,
>   and a little farther on still
>   these break beneath your feet. . . .[136]

Then, in measured tones:

If mortal catastrophe should overtake the British Nation and the British Empire, historians a thousand years hence will still be baffled by the mystery of our affairs. They will never understand how it was that a victorious nation, with everything in hand, suffered themselves to be brought low, and to cast away all that they had gained by measureless sacrifice and absolute victory — gone with the wind!

Now the victors are the vanquished, and those who threw down their arms and sued for an armistice are striding on to world mastery. That is the position — that is the terrible transformation that has taken place. . . . Now is the time at last to rouse the nation. . . . We should lay aside every hindrance and endeavour by uniting the whole force and spirit of our people to raise again a great British nation standing up before all the world; for such a nation, rising in its ancient vigour, can even at this hour save civilisation.[137]

As he took his seat, the House broke into a hubbub of noise; members rattled their papers and shuffled their way to the lobby. Virginia Cowles was in the House lobby, awaiting a prominent Conservative MP who had invited her to tea. As he strode up she asked him his opinion of Winston's speech. He replied: "Oh, it was the usual Churchillian filibuster; he likes to rattle the sabre and he does it jolly well, but you always have to take it with a grain of salt." She recalls: "That was the general attitude of the House of Commons in those days." Even Churchill realized that Chamberlain's determination not to "rouse the nation" was echoing the mood of countrymen who did not want to be roused. Fleet Street, in step with its readers, ignored Churchill's speech and reported Chamberlain's. The liberal *Manchester Guardian* declared, "Mr. Chamberlain has overcome the enemies in his own camp," and in the *New Statesman* John Maynard Keynes urged the Czechs to negotiate a settlement with Hitler. The Chamberlains and the Cadogans drove to Cliveden for a weekend party with, as Cadogan put it, an "ordinary sort of crowd." The P.M. won the after-dinner game of musical chairs every time. They always let him win. It meant so much to him.[138]

The morning after his dire warning to the House, Churchill received an unexpected, dismaying, and most unwelcome letter from the editor of Beaverbrook's *Evening Standard,* terminating his contract — in effect, firing him. Thus ended two years of fortnightly columns, depriving him of his most valuable public rostrum, because, the editor wrote, "it has been evident that your views on foreign affairs and the part this country should play are entirely opposed to those held by us." Winston replied that his "divergence from Lord Beaverbrook's policy" had been "obvious from the beginning, but it clearly appears to me to be less marked than in the case of the Low cartoons." Then, scathingly: "I rather thought that Lord Beaverbrook prided himself upon forming a platform in the *Evening Standard* for various opinions including of course his own."[139]

It was a setback, an annual loss of £1,820 — about $9,000 at the then prevailing rate of exchange — and the timing could scarcely have been worse. He was broke. He sat in his Chartwell study, staring at columns of figures which should have made him blush. As chancellor of the Exchequer in the 1920s he had presided over England's fiscal affairs for nearly five years, yet his personal finances were hopelessly muddled. Few writers could match his income; during the past eight years he had earned £102,102, an annual average of £12,763, the equivalent of about $62,000. Chartwell, his London flat, and general expenses alone exceeded £10,000 each year, and his travels, secretaries, researchers, and the lavish lunches and dinners he gave for colleagues and visitors from the Continent drove him deeper and deeper into the red.[140]

The year before, he had faced his first real financial crisis. His letters to Clementine in the first weeks of 1937 are shadowed by a veiled and then explicit preoccupation with money which was wholly out of character — small attempts at economizing while he spread himself elsewhere. He had set up Randolph and Sarah in Westminster Garden flats and had "told Sarah I will give her £200 toward expenses." But, he added defensively, he was only fulfilling promises made long before. Fuel for Chartwell, delivered "in five ton batches at £9.11.0 each . . . used to last a fortnight," he reminded her, but the last load kept them warm for three months, despite weather that was "raw and generally damnable." Moreover, he had lost only £12 at bezique, he wrote, and "the wine has been very strictly controlled and little drunk." Also, telephone bills showed "a marked reduction. We are having fortnightly accounts from the Post Office which enables us to check it." Finally, he wrote, on a note of triumph, "I am not taking Inches with me abroad."[141]

Clemmie knew that the little saved by leaving his valet behind would shrink to insignificance beside his Riviera expenses. And indeed, he glumly wrote on February 2 that he had been talking to a Mr. Frank Capon, a real estate agent. Capon "tells me," he wrote, "that there is a lady nibbling around for a house like Chartwell, and even mentioning Chartwell." The agent said he would "on no account mention any figure less than £30,000. If I could see £25,000 I should close with it. If we do not get a good price we can carry on for a year or two more. But no good offer should be refused, having regard to the fact that our children are almost all flown and my life is probably in its closing decade."[142]

Experience had taught him that budgets did not work with his family. The reason — though he would never have acknowledged it — was that *he* was the family spendthrift. Nevertheless, in April he drew up a balance sheet cutting their personal expenses to £6,000, solemnly telling them: "This cannot on any account be exceeded." In that year, as in the years preceding, it was exceeded by over £4,000. The flaw in the budget was that the head of the household was exempt; and Churchill had no intention of curtailing his own extravagant life-style. Indeed, no one except Clemmie dared raise the question. By the process of elimination, therefore, he concluded that he would have to work harder. He wouldn't rattle a tin cup, but he could no longer turn his back on lecture fees, though earning them meant a loss of time better spent working toward the strengthening of England's defenses.[143]

Now, a year later, he seemed to have no choice — his home and its eighty acres must be sold. Even so, it appeared he would have to quit Parliament to make money, as a writer, lecturer, and/or businessman. His security had lain in his reserve of American stocks. It was from there, where he felt safest, that the blow fell. Early in March 1938 the U.S. recession hit Wall Street. Stock prices plummeted so swiftly, and so deeply, that Churchill's brokers, Vickers da Costa, told him that his American investments had been wiped out. In fact, it was worse than that — his share account owed the brokerage firm £18,000. Where could he find so tremendous a sum? After his *History of the English-speaking Peoples* was finished — but only then — he would be paid £15,000. Even so he would be £3,000 in the red. His earnings as a journalist were high; but they weren't large enough to meet Britain's income tax and supertaxes. Chartwell must be put on the market.

In his youth Churchill had been the highest-paid correspondent in the Empire; perhaps the world. His articles still brought premium rates from newspapers and magazines, but he knew little of modern journalism. He decided to buy a full page from *The Times* to advertise Chartwell's attractions and availability. It was scheduled to run on April 2. He expected, at most, that the fact of his putting up his home for sale might merit a discreet paragraph in *The Times*'s "Londoner's Diary." But famous writers often forget that they are famous, and the malice of political enemies slips the memory of statesmen who hold no grudges themselves. Thus Winston was unprepared for what actually happened. Beaverbrook's *Daily Express* picked up the story immediately, and Winston's once and future friend, now a devout appeaser, managed to insinuate that Churchill was irresponsible, telling the *Express*'s readers that he was auctioning off his home while attempting to sabotage Chamberlain's thrifty budgets. The paper's March 17 headline read: "CHURCHILL FOLLOWING L.G. TO PARIS." To the Beaver, Paris meant intrigue with a weak ally when the sound course was to embrace virile Nazi Germany. The story beneath the head drove in this long needle: "In some quarters there has been a disposition to question the desirability of British politicians visiting Paris at this juncture." Hearst never sank lower. And *The Times* ran an account on its main news page — in those days its front page was still all ads — headed: "MR CHURCHILL'S HOME IN KENT FOR SALE," and including personal details which deeply offended Winston.[144]

Meantime he moved to close one hole in his dike — the loss of earnings from the *Standard*. He wrote Lord Camrose, proprietor of the *Daily Telegraph*, explaining the circumstances of his departure from the *Standard* and proposing to write now for the *Telegraph*. Attached to his letter were three lists of newspapers which carried his syndicated columns: the first list was of papers in Great Britain, the second of English-language papers around the world, and the third of papers which published them in translation. His agent, Imre Revesz, had drawn up the last list; they meant that Churchill's views and disclosures — chiefly from his intelligence net — reached readers in seventeen languages. "As you will see it is a very fine platform," he noted dryly, "though as Nazi power advances, as in Vienna, planks are pulled out of it." Camrose agreed to a six-month trial, paying Winston £70 a piece. The arrangement continued for fourteen months, until the *Daily Mirror* offered him better terms.[145]

This was an important step but in itself would not have been enough to save Chartwell. The fact is that Churchill never understood money and was awed by those who did. They in turn were captivated by him, which was fortunate, for his profligate ways would have driven him from Parliament long before he became the only man who could save England. Bernard Baruch had rescued him in 1929, but Winston couldn't go to the same well twice. Besides, Baruch was in America. The only wealthy member of his inner circle was Brendan Bracken, and the origin and extent of Bracken's holdings were unknown; he cultivated his reputation as a man of mystery. In any event, few men possessed the enormous liquidity Churchill needed, and Brendan wasn't one of them.

But he knew men who *did*. The day after the *Daily Express* story Winston told Bracken that he wanted someone to take over his portfolio for three years, with the power to buy or sell holdings, provided his debt not deepen. He expected to pay interest on the loan — about £800 a year. Afterward he wrote Bracken: "If it were not for public affairs and my evident duty I shd be able to manage all right." He thought it "unsuitable as well as harassing" to have to follow the market "from day to day when one's mind ought to be concentrated upon the great world issues now at stake. I shd indeed be grateful if I cd be liberated during these next few critical years from this particular worry, wh descended upon me so unexpectedly [and to] which I shall certainly never expose myself again. I cannot tell you what a relief it would be if I could put it out of my mind; and take the large decisions wh perhaps may be required of me without this distraction and anxiety."[146]

Bracken was alarmed. Austria had just fallen; Czechoslovakia lay between the Nazi jaws; Chamberlain was rejecting defense spending, which Berlin might misunderstand. To Brendan — and he knew he was not alone — Churchill was the one leader standing against the black tide, contemptuous of HMG, Cliveden, and Blickling Hall. The thought of him spending his energy on potboilers for *Collier's* and *News of the World*, leaving his corner seat in the House of Commons to speak in provincial lecture halls — of Churchill absent from the center of action when the future of civilization hung in the balance — was unbearable. Among Bracken's acquaintances in the City were wealthy men — many, but not all, Jews — who were outraged by Chamberlain's policy of courting Hitler. He circulated a memorandum among them, explaining Churchill's quandary. If Winston absented himself from public life he could pay his debts and build an estate. "But how is he to do this," Brendan asked, "while events run at this pitch?" One man took him aside; they talked quietly and shook hands; it was done.[147]

Told of the transaction, Churchill sent Brendan a note: "Enclosed is a letter wh you can show to our friend. This is only to tell *you* that as Hitler said to Mussolini on a recent and less worthy occasion, 'I shall never forget' this inestimable service." The "friend" was Sir Henry Strakosch, an industrialist in the City, who had been mining gold in South Africa for over forty years. Winston knew him; he was part of Churchill's intelligence net; since the Führer's decision to rearm the Reich, the expatriated South African tycoon had been an invaluable source of facts and figures in Germany's military budgets. Churchill's pride prevented him from begging; therefore Bracken, his most loyal follower, had done it for him. Strakosch agreed to cover Churchill's losses, buying his deflated U.S. securities at the price he had paid for them. He wrote Winston that he would "carry this position for three years, you giving me full discretion to sell or vary holdings at any time, but on the understanding that you incur no further liability."[148]

Chartwell had been saved (the *Times* advertisement was withdrawn after a single appearance) and Churchill had been granted a reprieve — not a gift, but a loan. He would have refused charity, and Strakosch had not amassed his fortune by playing the samaritan to improvident statesmen. Winston could remain a member of Parliament, provided he met his publishing deadlines — chiefly those for the last volume of his Marlborough biography and for *A History of the English-speaking Peoples* — and sent payments to Strakosch as they came due.

As Europe toiled slowly toward its next butchery — never was there a war so hard to start, nor a warlord more frustrated than the *Kriegsherr* in Berlin — the quintessential Churchill, the Winston the public never saw, prowled his study night after night, an inner shutter drawn in a private blackout of the mind, excluding everything but the topic before him. His prose grew in intensity as though controlled by a rheostat, as he used the language to express his wrath, a fury matched only by that of Hitler, who was free to act while Churchill, who couldn't even control his own spending, saw himself approaching senescence with no prospect of any change in his reputation as the leper of Parliament.

Meantime, he limited his attendance in Westminster to great debates and crucial votes. While his colleagues slept in London, in Kent he paced about in his loud dressing gown, scanning précis from his researchers, dictating, sending the typed manuscript to the printer by courier, and revising the galleys in red ink — "playing with the proofs," as he called it, a very expensive amusement, since extensive changes in the galleys were charged to the author. The grammar and spelling were subjected to a final, rigorous check by Eddie Marsh, his private secretary in earlier years, now recently knighted; then the courier reappeared and the job was done. The front bench was often critical of Churchill's absenteeism, but had he been faithful in his attendance, what would he have accomplished? In November and December of 1937 he had been completely absorbed in writing his Marlborough biography. During that time the prime minister and his cabinet had, in the name of economy, permitted England's military strength to lag farther and farther behind Germany's. Yet had Churchill been in Parliament he could have done nothing; His Majesty's Government did not need the approval of the House; it was under no obligation even to inform Parliament, and it didn't. Much of the caviling about Winston's truancy was disingenuous; when he was at Chartwell, they were safe from his biting wit. Writing Maxine Elliott in February 1938 he said he was determined to finish the book "by the end of the month. I am therefore not paying much attention to the House of Commons, at which I expect the Ministers will not be at all vexed!"[149]

Furthermore, his was the most persuasive rhetoric in England, and while speeches in Parliament were heard only by those within earshot, the written word may reach anywhere. Years later the White House revealed that a copy of *While England Slept*, the American edition of Churchill's *Arms and the Covenant*, had lain on President Roosevelt's bedside table, with key passages, including an analysis of the president's peace initiative, underscored. Churchill's prose, so rhythmic that it can be scanned, was vibrant with the terrific energy that can hold and sway vast audiences. Its vitality is remarkable, and in the late 1930s, because of his continuing financial obligations, his output became prodigious. In late 1937 he published *Great Contemporaries,* which was published in a revised and expanded edition the following year, along with *Arms and the Covenant* and the fourth and last volume of *Marlborough: His Life and Times. Step by Step* appeared in mid-1939. During 1938, while working on his four-volume *History of the English-speaking Peoples,* he also turned out fifty-nine magazine articles on subjects as diverse as "Would I Live My Life Again?" and "Women in War." Two of the books — *Great Contemporaries* and *Step by Step* — were collections of pieces written for newspapers and magazines, and *Arms and the Covenant* presented key foreign policy speeches; but even they required revision and rewriting. After reading the fourth volume of *Marlborough,* Maxine Elliott wrote him from the Riviera: "It is incredible to me that one man can possess the genius to write a book like this and at the same time pursue his ordinary life which is a thousand times fuller of grave duties and obligations than that of lesser men."[150]

He paid a price. In a life crowded with incident, familial obligations, recreation, and public service, he published forty-four books, five of them during Victoria's reign, when both his writing style and political philosophy were formed. Except for the small legacy which he had used to buy

Chartwell, writing had been his sole source of income, but he had never written under such pressure, and at an age when other writers slow down or retire altogether.

At times the sheer volume of his research notes and the goading of his agent, his publishers, and magazine editors were exasperating. "I am toiling double shifts," he wrote Clementine, away on holiday; "it is laborious: & I resent it and the pressure." Like any other writer, he hoped for windfalls. Now and then an unexpected check arrived, to be greeted with a radiant grin and instructions to Mrs. Landemare for a lavish spread that evening. But at least once he was cruelly disappointed. He had written Clemmie: "Tomorrow the Daily Herald begin distributing the new cheap edition of the World Crisis wh Odham's have printed. It can be sold for 3/9 for each of two volumes — a miracle of mass production. They expect to sell 150,000! I like to feel that for the first time the working people will hear my side of the [Gallipoli] tale." The royalty check, which would have exceeded £1,000, would have been equally welcome, but the cheap book was not an idea whose time had come. The workmen remained unenlightened and Churchill uncompensated. So he returned to double shifts. He was irked by deadlines, believing he could do a better job if given more time. He wrote Clemmie: "I should be able to do my books more slowly and not have to face the truly stupendous task like Marlborough IV being finished in 4 or 5 months," only to face another urgent date for the *History*, "worth £16,000, but entailing an immense amount of reading and solitary reflection if justice is to be done to so tremendous a topic."[151]

The consequences of such a grind have not enhanced his literary reputation. His masterpiece is *The World Crisis,* published over a period of several years, 1923 to 1931, a six-volume, 3,261-page account of the Great War, beginning with its origins in 1911 and ending with its repercussions in the 1920s. Magnificently written, it is enhanced by the presence of the author at the highest councils of war and in the trenches as a battalion commander. "After it," the British historian Robert Rhodes James writes, "anything must appear as anticlimax."[152]

Certainly *Marlborough* and *A History of the English-speaking Peoples* are heavy with what Philip Guedalla called "the lullaby of a majestic style." The second Lord Birkenhead, son of Churchill's old friend F.E., deplored "his lack of historic objectivity, of the fact that he is usually justifying a policy or a cause, and that his perception of the feelings and motives of others is dim and uncertain." Ironically, it was Churchill himself who had diagnosed part of his difficulty when, as a young man, he had written: "Few authors are rich men. Few human beings are insensible to the value of money. . . . Hurried style, exaggerated mannerisms and plagiarism replace the careful toil. The author writes no more for fame but for wealth.

Consequently his books become inferior. All this is very sad but very true." In his contributions to periodicals, however, it is fair to add that he may have had a second, higher motive. Events were moving swiftly in Europe; lacking power in Parliament, he made the press his megaphone. He believed he could arouse the nation by his prose, even though it was not his best. He was right. He did.[153]

❧   ❧

After the slaughter of ten million young men twenty years earlier, a renewal of the struggle seemed incomprehensible. The German people hated war as passionately as their once and future enemies, but in the Reich public opinion was forged by the state to an unprecedented degree. The Nazi Reichskulturkammer determined what was taught in the schools, the music people heard, the content of radio broadcasts, the books they read, what was published in newspapers, the churches they attended, and the plays and films they saw. The Führer, they were told over and over, was working toward noble goals and making a supreme effort to save the peace. Those who threatened it, who hated Germans because the Aryan race was superior to their own, were unmasked each year on the anniversary of the Nazi party — the Nuremberg *Reichsparteitag*, held in September.

The average Briton was better informed. To be sure, *The Times* was not the only paper in which rogue editors disgraced their craft by the distortion or outright suppression of the facts. Nevertheless the truth was there for those who cared to know. A majority chose to ignore it. Confronted with the prospect of another world war, they sought refuge in escapism. Londoners whose dreams were haunted by Nazi storm troopers could leave their nightmares in the checkroom at the St. James's Theatre, while they watched Terence Rattigan's *After the Dance*; or at the Duchess, where Emlyn Williams's *The Corn Is Green* was playing to packed houses; or at His Majesty's Theatre, where the high point of the evening would be hearing a quartet sing "The Stately Homes of England" in Noel Coward's *Operette*, which ran through 133 performances.

If you wanted to forget Japanese aggression in China and mutual aggression in Spain, a smorgasbord of entertainment lay before you: Len Hutton scoring 364 runs against Australia in the Oval Test Match; or, in the book department of Harrods, P. G. Wodehouse's *The Code of the Woosters*, Evelyn Waugh's *Scoop*, and Graham Greene's *Brighton Rock*. From across the Atlantic came new works by Faulkner, Hemingway, Steinbeck, and Nathanael West. The United States also presented, to enthusiastic theatre audiences, *Life with Father* and Rodgers and Hart's

The Boys from Syracuse; and, on what was then called the silver screen, *Gone With the Wind, The Wizard of Oz,* and Walt Disney's *Snow White and the Seven Dwarfs.*

In 1938, the year of the Anschluss and Munich, the British produced a tune and a dance step that swept all Europe and the United States:

> *Any time you're Lambeth way,*
> *Any evening, any day,*
> *You'll find us all*
> *Doin' the Lambeth walk.*
> *Hey!*

But Britain's greatest accomplishments in the lively arts would follow World War II. In the 1930s her entertainers remained loyal to the traditional, rollicking music hall songs. Yet the huge halls were barely half full now, relics, really; houses haunted by memories of Harry Lauder, Lillie Langtry, and George "Champagne Charlie Is My Name" Leybourne. The brash Americans rushed into the vacuum. *Snow White* alone provided three hit songs; other imported popular songs of 1938–1939 were "Over the Rainbow," three inanities — "Three Little Fishes," "A-Tisket A-Tasket," "Flat Foot Floogie with the Floy Floy" — and "Are You Having Any Fun?"[154]

Among those not having any fun were over two-thirds of Czechoslovakia's population. The country's prominence in the news from May 1938 to March 1939 may explain the immense popularity of an old Czech drinking song, "Roll Out the Barrel." In the popular view, World War II had not yet begun, but that would have been news to the Chinese, the Ethiopians, and the Spaniards. The greatest sufferers, of course, were the Jews. Nicolson, meeting an Austrian "who had just got away from Vienna," set down the man's account:

They rounded up the people walking in the Prater on Sunday last, and separated the Jews from the rest. They made the Jewish gentlemen take off all their clothes and walk on all fours on the grass. They made the old Jewish ladies get up into the trees by ladders and sit there. They then told them to chirp like birds. The Russians never committed atrocities like that. You may take a man's life; but to destroy all his dignity is bestial. This man told me that with his own eyes he had seen Princess Stahremberg washing out the urinals at the Vienna railway-station. The suicides have been appalling. A great cloud of misery hangs over the town.[155]

The situation of the German Jews was desperate. In every community, posters declared that they had been stripped of their civil rights and were forbidden to seek employment of any kind; Jewish shops and homes were plundered by Nazi storm troopers. Among the victims were the parents of Herschel Grynszpan, a seventeen-year-old refugee living in Paris. On November 7, 1938, after learning of this, Grynszpan murdered Ernst vom Rath, a third secretary at the German embassy in Paris. Senior Nazis, SS officers, and Gestapo agents instantly saw this as an outrageous opportunity. On November 9 Goebbels issued instructions that "a spontaneous demonstration of the German people" (*"eine spontane Reaktion des deutschen Volkes"*) was to be "organized and executed" that night. No one knows how many acts of murder, rape, and pillage were carried out during *die Kristallnacht*, as it came to be called — Crystal Night, or the Night of Broken Glass — but the pogrom was the greatest in history. Reinhard Heydrich, Heinrich Himmler's second in command at the SS, reported that the number of Jewish shops smashed and looted was 7,500.[156]

On May 10, 1938, Ambassador Henderson's first secretary, Ivone Kirkpatrick, lunched with Prince Bismarck. Kirkpatrick had a specific proposition, of which the French, he said, were unaware. In his report to Ribbentrop, Bismarck quoted Kirkpatrick as saying: "If the German Government would advise the British Government confidentially what solution of the Sudeten German question they were striving after, the British Government would bring such pressure to bear in Prague that the Czechoslovak Government would be compelled to accede to the German wishes."[157]

If one assumes that men in public life are guided by patriotism, reason, or even political survival, the conduct of His Majesty's foreign policy defies understanding. It makes sense, however, if one grasps the fact that HMG and the key diplomats who owed their rise to the men in Downing Street believed that England should sever her bonds with leftist France and form a new alliance with Hitler's Germany, thereby forming a solid front against the Soviet Union. It is a historic irony that Churchill, Britain's original anti-Bolshevik, should have fought them every inch of the way.

He could do little beyond sending Bill Deakin as his personal representative, to ask Prague whether the Czech government approved of his plan for a Grand Alliance — which it did — and to inquire about reports of disorders in the Sudetenland. In the spring of 1938 the Czechs were breaking up the Sudetendeutsche riots but treating the ringleaders with kid gloves, determined to give the Reich no excuse for intervention. On March 12 — the day Hitler annexed Austria and Churchill unsuccessfully urged Halifax to protest his conquest in Geneva — the Czech foreign minister, Dr. Kamil Krofta, instructed his ambassadors "to avoid all unnecessary criticism, and to make every effort to avoid being involved." His envoy in London was Jan Masaryk, the son of Tomáš. Jan was worried about London's vocalizing its support of the Czech cause. On the evening of March 13, a crowd gathered in Trafalgar Square and cheered a proposal that they stage a sympathetic demonstration outside his home in Grosvenor Place. He protested that he was "a good deal disturbed," and the demonstration was quietly canceled. It was a measure of Hitler's power that the mere possibility of annoying him was enough to quash a peaceful show of friendship — for a country he had not yet threatened — in the capital of the world's greatest empire.[158]

In newspaper accounts of the Czech disturbances, the German führer was reported to be upset by them. The British public did not suspect his complicity. For better or for worse, but mostly worse, Woodrow Wilson had sown the seed of self-determination at Versailles, and enlightened Europeans sympathized with the discontented Sudeten Germans. If German observers were to be believed — and German credibility was very high among those determined never to fight another war — the Czech government was subjecting the demonstrating Sudetendeutsche to outrageous brutality. As Harold Macmillan later pointed out: "It is a falsification of history to suggest that appeasement up to the time of Munich was not widely supported, either openly or by implication. It was only as the relentless march of events revealed the true character of the man who had seized control of Germany that opinion in Britain began to change."[159]

It was going to take a lot of havoc to turn people around, and except for Churchill few were trying. The London press was disenchanted with the French. The *Observer* commented: "We cannot allow the British Empire to be dragged down to disaster by the separate French alliances with Moscow and Prague." Kingsley Martin, then editor of the liberal *New Statesman*, later reflected on the pessimism in Whitehall and at No. 10. It began, he thought, toward the end of the 1920s, when Germany was still ruled from Weimar and almost every well-informed Englishman "regarded the French notion of keeping Germany as a second-class power as absurd, and agreed that the Versailles Treaty must be revised in Germany's favor." But France wouldn't have it, and Weimar, unarmed but still suspect, was impotent. By 1938, however, Martin felt that "things had gone so far that to plan armed resistance to the dictators was now useless. If there was a war we should lose it. We should, therefore, seek the most peaceful way of letting them gradually get all they wanted."[160]

One of the most outspoken of the appeasers was an Anglican bishop, the Reverend Morley Headlam, who defended Hitler's suppression of religious freedom before a church assembly, arguing that it was "only fair to realize that a great majority" of the Nazis believed that their cause "represented a strong spiritual influence" and looked upon it as "a real representation of Christianity." A visiting Nazi told the Anglo-German Fellowship: "Herr Hitler has given the Church a free hand . . . he is a very religious man himself." There was "no persecution of religion in Germany," said Bishop Headlam, merely "persecution of political action." Geoffrey Dawson published the bishop's sermons in full while consigning dispatches from his own Berlin correspondent, describing the imprisonment of German clergymen, to the wastebasket.[161]

The curtain rose on what would be the first Czech crisis when Konrad Henlein addressed a Sudeten German party rally in Karlsbad on April 24. He read a list of eight demands for action in Prague. They bore Hitler's stamp; two weeks after the Anschluss, on March 28, Henlein had been rushed to Berlin for a three-hour session in which he was coached by Hitler and his foreign minister. Hitler's closing words to the SDP leader were found among the Wilhelmstrasse debris in 1945 and submitted as an exhibit in Nuremberg. The Führer had told his Sudeten puppet that "demands should be made by the Sudeten German party which are unacceptable to the Czech government." Accordingly, sandwiched between innocuous demands at Karlsbad were two which any Prague government would reject. One was the recognition of the Sudeten Germans as autonomous within the state, and the other provided them "complete freedom to profess adherence to the German character and ideology." Later Henlein added another demand: a revision of Czech foreign policy, which had "hitherto placed the [Prague regime] among the enemies of the German people" and had considered it "the particular task of the Czech people to form a Slav bulwark against the so-called *Drang nach Osten,*" the Reich's "thrust to the east."[162]

This was provocative and, at the time, puzzling. If Hitler had the best interests of the Sudeten Germans at heart, or even if he intended to annex the Sudetenland — in short, if he intended anything except the incitement of riot leading to bloodshed — he was going about it the wrong way. Two days earlier President Beneš had told the British minister, Basil Newton, that he planned to open "serious negotiations" with Henlein and his party during May and June and, once they had reached an agreement, to pass the necessary legislation through the Czech legislature in July. Now Prague canceled this program. The Czech press was outraged. Foreign Minister Krofta called Henlein's program "far-reaching and dangerous"; among other things, it could be used to restrict equality and freedom for other minorities — specifically Jews. The demand that the Sudeten Germans be given a separate "legal personality," he added, was totally unacceptable. Nevertheless, the coalition government led by Premier Milan Hodža, a Slovak with broad popular support, left the door to negotiations ajar, though he told Newton that he doubted anything "serious" would be possible until after the local elections.[163]

Another French government had fallen in mid-April, and on April 28, four days after Henlein's Karlsbad speech, the new premier arrived in London for two days of conferences between the allies of the last war. He was Édouard Daladier. Accompanying him was Georges Bonnet, France's tenth foreign minister in less than six years. Daladier — not yet defeatist — was determined to honor his country's commitment to the embattled Czechs. Like Churchill, he believed Hitler's objective was nothing less than the "destruction of the present Czechoslovakian State." To block him Daladier wanted a joint declaration, putting the Führer on notice that a Nazi invasion of Czechoslovakia would trigger declarations of war in Paris and London. But when he arrived at No. 10 Downing Street he found that if he wanted to form a solid anti-Nazi front he had come to the wrong address. On March 20 Chamberlain had written his sister Ida: "I have therefore abandoned any idea of giving guarantees to Czechoslovakia, or the French in connection with her obligations to that country." He repeated this to Daladier, who left disappointed.[164]

Bonnet, whom Churchill called "the quintessence of appeasement," was secretly delighted, and, in fact, he represented the mood of French politicians and the Paris press. The Army of the Third Republic was ready to fight the Boche; so were the people, with their bitter memories of 1914–1918. But their leaders and their journalists were preparing to turn them round. Professor Joseph Barthélemy, who later served in Pétain's Vichy government as minister of justice, argued in *Le Temps* that the frequent violations of Locarno freed France from her treaty commitments. *Paris-Soir, Le Matin, Le Figaro, Paris-Midi, Information, L'Action Française, Le Temps, Petit Parisien*, the Socialist *Le Populaire* — every daily in the capital except the chauvinist *Epoque* and the Communist *L'Humanité* — opposed defending democratic Czechoslovakia.[165]

※   ※

Churchill's financial straits kept him at Chartwell most of the time, working to keep faith with Sir Henry Strakosch. Chamberlain's tenure faced no strong challenge, and his most visible rival was the "Eden

Group," as Fleet Street called them, between twenty and thirty MPs who met regularly at various homes with Eden presiding. Churchill's followers were the "Old Guard," never more than four or five at this time. His absences from London were too frequent and too long to attract and hold a large number of supporters, while "Eden's resignation," as Harold Macmillan recalled, "had at least produced a pivot round which dissenting members of the Conservative Party could more readily form."[166]

Visitors to Chartwell, correspondence, and frequent telephone conversations brought Churchill abreast of developments in the capital, however, and since public men of that generation kept meticulous accounts of public activities and personal impressions, Churchill's growing role in British affairs can be traced and documented with confidence. His intellect and will had been recognized since his first years in Parliament nearly forty years earlier, yet his contemporaries continued to charge that he lacked sound judgment. Isaiah Berlin later commented: "When biographers and historians come to describe and analyse his views . . . they will find that his opinions on all these topics are set in fixed patterns, set early in life and lately only reinforced."[167]

Whenever he was in London, Winston stopped in Whitehall to see Vansittart. Though stripped of power and influence, Van kept in touch with his sources abroad and accumulated inside information in Whitehall through friends and former subordinates. He was troubled, as was Winston, by the rot of defeatism among Englishmen, particularly among British diplomats. In Paris, Sir Eric Phipps told Bonnet that the Czechs, by declaring they would fight if invaded, had "put themselves in the wrong." Basil Newton, in Prague, consistently supported Nazi demands. If the French believed it "worthwhile to try to perpetuate the *status quo* in [their] own interests," he advised the FO, Britain should stand aside. As early as March 13, 1938, the day after the Anschluss, Newton counseled London: "If I am right in thinking that Czechoslovakia's present political position is not permanently tenable, it will be no kindness in the long run to try to maintain her in it."[168]

The most egregious of all His Majesty's emissaries was Sir Nevile Henderson. Duplicity had won him his appointment in Berlin, and any other foreign secretary — or prime minister — would have dismissed him long before he could inflict a mortal wound on European peace. When, in the House of Commons, Duff Cooper described him as "violently anti-Czech and pro-German," no one rose to Henderson's defense; no other interpretation of his record was possible. He described the Czechs as "a pigheaded race"; Beneš, their president — a graduate of the universities of Prague, Paris, and Dijon — was "the most pigheaded of the lot." As His Britannic Majesty's official representative, he informed the Germans:

"Great Britain would not think of risking even one sailor or airman for Czechoslovakia and . . . any reasonable solution would be agreed to, so long as it were not attempted by force."[169]

Putting all other work aside to back the Czechs, Churchill was writing and speaking in their behalf at Manchester, Bristol, Sheffield, and Birmingham, trying to rouse Britain to the great peril Chamberlain and those around him could not see. In the May 1, 1938, issue of the *News of the World* he opened a new series of articles with a piece on "Future Safeguards of National Defence." Predicting that Britain's chances of surviving the approaching conflict depended upon the extent and efficiency of her air-raid precautions, he called for a crash program to bring nearer the day "when the accursed air-murderer, for such I must judge the bomber of civilian populations, meets a sure doom." The "greatest safety," he argued, "will be found in having an air force so numerous and excellent that it will beat the enemy's air force in fair fight"; therefore continued study, expenditures, and preparations were essential. Chamberlain was infuriated; he regarded the article as an attack on His Majesty's foreign policy, a foul blow at the fragile arch of understanding the prime minister and foreign minister were trying to build between London and Berlin.

Recriminations over what had been done and what had been left undone were futile. Unlike Baldwin, Chamberlain believed in rearmament within limits. The chief limitation arose from his greater concern for Britain's economic prosperity. As he saw it, the practice under which the cabinet approved estimates submitted by the three services endangered the country's fiscal security. His solution was to fix a ceiling for defense spending and then let the services distribute it among themselves.

This was a businessman's way of defending a nation, but to others it made no sense. Duff Cooper attacked "the absurd new system of rationing the defence departments"; the "sensible plan," he argued, "must be to ascertain your needs for defence first, and then inquire as to your means for meeting them." Soldiers were even more vehement. Lieutenant Colonel Henry Pownall of the Committee of Imperial Defence wrote in his diary that the prime minister's theory of "limited liability in war" was "a most dangerous heresy"; the politicians "cannot or will not realize that if war with Germany comes again . . . we shall again be *fighting for our lives*. Our efforts *must* be the maximum, by land, sea, and air. . . . In God's name let us recognize that from the outset — and by that I mean *now*."[170]

Chamberlain told his cabinet that British production could not match Germany's "unless we are prepared to undertake the tremendous measure of control over skilled labour, as in Germany." He preferred "voluntary" cooperation by arms manufacturers, though such firms had not been noted in the past for their patriotism. The fact was that the bill for years of neglecting the nation's defenses, most of it during the ministries of Mac-Donald and Baldwin, was coming due. The people were uneasy; a scapegoat was needed, and the prime minister's eye fell on the secretary for air, Lord Swinton, who had neglected to show enthusiasm for appeasement policies. Later Churchill wrote of an Air Defence Research Committee meeting of May 12, 1938, at which "we were all busily engaged" discussing "technical problems, when a note was brought in to the Air Minister asking him to go to Downing Street." Swinton left at once and "never returned. He had been dismissed by Mr. Chamberlain."[171]

There was speculation, though not among those in a position to know, that Churchill might be appointed in his place. Instead, the prime minister announced a reshuffling of his cabinet, with Swinton replaced by Minister of Health Sir Kingsley Wood, the P.M.'s oldest and most faithful supporter, a Francophobe and the most fervent of appeasers, more eager even than Chamberlain for friendship with Nazi Germany. Kingsley Wood had never worn a uniform; his career had been devoted to health, education, and welfare. Nicolson wrote Vita: "We had an excitement yesterday, Swinton sacked. At once I telephoned or rather got Duncan [Sandys] to telephone to Winston. . . . How silly the whole thing is! Here we are at the greatest crisis in our history, with a genius like Winston doing nothing and Kingsley Wood as our Minister for Air." Other changes in the cabinet seemed just as baffling, Nicolson wrote. He blamed Chief Whip David Margesson ("not . . . a good Cabinet-maker") but conceded in the end that in such a hodgepodge it was impossible to assign responsibility. (He overlooked the prime minister.) "Nobody understands anything," he concluded. "There is a real impression that the whole show is going to crack up. This view is held, not only by protagonists like Winston, but by the silent useful members of whom nobody ever hears. They think that a new Government will emerge on a far wider basis, possibly a Coalition Government." Nicolson was two years — almost to the day — ahead of time.[172]

The RAF leadership, first under Sir Hugh ("Boom") Trenchard and then under Lord Weir, still held sacred the doctrine that "the bomber will always get through." Holding this principle sacred, Trenchard and Weir believed that Britain's only hope of survival lay in devastating retaliation against an enemy. Every RAF plan had called for two or three times as many bombers as fighter planes. Since bombers cost more, and required larger crews, both in the air and on the ground, the waste, in retrospect, is obvious. In the spring of 1938 Dowding's reply to this theory — radar and fast fighters to intercept hostile bombers — won acceptance. Before the shift could be reflected in the sky, however, Britain was confronted with a surplus of bombers and a scarcity of Spitfires and Hawker Hurricanes.

The imbalance, the loss of faith in their striking force of heavy bombers, wild exaggerations of Luftwaffe strength, and the deleterious implications of rationing on the service which most needed reequipment crippled RAF morale. It seemed at its lowest point in 1938, urged there by the most famous aviator of his time. Colonel Charles Lindbergh's impact had first begun to be felt in early 1936; he had just left Germany and was reappearing in London at the invitation of U.S. ambassador Joseph Kennedy, who squired him around as he shared his views with Chamberlain, his cabinet, Fleet Street, and virtually every other Briton who possessed power and made decisions. Göring, General Ernst Udet, and the rest of the Luftwaffe hierarchy had done a job on the Lone Eagle, but there had been more to it than that. Like many other visitors to Berlin, he and his wife had been impressed by the energy and self-confidence of the Führer and his people. She wrote: "There is no question of the power, unity, and purposefulness of Germany. It is terrific." Nothing they learned in subsequent visits to the Reich caused them to change that opinion. In April 1938 Lindbergh wrote in his diary: "England seems hopelessly behind in military strength in comparison to Germany" and "the assets in English character lie in confidence rather than ability; tenacity rather than strength; and determination rather than intelligence. . . . It is necessary to realize that England is a country composed of a great mass of slow, somewhat stupid and indifferent people, and a small group of geniuses."[173]

At the American embassy in September he told a select group of Englishmen, presumably those he would include among the geniuses (Kennedy had not invited Churchill), that they couldn't "realize the change aviation has made" and that "this is the beginning of the end of England as a great power." He thought that "German air strength is greater than that of all other European countries combined" and that "she is constantly increasing her margin of leadership." England and France, he believed, "are far too weak in the air to protect themselves. . . . It seems to me essential to avoid a general European war in the near future. I believe that a war now might easily result in the loss of European civilization."[174]

At Cliveden, where Lindbergh was guest of honor, Thomas Jones and Lord Astor said it was "necessary for England to fight if Germany moves into Czechoslovakia." The others, led by Nancy, shouted them down. Later Jones wrote that after reflecting upon what Lindbergh had said, "I've sided with those working for peace at any price in humiliation, because of the picture of our relative unpreparedness in the air and on the ground which Lindbergh painted, and because of his belief that the democracies would be crushed absolutely and finally."[175]

After Roosevelt had publicly branded him "defeatist," Lindbergh's prestige began to shrink, and when Wilhelmstrasse documents became available to historians during the war crimes trials at Nuremberg, his prewar evaluation of Nazi air strength was discredited. It is a measure of Lindbergh's prewar renown, however, that Roosevelt found it necessary to take such a step. In 1938 he was at his peak. A. L. Rowse recalls: "Great play in those days, I remember, was made of Lindbergh, treated as omniscient in air matters. . . . Dawson quoted Lindbergh to me: he was made much of by the Cliveden set." As Sheila Grant Duff reported to Churchill from central Europe, Lindbergh buttressed the German conviction that England "would be neutral if they attacked Czechoslovakia." On October 18, 1938, three weeks after the Munich Agreement, Hitler would decorate the American aviator with the highest award Germany could confer upon an *Ausländer* — the Service Cross of the German Eagle with Star — accompanied by a citation declaring that he "deserved well of the Reich." The Lone Eagle had earned his Nazi medal.[176]

❦   ❦

On Friday, May 6, when America's 1938 recession touched bottom and Churchill found his wallet empty, Lord Rothermere told readers of his *Daily Mail* that "Czechoslovakia is not of the slightest concern to us. If France likes to burn her fingers there, that is a matter for France." Bonnet, who was prone to nausea, read it over breakfast and became ill. On Saturday, May 7, French and British diplomats in Prague presented a formal demarche to Foreign Minister Krofta. Hitler already knew the gist of it; four days earlier Halifax had told the new German ambassador to the Court of St. James's, Herbert von Dirksen, that the demarche would "aim at inducing Beneš to show the utmost measure of accommodation to the Sudeten Germans." (The foreign secretary had not extended the same courtesy to Czechoslovakia's Ambassador Masaryk.) The Czechs were asked to make a "supreme effort" to go to "the utmost limit" to meet the Henlein demands of April 24, with the hope of reaching a "comprehensive and lasting settlement" with the Sudetendeutsche. Dirksen reported to the Wilhelmstrasse that Chamberlain and his government regarded the possibility of military action "doubtful," though the French, more optimistic, were ready to march.[177]

Henderson gave the Germans his personal view: "France is acting for the Czechs and Germany for the Sudeten Germans. Britain is supporting Germany." He "urgently hoped" that the Führer would "not refuse some kind of cooperation with Britain in this matter, which might then, perhaps, lead to cooperation in other matters also." Ribbentrop quickly replied that after this question was solved, the Reich would be *"durchtränkt"* — saturated.[178]

Any doubts about HMG's position were resolved by the prime minister. Lady Astor had given Chamberlain a luncheon on May 10; his fellow guests were American and Canadian foreign correspondents. The P.M. was accustomed to the deference of British newspapermen. He also put some of his remarks on the record and some off, a dangerous format, vulnerable to misunderstandings. On May 14 the *Montreal Star* and the *New York Times* broke the story, the *Star* reporting, "Nothing seems clearer than that the British do not expect to fight for Czechoslovakia. . . . That being so, then the Czechs must accede to the German demands, if reasonable." The *New York Times* man, formerly a diplomatic correspondent for *The Times*, went further: "Mr. Chamberlain today . . . certainly favors a more drastic measure — namely, separation of the German districts from the body of the Czechoslovak Republic and the annexation of them to Germany."[179]

The British press picked the story up. In less than a week the German embassy learned that the articles had been based on the P.M.'s remarks at Nancy Astor's luncheon. Dirksen advised Berlin that Chamberlain would approve of the Sudetenland's secession from Czechoslovakia, provided the wishes of the people were determined in a plebiscite "not interrupted by forcible measures on the part of Germany."

Hitler had hesitated to threaten Czechoslovakia. The Anschluss, he knew, had been much simpler. Austria had lacked allies and a strong military presence; nor did she have a defensive position which, if forfeited, would undermine Anglo-French security. Because the Czechs had all these, deliberate provocation of a crisis would risk a general European war or a humiliating withdrawal. Everything would depend on speed. He needed a fait accompli, before sympathy for the underdog mounted in the democracies, where public opinion counted, and the Russians seized the opportunity to become a European power through intervention. Hitler had wanted reassurance before he took such risks. And now he had it — from Britain.

Although Chamberlain had eased Hitler's doubts, the Führer had a backup plan. Colonel Malcolm Grahame Christie was an enigmatic figure similar to those found in Eric Ambler novels and Alfred Hitchcock films of the time. Educated in Germany and trained as an engineer, he had been a British fighter pilot in the last war and, afterward, an embassy attaché in Washington and Berlin, where he had become a friend of Göring. In 1930 he had retired from the RAF, ostensibly to become a businessman whose work required frequent trips to Germany. Actually, he was an intelligence officer gathering data on the Luftwaffe and the Reich's military plans.

Vansittart —kicked upstairs, but still serving the FO in an advisory role — was his control. When Van received a message from Henlein, asking for an interview, he asked Christie to make arrangements for him to visit London and return. If shown British resolve, Van reasoned, the Sudeten Germans might think twice before flouting Prague again. He seems not to have considered the possibility that Henlein, an ardent Nazi, might be acting on orders from Berlin.[180]

He was. On May 12, exactly two months after the Anschluss, he had stopped at Berlin on his way west, was admitted to the Foreign Ministry through a seldom-used door, and was ushered into the office of Baron von Weizsäcker, Ribbentrop's under secretary, for his final instructions. Most important, said Weizsäcker, would be British questions suggesting, or assuming, that he had been briefed by anyone in the government of the Third Reich, such as, say, Weizsäcker. Great weight was attached to his meeting with Churchill. The Führer believed that either Churchill or Eden would head the next government in England. Lastly, and this was a matter of judgment, he was expected to determine the temper of the men now in office. Were they as weak and incompetent as they seemed? Or was it all a trap? The Führer, himself a builder of traps, often thought he saw them in other countries, always with himself as their purported victim.[181]

Van minuted for the FO record afterward that as "it was impossible for members of the Government to see Herr Henlein lest some sort of negotiations be suspected, it was necessary to arrange that Herr Henlein should see not only myself but some persons of consequence in the House of Commons." Here Churchill was indispensable. The visitor wanted to sample British opinion; a meeting with Winston might persuade him that the British lion could still roar. Churchill, told of the plan, agreed to give Henlein a lunch at Morpeth Mansions. "His visit is being kept a secret," Winston wrote Archibald Sinclair. "His wish to come to London to see Van and a few others is a hopeful sign." The other guests were Sinclair, Christie, and the Prof, who served as interpreter and took notes.[182]

Henlein's theatrical talents were effective. They listened gravely, nodding in approval as he told them the excessive demands in his Karlsbad speech were not to be taken seriously; they were "bargaining points" from which he was "prepared to recede." He felt he was entitled to embrace the Nazi ideology but not "to impose it on others." Questioned over whether he might be used as a pawn in Hitler's *Drang nach Osten*, he swore on his word of honor that he had never received orders, or even "recommendations" ("*Weisungen*"), from Berlin. Asked whether he had claimed a veto power in Czechoslovakia's foreign policy, he vigorously denied it. Churchill wondered whether he realized that an incident in the Sudetenland "might easily set Europe alight" — that "if Germany marched," for example, "France would come in and England would follow."

Henlein replied that he had known that from the outset and had, in fact, avoided incitements, even when he "believed he was in the right." Looking ahead, he saw three paths: "Autonomy within the Czech State," a plebiscite which would probably lead to an Anschluss, and war. His followers, who were "impatient," preferred an Anschluss. If Prague ignored their appeals, they would ask Europe's great powers for a plebiscite "under international supervision."[183]

Police, railway, and postal workers in the Sudetenland would be required to speak German and the Sudeten Germans would be entitled to their own town and county governments, but "the frontier fortresses could be manned by Czech troops, who would, of course, have unhindered access thereto." As he left — not for his homeland, as his hosts assumed, but for Berchtesgaden, where he would report to Hitler — one of the others called out: "We hope you're not another Seyss-Inquart!" Over his shoulder he called back: "No chance of that!" Churchill immediately laid Henlein's terms before Jan Masaryk, who, as Winston later noted in his memoirs, "professed himself contented with a settlement on these lines." On May 16, three days after his luncheon for Henlein, Churchill told an audience in Bristol that he saw "no reason why the Sudetendeutsche should not become trusted and honored partners in what is, after all, the most progressive and democratic of the new States of Europe."[184]

Weizsäcker's coaching of Henlein — exploiting Britain's traditional championing of fair play — had been brilliant. The issue in Czechoslovakia had previously been depicted simply, as an unequal struggle in which the huge Reich was intimidating a plucky but outgunned neighbor. Now there was concern over a minority whose rights were being ignored or trammeled by insensitive Prague. In the Berghof, Henlein told Hitler that "no serious intervention in favor of the Czechs was to be feared from England or probably from France."[185]

The lunch in Morpeth Mansions had been on Friday, May 13, and Churchill had spoken in support of Henlein on the following Monday. Now, on Wednesday, a Leipzig newspaper published an account of Wehrmacht assault divisions moving into position on the Czech frontier. Thursday the British consulate in Dresden reported that there was "strong reason to believe that German troops are concentrating in southern Silesia and northern Austria." Later in the day a similar report arrived from Bavaria, together with a cable from Henderson adding: "My French colleague has also heard rumors of concentration of troops on the [Czech] frontier." The following day Krofta, alarmed, phoned Ernst Eisenlohr, the German minister in Prague, to protest; on his desk were several reports, each confirming the others, of heavy German troop concentrations in Saxony. Thus the stage was set for the May crisis.[186]

Czech municipal elections were to be held on Sunday. Since Henlein's return the Sudetenland had been chaotic. Gangs of Sudetendeutsche youths wearing swastika brassards had attacked neighbors of Slavic descent, marched through streets carrying torches, and held rallies which culminated in chants of *"Sieg Heil!"* and *"Wir wollen heim ins Reich!"* ("We want to go home to the Reich!"). Goebbels, meantime, had stepped up his denunciation of "Czech terror." The parallels with Austria were unmistakable. Any incident might touch off an invasion, and Friday, May 20, one made to order occurred when two Sudeten German motorcyclists were shot dead after ignoring a Czech policeman's whistle. After an emergency cabinet meeting in Hradschin Palace, President Beneš approved an urgent recommendation of the Czech General Staff, calling up reservists and specialist troops to man the Sudetenland garrisons.

In Berlin Ribbentrop heatedly denied hostile Wehrmacht concentrations, but when Eisenlohr and his military attaché called on General Ludvik Krejcí, the Czech chief of staff, they were shown an impressive collection of what he called "irrefutable evidence that in Saxony a concentration of from eight to ten divisions has taken place," with another twelve on the Czech frontier "ready to march within twelve hours." All the pieces of what had seemed a puzzle were falling into place. Krejcí's army believed it could hold the Wehrmacht in check long enough for France, Britain, and the Russians to intervene, provided its fortress line was manned and ready. The country would, however, be particularly vulnerable to a surprise attack by Nazi forces assembled and deployed under what Beneš's General Staff called "the guise of training purposes."[187]

"Training" was indeed the explanation the German high command (OKW) gave Weizsäcker, who passed it on to a skeptical world. But for once it was true. The Wehrmacht wasn't ready. A scrupulous examination of OKW and German foreign policy documents at Nuremberg after the war revealed that there had been no aggressive concentrations in Silesia or Austria that May. The OKW's statement that the Nazi troops along the Czech border were assembled for "peacetime maneuvers" was accurate. To foreigners the number of German soldiers near the frontier would have been disquieting, but such numbers could be seen nearly anywhere in the Reich. Germany had become a highly militarized nation; its economy was on a war footing. Hitler did intend to invade Beneš's country. And these were the soldiers who would form the point of his spearhead. But not yet.

In the spring of 1938, however, the truth was unknown. In Paris and London the men responsible for crucial decisions had every reason to believe that Hitler might be poised to unleash another bolt of lightning from his aerie above Berchtesgaden. Daladier staked out the French position by inviting the German ambassador to his home and speaking "frankly as a French ex-serviceman to his German comrade," warning him that should Hitler invade Czechoslovakia "the French would have to fight as they did not wish to be dishonored," and that the result could be the utter destruction of European civilization. Halifax, out of character but acting in the finest tradition of British diplomacy, sent the unhappy Henderson to the Wilhelmstrasse twice with personal messages from him to Ribbentrop. In the first he declared that "His Majesty's Government could not guarantee that they would not be forced by circumstances to become involved" if France, following her treaty obligations, intervened. The second note warned that if the Nazis resorted to force, "it is quite impossible for me to foretell results that might follow, and I would beg him not to count on this country being able to stand aside."[188]

Now there was no way Germany could avoid an enormous loss of face. Because the Wehrmacht was unprepared, Hitler could not attack, and since he did not, the Allies concluded that he had backed down. That was Churchill's interpretation. The Czechs, he wrote in the *Daily Telegraph* of June 23, had seemed doomed "to be swallowed whole by Berlin and reduced to shapeless pulp by the close-grinding mandibles of the Gestapo." Now Hitler knew Czechoslovakia would not "be left to struggle week after week against an avalanche of fire and steel."

Churchill thought the incident a triumph for England, but His Majesty's Government did not see it that way. For men who had presumably won a victory of diplomacy, they took no heart from it. In fact, they were badly frightened. Still convinced that the Germans had been intent on military action, they thought of the peril they had skirted and mopped their brows. Chamberlain wrote his sisters: "The more I hear about last weekend, the more I feel what a damned close run thing it was." In another letter to them, he wrote, "The Germans, who are bullies by nature, are too conscious of their strength and our weakness, and until we are as strong as they are" (which, if his defense policies were unaltered, would be never) "we shall always be kept in a state of chronic anxiety." After reviewing the cable traffic, Halifax and Cadogan vowed never again to approach the brink and, accordingly, sent Paris a telegram warning the French not to be "under any illusion" about the possibility of British help "against German aggression."[189]

The May crisis had arisen from a misunderstanding; if the Führer had been a sane man, he would have counted himself lucky to be out of it. Hitler, not sane, personifying the underside of the Teutonic character and four horrible years which had ended in the defeat, not just of Germany, but of *him,* saw a wrong crying for redemption. The fact that he had been planning the invasion of Czechoslovakia — that the only real misunderstanding in May had been over timing — somehow made it worse. "Injustice is relatively easy to bear," wrote Mencken. "What stings is justice." On May 28 the Führer suddenly appeared in Berlin and summoned the hierarchies of the OKW, the party, and the government to the chancellery. His voice still choking with rage, he said that the Sudeten question would be solved "once and for all, and radically." Preparations for military action must be completed by October 2, the Siegfried Line would be extended by workers toiling around the clock, and ninety-six divisions were mobilized immediately. The execution of *Fall Grün* "must be assured by October 1, 1938, at the latest." In his hoarse, staccato delivery, his voice sounding like a bearing about to go, he roared: *"Es ist mein unerschütterlicher Wille, die Tschechoslowakei von der Landkarte auszulöschen!"* ("It is my unshakable will to wipe Czechoslovakia off the map!").[190]

Churchill, unaware of Hitler's resolution, shared a fresh sense of relief with his *Daily Telegraph* readers on July 6. The Anschluss, he had decided on reflection, was not the Nazi triumph it had seemed to be. At the time, he recalled, he had told Parliament that

after a boa-constrictor has devoured a goat or a deer it usually sleeps the sleep of repletion for several months. It may, however, happen that this agreeable process is disturbed by indigestion. . . . If the prey has not been sufficiently crushed or covered with slime beforehand, especially if it has been swallowed horns and all, very violent spasms, accompanied by writhings and contortions, retchings and gaspings, are suffered by the great snake. These purely general zoological observations . . . suggest a parallel — no doubt very remote — to what has happened since Austria was incorporated into the German Reich.

Extrapolating from "a continuous stream of trustworthy information" he said that the German Nazis were bedeviled by "Jews in very large numbers . . . Catholics by the million . . . Monarchists faithful to a Hapsburg restoration . . . strong Socialist and Left-wing elements in every working-class district . . . numerous remnants of what was once the high society of the Austro-Hungarian Empire." There was also, in Austria, "the strongest and the only covert resistance to the Nazification" which "oddly enough" came from the "Austrian Nazis who were the prime cause and pretext of the invasion." Churchill was delighted to describe their fury at finding themselves "excluded from all positions of power, profit, and control," and their resulting rebellion.

By custom, newspaper columnists are entitled to an occasional romp in fantasy, and Churchill's optimistic picture of the Austrian situation was, unfortunately, that. On the whole, Churchill was a highly reliable journalist. His innumerable informants assured the accuracy of his information, at least eventually. In his *Daily Telegraph* piece of July 6 he was, however, guilty of another lapse, flagrant now but invisible at the time. "A settlement and reconciliation in Czechoslovakia would be no humiliation to Herr Hitler," he wrote. The Führer could take pride in having won for the Sudeten Germans "honorable status and a rightful place in the land of their birth," reforms which would have "strengthened rather than shaken the foundations of European peace." Churchill had been Konrad Henlein's mark in a kind of diplomatic confidence game, generating Churchillian warnings to Prague over its treatment of the restless citizens in the Sudetenland and this mild assessment of Hitler's goals. As late as July 26, Churchill was still lecturing Prague, writing in the *Daily Telegraph* that "The Czech Government owe it to the Western Powers that every concession compatible with the sovereignty and integrity of their State shall be made, and made promptly." Englishmen who demanded that "Germany not stir up strife beyond her border" should, to be consistent, offer "no encouragement to obduracy on the part of a small state."

In midsummer Sheila Grant Duff put Churchill straight. She wrote him of "the use which the Germans and Sudeten Germans are making of your words and actions. They claim to have your support against the Czechs and this is used by the more extreme to force the more moderate to raise their claims." She reminded Winston that Henlein had "shown himself to be most moderate in his conversation with you and that he had told you that the fulfillment of *all* his Carlsbad [*sic*] demands was not the necessary condition of agreement with the Czechs." But, "since his return to Prague," she wrote, "he has in fact raised his original demands." She believed Churchill was "the one British statesman of whom the Germans are afraid. If you are conciliated, they consider that they can expect much greater support from the British Government, whom they think are afraid. . . . Henlein is much more radical since he saw you." Indeed he was. Under great pressure from Halifax, Beneš offered the Sudetens "cantonal self-government" — a concession far exceeding the Sudeten German leader's most extravagant hopes when he had laid his case before Churchill in Morpeth Mansions. His followers rejoiced, but after conferring with Hitler at Berchtesgaden, Henlein rejected the offer, insisting on full independence, including sovereignty over the Czech fortress line in the Sudeten Mountains.[191]

Churchill's informants continued to be of a much higher caliber than the government's. Men unavailable to any other correspondent came to Chartwell to be interviewed by him. As early as July 14, 1938, less than eight weeks after the May crisis and a year before Hitler got round to Poland, Winston interrogated Albert Förster, *Gauleiter* (Nazi district leader) of Danzig and the Führer's man, in his sitting room. Many of Chartwell's visitors came at grave personal risk, though none graver than Major Ewald von Kleist-Schmenzin.

On August 18, 1938, Major von Kleist, in mufti, registered incognito at the Park Lane Hotel and was driven to Kent by Frank Jenner, the Westerham taxi driver. As the German talked, Randolph took notes; his father listened and interrupted from time to time with comments and questions. Kleist described an attack on Czechoslovakia as "imminent." He believed it would come between the annual Nazi rally at Nuremberg in the first week of September and the end of the month. "Nobody in Germany," Randolph's notes read, "wants war except H." The generals were for peace, "convinced that an attack upon Czechoslovakia would involve Germany in war with France and Britain." They were prepared to disobey the Führer, even overthrow him, but needed "a little encouragement." Churchill replied that though many Englishmen were unprepared to advocate war "in cold blood," few would "stand by idly once the fighting started." He emphasized that he and those who shared his view on this point were "anti-Nazi and anti-war but not anti-German." Kleist replied that he would share this message with his friends and colleagues but would welcome some gesture, even from "private members of Parliament," to help consolidate the "universal anti-war sentiment in Germany." After Kleist departed Chartwell, his host consulted Halifax, and when Kleist left London on August 23, he carried with him a letter signed by Churchill declaring that the crossing of the Czech frontier by German troops or warplanes "in force" would mean the renewal of the world war, which would be fought out "to the bitter end," with all the nations engaged in the struggle fighting on "for victory or death."[192]

When Winston received information that could not be published, he usually sent it to men in power. Usually they disregarded it. Kleist could have been invaluable, but when a summary of his message reached the prime minister, Chamberlain waved it away, saying, "I take it that von Kleist is violently anti-Hitler and is extremely anxious to stir up his friends in Germany to make an attempt at its [*sic*] overthrow. He reminds me of the Jacobites at the Court of France in King William's time, and I think we must discount a good deal of what he says."[193]

Like Churchill, who also traveled armed now, Hitler worried that before he could play out his role in history "something might happen" to him. It would be tragic, he told his generals, if, after so much toil in so just a cause, the war were to be fought without him. He knew they were worried about war on two fronts, and so on June 18, when he had drawn up his final directive for the invasion of Czechoslovakia, he had assured Field Marshal Wilhelm Keitel, chief of the OKW, that he would sign the order to march "only if I am firmly convinced, as in the case of the [Rhineland] demilitarized zone and the entry into Austria, that France will not march, and that therefore England will not intervene."[194]

Keitel was a lickspittle, but other OKW commanders were not reassured. On June 12 Daladier had renewed France's 1924 guarantee of Czech borders, saying it was "sacred and cannot be evaded." The commanders were depressed further by Kleist's failure in August in England; the letter Churchill had given Kleist had been invigorating, but he was out of power and likely to remain there. Hitler therefore gave his General Staff additional grounds for concern at the Kummersdorf Proving Ground, delivering one of his fulsome autopanegyrics: "Fortune must be seized when she strikes, for she will not come again! . . . I predict that by the end of the year we will be looking back at a great success!" The Siegfried Line, growing stronger with each passing hour, could hold the French and British in check, if it came to that, while they and their men overran Czechoslovakia. The man who couldn't hold the line against odds was "a scoundrel." At this point Major Helmuth Groscurth, an intelligence officer, scribbled in his diary that the Führer was spouting *"völliger Unsinn"* ("total nonsense").[195]

Europe's statesmen, if frozen in time during that late summer and early fall period in 1938, would resemble characters in a grotesque Friedrich Dürrenmatt play, each acting on assumptions the others would find startling or even preposterous. In Paris the prospect of another great war dismays Daladier, but he has faith in his British ally and the greatness of his army, and the mere suggestion that France might break her word is unthinkable. Bonnet, who breaks his own word almost daily, thinks of little else. In London His Majesty's Government still dreams of scuttling France and forming a new alliance with the Germans. Many powerful Germans would like to reciprocate, but only one of them counts and he is demented. He has told Keitel that the Western democracies won't fight, but even he doesn't believe it, and neither does the chief of the German General Staff, General Ludwig Beck, who resigns on August 27. Unless one shares the Führer's superstitious belief in intuition, his plans are ludicrous. In Beck's words, he has put himself in an "untenable position." William L. Shirer will write: "Germany was in no position to go to war on October 1, 1938" — the date Hitler had set, and would cling to — "against Czechoslovakia *and* France and Britain. . . . Had she done so, she would have been quickly and easily defeated, and that would have been the end of Hitler and the Third Reich."[196]

It wouldn't even have gone that far. Conspirators in the OKW would have intervened. At Nuremberg eight years later Field Marshal Keitel was asked to describe the Generalstab's reaction to Chamberlain's Munich sellout, and replied: "We were extraordinarily happy [*ausserordentlich glücklich*] that it had not come to a military operation because . . . we had always been of the opinion that our means of attack against the frontier fortifications of Czechoslovakia were insufficient." General Franz Halder, interrogated by an American officer toward the end of the Nuremberg trials, testified that the Czech issue inspired the German generals' plot against Hitler. Had the Führer ordered the attack in 1938, he said, "It had been planned to occupy by military force the Reich Chancellery and those government offices, particularly ministries, which were administered by party members and close supporters of Hitler, with the express intention of avoiding bloodshed and then trying the group before the whole German nation."[197]

Meanwhile, the Czechs, trusting their formidable defenses and their two fellow democracies in the west, were ready for anything — anything, that is, except betrayal by those two. The Poles and the Hungarians were plotting ignobly; if the Germans took part of Czechoslovakia, they wanted some, too. In Rome, Mussolini imagined that the others were wondering which way he would pounce. Actually, they weren't thinking of him at all. Since the Ethiopian fiasco the Duce's legions had been heavily discounted.

But what of the Russians? The fate of Czechoslovakia had the highest strategic consequences for the Soviet Union. If Hitler seized the Sudeten-land and the Czech fortifications, the Soviets would lose the outer bastion of their defense system. Hitler understood that; he called Beneš's country "the Soviet Russian Aircraft Carrier." The Foreign Office in Whitehall was aware of these implications; its career diplomats had repeatedly urged their political overseers to open "conversations" with the Russians, but although Litvinov had been trying to shoulder his way into an anti-Nazi alliance since the fall of Austria, the appeasers kept pretending the U.S.S.R. didn't exist.[198]

One incident reveals how far certain men in London and in France would go to stifle an alliance with the Soviet Union. Speaking to the French chargé d'affaires in Moscow, Litvinov proposed "immediate staff talks between the Soviet, French and Czech experts." Bonnet buried the chargé's report in a locked file and mentioned it to no one. Two days later he misled the British ambassador in Paris, telling him that the Rumanians would not permit Russian warplanes to violate their air space in support of the Czechs. But the secretary general at the Quai, the incorruptible Alexis Léger, had already informed Phipps that permission *would* be granted. Despite Bonnet, the facts reached R. A. Butler, Halifax's young new under secretary, who promptly spiked them, remarking, "Let us hope no more will come of this idea."[199]

Churchill prayed that something *would*. Hitler had massed at least 1.5 million soldiers on Czechoslovakia's borders and Churchill felt Russia's help was essential. On the last day of August he wrote Halifax to advise delivery of "a joint note" to Hitler from Britain, France, and Russia expressing their "desire for peace," their "deep anxiety at the military preparations of Germany," their common interest in "a peaceful solution of the Czechoslovak controversy," and their conviction that "an invasion by Germany of Czechoslovakia would raise capital issues." Ambassadors for the three powers, he said, should hand the note to President Roosevelt, "and we should use every effort to induce him to do his utmost upon it." To Winston it seemed "not impossible" that the president "would then address H. emphasising the gravity of the situation . . . saying that a world war would inevitably follow from an invasion of Czechoslovakia, and that he earnestly counselled a friendly settlement." The "peaceful elements in German official circles" — and no one in the Foreign Office was more aware of their strength — would "make a stand," forcing the Führer to "find a way out for himself by parleying with Roosevelt." This sequence of events was conjectural, Churchill granted; "one only sees them as hopes." But any hope was better than none.[200]

He drove to Whitehall and handed his letter to Halifax, who went across Downing Street to No. 10. There, like every other communication to the prime minister, including those bearing the royal seal, it came under the shifty eyes of Sir Horace Wilson. At his peak Rasputin was known to all Moscow. Wilson was more like one of the burrowing insectivores. A nation in peril, with hundreds of thousands of lives in jeopardy, does not refuse to answer the doorbell when a well-muscled neighbor, feeling his own future darkened by the same shadow, comes to make common cause. But that, in effect, was Horace Wilson's advice to his patron. When Churchill's proposal reached Chamberlain, attached to it was an admonition in his seneschal's neat handwriting condemning it in every particular. Wilson described it as "a mixture of diplomacy and threat" which would enrage Hitler by including Russia in the coalition confronting him. He predicted that if Winston's proposal were adopted, England would be carried closer to a situation in which "we might find ourselves . . . tackling Germany single-handed" — which was, of course, the one thing it would *not* have done.[201]

Winston, meantime, was receiving confirmation that his plan would have had a warmer reception elsewhere. On September 2 the Russian ambassador sent Chartwell word that he would like to drive down and discuss "a matter of urgency." Maisky's mission was to inform him of conversations which had taken place in Moscow the previous day between the French chargé d'affaires and Foreign Commissar Litvinov, the essence of which was that the Soviet Union wanted to stand shoulder to shoulder with the British and French against Hitler. Churchill later recalled: "Before he had got very far, I realized that he was making a declaration to me, a private person, because the Soviet Government preferred this channel to a direct offer to the Foreign Office which might have encountered a rebuff." He felt this implication strengthened, he wrote after the Russian had left, "by the fact that no request for secrecy was made." Considering the matter of signal importance, Winston composed a detailed account of the conversation for Halifax, taking special care not to use language which might "prejudice its consideration by Halifax and Chamberlain." This report, too, was received unenthusiastically by HMG; Halifax replied, Winston later wrote, "in a guarded manner, that he did not feel that action of the kind proposed . . . would be helpful, but that he would keep it in mind."[202]

Nonetheless, when Churchill's August 31 proposal was returned to the Foreign Office with Wilson's comment endorsed by Chamberlain, Halifax had been uneasy. If Hitler was Britain's enemy, then so was time; the government should make some clear statement of policy before the Reich chancellor delivered another of his incendiary speeches to the Reichstag, touching off rioting among Henlein's Sudeten Nazis. To restore order Prague would be obliged to use force; Hitler would rant about Czech police brutality, and the cycle would be repeated again, until a single swing of an impatient policeman's club could bring the Wehrmacht surging across the border. Therefore, the foreign secretary decided he himself should speak, establishing Britain's disapproval of Sudeten German incidents. He sent his text across the street, and back it came, with its own Wilson critique embellished by the prime minister's approval.

Wilson liked this even less than Winston's. He declared that "any intelligent journalist . . . could draw but one deduction, namely that we were threatening Germany." Patiently, Halifax sent over a new draft. Chamberlain himself commented on this one, and he could find nothing good to say about it. One paragraph was sure to "draw protests from the Dominions," another was "clearly a threat"; all in all it was "out of place till after Nuremberg." The whole point of it had been to put His Majesty's Government on record *before* the Führer's annual diatribe at the Nazis' September rally. Ambassadors Henderson and Newton were also critical, and Halifax wrote Henderson that he had "more or less given up the idea of making a public speech."[203]

Others, even champions of the new Germany, shared his concern.

Henderson reported that Ribbentrop believed England would not "move under any circumstances," and Under Secretary Weizsäcker had pointedly remarked that "war in 1914 might possibly have been avoided if Great Britain had spoken in time." In a general FO discussion on September 4, support grew for what one participant called "a *private* warning" to the Führer, a plain statement "that we should have to come in to protect France." Cadogan thought this had merit because "Hitler has probably been persuaded that our March and May statements are bluff, and that's dangerous." Yet nothing was done. They drifted.[204]

British policy had evolved subtly since late March, when the prime minister had barred commitments to, or even concern over, political events in Europe. Chamberlain was now concentrating on two objectives which were mutually exclusive: establishing a special relationship with the Reich and, at the same time, preserving England's longtime friendship with France. Together they were impossible, but *some* tie with the Continent was necessary. Otherwise England was merely an island country off the Continent's coast, at the mercy of any dominant continental power. So now, when Lord Maugham, Somerset Maugham's brother, said that "no vital British interest is involved" in the Sudetenland, Duff Cooper fiercely reminded him that "the main interest of this country has always been to prevent any one power from obtaining undue predominance in Europe," that in Nazi Germany they faced "the most formidable power that has ever dominated Europe," and that resistance to power "is quite obviously a British interest." No one in the cabinet disagreed. Yet as the crisis escalated, no statement of policy was made, publicly or through private diplomatic channels.[205]

The one British voice which had been heard through the summer was Geoffrey Dawson's. On June 3, in his lead editorial he had pondered the advisability of permitting "the Germans of Czechoslovakia — by plebiscite or otherwise — to decide their own future, even if it should mean secession to the Reich." Indeed, he wondered whether it might be sensible to allow other minorities inside the country to take the same course. It would be, he acknowledged, "a drastic remedy for the present unrest, but something drastic may be needed."

Drastic was not the word; it would be catastrophic. The nation Beneš and Masaryk had founded was a polyglot state, a reflection, in microcosm, of the Austro-Hungarian Empire from which it had derived. Within its borders were communities of Czechs, Slovaks, Germans, Magyars, Ruthenians, Poles, and Bohemians. That hardly meant that it was doomed. Dawson was writing *völliger Unsinn*. But many Europeans had once more concluded that *The Times* was the voice of Downing Street, and as September 1938 opened, no spokesman of His Majesty's Government denied this. Since no one in Whitehall was making foreign policy, a newspaper editor had done it.

The prime minister was assigning greater priority to an exercise in personal diplomacy.

❦   ❦

There is something almost touching about Neville Chamberlain's faith in his cherished Plan Z, a simple scheme, redolent of those *Chatterbox* volumes in which the Chamberlain boys, like so many young Victorians of their class, had lost themselves on long Saturday afternoons when there were no playmates and Nanny was busy elsewhere. Pen-and-ink drawings identified the handsome, mesomorphic heroes, the helpless but winning heroines, and the scowling ruffians doomed, in issue after issue, to be foiled in the last paragraph. And how had they been outwitted? By Plan Z! Or Plan X, or Q, or whatever — a simple ruse, harmless to others but fatal for the wicked. The first we know of its reappearance in the mind of Neville, grown up and grown old, is a memorandum by Sir Horace Wilson, written after the adjournment of a cabinet meeting on August 30, 1938. He and the prime minister had discussed the matter two or three days earlier, and now he wrote: "There is in existence a plan, to be called 'Plan Z,' which is known only to the Prime Minister, the Chancellor of the Exchequer, the Foreign Secretary, Sir Nevile Henderson and myself."[206]

The procedure's success, he continued, depended upon "its being a complete surprise, and it is vital nothing should be said about it." A second Wilson memorandum, filed the following day, gives the whole thing away: "On being told that Plan Z is emerging, Henderson will ascertain where Hitler is, but will not say why he wants to know." If time permitted, HM's ambassador in Berlin would receive another message indicating time of arrival; he would pass this along to Ribbentrop. Again, time permitting, "we would like to do this before we make public announcement here that Plan Z has been put into operation. Place of arrival must be Berlin connecting with Henderson and Ribbentrop. (Schmidt is reliable.)"[207]

Wilson's emphasis on time is subject to but one interpretation; the plan anticipated a supreme crisis, with a German invasion of Czechoslovakia imminent — perhaps but a few hours away. The need to know Hitler's whereabouts, and the reference to Paul Otto Schmidt, the Führer's personal interpreter, contemplated a surprise call on him — uninvited, with no prior arrangements. Presumably the P.M. planned to land in Germany and tell wide-eyed Germans, "Take me to your leader," though that would have been difficult because he, like Hitler, spoke only his native language.

On September 3 Chamberlain wrote his sister Ida: "I keep racking my brains to try and devise some means of averting catastrophe, if it should seem to be upon us. I thought of one so unconventional and daring that it rather took Halifax's breath away. But since Henderson thought it might save the situation at the 11th hour, I haven't abandoned it, though I hope all the time that it won't be necessary to try it." If, as Horace Wilson had written, success of the operation depended upon "complete secrecy," its chances were slim, since Henderson was notorious for sharing confidences with his Nazi friends Göring and Ribbentrop. The circle of those informed widened; Hoare and Simon were also told of it. No one remembered that it was illegal for a prime minister to leave the country without the King's permission, but the matter of cabinet approval arose. It was, they decided, unnecessary. Chamberlain's power to commit his country was beginning to rival Hitler's.[208]

The year which had begun with Vansittart's dismissal and Eden's resignation had now reached the first lovely week of September, and if the Wilhelmstrasse of 1914 had been confused by England's intentions, the Nazi generation was utterly baffled. The Quai d'Orsay had made it as clear as diplomats can that the French would fight if the Czech frontier were ruptured, and Britain was France's ally. Yet, after a long cabinet meeting in Downing Street, Henderson told Ribbentrop that "the Sudeten Germans and the Czechs are a matter of complete indifference to Great Britain. Great Britain is only concerned with the attitude of France."[209]

It was time to read *The Times* again. It is in keeping with the bizarre patterns of the Big Czech Crisis, now looming, that the author of the paper's September 7 leader has never been identified. Dawson would spend the rest of his life explaining that he had returned late from his country weekend, insisting that he didn't reach the office until late Tuesday afternoon, September 6. He read an incomplete draft of an editorial on Czechoslovakia, cut a paragraph, ordered it rewritten, and, apparently exhausted by this effort, left for dinner. Returning at 11:45 P.M. he had misgivings. A Francophile colleague, solicited for advice, urged further surgery. It would have been more useful, for those who wanted to avoid another great war, if they had burned every copy of the paper and then burned the building. One paragraph, in the words of Martin Gilbert, "gave its support to what was, in effect, the extreme Henlein position, unacceptable not only to Beneš, but also to that large number of Sudeten Germans for whom union with Germany would mean the loss of all liberty, swift imprisonment, forced labour, and death." It ran:

If the Sudetens now ask for more than the Czech Government are ready to give . . . it can only be inferred that the Germans are going beyond the mere removal of disabilities for those who do not find themselves at ease within the Czechoslovak Republic. In that case it might be worth while for the Czechoslovak Government to consider whether they should exclude altogether the project, which has found favour in some quarters, of making Czechoslovakia a more homogeneous state by the cession of that fringe of alien populations who are contiguous to the nation to which they are united by race.[210]

Considering the unique relationship between *The Times* and the government, it would be difficult to find a more irresponsible passage in the history of journalism. The unknown author — his identity shielded by Dawson, who either wrote it himself or knew who did — betrayed a staggering ignorance of geography, history, and both the ethnic diversity and range of political persuasions of the people living in the shadow of the Sudeten Mountains. As Churchill wrote the following day, in a letter which Dawson refused to publish, *The Times*'s proposal "would have the effect of handing over to the German Nazis the whole of the mountain defence line which marks the ancient boundaries of Bohemia, and was specially preserved to the Czechoslovak State as a vital safeguard of its national existence." German propaganda had created the impression that everyone living in the Sudetenland was German, and that Henlein was their spokesman. Neither was true; four other political parties strongly opposed his Sudetendeutsche Nazis, and at least a quarter-million voters were German fugitives from the Third Reich. Like their Austrian comrades in terror, they knew that the names of their leaders were on Gestapo lists. For them, the *Times* editorial was at the very least the first draft of a death warrant.[211]

Jan Masaryk had to pay two visits to Whitehall that morning before the Foreign Office agreed to announce that the *Times* proposal "in no way represents the view of His Majesty's Government." By then every capital in Europe was convinced that it did. In Blackpool the Labour party's National Executive issued a formal statement declaring that "the British Government must leave no doubt that they will unite with the French and Soviet Governments to resist any attack on Czechoslovakia." Halifax agreed — he was vacillating, not for the last time, on the Czech issue, and like many appeasers he was occasionally discomfited by flecks of doubt about the wisdom of endlessly yielding to Hitler's demands.[212]

By now the Czech border was swarming with German assault troops, and London knew that this time they weren't there for maneuvers. Theodor Kordt, the chargé d'affaires at the German embassy in the absence of Dirksen, had arrived in Downing Street the night of September 6 and entered No. 10 through the garden gate and the Horse Guards Parade. There he told Horace Wilson, and then Halifax, who came hurrying over from the FO, that he had come, "putting conscience before loyalty," as "a spokesman for political and military circles in Berlin who desire by every means to prevent war." He and his associates wanted a blunt warning that England would fight for the Czechs. "Hitler," he said, had "taken his decision to 'march in' on the nineteenth or twentieth."[213]

Kordt was confirmed by an equally sensational development. Dr. Karl Burckhardt of the League of Nations had given the British ambassador in Berne a message from Weizsäcker, second only to Ribbentrop in the Wilhelmstrasse, confirming Kordt in every particular and underscoring the need to warn the Führer that the invasion of Czechoslovakia meant war. Halifax, with Chamberlain's reluctant approval, drafted a sharply worded note for delivery to the German government: if the Czech frontier were breached France would declare war on Germany, touching off "a sequence of events" resulting in "a general conflict from which Great Britain could not stand aside." But Ambassador Henderson — who had no authority whatever to pass judgment on the foreign secretary's instructions — refused to deliver the note, on the ground that it would only inflame the Führer. Besides, he said, he had already made the British position "as clear as daylight to people who count." With this assurance, and because of the difficulty of communicating with Henderson, who was living aboard a train for five days while he attended the Nuremberg rally, Halifax, "on understanding that you have in fact already conveyed to Herr von Ribbentrop . . . [the] substance of what you were instructed to say," agreed that Henderson need make no further representation.[214]

Precisely what His Majesty's ambassador to the Reich may have said to Ribbentrop is unrecorded; but the SS officer who served as Henderson's escort at Nuremberg later said that during his stay he "remarked with a sigh that Great Britain was now having to pay for her guilty part in the Treaty of Versailles" and "expressed his aversion to the Czechs in very strong terms."[215]

On the third day after the *Times* editorial, Göring spoke to the vast, hysterical mass at Nuremberg, calling the Czechs a "miserable pygmy race . . . oppressing a cultured people" and fronting for "Moscow and the eternal mask of the Jew Devil." The Führer's turn at the rostrum came, as always, on the last night of the rally, Monday, September 12. Bathed in spotlights, pausing after each scream of invective as the huge, packed stadium roared, "*Sieg Heil! Sieg Heil! Sieg Heil!*" he shouted his distorted version of the May crisis, raging at the recollection of Germany's humiliation then, which he blamed on Beneš and his "Jew plotters." Sweating till his cowlick was plastered across his forehead, he called Czechoslovakia a "monstrous formation" and demanded that the Sudetendeutsche be granted the "right of self-determination" and "justice" ("*Gerechtigkeit*"), adding in a flash of arrogation: "Germans of Austria know best how bitter a thing it is to be separated from the Fatherland. They will be the first to recognize the significance of what I have been saying today." They would indeed. And so would Winston Churchill. According to the cabinet minutes, Halifax reported that he and the prime minister had seen Churchill on the previous day (Sunday), and said that "Mr. Churchill's proposition was that we should tell Germany that if she set foot in Czechoslovakia we should at once be at war with her. Mr. Churchill agreed that this line of action was an advance on the line of action which he had proposed two or three weeks earlier, but he thought that by taking it we should incur no added risk."[216]

Yet while Winston saw an Anschluss replay thundering toward them, the edgy cabinets in Paris and London, listening to Hitler's Nuremberg speech over radios, heard only wind. They awaited what the FO called "triggers," vows and demands which could only be resolved by German bayonets slashing toward Prague. Since the Führer was unspecific, however, the prime minister, the premier, and their ministers felt relieved. Misunderstanding him and his genius, they erred. This was his milieu, and he knew, as they did not, that his wild gestures and mindless raving were enough to set off bloody rioting in the Sudetenland. Prague declared martial law and rushed in convoys of troops. *"SCHRECKENHERRSCHAFT!"* ("REIGN OF TERROR") shrieked *Der Angriff*, and Henlein fled into Germany. Then, abruptly, the storm ended. Thursday morning everything in the Sudetenland was normal.[217]

At No. 10 Downing Street and the Paris home of the French premier, things were not. Premier Daladier wired Chamberlain, proposing that France, Britain, and Germany convene for a discussion *à trois*. But the P.M. had anticipated him. With the Sudetenland rioting approaching its peak, Chamberlain decided the time for Plan Z had arrived. Bypassing Henderson, he cabled Hitler during the night of September 13 that in the light of "the increasingly critical situation I propose to come over at once to see you with a view to trying to find a peaceful solution." He intended to fly, could "start tomorrow," asked for the "earliest time" they might meet and "a very early reply." Chamberlain was eager. And anxious. It was the sort of mood that sales clerks recognize in the customer who has decided to buy even before entering the store, and to pay any price.[218]

Churchill's *Daily Telegraph* column of September 15 predicted bloodshed; the Czechs, he wrote, possessed "an absolute determination to fight for life and freedom." If not "daunted by all the worry and pressure to which they have been subjected," they would inflict 300,000 or 400,000 casualties, but the world would hold them blameless. It was German aggression which would be condemned; "from the moment that the first shot is fired and the German troops attempt to cross the Czechoslovakian frontier, the whole scene will be transformed, and a roar of fury will arise from the free peoples of the world, which will proclaim nothing less than a crusade against the aggressor."

He could still sound his bugle, but the rest of the orchestra was following a different score. In the Foreign Office, Oliver Harvey wrote: "British press receives news of PM's visit with marked approval. City is much relieved. Reaction in Germany also one of relief. In America it looks as if it were regarded as surrender. Winston says it is the stupidest thing that has ever been done." Churchill knew what the prime minister was planning. He had learned that nearly a year earlier Chamberlain had written what he really wanted to tell the Nazis: "Give us satisfactory assurance that you won't use force to deal with the Austrians and Czecho- slovakians and we will give you similar assurance that we won't use force to prevent the changes you want, if you can get them by peaceful means." Declining Lord Moyne's invitation to join him on a Caribbean cruise, Winston wrote: "Alas, a cloud of uncertainty overhangs all plans at the present time. . . . We seem to be very near the bleak choice between War and Shame. My feeling is that we shall choose Shame, and then have War thrown in a little later on even more adverse terms than at present."[219]

The prime minister, of course, saw matters differently. In his eyes the choice lay between peace and devastation, and he saw nothing shameful in buying peace by coercing a pretentious little state on the far side of Germany. Late in life R. A. Butler, who had watched him prepare for his historic trip, described his mood as "exalted." Some Britons were worried by the loss of a strong ally — Czechoslovakia, whose army was described by the British military attaché in Prague as "probably the best in the smaller states of Europe," could field thirty to forty divisions after man- ning her fortress line. Others were troubled by the moral implications, and by the sloughing off of British pride. Winston's sixteen-year-old daughter, Mary, wrote him: "I have been following the Czechoslovakian problem with keen interest. I think we are making things more difficult by declar- ing such a feeble policy."[220]

Chamberlain, who distrusted public opinion, the press, and to some extent, the House of Commons and even the cabinet, had taken steps to free himself of unwanted advice while he practiced his personal diplomacy. Parliament was not sitting and would not convene in the immediate future. (They were "being treated more and more as a kind of Reichstag," Harold Macmillan complained.) The cabinet's Foreign Policy Committee had last met three months before; the next meeting was a month away.[221]

Those familiar with later conferences between world leaders, particu- larly Churchill's, may be surprised by the fact that apart from two typists and two bodyguards — who would travel in a separate plane — the prime minister took with him only three companions: the ubiquitous Sir Horace Wilson and two young FO diplomats. Like their leader, none in the party spoke a word of German. Henderson, who would join them in Munich, was fluent in German, but of course he also spoke in tongues. Chamberlain and Hitler would talk *à deux,* aided only by an interpreter. The prime minister had no strategy, no proposals, no conversational lines to fall back upon if confronted by an unexpected proposal requiring thought. As he said afterward, he regarded himself as a one-man mission of inquiry to determine "in personal conversation whether there was any hope of saving the peace." Horace Wilson had made some notes on reciprocal suggestions, but the P.M., it seems, was prepared only to accept the Führer's terms. This was his virgin flight, and he had been told to anticipate a bumpy three-hour trip to Munich. Understandably he was nervous, and he had therefore asked Geoffrey Dawson to ride with him to Heston airstrip. At such a time it was comforting to be accompanied by a friend who would console you with reasonable answers to unreasonable doubts, someone who understood you, someone you could trust.[222]

Hitler was guilty of treason, incest, incitement to riot, and the murder of millions. In small matters, however, he was a prig: a vegetarian who scorned nicotine, and was offended by foul language. *"Um Himmel willen!"* ("For heaven's sake!") was about as strong as he got, and he fairly sputtered it when told that the prime minister of Great Britain, the leader of the greatest empire in history, was coming to him, like the English pilgrims in the early days of the Third Reich. Landing at Munich about noon on September 15, Chamberlain enjoyed reviewing an honor guard whose members, Wilson noted without comprehension, wore skulls and crossbones on their caps. Though none of the English visitors knew it, these were members of the *Totenkopf* (Death's Head) SS, recruited from Dachau guards. It was not an auspicious greeting.

Chamberlain wrote Ida that he "felt quite fresh" during the ride from the airport to the train station, and was "delighted with the enthusiastic welcome of the crowds . . . all the way to the station." A three-hour train ride brought him to Berchtesgaden; then he and his entourage were driven up to the Berghof. There, Chamberlain later wrote, "Halfway down [the] steps stood the Führer, bareheaded and dressed in a khaki-coloured coat of broadcloth with a red armlet and a swastika on it, and the military cross on his breast." Except for this costume, the prime minister thought, "he looks entirely undistinguished. You would never notice him in a crowd, and would take him for the house painter" — Chamberlain had swallowed this whopper — "he once was."[223]

The prime minister had been traveling since dawn, and it was nearly 5:30 P.M. when, after tea, he and the Führer, accompanied by Schmidt, Hitler's interpreter, climbed the stairs to the Berghof's study, where Schuschnigg had been browbeaten seven months before. Hitler dominated the conversation, running on and on about how he had vowed to solve the Czech issue "one way or another." The Sudetenland's three million Germans must "return" ("*zurückkehren*") to the Reich. He was "prepared to risk a world war rather than allow this to drag on." Chamberlain had tried again and again to comment; now he succeeded in interrupting Hitler — something one did not *do* — and said that if the Führer had decided to resolve the issue by force, "why did you let me come? I have wasted my time." Hitler calmed down and suggested they examine "the question of whether a peaceful settlement is not possible after all." Would Britain agree to a *"Loslösung"* ("liberation") of the Sudetenland, one based on the right of *"Selbstimmungsrechts der Volker"* ("self-determination")? That was the trap. Chamberlain went for it. He was pleased, he said, that they "had now got down to the crux of the matter." Of course, he would have to sound out his cabinet and confer with the French, he said, adding, according to Schmidt's shorthand notes, that "he could personally state that he recognized the principle of the detachment of the Sudeten area. . . . He wished to return to England to report to the Government and secure their approval of his personal attitude." That, so to speak, was the ball game. The prospect had been hooked.[224]

At Chartwell, Winston was writing A. H. Richards, general secretary of the Anti-Nazi Council, "If, as I fear, the Government is going to let Czechoslovakia be cut to pieces, it seems to me that a period of very hard work lies before us all." Hard work lay ahead for Chamberlain, too. The betrayal of a nation requires just as much paperwork, conferring, and arguing over obscure points as its salvation. But the prime minister believed that *he* was the savior. He asked for, and was given, Hitler's promise that Germany would launch no attack until they had held a second summit sometime in the next few days. Departing Berchtesgaden, Chamberlain later wrote Ida, he felt he had "established a certain confidence, which was my aim, and, on my side, in spite of the hardness and ruthlessness I thought I saw in his face, I got the impression that here was a man who could be relied upon when he had given his word."[225]

In London on September 17 Chamberlain described Hitler to the cabinet as "the commonest little dog," and a "most extraordinary creature," but repeated his conviction that he would be "rather better than his word," adding that he had been told (presumably by Henderson) that the Führer had been "most favourably impressed." This, he said, was "of the utmost importance, since the future conduct of these negotiations depends mainly upon personal contacts." Hitler had assured him, he emphasized, that he wanted "no Czechs in the Reich"; he would be satisfied once he had included the Sudeten Germans. "The impression left on me was that Herr Hitler meant what he had said. . . . My view is that Herr Hitler is telling the truth."[226]

Having given this testimonial to the Führer, the P.M. assumed that his ministers would approve of ceding the Sudetenland to the Reich. To his surprise and dismay, several declined endorsing the German claim pending further discussion. In Paris there was also what Phipps described as "considerable heart-burning." Léon Blum wrote in *Le Populaire* that war would probably be avoided, but "under such circumstances that I, who for many years dedicated my life to [the struggle for peace], cannot feel joy. I feel myself torn between a sense of cowardly relief and shame."[227]

Churchill's feelings were unmixed; he was outraged. He sent his agent, Revesz, a statement for distribution to the European press. "The personal intervention of Mr Chamberlain and his flight to see Herr Hitler," he wrote, "does not at all alter the gravity of the issue at stake. We must hope that it does not foreshadow another complete failure of the Western Democracies to withstand the threats and violence of Nazi Germany." Phipps reported to Halifax that Churchill had telephoned the Quai d'Orsay, noting caustically that Winston "presumably . . . breathed fire and thunder in order to binge Bonnet up."[228]

But France was already committed to the Chamberlain solution. A delegation headed by Daladier and Bonnet reached Whitehall on September 18. The French premier's chief concern was to avoid the proposal of a plebiscite, "a weapon with which the German Government could keep Central Europe in a constant state of alarm and suspense." Chamberlain assured him that he had discarded that possibility — he knew Hitler would reject it since if the polling was supervised, he might lose. Yet the French were still uneasy; they could not walk away from their treaty with the Czechs. They wanted the British to join them in guaranteeing the borders of the mangled Czechoslovakia that the cession would leave. Chamberlain and Halifax tried to avoid that, but after nearly three hours of discussion they yielded, the P.M. taking consolation in Hitler's Berghof assurance that he was solely interested in the Sudeten Germans. The issue was absurd. If England had been unwilling to fight for a defensible Czechoslovakia, why should she agree to rush to the aid of the indefensible remnant? Beneš saw that; when the Anglo-French proposal was presented to him by Basil Newton, he rejected it, on the ground, reported Newton, that "guarantees which he already possessed had proved valueless."[229]

The Times, on September 20, in massive understatement, observed that the Anglo-French proposal, giving Hitler what he would otherwise have found very expensive, "could not, in the nature of things, be expected to make a strong *prima facie* appeal to the Czech Government, and least of all to President Beneš." It didn't, and at 8:00 P.M. on the twentieth the Czech government refused to agree to the annexation of its sovereign territory, explaining that as leaders of a democracy they could not make such an enormous decision without the approval of their parliament. Furthermore, they declared, submission to the Führer's demands would not solve the "question of peace" because they would face minority unrest elsewhere in their country. Lastly, Europe's "balance of power would be destroyed."[230]

This was one of those mysterious historical moments in which events acquire a momentum all their own and begin to exert an irresistible pressure. There was no reason to hurry; Ribbentrop told Paris, London, and Prague that the Führer could wait, and at his suggestion the next Hitler-Chamberlain meeting was postponed from Wednesday, September 21, to Thursday. Nevertheless, Phipps suggested to Bonnet that they tell Beneš that unless his reply constituted a complete, immediate acceptance of what amounted to an Allied ultimatum, England and France would "wash their hands of Czechoslovakia in the event of a German attack."[231]

In Prague the British minister, Newton, advised Whitehall that if he could deliver an "ultimatum to President Beneš," then "he and his Government will feel able to bow to a *force majeure*." That, more or less, is what happened. At 2:00 A.M. on the twenty-first Newton and his French counterpart, Victor de Lacroix, delivered a démarche informing Beneš that surrender of the Sudetenland to the Reich was "the only means of averting war and the invasion of Czechoslovakia," and that if he persisted in refusing it he would "bear the responsibility for the war," which would divide France and England, because the English would declare themselves neutral. British neutrality meant further that when "war starts, France will not take part, i.e. she will not fulfill her treaty obligations." They argued with the old man for an hour and a half; then he threw in his hand. Jan Masaryk sent the text of the Anglo-French ultimatum to Hugh Dalton, a Labour MP and a Churchill ally. When Dalton read it in the House of Commons, Sir Samuel Hoare solemnly replied that it was "in almost every respect a totally inaccurate description of the representations that we made to the Czechoslovak Government." Among the signs of moral disintegration in Chamberlain's clique was the adoption, by Hitler's British admirers, of the Big Lie.[232]

Roosevelt, summoning the British ambassador in Washington, told him that the Anglo-French proposal was "the most terrible remorseless sacrifice that has ever been demanded of a State" and predicted that it would "provoke a highly unfavorable reaction in America." The president again suggested a conference of world leaders — not in Europe, but in the Azores or some other Atlantic island — which he would attend. Roosevelt's proposal was swept from the prime minister's desk into his wastebasket.[233]

The P.M. was equally unresponsive to FDR's humanitarian appeal for the Czechs who would be dispossessed and were already well into the early stages of panic. The Sudetenland's anti-Nazis were hopelessly trapped. Wednesday evening Wenzel Jaksch, the leader of Czechoslovakia's 400,000 German Social Democrats, told John Troutbeck, the first secretary of the British embassy in Prague, that his followers had nowhere to go; the Czechs, overwhelmed by the mass of Sudeten refugees of their own race, were turning Sudeten Germans away. Therefore, Jaksch told Troutbeck, they "must lay their lives in the hands of the British and French Governments and ask for advice as to what was to be done for them." But the Allied embassies were mute. It was Vienna all over again. Jaksch's followers applied for British and French visas and were rejected. They returned to their homes to await the Gestapo, which would not keep them waiting long.[234]

Churchill had been active from the beginning of the crisis, using every weapon he could lay hands on to subvert Chamberlain. He tried to work behind the scenes, but in a nation with a free press, that was impossible; on Tuesday, September 6, to his chagrin, the *Daily Express* had reported that Heinrich Brüning, the former Weimar chancellor, had visited Chartwell, asking his host to urge His Majesty's Government to "speak plainly to Hitler." After *The Times* ran its disastrous editorial of September 7 proposing a partition of Czechoslovakia, Winston had repeatedly called on Halifax, trying to find out what was happening and then to influence policy. On Thursday, September 15, when Chamberlain departed for Berchtesgaden, Winston devoted his *Daily Telegraph* column to the Czechs.[235]

He bitterly rued his resignation, on a matter of principle, from the Conservative party's hierarchy in 1931. Like his father, who had surrendered his seals as chancellor of the Exchequer fifty years earlier on another issue, he had been ostracized ever since. Now he was alarmed by news that two strong members of Daladier's cabinet, Paul Reynaud and Georges Mandel, planned to quit their offices unless France honored her pledges to the Czechs. Churchill had immediately flown over on September 20 to point out that if they quit they would forfeit their roles as shapers of another, more rational foreign policy. Either the force of his argument, his powerful presence, or his position as Hitler's greatest enemy in Europe — or perhaps all three — brought them round. They agreed to stick it out.[236]

His plane brought him back on September 21. Upon returning to Morpeth Mansions he issued a statement denouncing plans to balkanize Czechoslovakia. Partition, he said, would amount "to the complete surrender of the Western democracies to the Nazi threat of force," putting England and France in an "ever weaker and more dangerous situation." A neutral Czechoslovakia would free at least twenty-five German divisions to threaten France and the Low Countries while opening up "for the triumphant Nazis the road to the Black Sea." It was "not Czechoslovakia alone which is menaced," he said, "but also the freedom and the democracy of all nations." The conviction that security could be bought "by throwing a small State to the wolves" was "a fatal delusion."[237]

On the twenty-second Chamberlain was on his way to his second airplane trip, with Dawson again alongside to see him off. At Heston Airport the prime minister was irritated by the presence of a small group which had gathered there, not to wish him well, but to boo. The German crowds were friendlier. The second summit was to be held in the small town of Godesberg, on the Rhine, and at the Petersberg Hotel elegant suites overlooking the river had been reserved for *die Engländer* — the P.M. and his small entourage, which included two British diplomats who had met his plane: Ambassador Henderson and Ivone Kirkpatrick. All that the German people knew of Chamberlain was that he was trying to preserve the peace, but it was enough; they had brought a band, and standing beneath his windows they serenaded him with the rollicking London hit:

> *Kommt ihr je nach Lambeth-Stadt*
> *Nich nur abends, auch em Tag,*
> *Findet ihr uns dabei,*
> *Beim tanzen des "Lambeth Walks,"*
> *Hei!*

Even as the P.M., Kirkpatrick, and Henderson crossed the Rhine for talks with Hitler in the Hotel Dreesen, Churchill, having left Downing Street, was hailing a cab for 11 Morpeth Mansions. He had called at No. 10 to ask precisely what Chamberlain would propose at Godesberg, and five peers along with three MPs — Bracken, Sinclair, and Nicolson — were gathering in his flat to hear what he had learned. Nicolson, the last to arrive, was waiting for the lift when Winston paid the cabbie and hurried in. As they ascended together, Nicolson said: "This is hell." Churchill muttered: "It is the end of the British Empire." According to Nicolson's diary, Churchill told the group that the cabinet had demanded "a firm stand" on Chamberlain's part, insisting on German demobilization, supervision of the Sudetenland transfer by an international commission, a refusal to discuss Polish or Hungarian claims on Czech territory, and a German guarantee of the new Czech borders. Almost in chorus, his guests said: "But Hitler will never accept such terms!" Winston replied, "In that case, Chamberlain will return tonight and we shall have war." In that event, one peer pointed out, "It will be inconvenient having our Prime Minister in German territory." Winston shook his massive head and growled, "Even the Germans would not be so stupid as to deprive us of our beloved Prime Minister."[238]

Hitler neither accepted nor rejected the cabinet's terms, because Chamberlain never gave them to him. He never had a chance. Expecting to please the Führer, he told him of the Anglo-French agreement to the Sudeten annexation. To his dismay, Hitler replied brusquely, *"Ja, es tut mir leid, aber das geht nicht mehr"* ("Yes, I am very sorry, but that is no longer possible"). He had decided to raise the stakes, indifferent to the outcome; war was his objective, and this old man was obstructing that. The Führer now said he thought Warsaw and Budapest were right in advancing claims on Czech territory, and peace could "not be firmly established until these claims had been settled." Furthermore, the Sudetenland problem must be completely solved by October 1 — there would be no time to adhere to the idea of self-determination. The Führer produced a marked map defining the area which must be occupied at once by German troops. Chamberlain, Kirkpatrick's notes recorded, professed himself "disappointed and puzzled." He had, he told Hitler, "risked his whole political career" to obtain his cabinet's approval of the principles agreed to at Berchtesgaden. After three hours of inconclusive and, as Chamberlain reported by telephone to London that night, "most unsatisfactory" talks, the meeting was adjourned, to be resumed the next day.[239]

Meanwhile, German troops were reported to have entered Egerland, on the Czech side of the Ohre, and Prague wanted to mobilize. As a sovereign power, Czechoslovakia needed no one's permission to take defensive measures, but Beneš sought the advice of the two great democracies, if only because alienating them was unthinkable. The Czech request to mobilize was forwarded to Godesberg and answered by Henderson, who, predictably, replied: "Wait awhile." The exchange had been relayed to London, however, and the cabinet, overruling Henderson, gave Beneš a green light. It was promptly changed back to red on instructions from Sir Horace Wilson in Godesberg, who had consulted no one. But the French told the Czechs to proceed. Prague, understandably confused, hesitated.

Phipps, in Paris, was indignant. "All that is best in France is against war," he wired Whitehall. "His Majesty's Government should realize extreme danger of even appearing to encourage small, but noisy and corrupt war group here." Cadogan, in the unaccustomed role of a hawk, angrily rebuked him: "By war group you surely do not include all those who feel that France must carry out her treaty obligations to Czechoslovakia." Phipps, equally angry, answered wildly: "I meant the communists who are paid by Moscow and have been working for war for months."[240]

Halifax was not a Communist, but he had begun to think seriously about approaching the Russians. In London he was encouraged by Winston Churchill, uninvited but nevertheless welcomed in this anxious hour when all lines to Godesberg seemed dead. The talks between the Führer and the prime minister had been suspended until Friday the twenty-third. War seemed very near. At 1:15 P.M. on Friday the foreign secretary instructed Butler, in Geneva: "It would be useful if you would have a conversation with M. Litvinov on the present situation, and endeavour to elicit from him anything concerning the views and intentions of his Government."[241]

At 10:00 P.M. Halifax, with the approval of the cabinet, sent Chamberlain word that the "great mass of public opinion seems to be hardening in sense of feeling that we have gone to the limit of concession and that it is up to the Chancellor to make some contribution. . . . From point of view of your own position, that of Government, and of the country, it seems to your colleagues of vital importance that you should not leave without making it plain to Chancellor if possible by special interview that, after great concessions made by Czechoslovak Government, for him to reject opportunity for peaceful solution . . . would be an unpardonable crime against humanity." Godesberg was again quiescent. An hour passed; two hours. Then, to Halifax's astonishment, Chamberlain sent him a brief report, assuring the nervous FO that Hitler's demands and a lasting European peace were reconcilable. Whitehall wondered what had happened. The answer was that the prime minister had been duped.[242]

The Friday meeting between Chamberlain and Hitler, originally scheduled to begin at 11:30 A.M., had been several times delayed while the two exchanged letters and notes laying out their positions. It was not until 10:30 P.M. that Chamberlain again crossed the Rhine; the German chancellor was waiting at the water's edge to meet the ferry and accompany the prime minister into the hotel lounge. But the cordial atmosphere soon evaporated as the British party studied the lengthy memorandum the Germans had prepared detailing the Führer's final position.

The document demanded that the Czechs begin evacuating the Sudetenland at 8:00 A.M. September 26, with the process to be completed two days later. Any who remained would be arrested or shot as trespassers, because the region would be Reich soil. During the two days of evacuation

German troops would be moving in to "protect" the area and to "restore order."[243]

Chamberlain was appalled; the talks became agitated and had reached an impasse when an adjutant entered with word that Beneš had just announced Czech general mobilization over the radio. According to Schmidt, the room was "deadly still" (*"totenstill"*). Suddenly, it erupted in furious argument. One of the few German words the prime minister knew was *Diktat*, and after rereading Hitler's memorandum and conferring with Schmidt about the translation, which was still incomplete, he said heatedly: "But this is an ultimatum!" Not at all, snapped the Führer. Pushing the paper under the P.M.'s eyes, he invited him to see for himself. It wasn't a *Diktat* at all, he said: *"Es steht ja 'Memorandum' darüber"* ("It is headed by the word 'Memorandum' "). Chamberlain ignored this childish duplicity and rose, saying he would fly home with a heavy heart. Hitler, determined to keep him hooked, quickly offered a *Konzession*, something, he said, he had never done before. The Czech evacuation needn't end till October 1. This was flimflam; Chamberlain did not know that the Generalstab had told the Führer that they couldn't possibly move in before the first of the month. But the prime minister was impressed, and expressed his appreciation. When the meeting broke up about 1:30 A.M., noted Schmidt, "Chamberlain bid a hearty farewell to the Führer." As he left the Dreesen, a newspaperman intercepted him to ask: "Is it hopeless, sir?" Chamberlain replied: "I would not like to say that. It is up to the Czechs now." In other words, peace was possible unless the Czechs stubbornly insisted on defending their homeland.[244]

When the Führer's terms became known in London, they were met with consternation. "Hitler's memo. now in," wrote Cadogan in his diary. "It's awful." Over the past week, he noted, they had "moved from 'autonomy' to cession," and "we salved our consciences, at least I did, by stipulating it must be an 'orderly' cession." This meant "safeguards for the exchange of populations, compensation, etc. Now," Cadogan continued, "Hitler says he must march into the whole area *at once* (to keep order!) and the safeguards — and plebiscites! can be held *after!* This is throwing away every last safeguard we had. The P.M. is transmitting this 'proposal' to Prague. Thank God he hasn't yet recommended it for acceptance."[245]

The prime minister arrived in London on Saturday afternoon, carrying with him Hitler's memorandum, a map showing which regions would pass into the hands of the Wehrmacht (followed by the Gestapo), and an evacuation timetable for the Czechs. At 5:30 P.M. he met with an anxious cabinet. At first, he told them, he had been "indignant" that Hitler was "pressing new demands on me." Eventually, however, "I modified my view on this point." The prime minister added that he thought he had "established some degree of personal influence over Hitler," who had told him, " 'You are the first man for many years who has got any concessions from me.' " Hitler had told him, he said, that if they "solved this question without conflict, it could be a turning-point in Anglo-German relations." The Führer had voluntarily added that (as he had already said several times) the Czech problem was "the last territorial demand" which he had to make in Europe. The prime minister thought this so important that he had instructed a bilingual young diplomat to write it out in German, and here it was: *"die letzte territoriale Forderung."* Chamberlain stressed that the Führer had not been prompted and had spoken "with great earnestness." (As Eden said later, "Chamberlain knew that Hitler lied. He just could not believe that Hitler would lie to *him."*) Now it was Chamberlain's conclusion that "We should accept those [Hitler's] terms and should advise the Czechs to do so."[246]

Duff Cooper protested. Hitherto, he said, they had faced the unpleasant alternatives of peace with dishonor or war. He now saw "a third possibility, namely war with dishonor, by which I mean being kicked into war by the boot of public opinion when those for whom we were fighting have already been defeated." But the other ministers endorsed the prime minister's view.

Czechoslovakia's leaders could hardly believe that Chamberlain had done what he had done. In France, Daladier was still troubled by "the moral issue," as he called it. Churchill wanted him to stay on that course. On Monday, September 26, Winston called on Halifax at the FO, asked that Rex Leeper be summoned, and with the foreign secretary's tacit agreement, stood over Leeper dictating a Churchillian communiqué: "If . . . a German attack is made upon Czechoslovakia . . . France will be bound to come to her assistance, and Great Britain and Russia will certainly stand by France." It is a measure of Churchill's powerful presence that Halifax then "authorized" the communiqué. As A. J. P. Taylor has observed, Halifax approved this announcement "but did not sign it. In this roundabout way, he secured his position both present and future: he retained Chamberlain's confidence, yet was later the only 'Man of Munich' who continued to stand high in favor with Churchill."[247]

The communiqué was ineffective. In Paris, Bonnet dismissed it as a forgery, and Chamberlain quashed it that evening by issuing a statement reaffirming his vow to meet all Hitler's demands. On Sunday an FO minute had set forth Britain's new stance vis-à-vis the Czechs: "It can be taken for granted that the only hope of preventing or at least localizing war is for His Majesty's Government . . . to make it absolutely clear that they [the Czechs] must accept German plan or forfeit claim to further support from Western Powers." Nevertheless, Jan Masaryk formally rejected the memorandum that Hitler had handed to Chamberlain, describing it as "a *de facto* ultimatum of the sort usually presented to a vanquished nation and not a proposition to a sovereign state. . . . The nation of St. Wenceslas, John Hus and Thomas Masaryk will not be a nation of slaves." Chamberlain sent Horace Wilson to Germany on Monday as his personal envoy, asking that the details of the annexation be settled by a commission of Germans, Czechs, and English. If Hitler rejected this proposal, Wilson was authorized to inform him that France and England would fight with the Czechs. The request was a bad idea. In his one concession at Godesberg, the Führer had specified that the annexation be complete by October 1. When Sir Horace brought up the commission, Hitler told him that acceptance of the memorandum was a precondition and must be received by 2:00 P.M. on Wednesday, September 28. Wilson called this a "very violent hour." To his horror Hitler fell to the floor, writhing in one of his famous fits. Henderson, who had accompanied Wilson, noted that the Reich chancellor "shrieked a good deal." It was effective. Following Henderson's example, Sir Horace decided not to deliver Chamberlain's warning.[248]

That night Hitler, still raging, delivered a venomous attack on Beneš in Berlin's Sportpalast. William L. Shirer thought he had "completely lost control of himself." On orders from the Czech president, the Führer charged, "whole stretches of country were depopulated, villages burned down, attempts were made to smoke out Germans with hand grenades and gas." He paused. "Now two men stand arrayed against one another: there is Mr. Beneš and here stand I." Another pause. Then: "Now let Mr. Beneš make his choice."[249]

Chamberlain's reaction to the Sportpalast speech was, even for him, extraordinary. Hitler had referred to him in passing, and now he told the press: "I have read the speech of the German Chancellor and I appreciate his references to the efforts I have made to save the peace." He stood ready, he said, to make further efforts. Wilson paid a farewell call on the Führer on Tuesday, and, according to Schmidt, the interpreter, he told him: "I will try to make those Czechos sensible." Hitler, in turn, handed him the Reich's final concession to England, a letter to Chamberlain offering a formal guarantee from him, as Führer, of truncated Czechoslovakia's new frontiers. That evening of the twenty-seventh the prime minister spoke to the country over the BBC, a speech most memorable for a single sentence which might be called the epitome of defeatism. "How horrible, fantastic, incredible it is that we should be digging trenches and trying on gas masks here because of a quarrel in a faraway country between people of whom we know nothing."[250]

*   *   *

If Chamberlain knew nothing of Czechoslovakia after the past five months, he was a very slow learner. And, as Harold Macmillan later pointed out, "In this message to the nation, nothing was said of the sufferings of the Czech people, only sympathy with Hitler 'and his indignation that German grievances had not been dealt with before this,' together with an offer to 'guarantee' that the Czech Government would 'carry out their promises.' "[251]

The people of Britain and France, conditioned by ghastly descriptions of what another European war would be like, were genuinely frightened. Macmillan recalled that "In the last few days of September — the five days that followed Chamberlain's return from Godesberg — they were grimly . . . making up their minds to face war," the "unthinkable" which was now "round the corner." Air attacks, they had been told, would wreak destruction "beyond all imagination," and they must "expect civilian casualties on a colossal scale." Baldwin had predicted sixty thousand Londoners dead after the first Luftwaffe offensive. (In fact, ninety thousand Britons were killed by Nazi bombers during the entire war.) Given these astounding figures, the mind-set of Londoners and Englishmen living in the great industrial cities of the Midlands can be compared to that of Americans in the 1980s if told that missiles with nuclear warheads were on their way to major U.S. cities. His Majesty's Government did not handle it well. Panic was the inevitable consequence of official notice instructing parents of infants under two years to bring their children to designated centers where they would be "fitted with helmets for protection against the effects of gas." There were even rumors, some of which found their way into print, that trenches were being dug in Hyde Park.[252]

As September 28 dawned, war seemed very near; the Führer's ultimatum would expire at 2:00 P.M. But late that morning, Chamberlain, through his ambassador in Rome, asked Mussolini to save the peace by intervening. The Duce telephoned Berlin, and within an hour Hitler had agreed to see the British prime minister again. He invited Mussolini to join them, and the Duce, flattered, replied that he was "willing to be present."[253]

The scene in Parliament later in the day was a piece of stage management from the people who had brought Britain to the brink of catastrophe. At about noon Hitler's invitation to Chamberlain had reached the German embassy in London, where it was immediately decoded and dispatched to No. 10. Three hours passed. Chamberlain, addressing the House of Commons in its first session since the August adjournment, was describing the tangled diplomatic skein when a messenger arrived. Normally so important a dispatch would have been taken straight to the front bench. This one was delivered to Halifax, seated in the Peers' Gallery. He passed it down to Simon, who read it and pushed it in front of the prime minister. The House watched all this with mounting interest. In a voice that could be heard throughout the hall, Chamberlain asked: "Shall I tell them now?" and, when Simon smiled and nodded, announced: "Herr Hitler has just agreed to postpone his mobilisation for twenty-four hours and to meet me in conference with Signor Mussolini and [Monsieur] Daladier at Munich." One independent MP, a diarist, described what followed as "one of the most dramatic moments which I have ever witnessed. For a second, the House was hushed in absolute silence. And then the whole House burst into a roar of cheering, since they knew that this might mean peace." Harold Macmillan remembered that "I stood up with the rest, sharing the general emotion."[254]

Some were undeceived by the contrivance. Macmillan recalled that "Eden just could not bear it; he got up and walked out of the Chamber. Another Member sat bravely still and refused to rise. It was Harold Nicolson." Amery also remained in his bench, arms folded. Men all round them were shouting "Get up! Get up!" and "Thank God for the Prime Minister!" Then, Macmillan recalled, "I saw one man silent and seated — with his head sunk on his shoulders, his whole demeanour depicting something between anger and despair. It was Churchill." But Winston, ever magnanimous, rose as Chamberlain passed him, shaking his hand, wishing him "Godspeed."[255]

The German army's anti-Nazi conspirators had been about to spring. The order to arrest Hitler and occupy all government buildings, including the chancellery, had been on General Franz Halder's desk at noon, and General Erwin von Witzleben was standing by to witness his signature, when his orderly entered with a bulletin: Chamberlain and Daladier would travel to Munich for further talks. Halder later testified: "I therefore took back the order of execution because, owing to this fact, the entire basis for the action had been taken away." The next day, as Telford Taylor writes, "the four men of Munich danced their quadrille."[256]

❧   ❧

Webster defines "munich" as "an instance of unresisting compliance with and capitulation to the demands of an aggressor nation." Actually, nothing of great consequence happened at the Munich Conference. The Czechs' fate had been decided at Berchtesgaden and Godesberg. Britain's participation was a gross violation of parliamentary government. Unnoticed after the prime minister had been swept out of the chamber by hysterical MPs was a singular omission. His (and Horace Wilson's) inconclusive, ambiguous, highly questionable exchanges with the German führer had never been subjected to a House debate. The entire cabinet assembled at the airport the next morning to wish him luck, but neither the cabinet (including the foreign secretary) nor Parliament had shared in the formation of the policy that led to Munich.

At Munich the prime minister was clearly delighted to see Hitler again, eager to stand at his side. Here he made a cardinal error. Afterward he happily wrote his sister that the Astors' son William, recently returned from a trip to Berlin, had the impression that "Hitler definitely liked me & thought he could do business with me." This was true in the sense that an armed robber thinks he can do business with a bank teller. In fact, Hitler had taken a strong personal dislike to Chamberlain, who impressed him as an "insignificant" man. The Führer dealt with him because he believed him to be infinitely malleable. Other men in Parliament, he knew, were dangerous. On the eve of Munich he said he was "fully aware" that one day Chamberlain might be replaced by Churchill, whose "aim would be to unleash at once a new world war against Germany."[257]

The Führer was right. He had never met Churchill, but he understood him, as Winston understood Hitler. Walter Lippmann observed that the supreme qualification for high office is temperament, not intellect, and on that level the two men had more in common than either would have acknowledged. The countless millions spellbound by Winston's genius would angrily reject any comparison of the two. Nevertheless they were mirror images of one another. Since the embattled defender of Western civilization was the one who was ultimately successful, his vision has prevailed. What would have happened had victory gone to the Nazi leader doesn't bear thinking about. In the mid-1980s a poll reported that a large majority of *Germans* believe the worst thing that could have happened to them would have been the triumph of the Third Reich.[258]

Satan was once angelic; he and God had much in common. Similarly, both the Führer and his English nemesis were born demagogues. Each believed in the supremacy of his race and in national destiny; each had artistic talent — Churchill had more, but Hitler, though dismissed as a shallow painter of picture postcards, was a charismatic figure moved by dark but profound passions, the man whose voice at Nuremberg inspired men to lay down their lives, shouting *"Heil, Hitler!"* as they died. The inescapable fact is that Hitler and Churchill both were ruled not by reason but by intuition.

Chamberlain, the businessman, accustomed to the friendship of other good fellows who met on the level and parted on the square, understood neither man. The P.M. respected success. He assumed that any man who had risen to rule the most powerful nation on the Continent was a man with whom he could deal. Neville seems to have been oblivious to the fact that nearly everyone who had tried to bargain with this extraordinary man had been murdered, sent to a concentration camp, or hounded into exile.

Chamberlain could not have comprehended the depth of the horrors plumbed by the Third Reich. The Führer vowed that restoring their beloved homeland to the mistreated Sudetendeutsche was his last claim, and Chamberlain believed him. The P.M. had not been deceptive in his "faraway country" broadcast. Although the "Czech problem" had been on his desk for months, to him Czechoslovakia remained precisely that: a problem, not a land inhabited by real people. He knew nothing of eastern European geography, not to mention the Serbs, Croats, Slavs, Slovaks, Czechs, Poles, and gypsies inhabiting the region; he disregarded all the warnings of the FO and swallowed everything he was told by the Reich's *Kriegsherr*.

Churchill knew better. He had studied Adolf Hitler's career with intensity, and remembered his remarkable history of broken promises. When the Führer broke the Versailles treaty he promised to honor Germany's signature on Locarno; when he broke the Locarno Pact — long before the Sudetenland became a synonym for crisis — he had sworn that the Rhineland would be his last territorial claim. When he sent Wehrmacht bayonets into Austria he grandly guaranteed Czechoslovakia's borders. His position had subtly evolved; he was interested only in Germans, he said — including, of course, Germans living beyond the borders of the Reich. But over the past two thousand years Europe had become a mix, racially, culturally, and ethnically. As Duff Cooper observed, "There are Germans in Switzerland, in Denmark, and in Alsace; I think that one of the few countries in Europe in which there are no Germans is Spain, and there are rumors that Germany has taken an interest in that country."[259]

Churchill's sources in the Reich reported that the great Ruhr munitions factories, on orders from Berlin, continued to work around the clock. In Kiel and Hamburg new U-boats slid into the water like the litters of an incredibly fertile sea monster; Luftwaffe observation planes, equipped with long-range cameras, overflew eastern Europe, Scandinavia, the Low Countries, even France. Churchill carried graphs when he entered the House of Commons now. They revealed that the gap between British and German arsenals was widening. Since fighting was inevitable, he argued, better that it come now, with France prepared to meet her treaty obligations to Czechoslovakia, thus confronting German strategists with the specter of a two-front war.

Now the crisis had reached its climax. Violet Bonham Carter recalled Churchill's mood then. "He rightly mistrusted Chamberlain, who, he was convinced, was still searching desperately for a way out" when no honorable way existed. That same September 29, as the so-called Four-Power Meeting began in Bavaria, the Focus group lunched in the Savoy's Pinafore Room. Violet saw that "Winston's face was dark with foreboding. I could see he feared the worst, as I did. I finally suggested that during the afternoon a few of us should draft a telegram to the Prime Minister adjuring him to make no further concessions at the expense of the Czechs and warning him that if he did so he would have to fight the House of Commons on his return." The wire was to be signed by, among others, Churchill, Lord (Robert) Cecil, Attlee, Archie Sinclair, Eden, Liddell Hart, Lloyd George, and Lord Lloyd.[260]

It was drafted — after eliminating the threat — and at 7:00 P.M. they again met at the Savoy. Winston then called for the signatures, and Sinclair, Lloyd, and Cecil came quickly forward. But some who had said they would come had not. Eden, reached by telephone, declined to permit the use of his name. Attlee was then phoned. He, too, refused; he said he would need the approval of his party. As Nicolson wrote in his diary, they "sat there gloomily realising that nothing could be done. Even Winston seemed to have lost his fighting spirit. . . . So far as one can see, Hitler gets everything he wants."[261]

It was decided to send no telegram. One by one the group drifted away. Violet wrote: "Winston remained, sitting in his chair immobile, like a man of stone. I saw the tears in his eyes. I could feel the iron entering his soul. His last attempt to salvage what was left of honor and good faith had failed." She spoke bitterly of those who refused to put their names to their principles. Then Churchill spoke. He said: *"What are they made of? The day is not far off when it won't be signatures we'll have to give but lives — the lives of millions. Can we survive? Do we deserve to do so when there's no courage anywhere?"*[262]

Shortly after noon that Thursday — as Churchill, heavy with despair, lunched at the Savoy — Hitler led his guests from a buffet at the Führerbau (the working headquarters of the Nazi party) and into his private office, to determine the future of a country in a conference from which that nation's elected leaders had been excluded. Two Czechs — Hubert Masařík and Vojtech Mastny — were in the city as "observers" attached to the British delegation, but when Chamberlain weakly suggested they attend the discussions the Führer had said *"Nein!"* The issue was then dropped, with the tacit understanding that the delegation from Prague would be informed of the Hitler-Chamberlain-Mussolini-Daladier decisions later.

"O Oysters, come and walk with us!"
The Walrus did beseech.

"A pleasant walk, a pleasant talk,
Along the briny beach."

Mussolini produced a memorandum, ostensibly drawn up by him but actually the work of Göring, Neurath, and Weizsäcker. The Englishmen — Horace Wilson had again accompanied Chamberlain — assumed that it was a base for negotiations, but Hitler did not negotiate. He simply repeated, over and over, what he was going to take, when he would take it, and what he might or might not do with it. Nevertheless, the men from Paris and London kept battering away, through the evening and past midnight. At 1:00 A.M. Chamberlain capitulated. Virtually all of the claims Hitler had made in the past were accepted, including many he could never have won by force of arms. He now held the strategic center of Europe. The agreement signed in the early hours of September 30 (though it was dated September 29) specified that Czechoslovakia should begin evacuation of the Sudetenland at once. All Czechs in the Sudetenland must be gone — no one thought to ask where they might go — by October 10. Their departure would be supervised by an international commission which would also decide when plebiscites should be held, determine where the borders of the rump Czech state should be drawn, and see to it that all "existing installations" remain intact in Czechoslovakia's lost territories. Poland, exploiting the turmoil, was placated by a slice of the pie, some three hundred square miles of Teschen Silesia. If other "problems of Polish and Hungarian minorities in Czechoslovakia" were not settled by negotiations with Prague, they would "form the subject" of another four-power meeting.[263]

The proceedings ended briskly, with efficient young German diplomats tidying up and disposing of loose strings. It had been a disgraceful business, but only Daladier and François-Poncet saw it for what it really was. The French premier was glum and silent; his ambassador to Germany, mortified by his country's sellout of a faithful ally, was overheard by Ciano as he spoke in a voice broken by shame: *"Voilà comme la France traite les seuls alliés qui lui étaient restés fidèles."* ("See how France treats the only allies who remained faithful to her.")[264]

As they were about to break up Horace Wilson gave a little start and asked: "What to do about the Czechs?"[265]

> *"But wait a bit," the Oysters cried,*
> *"Before we have our chat;*
> *For some of us are out of breath,*
> *And all of us are fat!"*

While others discussed who was to inform the Czechs and how to assure their cooperation, the P.M. and Hitler discussed the Reich's economic difficulties. Then the Führer consented to glance at a joint declaration regarding future Anglo-German relations which the prime minister had brought with him. This, for Chamberlain, was the high point in the conference. According to him, "As the interpreter translated the words into German, Hitler frequently ejaculated 'Ja, Ja,' and at the end he said, 'Yes, I will certainly sign it; when shall we do it?' I said 'Now,' and we went at once to the writing table, and put our signatures to the two copies which I had brought with me." Neither Schmidt nor Alec Douglas-Home, Chamberlain's parliamentary private secretary, who were looking on, shared the prime minister's conviction that the Führer was as elated as Chamberlain thought him to be. Schmidt wrote afterward that Hitler agreed to sign "with a certain reluctance," because the wording was too vague to be described as a commitment, and "to please Chamberlain." Douglas-Home thought he signed "perfunctorily." Compared with his signature on other documents, this one was careless, even sloppy.[266]

At 2:30 A.M. the P.M. joined a delegation to tell the Czechs — who were being held in the Regina Hotel, prisoners, in effect, of the Gestapo — the fate of their country. Hubert Masařík, who was given the text to read aloud, later said that the French seemed "embarrassed." Certainly the agreement was an occasion for Allied embarrassment. To the Czechs the terms were shocking. Yet Chamberlain, according to Masařík, "yawned without ceasing and with no show of embarrassment." Both he and Daladier said Czech approval was not, strictly speaking, necessary. It was indeed irrelevant; the agreement was final. According to Horace Wilson's later notes, Mastny was given "a pretty broad hint that . . . the best course for his Government was to accept what was clearly a considerable improvement upon the German Godesberg memorandum." It wasn't. Hitler had yielded nothing. Every outrageous demand he had made at Godesberg had been meekly met.[267]

As the Czechs were facing those who had betrayed them, Churchill had returned to the Savoy, joining fellow members of the Other Club for a very late dinner, to be followed by a meeting. Sleep was out of the question. According to Colin Coote, a member of the Other Club and also a member of the *Times* staff, they were awaiting the first editions of London's newspapers, which were expected to be carrying the Munich settlement. In the meantime, Coote remembered, discussion of the Godesberg terms and whether the P.M. would succeed in modifying these demands sparked "a violent argument. One began to understand why, in the House of Commons, a red line on the carpet, just beyond rapier reach of the opposite bench, marks the limit beyond which the speaker must not stray." One defender of Chamberlain was insulted so grossly that he left the table and, upon reaching home, sent a letter of resignation from the club.[268]

"Winston," Coote remembered, "was snarling and clawing at the two unhappy ministers [First Lord Duff Cooper and Walter Elliot, secretary for Scotland]. . . . One could always tell when he was deeply moved, because a minor defect in his palate gave an echoing timbre to his voice. On this occasion it was not an echo, but a supersonic boom." He asked them: "How could honourable men with wide experience and fine records in the Great War condone a policy so cowardly? It was sordid, squalid, sub-human, and," he said, "suicidal. . . . The sequel to the sacrifice of honour" would be "the sacrifice of lives, our people's lives." In his memoirs Cooper charges, quite rightly, that Churchill was fouling him. He agreed with Winston, but since he was still a cabinet minister, he felt it was "honorable to defend them for the last time."[269]

At last one man produced his watch and remarked that the early papers must be on the streets. The member pocketed his watch, left, and returned with a stop press. Duff Cooper snatched it from him and read the terms out loud, according to Coote's account "with obvious anger and disgust." Then he rose and departed without a word. Behind him he left silence. In Coote's words: "Nobody attempted to defend them. Humiliation took almost material shape." Churchill left with Richard Law, a young Tory MP. They passed the open door of a restaurant, from which issued the sounds of loud laughter. It was "packed," Law remembered long afterward, "and everyone was very gay. I was acutely conscious of the brooding figure beside me." As they turned away Winston muttered: "Those poor people. They little know what they will have to face." In the darkness they may have passed E. M. Forster, an English writer who resembled Churchill in only two traits: both possessed genius and remarkable intuition. Forster heard of the agreement in Munich and wrote that he "trailed about reading the notices, some of which had already fallen into the gutter." It was "good news," he wrote, "and it ought to have brought great joy; it did bring joy to the House of Commons. But unimportant and unpractical people often foresee the future more clearly than do those who are engaged in shaping it, and I knew at once that the news was only good in patches. Peace flapped from the posters, and not upon the wings of angels."[270]

Later in the morning, still September 30, Winston, Clemmie, and Lord Cecil seriously discussed gathering a group of friends who shared their wrath, marching to No. 10, and heaving a brick through a window. By then the two Czech delegates in the Regina had agreed not to fight. The need for their approval was urgent. By 5:00 P.M. that day an international commission would convene in Berlin to fix the details for evacuation of the first zone of the Sudetenland, which was to commence October 1, and the transfer of policing power from local officials to the German Wehrmacht.

The Czechs were angry, of course — they would have been certifiable otherwise — and the Frenchmen were the focus of their wrath. Chamberlain, to them, was contemptible. Masařík's narrative concluded: "The atmosphere was becoming oppressive for everyone present. It had been explained to us in a sufficiently brutal manner, and that by a Frenchman, that this was a sentence without right of appeal and without possibility of modification. Mr. Chamberlain did not conceal his fatigue. After the text had been read, we were given a second slightly corrected map. We said 'Good-bye' and left. The Czechoslovak Republic as fixed by the frontiers of 1918 had ceased to exist."[271]

> "I weep for you," the Walrus said:
> "I deeply sympathize."
> With sobs and tears he sorted out
> Those of the largest size,
> Holding his pocket-handkerchief
> Before his streaming eyes.

Masařík had not, however, formally accepted Czechoslovakia's subjugation. Nor could he; that decision had to be made in Prague. But he knew all hope had fled. The Führer didn't even have to send an ultimatum to Prague — Englishmen did it for him. Frank Ashton-Gwatkin, the member of the British delegation who had been given this dubious honor, arrived from Munich September 30, breakfasted with Lieutenant Colonel H. C. T. Stronge, the British military attaché, and showed him the Munich Agreement. Stronge said Czechoslovakia could never accept such terms; it would mean a sacrifice of their defenses, leaving them helpless. Ashton-Gwatkin said they *had* to accept. Stronge, to use his own word, was "staggered."[272]

Later in the day, after heated arguments with his advisers, military and civilian, Beneš capitulated. He also resigned five days later, but decided, at the urging of his ministers, to speak to the entire nation in a 7:00 P.M. broadcast, telling them what lay in the hearts of those they had elected to govern them. "They wished," Churchill later wrote, "to register their protest against a decision in which they had no part." On the air Beneš said that he remained "what I have always been, a convinced democrat." That was why he was stepping down; he thought it "best not to disturb the new European constellation which is arising." (He would be succeeded by an anti-Semitic banker who, in the words of one newspaper, "enjoys the confidence of Germany.") Beneš said: "Do not expect from me a single word of recrimination. But this I will say," — here he came as close to bitterness as a gentle man could — "that the sacrifices demanded from us were immeasurably great, and immeasurably unjust. This the nation will never forget, even though they have borne these sacrifices quietly." He departed to set up a government-in-exile in London. The SS moved in swiftly. No one knows how many Czechs were murdered in the week that followed, though it has been estimated that more than half of them were Jews. Exact figures were unavailable; with the Führer's men reigning over the Sudetenland, the news blackout was absolute.[273]

> *But answer came there none —*
> *And this was scarcely odd, because*
> *They'd eaten every one.*

The German generals, who had been sweating blood, could scarcely believe their good luck. They were unanimously agreed that had the British and French stood up to Hitler, and had Hitler invaded Czechoslovakia, the Reich would have been swiftly defeated. All this came out at Nuremberg. Keitel, chief of the OKW, testified: "From a purely military point of view we lacked the means for an attack which involved the piercing of the [Czech] frontier fortifications." Fritz Erich von Manstein, Germany's most brilliant field commander (and not a defendant at Nuremberg), said that "had Czechoslovakia defended herself, we would have been held up by her fortifications, for we did not have the means to break through." And Alfred Jodl, the key general at OKW, taking the witness stand in his own defense, told the International Military Tribunal: "It was out of the question with five fighting divisions and seven reserve divisions in the western fortification [Siegfried Line] . . . to hold out against 100 French divisions. That was militarily impossible." Churchill later wrote that he had "always believed that Beneš was wrong to yield. He should have defended his fortress line. Once fighting had begun, in my opinion at that time, France would have moved to his aid in a surge of national passion, and Britain would have rallied to France almost immediately." The chance had been tragically missed.[274]

Nevertheless, Hitler, returning from Munich on his private train, was not rejoicing. To his SS honor guard he ranted that Chamberlain had *"meinen Einzug in Prag verdorben"* ("spoiled my entry into Prague"). In his grand strategy the seizures of Austria and Czechoslovakia were to be the opening moves in a tremendous campaign for lebensraum in the east, to be followed in the west by the conquest of the Low Countries and France.

Only ten days earlier he had told the Hungarian prime minister that the wisest course was *"die Tschechoslowakei zu zerschlagen"* ("to destroy Czechoslovakia"). The sole danger was that the Czechs might buckle at the first threat. Now the British had done the buckling for them; Chamberlain had deprived the *Kriegsherr* of his first battlefield victory.[275]

On his flight home Daladier was also out of sorts, desolate and despairing. He later told Amery that as they landed in Paris and taxied toward the terminal he turned up his coat collar, to protect his face from the rotten eggs he expected when he came within range of the crowd. To his astonishment there were no eggs, no offensive shouts of *"Merde!"* and *"Nous sommes trahis!"* He paused halfway down the steps, dumbfounded. They were actually cheering him — shouting *"Vive Daladier!" "Vive la Paix!" "Vive la France!"* — greeting him as though he had won a great victory. Daladier was a man completely without vanity. He turned to Léger and whispered, *"Les cons!"* ("Fools!"). There were a few grumblers; one man muttered, *"Vive la France malgré tout."* Yet for the most part the gaiety was unqualified. It was also mindless. Because the Reich no longer need face the formidable Czech army in the east, Munich had been a catastrophe for France. Hitler's empire had increased its strength, and could quickly field twice as many soldiers. Nevertheless, the Chamber of Deputies ratified the Munich Agreement 535 to 75. Bonnet told an interviewer: "Yes, we have a treaty with the Czechs, and France remains faithful to her sacred word. Czechoslovakia wasn't invaded, was she?"[276]

Nestling in Chamberlain's pocket was the document he prized; today it lies in an obscure file at the Imperial War Museum, possibly the last place he would have had in mind. At the time that it was famous, Harold Nicolson denounced it in Parliament as "that bit of paper" which had betrayed the Reich's neighbors and threatened the security of England. In reality the document was meaningless. That was why Hitler had signed it. The first paragraph declared that Anglo-German relations were "of the first importance for the two countries and for Europe"; the second that the Munich Agreement and the Anglo-German Naval Agreement of 1935 were "symbolic of the desire of our two peoples never to go to war with one another again"; and the third that both the prime minister of Great Britain and the Führer of the Third Reich intended to use the "method of consultation" in questions "that may concern our two countries," because of their mutual determination "to continue our efforts to remove possible sources of difference, and thus to contribute to assure the peace of Europe." That is all. It lacked even the ringing affirmation of nonaggression treaties; instead it expressed the *desire* of their peoples not to war on one another. But for a few days in the quirky autumn of 1938 — the same season that Orson Welles's radio drama of Martians landing in New Jersey sent thousands of Americans heading for the hills — people believed that Chamberlain had done rather a good thing. Britons, haunted by the dread that war might be declared at any hour, felt that they had been granted a reprieve. They cast about for ways to express their gratitude. Some became hysterical.[277]

The P.M. had been "pleasantly tired" during the flight home, but once he saw the size of the crowd awaiting him at Heston Airport, he felt as though he had shed fifty years. To his entourage he seemed as excited and energetic as a youth returning from an adventure. They cheered. He read his three pitiful paragraphs, and they cheered louder, shouting, "Good old Neville!" and singing, "For he's a jolly good fellow." Then a courier wearing royal livery appeared and handed him a message from the King, asking him to come straight to Buckingham Palace, "so that I can express to you personally my most heartfelt congratulations. . . . In the meantime, this letter brings the warmest of welcomes to one who, by his patience and determination, has earned the lasting gratitude of his fellow-countrymen throughout the Empire." Afterward, Neville wrote Ida: "Even the descriptions of the papers give no idea of the scenes in the streets as I drove from Heston to the Palace. They were lined from one end to the other with people of every class, shouting themselves hoarse, leaping on the running board, banging on the windows, and thrusting their hands into the car to be shaken."[278]

But it was in Downing Street that the adulation peaked, and there — though it was not immediately obvious to the crowd — Chamberlain overreached himself. In the lore of every nation there are scenes, phrases, and deeds which live in the popular imagination. But an event, a speech, or a legend can never be repeated, for part of its appeal is that it is unique. That is why there cannot be another Arthur, another Joan of Arc, another Lincoln. It also explains why Chamberlain's last public act on his day of glory was a blunder.

Benjamin Disraeli's supreme diplomatic triumph came in 1878, at the Congress of Berlin. Unlike Chamberlain's Munich, Berlin was a genuine contribution to European peace. The states of eastern Europe were at each other's throats; the Russian diplomats were bumbling from bad to worse; even Bismarck couldn't broker a general settlement. Disraeli could and did. His mastery of divergent cultures permitted him to take the map apart and rebuild it, throttling several wars before they could break out and ending a full-fledged conflict between the Russians and the Turks. The memory of that feat sixty years earlier was on many minds that fall evening in 1938, including Chamberlain's. He wrote his sister that he spoke to the great crowd below "from the same window, I believe, as that from which Dizzy announced peace with honour 60 years ago." (He was wrong;

Disraeli's declaration was made in the House of Commons on July 16, 1878.) Now his wife said, "Neville, go up to the window and repeat history by saying peace in our time." He replied icily, "No, I do not do that kind of thing." Then he did it. Waving the piece of paper he and Hitler had signed, he called to the dense throng below: "My good friends, this is the second time in our history that there has come back from Germany to Downing Street peace with honor. I believe it is peace for our time." On the whole, public men are wise to avoid extravagant predictions. Very soon Chamberlain would have reason to regret this one.[279]

Meanwhile, however, the combers of admiration and praise continued to break at his feet. "No conqueror returning from a victory on the battlefield," *The Times* trumpeted, "has been adorned with nobler laurels." *Paris-Soir* offered him "a corner of French soil" where he could cast for trout, his favorite sport, than which "there could be no more fruitful image of peace." Fifty Englishmen wrote to Printing House Square, calling for a national fund in Chamberlain's honor. Those who had cheered his departure for Munich felt vindicated. Nicolson wrote of an exchange with Margot Asquith. She had said: "Now, Harold, you must agree that he is a great man." He replied, "Not at all." "You are as bad as Violet," she snapped; "he is the greatest Englishman that ever lived." Yet even Nicolson confessed in his diary that he momentarily felt "an immense sense of *physical* relief, in that I shall not be afraid tonight of the German bombs."[280]

But, he added "my moral anxieties are in no way diminished." After the cheering, a few thoughtful men, in the quietude of reflection, read the terms of Munich and were troubled. Halifax had sensed what was coming; in the triumphant ride from Heston he had astounded the prime minister by suggesting that he form a national government, bringing Churchill and Eden back and inviting Labour to join. Chamberlain replied that he would "think it over," but there is no evidence that he did. Lord Lloyd, who had been in the roaring throng outside No. 10, remembered feeling "elated" until Chamberlain said "peace with honor." Then "my heart sank; it was the worst possible choice of words, for I realized that he had sold honor to buy peace."[281]

The most sensational defection from Chamberlain's entrenched majority was that of his first lord of the Admiralty, Alfred Duff Cooper, "the pioneer," Conservative backbencher Vyvyan Adams called him, "along the nation's way back from hysteria to reason." Revolted by Chamberlain's fawning over Hitler, his sellout of the Czechs, and his smug pride in the piece of trumpery he and Hitler had signed, on Saturday, October 1, the day after the prime minister's return, Cooper resigned. Chamberlain, Duff Cooper wrote, was "as glad to be rid of me as I was determined to go." Lady Diana Cooper recalled that she "telephoned the news to Winston. His voice was broken with emotion. I could hear him cry." Churchill exulted that "one minister alone stood forth. . . . At the moment of Mr. Chamberlain's overwhelming mastery of public opinion, he thrust his way through the exulting throng to declare his total disagreement with its leader." [282]

The first doubts were struggling to the surface, but it was too soon for them to coalesce. Although some MPs were already wrestling with their consciences, they would have to put themselves on record in just five days, the evening of October 5, at the close of a three-day debate, when the issue before them would be: "That this House approves the policy of His Majesty's Government by which war was averted in the recent crisis and supports their efforts to secure a lasting peace." The vote was never in doubt, with the huge Conservative margin Baldwin had won three years earlier. But even those Conservatives who had remained doggedly faithful to their leader were becoming troubled. After the vote, Sir Alan Herbert, an independent member, wrote: "My soul revolted at the thought of another, and, I was convinced by many expert opinions, a much worse war. . . . But, 'wishful thinker,' 'anxious hoper,' 'old soldier,' or 'Christian believer' — what you will — I wanted Mr. Chamberlain to be right, and keep the peace successfully. . . . I voted sadly for Munich; and the whole thing made me ill."

PART FOUR

VORTEX

ON the Saturday before Parliament's Munich debate, Winston was at Chartwell, vigorously slapping bricks into place and awaiting a visitor, a twenty-six-year-old BBC producer, unknown then but destined to become infamous in the early 1950s. He was Guy Burgess, who with Kim Philby and Donald Maclean — all three upper class, all Cambridge men — would be cleared to review the U.S. government's most sensitive documents, including the Central Intelligence Agency's daily traffic and dispatches from Korea. In fact they would be Soviet intelligence agents. Burgess's notoriety lay far in the future that sunbright morning, however, when Churchill, in a blue boilersuit (a forerunner of his wartime "siren suit"), left his bricks to greet his visitor, a trowel still in one hand. The meeting was purposeless; Winston had been scheduled to give BBC listeners a half-hour talk on the Mediterranean, but when the Czech crisis erupted he had asked that the program be canceled. Burgess was keen to meet him anyhow, however, and Churchill, feeling that was the least he could do, had agreed.

In the beginning he was gruff. He complained, Burgess recollected afterward, that he had been "very badly treated in the matter of political broadcasts and that he was always muzzled by the BBC. . . . He went on to say that he would be even more muzzled in the future, since the BBC seemed to have passed under the control of the Government." According to Burgess, Winston said he had just received a message from Beneš — he always called him "Herr Beans" — asking for his "advice and assistance." But, he asked, "what answer shall I give? — for answer I shall and must. . . . Here am I, an old man without power and without party. What advice can I give, what assistance can I proffer?" Burgess stammered that he could offer his eloquence. Pleased, Winston said: "My eloquence! Ah, yes . . . that Herr Beans can rely on in full and indeed" — he paused and winked — "some would say in overbounding measure. That I can offer him. But what else, Mr. Burgess, what else can I offer him?" Burgess, usually garrulous, was tongue-tied. Moment succeeded moment, but he could think of nothing to say. He saw a great man, the scourge of fascism, caged by frustration. Then Churchill spoke. "You are silent, Mr. Burgess. You are rightly silent. What else can I offer Herr Beans? Only one thing: my only son, Randolph, who is already training to be an officer."[1]

Throughout 1938 Churchill's warnings had grown more and more persistent, and less and less effective. His mots were seldom passed along now because his targets, the "Men of Munich," as Fleet Street called them, were believed to have prevented a general European war. In almost any gathering, it would have been indiscreet to remark: "Have you heard what Winston says about Neville? 'In the depths of that dusty soul there is nothing but abject surrender.' " Or: "Churchill says the Government had to choose between war and shame. They chose shame. They will get war, too." Yet some hit home. Malcolm MacDonald, son of Ramsay and minister for the colonies and Dominions under Chamberlain, recalls with discomfort but also amusement how, during a speech on the future of Palestine, he was moved to say that "I cannot remember a time when I was not told stories of Jerusalem and Bethlehem, the birthplace of the Prince of Peace." And as he paused for breath Churchill muttered: "I always thought he was born in Birmingham."[2]

At 3:34 P.M. on Monday, October 3, 1938, Parliament opened its debate on the Munich Agreement. In the observance of custom, Duff Cooper, as a resigning minister, spoke first. "The Prime Minister," he said, "has believed in addressing Herr Hitler through the language of sweet reasonableness. I have believed that he was more open to the language of the mailed fist. . . . We have taken away the defences of Czechoslovakia in the same breath as we have guaranteed them, as though you were to deal a man a mortal blow and at the same time insure his life."

Chamberlain, he noted, attached "considerable importance" to the document he and Hitler had signed at Munich. "But," he asked, "what do those words mean? Do they mean that Herr Hitler will take 'no' for an answer? He has never taken it yet. Or do they mean that he believes that he will get away with this, as he has got away with everything else, without fighting, by well-timed bluff, bluster and blackmail? Otherwise it means very little." Duff Cooper ended: "I have ruined, perhaps, my political career. But that is a little matter. I have retained something which is to me of great value. I can still walk about the world with my head erect."[3]

The House was deeply moved by Cooper's resignation speech. Antony Winn, the *Times* lobby correspondent, reported that it had been well received. Dawson, who hadn't been there, tore up Winn's piece and wrote an account of his own, dismissing the speech as "a damp squib," and headed the story "From our lobby correspondent." Winn resigned.[4]

The prime minister, following Duff Cooper, paid ritualistic tribute to him and ignored his arguments. Chamberlain had already set forth his own views to the cabinet earlier in the day, and the kindest interpretation of his position is that he had forgotten he was prime minister and thought himself once more watchdog of the Treasury. Ever since his stewardship as chancellor of the Exchequer, he had told the cabinet, he had been haunted by the possibility that "the burden of armaments might break our backs." Therefore he had sought "to resolve the causes . . . responsible for the armaments race." Now, after his agreement with the German führer, England was in "a more hopeful position." The next steps would be further agreements "which would stop the arms race." The effort to strengthen the country's defenses should proceed, but that was "not the same thing as to say that as a thank offering for the present détente we should at once embark on a great increase in our armaments programme." His goal, he now told the House, had been "to work for the pacification of Europe, for the removal of those suspicions and those animosities which have so long poisoned the air. The path which leads to appeasement is long and bristles with obstacles." Czechoslovakia had been "the latest and perhaps the most dangerous" of these obstacles, but "now that we have got past it, I feel that it may be possible to make further progress along the road to sanity."[5]

The House did not hear him in silence. When he spoke proudly of the release by the Czechs of Sudetendeutsche prisoners, one MP called: "What about the kidnapped Czechs?" When he spoke of his "profound feeling of sympathy" for Czechoslovakia, several members cried, "Shame!" He replied: "I have done nothing to be ashamed of. Let those who have, hang their heads. We must feel profound sympathy for a small and gallant nation in the hour of their national grief and loss." A backbencher interrupted him: "It is an insult to say it." He told the House that "the real triumph" of Munich "is that it has shown that representatives of four great Powers can find it possible to agree on a way of carrying out a difficult and delicate operation by discussion instead of by force of arms, and thereby they have averted a catastrophe which would have ended civilisation as we have known it."[6]

Watching the prime minister, Harold Nicolson thought: "He is obviously tired and irritable and the speech does not go down well. Then up gets Anthony Eden. I felt at first that he was not coming out strongly enough, but he was getting the House on his side before opening the attack. When it came, it was superb." Eden doubted that "the events of the last few days . . . constitute the beginning of better things, as my right honorable friend [Chamberlain] hopes." Instead, he believed, "they only give us a breathing space, perhaps of six months or less, before the next crisis is upon us."[7]

Attlee, coming next, declared that they were "in the midst of a tragedy. We have felt humiliation. This has not been a victory for reason and humanity. It has been a victory for brute force." Sinclair noted that the P.M. had called the Munich terms a victory for self-determination; it was, he said, "a plain travesty of self-determination," because although the areas ceded were inhabited by "a substantial minority" of Germans, they *were* a minority, and many of them wanted no part of the Reich. The "irruption of German troops," he predicted, accurately, "will sweep before them a whole crowd of refugees who certainly would have been in favour of remaining in those territories. There is no justice or self-determination about that." Attacks on the settlement by Amery, Macmillan, and Bracken followed.[8]

Churchill sat, silent and immobile, for nearly three days of debate. He was scheduled to speak Wednesday after Sir John Simon, the chancellor of the Exchequer, wound up for the government. Simon declared that Chamberlain would be vindicated by time: "It can only be for history to decide hereafter whether the things done in Munich the other day lead . . . to better things, or whether the prognostications of increasing evil will prove to be justified." The crisis, he said, had been a splendid experience for the British people. Next time they would know precisely what to do. The Munich terms were "a vast improvement over the Godesberg Memorandum," he insisted. Everyone in the chamber knew that was untrue, and he finally acknowledged that His Majesty's Government was "deeply conscious today that while war has been avoided, Herr Hitler has again achieved the substance of his immediate and declared aim without declaring war."[9]

It was 5:10 P.M. when the Speaker recognized Churchill, and as Winston rose the mood of the House resembled that of Spaniards when the bull lunges into the arena. Before he had spoken a dozen words the turmoil began, and because nothing he said was conciliatory, it continued throughout the forty-nine minutes of his speech, led by Nancy Astor's cries of "Rude! Rude!" Sweeping the House with a hard stare, chin down, thumbs in his waistcoat pockets, feet solidly planted far apart, he declared that he would begin by saying "the most unpopular and most unwelcome thing. . . . We have sustained a total and unmitigated defeat, and . . . France has suffered even more than we have." Nancy called out, "Nonsense," and he whirled on her: "When the Noble Lady cries 'Nonsense' she could not have heard the Chancellor of the Exchequer admit in his illuminating and comprehensive speech just now that . . . the utmost . . . the Prime Minister has been able to secure by all his immense exertions, by all the great efforts and mobilisation which took place in this country, and by all the anguish and strain through which we have passed in this country, the utmost he has been able to gain has been —" He was interrupted by cries of "Peace!" ". . . the utmost he has been able to gain for Czechoslovakia and in the matters which were in dispute has been that the German dictator, instead of snatching his victuals from the table, has been content to have them served to him course by course." He saw no point in distinguishing between the positions reached at Berchtesgaden, Godesberg, and Munich. "They will be very simply epitomized, if the House will permit me to vary the metaphor. One pound was demanded at the pistol's point. When it was given, two pounds were demanded at the pistol's point. Finally, the dictator consented to take one pound, seventeen shillings and sixpence and the rest in promises of good will for the future." The terms Chamberlain had brought back with him could have been reached "through the ordinary diplomatic channels at any time during the summer. And I will say this, that I believe the Czechs, left to themselves and told they were going to get no help from the Western Powers, would have been able to make better terms than they have got."

He reviewed Hitler's successive aggressions and why all efforts to check him had failed: "There can never be absolute certainty that there will be a fight if one side is determined that it will give way completely." He himself had "always held the view that the maintenance of peace depends upon the accumulation of deterrents against the aggressor, coupled with a sincere effort to redress grievances." France and Britain — "especially if they had maintained a close contact with Russia, which certainly was not done" — could have influenced the "smaller States of Europe, and I believe they could have determined the attitude of Poland." Indeed, their impact would have been felt in the Reich, giving "strength to all that intense desire for peace which the helpless German masses share with their British and French fellow men, and which, as we have been reminded, found a passionate and rarely permitted vent in the joyous manifestations with which the Prime Minister was acclaimed in Europe."

Alliances and deterrents "of Powers, great and small, ready to stand firm upon the front of law and for the ordered remedy of grievances . . . might well have been effective." He did not "think it fair to charge those who wished to see this course followed, and followed consistently and resolutely, with having wished for immediate war. Between submission and immediate war there was this third alternative, which gave a hope not only of peace but of justice." Naturally, for such a policy to succeed, Britain "should declare straight out and a long time beforehand that she would, with others, join to defend Czechoslovakia against an unprovoked aggression." His Majesty's Government refused to give that guarantee when it would have saved the situation, yet in the end they gave it when it was too late, and now, for the future, they renew it when they have not the slightest power to make it good.

> All is over.
> Silent, mournful, abandoned, broken,
> Czechoslovakia recedes into darkness.

> She has suffered in every respect
> by her association with the Western democracies.

Plebiscites, he said, as defined in Hitler's Munich office, could not "amount in the slightest degree to a verdict of self-determination. It is a fraud and a farce to invoke that name. We in this country, as in other liberal and democratic countries, have a perfect right to exalt the principle of self-determination, but it comes ill out of the mouths of those in totalitarian States who deny even the smallest element of toleration to every section and creed within their bounds." In any event "this particular block of land, this mass of human beings to be handed over, has never expressed the desire to go under Nazi rule. I do not believe that even now, if their opinion could be asked, they would exercise such an option."

He asked: "What is the remaining position of Czechoslovakia? Not only are they politically mutilated, but, economically and financially, they are in complete confusion." Their banking and railroad nets were "severed and broken, their industries are curtailed, and the movement of their population is most cruel." He gave an example: "The Sudeten miners, who are all Czechs and whose families have lived in that area for centuries, must now flee into an area where there are hardly any mines left for them to work." He doubted — prophetically — that "in future the Czechoslovak State" could be "maintained as an independent entity. You will find that in a period of time which may be measured by years, but may be measured only by months, Czechoslovakia will be engulfed by the Nazi regime."

As a true Conservative, Churchill sought guidance "in the wisdom of the past, for all wisdom is not new wisdom." On holiday he had studied the reign of King Ethelred the Unready, and particularly "the rugged words of the Anglo-Saxon Chronicle, written a thousand years ago." He quoted a sentence: "All these calamities fell upon us because of evil counsel, because tribute was not offered to them at the right time nor yet were they resisted; but when they had done the most evil, then was peace made with them." So it was now: "We are in the presence of a disaster of the first magnitude which has befallen Great Britain and France. Do not let us blind ourselves to that. It must now be accepted that all the countries of Central and Eastern Europe will make the best terms they can with the triumphant Nazi Power." The democracies' loss of prestige, he told the House, beggared description. In Warsaw the British and French ambassadors sought to visit Colonel Józef Beck, Poland's foreign minister. "The door was shut in their faces." And what, he wondered, would be "the position of France and England this year and the year afterwards?" The German army probably outnumbered that of France now, "though not nearly so matured or perfected." There were, he said, unexplored options; unfortunately, none were encouraging. But what he found "unendurable" was "the sense of our country falling into the power, into the orbit and influence of Nazi Germany, and of our existence becoming dependent upon their good will or pleasure. . . . In a very few years, perhaps in a very few months, we shall be confronted with demands" which "may affect the surrender of territory or the surrender of liberty." A "policy of submission" would entail "restrictions" upon freedom of speech and the press. "Indeed, I hear it said sometimes now that we cannot allow the Nazi system of dictatorship to be criticised by ordinary, common English politicians."

He did not "grudge our loyal, brave people . . . the natural, spontaneous outburst of joy and relief" when they learned that war was not imminent, "but they should know the truth. They should know that there has been gross neglect and deficiency in our defences; they should know that we have sustained a defeat without a war, the consequences of which will travel far with us along our road; they should know that we have passed an awful milestone in our history, when the whole equilibrium of Europe has been deranged, and that the terrible words have for the time being been pronounced against the Western democracies: 'Thou art weighed in the balance and found wanting.' "

And do not suppose that this is the end.
This is only the beginning of the reckoning.

This is only the first sip —
    the first foretaste of a bitter cup
        which will be proffered to us year by year —

Unless —
    by a supreme recovery of our moral health and martial vigour,
        we arise again and take our stand for freedom,
            as in the olden time.[10]

Lord Maugham called Churchill an "agitator" who should be "shot or hanged." *The Times* reported that Churchill had "treated a crowded House to prophecies which made Jeremiah appear an optimist" and referred patronizingly to his "dismal sincerity." His speech, according to the *Daily Express*, was "an alarmist oration by a man whose mind is soaked in the conquests of Marlborough," and his failure to support the government "weakens his influence among members of the Conservative Party." It did indeed; Robert Rhodes James notes that "the feeling against him in the party was now intense."[11]

Parliament was still dominated by the privileged classes and their dread of the Soviets, a fear which Hitler played like a Stradivarius, repeatedly citing as his principal aim *"zur Bekämpfung des Bolschewismus"* ("the fight against bolshevism"). But out beyond Westminster and Whitehall — in the Midlands, the mines, the Lake District; the tributaries of the Thames, Humber, and Severn; and the commercial cities of Liverpool, Manchester, Birmingham, Sheffield, Leeds, and Bristol — there, once the first flush of gratitude for peace had passed, Munich became more controversial. In the House of Commons, once the big guns of Chamberlain's critics had ceased fire — Duff Cooper, Eden, and Churchill as anchor man — the debate would proceed languidly.

In humbler neighborhoods it was another story, now that Spain had taught rank-and-file workmen that fascism could not be stopped without bloodshed. This awareness was by no means confined to them. In Mayfair, Park Lane, and Bloomsbury, the wives of many Conservative MPs denounced their husbands' support for Chamberlain's appeasements.

These heated exchanges were not confined to the United Kingdom — England, Scotland, Wales, and Northern Ireland. Britain was still the world's sole superpower. The repercussions of decisions made in Whitehall and Downing Street were felt almost everywhere — throughout the Dominions and even in the United States, which was bumbling about, playing blindman's buff with the twin games of pacifism and isolationism. Churchill afterward wrote: "Among the Conservatives, families and friends in intimate contact were divided by a degree the like of which I have never seen. Men and women, long bound by party ties, the social amenities, and family connections, glared at one another in scorn and anger." His daughter Mary remembers: "Looking back, it is difficult to describe the feelings of anger, shame, and bitterness felt by those who opposed the Munich Agreement." And Lady Diana Cooper recalled that "husbands and wives stopped speaking to one another, fathers and sons said unforgivable things to one another; it was as if the entire country was in labor, straining to give birth. And in a way it was."[12]

Harold Macmillan believed that the new, proud Britain was two years in gestation and had been conceived in the summer of 1938, when dissident Tories, mostly young, began to form factions critical of the Chamberlain government. The followers of Leo Amery were stronger once he broke with HMG, but the most visible group was still Eden's. Eden's followers were pursued by the press; many of their leaders had distinguished themselves in the war, and they were commonly regarded as the next generation of ministers. Taken as a whole, however, they were altogether too civil, too respectful of their elders, too reluctant to take firm stands, and far too unimaginative to acquire the élan and vigor of successful Young Turks. They avoided offending the prime minister; they carefully disassociated themselves from Churchill and his tiny band; when Duncan Sandys expressed interest in attending one of their meetings, he was told that his presence was not required. In these weaknesses they reflected the flaws of their leader. Eden's departure from the Foreign Office had been the political sensation of the season, but his resignation speech was so crafted to avoid affronting anyone that, as Macmillan noted, it "left Members somewhat uncertain as to what all the row was about." At a Queen's Hall rally protesting Munich, Eden's discretion, according to Liddell Hart, irritated the audience, which grew restless. As he sat down, Violet Bonham Carter proposed the ritualistic vote of gratitude, but later she said she felt more like moving a vote of censure. Eden's chief asset then was that he was neither Neville Chamberlain nor Winston Churchill.[13]

In retrospect it seems that once Britain had grasped the price Chamberlain paid for Hitler's signature, the people should have turned to Churchill. In time they did, but public opinion is slow to coalesce, and as winter deepened and 1939 arrived, England vacillated. Certainly the average Briton was appalled by the Czech sellout. A poll taken after Godesberg showed that two out of every three Englishmen had disapproved of the Anglo-French proposals as too generous to Germany. Walking home on the evening of September 22, Duff Cooper had encountered a "vast procession . . . marching down Whitehall crying 'Stand by the Czechs' and 'Chamberlain must go.' " Yet England was not ready for Churchill. Capitulation to Hitler was unpopular, but the revulsion against a renewal of trench warfare remained. Although Winston's repeated calls for a defense buildup had been intended to avoid war, it was clear to all that, once committed, he would relish a good fight. As a Labour candidate had charged in 1923, he was "militant to the fingertips." In the wake of Munich a House critic effectively quoted A. G. Gardiner's comment made thirty years earlier: "Churchill will write his name in history; take care that he does not write it in blood."[14]

Macmillan recalled that "Everyone knew that so great was the strength of the Government in the country that nothing could seriously shake them in Parliament. At our almost daily conferences with our friends, we had the gloomiest forebodings. The tide was, at present, too strong. It was flowing against us — especially Churchill." Increasingly the dissidents' meetings were furtive, almost conspiratorial. Nicolson confided to his wife that he had attended "a hush-hush meeting" of a dozen MPs, including Eden, Amery, Macmillan, Sidney Herbert, and Duff Cooper. They had "decided that we should not advertise ourselves as a group or even call ourselves a group." It is difficult to understand what they hoped to accomplish; they would "merely meet together from time to time, exchange views, and organise ourselves for a revolt if needed." But they were too timid and far too respectable to rebel; Nicolson characterized them as "all good Tories and sensible men. This group is distinct from the Churchill group. . . . I feel happier about this."[15]

Part of Churchill's particular alienation may be traced to his megalomania, a source of strength in public life but distasteful to many in private. Boothby remarked that " 'Thou shall have no other gods but me' has always been the first, and the most significant, of his Commandments." Desmond Morton wrote a journalist long afterward: "The full truth, I believe, is that Winston's 'friends' must be persons who were of use to him. The idea of having a friend who was of no practical use to him, but being a friend because he liked him, had no place." To be sure, Morton's comment was made late in life, when he had become embittered because Churchill had not given him a more prominent role in the wartime government. But even Violet Bonham Carter, who adored Winston, conceded that "He demanded partisanship from a friend, or, at the worst, acquiescence."[16]

However, that was not why parliamentarians who had come to share his views avoided him in the House. Churchill was considered dangerous. If an MP had ministerial ambitions, association with Winston could kill his chances, and what could be the point of that? Because Churchill always seemed confident, strong, and self-assured, it never occurred to them that he might welcome a pat on the back, or a few pleasant words commending him for a great speech, despite the editorials, despite the lord chancellor's opinion that he should be introduced to a firing squad, or the noose of hemp, for having delivered it. The prime minister might notice, or hear of it. Since his acclamatory reception at the airport and at Downing Street, Chamberlain had acquired messianic airs.

On Thursday, the day after Churchill had spoken, the prime minister moved for an adjournment of the House until November 1. Attlee, Sinclair, and several Conservatives — Macmillan the most vehement of them — strongly protested. Churchill urged a two-day session in mid-October; it was "derogatory to Parliament," he said, "that it should be thought unfit, as it were, to be attending to these grave matters, that it should be sent away upon a holiday in one of the most formidable periods through which we have lived." Chamberlain replied shabbily that the Speaker decided when the House would be recalled, to which Winston instantly retorted: "But only on the advice of His Majesty's Government." Every MP knew that. Chamberlain called his remark "unworthy . . . tittle tattle," and now it was between the two of them; Winston, desperately in need of support, got none. He wrote No. 10, protesting the prime minister's slur, and the P.M. responded: "I am sorry if you think my remarks were offensive, but I must say that I think you are singularly sensitive for a man who so constantly attacks others. I considered your remarks highly offensive to me and to those with whom I have been working. . . . You cannot expect me to allow you to do all the hitting and never hit back."[17]

Churchill returned to Chartwell profoundly depressed. He canceled a lecture at the Imperial Defence College, explaining, "I am so distressed by the change in the situation that I haven't the heart to address myself to the task to which you invited me at present." Paul Reynaud and Georges Mandel, outraged by Munich, had resigned from the French cabinet, and Winston wrote Reynaud: "I cannot see what foreign policy is now open to the French Republic. No minor State will risk its future upon the guarantee of France. I am indulging in no pretensions upon our own account. . . . Can we make headway against the Nazi domination, or ought we *severally* to make the best terms possible with it — while trying to rearm? Or is a common effort still possible?" His nephew John George Churchill later told Martin Gilbert: "The gloom after Munich was absolutely terrific. At Chartwell there were occasions just alone with him when the despondency was overwhelming." To an old Canadian friend Winston wrote on October 11: "I am now greatly distressed, and for the time being staggered by the situation. Hitherto the peace-loving Powers have been definitely stronger than the Dictators, but next year we must expect a different balance."[18]

He thought he had touched bottom when Edward abdicated, but this was worse. *That*, however, was part of *this*. In 1936, A. J. P. Taylor writes, "Churchill had seemed the rallying point for patriotic and democratic opinion," but Winston's ambiguous position on the Spanish Civil War and his championing of a discredited monarch eroded his support, and "his prestige ran downhill," particularly on the left. The conventional explanation for his continued isolation is that he had outraged Parliament by his long losing battle for the Indian Raj; but Chamberlain had deplored the parliamentary maneuvers which led to dominion status for India. Labour approved of Winston's support of the League of Nations but recoiled from his calls for collective security. He "estranged the idealists," as Taylor puts it, "and so remained until the outbreak of war a solitary

figure, distrusted by both sides." After Britain's disillusionment with
Munich — and the "first ecstasy," noted Muggeridge, "soon passed" when
Englishmen realized that the agreement would "involve still further concessions to Germany" — reasonable men might at the very least have
acknowledged that Churchill had been right. But politics is never reasonable. Having denied, ridiculed, and scorned his accusations and impeach-
ments, the cabinet could not indemnify him without confessing to its own
incompetence.[19]

As the last weeks of 1938 skulked away, anyone wagering that the member
from Epping would still be in his corner seat a year hence would have been
entitled to ask for odds. Two exits were available. He could quit, or his
constituents could recall him. He had hung on for nine years, hoping for
a responsible post, but the chances of that were as remote as ever. He was
still urging the strengthening of Britain's defenses, and that, in the eyes of
the appeasers, was enough to disqualify him, despite his great abilities.
Furthermore, as Chamberlain noted in his diary, recognition of Churchill
was out of the question as long as friendship with Hitler and Mussolini
seemed possible: "I wouldn't risk it by what would certainly be regarded by
them as a challenge." Macmillan told Hugh Dalton that in Parliament or
out, Churchill was "in danger of relapsing into a complacent Cassandra. He
would say: 'Well, I have done my best. I have made all these speeches.
Nobody has paid any attention. All my prophecies have turned out to be true.
I have been publicly snubbed by the Government. What more can I do?' "[20]
    In London it seemed inconceivable that Churchill could be forced to
resign his seat in Parliament. But in the aftermath of Munich, during
those weeks in which it seemed that Chamberlain had actually succeeded in
buying peace, the rank and file of Conservative voters, proud of the party's
leader, were aroused by any criticism of him. In this political climate the
Sunday Express ran a brief item under the head: "Trouble is being made for
Churchill in Epping. The campaign is strong, the campaigners determined." Winston sent Beaverbrook a note of protest; the story, he wrote,
was "misleading as to the true state of affairs: & certainly most unhelpful
to me." It was unhelpful, but it was also accurate. Two of his loyal
constituents, Sir Harry Goschen and Sir Colin Thornton-Kemsley, had
been dismayed by his Munich speech. Goschen wrote to the chairman of
the Epping Conservative Association, Sir James Hawkey, that he could not
"help thinking it was rather a pity that he broke up the harmony of the
House by the speech he made. . . . I think it would have been a great deal
better if he had kept quiet and not made a speech at all."[21]
    Goschen decided to stick with Churchill; but Thornton-Kemsley
wanted him repudiated and replaced by someone who would "support the

Conservative administration, not . . . discredit them." On November 4, in a public meeting, Churchill defended his position on Munich. Then Thornton-Kemsley spoke, arguing that Winston's attempts to contain Germany with a "ring of strongly armed powers" had foundered. There was, he said, no conflict between British and German goals, and if the four nations represented at Munich could "agree upon a policy of friendship," no other nation would dare touch off a war. The audience seemed equally divided, but Hawkey lent his support to Winston, and his constituents passed a resolution regretting the failure of His Majesty's Government to respond to their member's warnings "given during the last five years" and declaring that had the prime minister and his cabinet followed Churchill's advice, Chamberlain "would have found himself in a far better position to negotiate with the heads of the dictator States."[22]

Churchill was once more secure in Epping — or so it seemed in November 1938 — but as Sarah later wrote him: "What price politics since they won't listen to you?" The one who listened least was the one who mattered most.[23]

Neville Chamberlain believed that Munich was the triumph of his career. Intolerant of dissent, a believer in strong party discipline, he was vain, rude, and vindictive. These unattractive traits were balanced by terrific energy, a powerful intellect, and an even stronger gift for command. William Strang, of the Foreign Office, who was outraged by the Munich settlement, nevertheless saw him as "a man of cool, calm mind, strong will, decisive purpose, wholly devoted to the public cause and with a firm confidence in his own judgment."[24]

If he had a sense of humor, it is unrecorded. In any event, he did not think public business and national institutions subject to levity. He had detested Rugby as much as Winston had Harrow; nevertheless, he believed that public schools were part of the social order and should not be mocked. When Churchill told the House that "Britain is like a Laocoön strangled by old school ties" and compared England's public school system to "feeding sham pearls to real swine," Neville scowled. An incapacity for the droll and the whimsical is typical of fanatics — and the prime minister now resembled a skipper who has set his bearing and lashed himself to the wheel. After Munich he should have given England's security overriding priority, but on Christmas Day, 1938, Oliver Harvey, a senior civil servant in the Foreign Office, noted despondently in his diary that Chamberlain was not pressing on with rearmament, that under Inskip the Committee of Imperial Defence "goes slower and slower," and that "Inskip must certainly go. A much more vigorous and imaginative man should be there. Winston is the obvious man, but I believe the PM would rather die than have him."[25]

That much seemed clear. In November, addressing the House of Commons from the front bench, the P.M. had scorned Winston, repeating the old accusation of Churchillian instability. It was the same old wine from the same dirty bottles, but no one could remember a British prime minister turning on one of his own party's private members. It simply wasn't done. And it was particularly unwise to do it to Churchill, as Chamberlain learned when Winston, speaking to 1,200 of his constituents in Chingford on December 9, noted that the P.M. had told Parliament "that where I failed, for all my brilliant gifts, was in the faculty of judging. I will gladly submit my judgement about foreign affairs and national defence during the last five years in comparison to his own."[26]

It was a devastating speech. In 1934, he recalled, Chamberlain had been chancellor of the Exchequer when Winston warned Stanley Baldwin that "the Germans had a secret Air Force and were rapidly overhauling ours. I gave definite figures and forecasts. Of course, it was all denied with all the weight of official authority." He had been derided as a "scaremonger." In less than six months, he reminded his audience, Baldwin "had to come down to the House and admit he was wrong and he said, 'We are all to blame.' " Baldwin had "got more applause for making this mistake, which may prove fatal to the British Empire and to British freedom," than most Englishmen who rendered a great service to the nation. "Mr Chamberlain was, next to Mr Baldwin, the most powerful Member of that Government. . . . He knew all the facts. His judgement failed just like that of Mr Baldwin and we are suffering from the consequences of it today." That blunder had been only the beginning. A year later Winston had asked that the RAF be doubled and redoubled, which prompted Lord Samuel, who shared Chamberlain's faith in appeasement, to say he thought "my judgement so defective that he likened me to a Malay running amok. It would have been well for him and his persecuted race if my advice had been taken. They would not be where they are now."

He then turned to Chamberlain's record as prime minister over the past two years. In his early days at No. 10 "the Prime Minister made a heart-to-heart settlement with Mr de Valera, and gave up to him those fortified ports on the South Coast of Ireland which are vital to our food supply in time of war." The P.M. led Englishmen to believe that "the country now called Eire were reconciled to us in friendship, but I warned him with my defective judgement that if we got into any great danger Mr de Valera would demand the surrender of Ulster as the price of any friendship or aid." And this, he said, "fell out exactly." Recently De Valera had announced that he could give England neither friendship nor aid while any British troops remained in Northern Ireland.

Next, in February 1938, Churchill continued, Chamberlain had said that

tension in Europe had greatly relaxed. A few weeks later Nazi Germany seized Austria. I predicted that he would repeat this statement as soon as the shock of the rape of Austria passed away. He did so in the very same words at the end of July. By the middle of August Germany was mobilising for those bogus manoeuvres which after bringing us all to the verge of a world war, ended in the complete destruction and absorption of the Republic of Czechoslovakia. At the Lord Mayor's Banquet in November at the Guild-hall, he told us that Europe was settling down into a more peaceful state. The words were hardly out of his mouth before the Nazi atrocities upon the Jewish population resounded throughout the civilised world.

These "proved errors of judgement in the past," Winston ended, should be weighed carefully when pondering "some of the judgements which have been passed upon the future, the results of which have not yet been proved."[27]

The Treasury Bench excepted, Churchill *did* have an attentive audience in Parliament, and they were its elite, men of eminence and accomplishment in other fields, backbenchers many of them, not because they lacked ministerial talent but because their time for public affairs was limited. In the division over the Munich Agreement, MPs, following their ancient ritual, had left the chamber to vote for or against it. Thirty eminent Conservatives remained seated, however, signifying abstention. This, wrote Nicolson, "must enrage the Government, since it is not our numbers that count but our reputation." Among the abstainers were Churchill, Eden, Duff Cooper, Leo Amery, Roger Keyes, Macmillan, Sandys, Bracken, and Boothby. This was a sign of party disarray. Rank and file MPs, Nicolson noted, realized that these dissidents "know far more about the real issue than they do." It was clear that "the Government were rattled by this. . . . The House breaks up with the Tories yelling to keep their spirits up. But they well know that Chamberlain has put us in a ghastly position and that we ought to have been prepared to go to war and smash Hitler. Next time he will be far too strong for us." On November 17 Churchill wrote in the *Daily Telegraph:* "Everyone must recognize that the Prime Minister is pursuing a policy of a most decided character. . . . By this time next year we shall know whether the Prime Minister's view of Herr Hitler and the German Nazi Party is right or wrong. By this time next year we shall know whether the policy of appeasement has appeased, or whether it has only stimulated a more ferocious appetite." Privately he wrote Lord Wolmer on December 12: "Neville leads us from bad to worse."[28]

Certainly he had presided over a series of disastrous defeats in 1938, altering the European balance of power and putting in jeopardy nations in eastern Europe which were friendly to France and Britain. The Anschluss and Munich had swollen the Reich's population by 10,250,000 — conscripts for the Wehrmacht, toilers in arms factories, drudges for the expanding empire. But it had already become clear that the safeguards adopted at Munich — the international commission and the guarantee of Czechoslovakia's new borders — were worthless. The commission met in the Wilhelmstrasse, under Ribbentrop's eye; the British and French delegates were under instructions, from Halifax and Bonnet, to yield to Hitler whenever possible. Their request for a definition of the impossible was unanswered. And Churchill's prediction that the Czech state could not survive the butchery of its frontiers in the Führerbau had been swiftly realized. With Beneš gone, the Czech defensive forts in Nazi hands, and ethnic minorities at each other's throats, the only democracy in eastern Europe was disintegrating. The Slovaks made the first move toward autonomy on October 6; three days later the Ukrainians followed their example; and on November 2 German and Italian arbitrators awarded Hungary nearly 4,600 square miles of Czechoslovakian soil. That left the Czech rump of Bohemia and Moravia, vaguely associated with the independent governments of Slovakia and Ruthenia.

At Chartwell, Churchill read reports of anti-Nazi fugitives from the Sudetenland. They echoed the tales Viennese had told earlier: midnight arrests, Gestapo firing squads, respectable leaders of their communities vanishing into concentration camps. On October 7 Halifax sent Berlin a note citing press accounts of such ill-treatment; he would be grateful, he said, for information "to combat such assertions, the spreading of which might in fact hamper the advocates of Anglo-German relations in the realisation of their aspirations." Hitler's response gave Britain's foreign secretary a lesson straight from *Mein Kampf:* anyone who agreed to negotiate with Nazis emerged a loser, his wounded pride treated with vigorous applications of salt. Speaking at Saarbrücken two days later, the Führer angrily declared: "We cannot tolerate any longer the tutelage of governesses. Inquiries of British politicians concerning the fate of Germans within the frontiers of the Reich — or of lands belonging to the Reich — are none of their concern."[29]

On the last evening of 1938 Nicolson wrote: "It has been a bad year. . . . A foul year. Next year will be worse." Churchill, more optimistic, told his constituents in January that while Englishmen like himself doubted that Munich had "purchased a lasting peace," they felt that at least a "breathing space" had been won. He said: "Let us make sure that this breathing space is not improvidently cast away." Later, after the Men of Munich had been discredited, that became the keystone of their cover-up; they had, they said, bought time to rearm. It wouldn't wash. The day after Churchill's speech, Chamberlain rejected Secretary for War Hore-Belisha's request for a larger army budget, playing the same weary tune the cabinet had heard so often before, telling them that "finances cannot be ignored, since our financial strength is one of our strongest weapons in any war which is not over in a short time." As a former chancellor, he said, he thought Britain's financial position looked "extremely dangerous." Other ministers argued that Hitler would be shocked by British rearmament, interpreting it as inconsistent with the spirit of Munich, asking why, if the two countries were trusted friends, England was arming to the teeth. Hore-Belisha proposed conscription. He was denied it. Kingsley Wood wanted air parity with Germany. His request was also denied, but because he invested everything he was given in new, superior fighter planes — while the bloated Luftwaffe remained content with what it had — the number of Spitfire and Hurricane squadrons jumped from five to forty-seven in a year. Antiaircraft batteries also multiplied, but "these improvements," as Churchill later wrote, "were petty compared with the mighty advance in German armaments."[30]

In every other category — artillery, tanks, and equipped divisions — Nazi gains were overwhelming. While Chamberlain was lecturing his ministers on the military value of stocks and bonds and spending £304 million on arms, German arms expenditures exceeded £1.5 billion — a fivefold gap. The number of Nazi divisions jumped from seven to fifty-one. By calling up trained reserves, the Reich could field an army of over seven million men, outnumbering the armies of France and England combined, and the Führer, unlike the democracies, did not have troops tied down in colonial possessions overseas. Vis-à-vis France, Churchill found, with every month that passed from 1938 onward the German army not only increased "in numbers and formations . . . but in quality and maturity." He believed that "in morale also the Germans had the advantage," and he attributed the ebbing of French martial resolve to Munich: "The desertion of an ally, especially from fear of war, saps the spirit of any army."[31]

※　※

Less than two months after Munich, Churchill entered his sixty-fifth year, and some parliamentarians, including friends, thought he was beginning to show his age. On Monday, December 5, the House of Commons received its long-awaited report on the preposterous attempt to court-martial Duncan Sandys. Everyone was exonerated; "misunderstandings" were blamed. Churchill rose. He started brilliantly, and everyone, Nicolson wrote, was "expecting a great speech." Then:

He accuses Hore-Belisha of being too complacent. The latter gets up and says, "When and where?" Winston replies, "I have not come unprepared," and begins to fumble among his notes, where there are some presscuttings. He takes time. He finds them. But they are not the best cuttings, and the ones he reads out tend to excuse rather than implicate Hore-Belisha. Winston becomes confused. He tries to rally his speech, but the wind has gone out of his sails, which flop wretchedly. "He is becoming an old man," says Bill Mabane beside me.[32]

It wasn't age, and he was capable of rebounding. The fact is that he was simply attempting to do too much. Indeed, the wonder is that he found time to appear in the House at all. His writing schedule continued to be punishing, and even as he struggled to meet it, Grace Hamblin recalls, Chartwell was being inundated by a blizzard of invitations to speak. As the taste of Munich turned to ashes, people wanted to see and hear the vindicated Ishmael. He was sensible enough to decline these, though some were tempting: the League of Nations Union, the Oxford Union (from its young president Edward Heath, a future prime minister), and a Jewish Youth Rally for National Service ("because of your courageous defence of freedom and denunciation of Nazi-ism [sic] you are held in the very highest esteem by all sections of Jewry"). He even turned down a dinner invitation from General Edward L. Spears, a fellow officer in Flanders twenty years earlier, explaining that "It is absolutely necessary for me to be in the country every possible night this year in order to complete the history I am writing."[33]

By day, however, he entertained visitors: French politicians, men who had held high posts in Vienna and Prague, and German anti-Nazis, many of them, like Count Lutz Schwerin von Krosigk, the Führer's finance minister, members of the old Wilhelmine aristocracy. In January a high French source sent Chartwell, in great confidence, information unknown to anyone in the British government. Deuxième Bureau agents were reporting that German munitions convoys were moving across Czechoslovakia, from the Sudetenland to the Hungarian frontier. Churchill immediately took this to the Foreign Office, where it was confirmed and then dismissed as part of a program to execute maneuvers and rearm the Austrian army on "the German scale and with German weapons."[34]

Of course, Winston could not hew to a spartan regimen. No one could work harder — while writing longer and more strenuously than ever before, he was also in one of his periods of intense bricklaying — but he had no intention of abandoning his sybaritic life-style. In the House of Commons he defended it with wit. Among the unhappiest victims of his gibes was Sir Stafford Cripps. Cripps was one of the very few on Labour's side of the House who shared Churchill's contempt for appeasement; he begged the front bench to rearm before Hitler struck. But he was also ascetic, a vegetarian, a man who shunned coffee and tea and quit smoking cigars because he thought the habit vulgar. "My God," said Churchill when told of this. "Cripps has cut his last tie with human civilization." On another, later occasion, Churchill was airborne over the Sahara Desert when his plane had to land for an emergency repair. Winston stretched his legs and gazed in all directions. "Here we are marooned in all these miles of sand — not a blade of grass or a drop of water or a flower," he said. "How Cripps would have loved it."[35]

Churchill did not propose to slacken his pace, but experience had taught him that he could be equally productive, and more comfortable, on the Riviera. Thus, in the first week of January 1939, after an interview with Kingsley Martin of the *New Statesman* — "War is horrible," he told Martin, "but slavery is worse, and you may be sure the British people would rather go down fighting than live in servitude" — he was off for Maxine's Château de l'Horizon. Changing trains in Paris, he read in the papers that the Germans had announced a vast plan to expand their submarine fleet. Before unpacking in Cannes he wrote and cabled home a *Daily Telegraph* column, calling the Nazi U-boat program "a heavy blow to all international cooperation in support of public law." It meant, he said, that England was imperiled by an "avoidable danger" which could only be mastered after great "loss and suffering." The *Telegraph* was unread in Cannes, but a local newspaper subscribed to his syndicate, and there was a stirring in the lush villas when the same paper ran an earlier piece in which Churchill pondered an Anglo-Soviet détente. Among its readers was the quondam king of England, now Duke of Windsor, and he was splenetic.[36]

To Churchill, Edward's wrath, once majestic, now seemed more like petty whining. By now Winston had shed all illusions about the man he had championed, at such cost to his career and the cause he led. There was, he noted, no depth to the man; he never read a serious book, never gave the world's affairs profound thought, and what he presented as opinion was merely narrow, ill-informed prejudice. He doted on his wife, who ordered him about, apparently to his delight. Winston was amused by Wallis's sartorial influence on her husband. On the memorable night when the Duke crossed swords with Churchill in Maxine's white-and-gold dining room he was wearing a Stuart tartan kilt. He was lucky Winston didn't leave him without a fig leaf, according to the account of Vincent Sheean, who kept notes when, as he wrote,

the Duke of Windsor and Mr. Churchill settled down to a prolonged argument, with the rest of the party listening in silence. . . . We sat by the fireplace, Mr. Churchill frowning with intentness at the floor in front of him, mincing no words, reminding HRH of the British constitution on occasion — "When our kings are in conflict with our constitution, we change our kings," he said — and declaring flatly that the nation stood in the gravest danger of its long history. The kilted Duke . . . sat on the edge of the sofa, eagerly interrupting whenever he could, contesting every point, but receiving — in terms of the utmost politeness as far as the words went — an object lesson in political wisdom and public spirit. . . . There was something dramatically final, irrevocable about this dispute.[37]

According to Sheean and their hostess, those who thought of Winston as doddering should have been there that evening. Afterward Maxine wrote Churchill, "Never have I seen you in such good form. . . . You are the most enormously gifted creature in the whole world and it is like the sunshine leaving when you go away." England was not like sunshine to him. "People talk of how brave Winston was in 1940," Lady Diana Cooper observed, "but his highest courage, and it was his *moral* courage, shone through when he saw war coming, England virtually helpless, and himself impotent — when he spoke the truth and men he had entertained in his home cut him in Parliament Square." He took it; he had to take it, but he didn't have to like it. Writhing in the bonds of his frustration he reminded Virginia Cowles of "a mighty torrent trying to burst its dam."[38]

That was one aspect of him, and to all but the few close to him it was the intrinsic Churchill, his quiddity and diathesis. Most public men have one personality for the world and another in private. Winston Churchill was an exception. In his greater speeches he could hold Parliament spellbound; at Chartwell his guests were entranced as he used the same language, mannerisms, and expressions. He could reminisce with old comrades, and the emotional undercurrent was always there. His eyes would fill, but like a sun shower the misty moment passed. The only people who saw the intimate Churchill — who knew the power and depth of his love, which lay within him like a vast reservoir eternally replenishing itself, available to them in boundless measure when they were parched or careworn — those few whom he cherished, were his family. His awareness of them was constant. In the middle of a letter on another topic in early

1939, he interpolated: "Mary has been . . . vy sweet to me and is growing into her beauty." His son had tried him as few fathers have been tried; nevertheless, it was understood that once Randolph married and began his own family, Chartwell would be his: his parents would move into more modest quarters. Creating those quarters was the impulse behind Churchill's renewed interest in bricklaying. Some diversion from his writing was essential, and he was aware of it. There were only so many productive working hours in a day; anything written beyond that was chaff. So he painted, fed his goldfish, savored his Pol Roger, and laid his bricks, letting his mind drift and rejuvenating his powers of thought.[39]

As usual, he had a new Chartwell improvement in progress. He was, he wrote Clemmie on January 28, supervising the tiling of roofs, putting down new floors, and "the joinery of the doors, cupboards, etc." Any other country squire at his age might have been overseeing such projects. But Churchill, as always, had grander plans. He was already building one cottage on the grounds with his own hands and planning another — for Clemmie and himself — when he retired and Randolph became Chartwell's householder. He wrote her: "In the summer when I am sure the book will be finished, I think I will build a house." It would stand on ten acres far from the mansion, he wrote, and would "cost about three thousand pounds." This was reasonable. Assuming he met the terms of his continuing contract for the *English-speaking Peoples* and completed assignments for *Collier's, News of the World,* the *Daily Mirror,* and his fortnightly syndicated columns, his literary earnings for 1939 would be £15,781. But knowing her dread of debt, he assured her that "we could sell it for five or six thousand pounds." After he had met all his writing deadlines he planned to ask Sir Edwin Lutyens, the eminent architect, for appraisals and opinions, hastily adding: "He will do this for nothing, I am sure, as he has always begged to give advice." For Winston the immediate value of the construction would be recreational: "It would amuse me all the summer and give me good health." To further soothe her he promised that "downstairs you will have one lovely big room" and "you may be sure that nothing will be done until you have passed the plans. I have at least two months work ahead on the present cottage." He had already christened it "Orchard Cottage."[40]

This letter reached her in Barbados. The year just passed, so disastrous for British diplomacy, had also been wobbly for her. A succession of minor ailments discouraged activity, and in July she had spent nearly three weeks alone in the French Pyrenees "taking the cure." In Paris she had broken her toe, a minor affliction but painful and slow to heal. Then came Munich and Winston's denunciation of it. Early in their marriage, as the wife of a politician who took unpopular stands, she had known that part of the price he paid — social opprobrium — must be shared by her. At first, when old acquaintances crossed the street to avoid greeting her, she had been shocked and hurt. She had been young and resilient then, however; tempered by her own anger, she had learned to take such shabby partisanship in her stride. It had seemed a small sacrifice; she shared her husband's convictions and was proud to be his wife. The pride was still there, but she was older now, and slights were harder to bear. Her spirits were at their lowest when deliverance, or what looked like it, appeared in the form of an invitation from Lord Moyne, suggesting that she join him and his friends for another voyage on the *Rosaura,* this time in the Caribbean. She loved the yacht and loved the idyllic islands, but her hopes of recapturing the ecstasy of their South Seas cruise four years earlier were crushed. As an unreconstructed Liberal she was outraged by conditions in the British West Indies. "These islands," she wrote Winston, "are beautiful in themselves but have been desecrated & fouled by man." Starchy food kept the population "alive but undernourished — eighty percent of the population is illegitimate, seventy percent (in several islands) have syphilis and yaws." There was no sanitation of any sort, not even earth latrines. "And this," she bitterly concluded, "is a sample of the British Empire upon which the sun never sets."[41]

She felt he was neglecting her. In the past, when they were parted he had sent her long, clever holographs, decorated with drawings of pigs or pug dogs. Now, preoccupied with his manuscripts, avalanches of mail, and the recurring crises in Parliament, he dictated notes or cables. She responded tartly: *"Please* don't telegraph — I hate telegrams just saying 'all well rainy weather love Winston.' " The news he did send was worse than none: an obituary of Sir Sidney Peel, who had fallen in love with her when she was eighteen, just after the turn of the century. She had nearly married him; twice they had been secretly engaged. Winston commented: "Many are dying that I knew when we were young. It is quite astonishing to reach the end of life & feel just as you did fifty years before. One must always hope for a sudden end, before faculties decay." By the time the *Rosaura* approached Nelson's old dockyard on Antigua, Clemmie was plainly homesick. "I miss you & Mary & home terribly," she wrote, "& although it is a boon to miss the English Winter & to bask in this warmth, I really think I should come home — only that I hope this prolonged voyage in warm weather will really set me up in health — I do not yet feel very strong, but I am sure I shall."[42]

She found strength when, following the news and reading Winston's letters — now frequent, long, and penitent — she realized how lonely and embattled he must be. In the February 9 *Daily Telegraph* he had ruefully conceded that support for a firm stand against Nazi aggression was still weak, that "ripples of optimism" to the contrary were, "alas," based on "insufficient justifications." He pointed out that the press had reported long troop trains passing through Vienna and Munich and asked "What is their destination? What is their purpose?" Obviously, the British public didn't care. Mussolini was mobilizing for an invasion of Albania, and Hitler had announced that Germany would support the Duce: "Indeed, it is clear that the German dictator could not afford to witness the downfall of his Italian colleague."

Nevertheless, England remained lethargic. In an attempt to rouse it, he had left his Disraeli desk for a whirlwind lecture tour, but his audiences had been small and tepid. To a friend he wrote: "Nothing but the terrible teaching of experience will affect this all-powerful, supine Government. The worst of it is that by the time they are convinced, or replaced, our own position will be frightfully weakened." Hitler appeared determined to fight on one issue or another; it hardly seemed to matter which. And each fresh concession by Chamberlain and Halifax debilitated Britain as the inevitable showdown approached.[43]

In the middle of one letter home Clementine blurted out, "O Winston, are we drifting into War?" England, it seemed, yearning for peace and all but defenseless, was nevertheless tottering toward the brink "without the wit to avoid it or the will to prepare for it." Then she scrawled across the page: "God bless you my darling." Thus clouds were gathering within her, and sooner or later Clementine's overcast moods led to an outburst. One that entered Churchill family lore occurred when Moyne and his guests were listening to a BBC political broadcast. The speaker was vehemently pro-appeasement — Sir John Reith banned any arguments from the other side — and when Churchill was attacked by name, Lady Vera Broughton, another member of the party, cried: "Hear, Hear!" Clementine awaited a conciliatory word from her host, but he compressed his lips and remained silent. That put the wind in her sails. She flew to her cabin, wrote him a note of explanation, and packed. Lady Broughton arrived, begging Clemmie to stay, in vain; Winston Churchill had been insulted, and Mrs. Winston Churchill would accept no apologies. Ashore, she booked a berth on the *Cuba*, which was sailing for England in the morning.[44]

As she entered Chartwell's front hall she cried their old mating call: "Wot!" And from deep within the mansion came the delighted echo: *"Wot!"* He embraced her, heard her story with pride and pleasure, described his progress on the manuscript, and then broke the news, as gently as possible, of a new attempt to expel him from Parliament. This second campaign, four months after the first, was again led by Thornton-Kemsley. But "Peace for our time," which had pealed across the land then, now had a hollow ring. Winston knew he had but to hire a hall or two, give tongue to what was in his heart, and his constituents would come gamboling to him.

That was his strategy, and it worked, first in Chigwell, on March 10, 1939, and then at Waltham Abbey four days later. He was in fine, fiery form at Chigwell, repeating his indictment of Munich ("I do not withdraw a single word"), declaring that he would "cordially support" larger defense appropriations, approved of a recent Chamberlain call at the Soviet embassy "to show the world" that Britain was prepared to cooperate with Moscow "so long as Russia continues to show herself an active friend to peace," and — this was mendacious — saying, "I have been out of office for ten years, but I am more contented with the work I have done in these past five years as an Independent Conservative than of any other part of my public life." He asked them: "What is the use of Parliament if it is not the place where true statements can be brought before the people?"[45]

Winston was confident, and no wonder. In the months following Munich, Hitler himself had entered the fray on behalf of those working against Churchill. No doubt the Führer had felt provoked: "When you look long into an abyss," Nietzsche wrote, "the abyss also looks into you." Churchill had been glaring at the Reich since the birth of the Nazi regime, and as the Führer looked up and their eyes locked, staring across the North Sea, Hitler impulsively decided to hound his gadfly from public life. The Führer had been nettled by the attempts of Britons, and particularly Winston in his syndicated columns, to arouse anti-Nazi Germans. Speaking at Weimar he said: "If Mr. Churchill had less to do with traitors and more with Germans, he would see how mad his talk is, for I can assure this man, who seems to live on the moon, that there are no forces in Germany opposed to the régime — only the force of the National Socialist movement, its leaders and its followers in arms." If Churchill returned to office, he predicted that his "aim would be to unleash [*loslassen*] at once a new world war against Germany."[46]

Churchill immediately issued a statement expressing surprise that "the head of a great State" should attack private members of Parliament "who hold no official position and who are not even leaders of parties." He said: "Such action on his part can only enhance any influence they may have, because their fellow countrymen have long been able to form their own opinions about them, and really do not need foreign guidance." As A. J. P. Taylor puts it, Hitler tried to "split British opinion." Assuming that Englishmen could be manipulated like Germans, he believed that advocacy of British rearmament would raise opposition among England's pro-Germans — whose number he vastly exaggerated, and whom he expected to sway by denouncing Winston as a "warmonger" (*"Kriegshetzer"*).

This, he thought, would be Churchill's undoing. It was a *kolossal* error. The voters, in Taylor's words, "resented Hitler's interference in their affairs. They believed in non-interference. Hitler could do what he liked in Eastern Europe; he could demolish Czechoslovakia or invade the Ukraine. But he must leave British politicians alone." His demands that Churchill be routed gave the English *Kriegshetzers*, Taylor observes, "a popularity which they could not have won for themselves."[47]

One wonders who, or what, was behind the challenges to Churchill. Obscure backbenchers are voted in and out of the House, but no one could remember a concerted attempt to unseat an eminent statesman known and respected in every European capital. There was gossip of German money being distributed among Winston's critics, but this lurid version is wholly without evidence. Thornton-Kemsley hinted at a more plausible source of support when he said that unless Winston was prepared to work with "our great Prime Minister, he ought no longer to shelter under the goodwill and name which attaches to a great Party." Later he added: "It was made clear to me that the growing 'revolt' in the Epping Division . . . was welcomed in high places."[48]

How high he did not say, but it was hardly a secret that the P.M. would be glad to see his eloquent critic retired; he had written his sister that Winston was "carrying on a regular campaign against me with the aid of [Jan] Masaryk, the Czech minister. They, of course, are totally unaware of my knowledge of their proceedings." He said he had "information of their doings & sayings which for the nth time demonstrated how completely Winston can deceive himself when he wants to, & how utterly credulous a foreigner can be when he is told the things he wants to hear." It seems unlikely that Chamberlain would instigate a plot against Churchill, but it is even unlikelier that Tories "in high places" would encourage Thornton-Kemsley without the knowledge and even the support of the party's national leader. Viewed in any light, the effort to unseat Churchill is depressing, a symptom of the squalid political intrigues which afflicted England as her hour of peril approached — and a direct consequence, ironically, of a selfless but mindless crusade for peace.[49]

Entering Waltham Abbey for his speech on March 14, Winston was handed a report that Nazi troops were massing along the frontiers of mutilated Czechoslovakia. At the lectern he departed from his notes to say: "The Czechoslovakian Republic is being broken up before our eyes. They are being completely absorbed; and not until the Nazi shadow has finally been lifted from Europe — as lifted I am sure it will eventually be — not until then will Czechoslovakia and ancient Bohemia again march into freedom." But, he added, to suppose that this new aggression did not threaten England was "a profound illusion." Although Britain could "do nothing to stop it," Britons would suffer "on a very great scale." Not only would they have to make financial sacrifices, which "would have been unnecessary if a firm resolve had been taken at an earlier stage," but English lives would be forfeit, and for the same reason.[50]

Late that night, after a BBC broadcast announced that Hitler had annexed Bohemia, Churchill — who was at the time writing about the late seventeenth century — told his son: "It's hard to take one's attention off the events of today and concentrate on the reign of James II — but I'm going to do it." It was perhaps the most remarkable example of his genius for concentration. Randolph stared in astonishment as his father rose and plodded up the stairs to his study. The reports were, in fact, extraordinary, and the following day they were confirmed. Barely three years earlier, in the *Friedensrede* following his Rhineland coup, the Führer of the Third Reich had assured the world that he had "no territorial demands" to make in Europe, and that "Germany will never break the peace!" At Munich he had told Chamberlain that he wanted no Czechs in his realm and had even joined the British prime minister in guaranteeing the frontiers of the truncated Czech state. Now, on March 15, he was entering its capital at the head of his troops, standing erect in an open Mercedes, beaming and extending a stiff-armed *Hitlergruss*. But here, unlike Vienna and the Sudetenland, few arms rose in response. The Czechs were stunned. So was all Europe. So was Neville Chamberlain.[51]

🦁   🦁

"**H**ITLER IN PRAGUE!**" screamed the newspaper posters on kiosks throughout England. What, outraged Englishmen asked one another, was he doing there? They had read his personal pledges to Chamberlain at Munich and his promise to be guided by the international commission, which would recognize Reich sovereignty only in "predominantly German" areas. Most Britons were unaware that Germany had ignored the commission with the connivance of London and Paris, unaware of Czechoslovakia's slow disintegration, unaware that the Nazis had, in defiance of the Munich Agreement, "awarded" Hungary and then Poland large tracts of Czech territory, inhabited by over one and a quarter million citizens of Czechoslovakia, none of them German, now made citizens of other states. These ominous events, heavy with implications, had been reported in the British press, but only briefly and obscurely.

His Majesty's Government had not prepared their countrymen for this blow. The fact is that they, too, were unprepared for the Prague invasion. In Hitler's most recent speech he had reflected upon how fortunate the world would be if Britons and Germans could unite "in full confidence with one another." On March 10, only five days before Hitler's Prague coup, the P.M. had told the House of Commons that the Continent was now "settling down to a period of tranquillity." Hoare, speaking next, had predicted that if Hitler, Mussolini, Franco, Chamberlain, and Daladier were to work in tandem they could banish nightmares of war and burdens of armament and thus "in an incredibly short space of time transform the whole history of the world." As a consequence of this joint effort, Hoare had envisioned a new "Golden Age," whose promise would be realized if the "jitterbugs" — singling out those who had appealed for a stronger British military presence: Churchill, Eden, Duff Cooper, Bracken, Amery, Boothby, Sandys, Nicolson, Macmillan, and Keyes — were denied their goals.[52]

A backbencher softly quoted Shakespeare:

> *That England, being empty of defense*
> *Hath shook and trembled at the ill neighborhood. . . .*

Hoare was fatuous, and Churchill knew it, but he could not deliver a plausible rebuke without exposing informants already being tailed by the Gestapo. Two weeks after Munich, Hitler had summoned Frantisek Chvalkovsky, Prague's new pro-German foreign minister, and told him that Czechoslovakia must abandon her cordial relationship with Britain and become reconciled to her "proper place" as a colony of the Reich. The Czechs must "not play any tricks with Germany." If they did, "in twenty-four hours — no, in eight hours — I'll finish her off [*mache ich Schluss*]!" The following month one of Winston's sources sent him a secret memorandum in which the Führer had described the next phase of his foreign policy to Ribbentrop and Weizsäcker. Britain, he had said, "must be attacked with speeches and in the press . . . first the Opposition, and then Chamberlain himself." Munich had taught him "how to deal with the English — one had to move aggressively [*vor den Bauch treten*]." His objective, he declared, was "to overthrow Chamberlain." The Opposition, he assumed — an absurd assumption, revealing his ignorance of parliamentary rule — "would not then be capable of forming a new government, and the same would occur as in France. The political strength of Great Britain would be paralyzed" and "Fascism would gain the upper hand."[53]

On March 12, three days before Hitler's rape of the rump Czech state, Chartwell had received another report from an agent in Brno, Moravia. "Hitler," Winston had learned, "is coming to Vienna" — fifty miles from Prague — "this week." Swastika banners "lavishly decorated" a "great many public buildings," and each evening Czech Nazis "gathered in or around the Deutsches Haus to sing and demonstrate." One night a procession of anti-Nazis paraded by the German House; the men wearing the hakenkreuz brassards shouted *"Sieg Heil!"* and sang the "Horst Wessel Song." These Nazis had been told that "Hitler will come on March 15 and the greeting 'Heil Marz!' instead of 'Heil Hitler!' has been quite common for some weeks."[54]

On the morning of March 14 the Slovakian legislature, which had been quarreling with the national government in Prague, had declared its independence. This presented the Führer with his opportunity. Obviously, he declared, Prague could not control its people. The Czechs were informed of his displeasure by Ribbentrop, who stressed the need for an immediate solution. At 10:40 P.M. — just as Churchill's meeting at Waltham Abbey was breaking up — a train bearing Chvalkovsky and Dr. Emil Hácha, formerly a judge of Czechoslovakia's supreme court and now the country's president, drew into Berlin's Anhalt Station. An SS guard of honor escorted them to the Hotel Adlon and then the Reich Chancellery, where the Führer kept them waiting until 1:15 A.M. Hácha was no Masaryk, no Beneš; he had come prepared to grovel. He denounced his great predecessors and actually said that after Munich "I asked myself whether it was a good thing for Czechoslovakia to be an independent state at all." He realized that the destiny of his country lay "in the Führer's hands, and I believe it is in safekeeping in such hands." He knew that the Czechs had a bad reputation in the Wilhelmstrasse. His explanation was that "there still exist many supporters of the Beneš regime." But, he was "trying by every means to silence them." He meekly added that he hoped the Führer "will understand my holding the view that Czechoslovakia has the right to live a national life."[55]

Hitler didn't understand it, however. Hácha's "Rump State" (*"Restbestand"*), he said, owed its very existence to his indulgence. At Munich he had hoped that the Czechs, under new leadership, would mend their ways, but he had also resolved that "if the Beneš tendencies did not completely disappear he would completely destroy this state." It was now obvious that they had not disappeared. Therefore, last Sunday, March 12, *"die Würfel waren gefallen"* ("the die was cast"). He had issued the orders for the invasion by German troops and for the incorporation of Czechoslovakia into the German Reich. Schmidt, his interpreter, noted that the Czechs "sat as though turned to stone. Only their eyes showed that they were alive." Hitler told them that at 6:00 A.M., on his orders, his armies would cross their borders near points where the Luftwaffe had already seized Czech airfields. Any attempts at defense would be broken by *"rohe Gewalt"* ("brute force"). He paused. Of course, he said, they had a choice. If the

defenders laid down their arms the Führer would treat them with generosity, assure their autonomy, and even grant them a certain measure of
freedom. He suggested they step into the next room and talk it over.[56]

Awaiting them there were Göring and Ribbentrop, who literally chased
them around a table strewn with documents, thrusting the papers at them,
pushing pens into their hands, shouting that if they refused to sign, within
two hours half of Prague would be bombed to ruins and their families
slain. Suddenly Schmidt heard Göring shout: *"Hácha hat einen Schwächean-
fall bekommen!"* Hácha, who had a heart condition, had indeed fainted, and
a single thought crossed the minds of the Germans: the world would say
that Czechoslovakia's president had been murdered in the Reich Chancellery. Then Dr. Theodor Morell — Hitler's personal physician, whose
strange drugs later addicted the Führer — gave Hácha an injection. A
special telephone line to Prague had been rigged up; over it, in a slurred
voice, the revived president advised the cabinet to capitulate. Morell gave
him another shot, and both Czechs signed the papers. It was 3:55 A.M.
Two hours later German troops swarmed over the shrunken Czech frontier. Hácha was appointed governor of the German Protectorate of Bohemia and Moravia. But the world already knew who really ruled the country
now. Hitler had told them. Before retiring for the night in Hradschin
Palace he issued a triumphant statement: *"Die Tschechoslowakei existiert
nicht mehr!"* — "Czechoslovakia has ceased to exist."[57]

That evening, as Hitler slept in his hijacked palace, Churchill dined at the
Grillions Club with Sir Horace Rumbold, formerly His Majesty's ambassador to Berlin, who had been dismissed after the Nazis, opening his
pouches, found he was reporting the facts about Hitler's regime and
demanded an envoy more sympathetic to the Führer's policies. Rumbold
was in low spirits. Learning that Hitler was in Prague, he concluded that
"Even Chamberlain's eyes must now be opened to the fact that Hitler's
statements and assurances are not worth the breath with which they have
been uttered. . . . I confess that I have never in my life been so disheartened as I am now." He was angry that the Foreign Office had ignored his
warnings six years before and that Chamberlain had been so gulled by
Hitler. Over the past few months, however, he had begun to note "increasing disgust with Germany" on all levels of British society and "a
growing conviction that there is nothing to be done with the Nazis."

This, he told Churchill, gave him a flicker of hope. And yet there were
Englishmen who were still working toward an Anglo-German alliance.
One, he said, was Lord Brocket, whom he regarded as "among the most
gullible of asses." Brocket had been shooting with Göring. Göring had
entrusted him with news of great importance: "Neither he [Göring] nor

Hitler had any knowledge of the recent Nazi action against the Jews." On reflection Rumbold became convinced that further aggression by Nazis in 1939 was inevitable. The following day he wrote to his brother: "This year . . . is their last opportunity of doing so with any chance of success." There was a general feeling of uneasiness, he wrote Churchill that same afternoon. "You asked me last night what I thought of the present situation. I replied that I was profoundly disheartened. This was an understatement. . . . I have never felt so depressed or so nauseated as I feel now and this because it seems to me that our Government have, for a year or more, failed to look ahead or to understand the character of the man with whom they are dealing. . . . I only hope that it will not enter into the PM's head to pay Hitler another visit." On March 20 Churchill replied, thanking Rumbold for his letter and adding: "Since you wrote it events have told their unanswerable tale."[58]

"The blow has been struck," Churchill told his readers on March 24. Hitler had "broken every tie of good faith with the British and French who tried so hard to believe in him. The Munich agreement which represented such great advantages for Germany has been brutally violated." British confidence in the Nazi hierarchy

can never again be mended while the present domination rules in Germany. . . . A veritable revolution in feeling and opinion has occurred in Britain, and reverberates through all the self-governing Dominions. Indeed, a similar process has taken place spontaneously throughout the whole British Empire. This mass conversion of those who had hitherto been hopeful took place within a single week, but not within a single day. It was not an explosion, but the kindling of a fire which rose steadily, hour by hour, to an intense furnace heat of inward conviction.[59]

That, or something like it, had indeed happened. A profound shift in public opinion was noted all over Britain. Hitler's Prague coup — which was followed, in a week, by his annexation of Memel, part of Lithuania — was the pivotal event in turning round British public opinion. The spirit of friendship between London and Berlin, which Chamberlain believed had been the fruit of Munich, had, in A. J. P. Taylor's phrase, "lost its glitter." And Robert Rhodes James, after reviewing the period, concludes:

All that can be said, and said with absolute justice, is that after the annexation of Czechoslovakia in March 1939, the possibility of averting war with Germany was entertained only by a minority in Britain. By some strange process which is inexplicable to those who were not alive that year, the fear of war which had been so evident in 1938 seemed to evaporate. The British did not want war, but . . . there was a weariness with procrastination, an aversion to false promises and wishful thinking, and a yearning for a simple, clear solution.[60]

Later in the year a scrap-iron drive was launched, but an exception had to be made for Lord Baldwin; the wrought-iron gates leading to his estate were needed to control angry men who, only two years before, had cheered his every appearance. Malcolm Muggeridge bitterly recalled Chamberlain's return from Munich and his response to the airport crowd: "He showed them the very document, pointed to the signature upon it; then told them to go home and sleep quietly in their beds, confident that they were secure against molestation, not just for that night and tomorrow night, but for many nights, perhaps for ever. Peace in our time; peace in his time — not even that. The first ecstasy soon passed."[61]

Muggeridge was considered a crank and was disregarded by the House because of his contempt for everything trendy. But for once he was in the mainstream; MPs knew it because their constituents told them so in every mail delivery. Only the prime minister remained blind to the shift in the national mood. Addressing the House of Commons on March 15 he ignored the Nazis' exploitation of ethnic feuds which had always riven eastern Europe. Slovakia, he solemnly noted, had proclaimed her "independence." What had happened in Bratislava hardly resembled the American Declaration of Independence — in fact the proclamation had been issued by an extremist band of Slovakian Fascists — but you would never have known it from the prime minister's remarks to the House. He said: "The effect of this [Slovakian] declaration put an end by internal disruption to the State whose frontier we had proposed to guarantee. His Majesty's Government cannot accordingly hold themselves any longer bound by this obligation."[62]

Back in Downing Street his ministers told him this made no sense. He turned away, refusing to concede that the issue which had made him a national hero had boomeranged. But his cabinet persisted, and he was under growing pressure from his whips, his closest colleagues, even from the King. Finally, on March 17, Chamberlain grasped the humiliating fact that the Führer had deceived him, exposing the paper they had signed for the placebo it was.

Another statesman might have abandoned his discredited policies, and at first it seemed that the P.M. had decided to do precisely that. Actually his commitment to appeasement lay too deep, and he could never entirely relinquish his conviction that the path to enduring peace lay through continuing compromise. So his public positions became schizoid, swinging from one extreme to another. That Friday he was decidedly hawkish. The Prague betrayal had angered him, and speaking before a large crowd in Birmingham, the arena most sympathetic to Joe Chamberlain's son, he executed what was, for the moment at least, an about-face. He believed, he said, that most Englishmen had not only approved of the Munich Agreement but had "shared my honest desire that that policy be carried further." Now he shared "their disappointment," their "indignation." Hitler claimed that his ingestion of what was left of Czechoslovakia was "justified by disturbances [there]. Is this the last attack upon a small state or is it to be followed by another? Is this in fact a step in the direction of an attempt to dominate the world by force?" If so, he said, Britain would take part "in resisting the challenge to the utmost of her power."[63]

Halifax told Dirksen: "In Anglo-German relations the clocks [have] been put back considerably." But Chamberlain did not let a formal protest leave the FO until March 18, three days after the occupation of Prague. Bonnet, having been put under similar pressure, did the same. Couriers from the French and British embassies sped along the Wilhelmstrasse bearing stiffly worded notes protesting the "denial of the spirit of Munich" to the Foreign Ministry. Ribbentrop discarded them unread.[64]

Ribbentrop's contempt was deserved. There had been so many such notes, deploring Hitler's seizure of the Rhineland and then its fortification, objecting to the Anschluss, remonstrating against the *Kristallnacht* and subsequent anti-Semitic pogroms. Ribbentrop knew the drill. Presently Henderson would appear and explain that friendship between the two countries must not be jeopardized, that mistakes would be resolved by negotiation. And, sure enough, the British envoy arrived within the hour. Meantime a meeting in Düsseldorf between British and German industrialists had been scheduled to open on March 15. It went ahead as planned. Even as Hitler rode through Prague, the participants signed a preliminary agreement, one clause of which permitted Germany to spend the foreign exchange resources of the country he had just seized — in short, providing the Reichsbank with stolen funds to finance Hitler's regime.[65]

The disposition of Czech gold deposited abroad soon became the focus of heated disagreement in England. Though the Bank of England quickly froze its Czech assets, some of the Czech gold it held — six million pounds' worth — was controlled by the Bank for International Settlements, which wanted it transferred to the Reichsbank. By mid-May rumors were rife that a German representative was in London to conclude negotiations — and HMG was refusing to intervene. The House of Commons erupted on May 26. Where, indignant MPs asked, was the six million pounds in gold? Why was the government willing to permit its transfer to Germany? Chancellor of the Exchequer Simon replied that he was not sure he was even entitled to ask the bank about Czech deposits. But MPs were persistent. After the Anschluss, Vienna's Threadneedle Street had been a gold mine for Hitler, transferring all Austrian assets to the Nazis, and Parliament wanted no encore. "Really," said Bracken, "this is the most squalid form of appeasement . . . appeasing the Germans with the money of the unfortunate Czechs."[66]

Chamberlain was evasive, Churchill apoplectic. British rearmament was picking up speed; the lag with the Germans continued, but an effort had begun at last. He told the House:

Here we are going about urging our people to enlist, urging them to accept new forms of military compulsion; here we are paying taxes on a gigantic scale to protect ourselves. If at the same time our mechanism of government is so butter-fingered that this £6,000,000 can be transferred to the Nazi Government of Germany, which only wishes to use it and is only using it, as it does all its foreign exchange, for the purpose of increasing its armaments, if this money is transferred out of our hands, to come back in certain circumstances quicker than it went, it stultifies the efforts people are making in every class and in every party to secure National Defence and rally the whole forces of the country.[67]

The prime minister flushed when Winston added that he could not understand how this matter could have escaped him. Churchill demanded that he put a halt to "the transference of this £6,000,000 of Czech money into the hands of those who have overthrown and destroyed the Czech republic." This, in Chamberlain's view, was another example of Churchill's lack of judgment, of his misunderstanding of the business world. Sentiment had no place in the City. The government in Prague had changed legally, since the Czech government had signed Hitler's documents, and Hácha had a perfect right to the gold Beneš had deposited here in the name of Czechoslovakia.[68]

Because of legerdemain — a hasty change in the Bank of England's bookkeeping methods — and the fact that vital Reichsbank records were later lost in the bombing of Berlin, to this day no one knows the degree to which the Nazis succeeded in obtaining these Czech assets. Gilbert and Gott state that Germany "never claimed the gold." But even if Nazi Germany lost a windfall, the Reich kept most of its powerful British friends.[69]

*   *   *

In London, Hitler was praised — praise which was entirely unmerited — for his generosity and restraint in suppressing violence in Prague. During the months following his entry into the city, 250,000 Czechs were killed, over half of them Jews. That was unknown at the time, for it was extremely difficult to get precise accounts of German behavior in Prague. The Nazi grip there had begun to tighten even before the coup. "Everywhere the Nazi salute and 'Heil Hitler' are to be found," one of Churchill's sources had written, "with pictures of the Führer in German restaurants." Nazis insulted young Czechs and clubbed them, Jews were required to register, and — a glint of black humor — "At the Capitol Cinema here [he was reporting from Brno] the German film 'Olympia' is showing. All the Nazis are itching to go, but there is a Nazi picket outside . . . because the cinema is owned by a Jew!" The same source described the Nazis' arrival: "I saw the first German troops entering the town. . . . The local Germans were very enthusiastic, but the rest of the population has been extremely and amazingly quiet. Everything is now draped in swastikas. Yesterday morning Hitler paid a surprise visit; the reception was very cool, and he drove straight back and did not make his intended speech here this evening. Few people saw him or even recognized him."[70]

Although the full scope of Nazi atrocities in Czechoslovakia was concealed from foreign correspondents, they could not be prevented from witnessing clubbings, the persecution of Jews, and the disappearance of Czech intellectuals once concentration camps had been built, wired, and equipped with watchtowers for machine guns and searchlights. There was no blinking the fact that this time Hitler had acted not as the champion of Germans living in a neighboring country but as a Genghis Khan bent upon pillage, enslavement, slaughter, and destruction. The Czechs were the first Slavs he had subjugated. He frequently broke his promises; his threats he always made good. In a secret *Führerordnung* he decreed that the Czechs were to be *"assimiliert,"* chiefly as *"Sklavenarbeit"* ("slave labor") in the Reich; the others, *"besonders die Intellektuellen"* ("particularly the intellectuals"), were to be *"entmanntet und ausgeschaltet "* ("castrated and eliminated"). All this had been set forth in *Mein Kampf,* the best-seller read by few and dismissed by most of them as ravings. Churchill, virtually the only public man who had taken Hitler at his word, published a collection of his own *Evening Standard* and *Daily Telegraph* columns under the title *Step by Step.* Clement Attlee wrote him, "It must be a melancholy satisfaction to see how right you were," and Lord Wolmer wrote: "The book is a record of perspicacity and courage on your part."[71]

Powerful Nazis had become British celebrities, however. On March 18, R. H. S. Crossman, a future cabinet member, spoke in the House of

Göring's "courage and capability." "Apart from Hitler," he said, "he is the only statesman of any caliber in the Third Reich. . . . Moreover, it was his energy in reorganizing the Prussian police and establishing the Gestapo which enabled Hitler to consolidate his position in 1933, and since then the triumphs of the Nazi foreign policy would have been impossible without his work."[72]

Parliament's indifference to the lot of the Czech Jews infuriated Churchill. Dispossessed by the Nazis, they wandered the roads of eastern Europe. Photographs of their ordeal were profoundly moving, but Dawson refused to run any of them in *The Times;* he couldn't help the victims, he explained to his staff, and if they were published Hitler would be offended. Then, nine weeks after Prague, the Chamberlain government announced that British policy in Palestine had been changed. Unlimited Jewish immigration was over; strict limits would be imposed on the number entering Palestine for the next five years, and after that all Jews would be turned away "unless the Arabs of Palestine are prepared to acquiesce in it." This closed the chief refuge for European Jews fleeing the growing Nazi empire, and it gave the Arabs veto power over the eventual establishment of a Jewish state.[73]

This was popular in the Reich. But it was also a renunciation of the Balfour declaration, which in 1917 had promised British support in "the establishment [in Palestine] of a national home for the Jewish people." To Churchill, who had been a Zionist for thirty years, it constituted a shocking act of treachery and a violation of his personal honor. In 1921, as colonial secretary, he had committed Britain to the founding of a homeland for the Jews; it would be called "Judea" or "Israel." And in 1937, he had reaffirmed his support of such a nation publicly and, privately, to Chaim Weizmann, president of the World Zionist Organization, who had become a close friend. In May 1939, the new Middle Eastern policy was defended in the House by Malcolm MacDonald, who now presided over the Colonial Office. Amery denounced it in blistering terms, and Churchill, after reviewing his speech with Weizmann (who said he wouldn't change a word; he thought it perfect), addressed the issue in Parliament on May 22.

As one "intimately and responsibly concerned in the earlier stages of our Palestine policy," he could not "stand by and see solemn engagements into which Britain has entered before the world set aside." Perhaps the government's purpose was "administrative convenience." It was unlikely. No one had suggested it. Or perhaps — and here Winston hinted at the darker, more obvious, and most reprehensible motive, an attempt by His Majesty's Government to ingratiate itself with the Führer — it was being done "for the sake of a quiet life," which, he predicted, would be "a vain hope." Of the Arab veto he said, "There is the breach; there is the violation of the pledge; there is the abandonment of the Balfour Declaration; there is the end of the vision, of the hope, of the dream." He asked: "What will our potential enemies think? . . . Will they not be tempted to say: 'They're on the run again. This is another Munich.' " At the end he stared straight at the prime minister's eyes and recalled that twenty years earlier, in this chamber, Chamberlain had said — he was quoting him directly — "A great responsibility will rest upon the Zionists, who, before long, will be proceeding, with joy in their hearts, to the ancient seat of their people. Theirs will be the task to build up a new prosperity and a new civilisation in old Palestine, so long neglected and misruled." Churchill closed with three shattering sentences: "Well, they have answered his call. They have fulfilled his hopes. How can he find it in his heart to strike them this mortal blow?"[74]

※   ※

The House witnessed its first sign of revolt by Tory MPs against their leadership on March 28, when thirty distinguished Conservatives — among them Churchill, Eden, Duff Cooper, and Macmillan — appealed for a new national government, with ministers drawn from the benches of all three parties.

Chamberlain, a better politician than a statesman, was ready for them. He knew the country no longer shared his faith in Munich. Indeed, it was apparent to all the appeasers that they could not survive another such sellout. Daladier told a secret meeting of his Foreign Affairs Commission that all agreements between France and Germany were *"en ruines."* He said that "if France does not face up to the consequences there will be a stampede among friendly countries which until now have been firm. It will be a rush toward servitude [*à la servitude*]. And we must have no illusion as to what will happen thereafter. New invasions will come to our country and threaten to submerge it [*risqueront de le submerger*]." At both No. 10 and in the Élysée Palace it was agreed that the Führer's next victim must be identified and bound to the democracies in a tight military alliance.[75]

It is a marvel that the Third Reich, now in its seventh year, had survived without precipitating a general conflict. It was coming now; historian Brian Gardner recalls that "While nations busily armed themselves for the war which statesmen said they had averted, there was a sort of political hush in Europe. Where would Hitler strike next, and when?" Appropriately, the answer found in London and Paris reflected their diplomatic incompetence. They picked the wrong country.[76]

*   *   *

Less than two weeks after the Führer had devoured Czechoslovakia the prime minister wrote one of his sisters: "There is always the possibility that Germany will act more cunningly & that instead we shall be faced with a new 'commercial agreement' which in effect puts Roumania at her mercy." Although the Rumanians shared no common border with the Reich, Hungary did; the government in Budapest was hostile toward Bucharest and would not object — in fact, would not *dare* object — if Nazi panzers raced across Hungarian soil to penetrate Rumania, a primitive Balkan country which was nevertheless rich in oil and controlled the mouth of the Danube.[77]

In Paris, Phipps asked Bonnet whether he thought Rumania would be "the next course on the Nazi menu." Bonnet told the British ambassador that he thought it "very likely." He was in fact convinced of it; his prediction was later found in Quai d'Orsay files. Henderson agreed that Hitler's next target would be "domination by force of the whole Danube basin." All this seemed supported by Virgil Tilea, the Rumanian minister in London. Tilea called at the Foreign Office on Thursday, March 16, the day after Prague fell. He told his tale to an FO assistant under secretary, then to Halifax and Cadogan — and, going public, to *The Times* and the *Daily Telegraph*. The gist of it was that his government, "from secret and other sources," had learned that the Germans planned to overrun Hungary and "disintegrate Roumania in the same way as they had disintegrated Czechoslovakia . . . establishing a German protectorate over the whole country." Their greatest prize would be the oil fields at Ploesti. He asked for a loan of ten million pounds to strengthen his country's defenses, emphasizing the "extreme urgency" of a "precise indication" of Britain's position "in the event of Roumania becoming a victim of German aggression." The "gravity" of the "imminent danger" was heightened by new German demands that the Reich receive preferred treatment in trade between the two countries, terms set forth in such language that they "seemed very much like an ultimatum," an impression reinforced by Wehrmacht troop movements along the Rumanian border. The eruption of hostilities "might possibly be a question of days."[78]

Halifax was alarmed. He seems to have accepted the Rumanian minister's apprehension at face value. But Tilea's account should have been examined more carefully. Had the Wilhelmstrasse conceived so bold a stroke, Rumania's government would have known of it, and an appeal to Britain would have been made on the very highest level. Instead, Halifax and Cadogan — without consulting first with Sir Reginald Hoare, their envoy in Bucharest — sent cables to Britain's ambassadors in Paris, Moscow, Warsaw, Ankara, Athens, and Belgrade, spreading Tilea's story and instructing them to ask what the leaders in these capitals would do if events confirmed it. Sir Reginald, when informed of Tilea's story, requested that these distress signals be withdrawn; he found the tale "utterly improbable" and the Rumanian foreign minister denied it in every particular. Sir Howard Kennard, His Majesty's ambassador to Warsaw, cabled that Poland's Ministry of Foreign Affairs was "highly skeptical," and so, it developed, were other foreign ministries throughout Europe.[79]

Tilea had been discredited. Nevertheless, he retracted nothing, and the response of His Majesty's Government was exactly what it would have been had he been confirmed. Chamberlain convened an emergency meeting of the cabinet on Saturday, the eighteenth. Halifax reported that Rumania's foreign minister, Grigore Gafencu, denied that there was a word of truth in what Tilea had said and affirmed that relations between his government and the Reich were "proceeding on completely normal lines as between equals." Therefore, said the foreign secretary, the matter was "probably" not "immediately threatening," as they had thought. But, as they all knew, he continued, the Führer was capable of anything. He proposed that they anticipate the next crisis and ponder what HMG's position should be. His own opinion was that "if Germany committed an act of naked aggression on Roumania, it would be very difficult for this country not to take all the action in her power to rally resistance and to take part in that resistance herself."[80]

They discussed how to go about ascertaining which countries might be willing to join Britain in standing up to Nazi Germany. At the time that Churchill had urged a Grand Alliance in Parliament, such a coalition had been feasible, but since Munich Britain had few friends in eastern Europe. His Majesty's Government simply wasn't trusted. Other ministers suggested the obvious course — to court the Soviet Union, Nazi Germany's sworn enemy and the most powerful military force in eastern Europe. But Chamberlain, as he wrote his sister, held "the most profound distrust of Russia." He concluded that Saturday meeting by saying that "the real point at issue" was whether Britain could persuade "sufficient assurances from other countries" to justify "a public pronouncement that we should resist any further act of aggression on the part of Germany."[81]

It was Tilea who suggested that Britain's position would be strengthened if Poland joined them as a third ally. Halifax and Chamberlain found the prospect appealing. Poland shared a common border with Rumania and, according to British intelligence (whose agents cannot have been on speaking terms with Churchill's informants), was "in a strong position with regard to Germany." The governments in Warsaw and Berlin were much alike. Both persecuted Jews; both despised Soviet Russia; both had conspired against the Czechs — during the Munich crisis and its aftermath

Ribbentrop had worked in tandem with Colonel Józef Beck, Poland's foreign minister. The Poles had left nothing undone to weaken Prague's position and, with Hitler's approval, had annexed Czech territory. In 1934 the Reich and Poland had signed a ten-year nonaggression treaty proclaiming mutual respect for existing territorial rights, the first breach in France's structure of alliances in eastern Europe. Since then Beck had toiled strenuously — and, it seemed, successfully — to remain on the best possible terms with Germany.[82]

To be sure, the port of Danzig was a potential sore spot. But the city's Polish commissioner, asked about the possibility of a German coup, "definitely" discounted it. In London, Dirksen, the German ambassador, assured Halifax that although the Reich intended to pursue a new role for the city, Hitler's means would entail neither threats nor violence. Instead, he would propose "consultation with the Polish government." (The anesthetic effect of German promises to negotiate in these years was extraordinary. Hitler never negotiated. He lied, he bluffed, he blackmailed, but serious negotiation was a skill he despised, a refuge for weaklings.) The last and decisive card in Poland's deck was her military reputation. Unlike her neighbors — and Great Britain — she boasted a field strength that was, at least on paper, immense: a million men under arms and another 800,000 reserves.[83]

The man who might well determine if these troops would be sent into battle was an enigmatic Polish colonel who in some ways resembled the Führer. No one questioned Józef Beck's ability. His remarkable diplomatic skills had led to his appointment, at the age of thirty-eight, as Poland's foreign minister. Respected for his intellect and powerful will, he was also distrusted — even detested — for his duplicity, dishonesty, and, in his private life, depravity. In Rome, where he had spent an extended visit-cum-vacation, the Princess of Piedmont had said of him that he had "the sort of face you might see in a French newspaper as that of a ravisher of little girls." Ciano thought him "an unsympathetic character who produces a chill around him." On one of his visits to London that spring, HMG gave him a lunch at the Savoy. Churchill thought him "cynical" and "coldhearted." Winston was watching him carefully, because he knew more about the strain between Warsaw and Berlin than anyone else there except the guest of honor. He casually asked Beck: "Will you get back all right in your special train through Germany to Poland?" The colonel gave him a sharp look and replied quietly: "I think we shall have time for that."[84]

Léger had advised the FO not to trust Beck because, to deflect Hitler southward, "he betrayed Rumania or is in the process of doing so." The very premise of Halifax's stratagem was false; it was Beck who fostered the notion that Poland was safe from Germany and did all he could to make it plausible. His ambassador in London told Halifax that Beck would "go a long way" to avoid a quarrel with the Reich. Beck himself, in conversation with Halifax, said that he and Ribbentrop would soon open negotiations over Danzig and he had decided to offer the Germans "magnanimous" terms. It would be his posture to do "nothing provocative." Pressed for details, he replied that he "did not propose to trouble" the British with an analysis of the Danzig dilemma. The problem was local, he said, and easy to solve; the possibility that it might grow into an international issue was inconceivable.[85]

Polish support of Rumania was indispensable, Halifax believed; however, on March 19, when he asked Beck to join a four-power declaration to warn the Germans against aggression in eastern Europe — the four being Britain, France, Poland, and Russia — Beck declined. Such a move would only provoke Germany, he said, and Poland did not want to associate herself in any way with the Soviet Union. In Warsaw, Ambassador Kennard asked Beck to "ponder" the matter, and within five days the Polish foreign minister came back with a counterproposal, relayed to Halifax by Beck's London ambassador, Count Edward Raczyński. Beck suggested that the two countries sign a bilateral convention that would call for Britain and Poland to "consult" in the event Germany threatened Poland. This should be kept a secret, Raczyński said, to avoid antagonizing the Reich. Halifax and Chamberlain were cool to the idea. For one thing, it made no mention of Rumania, which was the locus of Britain's concern. Besides, a secret convention would offend the French, whom the British had been consulting regularly, and would have no impact as a deterrent to the Nazis. A public pronouncement was needed.[86]

Halifax now conceived of another approach, which he proposed to the P.M.: What if Britain took matters a step further and offered to guarantee Poland? That might persuade Beck to reciprocate by joining Britain in guaranteeing Rumania. Chamberlain thought it was worth a try; after all, the Führer had no designs on territory governed by the Poles. What could be the harm? On his instructions, therefore, Halifax, Cadogan, and Butler spent the evening drafting a declaration of England's commitment. After consultation with the Quai d'Orsay, the consequence was an Anglo-French offer to rescue Poland or Rumania if either were attacked by Germany and resisted, although the commitment to Bucharest was contingent upon Warsaw's also agreeing to intervene — support the P.M. and his foreign secretary were confident they could secure. On March 27 the proposal was transmitted to Warsaw and Bucharest.[87]

As soon as reactions were received from these capitals, it was thought, negotiations to refine the details could proceed apace. The Continent was quiet. Nothing seemed particularly urgent. And then, suddenly, everything did. One reason was Chamberlain himself. Despite his hard-headed businessman's approach to issues, he had a hidden mercurial streak; he blew hot and cold, destroying a defensible Czechoslovakia one year and now guaranteeing Poland — which would prove far less defensible — the next. He had been misled by rumors all month, and this was dangerous, because his decisions were often based on fragile, unconfirmed evidence. Tilea's false alarm was one example.

Ian Colvin's warning was another, and in this instance the consequences were far graver. Colvin, Berlin correspondent for the London *News Chronicle,* was among the most astute newspapermen in Europe. His sources lay deep in the Nazi hierarchy; he was, indeed, part of Churchill's intelligence net. More than once he had sent to Chartwell directives from the Führer that were distributed to only three or four Nazi leaders. Repeatedly the correspondent's prophecies had proved true, and when he flew to London and conferred with Halifax and Cadogan late in the afternoon of Tuesday, March 28, he had their undivided attention.[88]

In January, he told them, "a victualling contractor to the German army" had received instructions to provide "the same amount of rations he had supplied in September 1938, and to have them ready by March 28, 1939." They were to be delivered "in an area of Pomerania which forms a rough wedge pointing to the railway junction of Bromberg [Bydgoszcz] in the Polish corridor." That was sinister enough, but Colvin's flight to London had also been inspired by the previous day's issues of *Völkischer Beobachter, Der Angriff,* and the *Berliner Tageblatt.* All had carried inflammatory accounts of "incidents" on the German-Polish frontier, assaults on Reich customs posts and even German civilians by Polish *Schweine,* some of whom had confessed they had been acting on orders from Warsaw. No one in the Foreign Office needed to be reminded that the Nazis had manufactured similar border clashes before each of their earlier invasions. Colvin was taken across Downing Street; Chamberlain heard his tale and agreed with the FO's recommendation — an immediate public declaration binding Britain to the defense of Poland.[89]

In the morning the cabinet cabled an approved text to the Poles and the French, who promptly endorsed it. Parliament was less docile. Critical MPs elicited acknowledgment that British intelligence had found nothing to confirm Colvin's suspicions. This was no reflection on him; the standards for a good newspaper story are quite different from those required of a prime minister committing his country's military forces. As it happened, Colvin had misinterpreted his data. The facts were right, but they were part of a German contingency plan whose date had since been set back. The spurious "incidents" were meant to build a case against Poland, and Hitler was indeed planning to move against the Poles; but his Wehrmacht directive specified action in September, not March. He wasn't ready now; after touring Memel, his latest conquest, he had stopped briefly in Berlin and entrained for Munich, leaving the OKW various instructions, including: "The Führer does not wish . . . to solve the Danzig problem forcefully. He does not wish thus to drive Poland into England's arms. . . . However, it should now be worked on. A solution in the near future would have to be based on especially favorable political conditions. In that case Poland shall be knocked out so completely that it will not be a political factor for the next decades."[90]

His staff knew he meant to hoist the hakenkreuz over all Poland before the first snow fell. Chamberlain was therefore aiming at the right target — though both his weapon and his ammunition were pitifully small — when he told the House on March 31:

I now have to inform the House that . . . in the event of any action which clearly threatens Polish independence, and in which the Polish Government accordingly considers it vital to resist with their national forces, His Majesty's Government will feel themselves bound at once to lend the Polish Government all support in their power. They have given the Polish Government an assurance to this effect. I may say that the French Government have authorised me to make it plain that they stand on the same ground in this matter as do His Majesty's Government.[91]

Thus Chamberlain reversed the British policy, adopted in 1918, of avoiding continental commitments. He had not — yet — signed a formal military alliance, but he had taken a long step in that direction. All evidence to the contrary, he believed he could discourage Hitler from forcing himself upon the Poles. He was also convinced that Poland was a powerful military nation. In both instances he was wrong.

France, already committed to Poland's defense, was greatly relieved. But Englishmen who possessed strategic vision were, with few exceptions, appalled. Boothby told Churchill: "This is the maddest single action this country has ever taken." Not only was the policy crazy, he said; so was the man with whom they were dealing. He had talked with Hitler for over an hour, and when the Führer told him that the Reich meant to use Poland as a staging area for a Nazi invasion of the Soviet Union, he said he saw in Hitler's eyes "the unmistakable glint" of dementia. The Führer had assured Boothby that he did not "wish to attack Britain and the British Empire but of course if England became a Polish or Russian ally, he would have no choice." Now, to Boothby's horror, Chamberlain had given "a sudden, unconditional guarantee to Poland, without any guarantee of Russian support." Basil Liddell Hart agreed that the Polish guarantee was "foolish, futile, and provocative . . . an ill-considered gesture" which "placed Britain's destiny in the hands of Poland's rulers, men of very dubious and unstable judgment." To dramatize his protest, he resigned as military correspondent of *The Times*. In the House, Lloyd George asked, and was not answered, whether the General Staff had agreed to defend this country which they could not reach under any conceivable circumstances. Duff Cooper noted in his diary: "Never before in our history have we left in the hands of one of the smaller powers the decision whether or not Britain goes to war."[92]

Churchill's reaction to the Polish guarantee was ambivalent. In his postwar memoirs he wrote of Poland's "hyena appetite" in joining in the "pillage and destruction of the Czechoslovak State." In 1938, with the Czechs as allies, fighting would have made sense, he said; now, after six years of "placatory appeasement," they were asking their young men "to stake their lives upon the territorial integrity of Poland." He wrote: "Here was decision at last, taken at the worst possible moment and on the least satisfactory ground, which must surely lead to the slaughter of tens of millions of people." That is not what he said at the time, however. He told the House of Commons: "The preservation and integrity of Poland must be regarded as a cause commanding the regard of all the world," and added that Chamberlain's declaration meant there was "almost complete agreement" between the prime minister and critics of his foreign policy: "We can no longer be pushed from pillar to post." This approached a blanket endorsement. The most generous explanation for the chasm between these two Churchillian positions is that in 1939 he was inspired by the discovery that Chamberlain would fight for *something*. It is also fair to add that within a week Winston was raising doubts about the Polish guarantee.[93]

Poland, Chamberlain had told the cabinet, was "very likely the key to the [European] situation." But Poland wasn't. It was true that the Poles were brave beyond belief, and that the million men in uniform, splendidly uniformed, were formidably organized in thirty infantry divisions and twelve large cavalry brigades — gallant horsemen all. Unfortunately, they would be useless against Nazi panzers. The Germans planned to invade Poland with ninety-eight divisions. They were the best fighting men in Europe, and their leaders understood the mobile, armored warfare of the future. Halifax, according to Liddell Hart, "believed that Poland was of more military value than Russia, and preferred to secure her as an ally." Actually, Liddell Hart continues, Poland's generals "still pinned their trust to the value of a large mass of horse cavalry, and cherished a pathetic belief in the possibility of carrying out cavalry charges. In that respect . . . . their ideas were eighty years out of date, since the futility of cavalry charges had been shown as far back as the American Civil War."[94]

Nevertheless, Józef Beck carried himself as though he were — and doubtless he believed himself to be — the representative of a first-rate military power. Swaggering, chain-smoking, and leering at young women, he arrived in London on April 3 to negotiate the details of Britain's new pledge to Poland. Though HMG expected that it would lead to a Polish guarantee of Rumania's frontiers, the FO had not secured an assurance from Warsaw on this point. Now, alone with Beck in Whitehall — Chamberlain, after welcoming his guest, had stepped across Downing Street to No. 10 — Halifax brought it up.

To his dismay Beck declined to commit himself. Any such maneuver by Poland, he said, would increase tension in eastern Europe; it would, moreover, "automatically" link Hungary and Germany in a military alliance. Halifax heatedly replied that the link was already there, de facto if not de jure, and with the menacing cloud of approaching conflict already darkening the Continent, "the lack of 'concerted plans' would be calamitous." Beck suavely countered by paraphrasing a recent Chamberlain warning in the House against the establishing of "opposing blocs" of nations; "rigid political systems," he said, were equally dangerous. At this point the prime minister rejoined them, and the more he listened to Beck the more alarmed he became. Poland alone was pointless, the P.M. said; Rumania was the "vital spot." The colonel lit a cigarette and repeated his objection to "too rigid a system." The prime minister tried to scare him. If Nazi troops occupied Rumania, he said, "Poland would have a longer frontier with Germany." Beck smoothly replied that "the additional frontier would be quite short," adding that it would be in the mountains, which could be held "with quite a small force."[95]

Chamberlain — apparently grasping, for the first time, the implications of Britain's commitment to Warsaw — expressed anxiety that a German invasion of Poland might involve Great Britain. Beck said nothing; there was nothing to say. Chamberlain naively asked where Hitler would strike next. The Pole sardonically replied that if Nazi statements were to be believed, "the gravest question is the colonial question." Chamberlain asked about Russia, pointing out that the Reich and the U.S.S.R. shared no common border; to fight Nazis the Red Army would have to cross Polish or Rumanian soil. Beck replied that "any association between Poland and Russia" would mean war between Poland and the Reich; whatever Britain and the Soviet Union decided to do, Poland would "keep clear." The issue of Rumania was raised for the third time, and Beck declared that

Rumania should be left to her own devices "until the Danubian problem has cleared itself up." He then reeled off a series of outright fabrications. Germany had "never contested" Polish rights in Danzig; indeed, Ribbentrop had "recently reaffirmed them." He doubted that the Führer would "risk a conflict" over "local matters," or that "any serious danger" of Nazi aggression existed. The prime minister suggested that Poland had been weakened by Germany's seizure of Czechoslovakia's Skoda Works. Beck replied that Poland was "not at all" dependent on Skoda's factories. In munitions she was "largely self-supporting"; indeed, the Poles exported weapons and "even supplied guns to Great Britain."[96]

That was too much for Chamberlain. As a man of commerce, he kept a sharper eye on England's trade balance than any prime minister in memory. He knew what Britain imported, where it came from, the quantities and the prices, particularly goods bought by His Majesty's Government. Polish arms weren't on the list. The illustrious Colonel Beck was a liar. Chamberlain and Halifax were beginning to understand why this man was a legend. They had been had. HMG's negotiations with him, and the culminating guarantee, had been a blind. Europe's security had not been strengthened. Instead Britain's vulnerability had grown.[97]

In politics the squeaky wheel gets little grease. This is particularly true when a public figure challenging the leader carries a controversial reputation in train. The mass distrusts controversy. Reluctant to reconsider its convictions, superstitions, and prejudices, it rarely withdraws support from those who are guiding its destinies. Thus inertia becomes an incumbent's accomplice. So does human reluctance to admit error. Those who backed the top man insist, against all evidence, that they made the right choice.

Chamberlain was still basking in the glow of the reception that had greeted his return from Munich. Having saved the peace then, he believed he could do it again. And in their hearts Englishmen still yearned for abiding peace. Chamberlain thought he had time. He could avoid a general election until 1942. By then, his loyal admirers believed, the old man could pull one more rabbit out of his hat, and the old man thought so, too. Something had gone wrong. If he could identify it and find it, he could set the world right again. But he was puzzled. What was it? Where had it gone?

The source of his greatest anxiety could be found in the Reich Chancellery, but now Hitler's fellow dictator in Rome had decided that he had better start grabbing while the grabbing was good. Brooding on his balcony above the huge sign *"Il Duce ha sempre ragione!"* ("The Duce is always right!") Mussolini had decided the Führer had been upstaging him.

The surest way to reach the world's front pages was to break the peace. Therefore, the Duce would dazzle the international press by avenging a personal insult: the Albanians, under King Zog, had objected to the bullying tactics of the local Fascist party. The tattered banners that Italian legions had dragged through Ethiopia were unfurled and mended; Italian warships bombed Zog's coast, causing him and his queen to flee to Greece first, and then to Turkey. On April 7, Good Friday, the first wave of legionnaires waded ashore, some of them drowning in a treacherous undercurrent, and the natives fled inland. Enough of them were assembled to vote for union with Italy. King Victor Emmanuel reluctantly accepted the crown. It was an infamous victory.

Churchill dryly observed: "The British habit of the week-end, the great regard which the British pay to holidays which coincide with festivals of the Church, is studied abroad." He then pointed out that this was not all opéra bouffe. Despite its Ruritanian appearance, the mountainous little country was a strategic springboard for an invasion of Greece. Mussolini's operation had been anticipated for weeks — every Italian embassy was like a sieve — but Churchill was the only English statesman who had worked out what he regarded as England's most appropriate response. The evening before the Duce launched his Albanian adventure, Winston had dined at Cherkeley, Beaverbrook's country home near Leatherhead. While the others were playing backgammon, he had approached a fellow guest — Arthur Christiansen, editor of the *Daily Express* and until now a stranger to him — to talk. He was feeling histrionic, and, as Christiansen put it in his memoirs, he seemed to be "rolling the words around his palate and licking them before they [were] uttered." He asked: "Where is the — ah — the British Fleet tonight? It is lolling in the Bay of Naples. No doubt the — ah — the Commander of the British ships at Naples is — ah — being entertained ashore, entertained no doubt on the orders of — ah — Mussolini himself at the Naples Yacht Club." Winston's demeanor changed; he glowered, chewed his cigar, then growled: "And where *should* the British Fleet be tonight? On the other side of that longheel of a country called Italy, in the Adriatic Sea, not the Mediterranean Sea, to make the rape of Albania impossible."[98]

At dawn the Duce's men were on the beaches. Churchill was at home in Kent when news of the Italian assault reached Chartwell. He sent word to No. 10: "Hours now count." Parliament, he wrote, ought to be "recalled at the latest on Tuesday," and he hoped Chamberlain would form a united parliamentary front, "as in the case of the Polish Agreement." As Churchill saw it, "It is imperative for us to recover the initiative in diplomacy. . . . What is now at stake is nothing less than the whole of the Balkan Peninsula. If these states remain exposed to German and Italian pressure while we appear, as they may deem it, incapable of action, they will be forced to make the best terms possible with Berlin. How forlorn then will our position become!"[99]

He proposed, as a first step, a British occupation of the Greek island of Corfu, "of course with Greek consent." If the Royal Navy were there first, an Italian attack "even upon a few British ships would confront Mussolini with beginning a war of aggression upon England. This direct issue gives the best chance to all the forces in England which are opposed to a major war with England. So far from intensifying the grave risks which are now open, it diminishes them. But action ought to be taken tonight." Chamberlain replied that this maneuver had found no support in the cabinet. Winston was not easily put off; the following week the P.M. wrote his sister that Churchill had been "at the telephone all day urging that Pmt should be summoned for Sunday & that the Fleet should go & seize Corfu that night!" If Winston were given an office, "would he wear me out resisting rash suggestions of this kind?"[100]

It was in fact rash. Churchill had proposed a classic exercise of sea power, ignoring the havoc Italian warplanes could wreak upon the British Fleet. Later he would learn not to underrate air power at sea. But the cardinal point is that he was urging action — while the prime minister was above all a man of inaction who would move only when, as at Munich, he was menaced by the threat of greater involvement. Harold Macmillan, a luncheon guest at Chartwell that Good Friday, later recalled, "It was a scene that gave me my first picture of Churchill at work. Maps were brought out; secretaries were marshalled; telephones began to ring." The estate had been transformed into a state within a state, with advisers, researchers, filing cabinets, and mounted charts. Approaching the end of his life, Macmillan would remember: "I shall always have a picture of that spring day and the sense of power and energy, the great flow of action, which came from Churchill, although he then held no public office." In London's ministries everyone seemed indecisive, vacillating. But not here with the master of Chartwell. To Macmillan, "He alone seemed to be in command, when everyone else was dazed and hesitating."[101]

Winston's proposals to Chamberlain seemed presumptuous, but no other living Englishman, in uniform or mufti, possessed so profound a knowledge of the Royal Navy. The effort which dazzled Macmillan continued to annoy Chamberlain, however. To his sister the P.M. complained that "It doesn't make things easier to be badgered . . . by the two Oppositions & Winston who is the worst of the lot, telephoning almost every hour of the day."[102]

Actually the prime minister ought to have been seeking advice; he had a great deal at stake in the Adriatic. Ever since moving into No. 10 he had been courting Mussolini, trying to drive a wedge between the Duce and the Führer. In January he and an FO entourage had journeyed to Rome and appealed for the good offices of "Musso," as Chamberlain called him in his diary. Specifically, he hoped that the Duce could be persuaded "to prevent Herr Hitler from carrying out some 'mad dog' act." Mussolini asked the P.M. whether he wanted to raise any specific point. Chamberlain replied that German rearmament and Wehrmacht troop moves were "giving rise to a great deal of anxiety and doubt . . . all over Europe." According to Ciano, his father-in-law thought this sounded like a whine; he had been listening for a trumpet call, but that was an instrument Neville Chamberlain did not know how to play. "The talks with the English are finished," wrote Ciano, dismissing them as "nothing of consequence." Churchill had anticipated Chamberlain's failure. Earlier, dining with Vansittart and Duff Cooper, he had remarked: "Mussolini, like Hitler, regards Britannia as a frightened, flabby old woman, who at worst would only bluster, and was anyhow incapable of making war. She certainly looks the part."[103]

Bismarck, when told that Romans dreamed of a second empire, remarked: "The Italians have a big appetite and poor teeth." That was rather brutal, but it described Musso to a T. Tiny Albania, like tiny Ethiopia, was about all that the new Italian army, straining every muscle and summoning that last desperate erg of effort, could manage to conquer. Still, his attack on King Zog's realm was aggression and therefore had to be condemned by Parliament, ending the possibility, once real, that Italy might again march with the democracies. This was a good time for wise British statesmen to say nothing. But Chamberlain, who brandished an olive branch when the flashing blade of a saber was needed, had a genius for flexing Britannia's muscles at the wrong time. On the following Thursday, April 13, he informed a startled House of Commons that His Majesty's Government had decided to guarantee the frontiers of Greece, Turkey, and, once more, Rumania.

Winston was already having second, third, and fourth thoughts about the Polish guarantee, in part because he learned that the prime minister was also having them. On Monday, April 3, three days after Chamberlain had announced Britain's new relationship with the Poles, Churchill had told the House that "this is no time for negotiation. After the crime and treachery committed against Czechoslovakia, our first duty is to reestablish the authority of law and public faith in Europe." Members were beginning to wonder about the relevance of this when he drew their attention to "a sinister passage in *The Times'* leading article on Saturday, similar to that which foreshadowed the ruin of Czechoslovakia." Dawson had written: "The new obligation which this country yesterday assumed does not bind

Great Britain to defend every inch of the present frontiers of Poland. The key word in the statement is not 'integrity' but 'independence.' " The prime minister's statement, the editorial continued, "involves no blind acceptance of the *status quo.* . . . This country" — the confidence of *The Times*'s editor in assuming that he always spoke for Britain is a source of endless amazement — "has never been an advocate of the encirclement of Germany, and is not now opposed to the extension of Germany's economic pressure and influence, nor to the constructive work she may yet do for Europe."[104]

Churchill was unaware that this passage actually reflected Chamberlain's views. Earlier that same Monday, before Winston spoke, the prime minister had written his sister that his statement linking England's fortunes with Poland was "unprovocative in tone, but firm, clear but stressing the important point (perceived alone by *The Times*) that what we are concerned with is not the boundaries of States, but attacks on their independence. And it is we who will judge whether this independence is threatened or not." Reports that appeasement was dead, it seemed, had been greatly exaggerated. But it was dying. Only a few weeks earlier Margot Asquith had declared that anyone "who is against the Gvts. Peace policy" was guilty of treason. But she had been among those who were completely turned round by the Nazi rape of Prague. After the prime minister's Birmingham speech protesting Hitler's betrayal of the Munich accord, she had written to Winston: "We are *old* friends (I, *very* old!). I think you sd go to 10 Downing Street & offer yr services, in whatever the PM wishes to place you. We *must* show Germany that we are united against her wish to dominate Europe."[105]

If so proud a woman could be humbled by Prague, as she was, if she could reject her convictions of yesterday and campaign for stronger British defenses, a hard line with Hitler, and, above all, Churchill's return to power — if that single event could reconcile Margot and her stepdaughter Violet, who had long believed Churchill alone could save England, to the point that they wept and embraced — then it is hardly surprising that their reconciliation was repeated in millions of homes, as those who had believed Munich meant "peace for our time" turned volte-face, boxing the compass as their long winter of feuding ended. Churchill, then Chamberlain, and then Margot prayed for "unity," for "union" — an end to the dissension which enervated England and succored only Hitler.

Their yearning for a single national purpose was not self-fulfilling. England was not marching in lockstep toward a single goal. Democracies do not work that way. Churchill's proposed policies, in the prime minister's view, would split the country into flinders. Nevertheless, one or the other must prevail. The question was which, and as England struggled toward a consensus, Englishmen had a lot of catching up to do. For six lost years the British public had been misled and misinformed. To be sure, it had been a public willing, even eager, to be deceived, but leaders bred in British public schools were expected to achieve more than popularity. Now, and throughout 1939 and into 1940, as the transfiguration of an England disenchanted with appeasement picked up momentum, the long pendulum swung back toward honor.

※   ※

The swing was neither smooth, swift, nor uninterrupted. A vague uneasiness had been perceptible even before Munich; after the prime minister departed London for his confrontation with the Führer at Godesberg, the German chargé d'affaires had wired the Wilhelmstrasse: "Chamberlain and his party have left under a heavy load of anxiety. . . . Unquestionably opposition is growing to Chamberlain's policy." But then the P.M. had brought back what the British public thought was peace with honor, and the pendulum had been arrested. After Prague, its motion resumed, only to slow when the Polish guarantee was announced.[106]

It went like that, in fits and starts. The British people remained deeply respectful of authority, and Neville Chamberlain continued to control the institutions of government. Fleet Street, in the beginning, was deeply divided. And those who wanted to see His Majesty's Government replaced could not agree on who should lead them. In retrospect Churchill seems to have been inevitable, but that was not so at the time. As the prime minister's popularity ebbed, senior Conservatives, led by David Margesson, the chief Tory whip, began casting about for a successor. Almost to a man, they preferred Halifax. Chamberlain himself favored his foreign secretary; so did the King; so did *The Times*. Outside the establishment, however, Halifax was discredited. If a new tenant were to move into Downing Street, most of the great London dailies — and, if the polls were accurate, most Englishmen — wanted a man untainted by a record of truckling to Hitler and unstained by responsibility for the shabby state of Britain's defenses.

The shoe fitted Winston, and he was an obvious candidate. Yet claims were advanced for others. Eden and Duff Cooper, disillusioned, had resigned from the cabinet. Amery was also fearless. Nevertheless, each of Churchill's rivals was vulnerable. Eden and Cooper had waited too long to quit. And Amery, who had misjudged the Führer in the beginning, had gone along with Baldwin's draconian cuts in Britain's defense estimates during the years when rearmament was vital.

Those who wanted a new broom in Downing Street sought a man of political stature who had opposed HMG's policies and attempted to reverse their course. Eden in particular had problems here. Even before his appointment as foreign secretary, he had been an ardent appeaser. To his mortification, his role in forfeiting the Rhineland, which he had thought forgotten, was exhumed. Duff Cooper, on the other hand, was unpredictable and guilty of lapses in judgment. As relations deteriorated between Whitehall and the Wilhelmstrasse he wrote seventy-two-year-old Earl Baldwin of Bewdley, the one man no other Conservative wanted to remember, with a singular proposal. "If the international situation deteriorates, which I believe it will," he wrote, "we shall be forced to have a Coalition Government." Duff Cooper doubted "that Neville could ever lead such a Government," and then dealt with the two likeliest successors — "Halifax or Winston." He didn't believe the first was "up to it," and Churchill "has too many and such violent enemies." Many Englishmen, he added, "don't trust him." Having set up the retired P.M., who was even more responsible than Chamberlain for the neglect of the country's defenses, Duff Cooper propositioned him: "I am wondering whether after two years' rest you feel you could come back." Since Earl Baldwin of Bewdley's image had been tarnished beyond restoring, he replied that no, he did not think he could.[107]

But there were doubts about Churchill, too. Amery, Eden, and Duff Cooper at least spoke in the idiom of their time, and until now each had attracted more supporters in Parliament than the lonely, eccentric genius whose star was just beginning to rise. In 1932 Nancy Astor had written him off as "finished"; his denunciation of Munich had been regarded as political suicide. Moreover, at this time the fall of Chamberlain, though in many minds, was not an immediate issue. Because of his party's large majority, only an uprising among Conservative backbenchers could drive him from No. 10. He was in trouble, but not that much trouble. Those who wished him ill could not move until he had suffered an accumulation of defeats. And the House knew that Churchill would not be satisfied with a cabinet post. He wanted office only as a springboard to the premiership, which raised other questions. On a superficial level, Churchill in the 1930s seemed almost vestigial. Approaching his late sixties, eligible for a pension, he was anachronistic in manner, dress, and speech. He could actually remember Gladstone recalling youthful memories of the bonfires celebrating Waterloo. Churchill's eclipse in the party, indeed, had been a direct consequence of his conviction, an article of faith in the nineteenth century but widely disputed in the twentieth, that the British Raj should continue to rule India.

Since his exile from power, he had campaigned against his own party's imperial, defense, and foreign policies, with a signal lack of success. To a people still haunted by the slaughter of trench warfare he had called for rearmament, declared that courage on the battlefield was a virtue, and gave "the world at large," in Samuel Hoare's words, the impression that he was "the very embodiment of a policy of war." He was also immovable. Any other politician twice faced with uprisings in his own constituency would have trimmed his sails, if ever so slightly. Churchill had known that the Munich Agreement, before the seizure of Prague, was popular. But he wouldn't retract a word. He delivered scathing speeches on appeasement and HMG's failure to rearm to audiences who felt otherwise, and whose votes he needed if he was to keep his seat. He didn't enjoy it. More than most public men, he reveled in applause. He just didn't know how to compromise. In *Great Contemporaries* he had written: "Politicians rise by toil and troubles. They expect to fail; they hope to rise." Perseverance is the worthiest of political traits, and certainly the most difficult; a British historian who takes a jaundiced view of Winston acknowledges that "To persist in a political career that appears to others, and even on occasion to the politician himself, as finished, demands exceptional strength of character in a sensitive and proud man." As Ralph Waldo Emerson pointed out, there is a distinction between intellect and character. Intellect had won Churchill acclaim; character prevented him from exploiting it. He yearned for a ministry, but only on his own terms. Had his constituents rejected him, his response would have echoed an Emerson couplet: "Good-bye, proud world! I'm going home; / Thou art not my friend and I'm not thine."[108]

Yet Prague had undeniably transformed Churchill's political weaknesses into strengths. The policies he had attacked were exposed, overnight, as bankrupt. England had been hoodwinked, and Englishmen wanted no Dear Vicar or Good Old Neville. Martin Gilbert observes: "With the shock of Hitler's occupation of Prague, pressure mounted for . . . a decisive change in British policy." Britons listened with a thirsty ear for a call to arms, but Chamberlain, like Baldwin before him, lacked the voice for that. They heard it loud and clear in Churchill's rhetoric, however, and his appeal for a "recovery of moral health." As a contributor to the *Yale Review* has pointed out, this was "his way of saying that the English after Munich had to learn all over again to recognize evil. They had lost the sense of villainy; they had no solid principles, unshakable convictions."[109]

Chamberlain still held the House of Commons. It is a peculiarity of the British parliamentary system that in insulating Parliament from mass hysteria or chimerical shifts in the public mood, the House may also ignore an aroused electorate and remain loyal to its leader, particularly if he is strong, determined, and clever. Each MP could be held accountable only to his constituency, and then only in general elections. Hitler had touched a nerve when he said on November 8, 1938: "After all, Churchill may have 14,000, 20,000, or 30,000 votes behind him [actually he had 34,849] — I am not so well informed about that — but I have 40,000,000 behind me." Since he had banned elections, there was no way to confirm that. Yet even in democratic England, Tory MPs were subject to pressure, not from the voters, but from Margesson and his fellow whips, who worked at No. 12 Downing Street and received their instructions from No. 10.[110]

Eventually, of course, the House must reckon with the public temper. So must a prime minister, though a stubborn man, which Chamberlain was, may act without parliamentary approval — even without the approval of his cabinet. After Prague, the tide of opposition to the P.M. rose throughout 1939, and it began with Churchill's readers, whose number multiplied week by week. His pieces were appearing in the *Daily Telegraph*, *Picture Post*, the *Illustrated London News*, the *Daily Mail*, and — in the United States, where he was sowing the seeds of a future alliance — *Collier's*. The titles speak for themselves: "Let the Tyrant Criminals Bomb!" "What Britain's Policy Should Be," "War, Now or Never," "Towards a Pact with Russia," "Bombs Don't Scare Us Now," "Germany's Use of Tactics of Encirclement," and "No Blood Will Flow Unless . . . ."

Churchill's prose was but one of many forces hammering on the consciences of the British public — Hitler's actions were the most effective — but the phenomenon of a militant Britain could not have been shaped as it was without him. The "gathering storm," as he later called it, became apparent to men in pubs, women pushing prams, greengrocers, drummers, lorry drivers, businessmen, shop stewards; to everyone, in short, except the oligarchy in power, which need not face the voters again for three years. Slowly the prevailing opinion of fifty million Englishmen would turn round until Britain became a mirror image of the country whose throne Edward VIII had rejected, a valiant nation glorying in everything it had scorned after Munich. This reversal was far more profound than the Führer's arousal of his *Volk* earlier in the decade. The Germans, after all, had been belligerent for two thousand years; British public school boys were taught that "Civilization stops at the Rhine and the Danube, the frontiers of the Roman Empire," or, as Winston put it, "A Hun alive is a war in prospect." In the past seventy years Germany had writ her name large on battlefields, while the British Empire had endeavored to impose a Pax Britannica on the world.[111]

Once appeasement was discredited, the scapegoating began. Like Gallipoli it became a political weapon, a lash to flog the Conservative party. Michael Foot and two collaborators later published a devastating Labour attack on the appeasers. Titled *Guilty Men*, it singled out fifteen Tories, among them Chamberlain, Simon, Hoare, MacDonald, Halifax, and Baldwin, indicting each for neglecting England's defenses and failing to alert and prepare the country for the inevitable conflict. *Guilty Men* received an enthusiastic press. The *Atlantic Monthly* called it an irrefutable exposure of Baldwin's "blunder and blindness"; the *Spectator* thought it persuasive evidence that coalition and Conservative ministries "were deceived by Hitler and did not, when awakened to realities, apply themselves with vigour to the task of restoring our defences"; and the *Boston Transcript* found the book's arguments "unanswerable."[112]

But they weren't. Throughout the 1930s Foot, a socialist who had cheered pacifist speeches, following Attlee's pacifist lead, had opposed *any* appropriations for the British army, the Admiralty, and the RAF. If the Tories had taken his line, Britain would have faced the Nazis naked. The MacDonald-Baldwin-Chamberlain triumvirate never went that far. At least they left the infrastructure intact. Indeed, it may almost be said that *Guilty Men* was written by guiltier men.

Churchill was still beleaguered by both sides of the House as the sands ran out, but "the public," as Brian Gardner notes, "were beginning to think otherwise; for someone who was meant to be an adventurer, his warnings had been going on a remarkably long time, and with strange consistency, determination, and integrity." J. B. Priestley, whose politics lay in deep left field, wrote that there were three urgent reasons for appointing Churchill to the cabinet: his "outstanding ability and experience," which Chamberlain's ministers conspicuously lacked; the emerging realization that "the people want him there"; and the fact that "his presence will at least do something to show the world, which has no confidence whatever in our statesmen, that we are in earnest."[113]

In a country enjoying freedom of speech, shifts in public opinion are first sensed by the press. Lord Boothby believed that until the great awakening which followed Prague most of the London press, "with the shining exception of the *Daily Telegraph*, was bright yellow," with editors following Geoffrey Dawson's lead. "Fleet Street," according to Boothby, "did everything in its power to help Neville Chamberlain and his wretched Government turn the whole country yellow." The campaign to depict Chamberlain as heroic and Churchill as a blackguard peaked in the weeks immediately following Munich. Even Kingsley Martin, the left-wing editor of the *New Statesman*, who had indicted His Majesty's Government for failing to stand up to Fascist and Nazi aggressors, was deceived by the

Munich hoax and later felt shame. Sir John Reith at the BBC continued to gag Hitler's critics — Sir Horace Rumbold and Harold Nicolson were denied airtime because they were "anti-German."[114]

Nevertheless, London newspapermen remained objective. Jaded by their government's duplicity, half-lies, and distortion, and by the gullibility of their readers, they were surprised to find growing support for Churchill among the middle, lower middle, and working classes — the yeomanry of England, and now, it seemed, her spine. These people wanted Winston in the government, with power to act and persuade — in short, with a ministry. His supporters could even be found in the cabinet. Malcolm MacDonald recalls that "the government was divided over whether Churchill should come in. On balance the younger members were for him, the older members skeptical. . . . We had begun to think this is war, we must get Churchill in, not as P.M. but as a very important war minister, or war-to-be minister, but Neville was reluctant."[115]

Chamberlain believed war ministers unnecessary because he remained convinced that he had brought Englishmen peace in their time, and this became clear as debate over establishment of a ministry of supply — first proposed by Churchill three years earlier, on April 23, 1936 — approached its climax. Without such a minister, an economic czar empowered to mobilize British industry and provide a national arsenal, future recruits would lack rifles, even uniforms. It was no longer enough for a nation to spring to arms. Artillery, tanks, and warplanes, decisive in modern war, must also be there. Such complicated weapons required lead time. On October 28, a month after Munich, the Air Ministry's director of plans had expressed doubts that RAF reserves would "last for more than a week of warfare on a modern scale." Churchill's intelligence net had seen to it that a copy of this report reached Chartwell, and he had written a friend that such failure "strips Ministers of all credentials to be judges of the national interests."[116]

Two days earlier the prime minister had told his cabinet he was ruling out a ministry of supply. No one could shake his faith in appeasement, not even Adolf Hitler. On November 14 Halifax, at a meeting of the cabinet Committee on Foreign Policy, had quoted the Führer as saying: "If I were Chamberlain I would not delay for a minute to prepare my country in the most drastic way for a 'total' war and I would thoroughly organize it. If the English have not got universal conscription by the spring of 1939 they may consider their world empire as lost. It is astounding how easy the democracies make it for us to reach our goal." The P.M., after a moment of stony silence, took up the next item on the agenda.[117]

To Churchill the need for the new ministry was compelling. That same week he had risen in the House of Commons to propose an amendment calling for its immediate establishment: "I put it as bluntly as I possibly can. If only fifty members of the Conservative Party went into the Lobby tonight to vote for this amendment, it would not affect the life of the Government, but it would make them act." The rapid production of munitions, he declared, should have begun long ago, and on a scale immensely greater than anything the War Office now contemplated. HMG's reply was that a ministry would "seriously dislocate" British industry, that it was wiser "to trust to cooperation than to compulsion." The House was still Chamberlain's, and Winston's rebuff was stunning. Not fifty MPs, but just two — Bracken and Macmillan — joined him. Berlin rejoiced. "GREAT DEFEAT OF CHURCHILL!" read one Nazi headline. Another trumpeted: "CHURCHILL'S INTRIGUES COLLAPSE / EVEN DUFF COOPER AND EDEN COULD NOT BE ROPED IN."[118]

As late as March 2, 1939, the prime minister's own secretary for war, Leslie Hore-Belisha, told him that if the government was serious about defending the country, something had to be done to arm and equip its fighting men, and Britain's industrial titans would listen to no one without a seat at the cabinet table. Wearily the P.M. cut him off in mid-argument. They were already "getting the goods," he said, and "now that public opinion is becoming satisfied on this point I think the demand for a Ministry will die down."[119]

But it didn't, and Hore-Belisha kept hammering away at cabinet meetings, citing desperate, unmet needs and how a supply minister could resolve them. He met Churchill in Morpeth Mansions for strategy meetings, and once, when Winston had hurt his foot in yard work, he drove to Chartwell for advice. This was risky; in a cabinet dominated by sycophants, the rebellious war minister was isolated.

Yet the Ministry of Supply had become inevitable, and presently even Chamberlain knew it. In April 1939, after the German occupation of Prague, his panel of industrialists — the men he admired most and had sought to shield from bureaucracy — reported that their chief recommendation, an urgent question to be met squarely "at the first possible opportunity," was "the establishment of a Ministry of Supply." Brendan Bracken wrote Bernard Baruch: "Winston has won his long fight. . . . No public man of our time has shown more foresight, and I believe that his long, lonely struggle . . . will prove to be the best chapter in his crowded life."[120]

It had been assumed by the public, Fleet Street, Parliament, and most of the cabinet that Churchill would be the man appointed to the new office. No one in the country could match his experience as the czar of war industry twenty years earlier. On April 19 Nicolson wrote in his diary: "The feeling that Winston is essential is gaining strength, and we shall probably see him in the Cabinet within a short time." Writing Winston, Lord Rothermere predicted "a great responsibility" falling on his shoulders "at an early date" and offering him £600 if he quit drinking brandy for a year; all England, he added, "including especially myself, will wish you to be in the finest fettle when the day arrives."[121]

The new post went, however, not to the superbly qualified man who would have served England best, but to Leslie Burgin, the minister of transportation, an obscure man whose only other appointment had been parliamentary secretary to the Board of Trade. Nicolson set down two reactions in the House of Commons: "a gasp of horror" and "a deep groan of pain." The *British Weekly* noted: "There was much disappointment on both sides of the House that the changes in the Cabinet did not include such out-standing figures as Mr. Winston Churchill and Mr. Anthony Eden." Samuel Hoare later attributed Churchill's exclusion to his repeated calls to arms, which had stigmatized him as a warmonger, and the prime minister, according to his biographer, was "anxious that Hitler not think of [Winston] as a spokesman for His Majesty's Government."[122]

Chamberlain's decision to bypass Winston and appoint Burgin had been made with an eye on the Wilhelmstrasse, and in his diary the prime minister justified it: "If there is any possibility of easing the tension and getting back normal relations with the dictators, I wouldn't risk it by what would certainly be regarded by them as a challenge." But he paid a price in Parliament. There, Nicolson noted, the general "impression was deplorable." Independent MPs, he wrote, had "hoped that the P.M. would take this opportunity of broadening the basis of his Cabinet. There is a very widespread belief that he is running a dual policy — one the overt policy of arming, and the other the *secret de l'Empereur,* namely appeasement plus Horace Wilson. Chamberlain's obstinate refusal to include any but the yes-men in his Cabinet caused real dismay."[123]

On March 18 Neville Chamberlain celebrated his seventieth birthday. He was exhausted, and the seeds of personal tragedy were beginning to take root. After two grueling years at No. 10, signs of stress were evident. Rab Butler had been in the country on Good Friday. Learning that the Italians had invaded Albania he hurried to Downing Street, and long afterward he recalled being led upstairs to a small room overlooking a garden, which the P.M. used as a study. The window was open; bird food was strewn on a shelf outside. Chamberlain appeared annoyed by Butler's arrival and expressed amazement at his distress. He said: "I feel sure Mussolini has decided not to go against us." Butler recalled: "When I started to talk about the threat to the Balkans, he dismissed me with the words: 'Don't be silly. Go home and go to bed,' and continued to feed the birds."[124]

Writing his sister of the Duce's Albanian adventure, Chamberlain complained, not of Italian aggression, but of duplicity: "What I had hoped when I went away on Thursday was that Musso would so present his coup as to make it look like an agreed arrangement & thus raise as little as possible questions of European significance." In a strange admission — coming so late, after so many broken promises in Rome and Berlin — he wrote: "Such faith as I ever had in the assurances of dictators is rapidly being whittled away."[125]

Before Parliament's Albania debate, on April 13, the P.M. sent for Winston "in the hope of keeping the House as united as possible." In the debate Churchill did endorse Chamberlain's guarantee to Rumania and Greece and said he anticipated "even more effective arrangements with Turkey." If a "great design" of binding alliances were achieved, he said, "even now, at the eleventh hour," the world could be spared "the worst of its agonies." At the same time, however, he wondered how His Majesty's Government could make such wide-ranging commitments when Britain's defenses were so weak — how they could speak so loudly when carrying so small a stick. At the very least, he argued, Parliament should be asked to approve the conscription of British youth. He could not understand why the government had remained silent on this pressing issue. He asked: "How can we bear to continue to lead our comfortable, easy lives here at home, unwilling even to pronounce the word 'compulsion,' unwilling even to take the necessary measure by which the armies that we have promised can alone be recruited and equipped?"[126]

He then raised an issue which MPs had discussed among themselves in the smoking room or lobby, but never in the chamber itself. It was the unique position of Sir Horace Wilson, known to insiders for his influence on Chamberlain, his sympathies for the Third Reich, and his unscrupulous intervention between the prime minister and other government advisers, including senior members of the cabinet. Without naming names, Churchill wondered how anyone on the Treasury Bench could indulge in "sunshine talk," predicting "the dawn of a Golden Age" only five days before Hitler raped what was left of Czechoslovakia. Yet it was now obvious that "something of a very exceptional character, the consequences of which could not be measured, was imminent." Why, then, was the government unprepared? "After twenty-five years' experience in peace and war, I believe the British Intelligence Service to be the finest of its kind in the world. Yet we have seen, both in the case of the subjugation of Bohemia and on the occasion of the invasion of Albania, that Ministers of the Crown had apparently no inkling, or at any rate no conviction, of what was coming. I cannot believe that this is the fault of the British Secret Service."

Churchill knew "very well," he continued, "the patriotism and sincere desire to act in a manner of perfect rectitude which animates Ministers of the Crown, but I wonder whether there is not some hand which intervenes and filters down or withholds intelligence from Ministers." More than once "the facts were not allowed to reach high Ministers of the Crown until they had been so modified that they did not present an alarming proposition."[127]

Chamberlain was vexed. April was turning into the cruelest month of his prime ministry. He had expected an altogether different sequel to Munich: growing friendship with Germany and Italy, trade agreements reviving British industries still sunk in the Depression, and, once Hitler and the Duce realized that the British could be trusted, worldwide disarmament. Instead, he had seen his diplomatic strategy collapse with the Nazi conquest of Czechoslovakia, the Italian invasion of Albania, threats to the Balkans, intrusions into Europe's affairs by Russia, and, most alarming of all, Nazi pressure on Poland, England's one hostage in eastern Europe — pressure suspiciously like Hitler's modus operandi in the opening moves of the Anschluss and the Czech crisis.

Moreover, Roosevelt had interceded. The American president's concern over Europe's murky future had been crystallized by the Italian landings in Albania. The week after the invasion the president had sent a personal message to Mussolini and Hitler, asking them to pledge not to undertake further aggression for ten "or even twenty-five years, if we are to look that far ahead." Both dictators ridiculed it. The Duce called it "a result of infantile paralysis." Göring suggested that Roosevelt was "*im Anfangsstadium einer Geisteskrankheit*" ("in the early stages of a mental disease"), and on April 28 Hitler cruelly mocked the president before the Reichstag — and then renounced both the Anglo-German Naval Agreement of 1935 and the German-Polish agreement of 1934, charging that Poland and Britain were conspiring to encircle the Reich.[128]

Chamberlain's response to Roosevelt's initiative was to denounce "Yankee meddling." He was sympathetic toward Berlin, indifferent or hostile to Washington; he believed Hitler, not Roosevelt. As Sidney Herbert had written Churchill: "One of the things which the Prime Minister appears consistently to ignore is American public opinion." He also tried to disregard British opinion, but his choices were narrowing. Events were in the saddle, riding Neville Chamberlain and driving him toward the one measure he had vowed he would never take: conscription.[129]

Churchill had been accused of living in the past. Actually that was what HMG was doing; in dodging the draft the appeasers were ignoring Britain's altered status as a world power. For generations the Continent had listened to British prime ministers with respect and had given their advice great weight because behind them ranged the great British Empire, ready to spring to arms — as in 1914 — when the sovereign, on instructions and without consulting his dominions, committed his vast realm to global war. Victoria had spoken of those dwelling in imperial possessions as "my people." But her great-grandson's relationship with their great-grandchildren had been altered by parliamentary statute. Although the Dominions would probably declare war if England did, they couldn't be counted on.

This massive fact, together with the neglect of the island's armed forces by MacDonald, Baldwin, and Chamberlain, meant that Britain could no longer expect the Continent to catch cold when the prime minister sneezed. Chamberlain had treated the Czechs as pawns. In reality their military presence — forty trained, well-equipped divisions — had dwarfed Britain's. As of this moment, Europe's great standing armies were the French and Italians, each with about one hundred divisions; the Germans, with over two hundred; and the Red Army — which Chamberlain slurred — with three hundred. Britain's potential might was great, and had the front bench responded to Churchill's appeals over the past six years the country might have had a strong force-in-being. He had been ignored. If asked to field an expeditionary force now, the chief of the Imperial General Staff could have sent two regular divisions right away, another two later, and four divisions of territorials.

Even Chamberlain had to recognize the discrepancy. In late March he took a half step toward conscription, increasing the territorials by 210,000 (unequipped) and therefore, theoretically, doubling the army reserve. No one was deceived. Now, on April 24, after introducing the new Ministry of Supply, he renounced his past pledges and proposed a draft. The pressures of an aroused country, the press, his own party, and even the King had played roles in turning him around; but the main force goading him was the persistence of Hore-Belisha, who "took his political life in his hands," Winston later wrote. "Several of his interviews with his chief were of a formidable character. I saw something of him in this ordeal, and he was never sure that each day in office would not be his last."[130]

Churchill, the *Daily Telegraph* reported, "was in his most striking and effective form" during the conscription debate. "To hear him, Members hurried in, filling the Chamber and side galleries." He not only approved of the draft; he said it should have been introduced immediately after Munich. Pacifists had denounced the measure as "peacetime conscription." His eyes sweeping the benches, he asked, "Is this peace?" and answered his own rhetorical question: "We have had three disastrous campaigns and the battles, the actions of the war have gone not only against us but against the principles of law and freedom, against the interests of the peaceful and progressive democracies. Those battles already make a long catalogue —

the Rhineland, Abyssinia, Austria, Munich, Prague and Albania [Hon Members 'And Spain']. . . . We are all, then, agreed that circumstances are analogous to war actually prevailing."[131]

But now he saw "a common cause in this House," and, indeed, throughout Western Europe: "The impulse, the main impulse, to resist the Nazi principles comes from the mass of the people." Doubtless many members voting for the bill would feel a wrench inside. He, too, had reservations, but his were different. He thought the measure inadequate. It provided for the induction of 200,000 twenty-year-old youths, but they would be issued neither equipment nor supplies until the Ministry of Supply persuaded British manufacturers to turn them out. It was the story of the reserves all over again; young Englishmen were to surrender their liberty and later, perhaps, their lives, but the production schedules of English factories still had priority. In effect this bill was a gesture, Churchill said, and "a gesture is not sufficient; we want an army and we may want it soon." He said he believed that "everyone is baffled by the now rapid changes of policy upon fundamental issues" in the government, switches which suggested that decisions were being made, "not after mature planning, but in a hurry, not from design, conviction, or forethought," but in response to initiatives in Berlin and Rome. This was consistent with the theme he had been sounding for years, but Chamberlain now suspected malice in all Churchill's criticism of him. He had heard, he wrote his sister, that Winston "thought I was going to offer him the Ministry of Supply & he was therefore smarting under a sense of disappointment, only kept in check by his unwillingness to do anything which might prevent his yet receiving an offer to join the Govt."[132]

The relationship between the Duce and the Führer was warmer. Within a month of the conscription debate, Mussolini yielded to Hitler's cajoling and agreed to join Germany in a military alliance. On May 22, 1939, the two dictators signed their Pact of Steel, agreeing to use force in acquiring "living space" for their peoples. If one of the two went to war, the other would "immediately come to its assistance as an ally and support it with all its military forces on land, at sea, and in the air." In the event of war neither nation would conclude a separate armistice or peace. General Ironside told Churchill that England and France were "in for a bad time."[133]

❦   ❦

What the prime minister failed to grasp was that with all Europe rushing headlong into a maelstrom, the readings on traditional political barometers were meaningless. Normally, crises in public life peaked and passed, the issues quickly forgotten. Instead, all spring and throughout the summer Churchill and Chamberlain moved in elegant counterpoint, as though cast in one of those skillfully plotted Wilkie Collins novels in which the narrative moves among several sets of characters, some evil, some benign, with the reader unaware of which will win, or how. But among the British public in 1939 there was little doubt about which of the duelists aroused the greater enthusiasm. All over England, on posters, billboards, and cartoons, the theme echoed: *Winston must come back*.

The prime minister's manner toward Churchill was unchanged — civility masking hostility. This disturbed Churchill. It was not in the parliamentary tradition; Winston's differences with Neville's father had been many and had cut deep, yet outside the House chamber they had been on good terms, and had frequently dined together. The prime minister's coldness toward him derived in part from the reversal of their standing in the public opinion polls. Winston's popularity was rising; one letter to *The Times*, which even Dawson hadn't dared suppress, was signed by 375 professors, faculty members of every British university, "strongly urging" Churchill's appointment to an important cabinet post.

It is impossible to say precisely when the yearning for Churchill first took hold, but even before Prague the turning toward him had begun. His foreign policy views had been set forth in the February 25, 1939, issue of *Picture Post*, which predicted that "the greatest moment of his life is still to come." A second piece trumpeting him had appeared in the March 4 *Picture Post*, and in a third, on March 11, Churchill answered thirteen questions put to him by the magazine's editor, calling for a new government and cabinet seats for Labour. Newspapers ran letters or even editorials calling him "The Only Man"; an *Evening Advertiser* cartoon had depicted him camping outside No. 10, awaiting appointment as minister of supply.

By April demands that he be brought into the government were being published almost daily. On Friday, April 21, the *Daily Telegraph* ran an especially poignant one from an Oxford don whose father had been killed at Gallipoli. Saturday's *Evening News* called for his appointment "as soon as possible," and the day after that the *Sunday Pictorial* devoted its first two pages to Churchill, telling readers: "The jealousy and suspicion of others compel him to stand idly aside." On Tuesday the editor wired Chartwell: "Huge mail has reached me this morning following my Churchill article Sunday. Letters are overwhelmingly in your favour." Wednesday he sent word that he had received 2,400 responses from subscribers, 97 percent agreeing that Winston must return to office. Of the majority, he wrote: "I have never known such an unqualified response." They came from all classes: ex-soldiers, men still in uniform, and especially the young. Typical comments, he said, were "No more boot-licking to Hitler," and "We want a strong man who is not afraid." The editor ended: "Your name on our street placards aroused tremendous interest, and there is not the slightest doubt of the overwhelming view of the country on this issue."[134]

"WE NEED CHURCHILL." cried a page-one headline in *Time and Tide* on May 6. Four days later the *News Chronicle* published the results of a straw vote reporting that 56 percent of those polled wanted Winston in the cabinet, 26 percent were opposed, and 18 percent expressed no opinion. Horace Wilson destroyed No. 10's copy of this edition before it reached the prime minister's desk. It was a futile gesture; there was no way to keep Chamberlain ignorant of the massive shift in Fleet Street's coverage of Churchill. After Munich speeches praising him had frequently gone unreported; all were covered now, and often published on front pages. On July 1 Archibald Sinclair told an enthusiastic audience that the prime minister should bring Churchill and Eden into his "inner counsels." The *Yorkshire Post* carried a full account of the meeting. The *Star* assumed Winston's appointment to office — "Mr Chamberlain will shortly strengthen his Cabinet. It is expected that he will invite Mr Churchill to join the Government" — and reported that Margesson, taking "soundings" among Tory backbenchers, had found that "in nearly every case the Chief Whip was told that the appointment of Mr Churchill to one of the key posts in the Cabinet would create fresh confidence." The *Sunday Graphic* on July 2 predicted that Churchill would be named first lord of the Admiralty.[135]

Editorials became bolder. The *Observer* thought it incredible that Churchill, with "so firm a grasp of European politics," should be excluded from office, adding that the phenomenon "must be as bewildering to foreigners as it is regrettable to most of his own countrymen." On July 3 the *Manchester Guardian* urged the prime minister to put patriotism above personal rancor and use Winston's gifts "in any capacity," because England needed "Ministers of vision and power as well as administrators." The *Daily Telegraph* agreed. That same week calls for Churchill's return to office appeared in the *Daily Mirror*, the *Evening News*, the *News Chronicle*, and even the *Daily Worker*, on the ground that Churchill had been "the outstanding opponent of the 'Munich policy.' " The *Mirror* described Winston as "the most trusted statesman in Britain . . . the watchdog of Britain's safety. For years he warned us of dangers which have now become terrible realities. For years he pressed for the policy of STRENGTH, which the whole nation now supports." The following day the *Daily Mail* and the *Evening Standard* joined the recruits; so, on July 7, did the *Spectator*, declaring that giving Churchill and Eden seats at the cabinet table would constitute "a decisive contribution to our cause" and might persuade Hitler to pause before sending his troops into yet another country.[136]

"Oh Winston dear," Maxine Elliott wrote from the Riviera, "was there ever such a triumph for a public man! Press and public alike hotly demanding its one man who has told them the frightening truth all these years and now they run to him to try and pull their burning chestnuts out of the fire." Leo Amery wrote him that he hoped the newspaper push "will result in your being brought in to the Government," and Stafford Cripps asked: "Could you not make a public statement . . . stating your preparedness to give your services to the country. . . . I feel it would make a tremendous impact just now on the country and would intensify enormously the demand that is growing everywhere for your inclusion in the Government."[137]

But Churchill replied that he was "quite sure that any such demarche would weaken me in any discussion I might have to have with the gentleman in question." And he was right. In Hoare's words, Chamberlain "resented outside pressure. The more, therefore, the Press clamoured for Churchill's inclusion, the less likely he was to take any action." Colin Coote at *The Times* — Winston called him his "friend in the enemy's camp" — wrote Boothby that the "agitation" favoring Churchill would fail: "I will offer you a small bet that the other Mr. C. won't listen to it for a moment; for his motto is still peace at any price except loss of office, and he is rightly sure that the inclusion of Winston means his own proximate exclusion."[138]

Probably nothing would have stopped Hitler at this point. By the first anniversary of Munich he would have 7,188,000 Germans in Wehrmacht and Luftwaffe uniforms. Orders for the destruction of Poland had been cut, and although rebel generals were still scheming against him, five years would pass before they made their move. But Winston was the last Englishman the Führer wanted in office. In the early summer of 1939 the Foreign Office received an account of a conversation between James Marshall-Cornwall, a British general, and Count Schwerin von Krosigk, Reich finance minister and a member of the German cabinet. Krosigk had told the general that Chamberlain should "take Winston Churchill into the Cabinet. Churchill is the only Englishman Hitler is afraid of." Marshall-Cornwall added that Krosigk had said that Hitler "does not take the PM and Lord Halifax seriously, but he places Churchill in the same category as Roosevelt. The mere fact of giving him a leading ministerial post would convince Hitler that you really mean to stand up to him."[139]

But Chamberlain still did not believe in standing up to him. All evidence to the contrary, he remained convinced that if the Führer were treated with generosity, he could become Britain's best friend. Therefore

Churchill remained in Coventry. Lord Camrose, proprietor of the *Daily Telegraph*, called at No. 10 to state the case for Winston. The press lord did not represent himself alone. He spoke for a select group of the most astute and distinguished Conservatives and independents, all of them known to Chamberlain and most of them friends of his. One of them was Harold Nicolson, a disaffected National Labour member, and on June 30, four days before Camrose's meeting with the P.M., he had noted in his diary: "The vital thing is to bring into the Cabinet people who are known abroad to be pledged to a policy of resistance and whose willingness to enter the Cabinet would show to the whole world that there can be no further Munichs." Briefing Camrose, the group had discussed "how far the Prime Minister would be opposed to bringing in Winston Churchill and Anthony Eden. . . . Camrose says that Winston is the vital figure. . . . The difficulty is that the Prime Minister himself, as well as Hoare and Simon, are terrified of Winston and will put up the strongest resistance. It would be much easier for them to accept Anthony, Amery or Duff Cooper." Camrose, however, was adamant. "You must have Winston," he said, and a majority of the group agreed.[140]

That was the centerpiece of the case he put to Chamberlain. According to Camrose's account, the prime minister replied that "while he appreciated Churchill's ability, his own experience in Cabinet work with him had not been such as to make him feel that his (Churchill's) inclusion in the Cabinet would make his own task any easier." Over the years, Chamberlain said, "he had had two discussions with him which had ended in rather violent disagreement." Anthony Eden's name had also been put forward, Camrose reminded the P.M. "Well, Winston was Public Enemy No 1 in Berlin, and Eden was the same in Italy. Their inclusion in the Cabinet might strike both ways." Chamberlain was cautious about Eden; his case was "not of the same consequence as that of Winston." Ministers, he conceded, made mistakes. "Simon's judgment, and Hoare's, might have been wrong at times, but Winston's was notorious." Camrose did not mention the notoriety of Hoare's deal with Laval, a far greater blunder than anything in Churchill's career.[141]

By the third week in July the Men of Munich thought "the Churchill flurry," as they called it, had ended. Halifax's chief aide wrote in his diary: "Pro-Churchill campaign dying down; no sign whatever of a move in No 10." Chamberlain wrote his sister: "As for the Churchill episode it has in Joe Kennedy's picturesque phrase 'Fallen out of bed.' . . . Even Camrose has now dropped it in the Telegraph." In another letter he wrote Ida that "the drive to put Winston in the government" had merely "enlivened" the week. "Anyway they have as usual over-played their hand," he said, and Hoare, echoing him in a letter to Lady Astor's son — she had startled

Parliament by coming out for Churchill — wrote that "I was convinced that the attempt would fail. Anything that Winston attempts is overdone, and in this case it was so overdone that it has stirred up a great reaction against him."[142]

Winston hadn't had a thing to do with it; despite pleas from his supporters, he had remained aloof. At one point he drafted a statement: "I have taken no part in the movement in favour of broadening His Majesty's Government, in which my name has been mentioned." On second thought he decided not to make it public. On April 24, before the press campaign to put him in the cabinet had picked up momentum, he had spoken to a large gathering of city workers in the East End: "Those who now come forward to join the Territorial Army are discharging the highest duty of citizenship." That was hardly incendiary, but once the press lords had tossed his hat in the ring he canceled all public addresses and spoke only in the House of Commons.[143]

Actually, he had no time to mount a major political campaign. He faced publishing deadlines, and the need to meet them was more urgent than ever. His income from newspaper syndication had dropped sharply, and the blow was not softened by the fact that Hitler was to blame. As the Axis empire grew — and the smaller states bordering the bloated Reich frantically followed pointed advice from the Wilhelmstrasse — editors dropped Winston's column. Since the fall of Albania, for example, the government in Athens had prohibited publication of any article criticizing fascism or Nazism — this despite Britain's guarantee of Greece's frontiers. In Rumania, Imre Revesz wrote him in May, twenty-two newspapers were "controlled directly by the Propaganda Ministry in Berlin." Poland was now Britain's ally, but Warsaw authorities had suppressed his piece on the Nazi threat to the Poles. Churchill sent an account of all this to Cadogan at the Foreign Office. He was not the only victim of Goebbels's strategy: articles by Duff Cooper, Attlee, Eden, and Henry Wickham Steed, Dawson's predecessor at *The Times*, had also been rejected. It was "a serious matter," Winston submitted to Cadogan. "A net is closing round our activities," he wrote to Revesz, "through fear of Germany." The literary agent, ever resourceful, opened negotiations with American networks for ten-minute Churchill broadcasts once or twice a month. Responding to this news, Winston wrote him on May 8, congratulating him for having "called in the New World to redress the balance of the Old." In little more than a year his use of that cluster of prepositional phrases, slightly altered, would arouse an embattled free world.[144]

As the dreary decade approached its close, Winston's main effort, the key to his financial survival, was directed toward completion of his *History of the English-speaking Peoples*, the linchpin of his agreement with Sir Henry Strakosch. The grand design was totally Churchillian: "I have all that in my head," he explained to one researcher. So was the prose; the entire text came from his muttering lips or, if he was revising galleys, from his fountain pen. He needed a supporting cast, of course, and he picked a first-rate troupe — Bill Deakin, Maurice Ashley, C. C. Wood, Ridley Pakenham-Walsh, John Wheldon, and three scholars who would one day become illustrious biographers of his most famous foes: Keith Feiling (Neville Chamberlain), Alan Bullock (Hitler), and G. M. Young (Stanley Baldwin, perhaps the most hostile official biography ever published). Eddie Marsh once more came aboard to read proofs and make general comments on syntax and grammar; Brigadier Sir James Edmonds, the official historian of the Great War, was recruited because his knowledge of the American Civil War was profound. Considering their skills and the immense amount of time each devoted to his assignments, they can scarcely be said to have been overpaid; the researchers received fifty pounds a month and Marsh twenty pounds per 100,000 wôrds — less than twenty-eight cents a page. But, of course, they weren't in it for the money. Other scholars would have done it for nothing.[145]

Winston's correspondence during these months reveals a quicksilver gift for bounding back and forth across nearly twenty centuries, from 55 B.C., when "the Proconsul of Gaul, Julius Caesar, turned his gaze upon Britain," to the Boer War, an adjournment chosen, perhaps, because it was then that the author himself appeared as a historical figure. Churchill opened with the broadest of themes:

> Our story centres in an island, not widely sundered from the Continent, and so tilted that its mountains lie all to the west and north, while south and east is a gently undulating landscape of wooded valleys, open downs, and slow rivers. It is very accessible to the invader, whether he comes in peace or war, as pirate or merchant, conqueror or missionary. Those who dwell there are not insensitive to any shift of power, any change of faith, or even fashion, on the mainland, but they give to every practice, every doctrine that comes to it from abroad, its own peculiar turn and imprint. . . .[146]

To an exceptional degree he enjoyed writing and was even invigorated by it. Few writers of depth are actually exhilarated by creativity; it drains them; at the end of a session most are exhausted. In many ways he was an exception. "Writing a long and substantial book," he said, "is like having a friend and companion at your side, to whom you can always turn for comfort and amusement, and whose society becomes more attractive as a new and widening field of interest is lighted in your mind." His letters seem to reflect the excitement of a writer rejoicing in the power of his inimitable style; to Clementine, skiing in Austria, he wrote: "The days pass quickly for I have so much to do."[147]

One senses his delight in his own virtuosity as, moving from informal to formal English, he shifts tone and syntax. Writing Clementine of his progress with the *History*, he tells her:

I have just finished writing about Joan of Arc. I think she is the winner in the whole of French history. The leading women in those days were more remarkable and forceful than the men.

Then, in his manuscript, we see the magic, his bold strokes, the might he could always invoke:

There now appeared on the ravaged scene an Angel of Deliverance, the noblest patriot of France, the most splendid of her heroes, the most beloved of her saints, the most inspiring of all her memories, the peasant Maid, the ever-shining, ever-glorious Joan of Arc.[148]

Eden wrote that he read Winston's accounts of the past "to forget the haunting apprehensions of our present days." His historical works appeared to offer Churchill the same asylum. "It has been a comfort to me in these anxious days," he wrote Mortimer Wheeler, keeper of the London Museum, "to put a thousand years between my thoughts and the twentieth century." On July 10, 1938, he had written Keith Feiling:

I have definitely plunged into the "English Speaking Peoples" and am now rollicking with the "Piltdown Man," Cassivalanus, Julius Caesar, the Scribe Gildas, the Venerable Bede and other hoary figures. How to make anything of this that is (a) readable, (b) original, (c) valuable and (d) true, is known only to the presiding genius of Britain who has not yet imparted his secrets to Yours most sincerely, Winston S. Churchill.[149]

And yet . . .

It was anything but a lark. Ten days later he wrote Eddie Marsh, "I am staggering along to the end of this job, and am glad to have found the strength to have accomplished it." Over half the present volume was in galleys, but ahead lay the insertion of special studies by Deakin and Bullock, checking facts, and soliciting comments from scholars who were expert in various areas. "I have had to work very hard," he wrote his publisher, "and many a night have sat up until two or three in the morning." In early 1939 he wrote Clemmie, "I have been leading a life of unbroken routine at Chartwell — and have now got into print no less than 220,000 words i.e. 63 days ahead of the vy hard task I prescribed of 1,000 a day from August 1. At this rate I shd cover the whole ground by May, wh wd leave 7 months for polishing. It is a formidable grind; but if accomplished will put things in a vy satisfactory basis."[150]

The strain was evident to those closest to him. Grace Hamblin recalls him as "a very hard taskmaster. He drove us." Kathleen Hill recollects that he "could be very ruthless." But he was exciting, too. Mrs. Hill was now living at Chartwell, and she remembers her first impressions of it: "I had never been in a house like that. It was alive, restless. When he went away it was still as a mouse. When he was there it was vibrating." In retrospect she sees him as "a disappointed man who was waiting for the call to serve his country."[151]

Pride and drive, that inner gyroscope which never failed, spurred him on. His remarkable output is even more extraordinary when seen in the context of the time. As events accelerated in central Europe he continued to be the best-informed private citizen in the country. Following his instructions, foreigners arriving in London would take the Oxted train from Victoria Station and detrain to find Winston himself there to greet them. Flattered, they would enter his car, sublimely unaware that they were putting their lives in the hands of the worst driver in the British Empire.

Vansittart, fuming under the meaningless title Chief Diplomatic Adviser to the Foreign Secretary, had become his silent partner. But Van remained on His Majesty's payroll; he had no establishment to support and could devote all his working hours to gathering and analyzing the European situation, which grew in complexity and frightfulness after the Anschluss, as Hitler led the Continent from crisis to crisis. Somehow Churchill kept all that in one part of his mind and his work in another. Only the first Queen Elizabeth could check his creative flow. In August 1939 he wrote to G. M. Young, the Oxford historian and Fellow of All Souls College. Young had agreed to vet parts of the work, and Winston now wondered "how you are getting along with the proofs I sent you." He himself, he added, had "completed the Commonwealth story (Lambeth and Monk), but have still not cleared away the Queen Elizabeth block. I am now working on the Chatham period, which is very inspiriting." He overcame the Queen's intimidation after the war, when his work was published. And that block stands alone. If in his long career he ever again struggled with anyone more complex, there is no record of it. And if he had, there would be.[152]

*   *   *

The Lambeth Articles of 1595 can scarcely be regarded as possessing great historical significance. There were nine articles, and they were meant to express Calvinist doctrine in such weighty matters as predestination and justification. Since they were never adopted by the church in any synod, they lacked ecclesiastical authority and are interesting to us only because they interested Churchill. Nor could George Monk, a Devonian soldier, be regarded a key figure in the vastness of history, though he was certainly more engaging. At the outbreak of the English Civil War he fought for the King; captured by Roundheads, he was imprisoned in the Tower for two years, emerged as an admirer of Cromwell, fought hard for him while intriguing for the reestablishment of the monarchy, and became a duke. During the plague of 1665 and the great fire a year later, he restored order in London; he wound up fighting the Dutch as a British admiral. In the long reach of history, he deserves a footnote at most; his prominence in Churchill's work is startling.

But history, like beauty, lies in the eye of the beholder. If it happened, and if the writer believes it to be consequential, in it goes. To the dismay of the dons advising him, Churchill overruled their recommendation that he cut the tale of King Alfred burning the housewife's cakes, on the ground that myths are as important as facts in the memory of a people. Actually, the weight of four thousand years was on his side. In ancient Greece and Rome historical accuracy was subordinate to style and dramatic tone. During the millennium which followed, theological historians — there were no others — sought evidence of divine motives, intervention, and design. This was the evocation of Saint Augustine's *City of God* and, in 1681 — a thousand years later — Jacques-Bénigne Bossuet's *Discours sur l'histoire universelle*. Interpreting human experience was considered the function of religion or philosophy — even of poetry or other imaginative works. Modern historiography, constructing a documented record of mankind's activities and then interpreting it, did not emerge until early in the nineteenth century. By 1900, however, it had emerged as a distinct discipline, the preserve of academicians who, jealous of their hard-won recognition, regarded interlopers like Churchill as trespassers.

Yet despite jeers that Churchill was shallow, volatile, the Barnum of politics, Sir Isaiah Berlin, singling out a 1928 condemnation of Winston's style, comments that "the stern critic and his audience were . . . mistaken. What he and they denounced as so much tinsel and hollow pasteboard was in reality solid; it was this author's natural means for the expression of his heroic, highly coloured, sometimes over-simple and even naive, but always genuine, vision of life." Both as a politician and as a historian he was an unrepentant romantic. He did indeed divide those of whom he wrote into white hats and black hats. But that is how he saw life, as a struggle between the forces of light and the powers of darkness. He never tried to hide it, or veil it, or hoodwink or mystify or dupe his audiences. It was an authentic view of life; there was and is no need to justify it.[153]

His grand vision, as the *History* testifies, was of an expanding British Empire governed by Great Britain and the United States, ruling in tandem. A. J. P. Taylor comments that while this theme "has a few merits . . . he never considered how far England and America had been associated, which was very little, and — particularly — how far they could be associated in the future." To Churchill, it is clear, the great thing, apart from the fact that the two countries shared the same language, was that they had fought side by side. Wars, to Winston, were of immense historic importance; like Carlyle and Nietzsche, he believed that armed conflict was a natural state of man. Although one may argue that events since 1945 have vindicated him, this viewpoint put him on a collision course with mainstream intellectuals of his time. His derogators declared that he was a boy who had never outgrown playing with toy soldiers. This denied him not only maturity but also the high seriousness to which he was entitled.[154]

Nevertheless, his zest for combat *was* excessive. In a revealing comment to Lord Moran he complained that 1830–1860, when England and the United States were at peace, were "thirty years when nothing happened." So marked was his lack of balance that in his second part, dealing with the era between 1485 and 1688, Shakespeare was not even mentioned in the index, and in the third the Industrial Revolution was disposed of in a single paragraph. His trivial dismissal of those who abhor war is jarring, as is his later remark, in the 1940s, to a British general: "Cheer up! We can't have a war every day." It was Crane Brinton, an American historian, who observed that the fourth part, covering the years between Waterloo and the end of the nineteenth century, gave "disproportionate attention" to the bloody struggle between America's North and South, while the development of the British Dominions received "comparative brevity."

In part this imbalance was a reflection of the tumultuous times in which he lived. Moreover, he was writing — particularly toward the end of the *History* — under tremendous pressure. And in fact it would not be published until after the coming war. But the wonder is not that his text was incomplete and flawed, but that he got most of the job done when he did. Part of the explanation was his skill in dictation; part was his memory, which one survivor of those days calls "Napoleonic"; part his prowess in commanding his team of researchers; and part his proficiency in gathering a chaos of material in his mind, mastering it, assembling it in an inner prism, and then refracting it in a terrific, blinding beam. Of course, he could have improved upon it had he had time, but with an eye on central Europe he did his best, and Churchill's best was very, very good. If his reach exceeded his grasp, it was because he was intent upon more than literary achievement in the first eight months of 1939. Had he not been the preeminent leader in the struggle against Hitler during this time, the results would doubtless have been very different.

Certainly his understanding of Britain's political history was remarkable. In the first week of January his mind had leaped nimbly back 216 years from Joan of Arc's execution to the Magna Carta (1215), then leapfrogged four centuries to the Petition of Right (1628) and the Habeas Corpus Act (1679). In sending Wheldon a check for £52.10 he asked him to read, "for a similar fee," chapters he had written spanning 1455 to the death of Henry VIII in 1547. Back at Chartwell on April 6, the eve of Mussolini's invasion of Albania, he wrote Wheldon: "I send you herewith Richard III, Henry VII, Edward VI, Mary and Elizabeth." All except Elizabeth were in a "very rudimentary form"; he would be "most grateful" for "any improvements and expansions you can make to them." The manuscript was moving swiftly between the 1400s and 1500s at a time when events in the 1930s begged for his attention, and it was a strain, even for him. On March 24, when Hitler wrenched Memel from Lithuania, he wrote Ashley: "It is very hard to transport oneself into the past when the future opens its jaws upon us."[155]

April had brought conscription, Roosevelt's appeal to Hitler and Mussolini, and the introduction of anti-Semitic laws, based on those of the Reich, in Hungary. Winston was asking Bullock for "two or three thousand words" of English social history which "I could then interweave . . . with the text as it stands"; he was also thanking G. M. Young "for your invaluable notes on the Stuart period," and sending him five thousand words on the opening of Charles II's reign, including an analysis of the Protestant status under the Clarendon Code.[156]

In May the Axis powers had signed the Pact of Steel, while the Japanese, threatening British communications between Hong Kong and Singapore, blockaded the British and French concession at Tientsin, and demanded British withdrawal of support for the Chinese. Winston sent Young revisions of his seventeenth-century chapters, including one on the Restoration (1660) but "omitting the Cromwell period which I am going to reconsider later." A week later he executed a mighty leap, in time and place: "I have the American Civil War on my hands now, which should take me about a fortnight." Actually four weeks passed before he reported again. It was June 11 — Britain and France were trying to form a "peace front" against Nazi aggression — before he sent Civil War galleys to Brigadier Edmonds, and even then he had only reached the Battle of

Chancellorsville (1863). He hoped, however, "to complete the tale to the death of Lincoln in 40,000 words." Simultaneously, he was revising the text on the 1400s, four centuries earlier. Even as he wrote about Gettysburg, he was dictating passages on the Norman Conquest of 1066. And four days later he was deep in chapters on the reigns of King John (1199–1216), Edward the Confessor (1042–1066), and Canute (1016–1035).[157]

By July the war fever had reached Washington, and Churchill's determination to stand by his Disraeli desk night after night approached the heroic. Roosevelt had asked Congress for a repeal of the arms embargo and revisions in the Neutrality Act; at the same time he announced that he would abrogate the U.S. 1911 trade treaty with Japan. Chamberlain maundered on, defending his foreign policy. The urge to shred it in a major speech was almost irresistible, but Churchill could do nothing for England if broke. Nevertheless, he attended all significant sessions of Parliament; his presence was felt in the service ministries, the Foreign Office, on the Continent, and even in Washington and Moscow.

His manuscript, however, had absolute priority, and he believed he was going to meet his deadline. On July 9 he wrote his publisher: "You will be glad to know that the 'Story of the English Speaking Peoples' is now practically complete. Four hundred and sixty thousand words are actually in print" — Churchill used galley proofs when a thriftier writer would use typists — "and more than half has gone a second revise. I hope, therefore, to let you have the work ready for publication in plenty of time before the end of the year." He thought the "American side has been very well treated, and the story of the American Civil War is a small book in itself." But he had far to go. The following day he was back in the 1300s with John Wycliffe and Richard II, then in the 1200s with Henry III and Edward I. A week later he decided to redraft forty-seven thousand words; then he sent Bullock his Henry III galleys, asking him to "kindly read it again for accuracy, challenging any points on which you do not agree." Style ("Will you think over some rules to be given to the printer about Capitals?") had to be settled with Eddie Marsh. It was mid-August before his treatment of the Victorian Age was complete, and at the end of the month he confronted Deakin with a major problem, the organization of the work. "What we want is a chronological account of the Seven Years War, featuring the rise of Chatham. This will include the 'Continental Struggle' and 'Frederick the Great.' . . . Will you let me have some books on the period covered by Chapter VII 'The Great Pitt'? While you are sending them to me, I am going on with 'Queen Elizabeth.' "[158]

It may be argued that if Churchill had not been a virtual prisoner in his Chartwell study during those critical months, England might have been better prepared in September, but he was still far from power, virtually impotent in the House of Commons. Only catastrophe could place England's fate in his hands. Yet because of the very men who had ignored or mocked him in the years since Hitler became Reich chancellor and führer, catastrophe was ineluctable. Some of the appeasers showed signs of uneasiness. Even *The Times,* while belittling public support for him, nevertheless commented on July 13: "Mr Churchill may well be needed in a Government again."

To Chamberlain this was heresy; his conviction that he would be vindicated was unshakable. Two days later, on July 15, he wrote his sister Ida: "If I refuse to take Winston into the Cabinet to please those who say it would frighten Hitler, it doesn't follow that the idea of frightening Hitler or rather of convincing him that it would not pay him to use force need be abandoned." On July 23 he again wrote her: "One thing is I think clear namely that Hitler has concluded that we mean business and that the time is not ripe for the major war. Therein he is fulfilling my expectations. Unlike some of my critics I go further and say the longer the war is put off the less likely it is to come at all as we go on perfecting our defences and building up the defences of our allies. That is what Winston and Co never seem to realise."[159]

They didn't realize it because it wasn't true. Churchill knew that Hitler's huge army and the Ruhr's smokestack barons were widening their lead over Britain and France. He wasn't speculating; he had the facts, and was sending them to the P.M. and the cabinet, hoping to rouse them before the blow fell. He was still recruiting new informants in Whitehall or the Wilhelmstrasse. A March 21 letter to Chamberlain urging a crash anti-aircraft program, for example, had been provoked by Major F. L. Fraser, who probably knew more about AA than anyone else in England. Fraser's reason for joining the net sheds light on why career officers volunteered to flout the Official Secrets Act. "In 1916 when you were commanding a battalion of the Royal Scots Fusiliers," he had written Winston on March 15, "I was GSO 3 of the 9th Division; in 1917, when I was wounded, you were kind enough to come & see me in hospital. . . . I am now Chief Intelligence Officer of the ARP [Air Raid Precautions] Dept and have been with the Dept since 1936. I should be most grateful if you could spare me a few minutes, as I should like to discuss certain matters with you." Chamberlain's chief accomplishments during the Great War had been serving as lord mayor of Birmingham and then as director-general of National Service. He had no concept of the bond between men who have worn the same uniform and survived heavy fighting together.[160]

In June the secretary for air, Kingsley Wood, offered Churchill a tour of airfields where radar was being installed. After inspecting the towers at Biggin Hill, Bawdsey, and Martlesham, Churchill wrote Wood that his trip had been "profoundly interesting, and also encouraging." He then anticipated Hermann Göring by over a year by noting: "These RDF stations require immediate protection." He had thought of "erecting dummy duplicates and triplicates of them at little expense" but "on reflection it seems to me that here is a case of using the smoke-cloud." He ended: "We are on the threshold of immense securities for our island. Unfortunately we want to go further than the threshold and time is short."[161]

The prime minister, too, was concerned about time, but he lacked Winston's sense of urgency. Chamberlain wrote his sister: "As always I want to gain time for I never accept the view that war is inevitable," and, in a letter to the Archbishop of Canterbury, he predicted that "some day the Czechs will see that what we did was to save them for a happier future." Sacrificing them, he believed, had "at last opened the way to that general appeasement which alone can save the world from chaos." Halifax, addressing the House of Lords in early June, declared that "the really dangerous element in the present situation . . . is that the German people as a whole should drift to the conclusion that Great Britain had abandoned all desire to reach an understanding with Germany and that any further attempt at such a thing must be written off."[162]

Winston wrote Halifax that he had been "a little disturbed" by his remarks, which suggested more appeasement. He called the foreign secretary's attention to the "very bad reports" of "bloody episodes," including "oppression and terrorism" in Bohemia, Moravia, and Slovakia. Because of these outrages, he continued, "I am sure you realise that to talk about . . . *lebensraum,* or any concession, while nine million Czechs are still in bondage, would cause great division among us." But defeatism seemed to lie over Whitehall like a dense pea-souper. In public appearances Joseph Kennedy, Hitler's best friend in the diplomatic community, was loudly cheered by Londoners. Churchill was confronted by the American ambassador's views at a dinner party given by Harold Nicolson and his wife, Vita Sackville-West. The American publicist Walter Lippmann, a fellow guest, recounted his afternoon with Kennedy, who had left the impression that he was pro-Nazi, anti-Semitic, and convinced that war was inevitable, and that Britain would be defeated. Nicolson noted: "Winston is stirred by this defeatism into a magnificent oration. He sits hunched there, waving his whisky-and-soda to mark his periods, stubbing his cigar with the other hand." According to his host's diary, Churchill said:

It may be true, it may well be true . . . that this country will at the outset of this coming and to my mind almost inevitable war be exposed to dire peril and fierce ordeals. It may be true that steel and fire will rain down upon us day and night scattering death and destruction far and wide. It may be true that our sea-communications will be imperilled and our food-supplies placed in jeopardy. Yet these trials and disasters, I ask you to believe me, Mr Lippmann, will but serve to steel the resolution of the British people and to enhance our will for victory. No, the Ambassador should not have spoken so, Mr Lippmann; he should not have said that dreadful word. Yet supposing — as I do not for one moment suppose — that Mr Kennedy were correct in his tragic utterance, then I for one would willingly lay down my life in combat, rather than, in fear of defeat, surrender to the menaces of these most sinister men. It will then be for you, for the Americans, to preserve and maintain the great heritage of the English-speaking peoples. It will be for you to think imperially, which means to think always of something higher and more vast than one's own national interests. Nor should I die happy in the great struggle which I see before me, were I not convinced that if we in this dear dear island succumb to the ferocity and might of our enemies, over there in your distant and immune continent the torch of liberty will burn untarnished and — I trust and hope — undismayed.[163]

But Churchill was always more than a rhetorician. Lippmann had been seated beside him at dinner, and the American's notes made later that night reveal Winston's grasp of global politics and his plan for victory:

Would cut losses in Far East; no dispersion of the fleet; settle with Japan after the war. Central Europe mobilized as a unit in 1914. Then Germany had ten divisions from Czechoslovakia; now they need six to hold it. Hungary, Jugoslavia, Rumania, dangerous and unreliable. Poland, a new force, and behind it the Russian pad. No use to say to Germany they are not being encircled. Better to overwhelm them with righteous indignation. Only argument that counts is force. No use shaping policy in accordance with Goebbels' propaganda. Take your own line and make them follow. In event of German mobilization, mobilize fleet; at first provocative action, cut German railway communication with Europe and defy them to do anything about it. . . .[164]

It is impossible to put a good face on war, but war, Churchill argued in the *News of the World* on June 18, did not mean annihilation. Even the "atrocity" of bombing civilians could be met by evacuations, RAF attacks on the bombers, antiaircraft — he couldn't mention radar, which was still highly secret — and shelters. Nevertheless, defeatism and the policy to which it gave voice — peace at any price — still flourished at the highest levels of English society. Hitler had betrayed Chamberlain in Prague and Chamberlain had struck back blindly, but appeasement remained his faith. He was also a loyal subject of the Crown, and this was one of those rare moments when a constitutional monarch could have influenced policy. Victoria had done so repeatedly, simply by speaking out forcefully. But this chance was missed. George VI, reticent, said little, and his sympathies lay with Chamberlain. The Queen Mother, in a letter to the King, had expressed the Royal Family's reaction to Munich: "I'm sure you feel as angry as I do at people croaking as they do at the P.M.'s action; for once I agree with Ly. Oxford who is said to have exclaimed as she left the House of Commons yesterday, 'He brought home Peace, why can't they be grateful?' "

Churchill yearned to finish his manuscript and do things which ought to be done and no one else was doing. He knew, from his informants in Whitehall, that the prime minister and his foreign secretary had been treating their French ally shabbily, dealing directly with Hitler and Mussolini without even informing the French. To be sure, those holding political power in Paris almost seemed to encourage this. At Munich, Daladier had played second fiddle to Chamberlain. The agreement had dismayed him but he failed to protest, despite the fact that he was among the more assertive premiers of the tottering Third Republic. But if war came again, poilus, not Tommies, would bear the heavier burden on the battlefield. Winston felt that it was time fences between the allied democracies were mended. Chamberlain and Halifax, however, still dreamed of a London-Berlin-Rome axis.

PART FIVE

SURGE

CHASING deadlines, Churchill was pushing himself and his secretaries ruthlessly, but when an important guest arrived he gave them, their silent typewriters, and himself a rest. As Chartwell moved through spring and high summer, it became the chief watering place for parliamentarians, flag officers, generals, air marshals, members of the established government, and even cabinet ministers haunted by nightmares of triumphant Nazis marching through the streets of London.

Among those who put their careers at risk to seek Winston's advice was a future chief of the Imperial General Staff, Tiny Ironside, now Sir Edmund Ironside, inspector-general of overseas forces. The general not only shared his host's concerns; they had been friends since the Boer War, and he regarded him with genuine affection. In his diary he wrote that the two of them "made a night of it"; after dining alone they "sat talking till 5 am this morning." The talk was of this and that. Churchill said he would have to "pull in my horns considerably" if he were returned to office, because he "would have to cease making money by writing." Ironside speculated that had last year brought war instead of Munich, his host would at the very least be first lord or war minister, and possibly P.M. But Winston had made friends in the cabinet, particularly "Belisha because . . . it was Belisha who got conscription through." They agreed that "Neville Chamberlain is not a war Prime Minister. He is a pacifist at heart. He has a firm belief that God has chosen him as an instrument to prevent this threatened war." In Winston's opinion, the general noted, it was "now too late for any appeasement. The deed was signed and Hitler is going to make war." Ironside concurred, and the prospect troubled him, for he knew that despite Hore-Belisha's efforts the General Staff had "no considered plans, no plans to deal with the war in general."[1]

Unlike the War Office, Churchill had plans. In a paper he had written on stratagems for the Royal Navy, he proposed, among other moves, that the Admiralty put "a Squadron of battleships into the Baltic. It would paralyse the Germans and immobilise many German divisions." The following day Ironside noted: "It ran through my head that here was a grand strategist imagining things, and the Navy itself making no plans whatever." When the present first sea lord had commanded the Mediterranean Fleet, Ironside had asked him for "any offensive plan for dealing with Italy." He had none then, and, the general added: "I am sure there is none now."[2]

Insofar as England's political leaders had plans, many surmised that Germany and Britain were virtually allied. One of them was Lord Kemsley, brother of Lord Camrose and a Fleet Street tycoon in his own right. Even as Winston and Ironside parted after a hearty breakfast, Kemsley was in Germany meeting a series of Nazi leaders, including Alfred Rosenberg, editor of the anti-Semitic Nazi *Völkischer Beobachter*, and Baron von Weizsäcker at the Foreign Ministry. Both asked about the strength of Chamberlain's critics in England, particularly Mr. Winston Churchill. On Thursday, July 27, when Hitler received Kemsley at Bayreuth, he, too, asked about Churchill "and his powers of expression." According to Kemsley's notes, he replied that in his opinion "far more notice was taken abroad of the Opposition than in England," and he reminded the Führer that "Mr. Churchill had been unfortunate in his campaigns on at least four occasions in the past, starting with the Abdication of King Edward VIII."[3]

This is shocking, and it served England ill, encouraging the Nazi conviction that England would not fight under any circumstances — that Churchill was an eccentric without a following, who spoke only for himself. A few months earlier that had been true. But as a publisher of newspapers Kemsley must have known how public opinion had changed since Prague, and how Churchill's stock had soared. It was now summertime 1939. By now Winston could have spoken anywhere in England, on any topic, for any fee. Ironside wrote in his diary on July 27: "I keep thinking of Winston Churchill down at Westerham, full of patriotism and ideas for saving the Empire. A man who knows that you must act to win. You cannot remain supine and allow yourself to be hit indefinitely. Winston must be chafing at the inaction. I keep thinking of him walking up and down the room."[4]

※   ※

One of the more insidious consequences of Munich was a sharp erosion in Britain's credibility, a suspicion on the Continent that His Majesty's Government would respond to future Nazi demands by diplomatic talks leading to capitulation. Churchill warned the House that "the slightest sign of weakness will only aggravate the dangers which concern not only us, but the whole world." He begged the prime minister: "Do not yield another yard."[5]

Britain's guarantee to the Poles was, he felt, one promissory note which was certain to be called. "The glare of Nazi Germany," he predicted in the *Daily Telegraph*, would soon "be turned on Poland." His great worry was that Chamberlain would refuse to redeem his pledge. The prime minister's betrayal of the Czechs had established a pattern. The first transgression is always the most difficult; the second is relatively easy. If forced to choose between breaking his word and breaking the peace, the P.M., Winston suspected, would not hesitate to scuttle his vow to rescue Poland, and that, Churchill believed, would lead to an irrevocable disaster. Britain's honor would be forfeit. Hitler's mastery of the Continent would be absolute. Freedom would vanish from Europe.[6]

But what if the P.M. acted out of character? Suppose he kept his word, and took Britain and France into war? He could do it; the French had permitted the initiative to pass to London and were a silent, acquiescent partner. Then diplomatic problems would be replaced by strategic questions. At Chartwell, Churchill studied his map and recalled the lessons inherent in *The World Crisis*. During the first three years of trench warfare, the Allied armies had kept the enemy at bay only because the czar's huge forces had tied a million Germans down on the eastern front. After the Bolsheviks had overthrown the Romanov regime in 1917 and signed a draconian peace with the kaiser's generals, the million Germans on the eastern front, no longer needed there, were rushed to the west for a knockout blow. In 1918 they had nearly achieved total victory. Only the last-minute arrival of a huge American army had rescued the weary Allies from defeat.

Now the Americans were committed — legally, by an act of Congress — to a policy of neutrality. Churchill doubted that Poland could hold the Wehrmacht at bay. It would be 1918 all over again, except that the Western democracies would lack not only the Yanks but also the Italians. This time the Germans looked like winners, and the future would be an unsurpassed horror for any people who lost a war to Adolf Hitler.

The destruction of Czechoslovakia and the subsequent demoralization among her neighbors to the south had left Britain and France without any strong ally in the east. Poland by herself was inadequate. What the democracies needed, Churchill concluded, was an eastern European ally more powerful than Poland — a nation strong enough to hold the Wehrmacht at bay, forcing the Führer to fight a two-front war. They couldn't choose; only one great power lay east of the Reich. He would have preferred almost any other country, but the long years of appeasement, pacifism, defeatism, and threadbare military budgets had reduced the democracies to the role of beggars, or at any rate petitioners. Moscow, however, had every reason to be responsive to Western overtures. The Soviet Union lay directly in Hitler's path of conquest. He meant to crush her; *Mein Kampf* testified to his intent, reaffirmed in a hundred Führer speeches since.

To Winston the solution to the Anglo-French dilemma was obvious: détente with Russia should become Whitehall's primary goal. Yet he knew that the chances of persuading the men ruling Britain to embrace Bolsheviks were exceedingly small. Therefore, when Labour adopted a policy of recriminations, reciting all the ways in which Baldwin and Chamberlain had played into Hitler's hands, he aligned himself with the government. Opening a major address on Monday, April 3, he described the Polish guarantee as "splendid," declaring his "full support" for the prime minister's policies. Chamberlain eyed him warily. Such ringing Churchillian affirmations were often followed, not by sly attacks — his rhetoric was nothing if not straightforward — but by the introduction of a new proposal which the P.M. liked even less. Actually, Winston began by reintroducing an old proposal of his own; he quoted a passage he had delivered in this chamber a year earlier: "If a number of States were assembled around Great Britain and France in a solemn treaty for mutual defence against aggression; if they had their forces marshalled in what you may call a Grand Alliance; if they had their staff arrangements concerted . . . then I say that you might even now arrest this coming war."[7]

Since then "the situation has deteriorated." And one of Hitler's excuses for the enslavement of millions had been his paranoid claim that Germany's enemies were trying to "encircle" her. In fact, Churchill said, he and his supporters had been urging "the encirclement of an aggressor." Collective security reassured nations which felt threatened, and all were entitled to it, including the Third Reich: "If Herr Hitler feels that he will be overrun by Russia, that he will be fallen upon by Poland, that he will be attacked by Belgium, Holland, or Switzerland, he has only to declare his anxiety open to the world in order to receive the most solemn international guarantees. We seek no security for ourselves that we do not desire Germany to enjoy as well." But providing that security for all countries deserved absolute priority, he said; halfway measures were more dangerous than none: "To stop here with a guarantee to Poland would be to halt in no-man's-land under fire of both trench lines and without the shelter of either. . . . We must go forward now until a conclusion is reached. Having begun to create a Grand Alliance against aggression, we cannot afford to fail." Nor, he warned the House, could they exclude unsavory regimes, provided those who ruled them sought peace.

As the P.M. had feared, Winston was proposing a fresh policy, a British tie with the one great power Chamberlain detested. Churchill's loathing of bolshevism was more famous, and had certainly been more memorably expressed; he had described Lenin as a "plague bacillus"; he had denounced "the Bolshevik cancer eating into the flesh of the wretched being" and had reviled "the bestial appetites and passions" of Communist Russia, a "tyranny of the vilest kind," where "thousands of people have been executed or murdered in cold blood." But he had also declared that when the safety of Britain and her empire stood at risk, his conscience became "a good girl"; and it happened now. He wanted the five million men of the Red Army marching against the Wehrmacht, and he told the House of Commons why.[8]

"Russia," he said, "is a ponderous counterpoise in the scale of world peace. We cannot measure the weight of support which may be forthcoming from Soviet Russia." Labour had proposed that "the attitude of His Majesty's Government towards Russia" be summed up in the phrase "The maximum cooperation possible." Winston thought this "a very accurate and convenient phrase." But, he added, "to find any guidance as to where we stay with Russia, one must ask what is the interest of the Russian people." He asked: "Why should we expect Soviet Russia to be willing to work with us? Certainly we have no special claims upon her good will, nor she upon ours." The answer, he said, was that "Soviet Russia is profoundly affected by German Nazi ambitions." He reeled off Nazi objectives which menaced the U.S.S.R.: the Danube Valley, the Black Sea (a "conquest of the Ukraine by Nazi Germany, upon which such covetous eyes have been avowedly set, would be a direct assault upon the life of the Russian Soviet State"), and targets in the Far East. Thus, "No one can say that there is not a solid identity of interest between the Western democracies and Soviet Russia, and we must do nothing to obstruct the natural play of that identity of interest. . . . The worst folly, which no one supposes we should commit, would be to chill and drive away any natural cooperation which Soviet Russia in her own deep interests feels it necessary to afford." The wisest course was to forget the Bolshevik past and forge Britain, France, and Russia in a "Triple Alliance."[9]

The Men of Munich thought the folly was Churchill's. The prime minister, gazing into his foggy crystal ball, appraised potential Soviet military contributions in a war against Germany and wrote, in a private letter on March 26: "I have no belief whatever in her [Russia's] ability to maintain an effective offensive, even if she wanted to." And even if she wanted to and could, he wasn't sure he would welcome her help. In his mind Bolsheviks, not Nazis, were still the greater threat to Western civilization.

Here Chamberlain represented the opinion of Britain's ruling classes. As Winston later observed in the House, during his April 3 speech he "heard a sort of commotion behind me. I heard the Noble Lady the Member for the Sutton Division of Plymouth (Viscountess Astor) express her dislike of any contact with Bolshevik Russia." He asked pointedly: "Where was this dislike when she paid a visit to Soviet Russia with Mr Bernard Shaw?" Lady Astor interrupted: "I have had the great advantage of going to Russia and seeing it; you have only had the advantage of hearing about it from the outside." The point, Winston replied, was that "the time when she went to Russia and gave all her applause and credit to Russia was the time when the influence was deeply detrimental to the interests of this country."[10]

The need for a bond with the U.S.S.R. was "very serious," he said, "and I hope I shall be able to put it without any offense." Nevertheless, it *was* offensive; the thought of shaking hands with what he himself had once called the "bloody paws" of the czar's murderers shocked all the Conservatives from front bench to backbenchers. But he wasn't speaking to them now, or to Nancy Astor; or even, at that evening session, to the House of Commons. His audience was in the Kremlin. Ivan Maisky was in the gallery, and his presence cannot have been coincidental. It was customary, when foreign powers were being discussed, for His Majesty's Government to suggest that their envoys attend Parliament. For a private member to extend such an invitation was highly irregular, but that is the only way the Russian ambassador could have got one that Monday; he and Halifax were on the worst of terms. After Munich, the foreign secretary wrote, Maisky's "attitude seemed to me . . . one of some suspicion." The ambassador, for his part, had come to regard the appeasers as Hitler's "accomplices."[11]

In this he reflected the views of his superior in Moscow, Maksim Litvinov, the Soviet commissar for foreign affairs. Litvinov and Churchill had been thinking along the same lines, and on March 18, three days after the destruction of Czechoslovakia, the commissar had made his first diplomatic move toward rapprochement, proposing an immediate conference in Bucharest of six powers — Russia, Rumania, Poland, Britain, France, and Turkey — to form a "peace front" against the expanding Reich. In the Quai d'Orsay files there is no record of any response from Bonnet, and the Soviet overture is not even mentioned in his capacious (and self-serving) memoirs. Halifax and Chamberlain read the Litvinov initiative, but the prime minister dismissed the plan as "premature" and the Foreign Office told the Russians that it was "not acceptable." On March 19 Maisky called at the FO to ask why. Halifax told him that he was short-handed; no minister of the Crown could be spared for the Bucharest meeting. Even though Litvinov had issued a public statement explaining that no Soviet guarantees of Poland and Rumania would be forthcoming unless their

Churchill votes in the General Election, November 14, 1935. The Baldwin victory keeps him in political exile.

King George V dies on January 20, 1936. His son succeeds him as King Edward VIII.

The new king stands somberly at the Cenotaph, November 11, 1936.

Edward VIII insists upon marrying an American woman with a tarnished past. Churchill, in a highly unpopular stand, supports him. Lord Beaverbrook's *Daily Express* tells the tale.

DAILY EXPRESS DECEMBER 12, 1936   TELEPHONE—CENTRAL 8000—PRIVATE EXCHANGE

LAST GUEST OF KING EDWARD AT THE FORT

Mrs. SIMPSON OVERWHELMED AS SHE HEARS EX-KING TELL OF HIS LOVE

Daily Express Staff Reporter
CANNES, Friday Night.

MRS. SIMPSON was quite overcome when she heard "Prince Edward's" broadcast.

The text was a surprise to her. The little group in the villa Lou Viei, Cannes, where Mrs. Simpson is staying, gathered round the radio after dinner.

At first reception was poor, but as the time approached for the broadcast reproduction was perfect.

Historic Toast

The toast of "His Sovereign Lord King George the Sixth" was first given in London last night at the dinner of the Dorchester Hotel of the Anglo-Baltic Society. "In all history no man has ever given up the pain of a quarter of the world for the gain of a woman," said Sir A. C. Bossom, M.P.

When the voice came through Mrs. Simpson, sitting received to the act, was gradually overwhelmed.

She went straight to her room afterwards. Could say nothing to any one, and went to bed. The afternoon a large bouquet of red roses and mimosa was delivered to Mrs. Simpson.

There was no word with the flowers, which would seem to indi-

MR. WINSTON CHURCHILL LUNCHED WITH KING EDWARD AT FORT BELVEDERE YESTERDAY; DROVE BACK TO LONDON WITH MR. WALTER MONCKTON, K.C., ATTORNEY-GENERAL TO THE DUCHY OF CORNWALL.

Hermann Göring *(right)* **with one of his warmest admirers, Sir Nevile Henderson, His Majesty's ambassador to Nazi Germany.**

As Hitler overruns the Rhineland, Sir John Simon, Anthony
Eden, and Sir Robert Vansittart follow the coffin of Leopold von
Hösch, the German ambassador to Britain.

Discussing Hitler's Austrian Anschluss, Churchill and Foreign Secretary Lord Halifax walk from the Foreign Office to Parliament, March 29, 1938.

Alfred Duff Cooper, First Lord of the Admiralty, resigns from Chamberlain's cabinet in disgust over Munich.

At the peak of the Munich crisis, September 1938, Winston Churchill gloomily leaves No. 10 Downing Street after conferring with Prime Minister Neville Chamberlain.

At Chartwell in early 1939 Winston nails tiles to the roof of Orchard Cottage, which he designed and largely built as a retirement home for Clementine and him.

Clementine in 1939 with one of Chartwell's two fox cubs, Charles-James and Victoria. With war imminent, both cubs were turned loose in the wild.

**As Honorary RAF Commodore, Winston flies as copilot at
Kenley, April 16, 1939.**

Why Not Mr. Churchill?

In an article in this page on Thursday last, Percy Cater, "Daily Mail" Parliamentary Correspondent, asked the question, "Why Not Mr. Baldwin?" and contended that he was the best leader of the country at the present time.

To-day F. G. Prince-White, "Daily Mail" Special Correspondent, retorts with "Why Not Mr. Churchill?"

★

IT has been said of William Pitt that he became Prime Minister at the moment when his leadership was a *tactical* necessity.

Great tasks awaited the hands of Chatham's brilliant son; there were vast responsibilities to be borne. England was soon to be shaken by the convulsions of a politically epileptic Europe. The timber for the tumbrils of the French Revolution was sea-

By
F. G.
PRINCE-WHITE

soned; in Paris the Little Corsican was finishing his military studies, oblivious yet of his dazzling destiny.

At such a time no ordinary voice could speak the country's will — nor could a weakling's hand steady the State in the fast oncoming day of upheaval among the neighbour nations.

have been errors inseparable from the exercise of great gifts. And even Mr. Churchill's bitterest opponents cannot but own that he is uncommonly gifted.

To younger students of politics it is a most puzzling mystery that Mr. Churchill was not Prime Minister long ago. They look at his record and discover that he has occupied almost every other Government position.

In 1906, when he was only 32, he was given the post of Under-Secretary of State for the Colonies. Two years later he was President of the Board of Trade, and two years after that found him Home Secretary. From 1911 until 1915 he was First Lord of the Admiralty, from which office he passed to that of Chancellor of the Duchy of Lancaster.

In 1917 he followed Mr. Lloyd George in that supremely important Department, the Ministry of Munitions. Next he figured on the Governmental stage as Secretary for War and for Air, and after that as Secretary of State for the Colonies

For five years—from 1924 to 1929—he was Chancellor of the Exchequer.

Here is no mediocre experience, but such as might well stand a Prime Minister in good stead.

Brilliant Oratory

IT has been Mr. Churchill's incomparable eloquence in the House of Commons that has crystallised most perfectly the nation's inmost thoughts and feelings in this prolonged season of international fear and distrust.

One could have believed, listening the other day to the climax of his speech on the Budget, that his voice belonged to one of the great masters of oratory and statecraft whose statues now stand silently amid Westminster Abbey's shadows :

" *Either there will be a melting of hearts and a joining of hands between great nations, and they will set out on realising the glorious era of prosperity and freedom now within the grasp of millions of toiling people, or there will be an explosion and catastrophe the course of which no imagination can measure,*

Demands that Churchill be brought into the government had been swelling for three years. The *Daily Mail* ran this article on May 11, 1936, in reaction to Hitler's seizure of the Rhineland.

"BRING HIM BACK — IT'S YOUR LAST CHANCE"

By the spring of 1939, the dictators were overrunning Europe; Memel, Albania, and what was left of independent Czechoslovakia fell to Hitler and Mussolini. Now most of Fleet Street sounded the alarm.

Churchill appeals for Territorial Army recruits at the Mansion House, April 24, 1939.

The press heightens its demands; this cartoon appeared in the
***Daily Express* on July 6, 1939.**

Six days later
this cartoon
appeared in
Punch.

In the turmoil of the 1930s Churchill often found sanctuary in painting.

On July 24, 1939, a huge sign, paid for by an anonymous backer of Churchill, appears on the Strand.

War is imminent in late August 1939, as Churchill and Anthony Eden walk down Whitehall to the House of Commons. Both are still treated as lepers by Chamberlain.

On September 1, 1939, the Germans invade Poland, and that same day Chamberlain appoints Churchill First Lord of the Admiralty. On September 3 Britain declares war on Germany. This photograph was taken on September 4, Churchill's first full day at the Admiralty.

In the first month of the war Randolph, serving in his father's old regiment, the 4th Hussars, marries Pamela, the daughter of Lord and Lady Digby.

"All the News That's Fit to Print."

The New York Times.

LATE CITY EDITION

VOL. LXXXIX...No. 30,058.   NEW YORK, SATURDAY, MAY 11, 1940.   PPP   THREE CENTS

DUTCH AND BELGIANS RESIST NAZI DRIVE; ALLIED FORCES MARCH IN TO DO BATTLE; CHAMBERLAIN RESIGNS, CHURCHILL PREMIER

COALITION ASSURED

Labor Decides to Allow Leaders to Join New National Cabinet

OLD MINISTERS STAY

Churchill Asks Them to Remain Until They Can Be Replaced

The International Situation

The War in the Low Countries

AID IS SENT AT ONCE

French Enter Belgium— Britons Cross Sea to Netherlands

CONTACT SOON MADE

Allies Help Low Countries Meet First Thrust of 29 German Divisions

THE FIRES OF WAR LEAP ACROSS THE LOW COUNTRIES

HOLLANDERS FIRM

Report 100 Nazi Planes Shot Down as Troops Strike at Invaders

BOMBERS RANGE LAND

Air Attacks Continuous —Parachutists Land at Strategic Spots

BELGIUM REPORTS NAZIS ARE HALTED

Leopold Is at Front as Active Commander—41 Killed, 82 Wounded in Brussels Raid

Bulletins on European Conflict

New York Times, May 11, 1940.

As France collapses and all seems lost, Winston Spencer
Churchill becomes Prime Minister of Great Britain.

governments asked for them — they didn't ask; they were terrified by the prospect of Nazi reprisals — Chamberlain told the House of Commons on March 23 that His Majesty's Government took a dim view of establishing "opposing blocs" in Europe, the very argument Beck would use in refusing to guarantee Rumania. After a frustrating session with Halifax, Maisky told Boothby that this rebuff to the Russian proposal had dealt "another smashing blow to the policy of collective security."[12]

Churchill's relationship with the Soviet envoy was very different. They had been meeting regularly for seven years to discuss diplomatic moves which could contain or discourage Nazi aggression. After Churchill concluded his speech suggesting British overtures to Moscow, the House broke up, and Maisky came down to the smoking room to talk to Churchill and other MPs he knew. According to Nicolson's diary: "The House rises at 10.50 pm and I am seized upon by Winston and taken down to the lower smoking room with Maisky and Lloyd George. Winston adopts the direct method of attack [upon Maisky]. 'Now look here, Mr Ambassador, if we are to make a success of this new policy, we require the help of Russia.' " He said: "Now I don't care for your system and I never have, but the Poles and the Rumanians like it even less. Although they might be prepared at a pinch to let you in, they would certainly want some assurances that you would eventually get out. Can you give us such assurances?" Although the question was highly pertinent, it was not one an envoy could answer, and they were interrupted anyway. Nicolson noted: "Lloyd George, I fear, is not really in favour of the new policy and he draws Maisky on. . . . Winston rather objects to this and attacks Lloyd George. 'You must not do this sort of thing, my dear. You are putting spokes in the wheel of history.' "[13]

This does not ring true. It seems inconceivable that Churchill had not consulted Maisky, with whom he was on such close terms, before his speech. As early as February 9 Maisky had been entertaining writers and independent MPs, encouraging the belief that Britain and Russia should put aside ideological differences and face the common enemy together. Boothby, J. B. Priestly, and Nicolson had attended such a luncheon at the Soviet embassy, and Nicolson noted that evening: "Maisky says that Russia was obviously much wounded by Munich and that we can expect no advance from her side. But (and here he became serious) if *we* made approaches, we should not find Russia as aloof or offended as we might have supposed. Bob Boothby and I have an eye-meet like a tennis-ball across a net."[14]

After Prague the Russians had, in fact, made a major advance, the six-power proposal at Bucharest. Then, and throughout the spring and summer of 1939, Churchill's son was seeing a great deal of the Soviet ambassador — Chamberlain wrote his sister of "a regular conspiracy in which Mr Maisky has been involved as he keeps in very close touch with Randolph" — and it is reasonable to assume that when Winston rose on the evening of April 3 he had Russian assurances that his seed would not fall on barren ground. No doubt prodding from Maisky contributed to his proposal, though he alone would have been inadequate. Churchill would have sought, or been offered, encouragement from a Soviet leader of higher rank.[15]

Almost certainly it came to him from Litvinov. The Soviet Union's commissar for foreign affairs held a curious position in Kremlin intrigues. He had become a revolutionary in 1898, was arrested and imprisoned in 1901, but escaped to England and became a Bolshevik in 1903. As a party member he was actually senior to Stalin. But he had never been admitted to the Kremlin hierarchy. He was a Jew, he had been abroad during the 1905 uprising, his wife was British, and during the great revolt in 1917 he had been in London — as Lenin's representative, to be sure, but Communists with an eye on the future made sure they were seen on the barricades. Nevertheless, Litvinov had been foreign commissar since 1930. Stalin trusted him, and was persuaded by Litvinov's argument that the Soviet Union would be wiser to pursue closer ties with England and France than to seek Hitler's good graces. Hitler, Litvinov said, had none. Thus, in Harold Macmillan's words, it became Russian policy "to seek security through the League and by alliances with the western democracies."[16]

The Soviets' chief obstacle continued to be what Thomas Jones called Chamberlain's "Russian complex." Late in November 1938 Bernard Shaw had given a lunch at his flat for Maisky and Jones, and in his diary Jones set down Maisky's summary of the blows Litvinov — and his policy — had suffered during the year. Immediately after the Anschluss, he said, Litvinov had approached Paris, proposing a joint declaration, vowing to fight for Czechoslovakian independence. In the Quai d'Orsay his demarche had been ignored. The foreign commissar had tried again on September 2. Bonnet suppressed his note, whereupon Maisky went to Whitehall. There, too, he was disappointed. "Beyond expressing an interest in the views of Russia," Jones wrote, "Halifax made no sign." The Soviets' exclusion from the Munich Conference had meant an immense loss of prestige for Litvinov and Maisky in the Kremlin; the Anglo-French rejection of Litvinov's proposal for a six-power conference was a further blow. Nevertheless, Stalin permitted him to prepare another tremendous move in 1939, which was in its final stages when Churchill on April 3, knowingly or unknowingly, fired the first gun in Parliament.[17]

Ten days later, on Thursday, April 13, in the debate following the invasion of Albania, Winston fired a second gun, warning Parliament that the peril is "now very near. A great part of Europe is to a very large extent mobilised. Millions of men are being prepared for war. Everywhere the frontier defences are manned. Everywhere it is felt that some new stroke is impending." Should war come, he asked, "can there be any doubt that we shall be involved?" Three months earlier, Britain, free of commitments, could stand aloof, but now His Majesty's Government had provided guarantees "in every direction, rightly in my opinion, having regard to all that has happened." Before Munich, when prospects were brighter, Britain had backed away from the growing tension on the Continent. "Surely then," he said, "when we aspire to lead all Europe back from the verge of the abyss onto the uplands of law and peace, we must ourselves set the highest example." But if they were to "rescue our people and the people of many lands from the dark, bitter waters which are rising fast on every side," they must seize every opportunity, or create opportunities where none existed.

Turning again to the need for an approach to the Soviets, he said:

The other day I tried to show the House the great interest that Russia has against further Eastward expansion of the Nazi power. It is upon that deep, natural, legitimate interest that we must rely, and I am sure we shall hear from the Government that the steps they are taking are those which will enable us to receive the fullest possible cooperation from Russia, and that no prejudices on the part of England or France will be allowed to interfere with the closest cooperation between the two countries, thus securing our harassed and anxious combinations the unmeasured, if somewhat uncertain, but certainly enormous counterpoise of the Russian power."[18]

Two days later he got action — of sorts. England and France could not reject Russia's Bucharest proposal outright; it would have been bad manners, bad diplomacy, and bad politics — the British people were beginning to anticipate the time when they would need every friend they could get. On April 15, therefore, the Soviets received formal proposals from Whitehall and the Quai. They found them disappointing. The British merely asked Russia to follow their example and affirm the independence of Poland and Rumania. The French had wanted more. They had proposed that Britain, France, and the Soviet Union come to one another's aid should Germany make war on any one of them, but Chamberlain and Halifax weren't prepared to go that far.[19]

Litvinov wanted them to go much further. The following Monday he rocked the chancelleries of Europe by handing Sir William Seeds, the British ambassador in Moscow, a formal proposal which, if it succeeded, would assure that any Wehrmacht offensive in the east would be met not only by Poland but also by the much larger resources of the Soviet Union, including the Red Army. What Stalin's foreign commissar had submitted was, in fact, nothing less than a blueprint for a triple alliance — a re-creation of the entente which had declared war on the kaiser's Second Reich in 1914 and which would have defeated Germany and Austria, without American help, had the Bolshevik revolution not shattered it three years later.

In Litvinov's draft agreement, England, France, and Russia would not only provide mutual assistance if attacked by Hitler; the treaty would be backed by a specific commitment defining the strength and objectives of their armies, navies, and air forces. This alliance, which Poland could join if she chose, would bind the signatories to "render mutually all manner of assistance, including that of a military nature, in case of aggression in Europe" against any member of the alliance or against "Eastern European States situated between the Baltic and Black Seas and bordering on the U.S.S.R." Further, the signing parties would neither negotiate nor make peace "with aggressors separately from one another and without common consent of the three Powers."[20]

The encirclement of Germany, a myth spun by the Führer at Nuremberg rallies, would be real, and it would be awesome. Any Wehrmacht thrust, anywhere, would trigger retaliation from every country on the Reich's borders except Switzerland and Italy, whose legions, after their performances in Ethiopia and Albania, counted for very little. Swift action was essential, however; with Germany on a war footing Hitler could strike while the alliance was being negotiated. Moreover, Litvinov was aware that Stalin would be highly suspicious of Allied delay. Therefore the commissar stipulated that military conversations between the three powers begin immediately. It was his last bid for a united anti-Nazi front with the West. He was staking his career on it. And he believed it would work.[21]

In London the critics of the Chamberlain government agreed. Macmillan recalled: "This was Litvinov's last chance. It was also ours." Later Churchill summed up the situation: "If . . . Mr. Chamberlain on receipt of the Russian offer had replied: 'Yes. Let us three band together and break Hitler's neck,' or words to that effect, Parliament would have approved, Stalin would have understood, and history might have taken a different course. At least it could not have taken a worse." Robert Coulondre, formerly France's ambassador in Moscow and now her envoy in Berlin, thought Litvinov's offer was almost too good to be true. He cabled Paris, urging instant acceptance.[22]

His advice was rejected. As Thomas Jones wrote, in both Paris and London the Men of Munich were "much more optimistic than I am about the behavior of the dictators" — Hitler and Mussolini — and far more wary of the despot in the Kremlin. Jean Montigny, a Radical-Socialist, had warned the Chamber of Deputies on "the error and the illusion of any foreign policy based even partly on confidence in the power of the Russian army outside its frontiers and on the loyalty of the Soviet government." Many deputies were concerned about Poland's willingness to accept Soviet aid; as Poland's ally, France had to deal with it. Nevertheless, on April 22 the French cabinet, albeit without enthusiasm, agreed to Litvinov's proposal as a basis of negotiation, and so informed the British. The Quai declared, Whitehall delayed.[23]

On April 19 the cabinet's Foreign Policy Committee considered the Litvinov initiative. The Foreign Office was startled by its airtight language; by contrast — and by design — Britain's Polish guarantee was a sieve of loopholes. Litvinov took Horace Wilson's breath away; what if a copy of this document fell into the Führer's hands? Suppose he blamed England for it? The consequences didn't bear thinking about, and so, instead of thinking about them, Cadogan, in the absence of Halifax, described the Russian plan as "extremely inconvenient," suggested that Soviet military strength was trivial, and declared that "from the practical point of view there is every argument against accepting the Russian proposal." As a civil servant, however, the under secretary had to recognize that England had more than one party. Politically, the issue could become a quagmire. Thus, "there is great difficulty in rejecting the Soviet offer. . . . The left in this country may be counted on" to exploit a refusal. There was also a "very remote" possibility that the Russians might join hands with the Germans. Nevertheless, Cadogan ended, "on balance" Litvinov's offer should be turned down on the ground that it might "alienate our friends and reinforce the propaganda of our enemies without bringing in exchange any real material contribution to the strength of our Front." One wonders who, in Cadogan's opinion, England's "friends" and "enemies" were.[24]

The situation, as one cabinet member pointed out, was "very awkward." The French cabinet, however reluctantly, had voted to accept the plan. Churchill, Lloyd George, Eden, Duff Cooper, Labour, and the Liberals would raise Cain if His Majesty's Government rejected it. The Poles and the Rumanians, *per contra*, would be up in arms if Litvinov's offer were accepted. Finally — and this was decisive — Chamberlain, Halifax, Wilson, Cadogan, Inskip, and Simon were revolted by the prospect of an alliance with Bolsheviks. The Russians, as Thomas Jones wrote in his diary, "made our flesh creep." Looking for a way out, the

P.M. solicited the views of the Chiefs of Staff and seized upon one point in their report. The military support the U.S.S.R. could provide to Poland or Rumania, they wrote, "is not so great as might be supposed generally."[25]

Chamberlain ignored what followed, which was the chiefs' conclusion that "Russian cooperation would be invaluable in that Germany would be unable to draw upon Russia's immense reserves of food and raw materials and should succumb more quickly to our economic stranglehold." He also suppressed the chiefs' supplementary appraisal, which concluded:

A full-blown guarantee of mutual assistance between Great Britain and France and the Soviet Union offers certain advantages. It would present a solid front of formidable proportions against aggression. . . . If we fail to achieve any agreement with the Soviet, it might be regarded as a diplomatic defeat which would have serious military repercussion, in that it would have the immediate effect of encouraging Germany to further acts of aggression and of ultimately throwing the U.S.S.R. into her arms. . . . Furthermore, if Russia remained neutral, it would leave her in a dominating position at the end of hostilities.[26]

According to Cadogan, this passage "annoyed" Chamberlain. Privately he threatened to "resign rather than sign an alliance with the Soviet." Admiral of the Fleet Lord Chatfield, whose commitment to defend Britain eclipsed his hostility to bolshevism, pointed out that the chiefs were "very anxious that Russia should not under any circumstances become allied with Germany. Such an eventuality would create a most dangerous situation for us." In the Foreign Office this minute was the source of great amusement. The admiral was informed that Communists and Nazis were as unlikely a combination as oil and water. If he would look after the Royal Navy, he was politely told, Whitehall would tend to foreign affairs.[27]

After a fortnight of silence from London, Stalin, not a man of great patience, lost the little he had. On the back page of *Pravda*'s May 3 issue a small item appeared in the "News in Brief" column: "M. Litvinov has been released from the Office of Foreign Commissar at his own request."

The significance of Litvinov's dismissal passed almost unnoticed in the Western democracies. Because of an intelligence failure in MI6 and the Deuxième Bureau, Allied governments did not know, as Churchill later wrote, that Vyacheslav Molotov, Litvinov's successor, "had always been favourable to an arrangement with Hitler," that he had been "convinced by Munich and much else that neither Britain nor France would fight until they were attacked, and would not be much good then." Like the FO diplomats, ordinary citizens never dreamed that a treaty binding Moscow and Berlin was possible. Eventually, it was assumed, the two would go to war.[28]

But it would not be Molotov who would make the final decision as to which way the Soviets turned; that power belonged exclusively to Joseph Stalin. Exploring the mind of a psychotic is impossible — the shortest distance between two points becomes a maze — yet as Churchill perceived, there was method in Stalin's dementia. In his own twisted way he was a patriot; like Winston he saw the peril in the Reich and wanted his country to survive it. That was his end. Any means was acceptable to him. He was quietly searching for one that would work.

Doubtless he would have preferred to avoid allies altogether. If he was viewed with suspicion in the capitals of Europe, his suspicions of their leaders ran to paranoia. Nevertheless, the necessity of making a choice, however distasteful, was becoming clear to him, and although Litvinov was in disgrace, an attachment to Britain and France was still preferable to a loathsome alliance with Berlin. Therefore the new foreign commissar, despite his Germanophilia, was instructed not to abandon discussions with Halifax and Bonnet.

Coulondre was encouraged by Molotov's accession. Molotov, he cabled' the Quai from Berlin, was chairman of the Council of People's Commissars and a "member of the Politburo, depositary of the thoughts of Stalin"; his appointment meant "Soviet foreign policy can only gain in clarity and precision, and France and England will have no reason to regret it." Bonnet wrote in his memoirs that he was "quite satisfied by the assurances" of the Russian ambassador in Paris that the switch in foreign commissars "does not denote any change in Soviet foreign policy," and that diplomatic discussions between envoys of the three nations could open whenever Britain and France were ready. Maisky brought the same message to Chamberlain and Halifax, who protested that they weren't ready.[29]

In fact, the democracies had every reason to regret the departure of their champion in the Kremlin. The Germans realized that they had gained ground. To drive the point home, the Russian chargé d'affaires in Berlin called at the Wilhelmstrasse to stress "the great importance of the personality of Molotov" — a curt, mulish man who spoke only Russian and held the Western Allies in contempt — and his "importance for future Soviet foreign policy." A dispatch from Warsaw reported that Litvinov had resigned after Marshal Kliment Voroshilov had told him that the Red Army was not prepared to fight for Poland and had denounced, in the name of the Russian General Staff, "excessively far-reaching military obligations." The *Frankfurter Zeitung* commented that Litvinov's fall was a

serious setback for Anglo-French plans to "encircle" the Reich. The German chargé in Moscow cabled the Wilhelmstrasse:

> Since Litvinov had received the English Ambassador as late as May 2 and had
> been named in the press of yesterday as guest of honour at the parade, his dismissal
> appears to be the result of a spontaneous decision by Stalin. . . . At the last Party
> Congress, Stalin urged caution lest the Soviet Union should be drawn into conflict.
> Molotov (no Jew) is held to be "the most intimate friend and closest collaborator
> of Stalin." His appointment is apparently the guarantee that the foreign policy will
> be continued strictly in accordance with Stalin's ideas.[30]

Some Englishmen were apprehensive. In London, Nicolson noted in
his diary that "the left-wing people" in particular were "very upset. . . .
They are not at all sure that Russia may not make a neutrality pact with
Germany. I fear this terribly." In his memoirs Churchill would write
scathingly of Litvinov's dismissal: "The eminent Jew, the target of German antagonism, was flung aside for the time being like a broken tool, and,
without being allowed a word of explanation, was bundled off the world
stage to obscurity, a pittance, and police supervision."[31]

The extent of Churchill's information about Kremlin infighting is
unknown. But the Soviet envoy Maisky was almost certainly his chief
confidant. It can hardly have been coincidence that he renewed his campaign for the triple alliance on May 4, the day after Litvinov was sacked.
The chief stumbling block, he knew, was Poland. The Poles were adamant
that Russian troops never be permitted to cross their territory, not even,
say, if Germany attacked France and the Red Army lunged westward to
support the French. Beck and his fellow officers in Warsaw not only
persisted in regarding the Russians as lepers; they resented anyone who
suggested that they be treated as anything else.

Churchill believed the moment must be seized despite the fears in
Warsaw. He pointed out in the *Daily Telegraph* that "Ten or twelve days
have passed since the Russian offer was made. The British people . . . have
a right, in conjunction with the French Republic, to call upon Poland not
to place obstacles in the way of a common cause." Hitler's prey needed not
only "the full cooperation of Russia" but also the three Baltic states, who,
with arms and munitions from the Soviet Union, could provide "perhaps
twenty divisions of virile troops." He appreciated the Polish policy of
"balancing between the German and Russian neighbour," but now that
"Nazi malignity is plain, a definite association between Poland and Russia
becomes indispensable." Otherwise, war would be certain, and a German
victory likely, with Poland in chains. The British and French could hold
the Wehrmacht in the west, he wrote, but without the Red Army, the

eastern front would collapse. He believed the Soviet Union would be responsive to overtures.

Russian interests are deeply concerned in preventing Herr Hitler's designs on Eastern Europe. It should still be possible to range all the states and peoples from the Baltic to the Black Sea in one solid front against a new outrage or invasion. Such a front, if established in good heart, and with resolute and efficient military arrangements, combined with the strength of the Western Powers, may yet confront Hitler, Goering, Himmler, Ribbentrop, Goebbels and Company with forces the German people would be reluctant to challenge.[32]

Unmentioned in his column, but of greater concern, was his knowledge that his own government was as hostile to the triple alliance as Beck. Britain had yet to issue a formal reply to Litvinov's proposal. That same day Lord Camrose, acting, in effect, as Winston's representative, called at the Foreign Office for a lord-to-lord talk with Halifax. Camrose reviewed all the reasons for establishing the peace bloc. After leaving the FO he wrote an account summing up the foreign secretary's counterarguments. Halifax thought such an alliance would be ill-received in Tokyo. Rumania, as well as Poland, would oppose it. England's Roman Catholics would be offended. Spain might react by joining the Axis, Italy would be alienated, the Portuguese might object, and Hitler might be driven into undertaking "desperate measures." Camrose had patiently replied that all these points were trivial or irrelevant — the Italians were already German allies — when balanced against the need to halt Nazi aggression in its tracks, defend Britain, and avert a general European war. Halifax listened politely but was unmoved.[33]

On May 8, three weeks after the Soviet Union had made its great move, London replied to it. "The response," William Shirer notes, "was a virtual rejection. It strengthened suspicions in Moscow that Chamberlain was not willing to make a military pact with Russia to prevent Hitler from taking Poland." His Majesty's Government did leave the door ajar — a few inches. The proposal would be restudied. A flame of hope gleamed, but it was faint and flickering.[34]

Chamberlain did not reveal his opinion of the Russian proposal in the House of Commons until May 19, and then only after Churchill, Lloyd George, and Eden had, in Winston's words, "pressed upon the Government the vital need for an immediate arrangement with Russia of the most far-reaching character and on equal terms." For an hour Lloyd George appealed for decision, a clear policy to succor England's friends and confound her enemies. Churchill described the prime minister's speech on the Soviet proposal as "cool, and indeed disdainful." Chamberlain's view, he later wrote, showed "the same lack of proportion as . . . in the rebuff to the Roosevelt proposals a year before." The P.M. insisted that "the suggestion that we despise the assistance of the Soviet Union is without foundation." If the government could "evolve a method by which we can enlist the cooperation and assistance of the Soviet Union . . . we welcome it; we want it; we attach value to it." It would be foolish, he said, to suppose that Russia, "that huge country, with its vast population and enormous resources, would be a negligible factor." Talks between British and Soviet diplomats had, he said, already begun. Unfortunately, they had bogged down. He acknowledged that he was reluctant to join hands with Moscow, but insisted that his position was based "on expedience and not on any ideological ground." There was, he said, "a sort of veil, a sort of wall, between the two governments which is extremely difficult to penetrate."[35]

Churchill thought the veil was in the P.M.'s mind. His skepticism was justified; two months earlier, commenting on the Soviet Union, Chamberlain had written his sister: "I must confess to the most profound distrust of Russia. . . . I distrust her motives, which seem to me to have very little connection with our ideas of liberty, and to be concerned only with getting everyone else by the ears. Moreover, she is both hated and suspected by many of the smaller States, notably by Poland, Roumania, and Finland." Significantly, he was untroubled by Nazi Germany's ideas of liberty, though at that time Hitler's concern with getting everyone by the ears had been far more conspicuous, and certainly more successful, than Stalin's. Colin Coote wrote Churchill that the prime minister "fundamentally wants Nazi ideas to dominate Europe, because of his fantastic dislike of Soviet Russia."[36]

French *députés* in Paris's *quartier des ministères* found an alliance with Moscow more attractive — no Channel separated them from the Wehrmacht — but ministers like Bonnet also regarded the Soviet Union as an evil empire, and made no effort to conceal it. In neither capital were the men in office aware that their personal opinions were irrelevant. Men who control great states must deal with their peers abroad, whatever their opinions of them; the Allies' studied rudeness toward the U.S.S.R. in the spring and summer of 1939, when Russia was offering them collective security, was inexcusable. Certainly it was no service to the millions they governed. It is arguable that Litvinov, had he met with civility and those supple conversations *à deux* in which trained diplomats excel, might have stopped the war that all Europe, with the exception of the Führer and his coconspirators, dreaded. The fact that they did not understand Litvinov's policy and the inner workings of the Soviet bureaucracy does not brighten their memory.

Winston, looking beyond ideologies, saw England in danger; her survival, for him, outstripped everything else. He doubted, he told the House on May 19, that Chamberlain's speech had contributed to the task before Parliament. "Nor has it, I venture to say, reassured those who feel deep misgivings about the present situation." He was, he said, "quite unable to understand what is the objection to making the agreement with Russia. . . . The alliance is solely for the purpose of resisting further acts of aggression. I cannot see what is wrong with that." Turning toward the front bench, he told the prime minister: "When you come to examine . . . the interest and loyalty of the Russian Government in this matter, you must not be guided by sentiment. You must be guided by a study of the vital interests involved. The vital major interests of Russia are deeply engaged in cooperation with Great Britain and France to prevent further acts of aggression." He asked: "If you are ready to be an ally of Russia in time of war" — as Chamberlain had said he was — "why should you shrink from becoming an ally of Russia now, when you may by that very fact prevent the breaking out of war? I cannot understand all these refinements of diplomacy and delay. If the worst comes to the worst you are in the midst of it with them, and you have to make the best of it with them. If the difficulties do not arise, well, you will have had the security in the preliminary stages."[37]

Of course, Winston told the House, there were complicated side issues in any treaty, but here, surely, the issue could hardly be simpler.

I should have thought that this plan of a triple alliance is a preliminary step, and an invitation to other countries in danger on this front to come under its protection, was the most straightforward and practical manner of approaching the subject. I do not know whether I can commend it to my right hon. Friend by adopting a simile selected as a special compliment to him. It is like setting up an armoured umbrella, under which other countries will be invited to take shelter as and when they seek to do so. But we cannot exclude from our minds the fact that we are in a deadlock at the moment. What are the differences? We have already given guarantees to Poland and Rumania, and the Government tell us that they would be glad if Russia would give similar guarantees. Consequently, if Poland and Rumania are attacked we shall be in the war, and so will Russia. It is almost axiomatic that those who are allies of the same Power are allies of one another.

"Clearly," he went on, "Russia is not going to enter into agreements unless she is treated as an equal, and not only treated as an equal, but has confidence that the methods employed by the Allies — by the peace front — are such as would be likely to lead to success." Vague policy and wavering leadership discourage nations otherwise attracted to a coalition, and Chamberlain "must realise that none of these States in Eastern Europe can maintain themselves for, say, a year's war unless they have behind them the massive, solid backing of a friendly Russia, joined to the combination of the Western Powers." Then Churchill raised what, for Englishmen, was the ultimate issue: "Unless there is an Eastern front set up, what is going to happen to the West? What is going to happen to those countries on the Western front to whom, if we have not given guarantees, it is admitted we are bound — countries like Belgium, Holland, Denmark, and Switzerland? . . . How are they to be defended if there is no Eastern front in activity?"

He ended:

It is a tremendous thing, this question of the Eastern front. I am astonished that there is not more anxiety about it. Certainly, I do not ask favours of Soviet Russia. This is no time to ask favours of countries. But here is an offer, a fair offer, and a better offer, in my opinion, than the terms which the Government seek to get for themselves; a more simple, a more direct and a more effective offer. Let it not be put aside and come to nothing. I beg His Majesty's Government to get some of these brutal truths into their heads. Without an effective Eastern front, there can be no satisfactory defence of our interests in the West, and without Russia there can be no effective Eastern front. If His Majesty's Government, having neglected our defences for a long time, having thrown away Czechoslovakia with all that Czechoslovakia meant in military power, having committed us without examination of the technical aspects to the defence of Poland and Rumania, now reject and cast away the indispensable aid of Russia, and so lead us in the worst of all ways into the worst of all wars, they will have ill-deserved the confidence and, I will add, the generosity with which they have been treated by their fellow-countrymen.[38]

Winston — and by now the weight of British public opinion — thought this reasoning unanswerable. Bowing to the storm of criticism, the prime minister on May 23 grudgingly agreed to negotiate with the Soviets on the basis of a British-French-Soviet alliance. He remained unpersuaded that such an alliance was necessary, however. And perhaps there was a certain logic in the argument that a strong ally on Germany's eastern front — or her western front, for that matter — was unnecessary if the intention was to meet Hitler's demands anyway. That, after all, had been the pattern; capitulation was inherent in the character of the British prime minister. The Führer's minister of propaganda, certain beyond doubt that the P.M. would yield, openly said so. The *Observer* quoted Goebbels as predicting that "Herr Hitler will secure peace with triumph because Mr. Chamberlain will force the Poles to give way."[39]

Give way where? Over what?

🐾   🐾

After Chamberlain's vow of support for Polish independence, Daladier had told his cabinet that the British now regarded the Vistula, not the Rhine, as their frontier. At the mouth of the Vistula stood the Free City of Danzig, a free state created by the Treaty of Versailles; the city's real significance arose from the fact that it lay on the Baltic Sea. Because the port could be approached through the Polish Corridor — another creation of Versailles — it gave the Poles access to the sea and world trade. Like almost every memorable Versailles gift, however, the transformation of the city's sovereignty had been made at the expense of the Germans. Until the 1919 peace treaty, it had been part of the Second Reich. Danzig, in fact, is a German name. After 1945 the Poles renamed it Gdańsk.

In 1939 it was not Polish territory, though *führertreu* readers of *Völkischer Beobachter* and *Der Angriff* had been led to believe that it was. The victors of 1918 had designated it a free state, to be administered by the Poles, but because the population remained overwhelmingly German, Germans dominated its legislative assembly. Even in the late 1920s friction between administrators and legislators had been frequent, and beginning in 1933, when Hitler moved into the Reich chancellery, it had intensified each year. Elected officials, proud of their membership in the local Nazi party, wore swastikas on their sleeves. On orders from Berlin, they could stage a full-fledged riot within an hour.

The dispute over Danzig was destined to launch World War II, but it had long lain quiescent, like a silent fracture in the earth's crust which, when it ruptures, will generate an earthquake. The Foreign Office had been largely unaware of the gravity of the problem until the spring of 1939, a shattering example of incompetence in both Whitehall and MI6, Britain's secret intelligence service. Danzig's tremors had been perceptible long before the *Volksdeutsche* made their grievances known in the Sudetenland; the Führer's plan to exploit them had been inscribed in *Mein Kampf*. Yet even after the issue emerged, His Majesty's Government believed it was manageable. It wasn't, because Hitler wasn't. The assumption that he was — the root of the government's foreign policy failures in the prewar years — was to persist through August 1939. Even after hostilities had actually begun, Chamberlain would cling to it, like an old dog worrying a naked bone.

The British might have been more alert had Colonel Beck not obscured the issue during his visit to London in April 1939. Danzig, the suave colonel had assured his hosts, was nothing to worry about; he would not even "trouble" them over it. Beck had been mendacious; the issue of the free city's future was in fact deeply troubling, and shadows had been darkening over it as early as November 5, 1937, when Konstantin von Neurath had told Józef Lipski, Poland's ambassador to the Reich, that "the Danzig question" would "permanently disturb German-Polish relations" until solved, and that the only possible solution would be "the restoration of German Danzig to . . . the Reich." The following year, in the aftermath of Munich, Ribbentrop had summoned Lipski to Berchtesgaden for a three-hour luncheon discussion about Danzig. It should, he said, be returned to Germany. In addition, Germany wanted extraterritorial rights in the Polish Corridor and a Polish denunciation of Russia. Chamberlain had committed himself to Poland initially because he thought Rumania was next on Hitler's hit list and he wanted the Poles to join him in pledging support of Rumanian independence. Actually, Poland had been — and still was — in far greater danger than Rumania.[40]

After Prague Ribbentrop had drawn the Poles deeper into the vortex of power politics. On Tuesday, March 21, he had again summoned Lipski, repeating his Danzig and corridor demands and adding complaints: anti-Nazi demonstrations by Poles must be crushed, and criticism of the Führer in Polish newspapers suppressed. The lack of a "positive reaction" to the Danzig issue had made "an unfavorable impression on the Führer," he said darkly; Hitler now "felt nothing but amazement over Poland's strange attitude on a number of questions." It would be wise, he suggested, for Colonel Beck to discuss these matters with the Führer, who might otherwise conclude that Poland "simply was not willing" to accommodate the Reich.[41]

Lipski had flown home, received instructions from Beck, and reappeared at the Wilhelmstrasse on Sunday with a memorandum from the colonel. Stripped of its elaborate periphrasis, it was a courteous rejection of all Hitler's demands, coupled with a refusal to visit Berlin until "the questions [have] been prepared, in advance, according to diplomatic custom." Ribbentrop, flushed with anger, replied that this response "could not be regarded by the Führer as satisfactory." If matters continued this way, he warned, "a serious situation might arise." Monday's papers carried accounts of anti-Nazi rioting in Bydgoszcz — a city in western Poland whose population was largely German. Ribbentrop exploited the disorders by summoning Lipski, implying that Bydgoszcz's Poles were to blame, and declaring that he could "no longer understand the Polish government." He added: "An evasive answer has been given to the generous proposal Germany made to Poland. . . . Relations between the two countries are therefore deteriorating sharply."[42]

The Foreign Office had first heard this ticking time bomb in the second week of April, when Goebbels spread rumors that Germany planned a

Danzig coup on the Führer's birthday, six days away. When this hear-say reached Halifax he wondered how Poland would respond to a staged "internal revolt" in the city, and asked HM's ambassador in Warsaw to clarify the question, which to him was "by no means clear." It seemed to him that if the Poles were "prepared to treat" with the Reich, they would "cut the ground from under the German Government by showing their disposition to negotiate." Beck curtly disagreed. He felt the time was not "opportune" for Warsaw to approach Berlin. If the Germans wanted to alter the status quo, they should take the initiative and state their claims; the Polish government would then consider them. It would not, however, agree to negotiate. Danzig, the Poles insisted, must remain a free city, their only major port, administered by them, as specified in the Versailles treaty. To turn it over to the Nazis would be interpreted as a sign of weakness and would invite further German claims. Halifax, unconvinced, continued to hint at the desirability of negotiations. Beck's principal private secretary told a British diplomat that these hints "tend to create an element of doubt as to the fixity of [Britain's] purpose." They evoked memories of Munich, he added, which was "not a good precedent."[43]

The Danzig crisis became public knowledge on the last Friday in April, when Hitler revealed to the Reichstag and the listening world — including the dismayed governments in London and Paris — that the Wilhelmstrasse had been negotiating with Beck over German claims against Poland for the past six months. Danzig was a German city, the Führer shouted; it must *"zurückkehren"* ("revert") to the Reich. He also demanded the right to build an autobahn and a double-track railroad across the Polish Corridor to East Prussia. Finally, Poland must join the Anti-Comintern Pact. Hitler called his Polish proposals "the greatest imaginable concession in the interests of European peace." Yet, he added in a sinister note, the Poles had refused "my one and only offer."[44]

All this was stage business. The OKW and the inner Nazi circle knew that the Führer had already decided to invade Poland whatever happened. Nearly a month earlier, he had issued to his high command copies of *Fall Weiss* (Case White), each numbered and labeled *Geheimhaltungsstufe* — Most Secret. "The task of the Wehrmacht," he had written, "is to destroy the Polish armed forces. To this end a surprise attack is to be aimed at and prepared." He added: "Surprise occupation of Danzig may become possible independently of Case White by exploiting a favorable political situation."[45]

He had created that situation by one of his cleverest strokes. Danzig now had the undivided attention of *Ausländspolitiker*. The free city, they were convinced, was his next objective. Meantime he would exploit their preoccupation as he prepared to achieve his real goal: the seizure of all Poland. He knew his Chamberlain. "Danzig at present is the danger spot," the prime minister wrote his sister, thrusting aside all warnings of a larger onslaught. He was "thinking of making a further proposal to Musso that he should move for a twelve months truce to let the temperature cool down." The Duce, eager to fuel the myth that Hitler took his advice seriously, wrote the Reich chancellor that "the British requests" for a cooling-off period over Danzig "contain the prerequisites . . . for reaching a solution favorable to Germany" which would not disturb the "rhythm of your splendid achievements . . . and you will add a fresh indubitable success to those you have already obtained."[46]

But a Danzig solution — incorporating the city in the Reich — would deprive Hitler of an excuse to invade Poland. On May 23 he summoned all OKW commanders in chief and Chiefs of Staff, each Generalstab officer with the distinctive red stripe running down his field gray trousers, to tell them they would "attack Poland at the first opportunity." There would be "no repetition of the Czech affair," the *Kriegsherr* warned them; instead, "There will be war." He was convinced that the British guarantee of Poland's frontiers was a bluff. Several weeks later in Zossen, twenty miles southeast of Berlin, where he had established General Staff headquarters and a small chancellery for himself, he assembled his generals and told them that they should not flinch "from solving the Eastern questions even at the risk of complications in the West," because he was sure the democracies would not fight, that such "complications" would never arise.[47]

Zossen thought him wrong, but he wasn't; throughout the summer of 1939 the appeasers remained in firm control of HMG's foreign policy. Lord Rothermere wrote Churchill on July 17: "Carefully handled I don't think there will be war over Danzig. Hitler left upon me the indelible impression that overtly he will never take the initiative in resorting to bloodshed. I suppose when I had my long talk with him he mentioned this matter at least a dozen times." Yet, he wrote, England was going on "arming night and day using up if necessary whatever available resources we can lay our hands on." Rothermere thought Hitler had been "badly handled. Instead of the language of reproach and rebuke constantly applied to him, I should have tried out the language of butter. . . . The language of guns may not go nearly as far as the language of butter." He ended, memorably, "I have never yet seen an authoritative statement made in England complimenting Hitler on his tremendous record of achievement in Germany."[48]

Churchill replied two days later: "You may well be right about Danzig; but does it really matter very much what the thing is called? Evidently a great 'crunch' is coming, and all preparations in Germany are moving ceaselessly to some date in August. Whether H. will call it off or not is a psychological problem which you can probably judge as well as any living man. I fear he despises Chamberlain, and is convinced that the reason he does not broaden his Government is because he means to give in once Parliament has risen [adjourned]." Plugging away at his book, Winston was, he said, "remaining entirely quiescent at the present time. . . . I have given my warnings, and I am consoled for being condemned to inaction by being free from responsibility." But of course he would never be free from responsibility. The pressure from without — to remain silent — was overpowered by the pressure from within. His conscience, his very essence, compelled him to shoulder his way into the public forum again and again.[49]

The first occasion was a 1900 Club dinner on June 21. Lord Londonderry, Winston's Germanophile cousin, was in the chair, and the guest of honor was Halifax. After his ritualistic, oleaginous tribute to those with whom he differed profoundly on the issues of the hour, Winston reminded Londonderry of "the flagrant and brutal manner in which the Munich agreement has been torn to pieces by the Nazi Government" and "the folly or villainy of the Nazi outrage" upon the rump Czech state. Summing up the case for the triple alliance, he concluded: "I believe most who are here tonight approve and endorse the willingness of His Majesty's Government to make an alliance with Soviet Russia, without which no effective stability can be created or long maintained in the East."[50]

Privately he was discouraged. Cripps visited him at his flat the following afternoon and stayed for over an hour. In his diary he noted that Winston "inveighed strongly against the PM, said he and Eden had been ready to join the Cabinet since Hitler went into Prague but would not be admitted as it would stop all possibility of appeasement." He agreed with Cripps that Parliament needed a coalition government "but despaired of any way of getting rid of or convincing Chamberlain." Cripps added with relish: "Amongst other things he pointed out that but for Chamberlain's shift on Foreign Policy after Prague, the Popular Front [left-wing] movement would have swept the country and I gather he could have supported it!" On Thursday, June 22, Churchill warned readers of the *Daily Telegraph* that reports of German troops massing on the Slovak frontier meant the Wehrmacht was intent on driving in Poland's "southern flank," and that Hitler wanted Danzig in order "to cut Poland [off] from the sea." The following day, Winston wrote G. M. Young: "I am afraid I continue to take a sombre view of our affairs," but in public he kept his spirits high. On Tuesday, June 27, he spoke to the Carlton Club before what the *Yorkshire Post* called "the largest audience ever gathered there on such an occasion" and appealed for "a full and solid alliance" with Russia. He told his audience that he wished he "could convince Herr Hitler of the fact that the British nation and, surely also, the British Empire, have reached the limit of their patience. We have receded and acquiesced time after time in breaches of solemn promises and treaties. Herr Hitler would make a profound mistake if he persuaded himself that all these retreats were merely the results of cowardice and degeneracy."[51]

However, that was precisely what Hitler thought. Moreover, successful criminals rarely change their M.O. — their method of operation. The Germans in the Sudetenland had led to Chamberlain's surrender at Munich, and there was a larger percentage of Germans in Danzig than in Czechoslovakia. He would stick to his M.O. He thought the British prime minister would come round to his way of thinking. And he was right. To Ida Chamberlain, Neville wrote that "should the [Danzig] issue come to a head now" he doubted that "any solution short of war is practicable," but if the Führer "would have a modicum of patience I can imagine a way could be found of meeting German claims while safeguarding Poland's independence and Economic Security." He listened again, with thirsty ear, for the cheers acclaiming his return from Munich. His M.O. had been established, too.[52]

Late in June another Goebbels rumor predicted a coup in Danzig for the weekend. He was testing British resolve, and he found it weak. Ribbentrop's under secretary, Weizsäcker, told Ambassador Coulondre: "We know you [France] would fight, but we are not sure about England." Daladier, disturbed, advised the British that "only a declaration couched in very energetic terms . . . will stop the Danzig coup," and in Warsaw a member of the ruling military junta told Clifford Norton, chargé d'affaires at the British embassy, that if Britain and France remained "unshaken," there would be no coup. At the same time, the British consul general in Danzig let the Foreign Office know that Germans there were saying that the Western Allies "will leave Poland in the lurch by not fighting on account of Danzig."[53]

The consul general recommended a strong stand by Britain, and Halifax dismissed him. The foreign secretary had no intention of fighting for Danzig. On July 1 the French, acting alone, informed Ribbentrop: "Any action, whatever its form, which would tend to modify the *status quo* in Danzig, and so provoke armed resistance by Poland, would bring the Franco-Polish agreement into play and oblige France to give immediate assistance to Poland." Bonnet suggested that Halifax take a similar step "at an early date." Halifax refused. In Parliament on July 10 Chamberlain declared that a Danzig coup "would involve a menace to Poland's independence which we have undertaken to defend," but added that future negotiations "ought to be possible . . . as the atmosphere cools."[54]

Churchill knew that the prime minister was putting pressure on the Poles; J. L. Garvin, editor of the *Observer,* had repeatedly accused him of it, and presently it became common knowledge. As Chamberlain wrote his sister on July 23, he had "heard last week that Hitler had told Herr Förster, the Danzig Nazi Leader, that he was going to damp down the agitation. True, the German claim that Danzig should be incorporated in the Reich was to be maintained, but that could wait until next year or even longer." Meantime "the city would be demilitarized and the press muzzled, but particular stress was laid on the need for secrecy at present and for restraint on the Polish side." Chamberlain had undertaken to send "all sorts of warnings to the Poles accompanied by exhortations to let nothing leak out." Unfortunately, the Germans had "let the cat out of the bag," giving "all my enemies" a chance "to say 'There I told you so. He means to sell the Poles,' and [making] it impossible for me to enter into conversations with Germans on any subject."[55]

That was shading the truth. He was talking to both the Germans and the Poles through Halifax, and he was consistently taking the Nazis' side, with his foreign secretary concurring. A remarkable example of their double standard arose when the Poles asked for a loan to buy arms. Colonel Adam Koc, a member of the Warsaw junta, had arrived in London on June 14 with a financial commission. The British had pledged a "general decision on principle," but during Koc's first ten days in England he was received but once by England's chief economic adviser, and that meeting was "purely nominal." Two weeks later the Treasury offered the Poles eight million pounds. It was far less than they needed, and was accompanied by so many strings that Koc returned to Warsaw alarmed and depressed. The Poles, after deliberations, decided with "great reluctance" that they could not accept the terms. Koc then requested a loan convertible into dollars, permitting Poland to buy weapons in the United States. Chancellor of the Exchequer Simon, who had been willing to let Czech gold slip through his "butterfingers," as Churchill called them, replied that because "this would seriously affect our own financial position," he "could not agree." Yet at the same time, as Gilbert and Gott found in their study of these transactions, "Treasury officials were offering the Germans widespread economic advantages in return for an Anglo-German nonaggression pact." Sir Orme Sargent, who had become the strongest Foreign Office opponent of appeasement since the fall of Vansittart, thought it lunacy to extend such privileges to Nazi Germany while Poland was so "roughly handled." During that summer one of those catchy, anonymous phrases which arise in times of great stress was heard on the lips of Englishmen who agreed with him: "It is better to die on your feet than live on your knees." Proud men all, His Majesty's Government never dreamed of living on their knees, but they believed that peace would be their reward if they answered the polemics of the Führer by keeping their other cheek turned and extending boundless generosity to Berlin. Meanwhile the Poles, who had been encouraged to entrust their independence to England, were consigned to march into battle carrying obsolete weapons and defective ammunition.[56]

❧   ❧

The present is never tidy, or certain, or reasonable, and those who try to make it so, once it has become the past, succeed only in making it seem implausible. Among the perceptive observations and shrewd conclusions of the Churchills and Sargents were clutters of other reports and forecasts, completely at odds with them. All of it, the prescient and the cockeyed, always arrives in a promiscuous rush, and most men in power, sorting through it, believe what they want to believe, accepting whatever justifies their policies and convictions while taking out insurance, whenever possible, against the possibility that the truth may lie in their wastebaskets.

Neville Chamberlain required a very large wastebasket, for he was stubborn and strong-willed, and long after his subordinates had abandoned their faith in appeasement he clung to the conviction that if he could just put the proper deal together, Hitler would buy it. "Hitler," Macmillan recalled, "was always regarded by British politicians as if he were a brilliant but temperamental genius who could be soothed by kindness or upset by hard words. It was this fearful misconception about the nature of dictators that was . . . the root-cause of much that went amiss in these tragic years." Somehow an excuse had been found for every wild threat and instance of extravagant behavior in the Reich Chancellery. Karl Burckhardt, the League of Nations high commissioner of Danzig, who later wrote *Meine Danziger Mission 1937–1939*, told Halifax that the Führer had said to him: "If the slightest incident happens now, I shall crush the Poles without warning in such a way that no trace of Poland can be found afterwards. I shall strike with the full force of a mechanized army, of which the Poles have no conception." Burckhardt thought the Führer's "boasting" arose from "fear," and Halifax accepted that explanation as reasonable.[57]

By the end of May virtually every powerful *Ausländpolitiker* in Europe had endorsed the triple alliance except the British prime minister. He wrote his sisters that Halifax had written that he had been "unable to shake Maisky on his demand for the 3 party alliance & Daladier had insisted that it was necessary, Poland had raised no objection. . . . It seemed clear that the choice lay between acceptance & the breaking off of negotiations," which "no doubt" would "rejoice the heart of Berlin & discourage Paris."

There was "no sign of opposition to the Alliance in the Press & it was obvious that refusal would create immense difficulties in the House even if I could persuade my Cabinet." Nevertheless, he still distrusted the Russians, still lacked faith in the Red Army, and still thought it disastrous to divide Europe into two armed camps. The only supporter he could find, he wrote, was "Rab Butler & he was not a very influential ally." The P.M. was searching for an escape hatch, instructing Horace Wilson to work out a plan which would give the Russians "what they want" but avoid "the idea of an Alliance" by substituting "a declaration of *intentions* in certain circumstances."[58]

That was on May 28, 1939. Churchill's repeated calls for swift execution of the alliance were a growing irritant to Chamberlain, a variant of the Chinese water torture; another of them appeared in the *Daily Telegraph* of June 8, and this time Winston struck a new, somber note. There was, he wrote, reason to doubt that His Majesty's Government was negotiating in good faith. This opinion seemed confirmed by HMG's response to a suggestion from the Kremlin that Britain send a special envoy to Moscow. Eden quickly volunteered. He would have been an excellent choice; he was a former foreign secretary, he had met Stalin several times under agreeable circumstances, and his resignation from the cabinet on a matter of principle had enhanced his prestige on the Continent. Instead, Chamberlain sent William Strang, "an able official," as Churchill described him, "but without any standing outside the Foreign Office." It was, as Winston called it, "another mistake. The sending of so subordinate a figure gave actual offence." The Russians were highly sensitive on matters of protocol, and the junior diplomat from Whitehall, having presented his credentials, was ignored by the new commissar for foreign affairs. On June 19 Nicolson wrote: "Strang has not seen Molotov again since Friday. Yet . . . Halifax told Winston yesterday that all was well. I confess I am most uneasy."[59]

In Parliament the prime minister repeated his pledge to stand by Poland if she were invaded. Nevertheless, Churchill felt a thickening sludge of defeatism. As so often in moments of despair, he looked westward across the Atlantic toward the one power which, if aroused and armed, could crush Nazi Germany without mortgaging Europe's future to Stalin. In *News of the World* on June 18, after outlining ways in which the "atrocity" of bombing civilian targets could be countered, he wrote: "Of these grievous events the people of the United States may soon become the spectators. But it sometimes happens that the audience becomes infuriated by a revolting exhibition. In that case we might see the spectators leaving their comfortable seats and hastening to the work of rescue and of retribution."

*   *   *

Britain and France, however, seemed to be losing their audience. The diplomatic conversations in Moscow were not revolting, but they had certainly become tiresome. The negotiations were wallowing. After a brief spurt of activity at the bargaining table, Halifax, on Chamberlain's instructions, permitted the talks to lapse again. This was dangerous, raising questions in other capitals over England's resolution and strength. On July 7 Mussolini, the poseur of machismo, summoned His Majesty's ambassador in Rome, Sir Percy Loraine, and said loftily, "Tell Chamberlain that if England is ready to fight in defense of Poland, Italy will take up arms with her ally, Germany."[60]

Actually, this was the hollowest of threats. Despite the Pact of Steel, the Italian end of the Axis was tin. Mussolini's men weren't ready. However, Whitehall was unaware of that (so was Hitler), and in any event Chamberlain's extravagant efforts to keep Italy in the Anglo-French entente had already failed.

The defection of Belgium was more serious. Three years had passed since the Belgians' announcement that they would no longer participate in staff talks with officers from the War Office and the French Ministère de Guerre. Instead they would, in any future conflict in Europe, remain strictly neutral. But Belgium now, as in 1914, did not enjoy the freedom to make that choice. If Hitler's powerful new Wehrmacht chose to knife through the Low Countries into France, it would drive a bloody blade into the same scar over the same wound the kaiser had opened a quarter-century earlier, and a nation which has been invaded cannot remain neutral. All the callow sovereign in Brussels had accomplished was to ease the task of Hitler's Generalstab. King Leopold III had reached his decision, Churchill commented, "in a spirit of detachment from the facts." He lived to see his people subjugated by the Wehrmacht, the young men forced to work as slave labor in Ruhr munitions factories, the old subject to execution as hostages whenever Belgian freedom fighters struck. They would still be bowed beneath the Third Reich's yoke when he died in 1944.[61]

Despite Hitler's shredding of the Munich Agreement, despite daily reports of Nazi outrages in Austria and shattered Czechoslovakia, and despite brutal incidents on the borders between Germany and Poland (the beatings of civilian Poles by Nazi thugs), Neville Chamberlain remained serene in his stateroom on the *Titanic*. And his troika — Halifax, Simon, and Hoare — was equally tranquil. Churchill, untranquil but helpless as Europe blundered toward the brink of war, toiled away at Chartwell or sat brooding by his fish pond, his hands in his lap, like weapons put to rest. The Chamberlain government ignored him, but he remained a public figure; J. L. Garvin wrote and published in the *Observer* an editorial stating that were Churchill taken into the cabinet the decision "would be accepted" throughout Europe as "conclusive proof of national efficiency and resolution." *Pravda,* arguing that the Baltic states must not fall into Nazi hands, noted on July 22 that "The security of such states" was of prime importance for Britain and France, "as even such a politician as Mr. Churchill has recognized."[62]

Churchill's rare disclaimers of ambition, his affecting to enjoy the squire's life in Kent, were merely the palaver expected of any political figure excluded from power. His lust for office remained undiminished. He yearned to be in the cockpit of action, not only for the excitement — though that would always be there, and was part of his charm; his expressions, gestures, and swings in mood evoked images of the mischievous small boy at Harrow. He relished the prospect of glory, and, if he made it to the top, of more decorations and honors, of audiences with his sovereign, and motorcycle escorts as he raced about serving the monarch and his people. But he was driven by deeper motives. He was, and proudly proclaimed himself to be, an egoist. He wanted, he *needed* power. He knew his worth, and suffered when he saw mediocrities, men without imagination, vision, or honor, betraying his England. Egoism and grandeur are so close that they may merge in one man, and he was such a man. Like Lord Chatham, prosecuting the Seven Years' War in the eighteenth century, Churchill could say: "I believe I can save this country and no one else can."[63]

Clearly Neville Chamberlain couldn't. His indifference to the Russian proposal proved that. The talks in Moscow remained stalled, and on July 13, nearly three months after the Soviet offer to Britain and France, Winston wrote in the *Daily Mirror* that there could be no excuse for the "unaccountable delay" in signing "a solid, binding, all-in alliance" between Moscow, Paris, and London. Such procrastination, he declared, "aggravates the danger of a wrong decision by Herr Hitler. It is lamentable indeed that this broad mainsail of peace and strength, which might carry the ship of human fortunes past the reef, should still be flapping half-hoisted in the wind."

The prime minister was unmoved. He wrote Ida: "I am so sceptical of the value of Russian help that I should not feel that our position was greatly worsened if we had to do without them." This was a stunning misjudgment. Hitler had told his interpreter that if Britain and France accepted the Soviet offer and formed the triple alliance which had been Litvinov's dream, he would be outmanned, outgunned, and outwitted; he would be forced to cancel his war plans and bide his time. Churchill later wrote that the three-power coalition "would have struck deep alarm into the heart of Germany." With "superior power on the side of the Allies," countries the Führer had marked as future victims would have regained the diplomatic initiative and "Hitler could afford neither to embark upon the war on two fronts . . . nor to sustain a check. It was a pity not to have placed him in this awkward position, which might well have cost him his life." Winston concluded: "Having got ourselves into this awful plight of 1939, it was vital to grasp the larger hope."[64]

Throughout July the three-power talks flickered, sputtered, and guttered, like the last candle in a darkening house. *Pravda* reported that "in the circles of the Soviet Foreign Ministry, results of the first talks are regarded as not entirely favorable." Actually Maisky had told the ministry that he believed the men from London "want the talks to fail," that Chamberlain was a creature of the "Cliveden set" whose only reason for entering negotiations had been to mollify his critics in Parliament. The distrust was mutual. Cadogan was developing a profound hatred for the Soviet delegation. Their chairman was particularly easy to hate. Churchill, who later encountered him at several official functions, described Molotov in vintage Chartwell prose: He was "a man of outstanding ability and cold-blooded ruthlessness. He had survived the fearful hazards and ordeals to which all the Bolshevik leaders had been subjected in the years of triumphant revolution. . . . His cannonball head, black mustache, and comprehending eyes, his slab face, his verbal adroitness and imperturbable demeanour, were appropriate manifestations of his qualities and skill. He was above all men fitted to be the agent and instrument of the policy of an incalculable machine. . . . I have never seen a human being who more perfectly represented the modern conception of a robot."[65]

But during the Moscow talks Molotov also had reason to fume. Cadogan wrote: "We give them all they want, with both hands, and they merely slap them." That was absurd; how could they be giving the Russian negotiators "all they want" when, despite repeated Soviet entreaties, they refused to exert pressure on Poland — whose best interests would be served, since the Poles would be trapped in any war between Russia and Germany — to become party to the agreement? The Anglo-French delegates rejected the simple, comprehensive Soviet proposal, suggesting instead unilateral guarantees by individual nations. The Englishmen parried and thrust, immunized to boredom by their profession and doubtful that Britain had anything to gain or lose here. Like Chamberlain and Halifax, most of them doubted that the Red Army would be any match for the Wehrmacht. And, like them, they believed nothing else was at stake.[66]

🦁   🦁

Here their error was not only spectacular, it was historic. Harold Macmillan, one of the handful who suspected what was coming, was puzzled by their blindness. In part they were victims of a distorted self-image, an illusion common among superpowers; like Americans a generation later, they assumed that all other countries held them in high regard. Actually, the men in the Kremlin bore malice toward the Western Allies, and with reason. Both England and France had intervened in the Russian Civil War after the Armistice of 1918 and had sent troops to fight the Bolsheviks; both had imposed diplomatic sanctions on Russia's new regime; and they had deprived the Soviet Union of Russian territories in postwar treaties. Postwar Germany had, on the other hand, shared in none of these actions. Even after the Nazi rise to power, Macmillan noted, "German-Russian relations had been good and even cordial." To be sure, "Hitler's violent and offensive anti-Communist propaganda no doubt angered Stalin, but he was not a man to be deterred by words from any action that he deemed advantageous."[67]

Yet what diplomatic action, in the growing European crisis, would be to Russia's advantage? War was coming, the Reich would be the aggressor, and Hitler did not wish Stalin well. If Russia allied herself with the democracies, the Führer would be forced to fight on two fronts. On the other hand, such a treaty would mean war between Germany and the Soviet Union. Britain and France could not guarantee Stalin peace — but Hitler could. A Nazi-Soviet nonaggression pact would mean peace for a Russia which chose to remain neutral, and would bring about, without the loss of a single Red soldier, the recovery of the lost lands surrendered to Rumania, Poland, and the Baltic states twenty years ago at the insistence of the Western powers. If he chose that course and the Allies were defeated, eventually he would have to face Germany alone. But Hitler might be dead by then, or overthrown; or Germany might be defeated. The temptation to withdraw from the imminent maelstrom, to buy time to arm, was enormous.

Meantime, the talks with the Allies were permitted to continue, in the hope that they would give him reason to turn away from what would, in the long run, be the greater peril. Long afterward, Churchill wrote: "It is not even now possible to fix the moment when Stalin definitely abandoned all intention of working with the Western democracies" and turned his attention to "coming to terms with Hitler." Maisky told Boothby he thought the die had been cast on March 19, when Halifax sandbagged Moscow's Bucharest conference, but the evidence strongly suggests that a firm Anglo-French commitment could have saved the triple alliance as late as mid-August. Nevertheless Stalin was keeping his German option open.[68]

How long had it been open? After the war Russian expatriates published *Notes for a Journal*, identifying the author as Maksim Litvinov. Establishing its authenticity is impossible, but according to this source, the

Soviet dictator had pondered a détente with Germany as soon as he read the Munich Agreement. He is quoted as having told Litvinov toward the end of 1938: "We are prepared to come to an agreement with the Germans . . . and also to render Poland harmless." According to a journal entry dated January 1939, Stalin had instructed Alexei Merekalov, the Russian ambassador in Berlin, to open talks with Weizsäcker, telling him "in effect" that "We couldn't come to an agreement until now, but now we can."[69]

Almost certainly this, or a variant of it, is close to the truth. If Munich had been a battle, it would have been among the most decisive in history. Walter Lippmann wrote: "In sacrificing Czechoslovakia to Hitler, Britain and France were really sacrificing their alliance with Russia. They sought security by abandoning the Russian connection at Munich, in a last vain hope that Germany and Russia would fight and exhaust one another." Stalin was aware of that. On March 10, five days before Prague, he had savaged the democracies for sacrificing Austria and Czechoslovakia and accused them of trying to "embroil" the Reich in a war with the U.S.S.R., "pushing the Germans further eastward, promising them an easy prey and saying: 'Just start a war with the Bolsheviks, everything else will take care of itself!' "[70]

Whitehall saw no shadows cast by coming events, but Gallic suspicions had begun well before Prague, when Coulondre had warned the Quai that a Nazi-Soviet rapprochement was in train; its objective, he said, would be to divide Poland between them. On May 9 he cabled the Quai: "For the last 24 hours Berlin is full of rumors that Germany has made, or is going to make, proposals to Russia leading to a partition of Poland." On May 22 he reported that Ribbentrop had said that Poland "sooner or later must disappear, partitioned again between Germany and Russia. In his mind this partition is closely linked with a rapprochement between Berlin and Moscow." Later Coulondre told Paris that the Führer "will risk war if he does not have to fight Russia. On the other hand, if he knows he has to fight her too he will draw back rather than expose his country, his party, and himself to ruin."[71]

Daladier, having studied the cable traffic from Coulondre, afterward wrote: "Since the month of May [1939] the U.S.S.R. had conducted two negotiations, one with France, the other with Germany. She appeared to prefer to partition rather than to defend Poland." Chamberlain seems to have been the last politician in Europe to discover that the Russians were keeping two sets of books. In late May, when the P.M. finally agreed to negotiate with the Russians largely on the basis of the terms embodied in Litvinov's original proposal, Dirksen, the Führer's envoy to the Court of St. James's, advised the Wilhelmstrasse that Chamberlain had taken this step "with the greatest reluctance," prompted by reports to the Foreign Office of "German feelers in Moscow." Chamberlain and Halifax, according to

Dirksen, were "afraid that Germany might succeed in keeping Soviet Russia neutral or even inducing her to adopt benevolent neutrality."[72]

By then the two dictators were in fact on the way to the altar. Churchill observed afterward: "It is a question whether Hitler or Stalin loathed it most." But marriages of convenience are not expected to be joyous. The one mot which won universal acceptance in the democracies and the United States was "They deserve each other." Certainly the Führer, until now regarded as the new Machiavelli, had met his match in duplicity. It was characteristic of Stalin's amorality that on the day after Litvinov had invited England and France to join Russia in an anti-Nazi alliance, Merekalov called on Ernst von Weizsäcker at the Wilhelmstrasse, ostensibly to discuss commercial issues arising from Czechoslovakia's incorporation into what was now known as *Grossdeutschland,* beginning with a request for sales to Russia from the Skoda Works, now a Nazi arsenal.[73]

In fact the ambassador's objectives transcended trade. His appearance in the office of Ribbentrop's under secretary marked the beginning of a dramatic shift in relations between the two dictatorships. On that day Weizsäcker responded to the Skoda issue first. He told his visitor that reports of Soviet negotiations with Britain and France, looking toward a military alliance, did not create "a favorable atmosphere for the delivery of war materials to Soviet Russia." But he knew that trade, even trade in arms, could not be the real reason for this visit. The ambassador had presented his credentials nearly a year ago, and this was the first time he had entered the Foreign Ministry. Weizsäcker, unlike Ribbentrop, was a trained diplomat; he had a pretty good guess at what was coming. To encourage Merekalov to get to the point, he remarked that the Russian press was not "fully participating in the anti-German tone of the American and some of the English papers."[74]

At that, his visitor spoke up: "Ideological differences of opinion had hardly influenced the Russian-Italian relationship," he said, "and they need not prove a stumbling block for Germany either. . . . There exists for Russia no reason why she should not live with Germany on a normal footing. And from normal, relations might become better and better." This ground-breaking ceremony was followed, first, by two meetings between Dr. Julius Schnurre of the Wilhelmstrasse and Georgi Astakhov, the Russian chargé d'affaires, and second, on May 20, by a long talk in Moscow between Molotov and Ambassador Friedrich Werner von der Schulenburg. Schulenburg found the foreign commissar *"sehr freundlich"* ("very friendly") and ready to discuss both economic and political agreements between the two powers. Thus the seeds were planted. They might never blossom. Russian diplomats were still courting Britain and France. But if those talks fell through, Stalin had established an alternative.[75]

*   *   *

On July 24 prospects for an accord between the Reich's three most powerful adversaries seemed to brighten. Molotov, summoning the British and French negotiators, was conciliatory; clearly he had received fresh instructions from the Kremlin. Since the political matters still to be thrashed out were technical, he said, he recommended that they draw up the related military convention spelling out the obligations of each nation, under the mutual assistance pact, in meeting Nazi aggression. The Foreign Office and the Quai were consulted; the French agreed enthusiastically, the British less so. Dirksen reported to the Wilhelmstrasse — now genuinely alarmed by the prospective alliance — that His Majesty's Government regarded the military talks "skeptically."[76]

Events swiftly confirmed the German ambassador. In diplomacy great importance is attached to the prestige of the men a nation sends to represent it. For these talks the Russians chose officers holding the highest ranks in the U.S.S.R.: Marshal Voroshilov, Russia's commissar for defense; the chief of the Red Army's General Staff; and the commanders in chief of the air force and the navy. To lead the French delegation Daladier picked General of the Army André Doumenc, formerly Maxime Weygand's deputy chief of staff, regarded throughout France as one of the most brilliant officers to serve under the tricolor. Chamberlain, however, repeated the Strang snub, deliberately offending the Kremlin. A month earlier, when Anglo-Polish military talks were held in Warsaw, Britain had been represented by Tiny Ironside. This time Tiny was kept home. Instead, an obscure and undistinguished British party was led by Admiral Sir Reginald A. R. Plunkett-Ernle-Erle-Drax, of whom Dirksen wrote that he was "practically on the retired list and was never on the Naval Staff."[77]

So slipshod were Whitehall's arrangements for the talks that Plunkett-Ernle-Erle-Drax wasn't even given written authority to negotiate — a serious breach of diplomatic courtesy — though he had been instructed to be discourteous anyway; British foreign policy documents reveal that he had been told to be vague and "go very slowly." As a final slight to the Russians, the British, who were handling transportation for the Allied teams, rejected the suggestion that they fly to Moscow, which would have taken a day. They boarded the nine-thousand-ton passenger-cargo ship *City of Exeter,* an ancient vessel whose top speed, Molotov's deputy foreign commissar found, was thirteen knots. They left England on August 5 and did not reach Leningrad until very late on August 9; they arrived in Moscow August 11. The *Queen Mary* would have brought them to New York in less time. And in this August, like that other August a quarter-century earlier, every hour counted. The triple alliance now had Hitler's undivided attention; he knew how formidable it would be and had ordered Ribbentrop to break it up. Joachim von Ribbentrop may have been only a wine salesman, but he had been a very good salesman, and he knew Molotov would be an eager customer. The only obstruction was Stalin. That was enough to discourage any diplomat except one who would have to return to the Führer empty-handed. The German's main hope lay in the possibility that the Anglo-French officers would bungle their assignment.[78]

That is precisely what they — or, more accurately, their governments — did. The military talks in Moscow got off to a wobbly start. Marshal Voroshilov was offended by the failure of Plunkett-Ernle-Erle-Drax to produce credentials signed by Chamberlain. Soviets put a premium on form; they interpreted the lapse as a sign that Britain did not regard the occasion as grave. General Doumenc, on the other hand, was on excellent terms with the Russians from the start. His *Ordre de Service*, signed by Daladier, was flawless; he had impressed the Red Army's leaders by his knowledge of Russian military traditions; he sympathized with their painful memories of Allied hostility to the Bolshevik cause in their struggle of 1918–1920 and was tactfully silent about Stalin's purges of the Red Army. In his determination to impress the Russians in their talks, he had, as one of his subordinates put it, "stretched the truth a little." The Maginot Line, he said, now extended "from the Swiss frontier to the sea." As any newspaper correspondent could have told the Soviets — and as their own intelligence service doubtless had — it was less than half that long. In Doumenc's defense, it should be noted that the French delegation, like Britain's, had been instructed by its senior officers to gloss over military weaknesses. The British were poorer liars. Their army spokesman blithely declared that Britain could field sixteen divisions "in the early stages of the war." The French were "astounded," one of their delegates later wrote; this was "three or four times" greater than Ironside's figure in the most recent Anglo-French staff talks. Voroshilov, suspicious, pressed the issue, asking, "How many divisions will you have if war breaks out soon?" The embarrassing answer was that England's standing army at present consisted of "five regular divisions and one mechanized division." At that moment, one French officer later wrote, "the Soviet delegation understood better than it had the immense weakness of the British Empire."[79]

The Russians' crucial question was asked by Voroshilov late in the afternoon of Sunday, August 13. The Soviet Union, he pointed out, had no common frontier with the Reich. What, he inquired, did the French and British General Staffs think the Red Army could do if Poland or Rumania were attacked, since the Soviet troops could not take action without entering "the territory of other states?" There was silence. Doumenc and Plunkett-Ernle-Erle-Drax replied that they would answer in the morning. That bought them a reprieve, but next day the marshal's questions were more specific: Would Soviet forces be allowed to move against the Wehrmacht through Poland's Wilno Gap and Polish Galicia? He said flatly: "We ask for straightforward answers to these questions. In my opinion, without an exact, unequivocal answer, it is useless to continue these military conversations." It was up to the Allies to secure permission for the passage of Russian troops, he said, because they, not the Soviet Union, had guaranteed Poland and Rumania. For the next two days the military talks got nowhere, as Allied diplomats sought to win the cooperation of the Poles. By the seventeenth Voroshilov had run out of patience. He demanded that the meetings adjourn until a definite reply from Warsaw had been received. The negotiators agreed to reassemble on Monday, August 21.[80]

The British and French ambassadors in Warsaw approached Beck on August 18. He told them that Soviet troops were of "no military value." The chief of the Polish General Staff agreed; he could see "no benefit to be gained by Red Army troops operating in Poland." Two days later the Polish foreign minister formally rejected the Anglo-French requests. Moreover, he added, he didn't want to hear any more about it: "I do not admit that there can be any kind of discussion whatever concerning the use of part of our territory by foreign troops." If Poland agreed, he said, "this would lead to an immediate declaration of war on the part of Germany." Hitler frightened him, but Stalin terrified him.[81]

The provocative question is why Paris and London did not put Beck to the ultimate test. Under these extraordinary circumstances they were entitled to declare that unless Poland agreed to let the Red Army help, Britain and France no longer felt bound to go to war in defense of Poland. Actually this dilemma had been anticipated in April when, four days after Chamberlain announced England's unilateral guarantee of Poland, Churchill and Lloyd George, speaking in the House, had both urged that the Soviet Union be encouraged to join an entente of countries threatened by Nazi aggression. Lloyd George, and then Churchill, had demanded that Chamberlain's guarantee be provisional, valid only if the Poles agreed to accept help from the U.S.S.R. Lloyd George had predicted:

If we are going in without the help of Russia, we are walking into a trap. . . . I cannot understand why, before committing ourselves to this tremendous enterprise, we did not secure beforehand the adhesion of Russia. . . . If Russia has not been brought into this matter because of certain feelings the Poles have that they do not want the Russians there, it ˙or us to declare the conditions, and unless the Poles are prepared to ˙pt the only conditions with which we can successfully help them, the ˙ponsibility must be theirs.[82]

The option was still there. The Anglo-Polish mutual security pact had not yet been signed. Britain's foreign secretary could have taken the simple step of making Beck's acceptance of Russian aid a condition of signature. Bonnet actually proposed this stratagem. Halifax sent Bonnet's proposal across Downing Street; Chamberlain frostily replied that he declined to be party to such a "maneuver." "Maneuver," like "creatures," was one of his pet pejoratives, but in this context it was meaningless. The prime minister had to have had another motive. The likeliest, though he did not cite it, was his visceral dislike of the Soviet Union.

Daladier, more tenacious and dismayed by the loss of a powerful ally on Germany's other front, was slow to accept diplomatic defeat. After a final appeal to Warsaw, which was brusquely rejected, the premier cabled Doumenc on the morning of August 21, instructing him to sign a military convention with Russia under the best terms possible, with the sole provision that it must be approved by the cabinet. The French premier also wired his ambassador in Moscow, authorizing him to tell Molotov that France approved "in principle" the right of Russian soldiers to cross Poland if Hitler attacked. But these telegrams did not arrive in the Soviet capital until late in the evening, and by then the drama was over.

Pressed to accept Soviet help in the event of trouble, the Poles were also being urged to yield on the Danzig issue, to placate the Führer and alleviate the mounting tension in Europe. In the final British negotiations over Danzig, a key figure, and at times *the* key figure, was Churchill's mirror image — the Nazis' favorite diplomat, Sir Nevile Henderson, His Majesty's ambassador to the Third Reich. Henderson defended the anti-Semitic pogroms of Danzig Nazis, opposed any link between London and Warsaw, thought the Poles should "talk a little less" about their courage and think "a little more" about the "realities" of their position on the eastern fringe of *Grossdeutschland*. He criticized his own country, telling Cadogan that England had led Poland "far up the garden path" by her pledges. Britain, he thought, should cede Danzig to Hitler. His great fear was that Beck, Koc, and their fellow colonels might arouse the German's temper. Danzig, he told Halifax in late July, ought to be declared a *"German* Free City," forcing Poles living there to leave. Until then, he predicted, "there will be no real peace" in eastern Europe.[83]

Clifford Norton, Britain's chargé in Warsaw, strenuously attacked Henderson in his dispatches. He thought it unlikely that "the present moment is a good one" for negotiations between Germany and the Poles. Before any talks began, he wrote, Poland's strength, and the justice of her cause, should be "visible and apparent not only to its partners, but also to its opponents." Actually, he doubted the value of negotiations under any

circumstances: "Even if Danzig were removed from the front of the stage
. . . there is little basis for hopes that such a settlement would introduce the
millennium." When Henderson criticized this as "rather hypothetical,"
Norton replied that the Führer and his Nazi hierarchy were "imbued with
the desire to dominate all Eastern Europe." That being true, he wrote, "no
difficulties . . . should be allowed to shake the firmness of the Anglo-
Polish alliance."[84]

Reading British foreign policy documents of that summer —
Henderson's dispatches, the memoranda of Halifax, the prime minister's
papers — it is startling to recall that Britain had made a commitment to
Poland, not Germany. Norton reminded the foreign secretary of that. In
consequence, Halifax tried to bypass him, and in Downing Street he was
dubbed "pro-Polish." It was meant as a slur. His Majesty's Government
was determined to prevent the Poles from embarrassing Britain by dragging her into war. Henderson thought that was their intention. Their
objective, he cabled home, was to "humiliate" the Third Reich.[85]

Clearly humiliation was to be the lot of *some* powers. Governments
were taking positions from which retreat without loss of face was impossible. Britain was committed to Poland; if the European balance of power
shifted dramatically, and the Polish position became untenable, England
would be in the soup. If that thought crossed Henderson's mind, he made
no record of it. Probably it didn't; as a diehard appeaser, he refused to
admit the possibility of a showdown, even to himself. If matters reached an
impasse, the disciples of appeasement reasoned, they would negotiate a new
settlement and their armies would stand down.

The Wehrmacht wasn't going to stand down. The Führer had made
that clear at Zossen. Germany was going to march into Poland, and the
dying would begin, whatever the diplomats did. The Reich's hopes for
victory, however, relied heavily on its chief diplomat. Ribbentrop was
doing both his best and his worst to achieve a pact with the Soviet Union,
though he had had problems with his führer. Hitler loathed Slavs almost
as much as he hated Jews, and while he had known a triple alliance would
present the gravest of threats to him and his Reich, he had vacillated
through May and June.

In late May the Führer had instructed the Wilhelmstrasse "to establish
more tolerable relations between Germany and the Soviet Union," and said
he wanted Count von der Schulenburg, his ambassador in Moscow, to
convey this to Molotov "as soon as possible." Four days later he canceled
this and said he preferred a "modified approach." Trade talks had begun,
but in June Hitler suddenly repudiated them. On July 18 they were
resumed after the Soviets had said they were prepared to extend and

intensify economic relations between the two countries. Hitler's munitions buildup was suffering from a lack of raw materials; he told Schulenburg to sign a trade agreement at the earliest possible moment and *"den Faden wiederaufnehmen"* ("again take up the thread") of political discussions with the foreign commissar. Suddenly, Russians and Germans began talking about power plays in Poland and the Baltic states — grabbing territories by joint aggression — coups elected leaders in democracies would not dare hatch, knowing that a free press and an aroused public would force them to withdraw.[86]

Englishmen were proud of their customs and traditions, some of which bordered on the eccentric. To Churchill's exasperation, Britain's ruling class continued "to take its weekends in the country," as he put it, while "Hitler takes his countries in the weekends." This was no small matter. It meant that crucial decisions could not be made because those with the authority to make them were beyond the reach of telephones. Suggestions that country weekends be shortened, or that provisions be made for emergencies, were met with icy stares. Britain's leaders detested being pushed; one of their chief complaints about Americans was that they always seemed to be in a hurry. Haste was somehow regarded as un-British. The ruling class was not called the leisured class for nothing.[87]

The timetable of events, as July melted into August, suggests the price England paid for Edwardian manners when trying to outwit and outmanipulate a twentieth-century Attila. On July 31, the day Chamberlain told Parliament that an Allied military mission would be sent to Moscow, the Reich's ambassador to Russia received an "urgent and secret" telegram from the Wilhelmstrasse, instructing him to see Molotov immediately. Three days later, *before the Anglo-French mission sailed for Leningrad,* the Russo-German talks became more specific. Ribbentrop, carrying out his *Blitzwerbung,* had told Schulenburg to present "more concrete terms . . . in view of the political situation and in the interests of speed." The Führer was no longer irresolute.[88]

He had scheduled his invasion of Poland for late August; the Wehrmacht had to overwhelm Poland before the October rains made the unpaved roads impassable for his panzers. He had to outbid the Allies in Moscow quickly, and price was no object. On August 12, toward the end of a meeting with the Italian foreign minister, Hitler said he had just received "a telegram from Moscow. The Russians have agreed to a German political negotiator being sent to Moscow."[89]

This may have been a trick to impress Ciano — no such cable was found among the German documents captured in 1945 — but other documents leave no doubt that on that same day Molotov agreed to discuss issues Schulenburg had raised, including Poland. The foreign commissar stressed the Soviet view that such talks must "proceed by degrees." When word of this was relayed to the Reich Chancellery, Hitler replied that protracted talks were out of the question. He didn't explain his reason — that German troops would march in less than three weeks. And the triple alliance was a harrowing possibility: that same afternoon in Moscow, Anglo-French military conversations with the Russians had begun.[90]

Hitler, in his summer headquarters on the Obersalzberg, made his great move on Monday, August 14. He told his court: "The great drama is now approaching its climax!" He was confident that neither Britain nor France would sacrifice a single soldier for Poland. The Quai d'Orsay was deferring to London, he said, and England "has no leaders of real caliber. The men I got to know at Munich are not the kind to start a new world war." Still, he knew how edgy his generals were about a two-front war, and so, on his instructions, Ribbentrop sent Schulenburg a "most urgent" cable directing him to "read it to Molotov."[91]

In his telegram to the Kremlin, Ribbentrop said the Reich was prepared to send him to Moscow to settle all outstanding problems "from the Baltic to the Black Sea." At the same time, he played to Stalin's paranoia. Britain and France, he said, were "trying to drive Russia into war with Germany" — Stalin, he knew, had used those very words in a speech to the Communist Party Congress. Tuesday evening Molotov greeted Ambassador Schulenburg warmly and asked whether the Nazis would join him in a joint "guarantee" of the Baltic states and — this was completely unexpected — a nonaggression treaty between the Soviet Union and the Reich. Hitler was ecstatic; Stalin was offering to play the role of spectator while the Wehrmacht took Poland. Wednesday Ribbentrop cabled the Führer's reply: "Germany is prepared to conclude a nonaggression pact with the Soviet Union . . . and to guarantee the Baltic States jointly." His foreign minister was ready, bags packed, to travel to Moscow "by airplane," bearing "full powers from the Führer . . . to sign the appropriate treaties."[92]

Stalin knew what he was giving Hitler. He also knew what he would get — all that Russia had lost at Versailles and more: vast tracts of Estonia, Latvia, Lithuania, Poland, Rumania, and what Ribbentrop's August 14 telegram had described as "Southeastern questions," i.e., the Balkans. The Western democracies couldn't match that. If the Russians signed the triple alliance Nazi panzers might rip through Poland and, without stopping, into the Soviet Union. Nevertheless, when Schulenburg passed along Ribbentrop's request that he be received on Friday, August 18, the foreign commissar, after consulting with the general secretary, replied this was too soon: the meeting would require "thorough preparation." But his manner was encouraging. He told the German envoy that he was "highly gratified" by the prospect of a visit by the foreign minister of the Reich; it stood, he said, "in marked contrast to England, which, in the person of Strang, has sent only an official of second-class rank to Moscow." Meantime, he was directing his military negotiators to ask the Allies, in effect, what Russia would get out of an alliance with Britain and France.[93]

The tyrant in Moscow continued to play with the tyrant in the Berghof. The Führer's eyes were on the calendar and on the clock. If the war was to start as planned, OKW orders had to be cut quickly: two huge army groups had to deploy on Poland's waters while fleets of U-boats sailed for British waters. Stalin and Molotov, sensing the Führer's anxiety, decided to let him hang. On the night of Friday, August 18, Schulenburg was sent another urgent cable from the Obersalzberg; he must insist that Molotov see Ribbentrop immediately, must refuse to take no for an answer, and must repeat that the German foreign minister had been authorized by the Führer "to settle fully and conclusively the total complex of problems." Ribbentrop was, for example, prepared "to sign a special protocol regulating the interests of both parties," including "the settlement of spheres of interest in the Baltic area."[94]

This cable arrived in the Reich's Moscow embassy at 5:45 A.M. on Saturday, and the German ambassador made a 2:00 P.M. appointment with Molotov. But when they met, the foreign commissar refused to make a date for Ribbentrop's trip; he repeated that "thorough preparations" would be required. Depressed, Schulenburg returned to his embassy, wondering how he could break the news to a despot who never accepted excuses and ruthlessly punished failure. So fearsome were the consequences that — blasphemous in a servant of the Führer — he prayed. And his prayers were answered. At 4:30 P.M. his telephone rang. It was Molotov, asking him to return. Emerging from the commissar's office, the elated ambassador returned to his embassy and sent the Wilhelmstrasse a triumphant wire. "The Soviet Government agree to the Reich Foreign Minister coming to Moscow," it began. The Soviet foreign commissar had stated that Ribbentrop "could arrive in Moscow on August 26 or 27. Molotov handed me a draft of a nonaggression pact." Hitler was elated, but he had by now set August 26 as the date for the attack on Poland. Drastic measures were necessary. Overcoming his distaste for Bolsheviks, on the twentieth the Führer sent a personal cable to Stalin, accepting the general terms of the nonaggression treaty and urging that final negotiations take place as soon as possible.[95]

Late the next night, Berlin radio interrupted a musical program for an announcement: "The Reich government and the Soviet government have agreed to conclude a pact of nonaggression with each other. The Reich Minister for Foreign Affairs will arrive in Moscow on Wednesday,

August 23, for the conclusion of the negotiations." It was nearly midnight, Monday, August 21, 1939. Europe had ten slaughterless days left.[96]

This conspiracy against peace — for that is what the pact amounted to — was a cynical deal, and Russia would pay a terrible price for it. But the British and French governments had played a sorry role. Over four months had passed since Litvinov had made his proposal to them. Had the opportunity been seized — had Eden, say, arrived in the Soviet capital with plenary powers — Hitler might never have had his chance. Russia needed peace; everyone knew that; but the democracies were insensitive to it. Three years later Stalin explained to Churchill: "We formed the impression that the British and French Governments were resolved not to go to war if Poland were attacked, but that they hoped the diplomatic line-up of Britain, France, and Russia would deter Hitler. We were sure it would not." Later Winston wrote: "Thus Hitler penetrated with ease into the frail defences of the tardy, irresolute coalition against him."[97]

Bonnet, as he later wrote in his memoirs, realized that *"pour France c'était un désastre."* At a bleak convocation of the Conseil de la Défense Nationale a pall of defeatism hung heavy over the council table. Gamelin, the most spineless generalissimo, said the army would not be ready for war until 1942; the most France could do now was mobilize, bringing "some relief to Poland by tying down a certain number of large German units on our frontier." Bonnet said flatly that they should ponder whether to ignore their treaty commitment and leave the Poles to their fate.[98]

Only Daladier's peasant strength suppressed Bonnet's pusillanimity. France's commitment to Poland, the premier reminded him, was a matter of honor and had been since Marshal Foch's secret military agreement with the Poles in 1921. If either a German hobnail or a Russian boot set foot on Polish soil, France had agreed, the Army of the Third Republic was pledged to attack the aggressor. Therefore, at the premier's insistence, the Conseil de la Défense decided that *"la seule solution"* in the present crisis was to adhere to *"nos engagements vis-à-vis de la Pologne."* In a public statement the French government reconfirmed its alliance with Poland, with each party guaranteeing the other "immediately and directly against any menace, direct or indirect, threatening their vital interest." The formal language of exchanges between governments could be no more precise.[99]

But the triple alliance which Russia had proposed and Churchill had enthusiastically endorsed — which conceivably could have averted war, or at the very least given the Germans less than an overwhelming margin — had become another of history's colossal Ifs. England and France were in the position of disappointed fiancées. The Soviets, in need of a spouse, had asked for their hand. They, also lacking a strong partner, had reluctantly approached the altar. There the ritualistic question had been raised: whether anyone had just cause to object to the union. And the Poles, at that crucial moment, had rudely spoken up, leaving the Russians in the embarrassing position of rejected suitors. Ribbentrop, having caught them on the rebound, rejoiced. His glee is understandable. The jubilation of Beck is harder to grasp, but he certainly felt triumphant. Ordinarily, he ran his office like a martinet, his face stiff and expressionless. But all that critical week his smile was vulpine, a smile of malice, the smile of a man who relished revenge. In the Russo-Polish War of 1920 the Bolsheviks had driven deep into Beck's homeland, to the gates of Warsaw. Now they had thought they could do it again, but he had outwitted them. This, he told his staff, was his greatest success. If he were to be remembered, it would be for barring the Red Army from Polish soil. He had saved Poland from the Communists.

So Nazis and Communists, until now sworn enemies, had been meeting secretly, frequently, and with growing confidence while the frustrated British public watched the Moscow-London-Paris entente, imaginatively conceived, struggling vainly to avoid stillbirth. Churchill's breathing spells from his book had been rare and brief. Any major issue brought him up to the House of Commons, however, and the prime minister created one when he decided to adjourn Parliament for two months — from August 4 to October 3. Chamberlain wrote his sister from Chequers that "all my information indicates that Hitler now realises that he can't grab anything else without a major war and has therefore decided to put Danzig into cold storage." If Parliament urged a show of Britain's growing military strength, however, the Führer would feel that "he must do something to show he is not frightened. I should not be at all surprised therefore, to hear of movements of large bodies of troops near the Polish frontier. . . . That is part of the war of nerves and [would] no doubt send Winston into hysterics." Provocative speeches in the House of Commons and demands for military maneuvers would, Chamberlain wrote, "play straight into Hitler's hands and give the world [the impression] that we are in a panic."[100]

Churchill — anxious, not panicky — feared, as a friend put it, "that Neville, having got rid of the House, proposed to do another Munich." Therefore, he decided to protest Chamberlain's decision to adjourn Parliament. General Spears, who had been staying at Chartwell that last weekend in July, told Harold Nicolson: "The old boy is determined to speak with great violence and to vote against, arguing, 'It is no good Chamberlain saying he will summon Parliament "if there is any change of situation." He must promise to summon if any cloud rises at all.' " Churchill told Spears that the motion for recess was a profound mistake because it would convince Hitler that Britain would be slow to act in a crisis, and give Russia the impression that Britain was not serious about collective security. "The scattering of Parliament," he wrote to Lord Wolmer, "is a serious snub."[101]

Most Tory critics of appeasement agreed, but thought the issue not worth another vote against their party leader. Harold Macmillan felt that way and phoned Churchill, asking him to reconsider. Winston bluntly refused. Eden also suggested that they let Chamberlain have this one and "toe the line," as Nicolson noted in his diary, adding: "I would do so were it not that Winston refuses, and I cannot let the old lion enter the lobby alone. But apart from this I do feel very deeply that the House ought not to adjourn for the whole of two months. I regard it as a violation of constitutional principle and an act of disrespect to the House."[102]

"This House," Churchill opened on August 2, "is sometimes disparaged in this country, but abroad it counts." Its debates and motions were particularly weighed by dictators "as a most formidable expression of the British national will and an instrument of that will in resistance to aggression." Winston had "the feeling that things are in a great balance." Certainly it was an "odd moment" for a parliamentary vacation "when the powers of evil are at their strongest." Berlin said the Reich had two million men under arms — the real figure was at least triple that — and another half million would be added this month.[103]

He had learned that public schools in large parts of Czechoslovakia, especially Bohemia, were being cleared and prepared for accommodation of wounded Germans. There was "a definite movement of supplies and troops through Austria towards the east" and a "strained situation in the Tyrol." The elements of crisis were there, and "all these are terribly formidable signs." Thus, he said, "At this moment in its long history it would be disastrous, it would be pathetic, it would be shameful for the House of Commons to write itself off as an effective and potent factor . . . against aggression." Then he delivered his heaviest blow:

It is a very hard thing, and I hope it will not be said, for the Government to say to the House, "Begone! Run off and play. Take your masks with you. Do not worry about public affairs. Leave them to the gifted and experienced Ministers" who, after all, so far as our defences are concerned, landed us where we were landed in December of last year, and who, after all — I make all allowances for the many difficulties — have brought us in foreign policy at this moment to the point where we have guaranteed Poland and Rumania, after having lost Czechoslovakia, and not having gained Russia.[104]

Amery and Macmillan joined in arguing against such a long adjournment, but Chamberlain was unmoved. Nicolson noted in his diary: "To the astonishment of the House the Prime Minister gets up and after saying that he will not give way an inch, he adds that . . . he wished it to be clearly understood that he regarded the vote as a vote of confidence in himself. . . . The general impression is that Chamberlain has in fact missed an opportunity and outraged the feelings of the House." Party strength prevailed, although forty Conservatives abstained; on that sour note the House dispersed for the summer.[105]

The following Tuesday Winston delivered a broadcast to the United States. Once more he was looking westward, convinced that the hope of England's security and, if it came to that, her deliverance lay across the Atlantic, in the vast untapped power of the United States. The fact that his mother had been American in no way diminished his loyalty to the Crown — he had been called "fifty percent American and one hundred percent British" — but he believed in bloodlines, was proud to have cousins across the sea, and admired the United States as Baldwin and Chamberlain did not. Furthermore, Franklin Roosevelt was president. Churchill would have regarded most occupants of the White House as lesser men than himself, but Roosevelt was not among them. Like Churchill, he was a great statesman. The two men were very different in other ways, but both possessed intellect, vision, courage, and the conviction that if civilization was to survive, Adolf Hitler must be destroyed. Roosevelt's handicap was that his people were overwhelmingly isolationist. Refugees from Europe, or descended from refugees, they wanted no part of "Europe's wars." Roosevelt and Churchill saw that the German demagogue was the enemy of freedom for all men. In his broadcast Churchill tried to plant the seed of that thought in the minds of his U.S. listeners, there to be nourished by Roosevelt.

His opening chord was unfortunate. In his hands the rapier of wit or the broadsword of ridicule was deadly, but on this occasion he was awkward, even embarrassing, with the hacksaw of sarcasm. He began heavily: "Holiday time, ladies and gentlemen! Holiday time, my friends across the Atlantic! Holiday time, when the summer calls the toilers of all countries for an all too brief spell from the offices and mills and stiff routine . . ." This went on. And on. He rumbled: "Let me look back — let me see. How did we spend our summer holidays twenty-five years ago?" Millions of listeners were too young to remember, and the rest had no recollection, as he had, of Germans "breaking into Belgium and trampling down its people." He had forgotten that the United States hadn't declared war on Germany until three years later, and that another year passed before U.S. doughboys, most of whom had never heard of Belgium, filed into the trenches.[106]

In the same vein of ponderous japery, he said that to believe Dr.

Goebbels, "you would suppose that it was . . . this wicked Belgium," with "England and the Jews," who attacked Germany, which in its righteous might fought manfully for four years and was about to win an overwhelming victory when "the Jews got at them again, this time from the rear. Armed with President Wilson's Fourteen Points they stabbed, we are told, the German armies in the back."

Dropping his caustic tone, Churchill became Churchillian once more, rousing and persuasive. Now, he said somberly, "There is a hush all over Europe, nay, over all the world." What kind of hush? "Alas, it is the hush of suspense, and in many lands it is the hush of fear." But, he said, almost whispering, if you listened carefully you could hear "the tramp of armies crunching the gravel of the parade grounds, splashing through rain-soaked fields, the tramp of two million Germans and over a million Italians." He recited their conquests — Austria, Czechoslovakia, Abyssinia, Albania — noting that the Duce and the Führer called them "liberations," and commented: "No wonder there is such a hush among the neighbors of Germany and Italy while they are wondering which one is going to be 'liberated' next."

Once more he appealed for collective security, once again he disposed of the Nazi charge of "encirclement." Then he drew a striking parallel between the American and British constitutions. "It is curious," he observed, "how the English-speaking peoples have always had [a] fear of one-man power," or "handing themselves over, lock, stock and barrel, body and soul, to one man, and worshipping him as if he were an idol." Tradition in the Reich was different: "In Germany, on a mountain peak, there sits one man who in a single day . . . can plunge all that we have and are into a volcano of smoke and flames." If that man "does not make war there will be no war. No one else is going to make war. . . . No one has ever dreamed of attacking Germany."

Approaching the end he said: "It is not, believe me, my American friends, from any ignoble shrinking from pain and death that the British and French peoples pray for peace." He was wallowing again; everyone shrinks from pain, and there is nothing ignoble about it. Yet, as always, he came on strong at the end:

But whether it be peace or war — peace with its broadening and brightening prosperity, now within our reach, or war with its measureless carnage and destruction — we must strive to frame some system of human relations in the future which will put an end to this prolonged hideous uncertainty, which will let the working and creative forces of the world get on with their job, and which will no longer leave the whole life of mankind dependent upon the virtues, the caprice, or the wickedness of a single man.[107]

Even when off his form, Churchill was a powerful broadcaster, and getting better all the time. By now informed Americans were beginning to realize it. As early as October 1938, he had told U.S. listeners why Munich had been a disaster and the perils it had spawned. Thomas Jones wrote a friend in the United States: "Churchill's speech to America, brilliant as it was in phrasing, is criticised here as not likely to be helpful on your side. I should have thought that for the present we ought to leave America alone."[108]

British opinion had reversed itself since Munich. Chamberlain, however, had not, and the country's new mood was not reflected in his policy. The public — even the House of Commons — knew very little of the decisions and commitments being made in the name of their king and affecting their future, or indeed, whether they would have one. Fleet Street had kept them informed of negotiations looking toward an alliance with the Soviets, because Litvinov had announced his plan to foreign correspondents. No Englishman — including, for a time, the country's leaders — knew of the talks between Berlin and Moscow, but England's Polish policy should have been known everywhere in Britain. At the very least it ought to have been debated in Parliament. In practice, it was conducted in secret by a handful of men, led by Chamberlain, Halifax, and Horace Wilson. They withheld news of the moves and countermoves in London, Warsaw, and Berlin because they knew their countrymen would disapprove. They were still the Men of Munich. Their higher loyalty was to appeasement. That policy continued to entail duplicity, lies, a stronger Reich, and a further weakening of the Führer's enemies in the coming conflict. His Majesty's Government had sold out the Czechs; now, if they thought it would keep them out of war, they would sell out the Poles, too.

Hitler and Stalin could gag their newspapermen; in the democracies that was impossible. Foreign correspondents from the United States and every European capital were aware of the developing tension between London and Warsaw, and although they only picked up fragments of the story, they gave the Poles a forum for their grievances, which were found to be completely justified when the forty volumes of *Documents on British Foreign Policy 1919–39* were published after the war. The issue was whether England would or would not fight for Poland. One of the first journalists to put it bluntly was Garvin, who noted in the *Observer* that summer that Chamberlain's reputation was reflected in the greeting now exchanged by passing acquaintances on the streets of Warsaw. They simply said: "Remember Munich."[109]

🦁   🦁

On Monday, August 14, the day Ribbentrop cabled Schulenburg that he wanted to fly to Moscow "in the name of the Führer" with the object of "restoring German-Russian friendship," Churchill left England for a three-day tour of the Maginot Line. His mission was an exercise in personal diplomacy, obsolescent then, illegal today, and rarely productive. At the time of Winston's departure, Chamberlain and his cabinet were unaware that he had left the country; only the Imperial General Staff, whose blessing he had, knew where he was going, and why. His name and his reputation were familiar to every Frenchman in authority.[110]

Political relationships between the two Western allies had soured; the Warsaw junta had driven a wedge between them. To Churchill's consternation, the rift between London and Paris was matched by chilliness on the military level. The Conseil Supérieur de la Guerre, France's high command, was altering its military plans, but Tiny Ironside had been provided with no details. He hoped they were better than Britain's.

Winston's prestige across the Channel made him an ideal choice to do what Britain's Imperial General Staff could not: talk to the French high command, question them, reassure them. In 1936, as their guest, he had toured Verdun, Metz, and the famous line named after André Maginot, a politician who believed good fences made neighbors who are not good friends keep their distance. Winston's letters then had been notable for their lack of opinion. To Clementine he had written: "There was nothing to see as all the troops were hidden in holes or under bushes. But to anyone with military knowledge it was most instructive." Now he was going to take a closer look. To Ironside he wrote that he was "off tomorrow" for the Rhine sector. "Generals Georges and Gamelin are very kindly going to come with me part of the time, and I expect we shall be able to have some talks on the matters we discussed."[111]

Accompanied by General Spears, he landed at Le Bourget and was greeted personally by Gamelin's deputy, General Joseph Georges, who had cleared his crowded calendar to serve as Churchill's guide. Winston was flattered; as he wrote Clementine that evening from the Ritz, "Georges will command the army in a war." After they had left the airport, he wrote, the general drove him and Spears "to the restaurant in the Bois where in divine sunshine we lunched & talked 'shop' for a long time." As they ate wood strawberries soaked in white wine, the French commander said the French thought "nothing will happen till the snow falls in the Alps & gives to Mussolini protection for the winter." Churchill agreed. "This looks like early or mid-September, wh wd still leave Hitler two months to deal with Poland, before the mud season in that country. All this of course is speculation, but also reasonable. It seems to fit the German programme so far as it has been published."[112]

As the tour progressed — they traveled, Winston proudly wrote Clementine, "in a special Michelin train of extreme speed, dining en route" and spent "2 vy long days on the line" — their host's feeling grew that hostilities were inevitable. According to Spears's notes, Georges said he was "convinced that war was almost upon us, and that the Germans, unless given all they wanted, were prepared to launch it." Spears wrote, "It emerged that there was no more doubt in General Georges' mind than in ours that it was the Germans rather than we who had benefited by the time gained at Munich, always supposing that they had really intended fighting then, which he doubted. He thought Hitler had been bluffing." A year ago, he told them, the Nazis had no elaborate defenses facing France; now they had built their *Westwall*, the Siegfried Line, "a formidable obstacle built according to modern ideas, in great depth, whereas the Maginot Line was linear." A year earlier, French artillery had been "incomparably superior"; the Germans, whose Munich spoils included Czechoslovakia's vast Skoda munitions works, were now masters of the big guns. Moreover, Georges said, the Nazis had built a long lead in the air, "and all we could do was to build and build, and place the largest possible orders in the United States."[113]

Churchill's second tour of the Maginot Line confirmed his new views of modern tactics and strategy. After he had lunched with General Gamelin, chief of the French General Staff and commander in chief–designate (Georges would be the field commander), Gamelin left instructions that Winston and Spears were to be shown parts of the intricate defense system never revealed before to any foreign visitor — strong points along the Rhine, ingenious new antitank obstacles, underground railroads opposite the *Westwall*, and, should Hitler decide to attack through Switzerland, heavy artillery sited on Swiss road junctions. And so it was that on Tuesday, August 15 — as Anglo-French diplomats tried in vain to get Poland to agree to let Soviet troops cross Polish territory — Churchill and Spears, led by Georges, began a grueling exploration of the line's eighty-seven "fortified" miles, completed four years earlier.

Shielded by ten feet of cement, each casemate housed grenade throwers, machine guns firing out of underground slits with a fifty-degree arc, and rapid-firing antitank guns. Every casemate was manned by twenty-five men who moved through tunnels and down elevators to sleeping quarters deep below the earth. Skillfully camouflaged, the casemates were invisible to intruders in the forest, save only for the two observation cupolas above each. Five miles behind these outer strong points, spaced every three to five miles, were steel-and-concrete forts housing as many as twelve hundred poilus, who were transported from their subterranean barracks to gun turrets by electric trains. Ventilation was provided by compressors which could screen out poison gas. A major fort consisted of from fifteen to eighteen concrete blocks, each bristling with guns — ranging from 37 millimeters to 135 millimeters — bolted to disappearing turrets. Each block was split into two sections linked by underground galleries, some over a mile long. If half the fort were captured, the other half could fight on, bringing down heavy fire on the enemy. At Verdun in 1916 two forts, Douamont and Vaux, had been lost to Germans who infiltrated their superstructures and fought their way downward. To prevent this, the designers of the Maginot Line had provided for "interval troops," special forces complete with their own field artillery, which could be shifted to any fort under heavy attack. "These," Alistair Horne explains, were meant "to compensate for what, by definition, the Line lacked: mobility."[114]

On Wednesday, August 16, accompanied by a *Times* correspondent, Winston and his party drove right up to the front line, within shouting distance of Nazi troops on the right bank of the Rhine. *The Times* reported that Winston was "amazed" to see an enormous sign opposite Neufbrisach reading: *"Ein Volk, ein Reich, ein Führer,"* and, on the left bank, a French billboard replying: *"Liberté, Égalité, Fraternité."* Churchill was amazed — but not by this very ordinary sport of idle soldiers. He was startled by the naked intent of the German deployment, invisible to the reporter's untrained eye but recognized immediately by him and his companion. "The trip," Spears wrote, "tore to shreds any illusion that it was not Germany's intention to wage war and to wage it soon. There was no mistaking the grim, relentless and barely concealed preparations she was making."[115]

That evening they joined French officers for a long discussion of the new threat posed by parachute troops, of tank traps, of assaults screened by artificial fog — Winston thought this very important — and of the need for heavier tanks, upon which all were agreed. As Spears listened, his mind drifted back to Vimy Ridge in 1915. Winston had earnestly explained his theory of "land cruisers" then to a French general and his staff. Spears had lingered after Churchill departed, and he remembered "how heartily they had laughed" at "this absurd idea." They had told Spears: "Your politicians are even funnier than ours."[116]

Thursday, when Ribbentrop's Luftwaffe pilot was instructed to prepare a flight plan for imminent departure to Moscow's Khodnynka Airport, Churchill and Spears were back in Paris, registering at the Ritz. Long afterward Spears said that what had impressed him most during their tour was "Winston's incredible vitality." Nearly sixty-five, he would have been entitled to bypass some of the line's lesser features, but he had insisted on stumbling over every pillbox in sight, scrutinizing antitank obstacles in front of the main line of resistance (repeatedly ensnaring himself on barbed wire), climbing in and out of antitank ditches, and striding in and out of the reinforced barracks, known as *maisons fortes*, for troops who must remain on the surface. He had been on the go for three days, hurrying through tunnels and sleeping bays, arguing over whether certain stretches could support the weight of tanks, and being manhandled down the slopes of the Rhine's banks so he could stand, arms akimbo, staring at the German soldiers on the far shore.

And he was not finished. In his room he prepared a report, to be dispatched by courier to the War Office. He thought it might be useful, he began, "to set down some of the points in my mind as a result of my long talks here." The coming war, he believed, ought to be better managed than the last, and to that end he recommended "a liaison between British and French supply organizations." In his opinion German regulation of industry "is the greatest advantage they possess." The Allies "should match it."[117]

He thought the possibility of any "heavy German effort" in the west during the "opening phase" of the war extremely unlikely. The Wehrmacht's strategy would be to crush Poland first. Preventing this was essential; if the Poles were overwhelmed the Germans could turn and hurl their full might against the Allies. Eventually France could put six million men in the field, but her present strength was only a fraction of Germany's. To "take the weight off Poland" the French should be prepared "to engage actively all along the line and . . . force the Germans to man their lines heavily." Since the German border on that front "extends so many miles, it ought to be possible to hold a very large number of German divisions in the West." The thought that England and France might remain idle, leaving the Poles to their fate in the hope of a negotiated peace with Hitler, never crossed his mind.[118]

However, his misgivings about the French static strategy were grave. The Paris dailies called the line "France's shield." But, Winston noted, the great advantage of a shield is that it may be moved to defend any part of the soldier's body. The Maginot Line was immovable. It was incapable of protecting the French from Germany's classic invasion route over the Belgian plains — "the pit of the French stomach," as Clausewitz had called it. Churchill recalled an old Whitehall joke: "The War Office is always preparing for the last war." Now, he thought, it was "certainly true of the French." In his report to Tiny Ironside he wrote that while "the French Front cannot be surprised . . . the flanks of this front . . . rest upon two small neutral states." He was satisfied that the French had "done everything in their power to prepare against an invasion through Switzerland," but "the attitude of Belgium," on the other hand, "is thought to be profoundly unsatisfactory. At present there are no military relations of any kind between the French and the Belgians."[119]

He had begun to understand the Maginot mind. It was the mind of a nation which did not want to lose a war, but didn't much want to win either. The French soldiers of 1914 had lusted for revanche, the return of Alsace and Lorraine, lost when their grandfathers had been overwhelmed in the Franco-Prussian War. The two provinces had been made French again at Versailles, and now the country had no war aims. In denying an appropriation to enlarge the republic's tank corps in 1935, the minister of war had asked a wildly cheering Chamber of Deputies, "How can we still believe in the offensive when we have spent milliards to establish a fortified barrier? Would we be mad enough to advance beyond this barrier upon God knows what adventure?" Yet everyone — including the Generalstab plotters meeting beneath the murmuring pines and hemlocks in Zossen — knew France's basic war plan. Because the minister of war had discounted the threat through Switzerland, the Maginot Line was expected to hold the enemy at bay while other poilus valiantly drove into Belgium to counterattack the attacking Germans. But if the counterattacking poilus lacked élan vital, their assault would fail. Feeling safe behind the line, "like the lotus-eating mandarins of Cathay behind their great Wall," as one writer put it, France had lapsed into languor, a spiritless lassitude which was the exact obverse of the lusty, singing, marching young Nazi soldiers across the border.[120]

During his tour of the line Churchill, like most visiting VIPs, confined his remarks to senior officers. Indeed, he would have given grave offense had he done otherwise. Spears tells us that he was "pleased with the aspect of the men. . . . He knew how to look every man in the eyes as he passed him, thus convincing him he had been recognised by someone already known, even in France, to be a very important person." But it is a pity Winston could not have talked to them, too, and later he said as much. The spirit of the Marne had, he realized, "exhausted its mission and itself in victory." It was as though the Third Republic had become a different country. Bravery, he noted, was now associated in the great majority of French minds with the futile butchery of 1914–1918. In metropolitan France alone 27 percent of the country's young men between the ages of eighteen and twenty-seven had not returned from the trenches. Simone de Beauvoir tells of a Dr. Lemair, who had operated on countless poilus under appalling conditions and who, on returning home, "took to his bed and never got up again."[121]

No one knew how many of the survivors of the war, the men who should have been guiding France in 1939, had been drained, exhausted, broken at the front. But the deterioration in the army's leadership had been shocking. The Conseil Supérieur de la Guerre, whose members would become senior generals when war broke out, was hopelessly entangled in red tape and bureaucratic muddle — *paperasse*, as the French call it. Tanks were despised (as mortars, machine guns, and warplanes had been despised in 1914). In 1921 Marshal Pétain, then supreme commander, had dismissed the future of armored warfare in nineteen words: "Tanks assist the advance of the infantry by breaking static obstacles and active resistance put up by the enemy." His successors endorsed this finding. As Charles de Gaulle had discovered in the early 1930s, no one in the Conseil Supérieur understood revolutionary air power and the implications of armored vehicles which could now "be made capable of withstanding artillery fire and could advance a hundred miles a day." Indeed, not a single French general had wanted to know. De Gaulle's memoranda had been returned to him unread, and when he published his controversial views in *Vers l'armée de métier* his name had been struck from the promotion list.[122]

During his glimpse of the Maginot Line in 1936, Churchill had thought the Conseil's doctrine sound. He later wrote that, lacking "access to official information for so many years," he had not comprehended "the violence effected since the last war by the incursion of a mass of fast-moving enemy armour. I knew about it, but it had not altered my convictions as it should have done."[123]

Indeed it should. He had fathered the tank in 1915, when it had been ridiculed as "Winston's Folly." And he was the last man in Parliament to plead backbencher lack of "access to official information." It is doubtful that any man at the cabinet table, including the prime minister, was as well-informed about the War Office, Admiralty, and RAF, all of which he had headed at one time or another, and whose staffs included officers who saw to it that he was kept abreast of the latest military developments. Moreover, as chancellor of the Exchequer he had witnessed the spectacular maneuvers of Britain's Experimental Armoured Force on Salisbury Plain in 1927, which vindicated advocates of high-speed tank forces. Nevertheless, as late as 1938 Churchill had written that "the tank has, no doubt, a great part to play; but I personally doubt very much whether it will ever again see the palmy days of 1918. . . . Nowadays the anti-tank rifle and the anti-tank gun have made such strides that the poor tank cannot carry thick enough skin to stand up to them."[124]

Other views had been suggested to him. The most imaginative came from Captain Basil Liddell Hart. After the Armistice, Liddell Hart had served on the team which drafted the new infantry training manual. Then, and later as military correspondent of *The Times,* he had set forth the first practical alternative to the entrenched, deadlocked siege warfare he had survived. In its place he proposed an "expanding torrent" offensive, spearheaded by swift, mobile masses of heavy tanks and backed by equally versatile self-propelled guns and infantry, bound for the enemy's rear aboard armored carriers. Liddell Hart urged abandonment of methodical siege techniques, which involved hitting the enemy where he was strongest. Instead, attackers would search for a weak spot in the foe's defenses and pour through it with mobile firepower, creating new fronts deep in the enemy's rear.

Churchill's French was weak, and he had not been exposed to de Gaulle. But he and Lloyd George had met Liddell Hart in Morpeth Mansions and heard him out. At least, Lloyd George had. In his memoirs Liddell Hart wrote: "It was . . . very noticeable that Churchill's mind was apt to focus on a phrase, while Ll. G. seized the point and followed on to the next point. . . . Moreover, Churchill liked to do most of the talking in any discussion." Winston was usually hospitable to military innovations. If he had been slow to grasp the new role of air power, he understood the fragility of England's air defenses. On the ground, however, he still clung to the continuous front school of military thought, remembering when it broke Ludendorff's line and forgetting the four years of heartbreaking, bloody failures before. Perhaps the answer to his inconsistency lay in his youth and his romantic idealization of it ("Twenty to twenty-five!" he often said. "Those are the years!"). Tanks were replacing horses, and at heart he remained a young officer of hussars. In a nostalgic chamber of his mind, Victorian colonial wars, with their negligible casualties — negligible, that is, for the British — would always glitter. He rejoiced in the memory of magnificence and turned away from the squalid, forgetting that the only moral judgments in war are made by the victors, and victorious armies are led by those who have mastered the latest, most efficient tools of their trade.[125]

Nevertheless, he possessed a rare gift for strategy, and he had been more attentive in Morpeth Mansions than Liddell Hart had thought. Spears's most vivid recollection of their eve-of-the-war examination of the Maginot Line, with long sessions of men bowed over map tables, was of Churchill spotting the great weakness in the French defense system. His mouth pursed, his gaze was fixed "as if," Spears wrote in his account, "he were crystal-gazing." He had been smiling; now the smile vanished and he shook his head ominously as he put his finger on the shoulder of the Maginot, where it ended near Montmedy and was extended by field works opposite the Ardennes forest. "He observed," recalled Spears, "that he hoped these field works were strong." He understood that Marshal Pétain had once remarked that the Ardennes was "impassable to strong forces." That view, said Winston, was now "very unwise." He asked Georges to "remember that we are faced with a new weapon, armour in great strength, on which the Germans are no doubt concentrating, and that forests will be particularly tempting to such forces since they will offer concealment from the air."[126]

Spears could not remember Georges's reply, but neither Georges nor Weygand acted upon, or even made note of, Churchill's advice. Yet in its heavily guarded headquarters outside Berlin, the German high command was studying that same spot in the Ardennes. Using tanks, the generals believed, they could outflank the Maginot Line, take Paris, and force the French to their knees — accomplishing in six weeks what their fathers had vainly sought in four years of bloody, frustrating siege warfare.

On Friday, August 18, when Ambassador Schulenburg was climbing walls in Moscow, trapped between his führer's demand for a windup of treaty negotiations with Russia and Stalin's dawdling, Spears and Churchill parted, Spears returning to London and Winston traveling fifty miles north of Paris to Dreux and the château of Consuelo Balsan, born a Vanderbilt and for twenty-six years a duchess of Marlborough. Her 1921 divorce from Charles ("Sunny") Marlborough had been amicable, and the door to her home was always open to Winston and his family. Churchill was aware that galleys and even page proofs were accumulating on his Chartwell desk, but despite his outward display of vigor, he was weary. Believing as always that "a change is as good as a rest," he had decided to paint. Clementine and Mary, now approaching her seventeenth birthday, awaited him there. Because they were "conscious that the sands of peace were fast running out," Mary recalls, their "appreciation of those halcyon summer days was heightened: there was swimming and tennis (so greatly enjoyed by Clementine) and *fraises des bois;* Winston painted a lovely picture of the exquisite old rose-brick house; we visited Chartres cathedral and were drenched in the cool blueness of the windows." As with a song that runs through one's mind, she kept remembering a line from Walter de la Mare: "Look thy last on all things lovely."[127]

Among Consuelo's other guests was Paul Maze, the professional painter and an old friend of Winston's. In his diary Maze noted: "We talked about his visit to the Maginot Line with Georges — very impressed by what he saw." At dinner he was cross, "but with reason," Maze thought, "as the assemblée didn't see any danger ahead. As [Sir Evan] Charteris was walking up the stairs to go to his bed he shouted to me, 'Don't listen to him. He is a warmonger.' " On two successive days he and Winston painted together. Maze wrote that as he worked alongside him, Churchill "suddenly turned to me and said: 'This is the last picture we shall paint in peace for a very long time.' What amazed me was his concentration over his painting. No one but he could have understood more what the possibility of war meant and how ill-prepared we were." As they worked, Winston would remark from time to time on the relative strength of the opposing armies. "They are strong, I tell you, they are strong." Then,

Maze wrote, "his jaw would clench his large cigar, and I felt the determination of his will. 'Ah,' he would say, 'with it all, we shall have
him.' "[128]

After three days at Consuelo's château Winston suddenly left. Later, in
his memoirs, he wrote that he "decided to go home, where at least I could
find out what was going on," promising "my wife I would send her word
in good time." It was August 22; the Germans and the Russians had
announced that final negotiations for their nonaggression pact would begin
tomorrow. Now it was official: the triple alliance was dead. The Allies
could expect no support from the U.S.S.R. The situation was even worse
than they thought. Not only would the pact provide that if either country
should "become the object of belligerent action by a third party," the other
country would "in no manner lend its support to this third power"; in a
secret protocol the signatories agreed to respect each other's "spheres of
influence in Eastern Europe" — the basis, a month later, for the division
of conquered Poland between the Soviet Union and the Reich. Even so, the
impact of the impending treaty on Englishmen may be roughly compared
to that of Pearl Harbor upon Americans. Nicolson, learning of it over the
6:00 P.M. BBC news, described Britain's shock: "This smashes our peace
front and makes our guarantees to Poland, Rumania and Greece very
questionable. How Ribbentrop must chuckle. I feel rather stunned. . . .
I fear that it means we are humbled to the dust." Malcolm Muggeridge
wrote: "Groping down darkened streets, dimly it was felt that a way of life
was failing, its comfortable familiarity passing away never to reappear."[129]

Churchill paused in Paris to lunch with Georges, who produced figures on the strength of the opposing armies, including their fighting spirit.
"The result impressed me so much," Winston later wrote, "that for the
first time I said: 'But you are the masters.' " The general replied: "The
Germans have a very strong army," adding cryptically: "We shall never be
allowed to strike first." French politics, in short, ruled out a French
preemptive strike into the Ruhr after war had been declared — Poland's
only hope and also, as it turned out, France's. Apparently Winston missed
these implications; he left Paris in a cheerful mood. Leaving Dreux, he
had seemed depressed, and Maze had given him a note to be read after he
was on his way: "Don't worry Winston. You *know* that you will be Prime
Minister and lead us to victory."[130]

❧   ❧

"That night," Churchill wrote in his memorandum of events, "I slept
at Chartwell." He did not sleep unguarded. In *The Gathering Storm* he

later wrote: "There were known to be twenty thousand organised German Nazis in England at this time, and it would only have been in accord with their procedure in other friendly countries that the outbreak of war should be preceded by a sharp prelude of sabotage and murder." In February he had spent six pounds, fifteen shillings, on his two guns, having them stripped, cleaned and oiled, fitted with new trigger blades and cross pins, and the two pairs of barrels rejointed. He had hired Inspector W. H. Thompson, the retired Scotland Yard detective who had served as his bodyguard in the 1920s, to resume his old duties. Thompson recalled that in the car on his way home from Croydon Airport, "Mr. Churchill grew graver and graver as he sat wrapped in thought, and then said slowly and thoughtfully: 'Before the harvest is gathered in — we shall be at war.' "[131]

Winston had not asked for official protection, as he wrote afterward, but "I had enough information to convince me that Hitler recognised me as a foe." At Chartwell he and Thompson planned vigils. "While one slept," Churchill wrote, "the other watched. Thus nobody would have had a walkover." He knew "a major burden" would fall upon him if war came — "and who could doubt its coming?" His wife and daughter had no doubts. They followed him to England a few days later, passing through Paris. "On that golden summer evening," Mary recalls, "the Gare du Nord teemed with soldiers: the French army was mobilizing."[132]

In the morning Churchill felt refreshed, and was off to London. Nicolson noted that he "has just returned from Paris and is in high fettle. The French are not at all perturbed by the Russo-German Pact and are prepared to support Poland nonetheless." Winston had "just rung up Paul Reynaud who asserts that all is going well: by which he means war, I suppose." He did, but only because there was no honorable alternative. A year ago the pied piper at No. 10 had thought there was. This new crisis was the bitter price they must pay for that error. Their exigency had worsened. There were no Czech divisions to march with them now, and the Russians — who had been ready to fight for Czechoslovakia — had shifted sides. Churchill believed that if the Allies had taken a firm stand at Munich, it "would have prevented war," and "if worse had come to worst, we should have been far better off than we may be at some future date."[133]

This was that future date. He devoted the night of his return to writing an article for the *Daily Mirror* — "At the Eleventh Hour" — which appeared on August 24. In the light of the "intrigue" between the Nazis and the Communists, he wrote, it was becoming "increasingly difficult to see how war can be averted." Events, he stated, were "moving forward from every quarter and along all roads to catastrophe. The German military preparations have already reached a point where action on the greatest scale is possible at any moment." That afternoon, August 24, Chamberlain recalled Parliament — to reach the House of Commons MPs had to pass through a line of pickets carrying signs bearing the single name CHURCHILL in a blue circle. The House approved an emergency war powers bill; the Royal Navy was ordered to its war stations, reservists were called up, twenty-five merchantmen were requisitioned for conversion to armed merchant cruisers, leaves were canceled, the Dominions alerted, and twenty-four thousand reservists ordered to man ack-ack batteries, radar stations, and balloon stations.

Britain was springing to arms, but not eagerly. In 1914, London, including Parliament, had thrilled with war fever. Now — and this was also true of Paris and Berlin — the mood was somber and resigned. Victor Cazalet wrote in his diary that the House had been "very full" and that Chamberlain had made "a good but not very impressive speech." Afterward, he added, "I sat in Smoking Room with LG and Winston. Both v anti-Chamberlain. Think he has led us into this mess. We ought never to have given guarantees to Poland unless they had consented to allow Russian army across their frontiers." Nicolson joined the group in the smoking room; he had heard rumors that the P.M. had offered to resign if war came and that the King would refuse to accept. That evening Churchill dined at the Savoy with Duff Cooper, Eden, Sandys, and Sinclair. In his diary Duff Cooper noted: "We were all very gloomy."[134]

On August 25, His Majesty's Government, recognizing the gravity of Poland's peril in light of the Nazi-Soviet Pact, signed a formal treaty of alliance with the Poles, turning a unilateral guarantee into a bilateral pact. Britain's obligation to Poland was now far more binding. The next Tuesday, after talking to Churchill on the telephone, Eddie Marsh noted in his diary that Winston had said "Hitler was evidently rattled, but he didn't see how he could climb down, which would cost him his life." That same day the FO also sent Berlin a note urging Germany not to attempt a Danzig coup. Churchill read it before it was sent — he always managed to be in the Foreign Office at critical moments, alerted by his informants there — and doubted that the message was strong enough. Duff Cooper, another diarist, noted that Vansittart had assured them that "HMG's note to Hitler was everything that could be desired. Winston rang up the Polish ambassador while we were there, who said that he was now completely satisfied with the support he was receiving from our Government."[135]

On Saturday, Ironside, driving down to Chartwell for lunch, had found Winston "full of Georges, whom he had seen over in France. I found that he had become very French in his outlook. . . . The burden of his song was that we must have a great Army in France, that we couldn't depend upon the French to do our effort for us." He wanted twenty British divisions across the Channel by Christmas. Before Ironside left Chartwell,

Winston observed that His Majesty's Government, in trying to sway European events, was taking a far more imperious pose than its military establishment warranted — that, as Ironside paraphrased him, "We were trying to get as much control in the conduct of affairs as if we had an Army of one and a half millions."[136]

Churchill thought HMG still did not fully appreciate that the great danger on the Continent required urgent measures. The prime minister and members of the cabinet, apparently believing this was just one more crisis which could be solved by deferring to the Führer, continued to be relatively passive as the week unfolded. With a few outstanding exceptions — Shirer, Colvin, Sheean, John Gunther, and the best of the London press corps — press dispatches from the Continent did not reflect a need for speed. One of Winston's most reliable sources was Geoffrey Parsons of the *New York Herald Tribune*. On Sunday Parsons wired Chartwell: "Send you this by telegraph since hours are numbered. Impossible to exaggerate confidence of Hitler and German people that British will capitulate. . . . Nobody has expected anything but swift easy victory over Poles, having been fed idea British would never fight over Danzig or Poland. . . . General cynicism toward British attitude amazes me after visit to London. But it exists in opinion of American observers in Britain."[137]

Chamberlain seems to have sensed as much, and, within the bounds of his desire to avoid offending the Führer, had been taking steps to counter this impression. On August 22 he had written a personal letter to Hitler, informing him that Britain was now on a war footing. This alert, he said, was the result of German troop movements and the assumption "in some quarters in Berlin" that since the announcement of Germany's agreement with Russia "intervention by Great Britain on behalf of Poland is no longer a contingency that need be reckoned with. No greater mistake could be made." Whatever the nature of Hitler's pact with Stalin, the P.M. wrote, "it cannot alter Great Britain's obligation to Poland, which His Majesty's Government have stated in public repeatedly and plainly, and which they are determined to fulfill."[138]

Ambassador Henderson flew to Berchtesgaden, arriving at Hitler's mountain retreat about noon on Wednesday, the twenty-third, to deliver the P.M.'s letter. Hitler was on edge — thirty Wehrmacht divisions were moving toward the Polish frontier — and his response, according to Henderson's cable to Halifax, was "excitable," couched in language "violent and exaggerated both as regards England and Poland." The situation of Germans in Poland had become intolerable, he shouted; *Polendeutsche* were even being subjected to *"kastrieren"* ("castration"). If Britain did not force the Poles to stop these outrages, the Reich would be forced to begin *"Gegenmassnahmen"* ("counter measures"). Later that day, he again received Henderson. This time his temper was under control, which made what he had to say all the more appalling. He was "fifty years old," he said, and "preferred war now" to when he "would be fifty-five or sixty." It was "surely quite clear to everyone that the World War would not have been lost" had he "been Chancellor at the time." In his formal, uncompromising reply to Chamberlain, he declared that the Reich had displayed "unparalleled magnanimity" in its attempts to settle the Danzig and Polish Corridor problems. Then, in what Churchill later called "a piece of lying effrontery," the *Kriegsherr* charged that England's "unconditional assurance" to Poland "could only be interpreted in that country as an encouragement henceforward to unloose, under cover of such a charter, a wave of appalling terrorism against the one and a half million German inhabitants living in Poland."[139]

In Danzig and Poland, local Nazis were following the modus operandi which had played so well in Austria and Czechoslovakia. Local Nazi storm troopers in uniform sacked stores owned by Jews, painted huge yellow swastikas on synagogues, and assaulted critics of their führer in the streets. In Polish communities where Germans were a majority, policemen cheered them on. Meantime German newspapers were telling their readers the exact opposite — that the victims were *Polendeutsche*, stalked by Polish terrorists. In Karlsruhe the daily paper carried the headline "WARSAW THREATENS BOMBARDMENT OF DANZIG — UNBELIEVABLE AGITATION OF THE POLISH ARCHMADNESS! [POLNISCHEN GRÖSSENWAHN]." "POLEN, GIB ACHT!" ("POLAND, LOOK OUT!") warned the *Berliner Arbeiterzeitung;* "ANSWER TO POLAND, THE RUNNER-AMOK [AMOKLÄUFER] AGAINST PEACE AND RIGHT IN EUROPE!" On Saturday, August 26, the *Zwölf-Uhr Blatt* reported: "THIS PLAYING WITH FIRE GOING TOO FAR — THREE GERMAN PASSENGER PLANES SHOT AT BY POLES — IN CORRIDOR MANY GERMAN FARMHOUSES IN FLAMES!" The banner headline in the *Berliner Arbeiterzeitung* that day read, "COMPLETE CHAOS IN POLAND — GERMAN FAMILIES FLEE — POLISH SOLDIERS PUSH TO EDGE OF GERMAN BORDER!" Goebbels saved his masterpiece for the Sunday *Völkischer Beobachter:*

ALL OF POLAND IN A WAR FEVER! 1.5 MILLION MEN MOBILIZED!
UNINTERRUPTED TROOP TRANSPORT TOWARD FRONTIER!
CHAOS IN UPPER SILESIA![140]

William L. Shirer notes dryly: "There was no mention, of course, of any German mobilization." Germany had been fully mobilized for two weeks, but the Poles, anxious to avoid provoking the Reich, and on British advice, had actually delayed their mobilization. Only thirty Polish divisions were in position to defend their frontiers. The Germans had massed fifty-six divisions, including nine armored, on Poland's borders. Two great pincer movements were prepared to overwhelm the defenders, troops whose leaders had no plan and cherished an absolute faith in the power of cavalry charges to defeat modern tanks.[141]

The Anglo-Polish Treaty of Mutual Assistance, as announced in London and Warsaw that last Friday in August, was a model of clarity. Article One clearly stated that should either country fall victim to aggression, the other would declare war on the offenders. To strengthen this, Article Two provided that this action would be triggered in the event of "any action by a European Power which clearly threatened, directly or indirectly, the independence of one of the contracting parties."

That was the way to handle Hitler. Yet despite Chamberlain's firm words in Parliament, the indecisiveness and yearning for German friendship were still there. When Hitler studied the text of the pact, he found no mention of Danzig. Since the free city was not Polish soil, he assumed that England was not committed to its defense. Actually England *was,* but Halifax had been unwilling to commit himself openly, and so — in an act of prodigious diplomatic incompetence — the guarantee to defend Danzig's status quo had been entered in a secret clause of the treaty. It would have been better to omit it entirely. As Duff Cooper had written in July: "Lack of decision is the worst fault from which a policy can suffer. So soon as a decision has been taken no time should be lost in announcing it. . . . It is of the first importance that we should know our own minds; it is of almost equal importance that the world should make no mistake about our intentions." Halifax, by clouding HMG's intentions, should have forfeited his office on this issue alone.[142]

Misunderstandings between the dictators and the democracies were inevitable anyhow; never, in the long reach of European history, had two more disparate cultures coexisted. The Nazis and Fascists were convinced that they were, as an admiring Anne Morrow Lindbergh called them, "the wave of the future." To celebrities from the West the societies created by the Duce and the Führer were impressive. They seemed efficient. There were no strikes, no demonstrations, no disrespect for authority. The *Gleichschaltung* — political coordination and the elimination of opponents — of Hitler's new order meant more productive assembly lines, organized holidays for workers, and an inspired, patriotic youth. It was heartening to see blond Aryan boys in short leather pants running through the fields hand-in-hand with blond, buxom Aryan girls, though visitors were seldom told why they were so enthusiastic. Once they were out of sight, the boy's lederhosen were shucked while his companion, as a loyal member of the Bund Deutscher Maedel, hoisted her skirts to enjoy Strength through Joy, pleasing the Führer by increasing the population of his Reich, which, he said, would always need soldiers. The young were the most ardent Nazis, but enthusiasm for the regime was found among Germans of every age and on every social level. They had always been a regimented people, and did not seem to mind the loss of personal freedom. They rallied to the slogans *"Gemeinnutz vor Eigennutz"* ("The Common Interest before Self-interest") and *"Kanonen statt Butter"* ("Guns instead of Butter"). Those who preferred liberty and butter absconded or remained silent. In the Third Reich *Gleichschaltung* wasn't for everybody, just everybody who wanted to live.

Nothing in the democracies, including the United States, matched the euphoria of this lusty carnival, these vigorous folk who never jaywalked, never argued with their superiors, who listened meekly when upbraided by policemen yet turned viciously on those they considered *Untermenschen*, their inferiors. They seemed to spend an inordinate amount of their time marching, and singing stirring songs as they marched: *"Die Wacht am Rhein," "Bomben auf Polen,"* the *"Horst Wessel Lied,"* and *"Deutschland über Alles"* (*". . . über alles in der Welt"*).

Since the United States was among *alles in der Welt,* and Franklin Roosevelt was determined not to see the swastika hoisted in Washington, the president asked Congress for $552 million to strengthen American defense. He also appealed to Hitler to keep his sword sheathed. The Führer ignored him; he held all democracies in contempt, seeing them as weak, indecisive, and easily bullied. Many in England, France, and the United States agreed with him. Each democracy now had its strong, local Fascist movement, and even those who scored dictatorships wondered whether their countrymen had gone "soft."

In the Nazis' book burning of May 10, 1933, Goebbels, who had struck the first match, had declared: "The soul of the German people can again express itself." Implicit here was the Nazi conviction that beneath the veneer of modern culture was the primitive vigor of a warrior race; of noble savages, supple and powerfully built; of those ancient Germans who, Tacitus had written, were conspicuous for their "fierce blue eyes, red hair, tall frames," and whose loyalty to their chieftain was absolute. Strip away that veneer, the Nazi ideologues told one another, and Germany, redeemed, would be invincible. What they overlooked was that it was true of all civilized nations. Deutschland was not the only European nation with proud military traditions. British soldiers had been winning battles, and the Royal Navy sinking ships, three centuries before Bismarck welded the three hundred states of central Europe into the German Empire. Churchill was putting it on record every night. It was Britain's misfortune, and the world's, that the men at the helm of His Majesty's Government in 1939 had lost England's compass and, lacking the wisdom of Caesar, thought you could strike a deal by shaking hands with barbarians.

Britain was by treaty committed to the defense of Danzig, but in fact HMG's position was very different. Immediately after signing the Anglo-Polish treaty on Friday, August 25 — the first day of the last week of peace — Halifax told the Polish ambassador that while he recognized "how vital to Poland was the position in Danzig," he did not feel that "if there were ever any opportunity of conversations being held about Danzig, the Polish Government would be right or wise to reject it." Indeed, he thought the Poles "would make a great mistake if they sought to adopt a position in which discussions of peaceful modifications of the status of Danzig were ruled out." Despite Daladier, members of the French government were frantically trying to abandon their ally in the east; a member of Daladier's cabinet said publicly: "There is nothing to be done but to allow Germany to have her way." To further enfeeble opposition to Hitler, England and France were trying to approach the Führer through Mussolini, although neither democracy was informing the other.[143]

The Poles, wary of yielding an inch to the Germans, believed that any concession over Danzig would lead to new Nazi demands. In Warsaw the British ambassador, Sir Howard Kennard, had returned from leave, to the relief of his exhausted chargé. Kennard was blessed with clearer vision than any senior diplomat in Whitehall except the shelved Vansittart. To the Foreign Office he explained that "if Hitler decides on war, it is for the sole purpose of destroying Polish independence."[144]

But HMG was sure Hitler could be bought off for less, if only they could get him to state his price. Hitler, too, with the invasion of Poland nearly at hand, needed to know what Britain would do. On August 25, the Führer summoned Henderson to the chancellery. There Hitler told him, as the ambassador afterward reported to Whitehall, that he "accepts the British Empire and is willing to pledge himself personally for its continued existence." Once "the problem of Danzig and the Corridor" was resolved, Hitler would convey "an offer" detailing how his few colonial demands could be "negotiated by peaceful methods." But first, HMG must inform him of its attitude toward the Polish problem.[145]

Meantime the Duce was trying desperately to stop the Nazi juggernaut from rolling into Poland, not to spare the Poles or avert another general war, but because, as Germany's ally, he was pledged to fight beside Hitler and couldn't do it. On the morning of August 25 he found himself in an unaccustomed state of acute embarrassment. The Führer had sent him an urgent personal letter, alerting him to the Wehrmacht's imminent plunge into Poland. The Führer had written: "In case of intolerable events in Poland, I shall act immediately."

Mussolini's reply reached Hitler at about 6:00 P.M. According to Schmidt, it staggered him. He had not asked for Italy's help; under the three-month-old Pact of Steel it was taken for granted. But Hitler and Chamberlain were not the only European statesmen prepared to break their word. In his answer to Hitler's letter, the Duce said flatly that if the Reich made war on the Poles, Italy must be counted out. "The Italian war preparations," he said, were not complete; he was unprepared to "resist the attack which the French and English would predominantly direct against us." It had been his understanding "at our meetings [that] the war was envisaged for 1942, and by that time I would have been ready." After Hitler read it, he summoned Keitel and shouted: "Stop everything! At once!" Thus the invasion of Poland — *Fall Weiss* — was postponed to September 1.[146]

As Europe slept, Churchill stood hunched over his Disraeli desk, correcting galleys, revising passages with his red pen, or dictating inserts to Mrs. Hill, who sat over the keyboard of a silent typewriter, her fingers at the ready. He was telling the tale of an earlier Britain, when, in time of war or the threat of war, pusillanimous officials were flogged or hung. He went back to the birth of Britain, to the Roman occupation, the departure of Rome's legions, and the chaos that followed in the fifth century when, as the Welsh monk Nennius recorded, invading Saxons ("Sessoynes") from Germany plundered the island's quilt of little kingdoms, raping, looting, and spreading disease. The desperate kings turned to a dux bellorum *— no monarch, but in those times something far more prestigious: a military commander of great gifts and courage — known to history as Arthur. Arthur brought England a century of peace by defeating the Saxons in twelve mighty battles, the greatest of which, "the crowning mercy," as Churchill called it, was fought on Mount Badon at some time between 490 and 503. Now in 1939, at Chartwell, he invested Arthur with a crown and wrote that his "name takes us out of the mist of dimly remembered history into the daylight of romance. There looms, large, uncertain, dim but glittering, the legend of King Arthur. . . . Somewhere in the Island a great captain gathered the forces of Roman Britain and fought the barbarian invaders to the death. Around him, around his name and deeds shine all that romance and poetry can bestow."*[147]

In London three days were devoted to preparing an official reply to Hitler's insolent offer to "accept" the British Empire once Polish problems were solved. Horace Wilson and Rab Butler completed the first draft that

Friday. Chamberlain reworked it until late in the evening. At 6:30 P.M. Saturday it was presented to the full cabinet, with Henderson present, presumably to offer the views of the German führer. There was, it turned out, nothing in it which he would have found objectionable. The reply was largely devoted to the need for Polish concessions, or the lack of them. Hitler had been insisting that they must give way, and HMG agreed. Hore-Belisha thought this first draft "fulsome, obsequious and deferential." He wrote in his diary that he had "urged that our only effective reply was to show strength and determination — that in no circumstances" should England "give the impression that we would weaken in our undertaking to Poland. Kingsley Wood supported me." Discussion continued awhile longer, then the group adjourned for the night.[148]

To Frenchmen it is *La Manche,* to Germans *der Ärmelkanal,* but Britons and Americans know it as the English Channel, and with some justification; it has long served the British as a formidable moat, the equivalent, in military terms, of perhaps a hundred divisions. It is not, however, unbridgeable. The Romans, Saxons, and Normans hurdled it. Philip II, Louis XIV, and Napoleon tried and came close. Concern about invasion fueled "isolationism," as the Victorians called it, three generations before Americans thought the concept theirs; and until Neville Chamberlain decided to chart his own foreign policy, it served as the keystone of British foreign policy in Europe. The island's safety, it was held, rested upon two stout principles. First, no nation possessing a great army would be permitted to seize the lowlands, Belgium and Holland. It was Germany's violation of Belgian territory which had triggered England's declaration of war in 1914. Second, power on the Continent would be shared by two or more nations. Chamberlain was the first prime minister to encourage domination by one, believing that Anglo-German friendship would guarantee peace, and — until Ribbentrop and Molotov signed their treaty of alliance in Moscow — that the Third Reich was a bulwark against Soviet imperialism. However, England's encouragement of balanced power in Europe had been challenged in every century, most frequently by France, but most memorably, perhaps, by Spain.

Prowling back and forth in his study — muttering while Mrs. Hill's fingers flew over her keyboard — Churchill reworked the story of Philip II's Great Armada. Philip II of Spain, envisaging his empire as the worldly arm of the Roman Catholic church, and himself as its sword, had plunged into all the religious wars of the time, guided by the faith that the Reformation could be undone and all Europe reunited in a single faith, regardless of the cost. Henry VIII had led England out of the church. Now his daughter Elizabeth was defending her father's Reformation. Philip, honing his blade, became obsessed with England, and when the northern Netherlands broke loose from Catholicism in 1581, he began building his "invincible Armada," over 132 vessels bearing 3,165 cannon and 30,000 men, intent upon the conquest of Britain. Lord Leicester could muster but 20,000 untrained men. This force could not defend the beaches, and the fate of the island therefore rested with the fleet.

If the British prevailed, rule of the seas would pass from Spain to England. There, too, however, prospects seemed dim. Only 34 of the Queen's ships were seaworthy, all of them smaller than the enemy's galleons. They were joined by 36 privately owned vessels. It didn't seem enough. But the Royal Navy was led by captains like John Hawkins and Francis Drake, the finest seamen the world had known. The size of their craft was misleading; based on his experience as a buccaneer in colonial waters, Hawkins had radically altered the design of English ships, cutting down the castles which had towered over decks, mounting heavier, long-range guns, and deepening keels and concentrating on seaworthiness and speed.

Perhaps the island's greatest weapon, however, was its sovereign. Now in her mid-fifties, she had ruled England for thirty years, as long as Philip had Spain, and was as skilled in the use of power. She knew how to wear the crown, how to use it, and, in this hour of national peril, how to arouse her people in its defense. "The nation was united in the face of Spanish preparations," Churchill wrote. "While the Armada was still off England Queen Elizabeth reviewed the army at Tilbury and addressed them in these stirring words:

"Let tyrants fear. I have always so behaved myself that, under God, I have placed my chiefest strength and safeguard in the loyal hearts and goodwill of my subjects; and therefore I am come amongst you, as you see, resolved, in the midst and heat of the battle, to live or die amongst you, to lay down for my God, and for my kingdom, and for my people, my honour and my blood, even in the dust. I know I have the body of a weak and feeble woman, but I have the heart and stomach of a king, and of a king of England too, and think foul scorn that Parma or Spain or any prince of Europe should dare to invade the borders of my realm; to which, rather than any dishonour shall grow by me, I myself will take up arms, I myself will be your general, judge and rewarder of every one of your virtues in the field."[149]

The first appeaser Hitler had laid eyes on had been Halifax, when the noble lord had visited the Berghof nearly two years earlier and had mistaken the master of the Reich for a servant. The Führer, skilled at taking a man's measure, told his guest that all SS men were shown the film *Lives of a Bengal*

Lancer because it depicted "a handful of Englishmen holding a continent in thrall." It was then that he had recommended that Gandhi be shot. Halifax's lack of enthusiasm, Hitler told his interpreter, triggered his first suspicion that the heirs to the British Empire were weak and irresolute. In mid-August, with the crisis over Poland growing, he had decided to probe. To Karl Burckhardt of the League of Nations he expressed "great sympathy" for Halifax: "I thought he was a man who saw things on a big scale and desired a peaceful solution. I hope one day to see him again." Burckhardt sent London an account of these remarks and Halifax began "considering" sending a member of His Majesty's Government to talk to the Führer. Another Munich seemed to be shaping up.[150]

On August 27 the P.M. met with Birger Dahlerus, a Swedish businessman and friend of Göring who served as an unofficial go-between that week. Dahlerus, who had arrived in London from Berlin that afternoon, told Chamberlain, Wilson, Halifax, and Cadogan that Danzig and the corridor were indeed Hitler's targets. To Dahlerus, Halifax emphasized the necessity of "direct discussions" between the Germans and the Poles. Now that HMG "knew" that Danzig was the Nazi objective, England could force Beck to yield it. This should be construed, the foreign secretary told Dahlerus, not as England's final position, "but rather to prepare the way for the main communication" — to establish, in short, a procedure for meeting further Nazi demands. In Berlin the Swede saw Göring that evening, but not the Führer: "Hitler too tired," he wired the Foreign Office. Halifax said he understood; the Führer had many burdens. In the morning — it was now Monday, August 28 — Dahlerus was granted an audience in the chancellery. To Halifax he quoted the chancellor: "Great Britain must persuade Poland to negotiate with Germany." It was "most important," Hitler said, that "Sir N. Henderson" bring him a statement affirming that England had undertaken to so persuade the Poles. The desirability of this was underscored after a cabinet meeting that afternoon, when the foreign secretary received a telegram from Sir George Ogilvie Forbes, counsellor in Britain's Berlin embassy. Ogilvie Forbes quoted Dahlerus as saying: "Herr Hitler suspects that the Poles will try to avoid negotiations. Reply should therefore contain a clear statement to the effect that the Poles have been strongly advised *immediately to establish contact* with Germany and negotiate." Halifax now took a step without precedent. He wired Kennard in Warsaw: "His Majesty's Government earnestly hope that . . . Polish Government . . . is ready *to enter at once into direct discussion* with Germany. Please endeavour to see M. Beck at once and telephone reply." Thus, without consulting or even informing the cabinet, Halifax turned a Nazi demand into British foreign policy, thereby weakening Britain's sole ally in the east. If the Wehrmacht crushed Poland,

Hitler could turn and hurl the full fury of his might against France, Britain's only ally in the west. Should France be overwhelmed, England would stand alone, facing the first European power in a century to threaten the very existence of Britain by vaulting the Channel.[151]

At Chartwell Churchill was writing Bill Deakin: "I have tried to fit these Galleys together. The present arrangement is quite impossible. I send you my own copies, where the Galleys are arranged more or less in chronological order. I see no use mixing up sections about Pitt and George III with separate studies of the American colonies." The Canadian section was "more or less complete"; so was the one on India. All that would be gathered together under the heading "The First British Empire," to be followed by a chapter called either "The Great Pitt" or "The Seven Years' War," describing "the position of the First British Empire as it stands at the Peace of Paris 1763." The next would be "The Quarrels of the English Speaking Peoples," covering "the reign of George III." George III is not remembered as an admirable sovereign, and not only because of his madness; but his years on the throne were marked by stirring events and the deeds of great men, among them the greatest military hero in the history of England. Winston had told his tale, and it lay in the galleys he was correcting before their dispatch to Deakin.[152]

By the autumn of 1805 Napoleon had massed his invasion barges at Boulogne. The Royal Navy's blockade of the Continent, built around nearly forty ships of the line, had frustrated French plans to cross the Channel in force, but now, Churchill wrote, "Napoleon . . . believed that the British fleets were dispersed and that the moment had come for invasion."

The decisive battle took place in the waters off Cape Trafalgar, Spain. Nelson was outnumbered and outgunned. At daybreak on October 21 he saw, "from the quarterdeck of the Victory, *the battle line of the enemy" — an advance squadron of twelve Spanish ships and twenty-one French ships of the line under Villeneuve. He signaled his captains to form for the attack in two columns. Then:*

Nelson went down to his cabin to compose a prayer. "May the Great God whom I worship grant to my country and for the benefit of Europe a great and glorious Victory. . . . For myself, I commit my life to Him who made me, and may His blessing light upon my endeavours for serving my country faithfully."

The fleets were drawing nearer and nearer. Another signal was run up upon the Victory, *"England expects every man will do his duty. . . ."*

A deathly silence fell upon the fleet as the ships drew nearer. Each captain marked down his adversary, and within a few minutes the two English columns thundered into action. . . . The Victory *smashed through between Villeneuve's flagships, the* Bucentaure, *and the* Redoutable. *The three ships remained locked together, raking each other with broadsides. Nelson was pacing as if on parade on his quarterdeck when at 1:15 p.m. he was shot from the mast-head of the* Redoutable *in the shoulder. His backbone was broken, and he was carried below amid the thunder of the* Victory's *guns. . . . In the log of the* Victory *occurs this passage, "Partial firing continued until 4.30, when a victory having been reported to the Right Hon. Lord Viscount Nelson, K.B. and Commander-in-Chief, he then died of his wound."*[153]

Chamberlain and Henderson were to die of cancer, Chamberlain in the autumn of 1940, Henderson two years later. Halifax spent the war years as Britain's ambassador in Washington, was created an earl in 1944, and died, aged seventy-eight, on December 23, 1959, thus surviving for over fourteen years the 357,116 Britons killed during the war.

🦁   🦁

The pressure on Warsaw worked. Two hours after receiving Halifax's wire, Kennard replied to the FO: "Poland is ready to enter at once into direct discussions with Germany." His instincts had told him that negotiations with the Nazis could lead only to disaster, but disaster lay at the end of every turning. Now, at last, HMG could give Hitler the reply he wanted, and that evening Ambassador Henderson met with Hitler to deliver the British note. Poland had given assurances that she was ready to "enter into discussions." The next step should now be to initiate negotiations between Germany and Poland. Instead of responding directly to the suggestion of negotiations, Hitler extended the limits of absurdity by asking whether Britain "would be willing to accept an alliance with Germany." An abler diplomat would have realized that Hitler was muddying the waters and raising a question of future policy while they were in the midst of a crisis requiring immediate solution. Beyond that was the fact, noted by Vansittart, that "an alliance means a military alliance if it means anything. And against whom should we be allying ourselves with such a gang as the present regime in Germany? The merest suggestion of it would ruin us in the United States." It would also have destroyed British credibility in countries to whom England was committed: France, Poland, Rumania, Turkey, and Greece. But Henderson's answer to the Führer, as he reported it to the FO, was that "speaking personally I did not exclude such a possibility."[154]

For an ambassador to express an opinion on such an issue was inexcusable. The FO sharply told Henderson that he had gone too far and turned the offer down. Incredibly, Henderson failed to tell the Führer that Britain had rejected his proposal. During their talk Hitler had spoken of "annihilating Poland," which ought to have alerted anyone, much less a diplomat, to the momentous fact that he would not be satisfied with Danzig. Yet Halifax ordered the reference deleted from the account of Henderson's meeting that was sent to Warsaw.[155]

Hitler wanted this problem, which he had created, to be resolved by bloodshed, but the Poles must be made to appear culpable. Receiving Henderson on Tuesday, the twenty-ninth, the Führer dispensed with the tact, civility, and outward show of mutual respect required in discourse between civilized nations. Instead, he demanded the appearance in Berlin of a Polish negotiator "with full powers" the following day.[156]

Even Henderson was astonished. He blurted out that this was *"ein Diktat."* Hitler and Ribbentrop, he later reported to Halifax, "strenuously and heatedly" denied it. The British ambassador left the chancellery "depressed by my own inadequacy" and "filled with the gloomiest foreboding." Danzig, he told Whitehall, "must revert to Germany."[157]

Halifax's response was a procedural suggestion. He, too, saw the Führer's demands as an ultimatum and suggested that instead they be called "proposals," offered as "a basis for discussion." Hitler agreed to this meaningless rephrasing, but it would still be necessary, he insisted, for a Pole qualified to speak for his government to appear in Berlin immediately. This was a problem. The Poles, under pressure and against their better judgment, had agreed to discussions with the Reich, but they balked at the Nazi demand that they send a negotiator, armed with full powers, on the next plane to Berlin. For them to do otherwise would have been madness; Hitler had yet to set forth formal proposals. Until he had, and until Warsaw had studied them, talks between the two sovereign powers would be meaningless — unless, of course, the Poles capitulated, which, they suspected, was what the Führer wanted.[158]

That the Poles continued to assert their rights was considered by Britain's ambassador to the Reich a sign of exaggerated "prestige" and *"amour propre."* Henderson advised Robert Coulondre, his French counterpart, "strongly to recommend" to Paris that France advise the Polish government "to propose the immediate visit of M. Beck as constituting in my opinion the sole chance now of preventing war." He "implored" the Polish ambassador in Berlin, Lipski, to ask the immediate dispatch of a negotiator from Warsaw, as commanded by the Führer and chancellor of the Greater German Reich.[159]

The pressure on the Polish government was becoming massive. At noon Wednesday Henderson, in one of his unauthorized trespasses into areas where he did not belong, approached the papal nuncio in Berlin and suggested that the pope put forward some "definite impartial solution," such as a neutral frontier patrolled by Catholic priests. The papal nuncio replied that he thought laymen would be more suitable. Unknown to either Henderson or the nuncio, the pope, after talking to Mussolini, was already in touch with Warsaw. He believed, he told the Poles, that prospects of peace would improve if they surrendered Danzig. Then, he reasoned, Hitler would be willing to negotiate over the corridor and minority problems. The pontiff thought this suggestion should receive the "most careful consideration of the Poles."[160]

Polish obstinacy, Chamberlain concluded, was the greatest obstacle to peace. Ambassador Joseph Kennedy wired the State Department: "Frankly he is more worried about getting the Poles to be reasonable than the Germans." At the cabinet meeting that Wednesday morning, only Hore-Belisha opposed pressing Beck to dispatch a negotiator to Germany. He thought it "important," he said, "to make it clear that we are not going to yield on this point," and he opposed any negotiations, anywhere, while the Führer was threatening Warsaw and massing his troops in Poland's borders. The cabinet agreed that Hitler's ultimatum was "wholly unreasonable." But the "really important thing," Halifax told them, was the German agreement to negotiate. The Polish government should "be prepared to do so without delay."[161]

Forcing the weak to submit is clearly easier than confronting the strong, particularly if you have persuaded yourself that the weak deserve what is coming to them. At Berchtesgaden, Godesberg, and Munich, Chamberlain had discovered flaws in the Czechs which had previously escaped his attention. So it was now with the Poles. Henderson worried that the Poles might provoke the Führer's wrath and "force" the Nazis to move against Poland. Actually, all the provocation had been on the other side, though the Nazis had gone to great lengths to make it appear otherwise. On Hitler's orders the Sicherheitsdienst, the SS security service, had dressed a dozen German prisoners in Polish uniforms. Identical uniforms were to be worn by SS men who would "lead" them in a simulated attack on a German radio station near the Polish border, holding it long enough for a Nazi fluent in Polish to announce Poland's invasion of the Reich. The criminals — whose code name was *Konserven* (Canned Goods) — would be given lethal injections by an SS doctor and then shot; their bloody bodies would be shown to the foreign press as evidence of Polish aggression.[162]

To the appeasers, efforts to avoid war were, ipso facto, virtuous, and they assumed that all sensible men would agree. But in Berlin making war was a virtue, and those who shrank from it were base. The Men of Munich never grasped this, and Henderson was staggered when the Nazis, whom he had regarded as his friends and future allies, decided that the time had come to humiliate him. On the evening of Wednesday, August 30, a German courier summoned Henderson to the Foreign Ministry. He expected the best. The Führer's diplomats were assumed to have drawn up proposals for a solution, and these, he hoped, would be the subject of their discussions.

There were no discussions. It was after midnight when Ribbentrop ordered him into his office. "From the outset," Henderson wrote in his memoirs, "his manner was one of intense hostility, which increased in violence. . . . He kept jumping up to his feet in a state of great excitement, folding his arms across his chest, and asking if I had anything more to say." He then interrupted each attempt to reply — though Henderson was trying to tell him that HMG had "consistently warned" the Poles against "all provocative action." The bewildered ambassador did manage to say that if the Reich's proposals were ready, HMG "could be counted upon to do their best in Warsaw to temporise negotiations." At this, the Nazi minister produced a long document and read it aloud "as fast as he could," Henderson wrote, "in a tone of utmost scorn and annoyance." There were sixteen points — the return of Danzig, a plebiscite in the corridor, sovereignty over Gdynia, a redrawing of boundaries, and on and on — but Henderson, as he wrote afterward, "did not attempt to follow too closely," assuming the paper would be handed to him at the end.[163]

It wasn't. Ribbentrop pocketed it, saying that since no Polish negotiator had come to Berlin, the proposals were "now too late." It was now the last day of August, the last day of peace. Henderson spent it frantically trying to get Beck, Lipski, or some senior Polish official to call on Ribbentrop. It is unlikely that any of them would have been received. Hitler admitted to Schmidt, his interpreter, that his offer to negotiate was a pretext. "I needed an alibi," he said, "especially with the German people, to show them that I had done everything to maintain peace." That, he said, explained his "generous offer" to settle *die Danziger und Korridor-Frage.* In any event, the Poles, proud and defiant, were not much interested in the advice of Henderson or any well-meaning go-between. Dahlerus told Horace Wilson that it had become "obvious to us" that the Poles were "obstructing" possible negotiations.[164]

Indeed they were. They didn't trust England anymore, though Wilson, Henderson, Halifax, and Chamberlain couldn't imagine why. Churchill could have told them, and later did. Ribbentrop's lies about Polish brutality had been believed; Beck's reports of Nazi atrocities rejected. Halifax and Chamberlain had confided in Dirksen, yet were evasive, not only with the Polish ambassador, Raczyński, but also with the French. They were violating, both in letter and spirit, solemn treaties they themselves had drafted and signed a few days earlier. The prospect of fighting was unthinkable to them, unimaginable and inconceivable, and it had unmanned them. In their desperate attempts to avoid it they had resorted to trickery and deception. And they were still in business. As Hoare had told the cabinet on Monday, should German troops invade Poland they could "always fulfil the letter of a declaration without going all out." In short, declare war but not wage it. The *dux bellorum* Arthur, Elizabeth I, Hawkins, Drake, and Nelson wouldn't have known what he was talking about, and Churchill would be slow to grasp it.[165]

As Henderson desperately tried to overcome what Chamberlain called "Polish stubbornness" and paced his embassy office struggling to remember the sixteen points the foreign minister had read to him at top speed, Churchill was at Chartwell dictating letters to Chamberlain, Kingsley Wood, his publisher, and G. M. Young ("It is a relief in times like these to escape into other centuries"). The note to Chamberlain urged him to take stern measures because there seemed to be no way "Hitler can escape from the pen in which he has put himself," but afterward Winston decided not to mail it. The caution was sound; the P.M. had become increasingly unresponsive to his suggestions, and if, as Churchill believed, his prospects of a cabinet seat were at last brightening, sending unsought advice to a suspicious prime minister was clearly impolitic.[166]

He could be frank with Secretary for Air Kingsley Wood, and he was. Flying home from Consuelo Balsan's château he had found that the buildings and concrete aprons at Croydon Airport had not been camouflaged, that airport authorities were "obstructing" the digging of trenches for pilots and crews during enemy air raids, and that construction of underground shelters was "proceeding far too slowly." Remarking upon these details was characteristic of him. So, at that time, was the lethargy of Croydon authorities and construction workers. British newspapers had reported the Nazi-Soviet Pact, and the public had been alarmed by it. But the ominous diplomatic exchanges between governments, and the growing momentum of the rush toward war, were known to very few. Only Chamberlain, Horace Wilson, and Halifax were in possession of all the facts, and the complete story of Hitler's actions, including the murders of the Canned Goods, would not emerge until the postwar Nuremberg trials, where Ribbentrop was candid, obsequious, and hanged. Civilians in England had not even been told that their government was committed to the defense of Danzig, that Danzig was in grave peril, and that war was therefore imminent.[167]

Churchill was probably better informed than anyone outside the inner circle, but the windup of his book preempted his attention. While Ribbentrop was affronting Henderson and telling him it was "too late," Winston was reworking his manuscript and writing Sir Newman Flower at Cassells, thanking him "for procuring this extra time for the Preface to the Life of Sir Austen Chamberlain" and adding:

I am, as you know, concentrating every moment of my spare life and strength upon completing our contract. These distractions are very very trying. However, 530,000 words [1,621 pages of manuscript] are now in print, and there is only cutting and proof reading, together with a few special points, now to be done.

You will understand, more than anyone else, how difficult it is for me to spend a night upon another form of work. However, I still hope I may be able to serve you.[168]

At 8:30 Friday morning Churchill was awakened by a telephone call from Raczyński, who told him that at 4:00 A.M. fifty-six German divisions, nine of them panzers, had crossed the Polish frontier in darkness from Silesia, Cracow, and the Carpathian flank. After he had bathed and breakfasted Winston received another call from Raczyński. Two Luftwaffe air fleets — sixteen hundred aircraft — had begun bombing Polish cities; civilian casualties were heavy. It was ten o'clock, and it occurred to Winston that the War Office might have fresh details. The War Office didn't even know Poland had been invaded. As Ironside noted in his diary, he reached "the Horse Guards as 10 A.M. was striking and was immediately rung up by Winston from Westerham who said 'They've started. Warsaw and Kracow are being bombed now.' " Ironside phoned Lord Gort, chief of the Imperial General Staff, "who didn't believe it." Ironside urged him to tell Hore-Belisha; Gort called back to report that "Belisha was seen rushing off to Downing Street." Ironside "rang Winston and he said he had the news definitely from the Polish Ambassador 1½ hours ago. . . . How could the War Office possibly be ignorant of this?"[169]

The answer was that Raczyński, a graduate of the London School of Economics and a twenty-year veteran of diplomacy, was familiar with the intricacies of English politics. He knew Winston could be trusted but was unsure of the others, and events swiftly confirmed him. Despite their treaty obligations, the unprovoked German invasion of Poland produced, not declarations of war by Britain and France, but an awful silence. On Hore-Belisha's return from No. 10 the War Office dispatched telegrams ordering full mobilization at 2:00 P.M., and France followed suit. But instead of planning to break through the Siegfried Line — a golden opportunity, for Hitler, confident that the democracies' fear would restrain them, had left only ten divisions to defend it — both Paris and London expressed their readiness to negotiate if the Führer's troops withdrew from Poland. For Berlin, this Allied betrayal of the Poles more than compensated for Mussolini's declaration of Italian neutrality less than an hour later.[170]

Churchill, outraged, was writing a blistering attack on the Chamberlain government. His voice counted now. Herbert Morrison, the leading Labourite, had once called him "a fire-eater and a militarist." But after Prague, Morrison saw him as England's last hope. The *Daily Telegraph*, *Manchester Guardian*, and *Daily Mirror* had become the most vehement forums demanding Winston's recall to the government. As long as the struggle between Churchill and his critics had remained confined to the House of Commons he was hopelessly outnumbered, but Fleet Street had laid his case before the people of England, who now saw him as their champion. That may have explained, at least in part, Chamberlain's call to Chartwell that noon. Parliament had been summoned for 6:00 P.M. Churchill would be driving up to London, and the prime minister said he would be grateful if, before entering the House of Commons, Winston would stop at No. 10 for a few minutes.

In the Cabinet Room, Chamberlain told Churchill that he saw "no hope of averting war." He proposed to form "a small War Cabinet of Ministers without departments" to conduct it. This would exclude the war, Admiralty and RAF ministers, which he thought wise. He had hoped to form a national coalition, but Labour had declined to join it. Churchill later recalled that the prime minister "invited me to become a member of the War Cabinet. I agreed to his proposal without comment, and on this basis we had a long talk on men and measures." The P.M. repeated that he had abandoned his long quest for peace. "The die," he said, "is cast." The Foreign Office had informed Berlin that unless the Germans suspended "all aggressive action against Poland" and were prepared "to withdraw their forces" already there, His Majesty's Government would fulfill its obligations to the Poles "without hesitation."[171]

This was considerably less than candid. Chamberlain had not abandoned hope of preserving the peace, did not believe the die was cast, and was prepared to hesitate indefinitely before fulfilling HMG's obligations to the Poles. To Parliament early that evening the prime minister announced that the government was preparing a White Paper which would "make it perfectly clear that our object has been to bring about discussions about the Polish-German dispute between the two countries themselves on terms of equality, the settlement to be one which safeguarded the independence of

Poland," an agreement buttressed "by international guarantees." The P.M. had his eye on history now; he was trying to launder it. His attempt was doomed. By drafting an apologia instead of fighting, he himself was flouting such guarantees. British and German foreign policy documents would provide a day-by-day account of his stewardship, and Churchill, not Chamberlain, was to be the first writer of that history. Furthermore, the last thing the Poles needed in this hour of desperation was a White Paper exonerating the Chamberlain government. Lacking tanks and divisions which could be moved on trucks, very short of antiaircraft and antitank guns, they had rashly decided to make their stand on Poland's frontiers, meeting the enemy columns with massed cavalry charges. The strongest enemy force, the army group under Field Marshal Gerd von Rundstedt, attacking from Moravia and Slovakia as well as Silesia, had overwhelmed the gallant but ill-starred defenders and was now roving through open country. Defiant but tragic Poles were being mashed beneath panzer treads of Generals Heinz Guderian and Paul von Kleist as the Wehrmacht drove across the corridor. The Poles' Field Marshal Edward Rydz-Smigly had no reserves because the corridor forced him to fight a two-front war, sending the reserves to check another German army group striking southward from East Prussia.[172]

At 10:00 A.M., as Churchill had been breaking the news to an incredulous Ironside, Raczyński had met his official obligation by calling on Halifax and delivering a formal notice of the Nazi invasion. It was, he said, "a plain case as provided for by the treaty." The foreign secretary replied that he had no doubt of the facts — he was reluctant to discuss the treaty — and at 10:50, after Raczyński had departed, Halifax summoned the German chargé d'affaires, Theodor Kordt, and asked if he had any news which might interest HMG. Kordt replied that he knew nothing of a German attack and had received no instructions from the Wilhelmstrasse. The foreign secretary murmured that reports reaching his desk "create a very serious situation." He said no more. Kordt reported their brief meeting to Berlin by phone at 11:45 A.M.[173]

In this new situation, one of the few civilians who seemed to be himself — if indeed he was a civilian — was Adolf Hitler. After describing the bogus Polish attack on the German radio station to the Reichstag, he received Göring, accompanied by the ubiquitous Dahlerus. The Führer had been at ease with the Reichstag, but now, Dahlerus thought, his manner was "exceedingly nervous and very agitated." He had always suspected that England wanted war, he said — believing his own lies — and now he knew it. He would crush Poland; he would crush England; he would destroy anyone who tried to stop him. The Führer "grew more and more excited and began to wave his arms," Dahlerus noted; he shouted, and the shout rose to a scream; the "movements of his body began to follow those of his arms," and "he brandished his fist and bent down so that it nearly touched the floor as he shrieked: *'Und wenn es erforderlich ist, will ich zehn Jahre kämpfen!'* ['And if necessary I will fight for ten years!']."[174]

Henderson was another exception to the rule. Everyone else in his embassy was anxious, but he followed the course that had contributed so much in leading Europe to the cataclysm now upon them. At 10:45 A.M., while the War Office in London was sending mobilization telegrams and Kordt was on his way to the FO, His Majesty's envoy in Berlin had phoned Halifax: "I understand that the Poles blew up the Dirschau bridge during the night." It was their bridge; they had the right to blow it, and, with German troops in their coal-scuttle steel helmets swarming on the far bank, would have been fools not to, but Henderson appears to have thought it aggressive. "On receipt of this news," he said, "Hitler gave orders for the Poles to be driven back from the border line and to Göring for destruction of the Polish Air Force along the frontier."[175]

The ambassador ended his report: "Hitler may ask to see me . . . as a last effort to save the peace." The fact that peace could no longer be salvaged — that World War II had begun, that borders guaranteed by his own government had been violated on a clumsy, vaudevillian excuse, that Poles of both sexes and all ages had been dying for nearly seven hours — was ignored. Josiah Wedgwood, an MP who despised appeasement and had visited Germany, recalled now in bitter contempt how Henderson had "smiled [and] fraternized with evil." Like Chamberlain, Halifax, and Horace Wilson, Henderson was among that group of Englishmen who had, in Wedgwood's words, mistaken Hitler "for a new crowned head at whose fancy cruelties they might giggle and from whom they might not differ with propriety."[176]

Hitler did not ask to see the British ambassador. After Britain's declaration of war Henderson would return to London and volunteer to serve His Majesty in another diplomatic post for which his experience made him suitable. The Foreign Office would reply that there was none.

🦁   🦁

In London parents of small children were studying a notice from the town clerk of Westminster instructing them to bring "infants up to two years of age" to designated centers "between the hours of 10.p [*sic*] and 6.0 p.m., to be fitted with helmets for protection against . . . gas." This time the gas threat was real. John Gunther, until recently the London correspondent of the *Chicago Daily News*, told Americans in an NBC broadcast that Friday evening, September 1: "It's a strange face that London wears tonight. It's a dark face. We're having a blackout here. The streets are black, the houses are black." In the entire length of Piccadilly he had seen fewer than a half-dozen cars; the only Londoners in sight were workmen carrying sandbags into position; indeed, already "the whole town looks sandbagged." Although "what may be the second world war began today," London was "quiet and confident. The British take even such a supreme moment of crisis as tonight with good humor, quietly. A few moments ago I saw something highly typical on the news ticker: 'The Football Association announces that a message received stated that the situation at present does not warrant the cancellation of tomorrow's matches.' "[177]

That sort of thing was taken as an illustration of British phlegm, and therefore encouraging. In fact, it was a sign that in their hearts and minds Britons were still at peace and expected to remain so. They were following their prime minister, matching their government's mood. Under the agreement Poland and Britain had signed the previous Friday, England was pledged to act "at once" with "all the support and assistance in its power," to make war on Germany. The status of Danzig alone was no longer an issue. Polish sovereignty had been violated. Without either an ultimatum or a declaration of war — shocking in those days — the Wehrmacht had invaded Poland on all fronts, and the Luftwaffe was bombing every Polish city, including Warsaw. No one could doubt now that the Führer's objective was the military conquest of the entire country. Legally, under her covenant, Great Britain had no choice; she was bound to declare war on Germany immediately. But she hadn't; the bold note to Berlin which Chamberlain had quoted to Churchill, and then in the House of Commons, was inadequate.[178]

Even so, there was less there than met the eye. Halifax sent Henderson, who would deliver the Foreign Office's message to Ribbentrop, a note explaining that it was "in the nature of a warning and is not to be considered as an ultimatum." At the same time, the Foreign Office asked Dahlerus: "Could you limit the hostilities until you had been to London?" Obviously, the invasion of Poland was not considered casus belli. Assured of some "limit," His Majesty's Government stood ready to negotiate. But any negotiations now would be cramped; the only alternative to declaring war was to insist that the Wehrmacht withdraw from Poland. Roger Cambon, of the French embassy, told Halifax that such a demand for a withdrawal "ought to be accompanied by a time limit." Halifax replied that it was an interesting question, but at this point the matter was "moot." How it could be moot confounded Cambon, but his position was weak. He couldn't be sure his own government would back him. France's response to the invasion of her ally had been waffly; the Quai d'Orsay had expressed its "willingness to negotiate" if the Wehrmacht pulled back but, like Whitehall, had specified no time limit.[179]

Churchill's situation was now uncomfortable. He had accepted a position in a War Cabinet, and this shackled him from public criticism of HMG's foreign policy. Shortly after midnight, in the early hours of Saturday, September 2, he wrote the prime minister from his Morpeth Mansions flat. It was a careful, crafted letter, opening with a minor issue and building toward his chief point. "Aren't we a very old team?" he asked at the outset. "I make out that the six you mentioned to me yesterday aggregate 386 years or an average of over 64!" Labour's refusal to join a coalition — which, though he did not mention it, was understandable; Chamberlain had not offered them a single cabinet post — meant "we shall certainly have to face a constant stream of criticism, as well as the many disappointments and surprises of which war largely consists." It was, therefore, "all the more important to have the Liberal Opposition firmly incorporated in our ranks," and because of Eden's popularity there, he suggested that a place on the front bench be found for him. Then Winston rolled up his heavy guns. "The Poles," he reminded the prime minister, "have now been under heavy attack for thirty hours, and I am much concerned to hear that there is talk in Paris of a further note. I trust you will be able to announce our Joint Declaration of War at *latest* when Parliament meets this afternoon." He closed: "I remain at your disposal."[180]

All day Saturday he awaited a summons from No. 10. Mrs. Hill recalls him "pacing up and down like a lion in a cage. He was expecting a call, but the call never came." At a suggestion from No. 10 Lord Hankey, who would also be included in the new cabinet, called at Morpeth Mansions for a visit. Hankey wrote his wife the following day: "As far as I can make out, my main job is to keep an eye on Winston! . . . He was brimful of ideas, some good, others not so good, but rather heartening and big. I only wish he didn't give one the impression that he does himself too well!"[181]

It was a time when men in public life — and their wives — kept diaries, wrote letters, and filed memoranda to themselves against the day they wrote their memoirs. Because of this, we know far more about their observations and opinions than future writers will know of ours. But it is important to remember that Churchill's popularity in the country was never matched in Parliament. In justifying him, events had discredited most of his colleagues. Being decent men, they tried to suppress their resentment. But they were not always successful. Hankey had been an appeaser. When Winston was down he had said hard things about him. Now Winston was up, and when Hankey told his wife about encountering him later that same day, his letter bore a faint taint of malice. In the House of Commons smoking room, Hankey wrote, "the amount of alcohol being consumed was incredible! Winston too was in a corner holding forth to a ring of admiring satellite MPs! He has let it get into the Press that he will be in the War Cabinet — to the great annoyance of many."

Certainly, Churchill had not kept the news of his impending appointment to himself. Lord Camrose's diary entry for that day opens, "Winston called me up at 11.30 and told me he had accepted a place in the Cabinet and was to be a Minister without portfolio." Telling a press lord was like making an announcement over the BBC. But to keep mum would have been wholly out of character for Churchill. Thirty years earlier, when he proposed to Clementine, he had promised to keep her acceptance secret until she could tell her mother; ten minutes later he had shouted it out to everyone within earshot. After ten years in the wilderness, he could hardly be expected to keep his new appointment to himself. The indiscretion, if any, was slight. It seems fairer to infer that the motives of those who were "greatly annoyed" are suspect.[182]

The real indiscretion that evening was historic, and it was committed by Neville Chamberlain. When the cabinet met at 4:30 P.M., the Poles' situation was desperate. The superior training, equipment, and strategy of the Germans had already brought Rydz-Smigly's troops to the brink of collapse. They had lost all the frontier battles. The Luftwaffe's Stuka dive-bombers were spreading chaos in the Polish rear, destroying communications and preventing the movement of replacements. German troops were already over the River Warta and approaching Cracow. In the north the Fourth Army, driving eastward, had linked up with another force, striking southward from East Prussia. If ever an embattled nation needed allies, it was Poland, and now. The French, fully mobilized, could have lunged into the Ruhr and the Saar upon the issuance of a single command. Hitler had rejected Anglo-French notes urging him to abort his attack; he blamed the British for encouraging the Poles in a policy of "persecution and provocation." Some French leaders, ever distrustful of perfidious Albion, believed him. Others, grasping at straws, found merit in Mussolini's proposal, earlier in the day, for a five-power conference. The French government, appalled at the prospect of facing the Wehrmacht alone, awaited a British initiative.

It was well that the MPs in the smoking room were fortifying themselves with drink. The session that lay ahead of them was going to be grim. In his note to Berlin, Halifax had been unwilling to set a time limit; now, in the Cabinet Room, he claimed this was the *French* position, though he supported it. The Germans, he thought, ought to be given till Sunday noon to accept or reject a conference with France and Britain. Raczyński, who had been waiting in an anteroom, was invited to address the ministers. The Polish ambassador told them that the Nazi offensives, slashing deep into his country from all sides, had been "violently resumed" at dawn, and since noon all large Polish cities had been subjected to "heavy bombing from the air."[183]

Hore-Belisha, deeply moved, spoke immediately after Raczyński's departure. As he recorded in his diary, he told his colleagues that "I was strongly opposed to further delay, which I thought might result in breaking the unity of the country. Public opinion was against yielding an inch." He proposed that His Majesty's Government immediately send Hitler an ultimatum which would expire at midnight. The discussion was lively, with several vehement conversations going on at once, but in the end all were won over, and Hore-Belisha recorded the final decision, binding on all ministers, including the prime minister: *"Unanimous decision was taken that ultimatum should end at midnight."* Halifax agreed to tell the Germans that what had been a warning was now in fact an ultimatum, and that it would end at the stroke of twelve. They rose. Parliament awaited them. The prime minister would make the announcement in the House. When the clock struck, Great Britain and Germany would be at war.[184]

The sequel to this meeting is baffling, even incomprehensible. With the exception of one telephone call, *no one outside the Cabinet Room was ever told of the decision.* Halifax, his faith in negotiations undiminished, broke his word to his colleagues and did nothing — did, in one instance, worse than nothing: he told Ciano that Britain saw her role as that of a "mediator" and, flatly contradicting the cabinet, repeated the line that HMG's warning "was *not* an ultimatum." The phone call was made by Cadogan. After the cabinet had adjourned he spoke to Bonnet in Paris and informed him of its resolution. Why he bypassed Ambassador Phipps is inexplicable. So is his choice of Bonnet, the arch appeaser (*"Votre Chamberlain, il est faible* [weak]," Georges Mandel told Duncan Sandys. *"Mais notre Bonnet, il est lâche* [a coward]."*) Bonnet did not repeat the conversation. He himself had not decided whether a conference of the great powers should be made conditional on the withdrawal of Nazi troops from Poland. The French cabinet, he had told Cadogan, was "going to deliberate" that point, but in any event they were "firmly decided" that any ultimatum "must be of forty-eight hours."[185]

At 7:30 P.M. a crowded House awaited the prime minister's announcement. Parliament, like the British press and public, was ready for war. The secret conduct of foreign policy was past. The country knew of HMG's commitment to Poland, knew how deeply the German army had penetrated the Polish defenses, knew England's delay in declaring war was responsible for Luftwaffe supremacy in the skies over Poland, and was ready to come to her aid. Spears had never seen Parliament "so stirred, so profoundly moved. . . . The benches were packed. The unbearable suspense was about to be relieved. One and all were keyed up for the announcement that war had been declared."[186]

To Churchill there was "no doubt that the temper of the House was for war. I even deemed it more resolute and united than in the similar scene on August 2, 1914, in which I had also taken part." As the prime minister rose another MP felt that "most [members of the House] were ready to show their intense relief that suspense was ended by cheering wildly."[187]

"But as we listened," Spears wrote, "amazement turned to stupefaction, and stupefaction into exasperation." Chamberlain was speaking, not of Nazi crimes, nor of suffering Poland, nor Britain's honor, but of "further negotiations," or rather of their possibility, since the German government had rejected HMG's last such proposal. But, the prime minister said to the staring, straining, immobile House, that was not necessarily a reason for discouragement. The Führer of the Reich was a very busy man. It was not impossible that he was pondering the Italian government's suggestion for a conference. Chamberlain affirmed HMG's demand that German troops leave Poland but — despite the unanimous vote of his own cabinet, and his pledge to report it here — he mentioned no deadline for their departure. "If the German Government should agree to withdraw their forces, then His Majesty's Government would be willing to regard the position as being the same as it was before the German forces crossed the Polish frontier." Then, he said triumphantly, "the way would be open to discussion" between Poland and the Reich, in which case Britain would be willing "to be associated with such talks."[188]

He sat down. No one cheered. Instead, Hugh Dalton heard what he called "a terrific buzz." Margesson signaled his whips to brace themselves for physical violence, and with reason. Duff Cooper and Amery, Dalton saw, were "red-faced and almost speechless with fury." Cooper himself had "never felt so moved." Spears saw the House "oozing hostility." Two MPs actually vomited. Churchill, for once understating the hostility to Chamberlain merely noted that "the Prime Minister's temporising statement was ill-received by the House," but Amery wrote that Parliament "was aghast. For two whole days the wretched Poles had been bombed and massacred," and here was the prime minister of Great Britain discussing how "Hitler should be invited to tell us whether he felt like relinquishing his prey! And then there were all these sheer irrelevancies about the terms of a hypothetical agreement between Germany and Poland." Amery wondered whether Chamberlain's "havering" was "the prelude to another Munich." On that occasion, Parliament had given the prime minister a standing ovation, but "this time any similar announcement would have been met by a universal howl of execration." When Arthur Greenwood rose to reply for the Opposition, Amery, fearing a "purely partisan speech" shouted, "Speak for England!" Greenwood, not known for his eloquence, stammered and said of Chamberlain, "I must put this point to him. Every minute's delay now means the loss of life, imperilling of our national interest — " He hesitated, and Boothby called: "Honour." Greenwood said: "Let me finish my sentence. I was about to say imperilling the very foundations of our national honour."[189]

Parliament adjourned, Amery wrote, in "confusion and dismay." In the prime minister's private room behind the Speaker's chair, Greenwood angrily told him that unless "the inevitable decision for war" had been announced before they gathered for tomorrow's session, "it will be impossible to hold the House." According to Ivone Kirkpatrick, Margesson, following on Greenwood's heels, confirmed him, "warning him," in the strongest possible language, that "unless we act tomorrow," Parliament would "revolt," and Spears wrote that Chamberlain could now entertain no doubts that "the House would accept no further procrastination." Chamberlain knew it. Back at No. 10 he phoned Halifax, who had been preoccupied with telegrams from his ambassadors. The prime minister said his statement "had gone very badly." Halifax hurried across the street and found him distraught. Later he wrote that he had "never known Chamberlain so disturbed." The P.M., insisting that he stay for dinner, said Parliament had been "infuriated"; if they were unable to "clear the position" by tomorrow, he doubted that his government would be able "to maintain itself."[190]

The foreign secretary was sympathetic. Yet even as Chamberlain recoiled from the House's hostility, Halifax had been pursuing the squalid policy which had led them to this dead end. Among the cables to reach his desk late that afternoon had been a report, from Ambassador Kennard in Warsaw, that Polish forces were severely handicapped by the Luftwaffe's mastery of the air. Beck had "very discreetly" suggested "some diversion as soon as possible in the west," hoping that the RAF would "draw off a considerable proportion of the German aircraft" at the eastern front. Kennard, endorsing this, thought that "every effort ought to be made to show activity on the western front." But there was no western front, and could be none until Britain and France, now neutral, became belligerents. The ambassador knew that. He ended: *"I trust I may be informed at the earliest possible moment of our declaration of war."*[191]

Halifax had ignored the telegram. Instead, he had instructed Henderson "immediately" to hand the text of the prime minister's statement in Parliament — the same statement which now threatened to split Chamberlain's government — "to certain quarters," among them Dahlerus and Göring. And now, despite the uproar in the House, and the abundant evidence to support the contrary position, Britain's foreign secretary returned to his office believing that the Nazi juggernaut could be halted and thrown into reverse gear by the prospect of conversations.

At ten o'clock that night he received the Polish ambassador, who told him that since noon the Luftwaffe had been bombing the center of Warsaw. "The position of Poland," Raczyński said, was "getting bad with the delay." What deadline, he asked, had Britain given the Germans? The noble lord replied that he was "not in a position" to divulge that information. The Pole was dumbfounded. If the Anglo-Polish alliance meant anything, the Poles were entitled to this vital information. He could not imagine why it was being withheld, never dreaming that a deadline could not be revealed because it did not exist. Yet Halifax knew the price of this last-ditch stand under the banner of appeasement, now stained with the blood of Austrians, Czechs, and Poles. To a fellow diplomat he acknowledged that "the moral effect of this delay on Poland [is] devastating."[192]

The Germans were fully aware of the situation — and of their thin line of field gray facing France. Saturday evening two of Dirksen's diplomats had approached Horace Wilson, asking what England's attitude would be if the Wehrmacht pulled back; specifically, whether Britain would approve of a German road across the Polish Corridor and the incorporation of Danzig into the Reich. Glossing over the situation in Poland, where, after forty-two hours of enemy assault, Polish casualties were approaching 100,000, Chamberlain's creature answered that once the Wehrmacht was back where it belonged, "the British Government would be prepared to let bygones be bygones." His visitors had told him that the question was not asked lightly. It was a formal "proposal" from the Wilhelmstrasse.[193]

It wasn't, nor could it have been; had Ribbentrop approved such a suggestion, and had Hitler heard of it, the Reich's ambassador to the Court of St. James's would have been repudiated, recalled, and sent to a *Konzentrationslager*. Why did Wilson not only listen to such tripe, but pass it along to the Foreign Office with an endorsement from No. 10? There is only one possible answer. It was still HMG's policy to believe anything the Germans said and disregard reports critical of them. Göring denied that his Luftwaffe was bombing cities, thereby killing or maiming civilians. Kennard, His Majesty's envoy in Warsaw, said it was happening all over Poland; he could see it from his embassy window. Halifax was doubtful. He asked for fuller accounts, adding: "In the meantime it is accepted Germans are attacking only military objectives."[194]

*   *   *

Among the deeply troubled men in London that Saturday evening was Duff Cooper, formerly first lord of the Admiralty and now, by choice, a private member. After Parliament broke up, Cooper and his wife — the striking Lady Diana, a public figure in her own right and much admired by Churchill — had walked along the Embankment to the Savoy. Cooper had dined here with Churchill the previous evening, and he was still fuming over an ugly exchange with the Duke of Westminster after they had parted. For over thirty years Winston and Bendor had been friends; but Westminster's virulent anti-Semitism and his admiration for Hitler had ruptured their friendship. Cooper had encountered him while leaving the Savoy, and in his diary he recorded that the Duke began by "abusing the Jewish race" and "rejoicing that we were not yet at war," adding "Hitler knew after all that we were his best friends." Infuriated, Cooper had replied: "I hope that by tomorrow he will know we are his most implacable and ruthless enemies."[195]

But this was tomorrow, and Duff Cooper's hope had been dashed. He lacked appetite. As he stared morosely at his plate two junior members of the government, Harold Balfour, the under secretary for air, and Euan Wallace, the minister of transport, passed the table. Cooper asked Balfour whether he was still in office; the answer was a gesture "of shame and despair." Wallace said nothing — later he explained that he was afraid that Cooper would cut him if he spoke — but he sent him word, via a waiter. The prime minister's statement, he said, had taken "the whole Cabinet by surprise," and they were demanding another meeting before midnight. Cooper was startled. The *whole* cabinet? Surely Wallace was exaggerating. Of course, there must have been some dissenters on the front bench, but it hardly seemed possible that the King's first minister would abrogate a commitment to another nation in defiance of a unified cabinet. Duff Cooper, like Eden, knew the strength of Neville Chamberlain's will, but Chamberlain was no Hitler. Wallace's implication didn't seem possible, Cooper thought, deciding that it wasn't. Shortly after 10:00 P.M. a messenger brought him another note: Conservative MPs distressed by the afternoon's events were meeting in Winston Churchill's flat opposite Westminster Cathedral; Churchill would like him to join them. Asking Diana to excuse him, Duff Cooper hurried to the turnaround in front of the Savoy and hopped into a cab: "Number eleven Morpeth Mansions."[196]

Eden, Sandys, Bracken, and Boothby were already there. Duff Cooper joined them "in a state of bewildered rage." Churchill himself afterward wrote that "all expressed deep anxiety lest we should fail in our obligations to Poland," but his account omits a basic disagreement over the course they should follow. If Churchill turned against the prime minister, Chamberlain's government would fall, and that was what his guests wanted. Boothby, Duff Cooper recorded in his diary, thought the prime minister had "lost the Conservative Party forever"; it was, he said, "in Winston's power to go to the House of Commons tomorrow and break him and take his place." If Winston failed to act, that would save Chamberlain, which was unthinkable; Churchill would be given office, but at an exorbitant price: "In no circumstances now should Winston consent to serve under him."[197]

The difficulty was that he already had, or thought he had. It was a nice point. The prime minister had offered him a place and he had accepted it. However, the place was to be in a *War* Cabinet. If there was no war there would be no office for Winston to hold; therefore he could not be part of the government and need not muffle his thunder. But Churchill, always sensitive about honor, believed that he must keep his word, even when, as in this case, it seemed unreasonable. His position was unmitigated by the fact that since their talk Chamberlain's behavior had been anything but gentlemanly. Drawing Duff Cooper aside, he told him, according to Cooper's diary, that he "considered that he had been very ill-treated, as he had agreed the night before to join the War Cabinet but throughout the day he had not heard a word from the Prime Minister." He said he had "wished to speak" to the House that afternoon, but "feeling himself already almost a member of the Government had refrained from doing so." Churchill's grievance was real. Nevertheless, he refused to split the country. The public images of political leaders were often volatile. Chamberlain was down now, but until recently he had been a national hero. He represented peace, and it was hard to quarrel with that; if overthrown now he would be martyred, and a divided England would be no match for Hitler.[198]

Outside, an electrical storm was rising. Distant thunder became less distant; suddenly, the cars parked outside were wrapped in sheets of heavy rain, and a servant hurried around closing windows. To the others Churchill seemed "very undecided," and Duff Cooper wrote that he "said that he had no wish to be Prime Minister, doubted his fitness for the position." This has a hollow ring. Churchill had never doubted his aptitude for Parliament's highest office and had been longing for it since the first decade of the century. It is, of course, very common for men confronted by the imminence of great responsibility to cloak themselves in humility. Winston, however, was not such a man. Perhaps Duff Cooper misunderstood him. It doesn't fit. It is a riddle without solution, but then, it had been a day of riddles, the greatest being the prime minister's behavior in the Commons.[199]

The men in Morpeth Mansions had many contacts, and they took turns phoning them. All cabinet ministers appeared to be unavailable. Churchill phoned the French embassy and "was told," one of his guests wrote, "that all was well — that we should see the situation from quite a different angle tomorrow which sounded very ominous to us." Whom Churchill had spoken to was unknown, but his source proved unreliable; at that hour no Frenchman, in the embassy or in France, knew what would happen in the morning. Other calls were made to senior civil servants. These yielded little. Eden, perplexed and disappointed, learned that he was scheduled to be Dominions secretary and excluded from the War Cabinet. According to Duff Cooper, "We all argued that Winston should refuse to serve unless Anthony was included in the War Cabinet as otherwise he would be a minority of one. Brendan pressed that he should also insist on my inclusion." At length Churchill left them all and withdrew into another room. He told them he was going to write Chamberlain. Before sending the letter to No. 10, he would read it to them.[200]

The letter began with a subtle reproach: "I have not heard anything from you since our talks on Friday, when I understood that I was to serve as your colleague, and when you told me that this would be announced speedily." In offering him office, he recalled, Chamberlain had said that war was inevitable. The recollection puzzled him: "I really do not know what has happened during the course of this agitated day; though it seems to me that entirely different ideas have ruled from those which you expressed to me when you said 'the die was cast.' " He realized that "with this tremendous European situation changes in method may become necessary," but felt "entitled to ask you to let me know how we stand, both publicly and privately, before the debate opens at noon." This was neither an ultimatum nor even a warning, but the steel beneath the velvet was unmistakable, and so was the time limit. Chamberlain might give Hitler forever to respond; Churchill was giving Chamberlain till lunch. He went on to offer advice. With both Labour and the Liberals "estranged," forming an effective war government would be "difficult." The only solution, it seemed to Winston, was to reconcile the other two parties by offering to share power with them.[201]

That brought him to the uproar in Parliament. There was a "feeling . . . in the House," he wrote, "that injury had been done to the spirit of national unity by the apparent weakening of our resolve." Winston did not "underrate the difficulties you have with the French" — this was a shrewd guess — but England must reach her decision "independently, and thus give our French friends any lead that may be necessary." To do that "we shall need the strongest and most integral combination" possible. Then came the final thrust: "I therefore ask that there should be no announcement of the composition of the War Cabinet until we have had our talk."

On Friday he had accepted Chamberlain's offer without comment, but only after the prime minister had told him that Britain was going to war. Now the situation had changed, and Churchill was commenting, making conditions. He would enter the cabinet only if assured — before the deadline — that Chamberlain's policy toward Nazi Germany was consistent with Churchillian principles. He added a final sentence: "As I wrote to you yesterday morning, I hold myself entirely at your disposal, with every desire to aid you in your task." Then he signed his name and rejoined his guests.[202]

Unknown and unsuspected by any of the men in Churchill's flat — including Duff Cooper, despite Wallace's hint at the Savoy — Chamberlain's cabinet was in a state of mutiny. To them his volte-face, coming only three hours after he had accepted their unanimous decision, was a gross betrayal. Everyone was in it, including Simon and Hoare. With the exception of Halifax, who had been absent during the afternoon meeting, they were the two most powerful men in the cabinet and the closest to the prime minister. As chancellor of the Exchequer, Simon, like Chamberlain, had a private room in Parliament. That was the mutineers' headquarters, and there they chose Simon as their leader. "The Cabinet," writes Robert Rhodes James, "was now in a state of acute tension." The prime minister's statement had left it, as one minister later recalled, "completely aghast." Hore-Belisha told them: "We are weakening on our undertaking to Poland and the French are ratting." The rebellious ministers intended to approach Chamberlain, but not to bargain with him; at No. 10 they had voted for an ultimatum to Germany, and they wanted it handed to Ribbentrop in Berlin *now.* Sir Reginald Dorman-Smith, minister of agriculture, later recalled that they voted to march on Downing Street and deliver "a plain *Diktat.*"[203]

Simon was on the phone, trying to get through to No. 10. He couldn't manage it. The house had been inhabited by prime ministers for over two hundred years, but now, it seemed, no one was home. The chancellor's room was crowded; in Dorman-Smith's words, "we got scruffier and sweatier," but "my colleagues . . . had decided they would not leave that room until such time as war had been declared. As we sat there and waited by the phone and nothing happened, I felt like a disembodied spirit. It didn't seem real; we were 'on strike' — like those poor little miners down there, you know." The dinner hour came and passed; there was no food, and the only water arrived in little cardboard cups borne by secretaries. At 9:00 P.M. Simon, Hore-Belisha, and two other ministers "sent PM a letter," as Hore-Belisha put it, "rehearsing our points." Eventually Simon was connected with Chamberlain, however, and they were all invited to

No. 10. Outside it was raining, hard. Some had cars, some found cabs, some actually hitchhiked. "By now," Dorman-Smith remembered, "*all* of us [were] actually scruffy and smelly, and it rather shook us to find Halifax, who had been dining with the PM, and Cadogan in evening clothes."[204]

Chamberlain had not dressed for dinner. He had been too busy, and as he led his ministers into the Cabinet Room they began to understand, from exchanges between him, Halifax, and Cadogan, why he had failed to answer Simon's calls. As late as 9:30 P.M., shortly after he had received the cabinet ultimatum signed by four senior members of his government, he had been on the phone with Rome, trying to turn Mussolini's proposal for a five-power conference into a reality, with the understanding that the talks could not begin until the German troops now in Poland were back in Germany. Ciano's final message had torpedoed the prime minister's hope. The Italians, the Duce's son-in-law had told him, "do not feel it possible" to ask the Reich to join such a conference; the British insistence on a Wehrmacht withdrawal would merely arouse the Führer's celebrated wrath. If Hitler decided "on his own" to pull out the Wehrmacht, Ciano said, "well and good," but Mussolini did not "feel able to press him to do so."[205]

This was the final blow to appeasement. Chamberlain bleakly acknowledged that his long struggle to keep the peace had failed. Halifax was not so sure, but the responsibility was not his, and he had not been in the House of Commons that afternoon. The decision was Chamberlain's, and, having made it, his next step was to inform Paris and arrange for a joint declaration of war. Shortly before 10:00 P.M., while dissident conservatives were conferring at Morpeth Mansions, the prime minister phoned Daladier and told him that there had been "an angry scene in the House of Commons," adding that his "colleagues in the Cabinet are also disturbed." The premier replied that the French government had decided to present the Germans with a forty-eight-hour ultimatum which would begin at noon tomorrow, Sunday, September 3. Out of the question, said the prime minister; if he agreed "it would be impossible . . . to hold the situation here." He wanted an Anglo-French ultimatum which would be issued at 8:00 A.M. tomorrow and expire at midday. Daladier, distressed, replied that he would confer with his ministers and reply through the Quai d'Orsay.[206]

In the Cabinet Room, Cadogan was also talking to Paris, telling Bonnet that His Majesty's Government would, of course, prefer simultaneous declarations of war by the two democracies, but England could not wait until noon Tuesday. If the German offensive maintained its momentum, Poland's position would be hopeless by then. Bonnet replied that it was all very well for England to set a Sunday deadline; the British had evacuated London's children to the country, but "we cannot get our young people out of Paris" on such short notice. This issue was new. The French could have followed the British example. They had overlooked it, and now, in the last-minute rash of calls to No. 10 and the Foreign Office, it obsessed them. According to Dorman-Smith's recollection they were "convinced Paris would be bombed as soon as war was declared . . . horrified and terrified at our determination for an immediate ultimatum and saying: 'Are you going to have all our women and children killed?' " HMG was unmoved. The French were indignant and surprised, and they sulked through most of Sunday. Yet their able ambassador in London, Charles Corbin, had alerted them to the fact that if HMG did not deliver an ultimatum in Berlin before Parliament met, "They risk overthrow," and French politicians, with their history of tumbling cabinets, should have understood that.[207]

In the past Chamberlain had tried to accommodate the French whenever possible, and he had usually found it possible. The renitent cabinet — representing, in Gilbert and Gott's felicitous phrase, England's "revolt of conscience" — had stiffened the backbones of its leaders. The decisive conversation was between the two foreign ministers. Halifax had crossed the street to take the call in his own office, but the prime minister, with an aroused Hore-Belisha at his elbow, had given him precise instructions. Chamberlain had not yet decided how he would yield to the cabinet, but he wanted the French to know that the British were prepared to act independently of Paris. Thus Halifax informed Bonnet that the British government would send Berlin an ultimatum, with a deadline, before they went to bed. They had no choice, "owing to the difficult position which has arisen in the House of Commons." And hesitation by Chamberlain now would make it "very doubtful" he could "hold the position" of His Majesty's Government. If France wanted to delay its ultimatum later than 8:00 A.M. that was up to the French. Great Britain would already be at war.[208]

Returning to No. 10 with Ivone Kirkpatrick, Halifax encountered Hugh Dalton and greeted him almost as a colleague; though Dalton represented Labour in Parliament, he was also a graduate of Eton, King's College at Cambridge, and the London School of Economics, and under MacDonald he had served two years as parliamentary under secretary in the FO. Halifax told him that France was vacillating and asked whether he thought Labour would "favor our declaring war alone." Dalton said he couldn't speak for the party, and in fact it was unnecessary; Greenwood had already gone on record with the prime minister. Kirkpatrick said he could speak for himself and then did. Public opinion, he said, was "bewildered and disturbed. Unless we go to war we are sunk."[209]

After a long meeting with Margesson — who once more advised that he could not answer for the consequences should Parliament meet tomorrow without a declaration of war — Chamberlain finally joined his ministers in the Cabinet Room. It was 11:00 P.M. They were hungry and tired, but none had left, or forgotten why they had come, or the strategy adopted in Simon's office. To Dorman-Smith "the PM was calm, even icy-cold." He told them of the French pleas and said they had not left him unmoved; he was, in fact, "terribly worried that Paris might indeed be attacked from the air." No one commented. However, when he pointed out that should an ultimatum be sent, they must agree on its timing, they broke their vow of silence. Hore-Belisha thought Henderson should deliver it at 2:00 A.M., less than three hours from now, and that it should expire four hours later. "The less time involved, the better," he argued. Many heads nodded in agreement, and Halifax left the room to cable Henderson: "I may have to send you instructions tonight. . . . Please be ready to act." But Chamberlain's implicit acceptance of war had dulled the edge of the mutineers' resolve. They were vulnerable to manipulation. In the end they agreed on a 9:00 A.M. delivery and an 11:00 A.M. expiration. Thus, by failing to stand by Hore-Belisha, Britain gave the advancing Nazi troops another five hours, and in the new mobile warfare that counted heavily. When time ran out and this final deadline passed, the Germans would be on the Vistula.[210]

It was nearly midnight. Outside, the storm was mounting, the lightning bolts coming ever closer; there was scarcely any interval now between the flash and the thunder pealing across St. James's Park. Simon and Sir John Anderson of the Home Office were in a corner, conferring. Chamberlain *seemed* determined, but he had seemed no less in earnest only seven hours earlier, in this very room, when he had approved of the "immediate fulfilment of British obligations to Poland" and declared his agreement with those in favor of a midnight ultimatum. This time they wanted his sworn word; either he promised to respect the decision of the cabinet now reassembled or they would carry their fight to the people. They approached him and told him that. Chamberlain nodded and said quietly: "Right, gentlemen. This means war."[211]

He had scarcely said it, Dorman-Smith recalled, "when there was the most enormous clap of thunder and the whole Cabinet Room was lit up by a blinding flash of lightning. It was the most deafening thunder-clap I've ever heard in my life. It really shook the building."[212]

The same stunning thunderclap shook Churchill's flat, and there, too, the timing was dramatic. Winston had just finished reading his letter to the prime minister aloud. Dazzled by the lightning bolt, his friends took a sharp breath, agreed that his message was splendid — and began arguing loudly over what should be added and what stricken out. This was scarcely practical, since the letter, if it was to be effective, must be sent to No. 10 immediately. Winston let them fuss. He had no intention of altering a comma. And he was quite pleased by the lightning. Its timing could scarcely have been improved upon.

Actually he was entitled to another dramatic moment. At intervals, between writing paragraphs, he had been placing more phone calls, and now he reached one of the insurgent ministers at No. 10. He told his guests that someone — he mysteriously described him as "a friend" — would call back and tell him what had been decided. "Unfortunately," Duff Cooper noted with amusement, "his secretary gave the show away by coming in and saying, 'Mr. Hore-Belisha is on the telephone.' Churchill was much annoyed. He came back with the information that it had been decided 'to deliver the ultimatum next morning.' " This changed the situation. The quarreling ended; the men in Morpeth Mansions recovered their poise. After a moment of reflection he decided to send his letter to Chamberlain anyway. Then he rooted around, producing items he had had the foresight to order a year earlier, before the Munich crisis. It was all on a list in his pocket: "1 Torch for Mrs. Churchill; dark material for door; Adhesive tape, gum and black paper." His departing guests had taken no precautions, "and so," Duff Cooper wrote, "we wandered through the dark streets."[213]

Halifax had cabled Henderson to request a 9:00 A.M. appointment with Ribbentrop, and then — since the ultimatum need not be drafted until morning — went to bed. To Kirkpatrick he had "seemed relieved" that the waiting was over and his role as an appeaser was finished. That was not true of his French counterpart. As the British foreign secretary slept, the French foreign minister made one last absurd attempt to avoid fighting Hitler's Germany. Telephoning Ciano, Bonnet asked whether *"un retrait symbolique"* ("a symbolic withdrawal") of German troops was possible. Ciano knew Hitler would scorn not only the idea, but also anyone who brought it to his attention. In his diary he wrote: "Nothing can be done. I throw the paper in the wastebasket without informing the Duce."[214]

Henderson delivered the ultimatum but he was heartbroken. Awaiting a reply that never came — Hitler would deliver his answer with his U-boats, now patrolling the sea lanes around Britain — he said farewell to Dahlerus, who noted that the British ambassador could not hide "his profound grief and disappointment." Dahlerus later wrote that "certain circles in England regarded him with scepticism and considered him susceptible to Nazi influence," but the Swede thought that unjust; he had "never found him a dupe of German policy." Since Dahlerus himself was a dupe, his judgment here carries little weight. But if Henderson's dreams lay in ruins, they were not only his dreams; they were shared by his superiors in London. He had not served King and Country well. Neither had they. And none of his acts diminishing England's prestige, and weakening her in the years before her people faced the greatest challenge in her history, would have been possible without the connivance and even the encouragement of Chamberlain, Halifax, and Cadogan.[215]

The British ultimatum expired (the French declaration of war would follow at 5:00 P.M., six hours later) and at 11:15 A.M. September 3 the prime minister spoke to the nation over the BBC, telling them that England and Germany were once again at war. His address was neither memorable nor inspiring; Boothby wrote Churchill: "Your immediate task seems to have been made much easier by the PM today. His was not the speech of a man who intended to lead us *through* the struggle." Winston and Clementine had heard over their Morpeth Mansions radio, and hardly had Chamberlain's voice died away than the piercing wail of air-raid sirens, later to become so familiar to an entire generation of Englishmen, sounded all over the city. Winston, Clementine, and Inspector Thompson hurried toward the door. "You know, you've got to hand it to Hitler," said Churchill — heading for the roof, not the shelter — "The war is less than a half-hour old, and already he has bombers over London." Actually, the alarm was false, though Churchill didn't know it as he gazed out, as he put it, "in the clear, cool September light" to watch "thirty or forty cylindrical balloons" slowly rising above the city. "It was with difficulty," Inspector Thompson recalled, "that we prevailed upon him to enter an air-raid shelter. He only agreed to go when it was pointed out to him that it was up to him to set an example. Down we went . . . the Old Man with a bottle of brandy under his arm."[216]

They made their way, Churchill wrote, "to the shelter assigned to us." It lay a hundred yards down the street, "an open basement, not even sandbagged," as he described it, already occupied by the tenants of a half-dozen flats. "Everyone was cheerful and jocular," he recalled, "as is the English manner when about to encounter the unknown." But according to Fritz Günther von Tschirschky, a German refugee, Churchill himself was less than jolly. Tschirschky remained outside the shelter, feeling a German would not be welcome, until Clemmie, who knew him, insisted he come down. There he found Churchill "in a great state of indignation, stamping his foot, complaining that there was no telephone and no portable wireless, and saying the Germans would have much better organized air raid shelters." Tschirschky volunteered that there was a portable radio in his flat, and Churchill said: "You Germans are so damned efficient — please be kind enough to fetch it." But just then the wailing was heard again. Churchill afterward remembered that he "was not sure that this was not a reiteration of the previous warning, but a man came running along the street shouting 'All Clear.' "[217]

Parliament met at noon, and as Churchill crossed the lobby he was handed a note from the prime minister asking him to call on him "as soon as the debate died down." It wasn't much of a debate. The issue which had divided them had been resolved. The prime minister, speaking first, called the day "a sad day"; then, having turned overnight from dove to hawk, added: "I hope I may live to see the day when Hitlerism has been destroyed." Greenwood, speaking for Labour, told the House that the "intolerable agony of suspense" had ended and saluted the gallant Poles, "now fighting for survival." More cheers. Churchill, scheduled as the third speaker, wrote afterward that "as I sat in my place, listening to the speeches, a very strong sense of calm came over me, after the intense passions and excitements of the last few days. I felt a serenity of mind and was conscious of a kind of uplifted detachment from human and personal affairs. The glory of Old England, peace-loving and ill-prepared as she was, but instant and fearless at the call of honour, thrilled my being and seemed to lift our fate to those spheres far removed from earthly facts and physical sensation. I tried to convey some of this mood to the House when I spoke."[218]

Parliament remembered his years of warnings, his denunciation of Munich, the countless scenes in which he had been hooted and jeered and mocked when he tried to tell them of Nazi Germany's growing military superiority and the threat to them and their island. He had anticipated this more than six years ago and never was a man more entitled to remind them that he had told them so. But his friends knew him incapable of that. "If we quarrel with the past," he had said, "we may lose the future." It is fair to add that he had high hopes of his imminent meeting with the prime minister. Bitterness now could sour his prospects then. So he began by declaring: "In this solemn hour it is a consolation to recall and to dwell upon our repeated efforts for peace. All have been ill-starred, but all have been faithful and sincere. . . . Outside, the storms of war may blow and the lands may be lashed with the fury of its gales, but in our own hearts this Sunday morning there is peace. . . . Our consciences are at rest."[219]

He warned them to expect "many disappointments, and many unpleasant surprises," but added, "We may be sure that the task which we have freely accepted is not one beyond the compass and strength of the British Empire and the French Republic." It was hardly true that Chamberlain had freely accepted it, and at hour four France was still at peace, but mention of the Empire was greeted with a murmur of approval; within the hour Australia and New Zealand had declared war on Germany while the other Dominions prepared to follow. Churchill noted that the prime minister had said it was "a sad day," and so it was, but "there is another note which may be present," a sense of gratitude that a new generation of Britons was "ready to prove itself not unworthy of the days of yore and not unworthy of those great men, the fathers of our land, who laid the foundations of our laws and shaped the greatness of our country."

Few cheered that. It was prophetic, but on that first day of the war the older generation's thoughts about England's youth were anxious thoughts. The Oxford Oath was still popular. Hitler was wicked; they knew that. He had forced this hated war on England. But fighting for the Union Jack, so powerful an incentive in 1914, had little appeal now. Vision was necessary, and in his closing remarks Churchill recognized that. Over the past few days, he observed, Parliament had passed bills entrusting "to the executive our most dearly valued traditional liberties," but they would be safe there; no British government would use them "for class or party interests"; it would instead "cherish and guard them." England's dream was of a world in which all governments could be so trusted, the dignity of all people respected.

This is not a question of fighting for Danzig or fighting for Poland. We are fighting to save the whole world from the pestilence of Nazi tyranny and in defence of all that is most sacred to man. This is no war of domination or imperial aggrandisement or material gain; no war to shut any country out of the sunlight and means of progress. It is a war, viewed in its inherent quality, to establish, on impregnable rocks, the rights of the individual, and it is a war to establish and revive the stature of man. . . . We look forward to the day, surely and confidently we look forward to the day, when our liberties and rights will be restored to us, and when we shall be able to share them with the peoples to whom such blessings are unknown.[220]

There was no standing ovation; whips on both sides of the House, wary of Churchill's rhetoric, had seen to that. But after Lloyd George had delivered the day's final speech, MPs of all parties surged toward Winston, their hands extended congratulating him. Comparison with the prime minister's remarks was inevitable. In his diary Amery described Chamberlain's address as "good, but not the speech of a war leader." He added: "I think I see Winston emerging as PM out of it all by the end of the year."[221]

If the prime minister overheard such invidious comparisons, he gave no sign of it. Cordially welcoming Churchill, he told him he had considered his letters and then told him the cabinet was being reshuffled. The Liberals had declined to join the government, and until now he had seen no role in the War Cabinet for the three service ministers. They had urged him to change his mind, however, and he had relented, which brought the average age of cabinet members — a matter which had troubled Winston — below sixty. Hore-Belisha would continue at the War Office, and Kingsley Wood would remain as secretary for air. However, Chamberlain proposed to transfer the Earl of Stanhope, now first lord of the Admiralty, to another post, and give the Admiralty to Churchill.

🦁   🦁

Thus, at a stroke, Winston was given a place in the War Cabinet and the responsibility of a ministry — the one he cherished most. He was "very glad of this," he wrote, "because, though I had not raised the point, I naturally preferred a definite task to that exalted brooding over the work done by others which may well be the lot of a Minister, however influential, who has no department." Had Chamberlain given him a choice between the War Cabinet and the Admiralty on Friday, he wrote, "I should, of course, have chosen the Admiralty. Now I was to have both." Clementine was waiting in the car outside No. 10, and Winston told her: "It's the Admiralty. That's a lot better than I thought."[222]

He would have preferred hurrying straight to his new post, because "the opening hours of war may be vital with navies," but the first meeting of the War Cabinet was scheduled for 5:00 P.M. It would be largely a formality; nevertheless, he had to be there. Thus he sent word to the Admiralty Board — "I shall take charge forthwith and arrive at six o'clock" — and headed for Downing Street. Newspaper opinion, led by *The Times,* had favored direction of the war by a small group, not more than five or six members. But counting the home secretary (Sir John Anderson) and the new Dominions secretary (Eden), Chamberlain's War Cabinet had eleven, the other nine being himself, Halifax, Hoare (privy seal), Simon (Exchequer), Hore-Belisha (war), Kingsley Wood (air), Hankey (without portfolio), Churchill, and Lord Chatfield (coordination of defense). Of these, Chamberlain, Halifax, Hoare, and Simon were still the Big Four; they had been in the public eye so long that if England's fortunes failed her, the British public would hold them accountable, even though the leaders had stayed in front by following public opinion. Every newspaper reader was familiar with them — Good Old Neville, as the crowds called him at his peak, the archetypical British businessman; Halifax, master of foxhounds, with the patrician's gift for backing into the limelight; dapper, fussy Hoare, the cabinet's fixer of Fleet Street opinion; Simon, the pedantic lawyer, of whom it was said that at the Exchequer he was chiefly concerned with making certain that Britain had enough money to pay the indemnity after losing the war.[223]

If, as Chamberlain put it a week later, righteousness was "a tremendous force on our side," no one else felt it. The British were depressed. *The Times* cheerfully reported that an eighty-six-year-old shepherd had presented the prime minister with a walking stick in the form of a rolled-up umbrella, whittled out of elm wood with a pocketknife; but shepherds were unthreatened by massive Luftwaffe bombings which, according to a Committee of Imperial Defence estimate, would last sixty days, leaving 600,000 dead and 1.2 million wounded. The committee had issued a statement, for reasons which defy understanding, that every possible precaution had been made: hospital beds had been prepared for the injured, thousands of papier-mâché coffins were stacked and then photographed for the press, and over a million burial forms were in the mail. The British public — remembering Baldwin's warning that "the bomber will always get through" — already lacked a once-more-into-the-breach spirit, and this did not develop it.

Winston's critics had predicted that if given a cabinet role he would be divisive, and now they observed with schadenfreude that he already was. The War Cabinet's first duty was to choose a new chief of the Imperial General Staff, since Secretary for War Hore-Belisha wanted to replace Gort. The War Office preferred Ironside, and so did Hore-Belisha. But Tiny had remained aloof from political maneuvering; other generals had courted ministers who now nominated them. Churchill intervened vigorously, and as Hore-Belisha wrote in his diary that evening, "There was some opposition to Ironside's appointment, but Winston came down on my side and strongly supported it; and that settled it." Churchill also asked for a survey of British gun production, and during the discussion Major General H. L. Ismay, secretary to the Committee of Imperial Defence, entered the room with an air reconnaissance report: a German *Flotte* — four or five battleships, four cruisers, and five destroyers — had weighed anchor and put out to sea. As first lord, Churchill was particularly alert to any threat, by submarines or surface ships, to merchant vessels, England's lifeline. If that was the *Flotte*'s mission, he said, they would be headed for the Baltic. Kingsley Wood, the air minister, agreed that the RAF could not ask for a "fairer target." An air attack was authorized, by twenty-seven Blenheim bombers and nine Wellingtons. But here, as in so many other ventures early in the war, nothing went right for the British. Sir Ian Jacob, then a field-grade officer seconded to No. 10, recalls that the RAF mission, which failed, "showed how ineffective and ill-designed our aircraft and bombs were against strong defences and well-armoured ships." Their mission unaccomplished, the British planes were downed by flak.[224]

The meeting over, Churchill headed for the Admiralty — which had already signaled the fleet: "Winston is back"— crossing the Horse Guards Parade with a young friend. Winston observed that to improve British morale, the public's conception of the country's military establishment must be revised upward. Between 1914 and 1918 London's chauvinistic press had elevated general and flag officers to the level of deities, and when the truth about the butchery in France and Flanders had eventually emerged, the crash in their status had been deafening. World War II restored dignity to the military profession, but it was not retroactive; it is still generally believed that during the interwar years English officers were insensitive, unimaginative Colonel Blimps. They weren't. Churchill had found them to be keen, anxious observers of the Luftwaffe and Wehrmacht buildups, and among them were the officers who, by coming to him, had risked their careers to prepare England for the ordeal they — but few civilians — knew was coming.

One of their projects, undertaken by those who anticipated the bombing of London, had been construction of a shelter for the country's leaders at Storey's Gate, two blocks south of Downing Street. Commonly described by the few who knew of it as the CWR, short for Cabinet War Room, it was actually an underground warren of drab rooms, including a bedroom for the P.M., whose sparse furnishings included a desk and a BBC microphone through which the P.M. could address the nation. Construction of this shelter — which might more properly be called a bunker, for its purpose, like that of the *Führerbunker* in Berlin, was to safeguard the leader's life — had begun in 1935, after the War Office pointed out that No. 10 was far too fragile to survive heavy bombardments undamaged. Millions of Londoners, allies, and an unknown number of enemy spies, passed the CWR daily without knowing it. The drab stone building above it, facing St. James's Park, bore a dull plaque reading CENTRAL STATISTICAL OFFICE.

Another precaution, anticipated long before the English public would even acknowledge a renewal of the conflict with Germany, was more conspicuous — was, indeed, spectacular. Every major governmental building was surrounded by huge concertinas of barbed wire — coils twelve feet high, with barbs as thick as a man's thumb. They had lain in warehouses for years and were produced when Britain's ultimatum was delivered in Berlin. The instant war was declared, up went the wire. The facade of Admiralty House was hidden by intervening buildings until Winston and his companion were almost upon it. Churchill and his companion turned a corner, and there it was, with its vast new concertinas and thousands of barbs gleaming in the late afternoon sun. "Great God!" said Winston's young friend. "What's *that* for?"

Churchill replied, "That's to keep me out."[225]

PART SIX

CATACLYSM

At the Admiralty he was expected, recognized, and saluted as he passed through a gap between concertinas. No guide was necessary, of course; the once and present first lord went straight to a concealed entrance where Kathleen Hill, summoned earlier by telephone, and Captain Guy Grantham, who would be his aide, awaited him. Inside, Churchill raced up the stairway, with Mrs. Hill and the captain panting at his heels, and burst into his old lair, the first lord's office, known to those who had served under Winston between 1911 and 1915 as "the private office." Swiftly crossing the room, he "flung open a hidden panel," as Mrs. Hill put it, revealing "a secret situation map" on which he had last plotted the locations of Allied and enemy ships on that long-ago day when he had last worked here. "The ships," Mrs. Hill remembers, "were still there" — exactly as he had left them on May 22, 1915, when his daring Dardanelles strategy was, as he later wrote, "ruined irretrievably" by incompetent subordinates, and he himself was generally regarded as a ruined politician. Now, he reflected, "a quarter of a century had passed, and still mortal peril threatened us at the hands of the same nation. Once again defence of the rights of a weak state, outraged and invaded by unprovoked aggression, forced us to draw the sword. Once again we must fight for life and honour against the might and fury of the valiant, disciplined, and ruthless German race. Once again! So be it."[1]

Churchill's early start at the Admiralty accomplished little; he was adrift in memories of the past — "filled with emotion," in the words of Rear Admiral Bruce Fraser, the third sea lord. That evening the first sea lord, Admiral Sir Dudley Pound, introduced him to the senior men with whom he would be working, and in the boardroom Winston took the first lord's chair, as of old. Pound formally welcomed him; Churchill, according to one of the admirals, "replied by saying what a privilege and honour it was to be again in that chair. . . . He surveyed critically each of us in turn and then, adding that he would see us all personally later on, he adjourned the meeting. 'Gentlemen,' he said, 'to your tasks and duties.' "

They left quietly. "Everybody," one of them later recalled, "realized what a wider responsibility he had" — his duties as a member of the War Cabinet and its Land Forces Committee, and his concern over the fighting in Poland and the strange lack of it in France.[2]

His original instinct had been correct; in the war at sea the early hours were crucial. Yet it is hard to see how anyone in the Admiralty could have prevented the war's first sea tragedy. When hostilities were declared late that morning, Admiral Karl Dönitz had thirty-nine U-boats cruising outside British seaports. One, the *U-30*, was lurking 250 miles off the Irish coast. At 7:45 P.M., as Pound was introducing Churchill to his fellow sea lords, the submarine's commander sighted the S.S. *Athenia*, no warship but an unarmed ocean liner carrying 1,103 passengers, most of them European refugees heading for asylum in the United States. Hitler had vetoed unrestricted submarine warfare in the early stages of the conflict, but the commander of the *U-30*, mistaking the liner for a British auxiliary cruiser, had torpedoed her. The 112 dead included 28 U.S. citizens. Two British destroyers and a Swedish yacht picked up the survivors, who signed affidavits testifying that the U-boat had circled the sinking steamship without offering assistance, though by then the sub's commander knew he had blundered. The Americans among them demanded transportation home shielded by a convoy of U.S. warships, which was not possible. Ambassador Kennedy sent his twenty-two-year-old son John F. Kennedy, a Harvard senior, to defuse their anger, reassure them, and find them safe passage to New York.

Hitler was indifferent to American public opinion, but Goebbels, as the Reich's minister of propaganda, could not be, particularly after Churchill publicly declared: "The *Athenia* was torpedoed without the slightest warning. She was not armed." Goebbels interrupted a Radio Berlin broadcast to call Churchill *"ein Lügenlord"* ("lying lord") and denied Nazi responsibility for the sinking, saying the only source for such reports was "your impudent lies, Herr Churchill, your infernal lies!" Learning that in English Winston's initials stood for what Germans called *Wasserklosett*, zealous Nazis painted them on latrines. Berlin announced that Churchill had personally ordered a bomb placed aboard the *Athenia*. "This falsehood," Winston noted, "received some credence in unfriendly quarters." In the House of Commons he said the passenger ship "was not defensively armed — she carried no guns and her decks had not even been strengthened for this purpose." He added that he had expressed his "profound sympathy with the relatives of those who may be bereaved by this outrage." Privately, he told the War Cabinet, "The occurrence should have a helpful effect as regards public opinion in the United States."[3]

*   *   *

He did not, however, expect a call from the White House. Nevertheless, in early October, while he was dining in Morpeth Mansions with two Admiralty guests, the phone rang, and a few moments later his valet-cum-butler entered to summon him. Churchill asked who was calling. "I don't know, sir," his man replied. "Well," said Winston, "say I can't attend to it now." To his surprise, the butler said: "I think you ought to come, sir." Annoyed, Churchill went, and it was his guests' turn to be perplexed, at his answers to his caller: "Yes, sir. . . . No, sir." One of them later recalled that there were "few people whom he would address as 'sir' and we wondered who on earth it could be. Presently he came back, much moved and said: 'Do you know who that was? The President of the United States. It is remarkable to think of being rung up in this little flat in Victoria Street by the President himself in the midst of a great war.' He excused himself, saying, 'This is very important. I must go and see the Prime Minister at once.' "[4]

Roosevelt had told him of a strange warning from Admiral Raeder, commander in chief of the Kriegsmarine. The *Grossadmiral* had informed the Americans that his agents had discovered a British plot: the U.S.S. *Iroquois*, which had sailed from Cork the day war was declared, would be sunk "in similar circumstances to the *Athenia*," which, according to the current Nazi line, meant by the Royal Navy, on Churchill's orders. The implication was that England would try to blame the Reich for the ship's loss and thus get the U.S. into the war. After consulting No. 10 and his sea lords, Churchill cabled the White House: "*Iroquois* is probably a thousand miles West of Ireland. . . . U-boat danger inconceivable in these broad waters. Only method can be time-bomb planted at Queenstown. We think this not impossible." Roosevelt agreed and warned the ship's commander, who quickly sought, and found, safe harbor. But a stem-to-stern search produced nothing. The British accused Germany of trying to spread propaganda against England, and Raeder was embarrassed. The truth is that despite all these hypotheses of Byzantine intrigue, no one in high position was to blame.[5]

The real significance of this minor contretemps was that Roosevelt had taken the initiative in establishing a bond with a belligerent power — despite official U.S. neutrality, a policy which enjoyed the overwhelming support of the American people — and had cooperated with the British to a remarkable degree, even following up the first lord's suggestion that the Germans might have smuggled a bomb aboard the ship. With few exceptions the British people, unfamiliar with U.S. politics and the mood of the American public, were unaware of how grave a political risk the president was taking. One British historian observes that from the outset

Roosevelt's idealism was clear-sighted. He was well aware that at least four out of five Americans were unwilling to be involved in what they saw as the Quarrel of European states, the very lands from which their ancestors had fled in search of freedom and prosperity. He was equally aware that the Nazi threat was of greater than local significance. . . . He was determined to spare nothing in his endeavors to sustain the West European democracies . . . and he had the vision to determine that whatever advice he might receive to the contrary from his Ambassador in London, Joseph P. Kennedy, Churchill was and would remain the standard bearer of resistance.[6]

In bypassing No. 10 Downing Street, the Foreign Office, and his own embassy in London, the president had established a direct tie with the only man, in his view, who could save Europe from Hitler. And since Roosevelt had made this extraordinary move entirely on his own, Churchill was the passive partner in the establishment of the most momentous relationship in his life. Of course, on their level each man was known to the other. Six years earlier, as a rapt admirer of FDR's New Deal, Winston had sent a copy of his first *Marlborough* volume to the White House, inscribed, on October 8, 1933: "With earnest best wishes for the success of the greatest crusade of modern times."[7]

Actually they had met once, at Gray's Inn, London, on July 29, 1918, when both were guests at a dinner for the War Cabinet, though Churchill — to FDR's annoyance — did not remember it. Roosevelt professed to have enjoyed Churchill's subsequent books, and, as noted earlier, he had read *While England Slept*, though the president rarely read anything except newspapers; he liked to learn the views of contemporary writers by inviting them to his home and listening to them. Considering Churchill's present responsibilities that was impractical now, but already Roosevelt was pondering ways to manage a rendezvous, the more dramatic the better. He never doubted he could do it. After overcoming his appalling paralysis to become the greatest figure in American political history, he felt he could do anything. If he wanted something, he reached for it. No president has ever had a broader reach, and now his hand was extended across the Atlantic.[8]

He knew he could buy peace for a generation of Americans, but the more he pondered the character of the regime in Berlin, the more convinced he became that the next U.S. generation would lie at Hitler's mercy. On September 1, as the Wehrmacht's panzer tracks chewed their way toward Warsaw, Phelps Adams of the *New York Sun* had asked FDR: "Can we stay out of it?" Privately, Roosevelt was doubtful, but after a long pause he had replied: "I not only sincerely hope so, but I believe we can, and every effort will be made by this Administration to do so." This amounted to duplicity, but the president could not become a great wartime leader unless he won a third term the following year. If he were blunt now he would lose then. However, on Sunday, the day Britain entered the war, he had sounded an unmistakable knell. It was "easy for you and me to shrug our shoulders," he told his countrymen in a fireside chat, and to dismiss "conflicts thousands of miles from the continental United States" as irrelevant to Americans. But "passionately though we may desire detachment, we are forced to realize that every word that comes through the air, every ship that sails the seas, every battle that is fought does affect the American future." In 1914 Woodrow Wilson had told the Senate that the "United States must be neutral in fact as well as in name. . . . We must be impartial in thought as well as in action." FDR now declared that impossible: "The nation will remain a neutral nation, but I cannot ask that every American remain neutral in thought as well. Even a neutral cannot be asked to close his mind and conscience."[9]

His own mind was open and his conscience at peace. In time his commitment would be clear to the entire world. He had already planned one of his bold, ingenious strokes, renouncing freedom of the seas for Americans. "Danger zones" would be proclaimed, and U.S. citizens and ships would be barred from them; there would be no *Lusitania* this time. The isolationism bloc could find no flaw in that. But if they mulled it over, they would see that the policy in effect gave a free hand to Britain and France, who were controlling the seas despite German submarines. A further step came in November 1939, when the U.S. Neutrality Act was amended to permit the sale of arms to belligerents on a cash-and-carry basis. Although theoretically applying equally to all, cash and carry in fact favored whoever dominated the seas; now the Allies could place large orders with American munitions manufacturers and then sail over to take delivery. The impact of cash and carry on the Reich would be anything but neutral, and the orders would mean thousands of jobs for Americans. In all events, FDR intended to intervene personally whenever he could help the democracies and hurt Hitler.[10]

If Roosevelt had judged him right, Churchill was the man with whom he could join hands. Even before his phone call to Morpeth Mansions, he had sent the Admiralty's first lord an overture via the American diplomatic pouch. Dated September 11 it began: "My dear Churchill: — It is because you and I occupied similar positions in the World War [FDR had been assistant secretary of the U.S. Navy] that I want you to know how glad I am that you are back again in the Admiralty." Winston — and of course Chamberlain, he added as an afterthought — should know that "I shall at all times welcome it, if you will keep me in touch personally with anything you want me to know about," sending "sealed letters through your pouch or my pouch." The president ended gracefully, "I am glad you did the Marlborough volumes before this thing started — and I much enjoyed reading them."[11]

To Winston, who had looked westward when the appeasers were looking to Berlin, this letter bore enormous implications. Laying it before the War Cabinet, he pointed out that the president, as commander in chief, controlled the movements of all American naval vessels and could "relieve the Royal Navy of a great load of responsibility." By executive order he could declare a safety belt around the Americas, which would make it impossible for the Germans to attack His Majesty's merchantmen "approaching, say, Jamaica or Trinidad, without risking hostilities with the United States." The War Cabinet approved his reply, the first of 1,688 exchanges between the two men. It opened, "The following from Naval Person," and that would continue to be his salutation until he took over the government of Great Britain, when he altered it to "former Naval Person."[12]

Now that he was first lord, Churchill saw no reason to alter his daily regimen. He knew that his late hours, a consequence of his siestas, were a trial for his subordinates. But most of them were career officers; they knew the need for sacrifices in wartime. He had followed the same schedule the first ten months of the last war, and the Admiralty had adjusted to it. He had been forty then; now, at sixty-five, he found the nap an absolute necessity, permitting him, he said, "to press a day and a half's work into one." Mary remembers that after an hour's rest he "awoke a giant refreshed." If he could work sixteen or seventeen hours a day, he reasoned, they could adjust to his eccentric hours. At one time or another all those officers directly under him tried to sleep in the early afternoon. Somehow they couldn't drift off. The only exception was the first sea lord. Pound developed a habit of sleeping while sitting bolt upright. The only difficulty was that it became involuntary. Winston would pace the private office, delivering precise, detailed instructions on a matter of considerable importance, only to discover that the Royal Navy's senior admiral of the fleet was, and for a time had been, dead to the world.[13]

Winston's typical Admiralty day began at six or seven in the morning and continued, broken only by his rest after lunch, through a two-hour evening conference and on until two or three the next morning. Of course, this was not Chartwell; his first visitor each morning was Captain Richard Pim, RN, arriving to brief the first lord on overnight developments in the war at sea. Pim always began by describing changes in the Admiralty's situation map. He did this slowly; Winston carried a rough map around in his head, and he needed time to switch, say, the little flag for this cruiser from here to there, or to remove — with great satisfaction — the pin representing a Nazi U-boat sunk by a British destroyer. Should Winston ever be captured by the enemy and successfully interrogated, using torture or drugs, the results would be catastrophic for the navy. Therefore, he never left Admiralty House without his pistol and a suicide pill in his pen.

During the first week of the war, while the first lord and his lady stayed in Morpeth Mansions, the Office of Works converted the nurseries and attics on the two top floors of Admiralty House into a flat for them. Clementine decided to keep the gay chintz curtains, hung by Lady Diana Cooper during Duff Cooper's tenure as first lord, but transformed the rest, as Lady Diana discovered when she came calling. In her diary she wrote: "O what a change . . . from my day!" She mourned her bed, which "rose sixteen feet from a shoal of gold dolphins and tridents; ropes made fast the blue satin curtains; round the walls Captain Cook was discovering Australia. Now all has suffered a sea change. The dolphins are stored away and on a narrow curtainless pallet bed sleeps the exhausted First Lord. My gigantic gold-and-white armoire holds his uniform. The walls are charts."[14]

First in Morpeth Terrace and then Admiralty House, Pim had to do a bit of shouting to make himself heard while Winston splashed about in his bath. The new first lord was eager to leave Morpeth Mansions; he disliked sleeping so far from his maps, framed in wood and hung on the walls of Admiralty House's elegant, 217-year-old library, which overlooked the Horse Guards Parade. This became the upper war room, a floor beneath the flat, created by Pim as directed in one of Churchill's first wartime orders. It was soon the nerve center of the navy. The maps — covered with black cloth to hide them from unauthorized Admiralty personnel passing through — bore small pins with flags which identified the last known position of His Majesty's warships, convoys, enemy vessels which had been spotted, and — with the help of Lloyd's of London — all British merchantmen. Details were at the fingertips of the Prof, who occupied an office next to the war room.[15]

This was in Lloyd's interest. Submarines were not the only peril awaiting British ships which left home waters. German raiders also lurked over the horizon: enemy warships and armed steamships disguised as peaceful freighters. A British skipper spotting a tramp steamer in the South Atlantic could send the Admiralty a coded inquiry and, within minutes, receive a reply telling him whether the vessel was registered and, if so, her mission and whether she was supposed to be where she was. "If a Raider was reported in any specific area," Pim wrote in his unpublished memoirs, "we were able in a few minutes to say what British ships were in the vicinity and what was their speed so that a wireless message could be sent ordering them, if necessary, to alter course to avoid the danger."[16]

Pim's assignment was formidable. Thousands of merchantmen flew the red ensign, feeding and arming England, and at any given moment at least half of them were at sea. Pim recalled how, when he believed the war room was ready, he sent word to the first lord. "Very good," said Churchill after inspecting it, "but the maps will all have to be replaced. When you know me better you will know that I only paint in pastel shades, and those strong colours under the lamps would give me and you a headache." Churchill required Pim and his staff to check the position of all known ships and convoys every twelve hours and replot them on the maps. The plotting was determined by a stream of signals, arriving around the clock, reporting losses of shipping to enemy attacks, details of attacks by Allied warships and aircraft, tonnage sunk by both sides, and graphs of imports arriving safely in England. If any signal of importance arrived after Winston was installed in his flat over the upper war room, Pim wrote,

a very few moments would elapse before he arrived in the War Room and was in complete possession of all the facts. I had always heard that he was an indefatigable worker and there is no other word to describe his activities. His day started with a visit in his multi-coloured dressing gown to the War Room generally soon after seven — although often it was a far earlier hour. . . . With the exception of about two hours' rest each afternoon he continued hard at it with a short respite for meals until one or two o'clock next morning when he used to pay us a final visit on his way to bed.[17]

The evening conference usually began at 9:00 P.M.; two hours later the first lord would start dictating speeches. ("Are you ready?" he might remark to his typist. "I'm feeling very fertile tonight.") The Prof would arrive in the private office around midnight, settle on a sofa in front of the fire, and remain until Churchill retired. Before bed Winston would tour the operational rooms in the basement — "terribly good for the naval staff," a private secretary recalls — and end his day with a final visit to the war room. Sir Geoffrey Shakespeare, parliamentary secretary to the Admiralty, writes that once, well after midnight, Winston asked a secretary, "Where is the OIL?" Baffled, the secretary replied, "What OIL?" Churchill said: "I want Admiral the OIL" — he meant "Earl" — "of Cork and Orrery." Shakespeare adds: "It was nearly 3 A.M. We were dropping with fatigue."[18]

Although the King waited patiently in Buckingham Palace, ready to present the Admiralty's seals to his new first lord, Churchill did not kiss hands until the third day after his appointment. He was far too busy. His prewar informants had kept him apprised of urgent naval issues, and as a critic of Anglo-German naval treaties, he had undertaken a detailed study of Raeder's new Oberkommando der Kriegsmarine (navy high command). But now he had to explore the whole of his new realm, launch projects, devise strategies, propose offensive operations, assign priorities, prepare defenses for the vast arsenal of challenges Raeder — after six years of planning aggressive naval war — was hurling at the Admiralty around the clock. Moreover, he had his other War Cabinet responsibilities, and was deeply involved in plans for the expansion of the army.

Nevertheless, if the Admiralty did not have his undivided attention, he gave it far more than any of Chamberlain's other ministers could have done. "His energy and stamina were prodigious," the historian Arthur Marder writes. "A stream of memoranda, virtually ultimata, issued from the Private Office covering every aspect of the war at sea and leaving the recipient in no doubt as to what the First Lord wanted." These memoranda became irreverently known as the First Lord's Prayers because they frequently opened with "Pray inform me . . ." or "Pray why has . . . not been done." Captain G. R. G. Allen recalls that the "one thing that remains firmly in my mind about Winston's arrival in the Admiralty was the immediate impact which his personality made on the staff at all levels, both service and civilian." Allen was among those who "began to receive little notes signed 'WSC' from the private office demanding weekly reports of progress direct to him. If the required report was a good one . . . one might get a reply in red ink: 'v.g. press on.' It was like the stone thrown in the pond, the ripples got out in all directions, galvanising people at all levels to 'press on' — and they did." He adds: "The same stimulation was at once felt in the fleet."[19]

The most fundamental source of conflict between Churchill and his staff would arise from polar opposites — his instincts and their traditional discipline. In peacetime the gravest sin a captain can commit is to lose his ship. If the vessel lost is a British or American warship, a court-martial is mandatory. Naval officers know that some ships must be lost in wartime, but their early training makes them cautious strategists, shrinking from risky plans and daring maneuvers. The battle of Jutland, in 1916, wasn't really a battle. On both sides the officers making the decisions were intent upon returning home with the fewest possible losses. Both succeeded — historians called Jutland a draw — because neither put up a real fight. If the man on the bridge believes, even on a subliminal level, that sinking is, for him, the ultimate disaster, he will remain secure in his command. He will also remain a cypher. Jellicoe and von Hipper, the commanders at Jutland, are forgotten. Nelson, Farragut, and Yamamoto will be remembered as long as fighting men go down to the sea in ships.[20]

Churchill loved risks and always sought ways to carry the war to the enemy. On the evening of his second day he again gathered his senior subordinates and subtly let them know, in a deceptively offhand talk, that his grasp of the Royal Navy was profound. His predecessor, the languid Lord Stanhope, had been a Gilbert and Sullivan first lord, celebrated for his ignorance of ships, of naval strategy, even of the sea. "Tell me," he once asked a sea lord, "what is a 'lee' *exactly?*" Winston's very language was nautical. He casually mentioned that after the naval treaties of 1930 and 1935, which he had opposed in Parliament, he had studied the design of the new German cruisers; and, as the admirals took notes, he reeled off figures and concise analyses of gunnery, engine room pressures, and keel design which would have been the envy of a flag officer lecturing at the Royal Naval College. He told them he was studying a convoy system to protect merchant shipping and was considering the laying of a mine barrage between Scotland and Norway; that he believed twelve destroyers could be "scraped" from other theaters for the Atlantic, where the enemy's "prime attack" could be expected, and that trawlers he had ordered reconditioned were being equipped with antisub devices, including Y-guns for firing depth charges. Since the Admiralty had assumed responsibility for the safety of merchantmen, they must faithfully follow zigzag courses to foil U-boats. Royal Navy officers would examine their logs and charts when they docked, and captains who had not zigzagged as instructed would be deprived of their papers. At present the war's big question mark was Italy. Her intentions were obscure. As long as they remained so, merchant shipping must avoid the Mediterranean by taking the long Cape route to India. But Mussolini could not drift forever. Churchill felt the Admiralty should "press" the government to bring the situation "to a head . . . as soon as possible." Rising, he said that "the First Lord submits these notes to his naval colleagues for consideration, *for criticism and correction.*" He wanted them treated as bases for discussion, he explained, not as direct orders.[21]

Admiral Sir William M. James thought Churchill displayed a "remarkable grasp of sea warfare," and that this mastery was also evident "in the numerous minutes he wrote." These memoranda, which would grow in fame as the war progressed, were described by one of his staff officers. "The First Lord," he wrote, "devised special red labels with just three words printed on them: 'ACTION THIS DAY.' This ensured that any important document . . . would be dealt with at once, and the reply was expected to be on not more than 'one sheet of paper.' " Winston also stressed that instructions from him were to be obeyed only if he put them in writing, immediately or immediately thereafter.[22]

🦁   🦁

During his years out of office, Churchill had, of course, been preoccupied with the widening gap between the Luftwaffe and the RAF. He had anticipated the need for an expanded army, and urged that plans be made to raise and equip one. The service which had troubled him least was the navy. It was still the most powerful fleet in the world, the "senior service" in an island nation which had dominated the high seas for over three centuries. When Stanley Baldwin, slashing naval estimates, had told Parliament that Britain's might at sea was an "expensive toy" and Churchill had rebuked him, for once in those lonely years he had heard an approving murmur of "Hear, hear" on both sides of the House. Winston had denounced the Anglo-German Naval Agreement of 1935, but its provision that the Nazi navy be permitted to build two warship tons for every seven built by Britain did not alarm the Royal Navy. Even the navies of other countries thought Admiralty hubris, though infuriating, was justified. On the first day of the new war Admiral Raeder had written that the Führer's Kriegsmarine was "in no way" prepared "for the great struggle with Great Britain." He thought his surface forces were "so inferior in number and strength to those of the British fleet" that they "can do no more than show that they know how to die gallantly"; and *"die U-bootwaffe"* — the submarine arm — was "still much too weak to have any *decisive* effect on the war."[23]

German admirals had always suffered from an inferiority complex; in their country the army was the senior service. But Hitler knew how dependent England was upon imports, and how close she had been brought to her knees in 1917, nearly starved into submission by German submarines lying athwart Britain's sea lanes and sinking all ships approaching England, regardless of nationality. To Birger Dahlerus he swore that he would create a great *U-bootwaffe* and destroy first the Royal Navy and then the merchant ships flying the red ensign. When the Swede looked skeptical, the Führer had given history one of its unforgettable moments. Flinging out his right arm and striking his breast with his left, he had cried: "Have I ever told a lie in my life?"[24]

If the Führer's confidant and the head of his navy expected little from the Reich's forces at sea, it is unsurprising that England's peril there was unknown to Churchill. He wasn't even aware of Germany's new naval strength. Here his intelligence had failed him. In the early summer of 1934 Hitler had given secret orders for the construction of the *Scharnhorst* and *Gneisenau*, battle cruisers of 26,000 tons, exceeding by 16,000 tons the limit imposed on Germany at Versailles. By 1939 the yards at Kiel and

Bremen had built three battleships, eight heavy cruisers, an aircraft carrier, thirty-four destroyers and torpedo boats, and, at Krupp's Germania shipyard, the first litter of the Kriegsmarine's newly designed U-boats, vastly improved over those of the last war. Two vessels of particular interest to *Jane's Fighting Ships*, the celebrity register of warships, were the *Graf Spee* and the *Deutschland*. The Germans called them *Panzerschiffe* (armored ships); to *Ausländer* they were "pocket battleships."

The *Panzerschiffe* were masterpieces of miniaturization. Powered by diesel engines, which gave them a range of 21,500 miles, each carried six eleven-inch guns and was capable of a 28-knot top speed. In the view of *Jane's*, they were mightier than almost any warship fast enough to overtake them. Moreover, at the outbreak of the war shifts of German shipbuilders were working around the clock to finish a battle cruiser, two battleships with tonnages of 41,700 — British, French, and American capital ships were limited to 35,000 tons — and the *Bismarck*, a superbattlewagon of 45,000 tons. Some military experts thought that in challenging Britain's naval superiority, the Führer was repeating the kaiser's mistake. They underestimated him. The British Admiralty's classic strategy had been the blockade. It had defeated Napoleon and the kaiser. The German counter to this was to sink ships provisioning Britain. Their argument was that sinkings were no more monstrous than a blockade which starved German children — they never answered the charge that leaving the survivors of the ships they sank to drown was another matter — and in any event they intended to launch torpedoes whenever they thought the loss of a target vessel would hurt England.[25]

One would have expected that the Royal Navy, after its harrowing duel with German submarines in the last war, would have been alert for signs that the Nazis were plotting a rematch. But all British naval glory seemed to lie in the past, and not the recent past. During the interwar years the sea lords had been refighting, not Jutland, but Trafalgar. They still glowed in anticipation of battles between ships of the line, firing broadsides that raked the enemy's decks and maneuvering to cross his T. The U-boat threat, they assured their civilian superiors, had been solved by surface ships in 1918, and, besides, they had a new secret weapon. This was the asdic, "the name," Churchill wrote, for "the system of groping for submarines below the surface by means of sound waves through the water which echoed back from any steel structure they met. From this echo the position of the submarine could be fixed with some accuracy." Lord Chatfield, the first sea lord, had driven him to Portland for a demonstration on June 15, 1938. Afterward Winston wrote excitedly, "I could see and hear the whole process, which was the sacred treasure of the Admiralty." He wrote Chatfield: "What surprised me was the clarity and force of the [asdic] indications. I had imagined something almost imperceptible, certainly vague and doubtful. I never imagined that I should hear one of those creatures asking to be destroyed. It is a marvellous system and achievement."[26]

It wasn't, not then. Later versions, which Americans came to know as sonar, fulfilled the promise of the primitive device Churchill saw and would prove valuable antisub weapons, but during Churchill's tenure as first lord the asdic was almost worthless. The clarity with which he had heard its unmistakable "ping" derived from the fact that its target subs were far from the transmitter. The shorter the range, the weaker the ping, and if a U-boat approached within fifteen hundred yards — the lethal range for torpedoes — the asdic signal was lost completely. U-boat commanders could hear the ping, too, and they would quickly learn how to take evasive action and approach at a deadlier angle. These problems challenged the most experienced asdic operators, of which there were very few in 1939; in the opening phase of the war at sea the transmitter-receivers would be in the hands of civilians who had been rushed through a three-month training course and assigned a task they simply could not grasp. Finally, the asdic could only be operated underwater. Admiral Karl Dönitz, a heroic submariner in the last war and now *Befehlshaber der U-boote*, simply ordered his commanders to attack at night from the surface. In the Royal Navy the asdic would be discredited, and its return to favor, like Churchill's, came slowly.

Dönitz, who knew the weaknesses of 1918 U-boats from personal experience — his had been sunk in the Mediterranean, and he had escaped drowning only to serve ten months of POW imprisonment — had devoted the 1920s to designing a tougher, more versatile underwater vessel. Ten days after the Anglo-German pact became effective in 1935 he had launched his new *U-1* from a tightly guarded shed in the Kiel shipyard. Unlike its predecessors, the *U-1* was equipped with heavy-duty batteries, which meant she could hide underwater for a much longer time. Of even greater importance was the revolutionary design of her torpedoes. Electrically powered, they left no telltale wakes, and each bore a magnetic firing mechanism which exploded it directly under the target vessel's keel, where a ship is most vulnerable.

If he had a fleet of a hundred U-boats, Dönitz believed, he could paralyze England by waging what he called a "tonnage war" — sinking all merchantmen carrying cargoes to England, whatever flag they flew. And with three hundred of them, organized in "wolf packs," he could sink over 700,000 tons of shipping a month in the Atlantic, even if the merchantmen sailed in convoys, escorted by warships. Events later in the war proved he could have done it in the first year of hostilities, but Dönitz was plagued by Hitler's chimerical moods and by interservice rivalry. Despite his vow to Dahlerus, the Führer blew hot and cold on submarine warfare. Yet sinking ships, particularly when civilians were aboard, appealed to the broad nihilist streak in him, and in that regard he found the reasoning of his *Befehlshaber der U-boote* flawless. In that last meeting with Dahlerus he had screamed: *"Ich U-boote bauen, U-boote bauen, U-boote, U-boote, U-boote, U-boote!"* ("I shall build U-boats, build U-boats, U-boats, U-boats, U-boats, U-boats!").[27]

Had he followed through and given Dönitz his three hundred submarines, it is hard to see how England could have avoided starvation. But the *Kriegsherr* liked the idea of powerful warships flying the swastika even more; when they sailed into European ports they contributed to the Third Reich's intimidating image. Furthermore, the senior admirals in Berlin, as in London, preferred to envision battles between surface ships, with enormous battleships trying to huff and puff and blow their enemies into submission. So Hitler let Britain's misfortune slip from his hands.

Even so, the war on the Atlantic shipping lanes opened with a series of savage, unexpected jolts for Britain. In the first week eleven merchantmen — 65,000 tons of shipping — were sunk, half the weekly losses of April 1917, the peak month of U-boat attacks that year, when England's Admiral John Jellicoe confided in his American counterpart that one freighter in four was going down, there was six weeks' supply of corn in the country, and he expected an Allied surrender by November 1. By the end of September 1939, twenty-six ships had been sunk by torpedoes. The fighting at sea, Churchill told the House of Commons on September 26, had "opened with some intensity," but, he assured the House: "By the end of October we expect to have three times the hunting force which was operating at the beginning of the war."[28]

At the same time, he felt he ought to inform Parliament that German *Schrecklichkeit* had reared its loathsome head. The Royal Navy had scrupulously observed the "long acquired and accepted traditions of the sea." When the RN sank enemy vessels, their crews were picked up. Even when German ships had deliberately sunk themselves to avoid the formalities of the prize court, the Royal Navy had rescued their crews, and no ship flying the flag of a neutral nation had been attacked. "The enemy, on the other hand," said Churchill, had behaved very differently; in their zeal to prevent supplies from reaching England, the Nazis had torpedoed Finnish, Dutch, Swedish, Greek, Norwegian, and Belgian vessels "on the high seas, in an indiscriminate manner, and with loss of life." Churchill acknowledged that "from time to time the German U-boat commanders have tried their best to behave with humanity. . . ." But many cruel and ruthless sea crimes had been committed. They all remembered the *Athenia*.

Her "tragic end" had been followed by the loss of the *Royal Sceptre,* "whose crew of 32 were left in open boats hundreds of miles from land and are assumed to have perished. Then there was the *Hazelside* — only the day before yesterday — twelve of whose sailors were killed by surprise gunfire, in an ordinary merchant ship." His Majesty's Government "cannot at all recognize this type of warfare . . . as other than a violation of the laws of war, to which the Germans themselves have in recent years so lustily subscribed." Such, he said, "is the U-boat war — hard, widespread and bitter, a war of groping and drowning, a war of ambuscade and stratagem, a war of science and seamanship."[29]

Speaking over the BBC a few days later, he described the first U-boat onslaught — how "they sprang out upon us as we were going about our ordinary business with two thousand ships in constant movement . . . upon the seas," and how, in consequence, "they managed to do some serious damage." But Britain was meeting the challenge with a threefold response: convoys, the arming of merchantmen and fast liners, and, "of course," the "British attack upon the U-boats." The *Athenia* had scarcely disappeared beneath the waves when "the Royal Navy . . . immediately attacked the U-boats and is hunting them night and day — I will not say without mercy, for God forbid we should ever part company with that — but at any rate with zeal and not altogether without relish."[30]

His voice vibrated with confidence, but in fact he was uneasy. Because the navy occupied a special place in the hearts of Englishmen, the Exchequer's knife, which had slashed so deeply into War Office and Air Ministry budgets in the 1930s, had been relatively gentle with Admiralty estimates. But since prime ministers, Fleet Street, and the public had been united in their scorn for all uniformed men, morale had slumped throughout the services. At the docks, ports, and naval bases Churchill inspected, he saw tarnished brass, scuffed shoes, and sagging coils of rope — insignificant in themselves but symptomatic of an institutional *défaillance*. If Nelson had relied on men like these he would have lost the battles of the Nile, Copenhagen, and Trafalgar, and Napoleon would have galloped up the Mall at the head of his *vieille garde* to demand the palace keys.

Nor was the fleet the force-in-being Churchill had ruled a quarter-century earlier. All that had been needed to keep it supreme had been hospitality to innovative ideas, supported by simple maintenance. The one new concept which both he and his admirals largely rejected was the enormous limits air power now placed on sea power. In all her wars till now, England had been able to control an island simply by stationing a warship offshore, or bottling up the enemy by sending a flotilla to bar a strategic strait. The kaiser's Kriegsmarine, for example, had been confined to the Baltic Sea during most of the last war because British warships had guarded the Skagerrak, the narrows separating the Baltic from the North Sea, thus keeping Germany from, among other possible objectives, the long coast of Norway. But if the fleet was vulnerable to Luftwaffe bombers, which the Admiralty would not concede, German ships could no longer be denied passage through the Skagerrak. Under an umbrella of Nazi planes, they could steam through unchallenged. Because the first lord and his sea lords would not fully accept this in 1939, within eight months the lesson would be forced upon them, and at a bitter price.

Maintenance was another matter. It seemed inconceivable that equipment vital to the navy should have been permitted to rust away, but that had happened. The sea lords blamed the small Admiralty appropriations under MacDonald, Baldwin, and Chamberlain. That wasn't good enough. During the 1930s their budgets had been large enough to build five new battleships, six aircraft carriers, and nineteen heavy cruisers. They just let small matters slide. In the first war Lord Kitchener of Khartoum, trying to console Winston in the dark hour of his dismissal from the Admiralty, had reminded him of his thorough preparations for the war. "There is one thing at any rate they cannot take from you," K of K had said. "The fleet was ready." This time, Churchill was discovering, the fleet was not.[31]

On the evening of September 15 he boarded a London train with Bracken, Sinclair, and Lieutenant Commander C. R. ("Tommy") Thompson, the first lord's flag commander. Their destination was Scotland and the sea anchorage of England's Home Fleet — the sea basin of Scapa Flow in the Orkney Islands. There, if anywhere, the Royal Navy should be buttoned up. Later he recalled how "on two or three occasions" in the autumn of 1914, most memorably on October 17, "the alarm was given that there was a U-boat inside the anchorage. Guns were fired, destroyers thrashed the waters, and the whole gigantic armada put out to sea in haste and dudgeon." Scapa was that important.[32]

Anxiety over the sea basin had returned, and this time the threat was real. In his lap lay a locked box of secret documents, among them a shocking report from the Chiefs of Staff Committee revealing that Scapa's defenses would not be ready until the spring of 1940. Arriving, he called on Sir Charles Forbes, the commander in chief, aboard H.M.S. *Nelson,* the admiral's flagship. Sir Charles confirmed that the basin's entrance channels were "not properly netted." The old steel webs had rusted, rotted, broken up, and drifted away. Winston immediately issued an order, stamped "urgent," calling for nets, booms, blockships (sunken ships barring entrance channels), antiaircraft guns, patrol craft, balloons, and searchlights. Until they were in place Scapa was insecure, an inviting target for daring German submarine commanders.[33]

And U-boat *Kapitäns*, so successful in sinking merchantmen, were now turning their periscopes toward Britain's ships of war. The enemy had actually laid a minefield across the mouth of the Thames, disabling one warship. After a second RN ship was sunk, the government, worried about civilian morale, had suppressed news of the loss. Two days before Churchill entrained for Scotland a U-boat had fired a salvo of torpedoes at H.M.S. *Ark Royal*, an aircraft carrier; they missed, and the carrier's destroyer escort sank the sub, but it was disquieting to know that Dönitz's vessels were lurking in British waters, capable of striking one of His Majesty's capital ships at any hour.

Indeed, it happened while Churchill was slumbering aboard H.M.S. *Nelson*, as he learned the next day. He and his party returned from Inverness to London aboard an overnight sleeper, and "as we got out at Euston," Winston wrote, "I was surprised to see the First Sea Lord on the platform. Admiral Pound's look was grave. 'I have some bad news for you, First Lord. The *Courageous* was sunk yesterday in the Bristol Channel.'" The ship had been an aircraft carrier, "a very necessary ship at this time," as Churchill wrote, and Bristol Channel, lying between South Wales and Somerset, was very close to home. Churchill told Pound, "We can't expect to carry on a war like this without these sorts of things happening from time to time. I have seen lots of this before." But within he was seething. He knew there would be questions in the House of Commons. To bring unconvoyed merchantmen into port he had been using carriers as escorts. *Courageous* had been attended by four destroyers, but two of them had been detached to hunt a Nazi submarine elsewhere. As the carrier turned into the wind to receive her aircraft, another U-boat *Kapitän* ran up his periscope and saw her naked flank in his cross hairs. He emptied his torpedo tubes and 518 Englishmen drowned, including the captain, who chose, as captains in those days did, to go down with his ship.[34]

Churchill's anxiety over Scapa Flow continued and mounted after His Majesty's Government spurned a peace feeler from Hitler. The offer had reached London via Birger Dahlerus. In Göring's presence, the Führer had proposed that a British representative — Ironside's name was mentioned — meet Göring "in some neutral country." Halifax on October 5 told the War Cabinet that "We should not absolutely shut the door"; Hoare suggested that Britain "damp down" her "anti-Göring propaganda"; Kingsley Wood also thought Göring the man to back, because "he would be glad to secure the removal of Herr Hitler." They had learned nothing, could not grasp the strength of the Führer's hold on his people, did not realize that the life expectancy of any German who moved against him would be measured in minutes. Churchill swiftly disposed of their arguments. If the overture was insincere its "real object might be to spread division and doubt amongst us"; if sincere, it had been inspired "not from any sense of magnanimity, but from weakness." The war, he suggested, might not be so popular in Germany as Goebbels insisted. On October 12 Chamberlain rejected the Nazi approach in the House. Winston had written the firmer parts of his speech, and afterward he told Pound that "one must expect a violent reaction from Herr Hitler. Perhaps quite soon." He ordered "special vigilance," suggested that "the Fleet at Scapa should be loose and easy in its movements," and concluded: "Pray let me know anything else you think we can do, and how best to have everything toned up to concert pitch. The next few days are full of danger."[35]

Danger appeared outside Scapa Flow at seven o'clock the following evening in the form of *U-47*, commanded by a thirty-one-year-old Dönitz protégé, Lieutenant Commander Günther Prien. In the first war, Dönitz knew, two U-boats had attempted to penetrate the deep, almost landlocked basin, and neither had returned. But studying aerial photographs of the anchorage, Dönitz reached the conclusion that an adroit navigator could thread his way past the three sunken ships meant to block Holm Sound.

Prien was his best U-boat *Kapitän*, and he almost failed. It took him nearly six hours to do it — at one point he seemed hopelessly ensnarled in a cable from one of the blockships — but at 12:30 on the morning of October 14 he was inside the basin. Dead ahead, at four thousand yards, lay the battleship *Royal Oak*. His first salvo missed, but the second time his spread of four torpedoes exploded in concert, mortally wounding the capital ship. In his log Prien wrote: "There is a loud explosion, roar and rumbling. Then come columns of water, followed by columns of fire, and splinters fly through the air." Thirteen minutes later *Royal Oak* rolled on her side and sank, carrying with her 833 officers and men, among them their captain and the rear admiral commanding the Second Battle Squadron.[36]

"Poor fellows, poor fellows," Churchill said when told, "trapped in those black depths." He wept, then thought of the unknown submariner's achievement and murmured: "What a wonderful feat of arms." It was not so wonderful for him, however. He "understood," he wrote, "how First Lords of the Admiralty are treated when great ships are sunk and things go wrong. If we were in fact going over the same cycle a second time, should I have once again to endure the pangs of dismissal? Fisher, Wilson, Battenberg, Jellicoe, Beatty, Pakenham, Sturdee, all gone!" He set down some lines of the nineteenth-century Irish poet Thomas Moore:

> *I feel like one*
> *Who treads alone*
> *Some banquet hall deserted,*
> *Whose lights are fled,*

Whose garlands dead,
and all but he departed.[37]

Hoare wrote His Majesty's ambassador in Washington: "Winston has been through some rough moments over the Scapa incidents. Being for the moment the war hero, he has come through it fairly well. I shudder to think what would have happened had there been another First Lord and he had been in Opposition." Exactly. Chamberlain could hardly dismiss the chief critic of the prewar governments which had been responsible for Scapa's vulnerability; the whole country knew that Winston bore no responsibility for the peacetime Royal Navy. Nevertheless, he took the setback personally, and took it hard. In the House he tried to balance the loss against the number of U-boats the navy had destroyed, but the books wouldn't balance. Germany's submarines were expendable; British warships were her lifeline. After informing the War Cabinet that the Home Fleet was being moved to the Clyde estuary in southwest Scotland as a "temporary disposition" prior to a move into an east coast base, Rosyth, he declared that the loss of the *Royal Oak*, "though an extremely regrettable disaster, does not materially affect the general naval position."[38]

It did, though. Germany was jubilant, Hitler ecstatic, Lieutenant Commander Prien a national hero. Even William L. Shirer was impressed, writing in his diary that the British battleship had been sunk in "the middle of Scapa Flow, Britain's greatest naval base!" Dönitz had scored a coup for *U-boote*. At the outset of hostilities the Führer had instructed U-boats to conform to the Hague Convention, which prohibited attacks without warning on enemy passenger and merchant ships. Prien's achievement opened Hitler's eyes to the possibilities of submarines and their lethal torpedoes. On October 16 Grossadmiral Raeder, speaking in Hitler's name, formally announced that "All merchant ships definitely recognized as enemy can be torpedoed without warning." So, it developed, could those flying neutral flags — except those of the United States — if their destinations were English ports. Neutral shipping had been sunk before, inadvertently or by reckless commanders. Now it was Kriegsmarine policy.[39]

All the billboards urging Englishmen to "Talk Victory" seemed to mock the Admiralty, and Clementine Churchill wrote her sister Nellie at Chartwell: "The war news is grim beyond words. One must fortify oneself by remembering that whereas the Germans are (we *hope*) at their peak, we have only just begun. Winston works night & day — He is well Thank God & gets tired only when he does not get 8 hours sleep — He does not need it at a stretch but if he does not get that amount in the 24 then he gets weary."[40]

*   *   *

England needed, not talk of victory, but the real thing. Any bright news would almost have to come from the high seas; there was no fighting, nor the prospect of any, on land or in the air. So out of this nettle, frustration, the navy must pluck this flower, triumph. The issue was not merely civilian morale. Captain Pim's maps told a sad tale, growing gloomier as autumn waned. Britain's loss of shipping would approach 745,000 tons by spring — over two hundred vessels. On November 21 H.M.S. *Belfast*, a new cruiser just launched, was gravely damaged by a mine in the Firth of Forth; two days later the British merchant cruiser *Rawalpindi*, armed with only four six-inch guns, was destroyed by the *Scharnhorst*, which then returned safely home with her sister ship, *Gneisenau*. But the Admiralty's greatest worry lay in the South Atlantic, where the pocket battleship *Graf Spee* was running amok. There, on the hundredth day of the war, an England famished for glory was about to be fed.

During the first weeks of the war Hitler had held back his fast, lethal *Panzerschiffe*, hoping to impose his peace terms upon a dispirited England. Once it became clear that His Majesty's Government meant to stay the course, he unleashed them as surface raiders. Of his two pocket battleships, *Deutschland* proved a disappointment. She was recalled after sinking only two merchantmen, one a neutral, and capturing a third, the U.S. freighter *City of Flint*, a prize Hitler did not need. *Flint* became the eye of a diplomatic storm which ended only after a Norwegian vessel intercepted her and returned her to her American crew. The tale of *Graf Spee* was very different, however. Commanded by Hans Langsdorff, a gallant, Wilhelmine anachronism, *Spee* had sent nine British cargo ships to the bottom without the loss of a single German life.

His adversary now was Commodore Henry Harwood, RN, and His Majesty's South Atlantic Fleet. Finding a single ship in so broad a vastness was almost impossible, but it was also crucial; *Graf Spee* was not only terrorizing merchant captains; the hunt for her was tying down over twenty Allied warships badly needed elsewhere, among them the carrier *Ark Royal*, the battle cruiser *Renown*, and the French battleship *Strasbourg*. Harwood believed that sooner or later Langsdorff would be irresistibly drawn to the fat, rich merchantmen emerging from the broad estuary of the River Plate, bound for England. He was right. Unfortunately, when the *Spee* hove into view at 5:52 on the morning of December 13, Harwood's force was no match for her. His heavyweights were elsewhere, too far to be recalled in time. He commanded three vessels: the British heavy cruiser *Exeter*, with six eight-inch guns; and two light cruisers, *Ajax* (his flagship) and the New Zealand *Achilles*, with six-inchers. The range of the German battleship's eleven-inchers was fifteen miles.

The commodore had issued a standing order to all RN vessels in the South Atlantic; should they find a Nazi battleship they were to "attack at once by day or night." Now, after scattering his small command so that Langsdorff would confront warships from three different directions, he sent *Exeter* racing toward Langsdorff at flank speed, 33 knots. Because the enemy was lunging forward at 28 knots, the two vessels were approaching one another at 50 miles an hour. *Ajax* and *Achilles* were also pouring it on, but *Exeter* was the first to come within range of Langsdorff's guns, and moments after she did, a 670-pound shell killed the crew manning the starboard torpedo tubes and crippled both communications and the ship's gun control.

But *Exeter* kept closing. Her gunners had just straddled the German ship when another huge shell demolished the wheelhouse and tore away one of the British gun turrets. Still she continued to close. The captain, though wounded, took a compass from one of the lifeboats and organized a line of tars to relay his orders to the helmsman abaft, where the strongest men in the crew, straining aching muscles, turned the cruiser's rudder by hand. They did it, to no avail; two more German shells hit the *Exeter,* one tearing up the deck and gouging out a huge gash on a flank, just above the waterline, while the other left a gaping wound in her port flank. Several fires had broken out in the ship; she was enveloped in smoke; fifty-one seamen lay dead. But *Exeter* had done her job, for *Ajax* and *Achilles* now had the *Panzerschiffe*. They were within range, their gunners were skilled veterans, and their six-inch shells were riddling the *Graf Spee*. After ninety minutes of continuous combat, with the pocket battleship swinging about, trying to decide which of the three attackers threatened her most, Harwood ordered his captains to make smoke and break off action.

The mauled *Exeter* headed for the Falkland Islands and repair. *Ajax* and *Achilles* were less battered, though the captain of the *Achilles* had been wounded in both legs and *Ajax*'s after gun turrets had been knocked out. The real loser, however, was Langsdorff. He himself had been hit by one British shell; his casualty list included thirty-seven men killed in action. His ship was a wreck. She had been hit eighteen times. Gaping holes had been opened in the deck and both flanks, several guns no longer functioned, her galleys were ruined, and she was almost out of ammunition. A voyage home was out of the question; even if unchallenged she could never make it. Repairs were essential. He limped into neutral — but anti-Nazi — Uruguay and asked for two weeks to put his ship in shape. He was given seventy-two hours. *Ajax* and *Achilles*, he knew, would be radioing for reinforcements. He did what he thought was sensible. His men were given berths on German freighters in the port, his ship was scuttled, and he himself, after wrapping himself in an old banner of imperial Germany — *not* the Nazi swastika — shot himself. He left a note: "For a captain with a sense of honor, it goes without saying that his personal fate cannot be separated from that of his ship."

The Royal Navy's triumph, wrote Churchill, "gave intense joy to the British nation and enhanced our prestige throughout the world. The spectacle of the three smaller British ships unhesitatingly attacking and putting to flight their far more heavily gunned and armoured antagonist was everywhere admired." His youngest daughter remembers: "It was a glorious victory, and brought a gleam of light into a dark December." Harwood was knighted and made an admiral. The sea lords proposed to leave *Exeter* in the Falklands, unrepaired, until the end of the war, but Winston would have none of it. Instead, he proposed to bring Sir Henry and his British ships home. He had not exaggerated the country's elation; acclaiming the heroes would guarantee their remembrance and give civilian morale a badly needed lift.[41]

By now Churchill had established his authority over the Admiralty. "Conveniently forgotten," one historian writes, was "his role in scaling down the navy's cruiser-building programme when Chancellor of the Exchequer in 1924–29. Remembered was his experience of the Admiralty, his love of the sea and the navy, his deep knowledge of the role of sea power in British history, and his reputation for getting things done." His weakness was his love of gadgetry and wildly improbable schemes. Admiral J. H. Godfrey notes: "Anything unusual or odd or dramatic intrigued him: Q ships, dummy ships, the stillborn operation 'Catherine' " (of this, more presently), "deception, sabotage, and, no doubt influenced by Professor Lindemann, the application of novel scientific methods."[42]

In retrospect some of his projects seem absurd. "White Rabbit Number 6," as he called it, was a "trench-cutting tank," capable of excavating an earthwork six feet deep and three feet wide at a rate of one mile an hour. Weighing 130 tons, standing eight feet tall, and stretching eighty feet long, it was to be used at night, penetrating the enemy's lines and taking him by surprise. The cabinet approved it; no one seems to have asked how surprise could be achieved by a device whose noise would be deafening. At the Admiralty, according to Godfrey, these schemes were regarded as outlets for the first lord's "demonic energy and extraordinary imagination," and generally tolerated, though some were considered "offensive." One pet project was an antiaircraft device which he called the Naval Wire Barrage (NWB). It looked like a large umbrella stand. In reality it was a multiple launcher into which were crammed fourteen three-inch projectiles, each carrying two thousand feet of wire with a small parachute at one end and a two-pound bomb at the other. Once the launcher had been rocketed aloft, the projectiles would be ejected at four thousand feet downward, their descent slowed by the parachutes. If an aircraft struck a wire, the bomb would be drawn upward and explode when it hit the plane's wing. It was the Prof's idea. Churchill thought NWBs marvelous, and despite his Ordnance Department's advice he ordered forty of the ungainly contraptions mounted on forty RN ships. They proved worthless. Rear Admiral R. D. Nicholls puts it bluntly: "The NWB was considered by everyone except Winston as plain crazy." Then he takes the larger view: "It was just part of the price — and not a very high one — that had to be paid to keep Winston going. Without him Britain and the Free World were sunk."[43]

In fact, as the war progressed, many of his ideas were to generate highly useful innovations: "Window" (strips of tinfoil dropped by bombers to confuse enemy radar), "Pluto" (a pipeline under the Channel), "Gee" (a device for guiding pilots), and "Mulberry" (the artificial harbors used in the D day invasion of Hitler's Europe).

What was needed now was a concept, a device, *something* that would make submarining so dangerous that Karl Dönitz would be walking the Kurfürstendamm looking for a job. Thus far, nothing had been found that surpassed the last war's answer to the U-boat, the destroyer. Unfortunately, the Royal Navy was incredibly short of destroyers — and the prospects for more were dim. "It is most disconcerting," Winston wrote Rear Admiral Fraser at the start of the war, "that we only get six destroyers in the present year, then no more for nine months, and only three more in the whole of 1940. Nine destroyers in sixteen months," he declared, "cannot possibly be accepted." Later, in his memoirs, he wrote: "Destroyers were our most urgent need, and also our worst feature."[44]

Here was a void that wanted filling. He hadn't forgotten the Nazi peril in the sky, so he called for the design and mass production of an "antisubmarine and anti-air vessel," built with "the greatest simplicity of armament and equipment" to free the few destroyers in commission for duty elsewhere. The ships he had in mind, he wrote in an Admiralty memorandum, "will be deemed 'Cheap and Nasties' (cheap to us, nasty to the U-boat)." Because they would be "built for a particular but urgent job," they would be useless once their mission was accomplished. Not to worry; the important thing was to "get the job done." The Prof, now working full time at the Admiralty, told him modern warfare could certainly be nasty, but never inexpensive. The *Unterseewaffe* threat would continue to grow. The Admiralty would have to fight back with its very thin line of destroyers.[45]

Most senior naval officers who worked with Winston allude to this quintessential Victorian trait — the late Victorians believed inventors could accomplish anything, and in the world of their limited imagination they were right. Yet these same officers had exaggerated claims for asdic before

Winston saw or heard it. And he and the Prof (whom the admirals had come to detest) *did* contribute to technological warfare. One early contribution was Britian's effective response to the magnetic mine. Here Churchill revealed the double standard found in all warriors; a weapon is admirable if his side has found it first, despicable if found first by the enemy. In a memorandum to Inskip a year earlier, he suggested that disabling the Kiel Canal would be a prime objective in any war with the Reich, and recommended that *"special fuses with magnetic actuation"* be considered. But while the British were still studying the problem, the Germans solved it. In the first weeks of the war their magnetic mines, dropped by parachute in shallow waters of channels and harbors and activated when a ship passed over them, became a nightmare for merchantmen.[46]

Winston was outraged. The "Nahrzees" (he was working on that idiosyncratic delivery, and each time, he came closer to making "Nazi" sound like an unspeakably vulgar moist petard) had stolen his idea. Briefly he persuaded himself that the device itself was criminal. The new mines, he said, were "contrary to the accepted rules of sea warfare," and he told the House of Commons: "This is about the lowest form of warfare that can be imagined. It is the warfare of the I.R.A., leaving the bomb in the parcels' office at the railway station. The magnetic mine . . . may perhaps be Herr Hitler's much vaunted secret weapon. It is certainly a characteristic weapon, and one that will no doubt be for ever associated with his name." Lacking a specimen of the mine, no counter could be devised. Then, as Churchill wrote, "fortune . . . favoured us." The night of November 22 a Nazi plane was seen dropping a large object, attached to a parachute, into the mud of the Thames estuary off Shoeburyness. Before dawn two RN officers skilled in underwater weapons retrieved the device, which, as suspected, turned out to be a magnetic mine. Here the Prof intervened, devising a method of demagnetizing ships by girdling them with an electric coil — degaussing, as it is called. Before the winter was out, Winston had his own magnetic mines and had forwarded a plan to sow the Rhine with ten thousand fluvial mines, only to have it vetoed in the spring by the French, who feared Nazi reprisals.[47]

Franklin Roosevelt later said: "Winston has fifty ideas a day, and three or four are good." He was no crank; when he hit the jackpot it was the mother lode. Although the Germans were the first to produce the magnetic mine, their very success demonstrated that his conception had been sound. Most of his schemes were politely discussed and then dropped. The difficulty was that his Admiralty staff was dealing with genius, with a man who thought in cosmic terms, and that the price for some of these excursions was beyond the grasp of career naval officers.

So it was with "Catherine," named after Catherine the Great, "because," he explained, "Russia lay in the background of my thought." Churchill introduced this proposed operation to his closest advisers in a five-page outline on September 12, Britain's tenth day at war. Unlike the rest of the Admiralty, Churchill had stopped speculating over where the Kriegsmarine would strike next and instead considered a Royal Navy counteroffensive. Thinking defensively, his admirals had assumed that if they could keep U-boat sinkings of Britain-bound merchantmen to a minimum and blockade enemy ports, they would have done their job, leaving it up to the soldiers to do theirs. But the first lord was taking a very different line. He was talking about a naval strategy which had never entered their minds, and as he talked, they wished it hadn't entered his. The command of the Baltic Sea, as he later pointed out in his memoirs, was "vital to the enemy. Scandinavian supplies, Swedish ore, and above all protection against Russian descents on the long undefended northern coastline of Germany — in one place little more than a hundred miles from Berlin — made it imperative for the German Navy to dominate the Baltic." Moreover, as he had noted earlier, an "attack upon the Kiel Canal" would render "that side-door from the Baltic useless, even if only at intervals."[48]

Churchill was contemplating an imaginative — and perilous — action: the seizure of the entire Baltic, the Reich's only sea link with Norway, Finland, and especially Sweden, the Ruhr's chief source of iron ore. He knew it would be difficult, but no one could doubt that success would bring Hitler to his knees. His source of raw materials for tanks, artillery, mortars, and rifles would be cut off.

A critical challenge lay in the narrow waters joining the North Sea and the Baltic; navigation of them by a strong fleet would attract swarms of Luftwaffe bombers. Winston had already discussed possible solutions with the Admiralty's director of naval construction. "It would . . . be necessary," he noted in his September 12 memorandum, "to strengthen the armour deck so as to give exceptional protection against air attack." He planned to commit two British battleships ("but of course 3 would be better") with fifteen-inch guns; "their only possible antagonists" would be the *Scharnhorst* and the *Gneisenau,* "the sole resources of Germany" in the battleship class. Both would be destroyed by the heavier guns of the British battleships, which would outrange them and "would shatter them." Escorting them, and shielding them, would be a dozen vessels yet to be built, "mine bumpers," he called them, with "a heavy fore end to take the shock of any exploding mine." Confiding only in Pound, he set down the five-page précis of his plan, marked "Most Secret." He wrote: "I commend these ideas to your study, hoping that the intention will be to solve the difficulties." Distribution of Catherine was confined to eight copies, "of which all except one," he wrote, "will be destroyed after the necessary examination has been made."[49]

Pound commented: "There can be little doubt that if we could maintain control of the Baltic for a considerable period it would greatly enhance our prestige." But the first sea lord saw difficulties. If the Soviet Union became a Nazi ally, the operation was doomed. The "*active* cooperation of Sweden" in providing a base, repair facilities, and oil must be assured, and the British ships committed must be expendable, "such that we can with our Allies at that time win the war without [them], in spite of any probable combination against us." Winston scrawled, "I entirely agree." To him Catherine had become "the supreme naval offensive open to the Royal Navy." Others receiving Winston's presentation studied it seriously and thought it feasible if . . . And then they, too, saw problems. The decisive problem was air power. Even admirals who underrated it had to consider the Luftwaffe threat. Battleships could be taken into the Baltic, but RAF fighters could not accompany them; the ships would be under constant, heavy attack from land-based enemy aircraft. Churchill dismissed the Luftwaffe. He wrote Roosevelt: "We have not been at all impressed by the accuracy of the German air bombing of our warships. They seem to have no effective bomb sights." In any event, he held, the ship's antiaircraft gunners could eliminate the air threat.[50]

He convinced no one. The support for Catherine, never strong, faded away. Moreover, it seems not to have occurred to Winston that the Nazis could occupy Denmark, move heavy artillery to the shore, and lay mines in the Kogrund Channel. Catherine died a slow, quiet, expensive death. Apart from preempting the time of Britain's best naval minds, twelve million pounds was spent on special equipment for the battleships' escorts. Churchill was disappointed, but because the entire plan had been highly classified he faced no barrage of criticism. Indeed, his reputation at the Admiralty shone as brightly as ever. The general verdict among the sea lords and other senior officials was that Catherine had been brilliantly conceived, that it could have ended the war if successful, but that too much had been at stake — and the ice too thin for skating.

Slowly the Admiralty came to realize that while the first lord might be dissuaded from this or that, he never lost because he never quit; his mind had many tracks, and if one was blocked, he left it and turned to another, the very existence of which was unknown until he chose to reveal it. Admiral Fraser, the flag officer responsible for naval construction, later wrote how Winston stunned him by asking him point-blank: "Well, Admiral, what is the navy doing about RDF?" Fraser was tongue-tied. Radar was the most closely guarded secret in the British military establishment, roughly comparable to America's Manhattan Project three years later. "A number of able officers were working on the problem," Fraser later wrote, "but to make any real progress a high degree of priority — especially in finance — was essential."[51]

Fully developed RDF had been a casualty of Chamberlain's cuts in military spending. England should have had a long lead with this extraordinary defensive weapon; Englishmen had discovered and perfected it, and Zossen didn't even know it existed. Yet not a single vessel in the Royal Navy had been equipped with it. After a long silence Churchill said, "Well, Admiral, it is very important," and later sent Fraser an instruction that all British warships, particularly "those engaged in the U-boat fighting," be provided "with this distinguishing apparatus." Fraser wondered how Churchill, a backbencher until the day England declared war on Germany, had heard about RDF. His bewilderment would have deepened had he known that Winston's knowledge of radar dated from July 25, 1935 — within twenty-four hours of Robert Watson-Watt's completion of experiments proving that the distance and direction of approaching aircraft could be pinpointed by using radio waves.[52]

If all the views of Churchill's months at the Admiralty are pooled — Winston seen in the letters, diaries, memoirs, and recollections of those who worked under him then and were close enough to reach informed judgments — a striking portrait emerges. It is distorted as Picasso's *Les Demoiselles d'Avignon* is distorted, complex and defying proportion but recognizable as the powerful image of an emerging warlord. The approval or disapproval of the witnesses is essentially irrelevant. They see him differently because he is different to each, possessing a plural, kaleidoscopic personality. His guise depends upon the man confronting him, and what he wants that man to see.

The first sea lord outranks the others and is closest to him. His admiration for Churchill is almost unqualified. No one in the Royal Navy can launch a direct attack on the first lord because Sir Dudley Pound, a great sailor and a man of absolute integrity, will deflect the blow. Pound's loyalty is reinforced by the first lord's popularity in the fleet. Captain S. W. Roskill, the distinguished naval historian, challenges this popularity, noting that "There was not one Admiral in an important sea command . . . whom Churchill, sometimes with Pound's support, did not attempt to have relieved." But admirals are not the fleet. Below decks, support for the first lord is strong. The ratings admire a fighter; they have heard of his concern for their welfare, which is genuine, and see him as a stimulating, inspiring first lord. Winston's constituency, then, is solidly behind him.[53]

He needs that support because a warlord, by definition, is a man with enemies. His natural aggression, curbed in peacetime, a stigma only a year earlier, is now a virtue. He cannot compromise, nor should he. Leaders in battle are guided less by reason than by instinct. He has always distrusted Eamon de Valera, and now in the War Cabinet he proposes that England reclaim her former bases in Eire, by force if necessary. Even Pound knows that the navy has no use for the bases and can easily deny them to the Germans. Churchill is wrong. Nevertheless, Englishmen approve, remembering: *Churchill stood up to the IRA*. Sir Andrew Cunningham, the RN's Mediterranean commander in chief, protests the first lord's repeated interference in tactical issues, telling him not only what to do, but how to do it. Commanders in chief in other theaters have the same grievance but wisely remain silent. Cunningham wins little sympathy in England. *Churchill has shown him who's in charge.* Winston has issued an order — "Plan R" — for strengthening the defenses at Scapa Flow. Contracts are signed. Nothing happens. He issues a general order to the Admiralty, reminding all hands of the time lag since Plan R was approved, and asks: "What, in fact, has been done since? How many blockships sunk? How many nets made? How many men have been in work for how many days? What buildings have been erected? What gun sites have been concreted and prepared? What progress has been made with the run-ways of the aerodrome? I thought we settled two months ago to have a weekly report. . . . Up to the present I share the Commander-in-Chief's anxieties about the slow progress of this indispensable work."[54]

That is on a Monday. On Tuesday Scapa is a hive of construction activity. R. D. Oliver, the officer responsible for Plan R, recalls: "With his backing it was amazing how bureaucratic obstruction melted." The impression: *Churchill gets things done.*[55]

In the House of Commons he consistently overstates the number of Nazi U-boats destroyed. His old adversaries make much of that, but this is war; facts are its first casualties. Leaders exaggerate the enemy's losses and inflate their own triumphs. To do otherwise would be interpreted, in the eyes of his people and his foes, as a sign of weakness. Donald McLachan, who understands this, writes afterward: "The First Lord had a morale role to play. The Navy was the only Service which was fully engaged at the time; it must not be discouraged by too rigorous a method of assessing 'kills'; it was essential that the nation should have some sense of action and success and achievement; and the only material that was readily available at that time came from the U-boat war. It was essential to make the most of what was happening [though] in the process truth suffered." Significantly, in less than a year the RAF will play faster and looser with *its* kill figures, but its records will go virtually unchallenged. There is no Churchill at the Air Ministry to incite critics.[56]

Nevertheless Churchill is disqualified, by temperament, from waging an effective campaign against U-boats. He has known from the beginning that if Britain loses the duel with Nazi submarines she cannot survive. The high priority he gives to converting trawlers into antisub vessels and his emphasis on destroyer production will contribute to the Admiralty's eventual success. The difficulty is that all this is *defensive,* and he is comfortable only when carrying the war to the enemy. He overrates the asdic. Worse, he withdraws destroyers from convoys to form "hunting groups" or "attacking groups," directing them to seek and destroy U-boats. This is "aggressive," he argues; convoy duty, on the other hand, is "passive." He minutes to Pound — who agrees — that "Nothing can be more important in the anti-submarine war than to try to obtain an independent flotilla which could work like a cavalry division." He is dead wrong; weakening convoys to permit offensive sweeps fails on both counts — no U-boats are sunk, and their elusive commanders, seizing opportunities while the destroyers are looking for them elsewhere, penetrate convoys with alarming results. Yet Churchill will stick to his "hunt 'em down" strategy after he becomes prime minister. Not until 1942, when the effectiveness of the convoy strategy has been demonstrated beyond all doubt, does he accept it without reservation.[57]

Meetings of the full cabinet, the War Cabinet, and the Land Forces Committee engage him in frequent and often lengthy colloquies with men against whom he has been waging parliamentary guerrilla warfare for the better part of a decade. He bears no grudges — "The only man I hate is Hitler," he says, "and that's professional" — but some of his adversaries are less generous. Although the year since Munich should have humbled them, humility is a rare virtue among men of this class, especially at this time. Sam Hoare was first lord in 1936 and 1937; he cannot evade some of the responsibility for the neglect of Scapa's defenses, without which Lieutenant Commander Prien's feat would have been impossible. Yet if Hoare has ever suffered a pang of guilt, no one has heard him acknowledge it. In the first days of the war he *was* heard describing Churchill as "an old man who easily gets tired," a judgment which would startle those at the Admiralty trying to match the old man's pace. According to John Reith, whom Chamberlain brings into the government as minister of information, the prime minister says Churchill's reputation is "inflated," largely "based on broadcasts." Reith, who would have prevented those broadcasts if Winston hadn't been a minister, agrees, and notes in his diary that there is "no doubt" about how the P.M. "feels about Churchill." Early in the war Hoare tells Beaverbrook that at meetings Winston is "very rhetorical, very emotional, and, most of all, very reminiscent." Actually, the Cabinet Papers show that Churchill, like everyone else at the time, is trying to understand what is happening in Poland.[58]

🦁   🦁

blitz · krieg . . . [G, lit., lightning war, fr. *blitz* lightning + *krieg* war]. . . .

So the word appears in *Webster's Third New International Dictionary*, presented as a term borrowed from the German. The anonymous journalist who first used it in an English periodical clearly agreed. "In the opening stage of the war," he wrote in the October 7, 1939, issue of *War Illustrated*, "all eyes were turned on Poland, where the German military machine was engaged in *Blitz-Krieg* — lightning war — with a view to ending it as soon as possible." In fact, the term "lightning war," like the concept itself, was of British origin. The bloody stalemate of 1914–1918 had bred pacifism and isolationism among civilians. Professional soldiers — and one statesman, Churchill — agreed that a reprise of trench warfare, with its adumbrations of stalemate and lethal attrition, was unthinkable.

They doubted, however, that it could be abolished; like Plato they believed that only the dead have seen the end of war. Therefore, men like Major General J. F. C. Fuller and Captain Basil Liddell Hart, searching for an alternative, studied Great War engagements in which tanks had been used successfully. Working out the theoretical possibilities of a totally mechanized offensive, they evolved the doctrine of mobile warfare, combining tanks and tactical aircraft. Commenting on the Wehrmacht's Polish campaign Liddell Hart wrote: "When the theory had been originally developed, in Britain, its action had been depicted in terms of the play of 'lightning.' From now on, aptly but ironically, it came into worldwide currency under the title of 'Blitzkrieg' — the German rendering."[59]

It might also have been christened *guerre d'éclairs*, for in Paris Colonel Charles de Gaulle, working independently, as always, had reached the same conclusion: "*la fluidité*" would be imperative on battlefields of the future and must be achieved, for "the sword is the axis of the world." But neither England nor France was interested in military innovation between the wars. Victors rarely are. Professional soldiers are wedded to tradition and resent change; politicians and the public flinch at the prospect of slaughter.[60]

The Conseil Supérieur had dismissed de Gaulle as an eccentric; Fuller, who had a knack for rubbing people the wrong way, was forced into early retirement; Liddell Hart was regarded as an entertaining writer with beguiling but impractical ideas.

Colonel Heinz Guderian, an enthusiastic reader of Fuller and Liddell Hart, was luckier. In the years before the Republic of Germany became the Third Reich, Guderian's superiors, like their fellow generals in England and France, were skeptical of mobile warfare. But he was among the ablest officers in the Reichswehr, the Wehrmacht's precursor, and so they threw him a sop — command of an armored battalion. He had no tanks, only automobiles with canvas superstructures identified by cardboard signs, PANZER or PANZERWAGEN, and aircraft had to be imagined. Then came Hitler. Like Churchill, the new Reich chancellor was fascinated by technical innovation. He first visited army maneuvers in the spring of 1933, and while other spectators were amused by Guderian's performance, Hitler instantly grasped its possibilities. He cried: "That's what I need! That's what I want!"[61]

Later Goebbels tried — with considerable success — to convince the world that every German division invading Poland was armored. Actually only nine were; the other forty-seven comprised familiar, foot-slogging infantrymen, wearing the same coal-scuttle helmets, the same field gray uniforms, and equipped much as their fathers had been on the Somme, in Flanders, and in the Argonne. That does not slight them; the Führer's soldiers were the best fighting men in Europe, and their morale was now at fever pitch. But it was the panzers which were terrifying. Each of Guderian's divisions was self-contained, comprising two tank regiments, self-propelled guns, and supporting units — engineers, reconnaissance companies, antitank and antiaircraft batteries, signalmen, and a regiment of infantry — transported on trucks or armored half-tracks. The Poles prayed for rain; commentators talked about "General Mud," as though World War II might be called off because of bad weather. But God wasn't riding at the Poles' stirrups that golden month. In 1870 and 1914 men in spiked helmets had talked of *Kaiserwetter*. Now it was *Hitlerwetter*, and Guderian's men found the dry, rolling plains of Poland ideal for maneuver.

The Poles were confident; they were overconfident; they were eager for battle, buoyed by Radio Warsaw, which played the national anthem, Chopin, and martial music, over and over. By the standards of 1920, when Poles had last seen action — against the Bolsheviks — they possessed a fine army: two million men under arms, with another million hurrying to the front. Twelve splendid brigades of horse cavalry were the pride of Poland. But they had only one armored brigade. Its tanks were obsolete. So were the air force's warplanes. And the battle plan of Marshal Edward Rydz-Smigly was a bad Polish joke. Since the Nazi occupation of Czechoslovakia had left the Poles with an immensely long frontier, it would have been prudent — it would have been sane — to assemble farther back. Instead, Rydz-Smigly decided to fight on the frontier, with no reserves behind his men and no defensive preparations. Their defense, he told incredulous military attachés from the Allied embassies, would be the counterattack.

Indulging his national pride, which his troops shared, over a third of his troops were concentrated in the Polish Corridor, exposed to Germans attacking from both east and west. Because of this stratagem, tracts more vital to Poland's defense were left thinly manned. Perhaps the mind-set of the Polish military on the eve of battle is best illustrated by Rydz-Smigly's high hopes for one unit, the crack Pomorska Cavalry Brigade. As the spearhead of Guderian's First Panzer Division appeared in the valley below, white-gloved officers signaled trumpeters, who sounded the charge. Down the slope rode the Pomorskas, sabers gleaming, pennons waving, moving at a steady gallop, their lances at the ready. And then, as they were preparing for the final irresistible surge, the Germans squeezed their triggers. The limbs, viscera, and skin — of men and horses, inextricably tangled — spewed gorily for over a mile. The few Polish survivors were taken prisoner. They were seen rapping hard on the tanks' armor. Somebody had told them German armor, like Guderian's mock panzers of 1933, was cardboard, and someone had been wrong.

Elsewhere Poles heard an ominous hum and looked up to see squadron after squadron of bombers — nearly four thousand of them — headed for Warsaw, where, by midafternoon, they annihilated the Polish air force, such as it was, on the ground. Poland's one million reservists never reached their units; the Luftwaffe blew up the railroad stations where they waited, or the trains they had already boarded. Then it bombed radio stations, bridges, factories, barracks, and public buildings. Before heading home to the Reich the bombers sowed incendiary and high-explosive bombs among the densest concentrations of civilians, including children's playgrounds. Farmers who had never held a weapon larger than a shotgun saw rapid-firing, self-propelled guns rolling down the rutted dirt roads at forty miles an hour. What they did not see, and would not have believed if they saw it, was the intricate communications net — telegraph, telephone, and radio — which coordinated the huge juggernaut.

The Polish soldiers on the frontier, each standing in front of a single hastily strung strand of barbed wire, each assuming that the high-level, Warsaw-bound bombers had been the entire Luftwaffe, were in for a shock. It was *half* the Luftwaffe. Now came the rest of it, meant for them, led by the Junkers 87 dive-bombers — the Stukas. The Stuka was more than a bomber; it was also an instrument of fear. Many had sirens attached to their undercarriages, and as the plane dove vertically, the ear-splitting siren convinced every Pole that it, and its bomb load, was headed straight for him. The Ju 87s left. It was time for the invading army to launch its ground attack. Guderian's panzers came in the first wave — motorcycles followed by armored cars, then tanks, then trucks bearing artillery and infantry. To the Poles' bewilderment, these Germans were not seeking a fight. They deliberately avoided pitting strength against strength, preferring to probe for soft spots. Eventually, given Rydz-Smigly's dispositions, they would find one, lunge through, and fan out, destroying communications, machine-gunning Poles who thought themselves safe behind the front, and — here tactics merged with strategy — splitting the Polish army into fragments, each out of touch with the others. When the marshal's headquarters tried to maneuver the troops, either the lines were dead or troop movement was impossible because panicky Polish civilians had choked the roads. This frenzy was encouraged by Nazis who, simulating Polish news programs with German commentators fluent in Polish, told the people to flee down the very roads Rydz-Smigly most needed. The Germans had enlarged the compass of military science. They had discovered how to exploit the very people defending armies are supposed to protect — the young, the aged, the women trembling at the prospect of rape — by encouraging them to ensnarl the defenders' rear.

By Sunday, September 3, when England and France finally declared war on Germany, the fighting in Poland was in its third day, and the situation of the defenders was critical. The Poles now had no air force. The country's railroad grid was in ruins. All bridges, except those which were useful to the Nazis, had been demolished. The Wehrmacht's troops, healthy and strong, were led by some of the greatest generals in German history — Gerd von Rundstedt, Heinz Guderian, Walter von Reichenau, Fedor von Bock, Paul von Kleist, Günther von Kluge, Georg von Küchler — all, indeed, except Erich von Manstein, who was planning the invasion of the Low Countries and France. Already the Polish frontier had been deeply penetrated by three great German drives, each advancing on Warsaw: eight divisions from East Prussia, twelve from Pomerania, and another seventeen — the main thrust, 886,000 men — heading straight for the capital from Silesia in the south. That Sunday, after the British declaration of hostilities but before France's, Kluge's 630,000 men had cut off the corridor and were advancing southeastward along both banks of the Vistula, toward the capital. All other commanders had reached their objectives and were engaged in complex envelopments, double envelopments, and encircling movements, incomprehensible to laymen in other countries, who nevertheless grasped their essence — that with the war less than seventy-two hours old, the defense of Poland was already disintegrating.

In London it was *hot*. Churchill could not recall a more pitiless heat wave. He wore a black alpaca jacket over a linen shirt and reflected that this was "indeed just the weather that Hitler wanted for his invasion of Poland. The great rivers on which the Poles had counted in their defensive plan were nearly everywhere fordable, and the ground was hard and firm for the movement of tanks and vehicles of all kinds." The War Cabinet, he wrote, stood "around the Cabinet table," witnessing the beginnings of "the swift and almost mechanical destruction of a weaker state according to Hitler's method and long design."[62]

It was hard to believe that the Poles actually had a quarter-million more men under arms than the invaders. "Each morning," Churchill later recalled, "the CIGS, General Ironside, standing before the map, gave long reports and appreciations which very soon left no doubt in our minds that the resistance of Poland would speedily be crushed. Each day I reported to the Cabinet the Admiralty tale, which usually consisted of a list of British merchant ships sunk by the U-boats." On Monday spearheads of Reichenau's panzers — which had jumped off from Jablunkov Pass in the Carpathian Mountains only three days earlier — reached and crossed the Pilica, fifty miles behind the Polish frontier. On Tuesday, the day Dönitz's submarines sank the *Royal Sceptre* and the *Bosnia,* Ironside told them that several panzer divisions had overrun the Poles' defenses at Czestochowa —a breakthrough "that might result in Germany capturing Poland's main industrial area" and the withdrawal of Rydz-Smigly's army to the line of the Vistula. Even now, however, no one in the Cabinet Room envisaged the disappearance of organized Polish resistance. They were remembering how the great German offensive of 1914 had been stopped in the Battle of the Marne and wondering when and where the Poles would roll back the field gray tide. But this was not 1914, and the Vistula was not the Marne.[63]

London newspapers on September 4 reported another bombardment of Warsaw; civilian casualties were said to be heavy. Labour MPs, remembering Guernica, were calling for British action. So, within the government, was Churchill. That morning, at the second meeting of the War Cabinet, he pointed out that the "main German effort" was against the Poles and proposed that "every means possible should be employed to relieve the pressure," starting with an immediate attack on the Siegfried Line carried out by French infantry and the RAF. The rest of the War Cabinet agreed that such a move was "a vital necessity."[64]

It was indeed. To do otherwise would be dishonorable; the world would conclude that pledges by His Majesty's Government and the Third Republic were as worthless as Hitler's. The first article of the Anglo-Polish treaty signed ten days earlier specified: "Should one of the contracting parties become engaged in hostilities with a European Power in consequence of aggression by the latter . . . the other contracting party will at once give the contracting party engaged in hostilities all the support and assistance in its power," and the second paragraph stipulated that each country was committed to the use of force even in the absence of aggression, in the event of "any action . . . which clearly threatened, directly or indirectly, the independence of one of the contracting parties."[65]

The rub was that Britain, an island, shared no border with Germany. It had the Royal Navy and the RAF, but the Poles had not been challenged at sea, and the limited range of aircraft then ruled out intervention by Britain-based warplanes in the skies over Poland. Poland needed an army, and England didn't have one. On land, writes Telford Taylor, Britain was "still almost in the position of a nineteenth-century Asiatic state challenging with the traditional arms of the past a European power armed with modern artillery and machine guns." In 1914 Churchill, as first lord, had ferried seven superbly trained British divisions across the Channel. He was preparing to repeat this feat, but it was impossible now; the men weren't there; Britain's standing army was so small as to be embarrassing. All the War Office could send now was four divisions. Winston noted that at best this could be called "a symbolic contribution." He had been appalled to find that although England had been "the cradle of the tank in all its variants," the "awful gap" in this symbolic contingent was "the absence of even one armoured division in the British Expeditionary Force."[66]

The War Cabinet's Land Forces Committee met September 7, on what Winston called a "sweltering afternoon," at the Home Office with Hoare in the chair, and decided, after hearing the views of the army's high command, to "forthwith begin the creation of a fifty-five division army," hoping that "by the eighteenth month, two-thirds of this . . . would either already have been sent to France or be fit to take the field." The Air Ministry protested; it planned to build an enormous air force in two or three years, and "the full army programme could not be realized in the time limits of two years without serious interference with the air programme." That took a moment to sink in. The protester — a veteran civil servant who had been permanent under secretary to the Air Ministry when Winston was its minister between 1919 and 1920 — was objecting to army expansion before 1942. Now, in 1939, it was too late to save Poland, but a gesture should be made. To leave the French army standing alone was unthinkable. London was blacked out; Britain could not tell when her turn would come, but expected a massive Luftwaffe raid at any time, and here were the service bureaucracies talking of three-year plans, five-year plans, unaware that by 1942 all London might be reduced to an unrecognizable, uninhabited scene of desolation. In a meeting of the full War Cabinet, Kingsley Wood repeated the Air Ministry argument: the RAF insisted upon priority; the army would have to wait. Churchill vigorously replied to this position and set down his thoughts in a secret memorandum: "I cannot think that less than twenty divisions by March 1, 1940, would be fair to the French army. . . . We must take our place in the Line if we are to hold the Alliance together and win the war."[67]

It was a sensible point, but Chamberlain's men had developed a habit of attributing the lowest motives to him. In his diary Hoare noted that one man had whispered to him, "He is writing his new memoirs," and Oliver Stanley, president of the Board of Trade — in a reference to *The World Crisis*, Churchill's history of the last war — said bitingly, "Why did he not bring his *World War?*" Chamberlain hesitated; he finally endorsed the recommendations of the Land Forces Committee, but the committee's report contained some disquieting predictions. The French army, it said, would probably "require assistance" in equipping its men "after the first four months of the war." And yet, the report went on to say that perhaps France could help in remedying certain of *Britain's* deficiencies. Clementine Churchill, reading the War Office's shopping list later, commented: "It shews the interminable distance we had to travel before we could fight."[68]

Before England could fight she needed, not only troops and arms but also a government of fighting ministers, men prepared — as soldiers must be — to sacrifice everything, including their lives, toward a great objective, the destruction of Nazi Germany. Churchill was such a man. Despite his membership in the cabinet, however, he was virtually alone. The rest of the government was schizoid. Their faith had failed; they were like simple folk who have been told yesterday that the world would end today and have found the prophecy a fraud. Nevertheless, they remained evangelists. The appeasers were still devout, still hopeful that the shopworn messiah at No. 10 would be vindicated. But now England was at war, a war she could lose — would certainly lose if their advice prevailed.

Friday morning, September 8, the war was five days old, and in his briefing Ironside told the War Cabinet that the Poles were "fighting well and had not been broken." Another War Office summary added that although the Poles were "not demoralized," their movements were "much impeded by the overwhelming German superiority in the air and in armoured vehicles." They wanted to know what their allies in the West were doing. The Air Ministry had already received a message from the Polish air attaché in London asking for the "immediate" bombardment of German industries and airports within reach of the RAF. He received no satisfactory reply. That same day Leo Amery approached Kingsley Wood and asked if the government was going to help Poland. Amery suggested dropping incendiary bombs on the Black Forest. "Oh, you can't do that," the air minister said, "that's private property. You'll be asking me to bomb the Ruhr next." Essen's Gusstahlfabrik, the flagship of the Krupp munitions works, should have been leveled already, Amery said, but Kingsley Wood told him that should he do so, "American opinion" would be alienated. In his memoirs Amery wrote that he "went away very angry."

Hugh Dalton raised the same question; Kingsley Wood replied that such a mission would be a violation of the Hague Convention, that the RAF must concentrate on "military objectives."[69]

It was still His Majesty's Government's policy to avoid offending Germany; although Great Britain and the Third Reich were at war, Reith's BBC was uncomfortable with criticism of the enemy regime. Reith, now minister of information, denied air time to eminent Englishmen on the ground that they were too critical of Germany. As a cabinet minister Hore-Belisha could not be denied BBC time, and in October he delivered a superb speech on British war aims. They were not fighting to reconstitute Czechoslovakia or Poland, he said: "We are concerned with the frontiers of the human spirit. . . . Only the defeat of Nazi Germany can lighten the darkness which now shrouds our cities, and lighten the horizon for all Europe and the world." Hore-Belisha's days were numbered. Next to Churchill he was the ablest member of the War Cabinet, advocating vigorous prosecution of the war; nevertheless, in January 1940 the prime minister asked for his resignation. Chamberlain wanted to offer him the Ministry of Information, but Halifax objected to the appointment; it would have a "bad effect among the neutrals," he said, "because HB [is] a Jew." Being a Jew was worse in Germany, of course, but under His Majesty's Government at the time it was no character reference.[70]

On Wednesday, September 6, His Majesty's Government assured the House of Commons that the Luftwaffe was bombing "only Polish military objectives." Yet three days earlier the Warsaw government had informed HMG that twenty-seven towns had been bombed by Nazi planes and over a thousand civilians killed. Edward Spears decided to raise in the House "the question of the lack of support we are giving the Poles," but changed his mind when Kingsley Wood told him the reply would involve "questions of strategy" and to discuss them in public would be "most dangerous." On Saturday, Beck cabled Raczyński, instructing him to raise the issue in Whitehall. On Monday, the Polish ambassador told Cadogan: "This is very unfair to us. The least that we can ask is, what are you prepared to do?" Cadogan promised him an answer by the end of the day. But Raczyński never heard from Cadogan, then or later.[71]

Chamberlain saw the growing anger in the House. He believed he fathomed it. "The Amerys, Duff Coopers, and their lot," he wrote, "are consciously swayed by a sense of frustration because they can only look on." He added: "The personal dislike of Simon and Hoare has reached a pitch which I find difficult to understand." There was a great deal he did not understand; he was neither the first nor the last leader to lose his touch, his feeling for the temper of his people. Once war has been declared, the slate is wiped clean. A leader's peacetime policies are forgotten, even those which led the country into a war it did not want, unless, of course, he is so unwise as to bring them up. Even after the fall of Poland, after Fleet Street had printed evidence of Nazi crimes in Poland — the random murders, then mass executions; the tortures and the seizure of Poles to work in German munitions factories — the prime minister seriously considered a negotiated peace with a Reich purged of the more extreme Nazis. He had a "hunch," he wrote, that the war would end in the spring of 1940. "It won't be by defeat in the field," he wrote, "but by German realization that they *can't* win and that it isn't worth their while to go on getting thinner and poorer when they might have instant relief." If negotiations were successful the Germans might "not have to give up anything they really care about." One pictures Neville Chamberlain in hell, sitting at one end of a table with Satan at the other, each checking off items on his agenda, and a slow, awful expression of comprehension crossing the late P.M.'s face as he realizes that he has just traded his soul for a promise of future negotiations.[72]

One issue which eluded him completely was that the plight of the Poles could not be relieved by Allied defensive warfare in the west. An offensive, or a series of offensives, should be launched, and launched *now*, while the Wehrmacht was committed in Poland. Blood had to be spilled in a drive against the Siegfried Line or in bombing the Reich. An infantry attack on the western front depended upon France. Although the British Expeditionary Force (BEF) was growing in strength every week, the overwhelming majority of the troops there were French, and their decisions would determine the Allied strategy there. The RAF could bomb, but here again France, because of her proximity to the Reich, could cast the decisive vote.

France did. The vote was a veto. The French had ruled out bombing, Chamberlain explained to the War Cabinet, because the Nazis might retaliate by an air attack on one of the Seine bridges. Churchill was aroused, but "I could not move them," he wrote. "When I pressed very hard, they used a method of refusal which I never met before or since. [On one occasion in Paris] M. Daladier told me with an air of exceptional formality that 'The President of the Republic himself had intervened, and that no aggressive action must be taken which might only draw reprisals upon France.' " In his memoirs, Winston commented:

This idea of not irritating the enemy did not commend itself to me. Hitler had done his best to strangle our commerce by indiscriminate mining of our harbours. We had beaten him by defensive means alone. Good, decent civilised people, it appeared, must never strike themselves till after they have been struck dead. In these days the fearful German volcano and all its subterranean fires drew near to their explosion point. There were still months of pretended war. On the one side endless discussions about trivial points, no decisions taken, or if taken, rescinded, and the rule "Don't be unkind to the enemy, you will only make him angry." On the other, doom preparing — a vast machine grinding forward ready to break upon us![73]

The prime minister, it developed, had decided to avenge the Poles killed in Luftwaffe raids on Warsaw, Cracow, and Katowice by punishing the Reich with "truth raids." In truth raids, leaflets were to be substituted for bombs. This strategy assumed that once Germans read the leaflets describing Hitler's atrocities, they would rise up and overthrow their Nazi leadership. After the first mission over Germany, Kingsley Wood revealed that this ingenious approach had been his inspiration, and that the Nazis in Berlin were deeply troubled by them. They were not without peril for the RAF; German antiaircraft gunners could not distinguish between Blenheims dropping explosives and those distributing the pamphlets threatening the stability of the regime in Berlin; hence British planes were lost. Hoare paid tribute to the truth-raiders. They wrote, he said, "a chapter of heroic bravery, of forlorn hopes, of brilliant improvisation."[74]

Ironside's optimistic briefing of the War Cabinet had been inspired more by the Poles' valor than their military prospects. Yet their élan *was* astonishing. That same Friday the Fourth Panzer Division, attacking Warsaw's southeastern suburbs, was thrown back and Polish divisions around Kutno rallied, counterattacked across the Bzura, and drove the German Eighth Army back for three straight days. It would be a long time before any troops, under any flag, would do anything like that again. They were inspired not solely by determination to preserve their honor — though their gallantry still gleams across a half century — but because they believed they were going to win. They knew they couldn't do it by themselves. That, they thought, was unnecessary. England and France were bound to them in ironclad military alliances. Both powers had declared war on Nazi Germany. The British, they assumed, had unleashed an all-out bombing of the Ruhr, and the French army, the world's strongest, must have penetrated deep into western Germany. If they pinned down the Wehrmacht here, the Poles reasoned, their allies would soon force Hitler to sue for peace.

RAF bombers had been rendered impotent by French fear of Luftwaffe reprisals. Where was the French army? Here the Poles' nemesis was the same officer who three and a half years earlier had, in effect, awarded Hitler the Rhineland by default. Gustave-Maurice Gamelin, a short, timid, rabbity man in his late sixties, was a former aide to Marshal Joseph-Césaire Joffre who had toiled his way upward through the maze of military politics to become *généralissime* of the enormous French army, constable of France, and leader of the combined Anglo-French high command. His rise had been extraordinary, not because he was eccentric — in mufti he was just another nondescript *fonctionnaire* — but because under pressure he became everything a commander ought not to be: indecisive, given to issuing impulsive orders which he almost always countermanded, and timid to and beyond a fault. Illustrative of his unpredictability was his proposal, at the outbreak of war, to invade Germany by lunging across neutral Belgium and Holland, and then, when a shocked cabinet rejected the plan, declaring that any French offensive would be doomed, that the poilus in the Maginot and their comrades above it should sit out the war. There would be more of this sort of thing later. And more. And more.

His performance during the Rhineland crisis should have revealed his incompetence to his civilian superiors. They had asked him for action then, and he had given them excuses. After that he ought to have been relieved of all responsibility for the defense of French soil. But like the rest of the senior officers in their army he had his *patron,* who in his case was Premier Daladier. So he had remained at his high post, and now the price must be paid, not by him, not by Daladier, but by the Poles. The issue of Polish survival was a matter of days, if not hours. France possessed the only force strong enough to save Poland by attacking Germany now. Furthermore, the Franco-Polish Military Convention of May 19, 1939, was more precise than Britain's agreement with the Poles. Drafted by Gamelin and two Polish generals, the convention provided that "the French army shall launch a major offensive in the west [*lancerait une grande offensive a l'ouest*] if the Germans attack Poland." The Poles had asked how many poilus would be available for this drive. "Between thirty-five and thirty-eight divisions," Gamelin had replied. The Poles had also wanted to know what form the attack would take. It was spelled out in the convention: the French army would "progressively launch offensive operations . . . the third day after General Mobilization Day." Yet that deadline had passed without action in Paris.[75]

On August 23, when the German invasion of Poland was imminent, the irresolute French commander in chief — without telling the Poles — had reappraised the military prospects of nations who offended the Führer. As a result, his faith in his army had been shaken, and his confidence in France's political leaders, and himself (this was justifiable), had shrunk. He hoped that by the spring of 1940, with British concurrence and the support of *"matériel américain,"* France would be capable of fighting, if necessary, *"une bataille défensive."* Then — this from a man who had promised the Poles offensive operations on the third day after mobilization — "My opinion has always been that we could not take the offensive before roughly 1941–1942." The French, in short, had unilaterally renounced the Franco-Polish Military Convention. Despite the fact that his signature was on the document, Gamelin concluded in his memoirs, "Our military protocol had no meaning and [did] not bind us." In his heart, therefore, he was *"satisfait."* Among other things, he had overlooked an earlier military treaty — still an absolute commitment by the French government — which Marshal Ferdinand Foch had negotiated with the Poles on February 19, 1921, pledging *"effectif et rapide"* support should Poland be confronted by German aggression.[76]

Generals are seldom afflicted by nagging consciences, but then, they seldom betray an embattled ally. Perhaps a pang of guilt moved this commander in chief to point out that French mobilization in itself would bring some relief to Poland "by tying down a certain number of large German units on our frontier." Daladier asked him how long the Poles, abandoned by their allies, could hold out. The *généralissime* replied that he believed they would put up *"une résistance honorable"* which would prevent *"la masse des forces"* of the Reich from turning against France until the English were *"effectivement à nos côtés"* — standing beside them, shoulder to shoulder.[77]

Between them the Poles and the French had 130 divisions against Germany's 98 — really 62, because 36, as Liddell Hart put it, were "virtually untrained and unorganized." Rydz-Smigly's army had but to hold up the Wehrmacht divisions on the eastern front; the French, meantime, could overwhelm the green, second-rate German divisions across the Rhine. The challenge should have daunted no one. Gamelin's forces in the west outnumbered the Germans by at least two to one — four to one, if one is to believe the Nuremberg testimony of OKW General Alfred Jodl, who told the International Military Tribunal that he had expected the Third Reich to collapse in 1939. He attributed its survival "to the fact that during the Polish campaign the approximately 110 French and British divisions in the West were held completely inactive against the 23 German divisions."[78]

Most of the Zossen generals were appalled at Hitler's gamble. To blitz Poland he had stripped the Siegfried Line defenses of armor, artillery, warplanes, and reliable troops, leaving a skeleton force to face Germany's ancient foe in the west. It seemed inconceivable that the French would let so golden an opportunity pass, knowing that a quick Nazi conquest of Poland would free the German Generalstab of its greatest nightmare — a two-front war — and permit the Führer to concentrate the full might of the Wehrmacht in a massive attack, knifing through the Low Countries, into France. Field Marshal Wilhelm Keitel, head of the OKW, recalled that "We soldiers always expected an attack by France during the Polish campaign, and were very surprised that nothing happened. . . . A French attack would have encountered only a German military screen, not a real defense."[79]

General Franz Halder agreed — up to a point. He testified: "The success against Poland was only possible by completely baring our western border." If the French had attacked, he added, "they would have been able to cross the Rhine without our being able to prevent it" and taken the Ruhr area, "the most decisive factor" in the German conduct of the war. Yet Halder, who had greater respect for Hitler's military intuition than his fellow members of the officer corps, was unsurprised by the inertia on the western front; on August 14 his first entry in his war diary noted that he considered a French offensive "not very likely," that France would not attack across the Low Countries "against Belgian wishes," and that the French would probably "remain on the defensive."[80]

At the time Halder was the only senior general in Zossen to endorse the Führer's prediction. On September 7, with the issue of whether to send Wehrmacht divisions to the west being discussed seriously, Halder's diary entry ended with a few lines summing up Hitler's views: "Operations in the West not yet clear. Some indication that there is no real intention of waging war." The Generalstab couldn't believe it. They remembered the indomitable poilus who had fought under Joffre and Galliéni in the early years of the last war, who had always counterattacked when attacked, whose line was never broken, whose *"Ils ne passeront pas"* denied Verdun to Germany's finest regiments through seven terrible months, and who paid an unprecedented price — four million casualties, one out of every four of them dead — for victory in 1918.[81]

But Joffre, Galliéni, Pétain, and Foch were gone, and in their place stood — though not particularly tall — Gamelin. As Halder recorded the Führer's thoughts, the French *généralissime* prepared to launch the only offensive of his career, a piece of opéra bouffe which mocked the memories of Verdun. *"L'offensive de la Sarre,"* as he grandly called it, was in fact a pitiful sortie. Of his 85 heavily armed divisions he committed 9 to an advance on a fifteen-mile front southeast of Saarbrücken. Moving slowly, taking every precaution, the infantry occupied twenty deserted villages and gained five miles. Here and there were reports of skirmishes, but the German response was to give ground, withdraw — and pray that the *généralissime* did not commit another fifty divisions to a full-scale attack. Of the Germans' total strength, all but eleven divisions were untrained and the rest lacked adequate arms and ammunition. Nevertheless, on September 12 Gamelin commanded a halt. He congratulated his men on their victory and instructed them to make preparations for a retreat into the security of the Maginot Line if a German offensive came roaring down through

Belgium. The next day the Polish military attaché, on orders from an alarmed Rydz-Smigly, asked Gamelin whether French warplanes had attacked their mutual enemy, and whether he could accelerate his infantry advance. Later that same day the architect of the Saar "offensive" replied mendaciously, in writing: "More than half of our active divisions on the northeast front are engaged in combat." The Boche, he said, were responding with *"vigoureuse résistance."* Interrogation of enemy prisoners revealed that the Germans were "pouring in reinforcements" — all of this, every word, pure fiction — and French warplanes had been in action from the outset, tying down *"une part considérable"* of the Luftwaffe. He had gone "far beyond" his pledge, he concluded. *"Il m'a été impossible de faire plus"* ("It has been impossible for me to do more").[82]

The ground gained in the Saar was lost when Gamelin, on September 30, ordered a retreat. The only achievement of his so-called Saar offensive was to reveal France's persistent confidence in outdated tactical ideas, notably the doctrine that any drive against a defended position must be preceded by a massive artillery bombardment, the "tin-opener," as it had been called in 1918. General André de Beaufre, then a captain, said that Gamelin's action, in character, had been a meaningless gesture (*"Voilà notre aide à la Pologne!"*), and Colonel de Gaulle dismissed *"l'offensive"* contemptuously as *"quelques démonstrations."*[83]

By the tenth day of fighting, the Polish cause was lost, and Rydz-Smigly, who had read the heartbreaking dispatches from Beck's diplomats in Paris and London, knew it. He ordered a general withdrawal into southeastern Poland, planning to organize a defensive position on a narrow front to prolong resistance. But the Generalstab had thought of everything. Already over half of the marshal's remaining forces had been trapped before they could retreat across the Vistula. Cut off from their bases, running out of ammunition, this remnant was caught in a vise between two German armies. And before Rydz-Smigly could reach his redoubt in the southeast, he, too, was encircled.

On September 17 two Soviet army groups, in accordance with the secret clause in the Nazi-Soviet Pact, invaded Poland from the east. Ribbentrop and Molotov had fixed the demarcation line along the river Bug, but there are always soldiers who don't get the word; shots were exchanged between some Germans and Russians, and a few men were wounded. Then all was quiet along the Bug. Both foreign armies were in Poland, but the Poles were forgotten; the fate of their homeland had been decided in the first three days of the Nazi invasion — actually, given the fourth color Gamelin had added to the French tricolor, before the fighting had begun.

By all precedents the Poles, in extremis, should have yielded once they found that they faced both the Wehrmacht and the Red Army. The Germans had them checked; now they were in checkmate. It was time to quit. They were victims of a squalid deal worked by two despots whose hands reeked of innocent blood, and they had been betrayed by two allies whose leaders had been regarded as honorable men. No indignity had been spared them. In London — where their cause found little sympathy — a cabinet minister had declared that after Nazi Germany had been crushed, "a Polish state would be reconstituted"; the Polish state to whose defense England had been committed was unmentioned. The Poles would gain nothing if they made a messy exit; they would merely forfeit the claims they had upon the world's compassion. It was far more sensible to go along quietly.

But the Poles didn't want pity, and while quietude may be good form among Anglo-Saxons in exigency, the Poles are traditionally noisy. Newspaper photographs showed German and Russian officers shaking hands, elated that the battle was over. Except that it wasn't; there were no pictures of Poles shaking hands with anyone. Their government and high command had left Warsaw for Rumania, leaving orders to fight to the bitter end. The Poles did; fueled by patriotic fervor, they barricaded streets with streetcars, stopping Reichenau's tanks; his infantry was forced into the ugliest and most dangerous close combat — house to house, room by room. By that mysterious process which telegraphs news throughout a country, even after its communications system has been destroyed, all Poland knew what was happening in Warsaw, and thousands of Poles followed its example. Guderian plunged deep through the Polish rear to Brest-Litovsk, but when he tried to storm the town's ancient citadel, he found an obsolete Renault tank had been jammed, and then welded, into the doorway. Warsaw, starving, lacking water, pounded around the clock by Nazi planes and artillery, finally capitulated ten days after the Russian invasion. Pockets of resistance fought on, though the last major stronghold — 17,000 men in Kock, a village southeast of the capital — did not lay down their arms until October 7. Meanwhile, 100,000 Polish soldiers and pilots had escaped to Rumania and made their way to England, where they would fight in Free Polish battalions beside the British, French, and later, the Americans; Polish destroyers and submarines reached the Orkneys and joined the Royal Navy.

Stalin left central Poland to Hitler. In return he got the eastern provinces, a free hand in Lithuania, and the oil fields of southeast Poland, with the understanding that he would ship thirty thousand tons of crude to the Reich every year. Hitler annexed part of Poland and established the rest as a Nazi vassal state, the General Government of Poland, whose governor-general was Hans Frank, a feisty, dapper young Nazi lawyer, the adoring father of five children, who began braiding his Nuremberg rope by announcing: "The Poles shall be the slaves of the Third Reich." He also became expert in carrying out programs whose euphemistic names masked some of the vilest crimes in history. Polish intellectuals, professional men, and anyone possessing leadership qualities — men and women who might subvert Frank's authority — were marked for slaughter. This operation, in which 3,500 persons were actually executed, persons who had committed no crime, who were singled out precisely because they had led distinguished careers, was encoded *Ausserordenliche Befriedigungsaktion* (Extraordinary Pacification Program). In another Frank campaign, all Jews were grouped together for his *Flurbereinigungs-Plan* (Housecleaning Plan). Later, after other code words had been tried, the Nazis settled on *Endlösung*, the Final Solution, to represent the destruction of the European Jews. Their time had come.[84]

And so had Western civilization's hour of maximum danger. Hitler was free now to turn the full fury of his might on England and France. Churchill had repeatedly spoken — mostly to empty seats — on the need to confront Nazi Germany with collective security. Above all, he had said, the Reich must be bracketed by strong nations, east and west, so that Hitler would know German aggression would mean a two-front war. When the Führer came to power the safeguards had seemed solid: France, England, and the Rhineland on the west, and Czechoslovakia and Poland to the east, with Russia, alienated by Nazi murders of German Communists and Hitler's anti-Soviet polemics, frowning behind them. One by one Hitler had eliminated these threats. He could not have done it alone. He had needed help — and found it in London and Paris. The Polish army had been a disappointment. But France, whose army was vital to the security of free peoples, hadn't even tried to exploit the period of grace — at least three weeks — when the German armies were tied down in the east. Now the democracies must face him alone — him and, in all probability, Italy, for the unprincipled Duce wanted to be on the winning side, and the Anglo-French alliance had been losing, losing, losing for nearly seven years. In England the iconoclastic General Fuller declared that France must be ruled by lunatics. There they had been in September, he wrote, with "the strongest army in the world, facing no more than twenty-six divisions, sitting still and sheltering behind steel and concrete while a quixotically valiant ally was being exterminated!" In Paris Léon Blum was recalling his conversation with a nonconformist French officer when they met in 1936. The Socialist leader had asked: "What would France do if Hitler should march on Vienna, Prague, or Warsaw?" Charles de Gaulle had replied: "According to circumstances, we shall have a limited call-up or full mobilization. Then, peering through the battlements of our fortifications, we shall watch the enslavement of Europe." Vienna, Prague, and Warsaw had fallen. Now Blum was wondering whether those battlements and fortifications were strong enough to save France herself from bondage.[85]

※   ※

Hitler had not expected France and England to go to war over Poland. After they had yielded the Rhineland, Austria, and Czechoslovakia, he had assumed that appeasement would continue to be the keystone of their foreign policy. He still doubted that they intended to fight. The French failure to attack the Siegfried Line when it was at its weakest had, in his view, confirmed him. The first inkling that he might have misjudged the British had been Churchill's appointment to the War Cabinet. Told of it, Hermann Göring had dropped into a chair and said heavily: "Churchill in the Cabinet. That means war is really on. Now we shall have war with England."[86]

The Nazi hierarchy had long been aware of Churchill. That included the Führer, which made Winston an exception. It is a remarkable fact that Hitler knew almost nothing of his enemies and even brushed aside information made available to him, preferring to rely on his instincts, which included contempt for all *Ausländer*. He did regard England as "our enemy Number One," however, and Churchill as the symbol of British militancy. After the fall of Poland he lost little time in singling him out. Making his ritualistic peace offering, the sequel to all Nazi conquests, he declared that Poland was dead; it would never rise again; therefore why fight about it? "I make this declaration," he said, "only because I very naturally desire to spare my people suffering. But should the views of Churchill and his following prevail, then this declaration will be my last. We should then fight. . . . Let those repulse my hand who regard war as the better solution!"[87]

As a cabinet minister, Churchill could now speak over the BBC whenever he chose, and on October 1, in his first wartime broadcast, he had told Britain: "Poland has again been overrun by two of the great powers which held her in bondage for a hundred and fifty years but were unable to quench the spirit of the Polish nation." The heroic defense of Warsaw had shown that "the soul of Poland is indestructible, and that she will rise again like a rock, which may for a spell be submerged by a tidal wave, but which remains a rock." He was more intrigued by "the assertion of the power of Russia." He would have preferred that the Russians "should be standing on their present line as the friends and allies of Poland instead of invaders. But that the Russian armies should stand on this line was clearly necessary for the safety of Russia against the Nazi menace." Ribbentrop, he noted, had been summoned to Moscow last week to be told that "the Nazi designs upon the Baltic States . . . must come to a dead stop." He continued:

> I cannot forecast to you the action of Russia.
> It is a riddle
> wrapped in a mystery
> inside an enigma;
>
> But perhaps there is a key.
> That key is Russian national interest.
>
> It cannot be in accordance
> with the interest or safety of Russia
> that Germany should plant itself
> upon the shores of the Black Sea
>
> Or that it should overrun the Baltic States
> and subjugate the Slavonic peoples
> of southeastern Europe.[88]

He announced with pride — not pardonable, because he still distrusted the convoy policy — that "a week has passed since a British ship, alone or in convoy, has been sunk or even molested by a U-boat on the high seas," and he closed with one of those passages which men in public life later wish could be expunged from the record. "Rough times lie ahead," he said, "but how different is the scene from that of October 1914!" Then the French front "seemed to be about to break under the terrible impact of German Imperialism. . . . We faced those adverse conditions then; we have nothing worse to face tonight."[89]

They faced something far worse, of course, but no one can hold a mirror up to the future, and the speech was well received in England. The prime minister's junior private secretary, Jock Colville, wrote in his diary that Churchill "certainly gives one confidence and will, I suspect, be Prime Minister before this war is over." Colville thought he might "lead us into the most dangerous paths. But he is the only man in the country who commands anything like universal respect, and perhaps with age he has become less inclined to undertake rash adventures." Hoare, another diarist, noted that Churchill seemed "very exhilarated" and that "the Press talked of him as Prime Minister." It was not just the press; Sir John Wheeler-Bennett was among those establishmentarians who, listening to

Winston, "first realized that Churchill was 'the pilot of the storm' who was needed to lead us through the crisis of the Second World War." That thought did not occur to Neville Chamberlain, but he was impressed; to his sister he wrote that he took "the same view as Winston, to whose excellent broadcast we have just been listening. I believe Russia will always act as she thinks her own interests demand, and I cannot believe she would think her interests served by . . . German domination in the Balkans."[90]

In Berlin, William Shirer wrote: "The local enthusiasm for peace a little dampened today by Churchill's speech last night." Goebbels suppressed references to Winston's comments on Russia, but his allusion to the Admiralty's success in shielding merchantmen from Nazi submarines had touched a nerve. Led by *Der Stürmer, Völkischer Beobachter,* and *Deutsches Nachtrichenbüro,* the German press had made a great thing out of the U-boat campaign; U-boat captains were the toast of the Reich, and cartoonists had pictured Winston as a battered, cornered prizefighter and as a drowning man surrounded by periscopes. His announcement that the subs had let a week pass without a victory enraged Hans Fritzsche, director of the Nazi broadcasting services. Fritzsche interrupted a program to deliver a thirteen-minute polemic denouncing Winston, quoting him and then raging: "So that is what the dirty gangster thinks! Who does that filthy liar think he is fooling? . . . So Mr. Churchill — that bloated swine [*aufgeblasenes Schwein*] — spouts through his dirty teeth that in the last week no English ship has been molested by German submarines? He does, indeed? . . . There you have the twisted and diseased mind of this infamous profiteer and specialist in stinking lying. Naturally those British ships have not been molested; they have been sunk."[91]

It is possible to be more overbearing in German than in any other tongue, but only if one has mastered it as Winston had mastered English. In any duel of denigration he was bound to leave Fritzsche far behind, and he did it in November, in his second wartime address over the BBC. Germany, he said, was more fragile than it seemed. He had

the sensation and also the conviction that that evil man over there and his cluster of confederates are not sure of themselves, as we are sure of ourselves; that they are harassed in their guilty souls by the thought and by the fear of an ever-approaching retribution for their crimes, and for the orgy of destruction in which they have plunged us all. As they look out tonight from their blatant, panoplied, clattering Nazi Germany, they cannot find one single friendly eye in the whole circumference of the globe. Not one![92]

Russia, he said, "returns them a flinty stare"; Italy "averts her gaze"; Japan "is puzzled and thinks herself betrayed"; Turkey, Islam, India, and

China "would regard with undisguised dread a Nazi triumph, well knowing what their fate would soon be"; and the "great English-speaking Republic across the Atlantic makes no secret of its sympathies." Thus "the whole world is against Hitler and Hitlerism. Men of every race and clime feel that this monstrous apparition stands between them and the forward move which is their due, and for which the age is ripe." The "seething mass of criminality and corruption constituted by the Nazi Party machine" was responsible for the power of its führer, "a haunted, morbid being, who, to their eternal shame, the German people in their bewilderment have worshipped as a god."[93]

Jock Colville wrote that he had "listened to Winston Churchill's wireless speech, very boastful, over-confident and indiscreet (especially about Italy and the U.S.A.), but certainly most amusing." If Colville was condescending, Harold Nicolson sometimes turned his thumb down on a Churchill broadcast. After listening to one of the early radio addresses, Nicolson observed in his diary that Winston "is a little too rhetorical, and I do not think that his speech will really have gone down with the masses. He is too belligerent for this pacifist age, and although once anger comes to steel our sloppiness, his voice will be welcome to them, at the moment it reminds them of heroism which they do not really feel."[94]

One hesitates to gainsay Harold Nicolson; he was one of the shrewdest observers of his time, and his lapses were rare. But this may have been one of them. Nicolson, with Amery and Spears, was a member of the Eden group and continued to attend their Carlton meetings well into 1940. More important, he — like Colville — belonged to the upper class, and carried all its paraphernalia with him. His credentials as an analyst of "the masses" are therefore thin; as he himself acknowledged, he misinterpreted the feelings of his own constituents. Now that the issue with Hitler was joined and English blood was flowing, Churchill had become the most overstated member of His Majesty's Government. Clearly that troubled Nicolson; men with his background prized understatement and recoiled from its opposite. Elsewhere on England's social spectrum, however, that was not true. Among the middle and lower classes, pacifism had begun to fade when Hitler entered Prague, and once war was declared it was replaced by patriotism. Before the war became dreary and stale, the signs of the nation's shift in mood had been unmistakable. The jubilant response to the naval victory off Montevideo had been one. Another had appeared when the people learned — from accounts of a Churchill speech in Parliament — that Luftwaffe pilots were machine-gunning the crews of unarmed fishing vessels and "describing on the radio what fun it was to see a little ship 'crackling in flames like a Christmas tree.' " Winston was swamped with mail from clerks and miners, waitresses and small businessmen, demanding reprisals. Of course, he refused; he was a gentleman. But *they weren't,* and they vastly outnumbered those who were.

There was talk — more out of Parliament than in it — of Churchill as prime minister. It was, and for thirty years had been, the only job which clearly suited him. That does not mean he was ineffectual elsewhere. He had always been able, and often brilliant, in other ministries, and even his Admiralty critics conceded that no other man in public life could match his performance in the private office. But given the broad reaches of his mind, his knowledge of the entire government, and his inability to hold his tongue in check, he often exasperated the cabinet by trespassing in departments which were the preserve of other men round the table. So it was in his BBC broadcasts. Although he began by confining himself to the war at sea, sooner or later he was bound to touch upon issues which could not be remotely construed as naval. If his touch had been light, the encroachment would have been ignored, but it was also characteristic of him that he was incapable of subtlety. His third major broadcast raised an issue which was clearly the special concern of the Foreign Office. He tore into Europe's neutral nations. By now none could doubt that the German führer had plans for their future, yet like Scarlett O'Hara they seemed to be promising themselves they would think about it tomorrow, while every tomorrow darkened their prospects. In a BBC broadcast on January 20, 1940, Churchill said:

> All of them hope that the storm will pass
>   before their turn comes to be devoured.
>   But I fear — I fear greatly —
>   the storm will not pass.
>
> It will rage and it will roar,
>   ever more loudly, ever more widely.
>   It will spread to the South;
>   it will spread to the North.
>
> There is no chance of a speedy end
>   except through united action;
>
> And if at any time, Britain and France,
>   wearying of the struggle,
>   were to make a shameful peace,
>
> Nothing would remain for the smaller states of Europe,
>   with their shipping and their possessions,
>   but to be divided between the opposite, though similar,
>   barbarisms of Nazidom and Bolshevism.[95]

Hoare commented in his diary: "Winston's broadcast to the neutrals. Bad effect." One consequence of the broadcast, unknown in London, was a *Führerordnung* to restudy possible operations in Scandinavia. Hitler guessed — correctly — that the first lord of the Admiralty had his eye on Norway. The Foreign Office was more concerned about the reaction in neutral capitals. In a pained note Halifax wrote Churchill: "I am afraid I think the effect of your broadcast in the countries which you no doubt had principally in mind has been very different from what you anticipated — though if I had seen your speech myself, I should have expected some such reactions." Among the newspapers which had bridled were *Het Handelsblad* in Holland, *Journal de Genève*, Denmark's *Politiken*, and Norway's *Morgenbladet*. Halifax complained that it "puts me in an impossible position if a member of the Gov. like yourself takes a line in public which differs from that taken by the PM or myself: and I think, as I have to be in daily touch with these tiresome neutrals, I ought to be able to predict how their minds will work." Churchill answered at once: "This is undoubtedly a disagreeable bouquet. I certainly thought I was expressing yr view & Neville's. . . . Do not however be quite sure that my line will prove so inconvenient as now appears. What the neutrals say is vy different from what they feel: or from what is going to happen." In fact Hitler had designs on most of them, and before spring ended the swastika would float over all their capitals but Switzerland's.[96]

Halifax had passed over the one paragraph in the broadcast with momentous implications. It was a reference to the fighting going on in Finland, part of a complex issue which no one in England, including Churchill, understood. The Russo-German marriage of convenience had scarcely been consummated in Poland before divorce proceedings were quietly begun. Stalin, anxious to guard his Baltic flank from a future Nazi attack, signed pacts with Estonia, Latvia, and Lithuania, permitting Moscow to garrison Red Army troops in each. He then turned to Finland. Among his objectives, all of which were defensive, was blocking the Gulf of Finland with artillery on both coasts, thus protecting the entrance to Leningrad. The Soviet Union offered Helsinki 2,134 square miles in exchange for the cession of 1,066 Finnish square miles. National sentiment — and fear of a German reprisal — barred an agreement. The Russians, desperate, offered to buy the territory. Helsinki still refused, and on November 30, 1939, the Red Army invaded Finland. To outsiders the invasion was an atrocity as black as the Nazi seizure of Poland. In retrospect, however, the difference is obvious. Russia's need to defend Leningrad is clear. The city came perilously close to conquest by the Germans later, and would certainly have fallen to the Nazis without the strip taken from the Finns.

The necessities of war modify principle; the hand of a country whose existence is threatened is not stayed by the rules of war. Churchill, at this very time, was telling the War Cabinet that "We must violate Norwegian territorial waters"; and Pétain, worried about the stretch of French frontier undefended by the Maginot Line, had told the Conseil Supérieur de la Guerre that if France was to remain faithful to the principle which had saved her in the last war ("the defensive and continuous front"), she must face the fact that the one stretch of her frontier unprotected by the Maginot Line was the classic invasion route followed by Germans for nearly two thousand years. Consequently, he concluded: *"Nous devons entrer en Belgique!"* — "We must go into Belgium!" Winston agreed that Belgium could not possibly remain neutral, that it was essential to erect "a shield along the Belgian frontier to the sea against that terrible turning movement" which had "nearly encompassed our ruin in 1914."[97]

To the astonishment of the world, tiny Finland threw the Russians back. Beginning with the Japanese conquest of Manchuria eight years earlier, the aggressor powers had repeatedly overwhelmed weak, poorly led defenders. Now a small country with one-fortieth the strength of the Soviet Union was humiliating a great power, sending the invaders reeling from the Mannerheim Line, named for their leader, Field Marshal Carl Gustaf Emil von Mannerheim. The Finn victories seemed miraculous, but there were several explanations. One was Mannerheim himself. Before the Russian Revolution, when Finland belonged to the czar, he had served as a lieutenant general; he had fought the Bolsheviks to a standstill then, and now, aged seventy-two, had come out of retirement to do it again. Stalin was holding his crack divisions in reserve should Hitler strike. He had sent the Red Army's poorest troops, ill-trained and sorely lacking in fighting spirit, against the Finns. Mannerheim led men fueled by the incentive of soldiers defending their homeland. He blinded the Russians with superior tactics, the use of superbly trained ski troops, a thorough knowledge of the lakes and forests constituting the terrain's natural obstacles, and a strategy peculiarly suitable to arctic warfare — cutting the enemy's line of retreat, waiting until the Russians were frozen and starved, and then counterattacking. The paralyzed invaders were not even properly clothed for the bitter Finnish winter. Churchill had spoken for tens of millions when, in his indictment of neutrals, he made an exception: "Only Finland — superb, nay, sublime — in the jaws of peril — Finland shows what free men can do. The service rendered by Finland to mankind is magnificent. They have exposed, for all the world to see, the military incapacity of the Red Army and of the Red Air Force. Many illusions about Soviet Russia have been dispelled in these few fierce weeks of fighting in the Arctic Circle."[98]

The British and the French — seeing the opportunity for a pretext to cross northern Sweden, and, in passing, to seize the Swedish iron mines at Gällivare, vital to the Third Reich's war effort — were about to send "volunteers" to aid the Finns when the tide turned. After two months of frustration the Russians secured their communications from the Leningrad-Murmansk frontier, which they should have done before the invasion, and launched a major assault on the Mannerheim Line with fourteen divisions of sledge-borne infantry supported by heavy artillery, tanks, and warplanes. The Finns stood up to it for five ferocious weeks, counterattacking the tanks with what Churchill called "a new type of hand-grenade" — bottles filled with gasoline and topped by wick, lit at the moment of hurling — which they audaciously christened Molotov cocktails. They gave ground slowly, but they gave it. Vyborg, vital to the defense, was threatened by frontal assault and, from the rear, by troops crossing the icebound Gulf of Finland and the icebound island of Hogland. On March 6, 1940, the Finns sued for peace and the Allies disbanded their expeditionary force. The repercussions of this — for England, and particularly for Churchill — were almost immediate. Winston felt he now had an excellent precedent for intervention in Scandinavia. The greatest sequel, however, was taking shape in the minds of Hitler and the German General Staff in Zossen. Like Britain's first lord of the Admiralty, they underestimated Soviet military strength "with," as Liddell Hart writes, "momentous consequences the following year."[99]

Churchill was not the first man in European public life to exploit the possibilities of radio. Hitler had been doing it for seven years. But Winston was the first British statesman to reach people in their homes and move them even more deeply than Roosevelt had in his fireside chats. Because the BBC had gone to great lengths to avoid controversy, its interwar programs were extraordinarily dull — "Arranging a Garden" and "Our Friends at the Zoo" were typical. So was Churchill's scheduled talk on the Mediterranean, which had brought Guy Burgess to Chartwell in 1938. Public issues had been discussed over the BBC, and earlier in the decade Winston had managed to get a word in now and then, but as the crises mounted on the Continent and tensions increased, Reith screened participants in debates, approving only those who presented bland views, offending no listeners, particularly those occupying the front bench in the House of Commons.

Until he entered the War Cabinet, Churchill's audiences had been largely confined to the House, lecture halls, and, during elections, party rallies. Suddenly that had changed. England was at war; the only action was at sea, and millions whose knowledge of Churchillian speeches had been confined to published versions heard his rich voice, resonant with urgency, dramatically heightened by his tempo, pauses, and crashing consonants, which, one listener wrote, actually made his radio vibrate. Churchill had been a name in the newspapers, but even his own columns lacked the power of his delivery. He found precisely the right words for convictions his audiences shared but had been unable to express. He spoke of "thoughtless dilettanti or purblind worldlings who sometimes ask us: 'What is it that Britain and France are fighting for?' To this I answer: 'If we left off fighting you would soon find out.' " His elaborate metaphors, simplistic but effective, fortified his argument, and were often witty: "A baboon in a forest is a matter of legitimate speculation; a baboon in a Zoo is an object of public curiosity; but a baboon in your wife's bed is a cause of the gravest concern."[100]

After the fall of Poland, when Hitler told the Western democracies to choose between a negotiated peace with him or "the views of Churchill and his following," Chamberlain gave him the official reply (which Churchill helped draft), but England heard Winston's, on the evening of November 12, 1939:

We tried again and again to prevent this war, and for the sake of peace we put up with a lot of things happening which ought not to have happened. But now we are at war, and we are going to make war, and persevere in making war, until the other side have had enough of it. . . . You may take it absolutely for certain that either all that Britain and France stand for in the modern world will go down, or that Hitler, the Nazi regime, and the recurring German or Prussian menace to Europe will be broken or destroyed. That is the way the matter lies and everybody had better make up his mind to that solid, somber fact.[101]

Like a thespian, Churchill began to receive critical notices. When he rose from the front bench to address the House of Commons, Beverley Baxter, an MP and a writer for the Beaverbrook press, compared him to "the old bandit who had been the terror of the mountain passes . . . the fire in him was burning low. His head was thrust forward characteristically, like a bull watching for the matador. He squared his shoulders a couple of times as if to make sure that his hands were free for the gestures that might come." When Winston told BBC listeners that "Now we have begun; now we are going on; now with the help of God, and the conviction that we are the defenders of civilisation and freedom, we are going on, and we are going on to the end," Virginia Cowles wrote that he was "giving the people of Britain the firm clear lead" they needed and "had not found elsewhere."[102]

In December, the war's fourth month, a public opinion poll reported that barely half of the British people had expressed confidence in Chamberlain — one disillusioned Conservative described him as "hanging onto office like a dirty old piece of chewing gum on the leg of a chair" — and Churchill, right behind him, was gaining. In the House of Commons smoking room, and in the lobby, predictions that Winston would succeed Chamberlain, once shocking, were no longer whispered; they were legitimate speculation. The theme is an undercurrent in Nicolson's diaries, returning whenever disaster looms. The first cluster of references begins early, as on September 17, when he writes, "At 11 am. (a bad hour) Vita comes to tell me that Russia has invaded Poland and is striking toward Vilna. . . . It may be that within a few days we shall have Germany, Russia and Japan against us." At the end of the entry, clearly a frightened man, he writes: "Chamberlain must go. Churchill may be our Clemenceau or our Gambetta. To bed very miserable and alarmed." Nine days later, in the House, Nicolson watches as "The Prime Minister gets up to make his statement. He is dressed in deep mourning. . . . One feels the confidence and spirits of the House dropping inch by inch. When he sits down there is scarcely any applause. During the whole speech Winston Churchill had sat hunched beside him looking like the Chinese god of plenty suffering from acute indigestion." Then Churchill rises. Nicolson is euphoric: "The effect of Winston's speech was infinitely greater than could be derived from any reading of the text. . . . One could feel the spirits of the House rising with every word. . . . In those twenty minutes Churchill brought himself nearer the post of Prime Minister than he has ever been before. In the Lobbies afterwards even Chamberlainites were saying, 'We have now found our leader.' " And then, in early October —at a meeting of the Eden group — Nicolson hears the second Lord Astor tell members that he "feels it is essential that the Prime Minister should be removed and that Winston Churchill should take his place."[103]

In Winston's place another ambitious politician hearing such praise — and it was coming to him from many sides — might have taken the pulse of the House, seeking to put together a coalition to topple the government and then form one of his own. Although members of this House of Commons, elected in 1935, were no longer reflective of the national mood, they too had built high hopes in the aftermath of Munich only to see them dashed; many felt betrayed; many others had heard from constituents who felt so. But plotting wasn't Churchill's style. He owed the Admiralty and his seat on the War Cabinet to the prime minister. Moreover, Chamberlain hadn't bullied him, called him on the carpet, or interfered in any way with his administration of the country's naval policy, though he may have been tempted; Winston, being Winston, had critics among naval officers of flag rank.[104]

Chamberlain did visit the upper war room frequently, but was always cordial and left expressing gratitude — if he knew that Sinclair and Beaverbrook were also shown the Admiralty maps (though neither was a member of the government), he kept it to himself. In the House Winston loyally supported the government's policies — was indeed their most forceful advocate — and praised the P.M. from time to time. In one of his broadcasts he said: "You know I have not always agreed with Mr. Chamberlain, though we have always been personal friends. But he is a man of very tough fiber, and I can tell you that he is going to fight as obstinately for victory as he did for peace." The war had, in fact, brought out an unexpected streak of belligerence in the prime minister. "Winston, for his part," Colville noted, "professes absolute loyalty to the P.M. (and indeed they get along admirably)," while Chamberlain wrote: "To me personally Winston is absolutely loyal, and I am continually hearing from others of the admiration he expressed for the P.M."[105]

It was the same in Churchill's private life. Virginia Cowles, lunching at Admiralty House, was startled by Winston's reaction when one of the children attempted a mild jest at Chamberlain's expense. In the past, she remembered, jokes at the prime minister's expense had been featured at almost every meal, but this time she saw "a scowl appear on the father's face. With enormous solemnity he said: 'If you are going to make offensive remarks about my chief you will have to leave the table. We are united in a great and common cause and I am not prepared to tolerate such language about the Prime Minister.' " Similarly, when he received Lady Bonham Carter, née Violet Asquith — "Well, here we are back in the old premises after a short interval of twenty-five years," he said in greeting — her criticism of "the old appeasers" still in the government sparked a Churchillian rebuke. In a vehement defense of Chamberlain, he said: "No man is more inflexible, more single-minded. He has a will of steel."[106]

On Friday the thirteenth of October, Churchill recorded, "my relations with Mr. Chamberlain had so far ripened that he and Mrs. Chamberlain came to dine with us at Admiralty House, where we had a comfortable flat in the attics. We were a party of four." During Stanley Baldwin's first prime ministry the two men had been colleagues for five years, yet they had never met socially. Churchill, "by happy chance" — one doubts that luck had anything to do with it — mentioned the Bahamas, knowing Chamberlain had spent several years there. Winston was "delighted to find my guest expand . . . to a degree I had not noticed before." Out came the long, sad story; Neville's father was convinced that the family fortune could be enriched, and an Empire industry developed, if his younger son grew sisal on a barren island near Nassau. Neville spent six years trying. Buffeted by hurricanes, struggling with inadequate labor, "living nearly naked," as Churchill paraphrased him, he built a small harbor, wharf, and a short railroad. But those were ancillary; his objective was to produce sisal, and although he tried every known fertilizer he found it could not be done, or at any rate not by him. "I gathered," wrote Winston, in one of his wonderfully wry curtain lines, "that in the family the feeling was that although they loved him dearly they were sorry to have lost fifty thousand pounds." And then a thought flashed across his mind: "What a pity Hitler did not know when he met this sober English politician with his umbrella . . . that he was actually talking to a hard-bitten pioneer from the outer marches of the British Empire!"[107]

But that was not the height of the evening. During dinner an officer came up from the war room immediately below them to report that a Nazi submarine had been sunk. He reappeared during dessert with news that a second U-boat had been sunk, and yet again, just before the ladies left the prime minister and first lord to their brandy, to announce, rather breathlessly, that a *third* sub had been sunk. Mrs. Chamberlain asked Winston: "Did you arrange all this on purpose?" Her host "assured her," as he put it, "that if she would come again we would produce a similar result."[108]

As ruler of the King's navy, Winston was paid £5,000 a year and found; Admiralty House was an absolute defense against creditors. Clementine felt like a young woman again. She hadn't christened a ship in over twenty-six years, but she remembered the drill when invited to launch the aircraft carrier *Indomitable* at Barrow-in-Furness. Winston was there, and a photograph — taken at the instant she was gaily waving the ship away — became his favorite picture of her; years later, when he returned to his easel, he sketched an enchanting portrait from it. Lord Fraser, watching him during the launching, observed first "his cheers" as the long vessel slid free of the ways, "and then the grave salute," perhaps prompted by thoughts of the ordeals *Indomitable* "would have to face in the future."[109]

Once the first lord and his lady had settled in topside at Admiralty House, Clementine's friends — and some acquaintances who weren't — came calling, wide-eyed ladies who could scarcely wait to see how she had done over the attics. Unwilling to offend them, she took them on tour, though she felt martyred; she had good taste, knew it, and didn't need confirmation. The only one qualified to judge was Diana Cooper, and she confined her criticisms to her diary. Even there she added that she was glad that the Churchills were in Admiralty House: "Winston's spirit, strength and confidence are . . . a chime that wakes the heart of the discouraged. His wife, more beautiful now than in early life, is equally fearless and indefatigable. She makes us all knit jerseys, for which the minesweepers must bless her."[110]

Winston hadn't time to miss Chartwell, but something had to be done; it was impractical to keep the mansion open and prodigal to continue paying servants when only maintenance was necessary. In the early days of the war it seemed destined for a humanitarian purpose. In anticipation of heavy, continuous bombing of British cities, the evacuation of over 1,250,000 women and children, particularly those living near London's East Side docks, had begun in August. Members of the upper class, their attitudes formed in abstract discussion of "the underprivileged" and "depressed areas," flung open the doors of their great country homes and received the evacuees with a compassion and a hospitality that was frequently, and swiftly, regretted. Two cultures clashed; the young strangers had never seen or even heard of underwear; many would neither eat at tables nor sleep in beds; they were accustomed to doorways and alleys. Others brought lice which often spread to a horrified hostess and her own children. The unbridgeable gap was reflected in the remark of a Whitechapel mother to her six-year-old: "You dirty thing, messing the lady's carpet. Go and do it in the corner."[111]

Chartwell had welcomed two East End mothers and their seven children. But like most other evacuees they drifted back to the docks, homesick and weary of the green country landscapes. Clemmie conferred with Winston. After two years' work he had nearly finished Orchard Cottage, to which they intended to retire while Randolph — who had joined his father's old regiment, the Fourth Hussars, and married the lovely Pamela Digby — moved into the big house. The cottage's three bedrooms were quite livable; if the first lord yearned for a weekend, they could stay there. Cousin Moppet agreed to serve as caretaker. She moved into what had been the chauffeur's cottage and was presently joined by Diana's two small children and their nannie. They had been evacuated but did not miss London, where their mother was serving as an officer in the Women's Royal Naval Service (WRNS). Duncan Sandys, Diana's husband, had been called up by his territorial unit and was stationed in London with an antiaircraft battery. Sarah and Vic Oliver had taken a flat in Westminster Gardens. "Darling Papa," Sarah wrote Winston,

. . . wherever I go, people rush up to me and shake me by the hand, congratulate me, and smile on me — because of you, and I felt I must pass on some of their wishes and good will to you.

There was such a lovely picture of you on the Newsreel the other day, and the buzz and excitement that swept through the theatre, suddenly made me feel so inordinately proud that I was your daughter, and it suddenly occurred to me that I had never really told you, through shyness and inarticulateness — *how much* I love you, and how much I will try to make this career that I have chosen — with some pain to the people I love, and not a little to myself — worthy of your name — one day — [112]

The note was signed, "Your loving Sarah." She was his favorite, and he needed her now. Security was so tight that every servant had to be investigated and cleared; even conversations with most friends and relatives were tense. Discussions of nearly everything now on Winston's mind was forbidden, so Clementine entertained less and less, grouping "outsiders," as the Churchills called them, together at dinner parties. Mary, seventeen and just out of school, lived with her parents, worked in a canteen and Red Cross workroom, and was enjoying her first taste of London society. Not everyone, she recalls, was barred from discussions of restricted information: "There was the small golden circle of trusted colleagues known to be 'padlock,' and to whom, of course, that trust was sacred." Nevertheless, the circle was very small. In wartime every cabinet member had to be careful in conversation, and this was especially true of the Admiralty's first lord. As Winston had said of Jellicoe in the first war, he was the only minister who could lose the war in an afternoon. Even the list of outsiders was short, excluding many with whom they had been close in the past. [113]

It certainly did not include Unity Mitford, who arrived back in England with a self-inflicted bullet wound in her neck. She had not cared to live through a war between her homeland and her beloved führer. The government did what it could to protect the privacy of her return, posting a guard with a fixed bayonet at the dock gate — "Nazi methods," fumed an *Express* reporter — but when her father protested that the whole family was being persecuted as Nazi sympathizers, Winston declined to intervene. Lord Redesdale and his talented daughters would have to muddle through on their own. [114]

The knitting bee into which Lady Diana had been drafted was only one of Clementine's projects. Life aboard the small boats which had been commandeered by the Admiralty and transformed into minesweepers was spartan and uncomfortable; therefore Clemmie made a successful public appeal for contributions to the Minesweepers and Coastal Craft Fund. She also served as a volunteer at the Fulmer Chase Maternity Home for officers' wives. By now she had become resigned, if not reconciled, to the company of Brendan Bracken and the Prof, and invited them to join other "padlock" friends, relatives, and "Chartwell regulars" in celebrating Christmas at Admiralty House. For Churchill it was a rare moment of relaxation; even so, he disappeared from time to time to check Pim's maps, aware that on this most sacred of holidays there were Britons who could not observe it, whose duties kept them at peril on the sea.[115]

🦁   🦁

In the United States thirty years later, Americans protesting the Vietnam War displayed bumper stickers asking: "What if they gave a war and nobody came?" The answer is that the war would become inconvenient, depressing, vexing, and, most of all, a bore — which is what Britons called World War II's first eight months: the Bore War. To Chamberlain it was the Twilight War, to Churchill the Sinister Trance, to Frenchmen the *Drôle de Guerre*, to Germans the *Sitzkrieg*, and to U.S. Senator William Borah and his fellow Americans the Phony War. But for the average Englishman it remained a bloody bore.[116]

In that strange lull following the fall of Poland a state of war existed between the Third Reich and the Anglo-French forces confronting them, but after Gamelin's *offensive de la Sarre* the only Allied casualty on the Continent was a British corporal who suffered a flesh wound while cleaning his rifle. Britain had been psyched up in September, ready for sacrifice; two stock comments at the time were, "We can't let old Hitler get away with it again, can we?" and "It's got to come, so we might as well have it and have done with it." An Englishwoman wrote that "we seemed to me to be going to war as a duty," because "it was the only wise course to take. . . . I began to hope (feeling very glad nobody knew) that the air raid would begin at once and the worst happen quickly." After Chamberlain's broadcast declaring war on Germany, a young office girl in Sheffield stood with her parents as the national anthem was played; she had "a funny feeling inside. . . . I know we were all in the same mind, that we shall and must win." A middle-aged schoolmistress noted: "At 11:15 I went up, and we sat round listening to Chamberlain speaking. I held my chin high and kept back the tears at the thought of all that slaughter ahead. When 'God Save the King' was played we stood."[117]

The country had braced itself to withstand a shock, believing its cause just, and then — nothing happened. As one Englishman put it: "The sense of mission turned sour." Chamberlain, demanding that the wage claims of workers be withdrawn, insisted that the wealthy had already made voluntary sacrifices. Audiences, even in Birmingham, laughed at him. Admiralty control of merchantmen often determined what was imported and what was not, and the first lord's ruling that all ships must zigzag to evade U-boats — a carryover from the last war — doubled the length of voyages. As a result there were shortages of everything: food, coal, and —

though the government had encouraged householders to keep backyard hens — grain to feed poultry. Sugar, bacon, ham, and butter were rationed: by the fifth month of the war forty-eight million ration books had been issued in the United Kingdom. Mutton, smoked to look like bacon, became known as "macon"; native and imported butter were lumped together and officially designated "nation butter." In London Gracie Fields bellowed out a new hit:

They can muck about
With your Brussels sprout,
But they can't ration love!

There was even a shortage of noise. Under the Control of Noises (Defence) Order, ambulance sirens, factory whistles, and automobile horns were prohibited. Later, church bells were added. The thought behind this was that such sounds might alarm citizens or confuse those responsible for defending the city. It does not seem to have occurred to the authorities that Britons who had been hearing these noises all their lives might find *silence* alarming. In the territorials ammunition for rifles and Bren guns was rationed, and frequently officers, whose only personal weapons were their pistols, were unable to fire a single practice round. MPs like Sandys who were also reserve officers were accosted, at officers' mess, with complaints and questions. One question which they themselves would have liked to raise in the House irked property owners, which many of them were. In the first week of the war the government had requisitioned private property for wartime use. Tenants were evicted, warehouses emptied, livestock ousted from barns which were then locked. Winter deepened, spring approached, and the housing, warehouses, and barns stood empty. What had the government wanted them for? And where were the evacuees, now streaming back into London, going to live?[118]

Doubt, suspicion, and distrust of authority — the mood known as "bloody-mindedness" in the British army — appeared and spread. The lower classes were especially restive. As late as May 3, when all continued quiet on the western front, Jock Colville's Downing Street diary noted "a somewhat alarming report from the Conservative Central Office. . . . It seems that the war is not popular among the lowest sections of the community, that there is a suspicion it is being fought in the interests of the rich, and that there is much discontent about the rising cost of living." He added perceptively: "This is but a slight foretaste of what we shall have to face after the war." But the discontent was everywhere. A public opinion poll found that 46 percent of the British people were gloomy, 20 percent saw "a dark future" which would eventually reveal "a silver lining," 22 percent were fatalistic, and only 12 percent were optimistic. Churchill belonged with those believing in a silver lining. At the end of the war's first week he wrote Ambassador Corbin that "if there is full comradeship I cannot doubt our victory"; and, in another letter, he reaffirmed his conviction that — quoting his Boer War captors, who had given him a lifelong maxim to live by — "all will come right if we all work together to the end."[119]

But Winston, whose home and office were in the same building, did not have to cope with the blackout, the most exasperating irritant of a war in which the enemy had yet to appear. On Christmas Day, King George VI, following precedent, addressed his people over the BBC. He had inherited his father's gift for tedium — "A new year is at hand," he said. "We cannot tell what it will bring" — and his closing remark was more appropriate than he knew. "Go out into darkness," he told them, "and put your hand into the hand of God. That shall be to you better than light, and safer than a known way." Englishmen knew bloody well they were going out into darkness, but they preferred the known way, believing it safer, and were convinced that after nightfall nothing was better than light.[120]

In the beginning the impenetrable darkness had been rather exciting, like Guy Fawkes Day. But it could also be dangerous. In January a Gallup poll reported that since the outbreak of war about one Briton in five had been hurt in blackouts: bowled over by invisible runners, bruised by walking smack into an Air Raid Precautions post, stumbling over a curb, or being knocked down by a car without lights when they were on a street or road and didn't know it. Criminals appeared in the Square Mile, the heart of London, and even sortied into the West End. Just before Christmas some shopping centers tested what was known as "amenity lighting" — equivalent to the glow of a single candle seen seventy feet away. It was judged more depressing than utter darkness. Youth had fun with it, as youth always does. In the tube they merrily sang bawdy music hall ballads popular when Churchill was a handsome young cavalry officer — "Knees Up, Mother Brown" was a hit once more. Mass Observation reported a new fashion; a young couple would enjoy "intercourse in a shop doorway on the fringe of passing crowds, screened by another couple waiting to perform the same adventure. It has been done in a spirit of daring, but is described as being perfectly easy and rather thrilling."[121]

When war broke out, or was reported to have broken out, Air Raid Precautions wardens had been popular. Usually they were kindly, avuncular neighbors, looking a bit sheepish at first in their helmets as they went from door to door testing gas masks and explaining that no chink of light should escape a dwelling. But as time passed people grew tired of waiting for the

Luftwaffe. One man told an interviewer that he felt like a patient in a dentist's waiting room: "It's got to come and will probably be horrible while it lasts, but it won't last forever, and it's just possible these teeth won't have to come out after all." It was just possible that Nazi Heinkels or Junkers would never appear in the night skies over England, so Mum or Dad might carelessly leave a shade up an inch or two, or a door ajar. Then the fatherly wardens turned into monsters. Their shining hour would come, and soon; in the Bore War, however, many of them were stigmatized to a degree which is puzzling today. But it should be remembered that in those days an Englishman's home was considered his castle; a premium was placed on privacy. And many men in tin hats were seen as a threat to it.[122]

In one remarkable instance a hundred-watt bulb had been left burning in an unoccupied house. The warden, a young, powerfully built man, found himself eyeball to eyeball with a double-locked mahogany door, framed in oak and set in concrete. He left, returned with a long iron bar, and, gathering his muscles for one heroic effort, burst into the room and turned off the lamp. The damage was fifteen pounds. An understanding magistrate reduced the usual two-pound fine to one pound. One outraged Londoner said he hated wardens more than Nazis and wanted to strangle them. If the German bombers had come it would have been different, but they hadn't. "What was the *point* of it?" asked Laurence Thompson, speaking for countless thousands. The English people, he wrote, were "a decent, puzzled, discontented people who had braced themselves to withstand Armageddon, and found themselves facing the petty miseries of burst water pipes, a shortage of coal, verminous evacuees, and the dim spiritual erosion of the blackout."[123]

The burst pipes, amounting to an epidemic, derived from the coldest European winter in forty-five years, an act of God which did not strengthen confidence in the King's endorsement of His benevolence. The coal shortage contributed to it, of course, but even without the inconveniences of wartime, Britain and the Continent would have suffered. Trains were buried under thirty-foot drifts; snowplows dug them out, but even so they were over twenty-eight hours late in reaching their destinations. Among civilians communications were often impossible. You couldn't phone, you couldn't send a wire; hundreds of miles of telephone and telegraph wires were down. In Derbyshire the drifts towered over cottage roofs. The Thames was solid ice for eight miles — from Teddington to Surbury. And the Strait of Dover was frozen at Dungeness and Folkestone. Afterward, one editorial surmised: "It is probable that on January 29, when chaotic transport conditions prevailed over a large part of England, due to snow and ice, Berlin had little idea of the extent of our wintry weather."[124]

It did not occur to that insular editor that the Continent might be sharing Britain's misery. Actually, the Continent was just as frigid. Even the Riviera was desolate, and Berlin, like London, was snowbound. The weather, which had not saved Poland, gave the Allies a reprieve. Seldom, if ever, have meteorological conditions so altered the course of a war, though the issue of who benefited most is debatable. Telford Taylor believes that because "the extremity of that bitter winter alone prevented Hitler from launching [an attack] against an ill-equipped and ill-prepared Anglo-French army . . . the weather saved the British army, which at that time had only half the strength it was to attain by spring." Certainly they felt blessed at the time. But afterward, when the OKW hierarchy was interrogated at Nuremberg, it became clear that during that arctic hiatus the Führer, in a brilliant stroke, completely changed his western strategy and thereby gained his margin of victory. How the Allies would have fared in the autumn of 1939 is moot. The fact that the French collapsed in the spring of 1940 is not, and the fewer troops the BEF had when France fell, the better, for in the ultimate crisis all of them had to be rescued.[125]

Hitler's military genius in the war's early years — his gift for reviewing the choices presented by *die Herren Oberbefehlshaber* (the commanders in chief) and unerringly selecting the right one — can hardly be exaggerated. Later, after his victories persuaded him that he was invincible, he provided the same generals with evidence to support their contention that his strategy was a succession of blunders. It wasn't; he achieved his remarkable triumphs despite them, in part because he understood them, and, more important, their soldiers, better than they did. Most of the world outside the Reich assumed that the Wehrmacht would rest after overwhelming Poland while the Führer digested his new conquest. Ironside disagreed. On September 15 — twelve days before the surrender of Warsaw — the CIGS told the War Cabinet that the French believed the Wehrmacht "would stage a big attack on the Western Front" within a month, and he himself thought a German offensive possible before the end of October. It seemed improbable. Even Churchill wrote Chamberlain later that same Friday that in his view a German attack on the western front "at this late season" was "most unlikely." A turn eastward and southward through Hungary and Rumania made more sense to Winston. He doubted that the Führer would turn westward until "he has collected the easy spoils which await him in the East," thereby giving his people "the spectacle of repeated successes."[126]

His vision was clouded there. However, no one outside the War Office and the Conseil Supérieur de la Guerre, and very few in them, matched his analysis of the Polish campaign. In that same letter he wrote that he was "strongly of the opinion that we should make every preparation to defend

ourselves in the West." In particular, French territory on the border
"behind Belgium should be fortified night and day by every conceivable
resource," including "obstacles to tank attack, planting railway rails upright, digging deep ditches, erecting concrete dolls, land-mines in some
parts and inundations all ready to let out in others, etc.," which "should be
combined in a deep system of defence." The panzers which were overrunning Poland, he wrote, "can only be stopped by physical obstacles defended
by resolute troops and a powerful artillery." If defenders lacked those, he
warned, "the attack of armoured vehicles cannot be resisted."[127]

Hitler shared Churchill's admiration for tanks, and for that very
reason he wanted to invade the neutral Low Countries before such obstacles
could be built. He also assumed — illustrating his ignorance of how
democracies work — that the Allies would soon occupy Belgium and Holland. Two days after Ironside's presentation to the War Cabinet and
Churchill's advice to the prime minister, the Führer told the OKW
commanders in Zossen that immediately after the Polish surrender he
wanted to move the entire Wehrmacht across Germany and strike at the
Allied forces. The Generalstab was shocked. They had been counting on
several months of positional warfare in the west while they retrained their
men and planned the army's order of battle. He was adamant; a few weeks
later, on October 10, he issued his Directive No. 6, ordering immediate
preparations for an attack through Luxembourg, Belgium, and Holland
"at as early a date as possible" with the objective of defeating the French
and establishing "a base for conducting a promising air and sea war against
England." To his staff he said he wanted the invasion under way by
November 12.[128]

Ten days after his directive, the generals submitted their plan for
invasion in the west. In Hitler's view, and in history's, it was remarkable
for its mediocrity and lack of imagination. They proposed a frontal assault
driving head-on across the Low Countries to the Channel ports. Six days
later the Führer suggested that the main thrust drive across southern
Belgium and through the forested Ardennes toward Sedan. Their reply
echoes Pétain's view; the hills and thick woods of the Ardennes were
"unmöglich" ("impossible"). The Führer made no further comment then.
He hadn't dismissed the idea, but had the fine weather held, the unimaginative attack would have proceeded. Although the Allied armies were not
up to strength, that was the plan they expected, and they would have met
it with everything they had. They did so seven months later, when they had
much more. Unfortunately, the German plan of attack had changed; while
they were rushing to bar the front door, the enemy slipped in the back.

The weather, responsible for the long delay, persuaded Hitler to
postpone his assault nine times. Each time, he reconsidered lunging

through the Ardennes with a panzer corps. His aides were instructed to bring him aerial photographs and detailed topographic maps of the terrain. Studying them, he felt confirmed; much of it was good panzer country, fields and roads; the forested areas which discouraged generals could be used to advantage, camouflaging tanks from aerial surveillance. In fact, although this was unknown to him, in 1939 when the Conseil Supérieur had staged a seven-division German drive in the French Ardennes with armored support, the "enemy" had put the defenders to flight. Field Marshal Walther von Brauchitsch, army commander in chief, was unconvinced, and protocol required the Führer to deal directly with him. However, a handful of his most gifted generals, Manstein, Rundstedt, and Guderian among them, believed that a massive panzer *Sichelschnitt* (scythe-cut) in the south, with a far stronger force than Hitler had proposed, could slice through the Ardennes, drive to the sea, and trap the Allied armies in the north, where the Germans were expected. On February 17, in a traditional ceremony, five generals promoted to corps commanders were invited to dine with the Führer. Manstein was among them. He gave his host a detailed account of the plan he, Rundstedt, and Guderian had developed. Hitler was ecstatic. At noon the next day he issued a new *Führerordnung*, incorporating all Manstein's points. By February 24, Hitler, Halder, and the OKW in Zossen, working round the clock, had completed the final orders for their Ardennes offensive. The blow would fall in May.

The British military presence in France, so slight before winter closed down Hitler's plan for a lightning stroke in the west, grew through the bitter winter, until Lord Gort, the BEF commander, had nearly 400,000 men dug in. Unlike their fathers in 1914, they were not eager to fight, but they were ready. Morale was high; the British spit-and-polish traditions were observed; so were training schedules; and officers organized games, the more vigorous the better, to keep the men fit. Gracie Fields's ration song was unheard here. The music halls had given the BEF a rollicking anthem which enjoyed tremendous popularity until events soured its lyrics.

We're gonna hang out the washing on the Siegfried Line.
Have you any dirty washing, Mother dear?

Soldiers given leave headed for Paris, where the season's hit shows were *Paris, Reste Paris,* at the Casino de Paris, starring Maurice Chevalier and Josephine Baker; Lucienne Boyer at her *boîte de nuit* in the rue Volney; and revivals of *Cyrano de Bergerac* and *Madame sans Gêne* at the Comédie Française. But on the whole Tommies found the City of Light disappointing. The attitude of the French puzzled them. They seemed surly, hostile, smoldering with grievances. And so they were. Some of their anger was intramural; they held their leaders in contempt. After the Russians had picked up their winnings in Poland and declared themselves at peace, France's powerful Communist party took the position that the war was a "capitalist-imperialist project" in which workers had no stake. At the other end of the political spectrum, the extreme French right still yearned for an understanding with the Reich; with Poland gone, they argued, the need for an anti-Bolshevik bulwark was all the greater. To them, German National Socialism was preferable to French socialism; their rallying cry was "Better Hitler than Blum." Lucien Rebattet, a gifted writer for the Fascist weekly *Je Suis Partout*, wrote that the war had been launched "by the most hideous buffoons of the most hideous Jewish and demagogic regime. . . . We are supposed once more to save the Republic, and a Republic worse than the one in 1914. . . . No, I do not feel the least anger against Hitler, but much against all the French politicians who have led to his triumph."[129]

However, the chief target of French discontent was Britain. Although the British were allies, they were treated with scorn. Until Tommies began manning sectors of the Maginot Line, a brigade at a time, most poilus were unaware that the British Expeditionary Force even existed. Certainly their newspapers didn't tell them. The Parisian press, reinforcing the public mood, was resentful not of Nazi aggression, the root cause of the war, but of *l'Albion perfide*. England, in the popular French view, had forced France into unnecessary hostilities, and there was widespread suspicion that the British had no intention of fighting — that when battle appeared imminent they would withdraw to their island, shielded by the Royal Navy, while poilus were slaughtered. Daladier told William Bullitt, the American ambassador, that he was convinced Britain intended to let the French do all the fighting. At the Quai d'Orsay, Alexis Léger spoke as though Britain were uncommitted, telling Bullitt: *"La partie est perdue. La France est seule."* Holding his first staff meeting as supreme commander of Allied troops, Gamelin revealed his opinion of his ally by neglecting to bring an interpreter and speaking so rapidly that less than half of what he said was understood by the British officers.[130]

> *We're gonna hang out the washing on the Siegfried Line*
> *'Cause the washing day is here.*

Churchill had been visiting France since childhood, and despite his atrocious accent, he spoke the language fluently. Hitler spoke only German. He had never been abroad. Yet Churchill's Francophilia was a romantic illusion, while the German führer's evaluation of the people who had been Germany's foe for over two thousand years was penetrating. "Hitler," Churchill later wrote, "was sure that the French political system was rotten to the core, and that it had infected the French Army." Whatever the reason, the rot was there. And Joseph Goebbels knew how to make it fester. The Luftwaffe, like the RAF, staged truth raids. They were, however, far more clever than England's. Their contribution to what one French officer called *"une guerre de confettis"* was not leaflets but single slips of paper that fluttered down round the French lines. Resembling colored leaves, they bore on one side the message: "In the autumn the leaves fall. So fall the poilus, fighting for the English." The obverse read: "In the spring the leaves come again. Not so the poilus."[131]

The leaflets were followed by beguiling enticements from French-speaking Germans using bullhorns and large signs taunting poilus at the front, asking why they should die for Danzig, the Poles, or the British (*"Ne mourez pas pour Danzig, pour les Polonais, pour les Britanniques!"*). Nazi propagandistic statements quoted by Molotov, effective among French Communists, assigned to *"la France et la Grande-Bretagne la responsabilité de la poursuite des hostilités."* On September 26, with Poland vanquished, the Germans opened a new propaganda campaign: "Why do France and Britain want to fight now? Nothing to fight about. Germany wants nothing in the West. [*L'Allemagne ne demande rien à l'ouest*]." The most effective line was the assurance that if the French didn't open fire, German guns would remain silent. *Time* reported a version of this: "We have orders not to fire on you if you don't fire on us." Soon poilus and *Soldaten* were bathing in the Rhine together. *Time* readers unfamiliar with the fighting spirit essential in infantry combat — not only for victory but also for the survival of the individual infantryman — might have thought this harmless. But it served the Führer in two ways. In the first week of the war civility between men on both sides would permit his thin screen of troops on the Reich's western front to hold while the Wehrmacht finished off the Poles. And idle soldiers, especially those doubtful of their cause, deteriorate under such circumstances; their combat efficiency loses whatever edge it had, and when the balloon goes up, they find it almost impossible to kill the likable, fair-haired youths on the far shore, which means the youths on the far shore, no longer under orders to appear likable, are far likelier to kill *them*.[132]

British soldiers appeared to be immune to the contagion. Their commanders were not defeatist, neither their great-grandfathers nor their fathers had been routed by German troops in 1870 and 1914 — and besides, whoever heard of Blighty losing a war?

What though the weather be wet or fine,
We'll just travel on without a care.

British officers, however, were worried. One of their strengths, and a source of impotent rage among those who lived under other flags and had to deal with them, was that Englishmen with their background could not be offended by pomposity because their own capacity for arrogance was infinite. In 1914 British officers had told their men, "The wogs" — a pejorative for subjects of the Empire — "begin at Calais." They were still saying it in 1939, distinctly pronouncing the final *s* in *Calais* while natives gnashed their teeth. Gamelin, reading French aloud at top speed, could never win playing this game with them. They had invented insolence and would leave his hauteur a thing of shreds and patches.

They were, however, concerned about the poilus' morale. If the Germans came — and despite enemy propaganda no one in authority doubted that they would — these French soldiers would be on the British right. Should they break, the BEF's flank would be left hanging on air, the ultimate horror of a generation of soldiers wedded to the doctrine of *le front continu*. Again and again they had been told that the French army was "matchless," a word, it now occurred to them, subject to two interpretations. Certainly few of them could recall seeing its equal in carelessness, untidiness, and lack of military courtesy. General Sir Alan Brooke, a future CIGS now commanding a BEF corps, attended a ceremony as the guest of General André-Georges Corap, commander of the French Ninth Army. In his memoirs he would recall taking the salute: "Seldom have I seen anything more slovenly and badly turned out. Men unshaven, horses ungroomed, clothes and saddlery that did not fit, vehicles dirty, and a complete lack of pride in themselves and their units. What shook me most . . . was the look in the men's faces, disgruntled and insubordinate looks, and although ordered to give 'Eyes left,' hardly a man bothered to do so." It would be a distortion, however, to indict the conscripted French soldier for his reluctance to defend the soil of France. The blight went all the way to the top. It was their *généralissime* who expressly forbade poilus from firing on German working parties across the river. *"Les Allemands,"* he said, *"répondront en tirant sur les nôtres"* ("The Germans would only respond by firing on us").[133]

Sumner Welles, the American under secretary of state, accepted an invitation to inspect the Allied front. Welles was touring Europe as a special emissary of FDR, and in Washington he reported that French officers had privately complained to him that their men were undisciplined; unless the Germans attacked soon, they predicted, the poilus would spontaneously disband and go home. If an army's leaders take a foreigner aside to criticize their own men, something is very wrong. Vigilant French leaders knew it. Not only was there no training; neither Gamelin nor General Georges, Churchill's friend, ordered exercises at divisional strength to make commanders familiar with the problems of handling large units in the field. General André-Charles-Victor Laffargue later wrote: "Our units vegetated in an existence without purpose, settling down to guard duty and killing time until the next leave or relief." Longer leaves were granted more frequently, recreation centers established, theatrical troupes summoned from Paris to entertain the troops.[134]

Nothing worked. Morale continued to decline. General Edmond Ruby, commander of the First Army, was alarmed to find "a general apathy and ignorance among the ranks. No one dared give an order for fear of being criticized. Military exercises were considered a joke, and work unnecessary drudgery." The next step down was alcoholism. It appears to have descended upon the whole army overnight. *"L'ivrognerie"* — drunkenness — "had made an immediate appearance," General Ruby noted, "and in the larger railroad stations special rooms had to be set up to cope with it — euphemistically known as 'halls of de-alcoholizing.' " So many men were so drunk in public that commanders began to worry about *civilian* morale.[135]

Although Churchill believed that the French army would never break, however strong the German assault, in January 1940 he crossed the Channel for a visit to the front. He did not return reassured. The French artillery, he was pleased to find, had been improved "so as to get extra range and even to out-range, the new German artillery." But he was deeply troubled by "the mood of the people," which "in a great national conscript force is closely reflected in its army, the more so when that army is quartered in the homeland and contacts are close." During the 1930s, he later wrote, "important elements, in reaction to growing Communism, had swung towards Fascism," and the long months of waiting which had followed the collapse of Poland had given "time and opportunity" for "the poisons" of communism and fascism "to be established." There could be "no doubt," he observed, that "the quality of the French army" was being "allowed to deteriorate during the winter." Sound morale in any army is achieved in many ways, "but one of the greatest is that men be fully employed at useful and interesting work. Idleness is a dangerous breeding-ground." He had observed "many tasks that needed doing: training demanded continuous attention; defences were far from satisfactory or complete, even the Maginot Line lacked many supplementary field works; physical fitness demands exercise." He had been struck by the "poor quality of the work in hand, by the lack of visible activity of any kind," and thought the "emptiness of the roads behind the line was in great contrast to the continual coming and going which extended for miles behind the British sector."[136]

Colonel de Gaulle also believed the troops needed training and exercise, and urged it in a vigorous report to his superiors. He thought programs should be both intensive and exhausting, partly because the men weren't fit but also to raise their spirits. Somewhere on its way up to high command his recommendation was lost, which was no surprise to those familiar with the system. In combat a leader's greatest need is information, and if he is competent he does everything possible to establish a communications system that will survive in the chaos of battle, and, if possible, at least one backup net, for what works well in peacetime maneuvers may disintegrate and vanish when great armies clash in the fog of war.

Gamelin seems not to have anticipated this obstacle. Indeed, it was almost as though he set out to frustrate his own chain of command and assure his isolation when he was most needed. Poring over documents in Vincennes, on the outskirts of Paris, he never established means of keeping in touch with field commanders. There was no radio at Vincennes. He could telephone Georges, the commander of all forces at the front, whose headquarters were at La Ferté-sous-Jouarre, thirty-five miles away, but he preferred to drive, an hour each way on roads swarming with suburban Paris traffic. In the age of radio and the teletype, it took six hours for an order from Gamelin to reach an air force command — by which time the target would be gone — and *forty-eight hours* to issue a general order to all commands. One French officer described his remote headquarters as a "submarine without a periscope," and later de Gaulle wrote bitterly: "There he was, in a setting as quiet as a convent [*silencieux comme un couvent*], attended by a few officers, working and meditating without mixing in day-to-day duties. In his retreat at Vincennes, General Gamelin gave the impression of a savant testing the chemical reactions of his strategy in a laboratory."[137]

Sir John Slessor of the Air Ministry, one of a series of visitors from London, described the supreme commander as a "nice old man not remotely equal to his enormous job." Why, then, didn't the British move to thwart the debacle that lay dead ahead? One reason was that the British troop commitment was much smaller than the French. Another was that in the last war it had taken four years to establish a unified command under Foch. Furthermore, Gamelin had served ably on Foch's staff. Most members of His Majesty's Government were Francophiles; they refused to credit the tales of Anglophobia across the water. All, Churchill included, retained their blind faith in the French army, which had taken the worst the Germans could throw at them between 1914 and 1918 and always came back. The poilus of this war were the sons of those in the last. Surely they had inherited the same fighting qualities. But they hadn't. Unlike their fathers, they preferred to live.

There was also the Maginot Line. Those whose memories do not reach back to the 1930s cannot grasp its enormous reputation before its hour struck. *La Ligne* was considered one of the world's wonders, and the French never lost an opportunity to polish its image. The French high command celebrated the first Christmas of the war by announcing that they had completed a staggering "work of fortification." Their goal had been "to double the Maginot Line" and it was "virtually complete. . . . From the first of this month our new line of fortifications seems to have removed any hope the enemy may have entertained either of crossing or flanking the Maginot Line."[138]

> *We're gonna hang out the washing on the Siegfried Line.*
> *Have you any dirty washing, Mother dear?*

An American foreign correspondent asked about the Ardennes. Every staff officer was aware that the forest was unfortified; Hitler knew; Manstein, Guderian, Halder, and Rundstedt knew; and Liddell Hart had known of it for over eleven years. But the American public, the British public, and the French public did not know. A majority were under the impression that the Maginot shielded France from every possible German thrust. At Vincennes an officer in a kepi and flawless uniform of sky blue quoted Pétain — *"Elle est impénétrable"* — with the proviso that "special dispositions" must be made there. The edges on the enemy side would be protected; some blockhouses would be installed. The war was nearly four months old, the Maginot Line had been doubled, but the dispositions were not complete. The American asked why. Because at this point the front would not have any depth, he was told, the enemy would not commit himself there. Finally: *"Ce secteur n'est pas dangereux."*[139]

> *We're gonna hang out the washing on the Siegfried Line*

Walter Lippmann was received as though he were a head of state; a dozen colonels took him on a tour of the Maginot Line, then accompanied him to Vincennes. Lippmann commented that there was only one thing wrong with the line: it was in the wrong place. The *généralissime* did not understand. What would happen, the American publicist asked, if the enemy attacked in the north, where the line ended at the Belgian frontier? Gamelin was glad he had asked. He was *hoping* the Germans would try that. "We've got to have an open side because we need a *champs de bataille*," he explained. "The Maginot Line will narrow the gap through which they can come, and thus enable us to destroy them more easily."[140]

'Cause the washing day is here.

Colonel de Gaulle was a *peste*. He had been repeatedly referred to the army manual *Les instructions pour l'emploi des chars* — tanks — which clearly stated that "Combat tanks are machines to accompany the infantry. . . . In battle, tank units constitute an integral part of the infantry. . . . Tanks are only supplementary means. . . . The progress of the infantry and its seizing of objectives are alone decisive." The role of the tank was to accompany infantry *"et non pour combattre en formations indépendantes."* Could anything be clearer? He was worse than the aviators, who at least had the decency to remain silent after General Gamelin had told them: "There is no such thing as the aerial battle. There is only the battle on the ground." Yet here was de Gaulle, turning up in Montry at general headquarters, where most of the General Staff and staff officers could be found, with another of his reports, this one on *les leçons* to be learned from the blitzkrieg in Poland. He wrote: "The gasoline engine discredits all our military doctrines, just as it will demolish our fortifications. We have excellent material. We must learn to use it as the Germans have."[141]

At present, de Gaulle pointed out, French tanks were dispersed for infantry support. It would be wiser, he submitted, to follow the example of the Germans, forming them in armored divisions as the Wehrmacht had done in its Polish campaign, and, indeed, before the Anschluss. His proposals were rejected by two generals — one of whom predicted that even if Nazi tanks penetrated French lines they would face *"la destruction presque complète."* To this snub the high command added mortal injury to the France de Gaulle loved. Despite the vindication of Guderian's prewar book *Achtung, Panzer!* in Poland, the French high command decided to sell its tanks abroad. The R-35 was a better tank than any German model. Of the last 500 produced before May 10, 1940, nearly half — 235 — were sold to Turkey, Yugoslavia, and Rumania, with the result that when the Germans struck only 90 were on the French front. Moreover, while Nazi troops, Stukas, and armored divisions were massing in the Rhineland for their great lunge westward, the generals charged with the defense of French soil gathered representatives of countries not regarded as unfriendly to France and auctioned off 500 artillery pieces, complete with ammunition, and 830 antitank guns — at a time when the French army was desperately short of both weapons.[142]

The French Ministry of War announced that 100,000 pigeons had been mobilized and housed inside the Maginot Line to carry messages through artillery barrages.

> *We're gonna hang our washing on the Siegfried Line —*
> *If the Siegfried Line's still there!*

🦁   🦁

The brief struggle in Finland had drawn the world's attention to Scandinavia, a development deplored by the Scandinavians, who, like other neutrals, hoped they would be overlooked until the war was over. Norway's yearning for obscurity — which was inevitably shared by Denmark, as it was situated between the Norwegians and the Reich — was frustrated by the Royal Navy on Friday, February 16, in an action which thrilled all England, widened the war, increased Churchill's popularity, and, in its sequel, almost led to his ruin.

Probably Oslo's desperate attempts to remain a spectator were doomed. A country's neutrality cannot always be determined by its own government. If it is violated by one warring power, the country is like the ravished maiden in the Nibelungenlied legend who immediately becomes available to all others, and the Germans had been exploiting Norway's territorial waters since the outbreak of the war. Swedish iron ore from Gällivare was "vital for the German munitions industry," as Churchill had told the War Cabinet on September 19, and while in summer German ships could transport this ore across the Gulf of Bothnia, between Finland and Sweden, in winter it had to be moved westward to Narvik, a Norwegian port, and then down the length of the Norwegian coast through the Leads, a deep-water channel running parallel to the shore. Germany wasn't the only country with U-boats; British submarines could have littered the floor of the North Atlantic with the sunken hulks of enemy freighters.[143]

It hadn't done so because their captains had remained within Norway's three-mile limit, and the government in Oslo, fearful of Nazi reprisals, had decided not to protest. If this use of Norwegian territorial waters could not be stopped "by pressure on the Norwegian government," said Churchill, it would be his duty to propose "the laying of mines" inside Norway's "territorial waters." There was precedent for this. The Admiralty had done it in 1917, and had successfully drawn the German ships out beyond the Leads. After the meeting broke up, he sent Pound a minute advising him that the War Cabinet, including Halifax, "appeared strongly to favor this action." Therefore, he wrote, he wanted Admiralty staff to study the minelaying operation, adding: "Pray let me be continually informed of the progress of this plan, which is of the highest importance in crippling the enemy's war industry." A further decision of the War Cabinet would be made "when all is in readiness."[144]

Pound had seen to it that all was soon in readiness, but other members of the cabinet had not really shared Churchill's sense of urgency, and when the project was mooted in Whitehall, the Foreign Office and the Dominions emitted sounds of alarm. After discussion a majority of the War Cabinet had decided that immediate action was unnecessary, and the matter had been set aside. This seemed to be the fate of every imaginative proposal Winston laid before them, and his sense of frustration is evident in a letter to a colleague. His "disquiet," he wrote, was mainly due to "the awful difficulty which our machinery of war conduct presents to positive action. I see such immense walls of prevention, all building and building, that I wonder whether any plan will have a chance of climbing over them."[145]

The issue had remained on Churchill's mind, however, and had been one of his motives in drafting Operation Catherine. Now in February a flagrant Nazi trespass inside the three-mile limit called for an instant response by the Admiralty. Before *Graf Spee*'s last battle, the captured crews of the British merchantmen she had sunk had been transferred to her supply ship, the *Altmark*. Over three hundred of these English seamen had been locked in *Altmark*'s hold, and they were still there, because after *Graf Spee* went down the smaller *Altmark* had escaped from the battered British warships. For nine weeks she had been hiding in the vastness of the South Atlantic; now, running out of fuel and provisions, with no safe haven elsewhere, she was bringing the British crews home to the Reich for imprisonment. On the morning of February 16 Winston was told that an RAF pilot had sighted her, hugging the Norwegian coast and heading south. Immediately he decided to rescue the men in her hold. Ordering all British warships in the area to "sweep northwards during the day," he directed them "to arrest *Altmark* in territorial waters should she be found. This ship is violating neutrality in carrying British prisoners of war to Germany. Surely another cruiser or two should be sent to rummage the Skagerrak tonight? The *Altmark* must be regarded as an invaluable trophy."[146]

That afternoon H.M.S. *Cossack*, Captain Philip Vian commanding, sighted the German vessel. She fled into Jösing Fjord. Vian blocked the mouth of the fjord and sent in a destroyer with a boarding party. Two Norwegian gunboats intercepted them, and the captain of one of them, the *Kjell*, arrived by barge on the *Cossack*. Vian wrote afterward that he told the Norwegian that he "demanded the right to visit and search, asking him to come with me." The Norwegian officer replied that the *Altmark* had been searched three times since her entry into Norwegian waters and that "no prisoners had been found. His instructions were to resist entry by force: as I might see, his ships had their torpedo tubes trained on *Cossack*. Deadlock."[147]

Vian signaled the Admiralty for instructions. Churchill had left word that any message concerning *Altmark* should be sent directly to him. The incident offers an excellent illustration of what General Sir Ian Jacob has called "the fury of his concentration." On such occasions, Jacob writes: "When his mind was occupied with a particular problem, however detailed, it focused upon it relentlessly. Nobody could turn him aside." Marder adds: "With a display of energy and his imagination, Churchill sometimes carried his offensive ideas too far. . . . The Baltic, and increasingly the Norwegian facet, became almost an obsession with him." There were those in the Foreign Office who thought his reply to Vian was too aggressive; they were the same people who, after his broadcast criticizing neutral countries, had issued a gratuitous statement declaring that the first lord had not represented HMG policy.[148]

In fact his instructions to Vian were almost flawless — "almost," because he should have sent them through Admiral Sir Charles Forbes, Vian's superior. He *did* phone Halifax and told him what he proposed to do. The foreign secretary hurried over to the Admiralty, where Winston and Pound lectured him on the "Law of Hot Pursuit" at sea. Halifax suggested giving the Norwegian captain an option — taking *Altmark* to Bergen under joint escort, for an inquiry according to international law. His suggestion was adopted, and then the order was radioed to *Cossack*. If the Norwegians refused to convoy *Altmark* to Bergen, Vian was told, he was to "board *Altmark,* liberate the prisoners, and take possession of the ship." If a Norwegian vessel interfered she should be warned off, but "if she fires upon you, you should not reply unless the attack is serious, in which case you should defend yourself using no more force than is necessary, and ceasing fire when she desists."[149]

That night, as the first lord and the first sea lord sat up in the war room — "in some anxiety," as Churchill wrote — Vian boarded *Kjell* and proposed the Halifax option. The Norwegian captain declined; he repeated that the German ship had been searched, that she was unarmed, and that she carried no British prisoners. These were all lies, but as Churchill pointed out, "Every allowance must be made" for the Norwegians, who were "quivering under the German terror and exploiting our forbearance." Already the Nazis "had sunk 218,000 tons of Scandinavian ships with a loss of 555 Scandinavian lives." Vian said he was going to board

Altmark. He invited the Norwegian officer to join him. The invitation was declined; henceforth he and his sister ship were passive spectators.[150]

So the *Cossack* entered the fjord alone, searchlights blazing, knifing through the ice floes until Vian realized that *Altmark* was under way and attempting to ram him. Luckily the German at the helm was a poor seaman. He ran his vessel aground. Vian forced his way alongside; his crew grappled the two ships together, and the British boarding party sprang across. The Nazi vessel *was* armed, with two pom-poms and four machine guns. The tars seized those and turned on *Altmark*'s crew; in a hand-to-hand fight four Germans were killed and five wounded; the others fled ashore or surrendered. No Norwegians had searched the ship. In battened-down storerooms and in empty oil tanks, 299 Britons awaited rescue. The boarding party was flinging open hatches; one of them called, "Are there any English down there?" There was a shouted chorus of "Yes!" and a boarder shouted back, "Well, the navy's here!" By midnight Vian was clear of the fjord, racing home to England.[151]

The news reached Admiralty House at 3:00 A.M., and Churchill and Pound were jubilant. Randolph's wife, Pamela, saw *Cossack* land the rescued prisoners at Leith, on the Firth of Forth, where doctors, ambulances, press, and photographers awaited them. She wrote her father-in-law: "You must have had a very thrilling & anxious night on Friday. It's comforting to know we can be ferocious." In his Downing Street diary, Jock Colville's Saturday entry began: "There was great excitement at No. 10 over the *Altmark* affair, news of which reached us early in the morning. It is a perfect conclusion to the victory over the *Graf von Spee*." The King sent a congratulatory note to his Admiralty's first lord, who replied at once: "It is a vy gt encouragement & gratification to me to receive Your Majesty's most gracious & kindly message. . . . By none is Your Majesty's compliment more treasured than by the vy old servant of Your Royal House and of your father & yr grandfather who now subscribes himself / Your Majesty's faithful & devoted subject / Winston S. Churchill."[152]

Arthur Marder speaks for RN professionals when he writes of the *Altmark* incident: "It was a minor operation of no significance save for its considerable moral effects." The episode had repercussions, as we shall see, but the casual reference to its impact on the British public reflects the attitude of military professionals. In wartime they are condescending toward civilians, although public opinion, as France was already demonstrating, can determine what kind of war will be fought, and, to a considerable extent, whether it will be won or lost. Blackouts without bombers were merely exasperating; it was after the *Altmark* that people began to hate. Not all the people — the well-bred still recoiled from the chauvinism without which great victories are impossible. As late as April 26, 1940, Jock Colville saw "a group of bespectacled intellectuals" in Leicester Square's Bierkeller "remain firmly seated while God Save the King was played. Everybody looked but nobody did anything, which shows that the war has not yet made us lose our sense of proportion or become noisily jingoistic." The lower classes were less tolerant, and the newspapers fed their wrath. Churchill had found the rescued men "in good health" and "hearty condition," but Fleet Street rechristened *Altmark* "The Hell-Ship"; those rescued were encouraged to exaggerate their ordeal, and their stories gained in the retelling. Public opinion was developing genuine hostility toward Nazi Germany. People *wanted* to believe in atrocities. Even after four of the men saved had appeared on a platform in the East End, looking well-fed and ruddy, a woman in the audience was quoted as saying: "If I saw a German drownding, I wouldn't save him. Not after that, I couldn't."[153]

Churchill, no hater, used the brief clash in the fjord to build patriotism and confidence in men like Vian and his crew. The House of Commons liked that. On Tuesday, February 20, Harold Nicolson noted: "Winston, when he comes in, is loudly cheered." Admiral Keyes had been in the war room that night, Nicolson's diary entry continued, and had told him how "Winston rang up Halifax and said, 'I propose to violate Norwegian neutrality.' The message was sent and they waited anxiously in the Admiralty for the result. What a result! A fine show. Winston, when he walks out of the House, catches my eye. He gives one portentous wink."[154]

Churchill wanted to squeeze every last drop out of it. The war hadn't been much of a war thus far. The Germans, he knew, were refitting for an offensive somewhere, and the Allies — who should have been giving them no rest — remained passive. He had no authority over the other services, but he could make the navy fight. The battle off Montevideo had given England its first real news to cheer about, and on February 15, just one day before the *Altmark* triumph, he had greeted *Exeter* as she arrived at Plymouth. Now, on February 23, he gathered the heroes of the River Plate in the great hall of the Guildhall, the focal point for the government of London for over a thousand years. There, beneath the Gothic facade, beneath the four fantastic pinnacles, the exuberant coat-of-arms, and the monuments to Chatham, Nelson, and Wellington, he reminded those present — and the nation beyond — that the brunt of the war thus far had been borne by sailors, nearly three thousand of whom had already been lost in the "hard, unrelenting struggle which goes on night and day." He said:

The spirit of all our forces serving on salt water has never been more strong and high than now. The warrior heroes of the past may look down, as Nelson's monument looks down upon us now, without any feeling that the island race has lost its daring or that the examples they set in bygone centuries have faded as the generations have succeeded one another. It was not for nothing that Admiral Harwood, as he instantly at full speed attacked an enemy which might have sunk any one of his ships by a single salvo from its far heavier guns, flew Nelson's immortal signal.[155]

He was gathering himself for the final flourish, shoulders hunched, brow lowered, swaying slightly, holding them all in his stern gaze. It wasn't a Bore War when Churchill spoke of it; it wasn't squalid or demeaning; it wasn't, in fact, like modern war at all. Destroying the Nazis and their führer became a noble mission, and by investing it with the aura of heroes like Nelson, men Englishmen had honored since childhood, he made the Union Jack ripple and St. George's sword gleam. To the action off the Plate, he said, there had recently been added an epilogue, the feat of "the *Cossack* and her flotilla," a gallant rescue, "under the nose of the enemy and amid the tangles of one-sided neutrality, of the British captives taken from the sunken German raider. . . . And to Nelson's signal of 135 years ago, 'England expects that every man will do his duty,' there may now be added last week's no less proud reply: *'The Navy is here!'* "[156]

The Guildhall exploded in a roaring, standing ovation.

In his diary Hoare grumbled about "Winston overbidding the market in his speeches," but it was a popular speech. No one had fewer illusions about combat than Siegfried Sassoon, who had been court-martialed for publishing his powerful antiwar poems while serving as a junior officer in the first war. Now he wrote Eddie Marsh: "What an apotheosis Winston is enjoying! I suppose he is the most popular — as well as being the ablest — political figure in England. He must be glorying in the deeds of the Navy, who are indeed superb. And W himself has certainly put up a grand performance."[157]

His last four words — "The Navy is here!" — wrote Laurence Thompson, "gripped the public mind. It was felt that, dull and unenterprising though the conduct of the war might be on land and sea, the navy was eternally there; and so it heroically was, bearing with the Merchant Navy the heaviest burden of the war." England had gone to war no more eagerly than the French, and as a people the British were less vulnerable to slogans and political melodrama. But as divisions deepened in Paris and the rest of France, Britons grew more united. If they had to fight they would. And though it seemed on that Friday that the Royal Navy had preempted the national consciousness, British soldiers were about to take the field against Nazi troops for the first time. It was to be an inauspicious opening.[158]

*   *   *

For Hitler the Royal Navy's coup de main in Jösing Fjord was *"unerträglich"* — "intolerable." He was enraged that the German seamen on the *Altmark* had not fought harder. According to Jodl's diary he raved, *"Kein Widerstand, Keine engl. Verluste!"* ("No resistance, no British losses!"). This seems hard on the four Germans who had been killed in the firefight, but the Führer had his own yardstick of valor; he reserved his approval for men who had been worthy of *him*. Two days later, on February 19, Jodl's diary reveals, "The Führer pressed energetically" for the completion of *Weserübung* — the code name for plans to occupy Norway — issuing orders to "equip ships; put units in readiness." To lead this operation he summoned a corps commander from the western front, General Nikolaus von Falkenhorst, who had fought in Finland at the end of the last war. Later, under interrogation in Nuremberg, Falkenhorst said he had the impression that it was the *Altmark* incident which led Hitler to "carry out the plan now."[159]

The origins of *Weserübung* were more ambiguous than might appear to be the case. In his war memoirs Churchill wrote that "Hitler's decision to invade Norway had . . . been taken on December 14, and the staff work was proceeding under Keitel." The only relevant event on December 14 had been a meeting between Hitler and Major Vidkun Quisling, a former Norwegian minister of defense, who had fallen under the Nazi spell and whose present ambition was to betray his country to the Reich. Admiral Raeder had urged the Führer to exploit this man's twisted allegiance, and Hitler had scheduled the interview because he wanted "to form an impression of him." Afterward, the Führer had put him on the payroll "to combat British propaganda" and strengthen Norway's Nazi party, an organization which existed almost entirely in Quisling's imagination. But *Weserübung* had not been Hitler's idea. In fact it was the only unprovoked Nazi aggression which wasn't. It was drawn up by the Oberkommando der Kriegsmarine on orders from Raeder alone, which also made it unique; the Wehrmacht high command and its Generalstab were not consulted, and Göring wasn't even told until the execution of the plan was hours away.[160]

Hitler was aware of it, of course; to embark on so ambitious a venture without keeping the chancellor fully informed would have been worth an officer's life. Hitler also knew how the kaiser's Imperial Fleet had been frustrated in the last war, bottled up in the Baltic by the British blockade, with no access to the high seas; and he knew his navy was determined to thwart the Royal Navy in any future conflict by establishing bases in Norway. In October, during a long report to the Führer on Kriegsmarine operations, Raeder had mentioned this objective, and according to Raeder's Nuremberg testimony, Hitler "saw at once the significance of the Norwegian operation." After the outbreak of the Russo-Finnish war several weeks later, the Führer also became alert to the danger implicit in reports that the Allies were forming expeditions to support the Finns, a pretext which threatened the lifeblood of his munitions factories in the Ruhr valley, where the smokestack barons needed fifteen million tons of iron ore every year and counted on Sweden for eleven million tons of it. The existence of *Weserübung* could be misinterpreted by civilians as proof of planned aggression. It wasn't; professional soldiers in every nation know that during peacetime general staffs draw up plans contemplating hostilities with other powers, even though the likelihood that they will ever be needed is very small. The War Department in Washington, for example, had drafted detailed instructions for invasions of virtually every country on the Continent.[161]

The fact — established beyond doubt at Nuremberg and in captured documents — was that Hitler did not *want* to occupy Norway. During his interview with Quisling, which was recorded in shorthand and transcribed, he said that he "would prefer Norway, as well as the rest of Scandinavia, to remain completely neutral"; he was not interested in schemes which would "enlarge the theater of war." A neutral Norway meant the Reich could import Swedish ore without British interference. There is strong evidence that he impressed this on Raeder; on January 13, the official war diary of the Kriegsmarine mentioned Scandinavia in passing and noted that "the most favorable solution would be the maintenance of Norway's neutrality." But both the Führer and his naval staff established caveats. "If the enemy were preparing to spread the war" in Scandinavia, Hitler said, he would "take steps to guard against that threat." Similarly, the Kriegsmarine's war diary expressed anxiety that "England intends to occupy Norway with the tacit agreement of the Norwegian government." The dubious source for this was Quisling, who also told Hitler that the *Cossack*'s boarding of the *Altmark* had been prearranged. The government in Oslo, he said, was England's willing accomplice; the Norwegian gunboats had been ordered to take no action, thereby hoodwinking the Third Reich and its führer. That was the kind of meat upon which this Caesar fed, but the records of his conferences with Raeder show that he was still hesitant, still convinced that "maintenance of Norway's neutrality is the best thing," and — this on March 9 — that so perilous an operation, pitting his small fleet against the legendary might of the Royal Navy, was "contrary to all the principles of naval warfare." Yet in that same conference he called the occupation of Norway *"dringend"* — "urgent." Ambivalence was not characteristic of the Reich's supreme *Kriegsherr*, but he seems to have been indecisive here.[162]

On the last Thursday in March William L. Shirer observed in his diary: "Germany cannot stay in the war unless she continues to receive

Swedish iron, most of which is shipped from the Norwegian port of Narvik on German vessels which evade the blockade by feeling their way down the Norwegian coast. . . . Some of us have wondered why Churchill has never done anything about this. Now it begins to look as if he may." It was reported in Berlin that "a squadron of at least nine of HM's destroyers was concentrated off the Norwegian coast and that in several instances Nazi freighters carrying iron had received warning shots." The Wilhelmstrasse told Shirer they would "watch" Churchill, and a key source assured him that "if British destroyers go into Norwegian territorial waters Germany will act." Act how? he wondered. "The German navy is no match for the British."[163]

Evidence that the Royal Navy was closing in had been accumulating since March 13, when a concentration of RN submarines had been reported off Norway. The next day the Germans had intercepted a message alerting all Allied transports to prepare to sail on two hours' notice; the day after that a party of French officers arrived in Bergen. Hitler did not reach his final decision, however, until Monday, April 1. Signals from Oslo, picked up by Germans monitoring all radio traffic in northern Europe, revealed that Norwegians manning coastal guns and antiaircraft batteries were being instructed to open fire on any unidentified vessels without asking permission from their superiors. Obviously Norway was expecting action and preparing for it. If *Weserübung* was to achieve surprise — essential to success — the Führer would have to move fast; the invasion was ordered to begin April 9. He prepared his explanation to the international audience: "The government of the Reich has learned that the British intend to land in Norway."[164]

The world outside the Reich, jaded by his *grosse Lügen*, would dismiss this new accusation as another absurd Nazi lie. But for once the Führer was telling the unvarnished truth.

Easter had arrived a week before Hitler's decision, and after the harsh winter England was celebrating an unseasonably warm four-day weekend. Traffic to Brighton was heavy. Over two hundred visitors were turned away from a hotel in Weston-super-Mare, and Blackpool landladies enjoyed one of their most profitable holidays in memory. Seaside resorts were unusually crowded; Britons hoped to hear warlike sounds over the water, the eruption of an exploding torpedo, perhaps, or the rattle of machine-gun fire. They heard none. Europe was at war but peaceful. The ominous news from Scandinavia attracted little attention. Hitler take Norway? With the Royal Navy barring the way? What a hope! And if he got it, what would he do with it? The British public, editors had learned, regarded Scandinavia as boring.

What they *did* want was summed up in a *Daily Express* story headed "COME ON HITLER! DARES IRONSIDE." The six-foot-four CIGS was in hiding, suffering the mortification of a man blindsided by a clever newspaperman. Reith's Ministry of Information had persuaded him to grant an interview to an American reporter, suggesting that he paint the rosiest possible picture. Tiny had thought he was talking off the record, and was staggered to learn that the *Express* owned British rights to whatever the American wrote. And so, to his horror, he found himself quoted as yearning for a clash with the Führer: "We would welcome a go at him. Frankly, we would welcome an attack. We are sure of ourselves. We have no fears." Actually, he spoke for millions of Englishmen weary of waiting for the monster to make his next move. At No. 10 Colville had wondered, a month after the fall of Poland, "whether all that has happened has been part of a gigantic bluff." Three months later he noted that a "number of people seem to be thinking that Hitler will not take the offensive, but may even be in a position to win a long war of inactivity — or at least to ruin us economically. . . . There is thus, for the first time, a feeling that we may have to start the fighting, and Winston even gave a hint to that effect in his speech on Saturday."[165]

In the teeth of vehement Foreign Office opposition, led by Halifax, Churchill since late September 1939 had sought cabinet approval of his plan to mine the Leads "by every means and on all occasions," as he later put it. The farthest his colleagues would go was on February 19, when they authorized the Admiralty "to make all preparations" to lay a minefield in Norwegian territorial waters so that, should he be given actual approval, "there would be no delay in carrying out the operation." But ten days later, the authorization was rescinded. The tide turned for Winston on March 28, when the Allied Supreme War Council approved the plan, and on April 1 — the day Hitler, unknown to them, gave the green light to *Weserübung* — the War Cabinet set April 5 for the operation. Churchill decided that because it was "so small and innocent," the mining operation should be called "Wilfred" — the name of a comic strip character in the *Daily Mirror*. He pointed out that the minelaying "might lead the Germans to take forcible action against Norwegian territory, and so give us an opportunity for landing forces on Norwegian soil with the consent of the Norwegian government"; and he proposed that "we should continue in a state of readiness to despatch a light force to Narvik." The Supreme War Council went farther; on April 8 a British brigade and a contingent of French troops would be sent to Narvik to "clear the port and advance to the Swedish frontier." Other forces would land at Stavanger, Bergen, and Trondheim "to deny these bases to the enemy."[166]

Had this schedule been followed, the Allies would almost certainly have scored a resounding triumph. On April 3 Oliver Stanley, who had succeeded Hore-Belisha at the War Office, received "a somewhat garbled account" that the Germans had "a strong force of troops" at the Baltic port of Rostock. Halifax noted that this "tended to confirm" the latest report from Stockholm, that large German troop concentrations were boarding transports at Stettin and Swinemünde. An assistant military attaché at the Dutch legation in Berlin passed along the same information to the Danes and Norwegians. The Danish foreign minister concluded that the Germans were headed for Norway but would bypass the Danes. The Norwegians believed the Nazis had decided to seize Denmark.[167]

On Saturday, April 6, Churchill later wrote, RAF reconnaissance pilots spotted "a German fleet consisting of a battle cruiser, two light cruisers, fourteen destroyers and another ship, probably a transport . . . moving towards the Naze across the mouth of the Skagerrak." Churchill wrote: "We found it hard at the Admiralty to believe that this force was going to Narvik. In spite of a report from Copenhagen that Hitler meant to seize that port, it was thought by the Naval Staff that the German ships would probably turn back into the Skagerrak."[168]

Actually, the British were involved in making adjustments to their plans because of a serious disagreement with the French, which had stalled Wilfred at a critical juncture. Churchill said that whatever the French did, England should proceed with the minelaying in Norway, and Chamberlain agreed. "Matters have now gone too far," he said, "for us not to take action." One more attempt would be made to reconcile differences with the French. If they continued to be fractious, Britain would go it alone.[169]

The row with France arose from French determination to avoid any move which might invite German retaliation. For over seven years they had been trying to wish Hitler away, and the habit was hard to break. Eventually they were bound to disagree with Churchill, who spent most of his waking moments trying to find new ways of making life miserable for the Nazis. One operation, whose potential exceeded Wilfred's, had been encoded "Royal Marine." During the winter he had studied mines. Among the various types, he had found, was a fluvial mine which floated just below the surface of water. The possibility of paralyzing all traffic on the Rhine — Germany's main artery of transport and communications — excited him. Among the river's many uses was sustaining the Reich's huge armies on the French frontier. Large numbers of fluvial mines which exploded on contact would be launched on that stretch of the river which lay just inside French territory, below Strasbourg. Among the targets would be tankers, barges, and floating bridges. Winston had conceived this scheme during his visit to the Rhine on the eve of war, but he had hesitated to lay it before the War Cabinet because neutral shipping also used the river. His mind had been changed by the "indiscriminate warfare" of U-boats, magnetic mines, and machine-gunning of crews in lifeboats, all of which had victimized neutrals as well as Britons. Then and later he insisted that, as he wrote General Gamelin, "the moral and juridical justification" for Royal Marine "appears to be complete." The Germans had "assailed the ports of Great Britain and their approaches with every form of illegal mining," had attacked unarmed fishing boats, and "waged a ruthless U-boat war on both belligerents and neutrals." Against such an enemy, he submitted, "stern reprisals are required." On November 19, 1939, he had proposed that "a steady process of harassing this main waterway of the enemy should be set on foot. . . . Not a day should be lost."[170]

Months, not days, were lost, for although the War Cabinet endorsed his recommendations "in principle" eight days later, the plan had to work its way through both the British and French bureaucracies. Meantime Royal Marine was expanding; by January the Admiralty had stockpiled ten thousand fluvial mines, the RAF had been brought into the picture as sowers of them, and not only the Rhine, but all major German rivers and canals were to be their targets. Churchill was captivated by his scheme; if padlock visitors called at the private office, one of his aides wrote, Winston would produce "a bucket full of water and insist that everyone should watch the model [of a fluvial mine] work." The War Cabinet finally approved Royal Marine on March 6, and detailed plans provided for floating the first two thousand mines; three hundred or four hundred would be loosed each night thereafter, and eventually the number would stabilize at two thousand a week. Admiral Jean Darlan, commander in chief of the French navy, declared himself "enthusiastically in favor" of the project and predicted that it would have "a decisive effect" on the war in less than a year. Only pro forma consent of the French government remained.[171]

It was not forthcoming. Daladier's government fell on March 20, several days after the Finnish surrender — he had been accused of tardy, inadequate aid to the Finns — and Paul Reynaud became premier. Though no longer premier, Daladier retained his post as minister of defense, and in that office he had the power, which he now exercised, of vetoing Royal Marine. According to gossip at No. 10, Daladier "does not want Reynaud to get the credit, or possibly . . . the French fear instant retaliation which they are not in a position to withstand." The second motive was the one given the British. The minister of defense, they were told, flinched from the possibility of reprisals in the form of Luftwaffe attacks on French air factories. The factories were especially vulnerable now. In two months they would be dispersed and the mines could be launched. On March 28, at the same meeting of the Supreme War Council at which Wilfred was approved, Chamberlain intervened, and his powerful promotion of Royal Marine persuaded the French to float the mines on April 4. Back in Paris they changed their minds and demanded a three-month postponement. Colville wrote, "Winston is going over to Paris to do a little personal persuasion. We are trying to blackmail the French by maintaining that we may not undertake the Norwegian territorial waters project unless we can combine it with the other."[172]

Churchill once observed: "There is only one thing worse than fighting with allies, and that is fighting without them." Yet it is hard to think of any substantial blow struck for Allied victory by the Third Republic. They were, of course, very *courtois* when Winston arrived in Paris the evening of April 4; the premier and most of his cabinet dined with the first lord at the British embassy. Unfortunately, the *ministre de guerre*, "the stumbling-block," as Churchill called him, did not find it convenient to attend. Next day Winston sought him out and cornered him in the rue St. Dominique. He "commented," as he later wrote, on Daladier's "absence from our dinner the night before. He pleaded his previous engagement." That was the war minister's last opportunity to say anything else for quite some time, for Churchill unloosed a torrent of arguments in favor of his project: melting snow in the Alps made this the most favorable time of year for the mines; the Rhine traffic was heavy; if the Germans possessed retaliatory weapons they would have used them by now. Nothing worked. The German reaction would be violent, Daladier said when Winston had finished, and the blow would "fall on France." Churchill reluctantly phoned London and told his colleagues he had decided that to press the French harder would be "a very great mistake." In reality, a far greater mistake had already been made. Operation Wilfred, the mining of Norwegian ports, had been scheduled for Friday, April 5, with Anglo-French landings to follow. Because of Winston's trip to Paris, the dates had been set back three days, to begin Monday, April 8. It is startling to read his postwar apologia: "If a few days would enable us to bring the French into agreement upon the punctual execution of the two projects, I was agreeable to postponing 'Wilfred' for a few days." Yet neither project was dependent upon the other; French reluctance to endorse one should not have held the other back, and "punctual execution" was precisely what his trip to Paris lost Wilfred.[173]

The delay proved fatal. Though each was only vaguely aware of the other, the British and the Germans were in a crucial race for Norway, and Falkenhorst and the Kriegsmarine won it in a photo finish. Hankey, then a member of the War Cabinet, later wrote that in their designs on Norway "both Great Britain and Germany were keeping more or less level in their plans and preparations. Britain actually started planning a little earlier. . . .

Both plans were executed almost simultaneously, Britain being twenty-four hours ahead in the so-called act of aggression, if the term is really applicable to either side." But Germany's final surge made the difference.[174]

Unaware of Nazi intentions, Chamberlain delivered a major political address on Thursday, the day Wilfred was put on hold while Winston traveled to Paris, ending it with four words which were to haunt him and, ultimately, to serve as powerful ammunition in the Tory uprising which would drive him from office. Germany's preparations at the war's outbreak, he told a mass meeting of Conservatives, "were far ahead of our own," and His Majesty's Government had assumed that "the enemy would take advantage of his initial superiority" and "endeavour to overwhelm us and France" before they could catch up. "Is it not a very extraordinary thing that no such attempt was made? Whatever may be the reason — whether it was that Hitler thought he might get away with what he had got without fighting for it, or whether it was that after all the preparations were not sufficiently complete — however, one thing is certain: he missed the bus."[175]

❦   ❦

Hitler had already boarded another bus, which followed its timetable with Teutonic precision on Tuesday, April 9, and at 4:10 A.M. began dropping off its passengers — elements from three Wehrmacht divisions — at their destinations: Denmark and the chief ports of Norway from Oslo right up to Narvik, twelve hundred miles from the nearest Nazi naval base and well above the Arctic Circle. Denmark was overrun in twelve hours. The Norwegian government was busy lodging protests against the British minelaying, which had begun a day earlier — and which Ribbentrop had called "the most flagrant violation of a neutral country [since] the British bombardment of Copenhagen in 1801" — but German landings there were not unopposed. At Oslo alone, shore batteries — ancient 28-centimeter guns built, ironically, by Krupp before the turn of the century — sank the heavy cruiser *Blücher*, permanently damaged the cruiser *Emden*, and destroyed auxiliary ships.

In London the first reaction to German audacity had been confusion and disbelief. That afternoon in Parliament, Chamberlain confirmed newspaper accounts of enemy landings at Bergen and Trondheim and added: "There have been some reports about a similar landing at Narvik, but I am very doubtful whether they are correct." It seemed unbelievable that Hitler could have committed himself so far north, particularly when he knew the Royal Navy was present in strength. The Admiralty suggested that "Narvik" must be a misspelling of Larvik, a community on Norway's south coast. But by evening they knew that forces of the Reich held all major Norwegian ports, including Narvik and Oslo, the country's capital. Two days later Churchill, his confidence in British sea power undiminished, told the House of Commons that it was his view, "shared by my skilled advisers," that "Herr Hitler has committed a grave strategic error," and that "we have greatly gained by what has occurred in Scandinavia." Having seized defenseless ports, the Führer "will now have to fight" against "Powers possessing vastly superior naval forces." Winston concluded: "I feel that we are greatly advantaged by . . . the strategic blunder into which our mortal enemy has been provoked."[176]

Liddell Hart comments: "The dream-castles raised by Churchill" were doomed to "come tumbling down." To be sure, in almost every surface battle the Royal Navy crippled the fleet Hitler had put at risk. But victory at sea was no longer determined solely by surface engagements. Churchill thought it still was, and so did Admiral Sir Thomas Phillips, who would sacrifice his life for this precept twenty months later in the waters off Malaya. Rear Admiral J. H. Godfrey comments: "Both W.S.C. and Tom Phillips were obsessed with the idea that a fleet or a big ship could provide complete aerial protection with its own A.A. guns." A vice admiral believes that Pound "was quite as ignorant as we all were before the Second World War as to what aircraft could do to ships. This was quite clear from the Norwegian campaign, where we intended . . . to send a squadron into Trondheim with no reconnaissance, and with the certainty that they would be bombed."[177]

Strategic thinking at the Admiralty had foundered on this reef — the conviction that in this war, as in the last, superior British sea power foreclosed a German invasion of the Norwegian coast. Admiral Forbes, commander in chief of the Home Fleet, discovered that "the scale of attack that would be developed against our military forces on shore and our naval forces off the Norwegian coast were grievously underestimated when the operations were undertaken." In the opinion of S. W. Roskill, the naval historian, those most blind in their conviction that Britannia's traditional sea power ruled the waves were the Chiefs of Staff, particularly Pound and Ironside. But the first lord of the Admiralty should be added to the list. Churchill, being Churchill, did not hesitate to assume command when he deemed it necessary. Godfrey refers to "Churchill's dictatorial behavior" and quotes a senior officer as saying that "Pound proved unable to prevent Winston from running wild during the Norwegian campaign." These, it should be noted, are the views of career officers, united in their loyalty to one another. Sir Eric Seal, who was Churchill's principal private secretary at the Admiralty, vehemently denies Admiral Godfrey's charges: "It is

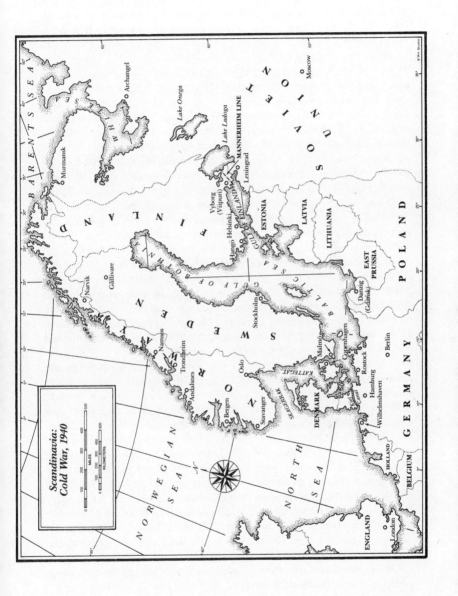

Scandinavia:
Cold War, 1940

MILES
0   100   200   300   400   500

KILOMETERS
0   100   200   300   400   500

BARENTS SEA

WHITE SEA

Murmansk

Archangel

Lake Onega

Lake Ladoga

MANNERHEIM LINE

Leningrad

SOVIET UNION

Moscow

FINLAND

Vyborg (Viipuri)

Hango   Helsinki

GULF OF BOTHNIA

ESTONIA

LATVIA

LITHUANIA

EAST PRUSSIA

Danzig (Gdansk)

POLAND

Gällivare

Narvik

BALTIC SEA

Stockholm

S W E D E N

N O R W A Y

Namsos

Trondheim

Andalsnes

Oslo

Bergen

Savanger

Malmö

Copenhagen

Rostock

Berlin

Hamburg

GERMANY

Wilhelmshaven

HOLLAND

BELGIUM

SKAGERRAK

KATTEGAT

DENMARK

Canal

NORTH SEA

NORWEGIAN SEA

ENGLAND

London

perfectly true that he spent a good deal of time in the War Room, which had a tremendous fascination for him. To infer from this that he assumed control is, in the circumstances, almost malicious. It is certainly unwarranted, and false."[178]

There was a bedrock issue here, and it transcended a clash of personalities, which can almost always be assumed in assessing relationships between Churchill and those who differed with him. War had changed. And those who had seen the Luftwaffe knew it in their bones. According to Gamelin, who was in London on April 26 for a meeting of the Supreme Council, Pound told him: "It is impossible to do anything against the enemy's superior air power." The first sea lord had told the *généralissime* that Polish tales of the Nazis' fearsome bomber fleet had not been exaggerated. The following day, Reynaud said, he found the Admiralty "terrorized by the effects of the bombing." In citing the Admiralty he cannot have included its first lord. Nevertheless, the Luftwaffe's performance had so impressed England's military establishment — less at sea than by its tactical support of Wehrmacht infantry — that they felt the French needed to prepare for it.[179]

But something else is wrong here. What the admirals say and write about air power in the Norwegian campaign is not consistent with what was done. Ships were *not* sacrificed to aircraft in the name of sea power. The Luftwaffe had confirmed conclusions already reached. With very few exceptions, Churchill among them, flag officers had been alert to the peril in the sky long before war was declared. Perhaps the most significant military event in the struggle for Norway was the decision — made in the first hours of the German attack — to send no British vessels except submarines into the Skagerrak. All German shipping had to pass through this channel between the Baltic and North seas. If it had been barred, neither supplies nor reinforcements could have been sent to German troops already committed. It is only seventy miles wide, and in Nelson's day, or even Jellicoe's, Britain's ships of the line would have annihilated them. But now in 1940 the Nazis quickly seized all usable Norwegian airfields, which meant that the Luftwaffe, with over a thousand planes committed to the operation, dominated the sky over the Skagerrak, and the admirals refused to risk their battlewagons to air power. In the 135 years since Trafalgar, sea power had permitted a small island to control its future and build the greatest empire in history. Now tiny little craft, hardly more expensive than ammunition for an 18-inch gun, could deny strategic waters to the mightiest navy the world had ever known.[180]

Weserübung, as conducted by Falkenhorst, was marked by meticulous planning, speed, and professionalism. German captains, entering Norwegian ports in the predawn darkness, answered gunners' challenges in

English. One parachute battalion floated down to take the airstrips at Oslo and Stavanger — the first use of paratroops in war, and it was very impressive. Narvik had been taken by what Colville called "a Trojan Horse manoeuvre"; freighters which usually bore iron ore carried Nazi soldiers in their holds. ("Very clever," said a cabinet minister, "and we were ninnies, we were ninnies!") Hitler's naval commitment had been large, but only 8,850 troops had been sent north in the first wave, and no landing was made by more than 2,000 men. Except for elements from a mountain division, none of Falkenhorst's soldiers came from elite units. Yet once dug in, they were almost impossible to dislodge. In Narvik 2,000 Austrian alpine troops, reinforced by another 2,000 German seamen, held off a British force — at one point 25,000 troops — week after week. In their lightning stroke the Nazis had not only occupied every major Norwegian airfield; they had also taken over the country's radio and telephone networks and seized all five major ports. The *Völkischer Beobachter* ran a banner headline in red ink and end-of-the-world type: "GERMANY SAVES SCANDINAVIA!" Churchill seemed stunned. He told Pound, "We have been completely outwitted." Thursday, April 11, he prepared an account of these tumultuous events for Parliament. The *Daily Mail* reported that "A thousand people packed the pavements outside the House of Commons. 'Where's Winnie?' they asked after other Ministers had arrived. 'Wonder if he'll be smiling. You can always tell what's in the air by Winnie's face.' " But when he appeared his expression was forbidding, and inside, as he arose, he faced what he later described as "a disturbed and indignant House of Commons." Nicolson, watching from his backbencher seat, wrote that the House

is packed. Winston comes in. He is not looking well and sits there hunched as usual with his papers in his hand. When he rises to speak it is obvious that he is very tired. . . . I have seldom seen him to less advantage. The majority of the House were expecting tales of victory and triumph, and when he tells them that the news of our reoccupation of Bergen, Trondheim, and Oslo is untrue, a cold wave of disappointment passes through the House. He hesitates, gets his notes in the wrong order, puts on the wrong pair of spectacles, fumbles for the right pair, keeps on saying "Sweden" when he means "Denmark", and one way and another makes a lamentable performance.[181]

Colville disagreed. Although Churchill was "less polished than usual," he wrote, he was "witty," causing "amusement by saying that Denmark had had most to fear from Germany of all the neutrals, because she had been the most recent to negotiate a non-aggression pact with her. He wisely damped down the absurd over-optimism of this morning's newspapers, but made a good case for the navy's achievements during the past few days." The public preferred the jingoism of Fleet Street, however, and was slow to accept the emerging truth. All they knew, or wanted to know, was that the Nazi navy was at loose along the thousand-mile Scandinavian peninsula, stopping here and there to leave contingents of troops, and the Royal Navy, led by Admiral Forbes, was in hot pursuit. No true Englishman could doubt which force would emerge triumphant. Even Churchill, rallying, told the War Cabinet, "We have the Germans where we want them." Colville noted: "The First Lord (who at last sees a chance of action) is jubilant and maintains that our failure to destroy the German fleet up to the present is only due to the bad visibility and very rough weather in the North Sea, while if the German ships fly for home they will leave their garrisons exposed to our expeditionary forces." *The Listener* quoted an enraptured Hoare as having told the nation over the BBC: "Today our wings are spread over the Arctic. They are sheathed in ice. Tomorrow the sun of victory will touch them with its golden light, and the wings that flashed over the great waters of the North will bear us homewards once more to the 'peace with honour' of a free people and the victory of a noble race."[182]

The Times was reminded of Napoleon's (Iberian) peninsula war. The *Express* wrote of the British storming of Narvik, which the British had not stormed, that it had "an Elizabethan ring to it. It ranks with Cadiz where we singed the King of Spain's beard." The *Daily Mirror* told its readers that despite the need for a speedy response to the German challenge, all cold-weather gear had been provided, including pack saddles for reindeer; and the *Daily Mail* reported: "The British Navy has embarked on a glorious enterprise. Hitler is shaken by the hammer blows of our sailors and airmen."[183]

In his memoirs Gamelin writes that upon hearing that German ships were on the move, he urged Ironside to hurry the dispatch of troops to Norway — Gamelin approved of fighting Germans anywhere except in France — but the CIGS replied: "With us the Admiralty is all-powerful; it likes to organize everything methodically. It is convinced that it can prevent any German landing on the coast of Norway." Churchill confirmed him. On the second day after the German landings, Shirer noted in his diary: "The BBC quotes Churchill as having said in the House of Commons today that 'Hitler committed a grave strategical error' and that the British navy will now take the Norwegian coast and sink all the ships in the Skagerrak and the Kattegat. God, I hope he's right." He was wrong. No one doubted that Raeder's fleet paled beside the Royal Navy, but the

Norwegian coastline is 2,100 miles long, deeply incised by fjords, some several miles deep, fringed with thousands of islands, and throughout April a heavy mist lay over all of it. Except in contested ports the RN couldn't *find* all the German ships.[184]

They found some, though, and the early days shone with tales of heroism. In the first confrontation between ships of the two navies, the Nazi heavy cruiser *Admiral Hipper* (13,000 tons) bore down on the British destroyer *Glowworm* (1,350 tons), all guns firing. In a magnificent beau geste the destroyer, hopelessly trapped, turned as if to flee, threw out a smoke screen, and when the *Hipper* charged into it, rammed her at flank speed, tearing away 130 feet of her armor belt and her starboard tubes. As the gallant *Glowworm* went down, her crew could see the huge heavy cruiser beginning to list under 500 tons of ingested seawater. And the British failure to take Narvik wasn't the navy's fault. On Wednesday, April 10, the day after ten German destroyers had taken Narvik and landed two battalions commanded by General Eduard Dietl, five British destroyers entered the harbor, sank two of the enemy destroyers, damaged the other three, and sank all but one of the Nazi cargo vessels. As they were leaving the harbor, the RN ships sighted the other five German destroyers. This time the British were outgunned. One of their destroyers was sunk, a second beached, and one of the three surviving vessels was damaged.

Three days later the Royal Navy was back, this time with a battleship and a flotilla of destroyers. Every enemy vessel still afloat was sent to the bottom. The commander of the RN task force radioed that Dietl and his men, stunned and disorganized, had taken to the hills. Since Narvik was wide open, he suggested, it should be occupied at once "by the main landing force." The next day an advance party of three infantry battalions arrived. Unfortunately, they were led by Major General P. J. Mackesy, a windy officer cast in the same mold as those who had lost Gallipoli in the first war. Mackesy decided landing at Narvik was too perilous; instead he went ashore at Harstad. There were no Germans in Harstad, only friendly Norwegians. But it was thirty-five miles north of Narvik, his objective.

The *Daily Mail*'s guess that Hitler had been badly shaken was not wide of the mark. Jodl's diary quivers with phrases describing Hitler's loss of self-control, his terror that he might lose his gamble, how he was always trembling on the verge of hysteria and sometimes plunged into it. *"Führer ist zunehmend beunruhigt über die englischen Landungen"* ("Führer is increasingly worried about the English landings") reads one of the milder entries. The Royal Navy's Narvik victory and the flight of Dietl, one of Hitler's old Bavarian cronies, led to "terrible excitement." Hitler demanded that Dietl and his men be "evacuated by air — an impossibility." Then: "Renewed crisis . . . an hysterical attack." "Chaos of leadership is again threatening."

"Each piece of bad news leads to the worst fears." Hitler never had been able to take the rough with the smooth, and as the war proceeded his violence increased. As campaigns go, *Weserübung* had entailed no great risks except to Raeder's surface vessels, which were considered expendable, and setbacks had been few. Between the lines of Jodl's diary one reads the anxious question: If the Führer carries on like this in what is almost a textbook victory, how might he behave in the face of defeat?[185]

In overplaying local successes and ignoring Britain's strategic dilemma, Fleet Street was merely following the line taken by briefing officers at the Admiralty, War Office, and Air Ministry — a press policy usually adopted by military men who are losing a struggle and cannot understand why. Totalitarian regimes can suppress bad news to the end, until the civilian comes to find his home in flames and his wife raped by an enemy he thought was about to surrender. In democracies the lid cannot be kept on long. Editors and publishers are willing to play the game in wartime, but when they send trusted correspondents to the front they will print their dispatches. And soldiers write home. Censors may cut military information which the enemy would find useful, but excluding details of the men's day-to-day life is impossible, and it was precisely there that the British people began to grasp the unwelcome fact that those responsible for the Norwegian campaign were mismanaging it.

Nearly three weeks of action had passed before Englishmen became aware of a cold, cruel shaft of light they recognized as truth. It arrived when several British newspapers quoted the distinguished U.S. foreign correspondent Leland Stowe. Stowe was in Norway, and he had described the plight of an English battalion dumped into Norway, untrained, poorly armed, lacking artillery, antiaircraft weapons, or fighter cover. After four days' fighting, half of the men had been killed, wounded, or captured by the Germans; the rest had fallen back. An officer had told Stowe, "We've simply been massacred." The War Office dismissed the dispatch as "an obvious distortion of the facts." But the English newspapermen in Norway also were talking to soldiers, and they were confirming the American.

Some of the unpleasant news was inherent in the War Office's disposition of forces, and it had little choice there. The country's trained troops were all in France. Those sent to Norway were largely territorials who had been called up only eight months earlier — salesmen, bank tellers, farmers, truck drivers, haulage contractors: men who knew very little about infantry combat. Their grievances were harder to explain. Along the line that started with the CIGS and descended to the rifle company commander, mismanagement had been, at times, scandalous. The territorials were equipped to fight Germans who had been under fire in Poland and carried complete equipment, including sealskin caps and uniforms lined with sheepskin. Pack saddles for reindeer may have been provided the Tommies (though they would have been useless, the reindeer having sensibly retreated inland) but no Tommy had been issued the one piece of gear essential in Norway: skis. Every Norwegian civilian, every enemy soldier had them. So did the French *Chasseurs Alpins,* trained for this sort of fighting, but once ashore they discovered that the navy had neglected to land their bindings, without which the skis were useless.

This kind of elementary error multiplied as time passed. Two territorial battalions were issued a dozen tourist maps of all Norway; their objective wasn't on them. Admiralty orders were often slow, hesitant, countermanded, reissued, and countermanded again. One cruiser squadron was about to depart Rosyth with an expeditionary force when the Admiralty learned Nazi battle cruisers had been spotted nearby; the squadron commander was ordered to put "the soldiers ashore, even without their equipment, and join the Fleet at sea." By the time the soldiers were reunited with their ships, their original objective was in enemy hands.

The worst blunders were committed in an operation Churchill had opposed, a stratagem designed by civilians sitting around the cabinet table fifteen hundred miles from the scene of action. The leadership in Whitehall had been weakened by divided counsel from the beginning, and basic disagreements surfaced over what Britain's chief military objective in Norway should be. Churchill argued that it had been, and should continue to be, Narvik. That was why the Germans were there; that was where the Allies wanted them out. But other members of the War Cabinet, and soon they were a majority, had favored throwing the Nazis out of Trondheim, Norway's ancient capital, nearly halfway between the peninsula's southern tip and Narvik. King Haakon VII and his government, fleeing from Oslo, begged the British to take Trondheim back, thereby giving them a rallying point to organize Norwegian resistance to the Nazi occupation. Halifax, as a peer, took royal requests very seriously. He buttressed his case: Trondheim would provide the Allies with a superb harbor, a base for the buildup of fifty thousand troops, a nearby airfield which would support several fighter squadrons, and direct railway contact with Sweden, which — a non sequitur he did not attempt to unravel — would "greatly improve the chances of Swedish intervention." The possibility of Sweden declaring war on the Reich was zero. Hitler had warned the Swedes of dire consequences if they abandoned strict neutrality and, Shirer wrote on Wednesday, April 10, "As far as I can learn the Swedes are scared stiff [and] will not come to the aid of their Norwegian brethren."[186]

On Saturday, April 13, with troop transports crossing the North Sea toward Narvik, Halifax told the War Cabinet they should be diverted to

Trondheim because "The most important point is to seize Trondheim and the railways leading from that port across the peninsula." Ironside vigorously disagreed; Churchill also opposed the switch, protesting that Trondheim, unlike Narvik, was "a much more speculative affair." But only Secretary for War Stanley supported him. Simon joined Halifax and Chamberlain; otherwise, Simon said, the Norwegians and Swedes would believe they were "only interested in Narvik." When the War Cabinet had decided to mine Norwegian territorial waters — clear evidence that Britain's intent in Norway was confined to crippling the Reich's war effort — Simon had not raised this novel proposition that public relations should play a role in fixing military objectives. He and his colleagues now rejected Churchill's proposal that no further commitment be made.[187]

The attack on Trondheim, it is now clear, derived from the lack of policy. At the outset, Britain's goal had been to stop the Swedish ore shipments. To reach their objective they needed Narvik. Implicit in the decision to take Trondheim was a decision to retake all Norway. The country's strategic value was small. And whether it could be conquered by anyone is doubtful; of its 119,240 square miles only 4 percent was inhabitable. Seizing its chief ports was one thing; keeping them, as Hitler was to discover, was another. That required the consent of the Norwegian people, and it was not forthcoming. The country had been taken by fewer than 10,000 German soldiers. Then the Norwegian underground began to organize, and it began its work by killing Nazi sentries. Despite the conquerors' policy of killing one hundred civilians for every murdered German, nearly 400,000 Nazi troops were tied down in Norway when Hitler's need for them elsewhere would be urgent.

"Although Narvik was my pet," Churchill wrote, he was serving "a respected chief and friendly Cabinet"; since they had decided to make the effort at Trondheim, he threw himself "into this daring adventure, and was willing that the Fleet should risk the weak batteries at the entrance to the fiord, the possible minefields, and, most serious, the air." The British ships' "very powerful antiaircraft armament" would be, he believed, equal to the Luftwaffe. But on April 18 the Chiefs of Staff, wary of the Luftwaffe, decided the risks of a frontal assault were too great. Therefore, Trondheim was to be enveloped by two forces already put ashore at ports still in Norwegian hands. One ("Sickleforce") was at Andalsnes, a hundred miles southwest of the city; the other ("Mauriceforce") at Namsos, far to the northeast. Originally they had been landed as diversions. Now, as Churchill wrote, they would "develop a pincer movement on Trondheim from north and south."[188]

Neither Trondheim pincer had a chance. The British were relying on the Norwegians for their information, and the Norwegians either blundered or were cleverly misled by the Germans, who were expecting an attack at this strategic harbor. Had the attackers known that Trondheim was now defended by 120,000 Nazi troops, outnumbering them six to one and reinforced with tanks and several Luftwaffe squadrons, they would have kept their distance. To do the job properly, six or seven divisions would have to have been withdrawn from France. Moreover, there were difficulties with the terrain. And the Germans were not likely to be deceived by the two-pronged attack; it was the textbook alternative to a frontal assault, and they knew where the British would be coming.

Reinforcing the small forces already ashore at Namsos and Andalsnes presented other problems. Namsos in particular looked forbidding. Later there would be questions in Parliament over why the troop transports did not carry the infantry all the way in to the Namsos docks; the implication was that the War Cabinet had overruled the navy. No one who had seen Namsos would have asked. Only one approach was possible: a fifteen-mile-long fjord, too narrow and winding for any ships but destroyers, to which the assault brigades were transferred. Furthermore, the transfer was an invitation to confusion, and confusion resulted. The transports departed with Mauriceforce's ammunition, rations, heavy weapons — and the brigade's commanding officer.

None of the planners seem to have given much thought to the weather at that latitude. Churchill did; Namsos, he found, was "under four feet of snow and offered no concealment from the air." Indeed, at each of their Norwegian objectives meteorologists forecast further "dense falls of snow" which could "paralyse all movement of our troops, unequipped and un-trained for such conditions." They were waging war in a very cold climate. The men had mistakenly been left with only two days' supplies. The distance was long, movement was clogged by snowdrifts, and the rein-forced German garrison, when told the British were ashore in force, landed parties to intercept them. Mauriceforce Tommies could only hope that Sickleforce's luck was better.[189]

It wasn't. It was worse. Afterward, Hoare said that one reason for the Trondheim operation was to secure airfields; but the Germans had taken them all, and therefore the RAF could not challenge the Luftwaffe. "In that case," Lloyd George acidly observed in the House of Commons, "we ought to have had picked men, and not a kind of scratch team . . . because the Germans had picked men, as is generally accepted. We sent there, I think, a Territorial brigade, which had not had much training." The territorials were in fact only part of the force put ashore at Andalsnes — a small fishing port unsuitable for the debarkation of soldiers and equipment — but their experience was typical. They lacked mortar am-munition, radios, accurate maps, or fire-control equipment for their antiaircraft weapons. Their orders called for a northward march toward Trondheim, but the Norwegian commander who met them, and who had participated in planning the mission in London, persuaded their brigadier to reinforce exhausted Norwegian forces in Lillehammer, eighty miles to the southeast. An eighty-mile march with combat gear is grueling for veteran infantrymen in suitable terrain. The territorials, whom one Norwegian officer described as looking like "untrained steel workers from the Midlands" — which some of them were — reached Lillehammer wearier than the men they were reinforcing. And before they could be billeted the Germans pounced on them.[190]

Quickly outflanked, they fell back. That night a panzer battalion seized Lillehammer. Once more they fell back, to the banks of a river, where the enemy tanks routed them. Once more the territorials retreated, forty-five miles this time, and along the way units became separated from the rest of the brigade. Their plight was pitiable. Now and then they would spot a lone Norwegian on a nearby crest, staring down, in amazement or contempt, at their lack of skis. Wading through the deep snow was like crossing a bog, and because they lacked compasses, they dared not leave roads, which sometimes took them in strange directions. In the early hours of April 20 two companies, staggering slowly through a dense snowstorm, reached a town which natives identified as Nykirke. The Norwegians produced a map. Studying it, the soldiers discovered that they were now two hundred miles from Trondheim, which they were supposed to capture, and were moving in the opposite direction.

Risking security, they phoned a hotel which the Norwegians told them was battalion headquarters. "Lucky you rang," said a cheerful English voice on the other end. "We were just wondering what was happening to you." Keeping in touch now, they set off with new instructions. Along the way they learned that the freighter carrying their transport and Bren carriers had been torpedoed and that the Royal Navy had been unable to prevent the Germans from landing tanks. They thought themselves lost again, but the panzers quickly tracked them down, whereupon they learned that their antitank gun, with its brutal kickback, did not penetrate enemy armor. They withdrew into a forest, but the enemy mortared them into the open, where the tanks machine-gunned them. Having achieved nothing, they had ceased to exist as a fighting force.

That was also true of the main body. Of the original force under his command, the brigadier could count only 300 soldiers and nine junior officers. He sent the survivors back to Andalsnes for evacuation. It was not that easy. The enemy followed the column, as vultures do; stragglers, moving in groups of two or three, roamed the hills, hoping to find sympathetic Norwegians, but most were found first by unsympathetic

Germans. A few reached Sweden and were interned. By now the War Cabinet and the Chiefs of Staff were aware of the disaster. Mauriceforce and Sickleforce had been in Norway ten days; neither had gained a yard; between them they had lost 1,559 men. Those who had succeeded in eluding capture were in danger. Those in London who had sent them there had no choice; as many as possible had to be evacuated. Thanks to the Norwegians — who paid a terrible price when the Nazis tracked them down — 1,800 Sickleforce troops stumbled aboard blacked-out transports on the night of April 30. In the morning, under constant Luftwaffe attack, another 1,300 men were picked up, and, that night, 1,000 more. Mauriceforce, more fortunate, had lost only 157 troops. But the sacrifice there had been equally pointless.

Hitler scorned Britain's Trondheim adventure as *"ein Fall von leichtsinnigem Dilettantismus"* ("a case of frivolous dilettantism"). At the Supreme War Council on April 27, Reynaud had predicted that an Allied failure in central Norway "would come as a great shock to public opinion," and might be followed by an Allied capitulation to the Reich. However, the council had agreed that the Trondheim plan must be abandoned because of the enemy's air superiority. On May 1 Nicolson noted having "a talk with Buck De la Warr and Stephen King-Hall in former's room at the House of Lords. Buck seems to think that if Norway is lost, the P.M. will have to resign." The next day, when the evacuation from Andalsnes was announced, Amery telephoned Hoare and angrily told him: "The government must go."[191]

On the western front of the Third Reich lay the greatest army Germany had ever mobilized to lunge into Belgium, Holland, and France: 136 divisions, ten of them panzer divisions, with virtually every aircraft in the Luftwaffe ready to darken the sky as the tanks and the infantry advanced. On May 1 the Führer, with his penchant for weekend invasions, set Sunday, May 5, as the day for *Fall Gelb* — Case Yellow — the assault on the Low Countries and France.

In Berlin, Shirer, listening to a 6:00 P.M. BBC news broadcast on May 2, heard "the bad news" that "Chamberlain had just announced in the Commons the awful [Scandinavian] reverse." Two days later he wrote in anguish: "The British have pulled pell-mell out of Namsos to the north of Trondheim, thus completing the debacle of Allied aid to the Norwegians in central Norway. Where was the British navy which Churchill only a few fortnights ago boasted would drive the Germans out of Norwegian waters?" And on May 4 Nicolson wrote that "there is grave suspicion of the Prime Minister. His speech about the Norwegian expedition has created disquiet. The House knows very well that it was a major defeat. But the P.M. said that 'the balance of advantage rested with us' and that 'Germany has not attained her objective.' . . . If Chamberlain believed it himself, then he was stupid. If he did not believe it, then he was trying to deceive. In either case he loses confidence."[192]

On May 3, a Friday, the day the men of Mauriceforce swung down an English gangplank, carrying the equipment they had never had a chance to use, Colonel Hans Oster of OKW intelligence (Abwehr) dined in the secluded Berlin suburb of Zehlendorf, at the home of one of his closest friends, Colonel G. J. Sas, military attaché in Holland's Zitadelle embassy and an ardent anti-Nazi. Oster had provided his host with earlier Nazi plans to overrun The Hague, and ten days before Germany's seizure of Denmark and Norway had given him OKW's plans and the exact date for *Weserübung*. Now Sas listened intently as the Abwehr colonel told him that fifty Wehrmacht divisions were concentrated on the Reich's western borders and the long-expected German offensive there would begin in a week — May 10. Actually, the offensive had been scheduled to begin in two days, but on that Friday the Führer set *der Tag* back to May 6, partly because of bad weather but also because the Foreign Ministry advised him that his pretext for invading the neutral Low Countries wasn't good enough. The Dutch attaché sent Oster's information home in the next day's pouch. It reached The Hague within an hour of another coded warning from Holland's envoy at the Vatican. The Dutch immediately passed this warning along to the Belgians, but not to the British or the French. Even at this late hour the Low Countries believed neutrality was possible.

How much of this information was in Churchill's hands is unknown, but over a month earlier he had warned Britain: "More than a million German soldiers, including all their active divisions and armored divisions, are drawn up ready to attack, at a few hours' notice, along the frontiers of Luxembourg, of Belgium, and of Holland. At any moment these neutral countries may be subjected to an avalanche of steel and fire." Ten days later he had written Admiral Forbes: "It seems to me very likely that the great land battle in the West will soon begin."[193]

On the French side of the Franco-Belgian border a brief argument enlivened the Sedan sector. General Charles Huntziger, responsible for it, was so convinced that the enemy would not strike there that he ordered the demolition of antitank obstacles which had been erected on the initiative of a major. Pierre Taittinger and another deputy, both members of the

Chamber of Deputies' Army Committee, inspected the position and were shocked at its vulnerability to enemy attack. In their report they wrote that the high command gave *"une importance exagérée"* to "the natural obstacles of the Ardennes forest and the Meuse river." They "trembled" they wrote, at the thought of what a German attack could do to this strategic position and recommended urgent measures to strengthen it. Huntziger replied: "I believe that there are no urgent measures to take for the reinforcement of the Sedan sector."[194]

On May 4 Hitler postponed *Fall Gelb* to May 7 and Premier Reynaud took the first steps toward dismissing General Gamelin from all his commands. Gamelin, though supreme commander of all Allied troops, had been completely ineffectual in the Norwegian campaign. Asked by the British how many troops he could send for the assault on Trondheim, he had replied, "One division per month." Reynaud exploded. He said: "It would be a crime to leave this gutless man [*cet homme sans nerfs*] as head of the French army."[195]

In parliamentary crises — one of which was shaping up in Westminster, though the prime minister didn't seem to realize it — precedents are worthless. A real political donnybrook bears less resemblance to *Robert's Rules of Order* than to a typhoon, in which water piles up behind a ship's keel, baffling the screws and forcing the helmsman to violate every principle of seamanship to avoid broaching to. Winston had never been a shrewd manipulator of votes. If he ever held a serious conversation with David Margesson, the chief Tory whip, one wonders what they could have discussed. At 11:00 P.M. on Saturday, April 27, he sent for Bill Deakin. Over the last several months he had done this often. Conscious of his contract with Cassell & Company and his obligation to finish his *History of the English-speaking Peoples* if possible, he had, according to Deakin, asked him "to spend an hour or so in the afternoon or in the early morning hours completing his chapters on the Norman Conquest and mediaeval England."[196]

This, surely, was unique in the history of statesmanship. That Saturday evening the Admiralty was sending ships to rescue the survivors of the ill-starred Trondheim expedition — "ramshackle" was Winston's word for it — while reinforcing the British force besieging Narvik. His Majesty's cruiser *Glasgow* was headed for Molde to evacuate King Haakon, his government, and Norway's gold reserves. The U-boats had sunk 101 merchant ships, and new corvette escort vessels intended to cut the German score — Winston's "cheap and nasties," nasty if not cheap — were doing the job, though the first lord was pondering, and would soon approve, closing the Mediterranean to normal British shipping. In the private office, Deakin recalls,

Naval signals awaited attention, admirals tapped impatiently on the door of the First Lord's room, while on one occasion talk inside ranged round the spreading shadows of the Norman invasion and the figure of Edward the Confessor who, as Churchill wrote, "comes down to us faint, misty, frail." I can still see the map on the wall, with the dispositions of the British Fleet off Norway, and hear the voice of the First Lord as he grasped with his usual insight the strategic position in 1066. But this was no lack of attention to current business. It was the measure of the man with the supreme historical eye. The distant episodes were as close and real as the mighty events on hand.[197]

Churchill knew the government was in trouble and might fall. His wisest course would have been to play the lonely role which had been his lot for so long, behaving correctly but keeping his distance from a prime minister who might be on his way out. He couldn't do it. Even when those in trouble were adversaries — for example, Hoare when his deal with Laval was exposed — Winston consoled them and, if it was in his power, helped them. He sensed that Chamberlain was in trouble. Plainly, the prime minister was overworked. When Chatfield resigned as minister for the coordination of defense his office was abolished; Churchill, at the prime minister's request, took up part of the burden, and since early April had presided over the War Cabinet's Military Coordination Committee. A *Daily Mail* headline on April 4 read: "MR CHURCHILL BECOMES SUPER WAR CHIEF," and a columnist wrote that Winston had become "in effect, Britain's Supreme Defence Minister." Berlin radio broadcast on April 3 that Winston had been "elevated from warmonger to grand warmonger." One of Churchill's oldest friends wrote him: "You have indeed great responsibility now, you are practically at the top of the tree." However, he went on: "What a terrible job you have Winston. Your helpmates do not strike me as being very good." Another friend, suspicious, wrote that he couldn't help "wondering whether it isn't deliberately calculated . . . so as to load you with work as to make things impossible."[198]

Separate forces were rallying round the prime minister and round his first lord, and there was very little either could do short of renouncing the premiership, which would have been absurd, since each felt himself the better man. One side whispered, *Gallipoli*; the other, *Munich*. On May 1 Harold Nicolson noted: "The Tapers and Tadpoles" — Taper and Tadpole were party hacks in Disraeli's novel *Coningsby* — "are putting it around that the whole Norwegian episode is due to Winston. There is a theory going round that Lloyd George may head a Coalition Cabinet. What worries people is that everybody asks, 'But whom could you put in Chamberlain's place?' " Clearly it would require someone who would take a sacred oath never to say that Hitler had "missed the bus." That slight remark rankled all England. Clementine called it "a monument to ignorance and obstinacy," and the rage it sparked seems to us now to be all out of proportion to the offense. The P.M. was simply a victim of very poor timing, over which he had no control.[199]

But the anger was there; a Gallup poll early in May, after the defeat in Norway, shocked No. 10. Chamberlain's supporters were vanishing. Only 32 percent of those polled backed him; 58 percent were vehement in their opposition. Nicolson went "to Arlington Street for the Watching Committee" and found "a glum crowd," he wrote on April 30. "The general impression is that we may lose the war. The tanks position is appalling and we hear facts about that. We part in gloom. Black Week in the Boer War can hardly have been more depressing."[200]

Henry Channon, a Tory MP loyal to Chamberlain, noted in the April 30 entry in his diary that he had heard "more talk of a cabal against poor Neville." Then, turning caustic: " 'They' are saying that it is 1915 all over again, that Winston should be Prime Minister as he has more vigour and the country behind him." On May 3 Ironside wrote in his diary: "I hear there is a first-class row commencing in the House, and that there is a strong movement to get rid of the PM." He added a backhanded endorsement of Churchill: "Naturally the only man who can succeed is Winston and he is too unstable, though he has the genius to bring the war to an end." This much was certain: Churchill's steadfast stand against Hitler was all that kept his candidacy alive — in Clementine's words, "Had it not been for your years of exile & repeated warnings re. the German peril, Norway might well have ruined you." Typically, a Liberal peer wrote him May 2: "You, I believe, are the only person in the Cabinet who is not responsible for this War. You are not tarred with the Munich brush. Your advice to re-arm went unheeded. You did not let down the small nations or throw our friends to the wolves."[201]

Later Winston wrote: "Failure at Trondheim! Stalemate at Narvik! Such in the first week of May were the only results we could show to the British nation, to our Allies, and to the neutral world, friendly or hostile. Considering the prominent part I played in these events . . . it was a marvel that I survived." Like Clemmie and others, he attributed his durability to "the fact that for six or seven years I had predicted with truth the course of events, and had given ceaseless warnings, then unheeded but now remembered."[202]

Churchill was trying desperately to salvage something from the wretched campaign in Norway, to depart with dignity and a small victory — something to justify the casualties, the anxieties, the expenses, and the hopes of England. He could not mourn Trondheim. He had been against it from the start. All he had ever wanted was Narvik. But although Winston was farsighted, his vision did not extend into the Arctic Circle, where Admiral of the Fleet Lord Cork and Orrery was trying to reconcile his own aggressive instincts, Churchill's prods, the lethargic general commanding the Tommies, and the fact that some of the general's reasons for his immobility were quite sound. Major General Pierse Joseph Mackesy had drawn up a battle plan which he considered flawless. He would wait until the snow melted and then attack. According to his calculations, that would happen sometime in the summer. Cork didn't believe that at this latitude the earth was ever entirely free of snow, though certainly it was too deep now. And it was growing deeper; more snow fell almost every day. It was "exasperating," he wrote Winston, "not being able to get on, & I quite understand your wondering why we do not, but I assure you that it is not from want of desire to do so."[203]

Taking Narvik became a matter of face, though after the major German offensive erupted across the Channel on May 10, no one in His Majesty's Government seriously considered trying to hold the town. On May 24 the cabinet voted to abandon it as soon as it was in Allied hands. That happened four days later, when it fell to British, French, and Polish troops. On Tuesday, June 4, the evacuation began; by Saturday the last Allied soldier had left. England scarcely noticed. Interest in Norway had dropped sharply; attention was riveted upon the Low Countries and northern France. In 1914, Churchill had written, the cabinet had been preoccupied by the Irish question when "a strange light began immediately, but by perceptible gradations, to fall and grow upon the map of Europe." Now that light had reappeared.[204]

In Berlin it was impossible to forget that one was in the capital of a nation at war. Bands blared *"Heil Hitler Dir,"* headlines preached rage, enormous banners displaying the hakenkreuz streamed down tall buildings from roofs to the street, and posters demanded *"Deutschland Erwache!"*, *"Die Fahne Hoch!"*, and *"Gemeinnutz vor Eigennutz!"* ("The Common Interest before Self-interest!"). On Saturday, May 4 — the day Hitler again postponed *Fall Gelb* — Shirer noted in his diary: "The German papers are full of accusations that *Britain* now intends to 'spread the war' in the Mediterranean or Balkans or *somewhere else,* by which I take it they mean Holland." May 5 was a Sunday, "and as the week began to unfold," Shirer later recalled, "it became pretty clear to all of us in Berlin that the blow in the West would fall within a few days."[205]

That same Saturday His Majesty's Loyal Opposition asked for a debate on the war situation. It was scheduled for May 7. The prime minister wasn't concerned or even particularly interested; on Saturday, May 4, he noted: "I don't think my enemies will get me this time." By "enemies" he meant his critics in the House of Commons, not Nazis, though a state of war had existed between Great Britain and the German Reich for eight months, and he himself had declared it. But in London it was easy to forget. Here there were no parading bands, no marching soldiers, no banners, and no posters. In the first weeks of the war people had talked of little else; now, except among those complaining about the blackout, it was scarcely mentioned.[206]

Winston in the cabinet was Winston gagged, so even politics was a bore. There was the usual maneuvering behind the scenes. The Watching Committee to which Nicolson had referred was led by Lord Salisbury, son of the turn-of-the-century prime minister. Now seventy-eight, the frock-coated marquess had been lord privy seal and the leader of the House under Baldwin. He was a man of convictions — his denunciation of Munich had been so savage that one of Chamberlain's supporters had physically assaulted him.

On May 5 the noble lord wrote: "The Sunday papers are excited, as I knew they would be, about Norway and the reconstruction of the Government. A good deal of this inspired by personal prejudice against the P.M. I fancy the movement for including Labour will grow, but whether they will serve under him [Chamberlain] or not remains to be seen." Actually, it was the other way round; the prime minister was not interested in leading a cabinet with Labour ministers. But Chamberlain's popularity had dropped so far and so fast that even Conservatives were speculating about his successor. Halifax was no speculator, not even in his diary, because his name was the one mentioned most often as the next prime minister. Geoffrey Dawson had been promoting him since March. And on Monday, May 6, the *Evening Standard* observed that "an all-party group of critics" wanted some ministers dropped and replaced by Liberals and Socialists. "If Mr Chamberlain refuses to make the changes," the *Standard* declared, "they say there should be a new Prime Minister. And the man they select is Lord Halifax." Halifax's only comment in his diary that evening was: "Considerable political clamour, but I doubt whether this, at present in all events, will amount to much."[207]

The following day was Tuesday, May 7, 1940.

🦁   🦁

The debate which opened that day was to be one of the most memorable in British history, but no one planned it so, or even expected it. Like a runaway grand jury, it was moved by forces deep within the House of

Commons, views vehemently held by individual MPs who had been unaware, till now, that so many fellow members shared them and felt just as strongly. They were to address the formal motion, "That this House do now adjourn," though in fact they would be debating the prosecution of the war. Chamberlain had chosen to open for the Conservatives; Churchill would close the following day. Labour had wanted Winston first — "We took the view that the First Lord was the Prime Minister's principal witness," Herbert Morrison said — but the prime minister knew Churchill was his most effective speaker and could draw all the government's arguments together as no other minister could.[208]

The government's most ineffective speaker was Chamberlain himself. "The House is crowded," Nicolson wrote, "and when Chamberlain comes in, he is greeted with shouts of 'Missed the bus!' He makes a very feeble speech and is only applauded by the Yes-men. He makes some reference to the complacency of the country, at which the whole House cheers vociferously and ironically, inducing him to make a little, rather feminine, gesture of irritation." As always Neville was coldly logical, but he seemed to lack his usual easy control of the House; his heart wasn't in it. Norway was no Gallipoli, he said — a comparison Winston may have wished he had found unnecessary, though the P.M. defended his first lord by dismissing as "unworthy and unfounded" the suggestion that one minister was more responsible than his colleagues for what had happened. Plainly, he was off his form. It may have been at this point that he realized for the first time that a shadow lay over his government.[209]

Attlee also made "a feeble speech" in Nicolson's opinion, but "Archie Sinclair a good one." Sinclair said the Norwegian operation had failed because "there had been no foresight in the political direction of the war and in the instructions given to the Staffs." He added: "In the first major effort of this war . . . we have had to creep back to our lairs, which is against the spirit of the men who are over the waters." Such damaging words were rarely heard in the Commons, but the pyrotechnics had only started. Another slashing speech followed, and yet another by the Labour MP Josiah Wedgwood, which was very odd. Nicolson wrote that he said "everything that he ought not to have said" and gave "the impression of being a little off his head. At one moment he suggests that the British Navy have gone to Alexandria since they are frightened of being bombed."[210]

This led to the first sign that a real tempest loomed. As Wedgwood wound up, Roger Keyes entered the chamber. At Duff Cooper's suggestion Keyes was in full uniform, gold braid up to his elbows and six rows of ribbons, topped by the Grand Cross of the Order of Bath, glittering on his chest. Here was a genuine naval hero, the man who had led the gallant raid against the German U-boat pens at Zeebrugge and Ostend in 1918.

Nicolson handed him a note quoting Wedgwood's remark about the navy. The old admiral immediately rose, went straight to the Speaker's chair, was recognized at once, and began by calling the previous speaker's remark "a damned insult" — unparliamentary language, but the Speaker did not call him on it, and the House, noted Nicolson, "roars with laughter, especially Lloyd George who rocks backwards and forwards in boyish delight with his mouth wide open."[211]

But Keyes had not come to amuse Parliament. He had brought a speech. His appalling delivery was known to everyone in the chamber, so at Harold Macmillan's suggestion he had written everything out. It was a devastating attack on the naval conduct at Narvik; the chamber was completely silent when he declared that a naval assault at Trondheim would have succeeded but had been canceled because of lack of nerve at the Admiralty. This was a blow at Churchill, doubly so because he and the admiral were old friends. It was probably unjustified; nevertheless, when Keyes sat down Chamberlain knew he was in real trouble. Nicolson described the reaction: "There is a great gasp of astonishment. It is by far the most dramatic speech I have ever heard, and when Keyes sits down there is thunderous applause."[212]

Now it was Leo Amery's turn. The Speaker called him during the dinner hour, and the House was no longer crowded, but Clement Davies, a Liberal MP and the unofficial whip of the dissident factions, toured the dining room, lobbies, and smoking room, drumming up an audience for him. They found him worth it. Amery was a senior parliamentarian; he had been an admirer of old Joe Chamberlain's and a friend of both Joe's sons. With great skill he moved the target of the government's critics away from the navy — and by implication, Churchill — and toward Chamberlain and the conduct of the war. "Somehow or other," he said, "we must get into the Government men who can match our enemies in fighting spirit, in daring, in resolution and in thirst for victory." Approaching the end he said: "Some 300 years ago, when this House found that its troops were being beaten again and again by the dash and daring of the Cavaliers, by Prince Rupert's cavalry, Oliver Cromwell spoke to John Hampden. In one of his speeches he recounted what he had said. It was this: 'I said to him, "Your troops are most of them old, decayed serving men and tapsters and such kind of fellows." You must get men of a spirit that are likely to go as far as they will go, or you will be beaten still.' "

Amery paused. He said: "We are fighting today for our life, for our liberty, for our all. We cannot go on being led as we are." Again he paused, assessing the mood of the House. He had them rapt. In his research he had come upon another quotation. It was brutal; he might lose his converts if he used it, but he was carried away, and looking toward the front bench he plunged ahead:

I have quoted certain words of Oliver Cromwell. I will quote certain other words. I do it with great reluctance, because I am speaking of those who are old friends and associates of mine, but they are words which, I think, are applicable to the present situation. This is what Cromwell said to the Long Parliament when he thought it was no longer fit to conduct the affairs of the nation:

"You have sat too long here for any good you have been doing. Depart, I say, and let us have done with you. In the name of God, go."[213]

In the opinion of some close to Chamberlain, Amery's pitiless attack shattered him. Churchill later wrote: "These were terrible words coming from a friend and colleague of many years, a fellow Birmingham Member, and a Privy Councillor of distinction and experience." In Nicolson's opinion the general impression left by the debate was that "we are unprepared to meet the appalling attack which we know is about to be delivered against us." The response was "something more than anxiety; it is one of actual fear, but it is a very resolute fear and not hysteria or cowardice in the least. In fact I have seldom admired the spirit of the House so much as I did today." He believed "there is no doubt that the Government is very rocky and anything may happen tomorrow." In his diary the loyal Henry Channon noted of the first day's debate: "The atmosphere was intense, and everywhere one heard whispers: 'What will Winston do?' "[214]

There is a jeu d'esprit that Frenchmen tell — though only to one another — of how, when God created the earth, he wanted one perfect place, so he made France. Then, seeing what he had done, he decided he had gone too far, so he made Frenchmen. At times foreigners also repeat the story, and it was enjoying an exceptional vogue in early May 1940. Anyone who has studied the fighting which was about to begin as the Wehrmacht surged into France cannot doubt that Reynaud was justified in his determination to cashier the indecisive, almost inaccessible Généralissime Gamelin. However, the premier's timing was poor. It may be that having no commander in chief was preferable to the French Hamlet in Vincennes, but the problem was larger than that. It was political, because Gamelin's champion, the republic's minister of defense, was Daladier, who wanted to be premier again and was awaiting only an opportunity to strike. Cashiering the *généralissime* would provoke Daladier's resignation and, therefore, a cabinet crisis. France could survive without a government now, but not if she were invaded. But Reynaud's mind was made up. By May 8 the document of indictment was ready; the premier called a cabinet meeting for the following day. The prospect, for everyone except Germans, was depressing. Marianne would face a powerful foe with her leaders quarreling among themselves. Once again poilus would reel backward shouting, *"Nous sommes trahis!"* and in a sense they would be right, though the betrayers would be *les députés* they had elected to office.

But Paris in the spring! In that second week in May the place God had made was a poem of beauty. The gardens of the Luxembourg and the Tuileries were in full blossom; so were the chestnut trees along the Seine; the overarching sky was unflawed by a single cloud, and on the boulevards and the Champs Élysées one could meditate or amuse oneself with friends in what Henri de Kerillis later remembered as "a bath of sun." The Duchess of Windsor worked at a canteen for poilus; Clare Boothe Luce, who had come to see her, thought the capital "insanely beautiful," with "unstartled birds singing in the gardens" and the flower market at the Madeleine "madly colorful." Theatres, cinemas, and nightclubs were packed; so were the stands at the Auteuil for spring racing; so were the halls of the Grand Palais, where the annual art exhibition was on display. In the rue de la Paix the windows of the great gem stores glittered with rubies, garnets, diamonds, jade, opal, sapphires, and emeralds, and business was brisk. On the Place Vendôme elegantly dressed women moved through the gilded corridors on their way to tea or lunch. Afterward de Kerillis would remember "how carefree and lighthearted" Parisians were.[215]

London is less celebrated for its beauty, though there are those who prefer it because, among other reasons, it never occurred to Londoners — and certainly not to Churchill — that England's capital should be surrendered rather than be submitted to the ravages of battle. The British were prepared to sacrifice London house by house, to be destroyed rather than dishonored. The French loved honor, but loved Paris more, as they would demonstrate before summer arrived. On Wednesday, May 8, the second day of the Norway debate in the House of Commons, Hitler set the final date for *Fall Gelb*. It would begin at 5:35 A.M. on Friday. This would be confirmed Thursday when he flashed the irrevocable code word "Danzig" to his commanders. Meantime, the Führer boarded his special train for his headquarters, Felsennest (Aerie), near Münstereifel, twenty-five miles southwest of Bonn. That Wednesday, as the House of Commons gathered, with its leaders feeling they were on the verge of something tremendous, though none could identify it, Shirer was cabling New York from Berlin. As he later wrote, he advised his home office "to hold one of our correspondents in Amsterdam instead of shipping him off to Norway, where the war had ended anyway." That evening his military censors "allowed me to hint in my broadcast that there would soon be action in the West, including Holland and Belgium." Only later did he learn why. The Nazis were deliberately focusing attention on the northern and western parts of the Low Countries, in the hope that no one would notice the German troop concentrations around the Ardennes.[216]

Wednesday morning Labour's leaders were busy. Hugh Dalton breakfasted with Hugh Gaitskell, who told him that "high Foreign Office officials are leaking very freely." Halifax, he had learned, had threatened to resign unless Trondheim were attacked, and Lord Cork and Orrery had said that "in the first twenty-four hours" — before the Germans arrived — "I could have taken Trondheim with my bare hands." His request to do so had been denied, not by Churchill, but by Whitehall.[217]

That morning's *Daily Herald*, the voice of Labour, reported that the party's Parliamentary Executive would meet before noon to determine its tactics in the concluding day of the debate. The *Herald*'s political correspondent, Maurice Webb, predicted "sweeping reconstruction of the Government, involving the possible resignation of Mr. Chamberlain . . . in the near future." Webb doubted, however, that events would "take this drastic turn at once. Indeed, as I have previously stated, the Government will get through the present debate without immediate disaster." He noted suggestions "that the Labour Party should either put down a vote of censure or force a division on a motion for the adjournment, a motion which, if passed, would bring the Government down." To his subsequent regret, he called this "an unwise tactic. . . . The view taken by the most experienced critics of the Government is that the debate should be allowed to end without any direct challenge."[218]

Herbert Morrison and Dalton had given Webb their assurance that there would be no call for a vote. However, he had not talked to Clement Attlee. Throughout Tuesday's session Attlee had kept a sharp eye on the benches opposite. He had observed the hostility toward their prime minister, and he meant to measure it. The leadership meeting, which he chaired, opened at 10:30 A.M., and he proposed that the Opposition force a division. Several of his colleagues were reluctant, arguing, as Dalton did, that "a vote at this stage" would "consolidate the Government majority," that it was precisely what Chamberlain and Halifax wanted. Nevertheless, Attlee's motion carried and was ratified at a later meeting of Labour backbenchers. Labour therefore prepared to make the first move when Parliament assembled. Morrison rose, as usual, to bait the front bench. At last, he observed, the prime minister had found a newspaper endorsement outside Britain and her commonwealth. It was the official organ of Franco's Spanish Falangists. He also read a few lines from Hoare's Norway speech from the BBC in *The Listener*. "Today our wings are spread over the Arctic. They are sheathed in ice. . . ." Hoare flushed crimson as the

House roared. Morrison said: "Hon. Members understandably laugh, but I am not quoting this for the purpose of arousing amusement, because it really is serious, for it is an indication of the delusions from which the Government are suffering." He then announced that "in view of the gravity of the events which we are debating . . . every Member has a responsibility to record his particular judgment upon them." Therefore, "we feel that we must divide the House at the end of our debate today." The Opposition was calling for a censure of the government.[219]

Chamberlain was startled, then angry. The cockiness of Morrison's manner — he always seemed to be lecturing a particularly stupid child — was enough to get under anyone's skin. Moreover, the prime minister had not expected this. There was an understanding between whips that if either party planned to ask for a vote, the other would be told, although recently Sir Charles Edwards, Labour's chief whip, had warned Margesson, his Tory counterpart, that he couldn't always carry out his side of the bargain, explaining apologetically, "It's a very difficult party to manage, you know."[220]

Thus taken unaware, the prime minister miscalculated. He jumped up and sputtered: "The words which the right hon. gentleman has just uttered make it necessary for me to intervene for a moment or two at this stage." Dalton thought he showed "his teeth like a rat" as he cried, "It may well be that it is a duty to criticise the Government. I do not seek to evade criticism, but I say to my friends in the House, *and I have friends in the House*" — here, according to Nicolson, his expression became "a leer of triumph" — "[that] no Government can prosecute a war efficiently unless it has public and parliamentary support. I accept this challenge. I welcome it indeed. At least I shall see who is with us and who is against us, and I call on my friends to support us in the Lobby tonight."[221]

Churchill described this as "an unfortunate passage"; his fellow Tories, he noted, "sat abashed and silenced." "Friends," in the context and idiom of the time and place, meant members of the P.M.'s party. Thus, in a partisan stroke, he had reduced the debate to the lowest level of politics, demanding that men belonging to the majority vote for him, regardless of how they felt about his prosecution of the war. It led to an unforgettable speech. Churchill called it "the last decisive intervention of Mr. Lloyd George in the House."[222]

He was now approaching eighty, and the awesome fire which had fueled the passion of the young Welsh crusader for justice had been reduced to embers. But Chamberlain, by cheapening the office Lloyd George had held in the last war, kindled them; in a final pyrotechnical display he evoked memories of the days when he was in his forties and Churchill in his thirties and the two radicals, the older as chancellor and the younger as president of the Board of Trade, had forged an alliance to emasculate the House of Lords and bring England a maximum work day for miners, pensions for the aged, free meals and free medical attention for all British schoolchildren, and insurance for the jobless and the sick. Violet Bonham Carter, whose father was then the prime minister, had watched them both, and now in 1940, sitting in the Strangers' Gallery, she thought this, Lloyd George's last bow, "the most deadly speech I have ever heard from him — voice, gesture, everything was brought into play to drive home the attack."[223]

He tried to exculpate Churchill — "I do not think the First Lord was responsible for all the things that happened in Norway" — but Churchill immediately interrupted him: "I take full responsibility for everything that has been done by the Admiralty, and I take my full share of the burden." After warning Winston not to allow himself "to be converted into an air-raid shelter to keep the splinters from hitting his colleagues," Lloyd George turned on Chamberlain:

It is not a question of who are the Prime Minister's friends. It is a far bigger issue. He has appealed for sacrifice. The nation is prepared for every sacrifice so long as the Government show clearly what they are aiming at, and so long as the nation is confident that those who are leading it are doing their best. *I say solemnly that the Prime Minister should give an example of sacrifice, because there is nothing which can contribute more to victory in this war than that he should sacrifice the seals of office.*[224]

Now the outcome of the House vote was a source of speculation. Labour could not win. They held 166 seats to the Conservatives' 387. Many men could not switch; commitments had been made, papers signed, obligations incurred. To many others, casting a Conservative vote was a sacrament. And still others knew that if they broke with the party they would be pariahs in their own constituencies, even their own homes. But Chamberlain, smug only yesterday, began to feel uneasy. If the great Tory majority thinned perceptibly, his problems could become grave. Keyes, Amery, and Lloyd George had stirred the House. He was lucky Churchill was on the front bench and would anchor the government's position in the last speech of the evening.

As the debate continued into evening it became obvious that Winston would not be called before 10:00 P.M. He wandered into the smoking room, and was poking a hole in a new cigar when he glanced up and saw Harold Macmillan. Macmillan recalled long afterward: "He beckoned to me, and I moved to speak to him. I wished him luck, but added that I hoped his speech would not be too convincing. 'Why not?' he asked. 'Because,' I replied, 'we must have a new Prime Minister, and it must be you.' He answered gruffly that he had signed on for the voyage and would stick to the ship. But I don't think he was angry with me."[225]

Churchill was, however, worried. After Lloyd George's valediction he had been heard to say to Kingsley Wood, "This is all making it damned difficult for me tonight," and to Walter Elliott that the old man had been "absolutely devastating." Nevertheless, when the Speaker recognized him shortly after ten o'clock, he squared away like a prizefighter, assuming his most pugilistic stance. He had taken the queen's shilling, had signed on for the cruise, and intended to give the captain his best possible performance. In his diary Channon observed, "One saw at once that he was in a bellicose mood, alive and enjoying himself, relishing the ironical position in which he found himself: i.e. that of defending his enemies, and a cause in which he did not believe." Channon called the speech "slashing, vigourous . . . a magnificent piece of oratory. I was in the gallery behind him, with Rab" — R. A. Butler — "who was several times convulsed with laughter."[226]

Winston said he understood Keyes's "desire to lead a valiant attack" but regretted "that this natural impulse should have led him to cast aspersions upon his old shipmates and his old staff officers, Sir Dudley Pound and Vice-Admiral Phillips." Then he turned on those who had deplored the prime minister's appeal to his friends. He had shared their dismay, but he wasn't going to let that prevent him from having fun with them. "He *thought* he had some friends," he said, "and I *hope* he has some friends. He certainly had a good many when things were going well." At one point he said that Allied shipping losses had almost been redeemed by new shipbuilding and the capture of German ships. "Oh!" cried Emanuel Shinwell, an exasperated socialist and a favorite Churchill target. Winston rounded on him. "I daresay the hon. Member does not like that. He would like me to have a bad tale to tell. That is why he skulks in a corner." A Labour MP, "rather the worse for drink," according to Channon, had never heard the word "skulks"; he thought Winston had said "skunks" and protested, with the support of several colleagues who had it aright, that he had used unparliamentary language. The brief exchange in Hansard is hilarious:

[*Interruption*]

Mr. Churchill: What are we quarreling about? [HON. MEMBERS: "You should withdraw that."] I will not withdraw it.

Mr. Sloan (South Ayreshire): On a point of order — [*Interruption*]

Mr. Maclean: On a point of order. Is "skulk" a Parliamentary word? The right hon. Gentleman used the word "skulk" and I am asking whether it is a Parliamentary word to use to another Member?

Mr. Speaker: It depends whether it applies accurately or not.

Mr. Maclean: Further to that point of order — [*Interruption*]

Mr. Churchill: Finally — [*Interruption*] — Hon. Members dare not listen to the argument.

Mr. Maclean: Are we to understand, Mr. Speaker, that a word becomes Parliamentary if it is accurate?

Mr. Churchill: All day long we have had abuse, and now hon. Members opposite will not even listen. . . .[227]

He had a knack for that — drawing them out and then playing the outraged injured party. "How much of the fire was real, how much ersatz, we shall never know," Channon wrote, "but he amused and dazzled everyone with his virtuosity." John Peck, a young civil servant who had recently joined Winston's staff, was fascinated — and troubled. Winston, he later wrote, "was constantly heckled by the Labour opposition, and he tore into them vehemently and often angrily. I had never heard him in action in the House of Commons and I was strangely uneasy." Somehow, he felt, "it did not ring entirely true." Actually, he reflected, it was impossible to offer "a completely sincere and heartfelt reply" to the attacks on the government. "Churchill knew that he was defending positions which were in many respects, indefensible. He knew that if the bitterest critics had their way, Chamberlain would resign. He knew that, in that case, he would probably become Prime Minister himself. But throughout the entire political crisis he never spoke or acted except in absolute loyalty to his Prime Minister." The fact was that the more eloquent his defense of Chamberlain, the more Chamberlain's chances shrank. After this no one would ask: "If not Chamberlain, who?"[228]

The House was blinded, and beguiled, by the skyrockets and pinwheels, but in solemn moments Churchill, though entertaining, was never a mere entertainer. He knew serious men would pore over Hansard, looking for a chain of logic, and he provided them with it. He did not lie, he did not distort. But it was sophistry all the same. He omitted certain facts; since they reflected well upon him, it would have been difficult for anyone to argue that he had deliberately remained mute. Among his omissions was the fact that he had spent seven months trying to persuade the War Cabinet that they must move on Narvik (though he *did* say, "My eye has always been fixed on Narvik"), nor did he reveal his original doubts about Trondheim. Once the Nazi invasion had begun, he said, no one could "dispute that we were bound to go to the aid of the Norwegians and that Trondheim was the place." Not a voice in the chamber cried:

"Why?" Yet that was his one weak point; had he been challenged here, the whole structure of his presentation could have collapsed.

But he got by it and was home free. He conceded that Trondheim had been "a hazardous operation," but could have succeeded had the Norwegians not neglected to blow key bridges, destroy railroad junctions, hold the mountain passes, or block the Nazi advance north of Oslo. All these delaying tactics having failed, the British commanders were left with a Hobson's choice: either evacuate their troops "or leave them to be destroyed by overwhelming force." Could they have been strengthened? They could — by ignoring the military maxim "Never reinforce failure" and by withdrawing divisions from the BEF in France. Escalation in Norway would have led to "a forlorn operation on an ever-increasing scale." Perhaps he was thinking of Gallipoli. Here he added a warning; he had not abandoned his illusion that sea power was omnipotent, but he foresaw the danger of recklessly committing the RAF unless the need for it became absolute: "We must be careful not to exhaust our air force, in view of the much graver dangers which might come upon us at any time."[229]

The prime minister was pleased and grateful. Then the House voted, and he was shocked to discover that over a hundred of those he had counted among his friends weren't friendly anymore. Despite the Conservative whips, 41 Chamberlain supporters had defected to the Opposition and another 60 had abstained — 26 of them Tories whose constituencies included the territorials martyred at Andalsnes. A united party vote would have given the P.M. a majority of 213. Instead, the final tabulation was 281 for the government, 200 against it — a majority of 81. It was a stinging rebuke, wholly unforeseen. And for many the decision had been excruciating. Duff Cooper saw "a young officer in uniform, who had been for long a fervent admirer of Chamberlain, walking through the Opposition lobby" — voting against the government — "with tears streaming down his face." Churchill had always voted as he pleased, but he was an exception; others faced punishment from Margesson and the party machine. They knew that if they appeared at No. 11 Downing Street's patronage office now they would be turned away. To abandon their leader had required considerable courage, but they had done it, and now he was in the deepest trouble of his political career.[230]

His spirits cannot have been raised by Parliament's response to the announcement of the vote. "Up to the last moment," Nicolson wrote, "the House had behaved with moderation," but "during the last twenty minutes . . . passions rose." The figures "are greeted with a terrific demonstration," he continued, "during which Joss Wedgwood starts singing *Rule Britannia*, which is drowned in shouts of 'Go, go, go, go!' " Some were waving handkerchiefs at the fleeing P.M. To counteract their jeers, Nicolson noted, "Margesson signals to his henchmen to rise and cheer the departing Prime Minister, and he walks out pale and angry." Hugh Dalton was asked: "What next?" He replied: "The Old Man must go to Buckingham Palace and hand them [the seals of office] in."[231]

At 11:13 P.M., May 8, 1940, when the House of Commons adjourned, thousands of Dutch, Belgians, and Luxembourgers had less than forty-eight hours to live, though they were unaware of it; in those days civilized nations mobilized, exchanged hostile notes, and then formally declared war. Nevertheless, guards on the borders of each of these small countries were puzzled and troubled by the total silence on the German side of their frontiers. Hitler had signed nonaggression pacts with each and repeatedly and solemnly reaffirmed them, vowing that not a single hobnailed Wehrmacht boot would ever touch their soil. They had taken little comfort from that; he had told too many *grosse Lügen*; his credibility had vanished and been replaced by fear. The Third Reich, possessing the most powerful military juggernaut Europe had ever known, was recognized as a terrorist nation, the very essence of *Schrecklichkeit*, the stuff of nightmares.

Luxembourg was not going to win this war. Her army comprised four hundred infantrymen and twelve cavalrymen. But she had already taken the first step in a campaign which would cripple the Wehrmacht in every conquered country. Luxembourgers had erected barbed wire barricades on frontier roads, evacuated border towns, and closed bridges across the duchy's river border with the Reich. They called it "passive defense," but the world would adopt the French name: *La Résistance*.

※　※

As he rose to leave the chamber, the prime minister had motioned to Churchill, an invitation to join him in his private room. There Winston "saw at once," as he later recalled, "that he took the most serious view of the sentiment of the House toward himself. He felt he could not go on. There ought to be a National Government. One party alone could not carry the burden. Someone must form a Government in which all parties would serve, or we could not get through."[232]

Churchill's reply was the last response one would have expected. He could have relished the moment. He had every right. "If [a prime minister] trips," he later observed, "he must be sustained. If he makes mistakes, they must be covered. If he sleeps he must not be wantonly disturbed. If he is no good he must be pole-axed." If ever a man deserved retribution, it was Neville Chamberlain. More than any man except Hitler — and Hitler could not have done it without him — he was responsible for the transformation of Germany into the most powerful military state in Europe, which had begun, with Teutonic efficiency, the destruction of all European Jews and had turned the Slavs in the vast lands it conquered into *Sklavenarbeiter* — slave laborers. Young Colville, who scorned those who condemned all Germans per se, had nevertheless reflected in March: "I suppose there is a natural strain of brutality in the German character and as great an insensitivity to human suffering as there is a sensitivity to beauty." The Nazis had unleashed the brutality, but had Chamberlain not embraced their führer at Munich, their government would have fallen as his was now falling.[233]

It would have been almost instinctive in any other member of Parliament to ponder the implications of the House vote for his own career. Every speech denouncing the government over the past two days had been an echo of the speeches Churchill had been delivering for years — often to empty seats. The awakening of Parliament's conscience had vindicated the torch he had held aloft, alone, at great personal cost. It was savage irony that he now found himself among the crew of a ship being sunk by torpedoes he had designed. Since he first won election to Parliament forty years earlier, his objective had been to become prime minister. Here, writhing on the rack of humiliation, was the man who had been his chief adversary during the three crucial years before the outbreak of the war. Knowing Neville, he was sure he would not throw in his hand voluntarily, but now the choice might no longer be his. Had Winston connived for office, as was his right — some would have said, his duty — he would have suggested various lines of action, or at the very least have remained silent.

But Churchill was never a rational man. His conduct often seemed to run at cross-purposes with what was best for him and best for England. His magnanimity, so often extended to those who least deserved it, might have led him to console Chamberlain by making some wildly generous, completely ruinous gesture, volunteering to accept, for example, blame that was not his. Instead, he yielded to another Churchillian impulse — to stand with Chamberlain, as though he were Horatius, to defend the indefensible bridge. "Aroused by the antagonisms of the debate," as he later wrote, he urged the prime minister to "fight on. 'This has been a damaging debate, but you have a good majority. Do not take the matter grievously to heart. . . . Strengthen your Government from every quarter, and let us go on until our majority deserts us.' " At midnight he left the P.M. unconvinced, uncomforted. Winston wondered why the man would "persist in his resolve to sacrifice himself." The answer was that although Chamberlain had never backed away from a fight, logic told him that if he were to survive this moral defeat, he would have to search for compromises. Churchill had never compromised. And in moments of crisis he sought guidance not by reasoning but by intuition.[234]

After baring his soul to Churchill, the prime minister reverted to type, trying to find a way out of the trap. Although it was midnight, the King readily agreed to see him. The audience was brief. Smiling, the prime minister said he had not come to resign; he hoped to restructure his government as a coalition, with Labour participation. Later a reliable source reported that George VI offered to intervene with Attlee. It seems implausible, a dubious move for Britain's constitutional monarch. In all events, the prime minister said that Attlee would have a better understanding of his party's attitude after its annual meeting, about to begin in Bournemouth. He had not yet grasped the nature of the crisis; he thought it would develop slowly, giving him time to negotiate.[235]

Chamberlain's critics have held that his sole object after the disastrous debate was to cling to office — "The Old Man is incorrigibly limpet," wrote Dalton, "always trying new tricks to keep himself firm upon the rock." It is unlikely that his motives were overtly selfish; able politicians always regard themselves as indispensable, and once Chamberlain realized that the country's fortunes were likely to improve under another leader, he devoted himself to an orderly transition. That light did not dawn on him until late Thursday morning, but he never sacrificed or bargained or wheedled to stay at No. 10, as Ramsay MacDonald had done ten years earlier.[236]

Churchill was shaving the following morning when Eden called at the Admiralty. Flourishing his safety razor, Winston predicted, as Eden wrote in his diary, that the P.M. would "not be able to bring in Labour and that a National Government must be formed." Eden returned early in the afternoon for lunch, and was startled to find that Kingsley Wood was also a guest. Just as Bracken was Churchill's satellite, so Wood was Chamberlain's. The prime minister trusted him and respected his advice; in turn, he had raised him from parliamentary secretary to cabinet rank, first as minister of health and now air minister. The RAF had doubled its strength during the past year, but that was not his doing; he was defeatist and had enthusiastically supported appeasement. Why was he at the Admiralty? He wanted to tell Churchill what Chamberlain had been doing. Eden was appalled. Churchill wasn't. With England in danger, personal loyalties went over the side. Winston may have assumed that his visitor was concerned about the nation's survival, not his cabinet seat, though later events demonstrated that his visitor's tale-bearing would not go unrewarded.[237]

The previous evening, it seemed, no member of the House had gone straight home. Factions and cabals had met in Westminster chambers,

Whitehall offices, and private apartments. The largest group, sixty rebel Conservatives, had elected Amery as their chairman and voted, unanimously, that none of them would join or support any government which did not include Labour and Liberals. Downing Street had been informed of this, of course, and at 8:00 A.M. Amery had been summoned to No. 10. Chamberlain had offered him the choice of any cabinet ministry — the Foreign Office and the Exchequer were expressly offered — if he would bring his rebels back into the fold. Amery had asked whether the rebuilt government would include members of the other two parliamentary parties. The prime minister had said bleakly: "I hope that will not be necessary." In that event, Amery had said, he could not accept the P.M.'s generous offer, and expressing his regrets he had departed.[238]

At 10:00 A.M., Kingsley Wood went on, Lord Halifax had appeared. There is something intriguing about the Halifax candidacy. The prime minister urged him to be his successor, implying that he would serve under him. Chamberlain's biographer leaves no doubt that the foreign secretary was his first choice. Back in his office Halifax dictated a note to Cadogan, commenting on the P.M.'s offer: "The evident drift of his mind left me with a bad stomach ache." Yet from the moment knowledgeable Englishmen had begun talking about a new prime minister, Halifax's name had led all the rest. On May 6, the day before the crucial two-day debate, he had quietly conferred with Morrison about the possibility of a Conservative-Labour coalition. His diary merely notes the appointment; neither his papers nor Morrison's mention what was said or decided. And the following day, before the debate began, the *Daily Mail* had published a letter from Sir Stafford Cripps, KC, which *The Times* had rejected. Signed "A British Politician," it had called for an all-party government, with a small cabinet — Churchill, Eden, Lloyd George, Morrison, and Attlee were mentioned — led by Halifax as prime minister.[239]

Dalton, like Morrison a member of the Labour hierarchy, was open in his support of Halifax. After Chamberlain's humiliation in the House, Dalton had told Rab Butler that "provided Chamberlain, Simon and Hoare disappeared" Labour might join a coalition, that if asked who should be the new P.M., "I thought, and a number of others shared this view, that there was much to be said for Halifax." Given the lopsided Tory majority in the House, the hard fact was that no one could form a government without the support of Tory backbenchers. Dalton told Attlee: "Given the strength of parties in the House, the P.M. *must* be a Conservative. He quite agreed. We thought it lay between Halifax and Churchill, and that either, if other conditions were right, would be a possible leader of a Coalition which we might join."[240]

Halifax had left the door ajar, or Chamberlain thought he had, and the

P.M., a man of heroic doggedness, refused to accept the noble lord's rejection. In any event, he himself would resign. In his diary Eden noted that at luncheon with Wood and Churchill, "They told me that Neville had decided to go. The future was discussed. Kingsley thought that W. should succeed, and urged that if asked he should make plain his willingness." But Wood warned Winston that the P.M. wanted Halifax and would ask Churchill to agree. "Don't agree," Wood said, "and don't say anything." In his memoirs Eden commented: "I was shocked that Wood should talk in this way, for he had been so much Chamberlain's man. But it was good counsel and I seconded it."[241]

For a party holding only 27 percent of the seats in the House, Labour was courted with extraordinary ardor. During the debates, Harold Macmillan later remembered, there was apprehension on the part of Churchill's supporters over Winston's role as the last speaker — concern that by giving a fighting speech, he might alienate Opposition leaders who would then veto his bid to succeed Chamberlain. "We were determined to bring down the Government," Macmillan recalled, but "if the chief issue of the first day had been the overthrow of the Government, the chief anxiety of the second was the rescue of Churchill." In fact, he wrote, Chamberlain was convinced that Winston's spirited defense of his government meant "Labour hostility to Churchill in forming a National Government." But Bracken, anticipating this, had entertained Attlee at dinner Tuesday evening. Attlee thought Halifax would move into No. 10 with Winston as his minister of defense. His people, he said, "have never forgiven Churchill for Tonypandy."*[242]

Bracken, on his own initiative, insisted that Churchill would never serve under Halifax, "incurring all the blame if things went wrong and with no real control of the situation." He then exacted a pledge from Attlee: if Churchill came to power, Attlee would not refuse to join the government. The irony here is that while Morrison and Dalton found Halifax acceptable — they barred only Chamberlain, Simon, and Hoare — the rest of the party leadership and virtually all the rank and file were less tolerant. On Thursday the ninth Clement Davies reported to Bob Boothby that "Attlee & Greenwood are unable to distinguish between the PM & Halifax & are *not* prepared to serve under the latter." That same evening Boothby — who had been in the House all day, drumming up support for Churchill — passed this information along to Churchill with the comment: "Opinion is hardening against Halifax as Prime Minister. I am doing my best to foster this, because I cannot feel he is, in any

---

* The location of a riot by striking Welsh miners in November 1910. Churchill, then home secretary, restored order and actually saved miners' lives. But "Tonypandy" had a memorable ring to it; union leaders made it pejorative and — like "Gallipoli" — it stuck.

circumstances, the right man." The Halifax boomlet was doomed; he could never have formed a coalition government — the only government that Parliament would accept.[243]

Kingsley Wood's visit was enormously useful to Winston. As Churchill put it, over lunch he "learned that Mr. Chamberlain was resolved upon the formation of a National Government and, if he could not be the head, he would give way to anyone commanding his confidence who could. Thus, by the afternoon, I became aware that I might well be called upon to take the lead. The prospect neither excited nor alarmed me. . . . I was content to let events unfold." He was back in his office, scanning staff reports, when the call came from No. 10. Arriving, he found Halifax with Chamberlain; very soon, the prime minister told him, Attlee and Greenwood, Labour's deputy leader, would arrive. The socialists arrived late, though they could scarcely reveal why. Stopping at the Reform Club, they had met with Clement Davies to review their position. A German attack on the Low Countries was believed imminent. Because of it, Attlee favored keeping Chamberlain in office until the crisis passed. The other two disagreed. Eventually they had brought him round, but it had taken them two hours. In the Cabinet Room he and Greenwood sat on one side, the three Tories on the other, Chamberlain in the middle.[244]

Chamberlain asked whether Labour would serve under him, or, if not, under another Conservative prime minister. Their formal response, they said, would depend upon the views of the party, now convening in Bournemouth, but they believed the reply to the first question would be "almost certainly, 'no' "; to the second "probably 'yes.' " Both Halifax and Churchill loyally urged support for Chamberlain, but just as Winston was beginning to work himself up toward a cadenza, Greenwood cut in: "We haven't come here to listen to you orating, Winston." Whatever their feelings, they said, they lacked the power to make decisions "because members of our party have got absolutely no confidence in the Prime Minister." Attlee was even more blunt: "I'm bound to tell you, Prime Minister, that in my view our party will not serve under you, nor does the country want you." Serving under another Conservative prime minister was another matter; they would lay it before the Labour Party Executive at Bournemouth tomorrow and Attlee would telephone yes or no. He and Greenwood then withdrew. Chamberlain, Halifax, and Churchill remained in the Cabinet Room; because this was a political matter, David Margesson joined them. If Kingsley Wood had been right, this was the time to be on the qui vive.[245]

Chamberlain told them he was now convinced that forming a national government was beyond his power. Attlee and Greenwood had tied the knot of that shroud. Margesson, asked for his opinion, agreed. Unity was indispensable, he said, and as long as Chamberlain remained in power it would be beyond reach. He added that he was not prepared — at the moment — to comment on the political strengths of Churchill and Halifax among Conservative backbenchers, at which, Halifax noted in his diary, "my stomach ache continued." Chamberlain's task now was to tell the King who should be sent for after he had surrendered the seals of office. He seemed calm, cool, almost detached. But he looked across the table at both of them.[246]

At this point we must choose between Churchill's recollection and Halifax's. Winston's account, the more engaging, has been almost universally accepted and presented in various stage, television, and film dramas. In this version he remembered Kingsley Wood's admonition to say nothing — advice far more difficult for Winston to follow than most men — and sat immobile while "a very long pause ensued. It certainly seemed longer than the two minutes which one observes in the commemorations of Armistice Day." Then, he tells us, Halifax said he couldn't possibly lead a government because, being a peer, he sat in the House of Lords.[247]

But Winston's tale, as it appears in *The Gathering Storm*, the first volume of his World War II history, does not bear close scrutiny. The meeting in the Cabinet Room occurred on May 9. He puts it on May 10. The difference between the two is huge; on May 9 the borders of France and the Low Countries were inviolate. The great surge of the Wehrmacht came on May 10, and Churchill tells us that upon returning to the Admiralty from the Cabinet Room, he found that "the Dutch Ministers were in my room. Haggard and worn, with horror in their eyes, they had just flown over. . . . Their country had been attacked without the slightest pretext or warning." The day before, when Chamberlain actually faced Halifax and Winston, Holland had been peaceful. Churchill got it wrong. And no wonder. He was dictating it six years after the event — six of the most crowded years any man had endured. To acquire some inkling of what that pressure did to his memory, one need only reflect upon what the first year did to it. Millions remember, and can recite, lines from his great speeches of 1940: "Their finest hour," "We shall fight on the beaches," and his tribute to the RAF after the Battle of Britain. Yet twelve months later, in 1941, Winston himself couldn't remember any of them.[248]

The more plausible account, and unquestionably the correct one, lies in these notes which Halifax scribbled upon returning to his office on the other side of Downing Street, and then turned over to Cadogan:

PM said I was the man mentioned as the most acceptable. I said it would be hopeless position. If I was not in charge of the war (operations) and if I didn't lead the House, I should be a cypher. I thought Winston was a better choice. Winston did *not* demur. Was very kind and polite but showed that he thought this right solution.

The PM, Winston, David Margesson and I sat down to it. The PM recapitulated the situation, and said he had made up his mind that he must go, and that it must be either Winston or me. He would serve under either. . . . I then said that I thought for the reasons given the PM must probably go, but that I had no doubt at all in my own mind that for me to take it would create a quite impossible position. . . . Winston, with suitable positions of regard and humility, said he could not but feel the force of what I had said, and the PM reluctantly, and Winston evidently with much less reluctance, finished by accepting my view.[249]

Margesson had been unwilling to comment on the popularity of the two among Tories until the decision had been made; now he could, and he observed that they had been "veering towards" Winston. Halifax had noted the same trend and remarked upon it to Cadogan, adding that if Chamberlain were to remain in the government, "as he is ready to do," his advice and judgment "would steady Winston." The prime minister had left them, explaining that he had to see someone else. The man who felt himself dispensable and the man who knew he was indispensable were left alone. They decided to have tea. "It was a bright, sunny afternoon," Churchill wrote, "and Lord Halifax and I sat for a while . . . in the garden of Number 10 and talked about nothing in particular." They then parted, each to his office. Winston knew Chamberlain could not move until Attlee called, and in the Cabinet Room he had said that he would "have no communication with either of the Opposition Parties until I had the King's commission to form a Government. . . . I then went back to the Admiralty."[250]

At "about 8 o'clock," Channon's diary entry read, he called at No. 10 and left with the impression that "Neville still reigns, but only just." A half-hour later, on the other side of the Horse Guards Parade, Churchill sat down to dinner in Admiralty House with four guests: the Prof, Bracken, Anthony Eden, and Archie Sinclair. He told them, Eden wrote, that he thought it "plain" that Chamberlain would advise the King to send for him, because Halifax, his only rival, "did not wish to succeed." As the evening lengthened, Winston slowly absorbed the massive fact of his position. During the evening Randolph called from his battalion, billeted in Northamptonshire, some seventy miles northwest of London. He asked if there was any news. His father replied: "I think I shall be Prime Minister tomorrow."[251]

On the evening of May 9, as Churchill entertained his friends at dinner, Labour's leaders in the palm courts of Bournemouth pondered whether to serve under him in an all-party government, and the London *News Chronicle* went to press with a banner story reporting that "Mr Chamberlain's early resignation is now certain" — the Bore War, in short, continued to bore. But developments across the Channel continued to foreshadow England's approaching peril.

On Germany's side of the Rhine, the Führer had assembled 136 divisions and their reserves — two million men, including a contingent wearing uniforms of the Netherlands army and fluent in the Dutch language. The Low Countries would be overwhelmed by vast surging waves of infantry and armor "unprecedented for size, concentration, mobility," Shirer wrote, which "stretched in three columns back for a hundred miles beyond the Rhine."[252]

The Führer's bold strategy deployed three great formations, one of which was meant to persuade the Allies that the Germans were following the Schlieffen Plan of 1914. In the north, the thirty divisions of Army Group B would strike into Holland and Belgium in a four-pronged assault. To meet what they were meant to think was the main threat, the best British and French troops would rush into Belgium, taking a stand along the Dyle River. In the south, Army Group C's nineteen divisions would feint toward the Maginot Line, keeping the poilus there tied up. The real Nazi blow would be delivered in the center, by Army Group A — forty-five divisions, including most of the Wehrmacht's panzers. Plunging through Luxembourg and the Ardennes, these motorized units would pour through the gap between the Maginot Line and the line of the Dyle, race westward to the Channel, and then pivot northward, joining Army Group B in the encirclement and destruction of the French and British troops.

Thus, the main body of the German army, cutting across the Allied rear, and using the panzers as it had in Poland, would exploit the new concept in warfare — deep penetration into enemy territory by mobile armored forces — a concept as revolutionary, Liddell Hart has pointed out, as "the use of the horse, the long spear, the phalanx, the flexible legion, the 'oblique order,' the horse-archer, the longbow, the musket, the [artillery] gun."[253]

On May 9, in the Berlin suburb of Zehlendorf, Colonel Oster of the Abwehr dined for the last time with his friend Colonel Sas, the Dutch military attaché. Oster once more confirmed that *Fall Gelb* would be unleashed at daybreak. To double-check, he drove them to OKW's Berlin headquarters in the Bendlerstrasse after their coffee and brandy. Sas waited

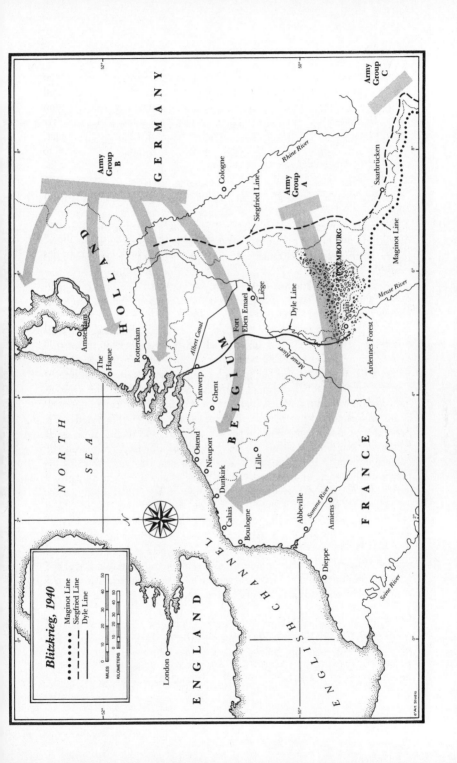

Blitzkrieg, 1940

Maginot Line ●●●●●
Siegfried Line ●- ●- ●-
Dyle Line ————

MILES
0 10 20 30 40 50

KILOMETERS
0 10 20 30 40 50

NORTH SEA

ENGLAND

London

ENGLISH CHANNEL

HOLLAND

Amsterdam
The Hague
Rotterdam

GERMANY

Army Group B

Cologne

Rhine River

Siegfried Line

Army Group A

LUXEMBOURG

Army Group C

Saarbrücken

Maginot Line

Meuse River

Ardennes Forest

Sedan

Dyle Line

Liège

Fort Eben Emael

Albert Canal

Antwerp
Ghent

BELGIUM

Ostend
Nieuport
Dunkirk
Calais
Boulogne

Lille

FRANCE

Abbeville
Amiens

Somme River

Dieppe

Seine River

© Art Studio

in the car while the Abwehr colonel inquired within. Returning, Oster said there had been no changes. He added: *"Das Schwein ist zur Westfront"* — "The swine [Hitler] has gone to the Western Front." They parted. Sas passed the new information to the Belgian military attaché, then crossed to his own legation and called The Hague to transmit, in simple code, the message: "Tomorrow at dawn!"[254]

At 10:20 that Thursday morning, when Chamberlain was offering the prime ministry of England to Halifax, Paul Reynaud announced that he would present the premiership of France to anyone who could form a government, unless his cabinet agreed with his indictment of Gamelin, commander in chief of the French army; supreme commander of the Allied forces, British as well as French; and the officer who presided over both the Conseil Supérieur de la Guerre and the Haut Comité Militaire. This was not Reynaud's first attempt to sack him — nor was Reynaud the first to try — but it was by far the most vigorous. The premier, though suffering a sore throat, spent over two hours reading his presentment. French military appointments were determined to a remarkable degree by an officer's politics and religion, and Gamelin had been a beneficiary of that *drôle* system, having served as France's senior soldier for five years. Afterward, after the calamitous spring of 1940, he and his officers bitterly complained that the Chamber of Deputies never gave them the arms to fight with. An audit revealed that each year Gamelin returned appropriations unspent — as much as 60 percent of his budget. He hated allies because they entailed the possibility of bloodshed, and would go to great lengths to avoid a fight, but the last straw, for Reynaud, had been the Norwegian operation. Gamelin had exercised none of his powers as supreme commander, and the first French force of any size — two demibrigades of *Chasseurs Alpins* and a third of foreign legionnaires — had not arrived in Norway until April 27, when the issue had already been decided. It is extraordinary to reflect that his name was never mentioned in newspaper accounts of the struggle there, never raised during the two-day debate in the House. He had participated in the plan to mine Norwegian waters. When the Germans swooped down on Norway, Reynaud had asked what he proposed to do. Mine the waters, Gamelin replied; that was the plan, and he meant to carry it out. The sudden appearance of the Germans was, to him, irrelevant.

Paul Baudouin, who kept the minutes, noted that throughout most of the premier's arraignment of the country's most prestigious military figure the cabinet observed *"un silence total. Personne ne dit mot."* As Reynaud went on and on, piling up his case, one minister whispered to another, *"C'est une exécution."* At 12:30 P.M. Reynaud finished, commenting that if

France continued with such a supreme commander, she was sure to lose the war. The minister of finance was convinced, he said, of *"l'impossibilité de laisser le général Gamelin à la tête des armées françaises."*[255]

Everyone turned to Daladier. He was minister of defense; he had defended Gamelin in the past. This was not the Daladier who had once been ready to fight for Czechoslovakia. He was defeatist now, infected with the spiritual corruption which had infected the government, the army, and virtually the entire infrastructure of French society. Replying to the premier, he blamed the British for the failure in Norway. Gamelin, he said, bore no share of the responsibility. He believed Gamelin was *"un grand chef militaire,"* a soldier with tremendous prestige and a fine military record. Everyone acknowledged his superior intelligence. True, he was seventy, but he was more active than many men his age. Daladier opposed "the desire of the premier to replace the generalissimo."[256]

Reynaud appealed to other ministers to speak up. Surely they had formed opinions; duty required that they voice them. But these were frightened little men. If one took a position, one might offend a powerful figure; by remaining silent, one lost nothing. Reynaud, however, wasn't going to let them off that easily. Their failure to speak, he said, meant they opposed him; since the government could not survive such a loss of confidence, therefore, "I consider the government as having resigned." They were dismayed. None had thought he would actually dissolve the government. Now they were all ex-ministers, as he was an ex-premier.[257]

During the afternoon Gamelin, glooming around in his Vincennes dungeon, learned of the bill of particulars Reynaud had drawn up against . him. Indignant, *he* resigned.

At 1:00 A.M. he was awakened. A French agent behind the German lines had sent an urgent signal: *"Colonnes en marche vers l'ouest"* — "Columns marching westward."

Hitler was on his way.

France had no government. The French army had no commander.

❦   ❦

The telephones began ringing in Whitehall as the first olive moments of daybreak revealed the majestic buildings towering against a darkling, still starry sky — vast cathedrals of an empire whose celebrants had been dwindling year by year since what had been called, and was now known to be, the Armistice.

Shortly after 5:30 A.M. Churchill was wakened and told the first, fragmentary reports. Before the mists of legend envelop him, before he comes to power and assumes leadership of the struggle to crush the monster in central Europe — while he is still, so to speak, Drake bowling when informed that the Armada has been sighted — it is useful to glimpse the entirely mortal Winston. The vision is less than inspiring; unlike some earlier heroes, Winston is engaged in no mundane but memorable act when the news arrives. Instead, wearing his blue dressing gown and carpet slippers, he stumbles down to the upper war room and is told that thus far the attack is "on Holland alone." Assuming, like everyone else in His Majesty's Government, that the main Nazi thrust will come here, he phones Charles Corbin, the French ambassador. He asks: Will the Allied armies move into Belgium on the strength of the little now known?

At 6:20 Corbin called back. German troops were now across the Belgian border, he said, and Brussels had "asked for help." Therefore, Gamelin had been told to invoke Plan D — the advance of the French Seventh Army and the British Expeditionary Force to the line of the Dyle River, there to join the Belgian and Dutch forces. Randolph Churchill, breakfasting in his camp, had heard a radio bulletin. He phoned his father, asking: "What's happening?" Winston replied: "Well, the German hordes are pouring into the Low Countries." He told him of the Allied counter-move, adding, "In a day or two there will be a head-on collision." His son asked him about his reference the previous evening to "you becoming Prime Minister today." Churchill said, "Oh, I don't know about that. Nothing matters now except beating the enemy."[258]

In this crisis Sam Hoare and Oliver Stanley, the other two service ministers, appeared with their chief advisers at Admiralty House. Later Hoare would remember, "We had had little or no sleep, and the news could not be worse, yet there he was, smoking his large cigar and eating fried eggs and bacon, as if he had just returned from an early morning ride." He was surrounded by yesterday's newspapers. The *Times* leader that morning rebuked Labour for dividing the House, since it had been obvious that Chamberlain intended to rebuild his cabinet when "the Labour Party ran up its flag," throwing the prime minister's plans "into confusion." The *News Chronicle* — which had championed Lloyd George — more accurately reported that since neither Liberal nor Labour leaders were willing to serve under Chamberlain, "a new Premier will thus have to be found. He is more likely to be found in Mr Winston Churchill than anyone else." Winston swept the papers to the floor with one vigorous arm, rose, and suggested they meet in the war room downstairs. There, with him in the chair, they agreed that two RAF squadrons should be sent to France "in accordance with the prearranged plan." Then orders to execute Royal Marine, his plan to mine the waters of the Rhine, were issued at long last.[259]

The first casualty of the Nazi offensive was the feud between Reynaud and Gamelin. The premier sent Vincennes a message: "The battle has begun. Only one thing counts: to win it." Gamelin agreed, replying: *"Seule la France compte"* — "Only France counts." His Majesty's Government, preoccupied with its own political crisis, had known nothing of the impasse in Paris. It had little meaning now anyway; what mattered was news of the enemy's penetration. Minute by minute information was accumulating. German paratroopers had landed in Belgium, the Luftwaffe was bombing airfields in France and the Low Countries, and the British and French were marching into Belgium — the last thing, we now know, that they should have done. The Führer's Army Group B had their undivided attention. Nothing much was happening to Army Group C, holding the frontier opposite the Maginot Line, and nothing was known of Rundstedt's Army Group A. Allied intelligence wasn't even aware that it was by far the largest, dwarfing the other two.[260]

During the night the first of Rundstedt's tanks had negotiated the minefields near the German-Belgian border, and at daybreak three panzer corps were driving hard, intent upon maneuvering through the wooded ravines of the Ardennes and crossing the Meuse near Sedan in forty-eight hours. Even the few French officers who doubted that the Ardennes were *impénétrable* believed the enemy could not possibly reach the river in less than ten days, by which time reinforcements could be brought up to dig in along the Meuse, swift and narrow, running between steep banks and therefore easy to defend. Yet already Rundstedt's armor had easily thrown aside the defense behind the mines — a thin screen of French cavalry, backed by light motorized forces. Thus, while the Allied right wing remained idle in the bowels of the troglodytic Maginot Line, and the left advanced toward what was expected to be the decisive encounter, the center was already gravely threatened. In the confusion of their rout the officers there neglected to send the bad news winging to Vincennes, La Ferté, or Montry. The fox was among the chickens, but the farmer, out in the pasture, didn't even know he had a problem.

At No. 10 the first of the War Cabinet's three meetings that day began with the Chiefs of Staff present. They were dazed, in the state of confusion which was the first reaction to blitzkriegs. Reports were accumulating faster than they could be skimmed. H.M.S. *Kelly* had been torpedoed off the Belgian coast. The Wehrmacht was in Luxembourg. Nazi paratroops had been dropped at three strategic locations, in the area between The Hague and Leiden, and near Rotterdam; Nancy had been bombed; the Luftwaffe was dropping magnetic mines in the Scheldt to disrupt Dutch and Belgian shipping. Churchill, the ministers were relieved to hear, had already sent sweeping gear to clear it.[261]

According to Reith's diary, Chamberlain "did not refer to Amery or any of the other Conservatives who had attacked him. He was in good form; the news from the Low Countries had stimulated him"; the German invasions had found him "ready for action if encouraged and authorized to act." He was a new man; he told his sister many of those who had voted against him had written to say "they had nothing against me except that I had the wrong people in my team." He had, indeed, convinced himself that in this crisis the country would be much better off if he remained as prime minister. Halifax noted in his diary: "The P.M. told the Cabinet . . . that he thought all would have to wait until the war situation was calmer." Privately he told his foreign secretary that "he had a feeling that Winston did not approve of the delay, and left me guessing as to what he meant to do."[262]

Reith's diary, which is confirmed by Eden's, notes that the prime minister had seen Attlee and Greenwood and understood that they were prepared to defer the political crisis, though the final decision would have to be made in Bournemouth. Hoare later wrote: "Chamberlain's first inclination was to withhold his resignation until the French battle was finished." Nicolson and his friends were among the outsiders who learned of this, and they were aghast. One of them phoned Salisbury, who replied, wrote Nicolson, "that we must maintain our point of view, namely that Winston should be made Prime Minister during the course of the day."[263]

Churchill's feelings about Chamberlain's switch of mood can only be imagined, but anxiety must have been among them. He was somewhat reassured by Kingsley Wood. At about 10:00 A.M. Wood once more crossed the Horse Guards Parade to report, as Winston later wrote, that the prime minister "was inclined to feel that the great battle which had broken upon us made it necessary for him to remain at his post." Hoare had encouraged him in this, but Wood's emphatic comment — which Horace Wilson, embittered, later damned as an act of "betrayal" — was that "on the contrary, the new crisis made it all the more necessary to have a National Government, which alone could confront it." Wood, wrote Churchill, had told him that Chamberlain had "accepted this view." But that was not the end of it. Shortly before the second meeting of the War Cabinet, at 11:00 A.M., Simon approached Eden and Hankey. He told them, Eden wrote, that he had heard that "despite the attacks in Flanders, Churchill was pressing for early changes in the Government." Simon was "indignant," but Hankey commented "quietly and firmly: 'Personally, I think that if there are to be changes, the sooner they are made the better.' "[264]

At this second meeting Winston pointed out that Roger Keyes was a close personal friend of the Belgian king; the admiral was eager to serve his country and might be useful in Brussels. The War Cabinet approved. The ministers were also pleased to learn that Churchill had given instructions "for the removal of the gold still left in Holland." They were less enthusiastic when Winston, explaining, "It won't take a minute," insisted that the war wait while they watch the Prof, who was sitting at a side table, demonstrate an antiaircraft homing fuse. According to Reith, "Ironside, very snotty," whispered to him, "Do you think this is the time for showing off toys?" This shirtiness sounds more like Reith than Ironside, who, noting the incident in his diary the following day, wrote of Churchill: "I have seldom met anybody with stranger gaps of knowledge or whose mind worked in greater jerks. Will it be possible to make it work in orderly fashion? On this much depends."[265]

During this second meeting of the War Cabinet, Chamberlain had continued to be very much the prime minister. Despite his assurance to Kingsley Wood he made no reference to surrendering his seals. Actually, the crucial decision could not be made by any member of His Majesty's Government. It rested with the men in Bournemouth; Chamberlain had agreed to abide by their finding. Labour's national executive, meeting in a basement room of the Highcliff Hotel, resolved that the party was "prepared to take our share of the responsibility, as a full partner, in a new Government, which, under a new Prime Minister, commands the confidence of the nation." Dalton was responsible for inserting "under a new Prime Minister." Some of the others doubted its necessity. He told them: "If you don't make it absolutely plain, the Old Man will still hang on." Attlee and Greenwood were about to drive to London with the signed document when the prime minister's private secretary phoned from Downing Street to ask whether Labour had reached a decision. Attlee read the resolution over the telephone.[266]

It was now 5:00 P.M. The War Cabinet's third meeting of the day had begun a half-hour earlier. The private secretary entered the Cabinet Room and handed the typewritten transcript of Labour's verdict to Horace Wilson, who read it and wordlessly slipped it in front of the prime minister. Chamberlain glanced at it and continued with his agenda. The Germans had bombed a dozen objectives and had dropped incendiaries in Kent; the Rotterdam airfield was in the hands of the Nazis, who were landing troop-carrying aircraft there; six Blenheims had been sent to intercept the troop carriers and five of them had been lost; the BEF had reached the line of the Dyle. After a lengthy discussion the ministers decided not to bomb the Ruhr. More paratroopers had landed in Belgium and the ministers decided to warn British troops in the United Kingdom "against parachutists attempting to land in this country." Then Chamberlain came to the last item on his agenda: the political situation.[267]

He read the Labour resolution aloud and said that "in the light of this answer" he had decided that he should "at once" tender his resignation to the King. It would be "convenient," he suggested, for the new prime minister to assume that "all members of the War Cabinet" were placing their resignations at his disposal, though there was no need "for this to be confirmed in writing." The minutes of the meeting ended: "The War Cabinet agreed to the course suggested." He had not told them whom he preferred as his successor, nor had he mentioned his meeting with Halifax and Churchill the day before. He proposed "to see the King this evening" — that was all.[268]

Actually, the prime minister, in his last act as prime minister, was on his way to the palace in less than half an hour. In his diary George VI recorded how he saw Chamberlain "after tea. I accepted his resignation, & told him how grossly unfairly I thought he had been treated, & that I was terribly sorry." They then talked informally about his successor. "I, of course, suggested Halifax," His Majesty wrote, "but he told me that H was not enthusiastic, as being in the Lords he could only act as a shadow or a ghost in the Commons, where all the real work took place." His royal host was "disappointed . . . as I thought H was the obvious man." Before the former prime minister could mention another name, George "knew that there was only one other person whom I could send for to form a Government . . . & that was Winston." He said so; Chamberlain confirmed his judgment. The King "thanked him for all his help to me, and repeated that I would greatly regret my loss at not having him as my P.M. I sent for Winston & asked him to form a Government."[269]

They didn't get to it straightaway. The monarch enjoyed a bit of regal byplay first. "His Majesty received me most graciously," wrote Churchill, "and bade me sit down. He looked at me searchingly and quizzically for some moments, and then said: 'I suppose you don't know why I have sent for you?' Adopting his mood, I replied: 'Sir, I simply couldn't imagine why.' He laughed and said: 'I want you to form a Government.' I said I would certainly do so." Since the King had made no stipulation about the government being national in character — apparently Chamberlain had not mentioned this, an unaccountable lapse — Winston felt his commission "was in no formal way dependent upon this point. But in view of all that had happened, and the conditions which had led to Mr. Chamberlain's resignation, a Government of national character was obviously inherent in the situation." However, if he failed to come to terms with the Liberal and Labour parties, he believed, "I should not have been constitutionally debarred from trying to form the strongest Government possible of all who would stand by the country in the hour of peril, provided that such a

Government could command a majority in the House of Commons."[270]

He told the King that he would "immediately send for the leaders of the Labour and Liberal Parties, that I proposed to form a War Cabinet of five or six Ministers, and that I hoped to let him have at least five or six names before midnight." On this he took his leave. His sole companion was his bodyguard, W. H. Thompson. As Thompson later recalled, their ride back to Admiralty House was made "in complete silence," but as the new prime minister was leaving the car he asked: "You know why I have been to Buckingham Palace, Thompson?" The former Scotland Yard inspector said he did and congratulated him, adding, "I only wish the position had come your way in better times, for you have an enormous task." Churchill's eyes filled. He said: "God alone knows how great it is. I hope that it is not too late. I am very much afraid that it is. We can only do our best."[271]

While Churchill had been with the King, Randolph found a message in the adjutant's office asking him to phone the Admiralty. He did, and asked why he was wanted. The private secretary in the private office replied: "Only just to say that your father has gone to the Palace and when he comes back he will be Prime Minister."[272]

Early in the evening Attlee, accompanied by Greenwood, called on Churchill. They talked easily; during the eleven years before the war's outbreak, Winston had crossed swords with the Conservative and national governments far more often than with Labour. He proposed that Labour should have "rather more than a third of the places, having two seats on the War Cabinet of five, or it might be six." He asked Attlee for a list of names — they could then discuss "particular offices" — and mentioned Labour MPs he admired: Morrison, Dalton, Ernest Bevin, and A. V. Alexander.[273]

As they conferred, Harold Nicolson was on his way to King's Bench Walk, passing posters saying "BRUSSELS BOMBED," "PARIS BOMBED," "LYONS BOMBED," "SWISS RAILWAYS BOMBED." That evening he joined his wife at Sissinghurst, their home forty miles southeast of London. They dined together and "just before nine, we turn on the wireless and it begins to buzz as the juice comes through and then we hear the bells" — the BBC identification signal. "Then the pips sound 9.0 and the announcer begins: 'This is the Home Service. Here is the Right Honourable Neville Chamberlain M.P., who will make a statement.' I am puzzled by this for a moment, and then realise that he has resigned." Addressing the nation, the fallen prime minister told the people that the events of the past few days had shown that a coalition government was necessary, and since the only obstacle to such a coalition was himself he had resigned. The King had "asked my friend and colleague, Mr. Winston Churchill, to form a truly National Government." For the moment, acting ministers "will carry on." He himself had agreed to serve under Churchill. Nicolson noted: "He ends with a fierce denunciation of the Germans for invading Holland and Belgium. It is a magnificent statement, and all the hatred I have felt for Chamberlain subsides as if a piece of bread were dropped into a glass of champagne."[274]

"Thus," wrote Winston, "at the outset of this mighty battle, I acquired the chief power in the State. . . . As I went to bed at about 3 A.M., I was conscious of a profound sense of relief. At last I had the authority to give directions over the whole scene." He felt, he said,

as if I were walking with Destiny, and that all my past life had been but a preparation for this hour and for this trial. Eleven years in the political wilderness had freed me from ordinary party antagonisms. My warnings over the last six years had been so numerous, so detailed, and were now so terribly vindicated, that no one could gainsay me. I could not be reproached either for making the war or with want of preparation for it. . . . Therefore, although impatient for the morning, I slept soundly and had no need for cheering dreams. Facts are better than dreams.[275]

🦁   🦁

Labour endorsed the decision of its leaders to support Churchill by a lopsided vote: 2,450,000 to 170,000 — a 93 percent victory — and when a pacifist MP demanded a division of the House on the question of whether Churchill should be prime minister, the vote was 380 to 0, the pacifist presumably abstaining. Winston possessed one great advantage which no other eminent parliamentarian could claim; as the historian Cyril Falls puts it, "His record was completely clean and satisfactory in those years when the Government had been hiding its head in the sand and . . . simultaneously voting against every attempt to arm the British forces." But his mood had not yet been synchronized with that of the powerful, including his sovereign. In his diary entry the following day — Saturday, May 11 — the King noted: "I cannot yet think of Winston as P.M. . . . I met Halifax in the garden" — the noble lord had been granted permission to walk through the palace garden en route from his Belgravia flat to the Foreign Office — "and told him I was sorry not to have him as P.M." George still felt uncomfortable with Winston. There was a generational gap between them. When they had first met in 1912 Winston was first lord of the Admiralty and the future monarch a young naval cadet. By normal reckoning Winston's political career ought to have ended ten years earlier. He had turned sixty-five the previous November; five months before he became prime minister he had been eligible to draw an old-age pension. Indeed, he was to be the senior statesman of the war — four years older than Stalin, eight years older than Roosevelt, nine years older than Mussolini, fifteen years older than Hitler. The King also liked Tories to be orthodox, conventional, loyal party men, and Churchill was none of those.[276]

That same Saturday, Margot Asquith, writing a letter to Geoffrey Dawson at *The Times*, told how, on impulse, she had taken a taxi to No. 10 the previous evening; she had looked at Chamberlain's "spare figure and keen eye and could not help comparing it with Winston's self-indulgent rotundity." R. A. Butler called Churchill "a half-breed American." And that evening young Colville, at No. 10, wrote in his diary: "There seems to be some inclination in Whitehall to believe that Winston will be a complete failure and that Neville will return." Long afterward Colville observed: "Seldom can a Prime Minister have taken office with the Establishment . . . so dubious of the choice and so prepared to have its doubts justified." Only a month earlier Eden's followers in Parliament had outnumbered Churchill's, and some of Winston's closest friends preferred Lloyd George as an alternative to Chamberlain.[277]

Among the general public it was different. Even so, the *News Chronicle* had reported that according to an opinion poll, his principal support was among "those in the lower income groups, those between 21 and 30, and among men." A prime minister should enjoy broader approval, particularly among the sophisticated, and a Conservative prime minister, in the House of Commons, ought to receive more cheers from Tory benches than from Labour. In his May 13 diary entry Nicolson noted: "When Chamberlain enters the House, he gets a terrific reception, and when Churchill comes in the applause is less. Winston sits there between Chamberlain and Attlee" — Attlee was now lord privy seal and, in effect, deputy prime minister — "[and then] makes a very short statement, but to the point." The only tribute to the new prime minister came from Lloyd George, who spoke of his "glittering intellectual gifts, his dauntless courage, his profound study of war, and his experience in its operation and direction." Winston wept.[278]

What Nicolson called Churchill's "very short statement" and Geoffrey Dawson described patronizingly as "quite a good little warlike speech from Winston" included five words now known to millions who were unborn at the time, who have never seen England, and do not even speak English.

I would say to the House,
  as I have said to those who have joined this Government:
    "I have nothing to offer but blood, toil, tears, and sweat." . . .

You ask, what is our policy?
  I will say: It is to wage war, by sea, land and air,

with all our might and with all the strength God can give us. . . .
That is our policy.

You ask, what is our aim?
I can answer in one word: It is victory,
victory at all costs, victory in spite of all terror,
victory however long and hard the road may be;
for without victory, there is no survival.[279]

The mighty Belgian fortress of Eben Emael, with its garrison of 1,200, fell on Saturday, May 11, the second day of the great Nazi offensive, captured by only 78 parachute-engineers led by a lieutenant. Landing in gliders on the unguarded roof, they blew up the armored cupolas and casemates of the fort's guns with a new, highly intensive explosive kept secret until now. Belgian frontier guards were prepared to blow up the bridges of the King Albert Canal, blocking the Nazi advance, but another small Nazi detachment, dropping silently out of the night sky, massacred them. In Holland the French Seventh Army engaged the Germans and was flung back. Liège fell to blond young Nazis shouting *"Heil Hitler!"* as they threw their bodies on the muzzles of Belgian machine guns, sacrificing themselves to maintain the blitzkrieg's momentum. On Tuesday, Rotterdam was the target of a massive Luftwaffe terror attack; thousands of 2,200-pound delayed-action bombs gutted the center of the city, destroyed 25,000 houses, and left 78,000 civilians homeless and a thousand dead. Rotterdam capitulated. The Dutch commander in chief surrendered his entire army. Queen Wilhelmina and the Dutch government fled to London.

That was the small shock. The great shock came in barely coherent dispatches from the Meuse. Guderian, leading mechanized spearheads of Rundstedt's army group, had been racing through Luxembourg and Belgium's Luxembourg Province. After rocking and tilting and pivoting their way through a seven-mile stretch of the Ardennes — they had been elaborately rehearsed in the Black Forest — these forces had entered France Sunday, right on schedule. Before Churchill had completed the formation of his cabinet, the Germans had seven tank divisions on the Meuse near Sedan. The heights on the far side of the Meuse were forbidding. The French had rushed heavy artillery there, and after firing a few rounds at the panzers, the artillery officer predicted that the Nazis would try to cross elsewhere. But the Germans had rehearsed this, too, and Rundstedt was a master at integrating his commands, including the use of tactical air. At first light on Monday, Stukas and low-level bombers began pounding the French batteries; by 4:00 P.M. every field piece, every enemy howitzer on the heights, had been destroyed. Nazi rubber boats reached the far shore unmolested; beachheads were established; pontoon bridges spanned the river, then heavy bridges — and finally, lumbering and growling, German tanks.

French tanks appeared to challenge them. They were superior to the Germans' in design and armament, and history's first great tank battle seemed imminent. But the outcome, to use a word that was on everyone's lips that week, was *une débâcle*. The French tank commanders weren't to blame. Their high command, having ruled that armor was to be used only in support of infantry, had gone to extraordinary lengths to discourage attacks by armored formations. The installation of radios in turrets had been forbidden. The French drivers, assembled from different units and unable to communicate with one another, could not coordinate a counterattack. In two hours Guderian's panzers had blown up fifty of them. The rest fled. Among the frustrated Frenchmen was Colonel de Gaulle. To his astonishment, dismay, and *effroi*, he saw shuffling mobs of poilus without weapons. The Germans had no time to take prisoners; they had disarmed the men and left them to blunder about. Meantime, the panzers had made a second crossing of the Meuse at Dinant. German armor was now pouring across the river. In Vincennes, however, concerned French officials calling upon Généralissime Gamelin found him still confident. He did ask if they had any news of the fighting. Apparently all the dispatches sent to him had gone astray.

Guderian's tanks had reached Montcornet, less than fifteen miles from Laon; they were plunging down the valley of the Somme toward Abbeville on the English Channel. Aghast, the Allied forces in Belgium, including the BEF, realized that the great German scythe slicing across France was slicing behind them. Already they were cut off from the main French armies in the south. On the nineteenth Reynaud dismissed Gamelin from all commands; his predecessor, seventy-three-year-old Maxime Weygand, was brought out of retirement to take over, but Weygand was helpless; events were beyond his control; the Nazis seemed to be everywhere, and everywhere victorious. Thus, only a few days after their advance into Belgium, the French and British divisions in the north disengaged and retreated behind the line of the Scheldt. Lord Gort was poring over a map, studying routes to the Channel ports, where the Germans planned to turn the last key in the last lock.

On May 19, Churchill addressed the nation over the BBC:

> I speak to you for the first time as Prime Minister
> in a solemn hour for the life of our country,
> of our Empire, of our Allies,
> and above all of the cause of freedom.

A tremendous battle is raging in France and Flanders.
The Germans, by a remarkable combination
of air bombing and heavily armoured tanks,
have broken through the French defences
north of the Maginot Line,

And strong columns of their armoured vehicles
are ravaging the open country,
which for the first day or two
was without defenders.

They have penetrated deeply
and spread alarm and confusion in their track.

Behind them there are now appearing
infantry in lorries,
and behind them, again,
the large masses are moving forward.

He had received, he said, "the most sacred pledges" from the leaders
of the French Republic, "and in particular from its indomitable Prime
Minister, M. Reynaud . . . that whatever happens they will fight to the
end, be it bitter or glorious." Then, a typical Churchill touch: "Nay, if we
fight to the end, it can only be glorious."

Since receiving the King's commission, he told the country, he had
formed a government "of men and women . . . of almost every point of
view.

We have differed and quarreled in the past;
but now one bond unites us all —
to wage war until victory is won,
and never to surrender ourselves to servitude and shame,
whatever the cost and agony may be.

If this is one of the most awe-striking periods
in the long history of France and Britain,
it is also, beyond doubt, the most sublime.

Side by side . . . the British and French peoples have advanced
to rescue not only Europe but mankind
from the foulest and most soul-destroying tyranny
which has ever darkened and stained the pages of history.

Behind them, behind us —
  behind the armies of Britain and France —
    gather a group of shattered states and bludgeoned races:
      the Czechs, the Poles, the Norwegians,
        the Danes, the Dutch, the Belgians —

Upon all of whom a long night of barbarism will descend
  unbroken even by a star of hope,
    unless we conquer, as conquer we must;
      as conquer we shall.[280]

Despite the "most sacred pledges" from Paris, the possibility loomed that France might not fight "to the end." The leaders of a nation verging on collapse cannot commit their countrymen if the army can no longer defend them. In capitals around the world leaders and newspapers wondered whether, if France fell, England would also quit. The prime minister again went on the air, on June 18, the day after Pétain sued for peace, to discount such speculation — to vow that England would continue the battle alone:

Upon this battle depends the survival of Christian civilisation.
  Upon it depends our own British life,
    and the long continuity of our institutions and our Empire. . . .

Hitler knows that he will have to break us on this island
  or lose the war.

If we can stand up to him all Europe may be free
  and the life of the world may move forward
    into broad, sunlit uplands.

But if we fail, then the whole world,
  including the United States,
    including all we have known and cared for,

Will sink into the abyss of a new Dark Age
  made more sinister, and perhaps more protracted,
    by the lights of perverted science.

Let us therefore brace ourselves to our duties,
  and so bear ourselves
    that if the British Empire and its Commonwealth
      last for a thousand years,

Men will still say:
  "*This* was their finest hour."[281]

Ｈe had come to power because he had seen through Hitler from the very beginning — but not, ironically, because his inner light, the source of that insight, was understood by Englishmen. Churchill's star was invisible to the public and even to most of his peers. But a few saw it. One of them wrote afterward that although Winston knew the world was complex and in constant flux, to him "the great things, races, and peoples, and morality were eternal." Isaiah Berlin, the Oxford philosopher, later observed that the Churchill of 1940 was neither "a sensitive lens, which absorbs and concentrates and reflects . . . the sentiments of others," nor a politician who played "on public opinion like an instrument." Instead Berlin saw him as a leader who imposed his "imagination and his will upon his countrymen," idealizing them "with such intensity that in the end they approached his ideal and began to see themselves as he saw them." In doing so he "transformed cowards into brave men, and so fulfilled the purpose of shining armour."[282]

Churchill's mood seemed to confirm this. He possessed an inner radiance that year and felt it. In his memoirs he wrote that "by the confidence, indulgence, and loyalty by which I was upborne, I was soon able to give an integral direction to almost every aspect of the war. This was really necessary because times were so very bad. The method was accepted because everyone realised how near were death and ruin. Not only individual death, which is the universal experience, stood near, but, incomparably more commanding, the life of Britain, her message, and her glory."[283]

To him, Britain, "her message, and her glory," were very real. At times he would address his country as though she were a personage. After he had comprehended the revolution wrought at Kitty Hàwk he said (to the astonishment of his companion, who had thought they were alone), "You came into big things as an accident of naval power when you were an island. The world had confidence in you. You became the workshop of the world. You populated the island beyond its capacity. Through an accident of airpower you will probably cease to exist." It sounded quaint, and it was. Churchill was not a public figure like, say, Roosevelt, who thought and spoke in the idiom of his own time. He was instead the last of England's great Victorian statesmen, with views formed when the British lion's roar could silence the world; he was the champion of the Old Queen's realm and the defender and protector of the values Englishmen of her reign had cherished, the principles they held inviolate, the vision which had illumined their world, which had steadied them in time of travail, and which he had embraced as a youth.[284]

He was ever the impassioned Manichaean, seeing life and history in primary colors, like Vittore Carpaccio's paintings of St. George; a believer in absolute virtue and absolute malevolence, in blinding light and impenetrable darkness, in righteousness and wickedness — or rather in the forces of good *against* the forces of evil, for the two would always be in conflict and be therefore forever embattled. He had been accused of inconsistency and capricious judgment. Actually, it was MacDonald and Baldwin and Chamberlain who tailored their views to fit the moment. Churchill's binnacle remained true. "Death and sorrow will be the companions of our journey," he told the House of Commons; "hardship our garment, constancy and valour our only shield."[285]

And, he might have added, grief as their reward. He was sure Britons could take it. Despite his high birth he had an almost mystical faith in the power of the ordinary Englishman to survive, to endure, and, in the end, to prevail. "Tell the truth to the British people," he had begged the shifty prime ministers of the 1930s; "they are a tough people, a robust people. . . . If you have told them exactly what is going on you have ensured yourself against complaints and reproaches which are not very pleasant when they come home on the morrow of some disillusion."[286]

But in those shabby years His Majesty's Governments believed that there were some things the country ought not to know, and that their policy of duplicity — which at times amounted to conspiracy — would be vindicated in the end. Chamberlain would be the scapegoat of appeasement, and before the year was out sackcloth would be his shroud, but he was only one of many. Baldwin, for example, bore a greater responsibility for weakening Britain's defenses while Hitler built his military juggernaut. The appeasers had been powerful; they had controlled *The Times* and the BBC; they had been largely drawn from the upper classes, and their betrayal of England's greatness would be neither forgotten nor forgiven by those who, gulled by the mystique of England's class system, had believed as Englishmen had believed for generations that public school boys governed best. The appeasers destroyed oligarchic rule which, though levelers may protest, had long governed well. If ever men betrayed their class, these were they.

Because their possessions were great, the appeasers had much to lose should the Red flag fly over Westminster. That was why they had felt threatened by the hunger riots of 1932. It was also the driving force behind their exorbitant fear and distrust of the new Russia. They had seen a strong Germany as a buffer against bolshevism, had thought their security would be strengthened if they sidled up to the fierce, virile Third Reich. Nazi coarseness, anti-Semitism, the Reich's darker underside, were rationalized; time, they assured one another, would blur the jagged edges of Nazi

Germany. So, with their eyes open, they sought accommodation with a criminal regime, turned a blind eye to its iniquities, ignored its frequent resort to murder and torture, submitted to extortion, humiliation, and abuse until, having sold out all who had sought to stand shoulder to shoulder with Britain and keep the bridge against the new barbarism, they led England herself into the cold damp shadow of the gallows, friendless save for the demoralized republic across the Channel. Their end came when the House of Commons, in a revolt of conscience, wrenched power from them and summoned to the colors the one man who had foretold all that had passed, who had tried, year after year, alone and mocked, to prevent the war by urging the only policy which would have done the job. And now, in the desperate spring of 1940, with the reins of power at last firm in his grasp, he resolved to lead Britain and her fading empire in one last great struggle worthy of all they had been and meant, to arm the nation, not only with weapons but also with the mace of honor, creating in every English breast a soul beneath the ribs of death.

SOURCE NOTES

PRIMARY BIOGRAPHICAL SOURCES

By far the largest single source for *les justifications*, as the French call scholarly citations, is the Churchill College Archives Centre at Cambridge University, the repository of 300 collections of private papers, including those of Baroness Spencer-Churchill (Clementine), Bracken, Violet Pearman, Bevin, Grigg, Keyes, E. L. Spears (partial), Hankey (partial), Phipps, Lord Lloyd, Lord Thurso (Sinclair), Christie, Page Croft, Margesson, Attlee, and Halifax (on microfilm — the originals are in the India Office Library, the Public Records Office, and the estate of his heir). Papers of Viscount Templewood (Hoare, partial), Baldwin, and Crewe may be found in the Cambridge University Library; those of Beaverbrook, Lloyd George, and Samuels —until their recent transfer to the Jerusalem Archive —were available in the House of Lords Library; those of Austen and Neville Chamberlain in the Birmingham University Library; those of Lothian and Margo Asquith in the National Library of Scotland, Edinburgh; Derby's in the Liverpool Public Record Office; Henry James Scrymgeours-Wedderburn's in the Dundee Archives; Hankey's (partial) in the Public Record Office; Marsh's in the New York Public Library; Dalton's diary and papers, as well as those of Cherwell (partial) in the British Library of Political and Economic Science; and Baruch's in the Princeton University Library.

Over a hundred collections of papers remain in private hands, including some of Spears's, Camrose's, some of Cherwell's, some of Halifax's, Amery's, Lord Lloyd's, Lord Southborough's, Butler's, Lothian's, Boothby's, Geoffrey Dawson's, J. L. Garvin's, Sheila Grant Duff's, Ironside's, Thomas Jones's, Harold Laski's, Paul Maze's, Harold Nicolson's, those of Viscount Norwich (Duff Cooper), Major General Pakenham-Walsh, Selborne, Vansittart, Weir, Chaim Weizmann, William Heinemann Ltd., Cripps, Rumbold, Salisbury, Swinton, Thornton-Kemsley, Ramsay MacDonald, Cecil, and the Blenheim Palace Archive.

PRIMARY HISTORICAL SOURCES

British Documents
British Cabinet Documents, Premier (Prime Minister), and Foreign Office Documents are catalogued at the Public Record Office in Kew, Richmond, Surrey, under "Records of Interest to Social Scientists." Guidance is necessary; the records of the Committee of Imperial Defence, for example, are filed under twenty-one different categories.

Published material may be found in *Documents on British Foreign Policy 1919–1939*, particularly the second and third series, edited by E. L. Woodward, MA, FBA, and Rohan Butler, assisted by Anne Orne, MA, and issued by Her Majesty's Stationery Office in 1952. Other unpublished official material concerning Churchill is in the archives of the Air Ministry, the Committee of Imperial Defence, the Treasury, Documents on International Affairs, and *Documents Concerning German-Polish Relations and the Outbreak of Hostilities between Great Britain and Germany*, London: His Majesty's Stationery Office, 1939 (The British Blue Book). Verbatim accounts of all proceedings in both the House of Commons and the House of Lords are published in *Parliamentary Debates* (Hansard), England's equivalent of America's *Congressional Record*.

French Documents

Le Livre Jaune Français. Documents diplomatiques, 1938–1939 (Paris: Ministre des Affaires Étrangères (The French Yellow Book).

Documents Diplomatiques Français, Première Série and *Deuxième Série: Les Événements survenus en France de 1933 à 1945*, a postwar investigation of French policy in the 1930s conducted by the *Assemblée Nationale* and published (a two-volume report supported by nine volumes of testimony) in 1947.

German Documents

Dokumente der deutschen Politik, 1933–1940; Akten zur Deutschen Auswärtigen Politik 1918–1945 (German Foreign Policy Documents), published jointly by the Foreign Office and the U.S. State Department; issued in Baden between 1950 and 1956. These documents are divided into *Serie C* (four volumes, covering January 30, 1933, to October 31, 1933) and *Serie D*, thirteen volumes which are arranged, not chronologically but by subject, but generally running from September 1937 to December 1941. There is an eleven-month gap here, but there are gaps in the Allied documents, too.

Nuremberg Documents (ND)

Nuremberg seems far in the future to those who have turned the last page of this book, but it was there that all the secret papers of the interwar years — some dating from 1919 — first appeared, and in documents which could not be explained away. They may be found in *Trial of the Major War Criminals:* forty-two volumes covering the proceedings and exhibits —mostly in German — before the International Military Tribunal; *Nazi Conspiracy and Aggression:* ten volumes of additional interrogation transcripts and affidavits, in English; *Trials of War Criminals before the Nuremberg Tribunals:* fifteen volumes of selected material from the twelve Nuremberg trials following the adjournment of the IMT.

Other Published Documentary Material

I documenti diploma italiani; Ottavo series, 1935–1939, Rome, Liberia della Stato, 1952–1953; *Official Document Concerning Polish German and Polish Soviet Relations 1933–1939*, London, 1939 (The Polish White Book); *Documents and Material Relating to the Eve of the Second World War*, 1937–1939, two volumes, Moscow, Foreign Language Publishing House, 1948; *Soviet Documents on Foreign Policy*, three volumes, London, Royal Institute of International Affairs, 1931–1953.

Citations from British manuscript collections are puzzling, or rather are a series of puzzles, because each archive makes its own rules. In some instances the archive is not large enough to require extensive cataloguing. With eminent men it is not so simple. However, there are certain constants. The figure or code to the left of the slash — e.g., "123" in "123/456" —identifies the section or shelf where a document may be found. The figure to the right usually identifies the specific box number, or, if the entry is large, such as a scrapbook, the file number which houses the document. See Janet Foster and Julia Sheppard, *British Archives: A Guide to Archive Resources in the United Kingdom* (London, 1982).

The first of the three major documents centers for this work is the Churchill College Archives Centre, Churchill College, Cambridge; Correll Barnett, the learned Keeper of the Archives, was ably assisted, during my early visits, by Archivist Marion Stewart, who has since been succeeded by Leslie James. The Centre contains 300 accessions of diplomatic, political, military, scientific, and naval papers, most of them twentieth-century. Everything has been done to make document retrieval simple; even so, the researcher must dig. To take one example, the Spears papers in the Centre comprise four sections. The first number following the code abbreviation gives the section number. Section 1 (300 files) is correspondence, A to Z. The second code number identifies the file number. The papers in Spears's code 2 (thirty-five files) pertain to personal and family matters. Section 3 (sixty-five boxes) has no material about Churchill and is restricted to scholars. Section 4 (seven files) contains miscellaneous papers.

The second mother lode of documents is the Public Record Office in Kew, Surrey, safe in the hands of Alfred Knightbridge, head of the search department. Here a letter code (CAB for cabinet papers, PrP for Prime Minister's papers, etc.) opens each citation. The second part, in numbers, breaks down the mass of materials by dates: the date of a cabinet meeting, or of events between meetings. The slash comes next, then the "piece number" identifying a given document.

The third trove of documentary material is the British Library's reference division in Great Russell Street (D. A. Clark and G. E. A. Raspin in charge). Much of the most valuable material here is kept in the Woolwich Repository; delivery is normally a day after application. British newspapers since 1801 are filed in the library's Newspaper Library, at Colindale Library, London.

Abbreviations and Short Titles Used in the Notes

BSCP	Papers of the Baroness Spencer-Churchill (Clementine Churchill).
CAB	British Cabinet Documents, Public Record Office, Kew.
ChP	Churchill Papers.
DBFP	*Documents on British Foreign Policy 1919–1939*, edited by E. L. Woodward and Rohan Butler, assisted by Anne Orne. London, 1952.
DDF	*Documents Diplomatiques Français, Première Série, Deuxième Série*.
DGFP	*Dokumente der deutschen Politik 1933–1940; Akten zur Deutschen Auswärtigen Politik 1918–1945*. Series C, D.
Événements	*Les Événements survenus en France de 1933 à 1945.*
FCNA	Führer's Conferences on Naval Affairs.
Hansard	*Record of Parliamentary Debates* (Hansard).
ND	Nuremberg Documents (see also NCA, TMWC, and TWC below).
NCA	*Nazi Conspiracy and Aggression*, 10 volumes of interrogation transcripts and affidavits; in English.
NYT	*New York Times.*
Prp	Premier (Prime Minister) Papers. Public Record Office, Kew.
Times	*The Times* of London.
TMWC	*Trial of the Major War Criminals*; 42 volumes covering the proceeding and exhibits (mostly in German) before the International Military Tribunal in Nuremberg.
TWC	*Trials of War Criminals before the Nuremberg Tribunals*; 15 volumes of selected material from the twelve Nuremberg trials following the adjournment of the International Military Tribunal.
WM/[name]	Author's interviews.

WSCHCS   *Winston S. Churchill: His Complete Speeches*, edited by Robert Rhodes James.

The Official Biography of Winston Spencer Churchill, by Martin Gilbert (Boston, 1966–), is cited as follows:

WSC V   Volume V. *The Prophet of Truth, 1922–1939* (biography)

CV V/1   Companion Volume V, part 1 (1922–1929, Documents)

CV V/2   Companion Volume V, part 2 (1930–1935, Documents)

CV V/3   Companion Volume V, part 3 (1936–1939, Documents)

WSC VI   Volume VI, *Finest Hour 1939–1941*

PREAMBLE

1. WM/Lady Soames (at Chartwell), 10/27/80; Robin Fedden, *Churchill and Chartwell* (Westerham, Kent, 1968), 13 ff.
2. Walter Henry Thompson, *Assignment Churchill* (New York, 1955), 92.
3. Walter Thompson, 183.
4. Mary Soames, *Clementine Churchill: The Biography of a Marriage* (Boston, 1979), 352; Adam Sykes and Iain Sproat, eds., *The Wit of Sir Winston* (London, 1965), 85.
5. WM/Lady Soames (at Chartwell), 10/27/80; Fedden, 25–26, 43–44. R. Howells, *Simply Churchill* (New York, 1965), 19.
6. WM/Grace Hamblin, 11/4/80, and letter of 9/12/87; Hamblin, letter to Martin Gilbert, 6/12/78; WM/Lady Soames (at Chartwell), 10/27/80; Fedden, 27; Kay Halle, *The Irrepressible Churchill: A Treasury of Winston Churchill's Wit* (New York, 1967), 109.
7. Howells, 41, 36; WM/Sir William Deakin, 10/5/80.
8. Howells, 36; Elizabeth Nel, *Mr. Churchill's Secretary* (New York, 1958), 33.
9. Norman McGowan, *My Years with Churchill* (London, 1958), 86–87; Howells, 19.
10. Howells, 19–20, 49; Halle, 313.
11. Winston S. Churchill, *The World Crisis*, 5 vols. and *The After-*math (New York, 1923–1931), V, Afterword.
12. Bruce West, *Churchill's Pilot: The Man Who Flew Churchill* (Canada, 1975), 6; McGowan, 93; Howells, 110.
13. Fedden, 50–51; Howells, 37–39; WM/ Lieutenant General Sir Ian Jacobs, 11/12/80; Sir John Wheeler-Bennett, ed., *Action This Day: Memoirs* by Lord Normanbrook, John Colville, Sir John Martin, Sir Ian Jacobs, Lord Bridges, Sir Leslie Rowan (London, 1968), 183; Charles Eade, ed., *Churchill by His Contemporaries* (London, 1953), 309.
14. Howells, 36, 138; McGowan, 92–93.
15. Howells, 20.
16. Howells, 138; CV I/2 996; Phyllis Moir, *I Was Winston Churchill's Private Secretary* (New York, 1941), 1, 89–90; WM/ Deakin; WM/Kathleen Hill, 11/4/80.
17. WM/Sir John Colville, 10/8/80; Sarah Churchill, *A Thread in the Tapestry* (New York, 1967), 38.
18. Fedden, 49.
19. Fedden, 49; Sir David Hunt, *On the Spot: An Ambassador Remembers* (London, 1975), 63; Colin Coote and Denvil Batchelor, *Maxims and Reflections* (London, 1947), 36; Viscount Chandos, *Memoirs* (London, 1962), 167; Howells, 150.
20. WM/Virginia Cowles, 10/15/80;

WM/ George Malcolm Thompson, 10/13/80; WM/Lord Geoffrey Lloyd, 11/27/80, WM/Deakin; WM/Lady Soames, 10/9/80; WM, personal information.

21. Wheeler-Bennett, ed., 87.
22. WM/Lord Lloyd; WM/Lord Boothby, 10/16/80.
23. WM/A. J. P. Taylor 12/1/80; WM, personal information.
24. Second Earl of Birkenhead, *The Professor and the Prime Minister* (Boston, 1962), 27–35, 36.
25. Birkenhead, 129–159 *passim*.
26. Sir John Colville, *Footprints in Time* (London, 1976), 100; WM/Colville.
27. Birkenhead, 38.
28. WM/Lady Soames, 10/9/80; Halle, 263; Wheeler-Bennett, ed., 25–28.
29. Kenneth Young, *Churchill and Beaverbrook: A Study in Friendship and Politics* (New York, 1966), 130.
30. Coote and Batchelor, 44.
31. WM/Cowles; WM/Kay Halle, 8/6/80; WM/Pamela Harriman, 8/22–23/80; Elizabeth Longford, *Winston Churchill: A Pictorial Life Story* (Chicago, 1974), 87, 130–131.
32. Sykes and Sproat, eds., 70, 71; Eade, ed., 307; Coote and Batchelor, 119–120.
33. Lord Moran, *Churchill. Taken from the Diaries of Lord Moran: The Struggle for Survival. 1940–1965* (Boston, 1966), 198; Halle, 152.
34. WM/Colville; Wheeler-Bennett, ed., 59–60.
35. McGowan, 72.
36. McGowan, 70; WM/Vanda Salmon, 11/26/80.
37. WM/Salmon; Martin Gilbert, *Winston Churchill: The Wilderness Years* (London, 1981), 28; Virginia Cowles, *Winston Churchill, The Era and the Man* (New York, 1953), 11.
38. Walter Thompson, 94; Eade, ed., 356–357; McGowan, 60.
39. John Paget, *The New "Examen"* (London, 1934).
40. Halle, 263; Soames, 323; Gilbert, *Wilderness*, 129.

41. Hunt, 77.
42. Soames, 301.
43. Eade, ed., 300, 309.
44. Eade, ed., 305.
45. Violet Bonham Carter, *Winston Churchill: An Intimate Portrait* (New York, 1965), 151, 152; Moran, 449.
46. Kenneth Young, *Churchill and Beaverbrook: A Study in Friendship and Politics* (New York, 1966), 26.
47. Soames, 305; WM/Deakin; Moran, 420; Winston S. Churchill, *Young Winston's Wars; The Original Despatches of Winston S. Churchill, War Correspondent 1897–1900*, edited by Frederick Woods (New York, 1972), xiii; WM/William L. Shirer, 7/20/74.
48. WM/Deakin.
49. WM/Cecily Gemmell, 7/10/80; Walter Thompson, 45.
50. Wheeler-Bennett, ed., 144; Harold Nicolson, *Diaries and Letters*, II, edited by Nigel Nicolson, 3 vols. (London, 1966), 320–321.
51. Peter Stansky, ed., *Churchill: A Profile* (New York, 1973), 38.
52. Robert Rhodes James, *Anthony Eden* (London, 1980), 229; Moran, 604.
53. WM/Hill, 11/4/80.
54. WM/Gemmell, 7/10/80.
55. Nel, 31.
56. Moir, 2, 58; Howells, 61.
57. Nel, 32; Moir, 88.

PROLOGUE

1. *Times* 11/12/32.
2. *NYT* 10/19/32; *Times* 10/31/32.
3. *NYT* 10/6/32, 10/25/32, 11/1/32; *Time* 11/7/32.
4. *Time* 11/14/32.
5. James Morris, *Farewell The Trumpets: An Imperial Retreat* (New York, 1978), 314, 311; Colin Cross, *The Fall of the British Empire* (New York and London, 1968), 216.
6. Morris, 313–314; *Time* 3/21/32.
7. Morris, 362; *Time* 4/11/32, 4/18/32.
8. Sir John Colville, *The Fringes of Power: 10 Downing Street Diaries,*

1939–1955 (New York, 1985), 71.

9. Morris, 335

10. *Times* 8/18/14; Robert Rhodes James, *Memoirs* (New York, 1970), 110.

11. *NYT* 11/18/29; *Nation* 2/12/30.

12. *Times* 1/22/29; *Book Review Digest* 433–434, 792–793; Siegfried Sassoon, *Siegfried's Journey, 1916–1920* (New York, 1946), 116–119.

13. Harold Nicolson, *Public Faces* (London, 1932), 16–17; Richard Kenin and Justin Wintle, eds., *The Dictionary of Biographical Quotations* (New York, 1958), 35.

14. Winston S. Churchill, *Amid These Storms: Thoughts and Adventures* (New York, 1932), 15–16; Telford Taylor, *Munich: The Price of Peace* (New York, 1979), 204.

15. Lincoln Steffens, *The Autobiography of Lincoln Steffens* (New York, 1931), 131.

16. Winston S. Churchill, *The World Crisis*, 5 vols. and *The Aftermath* (New York, 1923–1931), V, 66.

17. Hugh Dalton, *The Fateful Years* (London, 1957), 41–42.

18. William Manchester, *The Last Lion: Visions of Glory* (Boston, 1983), 76.

19. T. R. Fehrenbach, *F.D.R.'s Undeclared War 1939 to 1941* (New York, 1967), 22.

20. Telford Taylor, 107; Alistair Horne, *To Lose a Battle* (Boston, 1969), 22–23.

21. Churchill, *Crisis, The Aftermath*, 156.

22. William L. Shirer, *The Collapse of the Third Republic* (New York, 1969), 137.

23. Alistair Horne, *To Lose a Battle* (Boston, 1969), 56–57; Simone de Beauvoir, *La Force de l'âge* (Paris, 1961), 116–117.

24. Shirer, *Collapse*, 203; Beauvoir, 120–121; Horne, 57.

25. Beauvoir, 120–121.

26. Horne, 52; Beauvoir, 155.

27. Robert T. Elson and the editors of Time-Life Books, *Prelude to War* (New York, 1976), 47.

28. Elson et al., 74–79.

29. *NYT* 12/2/25.

30. *Berliner Tageblatt* 6/25/22.

31. *Frankfurter Zeitung* 12/2/25; *The New Encyclopaedia Britannica*, 15th ed. (Chicago, 1974), XIX, 966–967; *Berliner Tageblatt* 5/9/19; *NYT* 6/25/22.

32. WSCHCS 5197–5206; J. D. Scott, *Vickers: A History* (London, 1962), 86–87, 150–151; Otto Lehmann-Russbüldt, *Die blutige Internationale der Rüstungen* (Berlin, 1933), 50.

33. General Karl von Clausewitz, *On War*, trans. Col. J. J. Graham, 3 vols. (London, 1911), I, 5: Barbara Tuchman, *The Guns of August* (New York, 1962), 314.

34. Hugh Gibson, *A Journal from Our Legation in Belgium* (New York, 1917), 324.

35. Adolf Hitler, *Mein Kampf* (Munich, 1932), 369–370; Konrad Keiden, *Geschichte des Nationalsozialismus* (Berlin, 1932), 36.

36. *Living Age* 12/12/25; WM/Tilo Freiherr von Wilmowsky, 5/30/63 (Essen); *Der Spiegel* 6/5/63; Tilo von Wilmowsky, *Rückblickened möchte ich sagen . . .* (Hamburg, 1961), 178–181; *The New Encyclopaedia Britannica*, XIX, 969.

37. Hans Kohn, *The Mind of Germany, The Education of a Nation* (New York, 1960), 308; Franz L. Neumann, *Behemoth* (New York, 1942), 23.

38. *Süddeutsche Monatshafte* 12/21/24.

39. *Time* 8/22/32, 10/17/32.

40. *Time* 9/5/32, 11/28/32.

41. *Times* 2/2/32; Arnold Brecht, *Prelude to Silence* (New York, 1944), 35.

42. ND 203, 204, 37–25 PS.

43. André François-Poncet, *The Fateful Years: Memoirs of a French Ambassador in Berlin 1931–1938* (New York, 1949), 61.

44. *NYT* 3/25/33; Oswald Spengler, *Jahre der Entscheidung* (Munich, 1933), xiii.

45. Winston S. Churchill, *The Gathering Storm* (Boston, 1948), 84; Hansard 5/13/32, 7/11/32.

46. Churchill, *Storm*, 84; Ernst Hanf-staengl, *Hitler, The Missing Years* (London, 1957), 193–196.

47. Hansard 11/23/32; *Daily Mail* 10/17/32; WSC V, 627.

48. Günter Grass, *On Writing and Politics 1957–1983*, trans. Ralph Manheim (San Diego, 1985), cited in *NYT Book Review* 6/23/85.

49. *Times* 2/18/33.

50. *Times* 2/24/34; WSC V, 545; Christopher Hollis, *The Oxford Union* (London, 1955), 184–193.

51. Churchill, *Storm*, 85 fn.; WSC V, 504–505.

SHOALS

1. *Fodor's London 1984* (New York, 1984), 152.

2. WM, personal information (1/30/53).

3. WM, personal information (1/30/53); Sir John Colville, *The Fringes of Power: 10 Downing Street Diaries, 1939–1955* (New York, 1985), 36.

4. Sir David Hunt, *On the Spot: An Ambassador Remembers* (London, 1975), 30–31.

5. Lord Boothby, *I Fight to Live* (London, 1947), 38.

6. Telford Taylor, *Munich: The Price of Peace* (New York, 1979), 549, 550, 555.

7. WM/Lady Soames, 10/9/80.

8. Winston S. Churchill, *The Gathering Storm* (Boston, 1948), 83.

9. Thomas Jones, *A Diary With Letters, 1931–1950* (Oxford, 1954), 239–265.

10. Frank Owen, *Tempestuous Journey: Lloyd George, His Life and Times* (London, 1954), 737; *Daily Express* 9/16/36.

11. DBFP series 2, vol. IV, no. 265; Vernon Bartlett, *Nazi Germany Explained* (London, 1933), 517–522.

12. Telford Taylor, 217 fn.; *New York Herald Tribune* 5/19/33, 5/12/33.

13. *München Süddeutsche Zeitung* 9/26/30; *Frankfurter Zeitung* 9/26/30.

14. Fritz Hesse, *Hitler and the English* (England, 1954), 11–12; WM/R. A. Butler, 12/5/80.

15. *Strand* 11/35.

16. Sir John Wheeler-Bennett, ed., *Action This Day: Memoirs* by Lord Normanbrook, John Colville, Sir John Martin, Sir Ian Jacobs, Lord Bridges, Sir Leslie Rowan (London, 1968), 11.

17. Lord Vansittart, *The Mist Procession* (London, 1958), 482; WM/R. A. Butler.

18. *NYT* 7/30/31; Lord Moran, *Churchill, Taken from the Diaries of Lord Moran: The Struggle for Survival, 1940–1965* (Boston, 1966), 65; Virginia Cowles, *Winston Churchill; The Era and the Man* (New York, 1953), 285.

19. WM/A. J. P. Taylor, 12/1/80; WM/Harold Macmillan, 12/4/80; Harold Macmillan, *Winds of Change* (London, 1966), 291; Charles Eade, ed., *Churchill by His Contemporaries* (London, 1953), 67.

20. Elizabeth Longford, *Winston Churchill: A Pictorial Life Story* (Chicago, 1974), 84; Macmillan, 437; Victor Wallace Germains, *The Tragedy of Winston Churchill* (London, 1931).

21. WM/Lady Soames, 10/9/80; Macmillan, 113.

22. Kenneth Young, *Churchill and Beaverbrook: A Study in Friendship and Politics* (New York, 1966), 120–122.

23. WM/Malcolm Muggeridge, 11/25/80.

24. Hansard 11/23/32.

25. DBFP series 2, vol. IV, nos. 263, 30.

26. DBFP series 2, vol. V, nos. 5, 2229.

27. DBFP series 2, vol. V, no. 2229.

28. William E. Dodd, *Ambassador Dodd's Diary, 1933–1938*, edited by William E. Dodd, Jr., and Martha Dodd (London, 1941), 239 (4/15/35); Foreign Relations of the U. S., 1937, I, 84.

29. Jones, 180; Josiah Wedgwood, *Memoirs of a Fighting Life* (London, 1941), 225.

30. WM/William L. Shirer, 7/5/83.

31. WM/Shirer.

32. Vernon Bartlett, 242–243.

33. Churchill, *Storm*, 207.

34. Winston S. Churchill, *While England Slept* (New York, 1938), 35.

35. Claud Cockburn, *The Week*, No. 166, June 17, 1936; Martin Gilbert, *Winston Churchill: The Wilderness Years* (London, 1981), 165; CAB 23/86.

36. Stephen Roskill, *Hankey: Man of Secrets*, vol. III, *1931–1963* (London, 1974), 53.

37. A. L. Kennedy, *Britain Faces Germany* (London, 1937), 83–86; Gilbert, *Wilderness*, 136.

38. Hansard 6/29/31; Gilbert, *Wilderness*, 37.

39. Hansard 6/29/31.

40. WSC V, 445; *Daily Mail* 5/26/32.

41. ChP 18/75; *Daily Mail* 5/26/32.

42. Hansard 11/10/32.

43. Len Deighton, *Fighter* (New York, 1977), 39.

44. *Daily Mail* 11/17/32; 11/23/32.

45. Alistair Horne, *To Lose a Battle* (Boston, 1969), 22; WM/Lady Soames; WM/R. A. Butler.

46. ChP 9/103; *Times* 4/13/33.

47. Hansard 4/13/33.

48. *Birmingham Post* 4/19/33.

49. WSC V, 460–461.

50. Macmillan, 354; Hansard 3/23/33.

51. Hansard 3/23/33.

52. Hansard 11/5/29 (Lords); Telford Taylor, 249.

53. *Birmingham Post* 3/28/33.

54. Jones, 129; Murray Papers.

55. Martin Gilbert and Richard Gott, *The Appeasers* (Boston, 1963), 11.

56. ChP 2/266; *Times* 9/27/33, 6/17/36; J. R. M. Butler, *Lord Lothian* (London, 1960), Appendix IV, 354–362.

57. Cowles, 293.

58. *Times* 6/26/33.

59. *Times* 6/26/33.

60. Vernon Bartlett, 242–243.

61. Gilbert, *Wilderness*, 161; Norman Angell, *The Defence of the Empire* (New York, 1937), 183–184; Kennedy, 83–86.

62. Eade, ed., 44.

63. Kay Halle, *The Irrepressible Churchill: A Treasury of Winston Churchill's Wit* (New York, 1967), 37, 181, 323.

64. Halle, 268, 322.

65. Hansard 7/10/35, 6/25/41.

66. Colin Coote and Denvil Batchelor, eds., *Maxims and Reflections* (London, 1947), 53–54; Hansard 12/8/44.

67. Halle, 269; Coote and Batchelor, eds., 142.

68. Hansard 1/21/31; Halle, 125, 257.

69. Halle, 131, 133.

70. William Safire, "Banned Words," *NYT* 10/28/84.

71. Gilbert, *Wilderness*, 132.

72. Telford Taylor, 205; CAB 23/76.

73. John Baker White, *True Blue* (London, 1970), 161.

74. ChP 2/201.

75. BSCP 8/31/29.

76. Cowles, 296; Gilbert, *Wilderness*, 15.

77. Foreign Office Papers 371/16733.

78. *Harper's*, March 1946.

79. Gilbert, *Wilderness*, 120.

80. *The New Encyclopaedia Britannica*, 15th ed. (Chicago, 1974), VII, 4, 597.

81. DBFP series 2, vol. V, no. 127; *NYT* 2/17/85.

82. Vansittart, 478.

83. Gilbert, *Wilderness*, 118, 119.

84. Hansard 5/11/35; Sir John Colville, *Footprints in Time* (London, 1976), 95; WM/Sir John Colville, 10/8/80.

85. *Epping West Essex Gazette* 8/13/33; Hansard 8/23/33.

86. Horne, 38 *passim*.

87. Oswald Spengler, *Jahre de Entscheidung* (Munich, 1935), viii; TMWC XXXIV.

88. *Völkischer Beobachter* 5/18/33.

89. Hermann Rauschning, *Gespräche mit Hitler* (Munich, 1940), 55; Franz von Papen, *Der Wahrheit eine Gasse* (Munich, 1953), 330–333.

90. Beaverbrook Papers.

91. Blomberg's directive, TMWC, XXIV, 487–491.

92. William L. Shirer, *The Rise and Fall of the Third Reich: A History of Nazi Germany* (New York, 1960), 212.

93. Gottfried Benn, *Der neue Staat und die Intellecktuellen* (Stuttgart/Berlin, 1933), 576.

94. André François-Poncet, *De Versailles à Potsdam* (Paris, 1948), 107; ND 2001-PS; Alan Bullock, *Hitler —A Study in Tyranny* (New York, 1952), 199; ND EC-419.

95. Wolfgang Foerster, *Ein General kaempft gegen den Krieg* (Munich, 1949), 70–73.

96. NCA, VII, 335; Foerster, 122; *Völkischer Beobachter* 8/20/34; *Frankfurter Zeitung* 8/20/34; *Berliner Tageblatt,* 8/20/34.

97. ND C-100.

98. Telford Taylor, 205; CV V/1, 306, 307.

99. Robert Rhodes James, *Churchill: A Study in Failure, 1900–1939* (New York, 1970), 262; "How Wars of the Future Will Be Waged," *News of the World* 4/24/38.

100. Ronald H. Bailey and the editors of Time-Life Books, *The Air War in Europe, 1940–1945* (Chicago, 1981), 26.

101. PrP 1/237; Bailey et al., 43; Deighton, 78.

102. Churchill, *Storm,* 116, 127, 128.

103. WSC V, 553.

104. Hansard 3/11/35; Vansittart, 509.

105. Wheeler-Bennett, ed., *Action This Day,* 11.

106. Lord Eustace Percy, *Some Memories* (London, 1958), 187.

107. General Georg Thomas, *Basic Facts for a History of German War and Armament Economy* (mimeographed) (Nuremberg, 1945), cited in Shirer, *Rise and Fall,* 259; NCA, I, 827–830.

108. Walter Görlitz, *History of the German General Staff 1657–1945* (New York, 1953), 299.

109. Vansittart, 226; Gilbert, *Wilderness,* 108; Telford Taylor, 591–592; CAB 23/83–86.

110. ChP 2/271; WM/Kathleen Hill 11/4/80.

111. Templewood Papers.

112. *Times* 11/17/34; WSCHCS 5433 (verse form added).

113. Hansard 11/28/34.

114. Hansard 11/28/34.

115. Frances Stevenson, *Lloyd George: A Diary by Frances Stevenson,* edited by A. J. P. Taylor (New York, 1971), 294.

116. Hansard 11/28/34.

117. Hansard 3/8/34.

118. Telford Taylor, 246.

119. BSCP 3/8/35.

120. Foreign Office Papers 371/18828.

121. White Papers Cmd. 5107; BSCP 3/8/35.

122. Foreign Office Papers 371/18828.

123. *NYT* 3/17/35; Telford Taylor, 98; Shirer, *Rise and Fall,* 284.

124. *Strand* 11/35.

125. Hansard 3/19/35.

126. ChP 4/143.

127. Hansard 3/19/35.

128. Hansard 3/19/35.

129. Foreign Office Papers 371/18828.

130. BSCP 4/5/35.

131. Telford Taylor, 218.

132. Hansard 5/2/35.

133. Hansard 5/22/35.

134. Vansittart, 497–498.

135. BSCP 5/11/35, 5/13/35.

136. *Daily Telegraph* 4/26/35; *Daily Express* 5/3/35.

137. ChP 8/503; BSCP, 4/11/35.

138. Churchill, *Storm,* 126; Coote and Batchelor, 158–159.

139. Telford Taylor, 123.

140. *NYT* 5/23/35; *Times* 5/23/35.

141. John Evelyn Wrench, *Geoffrey Dawson and Our Times* (London, 1955), 361.

142. Shirer, *Rise and Fall,* 287–288.

143. Telford Taylor, 222–223; CAB 23/82, 6/19/35.

144. CAB 23/82, 6/19/35; Hansard 7/11/35.

145. Telford Taylor, 223.

146. Hansard 7/11/35.

147. *Daily Herald* 3/27/36; Halle, 299.

148. Telford Taylor, 97.

149. Telford Taylor, 222.

150. Hansard 3/19/35.

151. Churchill, *Storm,* 123.

152. Birla Papers; Martin Gilbert, *Churchill's Political Philosophy* (Oxford, 1981), 85–88; Peter Stansky, ed., *Churchill: A Profile* (New York, 1973), 201.

153. Robert Keith Middlemas and John Barnes, *Baldwin* (London, 1969), 868; WM/Macmillan; Macmillan, 395–397; A. W. Baldwin, *My Father: The True Story* (London, 1956), 242.

154. Middlemas and Barnes, 867; *Times* 11/1/35; L. S. Amery, *My Political Life*, 3 vols. (London, 1953), III, 75, 170; Middlemas and Barnes, 369.

155. *Strand* 11/35; Hansard 10/24/35.

156. *Strand* 11/35.

157. Foreign Office Papers 371/18878, 371/18880; ChP 2/237.

158. Foreign Office Papers 371/18880.

159. WSC V, 680; ChP 2/237.

160. Eade, ed., 171; DNB 11/8/38, 11/6/36, 9/9/38.

161. Henry Pelling, *Winston Churchill* (New York, 1974), 373; ChP 4/141.

162. Vansittart, 497.

163. Churchill, *Storm*, 128, 200; Baldwin Papers, 47, 113.

164. Hansard 5/2/35.

165. Wrench, 322.

166. Isaiah Berlin, *Mr. Churchill in 1940* (Boston, 1964), 16.

167. Jones, 157.

168. Jones, 203.

169. Brian Gardner, *Churchill in Power* (Boston, 1970), 6; WM/A. J. P. Taylor, 12/1/80; A. J. P. Taylor, *Origins of the Second World War* (New York, 1961), 116.

170. Churchill, *Storm*, 181; Longford, 86; Boothby, *I Fight to Live*, 137; WM/Lord Boothby 10/16/80.

171. Churchill, *Storm*, 181.

172. Robert T. Elson and the editors of Time-Life Books, *Prelude to War* (New York, 1976), 149.

REEF

1. Francis Paul Walters, *A History of the League of Nations* (New York, 1952), 648.

2. Harold Macmillan, *Winds of Change* (London, 1966), 383; Robert T. Elson and the editors of Time-Life Books, *Prelude to War* (New York, 1976), 150–151.

3. Hansard 10/24/35.

4. Lord Moran, *Churchill. Taken from the Diaries of Lord Moran: The Struggle for Survival, 1940–1965* (Boston, 1966), 692.

5. Macmillan, 386; Winston S. Churchill, *The Gathering Storm* (Boston, 1948), 133–134, 166–169.

6. Templewood Papers; Martin Gilbert, *Winston Churchill: The Wilderness Years* (London, 1981), 137.

7. Robert Rhodes James, *Churchill: A Study in Failure, 1900–1939* (New York, 1970), 286; *Times* 9/27/35.

8. Telford Taylor, *Munich: The Price of Peace* (New York, 1979), 233.

9. *Times* 10/4/35; Hansard 10/24/35.

10. Rhodes James, *Failure*, 283; Macmillan, 402; Elson et al., *Prelude*, 152; Earl of Avon, *Facing the Dictators* (Boston, 1962), 303.

11. *Paris-Soir* 12/9/35; Macmillan, 408; *Times* 12/18/35.

12. ChP 2/238.

13. Churchill, *Storm*, 183.

14. Vincent Sheean, *Between the Thunder and the Sun* (New York, 1943), 30, 42.

15. BSCP 12/30/35.

16. BSCP 1/7/36; Churchill, *Storm*, 181; BSCP 12/26/35.

17. Hansard 6/10/36; Telford Taylor, 232–233.

18. Telford Taylor, 169; *NYT* 11/2/36.

19. Templewood Papers; Avon, 355.

20. ChP 1/284.

21. Gilbert, *Wilderness*, 145; Harold Nicolson, *Diaries and Letters*, edited by Nigel Nicolson, 3 vols. (London, 1966), I, 228; WSC V, 709.

22. CAB 21/424; Templewood Papers; ChP 2/251.

23. BSCP 2/21/36, 2/27/36, 3/3/36.

24. Randolph Churchill Papers.

25. BSCP 1/8/36, 1/15/36; WM/Malcolm MacDonald, 11/6/80.

26. Beaverbrook Papers; ChP 2/28.
27. ChP 2/251; *Edinburgh Evening News* 2/13/36.
28. *Time* 3/16/36.
29. White Papers Cmd. 5107; WSC V, 711-712, 727; Hansard 3/10/36; A. J. P. Taylor, *Origins of the Second World War* (New York, 1961), 117.
30. Hansard 3/10/36; Churchill, *Storm*, 190.
31. Churchill, *Storm*, 191-192; *NYT* 5/22/35.
32. BSCP 1/17/36.
33. William L. Shirer, *The Collapse of the Third Republic* (New York, 1969), 251-252; General Maurice Gustave Gamelin, *Servir*, 3 vols. (Paris, 1947), II, 194-195; *Événements*, I, 138.
34. André François-Poncet, *The Fateful Years: Memoirs of a French Ambassador in Berlin 1931-1938* (New York, 1949), 188-189; ND C-159; William L. Shirer, *The Rise and Fall of the Third Reich: A History of Nazi Germany* (New York, 1960), 288, 291.
35. Shirer, *Collapse*, 253.
36. Shirer, *Collapse*, 250; Avon, 373, 376.
37. Avon, 373-376.
38. *Time* 3/16/36.
39. William L. Shirer, *Berlin Diary* (New York, 1941), 52-53.
40. Telford Taylor, 99-100; *NYT* 3/8/36.
41. Shirer, *Berlin Diary*, 51-54.
42. DGFP series D, vol. XI, no. 411.
43. Paul Schmidt, *Statist auf diplomatischer Buehne 1923-1945* (Bonn, 1949), 320.
44. Shirer, *Rise and Fall*, 294; TMWC XV, 352.
45. François-Poncet, *Fateful Years*, 192-193.
46. *NYT* 3/8/36.
47. *Événements*, III, 722.
48. *Événements*, I, 157-158; Gamelin, II, 212-218; Shirer, *Berlin Diary*, 49-50; *Événements*, I, 201; François-Poncet, *Fateful Years*, 190, 194-195.
49. Telford Taylor, 135.
50. Churchill, *Storm*, 193; *Événements*, I, 20.
51. DDF, I, Doc. No. 301, 413-414; I, Doc. No. 316, 426-427.
52. Avon, 385.
53. Avon, 388, 387.
54. *Événements*, III, 591-592.
55. *Times* 3/9/36.
56. Thomas Jones, *A Diary with Letters, 1931-1950* (Oxford, 1954), 180; Nicolson, I, 248-249.
57. Hansard 3/9/36.
58. Avon, 394.
59. Pierre-Etienne Flandin, *Politique française 1919-1940* (Paris, 1947), 202-204, 207-208.
60. Gilbert, *Wilderness*, 148-149; CAB 23/83.
61. CAB 23/83.
62. Shirer, *Rise and Fall*, 779, 828.
63. Churchill, *Storm*, 192-193.
64. Hansard 3/36.
65. N. Chamberlain Papers, diary; Hansard 3/36; *Evening Standard*.
66. WSC V, 712-713; Churchill, *Storm*, 195.
67. Foreign Office Affairs Comm. minutes; PrP 1/194.
68. N. Chamberlain Papers, diary, 3/12/36; WM/R. A. Butler, 12/5/80.
69. Gilbert, *Wilderness*, 152-153.
70. Gilbert, *Wilderness*, 152-153.
71. Churchill, *Storm*, 196.
72. Nicolson, ed., *Diaries and Letters*, I, 249-250.
73. Churchill, *Storm*, 195-196.
74. Churchill, *Storm*, 198, 197; Flandin, as quoted in Shirer, *Collapse*, 277; Shirer, *Berlin Diary*, 55; WM/William L. Shirer, 7/5/83; *NYT* 3/20/36.
75. Hansard 3/26/36.
76. Macmillan, 291; Elizabeth Longford, *Winston Churchill: A Pictorial Life Story* (Chicago, 1974), 84.
77. ChP 2/252.
78. Martin Gilbert and Richard Gott, *The Appeasers* (Boston, 1963), 48.
79. Alistair Horne, *To Lose a Battle* (Boston, 1969), 41.
80. Hansard 4/6/36.

81. Hansard 3/26/36; WM/Harold Macmillan, 12/4/80.

82. NCA, VII, 890; ND I-150.

83. Lord Vansittart, *The Mist Procession* (London, 1958), 497, 499; Gilbert, *Wilderness*, 268; Churchill, *Storm*, 152–153.

84. WSC V, 833–834.

85. Churchill, *Storm*, 198.

86. Churchill, *Storm*, 200.

87. Gilbert, *Wilderness*, 146; BSCP.

88. Sir Keith Feiling, *The Life of Neville Chamberlain* (London, 1946), 278.

89. Macmillan, 431; Iain Macleod, *Neville Chamberlain* (London, 1961), 193; Gilbert, *Wilderness*, 146.

90. Feiling, 278.

91. Feiling, cited by Churchill, *Storm*, 200; Macleod, 193; Brian Gardner, *Churchill in Power: As Seen by His Contemporaries* (Boston, 1970), 5.

92. Macmillan, 432; Macleod, 193; Robert Rhodes James, *Memoirs* (New York, 1970), 410; *Times* 3/16/36; Inskip, quoted in Gilbert and Gott, 365.

93. Churchill, *Storm*, 200.

94. Gardner, 5; Churchill, *Storm*, 200; Macmillan, 432; WM/Lord Geoffrey Lloyd, 11/27/80; ChP 2/330.

95. Churchill, *Storm*, 201; Gardner, 5; *Evening Standard* 5/4/36.

96. Hansard 3/26/36.

97. ChP 2/268.

98. Hansard 7/20/36; Nicolson, I, 269.

99. Hansard 4/23/36.

100. *Glasgow Forward* 10/3/36; *Times* 10/6/36.

101. *Times* 10/9/36. Ibarruri (born 1895) was still alive in 1988.

102. Hugh Dalton, *Memoirs, 1931–1945: The Fateful Years* (London, 1957), 97–104.

103. Peter Stansky and William Abrahams, *Journey to the Frontier. Julian Bell and John Cornford: Their Lives and the 1930s* (London, 1966), 315–316, 387, 390.

104. Macmillan, 436; WM/Macmillan; A. J. P. Taylor, *Origins*, 395; Wm/ A. J. P. Taylor, 12/1/80.

105. Telford Taylor, 538; Nicolson, I, 270; Avon, 453.

106. Macmillan, 438; Foreign Relations of the U.S., 1938, I.

107. Telford Taylor, 286.

108. Churchill, *Storm*, 214; *Evening Standard* 8/10/36.

109. Macmillan, 435.

110. Hansard 2/12/33.

111. Sheean, 59–60.

112. WM/Macmillan; Churchill, *Storm*, 144.

113. *Daily Telegraph* 12/30/38, 4/20/39; Hansard 4/14/37.

114. ChP 2/266.

115. PrP 1/193.

116. Jones, 233; Gilbert, *Wilderness*, 160–161.

117. Gilbert, *Wilderness*, 160–161; ChP 2/356.

118. Jones, 191.

119. CAB 23/86.

120. Alfred Duff Cooper, *Old Men Forget* (New York, 1954), 220.

121. ChP 2/271.

122. Hansard 11/11/36; Sir John Wheeler-Bennett, ed., *Action This Day: Memoirs* by Lord Normanbrook, John Colville, Sir John Martin, Sir Ian Jacobs, Lord Bridges, Sir Leslie Rowan (London, 1968), 242–243.

123. Hansard 11/12/36.

124. Hansard 11/12/36.

125. Nicolson, I, 278.

126. Hansard 11/12/36.

127. Nicolson, I, 278–279.

128. Hansard 11/12/36.

129. *Times* 11/1/35.

130. Hansard 11/12/36.

131. ChP 2/267; Churchill, *Storm*, 216.

132. Macmillan, 400; WM/Macmillan; Telford Taylor, 252–253, 254.

133. Telford Taylor, 535.

134. Eugen Spier, *Focus* (London, 1963), 9, 25; Gilbert, *Wilderness*, 153.

135. Gilbert, *Wilderness*, 156, 157, 158.

136. Winston S. Churchill, *While England Slept* (London, 1938), 302–303; ChP 2/283.

137. Churchill, *Storm*, 217; *Daily Telegraph* 3/1/65.

138. *Daily Telegraph* 3/1/65; Walter M. Citrine, *Citrine; Men and Work, An Autobiography* (London, 1964), 357.

139. Citrine, 357; *Daily Telegraph* 3/1/65.

140. Churchill, *Storm*, 217; *Daily Telegraph* 3/1/65.

141. Churchill, *Storm*, 217–218.

142. Macmillan, 441; WM/Macmillan; WM/ Lord Strauss, 10/13/80.

143. *Daily Telegraph* 3/1/65.

144. Kay Halle, *The Irrepressible Churchill: A Treasury of Winston Churchill's Wit* (New York, 1967), 132; WM, private information.

145. Hansard 6/28/1894.

146. WM/Anita Leslie, 10/1/84.

147. Duke of Windsor, *A King's Story: Memoirs of the Duke of Windsor* (New York, 1947), 237.

148. Francis F. Beirne, *Amiable Baltimoreans* (New York, 1951), 297, 119.

149. Robert Keith Middlemas and John Barnes, *Baldwin* (London, 1969), 280; Lord Birkenhead, *The Life of Walter Monckton of Trenchley* (London, 1969), 123.

150. ChP 2/264.

151. Lord Birkenhead, *Monckton*, 130; ChP 2/264.

152. ChP 2/264.

153. *NYT* 10/4/36, 10/15/36, 11/18/36; Telford Taylor, 541.

154. Macmillan, 440; WM/Macmillan.

155. Lord Beaverbrook, *The Abdication of King Edward VIII* (London, 1966), 37; WM/Lady Diana Cooper, 10/20/80.

156. ChP 2/264.

157. Middlemas and Barnes, 999; Gilbert, *Wilderness*, 169.

158. ChP 2/264; Kenneth Young, *Churchill and Beaverbrook: A Study in Friendship and Politics* (London, 1966), 123.

159. Macmillan, 440; WM/Macmillan.

160. *Times* 12/3/36; Duke of Windsor, 358.

161. Citrine, 328.

162. Mary Soames, *Clementine Churchill: The Biography of a Marriage* (Boston, 1979), 359; Telford Taylor, 542;

163. Nicolson, I, 282; Lord Moran, *Churchill*, 207.

163. *Daily Telegraph* 3/1/65; Hansard 12/9/36.

164. WSC V, 814; Channon Papers.

165. ChP 2/264; Duke of Windsor, 381.

166. *Times* 12/6/36.

167. WM/Lloyd; Walter Monckton, quoted in WSC V, 820; WSC V, 820; Boothby Papers 12/11/36.

168. WM/Lord Boothby, 10/16/80.

169. WM/Boothby; Nicolson, ed., *Diaries and Letters*, I, 283–284.

170. Boothby Papers; WM/Macmillan; WM/Boothby; WM/Lloyd; Macmillan, 441; WSC V, 821; Hansard 12/7/36.

171. Hansard 12/7/36; Nicolson, I, 284; Churchill, *Storm*, 218–219; WSC V, 822.

172. WM/Boothby.

173. Hansard 12/11/36.

174. Nicolson, I, 286; *Evening Standard* 12/28/36; Amery Papers.

175. Duke of Windsor, 407; ChP 2/264.

176. WM/Sir William Deakin, 10/5/80; Churchill, *Storm*, 219.

177. *Daily Telegraph* 3/1/65; Macmillan, 441.

178. ChP 2/264.

179. Soames, 360; ChP 2/264.

180. Macmillan, 441; Nicolson, I, 289, 284.

181. Young, 123; Bernard Baruch, "A Birthday Letter," Sir James Marchant, ed., *Winston Spencer Churchill: Servant of Crown and Commonwealth* (London, 1954), 166; ChP 2/312.

182. WSC V, 835–836 fn; Hankey Papers.

183. ChP 2/306; WSC V, 849–850.

184. Soames, 361 fn; Roberts Papers.

185. CAB 23/87.

UNDERTOW

1. WM/Virginia Cowles, 10/15/80; Virginia Cowles, *Winston Churchill: The Era and the Man* (New York, 1953), 307; Henry Pelling, *Winston Churchill* (New York, 1971), 410.

2. Winston S. Churchill, *The Gathering Storm* (Boston, 1948), 220; Harold Nicolson, *Diaries and Letters, 1930–1962*, edited by Nigel Nicolson, 3 vols. (London, 1966), I, 301; Lord Halifax, *Fullness of Days* (England, 1957), 182–183; Kay Halle, *The Irrepressible Churchill: A Treasury of Winston Churchill's Wit* (New York, 1967), 135.

3. Churchill, *Storm*, 221–222; Harold Macmillan, *Winds of Change* (London, 1966), 467.

4. L. S. Amery, *My Political Life*, 3 vols. (London, 1955), III, 226; Thomas Jones, *A Diary with Letters, 1931–1950* (Oxford, 1954), 350; Viscount Templewood, *Nine Troubled Years* (London, 1954), 257.

5. *NYT* 11/19/37; Martin Gilbert, *Winston Churchill: The Wilderness Years* (London, 1981), 210; Ivone Kirkpatrick, *The Inner Circle* (London, 1959), 97.

6. Hansard 12/21/37; Gilbert, *Wilderness*, 210–211.

7. Templewood Papers.

8. ChP 2/341, 2/328.

9. A. Chamberlain Papers.

10. Gilbert, *Wilderness*, 210; W. J. Brown, *So Far* (London, 1953), in Martin Gilbert and Richard Gott, *The Appeasers* (Boston, 1963), 377.

11. WM/Sir John Colville, 10/8/80; *Times* 6/1/37; Hansard 5/31/37; Channon Papers.

12. Nicolson, I, 328.

13. J. C. W. Reith, *Into the Wind* (London, 1949), 307–308.

14. CAB 27/623; PrP 1/27/38.

15. Churchill, *Storm*, 222–223; Earl of Avon, *Facing the Dictators* (Boston, 1965), 587–588.

16. R. W. Seton-Watson, *Britain and the Dictators* (Cambridge, 1938), 77; *Times* 10/28/37.

17. DGFP series D, vol. I, nos. 108, 104.

18. DGFP series D, vol. I, no. 131.

19. DGFP series D, vol. I, nos. 138, 148.

20. DGFP series D, vol. I no. 40; Sir Nevile Henderson, *Failure of a Mission: Berlin 1937–1939* (New York, 1940), 119.

21. *NYT* 7/12/36.

22. TWC XII, 761–764; Kurt von Schuschnigg, *Ein Requiem in Rot-Weiss-Rot* (Zurich, 1946), 109–111.

23. TWC XII, 761–764; NCA III, 409–413, NCA III, S. 690–693; NCA III, S. 716–717; NCA VII, S. 300; NCA V, S. 378; Paul Schmidt, *Statist auf diplomatischer Buehne, 1923–1945* (Bonn, 1949), 449.

24. Halle, 138; CAB 23/92.

25. Churchill, *Storm*, 251; David Dilks, ed., *The Diaries of Sir Alexander Cadogan O.M. 1938–1945* (New York, 1972), quoted in Telford Taylor, *Munich: The Price of Peace* (New York, 1979), 767 fn; Avon, 626.

26. Churchill, *Storm*, 254–255.

27. DDF-2e-V, no. 429; DDF-2e-VI, nos. 249, 482, 465; DDF-2e-VII, nos. 28, 137, 198.

28. Robert Rhodes James, *Anthony Eden* (London, 1986), 192–193; Telford Taylor, 566.

29. Rhodes James, *Eden*, 193–195, *Times* 2/14/38.

30. DGFP series D, vol. I, nos. 128, 750.

31. A. L. Rowse, *All Souls and Appeasement* (London, 1961), 28.

32. Churchill, *Storm*, 257–258.

33. Hansard 2/21/38.

34. Hansard 2/22/38.

35. WM/Kay Halle, 8/6/80; Sir John Colville, *The Churchillians* (London, 1981), 24; Harold Balfour, *Wings over Westminster* (London, 1973), 230; Mary Soames, *Clementine Churchill: The Biography of a Marriage* (Boston, 1979), 24.

36. Colville, *Churchillians*, 24; ChP 1/325.

37. WM/Colville; WM/Pamela Harriman, 8/22/80; Soames, 309.

38. Soames, 321–325; WM/Pamela Harriman; ChP 8/531.

39. WM/Lady Soames, 10/9/80, 6/25/85; Colville, *Churchillians*, 565; Soames, 325–326; BSCP 1/11/36.

40. Soames, 303.

41. ChP 1/344.
42. ChP 1/344.
43. WM/Lady Soames, 10/9/80; Soames, 339.
44. ChP 8/315.
45. Soames, 365, 369, 326.
46. Soames, 343–344.
47. WSC V, 589; Soames, 352–353.
48. Second Earl of Birkenhead, *The Professor and the Prime Minister* (Boston, 1962), 442; BSCP 1/1/35.
49. Soames, 345.
50. Soames, 345.
51. Soames, 347.
52. Soames, 349.
53. Willi Kerr, *Times Literary Supplement*.
54. Soames, 351, 354–355.
55. Soames, 356; WSC V, 933 fn; Gilbert, *Wilderness*, 209; ChP 8/551, 1/300.
56. William L. Shirer, *20th Century Journey: The Nightmare Years 1930–1940. A Memoir of the Life and the Times* (Boston, 1984), 311.
57. *Time* 2/13/39; Soames, 361.
58. Churchill, *Storm*, 222–224.
59. Churchill, *Storm*, 222–224.
60. ChP 2/303, 2/327.
61. Churchill, *Storm*, 236–237, WSC V, 853.
62. ChP 8/599.
63. ChP 2/304, 9/129.
64. Gilbert, *Wilderness*, 182–184; CAB 21/626; Hankey Papers.
65. ChP 2/304.
66. Churchill, *Storm*, 241; Avon, 447–448.
67. Gilbert and Gott, 69.
68. Dirksen Papers, vol. II. Appendix; DGFP series D, vol. I, nos. 95, 101; ChP 2/299, 2/302; Phipps Papers; Churchill, *Storm*, 241.
69. Quickswood Papers.
70. Hansard 6/30/38; WSC V, 952; John Harvey, ed., *The Diplomatic Diaries of Oliver Harvey* (London, 1970), 7/2/38.
71. Hankey Papers.
72. TMWC XXV, 402–13 (in German); DGFP series D, vol. I, nos. 29–39; William L. Shirer, *The Rise and Fall of the Third Reich: A History of Nazi Germany* (New York, 1960), 307.
73. DGFP series D, vol. II, no. 21.
74. Franz von Papen, *Der Wahrheit eine Gasse* (Munich, 1952), 456; DDF-2e-I, doc. 425, 549–552; Avon, 400, 402, 403; *Événements*, I, 157–158; Bernd Gisevius, *Bis zum bittern Ende* (Zurich, 1946), 229.
75. *Berliner Tageblatt* 2/21/38, and from Shirer's notes at the time.
76. *Evening Standard* 4/4/38; ChP 2/328.
77. ChP 2/328.
78. TMWC XVI, 193; WM/William L. Shirer, 7/20/80; Henderson, 120; Hansard 3/2/38.
79. *NYT* 2/25/38.
80. *Frankfurter Zeitung* 3/4/38.
81. ChP 2/328; Nicolson, I, 330.
82. Shirer, *Rise and Fall*, 335, 336, 343.
83. Henderson, 124.
84. WSC V, 910; DGFP series D, vol. I, no. 146.
85. Jones, 208.
86. Jones, 175.
87. Jones, 395–396.
88. Churchill, *Storm*, 271.
89. Winston S. Churchill, *The Grand Alliance* (Boston, 1950).
90. DGFP series D, vol. I, 273–275; Churchill, *Storm*, 271–272.
91. DGFP series D, vol. I, 273–275.
92. DBFP series D, vol. I, nos. 138–151, 578.
93. WSC V, 911.
94. Henderson, 124–125.
95. Nicolson, I, 330–331; Henderson, 311.
96. CAB 23/91; Templewood Papers.
97. PrP 1/238; CAB 23/91.
98. ChP 2/328; Shirer, *Rise and Fall*, 353.
99. WM/Shirer; Shirer, *Rise and Fall*, 351.
100. Winston S. Churchill, *Step by Step: 1936–1939 Articles* (London, 1939), 227; *NYT* 5/5/45; ChP 2/328.
101. DGFP series D, vol. II, no. 278.
102. NCA, I, 501–502.
103. Nicolson, I, 331; Hansard 3/14/38.
104. Dilks, ed., 3/12/38.

105. Dilks, ed., 2/12/38, 4/22/38.

106. Nicolson, I, 331; DBFP series 3, vol. I, no. 57.

107. Hansard 3/14/38.

108. Hansard 3/14/38.

109. Hansard 3/14/38; WM/Lord Boothby, 10/16/80.

110. Hansard 3/14/38.

111. NYT 3/18/38; DBFP series 3, vol. I, no. 107.

112. DBFP series 3, vol. I, no. 107; Dirksen Papers.

113. Nicolson, I, 331; Lord Boothby, *Recollections of a Rebel* (London, 1978), 134–135; WM/Boothby.

114. *Star* 3/15/35; Liddell Hart Memorandum, "Defence of Britain," 63–74, CAB 23/93.

115. Alfred Duff Cooper, *Old Men Forget* (New York, 1954), 218.

116. DGFP series D, vol II.

117. *Frankfurter Zeitung* 2/21/38.

118. Balfour Papers.

119. Hansard 5/31/35.

120. ChP 2/266.

121. ChP 2/307, 2/299.

122. CAB 23/93.

123. ChP 2/341.

124. WM/Shirer.

125. DBFP series 3, vol. I, no. 86; Foreign Office Studies, C 1865/132/18.

126. Foreign Office Studies, C 1865/132/18.

127. Foreign Office Studies, C 1865/132/18; Dilks, ed., 63; Sir Keith Feiling, *The Life of Neville Chamberlain* (London, 1946), 347–348; Robert Keith Middlemas and John Barnes, *Baldwin* (London, 1969), 188; DGFP series D, vol. II, 776.

128. *Times* 3/19/38. ChP 2/328.

129. *Evening Standard* 3/18/38.

130. CAB 53/27; Foreign Policy Committee Meeting 3/21/38.

131. CAB 27/623; CAB 27/627; Feiling, 347–348.

132. Duff Cooper, 218.

133. Duff Cooper, 218.

134. DBFP series 3, vol. I, nos. 106–110, 112, 116; CAB 27/623; Hansard 3/24/38.

135. WM/Cowles; Cowles, 308–309; Middlemas and Barnes, 206–207; Hansard 3/24/38.

136. Hansard 3/24/38 (verse form added).

137. Hansard 3/24/38.

138. WM/Cowles; Cowles, 308–309; Middlemas and Barnes, 206–207; Dilks, ed., 3/26/38.

139. ChP 8/600.

140. WSC V, 835.

141. BSCP 2/2/37.

142. BSCP 2/2/37.

143. BSCP 4/8/37.

144. *Daily Express* 3/17/38; *Times* 4/1/38, 4/2/38.

145. Camrose Papers.

146. ChP 1/328.

147. Lord Vansittart, *The Mist Procession* (London, 1958), 477, 499; ChP 1/328.

148. J. Baker White, *True Blue* (London, 1970), 161.

149. ChP 1/323.

150. Frederick Woods, *A Bibliography of the Works of Sir Winston Churchill KG, OM, CH* (London, 1963), 75–79, 83, 221–268; ChP 8/596.

151. Soames, 366; ChP 8/626; BSCP 2/2/37.

152. Robert Rhodes James, *Churchill: A Study in Failure, 1900–1939* (London, 1970), 340.

153. WM/John Grigg, 10/15/80; Rhodes James, *Failure*, 340.

154. WM/Lady Soames; WM/Lord Geoffrey Head, 11/19/80.

155. Nicolson, I, 347.

156. Shirer, *Rise and Fall*, 430–433.

157. DGFP series D, vol. II, no. 151.

158. Hansard 3/17/38; *NYT* 3/14/38.

159. Macmillan, 495.

160. *Observer* 11/29/37; Kingsley Martin, *Editor* (London, 1968), 50; Hugh Dalton, *Memoirs, 1931–1945: The Fateful Years* (London, 1957), 162.

161. *Times* 2/27/37, 6/23/37.

162. *NYT* 4/24/38; DGFP series D, vol.

II, nos. 197–198; ND 388-PS item 2.

163. DBFP series 3, vol I, no. 158.
164. DBFP series 3, vol. I, no. 164; Templewood Papers.
165. *Le Temps* 4/12/38; Telford Taylor, 778.
166. WM/Harold Macmillan, 12/4/80; Macmillan, 495–496.
167. Isaiah Berlin, *Mr. Churchill in 1940* (Boston, 1964), 16–17.
168. DBFP series 3, vol. I, no. 98.
169. DBFP series 3, vol. II, no. 337.
170. Telford Taylor, 638; Lieutenant General Sir Henry Pownall, *Chief of Staff*, vol. 1, *1933–40*, edited by Brian Bond (London, 1972), 80.
171. Churchill, *Storm*, 231–232.
172. Balfour, 99–110; Nicolson, I, 341–342.
173. Telford Taylor, 759; Anne Morrow Lindbergh, *The Flower and the Nettle: Diaries and Letters of Anne Morrow Lindbergh 1936–1939* (New York, 1976), 100; Charles A. Lindbergh, *The Wartime Journals of Charles A. Lindbergh* (New York, 1970), 22.
174. Charles Lindbergh, 73.
175. Jones, 409–411.
176. Telford Taylor, 851; Shirer, *Nightmare Years*, 238.
177. DBFP series 3, vol. I, nos. 171, 170.
178. DGFP series D, vol. II, no. 154.
179. *Times* 6/3/38; Shirer, *Rise and Fall*, 376.
180. ChP 2/329.
181. DBFP series 3, vol. I, no. 219, app. III.
182. Foreign Office Papers 271/1719; ChP 2/329.
183. ChP 2/340.
184. ChP 2/340; Churchill, *Storm*, 286; *Times* 5/17/38.
185. DGFP series D, vol. II, no. 13.
186. DBFP series 3, vol. I.
187. DBFP series 3, vol. I; DGFP series D, vol. II.
188. Telford Taylor, 392–393.
189. Telford Taylor, 655.
190. H. L. Mencken, *On Being an American*, 1923; NCA, V, 743–744.

191. *Daily Telegraph* 7/6/38, 7/26/38; ChP 2/330.
192. ChP 2/340, 2/331.
193. DBFP series 3, vol. II, app. IV.
194. ND II, 10.
195. Helmuth Groscurth, *Tagebücher eines Abwehroffiziers 1938–1940*, edited by Helmut Krausnick and Harold Deutsch (Stuttgart, 1970), 9/2/38; 9/4/38.
196. Shirer, *Rise and Fall*, 426.
197. TMWC X, 509.
198. Hermann Förtsch, *Schuld und Verhangnis* (Stuttgart, 1951), 173–174.
199. Dalton, 182.
200. ChP 2/331.
201. PrP 1/266.
202. Churchill, *Storm*, 293–294.
203. PrP 1/265.
204. Telford Taylor, 670; Dilks, ed., 95.
205. CAB 23/95.
206. PrP 1/266.
207. PrP 1/266.
208. Feiling, 357.
209. DGFP series D, vol. II, no. 42.
210. WSC V, 969; *Times* 9/7/38.
211. ChP 2/331.
212. Dalton, 174–175.
213. Dilks, ed., 95.
214. DBFP series 3, vol. II, nos. 775, 815, 818, 819, 823, 825; Dilks, ed., 96; Gilbert and Gott, 138; Harvey, 172–173.
215. DBFP series 3, vol. II, no. 482.
216. *Standard* 9/13/38; CAB 23/95.
217. Telford Taylor, 676–677.
218. DBFP series 3, vol. II, no. 862.
219. Harvey, 9/15/38; Feiling, 333; ChP 2/331.
220. WM/R. A. Butler 12/5/80; DBFP series 3, vol. I, no. 120; ChP 1/325.
221. WM/Macmillan.
222. Sir John Wheeler-Bennett, *Munich: Prologue to Tragedy* (New York, 1948), 108; Feiling, 366.
223. N. Chamberlain Papers, in Feiling, 366.
224. Shirer, *Rise and Fall*, 335, 386; DGFP series D, vol. II, no. 487.
225. ChP 2/343; N. Chamberlain Papers.
226. Duff Cooper, 229; CAB 23/95.

227. DBFP series 3, vol. II, no. 907; *Le Populaire* 9/20/38.

228. ChP 8/612; DBFP series 3, vol. II, no. 907.

229. DBFP series 3, vol. II, nos. 928, 951, 952, 961.

230. *Times* 9/20/38; DBFP series 3, vol. II, no. 978.

231. DBFP series 3, vol. II, no. 973.

232. Dalton, 196.

233. Foreign Relations of the U.S., 1938, III.

234. DBFP series 3, vol. II, no. 1008.

235. ChP 2/331.

236. ChP 4/92.

237. ChP 9/132.

238. Nicolson, I, 363–364.

239. Telford Taylor, 806 fn; DBFP series 3, vol. II, no. 1033.

240. DBFP series 3, vol. II, no. 1076.

241. DBFP series 3, vol. II, no. 1043.

242. DBFP series 3, vol. II, no. 1058.

243. DBFP series 3, vol. II, nos. 463, 773, 499–508.

244. Paul Schmidt, *Hitler's Interpreter* (New York, 1951), 95–102; Henderson, 156–162; *Times* 9/24/38.

245. Dilks, ed., 9/24/38.

246. CAB 23/95, Duff Cooper, 234.

247. Duff Cooper, 234; A. J. P. Taylor, *Origins of the Second World War* (New York, 1961), 177.

248. DBFP series 3, vol. II, no. 1092.

249. Shirer, *Berlin Diary*, 141–142.

250. *NYT* 9/28/38.

251. WM/Macmillan; Macmillan, 507.

252. Macmillan, 505, 507; WM/Macmillan; E. S. Turner, *The Phoney War* (London, 1961), 55.

253. DBFP series 3, vol. II, no. 1231.

254. *Times* 9/29/38; Kirkpatrick, 124–125; Nicolson, I, 370–371; Macmillan, 506.

255. Macmillan, 506; WM/Macmillan.

256. Shirer, *Rise and Fall*, 411; Telford Taylor, 897.

257. Templewood Papers; Peterpaul Donat, "*Das Munchener Abkommen vom 29. September 1938,*" *Deutsches Adelsblatt* no. 6 (1971), 82; Brian Gardner, *Churchill in Power: As Seen by his Contemporaries* (Boston, 1970) 11.

258. WM/Walter Lippmann, 10/10/64.

259. Hansard 10/3/38.

260. *Daily Telegraph* 3/1/65.

261. Nicolson, I, 372.

262. WSC V, 988.

263. Telford Taylor, 50–53.

264. Count Galeazzo Ciano, *The Ciano Diaries, 1939–1943,* edited by Hugh Wilson (New York, 1946), 166.

265. DBFP series 3, vol. II, no. 1210.

266. Feiling, 376.

267. Telford Taylor, 48–49.

268. Colin Coote, *A Companion of Honour: The Story of Walter Elliot* (London, 1965), 174.

269. Coote, 174.

270. Coote, 174; Gardner, 13.

271. Telford Taylor, 49.

272. WM/Shirer; Boothby, *Rebel,* 130.

273. G. E. R. Gedye, *Fallen Bastions* (London, 1939), 488–489; Churchill, *Storm,* 322.

274. International Military Tribunal, X, 572, 600, 772; Churchill, *Storm,* 302.

275. IMT, XIII, S. 4; ND 739–PS.

276. Amery, III, 337; J. P. Sartre, *The Reprieve* (London, 1947), 398.

277. Gilbert and Gott, 179; Middlemas and Barnes, 179; Telford Taylor, 64–65.

278. Shirer, *Berlin Diary,* 147–148; N. Chamberlain Papers.

279. Feiling, 376.

280. Nicolson, I, 371.

281. Halifax, 200; WM/Lord Lloyd, 11/27/80.

282. Rhodes James, *Failure,* 373; Duff Cooper, 243; ChP 2/350; Churchill, *Storm,* 234.

VORTEX

1. ChP 2/350; WSC V, 991–992.

2. Hugh Dalton, *Memoirs, 1931–1945: The Fateful Years* (London, 1957), 198; WM/ Malcolm MacDonald, 11/6/80; Hansard 11/24/38.

3. Hansard 10/3/38.

4. John Evelyn Wrench, *Geoffrey Dawson and Our Times* (London, 1955), 378.

5. CAB 23/95; Hansard 10/3/38.

6. Hansard 10/3/38.

7. Harold Nicolson, *Diaries and Letters, 1930–1962*, edited by Nigel Nicolson, 3 vols. (London, 1966), I, 374.

8. Hansard 10/3/38.

9. Hansard 10/5/38.

10. Hansard 10/5/38.

11. Brian Gardner, *Churchill in Power: As Seen by His Contemporaries* (Boston, 1970), 11; Robert Rhodes James, *Churchill: A Study in Failure, 1900–1939* (London, 1970), 373.

12. WM/Lady Soames, 10/9/80; Mary Soames, *Clementine Churchill: The Biography of a Marriage* (Boston, 1979), 363; WM/Lady Diana Cooper, 10/20/80.

13. WM/Harold Macmillan, 12/4/80; Harold Macmillan, *Winds of Change, 1914–1939* (London, 1966), 485; B. H. Liddell Hart, *The Memoirs of Captain Liddell Hart*, 2 vols. (London, 1965), II, 211.

14. Alfred Duff Cooper, *Old Men Forget* (London, 1953), 232.

15. WM/Macmillan; Nicolson, I, 377–378.

16. WM/Lady Soames.

17. Hansard, 10/6/38; ChP 2/332.

18. ChP 2/336, 2/332; WSC V, 1006.

19. A. J. P. Taylor, *The Origins of the Second World War* (New York, 1962), 123, 96, 116; Martin Gilbert, *Churchill's Political Philosophy* (Oxford, 1981), 910.

20. Sir Keith Feiling, *The Life of Neville Chamberlain* (London, 1946), 406; Dalton, 202.

21. Kenneth Young, *Churchill and Beaverbrook: A Study in Friendship and Politics* (New York, 1966), 128–129; WSC V, 1012.

22. WSC V, 1012, 1014–1015.

23. ChP 1/344.

24. Lord Strang, *Home and Abroad* (London, 1964), cited in Telford Taylor,

25. Kay Halle, *The Irrepressible Churchill: A Treasury of Winston Churchill's Wit* (New York, 1967), 140–141; Oliver Harvey, *The Diplomatic Diaries of Oliver Harvey 1937–1940*, edited by John Harvey (London, 1970), 12/25/38.

26. Hansard 11/17/38; WSCHCS 6046–6048.

27. WSCHCS 6046–6048.

28. Nicolson, I, 375–376; ChP 8/597.

29. DGFP series D, vol. IV, no. 249.

30. Nicolson, I, 384; CAB 23/97; Winston S. Churchill, *The Gathering Storm* (Boston, 1948), 329.

31. Churchill, *Storm*, 329–330.

32. Nicolson, I, 382.

33. WM/Grace Hamblin, 11/4/80; ChP 8/624.

34. Foreign Office Papers 371/22963.

35. Halle, 255.

36. *Daily Telegraph* 1/12/39.

37. Vincent Sheean, *Between the Thunder and the Sun* (New York, 1943), 73–74.

38. ChP 1/343; WM/Lady Diana Cooper; Virginia Cowles, *Winston Churchill: The Era and the Man* (New York, 1953), 307.

39. BSCP 1/8/39.

40. Perry Knowlton, Adam Deixel, and Iam Gonzales at Curtis Brown; ChP 1/344; WM/Lady Soames.

41. Soames, 364.

42. Soames, 367; BSCP 12/20/38.

43. ChP 2/378.

44. ChP 1/332; Soames, 368.

45. WSC V, 1044.

46. F. Nietzsche, *Beyond Good and Evil*, trans. Hellen Zimmern (London, 1923), IV, 146; *Frankfurter Zeitung* 11/5/38.

47. ChP 9/133; WM/A. J. P. Taylor, 12/1/80.

48. WSC V, 1043.

49. N. Chamberlain Papers.

50. WSC V, 1045.

51. Phyllis Moir, *I Was Winston*

Churchill's Private Secretary (New York, 1941), 100.

52. Martin Gilbert, *Winston Churchill: The Wilderness Years* (London, 1981), 248.

53. DGFP series D, vol. IV, nos. 55, 61; ChP 2/340.

54. ChP 3/12/39.

55. *NYT* 3/17/39.

56. William L. Shirer, *The Rise and Fall of the Third Reich: A History of Nazi Germany* (New York, 1960), 445–446.

57. Shirer, *Rise and Fall*, 445–446; Dalton, 226–227.

58. Martin Gilbert, *Sir Horace Rumbold: Portrait of a Diplomat* (London, 1973), 442.

59. Winston S. Churchill, *Step by Step: 1936–1939 Articles* (London, 1939), 302–303.

60. A. J. P. Taylor, 192; WM/A. J. P. Taylor; Rhodes James, *Failure*, 377.

61. Gardner, 9–10.

62. Hansard 3/15/39.

63. *Times* 3/18/39.

64. DGFP series D, vol. IV, no. 244.

65. Martin Gilbert and Richard Gott, *The Appeasers* (Boston, 1963), 209–210.

66. Hansard 5/26/39.

67. Hansard 5/26/39.

68. WM/Lord Boothby, 10/16/18; Hansard 5/26/39.

69. Gilbert and Gott, 212.

70. ChP 2/358.

71. ND USSR-172; ChP 8/628.

72. Hansard 3/18/39.

73. WSC V, 1069.

74. WSC V, 1070.

75. William L. Shirer, *The Collapse of the Third Republic* (New York, 1969), 418.

76. Gardner, 12.

77. N. Chamberlain Papers.

78. DBFP series 3, vol. IV, nos. 288, 298, 390, 397, 398, 395.

79. DBFP series 3, vol. IV, nos. 298, 390, 397, 398.

80. DBFP series 3, vol. IV, nos. 298, 390, 397, 398.

81. DBFP series 3, vol. IV, nos. 298, 390, 397, 398.

82. DBFP series 3, vol. IV, no. 395.

83. Leon Noël, *L'Agression allemande contre la Pologne* (Paris, 1946), 326 note 1.

84. Telford Taylor, 421; Churchill, *Storm*, 350.

85. DBFP series 3, vol. IV, no. 433.

86. DBFP series 3, vol. IV, nos. 433, 447; Józef Beck, *Final Report* (New York, 1957), 187–189.

87. Gilbert and Gott, 240; CAB 27/624; DBFP series 3, vol. IV, nos. 515, 516.

88. ChP 2/340.

89. Ian Colvin, *The Chamberlain Cabinet* (London, 1971), 194–198; Ian Colvin, *None So Blind* (New York, 1965), 298–311.

90. ND R-100, C-120.

91. Hansard, 3/31/39.

92. WM/Boothby; Lord Boothby, *Recollections of a Rebel* (London, 1978), 132; B. H. Liddell Hart, *History of the Second World War* (New York, 1971), 11; Alfred Duff Cooper, *The Second World War: First Phase* (New York, 1939), 320.

93. Churchill, *Storm*, 347; Hansard 4/3/39.

94. CAB 23/98; Liddell Hart, *Second World War*, 16.

95. Lord Halifax, *Fullness of Days* (London, 1957), 206.

96. Lord Vansittart, *The Mist Procession* (London, 1958), 430; Gilbert and Gott, 245.

97. DBFP series 3, vol. V, no. 207.

98. Churchill, *Storm*, 350, 352; Arthur Christiansen, *Headlines All My Life* (New York, 1962), 89.

99. Churchill, *Storm*, 350–351.

100. N. Chamberlain Papers.

101. Macmillan, 539; WM/Macmillan.

102. Templewood Papers.

103. N. Chamberlain Papers, diary; DBFP series 3, vol. III, nos. 477, 495, 496, 500, 502; Count Galeazzo Ciano, *The Ciano Diaries 1939–1943*, edited by

Hugh Wilson (New York, 1946), 1/11–14/39.

104. Hansard 4/3/39; *Times* 4/1/39.

105. N. Chamberlain Papers; Murray Papers; ChP 2/358.

106. Shirer, *Rise and Fall*, 341.

107. Gardner, 17.

108. Gilbert, *Political Philosophy*, 376.

109. Gilbert, *Wilderness*, 249; Reed Whittemore, "Churchill and the Limitations of Myth," *Yale Review*, Winter 1955.

110. WSC V, 1016.

111. Sir John Colville, *The Fringes of Power, 10 Downing Street Diaries, 1939–1955* (New York, 1985), 260, 264.

112. *Atlantic Monthly*, October 1940; *Spectator* 7/12/40; *Transcript* 9/26/40.

113. Gardner, 16, 17.

114. WM/Boothby; Lord Boothby, *Rebel*, 182; E. L. Spears, *Assignment to Catastrophe*, 2 vols. (New York, 1955), I, *Prelude to Dunkirk*, 38–39.

115. WM/MacDonald.

116. ChP 2/332.

117. CAB 27/624.

118. Hansard 11/18/38.

119. PrP 3/2/39.

120. PrP 1/358; Baruch Papers.

121. Nicolson, I, 398; ChP 2/360.

122. Nicolson, I, 398–399; *British Weekly* 4/27/39; Feiling, 386.

123. Feiling, 406; Nicolson, I, 399.

124. DGFP series D, vol. VI, no. 169; WM/R. A. Butler 12/5/80.

125. N. Chamberlain Papers.

126. Hansard 4/13/39.

127. Hansard 4/13/39.

128. Churchill, *Storm*, 355; *Frankfurter Zeitung*, 4/29/39.

129. ChP 2/322.

130. Churchill, *Storm*, 353.

131. *Daily Telegraph* 4/28/39; Hansard 4/27/39.

132. WSC V, 1065–1066; N. Chamberlain Papers.

133. *NYT* 5/23/39; Ironside Papers.

134. ChP 2/350, 8/264.

135. WSC V, 1068, 1080; WM/Butler.

136. WSC V, 1080, 1082, 1084.

137. ChP 2/371, 2/364, 8/628.

138. Viscount Templewood, *Nine Troubled Years* (London, 1954), 378; ChP 2/363.

139. Foreign Office Papers 371/22974.

140. Camrose Papers; Nicolson, I, 6/30/39.

141. Camrose Papers.

142. WSC V, 1086; N. Chamberlain Papers.

143. ChP 2/360, 2/343.

144. ChP 8/638.

145. ChP 8/217, 8/626.

146. Winston S. Churchill, *A History of the English-speaking Peoples*, 4 vols. (London, 1956–1958), I, 1.

147. ChP 2/302; BSCP 1/7/37.

148. ChP 1/325.

149. ChP 8/596, 8/597.

150. ChP 8/626.

151. WM/Hamblin; WM/Kathleen Hill, 11/4/80.

152. ChP 8/625.

153. Isaiah Berlin, *Mr. Churchill in 1940* (Boston, 1964), 9.

154. WM/A. J. P. Taylor.

155. ChP 8/626.

156. ChP 8/626.

157. ChP 8/626.

158. ChP 8/626.

159. N. Chamberlain Papers.

160. ChP 2/358.

161. Air Ministry Papers 19/26, 19/29.

162. *Yorkshire Post* 6/28/39; Hansard (Lords) 6/11/39.

163. ChP 2/359; Nicolson, I, 403.

164. Walter Lippmann notes, Lippmann Papers, as cited in WSC V, 1074–1075.

SURGE

1. Ironside Papers.

2. Ironside Papers.

3. PrP 1/332.

4. Ironside Papers.

5. Hansard 4/3/39.

6. *Daily Telegraph* 5/4/39.

7. Hansard 4/3/39.

8. *Sunday Express* 12/5/30; *Times* 1/21/27.

9. Hansard 4/3/39.

10. Keith Feiling, *The Life of Neville Chamberlain* (London, 1946), 603; Hansard 4/13/39.

11. DBFP series 5, vol. II, no. 1222, 623–624; Ivan Maisky, *The Origins of the Second World War*, broadcast talk, 1961, cited in Martin Gilbert and Richard Gott, *The Appeasers* (Boston, 1963), 31.

12. DBFP series 5, vol. II, no. 1221; DBFP series 5, vol. IV, no. 433; Hansard 3/23/39; WM/Lord Boothby, 10/16/80; Lord Boothby, *I Fight to Live* (London, 1947), 189.

13. Harold Nicolson, *Diaries and Letters, 1930–1962*, edited by Nigel Nicolson, 3 vols. (London, 1966), I, 394.

14. Nicolson, I, 391.

15. N. Chamberlain Papers.

16. Harold Macmillan, *Winds of Change* (London, 1966), 542.

17. Thomas Jones, *A Diary with Letters, 1931–1950* (Oxford, 1954), 418–419.

18. Hansard 4/13/39.

19. *Times* 4/16/39.

20. David Dilks, ed., *The Diaries of Sir Alexander Cadogan O.M. 1938–1945* (New York, 1972), 4/19/39; Lord Halifax, *Fullness of Days* (London, 1957), 206–207; DBFP series 3, vol. V, nos. 228, 229.

21. DBFP series 3, vol. I, no. 107.

22. WM/Harold Macmillan, 12/4/80; Macmillan, 542; Winston S. Churchill, *The Gathering Storm* (Boston, 1948), 365.

23. Jones, 418; *Le Monde* 3/28/39.

24. Dilks, ed., 175; CAB 23/98.

25. Jones, 210; CAB 27/624, 27/627.

26. CAB 27/624, 27/627.

27. Dilks, ed., 180; WM/Duncan Sandys, 11/7/80.

28. Churchill, *Storm*, 366.

29. Robert Coulondre, *De Staline à Hitler: Souvenirs de deux ambassades, 1936–1939* (Paris, 1950), 270;

Georges Bonnet, *De Munich à la guerre* (Paris, 1967), 184.

30. Telford Taylor, *Munich: The Price of Peace* (New York, 1979), 975; William L. Shirer, *The Collapse of the Third Republic* (New York, 1969), 428; Churchill, *Storm*, 366, 367; *Frankfurter Zeitung* 5/7/39.

31. Nicolson, I, 401; Churchill, *Storm*, 366.

32. *Daily Telegraph* 5/4/39.

33. Camrose Papers.

34. William L. Shirer, *The Rise and Fall of the Third Reich: A History of Nazi Germany* (New York, 1960), 481.

35. Churchill, *Storm*, 371, 373–374; Hansard 5/19/39; Feiling, 603.

36. Feiling, 603; ChP 2/332.

37. Hansard 5/19/39.

38. Hansard 5/19/39.

39. *Observer* 7/22/39.

40. Richard M. Watt, *Bitter Glory: Poland and Its Fate 1918–1939* (New York, 1974), 389–390; DBFP series 3, vol. VI, nos. 104–107; DGFP series D, vol. V, no. 13; Dilks, ed., 163–164; CAB 27/624.

41. Józef Beck, *Dernier Rapport: politique polonaise 1926–1939* (Neuchatel, 1951), 187–189; DBFP series 3, vol. IV, no. 518.

42. DGFP series D, vol. IV, no. 518.

43. DBFP series 3, vol. V, no. 163; vol. VI, no. 16.

44. *NYT* 4/29/39; Shirer, *Rise and Fall*, 455, 471.

45. NCA, VI, 916–928.

46. N. Chamberlain Papers; DGFP series D, vol. VII, no. 417.

47. DGFP series D, vol. IV, no. 513; vol. VII, no. 307, ND TC-73.

48. ChP 2/360.

49. ChP 2/367.

50. ChP 9/137.

51. ChP 4/19; *Yorkshire Post* 6/28/39; WSCHCP 6141–6142.

52. N. Chamberlain Papers.

53. DBFP series 3, vol. VI, nos. 289, 197, 198.

54. DBFP series 3, vol. VI, no. 212; Hansard 7/10/39.

55. N. Chamberlain Papers.

56. DBFP series 3, vol. VI, nos. 176, 222, 327; Gilbert and Gott, 256.

57. WM/Macmillan; Macmillan 542; DBFP series 3, vol. VI, no. 659.

58. N. Chamberlain papers.

59. *Times* 6/13/39; Churchill, *Storm*, 389; Nicolson, I, 404.

60. Churchill, *Storm*, 387–388.

61. DDF-2e-II, III, IV, V; Earl of Avon, *Facing the Dictators* (Boston, 1962), 547–548.

62. *Observer* 7/22/39.

63. WM/Boothby.

64. Templewood Papers; Churchill, *Storm*, 363.

65. *Pravda* 6/16/39; Churchill, *Storm*, 390, 365, 368.

66. Telford Taylor, 976; Dilks, ed., 189.

67. WM/Macmillan; Macmillan, 542.

68. Churchill, *Storm*, 363; Boothby, *I Fight to Live*, 189.

69. Shirer, *Collapse*, 428fn.

70. WM/Walter Lippmann, 10/10/64; "The Reminiscences of Walter Lippmann," 191–193, in Oral History Collection, Yale University Walter Lippmann Collection; Shirer, *Collapse*, 426.

71. *Le Livre Jaune Français. Documents diplomatiques, 1939–1940*, No. 120, 153–155.

72. Churchill, *Storm*, 367–370; DGFP series D, vol. VI, nos. 616–617.

73. Churchill, *Storm*, 393–394.

74. DGFP series D, vol. VI, no. 429.

75. ND 1526-PS, 084-PS, 288-P; *Nazi-Soviet Relations, 1939–1941. Documents from the Archives of the German Foreign Office* (Washington, 1948), 5–7, 8–9.

76. Shirer, *Rise and Fall*, 503.

77. DGFP series D, vol. VI, nos. 1033–1035.

78. Shirer, *Rise and Fall*, 673; DBFP, Appendix V, 763.

79. Shirer, *Collapse*, 454, 455–456; DBFP series 3, Appendix II, nos. 558–614; *Événements*, I, 39ff.

80. Shirer, *Collapse*, 454–456.

81. Shirer, *Rise and Fall*, 714.

82. Hansard 4/3/39.

83. DBFP series 3, vol. V, Appendix I (i); vol. VI, nos. 458, 460.

84. DBFP series 3, vol. VI, no. 461.

85. DBFP series 3, vol. VI, no. 585.

86. Shirer, *Collapse*, 451.

87. Several of the author's interviewees have cited WSC's quip about weekends.

88. Shirer, *Collapse*, 451–455.

89. DGFP series D, vol. VII, nos. 49, 58–59, nos. 13, 48.

90. Shirer, *Collapse*, 452.

91. ND 1618-PS; DGFP series D, vol. II, nos. 67–68.

92. DGFP series D, vol. VII, no. 75.

93. DGFP series D, vol. VII, no. 105.

94. Shirer, *Collapse*, 463; DGFP series D, vol. VII, no. 113.

95. DGFP series D, vol. VII, no. 125.

96. Shirer, *Collapse*, 465.

97. Churchill, *Storm*, 391, 380.

98. Bonnet, 301–302; General Maurice Gustave Gamelin, *Servir*, 3 vols. (Paris, 1946), I, 23–24.

99. DBFP series 3, no. 212; *Événements*, II (Docs.), 276–278; Bonnet, 305–308.

100. N. Chamberlain Papers.

101. Selborne Papers; Nicolson, I, 8/1/39; WSC V, 1095.

102. Nicolson, I, 407.

103. Hansard 8/2/39.

104. Hansard 8/2/39.

105. Nicolson, I, 407–408.

106. ChP 9/137.

107. ChP 9/137.

108. Jones, 419.

109. *Observer* 7/22/39.

110. DGFP series D, vol. VII, nos. 62–64.

111. ChP 2/365.

112. BSCP 8/14/39.

113. BSCP; E. L. Spears, *Assignment to Catastrophe*, 2 vols. (New York, 1955), I, 5.

114. Alistair Horne, *To Lose a Battle* (Boston, 1969), 29.

115. Spears, I, 9.

116. Spears, I, 10.

117. ChP 2/371.

118. ChP 2/371.

119. See Churchill, *Storm*, 474–475; ChP 2/371.

120. Shirer, *Collapse*, 186.

121. Spears, I, 9; Horne, 18; Churchill, *Storm*, 474; Simone de Beauvoir, *The Prime of Life*, trans. Peter Green (New York, 1962), 33.

122. Churchill, *Storm*, 474; Horne, 72.

123. Winston S. Churchill, *Their Finest Hour* (Boston, 1949), 36–37.

124. *News of the World* 4/24/38.

125. B. H. Liddell Hart, *The Memoirs of Captain Liddell Hart*, 2 vols. (London, 1965), I, 373.

126. Spears, I, 7.

127. WM/Lady Soames, 10/9/80; Consuelo Balsan, *The Glitter and the Gold* (New York, 1952), 298.

128. Maze Papers, Maze diary.

129. Churchill, *Storm*, 400; Nicolson, I, 411; Brian Gardner, *Churchill in Power: As Seen by His Contemporaries* (Boston, 1940), 18.

130. Churchill, *Storm*, 400–401.

131. Churchill, *Storm*, 401.

132. Churchill, *Storm*, 401; Mary Soames, *Clementine Churchill: The Biography of a Marriage* (Boston, 1979), 369.

133. Nicolson, I, 411; ChP 1/344.

134. Churchill, *Storm*, 396; CV V/3, 1597; Nicolson, I, 413; Norwich Papers.

135. WSC V, 1105; Norwich Papers, Duff Cooper diary.

136. Ironside Papers.

137. ChP 2/361.

138. Churchill, *Storm*, 396.

139. The British Blue Book, 98–104; DGFP series D, vol. VII, nos. 210–219; Churchill, *Storm*, 396–397.

140. Shirer, *Rise and Fall*, 564.

141. Shirer, *Rise and Fall*, 564; Churchill, *Storm*, 442–443.

142. C. Roberts, *The Nazi Claim to Colonies*, Introduction by Alfred Duff Cooper (London, 1939).

143. DBFP series 3, vol. VII, no. 309.

144. DBFP series 3, vol. VII, no. 367.

145. The British Blue Book, 120–123.

146. Shirer, *Rise and Fall*, 479–480.

147. Winston S. Churchill, *A History of the English-speaking Peoples*, 4 vols. (London, 1956–1958), I, 58–59.

148. R. J. Minney, *The Private Papers of Hore-Belisha* (London, 1960), 220.

149. Churchill, *English-speaking Peoples*, II, 125–126.

150. DBFP series 3, vol. VII, no. 3.

151. DBFP series 3, vol. VII, no. 349, note 7; no. 402, note 3; nos. 406, 411.

152. ChP 8/626.

153. Churchill, *English-speaking Peoples*, III, 306–308.

154. DBFP series 3, vol. VII, nos. 420, 426, 455.

155. DBFP series 3, vol. VII, no. 455.

156. DBFP series 3, vol. VII, no. 508.

157. DBFP series 3, vol. VII, no. 508; Sir Nevile Henderson, *Failure of a Mission: Berlin 1937–1939* (New York, 1940), 266.

158. DBFP series 3, vol. VII, no. 519.

159. DBFP series 3, vol. VII, nos. 501, 493; Henderson, 267–268.

160. DBFP series 3, vol. VII, nos. 523, 526.

161. Foreign Relations of the U.S., Kennedy to Hull, 8/30/39; Minney, 223–224; DBFP series 3, vol. VII, no. 539.

162. ND 2751-PS.

163. Henderson, 270.

164. Paul Schmidt, *Statist auf diplomatischer Buehne* (Bonn, 1949), 460; DBFP series 3, vol. VII, no. 589.

165. DGFP series D, vol. VII, no. 405.

166. ChP 2/364.

167. ChP 8/626, 8/624.

168. ChP 8/624.

169. Ironside Papers.

170. *Daily Mirror* 7/13/39; Churchill, *Storm*, 405.

171. Churchill, *Storm*, 405; Martin Gilbert, *Winston Churchill: The Wilderness Years* (London, 1981), 262.

172. Hansard, 9/1/39.

173. Shirer, *Rise and Fall*, 602.

174. Shirer, *Rise and Fall*, 500; Birger

Dahlerus, *The Last Attempt* (London, 1947), 120; TMWC IX, 471.

175. DBFP series 3, vol. VII, no. 644.
176. DGFP series D, vol. VII, nos. 509–510; Josiah Wedgwood, *Memoirs of a Fighting Life* (London, 1941), 225.
177. Gardner, 17–18.
178. Command Paper 6144.
179. DGFP series D, vol. VII, nos. 664, 639, 648.
180. ChP 4/96; Churchill, *Storm*, 406..
181. WM/Kathleen Hill, 11/4/80.
182. Camrose Papers; Hankey Papers.
183. Minney, 225.
184. Minney, 225, 226.
185. DBFP series 3, vol. VII, no. 731, 713.
186. Spears, I, 18.
187. Churchill, *Storm*, 406; Spears, I, 20.
188. Spears, I, 20; Hansard 9/2/39.
189. Hugh Dalton, *Memoirs, 1931–1945: The Fateful Years* (London, 1957), 264–265; Alfred Duff Cooper, *Old Men Forget* (London, 1953), 259; Spears, I, 21; Churchill, *Storm*, 406; L. S. Amery, *My Political Life*, 3 vols. (London, 1953), III, 324; Hansard 9/2/33.
190. Amery, III, 324; Ivone Kirkpatrick, *The Inner Circle* (London, 1959), 143–144; Spears, I, 22; Halifax, 210.
191. DBFP series 3, vol. VII, no. 734.
192. DBFP series 3, vol. VII, no. 751.
193. DGFP series D, vol. VII, no. 558.
194. DBFP series 3, vol. VII, nos. 740, 743.
195. Lady Diana Cooper, *The Light of Common Day* (Boston, 1959), 257; WM-/Lady Diana Cooper, 10/20/80.
196. WM/Lady Diana Cooper; Duff Cooper, 259.
197. Duff Cooper, 259; Churchill, *Storm*, 407; Norwich Papers.
198. Norwich Papers.
199. Norwich Papers.
200. Norwich Papers.
201. ChP 4/96; Churchill, *Storm*, 407.
202. ChP 4/96; Churchill, *Storm*, 407.
203. Minney, 226; *Sunday Times* 9/6/64; Robert Rhodes James, *Churchill: A Study in Failure, 1900–1939* (London, 1970), 379; Amery, III, 324.
204. *Sunday Times* 9/6/64; Minney, 227.
205. DBFP series 3, vol. VII, no. 739.
206. DBFP series 3, vol. VII, no. 740.
207. *Sunday Times* 9/6/64; Bonnet, 364.
208. Gilbert and Gott, 308; DBFP series 3, vol. VII, no. 741.
209. Kirkpatrick, 143–144.
210. *Sunday Times* 9/6/64; Minney, 227; DBFP series 3, vol. VII, no. 746.
211. *Sunday Times* 9/6/64.
212. *Sunday Times* 9/6/64.
213. Norwich Papers, Duff Cooper diary; ChP 8/639.
214. Kirkpatrick, 144; Bonnet, 363; Count Galeazzo Ciano, *The Ciano Diaries, 1939–1943*, edited by Hugh Wilson (London, 1946), 137.
215. Dahlerus, 109.
216. ChP 2/363; Churchill, *Storm*, 408; W. H. Thompson, *Sixty Minutes with Winston Churchill* (London, 1953).
217. W. H. Thompson; Martia Russell Papers; Churchill, *Storm*, 408.
218. Hansard 9/3/39; Churchill, *Storm*, 409.
219. Hansard 9/3/39.
220. Hansard 9/3/39.
221. Amery Papers, Amery Diary.
222. Churchill, *Storm*, 409; Gilbert, *Wilderness*, 267.
223. Churchill, *Storm*, 419–420; Laurence Thompson, *1940* (New York, 1966), 31.
224. CAB 65/1; Churchill, *Storm*, 442; Minney, 228–230; WM/Sir Ian Jacob, 11/1/80; Jacob to Martin Gilbert, 7/1/82.
225. WM/Lady Diana Cooper.

CATACLYSM

1. WM/Kathleen Hill, 11/4/80; Winston S. Churchill, *The Gathering Storm* (Boston, 1948), 409–410.
2. Churchill, *Storm*, 410; CAB 100/1; Admiral of the Fleet Lord Fraser of North Cape, "Churchill and the Navy," in Sir James Marchant, ed., *Winston Spencer Churchill: Servant of*

Crown and Commonwealth (London, 1954), 78–79; John Higham recollections in conversation with Martin Gilbert, 3/1/82.

3. Hansard 9/6/39; Churchill, *Storm*, 331; CAB 16/11.

4. Fraser, in Marchant, 81.

5. ChP 4/123.

6. Sir John Colville, *The Churchillians* (London, 1981), 88.

7. T. R. Fehrenbach, *F.D.R.'s Undeclared War 1939–1941* (New York, 1967).

8. Francis L. Loewenheim, Harold D. Langley, and Manfred Jonas, eds., *Roosevelt and Churchill: Their Secret Wartime Correspondence* (New York, 1975), 5.

9. *New York Sun* 9/2/39; *NYT* 8/20/14, 9/4/39.

10. Fehrenbach, 42–43.

11. Churchill, *Storm*, 440–441.

12. Admiralty Papers 199/1928; ChP 4/123.

13. Churchill, *Storm*, 421; WM/Lady Soames, 10/9/80; Mary Soames, *Clementine Churchill: The Biography of a Marriage* (Boston, 1979), 372.

14. Diana Cooper, *Trumpet from the Steep* (London, 1960), 37.

15. Pim Papers; Arthur Marder, *From the Dardanelles to Oran* (London, 1974), 29; Fraser, in Marchant, 87.

16. Pim Papers.

17. Pim Papers.

18. Recollections of Bernard Sendall in conversation with Martin Gilbert, 11/14/79; Shakespeare Papers.

19. Churchill, *Storm*, 411; Fraser, in Marchant, 79–80; Arthur Marder, "Winston Is Back: Churchill at the Admiralty," *English Historical Review*, Supplement 5 (Aberdeen, 1972), 2; Marder, *Dardanelles*, 106–107.

20. Turner Catledge, *My Life and the Times* (New York, 1971), 157.

21. Marder, *English Historical Review*, 2; Admiralty Papers 205/2.

22. Charles Eade, ed., *Churchill by His Contemporaries* (New York, 1954), 121; Fraser, in Marchant, 78–80.

23. Führer's Conferences on Naval Affairs, 1939 (mimeographed by British Admiralty, London, 1947), 13–14.

24. DBFP series 3, vol. VII, no. 283.

25. ND C-189, C-190.

26. Churchill, *Storm*, 163–164.

27. DBFP series 3, vol. VIII, no. 283.

28. Hansard 9/26/39.

29. Hansard 9/26/39.

30. WSCHCS 6160–6164 (10/1/39).

31. Winston S. Churchill, *The World Crisis, 5* vols. and *The Aftermath* (New York, 1923–1931), II, 391.

32. Churchill, *Storm*, 429.

33. Chiefs of Staff, 17 of 1939; CAB 79/1; Stephen Roskill, *The War at Sea, 3* vols. (London, 1954), I, 78–80.

34. Churchill, *Storm*, 433–444.

35. CAB 65/1; Admiralty Papers 205/2.

36. William L. Shirer, *The Rise and Fall of the Third Reich: A History of Nazi Germany* (New York, 1960), 646.

37. Churchill, *Storm*, 433.

38. Brian Gardner, *Churchill in Power: As Seen by His Contemporaries* (Boston, 1970), 27; Hansard 11/8/39; CAB 65/1.

39. William L. Shirer, *Berlin Diary* (New York, 1941), 237.

40. WM/Lady Soames; Soames, 372.

41. Churchill, *Storm*, 528, 527; Soames, 374; Templewood Papers.

42. Marder, *English Historical Review*, 2; J. H. Godfrey, *Naval Memoirs of Admiral J. H. Godfrey* (privately printed, 1964–1965), I, vi, 35.

43. Marder, *English Historical Review*, 9.

44. ChP 19/3; Churchill, *Storm*, 465.

45. ChP 19/3; Churchill, *Storm*, 465.

46. Captain J. S. S. Litchfield to the author; Marder, *English Historical Review*, 3; Churchill, *Storm*, 414.

47. Hansard 12/6/39; Churchill, *Storm*, 414, 505–508, 706–711; Marder, *English Historical Review*, 10, 28; CAB 65/6.

48. Admiralty Papers 199/1928; Churchill, *Storm*, 413–414.

49. Admiralty Papers 205/5, 199/19.

50. Admiralty Papers 199/1928, 205/5; Marder, *English Historical Review,* 31–38; WSC VI, 26–27, 37–38.

51. Fraser, in Marchant, 78.

52. Fraser, in Marchant, 78; ChP 19/3, 25/4; CAB 16/132; Weir Papers.

53. S. W. Roskill, "Marder, Churchill, and the Admiralty 1932–42," RUSI *Journal,* December 1972.

54. Admiralty Papers 205/6.

55. Vice-Admiral R. D. Oliver to the author; Marder, *English Historical Review,* 22.

56. Donald McLachan, "Naval Intelligence in the Second World War," RUSI *Journal,* 112, August 1967, 244.

57. CAB 66/1; Admiralty Papers 199/1928.

58. Charles Stuart, ed., *The Reith Diaries* (London, 1975), 249; CAB 132/33.

59. B. H. Liddell Hart, *The Memoirs of Captain Liddell Hart,* 2 vols. (London, 1965), II, 27.

60. Charles de Gaulle, *Le fil de l'épée* (Paris, 1932).

61. Robert Wernick, *Blitzkrieg* (New York, 1976), 24.

62. Churchill, *Storm,* 450, 442.

63. Churchill, *Storm,* 451.

64. CAB 61/11.

65. CAB 65/1; Command Paper 6144 (Treaty Series No. 58) 1939.

66. B. H. Liddell Hart, *History of the Second World War* (New York, 1971),18; William L. Shirer, *The Collapse of the Third Republic* (New York, 1969), 519; Churchill, *Storm,* 558.

67. Churchill, *Storm,* 451; CAB 83/3, 92/111; WSC VI, 15.

68. Hoare Diary, Templewood Papers; CAB 66/1; ChP 4/131.

69. CAB 65/1, 100/1; L. S. Amery, *My Political Life,* 3 vols. (London, 1953), III, 330; E. L. Spears, *Assignment to Catastrophe,* 2 vols. (New York, 1955), I 31–32; Hugh Dalton, *Memoirs, 1931–1945: The Fateful Years* (London, 1957), 274.

70. R. J. Minney, *The Private Papers of Hore-Belisha* (London, 1960), 251; Iain Macleod, *Neville Chamberlain* (New York, 1962), 286.

71. Hansard 9/6/39; Spears, I, 29; Dalton, 274, 277.

72. Sir Keith Feiling, *The Life of Neville Chamberlain* (London, 1946), 440.

73. Churchill, *Storm,* 574–575.

74. Dalton, 292; L. F. Ellis, *The War in France and Flanders* (London, 1953), 30–31; Viscount Templewood, *Nine Troubled Years* (London, 1954), 428.

75. General Maurice Gustave Gamelin, *Servir,* 3 vols. (Paris, 1947), II, 413–416, 424–425; Sir Lewis B. Namier, *Diplomatic Prelude* (London, 1948), 459–460.

76. Gamelin, I, 23–24; *Événements,* II, 276–278.

77. Gamelin, I, 24.

78. Shirer, *Rise and Fall,* 840.

79. TMWC XI, 350; TMWC X, 519.

80. TWC XII, 1086.

81. Franz Halder diary, 9/7/39.

82. Jacques Minart, *P.C. Vincennes Secteur 4,* 2 vols. (Paris, 1945), I, 19–20; Gamelin, III, 60–61, 55.

83. Général André Beaufre, *Le Drame de 1940* (Paris, 1965), 189; Général Charles de Gaulle, *Mémoires de Guerre,* 3 vols. (Paris, 1954), I, 22.

84. TMWC I, 257.

85. Shirer, *Rise and Fall,* 744.

86. A. J. P. Taylor, *The Origins of the Second World War* (New York, 1962), 228 fn. 4.

87. Virginia Cowles, *Winston Churchill: The Era and the Man* (New York, 1953), 313.

88. WSCHCS 6160–6164 (10/1/39; verse form added).

89. WSCHCS 6160–6164.

90. Sir John Colville, *The Fringes of Power: 10 Downing Street Diaries 1939–1955* (New York, 1985), 29; Templewood Papers; Chamberlain Papers.

91. Shirer, *Berlin Diary,* 229; *Time* 10/16/39.

92. WSCHCS 6171–6175 (11/12/39).

93. WSCHCS 6171–6175 (11/12/39).

94. Colville, *Fringes*, 50; Harold Nicolson, *Diaries and Letters, 1930–1962*, edited by Nigel Nicolson, 3 vols. (London, 1966), II, 59.

95. WSCHCS 6183–6186 (1/20/40; verse form added).

96. Hoare diary, Templewood Papers; ChP 23/3.

97. CAB 11/39; Général Paul-Emile Tournoux, "Les origines de la ligne Maginot," *Revue d'Histoire de la Deuxième Mondiale*, No. 33, January 1959, 14.

98. WSCHCS 6183–6186 (1/20/40).

99. Churchill, *Storm*, 541; Liddell Hart, *Second World War*, 45.

100. Kay Halle, *The Irrepressible Churchill: A Treasury of Winston Churchill's Wit* (New York, 1967), 153.

101. WSCHCS 6171–6175 (11/12/39).

102. B. Baxter, *Men, Martyrs, and Mountebanks* (London, 1940), 251; Cowles, 312–313.

103. Nicolson, II, 34–35, 37, 38.

104. Laurence Thompson, *1940* (New York 1966), 32.

105. WSCHCS 6171–6175 (11/12/39); Colville, *Fringes*, 108; N. Chamberlain Papers, diary.

106. Cowles, 311; Gardner, 21.

107. Churchill, *Storm*, 495.

108. Churchill, *Storm*, 494–495.

109. Soames, 374; Fraser, in Marchant, 81.

110. Soames, 374; Diana Cooper, 37; WM/Lady Soames; WM/Lady Diana Cooper.

111. Thompson, 24.

112. *Times* 10/5/39; ChP 1/355.

113. WM/Lady Soames.

114. Thompson, 17.

115. WM/Lady Soames.

116. Feiling, 424; Churchill, *Storm*, 549; Fehrenbach, 45.

117. T. Harrison and C. Madge, eds., *War Begins at Home* (London, 1940), 39; Margery Allingham, *The Oaken Heart* (London, 1941), 84; Thompson, 14.

118. *Time* 1/22/40.

119. Colville, *Fringes*, 116; Thompson, 15; ChP 19/2.

120. *Times* 12/26/39.

121. Thompson, 13–28 passim.

122. Thompson, 13–28 passim.

123. Thompson, 13–28 passim.

124. Thompson, 16.

125. Telford Taylor, *The Breaking Wave: The Second World War in the Summer of 1940* (New York, 1967), 39.

126. CAB 65/3.

127. ChP 19/2.

128. ND L-52; DGFP series D, vol. VIII, no. 224.

129. WM/William L. Shirer, 7/20/71; Emmanuel Beau de Loménie, *La Mort de la Troisième République* (Paris, 1951), 128–129.

130. Foreign Relations of the U.S., 1940, I, 107.

131. Churchill, *Storm*, 479.

132. *Time* 9/18/39; Shirer, *Berlin Diary*, 9/26/39.

133. Alphonse Goutard, *1940: La Guerre des Occasions Perdus* (Paris, 1956), 234.

134. Shirer, *Collapse*, 535–536.

135. Goutard, 132–133.

136. CAB 83/3; Churchill, *Storm*, 558–559.

137. *Événements*, III, 690, Beaufre, 232; Shirer, *Collapse*, 620–621.

138. Shirer, *Collapse*, 183–187.

139. *Time* 12/18/39.

140. Ronald Steel, *Walter Lippmann and the American Century* (Boston, 1980), 381.

141. Goutard, 131.

142. Goutard, 131; *Événements*, II, 281–282; Shirer, *Collapse*, 533–534.

143. CAB 65/1.

144. CAB 65/1; ChP 19/3; Eade, ed., 122.

145. CAB 65/1; ChP 19/3; Churchill, *Storm*, 554.

146. Churchill, *Storm*, 561–562.

147. Sir Philip Vian, *Action This Day: A War Memoir* (London, 1960), 26.

148. Marder, *English Historical Review*, 31 fn.

149. Churchill, *Storm*, 561–562; Nicolson, II, 59.

150. Churchill, *Storm*, 562, 564.
151. Churchill, *Storm*, 564; Vian, 26; ChP 19/5.
152. WSC VI, 154.
153. Churchill, *Storm*, 563; Marder, *English Historical Review*, 30; Thompson, 51.
154. Nicolson, II, 59.
155. ChP 9/143.
156. ChP 9/143.
157. Templewood Papers; ChP 8/658.
158. Thompson.
159. ND 004-PS; DGFP series D, vol. VIII, no. 663-33; ND C-63; NCA, Suppl. B, 1543-47.
160. Churchill, *Storm*, 564; ND C-66.
161. ND CD-170, C-166; FCNA, 1939, 27, 51.
162. FCNA, 1939, 51, 53-57; Jodl diary, 12/13/39; Halder diary, 12/14/39; Liddell Hart, *Second World War*, 54-55.
163. Shirer, *Berlin Diary*, 307.
164. Liddell Hart, *Second World War*, 56; ND 063-C; DGFP series D, vol. VIII, no. 644.
165. Thompson, 56; Colville, *Fringes*, 40, 76.
166. Churchill, *Storm*, 571-581; CAB 66/5, 65/11; Admiralty Papers 1/10795; CAB 65/12; Chief of Staff 64 (40); CAB 79/85; CAB 65/12.
167. John Elting and the editors of Time-Life Books, *Battles for Scandinavia* (Chicago, 1981), 47.
168. Churchill, *Storm*, 591-592.
169. Churchill, *Storm*, 582; CAB 65/12; Liddell Hart, *Second World War*, 58.
170. Admiralty Papers 205/2.
171. Admiralty Papers 116/4240; CAB 65/12.
172. Colville, *Fringes*, 94-95; CAB 65/6.
173. Churchill, *Storm*, 583, 582; Colville, *Fringes*, 95.
174. NCA, Supplement B, 1543-477; Liddell Hart, *Second World War*, 58.
175. *Times* 4/6/40.
176. Hansard 4/ 11/40.
177. Liddell Hart, *Second World War*, 52; Marder, *English Historical Review*, 55.

178. Roskill, *War at Sea*, I, 179; CAB 65/11; Sir Eric Seal's letter to the author, 9/8/71; Marder, *English Historical Review*, 57.
179. Gamelin, III, 866; Paul Baudouin, *The Private Diaries of Paul Baudouin* (London, 1953), 41.
180. Liddell Hart, *Second World War*, 62; Churchill, *Storm*, 624-627.
181. Shirer, *Berlin Diary*, 314; Admiralty Papers 116/4471; Churchill, *Storm*, 601; Nicolson, II, 79.
182. Colville, *Fringes*, 101; *The Listener* 5/6/40.
183. CAB 65/6; Colville, *Fringes*, 90; Thompson, 57; *Daily Mail* 4/11/40.
184. Shirer, *Berlin Diary*; Liddell Hart, *Second World War*, 59.
185. Jodl diary in Shirer, *Rise and Fall*, 709.
186. Churchill, *Storm*, 619; Shirer, *Berlin Diary*, 315, 320.
187. CAB 65/12, 21/1388; Churchill, *Storm*, 614.
188. Churchill, *Storm*, 624, 626-627.
189. Churchill, *Storm*, 623.
190. Hansard 5/8/40.
191. Shirer, *Collapse*, 569; Nicolson, II, 74.
192. CAB 99/3; Shirer, *Berlin Diary*, 324-326; Nicolson, II, 74-75.
193. Hansard 3/3/40; Seal Papers.
194. *Événements*, II, 359-360, 361-363.
195. Baudouin, 25.
196. WM/Sir William Deakin, 10/5/80; F. W. Deakin, "Churchill The Historian," *Schweizer Monatshefte* Nr. 4 (Zurich, 1970).
197. F. W. Deakin.
198. *Times* 4/4/40; *Daily Mail* 4/4/40; ChP 2/392, 2/395.
199. Nicolson, II, 74-75.
200. Nicolson, II, 74-75; ChP 4/131; Thompson, 70.
201. Robert Rhodes James, *Chips, The Diaries of Sir Henry Channon* (London, 1967), 243; Col. Roderick Macleod and Denis Kelly, eds., *The Ironside Diaries 1937-1940* (London, 1962), 293.
202. ChP 3/131, 2/393.

203. ChP 19/2.
204. ChP 1/99/1929; CAB 79/4.
205. Shirer, *Rise and Fall*, 944; WM/William L. Shirer, 7/20/80.
206. N. Chamberlain Papers, diary.
207. *Evening Standard* 5/6/40; Halifax Papers, diary.
208. Hansard 5/7/40.
209. Nicolson, II, 76; Hansard 5/7/40; Thompson, 80.
210. Nicolson, II, 76; Hansard 5/7/40.
211. Hansard 5/7/40; Nicolson, II, 77.
212. Nicolson, II, 77.
213. Hansard 5/7/40 (italics added).
214. Churchill, *Storm*, 659; Nicolson, II, 77; Rhodes James, *Chips*, 243, 245.
215. Henri de Kerillis, *Français, voici la vérité* (New York, 1942), 247; Clare Luce, *Europe in the Spring* (New York, 1940), 246, 126–127.
216. Shirer, *Rise and Fall*, 716.
217. Dalton, 304–305.
218. *Daily Herald* 5/8/40.
219. WM/Malcolm MacDonald, 11/6/80; Dalton, 305–306; Hansard 5/8/40.
220. Thompson, 82–83.
221. Nicolson, II, 78; Hansard 5/8/40.
222. Churchill, *Storm*, 659.
223. F. Owen, *Tempestuous Journey* (London, 1954), 748.
224. Hansard 5/8/40 (italics added).
225. WM/Macmillan; Harold Macmillan, *The Blast of War 1939–1945* (London, 1967), 74.
226. Dalton, 306; Rhodes James, *Chips*, 246; WM/R. A. Butler, 12/5/80.
227. Hansard 5/8/40; Rhodes James, *Chips*, 246.
228. Rhodes James, *Chips*, 246; John Peck, "Bull and Benediction," unpublished typescript, 96–97 (published in WSC VI, 298–299).
229. Hansard 5/8/40.
230. Alfred Duff Cooper, *Old Men Forget* (New York, 1954), 279.
231. Nicolson, II, 79–80; Dalton, 306.
232. Churchill, *Storm*, 661.
233. Adam Sykes and Iain Sproat, eds. *The Wit of Sir Winston* (London, 1965), 75; Colville, *Fringes*, 89.
234. Churchill, *Storm*, 661.
235. Thompson, 82, 83.
236. Dalton, 310.
237. Earl of Avon, *The Reckoning* (London, 1965), 96.
238. Dalton, 308; Thompson, 88.
239. Thompson, 89.
240. Thompson, 78–80; Dalton, 306–307, 309.
241. Avon, *Reckoning*, 96–97.
242. WM/Macmillan; Macmillan, *Blast*, 72; Amery, III, 361.
243. ChP 2/392.
244. Churchill, *Storm*, 661; Thompson, 91–92.
245. Churchill, *Storm*, 661–662; Thompson, 91–92.
246. Halifax Papers, diary, 5/9/40.
247. Thompson, 90; Churchill, *Storm*, 662–663.
248. Churchill, *Storm*, 662–663; WM/Viscount Head, 11/19/80.
249. Earl of Birkenhead, *Life of Lord Halifax* (London, 1965), 454.
250. David Dilks, ed., *The Diaries of Sir Alexander Cadogan O.M. 1938–1945* (New York, 1972), 280; Birkenhead, 454; Churchill, *Storm*, 662–663.
251. Rhodes James, *Chips*, 248; WM/Kathleen Hill, 11/4/80; ChP 2/413; Avon, *Reckoning*, 97; WSC VI, 305.
252. Shirer, *Rise and Fall*, 723.
253. Liddell Hart, *Second World War*, 66–67.
254. Allen Dulles, *Germany's Underground* (New York, 1947), 58–61. According to W. L. Shirer, Sas personally confirmed this account with him after the war.
255. *Événements*, IX, 2758–2760; Anatole de Monzie, *Ci-devant* (Paris, 1942), 44; Baudouin, 44–48.
256. Baudouin, 44–48.
257. Paul Reynaud, *Au Coeur de la mêlée, 1930–1945* (Paris, 1951), 412.
258. Churchill, *Storm*, 662; CAB 64/7; WSC VI, 306.
259. Templewood, 431–432; *Times, News Chronicle* 5/10/40; CAB 83/3.
260. Shirer, *Collapse*, 605.
261. CAB 65/7.

262. J. C. Reith, *Into the Wind* (London, 1949), 382; Halifax Papers, diary, 5/10/40.

263. Avon, *Reckoning*, 97–98; Templewood, 432; Nicolson, II, 82.

264. Churchill, *Storm*, 662; Avon, *Reckoning*, 94–98.

265. CAB 65/7; Stuart, 250; Macleod and Kelly, 303–304.

266. Dalton, 311–312.

267. CAB 65/7.

268. CAB 65/7; Avon, *Reckoning*, 98.

269. John W. Wheeler-Bennett, *King George VI, His Life and Reign* (London, 1958), 443–444.

270. Churchill, *Storm*, 665.

271. Churchill, *Storm*, 665; W. H. Thompson, *Sixty Minutes with Winston Churchill* (London, 1953), 44–45.

272. WSC VI, 311.

273. Churchill, *Storm*, 666.

274. Nicolson, II, 83–84.

275. Churchill, *Storm*, 666–667.

276. Reed Whittemore, "Churchill and the Limitations of Myth," *Yale Review*, Winter 1955; Wheeler-Bennett, *George VI*, 446.

277. John Evelyn Wrench, *Geoffrey Dawson and Our Times* (London, 1955), 415; Colville, *Fringes*, 122; WM/Sir John Colville, 10/8/80.

278. *News Chronicle* 1/1/40; Nicolson, I, 85.

279. Hansard 5/13/40 (verse form added).

280. WSCHCS 6220–6223 (5/19/40).

281. WSCHCS 6231–6238 (6/18/40).

282. ChP 4/194; Isaiah Berlin, *Mr. Churchill in 1940* (London, 1940), 26, 29.

283. Winston S. Churchill, *Their Finest Hour*, (Boston, 1949), 21–22.

284. Lord Moran, *Churchill. Taken from the Diaries of Lord Moran: The Struggle for Survival (1940–1965)* (Boston, 1966), 959.

285. Hansard 10/8/40.

286. Hansard 11/23/32.

INDEX

in Austria, 281; on Germany's position (1938, 1939), 324, 502; on Hitler, 345; on triple alliance, 457; on Scapa Flow, 561; on WSC's first wartime broadcast, 590; on Norway, 623–624, 634, 637, 641–642, 651; on Low Countries, 646, 651–652, 666

Siegfried Line, 491, 517, 583; WSC's knowledge of, 189; Hitler on, 321, 324, 588; German generals' view of, 324, 355; attack on, urged, 576, 580, 588; music hall song about, 608, 609, 614, 615, 616

Sign of the Cross, The (film) 23, 41

Silesia: German troops in, 318, 319, 502, 516, 518, 575; Poland receives portion of, 351

Simon, Sir John, 76, 416, 427, 579, 638; as foreign secretary, 81, 87, 90, 111, 112, 114, 128, 133, 134, 136, 240, 329, 470, (and German "parity") 92–93, 94, 142, 143; replaced, 151; as Chancellor of the Exchequer, 248, 470, 538–539, 579, 672, (and Czechoslovakia/Munich pact) 294, 330, 347, 366, (and Czech gold) 395, 467, (and loan to Poland) 467, (and Chamberlain's volte-face) 530, 531, 533; Russia as viewed by, 453; and coalition government, 661, 662

Simpson, Ernest, 223, 224

Simpson, Wallis Warfield Spencer, 223–228, 230, 232, 233, 236; as Duchess of Windsor, 161, 233, 255, 381, 651

Sinclair, Sir Archibald, 226, 340, 500, 558, 598, 665; as Liberal leader, 25–26, 131; opposes armaments, 139; supports WSC, 219, 230, 425; backs Sandys in information inquiry, 269; WSC letter to, 317; and Munich Agreement, 350, 366; protests House adjournment, 372; in Norway debate, 648

Singapore, 108, 144, 434

six-power conference. *See* "peace front"

Skaggerak, the, 558, 617, 626, 632, 634. *See also* Norway

Skoda Works. *See* Czechoslovakia

Slessor, Sir John, 613

Slovakia, 378, 437, 518; declares independence, 390, 393

Smith, F. E. *See* Birkenhead, Lord

Smuts, Jan Christiaan, 13

Snow White and the Seven Dwarfs (film), 306

Social Democrat Party (Czechoslovakia), 339

socialism, 54, 416, 587, 647; WSC and, 218; French view of, 609

sonar. *See* asdic

South Africa. *See* Boer War

Soviet Union, 74, 121, 134, 208, 316, 421; admired, 47, 84; Stalin and, 47–48 (*see also* Stalin, Joseph); and war reparations, 59; Germany as shield against, 59 (*see also* bolshevism); HMG policy toward, 75, 91, 100, 102, 218, 264, 307, 325–326, 367, 370, 400, 473, 683 (*see also* Chamberlain, Neville: AS PRIME MINISTER), (alliance with) 404–405, 451–453, 474 (*see also* and triple alliance, *below*; Grand Alliance), (and Russian sensitivity) 469, 472–473, 476, 482–483, 486; at Geneva Conference, 94; and Germany as enemy, 102, 125, 290, 307, 326, 327, 473, 567, (Locarno Pact and) 174, (British wishful thinking) 205, 400, 454–455, 590, (Hitler plans invasion) 404, 446, (and collective security) 449, 450, 587, (*see also* Communist party and communism [Nazism/Hitler vs.]); British agents for, 110, 363; French alliance with, *see* France: AS SOVIET ALLY; blamed for bombing of Guernica, 200; and Grand Alliance, 285–286; and Czechoslovakia, 290, 295, 319, 325–326, 331, 344, 474, (pact with) 141, 184, 450, 499, (FO and) 342; WSC on détente with, 381, 386, 446–447, 451, 465, 478; and Poland, *see* Poland: SOVIET UNION AND; and triple alliance, 447–460, 468–470, 471–472, 473–475, 479, 481, 482–485; and "peace front," 448; and collective security, 449, 458, 486; and Germany as ally, 453, 454–455, 456, (Rapallo Treaty) 59, 61, (Stalin's aversion to) 455, 473, 475, (and control of Baltic) 568; German nonaggression pact with, *see* Nazi-Soviet nonaggression pact; Allied rudeness toward, 458; post-World War I treaties with 473; as neutral, 473, 475; pact with Baltic states, 593; and Finland, 593–595, (WSC on) 594; military strength un-

COPYRIGHT ACKNOWLEDGMENTS